THE
B&B
GUIDE
2019

Published by AA Publishing, which is a trading name of AA Media Limited whose registered office is: Fanum House, Basing View, Basingstoke, Hampshire RG21 4EA. Registered number 06112600

49th edition published 2018

For queries relating to this guide, please contact:

lifestyleguides@theAA.com

Image credits:
The Automobile Association wishes to thank the following photographers and organisations for their assistance in the preparation of this book.

Abbreviations for the picture credits are as follows – (t) top; (b) bottom; (l) left; (r) right; (c) centre; (AA) AA World Travel Library.

3 Courtesy of Lindeth Fell Country House, Windermere; 4 AA/Stockbyte Royalty Free; 9 Courtesy of The Ship at Dunwich, Dunwich; 10 Courtesy of The Kings Arms, Sherborne; 12-16 BG Photodisc; 12 Courtesy of The Temple Bar Inn, Ewyas Harrold; 13l Courtesy of The 25 Boutique B&B, Torquay; 13r Courtesy of The Old Town Hall, Leyburn; 14l Courtesy of Cruickshanks Boutique B&B, Isle of Arran; 14r Courtesy of Rhedyn Guest House, Bulith Wells; 15l Courtesy of Causeway Lodge, Bushmills; 15r Courtesy of Long Melford Swan, Long Melford; 16 Fosse Farmhouse B&B; 24-25 AA/A Burton; 298-299 AA/J Henderson; 322-323 AA/M Sterling; 353 AA/M Bauer; 354-355 AA/C Hill.

Every effort has been made to trace the copyright holders, and we apologise in advance for any unintentional omissions or errors. We would be pleased to apply any corrections in a following edition of this publication.

Photographs in the gazetteer are provided by the establishments.

This guide was compiled by the AA Lifestyle Guides team and Servis Filmsetting Ltd, Stockport.

Cover design by Austin Taylor.

Maps prepared by the Mapping Services Department of AA Publishing.

Maps © AA Media Limited 2018.

Contains Ordnance Survey data © Crown copyright and database right 2018.

Ireland map contains data available from openstreetmap.org © under the Open Database License found at opendatacommons.org

A CIP catalogue record for this book is available from the British Library.

Printed in the UK by Bell & Bain.

ISBN: 978-0-7495-7982-1

A05602

Visit www.theaa.com/bed-and-breakfasts

Contents

Welcome to the AA B&B Guide 2019

From the most stylish and sophisticated urban boutique accommodation to family-run homes in the countryside; from ultra-chic luxury to charmingly rustic home-from-home comfort and many points between, *The AA B&B Guide* has it all.

Who's in the guide?

For almost half a century, our readers have been using *The AA B&B Guide* to find many different types of accommodation, for a multitude of reasons. As the AA inspects such a wide range of establishments, we hope that this guide will prove an invaluable asset in helping you to find the right place to stay.

Throughout the year, our specially trained team of expert inspectors are visiting, grading and advising the Guest Accommodation that appears in this guide. Each one is judged on its presentation, quality of accommodation, leisure facilities, breakfasts and evening meals, service, hospitality, conference facilities and cleanliness and housekeeping. They are then rated according to our classification system (pages 8 and 9).

Our inspectors also choose their Guest Accommodation of the Year for England, Scotland, Wales, and Northern Ireland, as well as the Friendliest B&B of the Year, the Unique B&B of the Year and the Restaurant with Rooms of the Year.

Gold Stars

All of the Guest Accommodation in this guide is of a high standard, but some are a cut above, and those with Gold Stars are in the top ten percent of their Star rating. At these establishments you can expect a little more of everything: more comfort, more extras, and more attention. From three to five Gold Stars, this is the best of British Guest Accommodation.

Silver Stars

These properties offer a superior level of quality within their Star rating, high standards of hospitality, service and cleanliness.

Premier Collection

All five-Star establishments, whether Gold, Silver or Black Stars, are part of the Premier Collection, and these entries are highlighted in the guide. This allows the reader to see at a glance those Guest Accommodations that have met all the criteria required by the Guest Accommodation Scheme and reached the highest rating possible.

Rosettes

Some of the B&Bs in this guide have their own restaurants, and many of them serve food that has been awarded AA Rosettes; including a few that have reached the four and five Rosette level, making them among the finest restaurants in the world. These are regularly visited by the AA Inspectorate who award Rosettes strictly on the basis of the inspector's experience alone.

Many establishments designated as Restaurants with Rooms have been awarded AA Rosettes for the quality of their food.

Anonymous inspection

Any Guest Accommodation applying for AA recognition receives an unannounced visit by one of the AA's professional inspectors to check standards. The inspector pays his or her own bill (rather than it being paid by the establishment).

After staying overnight at the Guest Accommodation, the inspector will make themselves known to a member of staff and ask to speak to the owner or manager. Once a rating is awarded, regular visits are made by our inspectors to check that standards are being maintained.

If the accommodation changes hands, the new owners must reapply for classification, as AA recognition is not transferable.

Tell us what you think

We welcome your feedback– you can email us at
lifestyleguides@theaa.com

The B&Bs are visited throughout the year by our team of inspectors. For the very latest updates visit
www.theaa.com/bed-and-breakfasts

Using the guide

1. | **CAMBRIDGE** | Map 12 TL45 |

Benson House

2. ★★★★ 🥚 GUEST HOUSE

5.

3. tel: 01223 311594 **24 Huntingdon Road CB3 0HH**
email: bensonhouse@btconnect.com web: www.bensonhouse.co.uk
4. dir: *0.5 mile northwest of city centre on A604.*

6. This popular guest house is well placed for the city centre and New Hall and Fitzwilliam colleges. Its pleasant bedrooms vary in size and style and all are well equipped with TV, clock radio, beverage tray and hairdryers. The delicious selection at breakfast includes kippers, and there is limited private parking behind the property. Benson House cannot cater for pets or children under 12 years of age.

7. **Rooms:** 6 en suite (1 GF) **S** fr £80 **D** fr £115 **Facilities:** FTV iPod docking station tea/coffee WiFi **Extras:** Welcome drink, speciality toiletries **Parking:** 5 **Notes:** No children 12 years Closed 31 December to 5 January

8.

9. **10.** **11.**

1. Location, map reference & name

Each country is listed in alphabetical order by county then location. The Channel Islands follow the England section and the Scottish Islands follow the Scotland section. Establishments are listed alphabetically in descending order of Stars, with Gold Stars appearing first in each rating.

The map page number refers to the atlas at the back of the guide and is followed by the National Grid Reference.

To find the location, read the first figure across and the second figure vertically within the lettered square.

You can find routes at **www.theAA.com** or **www.AAbookings.ie**. London has its own Plans (see end of atlas), and London establishments have a Plan number based on these.

2. Classification & designator

See pages 8 and 9 for more information on AA classifications and awards. Five-Star establishments are highlighted as

Premier Collection, and they are listed on pages 17–22.

🌹 **Rosettes** The AA's food award, see page 11.

🥚 **Egg cups and** 🥧 **pies** These symbols indicate that, in the experience of the inspector, either breakfast or dinner (or both) are really special, and have an emphasis on freshly prepared local ingredients.

3. Email address & website

Email and website addresses are included where they have been specified by the establishment. Such websites are not under the control of AA Media Limited, who cannot accept any responsibility or liability in respect of any and all matters whatsoever relating to such websites.

4. Directions & distances

Distances in **directions** are given in miles and yards, or kilometres and metres in the Republic of Ireland.

5. Photographs

Establishments may choose to include a photograph.

6. Description

Written by the inspector at the time of his or her visit.

7. Rooms

The number of letting bedrooms (rms), or rooms with a bath or shower en suite are shown. Bedrooms that have a private bathroom (pri facs) adjacent are indicated.

The number of bedrooms in an annexe of equivalent standard are also shown.

Charges are per night:

S minimum price for bed and breakfast per person

D minimum price bed and breakfast for two people sharing a room. If an asterisk (*) follows the prices this indicates 2018 prices.

If not including breakfast then 'room only' will be shown. Some prices include both breakfast and dinner – if unsure, check with the establishment.

The euro € is the currency of the Republic of Ireland.

Prices are indications only, so check before booking. Some places may offer free accommodation to children provided they share their parents' room.

8. Facilities

Most bedrooms will have a TV. If this is important to you, please check when booking. If **TV4B** appears, this means that there are TVs in four bedrooms.

If **Dinner** is shown, you may have to order in advance. Please check when booking.

For other abbreviations and symbols, see panel on the right of this page.

9. Extras

Anything the establishment offers in rooms that are more than expected e.g. speciality toiletries, trouser press, mineral water, home-made biscuits etc.

10. Parking

Parking is usually followed by the number of spaces. Motorists should be aware that some establishments may charge for parking. Please check when booking.

11. Notes

No children children cannot be accommodated, or a minimum age may be specified, e.g. No children 4yrs means no children under four years old.

Establishments with special facilities for children (**ch fac**) may include a babysitting service or baby-intercom system, playroom or playground, laundry facilities, drying and ironing facilities, cots, high chairs and special meals. If you have very young children, check facilities before booking.

Additional facilities such as lifts or any leisure activities available are also listed.

LB indicates that Short or Leisure Breaks are available. Contact the establishment for details.

Establishments are open all year unless **Closed** days/dates/months are shown. Some places are open all year but offer a restricted service (**RS**) in low season. If the text does not say what the restricted services are you should check before booking.

Civ wed 50 The establishment is licensed for civil weddings and can accommodate 50 guests for the ceremony.

Conference facilities Conf indicates that facilities are available. The total number of delegates that can be accommodated is shown, plus maximum numbers in various settings (theatre, classroom and boardroom).

Key to symbols and abbreviations

★★★	Classification (see page 8–9)
◉	AA Rosette award (see page 11)
A	Associate entry (see page 9)
U	Unclassified rating (see page 9)
	A very special breakfast, with an emphasis on freshly prepared local ingredients
	A very special dinner, with an emphasis on freshly prepared local ingredients
S	Single room
D	Double room (2 people sharing)
pri fac	Private facilities
fmly	Family bedroom
GF	Ground floor bedroom
LB	Short/Leisure breaks
*	2018 prices
ch fac	Special facilities for children
TVL	Lounge with television
Lounge	Lounge without television
TV4B	Television in four bedrooms
STV	Satellite television
FTV	Freeview television
WiFi	Wireless internet available
tea/coffee	Tea and coffee-making facilities
Conf	Conference facilities
rms	Bedrooms in main building
annexe rms	Bedrooms not in the main building
fr	From
RS	Restricted service
⚿	Secure storage
⊗	Indoor swimming pool
⊗	Heated indoor swimming pool
⚡	Outdoor swimming pool
⚡	Heated outdoor swimming pool
⚘	Croquet lawn
⚲	Tennis court
⚑	Golf

AA Inspected Guest Accommodation

The AA inspects and classifies more than 1,700 guest houses, farmhouses, inns and restaurants with rooms for its Guest Accommodation Scheme, under common quality standards agreed between the AA, VisitBritain, VisitScotland and VisitWales. AA recognised establishments pay an annual fee according to the classification and the number of bedrooms. The classification is not transferable if an establishment changes hands.

The AA presents several awards within the Guest Accommodation Scheme, including the **AA Friendliest B&B of the Year**, which showcases the very finest hospitality in the country; **AA Guest Accommodation of the Year Awards**, presented to establishments in England, Scotland, Wales, and Northern Ireland, **AA Unique B&B of the Year**, and **AA Restaurant with Rooms of the Year**. See pages 12-15 for this year's winners.

Stars

AA Stars classify guest accommodation at five levels of quality, from one at the simplest, to five offering the highest quality. In order to achieve a one-Star rating an establishment must meet certain minimum entry requirements. For example:

- A cooked breakfast or substantial continental option is provided
- The proprietor and/or staff are available for your arrival, departure and at all meal times
- Once registered, guests have access to the establishment at all times unless previously notified
- All areas of operation meet minimum quality requirements for cleanliness, maintenance and hospitality as well as facilities and the delivery of services
- A dining room or similar eating area is available unless meals are served in bedrooms

To obtain a higher Star rating, an establishment must provide increased quality standards across all areas, with particular emphasis in four key areas:

- Cleanliness and housekeeping
- Hospitality and service
- Quality and condition of bedrooms, bathrooms and public rooms
- Food quality

There are also particular requirements in order for an establishment to achieve three, four or five Stars, for example:

Three Stars and above

- access to both sides of all beds for double occupancy
- bathrooms/shower rooms cannot be used by the proprietor
- there is a washbasin in every guest bedroom (either in the bedrooms or the en suite/private facility)

Four Stars

- half of bedrooms must be en suite or have private facilities

Five Stars

- all bedrooms must be en suite or have private facilities

Establishments applying for AA recognition are visited by one of the AA's qualified accommodation inspectors as a mystery guest. Inspections are a thorough test of the accommodation, food, and hospitality. The inspector completes a full report, resulting in a recommendation for the appropriate Star rating. After this first visit, the establishment will receive a regular visit to check that standards are maintained. If the property changes hands, the new owners must re-apply for classification, as standards can change.

Guests can expect to find the following minimum standards at all levels:

- Pleasant and helpful welcome and service, and sound standards of housekeeping and maintenance
- Comfortable accommodation equipped to modern standards
- Bedding and towels changed for each new guest, and at least weekly if the room is taken for a long stay
- Adequate storage, heating, lighting and comfortable seating
- A sufficient hot water supply at reasonable times
- A full cooked breakfast. (If this is not provided, the fact must be advertised and a substantial continental breakfast must be offered.)

When an AA inspector has visited a property, and evaluated all the aspects of the accommodation for comfort, facilities, attention to detail and presentation, you can be confident the Star rating will help you make the right choice.

★ Gold Star Award

AA Gold Stars are awarded to the very best Guest Accommodation within the three, four, or five Star ratings.

★ Silver Star Award

Guest Accommodation with Silver Stars offer a superior level of quality within their Star rating, high standards of hospitality, service and cleanliness.

Accommodation Designators

Along with the Star ratings, six designators have been introduced. The proprietors, in discussion with our inspectors, choose which designator best describes their establishment:

Bed & Breakfast

A private house run by the owner with accommodation for no more than six paying guests.

Guest House

Run on a more commercial basis than a B&B, the accommodation provides for more than six paying guests and there are usually more services; for example staff as well as the owner may provide dinner.

Farmhouse

The B&B or guest house accommodation is part of a working farm or smallholding.

Inn

The accommodation is provided in a fully licensed establishment. The bar will be open to non-residents and can provide food in the evenings.

Restaurant with Rooms

This is a destination restaurant offering overnight accommodation, with dining being the main business, and open to non-residents. The restaurant should offer a high standard of food and restaurant service at least five nights a week. A liquor licence is necessary and there is a maximum of 12 bedrooms.

Guest Accommodation

Any establishment that meets the minimum entry requirements is eligible for this general category.

U Unclassified entries

A small number of establishments in this guide have this symbol because their Star classification was not confirmed at the time of going to press. This may be due to a change of ownership or because the establishment has only recently joined the AA rating scheme. For up-to-date information on these and other new establishments visit:
www.theAA.com/bed-and-breakfasts

A Associate entries

These establishments have been inspected and rated by VisitBritain, VisitScotland or VisitWales, and have joined the AA scheme on a marketing-only basis.

AA Advertised

These establishments are not rated or inspected by the AA, but are displayed for advertising purposes only.

Useful information

What follows is a selection of things we think it is worth bearing in mind when planning a stay. We hope you'll find them useful.

Arriving at the accommodation

There may be restricted access to some establishments, particularly in the late morning and the afternoon, so do check when booking.

Booking

Book as early as possible, particularly for the peak holiday period (early June to the end of September) and for Easter and other public holidays. In some parts of Scotland the skiing season is also a peak holiday period.

Some establishments only accept weekly bookings from Saturday, and some require a deposit on booking.

A very small number of establishments may not accept credit cards. If you plan on paying this way, then check when booking.

Prices

Minimum prices are shown for one (S) and two people (D) per night and include a full breakfast. If dinner is also included this is indicated in brackets (incl dinner). Where prices are for the room only, this is indicated.

Prices in the guide include VAT (and service where applicable), except the Channel Islands where VAT does not apply.

Where proprietors have been unable to provide us with their 2019 charges we publish the 2018 price as a rough guide (shown by an asterisk *). Where no prices are given, please make enquiries direct.

London prices

London prices tend to be higher than outside the capital, and normally only bed and breakfast is provided, although some establishments do provide a full meal service.

Cancellation

If you have to cancel a booking, let the proprietor know at once. If the room cannot be re-let you may be held legally responsible for partial payment; you could lose your deposit or be liable for compensation, so consider taking out cancellation insurance.

Food and drink

Some guest accommodation provides evening meals, ranging from a set meal to a full menu. Some even have their own restaurant. You may have to arrange dinner in advance, at breakfast or on the previous day, so do ask when booking.

Food allergies

From December 2014 an EU regulation came into force making it easier for those with food allergies to make safer food choices when eating out. There are 14 allergens listed in the regulation, and pubs and restaurants are required to list any of these that are used in the dishes they offer. These may be highlighted on the menus or customers can ask staff for full information. Remember, if you are allergic to a food and are in any doubt speak to a member of staff. For further information see:
www.food.gov.uk/safety-hygiene/allergy-and-intolerance

Dogs

Although many establishments allow dogs, they may be excluded from some areas of the accommodation and some breeds, particularly those requiring an exceptional license, may not be accepted at all. Under the Equality Act 2010, access should be allowed to guide dogs and assistance dogs. Please check the establishment's policy when making your booking.

If you book on bed, breakfast and evening meal terms, you may find that the tariff includes only the set menu. If there is a carte you may be able to order from this and pay a supplement.

On Sundays, many establishments serve the main meal at midday, and provide only a cold supper in the evening. In some parts of Britain, particularly in Scotland, high tea (i.e. a savoury dish followed by bread and butter, scones and cakes) is sometimes served instead of, or as an alternative to, dinner.

Farmhouses: Sometimes the land has been sold and only the house remains, but many are working farms and some farmers are happy to allow visitors to look around, or even to help feed the animals. However, you should always exercise care and never leave children unsupervised. Although the directory entry states the acreage and the type of farming, do check when booking to make sure that it matches your expectations. The farmhouses are listed under towns or villages, but do ask for directions when booking.

Inns: Traditional inns often have a cosy bar, convivial atmosphere, good beer and hearty pub food. Those listed in the guide will provide breakfast in a suitable room, and should also serve light meals during licensing hours. The character of the properties vary according to whether they are country inns or town establishments. Check before you book, including arrival times as these may be restricted to licensed opening hours. When it comes to coaches, Inns have well-defined legal obligations towards travellers; in the event of a query the customer should contact the proprietor or local licensing authority.

Facilities for disabled guests

The Equality Act 2010 details the legal rights of disabled people, including access to goods, services and facilities, and means that service providers may have to consider making adjustments to their premises. For more information about the Act see www.gov.uk/definition-of-disability-under-equality-act-2010 or www.gov.uk/government/policies/creating-a-fairer-and-more-equal-society

Under the Equality Act 2010, access should be allowed to guide dogs and assistance dogs. Please check the establishment's policy when making your booking.

We recommend that you always phone in advance to ensure that the establishment you have chosen has appropriate facilities. The establishments in this guide should be aware of their obligations under the Act.

Please note: AA inspectors are not accredited to make inspections under the National Accessibility Scheme. We indicate in entries if an establishment has ground floor rooms; and if a B&B tells us they have disabled facilities this may be included in the description.

AA Rosette Awards

The AA awards Rosettes to over 2,000 restaurants that we regard as the best in the UK and Ireland

◉

Excellent local restaurants serving food prepared with care, understanding and skill, using good quality ingredients.

◉◉

The best local restaurants, which aim for and achieve higher standards and better consistency, and where a greater precision is apparent in the cooking. There will be obvious attention to the selection of quality ingredients.

◉◉◉

Outstanding restaurants that demand recognition well beyond their local area.

◉◉◉◉

Among the very best restaurants in the British Isles, where the cooking demands national recognition.

◉◉◉◉◉

The finest restaurants in the British Isles, where the cooking compares with the best in the world.

AA Bed &Breakfast Awards 2018–19

Each year the AA celebrates the best that our Guest Accommodation Scheme has to offer. Our inspectors nominate those places that they feel to be a cut above the rest, and award winners are chosen. This year's awards recognised and rewarded almost 30 very deserving finalists.

THE FINALISTS

Friendliest B&B runners up

The Oasis, Llandudno, Conwy

The Ship Inn, Hesleden,
County Durham

Friendliest B&B finalists

Angel House B&B, Ludlow,
Shropshire

Bella Vista, Eastbourne, East
Sussex

Black Swan Inn, Pickering,
North Yorkshire

Bonnington Guest House,
Edinburgh

Bryn Derwen, Llandudno,
Conwy

Duke of York Inn, Cowes, Isle
of Wight

The Hideaway at Windermere,
Windermere, Cumbria

Lea House, Ross-on-Wye,
Herefordshire

The Leicester, Southport,
Merseyside

Newsham Grange, Thirsk,
North Yorkshire

The Old Presbytery Guest
House, Tadcaster, North
Yorkshire

The Park B&B, Weston-Super-
Mare, Somerset

Pricketts Place, Bolstone,
Herefordshire

Sherwood Guest House, Bath,
Somerset

Trecarne House, Liskeard,
Cornwall

Whashton Springs Farm,
Richmond, North Yorkshire

Waltons Guest House, Bath,
Somerset

Unique B&B runners up

The Old Railway Station,
Petworth, West Sussex

Slebech Park, Haverfordwest,
Pembrokeshire

**Restaurant with Rooms
runners up**

The Dog and Badger,
Medmenham,
Buckinghamshire

Windlestraw, Walkerburn,
Scottish Borders

FRIENDLIEST B&B OF THE YEAR

THE TEMPLE BAR INN ★★★★ ◎◎ ♀

EWYAS HARROLD, HEREFORDSHIRE, PAGE 138

Painstakingly restored, this handsome building was first licensed in the 1850s, but it has also served as a court house, a corn exchange, a school room and a stable. Today, it is very much the hub of the village community. The three smart bedrooms are well equipped for the modern guest – each has a TV, free WiFi and tea- and coffee-making facilities – and are complemented by stylish en suite bathrooms. There is a bustling bar area with oak beams, flagstone floors, comfy leather armchairs and a welcoming fire lit on cooler days; it is all too easy to linger a while with a pint of a local cider or ale. What was once the stable is now their 30-seater restaurant where the award-winning, weekly-changing menus offer quality, seasonal dishes based on local-sourced ingredients. As the inn is just a few miles from the Welsh border, it proves a popular pit-stop for walkers and cyclists who are exploring the Herefordshire Trail and glorious Black Mountains.

UNIQUE B&B OF THE YEAR

THE 25 BOUTIQUE B&B ★★★★★ ℮
TORQUAY, DEVON, PAGE 97

Andy and Julian have worked hard to transform this establishment from the relatively mainstream to the exceptional, and they continue to work tirelessly to create a unique guest experience. Their attention to detail is exacting, exemplified by the colour-matched Nespresso machines in the bedrooms – such touches are sure to make guests feel appreciated. The bedrooms have great personality and individuality and the smart, sparkling bathrooms certainly don't disappoint either. Quirky, flamoyant touches, like the zebra with sunglasses, are used judiciously to guarantee a smile, but they are never at the expense of comfort, ease of use or practicality. With Andy and Julian's great eye for design and lighting, guests experience a real sense of anticipation from the moment they step through the front door. It's worth noting that this B&B has had a real impact on the overall standards of other accommodation providers in Torquay – where they lead, others are following.

GUEST ACCOMMODATION OF THE YEAR FOR ENGLAND

THE OLD TOWN HALL ★★★★★ ℮
LEYBURN, NORTH YORKSHIRE, PAGE 283

Located in the heart of the Yorkshire Dales in the picture-postcard Wensleydale countryside, Louise and David Clarke offer their guests warm and genuine hospitality. In the cooler months, inviting open fires add to the charm and character of the property, but it is the luxury of the three individually designed bedrooms, with their lofty wooden ceilings, that proves nothing has been overlooked when it comes to providing their guests with a truly memorable experience. The large rooms have sumptuous beds with top quality linen, duck feather and down duvets, well-stocked hospitality trays, silent fridges, Temple Spa toiletries and oversized fluffy towels – these are just a few of the highlights. A stay is further enhanced by the home baking and the award-winning breakfasts where the extensive choices are based on locally-sourced, quality produce. Afternoon tea is served in the guests' lounge on arrival, with David's never-ending supply of tempting bakes ready to be sampled – guests are advised to arrive at The Old Town Hall feeling hungry.

AA Bed & Breakfast Awards 2018–19

GUEST ACCOMMODATION OF THE YEAR FOR SCOTLAND

CRUICKSHANKS BOUTIQUE B&B ★★★★★ 🏅
WHITING BAY, ISLE OF ARRAN, PAGE 320

First-time B&B owners Rob and Nanette took two years to restore their 19th-century home, overlooking Whiting Bay, to create luxury guest accommodation. They retained many of the original features while cleverly making the best use of the space available. The en suite bedrooms – Honeysuckle, The Whimsical Room and the Pearl Suite – have been appointed to a very high standard; each bed has a Hypnos mattress, Egyptian cotton bedding and a hypoallergenic duvet to ensure a comfortable night's sleep. There's WiFi, a smart TV, DAB clock radio with Bluetooth and beverage-making facilities too. As you would expect, great care and thought has gone into the breakfasts – Nanette's home-made muesli can be followed by a full Scottish breakfast, smoked haddock or pancakes with maple syrup and bacon. Guests are greeted on arrival with refreshments and home-baked cakes and before long they feel right at home beside the roaring wood-burning stove. The warm hospitality at this lovely B&B always shines whatever the Scottish weather has in store.

GUEST ACCOMMODATION OF THE YEAR FOR WALES

RHEDYN GUEST HOUSE ★★★★ 🏅 🍽
BULITH WELLS, POWYS, PAGE 346

Once a forester's cottage, this charming place dates back to the 1800s and offers a peaceful and relaxing home away from home on the edge of the beautiful Brecon Beacons National Park. The three bedrooms are deeply comfortable and individually designed, each is a successful blend of traditional and contemporary features – two are on the ground floor and have their own entrances. Owner, Muiread has had great fun furnishing the rooms, sourcing some quirky items such as the rhino wall lamps; returning guests will find that on each visit something will have changed. While there is a plethora of great things to do on the doorstep here, you'll find it hard to drag yourself away from Muiread and Ciaran's engaging hospitality – guests are treated like old friends. The food is also noteworthy – much of the produce is grown in the kitchen garden or sourced from local producers. Muiread creates the menus daily to showcase the best seasonal produce, so providing a truly memorable dining experience.

GUEST ACCOMMODATION OF
THE YEAR FOR NORTHERN IRELAND

CAUSEWAY LODGE ★★★★★ ☺
BUSHMILLS, COUNTY ANTRIM, PAGE 356

Causeway Lodge keeps going from strength to strength and owners Anne and Lyle Taggart continue to add more services and facilities for guests to enjoy whilst staying on the Antrim coast. There's a lot of interesting things to do in the area, and the lodge is located close to Bushmills Distillery and within easy reach of the National Trust's Giant's Causeway and Carrick-A-Rede Rope Bridge. Inside, every attempt has been made to anticipate the guests' needs – for instance, local and tourist information is readily provided in the lobby and atrium area. The purpose-built Wellness Centre is available to all guests and now boasts an outside hot tub, along with a shower area and gym. The stylish bedrooms are spacious and well-appointed – the beds are deeply comfortable and will ensure a wonderful night's sleep. Free WiFi, digital Freeview TVs, desks, dressing gowns and slippers come as standard. The world famous Irish hospitality will be evident from the minute you arrive until it is, sadly, time to leave.

RESTAURANT WITH ROOMS
OF THE YEAR

LONG MELFORD SWAN ★★★★★ ⊚⊚
LONG MELFORD, SUFFOLK, PAGE 238

This charming, family-run property, in the delightful Suffolk village of Long Melford, offers excellent, attentive service and warm hospitality. The village is situated close to the Essex border about 16 miles from Colchester and 14 miles from Bury St Edmunds. The Swan has been tastefully renovated throughout yet retains a wealth of charm and character including oak beams and original panelling. The business encompasses two properties – to the front of one is the Duck Deli with its array of high quality, artisan East Anglian produce and the provision of takeaway coffee, sandwiches and salads. To the rear is the welcoming bar, dining areas and outside terrace. In the adjoining building are seven oh-so-stylish en suite bedrooms with Hypnos beds, Egyptian cotton bed linen, walk-in showers, Noble Isle toiletries, fluffy towels and free WiFi to name but a few of their luxury facilities. Food is, of course, a major draw here – the ever-changing menus reveal confident cooking in dishes that offer innovative combinations created from tip-top ingredients.

AA B&B Story of the Year 2018–19

Sponsored by eviivo

Entrants for the AA B&B Story of the Year, told us about their journey to becoming the establishment that they are today. We chose the one we liked the best.

FOSSE FARMHOUSE B&B ★★★★ 🛏
CASTLE COMBE, WILTSHIRE, PAGE 266

Curiouser and Curiouser

How did a silver four-star AA B&B with just two guest bedrooms in the tiny village of Nettleton Shrub become the setting for the most famous anime (animated cartoon) on Japanese TV?

It all began in 1989 when the owner, Caron Cooper, met Japanese couple Shozo and Yasuko Mitani while selling antiques on London's Portobello Road. The Mitani's wanted to create an English-themed B&B in Japan, so Caron being naturally inquisitive invited them to tea the following day at her farmhouse B&B to find out why.

On arrival at the 200-year-old antique filled farmhouse deep in the Wiltshire countryside, they were both laughing uncontrollably. Caron enquired as to what was so funny and Shozo then replied that getting there was "just like falling through a tunnel in *Alice in Wonderland*". They enjoyed Caron's home baked scones delivered straight from the Aga and drank tea sitting under the cherry tree blossom in the garden.

Back in Japan, the Mitani's displayed photographs of Fosse Farmhouse in the reception of their own English themed B&B 'Tenkisu' in Hakuba – and the floodgates opened.

The editor of a popular Japanese ladies magazine *LEE* visited the Mitani's B&B and enquired if they could introduce her to Caron. They were more than happy to do so and the following month *LEE's* editorial team arrived in the UK to interview her. The glossy six-page feature was published in 1990 with circulation figures of 300,000, creating a huge amount of interest from Japanese office ladies requesting to stay at Caron's pretty B&B.

Then in 1992 Caron won an award for 'Best Tourist Accommodation' chosen by Japanese visitors as part of the 'Britain Welcomes Japan' campaign.

Next, the British Embassy in Japan invited her to bake scones for the Japanese Imperial family in Tokyo and in turn they came to stay at Fosse Farmhouse on a private visit in 1994.

Since then, Caron regularly visits Japan to host cream tea parties and discuss her busy B&B life in England.

Then, in 2012 a popular manga comic book *Kiniro-Mosaic* also known as *Kinmoza* was published in Japan. Based entirely upon Caron's life at Fosse Farmhouse, the story revolves around the main character, a teenage girl called Alice who lives there.

Genco animation approached Caron to film the TV series *KINMOZA!* at Fosse Farmhouse. The film footage was then converted into anime by studio artists and the series aired on Japanese TV in 2014 and 2015 reaching 5.5 million viewers on TV and DVD. In 2016, a movie of the TV series was released in Japan entitled *Pretty Days*. Caron was invited to the film premier in Tokyo and joined the red carpet guests with hundreds of fans queuing for her autograph.

Now anime fans worldwide head for Fosse Farmhouse to stay in the B&B bedrooms featured in the film.

Caron says 'My story is unbelievable but true and just like *Alice in Wonderland*, it's getting curiouser and curiouser.'
The End

★★★★★ The Premier Collection

ENGLAND

BERKSHIRE

HURLEY
Hurley House
The Olde Bell Inn

BRISTOL

BRISTOL
Berwick Lodge

BUCKINGHAMSHIRE

BEACONSFIELD
Crazy Bear Beaconsfield

BRILL
The Pointer

MEDMENHAM
The Dog and Badger

CAMBRIDGESHIRE

BARTLOW
The Three Hills

ELTON
The Crown Inn

CHESHIRE

BURWARDSLEY
The Pheasant Inn

CHESTER
Mitchell's of Chester
Stone Villa Chester

WARMINGHAM
The Bear's Paw

CORNWALL & ISLES OF SCILLY

BUDE
Pot and Barrel B&B

FALMOUTH
Anacapri

LAUNCESTON
Wheatley Farm

LOOE
The Beach House

LOSTWITHIEL
The Old Chapel B&B

MEVAGISSEY
Pebble House
Portmellon Cove Guest House

PADSTOW
Padstow Townhouse
St Petroc's Bistro
The Seafood Restaurant

PENZANCE
Camilla House

PERRANUTHNOE
Ednovean Farm

POLPERRO
Trenderway Farm

PORT GAVERNE
Port Gaverne

ST AUSTELL
Anchorage House

ST IVES
Downsfield Bed and Breakfast
The Gannet Inn
27 The Terrace

ST MELLION
Pentillie Castle & Estate

WADEBRIDGE
Wadebridge Bed and Breakfast

CUMBRIA

AMBLESIDE
Nanny Brow

ASKHAM
Askham Hall

BORROWDALE
Hazel Bank Country House

BROUGH
The Inn at Brough

CARTMEL
L'Enclume

CROSTHWAITE
The Punchbowl Inn
  at Crosthwaite

GLENRIDDING
Glenridding House

GRASMERE
Moss Grove Organic

KIRKBY LONSDALE
Plato's
The Sun Inn

LUPTON
Plough Inn

NEAR SAWREY
Ees Wyke Country House

NEWBY BRIDGE
The Knoll Country House

PENRITH
Brooklands Guest House
River Garth

WINDERMERE
Applegarth Villa & Restaurant
Hillthwaite
The Howbeck
Lindeth Fell Country House

Wheatlands Lodge
The Wild Boar Inn, Grill &
  Smokehouse

DERBYSHIRE

BELPER
Bridge Hill House
Dannah Farm Country House

BRADWELL
The Samuel Fox Country Inn

HOPE
Underleigh House

DEVON

AXMINSTER
Kerrington House

BRATTON FLEMING
Bracken House

CHILLATON
Tor Cottage

CULLOMPTON
Muddifords Court Country House

DARTMOUTH
Mounthaven
Strete Barton House

ERMINGTON
Plantation House

LYNMOUTH
The Heatherville

LYNTON
Highcliffe House

NEWTON ABBOT
Bulleigh Barton Manor

SIDMOUTH
The Salty Monk

TEDBURN ST MARY
Frogmill Bed & Breakfast

TIVERTON
Fernside Bed and Breakfast

TORQUAY
The Albaston
Babbacombe Bay
Cary Arms & Spa
Kingston House
Linden House
The Marstan
The 25 Boutique B&B
Tyndale B&B

TOTNES
Stoke Gabriel Lodgings -
   Badgers Retreat

DORSET

BROADWINDSOR
The Old George

CHRISTCHURCH
The Lord Bute & Restaurant

CRANBORNE
10 Castle Street

DORCHESTER
Little Court

SHERBORNE
The Kings Arms
The Rose and Crown Inn, Trent

SWANAGE
Swanage Haven Boutique B&B
2@2 Rabling Road

WIMBORNE MINSTER
Les Bouviers Restaurant
   with Rooms

ESSEX

DEDHAM
The Sun Inn

GREAT YELDHAM
The White Hart

WIX
Dairy House Farm

GLOUCESTERSHIRE

BARNSLEY
The Village Pub

CHELTENHAM
The Battledown Bed and
   Breakfast
The Bradley

CIRENCESTER
The Fleece at Cirencester

LOWER SLAUGHTER
The Slaughters Country Inn

STOW-ON-THE-WOLD
Old Stocks Inn
The Porch House

HAMPSHIRE

BARTON-ON-SEA
Pebble Beach

SOUTHAMPTON
Ennio's Restaurant
   & Boutique Rooms
THE PIG in the Wall

WINCHESTER
Giffard House

HEREFORDSHIRE

BOLSTONE
Prickett's Place

LEINTWARDINE
The Lion

LEOMINSTER
Hills Farm

ROSS-ON-WYE
Wilton Court Restaurant
   with Rooms

HERTFORDSHIRE

WELWYN
The Wellington

ISLE OF WIGHT

SHANKLIN
Haven Hall

VENTNOR
The Hambrough
The Leconfield

KENT

DEAL
Sutherland House

DOVER
The Marquis at Alkham

EGERTON
Frasers

GRAFTY GREEN
Who'd A Thought It

MAIDSTONE
Maiden's Tower at Leeds Castle

MARDEN
Merzie Meadows

TUNBRIDGE WELLS (ROYAL)
Danehurst House

WOODCHURCH
Brook Farm Bed & Breakfast

LANCASHIRE

BLACKBURN
The Millstone at Mellor

BURNLEY
Crow Wood

CLITHEROE
The Assheton Arms

COWAN BRIDGE
Hipping Hall

GREAT ECCLESTON
The Cartford Inn

ORMSKIRK
Moor Hall Restaurant
   with Rooms

LINCOLNSHIRE

HEMSWELL
Hemswell Court

HORNCASTLE
Magpies Restaurant with Rooms

HOUGH-ON-THE-HILL
The Brownlow Arms

MARKET RASEN
The Advocate Arms

STAMFORD
Meadow View

WINTERINGHAM
Winteringham Fields

LONDON POSTAL DISTRICTS

LONDON SW1
Georgian House

LONDON SW3
San Domenico House
Sydney House Chelsea

LONDON SW7
The Exhibitionist

LONDON W1
The Marble Arch by Montcalm
The Piccadilly London West End

LONDON W2
Park Grand London
  Lancaster Gate

NORFOLK

CLEY NEXT THE SEA
Old Town Hall House

HUNSTANTON
The Neptune Restaurant
  with Rooms

NORWICH
Brasteds
38 St Giles

SHERINGHAM
The Eiders Bed & Breakfast

THORPE MARKET
The Green House B&B

NORTHUMBERLAND

BELFORD
Market Cross Guest House

BERWICK-UPON-TWEED
The Captain's Quarters

STOCKSFIELD
The Duke of Wellington Inn

NOTTINGHAMSHIRE

ELTON
The Grange

NOTTINGHAM
Restaurant Sat Bains
  with Rooms

RETFORD
Blacksmiths

OXFORDSHIRE

ABINGDON-ON-THAMES
B&B Rafters

FARINGDON
Buscot Manor B&B

KINGHAM
The Wild Rabbit

OXFORD
Burlington House

SOUTH LEIGH
Artist Residence Oxfordshire

STADHAMPTON
The Crazy Bear

WITNEY
Old Swan & Minster Mill

WOODSTOCK
The Glove House

SHROPSHIRE

LUDLOW
The Charlton Arms
The Clive Bar & Restaurant
  with Rooms
Old Downton Lodge

MARKET DRAYTON
Ternhill Farm House

SHREWSBURY
Darwin's Townhouse

SOMERSET

AXBRIDGE
The Oak House

BACKWELL
The Rising Sun

BATH
Apple Tree Guest House
Apsley House
Chestnuts House
Dorian House
Haringtons

River House and Friary
  Coach House
Tasburgh House
Waterhouse
The Windsor Townhouse

CHEW MAGNA
The Bear & Swan

CORTON DENHAM
The Queens Arms

FIVEHEAD
Langford Fivehead

FLAX BOURTON
Blackwell House

FROME
Lullington House

HATCH BEAUCHAMP
Frog Street Farmhouse

HOLCOMBE
The Holcombe Inn

NORTH WOOTON
Crossways Inn

SOMERTON
Cartways Bed and Breakfast

WESTON-SUPER-MARE
Church House
The Park B&B

WITHYPOOL
Kings Farm

YEOVIL
Little Barwick House

SUFFOLK

BURY ST EDMUNDS
The Northgate

ELVEDEN
The Elveden Inn

LONG MELFORD
Long Melford Swan

MILDENHALL
The Bull Inn

NEWMARKET
The Packhorse Inn

ORFORD
The Crown & Castle

SOUTHWOLD
Sutherland House

STOKE-BY-NAYLAND
The Angel Inn

SUDBURY
The Black Lion

THORNHAM MAGNA
Thornham Hall

YAXLEY
The Auberge

SURREY

CHIDDINGFOLD
The Crown Inn

SUSSEX, EAST

BOREHAM STREET
Boreham House

DITCHLING
The Bull

EASTBOURNE
Ocklynge Manor

HASTINGS & ST LEONARDS
The Cloudesley
Stream House

LEWES
Broadacres

NORTHIAM
Knelle Dower B&B

RYE
Jeake's House
Manor Farm Oast

SUSSEX, WEST

CHICHESTER
Rooks Hill
The Royal Oak

CHILGROVE
The White Horse

LODSWORTH
The Halfway Bridge Inn

SIDLESHAM
The Crab & Lobster

WARWICKSHIRE

ILMINGTON
The Howard Arms

STRATFORD-UPON-AVON
Arden House

WEST MIDLANDS

SOLIHULL
Hampton Manor

WILTSHIRE

BOX
The Northey Arms

BURTON
The Old House at Home

CORSHAM
The Methuen Arms

DEVIZES
The Peppermill

EDINGTON
The Three Daggers

PEWSEY
Troutbeck Guest House
  at the Red Lion Freehouse

WORCESTERSHIRE

ABBERLEY
The Manor Arms

BEWDLEY
Kateshill House

BROADWAY
Abbots Grange
Russell's

**YORKSHIRE,
EAST RIDING OF**

BEVERLEY
Newbegin House

BRIDLINGTON
Marton Grange

SOUTH DALTON
The Pipe and Glass

YORKSHIRE, NORTH

AMPLEFORTH
Shallowdale House

ASENBY
Crab Manor

AUSTWICK
The Traddock

BAINBRIDGE
Yorebridge House

CLAPHAM
The New Inn

CRAYKE
The Durham Ox

FILEY
All Seasons Guesthouse

GOLDSBOROUGH
Goldsborough Hall

GRASSINGTON
Grassington House

HARROGATE
The Grafton Boutique B&B

HETTON
The Angel Inn

KIRKBY FLEETHAM
Black Horse Inn

KNARESBOROUGH
General Tarleton Inn

LEEMING BAR
Little Holtby

LEYBURN
Braithwaite Hall
The Old Town Hall

MIDDLEHAM
The Saddle Room

MIDDLETON TYAS
The Coach House

NORTHALLERTON
Woodlands Farm

OLDSTEAD
The Black Swan at Oldstead

OSMOTHERLEY
The Cleveland Tontine

PICKERING
17 Burgate

RIPON
Mallard Grange
The Old Coach House

SCARBOROUGH
The Plough Scalby

TIMBLE
The Timble Inn

WEST WITTON
The Wensleydale Heifer

YORK
The Judge's Lodging

YORKSHIRE, WEST

HUDDERSFIELD
315 Bar and Restaurant

KIRKBURTON
Woodman Inn

CHANNEL ISLANDS

JERSEY

ST AUBIN
The Panorama

SCOTLAND

ABERDEENSHIRE

ELLON
Aikenshill House

ANGUS

INVERKEILOR
Gordon's

ARGYLL & BUTE

BARCALDINE
Ardtorna

LOCHGOILHEAD
The Lodge on Loch Goil

OBAN
Blarcreen House

DUMFRIES & GALLOWAY

PORTPATRICK
Knockinaam Lodge

EDINBURGH

EDINBURGH
Kew House
21212
The Witchery by the Castle

FALKIRK

BANKNOCK
Glenskirlie House & Castle

FIFE

PEAT INN
The Peat Inn

HIGHLAND

BRACHLA
Loch Ness Lodge

CROMARTY
The Factor's House

DORNOCH
Links House at Royal Dornoch
2 Quail

GRANTOWN-ON-SPEY
The Dulaig

INVERNESS
Achnagairn Estate
Daviot Lodge
Trafford Bank

POOLEWE
Pool House

LOTHIAN, WEST

LINLITHGOW
Arden Country House

PERTH & KINROSS

ALYTH
Tigh Na Leigh Guesthouse

SCOTTISH BORDERS

MELROSE
Fauhope Country House

PEEBLES
Kingsmuir House

WALKERBURN
Windlestraw

STIRLING

STIRLING
Victoria Square Guest House

SCOTTISH ISLANDS

ARRAN, ISLE OF

WHITING BAY
Cruickshanks Boutique B&B

ISLAY, ISLE OF

GLENEGEDALE
Glenegedale House

SKYE, ISLE OF

STRUAN
Ullinish Country Lodge

WALES

ANGLESEY, ISLE OF

BEAUMARIS
The Bull - Beaumaris

CARMARTHENSHIRE

LLANARTHNE
Llwyn Helyg Country House

ST CLEARS
Coedllys Country House

CEREDIGION

ABERAERON
Feathers Royal

CARDIGAN
Caemorgan Mansion

EGLWYS FACH
Ynyshir

CONWY

ABERGELE
The Kinmel Arms

BETWS-Y-COED
Penmachno Hall

CONWY
The Groes Inn
Sychnant Pass Country House

LLANDUDNO
Bryn Derwen

RHOS-ON-SEA
Plas Rhos

TAL-Y-CAFN
Bodnant Welsh Food Centre

TREFRIW
Yr Hafod Country House

DENBIGHSHIRE

LLANDYRNOG
Pentre Mawr Country House

RUTHIN
Firgrove Country House B&B

ST ASAPH
Tan-Yr-Onnen Guest House

GWYNEDD

ABERDYFI
Penhelig Arms

CAERNARFON
Plas Dinas Country House

DOLGELLAU
Tyddynmawr Farmhouse

PWLLHELI
The Old Rectory

MONMOUTHSHIRE

USK
Newbridge on Usk

WHITEBROOK
The Whitebrook

PEMBROKESHIRE

EGLWYSWRW
Ael y Bryn

FISHGUARD
Erw-Lon Farm

HAVERFORDWEST
Roch Castle
Slebech Park Estate

ST DAVIDS
Penrhiw
Ramsey House

SOLVA
Crug Glas Country House

TENBY
Trefloyne Manor

POWYS

BRECON
Peterstone Court

★★★★★ The Premier Collection *continued*

MONTGOMERY
The Nags Head Inn

VALE OF GLAMORGAN

HENSOL
Llanerch Vineyard

PENARTH
Restaurant James Sommerin

NORTHERN IRELAND

COUNTY ANTRIM

BUSHMILLS
Causeway Lodge
Whitepark House

REPUBLIC OF IRELAND

COUNTY CLARE

LAHINCH
Moy House

COUNTY CORK

KINSALE
Friar's Lodge

SHANAGARRY
Ballymaloe House

DUBLIN

DUBLIN
Cliff Townhouse
Glenogra Town House
Harrington Hall

COUNTY GALWAY

GALWAY
Screebe House

COUNTY KERRY

DINGLE (AN DAINGEAN)
Castlewood House
Gormans Clifftop House
 & Restaurant

KILLARNEY
Fairview Guest House

KILLORGLIN
Carrig House Country House
 & Restaurant

COUNTY MEATH

SLANE
Tankardstown

COUNTY MONAGHAN

GLASLOUGH
The Castle at Castle
 Leslie Estate

COUNTY TIPPERARY

THURLES
The Castle

COUNTY WEXFORD

GOREY
Clonganny House

WEXFORD
Killiane Castle Country House
 & Farm

AA WALKING GUIDES

The 50 Best Walks of 2–10 Miles by Region and City

- Easy-to-follow directions with clear waypointed maps
- Colour-coded routes – pick from easy strolls through to more challenging walks
- Fascinating background reading for every walk
- Advice for dog owners
- Great for a full day out with recommended sights and attractions plus places to eat and drink

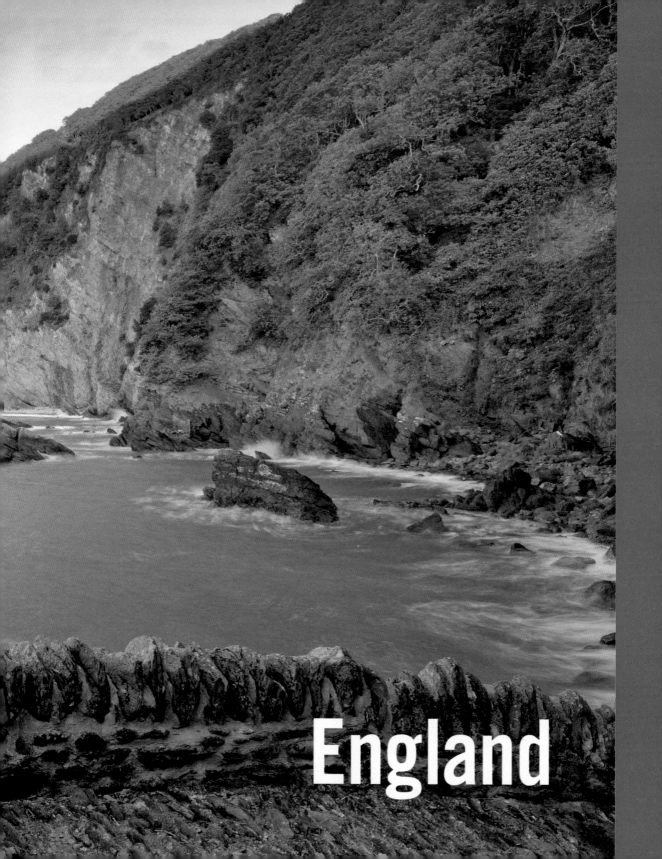

England

BEDFORDSHIRE

HENLOW
Map 12 TL13

The Crown

★★★★ ◉ ⚑ INN

tel: 01462 812433 **2 High Street SG16 6BS**
email: rooms@crownpub.co.uk **web:** www.crownpub.co.uk
dir: On B659 (High Street).

The Crown is situated on the High Street in Henlow with easy access from the A1. It's a traditional pub with a modern feel and an attractive beer garden where guests can relax in the summer. Bedrooms all have plenty of useful features such as smart TV, free WiFi, hair straighteners and Nespresso coffee machines. Guests can enjoy dinner in the restaurant which makes good use made of high quality, seasonal ingredients.

Rooms: 5 annexe en suite (1 fmly) (5 GF) **S** fr £105 **D** fr £105* **Facilities:** STV FTV Lounge tea/coffee Dinner available WiFi **Extras:** Speciality toiletries, mineral water, fresh milk **Parking:** 72 **Notes:** Closed 25–26 December

LEIGHTON BUZZARD
Map 11 SP92

The Heath Inn

★★★ INN

tel: 01525 237816 & 237390 **76 Woburn Road, Heath and Reach LU7 0AR**
email: enquiries@theheathinn.com **web:** www.theheathinn.com

Situated in the quiet village of Heath and Reach, close to Leighton Buzzard, this traditional inn offers comfortable accommodation. Good quality dishes and a range of cask ales are available in both the bar and restaurant.

Rooms: 16 en suite (5 fmly) (8 GF) **S** fr £65 **D** fr £75* **Facilities:** FTV TVL tea/coffee Dinner available WiFi 🚲 **Parking:** 50

BERKSHIRE

BEENHAM
Map 5 SU56

The Six Bells

★★★★ ⬚ INN

tel: 0118 971 3368 **The Green RG7 5NX**
email: info@thesixbells.co.uk **web:** www.thesixbells.co.uk
dir: Exit A4 between Reading and Newbury, follow signs for Beenham.

Not far from Thatcham and Newbury, The Six Bells is a friendly, traditional pub with comfortable, well-appointed bedrooms and good service. The restaurant serves a range of excellent, well-prepared dishes; dinner is recommended.

Rooms: 4 en suite **Facilities:** FTV tea/coffee Dinner available **Conf:** Max 40 Thtr 40 Class 40 Board 25 **Parking:** 20 **Notes:** No children 16 years

CHIEVELEY
Map 5 SU47

Crab & Boar

★★★★ ◉◉ ⚑ RESTAURANT WITH ROOMS

tel: 01635 247550 **Wantage Road RG20 8UE**
email: info@crabandboar.com **web:** www.crabandboar.com
dir: 1.5 miles west of Chieveley on B4494.

Part of The Epicurean Collection pub and inn group, the Crab & Boar has been appointed to a very high standard and bedrooms include a full range of modern amenities. Some ground-floor rooms have a small, private patio area complete with a luxury hot tub. The warm and cosy restaurant offers an extensive and award-winning range of dishes, using the best suppliers in the south. In summer, eating outside on the patio area, with its sweeping countryside views, is a delight.

Rooms: 9 en suite 5 annexe en suite (8 GF) **Facilities:** FTV tea/coffee Dinner available Direct dial WiFi Hot tub suites **Extras:** Home-made biscuits **Conf:** Max 14 Thtr 14 Class 14 Board 14 **Parking:** 80 **Notes:** LB

Ye Olde Red Lion

★★★★ ⬚ INN

tel: 01635 248379 & 07764 579808 **Green Lane RG20 8XB**
email: redlion@toucansurf.com **web:** www.yeolderedlion.com
dir: M4 junction 13 north towards Oxford for 300 yards, onto slip road signed Chieveley. Left at junction, 300 yards on left.

Situated in the quiet village of Chieveley, just five miles north of Newbury, this traditional inn offers comfortable en suite accommodation in the adjoining 15th-century house. The cosy pub offers a good range of real ales, and dinner can be enjoyed in the restaurant where good use is made of local and seasonal produce.

Rooms: 5 annexe en suite (3 GF) **S** fr £88 **D** fr £98 **Facilities:** FTV tea/coffee Dinner available WiFi **Parking:** 30 **Notes:** No children 14 years

EAST GARSTON   Map 5 SU37

Queens Arms
★★★★ INN

tel: 01488 648757 & 649590 **RG17 7ET**
email: info@queensarmseastgarston.co.uk **web:** www.queensarmseastgarston.co.uk
dir: *M4 junction 14 onto A338 to Great Shefford. Turn left signed East Garston and Lambourn. On right.*

The perfect choice for lovers of country pursuits, the Queens Arms is located in the beautiful Lambourn Valley. The individually themed bedrooms are well appointed and offer sumptuous beds, TVs and WiFi. Four-legged guests are welcomed too in both the bar and the rooms. The bar is well stocked, and the restaurant serves good British dishes created from local produce. The Queens Lodge, across the road, is perfect for weddings, private dinners and special occasions. There is ample parking at both venues.

Rooms: 7 en suite 5 annexe en suite (1 fmly) (5 GF) **S** fr £105 **D** fr £105*
Facilities: FTV tea/coffee Dinner available WiFi **Extras:** Speciality toiletries
Conf: Max 100 Thtr 70 Class 50 Board 30 **Parking:** 80

HUNGERFORD   Map 5 SU36

The Pheasant Inn
★★★★ 🍷 INN

tel: 01488 648284 **Ermin Street, Shefford Woodlands RG17 7AA**
email: info@thepheasant-inn.co.uk **web:** www.thepheasant-inn.co.uk
dir: *Phone for directions.*

The Pheasant Inn is located in a quiet spot with vast uninterrupted countryside views yet is easily accessible from the M4. All the bedrooms have been tastefully refurbished with modern decor and high-quality furnishings. Breakfast, lunch and dinner are available daily in the main bar and restaurant.

Rooms: 11 en suite (4 GF) **S** fr £115 **D** fr £135* **Facilities:** FTV tea/coffee Dinner available **Extras:** Bottled water **Parking:** 20

HURLEY   Map 5 SU88

Hurley House
★★★★★ 🌸🌸 🍷 RESTAURANT WITH ROOMS

tel: 01628 568500 **Henley Road SL6 5LH**
email: hello@hurleyhouse.co.uk **web:** www.hurleyhouse.co.uk
dir: *Phone for directions.*

Hurley House is a beautiful restaurant with rooms located in a quiet village. The 10 stunning bedrooms vary in size, but all have air conditioning, underfloor heating, a mini-bar, coffee machine and extremely comfortable king-size beds. The bathrooms are equipped to the same high standard and have luxurious towels and high-quality toiletries. A wood-burning stove, flagstone floors and plenty of comfortable seating of different styles help create a relaxing atmosphere. There is a popular, character bar with a snug and private dining areas. In the restaurant, the menu showcases the finest local produce in modern British dishes. Snacks are also available in the bar and outside areas which are covered and heated. Expect fine ales, beer, spirits and an excellent wine list. WiFi is available throughout, plus there is a treatment room and plenty of convenient parking.

Rooms: 10 en suite **Facilities:** Dinner available WiFi

The Olde Bell Inn
★★★★★ INN

tel: 01628 825881 **High Street SL6 5LX**
email: oldebellreception@coachinginn.co.uk **web:** www.theoldebell.co.uk
dir: *M4 junction 8/9 follow signs for Henley. At roundabout take A4130 to Hurley, turn right to Hurley Village, 800 yards on right.*

Dating in part to 1135, this charming coaching inn has lots of original features, with timber framed buildings and extensive landscaped gardens. Dinner can be enjoyed in the restaurant, and the kitchen uses some of the inn's own home-grown seasonal produce. There is a range of individually-styled bedrooms, each with a modern well-equipped bathroom. Both The Tithe Barn and Malthouse cater for functions and private parties, and there is a range of business facilities.

Rooms: 11 en suite 37 annexe en suite (21 GF) **S** fr £99 **D** fr £129*
Facilities: FTV tea/coffee Dinner available Direct dial WiFi 🌳 ♨ ⚓
⚓ **Conf:** Max 130 Thtr 130 Class 80 Board 52 **Parking:** 80 **Notes:** LB Civ wed 160

KINTBURY   Map 5 SU36

The Dundas Arms
★★★★ 🍴 INN

tel: 01488 658263 **53 Station Road RG17 9UT**
email: info@dundasarms.co.uk **web:** www.dundasarms.co.uk
dir: *A34 onto A4, turn left, signed Kintbury, into Station Road.*

Part of The Epicurean Collection, the inviting Dundas Arms sits right by the Kennet & Avon Canal and food and drinks can be served canalside. The en suite bedrooms are comfortable and well equipped; some have their own private waterside patio areas. Food is a highlight of the stay, with local produce featuring strongly on the menus. There are also extensive garden areas and ample parking.

Rooms: 8 en suite (2 fmly) (5 GF) **Facilities:** FTV Lounge tea/coffee Dinner available Direct dial WiFi Fishing **Conf:** Max 16 **Parking:** 60 **Notes:** LB

NEWBURY   Map 5 SU46

Rookwood Farm House
★★★★ GUEST ACCOMMODATION

tel: 01488 608676 & 07770 435621 **Stockcross RG20 8JX**
email: charlotte@rookwoodhouse.co.uk **web:** www.rookwoodhouse.co.uk
dir: *2 miles west of Newbury, at junction A4 and A34 onto B4000, 0.75 mile to Stockcross, 1st right signed Woodspeen, bear left, 1st on right.*

Rookwood Farm House enjoys wonderful views and is very much a family home. Bedrooms are attractively presented and feature fine pieces of furniture. Breakfast is served at one large table in the kitchen. The coach house has a kitchen and sitting room and, during the summer, visitors can enjoy the beautiful gardens and outdoor pool.

Rooms: 2 rms (1 en suite) (1 pri facs) 2 annexe en suite (1 fmly) **S** fr £80 **D** fr £110* **Facilities:** TVL tea/coffee WiFi 🌳 ♨ ⚓ **Conf:** Max 16 Board 16 **Parking:** 4 **Notes:** Civ wed 200

NEWBURY *continued*

Pilgrims Guest House

★★★★ GUEST ACCOMMODATION

tel: 01635 40694 **Oxford Road RG14 1XB**
email: office@pilgrimsgh.co.uk **web:** www.pilgrimsnewbury.co.uk
dir: *In Newbury exit A4 at Waitrose roundabout onto B4494 towards Wantage, 0.5 mile on left.*

Located close to the town centre, this smartly presented house has comfortable bedrooms with modern bathrooms; some rooms are located in an annexe. WiFi is provided throughout the property and breakfast is served in the bright dining room. Parking is available.

Rooms: 14 rms (10 en suite) (1 pri facs) 5 annexe en suite (2 fmly) (4 GF)
Facilities: FTV Lounge tea/coffee WiFi 🐾 **Parking:** 17 **Notes:** Closed 24 December to 2 January

| READING | Map 5 SU77 |

The French Horn

★★★★ ◎◎ RESTAURANT WITH ROOMS

tel: 0118 969 2204 **Sonning RG4 6TN**
email: info@thefrenchhorn.co.uk **web:** www.thefrenchhorn.co.uk
dir: *From A4 into Sonning, follow B478 through village over bridge, on right, car park on left.*

This long-established Thames-side establishment has a lovely village setting and retains the traditions of classic hospitality. The restaurant is a particular attraction and has been awarded two AA Rosettes. Bedrooms, including four cottage suites, are spacious and comfortable; many offer stunning views over the river. A private boardroom is available for corporate guests.

Rooms: 12 en suite 8 annexe en suite (4 GF) **Facilities:** FTV iPod docking station Lounge tea/coffee Dinner available Direct dial WiFi 🎣 Fishing 🐾 **Extras:** Speciality toiletries, safe, mineral water **Conf:** Max 14 Board 14 **Parking:** 43 **Notes:** Closed 1–2 January RS 25 December evening closed for dinner

| SLOUGH | Map 6 SU97 |

Furnival Lodge

★★★★ 🅰 GUEST HOUSE

tel: 01753 570333 **53–55 Furnival Avenue SL2 1DH**
email: info@furnival-lodge.co.uk **web:** www.furnival-lodge.co.uk
dir: *Just off A355 (Farnham Road), adjacent to BP garage.*

In operation for more than 20 years, Furnival Lodge offers modern and spacious rooms, complete with power showers in the en suite bathrooms. Bedrooms are pleasantly decorated and guests have the use of a comfortable lounge.

Rooms: 10 en suite (1 fmly) (3 GF) **Facilities:** TVL WiFi **Parking:** 7

| THATCHAM | Map 5 SU56 |

The Bunk Inn

★★★★ ◎◎ INN

tel: 01635 200400 **Curridge RG18 9DS**
email: info@thebunkinn.co.uk **web:** www.thebunkinn.co.uk
dir: *Phone for directions.*

The Bunk Inn is a quintessential English pub set in the pretty village of Curridge, close to Newbury Racecourse. The en suite bedrooms have plenty of character and offer impressive quality and comfort. Great beers and ales are served in peak condition in the characterful bar and great food is served, both at breakfast and at dinner, which has achieved two AA Rosettes. Private parties can be accommodated and there is plenty of parking.

Rooms: 9 en suite **Facilities:** tea/coffee Dinner available WiFi **Extras:** Speciality toiletries

| WINDSOR | Map 6 SU97 |

Rainworth House

★★★★ GUEST ACCOMMODATION

tel: 01753 856749 **Oakley Green Road SL4 5UL**
email: info@rainworthhouse.com **web:** www.rainworthhouse.com
dir: *Off A308 (Windsor to Maidenhead road). Take 1st left into Oakley Green Road.*

In well-kept grounds near Windsor, this smart property has six individually-styled bedrooms. The richly decorated rooms are well equipped and are ideal for both business and leisure guests. Public areas include a comfortable lounge, and the dining area is a sociable setting for breakfast. Parking is available.

Rooms: 6 rms (5 en suite) (1 pri facs) (2 fmly) **S** fr £70 **D** fr £98 **Facilities:** FTV Lounge tea/coffee Direct dial WiFi 🐾 **Parking:** 10

76 Duke Street B&B

★★★★ BED AND BREAKFAST

tel: 01753 620636 & 07884 222225 **76 Duke Street SL4 1SQ**
email: bedandbreakfast@76dukestreet.co.uk **web:** www.76dukestreet.co.uk
dir: *M4 junction 6 onto A332. Keep in left lane, take 1st slip road into Maidenhead Road. At roundabout turn left, at 1st set of lights turn left into Vansittart Road. Duke Street 1st turn on right, No 76 5th house on left.*

This is a Victorian property situated in a quiet residential area of Windsor, just 200 metres from the River Thames and a 10-minute walk along the riverside into the centre. A warm welcome can be expected and lots of thoughtful accessories are available along with free WiFi. Guests can enjoy a selection of freshly cooked items at breakfast, made with top quality ingredients.

Rooms: 1 rm (1 pri facs) **D** fr £85 **Facilities:** FTV Lounge TVL tea/coffee WiFi **Extras:** Chocolates, home-made biscuits/cakes, fresh fruit

Innkeeper's Lodge Old Windsor

★★★★ INN

tel: 03451 551551 **Staright Road, Old Windsor SL4 2RR**
email: info@innkeeperslodge.com **web:** www.innkeeperslodge.com
dir: *Phone for directions.*

Set back from the A308, this Innkeeper's Lodge is an easily recognisable building with its bright pink façade, and is conveniently located for access to the M4 and M25. Each bedroom has Freeview TV, a desk, tea-and-coffee making facilities and free WiFi as standard; family rooms are available. The on-site Toby Carvery meals are popular. Parking is provided.

Rooms: 15 en suite (2 fmly) (7 GF) **Facilities:** FTV tea/coffee Dinner available WiFi

The Windsor Trooper

★★★ INN

tel: 01753 670123 **97 St Leonards Road SL4 3BZ**
email: thewindsortrooper@live.co.uk **web:** www.thewindsortrooper.com
dir: *M4 junction 6, at roundabout follow signs for Windsor, then straight over next 2 roundabouts signed Staines-on-Thames, take 1st road on left.*

Located close to many popular attractions and within walking distance of the town centre, this traditional inn provides comfortable annexed accommodation, including a family room. Dinner is served in the bright and airy conservatory, where a range of daily specials is often available. A freshly prepared breakfast is served and limited secure parking is available.

Rooms: 4 en suite 4 annexe en suite (1 fmly) (3 GF) **Facilities:** FTV tea/coffee Dinner available WiFi **Extras:** Speciality toiletries **Parking:** 5 **Notes:** LB

WOKINGHAM   Map 5 SU86

Quarters

★★★★ GUEST ACCOMMODATION

tel: 0118 979 7071 **14 Milton Road RG40 1DB**
email: elaineizod@hotmail.com **web:** www.quarterswokingham.com
dir: *From town centre on A321 towards Henley and Twyford. Left at 1st mini-roundabout into Milton Road.*

Located just a short walk from the town centre, a warm welcome is assured at Quarters. Stylishly decorated bedrooms are well equipped and spacious. A hearty breakfast is served around the communal dining table.

Rooms: 3 en suite **S** fr £50 **D** fr £70 **Facilities:** FTV DVD iPod docking station tea/coffee WiFi **Notes:** No children 12 years

BRISTOL

BRISTOL   Map 4 ST57

Premier Collection

Berwick Lodge

★★★★★ ◎◎ RESTAURANT WITH ROOMS

tel: 0117 958 1590 **Berwick Drive, Henbury BS10 7TD**
email: info@berwicklodge.co.uk **web:** www.berwicklodge.co.uk
dir: *M5 junction 17, A4018 (Westbury-on-Trym). At 2nd roundabout 1st left (Westbury-on-Trym). At next roundabout double back on dual carriageway (signed M5 (M4)). Left after brown Clifton RFC sign. At crossroads straight on, follow Berwick Lodge signs.*

This delightful property was built in the late 1890s as a private manor house and is surrounded by rose and woodland gardens. It provides very high standards of quality and comfort throughout, with luxurious bedrooms and bathrooms offered in a range of shapes and sizes. Fine dining can be experienced in the opulent restaurant where both dinner and breakfast will be sure to delight even the most discerning guests.

Rooms: 12 en suite 2 annexe en suite (2 fmly) **S** fr £85 **D** fr £125* **Facilities:** STV FTV DVD Lounge tea/coffee Dinner available Direct dial Lift WiFi ◕ Beauty therapy treatments **Extras:** Robes, fruit **Conf:** Max 100 Thtr 100 Class 60 Board 30 **Parking:** 100 **Notes:** LB Civ wed 100

The Washington

★★★ GUEST HOUSE

tel: 0117 973 3980 **11–15 St Pauls Road, Clifton BS8 1LX**
email: washington@cliftonhotels.com
web: www.cliftonhotels.com/bristolhotels/washington
dir: *A4018 into city, right at lights opposite BBC, house 200 yards on left.*

This large terraced house is within walking distance of the city centre and Clifton Village. The bedrooms are well equipped for business guests. Public areas include a modern reception lounge and a bright basement breakfast room. The property has secure parking and a rear patio garden.

Rooms: 46 rms (40 en suite) (4 fmly) (10 GF) **Facilities:** FTV tea/coffee Direct dial Licensed WiFi Reduced rate pass at local health club and Bristol Zoo **Extras:** Fresh fruit – complimentary **Parking:** 16 **Notes:** Closed 23–31 December

BUCKINGHAMSHIRE

AMERSHAM   Map 6 SU99

The Crown

★★★★★ ◎◎ 🍷 INN

tel: 01494 721541 **16 High Street HP7 0DH**
email: reception@thecrownamersham.com **web:** www.thecrownamersham.com
dir: *M40 junction 2 onto A355, continue to Amersham. Onto Gore Hill, left into The Broadway.*

Once a coaching inn dating from the 16th century, The Crown now offers a mix of quirky, modern minimalist-style rooms spread over three buildings and designed by Ilse Crawford. These blend beautifully with the character of the original buildings. Deep beds, high quality bedding and the latest TV sound systems are on a list of available amenities. The award-winning Hawkyns Restaurant, overseen by acclaimed chef Atul Kochhar and his team, showcases local produce and flavours from the Indian continent, skilfully prepared and presented. The Courtyard Room is ideal for private functions; exclusive use of the inn is also an option. The Red House Spa offers treatments and resident guests have complimentary use of the gym.

Rooms: 29 en suite 16 annexe en suite (14 GF) **S** fr £120 **D** fr £120* **Facilities:** FTV tea/coffee Dinner available Direct dial WiFi ◕ 🔔 Spa facility access **Extras:** Speciality toiletries, snacks, wine – complimentary **Conf:** Max 30 Thtr 30 Class 18 Board 24 **Parking:** 38 **Notes:** Civ wed 60

The Potters Arms

★★★ 🍷 INN

tel: 01494 726222 **Fagnall Lane, Winchmore Hill HP7 0PH**
email: info@pottersarms.co.uk **web:** www.pottersarms.co.uk
dir: *From Beaconsfield on A355, left into Magpie Lane. Follow road to Winchmore Hill.*

Situated in a rural location in Buckinghamshire, close to Amersham, this traditional pub offers comfortable accommodation. A warm welcome is offered, and guests can enjoy a range of classic pub favourites in the bar and restaurant. The inn has become well known for its popular Comedy Nights, attracting top comedians.

Rooms: 4 en suite **Facilities:** FTV TVL tea/coffee Dinner available WiFi **Parking:** 20

ASTON CLINTON | Map 5 SP81

Innkeeper's Lodge Aylesbury (East)

★★★★ 🛏 INN

tel: 03451 551551 **London Road HP22 5HP**
email: info@innkeeperslodge.com **web:** www.innkeeperslodge.com
dir: *Phone for directions.*

This Innkeeper's Lodge, The Bell, in Aston Clinton offers bedrooms of different shapes and sizes in keeping with the age of the building. Each room has a TV, desk, tea- and coffee-making facilities and free WiFi as standard; family rooms are available. The wide-ranging menus feature something for everyone from light bites to traditional Sunday roasts. In the 1960s, The Bell was a place often frequented by the rich and famous – Elizabeth Taylor and Richard Burton once ate here, as did Jackie Onassis.

Rooms: 11 en suite (4 fmly) (3 GF) **Facilities:** FTV tea/coffee Dinner available Direct dial WiFi

AYLESBURY | Map 11 SP81

Innkeeper's Lodge Aylesbury (South)

★★★★ 🛏 INN

tel: 03451 551551 **40 Main Street, Weston Turville HP22 5RW**
email: info@innkeeperslodge.com **web:** www.innkeeperslodge.com
dir: *Phone for directions.*

At this Innkeepers' Lodge, The Five Bells in Weston Turville, there's a mix of traditional decor in the public spaces and modern amenities in the accommodation. The en suite bedrooms, in different shapes and sizes, come with TVs, desks and free WiFi as standard. A wide-ranging choice of dishes is offered on the seasonal menus. There's a beer garden to sit in when the weather's warm and free parking is provided

Rooms: 16 en suite (5 GF) **Facilities:** FTV tea/coffee Dinner available Direct dial WiFi

BEACONSFIELD | Map 6 SU99

Premier Collection

Crazy Bear Beaconsfield

★★★★★ ◉ 🍴 GUEST ACCOMMODATION

tel: 01494 673086 **75 Wycombe End, Old Town HP9 1LX**
email: enquiries@crazybear-beaconsfield.co.uk **web:** www.crazybeargroup.co.uk
dir: *M40 junction 2, 3rd exit from roundabout, next roundabout 1st exit. Over 2 mini-roundabouts, on right.*

Located in the heart of the old town, this former inn dating from Tudor times has an exciting and vibrant atmosphere. Award-winning cuisine in both the Thai and the English restaurants, classic cocktails and an extensive wine list can all be enjoyed. The Terrace and the Moroccan-style lounge offer a calm environment in which to relax. The bedrooms are individually appointed with unusual fabrics and dazzling colour schemes. Resident guests can also enjoy the swimming pool and jacuzzi. The Crazy Bear Beaconsfield is well equipped to cater for private parties, weddings and business meetings. Limited secure parking is available.

Rooms: 6 en suite 27 annexe en suite (2 GF) **Facilities:** STV Dinner available Direct dial Licensed WiFi 🐾 Jacuzzi **Extras:** Mineral water – complimentary
Conf: Max 100 Thtr 100 Class 100 Board 60 **Parking:** 12 **Notes:** Civ wed 100

BRILL | Map 11 SP61

Premier Collection

The Pointer

★★★★★ ◉◉ 🍴 RESTAURANT WITH ROOMS

tel: 01844 238339 **27 Church Street HP18 9RT**
email: info@thepointerbrill.co.uk **web:** www.thepointerbrill.co.uk
dir: *M40 junction 9, onto A41 signed Aylesbury. Right signed Brill, on left next to church.*

The Pointer is a stylish country pub and restaurant with rooms in the picturesque village of Brill near Aylesbury. Part of the business is a working organic farm and kitchen garden as well as an adjacent butcher's shop for pedigree meats. Inside, there are heavy low beams entwined with bare twigs and exposed, roughcast stone walls. In the restaurant, guests are treated to a range of crowd-pleasing dishes all served in a relaxed and informal setting. The four modern bedrooms, located just over the road, are spacious and attractively presented; all have coffee machines and extremely comfortable beds. The bathrooms are equipped to the same high standard and include luxurious towels and luxury toiletries.

Rooms: 4 en suite **D** fr £140* **Facilities:** FTV tea/coffee Dinner available WiFi
Extras: Home-made biscuits, Nespresso machine, still and sparking water, fresh milk, speciality toiletries **Parking:** 3 **Notes:** Closed 1st week of January

The Pheasant

★★★★ 🛏 INN

tel: 01844 239370 **39 Windmill Street HP18 9TG**
email: info@thepheasant.co.uk **web:** www.thepheasant.co.uk
dir: *M40 junction 7, take A329 Thame, A418 Aylesbury. At next roundabout take B4011, through Long Crendon, right signed Brill.*

The Pheasant is a popular pub with well-appointed bedrooms, some with views of the Grade II listed windmill. The mill is owned by the village and is open to the public at certain times of the year. At The Pheasant all the bedrooms have been nicely configured to offer comfort and practicality. Real ale and cocktails are served at the bar, while the restaurant offers simple, yet delicious dishes using local produce. Free parking and WiFi are available.

The Pheasant

Rooms: 2 en suite 2 annexe en suite (1 GF) **S** fr £90 **D** fr £120* **Facilities:** FTV Lounge tea/coffee Dinner available WiFi **Notes:** RS 25–26 December rooms available, no breakfast

See advert below

Poletrees Farm
★★★★ FARMHOUSE

tel: 01844 238276 **Ludgershall Road HP18 9TZ**
email: poletrees.farm@btinternet.com
dir: *Exit south from A41 signed Ludgershall/Brill, after railway bridge 0.5 mile on left.*

Located between the villages of Ludgershall and Brill, this 16th-century farmhouse retains many original features including a wealth of exposed beams. The bedrooms are in converted outbuildings, and the cosy dining room is the setting for a wholesome breakfast.

Rooms: 4 annexe en suite (2 fmly) (4 GF) **Facilities:** FTV TVL tea/coffee 🔒 **Parking:** 6 **Notes:** LB 110 acres sheep

CHALFONT ST GILES   Map 6 SU99

The Ivy House
★★★ 🍺 INN

tel: 01494 872184 **London Road HP8 4RS**
email: alfie@theivyhousechalfont.co.uk **web:** www.ivyhousechalfontstgiles.co.uk
dir: *Phone for directions.*

This popular traditional English inn is more than 250 years old and has retained some lovely period features. Situated in the heart of the Chiltern Vale surrounded by countryside it makes a popular venue for walkers or even for those heading to London, which is only 40 minutes away. Bedrooms are comfortably equipped, and guests can enjoy dinner in the attractive restaurant which also has a very good range of real ales and wines.

Rooms: 5 en suite **Facilities:** FTV tea/coffee Dinner available WiFi ♿ **Parking:** 40

DENHAM
Map 6 TQ08

The Falcon Inn
★★★★ ⬤ INN

tel: 01895 832125 **Village Road UB9 5BE**
email: mail@falcondenham.com **web:** www.falcondenham.com
dir: *M40 junction 1, follow A40 and Gerrards Cross signs. Approximately 200 yards, right into Old Mill Road, pub opposite village green.*

This 18th-century inn stands in the heart of the picturesque village of Denham, opposite the green. The en suite bedrooms, with smart shower rooms, are well equipped and display original features. Carefully prepared dishes, together with a good selection of wines, are served at both lunch and dinner in the cosy restaurant.

Rooms: 4 en suite **S** fr £89 **D** fr £99 (room only)* **Facilities:** FTV DVD tea/coffee Dinner available WiFi ⬤ ⬤ **Extras:** Fresh fruit, bottled water, speciality toiletries – complimentary **Notes:** LB No children 10 years Closed 24–26 December, 30 December to 1 January

GREAT MISSENDEN
Map 6 SP80

Nags Head Inn & Restaurant
★★★★ ⬤ INN

tel: 01494 862200 **London Road HP16 0DG**
email: goodfood@nagsheadbucks.com **web:** www.nagsheadbucks.com
dir: *North of Amersham on A413, left at Chiltern hospital into London Road signed Great Missenden.*

This delightful 15th-century inn, located in the picturesque Chiltern Hills, has a great reputation locally thanks to its extensive menu of local produce and carefully prepared dishes. Individually-designed bedrooms are comfortable with a modern twist ensuring a home-from-home atmosphere. Ample parking is available.

Rooms: 6 en suite (1 fmly) **S** fr £95 **D** fr £95* **Facilities:** FTV DVD tea/coffee Dinner available WiFi ⬤ **Extras:** Speciality toiletries, mineral water – complimentary **Conf:** Max 50 **Parking:** 40 **Notes:** Closed 25 December

HIGH WYCOMBE
Map 5 SU89

Fox Country Inn
★★★ INN

tel: 01491 638814 **Ibstone HP14 3XT**
email: info@foxcountryinn.co.uk **web:** www.foxcountryinn.co.uk
dir: *M40 junction 5 follow signs to Ibstone, 1.5 miles on left.*

This contemporary inn enjoys a peaceful rural location on the outskirts of High Wycombe. The bedrooms are attractively presented and have a host of thoughtful little extras. Free WiFi is available throughout. The contemporary and open-plan bar and restaurant retain some of the original features; food is served all day in the bar and on the terrace during the warm months of the year. Secure parking is provided.

Rooms: 16 en suite (1 fmly) (8 GF) **S** fr £65 **D** fr £75* **Facilities:** FTV Lounge TVL tea/coffee Dinner available Direct dial WiFi **Conf:** Max 25 Thtr 25 Class 20 Board 20 **Parking:** 23 **Notes:** Civ wed 50

MEDMENHAM
Map 5 SU88

Premier Collection

The Dog and Badger
★★★★★ ⬤ RESTAURANT WITH ROOMS

tel: 01491 579944 **Henley Road SL7 2HE**
email: thedogandbadger@oakmaninns.co.uk **web:** www.thedogandbadger.com
dir: *Phone for directions.*

The Dog and Badger is a beautifully restored restaurant with rooms located in the quiet village of Medmenham. The six stunning bedrooms are located in a separate cottage; all are spacious and highly comfortable with smart TVs, air conditioning, mini-bars and coffee machines provided as standard. The bathrooms are just as smart with soft fluffy towels and luxury toiletries. There is a popular feature bar which serves a great range of wines, spirits, beers and cocktails and throughout the property there's contemporary art which blends with original features such as exposed brick, wooden beams and decorative floor tiles. In the informal restaurant, guests are treated to a range of crowd-pleasing dishes. WiFi is available throughout plus there's outside seating and plenty of parking space. The Dog and Badger is an AA Restaurant with Rooms of the Year runner up for 2018–19.

Rooms: 6 en suite **Facilities:** Dinner available

NEWTON BLOSSOMVILLE
Map 11 SP95

The Old Mill
★★★ INN

tel: 01234 881273 **Clifton Road MK43 8AN**
email: enquiries@oldmill.uk.com **web:** www.oldmill.uk.com
dir: *M1 junction 14 onto A509 towards Wellingborough. In Emberton right into Newton Road, bear right into Clifton Road, The Old Mill on left.*

In the quiet and attractive village of Newton Blossomville, in the Borough of Milton Keynes, this traditional inn offers comfortable accommodation. The inn remains a friendly locals' pub and guests can also enjoy a game of skittles. A traditional pub menu offers a good range of dishes, and a selection of real ales is on offer.

Rooms: 5 en suite 1 annexe en suite (2 fmly) (1 GF) **S** fr £75 **D** fr £90* **Facilities:** FTV tea/coffee Dinner available WiFi ⬤ **Extras:** Bottled water, fresh milk **Notes:** LB

WADDESDON   Map 11 SP71

The Five Arrows

★★★★ ◎◎ ▢ RESTAURANT WITH ROOMS

tel: 01296 651727 **High Street HP18 0JE**
email: reservations@thefivearrows.co.uk **web:** www.waddesdon.org.uk/fivearrows
dir: *On A41 in Waddesdon. Into Baker Street for car park.*

This Grade II listed building with its elaborate Elizabethan-style chimney stacks stands at the gates of Waddesdon Manor and was named after the Rothschild family emblem. The individually styled, en suite bedrooms are comfortable and well appointed. Friendly staff are on hand to offer a warm welcome. Alfresco dining is possible in the warmer months.

Rooms: 8 en suite 8 annexe en suite (2 fmly) (3 GF) **Facilities:** FTV tea/coffee Dinner available WiFi ▢ **Conf:** Max 20 Thtr 20 Class 20 Board 20 **Parking:** 40
Notes: Civ wed 60

WOOBURN GREEN   Map 6 SU98

The Old Bell

★★★★ ▭ INN

tel: 01628 523117 **HP10 0PL**
email: oldbellwooburn@hotmail.co.uk **web:** www.oldbellwooburn.co.uk
dir: *M40 junction 2, A355 towards Beaconsfield. Take A40 through Beaconsfield. Left onto B4440 to Wooburn Green. At T-junction left into Town Lane. Old Bell on left.*

Dating back to the 16th century, this former coaching inn retains many original features, with low beams and real fires in the cosy bar. The Old Bell has a very good range of real ales, including guest brews, while the award-winning restaurant menus feature some excellent local produce. Bedrooms are very stylish and retain many of the period features that make this place unique. Free WiFi along with ample secure parking is available for guests.

Rooms: 6 en suite 1 annexe en suite (2 fmly) (1 GF) **Facilities:** FTV tea/coffee Dinner available WiFi ⚓ **Parking:** 14 **Notes:** LB Closed 1 January RS 25–26 December bar and restaurant closes at 4pm

CAMBRIDGESHIRE

BALSHAM   Map 12 TL55

The Black Bull Inn

★★★★ ◎ INN

tel: 01223 893844 **27 High Street CB21 4DJ**
email: info@blackbull-balsham.co.uk **web:** www.blackbull-balsham.co.uk
dir: *From south: M11 junction 9 towards Newmarket, exit signed Balsham, in centre of village. From north: M11 junction 10, A505 signed Newmarket (A11), exit signed Balsham.*

This privately owned 16th-century, Grade II listed free house is set in the pretty village of Balsham. There are five spacious en suite bedrooms located alongside the pub which provide very high levels of quality and comfort. Excellent food is served at lunch and dinner every day.

Rooms: 5 annexe en suite (1 fmly) (5 GF) **S** fr £95 **D** fr £129* **Facilities:** FTV DVD Lounge tea/coffee Dinner available WiFi ⚓ **Conf:** Max 30 Thtr 30 Class 24 Board 20 **Parking:** 20 **Notes:** LB

BARTLOW   Map 12 TL54

Premier Collection

The Three Hills

★★★★★ ◎◎ RESTAURANT WITH ROOMS

tel: 01223 890500 **Dean Road CB21 4PW**
email: info@thethreehills.co.uk **web:** www.thethreehills.co.uk
dir: *From A11 onto A1307 signed Haverhill. Pass Linton, turn right signed Bartlow. At crossroads, turn right, pub on left.*

This 17th-century, Grade II listed building in the heart of Bartlow has undergone a major refurbishment to create a delightful, modern restaurant with rooms with landscaped gardens leading down to the river. The stylish, contemporary bedrooms, in various sizes, have character and come with Egyptian cotton bed linen, soft lighting, a bath and/or power shower and luxury toiletries. The award-winning food served in the orangery is based on quality local produce and the dishes are created with skill and flair. Eating outside on the patio is possible in warm weather.

Rooms: 2 en suite 4 annexe en suite (2 GF) **D** fr £100* **Facilities:** FTV TVL tea/coffee Dinner available WiFi **Extras:** Speciality toiletries, Nespresso coffee machine **Parking:** 25

CAMBRIDGE

Map 12 TL45

Benson House

★★★★ ⓒ GUEST HOUSE

tel: 01223 311594 **24 Huntingdon Road CB3 0HH**
email: bensonhouse@btconnect.com web: www.bensonhouse.co.uk
dir: *0.5 mile northwest of city centre on A604.*

This popular guest house is well placed for the city centre and New Hall and Fitzwilliam colleges. Its pleasant bedrooms vary in size and style and all are well equipped with TV, clock radio, beverage tray and hairdryers. The delicious selection at breakfast includes kippers, and there is limited private parking behind the property. Benson House cannot cater for pets or children under 12 years of age.

Rooms: 6 en suite (1 GF) **S** fr £80 **D** fr £115 **Facilities:** FTV iPod docking station tea/coffee WiFi **Extras:** Welcome drink, speciality toiletries **Parking:** 5
Notes: No children 12 years Closed 31 December to 5 January

Hamden Guest House

★★★ GUEST HOUSE

tel: 01223 413263 & 07543 049010 **89 High Street, Cherry Hinton CB1 9LU**
email: info@hamdenguesthouse.co.uk web: www.hamdenguesthouse.co.uk
dir: *3 miles southeast of city centre. From M11 exit A1134 to Cherry Hinton; from A14 exit north on A1303 signed Cambridge and Cherry Hinton.*

Expect a warm welcome at this small, family-run guest house, which is just a short drive from the city centre. The pleasant bedrooms are generally quite spacious and

equipped with many thoughtful extras. Public rooms include a large kitchen-dining room where breakfast is served at individual tables.

Hamden Guest House

Rooms: 5 en suite (2 fmly) (1 GF) **S** fr £40 **D** fr £60 **Facilities:** FTV tea/coffee WiFi **Parking:** 6 **Notes:** LB No children 5 years

See advert opposite

The Alpha Milton Guest House

★★★ GUEST ACCOMMODATION

tel: 01223 311625 **61–63 Milton Road CB4 1XA**
email: info@alphamilton.com web: www.alphamilton.com
dir: *0.5 mile northeast of city centre.*

The Alpha Milton Guest House is in a residential area just a short walk from the city centre. The attractive lounge-dining room overlooks the rear garden, and all the pleasant bedrooms have a good range of facilities.

Rooms: 8 rms (7 en suite) (1 pri facs) (2 fmly) (2 GF) **Facilities:** FTV DVD tea/coffee WiFi **Parking:** 8

ELTON

Map 12 TL09

Premier Collection

The Crown Inn

★★★★★ ⓒ ⌂ INN

tel: 01832 280232 **8 Duck Street PE8 6RQ**
email: inncrown@googlemail.com web: www.thecrowninn.org
dir: *A1 junction 17, A605 west. In 3.5 miles right signed Elton, 0.9 mile, left signed Nassington. On village green.*

Expect a warm welcome at this delightful, 16th-century village pub, situated opposite the village green. It retains many original features such as a large inglenook fireplace and oak-beamed ceilings. The smartly decorated bedrooms are tastefully appointed and thoughtfully equipped. Public rooms include a large open-plan lounge bar, a small relaxed dining area to the front, and a tastefully appointed circular restaurant.

Rooms: 3 en suite 5 annexe en suite (3 fmly) (5 GF) **Facilities:** FTV tea/coffee Dinner available Direct dial WiFi ⌂ **Conf:** Max 40 Thtr 25 Class 40 Board 25 **Parking:** 15 **Notes:** RS Sunday evening, Monday (excluding bank holidays), 1st week January restaurant closed

ELY
Map 12 TL58

Lazy Otter Pub Restaurant

★★★★ INN

tel: 01353 649780 **Cambridge Road, Stretham CB6 3LU**
email: thelazyotter@btconnect.com **web:** www.lazy-otter.com
dir: *Phone for directions.*

The Lazy Otter enjoys an idyllic position, nestled on the banks of the River Ouse, ideally located between Cambridge and Ely. Comfortable bedrooms are all of a high standard. The restaurant overlooks the river with its boats and barges, and enjoys some lovely Fen scenery. The bar offers a range of real ales and guests can relax by roaring log fires in the cooler months. There is a very popular restaurant and the freshly cooked breakfasts are enjoyable. This is an ideal base from which to explore the countryside and delightful historic market towns.

Rooms: 3 en suite **Facilities:** FTV DVD iPod docking station tea/coffee Dinner available WiFi **Parking:** 60

The Anchor Inn

★★★★ INN

tel: 01353 778537 **Bury Lane, Sutton Gault CB6 2BD**
email: anchorinn@popmail.bta.com **web:** www.anchor-inn-restaurant.co.uk
dir: *West of Ely. Sutton Gault signed from B1381 at south end of Sutton.*

The Anchor is a traditional 17th-century inn situated outside the city of Ely in a quiet riverside location. Bedrooms are modern yet retain period charm, and guests can enjoy award-winning food in the restaurant.

Rooms: 4 en suite **Facilities:** FTV tea/coffee Dinner available Direct dial WiFi **Extras:** Bottled water, fresh milk – complimentary **Parking:** 10 **Notes:** Closed 25–26 December

The Three Pickerels

★★★★ INN

tel: 01353 777777 **19 Bridge Road, Mepal CB6 2AR**
email: info@thethreepickerels.co.uk **web:** www.thethreepickerels.co.uk

Situated in the tranquil village of Mepal on the outskirts of Ely, this property sits on the banks of the New Bedford River and has views of the surrounding area. Public rooms include a smart bar, a dining room and a lovely lounge overlooking the river. The smartly appointed bedrooms are comfortable and well equipped.

Rooms: 4 en suite (1 fmly) **Facilities:** FTV TVL tea/coffee Dinner available WiFi Fishing **Parking:** 40 **Notes:** LB

GREAT ABINGTON
Map 12 TL54

Three Tuns

★★★★ INN

tel: 01223 891467 **75 High Street CB21 6AB**
email: email@thethreetuns-greatabington.co.uk
web: www.thethreetuns-greatabington.co.uk
dir: *Phone for directions.*

Visitors are guaranteed a warm welcome at this charming 16th-century inn set in a prominent position in the heart of the pretty village of Great Abington. The very popular restaurant has a well-deserved reputation for its Thai cuisine and the bar has a good selection of real ales. The purpose-built bedrooms are beautifully presented and offer guests stylish and comfortable accommodation along with high quality bathrooms. Free WiFi is available throughout the property and secure parking is provided.

Rooms: 9 annexe en suite (1 fmly) (9 GF) **Facilities:** STV FTV tea/coffee Dinner available WiFi **Extras:** Speciality toiletries **Parking:** 20 **Notes:** Closed 1 January

HINXTON
Map 12 TL44

The Red Lion Inn
★★★★ @ INN

tel: 01799 530601 **32 High Street CB10 1QY**
email: info@redlionhinxton.co.uk **web:** www.redlionhinxton.co.uk
dir: *Northbound only: M11 junction 9, towards A11, left onto A1301. Left to Hinxton. Or M11 junction 10, A505 towards A11/Newmarket. At roundabout 3rd exit onto A1301, right to Hinxton.*

The Red Lion Inn is a 16th-century free house pub and restaurant set in the pretty conservation village of Hinxton that offers high quality, purpose-built accommodation. In the winter guests can relax by the well-stoked fire, while in summer they can enjoy the attractive walled garden which overlooks the village church.

Rooms: 8 annexe en suite (2 fmly) (8 GF) **S** fr £109 **D** fr £139* **Facilities:** FTV DVD Lounge tea/coffee Dinner available Direct dial WiFi 🔒 **Conf:** Max 20 Thtr 20 Class 15 Board 15 **Parking:** 43 **Notes:** LB

HUNTINGDON
Map 12 TL27

The Abbot's Elm
★★★★ @ INN

tel: 01487 773773 **Abbots Ripton PE28 2PA**
email: info@theabbotselm.co.uk **web:** www.theabbotselm.co.uk
dir: *A1(M) junction 13 onto A14 towards Huntingdon. At 1st roundabout straight on (A141 Spittals Way). Left at 2nd roundabout signed Abbots Ripton. 3 miles, in village centre.*

This Grade II listed thatched country inn is situated in the quiet village of Abbots Ripton, near the ancient market town of Huntingdon. Bedrooms are modern and comfortable, and guests can enjoy a range of real ales and fine wines in the spacious and smartly appointed bar and restaurant.

Rooms: 3 en suite 1 annexe en suite (4 GF) **S** fr £68 **D** fr £85 **Facilities:** STV Lounge tea/coffee Dinner available WiFi **Extras:** Robes; filtered water – complimentary **Parking:** 50

LITTLEPORT
Map 12 TL58

The Gate House
★★★★ 🥚 BED AND BREAKFAST

tel: 01353 863840 & 07940 120023 **2B Lynn Road CB6 1QG**
email: edna@thegatehousebandb.co.uk **web:** www.thegatehousebandb.co.uk
dir: *On A10 between Ely and King's Lynn. Cross railway line in Littleport, next right into Lynn Road, last house on left.*

This modern house has a range of beautifully presented, stylish bedrooms and is a short walk from Littleport railway station. Rear-facing rooms have lovely views of a spur on the River Great Ouse. The freshly-prepared breakfasts include award-winning local produce and shouldn't be missed. Both ample secure parking and free WiFi are available. Conveniently located close to Cambridge, Newmarket and Ely, The Gate House is an ideal base for exploring this lovely region.

Rooms: 3 rms (2 en suite) (1 pri facs) **Facilities:** FTV DVD Lounge tea/coffee WiFi **Extras:** Robes, slippers, home-made biscuits **Parking:** 4

MELBOURN
Map 12 TL34

Sheene Mill
★★★★ @@ RESTAURANT WITH ROOMS

tel: 01763 261393 **39 Station Road SG8 6DX**
email: reservations@sheenemill.com **web:** www.sheenemill.com
dir: *M11 junction 10 onto A505 towards Royston. Right to Melbourn, pass church on right, on left before old bridge.*

This 16th-century watermill is ideally situated just off the A10, a short drive from both Cambridge and Royston. The bedrooms are individually decorated and well equipped; some rooms overlook the mill pond and terrace. Public rooms include a comfortable lounge, a bar, conservatory and a delightful restaurant overlooking the pond.

Rooms: 10 en suite (4 fmly) **Facilities:** FTV Lounge tea/coffee Dinner available WiFi 🛗 Sauna 🔒 **Extras:** Speciality toiletries – complimentary **Conf:** Max 180 Thtr 120 Class 120 Board 60 **Parking:** 60 **Notes:** Civ wed 120

UFFORD
Map 12 TF00

The White Hart
★★★★ 🍴 INN

tel: 01780 740250 **Main Street PE9 3BH**
email: info@whitehartufford.co.uk **web:** www.whitehartufford.co.uk
dir: *Phone for directions.*

Just five miles from Stamford and 10 miles from Peterborough, this charming 17th-century inn is home to Ufford Ales, which are served in the bar. The property is built from local stone and retains many original features. The delightful bedrooms are tastefully furnished and thoughtfully equipped. Public rooms include a lounge bar, conservatory and restaurant.

Rooms: 4 en suite 8 annexe en suite (7 GF) **D** fr £80* **Facilities:** FTV tea/coffee Dinner available WiFi 🔒 **Conf:** Max 30 Thtr 30 Class 20 Board 20 **Parking:** 30 **Notes:** Civ wed 50

WHITTLESFORD
Map 12 TL44

The Red Lion at Whittlesford Bridge
★★★★ @ INN

tel: 01223 497070 & 497085 **Station Road, Whittlesford Bridge CB22 4NL**
email: reservations@hiexpresscambridgeduxford.co.uk
web: www.redlionwhittlesfordbridge.com
dir: *Phone for directions.*

A 13th-century coaching inn, with a wealth of charm and character, situated in close proximity to Duxford Air Museum, the major road networks (A11/M11), Cambridge and Whittlesford Parkway railway station. The individually designed bedrooms are well equipped and comfortable; the public areas include a large lounge bar, a restaurant, and a function suite as well as an outside dining area.

Rooms: 18 en suite **Facilities:** FTV iPod docking station Lounge tea/coffee Dinner available Direct dial WiFi **Conf:** Max 200 Thtr 200 Class 74 Board 40 **Parking:** 80 **Notes:** Civ wed 70

WOODHURST
Map 12 TL37

Falcon's Nest
★★★ GUEST ACCOMMODATION

tel: 01487 741140 **The Raptor Foundation, The Heath PE28 3BT**
email: info@raptorfoundation.org.uk **web:** www.raptorfoundation.org.uk
dir: *On B1040 between St Ives and Somersham.*

Located just a few miles from St Ives, Falcon's Nest is in the grounds of The Raptor Foundation estate. There are eight en suite rooms, all with kitchenette facilities. As a resident you are eligible for free entry to the Raptor Centre where there are many different birds of prey species. Breakfasts are available at an additional cost and served in the Silent Wings Tea Room.

Rooms: 8 en suite (1 fmly) (8 GF) **Facilities:** FTV DVD tea/coffee WiFi ⅃ Entry To The Raptor Foundation Bird of Prey Park **Parking:** 56 **Notes:** LB

CHESHIRE

ALDERLEY EDGE
Map 16 SJ87

Innkeeper's Lodge Alderley Edge
★★★★ INN

tel: 03451 551551 **5–9 Wilmslow Road SK9 7QN**
email: info@innkeeperslodge.com **web:** www.innkeeperslodge.com
dir: *Phone for directions.*

This Innkeeper's Lodge, The Merlin dating from the 1880s, is situated between Wilmslow and picturesque Alderley Edge and is only 12 miles from Manchester. The en suite, modern bedrooms have TVs, desks, free WiFi, tea- and coffee-making facilities as standard; family rooms are available. The cosy pub and restaurant offer a wide range of drinks and food. There is a beer garden and on-site parking.

Rooms: 11 en suite (3 fmly) **Facilities:** FTV tea/coffee Dinner available WiFi **Parking:** 50

BURWARDSLEY
Map 15 SJ55

The Pheasant Inn
★★★★★ ◎ INN

tel: 01829 770434 **Higher Burwardsley CH3 9PF**
email: info@thepheasantinn.co.uk **web:** www.thepheasantinn.co.uk
dir: *From A41, left to Tattenhall, right at 1st junction and left at 2nd Higher Burwardsley. At post office left, signed.*

This delightful 300-year-old inn sits high on the Peckforton Hills and enjoys spectacular views over the Cheshire Plain. Well-equipped, comfortable bedrooms are housed in an adjacent converted barn. Creative dishes are served either in the stylish restaurant or in the traditional, beamed bar where real fires are lit in the winter months.

Rooms: 2 en suite 10 annexe en suite (2 fmly) (5 GF) **Facilities:** FTV tea/coffee Dinner available Direct dial WiFi ⅃ **Parking:** 80

CHESTER
Map 15 SJ46
See also Malpas

Mitchell's of Chester
★★★★★ ⓖ GUEST HOUSE

tel: 01244 679004 **28 Hough Green CH4 8JQ**
email: welcome@mitchellsofchester.com **web:** www.mitchellsofchester.com
dir: *1 mile southwest of city centre. A483 onto A5104, 300 yards on right in Hough Green.*

A warm welcome is assured at this delightfully restored and elegant Victorian house, located on the south side of The Dee, within a 20-minute walk of the city centre. The very well equipped and delightfully furnished bedrooms have stylish en suite bathrooms. Guests have use of a beautiful lounge and dining room where sumptuous breakfasts, featuring lots of local produce, are served. Both these rooms reflect the house's Victorian heritage.

Rooms: 3 en suite **S** fr £75 **D** fr £95* **Facilities:** FTV DVD TVL tea/coffee Licensed WiFi **Extras:** Speciality toiletries – complimentary **Parking:** 5 **Notes:** LB No children 8 years Closed 13 December to 4 January RS Sunday to Wednesday closed

Stone Villa Chester
★★★★★ ⓖ GUEST ACCOMMODATION

tel: 01244 345014 & 07764 282015 **Stone Place, Hoole Road CH2 3NR**
email: info@stonevillachester.co.uk **web:** www.stonevillachester.co.uk
dir: *0.5 mile northeast of city on A56 (Hoole Road).*

Stone Villa Chester is a welcoming retreat, away from the bustling city, yet within walking distance of city centre attractions. Bedrooms have comfortable beds and a wealth of accessories which creates a home-from-home experience. Hearty breakfasts feature local produce and home-made jams. Secure parking is a bonus.

Rooms: 10 en suite (2 fmly) (3 GF) **S** fr £65 **D** fr £90* **Facilities:** FTV DVD iPod docking station Lounge tea/coffee Licensed WiFi ⓐ **Conf:** Max 10 Board 10 **Parking:** 16

Coach House Inn
★★★★ INN

tel: 01244 351900 & 351143 **39 Northgate Street CH1 2HQ**
email: info@coachhousechester.co.uk **web:** www.coachhousechester.co.uk
dir: *Phone for detailed directions.*

Ideally located in the centre of the city, this inn has been appointed to provide high standards of comfort and good facilities. Its sumptuous bedrooms have a wealth of thoughtful extras; some have views over the Town Hall Square and the cathedral. Staff offer and informal style of service and a warm welcome.

Rooms: 8 en suite (3 fmly) **Facilities:** FTV tea/coffee Dinner available Direct dial WiFi **Notes:** Closed 25 December

CHESTER *continued*

80 Watergate Street

★★★★ 🛈 BED AND BREAKFAST

tel: 01244 314879 & 07834 042278 **80 Watergate Street CH1 2LF**
email: 80watergatestreet@gmail.com **web:** www.80watergatestreet.co.uk
dir: *M53 junction 12 onto A56, then A5268. Continue to Watergate Street (A548), signed Watergate/Queensferry.*

This modern and quirky townhouse is situated in central Chester within a stone's throw of the famous racecourse. Guests can be assured of superbly well-equipped rooms, deeply comfortable beds dressed with fine linen and of course, a notable breakfast. The top-floor suite is particularly spacious. Personal attention is noteworthy – from tea and cake on arrival and having access to the goodies' cabinet through to a friendly chat at breakfast.

Rooms: 3 en suite **Facilities:** FTV iPod docking station Lounge tea/coffee WiFi
Extras: Snacks, coffee machine **Notes:** No children

Lavender Lodge

★★★★ GUEST ACCOMMODATION

tel: 01244 323204 **46 Hoole Road CH2 3NL**
email: bookings@lavenderlodgechester.co.uk **web:** www.lavenderlodgechester.co.uk
dir: *1 mile northeast of city centre on A56, opposite All Saints Church.*

A warm welcome is assured at this smart, late Victorian house located within easy walking distance of Chester's central attractions. The comfortable bedrooms are equipped with thoughtful little extras and have modern bathrooms. Hearty breakfasts are served in the attractive dining room.

Rooms: 5 rms (4 en suite) (1 pri facs) (2 fmly) (2 GF) **S** fr £50 **D** fr £80*
Facilities: FTV tea/coffee WiFi 🚗 **Parking:** 4 **Notes:** LB Closed 24 December to 2 January

The Boathouse

★★★★ INN

tel: 01244 328709 **21 The Groves CH1 1SD**
email: boathouse@jwlees.co.uk **web:** www.theboathousechester.co.uk
dir: *M53 junction 12, A56. Left into Canadian Avenue, at roundabout 2nd exit into Hoole Lane. Left at T-junction, right onto A51. Left into Dee Lane leading to The Groves.*

This property occupies an enviable river location along the River Dee – relaxing on the floating-barge seating area is just the place to be in the summer months. Once you've parked at The Boathouse, it is a moment's walk into the historic city. The bedrooms are in either the traditional annexe or the newly-built accommodation wing; all home comforts are catered for, and each room is designed with a rowing

and river theme. Local beers from the JW Lees brewery features here, whilst the hearty pub food, paired with daily-changing specials, proves popular.

Rooms: 21 en suite **Facilities:** FTV tea/coffee Dinner available WiFi **Parking:** 32

The Old Farmhouse B&B

★★★★ BED AND BREAKFAST

tel: 01244 332124 & 07949 820119 **9 Eggbridge Lane, Waverton CH3 7PE**
email: jmitchellgreenwalls@hotmail.com **web:** www.chestereggbridgefarm.co.uk
dir: *From A41 at Waverton left into Moor Lane, left into Eggbridge Lane, over canal bridge, house on right before shops.*

The Old Farmhouse, dating from the 18th century, is located in a village community three miles south of the city centre. The cosy bedrooms are equipped with a wealth of thoughtful extras, and the hearty breakfasts feature local and home-made produce.

Rooms: 2 rms (1 en suite) (1 pri facs) **S** fr £35 **D** fr £70* **Facilities:** FTV TVL tea/coffee WiFi 🚗 **Parking:** 6 **Notes:** LB No children 7 years Closed 13–28 February RS Christmas and New Year continental breakfast only

Innkeeper's Lodge Chester Christleton

★★★ INN

tel: 03451 551551 **Whitchurch Road CH3 6AE**
email: info@innkeeperslodge.com **web:** www.innkeeperslodge.com
dir: *Phone for directions.*

Innkeeper's Lodge Chester Christleton (locally known as The Cheshire Cat) offers comfortable bedrooms with classic decor and thoughtful amenities; some are in the main house and others in converted cottages alongside the canal. A popular lunch venue, the inn provides well-cooked meals served in cosy rooms, each with its own style, and most with a real fire. Large, attractive outside areas are available for dining in warmer weather, with access to the canal path to walk off your meal.

Rooms: 14 en suite (3 fmly) (4 GF) **Facilities:** FTV tea/coffee Dinner available Direct dial WiFi

Glen Garth

★★★ GUEST ACCOMMODATION

tel: 01244 310260 **59 Hoole Road CH2 3NJ**
email: glengarthguesthouse@btconnect.com **web:** www.glengarthguesthouse.co.uk
dir: *Exit M53 onto A56, 0.5 mile east of city.*

Situated within easy walking distance of the city, family-run Glen Garth provides well-equipped bedrooms, and hearty breakfasts served in the pleasant rear dining room. The friendly, attentive service is noteworthy here.

Rooms: 5 rms (3 en suite) (2 pri facs) (1 fmly) **S** fr £45 **D** fr £90 **Facilities:** FTV DVD tea/coffee WiFi 🛁 **Parking:** 5 **Notes:** LB

CONGLETON	Map 16 SJ86

The Plough Inn Eaton

★★★★ 🛈 INN

tel: 01260 280207 **Macclesfield Road, Eaton CW12 2NH**
email: enquiries@theploughinncheshire.com **web:** www.theploughinncheshire.com
dir: *On A536 (Congleton to Macclesfield road), 1.5 miles from Congleton town centre.*

In the traditional Cheshire mould of half-brick, half-timber, this rural inn offers modern accommodation and hearty pub food and drink. Bedrooms, in a separate annexe, are spacious and well equipped. The stunning 17th-century barn which serves as a function and wedding suite, was moved here piece-by-piece from Wales. A large garden to the rear is also available for dining or drinks.

Rooms: 17 annexe en suite (3 fmly) (8 GF) **S** fr £70 **D** fr £85 **Facilities:** STV FTV tea/coffee Dinner available Direct dial WiFi **Conf:** Max 115 Thtr 80 Class 80 Board 80 **Parking:** 90 **Notes:** Civ wed 85

CREWE
Map 15 SJ75

Corner Farm
★★★★ BED AND BREAKFAST

tel: 01270 841429 **2 Pit Lane, Hough CW2 5JQ**
email: leafarm@hotmail.co.uk **web:** www.cornerfarmathough.co.uk
dir: M6 junction 16 onto A500 towards Nantwich. 1st roundabout, take 1st left, 2nd roundabout follow signs to Hough. Over railway bridge, pass White Hart pub, left into Pit Lane, Corner Farm immediately on right.

This farmhouse enjoys beautiful scenic views beyond its own large landscaped gardens. It is conveniently situated to explore nearby Chester, and further afield for The Potteries. Bedrooms are very comfortably furnished and guests have access to a large, well-furnished lounge and also the gardens in warmer months. A genuine welcome and a hearty breakfast are assured.

Rooms: 3 en suite (1 fmly) **S** fr £42 **D** fr £66* **Facilities:** FTV DVD TVL tea/coffee WiFi **Extras:** Microwave available in dining room **Parking:** 8 **Notes:** Closed 25 December

MALPAS
Map 15 SJ44

Hampton House Farm
★★★★ FARMHOUSE

tel: 01948 820588 **Stevensons Lane, Hampton SY14 8JS**
email: enquiries@hamptonhousefarm.co.uk **web:** www.hamptonhousefarm.co.uk
dir: 2 miles northeast of Malpas. Exit A41 into Cholmondeley Road, next left.

Hampton House is located on a quiet farm and offers thoughtfully appointed accommodation and a warm welcome. Parts of the house are reputed to date from 1600, and its stylish decor highlights the many period features, including a wealth of exposed beams.

Rooms: 2 en suite **Facilities:** TVL tea/coffee WiFi **Parking:** 12 **Notes:** No children 12 years 180 acres mixed

MOBBERLEY
Map 15 SJ77

The Tens at Owen House Farm
★★★★ FARMHOUSE

tel: 07754 370721 & 01565 873555 **Wood Lane WA16 7NY**
email: stay@owenhousefarm.co.uk **web:** www.owenhousefarm.co.uk
dir: At crossroads of Wood Lane, continue on Small Lane. 50 metres on left.

Owen House Farm, as the name suggests, is a working farm which is being converted to a stunning wedding venue in the heart of the Cheshire countryside. Though you don't have to be at a wedding to stay! The Tens accommodation comprises spacious and very well-equipped double and family bedrooms in one of the farm's outbuildings; expect to find Nespresso machines, WiFi and Villeroy & Boch bathrooms. Breakfast in bed is the order of the day here with a hamper delivered to your door.

Rooms: 10 annexe en suite (2 fmly) (10 GF) **S** fr £75 **D** fr £75* **Facilities:** FTV tea/coffee Licensed WiFi **Extras:** Speciality toiletries **Parking:** 50 **Notes:** Civ wed 150 150 acres beef

PLUMLEY
Map 15 SJ77

The Golden Pheasant
★★★★ INN

tel: 01565 722261 **Plumley Moor Road WA16 9RX**
email: golden.pheasant@jwlees.co.uk **web:** www.goldenpheasantplumley.co.uk
dir: Phone for directions.

This 200-year-old rural inn has much to offer with traditional home-cooked food, a great range of ales and comfortable bedrooms that have great views of the Cheshire countryside. The individually styled bedrooms, one a four-poster suite, offer Freeview TVs, WiFi and tea- and coffee-making facilities as standard. Downstairs you'll find wood-burning stoves, cosy nooks, a large dining space and a bright garden room that looks out over the children's play area. Eating alfresco is possible in the beer garden in warmer weather.

Rooms: 9 en suite **Facilities:** tea/coffee Dinner available WiFi Riding **Parking:** 40

SANDBACH
Map 15 SJ76

Innkeeper's Lodge Sandbach, Holmes Chapel
★★★ INN

tel: 03451 551551 **Brereton Green CW11 1RS**
email: info@innkeeperslodge.com **web:** www.innkeeperslodge.com
dir: Phone for directions.

Peacefully located in rural Cheshire and close to Sandbach and Crewe, The Bear's Head, dating from 1624, is actually two adjoining buildings – one black-and-white-timbered and the other brick built. Inside there are real fires, old beams, flagstone floors, spacious dining areas and a wide choice of cask ales and food. The en suite, modern bedrooms have TVs, desks, free WiFi, tea- and coffee-making facilities as standard; family rooms are available. A continental buffet breakfast is complimentary for all guests.

Rooms: 25 en suite (6 fmly) (10 GF) **Facilities:** FTV tea/coffee Dinner available WiFi

TARPORLEY
Map 15 SJ56

Alvanley Arms Inn
★★★★ INN

tel: 01829 760200 **Cotebrook CW6 9DS**
email: info@alvanleyarms.co.uk **web:** www.alvanleyarms.co.uk
dir: M56 junction 10, follow signs for Whitchurch then A49.

This historic inn, bedecked with flowers in summer, dates back to the 17th century and the bar and dining areas still feature the original beams. Bedrooms are well equipped with complimentary WiFi access. The Alvanley Arms offers a wide choice of home-cooked meals that utilise local produce. The inn is perfectly placed for visiting the adjoining Shire Horse Centre and Countryside Park, which is popular with families, and also Delamere Forest Park and Oulton Park race circuit.

Rooms: 7 en suite **Facilities:** FTV DVD Lounge TVL tea/coffee Dinner available WiFi **Parking:** 30

WARMINGHAM
Map 15 SJ76

Premier Collection

The Bear's Paw

★★★★★ ◉ INN

tel: 01270 526317 **School Lane CW11 3QN**
email: info@thebearspaw.co.uk web: www.thebearspaw.co.uk
dir: *M6 junction 17, A534, A533 signed Middlewich and Northwich. Continue on A533, left into Mill Lane, left into Warmingham Lane. Right into Plant Lane, left into Green Lane.*

Located beside a small river in a rural Cheshire village, this fully modernised 19th-century, red-brick inn provides spacious boutique bedrooms that have a wealth of practical extras and feature deeply comfortable beds. The friendly team serves imaginative food, which makes use of quality seasonal produce, in an attractive open-plan dining room. Relaxed lounge areas are also available.

Rooms: 17 en suite (4 fmly) **Facilities:** STV FTV iPod docking station Lounge tea/coffee Dinner available Direct dial WiFi **Extras:** Apple TV – deposit required **Parking:** 75 **Notes:** LB

CORNWALL & ISLES OF SCILLY

BODINNICK
Map 2 SX15

The Old Ferry Inn

★★★ ⚲ ⬭ INN

tel: 01726 870237 **PL23 1LX**
email: info@oldferryinn.co.uk web: www.oldferryinn.co.uk
dir: *From Liskeard on A38 to Dobwalls, left onto A390. After 3 miles left onto B3359 signed Looe. Right at sign for Lerryn/Bodinnick/Polruan.*

The Old Ferry Inn has stood on the edge of the Fowey Estuary for over 400 years, overlooking the Bodinnick to Fowey ferry service. 'Ferryside', the childhood home of Daphne du Maurier, is at the bottom of the hill. There are plenty of coastal walks, historical buildings, fishing and wildlife nearby, with the famous Eden Project just a few miles away. A range of local beers and Cornish ciders is available, and meals can be enjoyed while gazing at the amazing river views.

Rooms: 12 rms (10 en suite) (2 pri facs) (1 fmly) **S** fr £80 **D** fr £80* **Facilities:** FTV Lounge TVL tea/coffee Dinner available WiFi **Parking:** 8 **Notes:** LB

BODMIN
Map 2 SX06

Mennabroom Farm

★★★★ ⚲ ⬭ FARMHOUSE

tel: 01208 821272 **Warleggan PL30 4HE**
email: enquiries@mennabroom.com web: www.mennabroom.co.uk
dir: *A30 take exit signed Colliford Lake. After 2.8 miles turn right signed Mennabroom Farm and Cottages, turn right into Mennabroom.*

In the heart of Bodmin Moor, this extremely comfortable farmhouse offers a haven of peace and tranquillity for visitors to the beautiful West Country. The bedrooms are well appointed with quality furnishings and very comfortable beds. Guests are welcomed with afternoon tea; dinner is available on request and breakfasts feature the farm's home-produced eggs, bacon and sausages. Self-catering cottages are also available.

Rooms: 2 en suite **S** fr £75 **D** fr £95 **Facilities:** FTV DVD Lounge tea/coffee Dinner available WiFi **Extras:** Speciality toiletries – complimentary **Parking:** 6 **Notes:** LB 40 acres sheep/pigs/beef

BUDE
Map 2 SS20

Premier Collection

Pot and Barrel B&B

★★★★★ ⚲ BED AND BREAKFAST

tel: 01288 355305 **Crooklets Beach EX23 8NE**
email: chris@potandbarrel.co.uk web: www.potandbarrel.com
dir: *From town centre follow signs for Crooklets Beach. Crooklets Inn on right, turn left towards sea, pass unmade track. Take sharp right hairpin bend, proceed up hill.*

Originally an elegant Edwardian gentleman's residence built 1910, the Pot and Barrel offers two well-appointed bedrooms, both furnished and decorated to a high standard. There is a guest lounge with a cosy fire in the winter months and a dining room with distracting coastal views; the sun lounge also boasts excellent views. A high-quality breakfast, with plenty of choice including daily changing specials, is on offer each morning.

Rooms: 2 en suite (1 GF) **D** fr £108* **Facilities:** FTV Lounge TVL tea/coffee WiFi ⚲ **Extras:** Robes, fresh milk – complimentary **Parking:** 3 **Notes:** LB No children 16 years

Bangors Organic

★★★★ ⚲ ⬭ GUEST HOUSE

tel: 01288 361297 **Poundstock EX23 0DP**
email: info@bangorsorganic.co.uk web: www.bangorsorganic.co.uk
dir: *4 miles south of Bude. On A39 in Poundstock.*

Situated a few miles south of Bude, this renovated Victorian establishment offers elegant accommodation with a good level of comfort. Bedrooms are furnished to a high standard with bathrooms worthy of special mention, being impressively spacious and luxurious. Breakfast and dinner, featuring organic, local and home-made produce, are served in the pleasant dining room. The establishment is certified as organic by the Soil Association.

Rooms: 2 en suite **Facilities:** TVL tea/coffee Dinner available Licensed WiFi ⚲ Badminton **Parking:** 10 **Notes:** No children 10 years

Pencarrol Guest House

★★★★ GUEST HOUSE

tel: 01288 352478 **21 Downs View EX23 8RF**
email: pencarrol21@gmail.com
dir: *0.5 mile north of Bude. North from Bude into Flexbury village.*

This cosy guest house is only a short walk from Bude centre and Crooklets Beach, and has glorious views over the golf course. Bedrooms are attractively furnished and there is a first-floor lounge. Breakfast is served at separate tables in the dining room.

Rooms: 5 rms (3 en suite) (2 pri facs) (2 fmly) **S** fr £35 **D** fr £74* **Facilities:** FTV tea/coffee WiFi ⚲ **Notes:** LB No children 10 years Closed November to February

Sea Jade Guest House

★★★ GUEST ACCOMMODATION

tel: 01288 353404 & 07737 541540 **15 Burn View EX23 8BZ**
email: seajadeguesthouse@yahoo.co.uk **web:** www.seajadeguesthouse.co.uk
dir: *From A39 follow signs for Bude and golf course.*

A warm welcome awaits at this popular establishment which is within a few minutes' walk of both the town and beaches. Bedrooms are light and airy with simple, contemporary styling; some have views across the golf course. Breakfast is a generous offering and guaranteed to get the day off to a satisfying start.

Rooms: 8 rms (7 en suite) (1 pri facs) (4 fmly) (2 GF) **S** fr £40 **D** fr £80*
Facilities: FTV TVL tea/coffee WiFi ⅃ ⏚ **Notes:** LB

CALLINGTON	Map 3 SX36

Woodpeckers

★★★★ 🍴 GUEST HOUSE

tel: 01579 363717 **Rilla Mill PL17 7NT**
email: alisonmerchant@talktalk.net **web:** www.woodpeckersguesthouse.co.uk
dir: *5 miles northwest of Callington. Exit B3254 at Upton Cross crossroads for Rilla Mill.*

Set in a conservation village, in a wooded valley, by a tumbling stream, this modern, detached house offers cosy, well-equipped bedrooms with numerous thoughtful extras. Home-cooked dinners, using the best local ingredients, are available by prior arrangement. The hot tub in the garden is an additional feature.

Rooms: 3 en suite **Facilities:** STV FTV tea/coffee Dinner available Gym ⏚ Spa/hot tub **Parking:** 7 **Notes:** LB

CAMELFORD	Map 2 SX18

Toppesfield House B&B

★★★★ 🍴 BED AND BREAKFAST

tel: 01840 211211 & 07789 462559 **26 Mill Lane PL32 9UF**
email: karenwilder9@aol.com **web:** www.toppesfieldhousebnb.co.uk
dir: *From High Street, turn into Mill Lane (opposite The Masons Arms). Up hill, pass Greenhills on left, fork right, 2nd house on right.*

With gardens overlooking Enfield Park, this bed and breakfast offers comfortable and inviting accommodation paired with warm hospitality. The well-presented en suite bedrooms, with garden views, are furnished to a high standard with many thoughtful extras. A good choice is offered at breakfast and makes a great way to start the day. Private parking is provided.

Rooms: 3 en suite **D** fr £95 **Facilities:** STV FTV tea/coffee WiFi ⏚ **Parking:** 3 **Notes:** No children 12 years

CRAFTHOLE	Map 3 SX35

The Little Fox

★★★★ 🍴 GUEST ACCOMMODATION

tel: 01503 230863 **PL11 3BD**
email: info@littlefoxhotel.co.uk **web:** www.littlefoxhotel.co.uk
dir: *Phone for directions.*

This attractive, historic 14th-century inn enjoys an imposing position in the rolling Cornish countryside. Bedrooms, many with pleasant views, have a homely feel – all are comfortable and have impressive modern facilities. Public areas have an engaging charm and the restaurant provides a relaxing environment with an impressive menu selection. Breakfasts are tasty and freshly cooked.

Rooms: 7 en suite 4 annexe en suite (5 fmly) (3 GF) **Facilities:** FTV Lounge TVL tea/coffee Dinner available Licensed WiFi ⅃ ⏚ **Conf:** Max 30 Thtr 30 Class 30 Board 30 **Parking:** 60 **Notes:** LB Civ wed 120

FALMOUTH	Map 2 SW83

Premier Collection

Anacapri

★★★★★ GUEST ACCOMMODATION

tel: 01326 311454 **Gyllyngvase Road TR11 4DJ**
email: anacapri@btconnect.com **web:** www.hotelanacapri.co.uk
dir: *A39 (Truro to Falmouth), straight on at lights. Over next 2 roundabouts into Melvill Road, down hill, 2nd right into Gyllyngvase Road, Anacapri on right.*

With stunning views out across the sea and beach, this well managed property offers friendly, attentive service from a young and upbeat team, with jolly managers Peter and June at the helm to oversee guest care. The smart and extremely comfortable bedrooms are spacious; many rooms enjoy splendid sea views. Public areas are varied and include a smart bar and lounge where guests can enjoy drinks and snacks, and ample seating is provided on the delightful sea-facing patio. This is a superb establishment where guests are made to feel very welcome and at home. The hosts are ready to offer all sorts of interesting and additional information on the location and region.

Rooms: 18 en suite (3 fmly) (2 GF) **Facilities:** FTV TVL tea/coffee Licensed WiFi ⏚ **Conf:** Max 50 Thtr 50 Class 40 Board 20 **Parking:** 18 **Notes:** LB

FALMOUTH *continued*

The Rosemary

★★★★ GUEST ACCOMMODATION

tel: 01326 314669 **22 Gyllyngvase Terrace TR11 4DL**
email: stay@therosemary.co.uk web: www.therosemary.co.uk
dir: *A39 (Melvill Road) signed to beaches and seafront, right into Gyllyngvase Road, 1st left.*

Just a short walk from the beach, this welcoming establishment is conveniently located for exploring the local area. All the well-equipped bedrooms provide impressive levels of comfort and quality, including speciality toiletries – many rooms have the added bonus of wonderful views across Falmouth Bay. Breakfast is a generous and tasty start to the day and is served in the light and airy dining room. Other facilities include a bar and guest lounge, while outside a decked area and rear garden are also available. Superfast broadband is available throughout. Dogs are allowed in some bedrooms.

Rooms: 8 en suite (2 fmly) **S** fr £50 **D** fr £79* **Facilities:** FTV Lounge tea/coffee Licensed WiFi 🐾 **Extras:** Superfast broadband, speciality toiletries, robes **Parking:** 2 **Notes:** LB Closed mid December to January

Melvill House

★★★★ GUEST ACCOMMODATION

tel: 01326 316645 **52 Melvill Road TR11 4DQ**
email: melvillhouse@btconnect.com web: www.melvill-house-falmouth.co.uk
dir: *On A39 near town centre and docks.*

Well situated for the beach, the town centre and the National Maritime Museum on the harbour, Melvill House is a family-run establishment with a relaxed atmosphere. Some bedrooms have four-poster beds, and breakfast is served in the smart dining room. Ample parking is provided.

Rooms: 7 en suite (2 fmly) (1 GF) **Facilities:** FTV TVL tea/coffee WiFi 🐾 **Parking:** 8 **Notes:** LB

Rosemullion

★★★★ GUEST ACCOMMODATION

tel: 01326 314690 **Gyllyngvase Hill TR11 4DF**
email: gail@rosemullionhotel.co.uk web: www.rosemullionhotel.co.uk
dir: *Phone for directions.*

Recognisable by its mock-Tudor exterior, this warm and friendly establishment is well situated for visiting both the town centre and the beach. Some of the comfortable bedrooms are on the ground floor, while a few rooms on the top floor have views to Falmouth Bay. Breakfast, served in the panelled dining room, is freshly cooked, and there is also a well-appointed lounge.

Rooms: 13 rms (11 en suite) (2 pri facs) (3 GF) **Facilities:** FTV Lounge tea/coffee WiFi **Parking:** 13 **Notes:** LB No children Closed 23 December to 3 January

Trevoil Guest House

★★★ GUEST HOUSE

tel: 01326 314145 & 07966 409782 **25 Avenue Road TR11 4AY**
email: alan.jewel@btconnect.com web: www.trevoilfalmouth.co.uk
dir: *Exit A39 (Melvill Road) left into Avenue Road, 150 yards from Maritime Museum.*

Located within walking distance of the town centre, the friendly Trevoil Guest House is a comfortable and relaxed place to stay. Breakfast is enjoyed in the light, pleasant dining room. Parking is available.

Rooms: 8 rms (4 en suite) (3 fmly) (1 GF) **Facilities:** FTV tea/coffee WiFi **Parking:** 7 **Notes:** LB

HAYLE	Map 2 SW53

The Penellen

★★★★ GUEST ACCOMMODATION

tel: 01736 753777 **64 Riviere Towans, Phillack TR27 5AF**
email: penellen@btconnect.com web: www.penellen.co.uk
dir: *From A30 onto B3301 through Hayle. Turn opposite petrol station, road bears left, into private road.*

Superbly situated at the water's edge, this personally run, friendly property has splendid views of the beach and coastline. Bedrooms are well equipped and comfortable, many with patio doors and stunning views to wake up to each morning. The cheerful hosts provide attentive service. The dining room is spacious with a bright and airy feel. Food is a strength, with good quality produce on offer. Parking is free.

Rooms: 5 en suite (2 fmly) **S** fr £80 **D** fr £80* **Facilities:** FTV tea/coffee WiFi **Parking:** 10 **Notes:** Closed November to February

LAUNCESTON   Map 3 SX38

Premier Collection

Wheatley Farm

★★★★★ 🛏 FARMHOUSE

tel: 01566 781232 **Maxworthy PL15 8LY**
email: valerie@wheatley-farm.co.uk **web:** www.farmstay-cornwall.co.uk
dir: From A39 at Wainhouse Corner follow signs to Canworthy Water. At T-junction, left and after 1.5 miles turn left at sign to Wheatley Farm. 1st farm on left.

This working dairy farm, in wonderful rolling countryside, dates back to 1871 and was originally part of Lord Bedford's estate; the family have been farming here for five generations. A pot of tea is always on offer for arriving guests, and every effort is made to ensure a relaxing and rewarding stay. The bedrooms provide high levels of comfort, likewise the modern bathrooms. Breakfast is a treat and is served in the lovely dining room complete with an original slate floor and imposing granite fireplace. Additional facilities include a guest lounge, heated indoor swimming pool, spa and sauna.

Rooms: 4 en suite **Facilities:** FTV DVD TVL tea/coffee WiFi 🏊 Sauna 🛁 Spa bath **Parking:** 4 **Notes:** LB No children Closed November to March 232 acres dairy

Bradridge Farm

★★★★ FARMHOUSE

tel: 01409 271264 & 07748 253346 **PL15 9RL**
email: angela@bradridgefarm.co.uk **web:** www.bradridgefarm.co.uk
dir: 5.5 miles north of Launceston. Exit B3254 at Ladycross sign for Boyton, Bradridge 2nd farm on right after Boyton school.

This late Victorian farmhouse stands in glorious countryside on the border of Devon and Cornwall. The well-presented bedrooms have many considerate extras, and the Aga-cooked breakfasts feature farm-fresh eggs.

Rooms: 4 rms (3 en suite) (1 fmly) **Facilities:** FTV Lounge TVL tea/coffee WiFi Fishing **Parking:** 6 **Notes:** LB Closed November to March 250 acres arable/beef/sheep/hens

Middle Tremollett Farm B&B

★★★★ 🛏 FARMHOUSE

tel: 01566 782416 & 07973 435529 **Coad's Green PL15 7NA**
email: btrewin@btinternet.com **web:** www.tremollett.co.uk
dir: A30 onto B3257, through village of Coad's Green. Turn right signed Tremollett, 1st on left at bottom of hill.

Genuine hospitality is assured at this delightful granite farmhouse surrounded with breathtaking views of the countryside. The bedrooms are individually furnished and decorated, and equipped with numerous extras. The delicious breakfasts use only the best local produce, and include home-made produce and the farm's own eggs.

Rooms: 2 en suite **Facilities:** FTV TVL tea/coffee WiFi ♿ 🛁 **Extras:** Speciality toiletries **Parking:** 3 **Notes:** LB No children 12 years Closed December to February 100 acres arable/beef/sheep

Tyne Wells House

★★★★ BED AND BREAKFAST

tel: 01566 775810 **Pennygillam PL15 7EE**
email: btucker@talktalk.net **web:** www.tynewells.co.uk
dir: 0.6 mile southwest of town centre. Exit A30 onto Pennygillam roundabout, house off roundabout.

Situated on the outskirts of town, Tyne Wells House has panoramic views over the countryside. There's a relaxed and friendly atmosphere and the bedrooms are neatly furnished. A hearty breakfast is served in the dining room which overlooks the garden.

Rooms: 3 rms (2 en suite) (1 pri facs) (1 fmly) **S** fr £40 **D** fr £65* **Facilities:** FTV DVD tea/coffee WiFi 🛁 **Extras:** Shared fridge **Parking:** 4 **Notes:** LB

Copper Meadow

[U]

tel: 01566 782239 & 07974 701250 **Trevadlock, Congdon Shop PL15 7PW**
email: barbara@trevadlock.co.uk **web:** www.trevadlock.co.uk
dir: Phone for directions.

Currently the rating for this establishment is not confirmed. This may be due to a change of ownership or because it has only recently joined the AA rating scheme.

Rooms: 2 en suite **S** fr £45 **D** fr £87.50 **Facilities:** FTV tea/coffee WiFi 🛁 **Parking:** 2 **Notes:** LB No children 5 years

LEEDSTOWN   Map 2 SW63

Little Pengelly Farm

★★★★ FARMHOUSE

tel: 01736 850452 **Trenwheal TR27 6BP**
email: maxine@littlepengelly.co.uk **web:** www.littlepengelly.co.uk
dir: From Hayle on B3302 towards Helston. Through Leedstown, after 2 miles at top of hill turn left. 1st house on right.

Little Pengelly Farm is situated in beautiful countryside about five miles from both the north and south coasts of the Cornish peninsula. B&B and self-catering accommodation are on offer, as well as a tea room serving freshly baked scones with home-made jam. The three guest rooms are bright and comfortable and enjoy views of the garden or courtyard. A farmhouse breakfast is served in the conservatory overlooking the gardens. A laundry service and free WiFi are available, and there is ample parking on site.

Rooms: 3 rms (2 en suite) (1 pri facs) (1 fmly) **D** fr £85* **Facilities:** FTV tea/coffee WiFi 🛁 **Extras:** Speciality toiletries – complimentary **Parking:** 10 **Notes:** LB Closed 23 December to 2 January 10 acres arable

LISKEARD
Map 2 SX26

See also Callington

Trecarne House

★★★★ ⬧ GUEST ACCOMMODATION

tel: 01579 343543 & 07950 262682 **Penhale Grange, St Cleer PL14 5EB**
email: trish@trecarnehouse.co.uk **web:** www.trecarnehouse.co.uk
dir: *B3254 north from Liskeard to St Cleer. 1st right after entering village, 3rd left after church, 2nd right, house on right.*

A warm welcome awaits at Trecarne House, a large family home, peacefully located on the edge of the village. The stylish and spacious bedrooms enjoy magnificent country views and have many thoughtful extras. The buffet-style breakfast offers a wide choice, which can be enjoyed in the dining room or bright conservatory overlooking rolling countryside.

Rooms: 3 en suite (2 fmly) (1 GF) **Facilities:** FTV DVD iPod docking station TVL tea/coffee Dinner available WiFi 🔒 Table tennis, trampoline **Extras:** Speciality toiletries **Conf:** Max 25 **Parking:** 8 **Notes:** LB

LIZARD
Map 2 SW71

Atlantic House B&B

★★★★ ⬧ BED AND BREAKFAST

tel: 01326 290399 **Pentreath Lane TR12 7NY**
email: atlantichse@btinternet.com **web:** www.atlantichouselizard.co.uk
dir: *A3083 to Lizard. Turn right at village green, right again into Pentreath Lane (no through road) signed Kynance Cove. House in 200 yards on right. (Park close to hedge on right side of lane).*

Located in a peaceful area of The Lizard, Atlantic House is within easy walking distance of the coastal path and many of the surrounding beaches. Service is the highlight of the stay ensuring that all needs and wants are catered for. The three guest bedrooms are en suite and offer a comfortable night's sleep. There is a south-facing sun terrace and garden, home-made afternoon teas and free WiFi. Full English breakfasts are offered daily in the delightful breakfast room.

Rooms: 3 en suite **S** fr £85 **D** fr £95* **Facilities:** FTV DVD tea/coffee WiFi **Extras:** Cornish cream tea for stays of three or more nights, speciality toiletries – complimentary **Parking:** 3 **Notes:** No children 16 years

LOOE
Map 2 SX25

The Beach House

★★★★★ ⬧ GUEST ACCOMMODATION

tel: 01503 262598 **Marine Drive, Hannafore PL13 2DH**
email: beachhouselooe@gmail.com **web:** www.thebeachhouselooe.co.uk
dir: *From Looe west over bridge, left to Hannafore and Marine Drive, on right after Tom Sawyers B&B.*

As its name would suggest, this property has panoramic sea views and is just a short walk from the harbour, restaurants and town. Some rooms have stylish hand-made furniture, and the bedrooms are well equipped and have many extras. Hearty breakfasts are served in the first-floor dining room, providing a good start for walking the South West Coast Path which passes right by the house.

Rooms: 5 en suite (4 GF) **D** fr £110* **Facilities:** FTV Lounge tea/coffee WiFi 🛥 Beauty treatment room **Extras:** Speciality toiletries, fresh fruit – complimentary **Parking:** 6 **Notes:** LB No children 16 years Closed Christmas

Bucklawren Farm

★★★★ FARMHOUSE

tel: 01503 240738 **St Martin-by-Looe PL13 1NZ**
email: info@bucklawren.co.uk **web:** www.bucklawren.co.uk
dir: *2 miles northeast of Looe. Off B3253 to Monkey Sanctuary, 0.5 mile right to Bucklawren, farmhouse 0.5 mile on left.*

This spacious 19th-century farmhouse stands in 400 acres of farmland just a mile from the beach. The attractive bedrooms, including one on the ground floor providing wheelchair access, are well equipped; the front-facing rooms have spectacular views across fields to the sea. Breakfast is served in the dining room with stunning views of the rolling countryside.

Rooms: 6 en suite (3 fmly) (1 GF) **S** fr £50 **D** fr £85 **Facilities:** FTV Lounge TVL tea/coffee WiFi ⛵ **Extras:** Speciality toiletries, fridge **Parking:** 6 **Notes:** LB No children 5 years Closed 20–27 December 400 acres arable/beef

Meneglaze Guest House

★★★★ GUEST HOUSE

tel: 01503 269227 & 07717 288497 **Shutta PL13 1LU**
email: dannycornwall@outlook.com **web:** www.meneglaze.com
dir: *A387, opposite railway station turn into Shutta, 100 yards on left.*

Built in 1860, this delightful guest house was formerly a sea captain's house. It has a private parking area and offers modern comfort and style just a five-minute, easy walk from the centre of Looe. Meneglaze maintains elements of its seafaring days with hints of the nautical throughout the decor. All bedrooms have tea- and coffee-making facilities, mini-bar fridges, sumptuous towelling gowns, Egyptian cotton bedding, Freeview TVs and free WiFi. Breakfasts are hearty and proudly Cornish. Expect the best quality home-made marmalades and jams and the finest (award-winning) Hog's Pudding available each morning.

Rooms: 4 en suite **Facilities:** FTV iPod docking station tea/coffee WiFi ⛵ **Extras:** Safe, fridge, fruit, home-made biscuits, sweets, flowers **Parking:** 6 **Notes:** LB No children

Trehaven Manor

★★★★ ⬤ ⬤ GUEST ACCOMMODATION

tel: 01503 262028 **Station Road PL13 1HN**
email: stay@trehaven.co.uk **web:** www.trehaven.co.uk
dir: *In East Looe between railway station and bridge. Trehaven's drive adjacent to The Globe public house.*

Run by a charming family, this former rectory is in a stunning location with magnificent views of the estuary. Many of the attractive bedrooms have views, and all are particularly well equipped. There is also a cosy lounge bar. Dinner, by arrangement, specialises in oriental cuisine, and breakfast features traditional fare; the meals are memorable.

Rooms: 7 en suite (1 fmly) (1 GF) **Facilities:** TVL tea/coffee Dinner available Licensed **Parking:** 8 **Notes:** LB

Tremaine Farm

★★★★ FARMHOUSE

tel: 01503 220417 **Pelynt PL13 2LT**
email: rosemary@tremainefarm.co.uk **web:** www.tremainefarm.co.uk
dir: *5 miles northwest of Looe. B3359 north from Pelynt, left at crossroads.*

Convenient for Fowey, Looe and Polperro, this pleasant working farm offers a relaxing and rewarding stay. The proprietors provide friendly hospitality and attentive service, and the spacious and stylish bedrooms are well equipped with impressive bathrooms. A hearty breakfast is served in the dining room and there is also a spacious and comfortable guest lounge.

Rooms: 3 en suite (1 fmly) **S** fr £45 **D** fr £80* **Facilities:** FTV DVD iPod docking station TVL tea/coffee WiFi **Extras:** Fridge **Parking:** 6 **Notes:** LB 250 acres arable/sheep

Trenake Manor Farm

★★★★ FARMHOUSE

tel: 01503 220835 & 07812 982775 **Pelynt PL13 2LT**
email: lorraine@cornishfarmhouse.co.uk **web:** www.cornishfarmhouse.co.uk
dir: *A38 onto A390 then B3359. Right at small crossroads, signed Trenake Farm.*

This welcoming 15th-century farmhouse is surrounded by countryside and makes a good base for touring Cornwall. Bedrooms have thoughtful finishing touches and there is a comfortable lounge. Breakfast, using local produce, is served in the cosy dining room, and you might see the milking cows passing the end of the garden.

Rooms: 3 en suite (1 fmly) **Facilities:** STV FTV Lounge TVL tea/coffee Dinner available WiFi ⛵ **Parking:** 10 **Notes:** LB 1000 acres dairy/beef/arable

Commonwood Manor

★★★★ ⬤ GUEST ACCOMMODATION

tel: 01503 262929 & 07795 258699 **St Martins Road PL13 1LP**
email: simon@commonwoodmanor.com **web:** www.commonwoodmanor.com
dir: *From centre of Looe, on A387, right onto B3253, 200 yards on right.*

Commonwood Manor is steeped in history, with high ceilings, grand fireplaces and panoramic views of the Looe Valley. Interior design respects the tradition and history of the building, but guests will find that all the modern comforts are provided. Despite the grand surroundings, the atmosphere is relaxed and friendly. The bedrooms are situated over three floors and offer great views. Breakfast is served daily in the family kitchen, a substantial offering that makes for a great start to the day.

Rooms: 7 en suite (3 fmly) **D** fr £90 **Facilities:** FTV Lounge tea/coffee Dinner available Licensed WiFi ⊗ ⛵ ⬤ **Extras:** Snacks **Conf:** Max 30 Thtr 20 Class 30 Board 12 **Parking:** 14 **Notes:** LB Civ wed 45

Little Harbour

★★★ GUEST HOUSE

tel: 01503 262474 & 07846 575262 **Church Street PL13 2EX**
email: littleharbour@btconnect.com **web:** www.littleharbour.co.uk
dir: *From West Looe harbour, right into Princess Square, guest house on left.*

Little Harbour is situated almost on Looe's harbour in the historic old town; it is in a pleasant and convenient spot and some parking is available. The proprietors are friendly and attentive, and bedrooms are well appointed and attractively decorated. Breakfast is served, freshly cooked, in the dining room.

Rooms: 5 en suite (1 fmly) **Facilities:** STV FTV TVL tea/coffee WiFi ⬤ Sauna Gym ⬤ **Conf:** Max 14 Thtr 14 Class 14 Board 14 **Parking:** 3 **Notes:** LB No children 5 years

LOOE *continued*

The Ship Inn

★★★ INN

tel: 01503 263124 **Fore Street PL13 1AD**
email: reservations@smallandfriendly.co.uk **web:** www.smallandfriendly.co.uk
dir: *Phone for directions.*

This lively family pub is located in the very heart of bustling East Looe and has a local following. The bedrooms are comfortable and equipped with all the expected facilities. A wide range of popular dishes is served at lunch and during the evenings, with light refreshments available throughout the day.

Rooms: 8 en suite (1 fmly) **Facilities:** FTV tea/coffee Dinner available WiFi
🔒 **Notes:** LB

LOSTWITHIEL   Map 2 SX15

Premier Collection

The Old Chapel B&B

★★★★★ 🍴 GUEST ACCOMMODATION

tel: 01579 321260 & 07979 234743 **West Taphouse PL22 0RP**
email: enquiries@theoldchapelbandb.co.uk **web:** www.theoldchapelbandb.co.uk
dir: *From Bodmin follow signs to Lostwithiel. In town, turn left onto A390. After 3 miles into West Taphouse, last property on left.*

Friendly hosts Greg and Kimberley offer a genuine welcome at The Old Chapel. The beautifully appointed bedrooms and bathrooms are well equipped with thoughtful touches including chocolates, shortbread biscuits and fresh milk for tea and coffee. The region has much to offer as sightseeing and activities are plentiful. The hosts have designed their own "Carless breaks" for those who wish to enjoy their trip with the option of leaving the car at home.

Rooms: 4 rms (3 en suite) (1 pri facs) **S** fr £65 **D** fr £70* **Facilities:** FTV DVD tea/coffee WiFi 🔒 **Extras:** Home-made biscuits, sweets, flowers – complimentary **Parking:** 6 **Notes:** LB No children 13 years

Penrose B&B

★★★★ GUEST ACCOMMODATION

tel: 01208 871417 & 07766 900179 **1 The Terrace PL22 0DT**
email: enquiries@penrosebb.co.uk **web:** www.penrosebb.co.uk
dir: *In Lostwithiel on A390 (Edgcumbe Road) into Scrations Lane, turn 1st right for parking.*

Just a short walk from the town centre, this grand Victorian house offers comfortable accommodation and a genuine homely atmosphere. Many of the bedrooms have the original fireplaces and all are equipped with thoughtful extras. Breakfast is a generous offering and is served in the elegant dining room, with views over the garden. WiFi access is also available.

Rooms: 6 en suite (3 fmly) (2 GF) **Facilities:** FTV DVD TVL tea/coffee WiFi
🔒 **Extras:** Speciality toiletries, robes, sweets – complimentary **Parking:** 8 **Notes:** LB

LUXULYAN   Map 2 SX05

Ivy Cottage

★★★★ BED AND BREAKFAST

tel: 01726 850796 & 07484 290206 **PL30 5DW**
email: liz.edwards1@btinternet.com **web:** www.ivycottage-luxulyan.co.uk
dir: *A30 exit at Innis Downs onto A391. Follow signs to Eden Project. At roundabout take 1st exit signed Luxulyan. Pass Kings Arms pub, over rail bridge to top of hill. Turn right and at church sharp left, 1st cottage on right.*

This welcoming cottage is surrounded by countryside and is an ideal base for touring Cornwall. Bedrooms have thoughtful finishing touches and there is a picturesque garden, with abundant wildlife, to relax in, and you can watch the friendly cows in the farmers' fields. Breakfast, prepared using local produce, is enjoyed in the cosy dining room. Private parking is provided.

Rooms: 2 en suite **S** fr £70 **D** fr £80* **Facilities:** FTV TVL tea/coffee Lift WiFi ⚓
🔒 **Parking:** 3 **Notes:** Closed 15 October to March

MARAZION   Map 2 SW53

The Marazion

★★★★ INN

tel: 01736 710334 **The Square TR17 0AP**
email: info@marazionhotel.co.uk **web:** www.marazionhotel.co.uk
dir: *In village square opposite Out of Blue gallery.*

Within 50 metres of one of Cornwall's safest beaches, this family-run establishment offers a relaxed atmosphere with friendly service. The individually furnished and decorated bedrooms are comfortable, and many have the benefit of stunning views across to St Michael's Mount. The Cutty Sark public bar is a great place to sit and enjoy a drink and listen to local banter, while the restaurant provides a wide range of meals to suit all tastes and budgets.

Rooms: 11 en suite (1 fmly) **Facilities:** FTV Lounge tea/coffee Dinner available WiFi
🔒 **Parking:** 20 **Notes:** Closed November

St Michael's Bed and Breakfast

★★★★ 🍴 BED AND BREAKFAST

tel: 01736 711348 **The Corner House, Fore Street TR17 0AD**
email: info@stmichaels-bedandbreakfast.co.uk
web: www.stmichaels-bedandbreakfast.co.uk
dir: *From A30 at Newtown roundabout, exit signed Marazion. At T-junction turn left, into Marazion, 800 metres on left next to methodist chapel.*

A relaxed yet professional approach together with comfortable accommodation make St Michael's the ideal place to stay when visiting the ancient market town of Marazion, the sandy beaches of Mount's Bay or St Michael's Mount. The top floor rooms enjoy sea views, and parking is available. The recommended breakfast includes a traditional Cornish option, which can be enjoyed in the sunny and spacious breakfast room.

Rooms: 6 en suite (1 GF) **Facilities:** FTV tea/coffee WiFi **Parking:** 6
Notes: No children 15 years

Glenleigh House

★★★ GUEST HOUSE

tel: 01736 710308 **Higher Fore Street TR17 0BQ**
email: glenleighbandb@hotmail.co.uk **web:** www.glenleigh-marazion.co.uk
dir: A394 to Penzance, opposite Fire Engine Inn.

Glenleigh House, overlooking St Michael's Mount and the sweeping panorama of Mount's Bay, has been owned and run by the Hales family for more than 30 years. With eight comfortable and well-appointed bedrooms (many with views to the Mount and the sea), you can be assured of a comfortable stay. Built in 1898 as the home of a prosperous farmer, the house retains its original Victorian charm while providing modern amenities such as free WiFi. Expect a filling breakfast of your choice to set you up for the day.

Rooms: 8 en suite (1 GF) **Facilities:** FTV TVL tea/coffee WiFi **Parking:** 8 **Notes:** LB No children 8 years Closed November to March

MEVAGISSEY
Map 2 SX04

Premier Collection

Pebble House

★★★★★ ◉ GUEST ACCOMMODATION

tel: 01726 844466 & 07973 714392 **Polkirt Hill PL26 6UX**
email: hello@pebblehousecornwall.co.uk **web:** www.pebblehousecornwall.co.uk
dir: B3273 to Mevagissey, into village and follow one-way system. Pass Ship Inn on right, up hill keeping sea on left to T-junction. Pebble House on right.

This property is affectionately known as 'THE house with THE view' which certainly provides an accurate description. Providing boutique-style accommodation, all the rooms are en suite and individual in design – contemporary, quirky and providing excellent comfort. You can buy pretty much everything you see in the house if you wish. Light snacks, picnics, cream teas and a range of drinks are available, along with a hearty breakfast featuring daily specials. Please note that Pebble House can only accommodate children aged over 16.

Rooms: 3 en suite (1 GF) **D** fr £170* **Facilities:** STV FTV DVD TVL tea/coffee Licensed WiFi ◉ **Extras:** Speciality toiletries, robes, bottled water **Parking:** 6 **Notes:** LB No children 16 years

Premier Collection

Portmellon Cove Guest House

★★★★★ ◉ GUEST ACCOMMODATION

tel: 01726 843410 & 07747 440002 **121 Portmellon Park, Portmellon PL26 6XD**
email: stay@portmellon-cove.com **web:** www.portmellon-cove.com
dir: A390 onto B3273 into Mevagissey. Through village, up Polkirt Hill. 1st left into Porthmellon Road, pass pub, right into Porthmellon Park, take 1st right then on right.

Portmellon Cove Guest House lies in a quiet, peaceful, sandy cove less than a mile from the pretty fishing village of Mevagissey. This well-run family property offers inviting sea-view rooms, free parking and WiFi. All three rooms are well equipped with a generous mini-bar and beverage tray. Award-winning breakfasts are served in the bright and airy dining room which enjoys views

across the garden and out to sea. Close to The Lost Gardens of Heligan, the Eden Project, the coastal path and cycleways, most of Cornwall's many attractions can be reached within an hour.

Rooms: 3 en suite **S** fr £99 **D** fr £99* **Facilities:** FTV DVD iPod docking station Lounge tea/coffee Licensed WiFi ↕ ◉ **Extras:** Mini-bar, snacks, robes, fridge, fresh milk – complimentary; Champagne, chocolates, flowers, fruit bowls, high/ cream teas – chargeable **Parking:** 5 **Notes:** LB No children 12 years Closed November to March

Stone's Throw Cottage

★★★★ BED AND BREAKFAST

tel: 01726 844605 **5 Polkirt Hill PL26 6UR**
email: info@stones-throw-cottage-mevagissey.com
web: www.stones-throw-cottage-mevagissey.com
dir: From St Austell take B3273 to Mevagissey.

A beautifully restored fisherman's cottage set in the centre of Mevagissey, a minute's walk from the quaint historic harbour, shops, bars and restaurants. The friendly host offers cheerful hospitality, alongside bedrooms and bathrooms that have been sympathetically appointed and well equipped. Comfort and quality is assured in the additional, thoughtful touches including chocolates, assorted teas and fresh milk for tea and coffee. Sumptuous beds ensure a good night's sleep.

Rooms: 3 rms (2 en suite) (1 pri facs) **Facilities:** FTV DVD tea/coffee WiFi **Extras:** iPads **Notes:** LB

MITCHELL
Map 2 SW85

The Plume of Feathers

★★★★ ⬛ INN

tel: 01872 510387 & 511122 **TR8 5AX**
email: theplume@hospitalitycornwall.com **web:** www.theplumemitchell.co.uk
dir: Just off A30 and A3076, follow signs.

The Plume of Feathers is a very popular inn, with origins dating back to the 16th century, situated close to Newquay and the beaches. The restaurant offers a varied menu which relies heavily on local produce. The stylish bedrooms are decorated in neutral colours and have wrought-iron beds with quality linens. The garden makes an ideal place to enjoy a meal or a Cornish tea. Staff are very friendly.

Rooms: 12 annexe en suite (3 fmly) (9 GF) **S** fr £75 **D** fr £100* **Facilities:** FTV tea/coffee Dinner available WiFi **Conf:** Max 65 **Parking:** 40 **Notes:** LB

NEWQUAY
Map 2 SW86

Lewinnick Lodge
★★★★ RESTAURANT WITH ROOMS

tel: 01637 878117 **Pentire Headland TR7 1QD**
email: thelodge@hospitalitycornwall.com **web:** www.lewinnicklodge.co.uk
dir: *From A392, at roundabout exit into Pentire Road then Pentire Avenue. Turn right to Lewinnick Lodge.*

Set above the cliffs of Pentire Headland, looking out across the mighty Atlantic, guests are guaranteed amazing coastal views here at Lewinnick Lodge. The bedrooms were designed by Guy Bostock and are modern, spacious, and offer many thoughtful extras; some have open-plan bathrooms. Modern British food (with an emphasis on fresh fish) is served all day.

Rooms: 17 en suite (1 fmly) **S** fr £116 **D** fr £155 (room only)* **Facilities:** FTV Lounge tea/coffee Dinner available Direct dial Lift WiFi 🛝 Surf board store **Extras:** Speciality toiletries, robes, bottled water – complimentary **Parking:** 50

The Lyncroft Bed & Breakfast
★★★★ BED AND BREAKFAST

tel: 01637 873812 & 07580 109443 **54 Tower Road TR7 1LU**
email: info@thelyncroftnewquay.co.uk **web:** www.thelyncroftnewquay.co.uk
dir: *A392 into Newquay (Trevemper Road/Gannel Road). At roundabout, 2nd exit into Higher Tower Road. On right opposite golf course.*

The Lyncroft is a 100-year-old, stone-built Cornish house with views out over Fistral Beach and along the Cornish coast. All the contemporary and relaxing bedrooms are appointed to a very good standard; all have en suite shower rooms, TVs and free WiFi. Five minutes' walk in one direction will take you to Fistral Beach, five minutes in the other and you will find Towan Beach and the town centre. Dogs are allowed on request; off-street parking is provided.

Rooms: 7 en suite (1 fmly) **Facilities:** FTV TVL tea/coffee WiFi 🛝 **Parking:** 6 **Notes:** LB

The Three Tees
★★★ GUEST ACCOMMODATION

tel: 01637 872055 **21 Carminow Way TR7 3AY**
email: greg@3tees.co.uk **web:** www.3tees.co.uk
dir: *A30 onto A392 signed Newquay. Right at Quintrell Downs roundabout signed Porth, over crossroads, 3rd right.*

Located in a quiet residential area just a short walk from the town and beach, this friendly family-run establishment is comfortable and well equipped. Guests have use of a lounge, a bar and a sun lounge, and breakfast is served in the dining room, where snacks are available throughout the day. The bar serves light snacks in the evenings. In addition to the bedrooms in the main house, a family annexe is also available which offers flexible, level-access accommodation.

Rooms: 8 rms (7 en suite) (1 pri facs) 1 annexe en suite (4 fmly) (2 GF) **D** fr £70*
Facilities: FTV DVD TVL tea/coffee Licensed WiFi 🛝 **Parking:** 9 **Notes:** LB
Closed November to February

Avalon
★★★ GUEST ACCOMMODATION

tel: 01637 877522 & 07870 320346 **4 Edgcumbe Gardens TR7 2QD**
email: enquiries@avalonnewquay.co.uk **web:** www.avalonnewquay.co.uk
dir: *From A30 at Quintrell Downs roundabout onto A3058 signed St Columb Minor. Left in 1 mile opposite Rocklands.*

Conveniently situated within walking distance of the town centre and the beaches, in a quiet residential area, Avalon provides comfortable accommodation, and enjoys the benefit of on-site parking. Guests can take advantage of the front-facing sun terrace during summer months.

Rooms: 6 rms (5 en suite) (1 pri facs) (1 fmly) **S** fr £30 **D** fr £60 **Facilities:** FTV tea/coffee WiFi 🛝 **Parking:** 6 **Notes:** LB

PADSTOW
Map 2 SW97

Premier Collection

Padstow Townhouse
★★★★★ ❦❦❦❦ 🍽 RESTAURANT WITH ROOMS

tel: 01841 550950 **16/18 High Street PL28 8BB**
email: stay@padstowtownhouse.co.uk **web:** www.paul-ainsworth.co.uk
dir: *Phone for directions.*

This cosy 18th-century townhouse offers six individually styled suites, providing all home comforts as well as some extra little luxuries. Each room has its own 40" curved TV complete with Apple TV, as well as free WiFi. Breakfast is served in Rojano's in the Square (one AA Rosette), and guests are welcome to dine there or at the four AA-Rosette restaurant, Paul Ainsworth at No.6 restaurant.

Rooms: 6 en suite **Facilities:** Dinner available WiFi **Extras:** Speciality toiletries

Premier Collection

The Seafood Restaurant
★★★★★ ❦❦❦ 🍽 RESTAURANT WITH ROOMS

tel: 01841 532700 **Riverside PL28 8BY**
email: reservations@rickstein.com **web:** www.rickstein.com
dir: *Into town centre, down hill (Station Road), follow signs to harbour car park, opposite car park.*

Food lovers continue to beat a well-trodden path to this famous restaurant. Situated on the edge of the harbour, just a stone's throw from the shops, The Seafood Restaurant offers chic and comfortable bedrooms that boast numerous thoughtful extras; some have views of the estuary and a couple have private balconies with stunning sea views. Service is relaxed and friendly; booking is essential for both the accommodation and a table in the restaurant.

Rooms: 16 en suite 6 annexe en suite (12 fmly) (3 GF) **S** fr £165 **D** fr £165*
Facilities: FTV DVD tea/coffee Dinner available Direct dial Lift WiFi 🛝 Cookery School **Extras:** Speciality toiletries, robes, mini-bar **Notes:** LB Closed 24–26 December RS 24 December limited restaurant service times

St Petroc's Bistro

★★★★★ ⑳ RESTAURANT WITH ROOMS

tel: 01841 532700 **4 New Street PL28 8EA**
email: reservations@rickstein.com **web:** www.rickstein.com
dir: *A39 onto A389, follow signs to Padstow town centre.*

One of the oldest buildings in town, this charming establishment is just up the hill from the picturesque harbour. Style, comfort and individuality are all great strengths here, particularly so in the impressively equipped bedrooms. Breakfast, lunch and dinner all reflect a serious approach to cuisine, and the popular restaurant has a relaxed, bistro style. Comfortable lounges, a reading room and lovely gardens complete the picture.

Rooms: 10 en suite (2 fmly) **S** fr £165 **D** fr £165* **Facilities:** FTV Lounge tea/coffee Dinner available Direct dial WiFi **Extras:** Speciality toiletries – complimentary; mini-bar, snack basket – chargeable **Notes:** LB Closed 24–26 December

The Old Mill House

★★★★ ⑳ GUEST ACCOMMODATION

tel: 01841 540388 **PL27 7QT**
email: enquiries@theoldmillhouse.com **web:** www.theoldmillhouse.com
dir: *2 miles south of Padstow. In centre of Little Petherick on A389.*

The Old Mill House is situated in an Area of Outstanding Natural Beauty, a couple of miles from the busy town of Padstow with its pretty harbour, many shops, bars and restaurants. This 16th-century property, a former corn mill house, has been sympathetically converted and is beautifully decorated and well equipped. Family-run, it offers good levels of comfort and quality. Dinner is served in the restaurant with a good selection of dishes to suits all tastes. Traditional afternoon teas may be served in the garden and a good hearty 'Full Cornish' breakfast is made with locally sourced produce and ingredients.

Rooms: 7 en suite (2 fmly) **Facilities:** FTV DVD Lounge tea/coffee Dinner available Licensed WiFi ⚿ Hot tub on request **Extras:** Sherry, fresh milk, snacks **Notes:** LB Closed 20 December to 1 February

Rick Stein's Café

★★★★ BED AND BREAKFAST

tel: 01841 532700 **10 Middle Street PL28 8AP**
email: reservations@rickstein.com **web:** www.rickstein.com
dir: *A389 into town, one way past church, 3rd right.*

Another Rick Stein success story, this is a lively café by day, restaurant by night, and offers good food and quality accommodation just a short walk from the harbour. Three bedrooms are available – each is quite different but all have high standards of comfort. Friendly and personable staff are always on hand.

Rooms: 3 en suite (1 fmly) **D** fr £113 **Facilities:** FTV DVD tea/coffee Dinner available Direct dial Licensed WiFi ⚿ Cookery school **Extras:** Speciality toiletries; mini-bar – chargeable **Notes:** LB Closed 24–26 December RS 24 December limited service times

---

PAR   **Map 2 SX05**

The Britannia Inn & Restaurant

★★★★ ⬭ INN

tel: 01726 812889 & 815796 **St Austell Road PL24 2SL**
email: info@britanniainn.com **web:** www.britanniainn.com
dir: *On A390 between Par and St Austell, next to Cornish Market World.*

This long-established inn is situated between Par and St Austell and is just a five-minute drive from The Eden Project. There is a very genuine welcome here and a collective effort to ensure guests are well looked after and enjoy their stay. A choice of bars is available, together with attractive gardens, a function room and range of dining options. The extensive menu features plenty of Cornish produce, with a range of daily specials also offered. The bedrooms offer contemporary style and comfort with impressive, high-quality bathrooms.

Rooms: 7 en suite (4 fmly) **Facilities:** FTV tea/coffee Dinner available Direct dial WiFi ⚿ **Conf:** Max 75 Thtr 60 Class 45 Board 50 **Parking:** 105 **Notes:** RS 25 December open 12–2 drinks only

Elmswood House

★★★★ GUEST ACCOMMODATION

tel: 01726 814221 **73 Tehidy Road, Tywardreath PL24 2QD**
email: info@elmswoodhouse.co.uk **web:** www.elmswoodhouse.co.uk
dir: *Right from Par station, then 1st left to top of hill, opposite village church.*

Elmswood House is a fine Victorian building set in the middle of the village opposite the church. Many guests return to stay here time and again. Bedrooms have quality furnishings and many extra facilities, and the attractive dining room and lounge overlook a beautiful garden.

Rooms: 4 en suite (2 fmly) (1 GF) **S** fr £70 **D** fr £75* **Facilities:** FTV Lounge TVL tea/coffee WiFi **Parking:** 6 **Notes:** No children 10 years Closed December to January

The Royal Inn

★★★★ INN

tel: 01726 815601 **66 Eastcliffe Road, Tywardreath PL24 2AJ**
email: info@royal-inn.co.uk **web:** www.royal-inn.co.uk
dir: *Adjacent to Par railway station.*

Situated next to the railway station on the edge of Tywardreath, this free house provides high standards of comfort and quality. Only five minutes from Par Sands and four miles from The Eden Project, it is an ideal base for exploring Cornwall. The open-plan bar area has slate floors and a large open fire; the atmosphere is relaxed and diners can choose from the bar menu or dine more formally in the restaurant or conservatory. All twin rooms have sofa beds (suitable for children under 14), and there is a suite which is suitable for families of four or five.

Rooms: 15 en suite (8 fmly) (4 GF) **Facilities:** STV FTV tea/coffee Dinner available WiFi **Conf:** Max 20 Thtr 8 Class 8 Board 20 **Parking:** 17 **Notes:** LB

Prospect House

★★★★ GUEST ACCOMMODATION

tel: 01326 373198 **Commercial Road TR10 8AH**
email: stay@prospecthouse-penryn.co.uk **web:** www.prospecthouse-penryn.co.uk
dir: *Exit A39 at Treluswell roundabout onto B3292, right at Penryn town centre sign. Left at junction to town hall, left into Saint Gluivas Street, at bottom on left.*

Prospect House is an attractive building close to the waterside and was built in 1820 for a ship's captain. The original charm of the house has been carefully maintained and the attractive bedrooms are well equipped. A comfortable lounge is available, and freshly cooked breakfasts are served in the elegant dining room.

Rooms: 3 en suite **Facilities:** FTV Lounge tea/coffee WiFi **Parking:** 4

Premier Collection

Camilla House

★★★★★ 🍴 GUEST ACCOMMODATION

tel: 01736 363771 **12 Regent Terrace TR18 4DW**
email: enquiries@camillahouse.co.uk **web:** www.camillahouse.co.uk
dir: *A30 to Penzance, at rail station follow road along harbourfront into Promenade Road. Opposite Jubilee Bathing Pool, Regent Terrace 2nd right.*

A warm welcome is assured at this charming Victorian property which is located in a quiet residential area facing the sea and only a short walk from Penzance's beach and town centre attractions. Bedrooms, some with views towards the coast, are spacious and attractively appointed. There's a stylish guest lounge with many homely features, and breakfast shouldn't to be missed. Secure parking is provided.

Rooms: 8 rms (7 en suite) (1 pri facs) (1 GF) **Facilities:** FTV DVD Lounge tea/coffee WiFi 🔒 **Parking:** 7 **Notes:** Closed November to March

Premier Collection

Ednovean Farm

★★★★★ 🍴 FARMHOUSE

tel: 01736 711883 **TR20 9LZ**
email: info@ednoveanfarm.co.uk **web:** www.ednoveanfarm.co.uk

(For full entry see Perranuthnoe)

Mount Royal

★★★★ 🍴 GUEST ACCOMMODATION

tel: 01736 362233 **Chyandour Cliff TR18 3LQ**
email: mountroyal@btconnect.com **web:** www.mountroyalpenzance.com
dir: *From A30 onto coast road into town.*

Part Georgian and part Victorian, the spacious Mount Royal has splendid views over Mount's Bay and is convenient for the town's attractions. There's a gracious elegance throughout with the impressive dining room retaining its original fireplace and ornate sideboard. Parking is available to the rear of the property.

Rooms: 6 en suite (1 fmly) (1 GF) **S** fr £120 **D** fr £130* **Facilities:** FTV Lounge tea/coffee WiFi 🔒 **Extras:** Speciality toiletries **Parking:** 8 **Notes:** LB No children 10 years Closed October to May

The Dunedin Guest House

★★★★ GUEST ACCOMMODATION

tel: 01736 362652 **Alexandra Road TR18 4LZ**
email: info@dunedinhotel.co.uk **web:** www.dunedinhotel.co.uk
dir: *A30 to Penzance, at rail station along harbour front into Promenade Road, right into Alexandra Road, Dunedin on right.*

The Dunedin is on a tree-lined avenue just a stroll from the promenade and town centre. The friendly proprietors provide a relaxed atmosphere, and bedrooms that are well equipped and smartly decorated to a high standard. Hearty breakfasts are served in the dining room.

Rooms: 8 en suite (2 fmly) (2 GF) **S** fr £68 **D** fr £75 **Facilities:** FTV DVD tea/coffee WiFi 🔒 **Extras:** Speciality toiletries **Notes:** LB No children 12 years Closed 31 October to February

The Dolphin Tavern

★★★ INN

tel: 01736 364106 **Quay Street TR18 4BD**
email: dolphintavern@tiscali.co.uk **web:** www.dolphintavern.co.uk
dir: *Opposite Penzance harbour.*

The Dolphin Tavern is a traditional inn just a few yards away from Penzance harbour, usefully located for the Scillonian ferry. Rooms are comfortable and well presented, and the staff are friendly and attentive. Food is available in the bar and restaurant daily from a wide menu which also offers daily-changing specials.

Rooms: 3 en suite **Facilities:** FTV tea/coffee Dinner available WiFi 🔒 Pool table in winter only

The Summer House

🅄

tel: 01736 363744 & 07768 608439 **Cornwall Terrace TR18 4HL**
email: reception@summerhouse-cornwall.com **web:** www.summerhouse-cornwall.com
dir: *A30 to Penzance, at rail station follow along harbour onto Promenade, pass Jubilee Pool, right after Queens Hotel. Summer House 30 yards on left.*

Currently the rating for this establishment is not confirmed. This may be due to a change of ownership or because it has only recently joined the AA rating scheme.

Rooms: 5 en suite **Facilities:** FTV DVD TVL tea/coffee Licensed WiFi **Extras:** Fresh milk, chocolates, mini-fridge **Parking:** 5 **Notes:** No children 16 years Closed October to Easter

PERRANUTHNOE   Map 2 SW52

Premier Collection

Ednovean Farm
★★★★★ ⬚ FARMHOUSE

tel: 01736 711883 **TR20 9LZ**
email: info@ednoveanfarm.co.uk **web:** www.ednoveanfarm.co.uk
dir: *Off A394 towards Perranuthnoe at Dynasty Restaurant, farm drive on left on bend by post box.*

Tranquillity is guaranteed at this 17th-century farmhouse which looks across the countryside towards Mount's Bay. The bedrooms are individually styled and very comfortable. The impressive Mediterranean-style gardens are ideal for relaxation and taking in the superb views. In addition to the sitting room, there is also a garden room and several patios. Breakfast is served at a magnificent oak table.

Rooms: 3 en suite (3 GF) **S** fr £120 **D** fr £120 **Facilities:** FTV DVD iPod docking station Lounge tea/coffee WiFi **Extras:** Speciality toiletries, slippers, robes **Parking:** 4 **Notes:** LB No children 16 years Closed 24–28 December 22 acres grassland/stud

POLPERRO   Map 2 SX25

Premier Collection

Trenderway Farm
★★★★★ ⬚ FARMHOUSE

tel: 01503 272214 **Pelynt PL13 2LY**
email: stay@trenderwayfarm.com **web:** www.trenderwayfarm.co.uk
dir: *Take A387 from Looe to Polperro, right at signpost to Pelynt. 3rd left at signed junction to farm. Continue down lane to gravel car park.*

Warm hospitality awaits at this delightful 16th-century farmhouse set on a 200-acre working farm. Stylish bedrooms, both in the farmhouse and in the adjacent barns, offer high levels of comfort and include WiFi. Hearty breakfasts are served in the conservatory overlooking the lake, and free-range eggs from the farm, as well as high quality local produce, are served.

Rooms: 2 en suite 5 annexe en suite (2 GF) **Facilities:** FTV DVD Lounge tea/coffee Licensed WiFi 🎣 Lakes Falconry school **Extras:** Speciality toiletries; mini-bar – chargeable **Conf:** Max 100 Thtr 100 Class 50 Board 15 **Parking:** 8 **Notes:** LB No children 16 years Civ wed 120 200 acres beef/sheep/orchards

Penryn House
★★★★ ⬚ GUEST ACCOMMODATION

tel: 01503 272157 **The Coombes, Polperro PL13 2RQ**
email: enquiries@penrynhouse.co.uk **web:** www.penrynhouse.co.uk
dir: *A387 to Polperro, at mini-roundabout left down hill into village (ignore restricted access). 200 yards on left.*

Penryn House has a relaxed atmosphere and offers a warm welcome. Every effort is made to ensure a memorable stay. Bedrooms are neatly presented and reflect the character of the building. After a day exploring, enjoy a drink at the bar and relax in the comfortable lounge.

Rooms: 12 en suite (3 fmly) **S** fr £50 **D** fr £85 **Facilities:** FTV Lounge tea/coffee Licensed WiFi 🅿 **Parking:** 13 **Notes:** LB Closed December to February

PORT GAVERNE   Map 2 SX08

Premier Collection

Port Gaverne
★★★★★ ◉◉ INN

tel: 01208 880244 **PL29 3SQ**
email: eat@portgavernehotel.co.uk **web:** www.portgavernehotel.co.uk
dir: *Phone for directions.*

You'll find antique furniture, nooks and crannies, a wonderfully comfortable bed and good food here. This traditional inn is located in a tiny and peaceful cove on Cornwall's dramatic north coast, one headland away and five minutes' walk from Port Isaac. The 15 en suite bedrooms are all comfortably furnished, well-maintained and spotlessly clean; no two are the same. All rooms come complete with full satellite TV, radio, direct-dial phone and coffee and tea-making facilities. Also available is a relaxing sitting room, outside terrace and sunny beer garden.

Rooms: 15 en suite (4 fmly) **Facilities:** STV FTV DVD iPod docking station Lounge tea/coffee Dinner available Direct dial WiFi 🎣 🅿 **Extras:** Speciality toiletries, Nespresso coffee machine, chocolates, bottled water **Conf:** Max 12 Board 12 **Parking:** 17 **Notes:** LB

Kota Restaurant with Rooms

★★★★ ◉◉◉ RESTAURANT WITH ROOMS

tel: 01326 562407 **Harbour Head TR13 9JA**
email: kota@btconnect.com **web:** www.kotarestaurant.co.uk
dir: *B3304 from Helston into Porthleven. Kota on harbour opposite slipway.*

Overlooking the water, this 300-year-old building is the home of Kota Restaurant ('kota' being the Maori word for 'shellfish'). The bedrooms are approached from a granite stairway to the side of the building. The family room is spacious and has the benefit of harbour views, while the smaller, double room is at the rear of the property. The enthusiastic young owners ensure guests enjoy their stay here, and a meal in the award-winning restaurant is a must. Food and drink is also served in the Kota Kai Bar & Kitchen. Breakfast features the best local produce.

Rooms: 2 annexe en suite (1 fmly) **S** fr £70 **D** fr £85* **Facilities:** FTV DVD tea/coffee Dinner available WiFi ⚓ ⚓ **Extras:** Fridge **Parking:** 1 **Notes:** Closed January to 10 February

The Lugger

★★★★ ◉◉ ⚲ INN

tel: 01872 501322 **TR2 5RD**
email: reservations.lugger@bespokehotels.com **web:** www.bespokehotels.com/thelugger
dir: *A390 to Truro, B3287 to Tregony, A3078 (St Mawes Road), left for Veryan, left for Portloe.*

This delightful inn enjoys a unique setting adjacent to the slipway of the harbour, where fishing boats still come and go. Bedrooms, some in adjacent buildings and cottages, are contemporary in style and are well equipped. There is a sitting room which reflects the original character of the property, with beams and open fireplaces creating a cosy atmosphere. The modern restaurant enjoys superb views, and in warmer months, a sun terrace overlooking the harbour proves a popular place to enjoy a meal.

Rooms: 5 en suite 17 annexe en suite (1 GF) **Facilities:** FTV Lounge tea/coffee Dinner available Direct dial WiFi **Parking:** 26 **Notes:** Civ wed 50

Old Railway Yard

★★★★ ⚲ ➣ BED AND BREAKFAST

tel: 01209 314514 & 07970 595598 **Lanner Hill TR16 5TZ**
email: g.s.collier@btinternet.com **web:** www.old-railway-yard.co.uk
dir: *A393 (Redruth/Falmouth road), at brow of hill before Lanner village, turn right into Tram Cross Lane, 125 metres on right.*

Warm, genuine service and hospitality awaits you at the Old Railway Yard where a friendly welcome is assured from Graham. Located in the heart of Cornwall, minutes away from the A30, this B&B is perfect for exploring all the region offers. Enjoy a complimentary Cornish cream tea during your stay. A superb full Cornish breakfast with home-made bread will set you up for the day ahead.

Rooms: 3 en suite (1 GF) **S** fr £70 **D** fr £80* **Facilities:** FTV DVD TVL tea/coffee Dinner available Licensed WiFi ⚓ Hot tub **Parking:** 8 **Notes:** No children 6 years

Lanner Inn

★★ INN

tel: 01209 215611 **The Square, Lanner TR16 6EH**
email: info@lannerinn.co.uk **web:** www.lannerinn.co.uk
dir: *2 miles southeast of Redruth. In Lanner on A393.*

Conveniently situated for access to Redruth and the A30, this traditional inn is situated in the centre of Lanner and has a good local following. The property has a dining room and a bar in addition to the comfortable bedrooms. This inn is owner-run and managed, and the team of staff are very friendly.

Rooms: 3 en suite 1 annexe en suite (2 fmly) (1 GF) **Facilities:** FTV tea/coffee WiFi ⚓ **Parking:** 16

RUAN HIGH LANES

Map 2 SW93

Trenona Farm Holidays

★★★ FARMHOUSE

tel: 01872 501339 & 07775 698953 **TR2 5JS**
email: info@trenonafarmholidays.co.uk **web:** www.trenonafarmholidays.co.uk
dir: A390 onto A3078, signed St Mawes. 6m on left.

Trenona Farm is located on the Roseland Peninsula, surrounded by rolling countryside and close to lots of beautiful sandy beaches. The area provides many attractions, great restaurants and pubs and is very popular with walkers. A warm welcome awaits guests (and well-behaved dogs). Well-equipped rooms are warm and comfortable and a good hearty farmhouse breakfast is provided in the attractive dining room.

Rooms: 4 rms (3 en suite) (1 pri facs) (2 fmly) **S** fr £45 **D** fr £65* **Facilities:** FTV TVL tea/coffee WiFi **Extras:** Fridge, fresh milk **Parking:** 8 **Notes:** LB Closed November to mid March 250 acres arable/beef

ST AGNES

Map 2 SW75

Driftwood Spars

★★★★ ⌂ GUEST ACCOMMODATION

tel: 01872 552428 **Trevaunance Cove TR5 0RT**
email: info@driftwoodspars.co.uk **web:** www.driftwoodspars.co.uk
dir: A30 to Chiverton roundabout, right onto B3277, through village. Driftwood Spars 200 yards before beach.

Partly built from shipwreck timbers, this 18th-century building attracts locals and visitors alike. The attractive bedrooms, some in an annexe, are decorated in a bright, seaside style with many interesting features. Local produce, including delicious seafood, is served in the informal dining room and in the restaurant, together with a range of hand-pulled beers.

Rooms: 9 en suite 6 annexe en suite (4 fmly) (5 GF) **Facilities:** FTV tea/coffee Dinner available Direct dial Licensed WiFi Table football **Conf:** Max 70 Thtr 70 Class 25 Board 20 **Parking:** 40 **Notes:** LB RS 25 December no lunch/dinner, no bar in evening Civ wed 76

Penkerris

★★ GUEST HOUSE

tel: 01872 552262 **Penwinnick Road TR5 0PA**
email: penkerris@gmail.com **web:** www.penkerris.co.uk
dir: A30 onto B3277 to village, Penkerris on right after village sign, just before the museum.

Set in gardens on the edge of the village, this Edwardian house has a relaxed and welcoming atmosphere. Period features abound, and the best possible use is made of space in the bedrooms. Home-cooked evening meals are served by prior arrangement. Ample parking is available.

Rooms: 7 rms (4 en suite) (3 fmly) **S** fr £25 **D** fr £50* **Facilities:** FTV TVL tea/coffee Dinner available Licensed WiFi Badminton, volleyball **Parking:** 9 **Notes:** LB

Premier Collection

Anchorage House

★★★★★ GUEST ACCOMMODATION

tel: 01726 814071 **Nettles Corner, Tregrehan Mills PL25 3RH**
email: info@anchoragehouse.co.uk **web:** www.anchoragehouse.co.uk
dir: *2 miles east of town centre off A390, opposite St Austell Garden Centre.*

Georgian-style Anchorage House is set in an acre of carefully landscaped gardens at the end of a private lane. Guests are met on arrival with afternoon tea, often served on the patio. The luxurious and elegant bedrooms are equipped to the highest standard with sumptuous beds, and include satellite TV, fresh fruit, magazines, bottled water and chocolates. Guests also have use of the indoor heated pool, hot tub and gym. The house is a short distance from many of Cornwall's major tourist attractions.

Rooms: 3 en suite 1 annexe en suite (1 GF) **S** fr £115 **D** fr £135* **Facilities:** STV FTV DVD Lounge tea/coffee WiFi ☜ Gym ♨ Hot tub **Extras:** Speciality toiletries **Parking:** 6 **Notes:** No children 16 years Closed November to March

Langdale House

★★★★ BED AND BREAKFAST

tel: 01726 71404 & 07764 531050 **1A Southbourne Road PL25 4RU**
email: stay@langdalehousecornwall.co.uk **web:** www.langdalehousecornwall.co.uk
dir: *On A390 (St Austell bypass), 0.5 mile south of town centre.*

Handy for the town centre, this is an ideal choice for both business and leisure guests and a great place to relax, unwind and re-charge the batteries. Quality and comfort levels are high throughout, both in the elegant bedrooms and the impressive bathrooms. The welcome is warm and friendly with every effort made to ensure an enjoyable and rewarding stay. Breakfast is served in the attractive dining room, with a good range of dishes offered. Super-fast WiFi is provided.

Rooms: 3 en suite **S** fr £50 **D** fr £85* **Facilities:** FTV tea/coffee WiFi **Parking:** 3 **Notes:** No children 5 years

Ancient Shipbrokers

★★★★ BED AND BREAKFAST

tel: 01726 843370 & 07732 073184 **1 Higher West End, Pentewan PL26 6BY**
email: shipbrokers1@btinternet.com **web:** www.pentewanbedandbreakfast.com
dir: *From St Austell on B3273, at Mill Garage turn left signed Pentewan, over bridge bear right and pass Ocean Sports. Next left into private road, Higher West End.*

The Ancient Shipbrokers overlooks Pentewan harbour and one of the best sandy beaches in Cornwall. The house has bags of history and character and has been decorated tastefully and sympathetically. A large area of the garden is dedicated to wild flowers and trees and there is also a kitchen garden. The dining room enjoys a wonderful view out across the harbour and the beach and is the ideal venue for home-cooked breakfasts. The en suite bedrooms have TVs, DVD players, free WiFi and tea- and coffee-making facilities. Private parking is available on-site or in the village car park; help with luggage is offered. There is also space for storing bicycles, surf boards and wetsuits. Self-catering is available too.

Rooms: 3 en suite **S** fr £66 **D** fr £90* **Facilities:** FTV DVD tea/coffee WiFi ♨ **Parking:** 3 **Notes:** LB Closed 20 December to 5 January

Polgreen Farm

★★★★ FARMHOUSE

tel: 01726 75151 **London Apprentice PL26 7AP**
email: polgreen.farm@btinternet.com **web:** www.polgreenfarm.co.uk
dir: *1.5 miles south of St Austell. Exit B3273, left on entering London Apprentice and signed.*

Guests regularly return for the friendly welcome at this peaceful establishment located just south of St Austell. The spacious and well-equipped bedrooms are divided between the main house and an adjoining property, and each building has a comfortable lounge. Breakfast is served in a pleasant conservatory overlooking the garden.

Rooms: 4 annexe en suite (1 fmly) (1 GF) **Facilities:** FTV Lounge TVL tea/coffee WiFi **Parking:** 8 **Notes:** LB Closed November to March 64 acres livestock

The Bugle Inn

★★★ INN

tel: 01726 850307 **57 Fore Street, Bugle PL26 8PD**
email: thebugleinn@gmail.com **web:** www.bugleinn.co.uk
dir: *A30 onto A391. In Bugle at crossroads.*

The Bugle Inn is a warm and inviting establishment, with its origins dating back to the 17th century. It's situated in the heart of the Cornish countryside, between Bodmin and St Austell, handy for The Eden Project. Traditional pub food and drinks are served in a characterful building with a lovely open fire. Bedrooms are attractive with a cosy feel.

Rooms: 5 en suite (1 fmly) **Facilities:** FTV tea/coffee Dinner available Direct dial WiFi

Tregurnow Farm

★★★★ ⚲ FARMHOUSE

tel: 01736 810255 **TR19 6BL**
email: tregurnow@lamorna.biz **web:** www.lamorna.biz
dir: *From Newlyn take B3315, after 4 miles follow black and white sign on left just past turn for Lamorna Cove.*

Tucked away near St Buryan, Tregurnow Farm offers traditional, quality farmhouse bed and breakfast and self-catering facilities. Peace and quiet, stunning views and hearty breakfasts are hallmarks of a stay here. Close to Mousehole, Minack Theatre and Penzance, this is a good base for touring the far southwest of the county.

Rooms: 3 en suite **Facilities:** FTV Lounge TVL WiFi ♨ **Extras:** Fridge **Parking:** 10 **Notes:** No children 5 years Closed Christmas 100 acres mixed

ST IVES
Map 2 SW54

Premier Collection

Downsfield Bed and Breakfast

★★★★★ GUEST ACCOMMODATION

tel: 01736 796659 **Longstone Hill TR26 2LJ**
email: sharonp27@hotmail.com **web:** www.downsfieldbnb.co.uk
dir: *On main road between Carbis Bay and St Ives.*

A warm welcome awaits you at Downsfield from the lovely hosts, Sharon and Phil. Decorated and furnished to an exceptionally high standard, this place will feel like a home from home. There is private parking, which is invaluable in St Ives during the summer. The bedrooms are spacious and well equipped with very good levels of comfort. The property is within walking distance of St Ives with its many unique shops and restaurants. This is a good choice for exploring the region and stunning coastal attractions.

Rooms: 8 en suite (1 fmly) (4 GF) **Facilities:** FTV TVL tea/coffee WiFi
Extras: Speciality toiletries, gowns, chocolate **Parking:** 6
Notes: No children 4 years

Premier Collection

The Gannet Inn

★★★★★ GUEST ACCOMMODATION

tel: 01736 795651 & 795311 **St Ives Road, Carbis Bay TR26 2SB**
email: info@thegannetinn.co.uk **web:** www.gannetstives.co.uk
dir: *From St Ives on A3074 in Carbis Bay.*

The Gannet Inn, near St Ives, has unique interiors with all the style and finesse of a boutique hotel, and is a warm and friendly place to pop in for a catch up or a bite to eat. Stylish, high-standard, en suite bedrooms, decorated in calming colours, range from 'cosy', 'quirky' and 'family' to 'spot the gannet' sea-view rooms. As part of The Carbis Bay Hotel, Spa & Estate, guests at The Gannet Inn are offered the use of all their leisure facilities throughout their stay.

Rooms: 16 en suite (4 fmly) **Facilities:** STV Lounge tea/coffee Dinner available Direct dial Licensed WiFi ✦ Fishing Leisure facilities available at sister hotel including a spa **Extras:** Speciality toiletries **Conf:** Max 100 Thtr 100 Class 70 Board 60 **Parking:** 30 **Notes:** Civ wed 100

Premier Collection

27 The Terrace

★★★★★ GUEST ACCOMMODATION

tel: 01736 797450 **27 The Terrace TR26 2BP**
email: stay@27theterrace.co.uk **web:** www.27theterrace.co.uk
dir: *A3074 through Carbis Bay into St Ives, past St Ives Bay Hotel on left, overlooking Porthminster Beach.*

Situated above Porthminster Beach with stunning views overlooking the beautiful waters of St Ives Bay, this Georgian property offers nine elegant and stylish en suite bedrooms in the main house and a studio apartment next door. There's a private walled garden with sun terrace to relax in and free on-site parking is provided. It's only a two-minute stroll into St Ives from here.

Rooms: 9 en suite (2 GF) **D** fr £115* **Facilities:** FTV iPod docking station TVL tea/coffee Licensed WiFi **Extras:** Nespresso coffee machine, honesty bar, robes and slippers in all deluxe rooms, binoculars in all sea view rooms **Parking:** 10
Notes: LB No children 13 years Closed January

Chypons Farm

★★★★ BED AND BREAKFAST

tel: 01736 740303 **Chypons Hill, Nancledra TR20 8NE**
email: chyponsfarm@gmail.com **web:** www.cornwallbnb.com
dir: *Phone for directions.*

Chypons Farm comprises a group of 300-year-old stone barns and self-catering cottages set around a courtyard and bordered by a small river and woodland. It is located on the side of a valley in the village of Nancledra, home to many artists who have escaped the hustle and bustle of nearby St Ives. There is a bus service into St Ives which saves parking in the town. The local pub is less than a mile away if you take the scenic walk through the fields or much less if you take the direct route along the road. Ample parking is available as well as the use of the well-kept gardens and summer house.

Rooms: 1 en suite **D** fr £87.50* **Facilities:** STV DVD WiFi **Notes:** No children 18 years

Lamorna Lodge

★★★★ GUEST ACCOMMODATION

tel: 01736 795967 & 07837 638620 **Boskerris Road, Carbis Bay TR26 2NG**
email: lamornalodge@gmail.com **web:** www.lamorna.co.uk
dir: *A30 onto A3074, right after playground in Carbis Bay, establishment 200 yards on right.*

A warm welcome is assured at Lamorna Lodge, which is just a short walk from Carbis Bay beach. Wonderful views over St Ives Bay to Godrevy Lighthouse can be enjoyed from the spacious lounge, a view also shared by some of the stylish bedrooms. Breakfast makes great use of local Cornish produce and is served in the elegant surroundings of the dining room. The stylish terrace enjoys lovely sea views.

Rooms: 8 en suite (2 fmly) (2 GF) **S** fr £60 **D** fr £100* **Facilities:** FTV Lounge tea/coffee Licensed WiFi **Conf:** Max 18 Thtr 18 Class 18 Board 18 **Parking:** 8 **Notes:** LB Closed 5 November to 10 March

The Nook

★★★★ GUEST ACCOMMODATION

tel: 01736 795913 **Ayr TR26 1EQ**
email: info@nookstives.co.uk **web:** www.nookstives.co.uk
dir: *A30 to St Ives left at NatWest, right at roundabout and left at top of hill.*

The Nook is an ideal base for exploring Cornwall's spectacular coastline, gardens and countryside. The comfortable bedrooms are furnished in a contemporary style and are equipped with numerous facilities. There is a wide variety on offer at breakfast, including full English, continental and dishes such as scrambled eggs with smoked salmon.

Rooms: 11 en suite (1 fmly) (1 GF) **Facilities:** FTV DVD TVL tea/coffee WiFi **Parking:** 10 **Notes:** LB

Thurlestone House

★★★★ BED AND BREAKFAST

tel: 01736 796369 & 07759 715595 **St Ives Road, Carbis Bay TR26 2RT**
email: thurlestoneguesthouse@yahoo.co.uk **web:** www.thurlestoneguesthouse.co.uk
dir: *A3074 to Carbis Bay, pass convenience store on left, 0.25 mile on left next to Carbis Bay Holidays Office.*

Built in 1843, this granite, former chapel now offers stylish, comfortable accommodation. The welcoming proprietors provide a relaxed environment, and many guests return regularly. The well-equipped bedrooms have modern facilities, some have sea views.

Rooms: 6 en suite **D** fr £80* **Facilities:** FTV tea/coffee WiFi **Extras:** Safe **Parking:** 5 **Notes:** LB No children Closed November to March

ST IVES *continued*

Count House Cottage B&B

★★★★ GUEST HOUSE

tel: 01736 798951 & 07399 592039 **Count House Lane, Carbis Bay TR26 2PZ**
email: info@counthousecottagebandb.co.uk **web:** www.counthousecottagebandb.co.uk
dir: *In Carbis Bay, on corner of St Ives Road and Count House Lane.*

Count House Cottage B&B is approximately a 10-minute drive from the A30, and
it's only a few minutes by car to St Ives. This modern property offers five bedrooms
with stunning en suite showers. Three of the rooms have sea views and one room is
on the ground floor.

Rooms: 5 en suite (1 GF) **Facilities:** FTV tea/coffee WiFi **Parking:** 5 **Notes:** LB
No children 16 years

The Rookery

★★★★ GUEST ACCOMMODATION

tel: 01736 799401 **8 The Terrace TR26 2BL**
email: therookerystives@hotmail.com **web:** www.rookerystives.com
dir: *A3074 through Carbis Bay, right fork at Porthminster Hotel, The Rookery 500 yards
on left.*

Aptly named, The Rookery stands in an elevated position overlooking the town and
sandy beach. The attractive bedrooms include one which is on the ground floor and
a luxurious suite, all of which are well equipped and offer a good level of comfort.
Breakfast is served in the first-floor dining room at separate tables.

Rooms: 7 en suite (2 fmly) (1 GF) **Facilities:** FTV tea/coffee WiFi 🐾 **Parking:** 7
Notes: No children 7 years

Coombe Farmhouse

★★★★ BED AND BREAKFAST

tel: 01736 740843 **TR27 6NW**
email: coombefarmhouse@aol.com **web:** www.coombefarmhouse.com
dir: *1.5 miles west of Lelant. Exit A3074 to Lelant Downs.*

Built of sturdy granite, this early 19th-century farmhouse is in a delightful location
tucked away at the southern foot of Trencrom Hill, yet convenient for St Ives. The
comfortable bedrooms are attractively decorated. There is a conservatory lounge,
and substantial breakfasts, featuring farm-fresh eggs, are served in the dining
room overlooking the garden.

Rooms: 3 rms (2 en suite) (1 pri facs) **S** fr £50 **D** fr £82* **Facilities:** FTV Lounge
tea/coffee WiFi **Extras:** Bottled water – complimentary **Parking:** 3
Notes: No children 16 years Closed December to February

The Mustard Tree

★★★★ GUEST HOUSE

tel: 01736 795677 **Sea View Meadows, St Ives Road TR26 2JX**
email: enquiries@mustard-tree.co.uk **web:** www.mustard-tree.co.uk
dir: *A3074 to Carbis Bay, The Mustard Tree on right opposite Methodist church.*

Set in delightful gardens and with sea views, this attractive house is just a short
drive from the centre of St Ives, and the coastal path that leads from Carbis Bay to
St Ives. The pleasant bedrooms are very comfortable and have many extras. A
splendid choice is offered at breakfast, with vegetarian and continental options.

Rooms: 9 rms (8 en suite) (1 pri facs) (1 fmly) (4 GF) **S** fr £49 **D** fr £74
Facilities: FTV DVD TVL tea/coffee WiFi 🐾 **Extras:** Guest PC available, fridge
Conf: Max 20 **Parking:** 9

The Old Count House

★★★★ GUEST HOUSE

tel: 01736 795369 & 07853 844777 **1 Trenwith Square TR26 1DQ**
email: counthouse@btconnect.com **web:** www.theoldcounthouse-stives.co.uk
dir: *Follow signs to St Ives, house between leisure centre and school.*

Situated in a quiet residential area with on-site parking, The Old Count House is a
granite building where Victorian mine workers once collected their wages. Guests
are assured of a warm welcome and an extensive choice at breakfast. The well-
equipped bedrooms vary in size. The town centre, with its many restaurants, is only
a five-minute walk away.

Rooms: 10 rms (9 en suite) (1 pri facs) (2 GF) **S** fr £55 **D** fr £85* **Facilities:** FTV DVD
Lounge TVL tea/coffee WiFi Sauna 🐾 Excercise equipment, massage chair
Parking: 8 **Notes:** LB No children Closed November, 20–29 December and February

Old Vicarage

★★★★ 🍽 GUEST HOUSE

tel: 01736 796124 **Parc-an-Creet TR26 2ES**
email: stay@oldvicarage.com **web:** www.oldvicarage.com
dir: *From A3074 in town centre take B3306, 0.5 mile right into Parc-an-Creet.*

This former Victorian rectory stands in secluded gardens in a quiet part of St Ives
and is convenient for the seaside, town and Tate St Ives. The bedrooms are
enhanced by modern facilities. A good choice of local produce is offered at
breakfast, plus home-made yogurt and preserves.

Rooms: 6 en suite (4 fmly) **S** fr £85 **D** fr £92* **Facilities:** FTV TVL tea/coffee Licensed
WiFi **Parking:** 12 **Notes:** LB Closed December to February Civ wed 30

The Regent

★★★★ GUEST ACCOMMODATION

tel: 01736 796195 **Fernlea Terrace TR26 2BH**
email: keith@regenthotel.com **web:** www.regenthotel.com
dir: *In town centre, near bus and railway station.*

This popular and attractive property stands in an elevated position that's
convenient for the town centre and seafront. The Regent has well-equipped
bedrooms, some with spectacular sea vistas, and the comfortable lounge also has
great views. The breakfast choices, including vegetarian, are excellent.

Rooms: 10 rms (8 en suite) (1 fmly) **S** fr £53 **D** fr £98 **Facilities:** FTV Lounge TVL tea/
coffee WiFi 🐾 **Parking:** 12 **Notes:** LB No children 16 years

The Sloop Inn

★★★ INN

tel: 01736 796584 **The Wharf TR26 1LP**
email: sloopinn@btinternet.com **web:** www.sloop-inn.co.uk
dir: *On St Ives harbour by middle slipway.*

This attractive, historic inn has an imposing position on the harbour. Each of the
guest rooms has a nautical name, many enjoy pleasant views, and all have
impressive modern facilities. A good choice of dishes is offered at lunch and dinner
in the atmospheric restaurant-bar.

Rooms: 22 en suite (6 fmly) (5 GF) **S** fr £86.25 **D** fr £120 **Facilities:** FTV tea/coffee
Dinner available WiFi 🐾 **Parking:** 8 **Notes:** LB

ST KEVERNE
Map 2 SW72

Gallen-Treath Guest House

★★★ ⬤ GUEST HOUSE

tel: 01326 280400 & 07813 920738 **Porthallow TR12 6PL**
email: gallentreath@btclick.com **web:** www.gallen-treath.com
dir: 1.5 miles southeast of St Keverne in Porthallow.

Gallen-Treath Guest House has super views over the countryside and sea from its elevated position above Porthallow. Bedrooms are individually decorated and feature many personal touches. Guests can relax in the large, comfortable lounge complete with balcony. Hearty breakfasts and dinners (by arrangement) are served in the bright dining room.

Rooms: 5 en suite (1 fmly) (1 GF) **Facilities:** FTV TVL tea/coffee Dinner available Licensed WiFi **Parking:** 6 **Notes:** Closed 22 December to 2 January

ST KEW
Map 2 SX07

Tregellist Farm

★★★★ BED AND BREAKFAST

tel: 01208 880537 & 07970 559637 **Tregellist PL30 3HG**
email: tregellistfarm@btinternet.com **web:** www.tregellistfarm.co.uk
dir: On B3314 between Pendoggett and St Endellion, take turn signed to St Kew and Tregellist Farm.

Tregellist Farm, located in beautiful countryside close to Port Isaac, is convenient for Lanhydrock, Pencarrow, The Lost Gardens of Heligan, Padstow and The Eden Project. All the bedrooms are en suite, with TVs and hospitality trays with fresh milk. Served at separate tables in the dining room, breakfast is sourced locally and includes fresh eggs from the farm.

Rooms: 2 en suite 2 annexe en suite (1 fmly) (2 GF) **Facilities:** FTV DVD TVL tea/coffee WiFi ⬤ **Parking:** 6 **Notes:** Closed Christmas and New Year

ST MARY'S (ISLES OF SCILLY)
Map 2 SV91

Crebinick House

★★★★ GUEST HOUSE

tel: 01720 422968 **Church Street TR21 0JT**
email: aa@crebinick.co.uk **web:** www.crebinick.co.uk
dir: House 500 yards from quay through Hugh Town; (airport bus to house).

Many guests return time and again to this friendly, family-run house close to the town centre and the seafront. The granite-built property dates from 1760 and has smart, well-equipped bedrooms; two are on the ground floor. There is a quiet lounge for relaxation.

Rooms: 4 en suite (2 GF) **S** fr £54 **D** fr £78* **Facilities:** FTV Lounge tea/coffee WiFi **Notes:** LB No children 10 years Closed November to March

ST MELLION
Map 3 SX36

Premier Collection

Pentillie Castle & Estate

★★★★★ ⬤ GUEST ACCOMMODATION

tel: 01579 350044 **Paynters Cross PL12 6QD**
email: contact@pentillie.co.uk **web:** www.pentillie.co.uk
dir: From A38 Saltash onto A388 to Callington and St Mellion. After 3.1 miles right to Cargreen and Landulph. 100 yards on left.

Pentillie Castle & Estate has a great deal to offer. For a start, it's in a peaceful location in the heart of the Tamar Valley on the Cornwall and Devon border. It has established gardens, formal lawns and breathtaking views stretching over 2,000 acres. The property has been lovingly renovated to reveal its former glory; the comfortable and well-equipped bedrooms are warm and inviting. Supper and breakfast are served in the elegant dining room that has views of the gardens. The beautifully-designed lounge and drawing room are the perfect setting for reading the paper or enjoying a glass of wine from the honesty bar.

Rooms: 9 en suite (1 GF) **S** fr £120 **D** fr £135* **Facilities:** FTV DVD Lounge TVL tea/coffee Dinner available Licensed WiFi ⬤ Games room **Extras:** Speciality toiletries, robes, slippers, home-made shortbread – complimentary **Conf:** Max 70 Thtr 70 Class 24 Board 24 **Parking:** 100 **Notes:** LB Civ wed 60

SALTASH
Map 3 SX45

Smeaton Farm

★★★★ ⬤ FARMHOUSE

tel: 01579 351833 & 07813 027657 **PL12 6RZ**
email: info@smeatonfarm.co.uk **web:** www.smeatonfarm.co.uk
dir: 1 mile north of Hatt and 1 mile south of St Mellion just off A388.

This elegant Georgian farmhouse is surrounded by 450 acres of rolling Cornish farmland, providing a wonderfully peaceful place to stay. Home to the Jones family, the atmosphere is relaxed and hospitable, with every effort made to ensure that guests have a comfortable and rewarding break. Bedrooms are spacious, light and airy. Enjoyable dinners often feature home-reared meats, and the sausages at breakfast come highly recommended.

Rooms: 3 en suite (1 fmly) **S** fr £65 **D** fr £80* **Facilities:** FTV DVD Lounge TVL tea/coffee Dinner available Licensed WiFi ⬤ Riding ⬤ Cornish maze Guided farm tours **Extras:** Speciality toiletries, snacks, fruit **Conf:** Max 10 Board 10 **Parking:** 8 **Notes:** LB 450 acres arable/beef/sheep

Hay Lake Farm Bed & Breakfast

★★★★ BED AND BREAKFAST

tel: 01752 851209 & 07989 426306 **Landrake PL12 5AE**
email: ianbiffen@hotmail.co.uk **web:** www.haylakefarm.co.uk
dir: A38 at Landrake turn into West Lane. 0.75 mile on left before crossroads.

This modern, comfortable bed and breakfast offers spacious and well-equipped en suite accommodation. Hay Lake Farm is ideal for those exploring both north and south coasts of Cornwall, and is within easy reach of many National Trust properties as well as The Eden Project. Stables are available.

Rooms: 3 en suite (2 fmly) (1 GF) **S** fr £50 **D** fr £85* **Facilities:** FTV DVD tea/coffee WiFi ⬤ **Extras:** Speciality toiletries – complimentary **Parking:** 6

SALTASH *continued*

Crooked Inn

★★★★ INN

tel: 01752 848177 **Stoketon Cross, Trematon PL12 4RZ**
email: info@crooked-inn.co.uk web: www.crooked-inn.co.uk
dir: *1.5 miles northwest of Saltash. A38 west from Saltash, 2nd left to Trematon, sharp right.*

The friendly animals that freely roam the courtyard add to the relaxed country style of this delightful inn. The spacious bedrooms are well equipped, and freshly cooked dinners are available in the bar and conservatory. Breakfast is served in the cottage-style dining room.

Rooms: 15 annexe en suite (5 fmly) (7 GF) **Facilities:** FTV tea/coffee Dinner available WiFi ⚡ **Extras:** Speciality toiletries, fresh milk **Conf:** Max 70 **Parking:** 45
Notes: Closed 25 December

ISLES OF SCILLY
See St Mary's & Tresco

TRESCO (ISLES OF SCILLY)   Map 2 SV81

New Inn

★★★★ INN

tel: 01720 422849 & 423006 **TR24 0QQ**
email: contactus@tresco.co.uk web: www.tresco.co.uk
dir: *By New Grimsby Quay.*

This friendly, popular inn is at the heart of its community on the privately-owned and beautiful island of Tresco. It offers bright, attractive and well-equipped bedrooms, many with splendid sea views. There is an extensive choice on the menu at both lunch and dinner – dishes are firmly based on island produce; meals can be enjoyed in either in the airy bistro-style Pavilion or the popular bar that also serves real ales. A heated outdoor pool is also available.

Rooms: 16 en suite (2 fmly) (2 GF) **Facilities:** FTV DVD Lounge tea/coffee Dinner available Direct dial WiFi ⚡ ♨ Fishing Use of local leisure spa **Extras:** Speciality toiletries, fresh ground coffee, home-made shortbread **Notes:** LB

TRURO   Map 2 SW84

Bodrean Manor Farm

★★★★ 🏠 FARMHOUSE

tel: 07970 955857 **Trispen TR4 9AG**
email: bodrean@hotmail.co.uk web: www.bodreanmanorfarm.co.uk
dir: *3 miles northeast of Truro. A30 onto A39 towards Truro, left after Trispen signed Trehane, farm drive 100 yards.*

This friendly farmhouse is located in peaceful countryside, convenient for Truro or as a touring base. It has all the charm of an historic house but is styled and fitted with modern facilities. Bedrooms are thoughtfully and extensively equipped, and the bathrooms are well provisioned with soft towels and a host of toiletries. The home-cooked breakfast is served around a large, communal table in the smartly appointed dining room. Storage for motorbikes and bikes is available.

Rooms: 3 rms (2 en suite) (1 pri facs) (1 fmly) **S** fr £50 **D** fr £76* **Facilities:** FTV TVL tea/coffee WiFi 🅿 **Parking:** 6 **Notes:** LB 220 acres mixed

Donnington Guest House

★★★ GUEST ACCOMMODATION

tel: 01872 222552 & 07787 555475 **43 Treyew Road TR1 2BY**
email: info@donnington-guesthouse.co.uk web: www.donnington-guesthouse.co.uk

A well located property, just 12 minutes' walk from the city centre. It is actually two houses operating as one, with breakfast being taken in the breakfast room of one of them. Well-appointed bedrooms, a friendly host and good off-road parking make this a very popular venue.

Rooms: 14 rms (12 en suite) (2 pri facs) (2 fmly) (2 GF) **Facilities:** FTV DVD tea/coffee ⚡ 🔒 **Extras:** Fridge **Parking:** 11

Resparveth Farm

★★★ FARMHOUSE

tel: 01726 882382 & 07929 234206 **Grampound Road TR2 4EF**
email: resparveth.farm@gmail.com **web:** www.resparveth.co.uk
dir: *A30 exit signed Fraddon/Grampound Road (B3275). Continue on A3058, through Grampound Road village, turn right at B&B sign.*

The young owners of this traditional farmhouse bed and breakfast do all they can to make a stay as comfortable as possible. The farm is in a handy location for St Austell, The Eden Project and Truro, and offers comfortable rooms. Freshly cooked breakfasts are served at one large table in the breakfast room that features an original Cornish range.

Rooms: 2 en suite **D** fr £69* **Facilities:** FTV DVD tea/coffee WiFi 🐎 Riding 🔒 Feeding of animals, farm experience **Conf:** Max 6 Thtr 6 Class 6 Board 6 **Parking:** 3 **Notes:** LB 60 acres beef/sheep/bees/pigs/chickens/arable

VERYAN Map 2 SW93

Elerkey Guest House

★★★★ GUEST HOUSE

tel: 01872 501261 & 501160 **Elerkey House TR2 5QA**
email: anne@elerkeyguesthouse.co.uk **web:** www.elerkeyguesthouse.co.uk
dir: *In village, 1st left after church and water gardens.*

This peaceful home is surrounded by attractive gardens in a tranquil village. The proprietors and their family provide exemplary hospitality and many guests return time and again. The pleasantly appointed bedrooms have many considerate extras.

Rooms: 4 en suite (1 fmly) **Facilities:** FTV DVD Lounge tea/coffee Direct dial WiFi 🔒 Art gallery and gift shop **Extras:** Mineral water **Parking:** 5 **Notes:** LB Closed December to January

WADEBRIDGE Map 2 SW97

Premier Collection

Wadebridge Bed and Breakfast

★★★★★ 🛏 BED AND BREAKFAST

tel: 01208 816837 & 07740 255092 **Orchard House, Elmsleigh Road PL27 7HA**
email: info@wadebridgebedandbreakfast.net
web: www.wadebridgebedandbreakfast.net
dir: *From Bodmin A389 into Wadebridge. Pass Trelawney Garden Centre on right, continue to roundabout. Exit onto A39. At next roundabout left into West Hill. After phone box on left, take next left into Elmsleigh Road, 1st house on left.*

This contemporary house is just a short walk from the town centre and provides an ideal base from which to explore the area. Bedrooms offer impressive levels of comfort and quality, and one has a balcony with lovely views over the town and countryside. Bathrooms offer all the expected mod cons with underfloor heating, invigorating showers and fluffy towels. Generous and tasty breakfasts are served in the dining room with a garden patio available for alfresco dining. Secure storage is available for bikes and surf boards.

Rooms: 3 en suite **S** fr £80 **D** fr £90* **Facilities:** FTV TVL tea/coffee WiFi 🔒 **Extras:** Bottled water, fresh milk, speciality toiletries **Parking:** 4 **Notes:** LB No children Closed January to February

CUMBRIA

AMBLESIDE Map 18 NY30

Premier Collection

Nanny Brow

★★★★★ 🛏 GUEST ACCOMMODATION

tel: 015394 33232 & 07746 103008 **Clappersgate LA22 9NF**
email: unwind@nannybrow.co.uk **web:** www.nannybrow.co.uk
dir: *M6 junction 36 onto A590 and A591 through Windermere. At lights bear left onto A593, left again at rugby pitch and left over bridge. Through Clappersgate, 0.5 mile on right.*

Nanny Brow provides high quality throughout. Each room is thoughtfully decorated with contemporary furnishings, antique furniture and original arts and crafts. The property is situated in Clappersgate, close to Ambleside, standing high above the road and overlooking the beautiful Langdale Valley. A drink from the bar menu can be enjoyed in the quiet guest lounge where you will find plenty of information about local walks.

Rooms: 12 en suite 2 annexe en suite (2 GF) **D** fr £130* **Facilities:** FTV DVD Lounge tea/coffee Licensed WiFi 🔒 **Extras:** Robes, champagne, chocolates, flowers – chargeable **Conf:** Max 26 Thtr 26 Class 12 Board 12 **Parking:** 15 **Notes:** LB No children 12 years Civ wed 32

AMBLESIDE *continued*

Riverside B&B

★★★★ ⊜ GUEST HOUSE

tel: 015394 32395 & 32440 **Under Loughrigg LA22 9LJ**
email: info@riverside-at-ambleside.co.uk **web:** www.riverside-at-ambleside.co.uk
dir: *A593 from Ambleside to Coniston, over stone bridge, right into Under Loughrigg Lane, Riverside 150 yards left.*

Riverside is a Victorian house situated on a quiet lane by the River Rothay below Loughrigg Fell. The owners offer a very friendly welcome. All the bedrooms have lovely views, are very comfortable and stylishly furnished and feature many thoughtful extras. A log-burning stove warms the lounge in winter. Guests can use the garden which has seating ideally placed for the morning and evening sun. An award-winning hearty Lakeland breakfast is a highlight of any stay and features local produce along with home baking and preserves.

Rooms: 6 en suite **S** fr £116 **D** fr £116* **Facilities:** FTV iPod docking station TVL tea/coffee Licensed WiFi ♨ **Extras:** Speciality toiletries **Parking:** 6
Notes: No children 10 years Closed 13 December to 22 January

Innkeeper's Lodge Ambleside, Lake District

★★★★ INN

tel: 03451 551551 **The White Lion, Market Place LA22 9DB**
email: info@innkeeperslodge.com **web:** www.innkeeperslodge.com
dir: *Phone for directions.*

A charming 18th-century inn situated in the heart of Ambleside close to Windermere and within easy reach of the M6. The modern, well-equipped bedrooms are very well appointed with a range of modern facilities. Public areas include a large open-plan lounge bar with a roaring open fire and a selection of seating options; both dinners and full English breakfasts are available in the smart dining room.

Rooms: 7 en suite (4 fmly) **Facilities:** FTV tea/coffee Dinner available WiFi
Conf: Max 20 **Parking:** 7

ASKHAM   Map 18 NY52

Premier Collection

Askham Hall

★★★★★ ◉◉ ⊜ GUEST ACCOMMODATION

tel: 01931 712350 & 07887 724857 **CA10 2PF**
email: enquiries@askhamhall.co.uk **web:** www.askhamhall.co.uk
dir: *South of Penrith, follow signs from B5320 to Askham and brown tourist signs.*

Askham Hall sits on the edge of the Lake District surrounded by the majestic Cumbrian countryside. This Grade I listed building dates back to the 14th century with only the restaurant being a modern addition to the building. Public areas are warm and welcoming with the open fire adding to the charm. Bedrooms and their en suites cater well for the modern guest – many thoughtful extras are provided as standard. The award-winning food uses produce from the kitchen gardens as well as the farms within the estate. The friendly, hands-on team add to the wonderful guest experience.

Rooms: 18 en suite (3 fmly) (2 GF) **S** fr £138 **D** fr £150* **Facilities:** STV FTV DVD Lounge tea/coffee Dinner available Direct dial Licensed WiFi ⚲ ⚑ Fishing Snooker Sauna ♨ Spa treatment room **Extras:** Speciality toiletries, mini-bar, fridge **Conf:** Max 150 **Notes:** Closed Christmas RS January to mid February group bookings only Civ wed 150

The Punchbowl Inn, Askham

★★★ ⬮ INN

tel: 01931 712443 **CA10 2PF**
email: info@punchbowlinnaskham.co.uk **web:** www.punchbowlinnaskham.com
dir: *From M6 junction 39 onto A6 towards Penrith. Continue through Hackthorpe, follow signs for Lowther and to Askham.*

An idyllic Lakeland village is the setting for this whitewashed country pub. It retains a great deal of original coaching house character with low oak beams and stone floors. The restaurant to the rear is more contemporary but just as comfortable. Bedrooms differ in size but all are well appointed and well presented. The food is noteworthy, and the bar boasts several local real ales and an open fire that adds to the charm in the colder months.

Rooms: 6 en suite **S** fr £50 **D** fr £50* **Facilities:** FTV Lounge TVL tea/coffee Dinner available WiFi **Notes:** LB

BORROWDALE — Map 18 NY21

Premier Collection

Hazel Bank Country House

★★★★★ ◉ ⬮ GUEST ACCOMMODATION

tel: 017687 77248 & 07775 701069 **Rosthwaite CA12 5XB**
email: info@hazelbankhotel.co.uk **web:** www.hazelbankhotel.co.uk
dir: *B5289 from Keswick towards Borrowdale, left after sign for Rosthwaite.*

Set on an elevated position surrounded by four acres of gardens and woodland, Hazel Bank Country House enjoys wonderful views of Borrowdale. The approach to this grand Victorian house is impressive, reached via a picturesque humpback bridge and a winding drive. Bedrooms are sumptuous and all are en suite. Carefully cooked dishes are served in the elegant dining room; the daily-changing, four-course menu features fresh, local ingredients. There is a friendly atmosphere here and the proprietors are very welcoming.

Rooms: 7 en suite (1 GF) **Facilities:** FTV iPod docking station Lounge tea/coffee Dinner available Licensed WiFi ⛵ **Extras:** Speciality toiletries, chocolates, bottled water **Parking:** 9 **Notes:** LB No children 12 years Closed 30 November to 30 January

BOWNESS-ON-WINDERMERE

See Windermere

BRAITHWAITE — Map 18 NY22

The Cottage in the Wood

★★★★ ⬮ RESTAURANT WITH ROOMS

tel: 017687 78409 & 07730 312193 **Whinlatter Pass CA12 5TW**
email: relax@thecottageinthewood.co.uk **web:** www.thecottageinthewood.co.uk
dir: *M6 junction 40, A66 west. After Keswick exit for Braithwaite via Whinlatter Pass (B5292), establishment at top of pass.*

This charming property sits on wooded hills with striking views of Skiddaw, and is conveniently placed for Keswick. The owners provide excellent hospitality in a relaxed manner. The food, freshly prepared and locally sourced, is served in the bright and welcoming conservatory restaurant with its stunning views. The comfortable bedrooms are well appointed and have many useful extras.

Rooms: 9 en suite **Facilities:** FTV Lounge tea/coffee Dinner available Direct dial WiFi **Parking:** 15 **Notes:** LB No children 10 years Closed January RS Monday closed

BRAMPTON — Map 21 NY56

Abbey Bridge

★★★★ ⬮ GUEST ACCOMMODATION

tel: 016977 3841 **Lanercost CA8 2HG**
email: tim@abbeybridge.co.uk **web:** www.abbeybridge.co.uk
dir: *M6 junction 43. A69 to Brampton, follow signs for Lanercost Priory. Through town, 2 miles on left, next to Lanercost Bridge.*

Abbey Bridge has a long history and is a beautifully presented property offering wonderful hospitality and high standards of comfort. Previously, an inn and pub but also a Temperance Inn until regaining its license in the 1970s; the property is currently fully licensed and comprises two buildings, The Blacksmiths and the main house. Walkers are well catered for, with a boot- and wet-kit room which even boasts boot-drying equipment. Located close to Hadrian's Wall and even closer to Lanercost Priory, it's an ideal base to tour the surrounding area with Edinburgh, Newcastle, the North Pennines and the Lakes all within easy reach as the A69 is just minutes away. Dinner is available by prior arrangement.

Rooms: 5 en suite 1 annexe en suite **S** fr £75 **D** fr £90* **Facilities:** FTV tea/coffee Dinner available Licensed WiFi **Parking:** 7 **Notes:** Closed November to March

The Blacksmiths Arms

★★★★ INN

tel: 016977 3452 & 42111 **Talkin Village CA8 1LE**
email: blacksmithsarmstalkin@yahoo.co.uk **web:** www.blacksmithstalkin.co.uk
dir: *B6413 from Brampton to Castle Carrock, after level crossing 2nd left signed Talkin.*

Dating from the early 19th century and used as a smithy until the 1950s, this friendly village inn offers good home-cooked fare and real ales, with two Cumbrian cask beers always available. Bedrooms are well equipped, and three are particularly smart. An extensive menu and daily specials are offered in the cosy bar lounges or the smart, panelled Old Forge Restaurant.

Rooms: 5 en suite 3 annexe en suite (2 fmly) (3 GF) **Facilities:** FTV tea/coffee Dinner available Direct dial WiFi ⛵ **Parking:** 20

BROUGH — Map 18 NY71

Premier Collection

The Inn at Brough

★★★★★ ◉ INN

tel: 01768 341252 **Main Street CA17 4AX**
email: enquiries@theinnatbrough.co.uk **web:** www.theinnatbrough.co.uk
dir: *M6 junction 38, A685 to Kirkby Stephen, then Brough. A66 exit to Brough and Kirkby Stephen.*

This 18th-century former coaching inn is located in the picturesque Eden Valley and enjoys easy access to the A66. Deeply comfortable bedrooms feature a host of luxury touches, while bathrooms boast Villeroy & Boch fittings and locally-made toiletries. There are contemporary touches throughout the bar and restaurant, and a function suite is available. Any stay here would not be complete without sampling the wonderful food on offer both at dinner and breakfast.

Rooms: 14 en suite 2 annexe en suite (2 fmly) (2 GF) **Facilities:** FTV DVD tea/coffee Dinner available WiFi ⛵ **Extras:** Robes, slippers, soft drinks, home-made biscuits **Conf:** Max 100 Thtr 60 Class 60 Board 30 **Parking:** 40 **Notes:** LB

CARLISLE   Map 18 NY35

See also Brampton

The Angus

★★★★ GUEST ACCOMMODATION

tel: 01228 523546 **14–16 Scotland Road CA3 9DG**
email: hotel@angus-hotel.co.uk **web:** www.angus-hotel.co.uk
dir: *0.5 mile north of city centre on A7.*

Situated just north of the city and built on the actual foundations of Hadrian's Wall, this family-run establishment is ideal for business and leisure. A warm welcome is assured and the accommodation is well equipped. Dinner is available by prior arrangement, providing enjoyable food and home baking. There is also a comfortable lounge available for the guests.

Rooms: 10 en suite (2 fmly) **Facilities:** FTV Lounge tea/coffee Dinner available Licensed WiFi **Notes:** LB

CARTMEL   Map 18 SD37

Premier Collection

L'Enclume

★★★★★ ◉◉◉◉◉ RESTAURANT WITH ROOMS

tel: 015395 36362 **Cavendish St LA11 6PZ**
email: info@lenclume.co.uk **web:** www.lenclume.co.uk
dir: *From A590 turn left for Cartmel before Newby Bridge.*

L'Enclume is a delightful 13th-century property in the heart of a lovely village, and offers incredible 21st-century cooking that draws foodies from far and wide. Once the village forge (l'enclume is French for 'the anvil') it's now the location for some of Britain's best food, and Simon Rogan's imaginative and adventurous cooking may be sampled in the stylish restaurant. Individually designed, modern, en suite rooms of varying sizes and styles are in the main property and dotted about the village only a few moments' walk from the restaurant.

Rooms: 5 en suite 11 annexe en suite (3 fmly) (2 GF) **Facilities:** STV DVD iPod docking station tea/coffee Dinner available Direct dial WiFi **Extras:** Mini-bar, speciality toiletries **Parking:** 3

CLIFTON   Map 18 NY52

George and Dragon, Clifton

★★★★ ◉ ⬤ INN

tel: 01768 865381 & 07887 724857 **CA10 2ER**
email: enquiries@georgeanddragonclifton.co.uk **web:** www.georgeanddragonclifton.co.uk
dir: *On A6 in village of Clifton.*

The George and Dragon is an 18th-century coaching inn located just south of Penrith, ideally located for the Lakes and surrounding areas. The restored property reflects its Georgian heritage and retains many original features and materials. The comfortable bedrooms are well appointed and cater well for the needs of the modern guest. The bar is warm and welcoming with several real ales on offer. The award-winning dishes use mainly local produce, much of which comes from the owners' estate. The hearty breakfast will provide a great start to the day.

Rooms: 11 en suite (2 fmly) **S** fr £85 **D** fr £100* **Facilities:** STV FTV Lounge tea/coffee Dinner available WiFi ⚲ Fishing **Extras:** Speciality toiletries
Notes: Closed 26 December

CROSTHWAITE — Map 18 SD49

The Punchbowl Inn at Crosthwaite

★★★★★ ◉◉ 🍷 INN

tel: 015395 68237 **Lyth Valley LA8 8HR**
email: info@the-punchbowl.co.uk web: www.the-punchbowl.co.uk
dir: *M6 junction 36 signed Barrow, on A5074 towards Windermere, turn right for Crosthwaite. At east end of village beside church.*

Located in the stunning Lyth Valley alongside the village church, this historic inn has been appointed to provide excellent standards of comfort and facilities. Its sumptuous bedrooms have a wealth of thoughtful extras, and imaginative food is served in the elegant restaurant or in the rustic-style bar that has open fires. A warm welcome and professional service is assured.

Rooms: 9 en suite **S** fr £85 **D** fr £110* **Facilities:** FTV Dinner available Direct dial WiFi 🔒 **Extras:** Speciality toiletries, home-made scones and jam **Parking:** 25
Notes: Civ wed 48

GLENRIDDING — Map 18 NY31

Glenridding House

★★★★★ 🍷 GUEST ACCOMMODATION

tel: 017684 82874 & 07966 486701 **CA11 0PH**
email: stay@glenriddinghouse.com web: www.glenriddinghouse.com
dir: *M6 junction 40 onto A66, then A592 to Glenridding. Turn sharp 2nd left.*

Glenridding House is a wonderful Georgian Lakeside villa which sits right on the shores of Ullswater. Used as a holiday home by Charles Darwin, this once derelict building has been lovingly restored. Bedrooms differ in size, and a number boast stunning views of the lake and surrounding fells. An excellent location for those touring this unspoilt area of the Lake District.

Rooms: 6 rms (6 pri facs) (1 GF) **Facilities:** FTV Lounge tea/coffee Dinner available Licensed WiFi Fishing 🔒 Packed lunches available **Conf:** Max 30 Thtr 30 Class 30 Board 30 **Parking:** 30 **Notes:** LB No children 18 years Civ wed 50

GRANGE-OVER-SANDS — Map 18 SD47

Birchleigh Guest House

★★★★ GUEST HOUSE

tel: 015395 32592 & 07527 844403 **Kents Bank Road LA11 7EY**
email: birchleigh@btinternet.com web: www.birchleighguesthouse.com
dir: *M6 junction 36, A590 signed Windermere, then Barrow. At Meathop Roundabout left onto B5277 to Grange-over-Sands. At 1st roundabout left, at 2nd roundabout right. At T-junction left into Kents Bank Road. 3rd house on left after car park.*

This homely and welcoming guest house is situated in the heart of the charming town of Grange-over-Sands, providing four comfortable and tastefully-decorated, modern bedrooms. Expect a hearty breakfast served in the well-appointed dining room.

Rooms: 4 en suite (1 fmly) **S** fr £65 **D** fr £83* **Facilities:** FTV tea/coffee WiFi 🔒 **Extras:** Fresh milk **Parking:** 2

GRASMERE — Map 18 NY30

Moss Grove Organic

★★★★★ 🍷 GUEST ACCOMMODATION

tel: 015394 35251 **LA22 9SW**
email: enquiries@mossgrove.com web: www.mossgrove.com
dir: *From south: M6 junction 36 onto A591 signed Keswick. From north: M6 junction 40 onto A591 signed Windermere.*

Located in the heart of the Lakes, this impressive Victorian house has been appointed using as many natural products as possible, as part of an ongoing dedication to cause minimal environmental impact. The stylish bedrooms, decorated with beautiful wallpaper and natural clay paints, feature hand-made beds and furnishings. Bose home-entertainment systems, TVs and luxury bathrooms add further comfort; one room even has a hot tub. Extensive continental breakfasts are served in the spacious kitchen, where guests can help themselves and dine individually or communally at the large wooden table.

Rooms: 11 en suite (2 GF) **Facilities:** STV DVD iPod docking station Lounge tea/coffee Licensed WiFi 🔒 **Extras:** Speciality toiletries – complimentary **Parking:** 11
Notes: LB No children 14 years Closed 24–25 December

HAWKSHEAD — Map 18 SD39

See also Near Sawrey

Ees Wyke Country House

★★★★★ ◉ 🍷 GUEST HOUSE

tel: 015394 36393 **LA22 0JZ**
email: mail@eeswyke.co.uk web: www.eeswyke.co.uk

(For full entry see Near Sawrey)

HAWKSHEAD *continued*

The Queen's Head Inn & Restaurant

★★★★ 🕸 INN

tel: 015394 36271 **Main Street LA22 0NS**
email: info@queensheadhawkshead.co.uk **web:** www.queensheadhawkshead.co.uk
dir: *M6 junction 36, A590 to Newby Bridge. Over roundabout, 1st right into Hawkshead.*

This 16th-century inn features a wood-panelled bar with low, oak-beamed ceilings and an open log fire. An excellent selection of quality dishes and local ales are served throughout the day. The smart accommodation is comfortable and stylishly decorated with modern amenities – walk-in showers, 32" TVs, teas- and coffee-making facilities and free WiFi. A family suite is available in a 16th-century annexe and there is a ground-floor room with its own entrance.

Rooms: 10 en suite 3 annexe en suite (1 fmly) (2 GF) **S** fr £75 **D** fr £90*
Facilities: FTV DVD iPod docking station tea/coffee Dinner available WiFi
🛁 **Extras:** Speciality toiletries, robes, slippers, coffee machine

Sun Inn

★★★★ 🕸 INN

tel: 015394 36236 **Main Street LA22 0NT**
email: rooms@suninn.co.uk **web:** www.suninn.co.uk
dir: *M6 junction 36 onto A591 (Ambleside). Follow signs to Hawkshead, in centre of village.*

The Sun Inn is a charming 17th-century building located in the heart of the peaceful village of Hawkshead on the quieter side of Windermere. It has retained a great deal of original character, with wooden panelling, oak beams, stone floors and exposed brickwork. Bedrooms differ in size but all are well appointed, with the locally hand-made furniture making the best of the available space. The food has been awarded an AA Rosette and the bar boasts a number of local real ales, with an open fire adding to the charm in the colder months.

Rooms: 8 en suite (1 fmly) **S** fr £70 **D** fr £100* **Facilities:** FTV tea/coffee Dinner available WiFi 🛁 **Extras:** Wine/champagne, flowers, chocolates – chargeable

Kings Arms

★★★ 🍸 INN

tel: 015394 36372 **LA22 0NZ**
email: info@kingsarmshawkshead.co.uk **web:** www.kingsarmshawkshead.co.uk
dir: *M6 junction 36, A591, left onto A593 at Waterhead. 1 mile, onto B5286 to Hawkshead, Kings Arms in main square.*

The Kings Arms is a traditional Lakeland inn in the heart of a conservation area. The cosy, thoughtfully equipped bedrooms retain much character and are

traditionally furnished. A good choice of freshly prepared food is available in the lounge bar and the neatly presented dining room.

Rooms: 8 en suite (3 fmly) **S** fr £75 **D** fr £105 **Facilities:** FTV tea/coffee Dinner available Direct dial WiFi 🛁 Fishing Riding 🎳 Bowls **Notes:** LB Closed 25 December

HOLMROOK — Map 18 SD09

The Lutwidge Arms

★★★★ INN

tel: 019467 24230 **CA19 1UH**
email: mail@lutwidgearms.co.uk **web:** www.lutwidgearms.co.uk
dir: *M6 junction 36, A590 towards Barrow. Follow A595 towards Whitehaven and Workington, property in village centre.*

This Victorian roadside inn is family run and offers a welcoming atmosphere. Its name comes from the Lutwidge family of Holmrook Hall, whose lineage included Charles Lutwidge Dodgson, better known as Lewis Carroll. The bar and restaurant offer a wide range of meals during the evening. Bedrooms are smart and comfortable, and the Orangery has transformed the garden and dining areas.

Rooms: 11 en suite 5 annexe en suite (5 fmly) (5 GF) **Facilities:** FTV TVL tea/coffee Dinner available WiFi 🛁 **Conf:** Max 20 Thtr 20 Class 20 Board 20 **Parking:** 30 **Notes:** LB No children 5 years

IREBY — Map 18 NY23

Woodlands Country House

★★★★ 🍸 GUEST HOUSE

tel: 016973 71791 **CA7 1EX**
email: stay@woodlandsatireby.co.uk **web:** www.woodlandsatireby.co.uk
dir: *M6 junction 40, A66, pass Keswick, at roundabout right onto A591. At Castle Inn right signed Ireby, 2nd left signed Ireby. Pass church on left, last house in village.*

Previously a vicarage, this lovely Victorian home is set in well-tended gardens that attract lots of wildlife. Guests are given a warm welcome by the friendly owner and delicious home-cooked evening meals are available by prior arrangement. A peaceful lounge and cosy bar with snug are also available. Bedrooms are attractively furnished and thoughtfully equipped.

Rooms: 4 en suite 3 annexe en suite (3 fmly) (3 GF) **Facilities:** FTV Lounge TVL tea/coffee Dinner available Licensed WiFi **Extras:** Home-made shortbread, sweets, mineral water – complimentary **Parking:** 11 **Notes:** LB

IRTHINGTON — Map 21 NY46

The Golden Fleece

★★★★ 🕸 🍸 INN

tel: 01228 573686 & 07766 736924 **Rule Holme CA6 4NF**
email: info@thegoldenfleececumbria.co.uk **web:** www.thegoldenfleececumbria.co.uk
dir: *M6 junction 44 onto A689 signed Brampton. 1 mile past Carlisle Airport, on left.*

The Golden Fleece is a rural inn set beside the A689, close to Carlisle and Hadrian's Wall. Public areas include a feature bar with local real ales on draught, and a cosy lounge area with a fire. The dining room is split between several areas helping to create a sense of intimacy. Bedrooms and bathrooms are all modern in appearance. The full Cumbrian breakfasts are not to be missed, and friendly staff provide a true Cumbrian welcome. There is ample parking.

Rooms: 8 en suite (4 fmly) **Facilities:** FTV DVD iPod docking station Lounge tea/coffee Dinner available WiFi ♨ Fishing 🛁 **Extras:** Speciality toiletries, home-made cakes **Conf:** Max 150 Thtr 120 Class 70 Board 70 **Parking:** 100 **Notes:** Closed 1–8 January Civ wed 100

KENDAL
Map 18 SD59

The Punch Bowl
★★★★ ⊜ INN

tel: 015395 60267 **Barrows Green LA8 0AA**
email: punch_bowl@hotmail.co.uk **web:** www.thepunchbowla65.com
dir: *M6 junction 36 onto A65 signed Kendal. After 4 miles, on left.*

Expect a warm welcome at this friendly pub that is within easy reach of transport links and perfectly situated at the gateway to the Lake District. The two tastefully decorated bedrooms are comfortable and well equipped for the modern guest. Dinner is traditional, wholesome 'pub grub', and breakfast is a hearty affair.

Rooms: 2 en suite **Facilities:** FTV Lounge TVL tea/coffee Dinner available WiFi 🔒 **Extras:** Bottled water, Kendal mintcake **Parking:** 40

KESWICK
Map 18 NY22

Amble House
★★★★ ⊜ GUEST HOUSE

tel: 017687 73288 **23 Eskin Street CA12 4DQ**
email: info@amblehouse.co.uk **web:** www.amblehouse.co.uk
dir: *400 yards southeast of town centre. Exit A5271 (Penrith Road) into Greta Street and Eskin Street.*

An enthusiastic welcome awaits you at this Victorian mid-terrace house, near the town centre and in an ideal location for exploring the Lakes. The thoughtfully-equipped bedrooms have co-ordinated decor and are furnished in pine. Healthy breakfasts are served in the attractive dining room.

Rooms: 5 en suite **S** fr £60 **D** fr £84* **Facilities:** tea/coffee WiFi 🔒 **Extras:** Speciality toiletries, USB chargers **Notes:** LB No children 16 years Closed 24–26 December

Badgers Wood
★★★★ ⊜ GUEST HOUSE

tel: 017687 72621 **30 Stanger Street CA12 5JU**
email: enquiries@badgers-wood.co.uk **web:** www.badgers-wood.co.uk
dir: *In town centre off A5271 (main street).*

Anne and Andrew extend a warm welcome to guests at their delightful Victorian terrace house, located in a quiet area close to the town centre. The smart, well-equipped bedrooms are furnished to a high standard and have lovely views; the attractive breakfast room at the front of the house overlooks the fells. Special diets are gladly catered for. Off-road parking is an added benefit.

Rooms: 6 en suite **Facilities:** FTV tea/coffee WiFi 🔒 **Parking:** 6
Notes: No children 12 years Closed November to January

Dalegarth House
★★★★ ⊜ GUEST ACCOMMODATION

tel: 017687 72817 **Portinscale CA12 5RQ**
email: allerdalechef@aol.com **web:** www.dalegarth-house.co.uk
dir: *Exit A66 to Portinscale, pass Farmers Arms, 500 yards on left.*

This friendly, family-run establishment stands on an elevated position in the village of Portinscale, and has fine views from the well-tended garden. The attractive bedrooms are well equipped, and there is a peaceful lounge, a well-stocked bar, and a spacious dining room where the resident owner-chef produces hearty breakfasts.

Rooms: 8 en suite 2 annexe en suite (1 fmly) (2 GF) **S** fr £46 **D** fr £92*
Facilities: FTV Lounge tea/coffee Licensed WiFi 🔒 **Extras:** Home-made cakes – complimentary **Parking:** 10 **Notes:** LB No children 12 years Closed 24 November to 1 March

The Edwardene
★★★★ ⊜ GUEST ACCOMMODATION

tel: 017687 73586 **26 Southey Street CA12 4EF**
email: info@edwardenekeswick.co.uk **web:** www.edwardenekeswick.co.uk
dir: *M6 junction 40, A66 follow 1st sign to Keswick, right into Penrith Road. Sharp left by war memorial into Southey Street, 150 metres on right.*

Located close to the heart of the town centre, this Victorian lakeland stone building retains many of its original features. Bedrooms are well equipped, with many thoughtful extras provided throughout. A comfortable lounge is available, and the generous Cumbrian breakfast is served in the stylish dining room.

Rooms: 11 en suite (1 fmly) **S** fr £56 **D** fr £98* **Facilities:** FTV Lounge TVL tea/coffee Licensed WiFi 🔒 **Extras:** Speciality toiletries **Parking:** 1 **Notes:** LB No children 2 years

The Royal Oak at Keswick
★★★★ INN

tel: 017687 74584 **Main Street CA12 5HZ**
email: relax@royaloakkeswick.co.uk **web:** www.royaloakkeswick.co.uk
dir: *M6 junction 40, A66 to Keswick town centre to war memorial crossroads. Left into Station Street. Inn 100 yards.*

Located on the corner of the vibrant market square, this large, friendly 18th-century coaching inn offers a wide range of meals throughout the day and evening. There is a fully stocked bar complete with well-kept cask ales. The bedrooms vary in size but all are contemporary, smartly presented and feature quality accessories such as LCD TVs. There is also a drying room.

Rooms: 19 en suite (2 fmly) **Facilities:** FTV tea/coffee Dinner available **Notes:** LB

Brundholme
★★★★ ⊜ GUEST ACCOMMODATION

tel: 017687 73305 & 07739 435401 **The Heads CA12 5ER**
email: bazaly@hotmail.co.uk **web:** www.brundholme.co.uk
dir: *Phone for directions.*

Centrally located and overlooking Hope Park, Brundholme is a Victorian property just a few minutes' walk from the town centre in one direction and the theatre in the other. The comfortable bedrooms are well appointed and some boast wonderful views of the surrounding fells. The well-cooked, traditional Lakeland breakfast will set you up for the day, and service is relaxed and friendly. Limited off-road parking is available.

Rooms: 4 en suite (1 GF) **Facilities:** FTV tea/coffee WiFi **Extras:** Fridges **Parking:** 6

Claremont House
★★★★ GUEST ACCOMMODATION

tel: 017687 72089 **Chestnut Hill CA12 4LT**
email: info@claremonthousekeswick.co.uk **web:** www.claremonthousekeswick.co.uk
dir: *A591 north into Chestnut Hill. Pass Manor Brow on left, Claremont House 100 yards on right.*

This impressive 19th-century house has commanding views over Keswick and beyond and is set in mature grounds where red squirrels regularly visit. It is within walking distance of the town and is ideal for walkers or those looking for relaxation. Guests can expect comfortable bedrooms, a hearty breakfast and friendly service with tea and cake on arrival.

Rooms: 6 en suite (1 fmly) (1 GF) **S** fr £50 **D** fr £60* **Facilities:** FTV tea/coffee WiFi 🔒 **Extras:** Flowers, wine, chocolate – chargeable **Parking:** 8 **Notes:** LB No children 8 years Closed 24–26 December

KESWICK *continued*

Damson Lodge

★★★★ 🍴 BED AND BREAKFAST

tel: 017687 73629 **25 Eskin Street CA12 4DQ**
email: damsonlodge@yahoo.co.uk **web:** www.damsonlodge.co.uk

Damson Lodge is situated in the heart of Keswick and only a short work from the centre of town. Well-appointed bedrooms offer comfort and cater well for the needs of the modern guest. The award-winning breakfast sources local produce and is further enhanced with the ever-changing specials which just may tempt you away from the traditional grill. Hospitality is warm and genuine, with Viri and Paul on hand to offer advice for places to see and to suggest maps for your walks.

Rooms: 3 en suite **S** fr £65 **D** fr £75* **Facilities:** FTV tea/coffee WiFi **Extras:** Home-made shortbread **Notes:** No children

The George

★★★★ 🍺 INN

tel: 017687 72076 **Saint Johns Street CA12 5AZ**
email: rooms@thegeorgekeswick.co.uk **web:** www.thegeorgekeswick.co.uk
dir: *M6 junction 40, A66, take left filter road signed Keswick, pass pub on left. At crossroads left into Station Street, 150 yards on left.*

Located in the centre of town, this property is Keswick's oldest coaching inn. There is an abundance of character with a wooden beamed bar, cosy seating areas and an atmospheric, candle-lit dining room. Food is a highlight, with a wide choice of freshly prepared dishes. Bedrooms are simply presented and comfortable. Parking permits and storage for bikes are available.

Rooms: 12 en suite (2 fmly) **Facilities:** FTV tea/coffee Dinner available 🅿 **Parking:** 4

Skiddaw Croft B&B

★★★★ GUEST ACCOMMODATION

tel: 017687 72321 **Portinscale CA12 5RD**
email: info@skiddawcroft.co.uk **web:** www.skiddawcroft.co.uk
dir: *A66 past Keswick, turn left signed Portinscale. Pass Farmers Arms pub, over brow of hill, 3rd property on left.*

Located in the peaceful village of Portinscale, just a few hundred metres from majestic Derwentwater, Skiddaw Croft was built in 1913 but has enjoyed extensive investment with numerous projects taking place inside and out. A warm, genuine welcome awaits all guests on arrival, with the offer of refreshments and home baking. Well appointed, modern bedrooms enjoy a variety of views – the lake and sometimes Cat Bells (depending on the time of year) from the front, while from the rear, Skiddaw is visible. Off-road parking is a bonus, and Portinscale is handy for the A66 and Keswick.

Rooms: 6 rms (4 en suite) (1 fmly) **S** fr £50 **D** fr £83* **Facilities:** FTV Lounge tea/coffee WiFi 🅿 **Extras:** Speciality toiletries – complimentary **Parking:** 5 **Notes:** No children 8 years Closed 18 December to January RS 1–17 December, 1–18 February open weekends only

Dorchester House

★★★★ GUEST ACCOMMODATION

tel: 017687 73256 **17 Southey Street CA12 4EG**
email: dennis@dorchesterhouse-keswick.co.uk **web:** www.dorchesterhouse-keswick.co.uk
dir: *200 yards east of town centre. Exit A5271 (Penrith Road) into Southey Street, 150 yards on left.*

Mr and Mrs Banner offer a warm welcome at Dorchester House, just a short stroll from the town centre and its amenities. The comfortably proportioned, well-maintained bedrooms offer pleasing co-ordinated decor and some have views of the surrounding fells. Hearty breakfasts are served in the attractive ground-floor dining room.

Rooms: 8 rms (7 en suite) (1 pri facs) (2 fmly) **Facilities:** FTV tea/coffee WiFi **Notes:** LB No children 6 years

Elm Tree Lodge

★★★★ GUEST ACCOMMODATION

tel: 017687 71050 & 07980 521079 **16 Leonard Street CA12 4EL**
email: info@elmtreelodge-keswick.co.uk **web:** www.elmtreelodge-keswick.co.uk
dir: *Exit A66, pass ambulance depot, left before pedestrian crossing, left into Southey Street. 3rd left into Helvellyn Street, 1st right into Leonard Street, property 3rd on right.*

Close to the town centre, Elm Tree Lodge is a tastefully decorated Victorian house that offers a variety of rooms. Bedrooms feature stripped pine, period furniture, crisp white linen and modern en suites or a private shower room. Hearty breakfasts are served in the charming dining room and feature local produce. A friendly welcome is guaranteed.

Rooms: 4 rms (3 en suite) (1 pri facs) **S** fr £45 **D** fr £65 **Facilities:** FTV tea/coffee WiFi 🅿 **Parking:** 2 **Notes:** LB No children 8 years

Hedgehog Hill Guest House

★★★★ GUEST HOUSE

tel: 017687 80654 & 07944 580959 **18 Blencathra Street CA12 4HP**
email: hedgehoghillkeswick@gmail.com **web:** www.hedgehoghill.co.uk
dir: *From A5271 (Penrith Road) via either Southey Street or Greta Street into Blencathra Street.*

At Hedgehog Hill Guest House expect high standards of hospitality along with great customer care. Like many properties in this area, this is a Victorian terraced house which affords great views from the bedrooms. It is just a short walk to the town centre, and many walks lead from the door. The bedrooms are comfortably equipped and offer thoughtful extras. Hearty breakfasts are served in the light and airy dining room; vegetarians are well catered for.

Rooms: 6 rms (4 en suite) (2 pri facs) **S** fr £38 **D** fr £78 **Facilities:** FTV tea/coffee WiFi 🅿 **Notes:** No children 12 years

Springs Farm B&B

★★★ FARMHOUSE

tel: 017687 72144 & 07816 824253 **Springs Farm, Springs Road CA12 4AN**
email: springsfarmkeswick@gmail.com **web:** www.springsfarmkeswick.co.uk
dir: A66 into Keswick, left at T-junction onto Chestnut Hill. After 200 yards right on Manor Brow, then left into Springs Road. 0.5 mile, at end of road.

Part of a working beef farm, the farmhouse was built around 150 years ago. Guests can expect comfortable accommodation and a well-cooked breakfast with eggs from the farm's own hens. Springs Farm B&B is ideally located in the heart of the countryside but surprisingly close to the town centre, which is an easy 10-minute walk away.

Rooms: 2 en suite **S** fr £48 **D** fr £90* **Facilities:** STV FTV DVD tea/coffee WiFi
🛁 Farm shop, tea room **Extras:** Fresh milk **Parking:** 6 **Notes:** LB Closed 19–29 December 180 acres beef

KIRKBY IN FURNESS   Map 18 SD28

Low Hall Farm

★★★★ FARMHOUSE

tel: 01229 889220 **LA17 7TR**
email: tracey.edmondson@btinternet.com **web:** www.low-hall.co.uk
dir: M6 junction 36 onto A590. At roundabout signed Workington follow A595, through Askam in Furness. After 2.5 miles turn right, signed Low Hall Farm then 1st left.

Low Hall is a lovely Victorian farmhouse owned by Holker Hall Estates and run by Peter and Tracey Edmondson. The farm rears beef cattle and sheep and is set in peaceful countryside with spectacular views of the Duddon Estuary and Lakeland fells. Low Hall is a very spacious farmhouse and all rooms offer high quality furnishings. English breakfasts are served in the bright and airy dining room, and there is a comfortable living room with a wood-burning stove. Ironing facilities are available too.

Rooms: 3 en suite **S** fr £45 **D** fr £70* **Facilities:** FTV TVL tea/coffee WiFi
Extras: Speciality toiletries – complimentary **Parking:** 4 **Notes:** No children 14 years 366 acres beef/sheep

KIRKBY LONSDALE   Map 18 SD67

Premier Collection

The Sun Inn

★★★★★ ◎◎ 🍴 RESTAURANT WITH ROOMS

tel: 015242 71965 **6 Market Street LA6 2AU**
email: email@sun-inn.info **web:** www.sun-inn.info
dir: From A65 follow signs to town centre. Inn on main street.

The Sun is a 17th-century inn situated in the destination market town of Kirkby Lonsdale and overlooks St Mary's Church. The atmospheric bar features stone walls, wooden beams and log fires with real ales available. Delicious meals are served in the bar or in the relaxed and modern restaurant. Traditional and modern styles are blended together in the beautifully appointed bedrooms with excellent en suites.

Rooms: 11 en suite (1 fmly) **S** fr £99.50 **D** fr £117* **Facilities:** FTV tea/coffee Dinner available Direct dial WiFi 🌐 ♨ **Extras:** Bath robes, speciality toiletries **Notes:** LB

Premier Collection

Plato's

★★★★★ 🍴 RESTAURANT WITH ROOMS

tel: 015242 74180 **2 Mill Brow LA6 2AT**
email: hello@platoskirkby.co.uk **web:** www.platoskirkbylonsdale.co.uk
dir: M6 junction 36, A65 Kirkby Lonsdale, after 5 miles at roundabout take 1st exit, onto one-way system.

Tucked away in the heart of this popular market town, Plato's is steeped in history. The bedrooms have a wealth of thoughtful extras and personal touches. Imaginative food is available in the elegant restaurant with its open-plan kitchen or downstairs in the vaulted cellar. The lounge bar has a more relaxed vibe with open fires and soft seating. A warm welcome and professional service is always assured.

Rooms: 8 en suite **S** fr £70 **D** fr £87* **Facilities:** FTV DVD iPod docking station TVL tea/coffee Dinner available WiFi ♨ **Notes:** LB

Pheasant Inn

★★★★ ◎ INN

tel: 015242 71230 **Casterton LA6 2RX**
email: info@pheasantinn.co.uk **web:** www.pheasantinn.co.uk
dir: M6 junction 36, A65 for 7 miles, left onto A683 at Devils Bridge, 1 mile to Casterton centre.

A friendly, family-run dining pub with rooms, this is perfectly situated near the picturesque market town of Kirkby Lonsdale. Real ales are a key feature here along with hearty but refined cooking served in the oak-panelled dining room. Spacious and comfortable accommodation is varied but always ship shape.

Rooms: 10 en suite (1 GF) **Facilities:** FTV Lounge tea/coffee Dinner available Direct dial **Parking:** 20 **Notes:** Closed January

The Copper Kettle

★★★ 🅰 GUEST ACCOMMODATION

tel: 015242 71714 **3–5 Market Street LA6 2AU**
email: gamble_p@btconnect.com **web:** www.copperkettlekirkbylonsdale.co.uk
dir: In town centre, down lane by Post Office.

Built between 1610 and 1640, The Copper Kettle is situated in the heart of this small quaint market town which is on the banks of the River Lune. The bedrooms, all of which retain their old world, 17th-century charm, are comfortable and atmospheric. Home-cooked meals and hearty breakfasts are served in the cosy restaurant.

Rooms: 5 en suite (2 fmly) **S** fr £40 **D** fr £68* **Facilities:** FTV tea/coffee Dinner available Licensed WiFi 🛁 **Parking:** 3 **Notes:** LB

LITTLE LANGDALE
Map 18 NY30

Three Shires Inn

★★★★ 🍴 INN

tel: 015394 37215 **LA22 9NZ**
email: enquiry@threeshiresinn.co.uk **web:** www.threeshiresinn.co.uk
dir: *Exit A593, 3 miles from Ambleside at 2nd junction signed Langdales. 1st left after 0.5 mile, 1 mile along lane.*

Enjoying an outstanding rural location, this family-run inn was built in 1872. The brightly decorated bedrooms are individual in style and many offer panoramic views. The attractive lounge features a roaring fire in the cooler months and there is a traditional bar with a great selection of local ales. Meals can be taken in either the bar or cosy restaurant.

Rooms: 10 en suite (1 fmly) **D** fr £115* **Facilities:** FTV Lounge tea/coffee Dinner available WiFi 🛁 Use of local country club **Parking:** 15 **Notes:** LB Closed 25 December RS December to January weekends and New Year only

LONGTOWN
Map 21 NY36

The Sycamore Tree

★★★★ 🍴 GUEST ACCOMMODATION

tel: 01228 791919 **40/42 Bridge Street CA6 5UD**
email: jfothergill2008@googlemail.com **web:** www.sycamoretreelongtown.co.uk
dir: *On A7.*

The Sycamore Tree is located on the high street of Longtown just four miles from Gretna and the Scottish border. Choose from a four-poster or a king-size family room. If you are staying over for one of the 'steak nights' be sure to reserve a table for dinner.

Rooms: 2 en suite (2 fmly) **S** fr £45 **D** fr £70* **Facilities:** FTV tea/coffee Dinner available Licensed WiFi **Extras:** Robes, slippers, bottled water – complimentary **Notes:** Closed 1st 2 weeks September and 26 December

LOWESWATER
Map 18 NY12

Kirkstile Inn

★★★★ 🍴 INN

tel: 01900 85219 **CA13 0RU**
email: info@kirkstile.com **web:** www.kirkstile.com
dir: *A66 onto B5292 into Lorton, left signed Buttermere. Follow signs to Loweswater, left signed Kirkstile Inn.*

This historic 16th-century inn lies in a valley surrounded by mountains. Serving great food and ale, its rustic bar and adjoining rooms prove to be a mecca for walkers. There is also a cosy restaurant offering a quieter ambiance. Bedrooms retain their original character. There is a spacious family suite in an annexe, with two bedrooms, a lounge and a bathroom.

Rooms: 7 en suite 3 annexe en suite (1 fmly) (2 GF) **S** fr £63.50 **D** fr £117* **Facilities:** TVL tea/coffee Dinner available WiFi **Parking:** 30 **Notes:** LB Closed 25 December

Grange Country House

★★★★ 🍴 GUEST ACCOMMODATION

tel: 01946 861211 & 861570 **CA13 0SU**
email: info@thegrange-loweswater.co.uk **web:** www.thegrange-loweswater.co.uk
dir: *Exit A5086 for Mockerkin, through village. After 2 miles left signed Loweswater Lake. Grange Country House at bottom of hill on left.*

The delightful Grange Country House is set in extensive grounds in a quiet valley at the north-western end of Loweswater and proves popular with guests seeking peace and quiet. It has a friendly, relaxed atmosphere and cosy public areas which include a small bar serving a great range of local beers, a residents' lounge and an attractive dining room where dinner is served by prior arrangement. The bedrooms are well equipped and comfortable, some have four-poster beds.

Rooms: 8 en suite (2 fmly) (1 GF) **Facilities:** FTV Lounge TVL tea/coffee Dinner available Licensed WiFi **Extras:** Speciality toiletries **Conf:** Max 25 Thtr 25 Class 25 Board 25 **Parking:** 20 **Notes:** LB

LUPTON
Map 18 SD58

Premier Collection

Plough Inn

★★★★★ 🏵 INN

tel: 015395 67700 **Cow Brow LA6 1PJ**
email: info@theploughatlupton.co.uk **web:** www.theploughatlupton.co.uk
dir: *M6 junction 36 onto A65 towards Kirkby Lonsdale. Through Nook, up hill, inn on right.*

This delightful inn's interior is open plan and a real delight; modern but with a rustic farmhouse appearance. There are large beams, and a log-burning stove in the lounge surrounded by comfortable sofas where you can relax and read the papers. The bedrooms are well proportioned and reflect the inn's high standards; all have feature bathrooms with roll-top baths and walk-in showers. The staff are excellent and guests are made to feel like part of the family. The inn is open all year and serves food every day.

Rooms: 6 en suite (1 fmly) **Facilities:** FTV Lounge tea/coffee Dinner available Direct dial WiFi 🛁 **Extras:** Speciality toiletries **Parking:** 50

NEAR SAWREY
Map 18 SD39

Premier Collection

Ees Wyke Country House

★★★★★ 🏵 GUEST HOUSE

tel: 015394 36393 **LA22 0JZ**
email: mail@eeswyke.co.uk **web:** www.eeswyke.co.uk
dir: *On B5285 on west side of village.*

A warm welcome awaits at this elegant Georgian country house with views over Esthwaite Water and the surrounding countryside. The thoughtfully equipped bedrooms have been decorated and furnished with care. There is a charming lounge with an open fire, and a splendid dining room where a carefully prepared five-course dinner is served. Breakfasts have a fine reputation due to the skilful use of local produce.

Rooms: 8 en suite (1 GF) **S** fr £59 **D** fr £90 **Facilities:** FTV Lounge tea/coffee Dinner available Licensed WiFi **Extras:** Sherry **Parking:** 12 **Notes:** LB No children 12 years

NEWBY BRIDGE
Map 18 SD38

Premier Collection

The Knoll Country House

★★★★★ ⬩ ⬩ GUEST ACCOMMODATION

tel: 015395 31347 **Lakeside LA12 8AU**
email: info@theknoll-lakeside.co.uk **web:** www.theknoll-lakeside.co.uk
dir: *A590 west to Newby Bridge, over roundabout, signed right for Lake Steamers, house 0.5 mile on left.*

This delightful Edwardian villa stands in a leafy dell on the western side of Windermere. Public areas have many original features, including open fires in the cosy lounge and dining room. The attractive and very stylish bedrooms vary in outlook. Proprietor and chef, Jenny Mead and her enthusiastic team extend a very caring and natural welcome. Jenny also prepares a good range of excellent dishes at breakfast.

Rooms: 8 en suite 1 annexe rm (1 pri facs) **S** fr £80 **D** fr £95 **Facilities:** STV FTV DVD iPod docking station Lounge TVL tea/coffee Direct dial Licensed WiFi ⬩ **Extras:** Fruit and wine in 1 room **Conf:** Max 30 Thtr 30 Class 18 Board 12 **Parking:** 9 **Notes:** LB No children 16 years Closed 24–26 December

PENRITH
Map 18 NY53

Premier Collection

Brooklands Guest House

★★★★★ ⬩ GUEST HOUSE

tel: 01768 863395 **2 Portland Place CA11 7QN**
email: enquiries@brooklandsguesthouse.com **web:** www.brooklandsguesthouse.com
dir: *M6 junction 40, follow sign for TIC, left at town hall, 50 yards on left.*

In the bustling market town of Penrith, this beautifully appointed house offers individually furnished bedrooms with high quality accessories and some luxury touches. Nothing seems to be too much trouble for the friendly owners and, from romantic breaks to excellent storage for bikes, all guests are very well looked after. Delicious breakfasts featuring Cumbrian produce are served in the attractive dining room.

Rooms: 6 en suite (1 fmly) **S** fr £45 **D** fr £88* **Facilities:** FTV iPod docking station tea/coffee WiFi ⬩ **Extras:** Speciality toiletries, fresh fruit – complimentary **Parking:** 2 **Notes:** LB No children 3 years Closed 24 December to 4 January

Premier Collection

River Garth

★★★★★ ⬩ GUEST HOUSE

tel: 01768 863938 & 07718 763273 **Eamont Bridge CA10 2BH**
email: rivergarth@hotmail.co.uk **web:** www.rivergarth.co.uk
dir: *M6 junction 40, A66 east towards Scotch Corner. At roundabout 4th exit to Shap, 150 yards over bridge and continue for 200 yards, turn right at "Keep Clear" road marking. Last bungalow facing river (with balconies).*

The River Garth is in an elevated position overlooking the River Eamont. The spacious and well-presented bedrooms cater well for guests' needs, and two rooms have balconies looking out on the river. The lounge dining room is comfortable and breakfasts use the finest local produce.

Rooms: 3 en suite (1 fmly) **Facilities:** STV FTV TVL tea/coffee WiFi ⬩ **Extras:** Speciality toiletries, bottled water, sweets – complimentary **Parking:** 6 **Notes:** LB

Albany House

★★★★ ⬩ ⬩ GUEST HOUSE

tel: 01768 863072 **5 Portland Place CA11 7QN**
email: info@albany-house.org.uk **web:** www.albany-house.org.uk
dir: *Left at town hall into Portland Place. 30 yards on left.*

A well-maintained Victorian house close to Penrith town centre. Bedrooms are comfortable and thoughtfully equipped. Wholesome breakfasts using local ingredients are served in the attractive breakfast room. Good quality dinners are served at the weekend – advance bookings are required.

Rooms: 5 rms (3 en suite) (2 pri facs) (1 fmly) **S** fr £45 **D** fr £75* **Facilities:** FTV tea/coffee Dinner available WiFi ⬩ **Extras:** Speciality toiletries, bottled water, chocolates **Notes:** LB

Glendale Guest House

★★★★ GUEST HOUSE

tel: 01768 210061 **4 Portland Place CA11 7QN**
email: info@glendaleguesthouse.com **web:** www.glendaleguesthouse.com
dir: *M6 junction 40, follow town centre signs. Pass castle, turn left before town hall.*

The Glendale Guest House is a friendly, family-run property, part of a Victorian terrace only a stroll from the town centre, and convenient for the Lakes and Eden Valley. Bedrooms vary in size, but all are attractive, well equipped, well presented and cater well for the modern guest. Hearty breakfasts are served at individual tables in the charming ground-floor dining room. Walkers and cyclists will be pleased to know that drying facilities are available.

Rooms: 7 en suite (3 fmly) **S** fr £35 **D** fr £60 (room only)* **Facilities:** FTV WiFi ⬩ **Notes:** No children 5 years

Stoneybeck Inn

★★★★ ⬤ INN

tel: 01768 862369 **Bowscar CA11 8RP**
email: reception@stoneybeckinn.co.uk **web:** www.stoneybeckinn.co.uk
dir: *Phone for directions.*

This inn enjoys panoramic views over the Cumbrian Fells and is ideally located for easy access to the M6 and as a base for touring the Lakes and beyond. Bedrooms are finished to an impressive standard with a number of luxurious touches. The inn has built up a strong following locally for both its food and drink; monthly pudding nights and the Sunday carvery should not be missed. Extensive conference and banqueting facilities are also on site, as well as complimentary parking.

Rooms: 7 en suite (2 GF) **Facilities:** FTV Lounge tea/coffee Dinner available WiFi ⬩ **Conf:** Max 200 Thtr 200 Class 130 Board 60 **Parking:** 50 **Notes:** Civ wed 200

POOLEY BRIDGE
Map 18 NY42

1863 Bar Bistro Rooms
★★★★ ❀ RESTAURANT WITH ROOMS

tel: 017684 86334 **High Street CA10 2NH**
email: info@1863ullswater.co.uk **web:** www.1863ullswater.co.uk
dir: *M6 junction 40 onto A66 towards Keswick. At roundabout take 2nd exit onto A592. Continue for 4 miles, at junction turn left onto B5320 signed Pooley Bridge. Continue to village, opposite St Paul's church.*

1863 Bar Bistro Rooms is located in the idyllic village of Pooley Bridge on the edge of the majestic Ullswater. Built in 1863, as its names suggests, it was once the village blacksmiths and then the post office before becoming an accommodation provider. All bedrooms are well appointed and comfortable with many modern extras including TVs, DVD players, WiFi and bathrobes provided as standard. A rolling refurbishment programme has introduced two new stylish suites, which like the other rooms, feature colourful Designer Guild wallpapers. The award-winning dishes use the best produce that the Cumbrian larder can offer and are served in relaxed surroundings.

Rooms: 7 en suite **Facilities:** FTV Lounge Dinner available WiFi
Notes: No children 10 years Closed 24–26 December, 2–13 January

The Crown Inn
★★★★ INN

tel: 017684 25869 **Finkle Street CA10 2NP**
email: relax@crowninnpooleybridge.co.uk **web:** www.crowninnpooleybridge.co.uk
dir: *Follow A592 from Penrith. Take B5320 to Pooley Bridge.*

The Crown Inn is part of the Thwaites Inns collection. Set by the river in the busy, seasonally popular village of Pooley Bridge at the head of Ullswater, it has beautiful views and easy access to the lakes and transport links. The extensive bar and restaurant space includes a first-floor terrace and bi-fold doors that lead onto a patio and the river. Local and guest ales are on tap at all times and a solid pub menu is on offer. Bedrooms are smart and contemporary.

Rooms: 17 en suite (3 fmly) (1 GF) **Facilities:** tea/coffee Dinner available WiFi
🛁 **Notes:** LB

RAVENGLASS
Map 18 SD09

The Inn at Ravenglass
★★★★ ☕ RESTAURANT WITH ROOMS

tel: 01229 717230 **Main Street CA18 1SQ**
email: gm@penningtonhotels.com **web:** www.theinnatravenglass.co.uk
dir: *Phone for directions.*

The Inn at Ravenglass enjoys picture-postcard views and is ideally located overlooking the estuary where the three rivers merge before entering the Irish Sea. This 17th-century inn not only offers great real ales but also good quality food in the upstairs, panoramic à la carte restaurant; in the downstairs pub guests will find more relaxed, comfort food. The inn shares some facilities with its sister hotel located a couple of doors away – this is where breakfast is served. The spacious, well-appointed bedroom has views of the estuary and village and has its own private entrance.

Rooms: 1 en suite **Facilities:** Dinner available

RAVENSTONEDALE
Map 18 NY70

The Black Swan
★★★★ ❀❀ ☕ INN

tel: 015396 23204 **CA17 4NG**
email: enquiries@blackswanhotel.com **web:** www.blackswanhotel.com
dir: *M6 junction 38. Black Swan on A685, west of Kirkby Stephen.*

Set in the heart of this quiet village, the inn is popular with visitors and locals alike and offers a very friendly welcome. The bedrooms are individually styled and comfortably equipped. There is an informal atmosphere in the bar areas and home-made meals can be taken in the bar or the stylish dining room. Guests can relax by the fire in the cooler months and enjoy the riverside garden in the summer.

Rooms: 10 en suite 6 annexe en suite (3 fmly) (3 GF) **S** fr £75 **D** fr £95*
Facilities: FTV iPod docking station Lounge tea/coffee Dinner available WiFi 🛁 ♨
Fishing Riding Snooker 🛁 **Extras:** Speciality toiletries, snacks, water, robes
Conf: Max 14 Thtr 14 Class 14 Board 14 **Parking:** 20 **Notes:** LB

The Fat Lamb
★★★★ ☕ INN

tel: 015396 23242 **Crossbank CA17 4LL**
email: enquiries@fatlamb.co.uk **web:** www.fatlamb.co.uk
dir: *On A683, between Kirkby Stephen and Sedbergh.*

Solid stone walls and open fires feature at this 17th-century inn. The bedrooms are comfortable, and all are en suite; an accessible ground-floor room with an en suite wet room is available. Guests can enjoy a choice of dining options – well-cooked dishes using local produce are served in either the traditional bar or the more formal dining room. There is also a beer garden.

Rooms: 12 en suite (4 fmly) (5 GF) **S** fr £76 **D** fr £112 **Facilities:** Lounge tea/coffee Dinner available WiFi ♨ 🛁 Private 5-acre nature reserve **Parking:** 60 **Notes:** LB

RYDAL

See Ambleside

SHAP
Map 18 NY51

Brookfield Guest House
★★★★ GUEST HOUSE

tel: 01931 716397 **CA10 3PZ**
email: info@brookfieldshap.co.uk **web:** www.brookfieldshap.co.uk
dir: *M6 junction 39, A6 towards Shap, 1st accommodation off motorway, on right.*

In a quiet rural location within easy reach of the M6, inviting Brookfield Guest House stands in well-tended, attractive gardens. Bedrooms are thoughtfully appointed and well maintained. There is a comfortable lounge, and a small bar area next to the traditional dining room where substantial, home-cooked breakfasts are served at individual tables.

Rooms: 4 rms (3 en suite) (1 pri facs) **Facilities:** FTV TVL tea/coffee Licensed WiFi
🅿 **Parking:** 20 **Notes:** No children 12 years Closed October to April

TEMPLE SOWERBY
Map 18 NY62

The Kings Arms
★★★★ 🛌 INN

tel: 017683 62944 **CA10 1SB**
email: enquiries@kingsarmstemplesowerby.co.uk
web: www.kingsarmstemplesowerby.co.uk
dir: *M6 junction 40, east on A66 to Temple Sowerby, Kings Arms in village.*

The Kings Arms is located in the peaceful village of Temple Sowerby, just a couple of minutes from the A66 bypass and a short drive from Center Parcs. The property dates back over 400 years and offers a good deal of charm and character. Quality food is served in the small restaurant or in the bar itself which has an open fire. Comfortable, well-appointed accommodation makes this an ideal base for touring this delightful area.

Rooms: 8 en suite (5 fmly) **S** fr £70 **D** fr £120* **Facilities:** FTV Lounge tea/coffee Dinner available WiFi Fishing 🅿 **Parking:** 20 **Notes:** LB

Skygarth Farm
★★★ FARMHOUSE

tel: 017683 61300 **CA10 1SS**
email: skygarth@outlook.com **web:** www.skygarth.co.uk
dir: *Exit A66 at Temple Sowerby for Morland, Skygarth 500 yards on right, follow signs.*

Skygarth is just south of the village, half a mile from the busy main road. The house stands in a cobbled courtyard surrounded by cowsheds, with gardens to the rear where red squirrels can be seen. There are two well-proportioned bedrooms and an attractive lounge where tasty breakfasts are served.

Rooms: 2 rms (1 en suite) (2 fmly) **S** fr £40 **D** fr £70* **Facilities:** FTV TVL tea/coffee WiFi 🅿 **Extras:** Bottled water, biscuits – complimentary; robes **Parking:** 4 **Notes:** Closed December to January 200 acres mixed

ULVERSTON
Map 18 SD27

Virginia House
★★★ ⊚⊚ RESTAURANT WITH ROOMS

tel: 01229 584844 & 07495 128499 **24 Queen Street LA12 7AF**
email: hello@virginiahouseulverston.co.uk **web:** www.virginiahouseulverston.co.uk
dir: *M6 junction 36 onto A590 towards Barrow-in-Furness. In Ulverston take 3rd exit at Tank Square roundabout and follow one-way system. 1st exit at mini-roundabout into King Street, then Queen Street. 200 metres on right.*

A warm, personal welcome is guaranteed at this family-run property where the restaurant is at the heart of the operation. The award-winning meals, based on very good quality local produce, are served in modern and comfortable surroundings. The gin parlour has a selection of over 100 gins to choose from. The bedrooms are comfortable and well appointed, and complimentary WiFi is available throughout. There is no parking on-site, but there is provision within a short walking distance.

Rooms: 8 en suite **S** fr £59 **D** fr £89* **Facilities:** FTV iPod docking station tea/coffee Dinner available WiFi 🅿 **Extras:** Speciality toiletries, home-made biscuits **Conf:** Max 30 Thtr 30 Class 11 Board 16 **Notes:** No children 18 years

WASDALE HEAD
Map 18 NY10

Wasdale Head Inn
★★★★ INN

tel: 019467 26229 & 26333 **CA20 1EX**
email: reception@wasdale.com **web:** www.wasdale.com
dir: *Exit A595 (towards south) at Santon Bridge or Gosforth. Follow signs for Wasdale Head.*

Wasdale Head is known as the birthplace of British climbing for good reason. The setting of this popular inn is breathtaking, surrounded by the fells with the brooding Wast Water close by. Inside, the decor is enhanced with objets d'art and photos of climbers and mountains. Bedrooms and public areas are comfortable, and the service is relaxed and informal. Real ales and good food are served in the rustic bar while a separate restaurant is available for residents.

Rooms: 11 en suite 9 annexe en suite (2 fmly) (5 GF) **S** fr £59 **D** fr £118* **Facilities:** FTV Lounge tea/coffee Dinner available Direct dial WiFi 🅿 **Conf:** Max 20 Thtr 20 Class 20 Board 20 **Parking:** 30 **Notes:** LB Civ wed 50

WINDERMERE
Map 18 SD49

Premier Collection

Applegarth Villa & Restaurant
★★★★★ 🍽 🛌 GUEST ACCOMMODATION

tel: 015394 43206 **College Road LA23 1BU**
email: info@lakesapplegarth.co.uk **web:** www.lakesapplegarth.co.uk
dir: *M6 junction 36, A591 towards Windermere. On entering town left after NatWest Bank into Elleray Road. 1st right into College Road, Applegarth on right.*

This period building in the heart of Windermere offers elegantly furnished accommodation with luxurious bathrooms in the main house. Seven suites in the adjacent, former coach house offer modern accommodation and features such as hot tubs on each balcony. The attractive conservatory dining room has stunning views of the mountains and serves locally sourced produce. Alternatively, the oak-panelled bar with its open fire is the perfect retreat to while away a winter's evening. Private off-road parking is guaranteed.

Rooms: 15 en suite 7 annexe en suite (2 GF) **S** fr £125 **D** fr £140* **Facilities:** FTV iPod docking station tea/coffee Dinner available Direct dial Licensed WiFi 🅿 7 suites with outdoor hot tubs **Extras:** Speciality toiletries, bottled water, fruit – complimentary **Parking:** 27 **Notes:** LB No children 18 years

WINDERMERE *continued*

Lindeth Fell Country House

★★★★★ ⚲ GUEST ACCOMMODATION

tel: 015394 43286 & 44287 **Lyth Valley Road, Bowness-on-Windermere LA23 3JP**
email: kennedy@lindethfell.co.uk **web:** www.lindethfell.co.uk
dir: *1 mile south of Bowness on A5074.*

Lindeth Fell offers luxury bed and breakfast accommodation, perfectly located overlooking Lake Windermere. This elegant, stylishly restored Edwardian country house is owned and managed by the Kennedy family, who combine a warm, friendly welcome with five-star service. The 14 individually-designed bedrooms have crisp Egyptian cotton bed linen, deluxe fluffy towels, robes, slippers, complimentary sherry, DAB radios, WiFi, TVs, tea trays and Nespresso coffee machines. Many rooms have superb lake views. Tea and home-made scones are offered in the elegant lounge on arrival. There are cosy log fires in winter, while in summer you can explore the stunning gardens, complete with a private lake.

Rooms: 14 en suite (1 fmly) (1 GF) **S** fr £100 **D** fr £200* **Facilities:** FTV iPod docking station Lounge tea/coffee Direct dial Licensed WiFi ⚓ ⚓ Use of leisure facilities at nearby hotel **Extras:** Speciality toiletries, robes, slippers, sherry – complimentary **Conf:** Max 12 Class 12 Board 12 **Parking:** 20 **Notes:** LB Closed January

Hillthwaite

★★★★★ ⚲ GUEST ACCOMMODATION

tel: 015394 43636 & 46691 **Thornbarrow Road LA23 2DF**
email: reception@hillthwaite.com **web:** www.hillthwaite.com
dir: *M6 junction 36, A591 Windermere, follow lane road through village A5074, left opposite Goodley Dale School, approximately 0.5 mile from A591.*

Family-owned Hillthwaite, set in landscaped gardens between Windermere and Bowness, offers panoramic views overlooking Lake Windermere and beyond to Langdale Pike, Crinkle Crags and Coniston Old Man. Individually designed rooms have seen much refurbishment and are maintained to a high standard. Public rooms on the ground floor include a brand new suite suite of lounges with a contemporary bar, conservatory with log stove and a comfortable restaurant where guests can also enjoy those impressive views at breakfast or over imaginative dinners.

Rooms: (4 fmly) (3 GF) **S** fr £79.50 **D** fr £129* **Facilities:** Dinner available ⟳ Sauna **Notes:** Closed 24–26 December Civ wed

The Howbeck

★★★★★ GUEST HOUSE

tel: 015394 44739 **New Road LA23 2LA**
email: relax@howbeck.co.uk **web:** www.howbeck.co.uk
dir: *A591 through Windermere town centre, left towards Bowness.*

The Howbeck is a delightful Victorian villa, convenient for the village and the lake. Bedrooms are well appointed and feature lovely soft furnishings, along with luxurious spa baths in some cases. There is a bright lounge with internet access and an attractive dining room where home-prepared hearty Cumbrian breakfasts are served at individual tables.

Rooms: 10 en suite 1 annexe en suite (3 GF) **Facilities:** STV FTV TVL tea/coffee Dinner available Licensed WiFi Free membership to nearby spa and leisure club **Parking:** 12 **Notes:** LB Closed 24–25 December

Wheatlands Lodge

★★★★★ BED AND BREAKFAST

tel: 015394 43789 **Old College Lane LA23 1BY**
email: info@wheatlandslodge-windermere.co.uk
web: www.wheatlandslodge-windermere.co.uk
dir: *Phone for directions.*

Tucked away from the main street though still in the heart of Windermere, this smartly appointed and modern B&B offers a great base for exploring the Lake District, now a designated World Heritage Site. Richard and Yvonne are consummate hosts who strive to make sure any stay is warm and welcoming. Bedrooms are comfortable with contemporary styling. Breakfast here features lots of home-made items and memorable local produce.

Rooms: 8 en suite (1 GF) **S** fr £95 **D** fr £115* **Facilities:** iPod docking station tea/coffee WiFi **Extras:** Speciality toiletries **Parking:** 8 **Notes:** LB No children 16 years

The Wild Boar Inn, Grill & Smokehouse

★★★★★ @ INN

tel: 015394 45225 **Crook LA23 3NF**
email: thewildboar@englishlakes.co.uk **web:** www.thewildboarinn.co.uk
dir: *2.5 miles south of Windermere on B5284. From Crook 3.5 miles, on right.*

Steeped in history, this former coaching inn enjoys a peaceful rural location close to Windermere. Public areas include a welcoming lounge and a cosy bar where an extensive choice of wines, ales and whiskies is served. The Grill & Smokehouse features quality local and seasonal ingredients. Bedrooms, some with four-poster beds, vary in style and size. Leisure facilities are available close by.

Rooms: 34 en suite (2 fmly) (9 GF) **Facilities:** FTV DVD tea/coffee Dinner available Direct dial WiFi Use of leisure facilities at sister hotel **Extras:** Speciality toiletries **Parking:** 60 **Notes:** LB Civ wed 100

Dene House

★★★★ GUEST ACCOMMODATION

tel: 015394 48236 **Kendal Road LA23 3EW**
email: denehouse@ignetics.co.uk **web:** www.denehouse-guesthouse.co.uk
dir: *From Lake Road, turn opposite St Martins Church into Kendal Road. 400 yards on right.*

A detached period property situated on the edge of the village just a short walk from pubs, restaurants and of course, Lake Windermere. Bedrooms are individually furnished and tastefully decorated. Deeply comfortable beds are crisply dressed; one room is situated on the ground floor for easy access. Breakfast is served at individual tables in the smart dining room and the property has a beautiful terrace garden.

Rooms: 7 rms (6 en suite) (1 pri facs) (1 GF) **S** fr £68 **D** fr £104* **Facilities:** FTV iPod docking station tea/coffee WiFi Use of pool and gym at nearby hotel – charges apply **Parking:** 7 **Notes:** LB No children 12 years

Fairfield House and Gardens

★★★★ GUEST HOUSE

tel: 015394 46565 **Brantfell Road, Bowness-on-Windermere LA23 3AE**
email: book@the-fairfield.co.uk **web:** www.the-fairfield.co.uk
dir: *Into Bowness town centre, turn opposite St Martin's Church and sharp left by The Arts Bar & Grill, house 200 metres on right.*

This Lakeland country house is tucked away in half an acre of secluded, peaceful gardens yet is in the heart of Bowness. The house combines Georgian and Victorian features with stylish, contemporary design. Guests are shown warm hospitality and can relax either in the bright lounge or gardens. Bedrooms are well furnished, varying in size and style, with some featuring luxurious bathrooms. An extensive cold buffet breakfast (eggs cooked on request) can be taken in the attractive dining room or on the terrace in warmer weather.

Fairfield House and Gardens

Rooms: 8 en suite (3 GF) **S** fr £69 **D** fr £89* **Facilities:** FTV DVD Lounge tea/coffee Licensed WiFi ⚓ ⚒ 🛎 **Extras:** Robes, rose petals and chocolates, wine, champagne – chargeable **Conf:** Max 20 Thtr 20 Class 10 Board 12 **Parking:** 10 **Notes:** LB No children 10 years Closed Christmas

Glenville House

★★★★ 🛎 GUEST HOUSE

tel: 015394 43371 **Lake Road LA23 2EQ**
email: mail@glenvillehouse.co.uk **web:** www.glenvillehouse.co.uk
dir: *At Windermere station/tourist info centre, turn left into village. Straight through, on right opposite vets' surgery.*

Glenville House is very conveniently located in a pleasant area, and good parking is a bonus. The house is well appointed and the bedrooms have comfortable beds and many accessories to make your stay relaxing and enjoyable. The friendly proprietors make guests welcome, and breakfast is taken in a pleasant room at individual tables.

Rooms: 7 en suite (1 GF) **D** fr £75* **Facilities:** FTV iPod docking station tea/coffee WiFi **Extras:** Mini-fridge **Parking:** 7 **Notes:** LB No children 18 years Closed 6–30 January

The Hideaway at Windermere

★★★★ 🛎 GUEST ACCOMMODATION

tel: 015394 43070 **Phoenix Way LA23 1DB**
email: eatandstay@thehideawayatwindermere.co.uk
web: www.thehideawayatwindermere.co.uk
dir: *Exit A591 at Ravensworth B&B, into Phoenix Way, The Hideaway 100 metres on right.*

Quietly tucked away, this beautiful Victorian Lakeland house is personally run by owners Richard and Lisa. Delicious food, individually designed bedrooms and warm hospitality ensure an enjoyable stay. There is a beautifully appointed lounge looking out to the garden, and the dining area is split between two light and airy rooms. Bedrooms vary in size and style; the larger rooms feature luxury bathrooms. Breakfast is freshly prepared using the best local ingredients and service is attentive and friendly. Afternoon tea with home-made cake is served every day.

Rooms: 10 en suite 1 annexe en suite **S** fr £80 **D** fr £90* **Facilities:** FTV Lounge tea/coffee Direct dial Licensed WiFi 🛎 **Parking:** 15 **Notes:** LB No children 16 years Closed January to mid February

WINDERMERE *continued*

The Haven

★★★★ ☺ BED AND BREAKFAST

tel: 015394 88583 **10 Birch Street LA23 1EG**
email: info@thehavenwindermere.co.uk **web:** www.thehavenwindermere.co.uk
dir: *On A5074 enter one-way system, 3rd left into Birch Street.*

Built from Lakeland slate and stone, The Haven is just a 50-metre stroll from the town centre and shops. The bright, spacious bedrooms offer en suite facilities and one has a Victorian brass bed. A hearty Cumbrian breakfast is served in a very well-appointed dining room. The Haven benefits from limited off-road parking, available on a first-come-first-served basis. The pretty hanging baskets and planters outside set the scene for a warm and genuine welcome from the owners.

Rooms: 4 en suite (1 fmly) **Facilities:** FTV DVD Lounge tea/coffee WiFi 🔒 **Parking:** 3
Notes: LB No children 7 years

Blenheim Lodge

★★★★ GUEST ACCOMMODATION

tel: 015394 43440 **Brantfell Road, Bowness-on-Windermere LA23 3AE**
email: enquiries@blenheim-lodge.com **web:** www.blenheim-lodge.com
dir: *From Windermere to Bowness village, left at mini-roundabout, left, and left again, to top of Brantfell Road, turn right.*

From a peaceful position above Bowness, Blenheim Lodge has stunning panoramic views of Lake Windermere. Bedrooms are well equipped and feature antique furnishings and pocket-sprung mattresses. Most beds are antiques and include two William IV four-posters and three Louis XV examples. There is a comfortable lounge and a beautifully decorated dining room.

Rooms: 11 rms (10 en suite) (1 pri facs) (1 fmly) (2 GF) **S** fr £66 **D** fr £91
Facilities: FTV TVL tea/coffee Licensed WiFi 🔒 Free fishing permits **Parking:** 11
Notes: LB No children 8 years Closed 25 December RS 24–27 December may open, phone for details

The Old Court House

★★★★ GUEST HOUSE

tel: 015394 45096 **Lake Road LA23 3AP**
email: alitheoch@gmail.com **web:** www.theoch.co.uk
dir: *On Windermere-Bowness road at junction Longlands Road.*

Guests are given a warm welcome at this attractive former Victorian police station and courthouse, located in the centre of Bowness. Comfortable, pine-furnished bedrooms offer a good range of extra facilities. Freshly prepared breakfasts are served in the bright ground-floor dining room.

Rooms: 5 en suite (2 GF) **Facilities:** FTV tea/coffee WiFi **Parking:** 6 **Notes:** LB
No children 10 years

Bonny Brae Guest House

★★★ GUEST HOUSE

tel: 015394 22699 & 07765 778046 **West Beck, 11 Oak Street LA23 1EN**
email: stay@bonnybraewindermere.com **web:** www.bonnybraewindermere.com
dir: *Phone for directions.*

A warm and genuine welcome awaits you at Bonny Brae, situated in the heart of Windermere village, just a short walk from cafés, shops and travel links. Accommodation is comfortable, and breakfast makes good use of local produce.

Rooms: 5 en suite (1 fmly) **S** fr £70 **D** fr £86* **Facilities:** FTV DVD iPod docking station tea/coffee WiFi 🔒 **Notes:** No children 7 years

Ellerdene Guesthouse

★★★ GUEST HOUSE

tel: 015394 43610 **12 Ellerthwaite Road LA23 2AH**
email: info@ellerdene.co.uk **web:** www.ellerdene.co.uk
dir: *M6 junction 36 follow signs for Kendal then Windermere (A591). Follow one-way system, take 2nd left after pedestrian crossing into Ellerthwaite Road. On right opposite Holly Road.*

Ellerdene is a welcoming guest house situated in the heart of Windermere, perfectly situated for all local amenities. The modern, stylishly designed bedrooms are comfortable and thoughtfully equipped. Expect a generous, freshly-cooked breakfast served in the bright and spacious dining room.

Rooms: 6 rms (5 en suite) (1 pri facs) (1 GF) **S** fr £36 **D** fr £75* **Facilities:** FTV DVD tea/coffee WiFi 🔒 **Extras:** Fridge **Notes:** LB No children 6 years Closed 8–25 November

Adam Place Guest House

★★★ GUEST HOUSE

tel: 015394 44600 & 07484 826762 **1 Park Avenue LA23 2AR**
email: adamplacewindermere@yahoo.co.uk **web:** www.adamplacelakedistrict.co.uk
dir: *Exit A591 into Windermere, through town centre, left into Ellerthwaite Road and Park Avenue.*

Located in a mainly residential area within easy walking distance of the lake and town centre, this stone-built Victorian house offers comfortable and homely bedrooms. Comprehensive breakfasts are served in the cosy dining room and there is a pretty patio garden.

Rooms: 5 en suite (2 fmly) **Facilities:** FTV DVD tea/coffee WiFi 🔒 **Notes:** LB
No children 6 years

Green Gables Guest House

★★★ GUEST HOUSE

tel: 015394 43886 **37 Broad Street LA23 2AB**
email: info@greengablesguesthouse.co.uk **web:** www.greengablesguesthouse.co.uk
dir: *A591 into Windermere, 1st left after pelican crossing, opposite car park.*

Aptly named, Green Gables is a friendly guest house looking onto Elleray Gardens. Just a short walk from the centre, the house is attractively furnished and offers bright, fresh and well-appointed bedrooms. There is a comfortable bar-lounge, and substantial breakfasts are served in the spacious dining room.

Rooms: 7 rms (4 en suite) (3 pri facs) (2 fmly) (1 GF) **Facilities:** FTV TVL tea/coffee Licensed WiFi **Notes:** LB Closed 23–27 December

WORKINGTON
Map 18 NY02

The Sleepwell Inn
★★★★ GUEST ACCOMMODATION

tel: 01900 65772 **Washington Street CA14 3AX**
email: info@washingtoncentralhotel.co.uk **web:** www.washingtoncentralhotel.co.uk
dir: *M6 junction 40, west on A66. At bottom of Ramsay Brow left into Washington Street, 300 yards on left opposite church.*

The Sleepwell Inn offers comfortable and well-appointed accommodation and is situated just 100 metres from its sister property, the Washington Central Hotel. Guests have full use of the Washington's facilities and that is where breakfast is served. The bedrooms differ in size and style at The Sleepwell – some inter-connecting rooms are available; a calming, natural colour scheme has been used in the bedrooms to create a chic, contemporary feel. Off-road parking is available to the rear.

Rooms: 24 en suite (4 fmly) (12 GF) **S** fr £58 **D** fr £85 (room only)* **Facilities:** FTV Lounge TVL tea/coffee Dinner available Direct dial Licensed WiFi ⚓ Facilities available at Washington Central Hotel **Parking:** 32 **Notes:** LB Civ wed 300

DERBYSHIRE

ASHBOURNE
Map 10 SK14

Compton House
★★★★ GUEST ACCOMMODATION

tel: 01335 343100 **27–31 Compton DE6 1BX**
email: jane@comptonhouse.co.uk **web:** www.comptonhouse.co.uk
dir: *A52 from Derby into Ashbourne, over lights at bottom of hill, house 100 yards on left opposite garage.*

Within easy walking distance of the central attractions, this conversion of three cottages has resulted in a house with good standards of comfort and facilities. Bedrooms are filled with homely extras and comprehensive breakfasts are served in the cottage-style dining room. Parking is available.

Rooms: 5 en suite (1 fmly) (1 GF) **Facilities:** FTV TVL tea/coffee WiFi ⚓ **Parking:** 5

Mercaston Hall
★★★★ FARMHOUSE

tel: 01335 360263 & 07836 648102 **Mercaston DE6 3BL**
email: mercastonhall@btinternet.com **web:** www.mercastonhall.com
dir: *Exit A52 in Brailsford into Luke Lane, 1 mile, right at 1st crossroads, house 1 mile on right.*

Located in a pretty hamlet, this medieval building retains many original features. The bedrooms are homely, and additional facilities include an all-weather tennis court and a livery service. WiFi is also available. This is a good base for visiting nearby stately homes, the Derwent Valley Mills and Dovedale.

Rooms: 3 en suite **S** fr £65 **D** fr £75* **Facilities:** FTV DVD Lounge tea/coffee WiFi ⚓ Fishing ⚓ **Extras:** Fridge **Notes:** Closed Christmas 60 acres mixed

BAKEWELL
Map 16 SK26

Wyeclose
★★★ BED AND BREAKFAST

tel: 01629 813702 **5 Granby Croft DE45 1ET**
email: wyeclosebnb@gmail.com **web:** www.wyeclosebnb.co.uk
dir: *From centre of Bakewell onto A6 (Matlock Street) left into Granby Road and 2nd right into Granby Croft.*

Located in a quiet cul-de-sac in the town centre, this Edwardian house provides thoughtfully furnished bedrooms with smart modern bathrooms, and an attractive dining room which is the setting for comprehensive breakfasts. Original family art is a feature in the ground-floor areas.

Rooms: 2 rms (1 en suite) (1 pri facs) **D** fr £75 **Facilities:** FTV DVD tea/coffee WiFi ⚓ **Parking:** 3 **Notes:** No children 8 years Closed Christmas and New Year

BEELEY
Map 16 SK26

The Devonshire Arms at Beeley
★★★★ ⑥ INN

tel: 01629 733259 & 01756 718111 **Devonshire Square DE4 2NR**
email: enquiries@devonshirebeeley.co.uk **web:** www.devonshirebeeley.co.uk
dir: *B6012 towards Matlock, pass Chatsworth House. After 1.5 miles turn left, 2nd entrance to Beeley.*

The Devonshire Arms at Beeley is a charming 18th-century village inn, located on the Chatsworth Estate, with Chatsworth House itself only a short drive away. With stylish and well-appointed rooms and suites, this is the ideal place to stay for exploring one of Britain's best-loved stately homes, the pretty villages on the estate, and the wild and natural beauty of the Peak District National Park. Local produce is fully evident on the menu, and the inn serves an array of dishes. Eat in the cosy bar area, The Malt Vault – a private seating area suited to groups of up to 12, or the contemporary, colourful Brasserie. In the summer months there is a terrace for alfresco dining too, with tables and parasols beside the brook.

Rooms: 4 en suite 14 annexe en suite (3 fmly) (7 GF) **Facilities:** FTV DVD tea/coffee Dinner available Direct dial WiFi **Extras:** Mini-bar – chargeable; speciality toiletries, Nespresso coffee machine **Parking:** 30

BELPER
Map 11 SK34

Premier Collection

Dannah Farm Country House
★★★★★ ⑤ GUEST ACCOMMODATION

tel: 01773 550273 & 550630 **Bowmans Lane, Shottle DE56 2DR**
email: slack@dannah.co.uk **web:** www.dannah.co.uk
dir: *A517 from Belper towards Ashbourne, 1.5 miles right into Shottle after Hanging Gate pub on right, over crossroads and right.*

Part of the Chatsworth Estates at Shottle, in an elevated position with stunning views, this impressive Georgian house and its outbuildings have been renovated to provide luxurious, individually styled bedrooms. Two have private hot tubs, one has a sauna, and there is a spa cabin and a 'Secret Garden' hot tub that can be booked separately. The elegant dining room is the setting for memorable breakfasts which make use of the finest local produce. Excellent supper platters are also available by prior arrangement.

Rooms: 8 en suite (1 fmly) (2 GF) **S** fr £95 **D** fr £165* **Facilities:** FTV DVD iPod docking station Lounge tea/coffee Licensed WiFi Sauna ⚓ Leisure cabin, hot tub **Extras:** Bath robes, speciality toiletries, honesty bar **Parking:** 20 **Notes:** LB Closed 24–26 December

BELPER continued

Bridge Hill House

★★★★★ 🍴 GUEST ACCOMMODATION

tel: 07931 931011 & 01773 599859 **34a Lodge Drive DE56 2TP**
email: info@bridgehillhouse.co.uk **web:** www.bridgehillhouse.co.uk
dir: *In town centre turn onto A517 signed Ashbourne. After 350 metres right into Belper Lane, then left into Lodge Drive. Continue up hill, right into drive alongside Number 34.*

Bridge Hill House is a modern property designed by its owners and built using local stone on what used to be part of the extensive Strutt family estate. Some evidence of its former life remains, including the ice house and underground arched tunnels which are now listed. A warm welcome is assured, and home-made afternoon bakes and cakes are not to be missed. Award-winning breakfasts are served in the open-plan family room which has far-reaching views across Belper and beyond. Attractively presented en suite accommodation is all on the ground floor, and rooms are decorated in soft tones with a host of thoughtful extras provided. Local guided tours by prior arrangement.

Rooms: 4 en suite (4 GF) **S** fr £80 **D** fr £90* **Facilities:** FTV Lounge tea/coffee WiFi 🛁 **Extras:** Mineral water, fresh milk, sweets, fruit – complimentary **Parking:** 4 **Notes:** LB No children 16 years Closed November to February

BIRCH VALE — Map 16 SK08

Ladygate Farm Bed and Breakfast

★★★★ 🍴 BED AND BREAKFAST

tel: 01663 745562 & 07885 593123 **Briargrove Road SK22 1AY**
email: liz@ladygatefarm.co.uk **web:** www.ladygatefarm.co.uk
dir: *From Marple Bridge follow signs to Mellor/New Mills. After 3 miles left into Briargrove Road, 0.5 mile on left at bottom of hill.*

Beautifully restored, this former farmhouse is both peaceful and homely, and is surrounded by picturesque Derbyshire countryside. Known as the location for the BBC drama *The Village*, Hayfield is just two miles away. Lyme House, Kinder Scout and the start of the Pennine Way are also within easy reach. Stylish bedrooms are well equipped with comfortable beds, a wealth of thoughtful extras and smart modern bathrooms. Served at the large dining table, Aga-cooked breakfasts include sausage and bacon from a local award-winning butcher. Hosts Liz and Dave will be happy to recommend a number of local dining options.

Rooms: 3 rms (2 en suite) (1 pri facs) **Facilities:** FTV DVD TVL tea/coffee WiFi 🛁 **Extras:** Robes, fruit, fresh flowers, speciality toiletries **Parking:** 3 **Notes:** LB No children 12 years

BRADWELL — Map 16 SK18

The Samuel Fox Country Inn

★★★★★ ◎◎ INN

tel: 01433 621562 **Stretfield Road S33 9JT**
email: enquiries@samuelfox.co.uk **web:** www.samuelfox.co.uk
dir: *M1 junction 29, A617 towards Chesterfield, A619 signed Baslow and Buxton, 2nd roundabout A623 for 7 miles, take B6049 to Bradwell, through village on left.*

Named after Bradwell's most famous son, industrial magnate Samuel Fox who built the steelworks at Stocksbridge, The Samuel Fox Country Inn is modern and stylish yet retains its rustic charm. The bedrooms are immaculately presented

and extensively equipped, and service is highly attentive. The restaurant has breathtaking views and serves modern British cuisine, awarded two AA Rosettes.

Rooms: 4 en suite **Facilities:** FTV tea/coffee Dinner available WiFi ♿ 🛁 **Extras:** Home-made chocolates, hand-made cookies, sherry **Conf:** Max 20 Thtr 12 Class 12 Board 10 **Parking:** 15 **Notes:** LB Closed 2–17 January

BUXTON — Map 16 SK07

Alpine Lodge Guest House

★★★★ GUEST HOUSE

tel: 01298 26155 & 07808 283408 **1 Thornsett, Hardwick Mount SK17 6PS**
email: sales@alpinelodgebuxton.co.uk **web:** www.alpinelodgebuxton.co.uk
dir: *A515 onto Hardwick Street. Take right fork into Hardwick Mount, just past church on left.*

Alpine Lodge is particularly welcoming to walkers and cyclists. It offers elegant, stylishly furnished accommodation on a tree-lined residential road, close to the town centre. All rooms have en suite shower facilities or private bathrooms with large baths, separate showers and luxurious toiletries. A hospitality tray with fresh milk is provided in each room. Non-allergenic duvets and pillows are available on request, and all beds have fresh crisp cotton sheets and duvet covers. Buxton Opera House and the tranquil Pavilion Gardens are a 10 minutes' stroll away. The Peak District National Park and Derbyshire Dales are on the doorstep.

Rooms: 5 rms (4 en suite) (1 pri facs) (1 fmly) **S** fr £65 **D** fr £85* **Facilities:** FTV tea/coffee WiFi 🛁 **Extras:** Speciality toiletries, bottled water – complimentary **Parking:** 4 **Notes:** No children 1 year

Roseleigh Guest House

★★★★ GUEST ACCOMMODATION

tel: 01298 24904 **19 Broad Walk SK17 6JR**
email: enquiries@roseleighhotel.co.uk **web:** www.roseleighhotel.co.uk
dir: *A6 to Morrisons roundabout, into Dale Road, right at lights, 100 yards left by Swan pub, down hill, right into Hartington Road.*

This elegant property has a prime location overlooking Pavilion Gardens, and the quality furnishings and decor highlight the many original features. The thoughtfully furnished bedrooms have smart, modern shower rooms, and a comfortable lounge is also available.

Rooms: 14 rms (12 en suite) (2 pri facs) (1 GF) **Facilities:** FTV Lounge tea/coffee WiFi **Parking:** 9 **Notes:** No children 6 years Closed 6 December to 20 January

CASTLETON — Map 16 SK18

Innkeeper's Lodge Castleton, Peak District

★★★ INN

tel: 03451 551551 **Castle Street S33 8WG**
email: info@innkeeperslodge.com **web:** www.innkeeperslodge.com
dir: *Phone for directions.*

This property, The Castle, enjoys an excellent location in the Peak District's Hope Valley and is surrounded by the wild moors and sheer rock faces. Dating back to the 1800s, this former coaching inn provides en suite, modern bedrooms, in different shapes and sizes, that have TVs, desks, free WiFi and tea- and coffee-making facilities as standard; family rooms are available. The welcoming lounge bar is a popular place to eat, with food served all day. There's an on-site car park.

Rooms: 15 en suite (4 fmly) (3 GF) **Facilities:** FTV tea/coffee Dinner available Direct dial WiFi

CHESTERFIELD　　　　　　　　　　　Map 16 SK37

Church Villa B&B

★★★ 🍴 BED AND BREAKFAST

tel: 01246 850254 **29 Church Lane, Temple Normanton S42 5DB**
email: churchvilla@btinternet.com **web:** www.churchvilla29.co.uk
dir: *M1 junction 29 onto A617. After 2 miles turn to Temple Normanton. Take 3rd right signed Holmewood, right again into Birkin Lane. Next right into Church Lane, opposite church notice board.*

Church Villa B&B is a charming cottage situated on the outskirts of Chesterfield, ideally placed for visiting the Peak District. It has comfortable, well-equipped bedrooms which come complete with many thoughtful extras. Breakfast and home-cooked dinners are served in the dining room, which has a 100-year old vine, and overlooks the country garden. A guest lounge is also available.

Rooms: 3 en suite **S** fr £54 **D** fr £64* **Facilities:** FTV DVD TVL tea/coffee Dinner available WiFi 🛁 **Extras:** Robes, speciality toiletries **Parking:** 3 **Notes:** LB

CHINLEY　　　　　　　　　　　Map 16 SK08

The Old Hall Inn

★★★★ 🅰 INN

tel: 01663 750529 **Whitehough SK23 6EJ**
email: info@old-hall-inn.co.uk **web:** www.old-hall-inn.co.uk

This 16th-century, family-run inn is located in some prime walking country. All the bedrooms are en suite and have TVs and WiFi; one has a balcony overlooking the garden. Breakfast comes as full English or continental style, while other meals can be eaten in the Old Hall's Minstrel Gallery restaurant. The bar features many ales from local breweries as well as an extensive wine list.

Rooms: 7 en suite 4 annexe en suite **Facilities:** FTV DVD tea/coffee Dinner available WiFi 🛁 **Conf:** Max 16 Board 16 **Parking:** 20 **Notes:** LB

CROMFORD　　　　　　　　　　　Map 16 SK25

Alison House

★★★★ GUEST ACCOMMODATION

tel: 01629 822211 **Intake Lane DE4 3RH**
email: info@alison-house-hotel.co.uk **web:** www.alison-house-hotel.co.uk
dir: *From A6, southeast of Cromford, right into Intake Lane.*

This well furnished and spacious 18th-century house stands in seven acres of well-tended grounds just a short walk from the village. Public rooms are comfortable and charming, and bedrooms come in a variety of sizes. All are furnished to a high standard, and The Arkwright Suite is a favourite with honeymooners.

Rooms: 15 en suite (2 fmly) (4 GF) **Facilities:** TVL tea/coffee Dinner available Licensed WiFi 🛁 **Conf:** Max 60 Thtr 60 Class 40 Board 40 **Parking:** 30 **Notes:** LB Civ wed 80

DERBY
Map 11 SK33

See also Belper and Melbourne

The Derby Conference Centre
★★★★ GUEST ACCOMMODATION

tel: 01332 861842 & 861831 **London Road DE24 8UX**
email: enquiries@thederbyconferencecentre.com
web: www.thederbyconferencecentre.com
dir: *M1 junction 25, A52 towards Derby. Filter left onto A5111 signed Ring Road. At Raynesway Park roundabout 3rd exit signed Ring Road/Alvaston. At next roundabout A6 towards Derby centre. Pass Wickes, left into entrance.*

Formerly a railway training centre, this Grade II listed art deco building has modern public areas, meeting rooms and accommodation, yet original features such as the wall paintings by Norman Wilkinson still remain. Extensive conference facilities include a lecture theatre. Complimentary WiFi and on-site parking are available.

Rooms: 50 en suite (10 GF) **Facilities:** FTV Lounge TVL tea/coffee Dinner available Licensed WiFi ♿ 🐾 **Conf:** Max 1000 Thtr 380 Class 60 Board 40 **Parking:** 200
Notes: Closed 22 December to 2 January Civ wed 380

EDALE
Map 16 SK18

Stonecroft Country Guesthouse
★★★★ GUEST HOUSE

tel: 01433 670262 **Stonecroft S33 7ZA**
email: enquiries@stonecroftguesthouse.co.uk **web:** www.stonecroftguesthouse.co.uk
dir: *From A6187 in Hope follow signs for Edale. After 4.5 miles, pass large car park on right, turn right (marked No Through Road). 3rd house after church.*

A warm welcome awaits at this beautifully located guest house in the quiet village of Edale. Bedrooms are comfortable and feature luxurious extras such as fluffy bathrobes and well-stocked beverage trays. Award-winning breakfasts are served around a communal breakfast table, and dietary requirements are especially well catered for. The large lounge area with a roaring log is perfect for chilly winter evenings. A limited amount of on-site parking is available.

Rooms: 3 rms (2 en suite) (1 pri facs) **S** fr £60 **D** fr £105* **Facilities:** FTV iPod docking station TVL tea/coffee WiFi 🐾 **Extras:** Robes, speciality toiletries, fruit, chocolates, fresh flowers **Parking:** 3 **Notes:** LB No children 15 years Closed Christmas

EYAM
Map 16 SK27

Barrel Inn
★★★ INN

tel: 01433 630856 **Bretton S32 5QD**
email: barrelinn@btconnect.com **web:** www.thebarrelinn.co.uk
dir: *From Baslow on A623, turn right signed Foolow. At next T-junction, turn left and immediately right opposite pond. 1 mile on left.*

Laying claim to be the highest pub in Derbyshire, the Barrel Inn dates back to 1597 and provides guests with a warm and homely base from which to explore the area. An oak-beamed ceiling and a flagstone floor are features in the bar area, while the restaurant offers a wide selection of meals. On a clear day it is possible to see five counties.

Rooms: 4 annexe en suite (1 fmly) (3 GF) **Facilities:** DVD tea/coffee Dinner available WiFi **Parking:** 20

FOOLOW
Map 16 SK17

The Bulls Head Inn
★★★★ INN

tel: 01433 630873 **S32 5QR**
email: wilbnd@aol.com **web:** www.thebullatfoolow.co.uk
dir: *Exit A623 into Foolow.*

Located in the village centre, this popular inn retains many original features and offers comfortable, well-equipped bedrooms. Extensive and imaginative bar meals are served in the traditionally furnished dining room or in the cosy bar areas. The inn welcomes well-behaved dogs in the bar (and even muddy boots on the flagstone areas).

Rooms: 3 en suite (1 fmly) **Facilities:** tea/coffee Dinner available ♿ 🐾 **Parking:** 20

FROGGATT
Map 16 SK27

The Chequers Inn
★★★★ ⊚⊚ INN

tel: 01433 630231 **S32 3ZJ**
email: info@chequers-froggatt.com **web:** www.chequers-froggatt.com
dir: *On A625 between Sheffield and Bakewell, 0.75 mile from Calver.*

The Chequers is a very popular 16th-century inn offering an extensive range of interesting, two AA Rosette-worthy dishes, with a clear focus on local produce. The bedrooms are comprehensively equipped with all modern comforts and the hospitality is warm and sincere. This is a good location for visiting Chatsworth and touring Derbyshire and the Peak District National Park.

Rooms: 7 en suite **S** fr £135 **D** fr £135* **Facilities:** FTV tea/coffee Dinner available WiFi **Parking:** 45 **Notes:** LB Closed 25 December

GREAT HUCKLOW | Map 16 SK17

The Queen Anne

★★★ 🍺 INN

tel: 01298 871246 **SK17 8RF**
email: angelaryan100@aol.com **web:** www.queenanneinn.co.uk
dir: *Exit A623 onto B6049 to Great Hucklow.*

Set in the heart of this pretty village, The Queen Anne has been a licensed inn for over 300 years and to this day acts a hub for the local community. Meals are served in the cosy bar and dining room which benefits from a wealth of original features. During summer months meals can be taken in the pretty garden with far reaching views across the Derbyshire countryside. The bedrooms are tucked away to the rear of the property in a separate building with direct access; they are comfortable and have modern en suite shower rooms. Ample parking and free WiFi are available.

Rooms: 2 annexe en suite (2 GF) **S** fr £63 **D** fr £75* **Facilities:** FTV DVD TVL tea/coffee Dinner available WiFi **Parking:** 20 **Notes:** LB No children 10 years Closed Christmas and New Year

HATHERSAGE | Map 16 SK28

The Plough Inn

★★★★ 🍽 INN

tel: 01433 650319 & 650180 **Leadmill Bridge S32 1BA**
email: sales@theploughinn-hathersage.co.uk **web:** www.theploughinn-hathersage.co.uk
dir: *1 mile southeast of Hathersage on B6001. Over bridge, 150 yards at Leadmill.*

This delightful 16th-century inn with beer garden has an idyllic location by the River Derwent. A selection of real ales and imaginative food is served in the spacious public areas, and original fireplaces and exposed beams have been retained. The attractive, well-equipped bedrooms include several luxury rooms, and WiFi is available throughout.

Rooms: 3 en suite 3 annexe en suite (3 fmly) (2 GF) **S** fr £85 **D** fr £110* **Facilities:** FTV DVD iPod docking station tea/coffee Dinner available Direct dial WiFi 🚶 **Extras:** Fruit, water – complimentary **Parking:** 50 **Notes:** LB Closed 25 December

HOPE | Map 16 SK18

Premier Collection

Underleigh House

★★★★★ 🍴 GUEST ACCOMMODATION

tel: 01433 621372 **Lose Hill Lane S33 6AF**
email: info@underleighhouse.co.uk **web:** www.underleighhouse.co.uk
dir: *From village church on A6187 into Edale Road, 1 mile left into Lose Hill Lane.*

Situated at the end of a private lane, surrounded by glorious scenery, Underleigh House was converted from a barn and cottage that dates from 1873, and now offers carefully furnished and attractively decorated bedrooms with modern facilities. Several rooms have private lounge areas and some also have access to the gardens. There is a very spacious lounge with comfortable chairs and a welcoming log fire. Memorable breakfasts are served at one large table in the dining room.

Rooms: 4 en suite (1 GF) **S** fr £75 **D** fr £95* **Facilities:** FTV DVD TVL tea/coffee Licensed **Extras:** Speciality toiletries, fruit, sweets – complimentary **Parking:** 6 **Notes:** LB No children 12 years Closed Christmas, New Year and January

Stoney Ridge

★★★★ 🍴 GUEST ACCOMMODATION

tel: 01433 620538 **Granby Road, Bradwell S33 9HU**
email: info@stoneyridge.org.uk **web:** www.stoneyridge.org.uk
dir: *From north end of Bradwell on B6049 into Gore Lane, uphill, pass Ye Olde Bowling Green Inn, left into Granby Road.*

This large, split-level bungalow stands in attractive mature gardens at the highest part of the village and has extensive views. Hens roam freely in the landscaped garden and their fresh eggs add to the hearty breakfasts. Bedrooms are attractively furnished and thoughtfully equipped, and there is a spacious, comfortable lounge to relax in.

Rooms: 4 rms (3 en suite) (1 pri facs) **S** fr £66 **D** fr £84 **Facilities:** STV FTV TVL tea/coffee WiFi **Extras:** Sweets, bottled water **Parking:** 6 **Notes:** LB No children 14 years RS November proprietors' holiday

Round Meadow Barn

★★★ BED AND BREAKFAST

tel: 01433 621347 & 07836 689422 **Parsons Lane S33 6RB**
email: roundmeadowbarn@gmail.com **web:** www.roundmeadowbarn.co.uk
dir: *Exit A625 (Hope Road) north onto Parsons Lane, over rail bridge, in 200 yards right into hay barnyard, through gates, across 3 fields, house on left.*

This converted barn, with original stone walls and exposed timbers, stands in open fields in the picturesque Hope Valley. The bedrooms are large enough for families and there are two modern bathrooms. Breakfast is served at one large table adjoining the family kitchen.

Rooms: 3 rms (1 en suite) (2 pri facs) (1 fmly) **Facilities:** FTV tea/coffee Direct dial WiFi **Parking:** 8 **Notes:** LB

MARSTON MONTGOMERY | Map 10 SK13

The Crown Inn

★★★★ INN

tel: 01889 591430 & 07860 342514 **Riggs Lane DE6 2FF**
email: enquiries@thecrowninnderbyshire.co.uk **web:** www.thecrowninnderbyshire.co.uk
dir: *Phone for directions.*

The Crown Inn in the village of Marston Montgomery was purchased by one of the villagers and has established a good reputation for food and accommodation. The contemporary interior, with traditional features retained, creates a friendly and comfortable environment. The bedrooms (all named after people that have lived in the village for a long time) are well furnished and come with TVs, Egyptian cotton bed linen, luxury toiletries and complimentary mineral water and biscuits. The menus are based on much locally-sourced produce and backed up by a choice of frequently-changing specials. The outdoor space provides a delightful area to sit – whatever the weather.

Rooms: 7 en suite 1 annexe en suite (3 fmly) **Facilities:** STV FTV tea/coffee Dinner available WiFi **Conf:** Max 30 Thtr 30 Class 30 Board 30 **Parking:** 20

■ MATLOCK   Map 16 SK35

Castle Green Bed and Breakfast

★★★★ BED AND BREAKFAST

tel: 01629 581349 & 07584 162988 **Butts Drive DE4 3DJ**
email: john@castlegreenbandb.co.uk **web:** www.castlegreenbandb.co.uk
dir: *A615 into Matlock, pass British Red Cross on left, opposite Castle Green and Butts Drive.*

Located in the peaceful grounds of the former Ernest Bailey mansion, the property sits in a wooded valley with views of Riber Castle; the house is within walking distance of Matlock. A warm welcome awaits and the accommodation is well equipped and very comfortable. Breakfast is served in the dining room on the ground floor. Other facilities include WiFi and on-site parking.

Rooms: 6 en suite (1 GF) **S** fr £60 **D** fr £95* **Facilities:** FTV tea/coffee WiFi
 Extras: Speciality toiletries, fridge, fresh milk, USB chargers **Parking:** 8 **Notes:** LB No children

---

The Pines

★★★★ BED AND BREAKFAST

tel: 01629 732646 & 07796 437333 **12 Eversleigh Road, Darley Bridge DE4 2JW**
email: info@thepinesbandb.co.uk **web:** www.thepinesbandb.co.uk
dir: *From Bakewell or Matlock take A6 to Darley Dale. Turn at Barringtons onto B5057, pass Square & Compass pub and The 3 Stags Heads, The Pines on right.*

Dating from the 1820s, this home as been authentically restored and stands in a secluded and pretty garden. Three spacious en suite bedrooms are stylishly furnished using rich fabrics. Comprehensive breakfasts, making use of quality local produce, offer a hearty start to the day. The Pines makes an ideal location for visiting the Peak District.

Rooms: 3 en suite **S** fr £50 **D** fr £80* **Facilities:** FTV DVD tea/coffee Dinner available WiFi **Extras:** Bottled water, fruit **Parking:** 5 **Notes:** LB

■ MELBOURNE   Map 11 SK32

The Coach House

★★★★ BED AND BREAKFAST

tel: 01332 862338 **69 Derby Road DE73 8FE**
email: enquiries@coachhouse-hotel.co.uk **web:** www.coachhouse-hotel.co.uk
dir: *Off B587 in village centre.*

The Coach House sits in the heart of a conservation area, close to Donington Park and East Midlands Airport. This traditional cottage has been restored to provide good standards of comfort and facilities. Bedrooms are thoughtfully furnished, and a lounge and secure parking are available.

Rooms: 6 en suite (1 fmly) (3 GF) **S** fr £54 **D** fr £75* **Facilities:** FTV TVL tea/coffee WiFi **Parking:** 5 **Notes:** LB

Harpur's of Melbourne

★★★★ ◉◉ INN

tel: 01332 862134 **2 Derby Road DE73 8FE**
email: info@harpursofmelbourne.co.uk **web:** www.harpursofmelbourne.co.uk
dir: *From A50 exit signed Melbourne/Swadlincote. Continue for 5 miles, in centre of Melbourne on left.*

Starting life back in the late 18th century as two houses, before becoming the Melbourne Hotel in the mid-19th century, Harpur's continues to welcome guests from far and wide. It's now a modern inn and restaurant with an increasingly strong following not only for its ales but also for its food; dishes use some of the finest local ingredients. Situated in the attractive Georgian town of Melbourne and steeped in history, Harpur's offers comfortably appointed en suite accommodation. The inn is within easy reach of the National Forest.

Rooms: 4 en suite **Facilities:** FTV tea/coffee Dinner available WiFi **Conf:** Max 50 Thtr 50 Class 30 Board 30 **Parking:** 20 **Notes:** LB

■ MICKLEOVER   Map 10 SK33

The Great Northern

★★★★ INN

tel: 01332 514288 **Station Road DE3 9FB**
email: greatnorthernderby@yahoo.co.uk **web:** www.thegreatnorthern.co.uk
dir: *From north – A38 to Markeaton Island, take 3rd exit. Then 2nd left into Radbourne Lane, 3rd left into Station Road.*

Bedrooms at The Great Northern are in a converted barn; the three boutique-style rooms are well appointed and thoughtfully equipped. This modern inn, with friendly staff, provides imaginative food and a selection of local cask ales. Free WiFi and ample parking are provided. A meeting room is available for small parties and can be used for private dining.

Rooms: 3 en suite (1 fmly) (1 GF) **S** fr £80 **D** fr £80* **Facilities:** FTV DVD tea/coffee Dinner available WiFi **Conf:** Max 80 Thtr 80 Class 50 Board 25 **Parking:** 80

■ NEW MILLS   Map 16 SK08

Pack Horse Inn

★★★★ INN

tel: 01663 742365 **Mellor Road SK22 4QQ**
email: info@packhorseinn.co.uk **web:** www.packhorseinn.co.uk

The Pack Horse Inn sits on the edge of the Peak District, ideally located within easy reach of Stockport, Manchester and Sheffield. Some bedrooms are in a converted barn and still have original oak beams; others are in the main building. The friendly bar has at least three hand-pulled, regularly-changing guest ales together with Tetley bitter. Traditional bar meals and snacks are available, or more formal meals are served in the dining room which overlooks the patio area where guests can eat and drink in the warmer weather.

Rooms: 7 en suite 5 annexe en suite **Facilities:** tea/coffee Dinner available WiFi **Extras:** Speciality toiletries, fruit, speciality teas **Parking:** 60

PILSLEY
Map 16 SK27

The Devonshire Arms at Pilsley
★★★ INN

tel: 01246 565405 **The High Street DE45 1UL**
email: res@devonshirehotels.co.uk **web:** www.devonshirepilsley.co.uk
dir: From A619, in Baslow, at roundabout take 1st exit onto B6012. Follow signs to Chatsworth, 2nd right to Pilsley.

Part of the Devonshire Hotels and Restaurants group, The Devonshire Arms at Pilsley is just two miles from Chatsworth House, and also a minute's walk from the Chatsworth farm shop which provides much of the food served. It is an intimate yet traditional 18th-century village inn with a selection of cosy bedrooms, some in the inn and some in the farmhouse next door.

Rooms: 7 en suite 6 annexe en suite (2 fmly) (3 GF) **S** fr £139.50 **D** fr £159*
Facilities: FTV Lounge tea/coffee Dinner available WiFi **Parking:** 16
Notes: RS 24–26 December and 31 December to 1 January Christmas and New Year packages

QUARNDON
Map 10 SK34

Kedleston Country House
★★★★ ● RESTAURANT WITH ROOMS

tel: 01332 477222 **Kedleston Road, Kedleston DE22 5JD**
email: kedlestonreception@derbybrewing.co.uk **web:** www.thekedleston.co.uk
dir: From Derby on Kedleston Road towards Allestree. Turn left (staying on Kedleston Road), on right before golf club.

Located on the outskirts of Derby and close to the Peak District, this Robert Adams designed Georgian property has been lovingly and tastefully restored to create five boutique bedrooms, along with a bar and snug, modern country restaurant and orangery. Service is friendly and attentive and you are assured of a warm welcome.

Rooms: 5 en suite (1 fmly) **S** fr £150 **D** fr £150* **Facilities:** Lounge tea/coffee Dinner available WiFi **Extras:** Speciality toiletries **Conf:** Max 80 Thtr 70 Class 80 Board 40 **Notes:** LB Civ wed 70

REPTON
Map 10 SK32

The Boot Inn
★★★★ ●● INN

tel: 01283 346047 **12 Boot Hill DE65 6FT**
email: info@thebootatrepton.co.uk **web:** www.thebootatrepton.co.uk
dir: From Repton Cross into Brook End, The Boot on right.

The Boot can trace its history back to the 17th century when it was a coaching inn; it was also used for legal sessions and proceedings prior to the completion of the Court House opposite, which now forms part of Repton School. It is a delightful village inn with a contemporary dining area and bar, made homely with attractive artwork, exposed original features and wood-burning stoves. The Boot also has its own micro-brewery, producing brews like Repton Cross, Tuffer's Old and Clod Hopper. The en suite bedrooms are individually decorated, each tastefully furnished with an emphasis firmly on comfort. Carefully prepared dishes make great use of quality, local produce at breakfast and dinner. Free WiFi and on-site parking are available.

Rooms: 9 en suite (4 fmly) **Facilities:** FTV DVD tea/coffee Dinner available WiFi **Parking:** 8 **Notes:** LB

WILLINGTON
Map 10 SK22

The Dragon
★★★★ ● INN

tel: 01283 704795 **11 The Green DE65 6BP**
email: info@thedragonatwillington.co.uk **web:** www.thedragonatwillington.co.uk
dir: At junction of A50/A38 follow signs for Willington. At mini-roundabout turn left, The Dragon on left.

Situated on the bank of the Trent and Mersey Canal, this village inn has been welcoming guests by land and water for over 150 years. It's ideally situated for those wishing to explore south Derbyshire's attractions and unspoilt countryside. The beautifully appointed en suite rooms are located in the neighbouring cottage and benefit from private parking and complimentary WiFi. A cooked breakfast includes award-winning local sausages which are a must.

Rooms: 7 annexe en suite (2 GF) **Facilities:** FTV tea/coffee Dinner available WiFi **Conf:** Max 50 Thtr 50 Class 45 Board 45 **Parking:** 20 **Notes:** LB

WINSTER
Map 16 SK26

Brae Cottage
★★★★ ▲ GUEST ACCOMMODATION

tel: 01629 650375 **East Bank DE4 2DT**
web: www.braecottagewinster.co.uk
dir: A6 onto B5057, driveway on right past pub.

Brae Cottage lies in the heart of this Peak District village, a stone's throw from the Old Bowling Green Inn. The bedrooms are in converted outbuildings and have a wealth of thoughtful extras. Comprehensive breakfasts, featuring home-made or local produce, are served at an antique table in the carefully furnished cottage.

Rooms: 2 annexe en suite (1 fmly) (2 GF) **S** fr £55 **D** fr £65* **Facilities:** tea/coffee **Extras:** Mineral water – complimentary **Parking:** 2 **Notes:** No children 11 years Closed November to February

YOULGREAVE
Map 16 SK26

The George
★★★ INN

tel: 01629 636292 **Church Street DE45 1UW**
dir: 3 miles south of Bakewell in Youlgreave, opposite church.

The public bars of the 17th-century George are popular with locals and tourists alike. The bedroom styles vary but all have en suite shower rooms. Breakfast is served in the lounge bar, and a range of bar meals and snacks is available.

Rooms: 3 en suite (1 fmly) **Facilities:** FTV DVD tea/coffee Dinner available WiFi Fishing **Parking:** 12 **Notes:** LB

DEVON

ASHBURTON
Map 3 SX77

Greencott

★★★★ GUEST HOUSE

tel: 01803 762649 **Landscove TQ13 7LZ**
web: www.stayawhile.co.uk/southwest/Greencott/Greencott.html
dir: *3 miles southeast of Ashburton. Exit A38 at Peartree junction, Landscove signed on slip road, village green 2 miles on right, opposite village hall.*

Greencott is in a peaceful village location and has superb country views. Your hosts extend a very warm welcome and there is a relaxed home-from-home atmosphere. The service is attentive and caring, and many guests return time and again. The bedrooms are attractive, comfortable and very well equipped. Delicious breakfasts are served around an oak dining table.

Rooms: 2 en suite **S** fr £30 **D** fr £60* **Facilities:** FTV TVL tea/coffee 🔒 **Parking:** 3 **Notes:** LB Closed 25–26 December

Gages Mill Country Guest House

★★★★ GUEST ACCOMMODATION

tel: 01364 652391 **Buckfastleigh Road TQ13 7JW**
email: katestone@gagesmill.co.uk **web:** www.gagesmill.co.uk
dir: *Exit A38 at Peartree junction, turn right then left at fuel station, Gages Mill 500 yards on left.*

Conveniently situated within easy reach of the A38, this Grade II listed building was formerly a woollen mill. Very much a family home, there is a relaxed and welcoming feel here and every effort is made to ensure a rewarding and memorable stay. The bedrooms provide good standards of comfort and many have lovely views across the surrounding fields. Breakfast provides a substantial and enjoyable start to the day, with plenty of choice for all appetites.

Rooms: 7 en suite (1 fmly) (1 GF) **S** fr £75 **D** fr £85* **Facilities:** iPod docking station TVL tea/coffee Licensed WiFi 🔒 **Parking:** 7 **Notes:** Closed November to February

ATHERINGTON
Map 3 SS52

West Down

★★★★ 🍸 🍽 FARMHOUSE

tel: 01769 560551 **Little Eastacombe EX37 9HP**
email: info@westdown.co.uk **web:** www.westdown.co.uk
dir: *0.5 mile from Atherington on B3227 to Torrington, turn right, 100 yards on left.*

Set within 25 acres of lush Devon countryside, this farmhouse makes a good base for exploring the area. A peaceful atmosphere and caring hospitality are assured. Bedrooms are equipped with a host of thoughtful extras, and every effort is made to ensure an enjoyable stay. One bedroom has wheelchair access and a large wet room. A choice of homely lounges is available; breakfast and very good dinners are served in the sun lounge.

Rooms: 1 en suite 2 annexe en suite (2 GF) **S** fr £57 **D** fr £90* **Facilities:** FTV Lounge TVL tea/coffee Dinner available WiFi 🔒 **Parking:** 8 **Notes:** LB 25 acres sheep/chickens

AXMINSTER
Map 4 SY29

Premier Collection

Kerrington House

★★★★★ 🍸 🍽 GUEST ACCOMMODATION

tel: 01297 35333 **Musbury Road EX13 5JR**
email: info@kerringtonhouse.com **web:** www.kerringtonhouse.com
dir: *0.5 mile from Axminster on A358 towards Seaton, house on left.*

This former Victorian gentleman's residence has been decorated and furnished to very high standards to make guests as comfortable as possible. Bedrooms and bathrooms include a range of welcome extras. Afternoon tea may be enjoyed in the comfortably furnished lounge or, in the warmer months, outside overlooking the landscaped gardens. Locally sourced produce is used both at breakfast and at dinner, which is available by prior arrangement.

Rooms: 5 en suite (2 fmly) (2 GF) **S** fr £85 **D** fr £130 **Facilities:** FTV DVD iPod docking station Lounge tea/coffee Dinner available Licensed WiFi 🔒 **Extras:** Speciality toiletries, sherry, chocolates – complimentary **Conf:** Max 12 Board 12 **Parking:** 6 **Notes:** LB

Tytherleigh Arms

★★★★ ⊚ INN

tel: 01460 220214 **Tytherleigh EX13 7BE**
email: info@tytherleigharms.com **web:** www.tytherleigharms.com
dir: *Phone for directions.*

This former coaching inn dates back to the 16th century and in recent years has been refurbished extensively. The result is a relaxed and welcoming inn with much engaging appeal. The stylish and comfortable bedrooms are located in an adjacent building which was once the stables; each room has a separate entrance allowing flexibility and freedom for guests. The accomplished cooking at breakfast and dinner shouldn't be missed – the dishes utilise excellent quality produce, much of it sourced locally.

Rooms: 6 annexe en suite (1 fmly) (6 GF) **D** fr £95* **Facilities:** FTV tea/coffee Dinner available WiFi **Extras:** Speciality toiletries, home-made biscuits, bottled water **Parking:** 50

BAMPTON — Map 3 SS92

The Swan

★★★★ ◉◉ INN

tel: 01398 332248 **Station Road EX16 9NG**
email: info@theswan.co **web:** www.theswan.co
dir: *Phone for directions.*

The Swan is a traditional hostelry offering good food, good beer and a wide selection of wines coupled with comfortable, well-equipped bedrooms and en suite bathrooms. Each bedroom has a TV and other modern media staples. Staff are very friendly and do all they can to make a stay comfortable. Breakfast is a hearty affair using good local ingredients, and the menu in the evening, which has been awarded two AA Rosettes, offers a great choice for all.

Rooms: 3 en suite **Facilities:** FTV iPod docking station tea/coffee Dinner available WiFi Fishing Riding Gym **Extras:** Speciality toiletries, espresso machine, snacks **Notes:** LB Closed 25–26 December

Weston House

★★★★ BED AND BREAKFAST

tel: 01398 332094 & 07958 176799 **6 Luke Street EX16 9NF**
email: peter@westonhousedevon.co.uk **web:** www.westonhousedevon.co.uk
dir: *On B3227, in village, opposite church.*

Located in the heart of Bampton within easy reach of many local attractions and gardens, Weston House offers comfortable, well-equipped bedrooms and hearty breakfasts using quality local ingredients. Owner Catherine Stott is an artist who teaches, and many of her pieces are tastefully displayed throughout the house. Public parking is available within a few minutes' walk.

Rooms: 3 rms (2 en suite) (1 pri facs) **S** fr £60 **D** fr £75* **Facilities:** FTV DVD tea/coffee WiFi **Drying facilities Extras:** Speciality toiletries, home-made biscuits – complimentary **Notes:** LB Closed 20–28 December

BARNSTAPLE — Map 3 SS53

The Spinney

★★★★ GUEST ACCOMMODATION

tel: 01271 850282 & 07775 335654 **Shirwell EX31 4JR**
email: stay@thespinneyshirwell.co.uk **web:** www.thespinneyshirwell.co.uk
dir: *From Barnstaple on A39, past hospital towards Lynton.*

This elegant 18th-century former rectory is located in the heart of north Devon, three miles from the historic market town of Barnstaple. The Spinney offers stylishly decorated, en suite accommodation in muted colours, with thoughtful extras. Local farm sausages feature at breakfast which is served in the conservatory. Ample private parking is available.

Rooms: 5 rms (4 en suite) (1 pri facs) (1 fmly) **Facilities:** FTV DVD Lounge tea/coffee WiFi **Extras:** Chocolates, water – complimentary **Parking:** 7 **Notes:** LB No children 10 years RS December to 1 March winter opening times may vary

BEESANDS — Map 3 SX84

The Cricket Inn

★★★★ ◉ INN

tel: 01548 580215 **TQ7 2EN**
email: enquiries@thecricketinn.com **web:** www.thecricketinn.com
dir: *From Kingsbridge follow A379 towards Dartmouth, at Stokenham mini-roundabout turn right for Beesands.*

Dating back to 1867, this charming seaside inn is situated almost on the beach at Start Bay. The well-appointed bedrooms have en suite walk-in shower rooms, comfortable beds, tea-and coffee-making facilities and TVs; five of the seven rooms have fantastic views of the bay. The daily-changing fish menu includes locally-caught crabs, lobster and perhaps hand-dived scallops.

Rooms: 7 en suite (3 fmly) **Facilities:** FTV tea/coffee Dinner available WiFi **Parking:** 30 **Notes:** Closed 25 December and January, closed for maintenance

BIDEFORD — Map 3 SS42

The Pines at Eastleigh

★★★★ GUEST ACCOMMODATION

tel: 01271 860561 **The Pines, Eastleigh EX39 4PA**
email: info@thepinesateastleigh.co.uk **web:** www.thepinesateastleigh.co.uk
dir: *A39 onto A386 signed East-the-Water. 1st left signed Eastleigh, 500 yards next left, 1.5 miles to village, house on right.*

This charming Grade II listed house is set in seven-acre grounds with lovely views across rolling farmland towards Lundy Island and Hartland Point. This makes a wonderful location from which to explore this beautiful area, and your welcoming hosts will help with any local information required. The bedrooms are located both in the main house and adjacent courtyard – all provide impressive levels of quality and comfort and have stylish bathrooms. Tasty breakfasts are served in the elegant dining room; a guest lounge, with an honesty bar, is also available.

Rooms: 4 en suite 5 annexe en suite (1 fmly) (5 GF) **S** fr £75 **D** fr £95* **Facilities:** FTV TVL tea/coffee Licensed WiFi **Games room Conf:** Max 25 Thtr 20 Board 20 **Parking:** 9 **Notes:** LB No children 9 years

BISHOPSTEIGNTON — Map 3 SX97

Cockhaven Arms

★★★★ INN

tel: 01626 775252 **Cockhaven Road TQ14 9RF**
email: contact@cockhavenarms.co.uk **web:** www.cockhavenarms.co.uk
dir: *From A381 follow brown tourist signs.*

Cockhaven Arms is a friendly, family-run inn that dates back to the 16th century. The bedrooms offer impressive levels of comfort and quality – all are well equipped and many enjoy views across the beautiful Teign estuary. A choice of dining options is offered – on the menus are traditional favourites and daily specials, and locally-caught fish is a speciality.

Rooms: 10 en suite (2 fmly) **Facilities:** FTV tea/coffee Dinner available WiFi **Conf:** Max 144 Thtr 100 Class 100 Board 24 **Parking:** 30 **Notes:** LB Closed 26 December Civ wed 80

BLACKAWTON
Map 3 SX85

The George Inn
★★★ INN

tel: 01803 712342 **Main Street TQ9 7BG**
email: tgiblackawton@yahoo.co.uk **web:** www.blackawton.com
dir: *From Totnes on A381 through Halwell. Left onto A3122 towards Dartmouth, turn right to Blackawton.*

Situated in the heart of Blackawton, this village local offers a warm welcome to all. A proper, unspoilt pub, it enjoys an engaging traditional atmosphere and a real sense of community. Bedrooms offer good levels of comfort and quality, likewise the modern bathrooms. Public areas have an inviting, rustic charm and a wide range of food options is offered, with local produce used as much as possible. Lovely views across the rolling countryside can be enjoyed from the terrace and garden.

Rooms: 4 en suite (1 fmly) **Facilities:** FTV DVD tea/coffee Dinner available WiFi
Parking: 12 **Notes:** LB

BOVEY TRACEY
Map 3 SX87

Courtenay House
★★★ BED AND BREAKFAST

tel: 01626 835363 & 07774 260446 **76 Fore Street TQ13 9AE**
email: info@courtenayhouse.co.uk **web:** www.courtenayhouse.co.uk
dir: *A38 from Exeter towards Plymouth. Follow B3344 Chudleigh Knighton signs. At T-junction in Bovey Tracey, right, follow Town Centre signs into Fore Street. House on left after Orchard Terrace.*

Courtenay House is located in the heart of the historic town of Bovey Tracey and is the perfect base to explore the area. The bedrooms are well furnished and equipped with a range of useful amenities. Freshly cooked breakfasts are served in the tea room just off the antique shop.

Rooms: 3 rms (2 en suite) (1 pri facs) (1 GF) **Facilities:** FTV tea/coffee WiFi **Notes:** LB No children 16 years Closed 24 December to 6 January

BRATTON FLEMING
Map 3 SS63

Premier Collection

Bracken House
★★★★★ BED AND BREAKFAST

tel: 01598 711810 & 07970 275881 **EX31 4TG**
email: info@brackenhouse.co.uk **web:** www.brackenhouse.co.uk
dir: *M5 junction 27, A361 to South Molton, right on A399 for 7 miles, left to Bratton Fleming for 2 miles. Sign at end of drive opposite Baptist chapel.*

Bracken House, a former Victorian rectory, has four en suite bedrooms and is situated on the edge of the popular north Devon village of Bratton Fleming. It is within easy driving distance of the spectacular north Devon coast, Exmoor and many other local attractions, including National Trust properties, the gardens at RHS Rosemoor, Castle Hill, Marwood and Tapeley Park. The drawing room, with its cosy open fire, has lovely views over the garden towards Hartland through the large bay window. The dining room, where a full English breakfast is served each morning, has a wood-burner which is lit on cooler mornings.

Rooms: 4 en suite (1 fmly) (1 GF) **Facilities:** FTV DVD Lounge tea/coffee WiFi
Extras: Speciality toiletries **Parking:** 6 **Notes:** Closed 23–26 December
Civ wed 20

BRIXHAM
Map 3 SX95

Anchorage Guest House
★★★★ GUEST HOUSE

tel: 01803 852960 & 07950 536362 **170 New Road TQ5 8DA**
email: enquiries@brixham-anchorage.co.uk **web:** www.brixham-anchorage.co.uk
dir: *A3022, enter Brixham, left at lights at junction with Monksbridge Road. Pass Toll House immediately on right.*

Conveniently located within walking distance of the town centre and harbour, this is an excellent choice for anyone looking to explore the many attractions of this popular holiday area. The dining room and the bedrooms have a light, bright contemporary style, with many extra facilities provided to ensure a comfortable stay. Guests are welcome to use the delightful garden, and on-site parking is a bonus.

Rooms: 7 rms (6 en suite) (1 pri facs) (4 GF) **Facilities:** FTV tea/coffee WiFi
Parking: 6

BUCKFAST
Map 3 SX76

Furzeleigh Mill
★★★ GUEST ACCOMMODATION

tel: 01364 643476 **Old Ashburton Road TQ11 0JP**
email: enquiries@furzeleigh.co.uk **web:** www.furzeleigh.co.uk
dir: *Exit A38 at Dartbridge junction, right at end slip road, right signed Ashburton/Prince Town (NB do not cross River Dart bridge), 200 yards right.*

This Grade II listed, 16th-century converted corn mill stands in its own grounds and is a good base for touring Dartmoor. Spacious family rooms are available as well as a lounge and a bar. All meals are served in the dining room and use local produce.

Rooms: 14 en suite (2 fmly) **Facilities:** FTV TVL tea/coffee Dinner available Licensed WiFi **Conf:** Max 20 Thtr 20 **Parking:** 32 **Notes:** LB No children 6 years Closed 23 December to 2 January

BUCKFASTLEIGH
Map 3 SX76

Kilbury Manor
★★★★ GUEST ACCOMMODATION

tel: 01364 644079 **Colston Road TQ11 0LN**
email: kilburymanor@gmail.com **web:** www.kilburymanor.co.uk
dir: *A38 onto B3380 to Buckfastleigh, left into Old Totnes Road, at bottom turn right, Kilbury Manor on left.*

Dating back to the 17th century, this charming Devon longhouse is situated in the tranquil surroundings of the Dart Valley with access to the river across the meadow. Bedrooms have an abundance of character and are located in the main house and in adjacent converted barns; all provide high levels of comfort. The stylish bathrooms are also appointed to impressive standards. Breakfast is served in the elegant dining room with local produce very much in evidence.

Rooms: 4 rms (3 en suite) (1 pri facs) (1 GF) **Facilities:** FTV DVD tea/coffee WiFi
Parking: 5 **Notes:** No children 7 years

CHILLATON
Map 3 SX48

Premier Collection

Tor Cottage
★★★★★ ⬒ GUEST ACCOMMODATION

tel: 01822 860248 **PL16 0JE**
email: info@torcottage.co.uk **web:** www.torcottage.co.uk
dir: *A30 Lewdown exit through Chillaton towards Tavistock, 300 yards after Post Office right signed 'Bridlepath No Public Vehicular Access' to end.*

Tor Cottage, located in its own valley with 18 acres of grounds, is a welcome antidote to the fast pace of everyday life. Rooms are spacious and elegant; the cottage-wing bedroom has a separate sitting room, and the garden rooms have their own wood-burners. The gardens are delightful, with a stream and heated outdoor pool. An exceptional range of dishes is offered at breakfast, which can be enjoyed either in the conservatory dining room or on the terrace.

Rooms: 1 en suite 3 annexe en suite (3 GF) **S** fr £98 **D** fr £150 **Facilities:** FTV DVD TVL tea/coffee WiFi ⬭ ⬤ **Parking:** 8 **Notes:** LB No children 14 years Closed mid December to beginning February

CHRISTOW
Map 3 SX88

Hyner Farm
★★★★ FARMHOUSE

tel: 01647 252923 & 07781 186133 **EX6 7NT**
email: preston916@btinternet.com **web:** www.hynerfarm-bandb-devon.co.uk
dir: *From A38 take exit signed Teign Valley. Follow brown tourist signs for Canonteign Falls. Turn sharp left signed No Through Road at Canonteign Falls exit.*

This beautiful, rural farmhouse located in the middle of the Teign Valley has three highly individual bedrooms, and grounds looking out onto the countryside. All the bedrooms are richly decorated and well equipped; ideal for business or leisure guests. Public areas include a comfortable lounge and a dining area with inglenook fire place – a sociable setting for enjoying breakfast. Parking is provided.

Rooms: 3 en suite **Facilities:** FTV DVD TVL tea/coffee WiFi ⬥ ⬤ **Parking:** 3 **Notes:** LB 120 acres beef/grass

CHULMLEIGH
Map 3 SS61

The Old Bakehouse
★★★★ ⬒ GUEST HOUSE

tel: 01769 580074 & 580137 **South Molton Street EX18 7BW**
email: holly@oldbakehousedevon.co.uk **web:** www.oldbakehousedevon.co.uk
dir: *A377 onto B3096 into village centre, left into South Molton Street, 100 yards on left.*

This 16th-century thatched house is situated in the centre of Chulmleigh, a hilltop town which stands above a beautiful river valley. The charming bedrooms are equipped with many extras such as DVD players (library available) and are located across a pretty, secluded courtyard garden in the former village bakery. A wealth of beams, thick cob walls and a wood-burning stove all contribute to the character and comfort. A generous choice is offered at breakfast with an emphasis on excellent local produce.

Rooms: 3 en suite (1 GF) **S** fr £60 **D** fr £90 **Facilities:** FTV DVD Lounge tea/coffee ⬥ ⬤ **Extras:** Home-made biscuits, cafetière, flowers **Notes:** LB No children 11 years

CLOVELLY
Map 3 SS32

East Dyke Farmhouse
★★★★ ⬒ FARMHOUSE

tel: 01237 431216 **East Dyke Farm, Higher Clovelly EX39 5RU**
email: helen.goaman@btinternet.com **web:** www.bedbreakfastclovelly.co.uk
dir: *A39 onto B3237 at Clovelly Cross roundabout, farm 500 yards on left.*

Adjoining an Iron Age hill fort, this working farm has glorious views of Bideford Bay in the distance. The farmhouse has a friendly atmosphere and the open fires, beams and stone floors add to its charm and character. The three bedrooms are spacious and furnished in co-ordinated fabrics with thoughtful little extras. A key feature here is the breakfast – local produce and delicious home-made preserves are served around one large table.

Rooms: 3 rms (2 en suite) (1 pri facs) (1 fmly) **S** fr £45 **D** fr £75* **Facilities:** FTV TVL tea/coffee WiFi ⬤ **Extras:** Fridge **Parking:** 6 **Notes:** Closed 10 December to 10 January RS December to February advance bookings only 350 acres beef/arable

Red Lion
★★★★ INN

tel: 01237 431237 **The Quay EX39 5TF**
email: stay@clovelly.co.uk **web:** www.clovelly.co.uk
dir: *Exit A39 at Clovelly Cross onto B3237. Pass visitor centre, 1st left by white rails to harbour.*

'Idyllic' is the word that best describes the harbour-side setting of this charming 18th-century inn, with the famous fishing village forming a spectacular backdrop. Bedrooms are stylish and enjoy delightful views. The inn's relaxed atmosphere is conducive to relaxation, even when the harbour comes alive with the activities of the local fishermen during the day.

Rooms: 17 en suite (5 fmly) (2 GF) **Notes:** Civ wed 70

New Inn
★★★ INN

tel: 01237 431303 **High Street EX39 5TQ**
email: newinn@clovelly.co.uk **web:** www.clovelly.co.uk
dir: *At Clovelly Cross, exit A39 onto B3237. Follow down hill for 1.5 miles. Right at sign 'All vehicles for Clovelly'.*

Famed for its cobbled descent to the harbour, this fascinating fishing village is a traffic-free zone. Consequently, luggage is conveyed by sledge or donkey to this much-photographed inn. Smartly presented bedrooms and public areas are appointed with quality, locally-made furnishings. Meals may be taken in the elegant restaurant or the popular Upalong bar.

Rooms: 8 en suite (1 fmly) (1 GF) **Facilities:** Lounge tea/coffee Dinner available Direct dial WiFi Sea fishing, diving and tennis can be arranged **Notes:** Civ wed 50

COLEFORD
Map 3 SS70

The New Inn
★★★★ INN

tel: 01363 84242 **EX17 5BZ**
email: enquiries@thenewinncoleford.co.uk **web:** www.thenewinncoleford.co.uk
dir: *Exit A377 into Coleford, 1.5 miles to inn (signed).*

Originally dating back to the 13th century, The New Inn is a charming thatched village inn with much to offer and is a relaxing base from which to explore this beautiful corner of Devon. Bedrooms are spacious, comfortable and well appointed with lovely beds and lots of period features. Roaring fires, flagged floors and 'Captain' the resident parrot all combine to create an engaging atmosphere. A choice of carefully prepared dishes is on offer in the restaurant and bar lounges, with local produce strongly featured.

Rooms: 6 en suite (4 fmly) (1 GF) **S** fr £68 **D** fr £90* **Facilities:** FTV DVD tea/coffee Dinner available Direct dial WiFi ⚓ **Extras:** Bottled water – complimentary **Parking:** 50 **Notes:** LB Closed 25–26 December

CREDITON
Map 3 SS80

The Lamb Inn
★★★★ ⚙ INN

tel: 01363 773676 **The Square, Sandford EX17 4LW**
email: thelambinn@gmail.com **web:** www.lambinnsandford.co.uk
dir: *Phone for directions.*

The Lamb Inn is the sort of quintessential local which any village would be proud to have. This is a proper, unpretentious pub with a very welcoming and engaging atmosphere, where good-natured banter will accompany a refreshing pint. Food must not be overlooked here, the accomplished cooking makes good use of quality, local produce, and the breakfasts are generous. Bedrooms and bathrooms offer impressive levels of quality with contemporary styling.

Rooms: 3 en suite 4 annexe en suite (3 fmly) **S** fr £69 **D** fr £95* **Facilities:** FTV Lounge Dinner available WiFi **Conf:** Max 25 Thtr 25 Class 25 Board 25 **Notes:** RS 25 December restaurant closed

CROYDE
Map 3 SS43

The Whiteleaf
★★★★ ⚜ ☕ GUEST HOUSE

tel: 01271 890266 **Croyde Road EX33 1PN**
email: bookings@thewhiteleaf.co.uk **web:** www.thewhiteleaf.co.uk
dir: *On B3231 entering Croyde, on left at 'Road Narrows' sign.*

A warm family welcome awaits guests at this attractive house within easy walking distance of the pretty village and the sandy beach. Each of the well-equipped bedrooms has its own charm, and three rooms have decked balconies. Ambitious and imaginative dinners, using fresh seasonal produce, are served in the elegant restaurant.

Rooms: 5 en suite (2 fmly) **S** fr £72 **D** fr £86* **Facilities:** FTV Lounge tea/coffee Dinner available Direct dial Licensed WiFi ⚓ **Extras:** Mini-bar **Parking:** 10 **Notes:** LB Closed 24–27 December

CULLOMPTON
Map 3 ST00

Muddifords Court Country House
★★★★★ ⚜ GUEST ACCOMMODATION

tel: 01884 820023 & 07890 273730 **Willand EX15 2QG**
email: info@muddifords.co.uk **web:** www.muddifordscourt.co.uk
dir: *M5 junction 27 onto A38 (Wellington). After 1 mile at roundabout right onto B3181, at roundabout (4 miles) right signed Halberton/Willand. Over mini roundabout, 500 metres turn right (Sampford Peverell). 200 metres on right.*

Muddifords Court is a high-quality establishment, with the added benefit of a range of flexible meeting space to accommodate weddings, conferences and special events. The bedrooms have been finished to a high standard and are sumptuously appointed; some haver attractive views over the Culm Valley and beyond. A choice of freshly prepared breakfasts is served in the main dining room. Self-catering huts are available in the private copse.

Rooms: 5 en suite 2 annexe en suite (1 GF) **Facilities:** FTV DVD TVL tea/coffee Licensed WiFi ⚓ **Extras:** Sherry **Conf:** Max 100 Thtr 100 Class 80 Board 60 **Parking:** 70 **Notes:** Closed 24 December to 2 January Civ wed 120

DARTMEET
Map 3 SX67

Brimpts Farm
★★★ GUEST ACCOMMODATION

tel: 01364 631450 **PL20 6SG**
email: info@brimptsfarm.co.uk **web:** www.brimptsfarm.co.uk
dir: *Dartmeet at east end of B3357, establishment signed on right at top of hill.*

A popular venue for walkers and lovers of the great outdoors, Brimpts Farm is peacefully situated in the heart of Dartmoor and has been a Duchy of Cornwall farm since 1307. Bedrooms are simply furnished and many have wonderful views across the moor. Additional facilities include a sauna and spa, and a children's play area.

Rooms: 10 en suite 3 annexe rms (3 pri facs) (2 fmly) (7 GF) **S** fr £45 **D** fr £75 **Facilities:** Lounge TVL tea/coffee Licensed WiFi Sauna ⚓ Farm walks and trails, hot tub **Conf:** Max 60 Thtr 60 Class 40 Board 25 **Parking:** 50 **Notes:** LB

DARTMOUTH
Map 3 SX85

Strete Barton House
★★★★★ 🍴 GUEST HOUSE

tel: 01803 770364 **Totnes Rd, Strete TQ6 0RU**
email: info@stretebarton.co.uk **web:** www.stretebarton.co.uk
dir: *From Dartmouth on A379, exit coastal road into village, just below church.*

This delightful 16th-century, former farmhouse blends stylish accommodation with original character. The bedrooms are very comfortably furnished and well equipped with useful extras. Breakfast makes good use of quality local produce and is served in the spacious dining room. Guests are also welcome to use the comfortable lounge, complete with a log-burning stove. The village lies between Dartmouth and Kingsbridge and has easy access to beautiful South Hams as well as many local pubs and restaurants.

Rooms: 5 rms (4 en suite) (1 pri facs) 1 annexe en suite **S** fr £110 **D** fr £110*
Facilities: FTV DVD iPod docking station Lounge tea/coffee WiFi ⅃
🔒 **Extras:** Speciality toiletries, guests' fridge **Parking:** 2 **Notes:** LB
No children 8 years

Mounthaven
★★★★★ BED AND BREAKFAST

tel: 01803 839061 & 07919 274751 **Mount Boone TQ6 9PB**
email: enquiries@mounthavendartmouth.co.uk
web: www.mounthavendartmouth.co.uk
dir: *A379, right into Townstal Road, opposite Royal Naval College gates. 1st left into Mount Boone, halfway down on right.*

Set on the hillside of Mount Boone, Mounthaven has a superb view of the town and the estuary yet is only a few minutes' walk from the town centre. The hosts are experienced and professional and a very warm welcome is assured. Bedrooms are individually decorated and each enjoys a view of historic Dartmouth or the sea.

Rooms: 3 en suite **D** fr £110* **Facilities:** STV FTV DVD TVL tea/coffee WiFi ⅃
🔒 **Parking:** 5 **Notes:** LB No children 16 years

Hill View House
★★★★ GUEST ACCOMMODATION

tel: 01803 839372 **76 Victoria Road TQ6 9DZ**
email: enquiries@hillviewdartmouth.co.uk **web:** www.hillviewdartmouth.co.uk
dir: *Phone for detailed directions.*

Centrally located, Hill View House is a five-storey, late Victorian townhouse. A warm welcome is guaranteed, and the house is located only minutes from the heart of Dartmouth. The bedrooms are comfortably furnished, appointed to a high standard and come equipped with a range of accessories. Breakfast is served in the light and airy dining room. Free WiFi is accessible throughout.

Rooms: 3 en suite **Facilities:** TVL tea/coffee WiFi ⅃ **Extras:** Speciality toiletries **Parking:** 2 **Notes:** No children 14 years

Bayards Cove Inn
★★★★ 🍴 🍺 INN

tel: 01803 839278 & 07704 188831 **27 Lower Street TQ6 9AN**
email: info@bayardscoveinn.co.uk **web:** www.bayardscoveinn.co.uk
dir: *Phone for directions.*

There's a real sense of history at this charming waterside establishment, once a Tudor merchant's house, that is located a few steps from where the pilgrims set sail on the *Mayflower* in 1621. Every effort is made to ensure guests have a relaxed and rewarding stay. A café and wine bar by day, the inn's evening opening times vary, with a tapas menu available on selected nights. The bedrooms are comfortable and individually styled; bathrooms provide all the expected modern necessities with cosseting towels and quality toiletries etc. Breakfast is a generous affair, with a range of continental and cooked options, all showcasing the best local produce.

Rooms: 7 en suite (2 fmly) **S** fr £95 **D** fr £110* **Facilities:** FTV DVD Lounge tea/coffee Dinner available WiFi ⅃ 🔒 **Extras:** Magazines, speciality toiletries – complimentary

Cherub's Nest
★★★★ GUEST ACCOMMODATION

tel: 01803 832482 & 07816 762799 **15 Higher Street TQ6 9RB**
email: cherubsnest4bb@aol.com **web:** www.cherubsnest.co.uk
dir: *From Lower Dartmouth ferry along Lower Street, left into Smith Street, left into Higher Street, Cherub's Nest 50 yards on left.*

Dating from 1710, this former merchant's house, bedecked with flowers during the summer, is located in the very heart of historic Dartmouth. Full of character, the individually decorated bedrooms vary in size, but all are attractive and well equipped. A choice of breakfasts is served in the cosy dining room.

Rooms: 3 en suite **Facilities:** FTV tea/coffee WiFi **Notes:** LB No children 10 years

DODDISCOMBSLEIGH
Map 3 SX88

The Nobody Inn
★★★★ ⬡ INN

tel: 01647 252394 **EX6 7PS**
email: reservations@nobodyinn.co.uk web: www.nobodyinn.co.uk
dir: *From A38 turn off at top of Haldon Hill, follow signs to Doddiscombsleigh.*

Dating back to the 16th century, this fascinating inn is something of a mecca for lovers of wine, whisky and local ale – the choices are extensive. Let's not forget the impressive food, much of which is sourced locally including an extensive cheese selection. Bedrooms and bathrooms have been appointed to provide high levels of quality, comfort and individuality. Reassuringly, the bars and lounges remain unchanged with charmingly mismatched furniture, age-darkened beams and an inglenook fireplace.

Rooms: 5 rms (4 en suite) (1 pri facs) **Facilities:** FTV DVD tea/coffee Dinner available Direct dial WiFi 🐾 **Extras:** Sherry **Conf:** Max 24 **Parking:** 25 **Notes:** No children 5 years Closed 25 December

DUNKESWELL
Map 3 ST10

The Old Kennels
★★★★ BED AND BREAKFAST

tel: 01823 681138 **Stentwood EX14 4RW**
email: info@theoldkennels.co.uk web: www.theoldkennels.co.uk

Located in the heart of the beautiful Blackdown Hills, on the Devon–Somerset border, The Old Kennels is in a quiet rural location and makes an ideal base for exploring this vibrant area. Accommodation includes a cosy two-bedroom loft apartment featuring antique furniture and vintage details, a compact lounge area and fully-fitted kitchen. A continental breakfast hamper is delivered to the apartment, allowing the flexibility to enjoy breakfast at your own pace, perhaps outside on the terrace with lovely views across the fields.

Rooms: 2 rms annexe (1 en suite) (1 pri facs) (1 fmly) **S** fr £85 **D** fr £100 (room only)* **Facilities:** FTV TVL tea/coffee WiFi ⬡ 🐾 25 acres of woodland, arts and crafts courses **Extras:** Fresh milk **Conf:** Max 12 Board 12 **Parking:** 10 **Notes:** LB

ERMINGTON
Map 3 SX65

Plantation House
★★★★★ ⬡⬡ 🍴 RESTAURANT WITH ROOMS

tel: 01548 831100 & 830741 **Totnes Road PL21 9NS**
email: info@plantationhousehotel.co.uk web: www.plantationhousehotel.co.uk
dir: *Phone for directions.*

Peacefully situated in the picturesque South Hams, this former rectory provides an intimate and relaxing base from which to explore the area. Quality, comfort and individuality are hallmarks throughout, with bedrooms offering impressive standards and a host of thoughtful extras. The stylish bathrooms come equipped with fluffy towels, robes and underfloor heating. A drink beside the crackling log fire is the ideal prelude to dinner, where skill and passion underpin menus focusing on wonderful local produce. Breakfast is equally enjoyable, with superb eggs provided by the resident hens.

Rooms: 8 en suite **S** fr £65 **D** fr £110 **Facilities:** FTV DVD iPod docking station Lounge tea/coffee Dinner available Direct dial WiFi ⬡ 🎣 Fishing Riding Massage and therapies **Extras:** Speciality toiletries, fruit, home-made cakes and biscuits, robes, mineral water, fresh milk **Conf:** Max 16 **Parking:** 30 **Notes:** LB

EXETER
Map 3 SX99

Chi Restaurant & Bar with Accommodation
★★★★ 🍴 RESTAURANT WITH ROOMS

tel: 01626 890213 **Fore Street, Kenton EX6 8LD**
email: enquiries@chi-restaurant.co.uk web: www.chi-restaurant.co.uk
dir: *5 miles south of Exeter. M5 junction 30, A379 towards Dawlish, in village centre.*

This former pub has been spectacularly transformed into a chic and contemporary bar, allied with a stylish Chinese restaurant. Dishes are beautifully presented with an emphasis on quality produce and authenticity, resulting in a memorable dining experience. Bedrooms are well equipped and all provide good levels of space and comfort, along with modern bathrooms.

Rooms: 5 en suite (1 fmly) **S** fr £55 **D** fr £70 (room only)* **Facilities:** FTV DVD Lounge tea/coffee Dinner available WiFi 🐾 **Parking:** 26 **Notes:** Closed Sunday to Monday

Innkeeper's Lodge Exeter, Clyst St George
★★★ INN

tel: 03451 551551 **Clyst St George EX3 0QJ**
email: info@innkeeperslodge.com web: www.innkeeperslodge.com
dir: *Phone for directions.*

This welcoming inn, The St George & Dragon, is just a short drive from the centre of Exeter and very convenient for access to the M5. Surrounded by rolling fields, this is an excellent base for exploring the east Devon coast, with Exmouth close by and Topsham also worth a visit. The en suite, modern bedrooms have TVs, desks, free WiFi, tea- and coffee-making facilities as standard; family rooms are available. The pub has a warm and inviting atmosphere with a crackling log fires and cosy hideaways. Free parking and a garden are available.

Rooms: 21 en suite (6 fmly) (8 GF) **Facilities:** FTV tea/coffee Dinner available Direct dial WiFi

Innkeeper's Lodge Exeter, Middlemoor Lodge

★★★ INN

tel: 03451 551551 **Rydon Lane, Middlemoor EX2 7HL**
email: info@innkeeperslodge.com **web:** www.innkeeperslodge.com
dir: *M5 junction 29 onto A30 towards Honiton/Exeter Airport. Right into Honiton Road,*
take 1st exit at next 2 roundabouts, then 2nd exit at next roundabout, property on left.

This conveniently located establishment is ideally suited for both business and
leisure guests. It's just a short drive from the city centre and is also close to the
airport and Digby and Sowton station. Contemporary bedrooms offer good levels of
comfort and quality. A Toby Carvery is adjacent.

Rooms: 1 en suite 37 annexe en suite (1 fmly) (28 GF) **Facilities:** FTV tea/coffee
Dinner available WiFi **Conf:** Max 40 **Parking:** 200

EXMOUTH   Map 3 SY08

The Devoncourt

★★★ GUEST ACCOMMODATION

tel: 01395 272277 **16 Douglas Avenue EX8 2EX**
email: enquiries@devoncourt.com **web:** www.devoncourt.com
dir: *M5/A376 to Exmouth, follow seafront to Maer Road, right at T-junction.*

The Devoncourt stands in four acres of mature, subtropical gardens, sloping gently
towards the sea and overlooking two miles of sandy beaches. It offers extensive
leisure facilities, and the smartly furnished bedrooms are exceptionally well
equipped. The spacious public areas are available to timeshare owners as well as
guests. For meals there is a choice between the informal bar and the restaurant.

Rooms: 52 en suite 2 annexe en suite (35 fmly) (8 GF) **Facilities:** FTV DVD TVL tea/
coffee Dinner available Direct dial Lift Licensed WiFi ⊗ ⚲ ⬟ ⚲ ⚲ Snooker
Sauna Gym Sun shower, Jacuzzi **Parking:** 50 **Notes:** LB Civ wed 100

HAYTOR VALE   Map 3 SX77

Rock Inn

★★★★ ◉◉ INN

tel: 01364 661305 & 661465 **TQ13 9XP**
email: inn@rock-inn.co.uk **web:** www.rock-inn.co.uk
dir: *A38 onto 382 to Bovey Tracey, in 0.5 mile left onto B3387 to Haytor.*

Dating back to the 1750s, this former coaching inn is in a pretty hamlet on the
edge of Dartmoor. Named after Grand National winners, each of the individually
decorated bedrooms has some nice extra touches. The bars are full of character
with flagstone floors and old beams, and offer a wide range of dishes, cooked with
imagination. The food has been awarded two AA Rosettes.

Rooms: 9 en suite **Facilities:** FTV DVD Lounge tea/coffee Dinner available Direct dial
WiFi 🔒 **Parking:** 10 **Notes:** LB Closed 25–26 December

HOLSWORTHY   Map 3 SS30

Barton Gate Farm Guesthouse

★★★★ BED AND BREAKFAST

tel: 07768 402640 & 07831 739206 **Pancrasweek EX22 7JT**
email: paularaefrancis@me.com **web:** www.bartongatedevon.co.uk
dir: *From Holsworthy take A3072 to Bude, 3.1 miles on right.*

This relaxed and welcoming establishment is ideally located for exploring the coast.
Every effort is made to ensure guests enjoy a rewarding stay, with plenty of local
information always on offer. Hospitality is also extended to animals, with anything
from a hamster to a horse being more than welcome. Bedrooms are in a converted
stable block – all offer good levels of comfort and the advantage of inter-
connecting doors to make extra space for families. A choice of continental or
traditional English breakfast is served in the light and airy dining room. Additional
facilities include a games room, lounge, nail bar and a large exercise field for dogs.

Rooms: 3 en suite (3 fmly) (3 GF) **Facilities:** FTV DVD Lounge TVL tea/coffee 🔒 4G
WiFi, table tennis **Parking:** 30 **Notes:** LB

HONITON   Map 4 ST10

Threshays

★★★ BED AND BREAKFAST

tel: 01404 43551 & 07811 675800 **Awliscombe EX14 3QB**
email: threshays@btinternet.com **web:** www.threshays.co.uk
dir: *2.5 miles northwest of Honiton on A373.*

A converted threshing barn, situated on a non-working farm, Threshays has
wonderful views over open countryside. With tea and cake offered on arrival, this
family-run establishment provides comfortable accommodation in a friendly
atmosphere. The lounge-dining room is a light and airy setting for enjoying
breakfasts. Ample parking is a bonus.

Rooms: 2 rms (1 fmly) **S** fr £40 **D** fr £70* **Facilities:** TVL tea/coffee WiFi **Parking:** 4

HOPE COVE   Map 3 SX64

Cottage

★★★★ ☕ GUEST ACCOMMODATION

tel: 01548 561555 **The Cottage TQ7 3HJ**
email: info@hopecove.com **web:** www.hopecove.com
dir: *From Kingsbridge on A381 to Salcombe. 2nd right at Marlborough, follow road to Galmpton into Hope Cove, left for Inner Hope.*

Glorious sunsets can be seen over the attractive bay from this popular establishment. Friendly and attentive service from the staff and management mean many guests return here frequently. The bedrooms, many with sea views and some with balconies, are well equipped. The restaurant offers an enjoyable dining experience.

Rooms: 32 rms (31 en suite) (1 pri facs) (5 fmly) (5 GF) **Facilities:** FTV DVD Lounge TVL tea/coffee Dinner available Direct dial Licensed WiFi ♪ ♣ Table tennis **Conf:** Max 70 Thtr 60 Class 60 Board 30 **Parking:** 50 **Notes:** LB Closed early January to early February

ILFRACOMBE   Map 3 SS54

Marine Court

★★★★ ☕ GUEST HOUSE

tel: 01271 862920 & 07791 051778 **Hillsborough Road EX34 9QQ**
email: info@marinecourthoteldevon.co.uk **web:** www.marinecourthoteldevon.co.uk
dir: *M5 junction 27, A361 to Barnstaple, continue to Ilfracombe.*

Marine Court is a well-established guest house offering comfortable, well appointed rooms in a handy location. Guests are assured a very warm welcome from the hosts who do all they can to ensure a comfortable stay. Guests have use of a small bar lounge where drinks can be served, and off-road parking is a bonus.

Rooms: 8 en suite **Facilities:** FTV DVD iPod docking station Lounge tea/coffee Licensed WiFi **Extras:** Mini-bar **Parking:** 8 **Notes:** No children 16 years Closed November to March

Collingdale Guest House

★★★★ ☕ GUEST HOUSE

tel: 01271 863770 & 07768 522323 **13 Larkstone Terrace EX34 9NU**
email: thecollingdale@gmail.com **web:** www.thecollingdale.co.uk
dir: *Take A399 east through Ilfracombe, on left past B3230 turning.*

Overlooking the harbour, this terraced Victorian guest house is within easy walking distance of the town centre and seafront. The well-presented bedrooms, many with sweeping sea views, are furnished to a high standard with many thoughtful extras. Two rooms have their own balcony. The comfortable lounge and elegant breakfast

room share the magnificent views. The breakfast features quality local produce. A cosy honesty bar is available for a tipple before bedtime.

Rooms: 9 rms (8 en suite) (1 pri facs) (2 fmly) **S** fr £55 **D** fr £82 **Facilities:** FTV Lounge TVL tea/coffee Licensed WiFi ♪ **Extras:** Mineral water, speciality toiletries – complimentary **Notes:** LB No children 8 years Closed November to February

LEWDOWN   Map 3 SX48

Lobhill Farmhouse

★★★★ BED AND BREAKFAST

tel: 01566 783542 & 07817 244687 **EX20 4DT**
email: jane.colwill@btopenworld.com **web:** www.lobhillbedandbreakfast.co.uk
dir: *Exit A30 at Sourton Cross, follow signs for Lewdown onto old A30. Lobhill 1 mile before Lewdown.*

Ideally and peacefully situated for easy access to moorland and the Devon and Cornwall coasts, this stone farmhouse dates back some 130 years. It offers impressive levels of quality yet it still retains a reassuringly traditional and homely feel. Bedrooms (including one on the ground floor with separate access) have free WiFi and views of the countryside. Tasty and satisfying breakfasts are cooked on the Aga and served either in the dining room or at the kitchen table. Guests are welcome to make use of the lovely gardens and summerhouse or explore the woodland walks.

Rooms: 4 en suite (1 fmly) (1 GF) **S** fr £55 **D** fr £85 **Facilities:** FTV DVD iPod docking station Lounge tea/coffee WiFi Fishing Riding ♣ Vineyard tours **Extras:** Home-made biscuits, local fudge **Parking:** 8 **Notes:** LB

LYNMOUTH   Map 3 SS74

Premier Collection

The Heatherville

★★★★★ ☕ ☕ GUEST ACCOMMODATION

tel: 01598 752327 & 753893 **Tors Park EX35 6NB**
email: theheatherville@aol.com **web:** www.heatherville.co.uk
dir: *Exit A39 into Tors Road, 1st left fork into Tors Park.*

This wonderful Victorian establishment stands high above Lynmouth, and the views across the wooded valley are quite superb. There is an abundance of charm and quality here at The Heatherville, and bedrooms are individually styled with comfort and character. Public rooms are also inviting with an elegant lounge and snug bar, while the dining room is the attractive venue for skilfully prepared dinners and substantial breakfasts.

Rooms: 6 en suite **D** fr £95* **Facilities:** FTV DVD Lounge tea/coffee Dinner available Licensed WiFi ♣ **Parking:** 6 **Notes:** LB No children 16 years Closed November to March

Rising Sun

★★★★ ◉◉ ☕ INN

tel: 01598 753223 **Harbourside EX35 6EG**
email: reception@risingsunlynmouth.co.uk **web:** www.risingsunlynmouth.co.uk
dir: *M5 junction 23, A39 to Minehead. On harbourside.*

The Rising Sun is a delightful thatched establishment, once a smugglers' inn, that sits on the harbour front. Popular with locals and guests alike, there is the option of eating in either the convivial bar or the restaurant; a comfortable, quiet lounge is also available. Bedrooms, located in the inn and adjoining cottages, are individually designed and have modern facilities.

Rooms: 10 en suite 4 annexe en suite (1 fmly) (1 GF) **D** fr £155* **Facilities:** FTV Lounge tea/coffee Dinner available Direct dial WiFi **Notes:** Closed 25 December

East Lyn House

★★★★ ☺ GUEST HOUSE

tel: 01598 752540 **17 Watersmeet Road EX35 6EP**
email: enquiries@eastlynhouse.co.uk **web:** www.eastlynhouse.co.uk
dir: *A39 Countisbury Hill into Lynmouth, 2nd left into Watersmeet Road. House on left.*

Just a short stroll from the centre of the village and the harbour, this is a perfect place to stay to enjoy this picturesque location. Bedrooms provide all the expected comforts with comfy beds ensuring a good rest before the day's activities. Public areas include a bar and lounge, while outside a wonderful terrace looks out over the River Lyn, with stunning views up the densely wooded valley. Breakfast is a tasty start to the day, and can be served on the terrace in summer months. Parking is also available.

Rooms: 8 en suite **S** fr £90 **D** fr £90* **Facilities:** FTV tea/coffee Licensed WiFi
♨ **Extras:** Speciality toiletries, variety locally blended teas **Parking:** 8
Notes: No children 18 years Closed November to 13 February

LYNTON Map 3 SS74

Premier Collection

Highcliffe House

★★★★★ ☺ BED AND BREAKFAST

tel: 01598 752235 & 07889 574005 **Sinai Hill EX35 6AR**
email: info@highcliffehouse.co.uk **web:** www.highcliffehouse.co.uk
dir: *From B3234 follow signs to Lynton (Castle Hill). Turn left into Sinai Hill, past The Crown on left.*

Highcliffe House prides itself in offering superb luxury accommodation. This Exmoor bed and breakfast promises boutique-style rooms and panoramic views of the north Devon coastline while you eat your breakfast.

Rooms: 6 en suite **S** fr £120 **D** fr £120* **Facilities:** FTV iPod docking station Lounge Licensed WiFi **Extras:** Robes, speciality toiletries **Parking:** 10 **Notes:** LB No children 18 years Closed 31 November to 10 February

Sinai House

★★★★ ☺ GUEST HOUSE

tel: 01598 753227 **Lynway EX35 6AY**
email: enquiries@sinaihouse.co.uk **web:** www.sinaihouse.co.uk
dir: *A39 onto B3234 through town, pass church, house on right overlooking main car park.*

Built in 1850 for the Lord Mayor of London, the house is on a hillside and offers lovely sea views. The bedrooms come in a range of shapes and sizes and most are en suite; free WiFi is available. Both the quiet guest lounge and the dining room overlook the sea and eating outside on the balcony is possible in the summer. The bar is well stocked and guests might like to relax with a drink in the secluded garden. Off-street parking is provided.

Rooms: 8 rms (6 en suite) (2 pri facs) **S** fr £50 **D** fr £85* **Facilities:** FTV DVD Lounge tea/coffee Licensed WiFi ♨ **Extras:** Bottled water **Parking:** 7 **Notes:** LB No children 12 years

Gable Lodge Guest House

★★★★ ☺ 🛏 GUEST ACCOMMODATION

tel: 01598 752367 & 07811 031270 **35 Lee Road EX35 6BS**
email: gablelodge@btconnect.com **web:** www.gablelodgelynton.co.uk
dir: *M5 junction 23 onto A39 to Lynmouth. Right, up hill to Lynton, right at top of hill signed Lynton. Continue through town, Gable Lodge on right.*

Gable Lodge is a Grade II listed, family-run Victorian establishment just a short stroll from the centre of this small town. The welcome is warm and genuine with plenty of local information, help and advice always available to help ensure a memorable stay. Bedrooms provide good levels of comfort and quality, with lovely views an added bonus. Generous breakfasts are served in the dining room, and evening meals are available on request. Additional facilities include a guest lounge and parking.

Rooms: 6 en suite (2 fmly) **S** fr £46 **D** fr £62* **Facilities:** FTV DVD iPod docking station TVL tea/coffee Dinner available Licensed WiFi ♨ **Extras:** Mini-fridge, fresh milk **Parking:** 5 **Notes:** LB Closed Christmas

Rockvale

★★★★ 🅰 GUEST ACCOMMODATION

tel: 01598 752279 **Hollerday Drive, Lee Road EX35 6HQ**
email: enquiries@rockvalelynton.com **web:** www.rockvalelynton.com
dir: *From A39 follow signs to Lynton, then town hall. In Lee Road, turn opposite Costcutter supermarket into Hollerday Drive.*

Rockvale was once the residence of a Victorian merchant, and now offers all the comforts of home, with accommodation to suit families, couples and single guests. Rockvale has a warm, friendly atmosphere, great views and good food, with a licensed bar. Guests have use of a lounge with a log fire, and evening meals are served at 7pm, although an earlier sitting can sometimes be arranged if necessary. This is an ideal base for exploring as it's close to the north Devon coast and with easy reach of the stunning countryside in Exmoor National Park.

Rooms: 7 rms (6 en suite) (1 pri facs) (3 fmly) **S** fr £35 **D** fr £65* **Facilities:** STV Lounge TVL tea/coffee Dinner available Licensed WiFi ♨ **Parking:** 7
Notes: Closed 31 October to 13 March

LYNTON *continued*

The Fernery

★★★ ☺ BED AND BREAKFAST

tel: 01598 753265 & 07970 857459 **Lydiate Lane EX35 6AJ**
email: info@thefernerylynton.com web: www.thefernerylynton.com
dir: *B3234 to Lynton into Castle Hill. Then Lee Road, turn left into Cross Street. Left into Lydiate Lane, 300 metres on right.*

Situated in a quiet street within a few minutes' walk of the town centre, The Fernery provides a comfortable, convenient base for exploring the north Devon coast and Exmoor National Park. The bedrooms are bright and have very comfortable beds, and breakfast features local, quality produce. There is on-street parking nearby and two public car parks not far away.

Rooms: 3 en suite **Facilities:** FTV DVD Lounge tea/coffee WiFi ☖

MEDDON   Map 2 SS21

The West Country Inn

★★★ INN

tel: 01237 441724 & 07977 496535 **Bursdon Moor EX39 6HB**
email: thewestcinn@aol.com web: www.westcountryinn.co.uk
dir: *On A39, south of Clovelly.*

Originally a coaching inn dating back to the 16th century, this traditional and welcoming establishment is ideally placed for exploring this picturesque area. The bedrooms provide good levels of comfort and have all that's needed to ensure a relaxing stay. The well-stocked bar has a range of local ales and provides a convivial focal point with plenty of good-natured banter always to be heard. A range of good, honest dishes is served either in the bar or adjacent dining room. Additional facilities include a spa and gym.

Rooms: 9 en suite (1 fmly) **S** fr £59 **D** fr £89 (room only) **Facilities:** FTV Lounge TVL tea/coffee Dinner available WiFi Gym ☖ Hot tub **Conf:** Max 100 Thtr 100 Class 70 Board 70 **Parking:** 100

NEWTON ABBOT   Map 3 SX87

Premier Collection

Bulleigh Barton Manor

★★★★★ ☺ BED AND BREAKFAST

tel: 01803 873411 & 07973 422678 **Ipplepen TQ12 5UA**
email: liz@escapetosouthdevon.co.uk web: www.escapetosouthdevon.co.uk
dir: *From A381 follow signs to Bulleigh and Compton Castle. Bear left along narrow lane, after 1.5 miles Bickley Mill signed on left, drive directly opposite turning.*

Warm hospitality and a genuine welcome are both hallmarks at this family-run establishment. This wonderful house dates back to the 1400s and is steeped in history. Today, it offers en suite bedrooms providing comfortable accommodation in a peaceful countryside location. Breakfast is a hearty affair featuring locally sourced produce.

Rooms: 3 en suite **S** fr £76.50 **D** fr £85.50* **Facilities:** FTV DVD Lounge tea/coffee WiFi ⤴ ☖ **Extras:** Home-made fudge and cakes, fresh milk – complimentary **Parking:** 4 **Notes:** LB No children 16 years

Bulleigh Park Farm

★★★★ ☺ FARMHOUSE

tel: 01803 872254 **Ipplepen TQ12 5UA**
email: southdevonaccommodation@gmail.com
web: www.southdevonaccommodation.co.uk
dir: *3.5 miles south of Newton Abbot. Exit A381 at Parkhill Cross, by petrol station, for Compton, 1 mile, signed.*

Bulleigh Park is a working farm – stock includes a rare breed of sheep, the Devon Closewool. Expect a warm friendly welcome at this family home set in glorious tranquil countryside, yet it is centrally located for the coast and Dartmoor. Home-made tea and cakes greet guests on arrival. The breakfasts are notable for their wealth of fresh, local and home-made produce, and the porridge is cooked using a secret recipe. An inn is just a short stroll away.

Rooms: 2 en suite (1 fmly) **S** fr £55 **D** fr £84* **Facilities:** FTV iPod docking station Lounge TVL tea/coffee WiFi ☖ **Extras:** Mini-fridge **Parking:** 6 **Notes:** LB No children 5 years Closed November to March 60 acres beef/sheep/hens

OKEHAMPTON   Map 3 SX59

See also Holsworthy

Meadowlea Guest House

★★★★ GUEST HOUSE

tel: 01837 53200 **65 Station Road EX20 1EA**
email: meadowlea65@btinternet.com web: www.meadowleaguesthouse.co.uk
dir: *From A30 onto B3260, after 2 miles left at lights, then 3rd right into Station Road. 200 yards on left.*

A well-presented period house, Meadowlea has been modernised over the years but still retains the essence of its Victorian heritage. A range of comfortably appointed rooms for all budgets, some with shared facilities, is offered. There is a well-appointed sitting room in which to relax, and local produce appears on the breakfast menu. Should you wish to eat in after a long day out, you are welcome to use the breakfast room which is suitably equipped. Secure storage for bikes is available.

Rooms: 7 rms (4 en suite) (1 fmly) **S** fr £35 **D** fr £70* **Facilities:** FTV Lounge tea/coffee WiFi ☖ Drying room for boots and coats **Extras:** Bottled water – complimentary **Parking:** 2

PAIGNTON   Map 3 SX86

Devon House Guest House

★★★★ GUEST HOUSE

tel: 01803 528080 & 07777 642340 **20 Garfield Road TQ4 6AX**
email: dhgh@btconnect.com web: www.devonhouseguesthouse.co.uk
dir: *In Paignton follow signs to seafront and Esplanade Road. Into Torbay Road, then Garfield Road.*

Devon House has been lovingly restored and is conveniently located to explore Paignton and its surrounding areas. All bedrooms offer comfortable beds and a range of facilities to meet the needs of a varied clientele, including families. Freshly cooked breakfasts are served in the attractive dining room on the ground floor.

Rooms: 8 en suite (2 fmly) **Facilities:** FTV tea/coffee WiFi

Two Beaches

★★★★ ♨ GUEST ACCOMMODATION

tel: 01803 522164 & 07787 517421 **27 St Andrews Road TQ4 6HA**
email: stay@twobeaches.co.uk **web:** www.twobeaches.co.uk
dir: *A380 onto A3022 signed Paignton seafront, Apollo complex on left. At end of road, turn right at roundabout, St Andrews Road 2nd on left. Two Beaches 400 yards on left.*

Quietly located in a residential area, this is an ideal base from which to explore the many delights of Paignton, Brixham and Torquay. A warm welcome is assured and there is always help on hand for suggestions for local days out. Bedrooms provide impressive levels of comfort with all the essentials required for a relaxing stay. Breakfast is a real treat with quality produce ensuring a tasty and satisfying start to the day. Additional facilities include a guest lounge, honesty bar and lovely garden. Private parking is available for all guests.

Rooms: 7 en suite (2 GF) **S** fr £50 **D** fr £90* **Facilities:** FTV Lounge TVL tea/coffee Licensed WiFi **Parking:** 7 **Notes:** No children 8 years Closed December to February

Beaches

★★★★ BED AND BREAKFAST

tel: 01803 665448 & 07854 940747 **9 Manor Road TQ3 2HT**
email: mikemitchell21@hotmail.com **web:** www.beachesbandb.co.uk
dir: *From A38 follow signs to Torquay, then Paignton, then Preston. Take one-way system at seafront, right into Manor Road.*

Situated just a few hundred metres from Paignton's seafront, this bed and breakfast offers bright, spacious, well-equipped rooms with comfortable beds. Breakfast is served in the light, airy breakfast rooms and guests have use of complimentary WiFi, a well-appointed guest lounge and free off-road parking.

Rooms: 6 en suite (2 fmly) **Facilities:** FTV TVL tea/coffee WiFi ♨ **Extras:** Speciality toiletries **Parking:** 4 **Notes:** LB RS October to January weekends only

Lazy Days

★★★★ ♨ GUEST ACCOMMODATION

tel: 01803 520854 & 07787 438172 **10 Queens Road TQ4 6AT**
email: irenewolf777@gmail.com **web:** www.lazydaysguesthousepaignton.co.uk
dir: *M5 junction 31, A38 then A380 to Torquay. After Newton Abbot, Torquay and Paignton signs follow Paignton seafront signs. Right after Vue cinema into Adelphi Road, left into Queens Road.*

Handily placed for access to the seafront and the town, this establishment is an ideal base exploring the area or venturing further afield to enjoy the delights of south Devon. A warm welcome is assured, and help is always on hand for planning day trips or finding the best places to eat locally. All bedrooms provide impressive levels of quality and comfort, with snuggly beds ensuring a peaceful night's sleep; bathrooms are modern and well appointed. Additional facilities include a lounge and a galley area where guests can make drinks and prepare light snacks if required. Breakfast is a treat, with a range of tasty options available.

Rooms: 6 rms (5 en suite) (1 pri facs) **S** fr £50 **D** fr £66 **Facilities:** FTV TVL tea/coffee WiFi **Extras:** Bottled water, sweets, fresh milk, microwave **Parking:** 2 **Notes:** No children 14 years Closed November to February

The Clydesdale

★★★★ GUEST HOUSE

tel: 01803 558402 & 07939 147013 **5 Polsham Park TQ3 2AD**
email: theclydesdale@hotmail.co.uk **web:** www.theclydesdale.co.uk
dir: *Exit A3022 (Torquay Road) into Lower Polsham Road, 2nd right into Polsham Park.*

Tucked away in a quiet residential area, this is an ideal location from which to explore the varied attractions of Paignton and the wider Torbay area. The welcome is warm and genuine, with every effort made to ensure a relaxed and rewarding stay. The bedrooms are well appointed and provide all the expected modern comforts. Breakfast is served in the dining room; a separate guest lounge is also available.

Rooms: 7 en suite (1 fmly) (2 GF) **Facilities:** FTV TVL tea/coffee WiFi ♨ **Parking:** 5 **Notes:** LB No children 3 years Closed Christmas and New Year RS November to February open by prior arrangement

Merritt House Bed & Breakfast

★★★★ ♨ GUEST ACCOMMODATION

tel: 01803 528959 **7 Queens Road TQ4 6AT**
email: bookings@merritthouse.co.uk **web:** www.merritthouse.co.uk
dir: *From Paignton seafront, right into Torbay Road, 1st left into Queens Road, house on right opposite Queens Hotel.*

Handily located for the town centre and the lovely beach, this is an ideal choice if exploring this popular holiday area. A warm welcome is assured along with a slice of cake, the perfect way to start a relaxing break. Bedrooms, including ground-floor rooms, provide good levels of comfort. Breakfast is a real treat, with a range of tantalising options on offer. Off-road parking is available.

Rooms: 7 en suite (3 GF) **Facilities:** FTV DVD tea/coffee WiFi ♨ **Parking:** 4 **Notes:** LB No children 12 years

PLYMOUTH   Map 3 SX45

Jewell's

★★★★ GUEST ACCOMMODATION

tel: 01752 254760 **220 Citadel Road, The Hoe PL1 3BB**
email: jewellsguest@btconnect.com **web:** www.jewellsguesthouse.com
dir: *A38 towards city centre, follow sign for The Barbican, then The Hoe. Left at lights, right at top of road into Citadel Road. Jewell's 0.25 mile.*

This smart, comfortable, family-run establishment is only a short walk from The Hoe and is convenient for the city centre, the Citadel and the Barbican. Bedrooms come with a wide range of extra facilities, and breakfast is served in the pleasant dining room. Some secure parking is available.

Rooms: 10 rms (7 en suite) (1 fmly) (1 GF) **Facilities:** FTV tea/coffee WiFi **Notes:** LB

PLYMOUTH *continued*

Rainbow Lodge Guest House

★★★★ GUEST HOUSE

tel: 01752 229699 & 07584 472723 **29 Athenaeum Street, The Hoe PL1 2RQ**
email: stay@rainbowlodgeplymouth.co.uk **web:** www.rainbowlodgeplymouth.co.uk
dir: *A38 onto A374. Follow City Centre signs for 3 miles. Bear left into Breton Side at lights, follow road, left into Athenaeum Street at Walrus pub.*

Located in a peaceful area of Plymouth, Rainbow Lodge Guest House is within easy walking distance of the town centre, The Barbican and the harbour. The service here is noteworthy and all guests' needs are catered for. All the guest bedrooms are en suite and provide a comfortable night's sleep. Free WiFi is available, and a full English breakfast is offered daily in the delightful breakfast room.

Rooms: 10 rms (6 en suite) (1 pri facs) (2 fmly) (1 GF) **Facilities:** FTV tea/coffee WiFi **Notes:** No children 5 years Closed 21 December to 1 January

The Firs Bed & Breakfast

★★★ BED AND BREAKFAST

tel: 01752 262870 & 300010 **13 Pier Street, West Hoe PL1 3BS**
email: thefirsguesthouseinplymouthdevon@hotmail.com
web: www.thefirsinplymouth.co.uk
dir: *A374 into city centre, follow signs to The Hoe. Continue on Hoe Road, with sea on left, 1st right at mini roundabout into Pier Street.*

A well located and well established house on the West Hoe with convenient on-street parking. Friendly owners and comfortable rooms make it a popular destination. Dogs are permitted in bedrooms by prior arrangement.

Rooms: 7 rms (3 en suite) (2 fmly) **Facilities:** FTV tea/coffee Dinner available WiFi ⚓ Fishing trips can be arranged **Notes:** LB

The Lamplighter

★★★ GUEST ACCOMMODATION

tel: 01752 663855 **103 Citadel Road, The Hoe PL1 2RN**
email: stay@lamplighterplymouth.co.uk **web:** www.lamplighterplymouth.co.uk
dir: *Near war memorial.*

With easy access to The Hoe, The Barbican and the city centre, this comfortable house provides a good base for leisure or business guests. Bedrooms, including family rooms, are light and airy and furnished to a consistent standard. Breakfast is served in the dining room which has an adjoining lounge area.

Rooms: 9 rms (7 en suite) (2 pri facs) (2 fmly) **S** fr £45 **D** fr £65* **Facilities:** FTV TVL tea/coffee WiFi ⚓ **Parking:** 4

SEATON	Map 4 SY29

Mariners

★★★★ ⬛ GUEST ACCOMMODATION

tel: 01297 20560 **East Walk Esplanade EX12 2NP**
email: mariners.hotel@btconnect.com **web:** www.marinershotelseaton.co.uk
dir: *Exit A3052 signed Seaton, Mariners on seafront.*

Located just yards from the beach and cliff paths, this comfortable establishment has a friendly and relaxed atmosphere. Bedrooms, some with sea views, are well equipped, and public rooms are light and airy. The dining room is the venue for enjoyable breakfasts that utilise quality local produce; afternoon teas are also available on the seafront terrace.

Rooms: 5 en suite **D** fr £85* **Facilities:** FTV tea/coffee WiFi ⚓ **Parking:** 5 **Notes:** LB No children 5 years Closed November to February

Beaumont Guest House

★★★★ GUEST HOUSE

tel: 01297 20832 & 07775 713667 **Castle Hill EX12 2QW**
email: beaumont.seaton@btconnect.com **web:** www.beaumont-seaton.co.uk
dir: *In Seaton, from Harbour Road west to Marine Place on seafront. Beaumont Guest House at beginning of Castle Hill.*

Dating back to the days of Victorian splendour, this elegant establishment is just a few steps away from the wonderful beach at Seaton. A warm and genuine welcome awaits, with plenty of helpful local advice always on offer. Bedrooms, including a ground-floor room, have great sea views and provide all the expected modern comforts. Breakfast, served in the attractive dining room, provides a tasty start to the day.

Rooms: 5 en suite (1 fmly) (1 GF) **S** fr £65 **D** fr £85* **Facilities:** FTV tea/coffee WiFi **Parking:** 6 **Notes:** LB Closed Christmas and New Year

SHALDON

See Teignmouth

SIDMOUTH	Map 3 SY18

Premier Collection

The Salty Monk

★★★★★ ◉◉ ⬛ RESTAURANT WITH ROOMS

tel: 01395 513174 **Church Street, Sidford EX10 9QP**
email: info@saltymonk.com **web:** www.saltymonk.co.uk
dir: *On A3052 opposite church in Sidford village.*

Set in the village of Sidford, this attractive property dates from the 16th century. There's plenty of style and appeal here and each bedroom has a unique identity. Bathrooms are equally special with multi-jet showers, spa baths and cosseting robes and towels. The output from the kitchen is impressive with excellent local produce very much in evidence, served in the elegant surroundings of the restaurant. A mini-spa facility is available.

Rooms: 5 en suite 2 annexe en suite (4 GF) **S** fr £85 **D** fr £135* **Facilities:** FTV Lounge tea/coffee Dinner available WiFi Sauna Gym ⚓ Outdoor hot tub, massage therapists **Extras:** Speciality toiletries, robes, bottled water, snacks, magazines – complimentary **Parking:** 20 **Notes:** LB Closed 1 week November and January

Mincombe Barn Bed & Breakfast

★★★★ ⬛ BED AND BREAKFAST

tel: 01395 597858 & 07753 747941 **Roncombe Lane, Sidbury EX10 0QN**
email: mincombebarn@outlook.com **web:** www.mincombebarn.com
dir: *North of Sidmouth on A375, through Sidbury, right to Roncombe (1.5 miles).*

Set in 20 acres of peaceful pasture and woodland, Mincombe Barn is midway between Honiton and Sidmouth, within the East Devon Area of Outstanding Natural Beauty, a UNESCO World Heritage Site, with the Blackdown Hills just to the north. Each bedroom is individually designed to be elegant, comfortable and practical; all rooms can be made to be either a twin or double. Breakfast feature ingredients sourced locally along with fresh eggs laid daily on site.

Rooms: 3 en suite (3 GF) **D** fr £110* **Facilities:** FTV Lounge tea/coffee WiFi ⬦ ⚓ **Extras:** Home-made biscuits, fridge, robes, slippers **Parking:** 8 **Notes:** LB

The Old Farmhouse

★★★★ GUEST ACCOMMODATION

tel: 01395 512284 **Hillside Road EX10 8JG**
web: www.theoldfarmhousesidmouth.co.uk
dir: *A3052 from Exeter to Sidmouth, right at Bowd crossroads, 2 miles left at roundabout, left at mini roundabout, next right, over hump-back bridge, bear right at corner.*

This beautiful 16th-century thatched farmhouse, in a quiet residential area just a stroll from the Esplanade and shops, has been lovingly restored. Bedrooms are attractively decorated, and the charming public rooms feature beams and an inglenook fireplace. The welcoming proprietors provide memorable dinners (by prior arrangement) using traditional recipes and fresh, local ingredients.

Rooms: 3 en suite 2 annexe en suite **D** fr £80* **Facilities:** FTV Lounge TVL tea/coffee Dinner available WiFi ♿ **Extras:** Speciality toiletries **Parking:** 4 **Notes:** LB No children 12 years Closed November to March

Glendevon

★★★★ GUEST ACCOMMODATION

tel: 01395 514028 & 07960 052475 **Cotmaton Road EX10 8QX**
email: enquiries@glendevonsidmouth.co.uk web: www.glendevonsidmouth.co.uk
dir: *A3052 onto B3176 to mini roundabout. Right, house 100 yards on right.*

Located in a quiet residential area just a short walk from the town centre and beaches, this stylish Victorian house offers neat, comfortable bedrooms. Guests are assured of a warm welcome from the resident owners.

Rooms: 8 en suite **S** fr £44 **D** fr £88* **Facilities:** FTV DVD TVL tea/coffee WiFi ♿ **Notes:** No children 10 years

---

SOURTON   Map 3 SX59

Collaven Manor

★★★★ ♟ ⬤ GUEST ACCOMMODATION

tel: 01837 861522 **EX20 4HH**
email: collavenmanor@gmail.com web: www.collavenmanor.co.uk
dir: *A30 onto A386 to Tavistock, 2 miles on right.*

This delightful 15th-century manor house is quietly located in five acres of well-tended grounds. The friendly proprietors provide attentive service and ensure a relaxing environment. The charming public rooms, with old oak beams and granite fireplaces, provide a range of comfortable lounges and a well-stocked bar. In the restaurant, a daily-changing menu offers interesting dishes.

Rooms: 7 en suite (1 fmly) **S** fr £89 **D** fr £108* **Facilities:** FTV Lounge tea/coffee Dinner available Direct dial Licensed WiFi ⛳ Bowls **Conf:** Max 14 Thtr 14 Class 14 Board 14 **Parking:** 50 **Notes:** LB Closed December to January

---

SOUTH BRENT   Map 3 SX66

Woodland Barton Farm

★★★ FARMHOUSE

tel: 01364 73460 & 07837 928588 **Avonwick TQ10 9EZ**
email: christine@woodlandbartonfarm.co.uk web: www.woodlandbartonfarm.co.uk
dir: *Exit A38 at Marleyhead junction, follow signs for South Brent, then signs for Avonwick. At Avon Inn turn right, 0.5 miles on right.*

Situated on the outskirts of Avonwick, this family farmhouse is the perfect choice for those wanting a base from which to explore the many attractions of south Devon. The welcome is warm and genuine with every effort made to ensure a relaxing and rewarding stay. Bedrooms offer good levels of comfort and have views over the farm and surrounding countryside; families can be accommodated. Breakfast, served in the dining room, includes fresh eggs from the resident hens.

Rooms: 2 en suite (1 fmly) **S** fr £40 **D** fr £80* **Facilities:** FTV DVD TVL tea/coffee WiFi **Parking:** 3 **Notes:** LB 400 acres beef/sheep

---

SOUTH MOLTON   Map 3 SS72

Sampson Barton Guest House

★★★★ ⬤ GUEST HOUSE

tel: 01769 572466 **Kings Nympton EX37 9TG**
email: mail@sampsonbarton.co.uk web: www.sampsonbarton.co.uk
dir: *From South Molton follow signs for George Nympton and Kings Nympton. Through George Nympton, down hill, over bridge, 1st right into lane signed Sampson and Sletchcott. Up hill, 0.75 mile on left.*

Dating back some 400 years, this charming former farmhouse is the perfect place to relax. A reviving cup of tea on arrival in front of the warming wood-burner sets the scene, with helpful local information always on hand. Bedrooms offer good levels of comfort, likewise the contemporary bathrooms. Dinner is a treat, with wonderful local produce on offer. Breakfast is also impressive and eggs are supplied by the resident hens. A stroll around the wonderful gardens is a must; find a peaceful vantage point and gaze over the rolling Devon countryside.

Rooms: 5 en suite (1 fmly) **S** fr £60 **D** fr £86* **Facilities:** FTV TVL tea/coffee Dinner available Licensed WiFi 🔥 **Extras:** Speciality toiletries – complimentary **Parking:** 6 **Notes:** LB Closed December to January

---

The Coaching Inn

★★★ INN

tel: 01769 572526 **Queen Street EX36 3BJ**
email: jayne.coach@googlemail.com web: www.thecoaching-inn.co.uk
dir: *In town centre.*

This long-established former coaching inn has been providing a warm welcome to weary travellers for many years. Situated in the heart of this bustling town, guests are assured of a relaxing stay in a genuine, family-friendly atmosphere. Bedrooms provide good levels of comfort. An extensive menu is provided with an emphasis on quality and value for money.

Rooms: 10 en suite (2 fmly) **S** fr £38 **D** fr £70* **Facilities:** FTV tea/coffee Dinner available WiFi 🔥 **Conf:** Max 100 Thtr 80 Class 50 Board 60 **Parking:** 40

SOUTH POOL
Map 3 SX74

The Millbrook Loft

★★★★ ⬡ INN

tel: 01548 531581 & 07967 046770 **The Millbrook Inn TQ7 2RW**
email: info@millbrookinnsouthpool.co.uk **web:** www.millbrookinnsouthpool.co.uk
dir: *Phone for directions.*

The fortunate folks who live in the idyllic South Hams village of South Pool are justifiably very proud of their local, The Millbrook Inn — a 'proper' local, unpretentious and charming. Low beams and stone floors add to the character and the good-natured chatter creates an engaging atmosphere. The food shouldn't be missed here — the top-notch, local produce is cooked with passion and precision resulting in flavoursome dishes. There's just one bedroom, The Millbrook Loft, which offers impressive levels of quality, style and comfort; it can be used as a self-catering unit or on a bed and breakfast basis; a continental breakfast is delivered to the room.

Rooms: 1 en suite **S** fr £135 **D** fr £150* **Facilities:** FTV TVL tea/coffee Dinner available WiFi **Notes:** LB No children over 2 years

SOUTH ZEAL
Map 3 SX69

The Oxenham Arms and Restaurant

★★★★ ⊛ INN

tel: 01837 840244 **EX20 2JT**
email: lyn@theoxenhamarms.com **web:** www.theoxenhamarms.com
dir: *From A30, follow signs for A382 Moreton Hampstead/Winkleigh/Torrington. Over mini roundabout towards South Zeal, after 2 miles, right into village, opposite village shop and post office.*

Dating back to the 12th century, there is a tangible sense of the past at this fascinating inn. Still very much the village local, it was first licensed in 1477 and boasts a standing stone dating back some 5,000 years. Today, the inn blends contemporary styling with historic features. Bedrooms have plenty of character and no two are alike; a number of the rooms have four-posters. The stylish restaurant offers accomplished cuisine with a range of dishes that make good use of high quality, local produce. In summer, meals can be taken in the extensive garden that has stunning views of Dartmoor.

Rooms: 7 en suite (4 fmly) **S** fr £108 **D** fr £108 **Facilities:** FTV DVD Lounge TVL tea/coffee Dinner available WiFi ⬡ ⅃ Fishing Riding **⬡** Free loan of bicycles **Extras:** Bottled water, cookies — complimentary **Conf:** Max 50 Thtr 30 Class 25 Board 40 **Parking:** 7 **Notes:** LB

STRETE
See Dartmouth

TAVISTOCK
Map 3 SX37

Premier Collection

Tor Cottage

★★★★★ ⬡ GUEST ACCOMMODATION

tel: 01822 860248 **PL16 0JE**
email: info@torcottage.co.uk **web:** www.torcottage.co.uk

(For full entry see Chillaton)

TEDBURN ST MARY
Map 3 SX89

Premier Collection

Frogmill Bed & Breakfast

★★★★★ ⬡ BED AND BREAKFAST

tel: 01647 272727 & 24088 **EX6 6ES**
email: frogmillbandb@btinternet.com **web:** www.frogmillbandb.co.uk
dir: *From A30 take exit signed Cheriton Bishop. Take Tedburn road, then left towards Crediton. After 1 mile left to Froggy Mill, 1 mile on left.*

Situated in the heart of Devon, this former mill house is as picturesque as can be, complete with thatch and a babbling brook. The grounds are spectacular, with around 10 acres of woodland and pasture. The welcome is just as impressive; a cream tea in the garden is offered on arrival. The comfortable bedrooms offer quality and individuality and include a separate, self-contained suite away from the main building; the bathrooms have soft towels and invigorating showers. Food is a real treat here — the eggs for breakfast are provided by the resident hens. In addition to the elegant dining room, a lounge, with deep leather sofas and a wood-burner, is provided.

Rooms: 2 en suite 1 annexe en suite (1 fmly) (1 GF) **S** fr £70 **D** fr £80* **Facilities:** FTV iPod docking station Lounge tea/coffee WiFi **⬡ Extras:** Fruit, chocolates — complimentary; robes **Parking:** 6

TEIGNMOUTH
Map 3 SX97

Potters Mooring

★★★★ GUEST ACCOMMODATION

tel: 01626 873225 **30 The Green, Shaldon TQ14 0DN**
email: info@pottersmooring.co.uk **web:** www.pottersmooring.co.uk
dir: *A38 onto A380 signed Torquay, B3192 to Teignmouth and Shaldon, over river, follow signs to Potters Mooring.*

A former sea captain's residence dating from 1625, Potters Mooring has been appointed to provide charming accommodation of a very high standard, including a four-poster room. The friendly proprietors make every effort to ensure an enjoyable stay, and the Captain Potter's breakfast features tasty local produce.

Rooms: 9 en suite

TIVERTON
Map 3 SS91

Premier Collection

Fernside Bed and Breakfast

★★★★★ ⬡ BED AND BREAKFAST

tel: 01884 860025 & 07885 192331 **Fernside Cottage, Templeton EX16 8BP**
email: ianthorington@hotmail.co.uk
web: www.fernsidecottage-bed-and-breakfast.co.uk
dir: *M5 junction 27, A361 signed Barnstaple. In approximately 12 miles at Stonelands Cross left signed Rackenford and Templeton. Left at T-junction signed Templeton. 2nd right. In Templeton Bridge at T-junction right signed Witheridge. B&B up hill on right.*

This charming thatched cottage is within easy reach of Tiverton and the M5, and sits in rolling countryside, a haven of peace and tranquillity. Expect high quality bedrooms with wonderful beds, smart bathrooms, Aga-cooked breakfasts and a really warm welcome from two very caring hosts.

Rooms: 2 en suite **Facilities:** FTV iPod docking station Lounge tea/coffee WiFi **⬡ Extras:** Speciality toiletries, robes, slippers, home-made biscuits, bottled water, chocolates, guest fridge **Parking:** 3 **Notes:** No children 18 years

TORBAY

See Brixham, Paignton and Torquay

TORQUAY

Map 3 SX96

Premier Collection

Cary Arms & Spa

★★★★★ ⊛ INN

tel: 01803 327110 **Babbacombe Beach TQ1 3LX**
email: enquiries@caryarms.co.uk **web:** www.caryarms.co.uk
dir: *A380 at Ashcombe Cross onto B3192 to Teignmouth. Right at lights to Torquay on A379, left at lights to Babbacombe. Left into Babbacombe Downs Road, left into Beach Road.*

Located on the water's edge at Babbacombe, this seaside retreat is very well appointed; the rooms have sea views and nearly all have terraces or balconies. Bedrooms and bathrooms are fitted to a high standard with many thoughtful extras and unique touches to make a stay memorable. This is a popular dining venue whether eating inside, or on the terraces that lead down to the water's edge. In summer there's a barbecue and wood-fired oven. The dedicated staff will assist in planning your day, or simply share local knowledge.

Rooms: 8 en suite 10 annexe en suite (4 fmly) (3 GF) **Facilities:** FTV Lounge tea/coffee Dinner available WiFi ⚓ Fishing Sauna Gym Spa, treatment rooms **Extras:** Speciality toiletries, sloe gin, confectionery **Conf:** Max 24 Thtr 24 Class 24 Board 24 **Parking:** 15 **Notes:** LB Civ wed 42

Premier Collection

Kingston House

★★★★★ ⊜ GUEST ACCOMMODATION

tel: 01803 212760 **75 Avenue Road TQ2 5LL**
email: stay@kingstonhousetorquay.co.uk **web:** www.kingstonhousetorquay.co.uk
dir: *From A3022 to Torquay, turn right at Torre Station down Avenue Road, Kingston House approximately 0.4 mile on left.*

Dating from around 1870, this elegant Victorian house, just a short stroll from the seafront, is well positioned for those visiting the area on business or leisure. There is always plenty of helpful advice and information readily available. Tea and cakes are served on arrival in the inviting guest lounge, an ideal way to start a relaxing break. Bedrooms offer impressive quality with wonderfully comfortable beds; likewise bathrooms come equipped with cosseting towels and robes. Breakfast offers a number of tasty options and is served in the well-appointed dining room.

Rooms: 5 en suite **S** fr £85 **D** fr £85* **Facilities:** FTV iPod docking station TVL tea/coffee WiFi **Extras:** Speciality toiletries, chocolates, home-made cakes, bottled water **Parking:** 5 **Notes:** No children 16 years Closed December to February

Premier Collection

The Marstan

★★★★★ ⊜ GUEST HOUSE

tel: 01803 292837 **Meadfoot Sea Road TQ1 2LQ**
email: enquiries@marstanhotel.co.uk **web:** www.marstanhotel.co.uk
dir: *A3022 to seafront, left onto A379 (Torbay Road and Babbacombe Road), right into Meadfoot Road, The Marstan on right.*

This elegant, mid 19th-century villa provides high levels of comfort and quality throughout. The hospitality and service are excellent, and every effort is made to

create a relaxed atmosphere. Public areas include an impressive dining room, a bar and a comfortable lounge. Outside, guests can enjoy a heated swimming pool and hot tub in the secluded garden.

Rooms: 9 en suite (1 fmly) (2 GF) **Facilities:** FTV iPod docking station Lounge tea/coffee Direct dial Licensed WiFi ⚓ Hot tub **Parking:** 8 **Notes:** LB

AA UNIQUE B&B OF THE YEAR 2018–19

Premier Collection

The 25 Boutique B&B

★★★★★ ⊜ BED AND BREAKFAST

tel: 01803 297517 **25 Avenue Road TQ2 5LB**
email: stay@the25.uk **web:** www.the25.uk
dir: *A3022 into Torquay, pass railway station and into Avenue Road. Just past lights.*

The 25 Boutique B&B is located within easy walking distance of Torquay's Abbey Sands beach, town centre and harbour. A warm and friendly atmosphere, attention to detail and attentive yet unobtrusive service is on offer from the proprietors. The six individually designed bedrooms and suites are named after local beaches – all have modern en suites, free WiFi and fridges with fresh milk and bottled water. The decor combines the latest trends with a classic twist to highlight the period features. A full English breakfast is served in the light and contemporary breakfast room. Off-street parking is available.

Rooms: 6 en suite **S** fr £99 **D** fr £125* **Facilities:** FTV DVD iPod docking station Lounge tea/coffee Licensed WiFi 🛁 **Extras:** Speciality toiletries, home-made biscuits, robes, slippers, Nespresso machine, fresh milk, sweets, iPad **Parking:** 6 **Notes:** LB No children 18 years Closed Christmas and New Year

Premier Collection

The Albaston

★★★★★ ⊜ GUEST ACCOMMODATION

tel: 01803 212100 **27 St Marychurch Road TQ1 3JF**
email: contact@albastonhotel.co.uk **web:** www.albastonhotel.co.uk
dir: *A380 to centre (Riviera Way), left onto B3119. Over 1st roundabout and 2nd double roundabout, right at lights into St Marychurch Road, 0.5 miles on left.*

The Albaston is a detached Victorian residence offering quality guest accommodation, suitable for either business or leisure guests. Located in the heart of Torquay, it's an ideal base for exploring the English Riviera – the town centre, harbour and beach are within walking distance, as is Babbacombe Bay. The Albaston is also close to the International Language Schools. On offer are a guest lounge, private south-facing Japanese-style decking area and Oscars bar serving local beers, lager and wine. Freshly cooked breakfasts, using locally sourced ingredients, are served in the dining room. CCTV-monitored parking and unrestricted on-street parking are available.

Rooms: 9 en suite **D** fr £75* **Facilities:** FTV DVD Lounge TVL tea/coffee Licensed WiFi **Parking:** 6 **Notes:** No children 14 years

TORQUAY *continued*

Premier Collection

Babbacombe Bay

★★★★★ GUEST ACCOMMODATION

tel: 01803 323509 **33-35 Babbacombe Downs Road TQ1 3LN**
email: reception@babbacombebayhotel.co.uk **web:** www.babbacombebayhotel.co.uk
dir: *Phone for directions.*

Ideally located in the centre of Babbacombe Downs with splendid views across Lyme Bay and beyond, this luxury accommodation has been refurbished to very high standards. Bedrooms and bathrooms come in a range of shapes and sizes with the larger suites being particularly impressive and having sea views. Guests are welcome to use the comfortable lounge or in warmer months to sit out and enjoy the views from the roof terrace. A good range of hot and cold dishes is provided at breakfast. In addition, a café is available throughout the day and a bistro menu is offered for dinner on Wednesday to Sunday evenings.

Rooms: 10 en suite (2 fmly) **D** fr £100* **Facilities:** FTV Lounge tea/coffee Dinner available Licensed WiFi **Notes:** Closed 20–30 December

Premier Collection

Linden House

★★★★★ GUEST ACCOMMODATION

tel: 01803 212281 & 07715 303951 **31 Bampfylde Road TQ2 5AY**
email: cmpw53@gmail.com **web:** www.lindenhousetorquay.co.uk
dir: *Phone for directions.*

This grand Victorian house has timeless elegance and charm, and offers impressive levels of contemporary comfort combined with stylish period features. Tea and cake is always available on arrival, along with a friendly welcome and the offer of help with local information and advice. Bedrooms and bathrooms offer high levels of quality with individual styling, and everything necessary to ensure a relaxing and rewarding stay. Spacious public areas include a lovely lounge with views over the garden; and the airy dining room is the venue for the wonderful breakfasts that are guaranteed to get the day off to a tasty and satisfying start.

Rooms: 6 en suite 1 annexe en suite (1 GF) **Facilities:** FTV Lounge tea/coffee WiFi **Extras:** Home-made chocolates, fridge **Parking:** 6 **Notes:** LB No children 16 years Closed 21 December to 6 January

Premier Collection

Tyndale B&B

★★★★★ BED AND BREAKFAST

tel: 01803 380888 **68 Avenue Road TQ2 5LF**
email: tyndaletorquay@btinternet.com **web:** www.tyndaletorquay.com
dir: *A380 onto A3022, follow seafront signs into Avenue Road, on right side of 1st lights.*

A warm and genuine welcome is extended to all guests arriving at Tyndale. The location is very convenient, being within walking distance of the town and beach, and with good off-road parking. Bedrooms offer impressive levels of comfort and quality, likewise the stylish bathrooms, complete with cosseting towels and snuggly robes. Breakfast is a real treat with a number of options to tantalise the taste buds.

Rooms: 4 en suite (1 GF) **S** fr £70 **D** fr £80* **Facilities:** FTV iPod docking station tea/coffee WiFi **Extras:** Speciality toiletries, chocolates, robes, slippers, fridge, bottled water, iPad **Parking:** 7 **Notes:** LB No children 15 years

The Cleveland

★★★★ GUEST ACCOMMODATION

tel: 01803 297522 **7 Cleveland Road TQ2 5BD**
email: info@clevelandbandbtorquay.co.uk **web:** www.clevelandbandbtorquay.co.uk
dir: *A3022 into Torquay, at lights by Torre Station take right fork. 1st left into Cleveland Road, at far end on left.*

Located in a peaceful area of Torquay, this family-run guest accommodation is within easy walking distance of Abbey Sands beach, town centre and harbour. Service is the highlight of any stay, ensuring that all needs and wants are catered for. The seven guest bedrooms are all en suite, and are ideal for a comfortable night's sleep. A south-facing sun terrace and garden are also available for guest use. There is also a fully licensed bar and lounge. Free WiFi and off-street parking are included, with a full English breakfast offered daily within a delightful breakfast room.

Rooms: 7 en suite (2 fmly) (1 GF) **S** fr £39 **D** fr £59 **Facilities:** FTV Lounge tea/coffee Licensed WiFi **Extras:** Bottled water, robes in suites, speciality toiletries, home-made fudge **Parking:** 7

The Downs, Babbacombe

★★★★ GUEST ACCOMMODATION

tel: 01803 328543 **41-43 Babbacombe Downs Road, Babbacombe TQ1 3LN**
email: manager@downshotel.co.uk **web:** www.downshotel.co.uk
dir: *From Torquay A379 to Babbacombe. Left into Princes Street. Left into Babbacombe Downs Road, 20 metres on left.*

Built in the 1850s, this elegant building forms part of a seafront terrace with direct access to the promenade and Babbacombe Downs. The warm welcome is matched by attentive service, with every effort made to ensure a rewarding and relaxing stay. Bedrooms offer impressive levels of comfort and most have spectacular views across Lyme Bay with balconies being an added bonus. For guests with limited mobility, assisted access is available to the first floor. Additional facilities include the convivial lounge/bar and spacious restaurant where enjoyable dinners and breakfasts are offered.

Rooms: 12 en suite (4 fmly) **Facilities:** FTV TVL tea/coffee Dinner available Direct dial Licensed WiFi **Parking:** 8 **Notes:** LB

Headland View

★★★★ BED AND BREAKFAST

tel: 01803 312612 **37 Babbacombe Downs Road, Babbacombe TQ1 3LN**
email: reception@headlandview.com **web:** www.headlandview.com
dir: *A379 into Babbacombe, follow signs for seafront. Into Babbacombe Downs Road.*

With a Victorian heritage, this elegant establishment in Babbacombe looks out over the stunning expanse of Lyme Bay. Many period features have been retained which add a sense of history and charm. Bedrooms are furnished for comfort with thoughtful extras and sumptuous beds; four rooms also have balconies offering spectacular sea views. Every effort is made to ensure a relaxed and rewarding stay, with many guests returning several times a year to de-stress and unwind. Breakfast features daily specials alongside the ever-popular and indulgent, traditional English offering. Off-road parking is available.

Rooms: 6 rms (4 en suite) (2 pri facs) **S** fr £60 **D** fr £70* **Facilities:** FTV iPod docking station Lounge tea/coffee WiFi **Parking:** 4 **Notes:** No children 13 years

Orestone Manor

★★★★ ◉◉ ☖ RESTAURANT WITH ROOMS

tel: 01803 328098 **Rockhouse Lane, Maidencombe TQ1 4SX**
email: info@orestonemanor.com **web:** www.orestonemanor.com
dir: *North of Torquay on A379, on sharp bend in village of Maidencombe.*

Set in a fabulous location overlooking the bay, Orestone Manor has a long history of providing fine food and very comfortable accommodation, coupled with friendly, attentive service. Log fires burn in cooler months, and there is a conservatory, a bar and a sitting room for guests to enjoy. AA Rosettes have been awarded for the uncomplicated modern cuisine which is based on quality local produce.

Rooms: 11 en suite 3 annexe en suite (6 fmly) (3 GF) **S** fr £95 **D** fr £110*
Facilities: STV FTV iPod docking station Lounge tea/coffee Dinner available Direct dial WiFi ☖ **Extras:** Speciality toiletries, robes, bottled water **Conf:** Max 90 Thtr 90 Class 60 Board 30 **Parking:** 38 **Notes:** LB Closed 3–29 January

Garway Lodge Guest House

★★★★ ☖ GUEST HOUSE

tel: 01803 293126 & 07711552878 **79 Avenue Road TQ2 5LL**
email: info@garwaylodge.co.uk **web:** www.garwaylodge.co.uk
dir: *On A3022, 100 metres past Torre Station on left.*

Garway Lodge is in the heart of Torquay and offers accommodation exclusively for adults. The bedrooms are spacious and stylish and include a ground-floor room. Business guests are particularly welcomed and there is free on-site parking and free WiFi. Residents have use of a small honesty bar, and an extensive breakfast menu is offered. The seafront and harbourside restaurants are a level walk away.

Rooms: 6 en suite (1 GF) **S** fr £35 **D** fr £68* **Facilities:** FTV DVD iPod docking station tea/coffee Licensed WiFi ☖ **Extras:** Speciality toiletries, honesty bar **Parking:** 6 **Notes:** LB No children

Kelvin House

★★★★ GUEST ACCOMMODATION

tel: 01803 209093 **46 Bampfylde Road TQ2 5AY**
email: kelvinhousehotel@hotmail.com **web:** www.kelvinhousehotel.co.uk
dir: *M5 junction 31, A380, A3032 (Newton Road) into Torquay. At lights at Torre Station right into Avenue Road. Bampfylde Road on left.*

This attractive Victorian house was built in the 1880s and sits on a lovely tree-lined road. It is a family-run property with a relaxed, friendly home-from-home atmosphere. All bedrooms are en suite and have been appointed to a high standard with many extras. A large elegant sitting room is available for guests, and hearty breakfasts are served in the dining room, or on the patio in good weather. Close to good transport links, it makes an ideal base for touring the Torquay Riviera.

Rooms: 8 en suite (1 fmly) (2 GF) **Facilities:** FTV TVL tea/coffee Licensed WiFi **Parking:** 6 **Notes:** LB No children 12 years

Kingsholm

★★★★ GUEST ACCOMMODATION

tel: 01803 297794 **539 Babbacombe Road TQ1 1HQ**
email: thekingsholm@virginmedia.com **web:** www.kingsholmhotel.co.uk
dir: *From A3022 left onto Torquay seafront, left at clock tower roundabout, Kingsholm 400 metres on left.*

An elegant, personally-run establishment situated in a conservation area, only 350 metres from the bustling harbour, this fine Edwardian house offers excellent accommodation that is appointed to a high standard; many rooms overlook Torwood Gardens. All bedrooms have Freeview TV, free WiFi, hairdryers and hospitality trays. There is also a guest lounge, a spacious dining room with separate tables and a licensed bar. Parking is free. Owners June and Carl offer a friendly welcome.

Rooms: 9 en suite **S** fr £40 **D** fr £60* **Facilities:** FTV TVL tea/coffee Licensed WiFi **Parking:** 9 **Notes:** No children 10 years Closed 17 November to 1 March

Peppers

★★★★ GUEST ACCOMMODATION

tel: 01803 293856 **551 Babbacombe Road TQ1 1HQ**
email: enquiries@hotel-peppers.co.uk **web:** www.hotel-peppers.co.uk
dir: *A3022 to seafront, left onto B3199 towards harbour. At clock tower roundabout, turn left, 250 metres on left.*

Dating back to the Edwardian era, Peppers has much to offer and is conveniently located just a short walk from the harbour. Hospitality is assured with every effort made to ensure a relaxing and rewarding stay. Bedrooms are elegantly appointed and all provide impressive levels of quality and comfort. Additional facilities include a spacious guest lounge and intimate bar. The contemporary dining room is the venue for tasty breakfasts with a generous choice on offer. At the rear of the property, a sun terrace leads to the car park.

Rooms: 10 rms (9 en suite) (1 pri facs) **S** fr £40 **D** fr £60* **Facilities:** FTV TVL tea/coffee Licensed WiFi **Extras:** Bottled water – complimentary **Parking:** 9 **Notes:** LB No children 10 years Closed 18 December to 18 January

The Robin Hill

★★★★ GUEST ACCOMMODATION

tel: 01803 214518 & 07940 559925 **74 Braddons Hill Road East TQ1 1HF**
email: reservations@therobinhill.co.uk **web:** www.robinhillhotel.co.uk
dir: *From A38 to seafront then left to Babbacombe. Pass theatre to Clock Tower roundabout, take 1st exit and through 2 sets of lights, Braddons Hill Road East on left after museum.*

Dating back to 1896, this fascinating building has character in abundance and is located a short stroll from the harbour and shops. Every effort is made to ensure a stay is enjoyable; assistance is readily available at all times. Bedrooms, in varying styles, provide all the expected necessities. Public areas include an inviting lounge, plus a light and airy dining room where breakfast is served.

Rooms: 12 en suite (3 fmly) (1 GF) **S** fr £60 **D** fr £70* **Facilities:** FTV iPod docking station Lounge TVL tea/coffee Licensed WiFi ☖ **Conf:** Max 32 Thtr 32 Class 32 Board 28 **Parking:** 10 **Notes:** LB Closed 20 December to 4 January

TORQUAY *continued*

Aveland House

★★★★ GUEST ACCOMMODATION

tel: 01803 326622 **Aveland Road, Babbacombe TQ1 3PT**
email: avelandhouse@aol.com **web:** www.avelandhouse.co.uk
dir: *A3022 to Torquay, left onto B3199 (Hele Road) into Westhill Road. Then Warbro Road, 2nd left into Aveland Road.*

Set in well-tended gardens in a peaceful area of Babbacombe, close to the South West Coast Path, beaches, shops and attractions, Aveland House is within easy walking distance of Torquay harbour and town. This family-run house offers warm and attentive service. The attractive bedrooms are well equipped, with free WiFi throughout. A pleasant bar and two comfortable TV lounges are available. Hearing-impaired visitors are especially welcome, as both the proprietors are OCSL signers. Evening meals and bar snacks are available by arrangement. Coeliacs and special diets can be catered for.

Rooms: 10 en suite **S** fr £60 **D** fr £88* **Facilities:** Lounge TVL tea/coffee Dinner available Licensed WiFi 🔒 **Parking:** 10 **Notes:** LB No children 12 years Closed 12 December to 6 January RS Sunday no evening meals

Babbacombe Palms

★★★★ GUEST HOUSE

tel: 01803 327087 **2 York Road, Babbacombe TQ1 3SG**
email: babbacombepalms@hotmail.com **web:** www.babbacombepalms.com
dir: *Phone for directions.*

Just a short stroll from the fabulous Babbacombe Downs, this warm and welcoming, family-run establishment provides a perfect base for exploring the local area and many popular attractions. Every effort is made to ensure guests have a relaxed and rewarding stay, and helpful advice about the area is always on offer if required. Bedrooms, including a family room, provide good levels of comfort. Breakfast is a treat with local produce very much to the fore, and is served in the stylish and elegant dining room. Other facilities include a bar and lounge area.

Rooms: 7 en suite **D** fr £55* **Facilities:** tea/coffee Licensed WiFi

Barclay Court Guest House

★★★★ GUEST ACCOMMODATION

tel: 01803 292791 **29 Castle Road TQ1 3BB**
email: enquiries@barclaycourt.co.uk **web:** www.barclaycourtguesthouse.co.uk
dir: *M5 onto A38 then A380 to Torquay. A3022 (Newton Road) left onto Upton Road, right towards Lymington Road. Right to Castle Circus, Castle Road on left.*

The delightful, personally-run Barclay Court is within easy walking distance of Torquay's attractions and offers a friendly, relaxed atmosphere. Individually decorated rooms vary in size, but all are en suite and well equipped. There is a games room on the lower-ground floor and the garden is a quiet retreat, especially in the summer months.

Rooms: 11 en suite (4 fmly) (3 GF) **S** fr £35 **D** fr £60* **Facilities:** FTV tea/coffee WiFi 🔒 **Parking:** 7 **Notes:** Closed November to March (excluding Christmas and New Year)

The Coppice

★★★★ GUEST ACCOMMODATION

tel: 01803 297786 & 211085 **Barrington Road TQ1 2QJ**
email: reservations@coppicehotel.co.uk **web:** www.coppicehotel.co.uk
dir: *From Torquay harbour take A379 (Babbacombe Road) towards Babbacombe. After St Matthias Church (on right) turn left into Barrington Road.*

Friendly and comfortable, The Coppice is a popular choice and occupies a convenient location within walking distance of the beaches and shops. In addition to the indoor and outdoor swimming pools, evening entertainment is often provided in the spacious bar. Bedrooms are bright and airy with modern amenities.

Rooms: 39 en suite (10 fmly) (28 GF) **S** fr £35 **D** fr £70* **Facilities:** FTV Lounge tea/coffee Dinner available Licensed WiFi 🕐 ⚡ ♨ Sauna Gym **Conf:** Max 60 Thtr 60 Class 60 Board 60 **Parking:** 20 **Notes:** LB

The Elmington

★★★★ GUEST ACCOMMODATION

tel: 01803 605192 **St Agnes Lane, Chelston TQ2 6QE**
email: mail@elmington.co.uk **web:** www.elmington.co.uk
dir: *At rear of rail station.*

Set in sub-tropical gardens with views over the bay, this splendid Victorian villa has been lovingly restored. The comfortable bedrooms are brightly decorated and vary in size and style. There is a spacious lounge, bar and dining room. Additional facilities include an outdoor pool and terrace.

Rooms: 19 en suite **Facilities:** FTV Lounge TVL tea/coffee Licensed WiFi ⚡ ♨ ♨ 🔒 **Parking:** 24 **Notes:** LB No children 6 years Closed November to March

Newton House

★★★★ GUEST ACCOMMODATION

tel: 01803 297520 **31 Newton Road TQ2 5DB**
email: newtonhouse_torquay@yahoo.com **web:** www.newtonhouse-tq.co.uk
dir: *From Torre station bear left at lights, Newton House 40 yards on left.*

You are assured of a warm welcome at Newton House, which is close to the town centre and attractions. The comfortable bedrooms, some on the ground floor, have thoughtful extras, and a lounge is available. Breakfast is enjoyed in the pleasant dining room.

Rooms: 9 en suite (3 fmly) (5 GF) **Facilities:** FTV Lounge tea/coffee WiFi 🔒 Drying room **Extras:** Snacks, chocolate, sweets – complimentary **Parking:** 15 **Notes:** LB

The Norwood

★★★★ 🅰 GUEST ACCOMMODATION

tel: 01803 294236 & 07444 741409 **60 Belgrave Road TQ2 5HY**
email: stay@norwoodhoteltorquay.co.uk **web:** www.norwoodhoteltorquay.co.uk
dir: *From Princess Theatre towards Paignton, at 1st lights right into Belgrave Road, over crossroads, 3rd building on left.*

The Norwood is just a short walk from the seafront, town centre and conference centre. All the individually decorated bedrooms are en suite and four-poster rooms are available. There are excellent choices at breakfast, from traditional full English to lighter options, and the hosts are happy to cater for special dietary requests. Packed lunches and takeaway breakfasts are also available.

Rooms: 9 en suite (5 fmly) (1 GF) **S** fr £42 **D** fr £62* **Facilities:** FTV tea/coffee WiFi **Extras:** Speciality toiletries – complimentary **Parking:** 3 **Notes:** LB

TOTNES
Map 3 SX86

Premier Collection

Stoke Gabriel Lodgings - Badgers Retreat

★★★★★ ⊜ BED AND BREAKFAST

tel: 01803 782003 & 07785 710225 **2 Orchard Close, Stoke Gabriel TQ9 6SX**
email: info@stokegabriellodgings.com **web:** www.stokegabriellodgings.com
dir: *In Stoke Gabriel, pass Baptist church, take left fork into Paignton Road.*
100 metres to entrance on left by public bench at top of hill on Orchard Close.

Stoke Gabriel Lodgings is an attractive property of contemporary architecture, positioned high above the River Dart just outside Stoke Gabriel, near Totnes – it was designed to take full advantage of its location. David and Helen offer a warm welcome as well as a delicious Devon cream tea on arrival. The bedrooms are spacious and lavishly furnished with comfortable seating, and the en suites have wet shower areas and heated towel rails. Patio doors open onto a private balcony overlooking the garden and countryside. Outside, the landscaped garden can be enjoyed from the large terrace or conservatory. Breakfast is a delight, and there are many local pubs and restaurants for lunch and dinner.

Rooms: 3 en suite (1 fmly) **S** fr £74.50 **D** fr £99 **Facilities:** STV FTV DVD iPod docking station Lounge TVL tea/coffee WiFi ⏹ ⏻ **Extras:** Speciality toiletries, fruit/snacks, mineral water **Parking:** 6

YARCOMBE
Map 4 ST20

The Belfry at Yarcombe

★★★★ ⊜ BED AND BREAKFAST

tel: 01404 861234 **EX14 9BD**
email: stay@thebelfryatyarcombe.co.uk **web:** www.thebelfrycountryhotel.com
dir: *On A30, in village of Yarcombe opposite church.*

Built in the late 1860s and originally the village school, The Belfry at Yarcombe now offers bright and clean accommodation. Six comfortable en suite rooms are on offer along with a pleasant guest lounge and south-facing terrace, views across the village and valley are a highlight. WiFi and off-street parking are available.

Rooms: 6 en suite (2 GF) **S** fr £60 **D** fr £90 **Facilities:** FTV TVL tea/coffee WiFi ⏻ **Extras:** Speciality toiletries, fresh milk, juice **Parking:** 7 **Notes:** LB No children 10 years

YELVERTON
Map 3 SX56

Tor Royal

★★★★ ⊜ BED AND BREAKFAST

tel: 01822 890189 & 07892 910666 **Princetown PL20 6SL**
email: stay@torroyal.co.uk **web:** www.torroyal.co.uk
dir: *A38 exit at Ashburton, follow signs to Princetown/Two Bridges. Turn right to Princetown and left opposite Country Charm shop, Tor Royal on right.*

This peacefully located Grade II listed former country house is a wonderfully relaxing base from which to explore the picturesque delights of Dartmoor. Parts of the house date back to the 17th century, but modern comforts are now in place, with bedrooms and bathrooms offering high levels of quality and character. Breakfast makes use of excellent local produce, served in the attractive dining room. Guests also have a lovely lounge at their disposal, with an open fire to keep the chill off in cooler months. There is also a large garden.

Rooms: 5 en suite (1 GF) **Facilities:** FTV DVD TVL tea/coffee WiFi ⏻ **Conf:** Max 30 Class 25 Board 20 **Parking:** 10 **Notes:** LB RS Christmas and New Year Civ wed 50

Burrator Inn

★★★★ ⊜ ⏻ INN

tel: 01822 853121 **Dousland PL20 6NP**
email: reservations@theburratorinn.co.uk **web:** www.theburratorinn.com
dir: *From Yelverton on B3212 to Dousland.*

This lively pub is located in the very heart of Dousland, near Yelverton, and has a good local following. The bedrooms are comfortable and equipped with all the expected facilities. A wide range of popular dishes is served all day, and the very cheerful and upbeat staff are ready and willing to meet the needs of their guests. A good selection of wines and local beers is offered. Great for all ages and families.

Rooms: 7 en suite (3 fmly) **Facilities:** FTV DVD tea/coffee Dinner available WiFi **Parking:** 40 **Notes:** Closed 25 December

Overcombe House

★★★★ ⏹ GUEST HOUSE

tel: 01822 853501 **Old Station Road, Horrabridge PL20 7RA**
email: enquiries@overcombehotel.co.uk **web:** www.overcombehotel.co.uk
dir: *Signed 100 yards off A386 at Horrabridge.*

Many guests return on a regular basis to enjoy this delightful, family-run establishment. Genuine hospitality is a great strength, and every effort is taken to ensure an enjoyable and memorable stay. Given its location, this is a perfect base for exploring the rugged beauty of the Dartmoor National Park, just on the doorstep. Bedrooms are neatly presented; many have lovely views across the countryside.

Rooms: 8 en suite (2 GF) **S** fr £72.50 **D** fr £82.50* **Facilities:** FTV DVD tea/coffee Licensed WiFi ⏻ **Parking:** 7 **Notes:** No children 12 years Closed 24 December to 2 January

DORSET

ASKERSWELL
Map 4 SY59

The Spyway Inn

★★★★ ⊜ ⏻ INN

tel: 01308 485250 **DT2 9EP**
email: spywaytim@hotmail.com **web:** www.spyway-inn.co.uk
dir: *From A35 follow Askerswell sign, then follow Spyway Inn sign.*

Peacefully located in the rolling Dorset countryside, this family-run inn offers a warm and genuine welcome. Bedrooms are spacious and well appointed with a number of extras provided, including bath robes. Real ales are on tap in the bar. Menus feature home-cooked food, with many dishes making use of local produce both at dinner and breakfast. The extensive beer garden, with wonderful views, is popular in summer.

Rooms: 3 en suite (1 fmly) **Facilities:** FTV tea/coffee Dinner available WiFi **Extras:** Robes **Parking:** 40 **Notes:** LB

BLANDFORD FORUM
Map 4 ST80

Portman Lodge
★★★★ BED AND BREAKFAST

tel: 01258 453727 **Whitecliff Mill Street DT11 7BP**
email: enquiries@portmanlodge.co.uk **web:** www.portmanlodge.co.uk
dir: *One-way system, follow signs from town centre to Shaftesbury and hospital. On right past Our Lady of Lourdes church (on left).*

A Victorian building once used as a music school, this substantial detached house now provides elegant accommodation and a warm welcome. All bedrooms and bathrooms are well decorated and comfortably furnished. Breakfast utilises good quality ingredients and is served at a communal table.

Rooms: 3 en suite 2 annexe en suite (1 fmly) **S** fr £70 **D** fr £85 **Facilities:** STV tea/coffee WiFi ♨ **Extras:** Speciality toiletries **Parking:** 8 **Notes:** No children 10 years

See advert opposite

BOURNEMOUTH
Map 5 SZ09

Washington House
★★★★ GUEST ACCOMMODATION

tel: 01202 556111 **3 Durley Road BH2 5JQ**
email: info@washingtonhousehotel.com **web:** www.washingtonhousehotel.com
dir: *Phone for directions.*

This Grade II listed Victorian villa has much to offer, not least of which a great location, just a short walk from the seafront and the Bournemouth International Centre. The bedrooms provide individuality, style and comfort, likewise the modern bathrooms. Public areas are equally impressive; the elegant dining room is the venue for breakfast, an extensive continental offering. A guest lounge is also provided, and there is parking available.

Rooms: 13 en suite (2 fmly) (4 GF) **Facilities:** FTV Lounge tea/coffee Licensed WiFi **Parking:** 12

Southern Breeze Lodge
★★★★ ♟ GUEST HOUSE

tel: 01202 427459 & 07806 950168 **20 Southern Road BH6 3SR**
email: enquiries@southernbreezelodge.co.uk **web:** www.southernbreezelodge.co.uk
dir: *From A35, at Pokesdown Station turn opposite into Seabourne Road. After 0.5 mile turn right into Chestnut Avenue. Cross Pine Avenue into Southern Road, 180 yards on left.*

Situated in a quiet location, close to Southbourne's popular shops and cafés, this warm and welcoming establishment provides an excellent base from which to explore the local area. Just a five-minute stroll from the cliff tops overlooking the Blue Flag beach, the views from which are superb, there is also a pathway down to the beach or alternatively the Cliff Lift. Bedrooms are furnished with appealing simplicity – light and airy with a focus on comfy beds. Breakfast is a generous offering with an impressive selection of both hot and cold options, a real taste of Dorset.

Rooms: 6 en suite **S** fr £65 **D** fr £75* **Facilities:** FTV tea/coffee WiFi **Extras:** Mini-fridge **Parking:** 5 **Notes:** LB No children 16 years Closed 6 January to 29 March

Trouville Lodge
★★★ GUEST ACCOMMODATION

tel: 01202 552262 **9 Priory Road BH2 5DF**
email: reception@trouvillehotel.com **web:** www.trouvillehotel.com
dir: *Phone for directions.*

Professionally run, this well-managed establishment offers an impressive standard of accommodation and facilities. The stylishly appointed and comfortably furnished bedrooms are situated in an annexe of the Trouville Hotel next door. Further facilities are to be found in the hotel. The Deauville restaurant offers a very good menu choice, and the well-stocked Le Café Bar provides an informal and pleasant environment. There is also a large pool and sauna as well as a resident beautician.

Rooms: 19 en suite (4 fmly) (4 GF) **Facilities:** FTV tea/coffee Dinner available Licensed WiFi ♨ Sauna Gym Leisure facilities available at Trouville Hotel **Parking:** 14 **Notes:** LB

BRIDPORT
Map 4 SY49

Oxbridge Farm

★★★★ FARMHOUSE

tel: 01308 488368 & 07766 086543 **DT6 3UA**
email: enquiries@oxbridgefarm.co.uk **web:** www.oxbridgefarmbedandbreakfast.co.uk
dir: *From A3066 (Bridport to Beaminster), after passing caravan site on left, take next left to Oxbridge. On left blind bend, in 1 mile.*

Oxbridge Farm sits in the rolling hills of west Dorset in an Area of Outstanding Natural Beauty. The bedrooms are well equipped and offer a very good level of comfort. A hearty breakfast is served in the attractive dining room which benefits from wonderful countryside views.

Rooms: 4 rms (3 en suite) (1 pri facs) (2 fmly) (1 GF) **S** fr £80 **D** fr £110
Facilities: FTV Lounge tea/coffee Dinner available WiFi ⅃ **Parking:** 6 **Notes:** LB
Civ wed 200 40 acres sheep

BROADWINDSOR
Map 4 ST40

Premier Collection

The Old George

★★★★★ ⚲ GUEST ACCOMMODATION

tel: 01308 868434 **The Square DT8 3QD**
email: theoldgeorge@gmail.com **web:** www.theoldgeorge-broadwindsor.co.uk
dir: *Phone for directions.*

Located in the peaceful and quintessentially English village of Broadwindsor, this comfortable, listed Georgian house was converted sympathetically from a pub to a family home 50 years ago, and is an ideal retreat for those seeking peaceful surroundings. King Charles II slept in the adjacent property in 1651. Each of the bedrooms has its own character and the range of thoughtful extras includes fresh flowers, bottled water and magazines. Home-cooked breakfasts are served in the comfortable dining room. A pub offering a selection of evening meals is just a stone's throw away.

Rooms: 3 en suite **Facilities:** FTV DVD TVL tea/coffee WiFi ⅃ ⚿ **Extras:** Speciality toiletries **Parking:** 2 **Notes:** LB

Portman Lodge

Built in 1873, *Portman Lodge* is the main wing and entrance into a large Victorian property, originally part of Lord Portman's estate. It is thought to have been a residence for choristers for St Martin's Church. Many of the original fixtures and fittings remain, in particular the attractive Victorian tiled floor in the entrance hall and corridor.

The individually decorated bedrooms, with twin, double or kingsize beds, are supremely comfortable, with en suite rooms, plentiful hot water, powerful showers and white fluffy towels.

Substantial cooked tasty breakfasts, including a varied range of locally sourced produce, are served around a large table in our lovely dining room.

There is a good choice of pubs and restaurants for lunch and dinner in the beautiful Georgian market town of Blandford, just five minutes' walk away, so no need to get into your car.

Recommended in the area: Kingston Lacy, Lulworth Cove, Jurassic Coast, Corfe Castle, Abbotsbury Swannery and Gardens

Whitecliff Mill Street, Blandford Forum, Dorset DT11 7BP
Tel: 01258 453727
Mobile: 07860 424235 (Gerry) • 07785 971743 (Pat)
Website: www.portmanlodge.co.uk
Email: enquiries@portmanlodge.co.uk

Map 4 SY49

The Anchor Inn

★★★★ 🍷 🍴 INN

tel: 01297 489215 **Seatown DT6 6JU**
email: contact@theanchorinnseatown.co.uk **web:** www.theanchorinnseatown.co.uk
dir: Exit A35 in Chideock into Duck Street, 0.75 mile down lane to sea.

This long-established inn has much to offer, not least because of its superb position, just a few steps away from the sea. There is a simple and rustic nautical style throughout the bars, combined with an engaging and good humoured atmosphere. Bedrooms are spacious with wonderful bathrooms and the added luxury of quality toiletries and cosseting robes. The food is not to be missed, a varied menu with excellent quality local seafood is always on offer. Breakfast also makes use of impressive local produce. Dogs are allowed in the public areas.

Rooms: 3 en suite (2 fmly) **S** fr £115 **D** fr £130* **Facilities:** FTV tea/coffee Dinner available Direct dial WiFi **Extras:** Speciality toiletries, slippers, gowns **Parking:** 8 **Notes:** Closed 24 December to 1 January

CHRISTCHURCH Map 5 SZ19

Premier Collection

The Lord Bute & Restaurant

★★★★★ 🌸🌸 🏅 GUEST ACCOMMODATION

tel: 01425 278884 **179-181 Lymington Road, Highcliffe on Sea BH23 4JS**
email: mail@lordbute.co.uk **web:** www.lordbute.co.uk
dir: A337 towards Highcliffe.

The elegant Lord Bute stands directly behind the original entrance lodges of Highcliffe Castle, close to the beach and historic town of Christchurch. Bedrooms have been finished to a very high standard with many thoughtful extras including spa baths. Excellent, award-winning food is available in the smart restaurant. Conferences and weddings are catered for.

Rooms: 9 en suite 4 annexe en suite (1 fmly) (6 GF) **D** fr £130* **Facilities:** FTV Lounge tea/coffee Dinner available Direct dial Licensed WiFi **Conf:** Max 25 Thtr 25 Class 15 Board 18 **Parking:** 40 **Notes:** LB RS Monday restaurant closed (open breakfast) Civ wed 120

Grosvenor Lodge

★★★★ GUEST HOUSE

tel: 01202 499008 **53 Stour Road BH23 1LN**
email: bookings@grosvenorlodge.co.uk **web:** www.grosvenorlodge.co.uk
dir: A35 from Christchurch to Bournemouth, at 1st lights left into Stour Road. Lodge on right.

Grosvenor House is a friendly and popular guest house near the centre of this historic town. The bedrooms are brightly and individually decorated and have lots of useful extras. Hearty breakfasts are served in the cheerful dining room, and there are many local restaurants for lunch and dinner.

Rooms: 7 en suite (2 fmly) (1 GF) **Facilities:** FTV DVD iPod docking station tea/coffee WiFi 🚲 **Parking:** 10 **Notes:** LB

Avon Breeze

★★★★ 🍷 BED AND BREAKFAST

tel: 01425 279102 & 07896 128026 **21 Fulmar Road BH23 4BJ**
email: info@avonbreeze.co.uk **web:** www.avonbreeze.co.uk
dir: A35 follow signs for Christchurch. At Sainsburys, follow signs for Mudeford. At Mudeford quay, turn into Falcon Drive, left and left again.

Avon Breeze is situated on the edge of the New Forest, a few minutes' level walk from the harbour, beach and local pubs. This contemporary home offers two comfortable en suite rooms as well as the use of a conservatory. Breakfast consists of locally-sourced, organic ingredients. Ample off-street parking is available.

Rooms: 2 en suite (2 GF) **Facilities:** FTV DVD iPod docking station tea/coffee WiFi 🚲 **Extras:** Bottled water, chocolate – complimentary **Parking:** 3 **Notes:** LB No children Closed October to March RS April one room only open

Riversmead

★★★★ GUEST ACCOMMODATION

tel: 01202 487195 **61 Stour Road BH23 1LN**
email: riversmead.dorset@googlemail.com **web:** www.riversmeadbb.co.uk
dir: A338 to Christchurch. Left turn to town centre, turn right over railway bridge.

Ideally located close to the town centre, beaches and the New Forest, with excellent access to local transport links, Riversmead is the perfect base for a short break or longer stay. This comfortable house offers a range of facilities including enclosed off-road parking, fridges in rooms and an excellent breakfast.

Rooms: 3 en suite (1 fmly) **D** fr £70* **Facilities:** FTV DVD tea/coffee WiFi
🔒 **Parking:** 9 **Notes:** LB No children 10 years

Brantwood Guest House

★★★ GUEST ACCOMMODATION

tel: 01202 473446 **55 Stour Road BH23 1LN**
email: brantwoodbookings@gmail.com **web:** www.brantwoodguesthouse.com
dir: A338 Bournemouth, 1st exit to Christchurch, right after railway bridge, cross lights, 200 yards on right.

Brantwood Guest House offers relaxed and friendly guest accommodation where the proprietors create a home-from-home atmosphere. Bedrooms and bathrooms are well decorated and comfortably furnished. The town centre is just a stroll away and off-road parking is available.

Rooms: 5 en suite (2 fmly) (1 GF) **Facilities:** FTV tea/coffee WiFi **Parking:** 5

CORFE MULLEN   Map 4 SY99

Kenways

★★★ BED AND BREAKFAST

tel: 01202 280620 **90a Wareham Road BH21 3LQ**
email: eileen@kenways.co.uk **web:** www.kenways.co.uk
dir: 2 mile southwest of Wimborne. Exit A31 to Corfe Mullen. Over B3074 roundabout, 0.3 mile on right.

Expect to be welcomed as one of the family at this homely bed and breakfast situated between Wimborne Minster and Poole. The spacious bedrooms are well provisioned with thoughtful extras, and breakfast is served in the pleasant conservatory overlooking attractive gardens.

Rooms: 4 rms (4 pri facs) (1 fmly) (2 GF) **S** fr £35 **D** fr £70* **Facilities:** FTV DVD TVL tea/coffee WiFi 🔒 Table tennis, snooker table **Parking:** 4

CRANBORNE   Map 5 SU01

Premier Collection

10 Castle Street

★★★★★ 🍽 GUEST ACCOMMODATION

tel: 01725 551133 **BH21 5PZ**
email: enquiries@10castlestreet.com **web:** www.10castlestreet.com
dir: From centre of village turn into Castle Street (B3078) signed Alderholt and Fordingbridge. On right.

This fine country mansion is situated in the tranquil Dorset village of Cranborne. Now refurbished, it's easy to unwind in the genuinely welcoming atmosphere. The team are sincere, helpful and unobtrusive and the bedrooms have individuality and charm, ensuring a good night's sleep, while the impressive bathrooms feature cosseting towels, robes and quality toiletries. Graceful public rooms are furnished for comfort and the gardens are quite superb.

Rooms: 9 rms (8 en suite) (1 pri facs) (2 fmly) **D** fr £195* **Facilities:** FTV iPod docking station Lounge tea/coffee Dinner available Direct dial Licensed WiFi 🛎 ⚲ 🔒 **Extras:** Speciality toiletries **Parking:** 30 **Notes:** LB Closed 25 and 31 December

The Inn at Cranborne

★★★★ 🍽 INN

tel: 01725 551249 **5 Wimborne Street BH21 5PP**
email: info@theinnatcranborne.co.uk **web:** www.theinnatcranborne.co.uk
dir: On B3078 in centre of village.

A delightful 17th-century inn, lovingly restored and full of special touches, The Inn at Cranborne is located in a peaceful village just a short drive from the New Forest and the Jurassic Coast. Nine comfortable and beautifully appointed en suite rooms are available. Breakfast (a real treat here), lunch and dinner are served in the bar and dining room areas. Off-street parking is available.

Rooms: 9 en suite (2 fmly) **Facilities:** FTV DVD iPod docking station Lounge TVL tea/coffee Dinner available WiFi ⚲ 🔒 **Extras:** Speciality toiletries, ground coffee, fresh milk **Conf:** Max 10 Thtr 10 Board 10 **Parking:** 25 **Notes:** LB

DORCHESTER   Map 4 SY69

Premier Collection

Little Court

★★★★★ 🍽 GUEST ACCOMMODATION

tel: 01305 261576 **5 Westleaze, Charminster DT2 9PZ**
email: info@littlecourt.net **web:** www.littlecourt.net
dir: A37 from Dorchester, 0.25 mile right at Loders Garage, Little Court 0.5 mile on right.

Built in 1909 in the style of Lutyens, Little Court sits in over four acres of attractive grounds and gardens, complete with tennis courts and swimming pool. The property has been appointed to a very high standard and the friendly proprietors are on hand to ensure a pleasant stay. A delicious breakfast, including home-grown produce, can be enjoyed in the stylish dining room.

Rooms: 8 en suite (1 fmly) **S** fr £99 **D** fr £129* **Facilities:** FTV Lounge tea/coffee Licensed WiFi ⚲ ⚲ ⚲ **Parking:** 10 **Notes:** LB Closed Christmas and New Year

DORCHESTER continued

Baytree House Dorchester

★★★★ BED AND BREAKFAST

tel: 01305 263696 **4 Athelstan Road DT1 1NR**
email: info@baytreedorchester.com **web:** www.bandbdorchester.co.uk
dir: 0.5 mile southeast of town centre.

Baytree House Dorchester is a friendly, family-run bed and breakfast situated in the heart of the town, not far from the village of Higher Bockham, birthplace of Thomas Hardy. The bedrooms are furnished in an appealing contemporary style and provide high levels of comfort. Breakfast is served farmhouse style in the open-plan kitchen/dining area. Parking is available.

Rooms: 6 en suite **Facilities:** FTV iPod docking station tea/coffee **Parking:** 3 **Notes:** LB

EVERSHOT — Map 4 ST50

The Acorn Inn

★★★★ ⑯ INN

tel: 01935 83228 **28 Fore Street DT2 0JW**
email: stay@acorn-inn.co.uk **web:** www.acorn-inn.co.uk
dir: From A37 between Yeovil and Dorchester, follow Evershot and Holywell signs, 0.5 mile to inn.

This delightful 16th-century coaching inn is located in the heart of the village. Many of the bedrooms feature interesting four-poster beds, and all the rooms have been individually decorated and furnished. The public areas retain many original features including oak panelling, open fires and stone-flagged floors. Fresh local produce is included on the varied menu.

Rooms: 10 en suite (2 fmly) **Facilities:** STV FTV TVL tea/coffee Dinner available Direct dial WiFi ♨ Use of spa opposite – chargeable **Extras:** Speciality toiletries, robes, home-made biscuits **Conf:** Max 30 Thtr 30 Board 30 **Parking:** 40 **Notes:** LB

FARNHAM — Map 4 ST91

The Museum Inn

★★★★ ⑯⑯ ⚑ INN

tel: 01725 812702 **DT11 8DE**
email: enquiries@museuminn.co.uk **web:** www.museuminn.co.uk
dir: Off A354 between Salisbury and Blandford Forum.

Part of The Epicurean Collection and located in a peaceful Dorset village, this traditional inn offers cosy log fires, flagstone floors and a welcoming bar combined with efficient service and a friendly welcome. Bedrooms include larger, stylish rooms in the main building or a selection of cosy rooms in an adjacent property. Food here, whether dinner or breakfast, uses the finest quality produce and really should not be missed.

Rooms: 4 en suite 4 annexe en suite (2 fmly) (4 GF) **Facilities:** FTV Lounge tea/coffee Dinner available Direct dial WiFi ♨ Fishing Riding **Extras:** Speciality toiletries **Conf:** Max 30 Thtr 30 Class 24 Board 20 **Parking:** 24 **Notes:** LB

HIGHCLIFFE

See Christchurch

LYME REGIS — Map 4 SY39

See also Axminster (Devon)

Old Lyme Guest House

★★★★ GUEST ACCOMMODATION

tel: 01297 442929 **29 Coombe Street DT7 3PP**
email: oldlymeguesthouse@gmail.com **web:** www.oldlymeguesthouse.co.uk

This historic 17th-century stone building is located in a quiet street and just a short stroll to the centre of town and the seafront. The welcome is warm and genuine with a relaxed 'home from home' atmosphere. Bedrooms have impressive levels of comfort with a simple and uncluttered style, sympathetic to the period architecture; bathrooms are equipped with power showers. Breakfast is served in the lovely dining room with a good choice of both hot and cold items offered, much is sourced locally. A guest lounge is also provided, ideal for snuggling up with a good book. Free parking is provided in the nearby public car park.

Rooms: 5 rms (4 en suite) (1 pri facs) (1 fmly) **S** fr £80 **D** fr £90*
Facilities: TVL tea/coffee WiFi **Extras:** Speciality toiletries, chilled filtered water **Notes:** No children 7 years Closed mid November to mid February

St Cuthberts

★★★★ BED AND BREAKFAST

tel: 01297 445901 **Charmouth Road DT7 3HG**
email: info@stcuthbertsoflyme.co.uk **web:** www.stcuthbertsoflyme.co.uk
dir: A35 from Dorchester, at Charmouth roundabout onto B3052 for 2 miles. Establishment on opposite side of road to "Welcome to Lyme Regis" sign.

Located just a 10-minute walk above the main town and harbour, this detached home is set within mature gardens and has its own parking. Bedrooms and bathrooms offer plenty of quality and comfort, as well as many thoughtful extras. A lounge with a log-burning stove and a decked terrace are available for guests. Breakfast, served around one large table, offers a varied choice including delicious pancakes with bacon and maple syrup.

Rooms: 3 en suite (1 GF) **Facilities:** FTV DVD TVL tea/coffee ♨ ♨ **Parking:** 6 **Notes:** No children 7 years

HIX Townhouse

★★★★ GUEST HOUSE

tel: 01297 442499 **1 Pound Street DT7 3HZ**
email: info@hixtownhouse.co.uk **web:** www.hixtownhouse.co.uk
dir: Phone for directions.

This elegant Georgian townhouse is handily located for all that Lyme has to offer and just a short stroll to the Hix Oyster & Fish House. There is a style and swagger in abundance here with an engaging individuality throughout all areas. No two rooms are the same, each themed to reflect owner Mark Hix's passions, examples being the Garden, Hunting and Sailing Rooms. Bathrooms also have personality with fluffy towels and robes to ensure a cosseting stay. A continental breakfast hamper is brought to the room in the morning to be enjoyed at leisure.

Rooms: 8 en suite **S** fr £95 **D** fr £135* **Facilities:** tea/coffee Dinner available Licensed WiFi **Extras:** Nespresso machine, fresh milk **Notes:** Closed 25–26 December, 7–20 January

Kersbrook

★★★★ ⬤ GUEST ACCOMMODATION

tel: 01297 442596 **Pound Round DT7 3HX**
email: alex@kersbrook.co.uk **web:** www.kersbrook.co.uk
dir: *Phone for directions.*

Just a stroll from the town centre and the famous Cobb, this thatched property provides an excellent base for exploring the fascinating delights of Lyme Regis. Dating back to 1790, there is character and charm in abundance, with facilities including a bar and lounge. Breakfast is a treat, the ideal start to a day of exploration. Bedrooms are traditionally styled, allied with modern bathrooms – an appealing combination.

Rooms: 14 rms (13 en suite) (1 pri facs) (1 fmly) (4 GF) **S** fr £55 **D** fr £110*
Facilities: FTV Lounge tea/coffee Licensed WiFi ⚓ Fishing 🅿 **Parking:** 13 **Notes:** LB

Dorset House

U

tel: 01297 442055 **Pound Road DT7 3HX**
email: info@dorsethouselyme.com **web:** www.dorsethouselyme.com
dir: *From A35 roundabout follow signs into Lyme Regis to seafront. Follow road up hill along Broad Street. Turn right into Silver Street. Dorset House on left, turn left into Pound Road.*

Currently the rating for this establishment is not confirmed. This may be due to a change of ownership or because it has only recently joined the AA rating scheme.

Rooms: 5 en suite (1 fmly) **S** fr £95 **D** fr £105* **Facilities:** FTV DVD iPod docking station Lounge tea/coffee Licensed WiFi **Extras:** Speciality toiletries, robes
Conf: Max 12 Board 12

MILTON ABBAS   Map 4 ST80

Hambro Arms

★★★★ INN

tel: 01258 880233 **DT11 0BP**
email: info@hambroarms.com **web:** www.hambroarms.com
dir: *From A354 follow signs for Milton Abbas, in village.*

The village of Milton Abbas is something very special. Much admired and featured on many a postcard, it is situated in the heart of Dorset. Identical thatched cottages that once housed the local estate workers line either side of the gently winding road. The Hambro Arms occupies one such thatched building and is a charming and quintessential village hostelry. Step inside for a genuine welcome and enjoy the bars, restaurant and lounge, all retaining their original character. Food demonstrates a genuine commitment to quality, local produce; likewise the tasty and substantial breakfast. Impressive bedrooms provide all the expected comforts combined with historic charm.

Rooms: 4 en suite (1 fmly) **Facilities:** FTV Lounge tea/coffee Dinner available WiFi
🅿 **Parking:** 15

MOTCOMBE   Map 4 ST82

The Coppleridge Inn

★★★ ⬤ INN

tel: 01747 851980 **SP7 9HW**
email: thecoppleridgeinn@btinternet.com **web:** www.coppleridge.com
dir: *Exit A350 to Motcombe, under railway bridge, 400 yards, right to Mere, inn 300 yards on left.*

This village inn, set in 15 acres, offers en suite bedrooms located in a pretty courtyard. All bedrooms have been appointed to a high standard and provide a very comfortable stay. Staff offer a warm welcome, and the inn serves good food with many daily specials. There are tennis courts and a boules court, plus a children's play area. Clay pigeon shooting can also be arranged.

Rooms: 10 en suite (2 fmly) (10 GF) **S** fr £70 **D** fr £100* **Facilities:** FTV DVD TVL tea/coffee Dinner available Direct dial WiFi ⬤ 🅿 Boules **Extras:** Mini-bar, home-made biscuits **Conf:** Max 60 Thtr 60 Class 60 Board 30 **Parking:** 100 **Notes:** LB
Civ wed 120

PLUSH   Map 4 ST70

The Brace of Pheasants

★★★★ ⬤ INN

tel: 01300 348357 **DT2 7RQ**
email: info@braceofpheasants.co.uk **web:** www.braceofpheasants.co.uk
dir: *A35 onto B3142, right to Plush 1.5 miles.*

Situated in the heart of Dorset, The Brace of Pheasants is a picturesque thatched pub that offers a warm and genuine welcome to both visitors and locals alike. Very much a traditional inn, its atmosphere is convivial with plenty of good-natured conversation. Bedrooms are split between the main building and the former skittle alley – all offer exceptional standards of comfort and individual style, with wonderful bathrooms. The food here should not be missed, with excellent local produce used to create an appealing menu.

Rooms: 4 en suite 4 annexe en suite (4 GF) **Facilities:** FTV tea/coffee Dinner available Direct dial WiFi **Conf:** Max 14 Board 14 **Parking:** 15 **Notes:** Closed 25 December Civ wed 130

POOLE   Map 4 SZ09

Seacourt

★★★ GUEST ACCOMMODATION

tel: 01202 674995 **249 Blandford Road, Hamworthy BH15 4AZ**
email: seacourtguesthouse@hotmail.co.uk
dir: *Exit A3049/A35 signed to Hamworthy.*

Within a short distance of the ferry port and town centre, this friendly establishment is well maintained and efficiently run. The comfortable bedrooms, some located on the ground floor, are nicely decorated and equipped with useful extra facilities. Breakfast is served in the pleasant dining room at separate tables.

Rooms: 5 en suite (1 fmly) (3 GF) **D** fr £70* **Facilities:** FTV DVD tea/coffee WiFi
Extras: Use of microwave and fridge **Parking:** 5 **Notes:** No children 5 years

PORTESHAM   Map 4 SY68

Kings Arms

★★★★ ≗ INN

tel: 01305 871342 **2 Front Street DT3 4ET**
email: info@kingsarmsportesham.co.uk **web:** www.kingsarmsportesham.co.uk
dir: On B3157 (coastal road).

Situated on the coast road, approximately half way between Weymouth and Dorchester, this long-established and popular village local is a great base from which to explore the area. The atmosphere is warm and welcoming with good natured banter at the bar. Local produce features on the menu that has a range of dishes for all tastes. The bedrooms are located to the side of the pub — all have level access and a private entrance.

Rooms: 3 en suite (1 fmly) (3 GF) **S** fr £75 **D** fr £110* **Facilities:** tea/coffee Dinner available WiFi **Extras:** Speciality toiletries **Parking:** 20

PORTLAND   Map 4 SY67

Queen Anne House

★★★★ GUEST ACCOMMODATION

tel: 01305 820028 **2/4 Fortuneswell DT5 1LP**
email: margaretdunlop@tiscali.co.uk **web:** www.queenannehouse.com
dir: A354 to Portland then Fortuneswell. House on left 200 metres past Royal Portland Arms.

This delightful, Grade II listed building is a charming and comfortable place to stay; particularly delightful are the Italianate gardens to the rear. Ideal for business and leisure guests, Queen Anne House is close to Portland Bill, Weymouth and Chesil Beach. The bedrooms are particularly attractive and pleasantly furnished. Breakfast, taken at one large table, offers a wide range of options.

Rooms: 3 en suite **S** fr £62.50 **D** fr £90* **Facilities:** FTV TVL tea/coffee WiFi **Parking:** 4

Portland Lodge

★★★ GUEST ACCOMMODATION

tel: 01305 820265 **Easton Lane DT5 1BW**
email: info@portlandlodge.com **web:** www.portlandlodge.com
dir: Follow signs to Easton/Portland Bill, at roundabout at Portland Heights Hotel 1st right. Portland Lodge 200 yards.

Situated on the fascinating island of Portland, this modern, lodge-style establishment provides comfortable accommodation including a number of ground-floor bedrooms. Breakfast is served in the spacious dining room with a friendly team of staff on hand. This is an ideal location for those wishing to explore the World Heritage coastline.

Rooms: 30 annexe en suite (15 fmly) (7 GF) **Facilities:** FTV tea/coffee WiFi **Parking:** 30 **Notes:** LB

PUNCKNOWLE   Map 4 SY58

Offley Bed & Breakfast

★★★★ GUEST ACCOMMODATION

tel: 01308 897044 & 07792 624977 **Looke Lane DT2 9BD**
web: www.offleybedandbreakfast.info
dir: Off B3157 into village centre, left after Crown Inn into Looke Lane, 2nd house on right.

With magnificent views over the Bride Valley, this village house provides comfortable, quality accommodation. Guests are assured of a warm, friendly welcome, and this is an ideal base from which to enjoy the numerous local attractions. There are several inns nearby; there's one in the village which is just a gentle stroll away.

Rooms: 3 rms (2 en suite) (1 pri facs) **Facilities:** FTV TVL tea/coffee WiFi ♨ **Extras:** Fruit, flowers — complimentary **Parking:** 4 **Notes:** LB Closed 1 week Christmas

SHAFTESBURY   Map 4 ST82

La Fleur de Lys Restaurant with Rooms

★★★★★ ⊛⊛ RESTAURANT WITH ROOMS

tel: 01747 853717 **Bleke Street SP7 8AW**
email: info@lafleurdelys.co.uk **web:** www.lafleurdelys.co.uk
dir: From junction of A30 and A350, 0.25 mile towards town centre.

Located just a few minutes' walk from the famous Gold Hill, this light and airy restaurant with rooms combines efficient service with a relaxed and friendly atmosphere. Bedrooms, which are suitable for both business and leisure guests, vary in size but all are well equipped, comfortable and tastefully furnished. A relaxing guest lounge and courtyard are available for afternoon tea or pre-dinner drinks. The excellent food has been awarded two AA Rosettes.

Rooms: 8 en suite (2 fmly) (1 GF) **S** fr £85 **D** fr £100* **Facilities:** FTV Lounge tea/coffee Dinner available Direct dial WiFi **Extras:** Home-made biscuits, fresh milk — complimentary **Conf:** Max 12 Board 10 **Parking:** 10 **Notes:** LB RS 1–21 January restaurant closed

The Fontmell

★★★★ ⊜ INN

tel: 01747 811441 **Crown Hill, Fontmell Magna SP7 0PA**
email: info@thefontmell.com **web:** www.thefontmell.com
dir: Phone for directions.

This warm and welcoming pub offers a stylish and comfortable environment, complete with a stream, Collier's Brook, that actually flows between the bar and the dining room. Relaxation here is guaranteed; it's a great place to linger over a pint at the bar or curl up on the sofa and peruse the papers. The bedrooms offer impressive quality and comfort, and each has its own unique identity. The kitchen presents a range of flavour-packed dishes, based on the best local, seasonal produce.

Rooms: 6 rms (6 pri facs) (1 fmly) **Facilities:** FTV DVD tea/coffee Dinner available Direct dial WiFi ♨ Fishing Riding **Extras:** Bottled water **Parking:** 20

See also Corton Denham (Somerset)

Premier Collection

The Kings Arms
★★★★★ ◉ INN

tel: 01963 220281 **Charlton Horethorne DT9 4NL**
email: admin@thekingsarms.co.uk web: www.thekingsarms.co.uk
dir: *From A303 follow signs for Templecombe and Sherborne onto B3145 to Charlton Horethorne.*

Situated in the heart of this engaging village, The Kings Arms offers impressive standards throughout. The experienced owners have created something for everyone with a convivial bar, snug and choice of dining environments, including the garden terrace with lovely countryside views. Bedrooms have individuality, quality and style with marble bathrooms, robes and wonderful showers. Food is taken seriously here, with an assured team producing a menu showcasing the best local produce.

Rooms: 10 en suite (1 fmly) **Facilities:** FTV DVD Lounge tea/coffee Dinner available Direct dial Lift WiFi 🐾 🕹 **Parking:** 30 **Notes:** Closed 25 December RS 26 December no dinner served

Premier Collection

The Rose and Crown Inn, Trent
★★★★★ ◉◉ INN

tel: 01935 850776 **Trent DT9 4SL**
email: info@theroseandcrowntrent.co.uk web: www.theroseandcrowntrent.co.uk
dir: *Just off A30 between Sherborne and Yeovil.*

The Rose and Crown dates from the 14th century and is a quintessential country inn with a long and interesting history. Packed full of character, this is a place where relaxation comes easily, with crackling fires adding to the atmosphere and charm. Bedrooms are accessed externally, and each has high levels of comfort and quality, with stylish bathrooms and cosseting extras. They also have patio areas with lovely views across the rolling countryside. Food is high on the agenda here and creative and flavoursome dishes are offered.

Rooms: 3 annexe en suite (3 GF) **Facilities:** FTV DVD iPod docking station Lounge tea/coffee Dinner available WiFi 🔒 **Extras:** Speciality toiletries, home-made cookies **Parking:** 30

The Alders
★★★★ BED AND BREAKFAST

tel: 01963 220666 **Sandford Orcas DT9 4SB**
email: info@thealdersbb.com web: www.thealdersbb.com
dir: *3 miles north of Sherborne. Off B3148 signed Sandford Orcas, near Manor House in village.*

Located in the charming conservation area of Sandford Orcas and set in a lovely walled garden, this delightful property offers attractive, well-equipped bedrooms. Guests have their own entrance leading from the garden. A large inglenook fireplace with a wood-burning stove can be found in the comfortable sitting room, which also features the owner's watercolours. Massage therapies are available.

Rooms: 3 en suite (1 fmly) **S** fr £60 **D** fr £75 **Facilities:** FTV TVL tea/coffee WiFi 🔒 **Parking:** 4

Premier Collection

Swanage Haven Boutique B&B
★★★★★ GUEST HOUSE

tel: 01929 423088 **3 Victoria Road BH19 1LY**
email: info@swanagehaven.com web: www.swanagehaven.com
dir: *Phone for directions.*

Swanage Haven is a boutique-style guest house close to the beach and the coastal path. Exclusively for adults, the accommodation is contemporary, with many extras such as fluffy robes, slippers, hot tub and WiFi. The hands-on owners provide excellent hospitality with a relaxed and friendly service. The breakfasts are superb – top quality organic and local produce are featured on the extensive menu.

Rooms: 8 en suite **S** fr £65 **D** fr £100* **Facilities:** FTV TVL tea/coffee Licensed WiFi 🔒 Hot tub **Extras:** Honesty bar – chargeable **Parking:** 7 **Notes:** LB No children 18 years Closed November to weekend nearest 14 February

SWANAGE *continued*

Premier Collection

2@2 Rabling Road

★★★★★ BED AND BREAKFAST

tel: 01929 423983 & 07803 182530 **2 Rabling Road BH19 1EE**
email: 2at2rablingroad@gmail.com **web:** www.visit-dorset.com/accommodation/2-rabling-road-bed-and-breakfast-p2073433
dir: *A351 into Swanage (Victoria Avenue), left into Northbrook Road. 1st right into Rabling Road, house on left.*

This 1930s house is situated just a short stroll from the beach and a level walk to the town centre, thus making a perfect base for exploring the many charms of Swanage. There is an engaging fusion of period features and contemporary style which contributes to a relaxing environment. A warm welcome is assured plus helpful advice, if required, about the local area. Each of the bedrooms provides impressive levels of comfort including spacious bathrooms with a bath, separate shower and cosseting bathrobes. Breakfast is a tasty start to the day, served within the elegant dining room, after which, perhaps a few minutes relaxation in the attractive garden may be in order, or a stroll along the beach.

Rooms: 2 rms (1 en suite) (1 pri facs) **Facilities:** FTV DVD iPod docking station tea/coffee Dinner available WiFi 🛁 Hot tub **Extras:** Home-made snacks, bottled water **Parking:** 2 **Notes:** No children over the age of 12 months Closed 30 October to March

Caythorpe House

★★★★ GUEST ACCOMMODATION

tel: 01929 422892 **7 Rempstone Road BH19 1DN**
email: enquiries@caythorpehouse.co.uk **web:** www.caythorpehouse.co.uk
dir: *A351 to Swanage. Right at lights opposite church, Caythorpe House at junction.*

Conveniently located just a short stroll from the seafront and town centre, this elegant Edwardian villa is a perfect place from which to enjoy the many delights Swanage has to offer. A warm and genuine welcome is assured, with every effort made to provide a relaxing and rewarding break whether for business or pleasure. The bedrooms are light and airy with all the expected comforts, and there's a variety of configurations to suit all needs. Breakfast is a satisfying start to the day and helpful advice on the area is always on offer. A guest lounge is also provided and there is ample off-road parking.

Rooms: 7 en suite (2 GF) **S** fr £50 **D** fr £90* **Facilities:** FTV DVD TVL tea/coffee WiFi 🛁 **Parking:** 6 **Notes:** No children 10 years Closed 17 October to 1 April

The Limes

★★★★ GUEST HOUSE

tel: 01929 422664 **48 Park Road BH19 2AE**
email: info@limeshotel.net **web:** www.limeshotel.net
dir: *Follow one-way system, signed to Durlston Country Park. Pass Trattoria restaurant on left, right into Park Road, 200 metres on right.*

Ideally located for both the town centre and the seafront, this comfortable establishment offers a variety of different bedroom shapes and sizes. In addition to the pleasant dining room, guests are free to use a small bar area and a popular games room.

Rooms: 12 rms (10 en suite) (7 fmly) **S** fr £48 **D** fr £99 **Facilities:** FTV DVD Lounge tea/coffee Licensed WiFi 🛁 **Conf:** Max 25 Thtr 25 Class 20 Board 16 **Parking:** 8 **Notes:** LB

Kingston Country Courtyard

★★★★ GUEST ACCOMMODATION

tel: 01929 481066 **Kingston, Nr Corfe Castle BH20 5LR**
email: relax@kingstoncountrycourtyard.com **web:** www.kingstoncountrycourtyard.com
dir: *Through Corfe Castle towards Swanage (A351), turn right onto B3069. Through village, up steep hill, sharp left bend, Kingston Country Courtyard 0.25 mile on left.*

Situated amid the beautiful Purbeck Hills, the views from this house include historic Corfe Castle and the distant shores of the Isle of Wight. A variety of comfortable guest bedrooms is on offer and breakfast is served in the spacious dining hall.

Rooms: 25 en suite (3 fmly) (21 GF) **Facilities:** FTV Lounge tea/coffee Licensed WiFi 🛁 **Conf:** Max 100 Thtr 100 Class 100 Board 50 **Parking:** 100 **Notes:** LB Closed 24 December to 3 January RS weekends may be closed due to weddings Civ wed 130

Worgret Manor

★★★★ GUEST ACCOMMODATION

tel: 01929 552957 **Worgret Road BH20 6AB**
email: admin@worgretmanor.co.uk **web:** www.worgretmanor.co.uk
dir: *A351 to Wareham. Take A352 signed Dorchester. 0.5 mile to manor on left.*

Worgret Manor is a grand Georgian house perfectly situated for exploration of this beautiful area, with the Saxon market town of Wareham just a mile away. Comfortable bedrooms provide good levels of space with period features adding to the character and charm. Breakfast provides a satisfying start to the day and friendly and helpful service is always on offer.

Rooms: 3 en suite (1 GF) **S** fr £75 **D** fr £95* **Facilities:** FTV tea/coffee Licensed WiFi 🛁 **Parking:** 8 **Notes:** No children 16 years

See also Portland

Swallows Rest

★★★★ 🛏 BED AND BREAKFAST

tel: 01305 785244 & 07747 753656 **Martleaves Farm, South Road DT4 9NR**
email: jane.furlong@btinternet.com **web:** www.swallowsrestselfcatering.co.uk
dir: *From Weymouth on Portland road, turn right into Parkmead road. Then turn left and immediately right into South Road.*

This beautiful, rural B&B with coastal views has highly individual bedrooms. Each is richly decorated and well equipped – ideal for any type of break. Public areas include a comfortable lounge and a dining area which is a sociable setting for breakfast. Parking is available, and there is also a campsite and self-catering apartments. The owners have their own pigs, chickens, ducks and alpacas, and the grounds are full of interest. Guests now also have the added luxury of a hot tub.

Rooms: 5 en suite (1 fmly) **S** fr £60 **D** fr £95 **Facilities:** FTV TVL tea/coffee WiFi
🛁 Hot tub **Extras:** Speciality toiletries, home-made cakes, chocolates **Parking:** 16
Notes: LB No children 5 years Closed 24–26 December Civ wed 30

The Esplanade

★★★★ ⬦ GUEST ACCOMMODATION

tel: 01305 783129 & 07515 657116 **141 The Esplanade DT4 7NJ**
email: stay@theesplanadehotel.co.uk **web:** www.theesplanadehotel.co.uk
dir: *On seafront, between Jubilee Clock and pier bandstand.*

Dating from 1835, this attractive property is located on the seafront and offers wonderful views from the elegant dining room and stylish first-floor lounge. There's a genuine enthusiasm here, with a warm welcome assured. The comfortable bedrooms are thoughtfully equipped, including Egyptian cotton sheets and towels, and many rooms have sea views. Breakfast is a showcase of local produce with an extensive menu.

Rooms: 11 en suite (3 fmly) (2 GF) **Facilities:** FTV TVL tea/coffee Licensed WiFi
Parking: 9 **Notes:** LB Closed November to February

Barnes's Rest Weymouth

★★★★ BED AND BREAKFAST

tel: 01305 779354 & 07582 707749 **165 Dorchester Road DT4 7LE**
email: barnessrest@hotmail.co.uk **web:** www.barnessrest.co.uk
dir: *A354 into Weymouth. At Manor roundabout 1st exit onto B3159 (Dorchester Road), on right just past doctors' surgery.*

This Victorian family home is ideally located for those visiting Weymouth for either business or leisure. The welcome is warm and inviting, and every effort is made to ensure a relaxing and rewarding stay. Its location means it's just a 10-minute stroll from the seafront. Bedrooms and bathrooms are light and airy with modern facilities and all the required necessities. Breakfast is served around the dining table with an ample choice for all appetites. Safe storage facilities are available for bikes and outdoor gear.

Rooms: 4 en suite (1 GF) **Facilities:** FTV tea/coffee WiFi 🛁 **Notes:** LB

Florian Guest House

★★★★ GUEST HOUSE

tel: 01305 773836 & 07460 442166 **59 Abbotsbury Road DT4 0AQ**
email: enquiryflorian@aol.com **web:** www.florianguesthouse.co.uk
dir: *At junction of A354 & A353 into Abbotsbury Road. 500 yards on left after church.*

Situated about a 10-minute walk from the town centre, beach and local attractions, this welcoming property offers bedrooms in a range of shapes and sizes and is ideally situated for a family seaside holiday or a short break. Breakfast is taken in the comfortably furnished downstairs dining area.

Rooms: 6 rms (5 en suite) (1 pri facs) (1 fmly) (1 GF) **S** fr £25 **D** fr £50*
Facilities: FTV DVD Lounge tea/coffee WiFi 🛁 Sea fishing **Extras:** Fridge, microwave
Parking: 4 **Notes:** LB Closed January

Kingswood

★★★★ GUEST ACCOMMODATION

tel: 01305 784926 & 07899 770920 **55 Rodwell Road DT4 8QY**
email: info@kingswoodhotel.com **web:** www.kingswoodhotel.com
dir: *On A354 up hill towards Portland from inner harbour, on left after lights.*

Handily located for both Weymouth and Portland, this welcoming establishment provides spacious guest accommodation, including larger suites with jacuzzi baths; most rooms have fridges. The building has a long and interesting history, including a period when it was commandeered for American officers during World War II. The bedrooms are well appointed and comfortable, as are the public areas. Breakfast is served in the attractive dining room. Just a stroll away is Brewers Quay, a lovely area in which to while away an hour or two.

Rooms: 10 rms (9 en suite) (1 pri facs) (2 GF) **Facilities:** FTV Lounge tea/coffee WiFi
Parking: 20 **Notes:** LB No children Closed November to February

St John's Guest House

★★★★ GUEST HOUSE

tel: 01305 775523 **7 Dorchester Road DT4 7JR**
email: stjohnsguesthouse@googlemail.com **web:** www.stjohnsguesthouse.co.uk
dir: *Opposite St John's Church. The car park is in Grange Road.*

Located just 70 yards from the beach, St John's is an elegant building from around 1880. Hospitality here is warm and genuine, and the property has an appealing, uncluttered and refined style. Standards are high throughout with comfy bedrooms being well equipped with such extras as DVD players and WiFi access. Breakfast is served in the light and airy dining room, a satisfying and tasty start to the day.

Rooms: 8 en suite (2 fmly) (2 GF) **Facilities:** FTV DVD tea/coffee WiFi **Parking:** 10
Notes: LB No children 4 years

Wadham Guesthouse

★★★ GUEST HOUSE

tel: 01305 779640 & 07375 914381 **22 East Street DT4 8BN**
email: shirleystephenson@btconnect.com **web:** www.wadhamhouse.co.uk
dir: *Off south end of A353 (The Esplanade).*

This pleasant town centre property offers a range of rooms, and is a good base for touring or for a short stay. The comfortable bedrooms are attractively decorated, and home-cooked breakfasts are served in the ground-floor dining room. Parking permits are available.

Rooms: 8 en suite **S** fr £40 **D** fr £72* **Facilities:** FTV tea/coffee WiFi
Notes: No children 10 years Closed Christmas, New Year, January, February
RS March limited rooms available

WEYMOUTH *continued*

The Edenhurst

★★★ GUEST HOUSE

tel: 01305 771255 **122 The Esplanade DT4 7ER**
email: enquiries@edenhurstweymouth.com **web:** www.edenhurstweymouth.com
dir: *Phone for directions.*

Just a step across the road from the beach and within walking distance of the railway and bus stations, this smartly presented establishment is a perfect base from which to explore the local area. Several bedroom styles are offered – some have balconies and wonderful sea views, all have modern bathrooms. Breakfast is served in the elegant, sea-facing dining room, and a guest lounge is also provided.

Rooms: 12 rms (11 en suite) (1 pri facs) (4 fmly) **S** fr £41 **D** fr £80* **Facilities:** FTV TVL tea/coffee WiFi **Extras:** Bottled water – complimentary **Notes:** LB

Beaufort Guesthouse

★★★ GUEST HOUSE

tel: 01305 782088 **24 The Esplanade DT4 8DN**
web: www.beaufortguesthouse.co.uk

Just a few steps from the sandy beach, this friendly, family-run establishment is ideally located for a seaside break. Bedrooms are soundly appointed with all the necessary essentials, likewise the modern showers. Some of the rooms have the added bonus of sea views. Breakfast is served in the lounge diner, which also has a bar to refresh and revive guests after a hard day enjoying the many and varied local attractions.

Rooms: 6 rms (5 en suite) (1 pri facs) (2 fmly) **S** fr £30 **D** fr £60* **Facilities:** FTV tea/coffee Licensed WiFi **Notes:** LB No children 6 months Closed 23 December to 1 January

WIMBORNE MINSTER
Map 5 SZ09

Premier Collection

Les Bouviers Restaurant with Rooms

★★★★★ ◉◉ RESTAURANT WITH ROOMS

tel: 01202 889555 **Arrowsmith Road, Canford Magna BH21 3BD**
email: info@lesbouviers.co.uk **web:** www.lesbouviers.co.uk
dir: *A31 onto A349. Left in 0.6 mile. In approximately 1 mile right into Arrowsmith Road. Establishment approximately 100 yards on right.*

Les Bouviers is an excellent restaurant with rooms in a great location, set in five and a half acres of grounds. Food is obviously a highlight of any stay here, as is the friendly, attentive service. Chef patron Leonard James Coward and his team turn out impressive cooking, which has been recognised with two AA Rosettes. The bedrooms are extremely well equipped, and the beds are supremely comfortable. Cream teas can be taken on the terrace.

Rooms: 6 en suite (4 fmly) **S** fr £70 **D** fr £80* **Facilities:** FTV DVD Lounge tea/coffee Dinner available Direct dial WiFi All bathrooms have steam showers or air baths **Extras:** Robes, slippers, mineral water **Conf:** Max 120 Thtr 100 Class 100 Board 100 **Parking:** 50 **Notes:** LB RS Sunday evening restricted opening and restaurant closed Civ wed 120

St Algars B&B

★★★★ BED AND BREAKFAST

tel: 01202 883325 & 07986 423457 **Holt Lane, Holt BH21 7DQ**
email: davieskimberly@googlemail.com **web:** www.dorsetbedandbreakfast.vpweb.co.uk
dir: *North from Wimborne on B3078, follow signs for Cranborne. Turn right, signed Furzehill, Holt and Horton. Through Furzehill, 4th house on left after Holt village sign.*

Situated in the picturesque village of Holt, just 2.5 miles from Wimborne Minster, this warm and welcoming establishment provides comfortable accommodation and a relaxed, homely atmosphere. Bedrooms are well appointed and include one on the ground floor with level access. Breakfast is served around the dining table with lovely views across the garden to the fields beyond. There is much to see and do in the area with the New Forest and Bournemouth's beaches within a short drive; it's a popular location for walkers and cyclists.

Rooms: 2 en suite (1 fmly) (1 GF) **S** fr £40 **D** fr £75* **Facilities:** FTV DVD TVL tea/coffee WiFi ⊛ **Parking:** 3 **Notes:** LB No children 11 years

COUNTY DURHAM

CHESTER-LE-STREET
Map 19 NZ25

The Lambton Worm

★★★★ ⊜ INN

tel: 0191 387 1162 **North Road DH3 4AJ**
email: info@thelambton.com **web:** www.thelambton.com
dir: *A1(M) junction 63 onto A167, 0.7 mile on left.*

Named after a local legend that inspired Bram Stoker's 1911 novel, *The Lair of the White Worm*, this boutique inn offers comfortable and well-appointed bedrooms. Real ales come from the local parent company, Sonnet 43 Brew House, while the excellent food is locally sourced and of a very good standard. The team are friendly and helpful, making this property a real little gem.

Rooms: 14 en suite (2 fmly) **Facilities:** FTV iPod docking station Lounge tea/coffee Dinner available WiFi ⅃ ⊛ **Parking:** 24 **Notes:** LB

DURHAM
Map 19 NZ24

The Old Mill

★★★★ ⊜ INN

tel: 01740 652928 **Thinford Road, Metal Bridge DH6 5NX**
email: office@oldmilldurham.co.uk **web:** www.oldmilldurham.co.uk
dir: *5 miles south of Durham. A1(M) junction 61, A688 south for 1.5 miles, left at roundabout, sharp right.*

This traditional, family-owned inn is in a countryside setting yet is only a mile from the A1(M). There is a friendly atmosphere and the bar and dining areas are full of character. Food is served throughout the day and evening, with the vast menu displayed on blackboards. Bedrooms are spacious and well equipped. Complimentary WiFi is provided.

Rooms: 12 en suite **Facilities:** STV FTV DVD tea/coffee Dinner available Direct dial WiFi ⊛ **Conf:** Max 40 Thtr 40 Class 40 Board 25 **Parking:** 40 **Notes:** Closed 26 December RS 25 December bookings only

The Kingslodge Inn

★★★ ⌷ INN

tel: 0191 370 9977 **Waddington Street, Flass Vale DH1 4BG**
email: enquiries@kingslodgeinn.co.uk **web:** www.kingslodgeinn.co.uk
dir: *Phone for directions.*

The Kingslodge Inn is situated by woodland in a peaceful location yet is just minutes away from the city centre. Service and hospitality are both warm and genuine. The modern, well-appointed bedrooms offer quality and comfort. The menu, as with the other properties within The Inn Collection group, is very appealing with a wide choice of dishes; real ales are always on tap. Outdoor seating in the gardens is an added benefit as is the off-road parking.

Rooms: 23 en suite (3 fmly) (2 GF) **Facilities:** FTV tea/coffee Dinner available WiFi **Parking:** 25

HESLEDEN   Map 19 NZ43

The Ship Inn

★★★★ ⌷ INN

tel: 01429 836453 & 07760 767448 **High Hesleden TS27 4QD**
email: sheila@theshipinn.net **web:** www.theshipinn.net
dir: *A19 onto B1281 signed Blackhall. Follow Hesleden signs to High Hesleden.*

The Ship Inn has some wonderful sea views from its well-appointed and comfortable bedrooms. The bar is cosy and welcoming and has an impressive selection of well-kept real ales. Dinner is served in the spacious, comfortable restaurant and log fires burn brightly on cooler evenings. Sympathetically restored over a number of years, many of the original features of this fine old property are still in place. Free WiFi and secure parking are provided. The Ship Inn is an AA Friendliest B&B of the Year runner up for 2018–19.

Rooms: 6 en suite 3 annexe en suite (3 fmly) (6 GF) **S** fr £85 **D** fr £85*
Facilities: STV FTV DVD tea/coffee Dinner available WiFi 🔒 **Extras:** Fruit – complimentary **Conf:** Max 45 Thtr 45 Class 25 Board 25 **Parking:** 25
Notes: RS Monday

LANCHESTER   Map 19 NZ14

The Old Post Office

★★★★ GUEST HOUSE

tel: 01207 528420 & 07917 108481 **27 Front Street DH7 0LA**
email: keithgill51@talktalk.net **web:** www.theoldpostofficelanchester.com
dir: *From Durham on A691, follow signs to Consett. Turn left signed Lanchester village centre, then immediately right into Front Street. On right by post box.*

Located in the historic town of Lanchester, this Grade II listed building dates back to 1788 and has been lovingly restored by the current owners. Bedrooms are spacious and very comfortable, with thoughtful extras provided as standard. Great care is taken when choosing suppliers for breakfast items. The delightful gardens to the rear add to the quality of this wonderful property.

Rooms: 3 en suite (1 fmly) **Facilities:** FTV Lounge tea/coffee WiFi 🔒 **Extras:** Speciality toiletries, chocolate, home-made biscuits – complimentary **Parking:** 3

PETERLEE   Map 19 NZ44

The Bell Guest House

★★★★ GUEST HOUSE

tel: 0191 586 3863 **Sunderland Road SR8 4PF**
email: info@thebellguesthouse.com **web:** www.thebellguesthouse.com
dir: *From A19 onto A1086 (Sunderland Road).*

The Bell Guest House is located in Horden just a few minutes from the sea. The house gets its name from the previous owner, Henry Bell, who purchased the property back in 1925 – retains plenty of charm and character. The bedrooms are well appointed and comfortable, while the coach bar and lounge are warm and welcoming. This guest house is ideally located for Hartlepool, Sunderland, Newcastle and Durham.

Rooms: 9 en suite (2 fmly) **Facilities:** FTV TVL tea/coffee Licensed WiFi
🔒 **Notes:** Closed 24–26 December

SEAHAM   Map 19 NZ44

The Seaton Lane Inn

★★★★ ⌷ INN

tel: 0191 581 2038 **Seaton Lane, Seaton Village SR7 0LP**
email: info@seatonlaneinn.com **web:** www.seatonlaneinn.com
dir: *A19 south of Sunderland on B1404 between Seaham and Houghton.*

Newly refurbished, this popular inn in Seaton is just off the A19, close to Seaham and within easy reach of Sunderland, Durham and Newcastle. A contemporary, botanical theme, where outdoors meets indoors, runs throughout the property. The emphasis is on food here and guests can dine on home-made dishes and enjoy a drink in the inn's orangery. The comfortable bedrooms are modern, spacious and smartly furnished.

Rooms: 18 en suite (9 GF) **Facilities:** FTV TVL tea/coffee Dinner available Direct dial WiFi ♿ **Parking:** 36

WHORLTON   Map 19 NZ11

Fernaville's Rest

★★★★ ⌷ INN

tel: 01833 627341 **Whorlton DL12 8XD**
email: thomas@fernavilles.com **web:** www.fernavilles.com
dir: *Phone for directions.*

Fernaville's Rest is a Grade II listed inn located in the quiet village of Whorlton which is within easy striking distance of Barnard Castle. This family-run operation offers well-appointed, en suite bedrooms. Hospitality from the hands-on owners and team is noteworthy and makes for a wonderful guest experience. Dinner menus showcase local quality produce which is accurately cooked and well presented. Real ales, including a 'dog beer', are served in the bar and in winter can be enjoyed in front of the open fire.

Rooms: 6 en suite **S** fr £50 **D** fr £75* **Facilities:** FTV Dinner available WiFi 🔒

ESSEX

CHELMSFORD
Map 6 TL70

The Lion Inn
★★★★ 🛏 INN

tel: 01245 394900 **Main Road, Boreham CM3 3JA**
email: info@lioninnhotel.co.uk web: www.lioninnhotel.co.uk
dir: *A12 junction 19 onto B1137 to Maldon. 0.75 mile on right.*

The Lion Inn offers stylish and comfortably appointed accommodation; well-equipped with TVs, free WiFi and full air conditioning it appeals to leisure and business guests alike. Many rooms benefit from balconies or direct access to the private garden. The spacious bar and restaurant are open-plan with additional seating in the Victorian conservatory. Guests can enjoy a wide selection of good classic pub dishes with a continental twist; a cooked and continental breakfast is served daily.

Rooms: 15 en suite 8 annexe en suite (1 fmly) (9 GF) **Facilities:** FTV tea/coffee Dinner available Direct dial WiFi **Conf:** Max 150 Thtr 150 Class 50 Board 20 **Parking:** 150 **Notes:** Closed 24–26 December RS All bank holidays Civ wed 150

CLACTON-ON-SEA
Map 7 TM11

The Chudleigh
★★★★ GUEST ACCOMMODATION

tel: 01255 425407 **13 Agate Road, Marine Parade West CO15 1RA**
email: chudleighhotel@btconnect.com web: www.chudleighhotel.com
dir: *With sea on left, cross lights at pier, turn into Agate Road at mini roundabout.*

Conveniently situated for the seafront and shops, this immaculate property has been run by the friendly owners Peter and Carol Oleggini for more than 50 years. Bedrooms are most attractive with co-ordinating decor and well chosen fabrics. Breakfast is served in the smart dining room and there is a cosy lounge with plush sofas.

Rooms: 10 en suite (2 fmly) (2 GF) **S** fr £60 **D** fr £75* **Facilities:** FTV TVL tea/coffee Direct dial Licensed WiFi 🍴 **Extras:** Speciality toiletries, chocolates – complimentary **Parking:** 6 **Notes:** No children 18 months Closed October RS 1 week March/April

COLCHESTER
Map 13 TL92

Black Bond Hall Bed and Breakfast
★★★★ BED AND BREAKFAST

tel: 01206 735776 & 07909 516013 **Lodge Lane, Langenhoe CO5 7LX**
email: gill@blackbondhall.co.uk web: www.blackbondhall.co.uk
dir: *A12 junction 26 signed to Mersea (B1025). Through Abberton and Langenhoe pass crossroads and garage, 1st left into School Road and Fingringhoe Range. 1st right into Lodge Lane, on right.*

Black Bond Hall is ideally situated for Colchester and attractions such as The Beth Chatto Gardens, Dedham, Rowhedge, Abberton Reservoir, Mersea Island and Fingringhoe Nature Reserves. The two comfortable double rooms provide tea- and coffee-making facilities, TV, WiFi and hairdryer. Guests can expect a warm welcome, with home-made cake on arrival, as well as tea and coffee. Breakfast is made from local produce and is served in either the modern breakfast room overlooking the garden or in the traditional dining room. There are pubs nearby for evening meals.

Rooms: 2 en suite **S** fr £65 **D** fr £90* **Facilities:** FTV tea/coffee WiFi 🍴 🔒 **Extras:** Snacks **Parking:** 8 **Notes:** LB No children 12 years

DEDHAM
Map 13 TM03

Premier Collection

The Sun Inn
★★★★★ 🏵🏵 🍷 INN

tel: 01206 323351 **High Street CO7 6DF**
email: office@thesuninndedham.com web: www.thesuninndedham.com
dir: *In village centre opposite church.*

The Sun Inn is a charming 15th-century coaching inn situated in the centre of Dedham, opposite the church. The carefully decorated bedrooms include four-poster and half-tester beds, along with many thoughtful touches. The open-plan public rooms have a wealth of character with inglenook fires, oak beams and fine oak panelling, and the food in the restaurant has been awarded two AA Rosettes.

Rooms: 7 en suite **S** fr £90 **D** fr £145* **Facilities:** FTV DVD iPod docking station Lounge tea/coffee Dinner available WiFi 🔒 **Extras:** Speciality toiletries, mineral water **Parking:** 15 **Notes:** LB Closed 25–28 December

GREAT TOTHAM · Map 7 TL81

The Bull & Willow Room at Great Totham

★★★★ ◉◉ RESTAURANT WITH ROOMS

tel: 01621 893385 & 894020 **2 Maldon Road CM9 8NH**
email: reservations@thebullatgreattotham.co.uk **web:** www.thebullatgreattotham.co.uk
dir: *Exit A12 at Witham junction to Great Totham.*

A 16th-century, former coaching inn located in the village of Great Totham, The Bull is a very stylish restaurant with rooms that offers en suite bedrooms with satellite TVs with Freeview; WiFi is available throughout. Guests can enjoy dinner in the gastro-pub or in the two AA Rosette award-winning fine dining restaurant, The Willow Room.

Rooms: 4 annexe en suite (2 GF) **S** fr £80 **D** fr £90* **Facilities:** STV FTV TVL tea/coffee Dinner available WiFi ⚐ **Conf:** Max 75 Thtr 40 Class 40 Board 16 **Parking:** 80 **Notes:** LB

GREAT YELDHAM · Map 13 TL73

Premier Collection

The White Hart

★★★★★ ◉◉ ⚐ INN

tel: 01787 237250 **Poole Street CO9 4HJ**
email: restaurant@whitehartyeldham.com **web:** www.whitehartyeldham.com
dir: *On A1017 in village.*

The White Hart is a large timber-framed character building that includes the main restaurant and bar areas while the bedrooms are located in the converted coach house; all are smartly appointed and well equipped with many thoughtful extras. The comfortable lounge and bar and the beautifully landscaped gardens provide areas for relaxation. Locally sourced produce is used on menus in the main house restaurant which is popular with local residents and guests alike.

Rooms: 13 en suite (2 fmly) (6 GF) **Facilities:** FTV TVL tea/coffee Dinner available Direct dial WiFi **Conf:** Max 200 Thtr 200 Class 200 Board 50 **Parking:** 80 **Notes:** LB Closed 1–18 January Civ wed 130

HARWICH · Map 13 TM23

The Goodlife Guesthouse

★★★ GUEST ACCOMMODATION

tel: 01255 556565 & 242440 **162 High Street, Dovercourt CO12 3AT**
email: mike@clickyourfingers.com **web:** www.goodlifehotel.co.uk
dir: *On Dovercourt High Street, opposite park.*

This seaside establishment is located in the centre of Harwich. The accommodation is modern in style and very spacious, as are the main dining and lounge areas. There is a private car park on site, and directly opposite there's a park with good views of the sea which is only 150 metres from the house. A cooked breakfast is served daily in the dining area.

Rooms: 10 en suite (2 fmly) **Facilities:** STV FTV TVL tea/coffee Lift Licensed WiFi ⚐ Snooker 🔒 **Parking:** 24

HATFIELD HEATH · Map 6 TL51

Lancasters Farm

★★★★ FARMHOUSE

tel: 01279 730220 **Chelmsford Road CM22 7BB**
email: lancastersfarm@btconnect.com **web:** www.lancastersfarm.com
dir: *A1060 from Hatfield Heath for Chelmsford, 1 mile left on sharp right bend, through white gates.*

Guests are made to feel at home at this delightfully spacious house, which is at the heart of this large working arable farm close to Stansted Airport. Bedrooms vary in size and style, but all are smartly decorated and thoughtfully equipped. Garaging can be arranged, as can transport to and from the airport.

Rooms: 4 rms (3 en suite) (1 pri facs) **S** fr £50 **D** fr £100* **Facilities:** FTV Lounge tea/coffee WiFi **Parking:** 6 **Notes:** No children 12 years Closed 14 December to 4 January 260 acres arable

MALDON · Map 7 TL80

The Bell

★★★ ⚐ GUEST HOUSE

tel: 01621 843208 **2 Silver Street CM9 4QE**
email: info@thebellmaldon.co.uk **web:** www.thebellmaldon.co.uk
dir: *Phone for directions.*

Centrally located for exploring the historic town of Maldon and surrounding areas, this attractive guest house used to be a pub in a previous life and many original features can still be found around the property. The bedrooms offer good accommodation, while breakfast is served in the former cellar. Limited parking is available.

Rooms: 4 rms (2 en suite) (2 pri facs) **Facilities:** FTV DVD TVL tea/coffee Direct dial WiFi ⚐ 🔒 **Parking:** 2 **Notes:** LB No children 6 years

MANNINGTREE · Map 13 TM13

Premier Collection

Dairy House Farm

★★★★★ FARMHOUSE

tel: 01255 870322 & 07749 073974 **Bradfield Road CO11 2SR**
email: bridgetwhitworth353@gmail.com **web:** www.dairyhousefarm.info

(For full entry see Wix)

SAFFRON WALDEN   Map 12 TL53

Bendysh Hall Bed & Breakfast

★★★★ FARMHOUSE

tel: 01799 599220 & 07950 750684 **Ashdon Road, Radwinter CB10 2UA**
email: info@bendyshhallbedandbreakfast.co.uk
web: www.bendyshhallbedandbreakfast.co.uk
dir: *From Saffron Walden on B1053 towards Radwinter, through village, turn left signed Ashdon. Bendysh Hall 1 mile on right.*

Bendysh Hall Bed & Breakfast is located close to Saffron Walden in a quiet spot that results in a comfortable night's sleep. It is a beautiful Grade II listed building, on a 300-acre farm, that has been thoughtfully renovated over the years to retain some of the original period features. The hearty breakfasts make good use made of high quality ingredients and eggs from the farm. Guests are welcome to take a walk or cycle through the woods.

Rooms: 3 rms (2 en suite) (1 pri facs) **Facilities:** FTV DVD Lounge TVL tea/coffee WiFi Fishing **Extras:** Snacks – complimentary; robes **Parking:** 10 **Notes:** LB No children 10 years 300 acres arable/poultry

The Crown Inn

★★★ INN

tel: 01799 522475 **Little Walden CB10 1XA**
email: pippathecrown@aol.com **web:** www.thecrownlittlewalden.co.uk
dir: *M11 junction 9 follow signs for Saffron Walden. In Saffron Walden, left at lights signed Thaxted. At mini roundabout left towards Little Walden (B1052).*

This charming country inn enjoys a prominent position in the pretty village of Little Walden and has a choice of three cosy, comfortable bedrooms. All are individually styled and well equipped. Free WiFi is available throughout the property and there is secure parking for guests. There's a great atmosphere in the authentic bar, and an extensive choice of home-cooked meals on the evening menu.

Rooms: 3 en suite **Facilities:** FTV DVD tea/coffee Dinner available WiFi **Conf:** Max 40 Thtr 40 Class 30 Board 30 **Parking:** 30

SOUTHEND-ON-SEA   Map 7 TQ88

The Ilfracombe House

★★★★ GUEST ACCOMMODATION

tel: 01702 351000 **9–13 Wilson Road SS1 1HG**
email: info@ilfracombe-hotel.co.uk **web:** www.ilfracombe-hotel.co.uk
dir: *500 yards west of town centre. Exit A13 at Cricketers pub into Milton Road, 3rd left into Cambridge Road, 4th right, car park in Alexandra Road.*

The Ilfracombe House lies in Southend's conservation area, just a short walk from the cliffs, gardens and the beach. The public rooms include a dining room, lounge and a cosy bar, and the well-equipped bedrooms include deluxe options and two four-poster rooms.

Rooms: 20 en suite (4 fmly) (2 GF) **Facilities:** STV FTV DVD TVL tea/coffee Dinner available Direct dial Licensed WiFi **Extras:** Mini-fridge **Conf:** Max 15 **Parking:** 9 **Notes:** LB

STANSTED AIRPORT   Map 6 TL52

See also Bishop's Stortford (Hertfordshire)

The White House

★★★★ GUEST ACCOMMODATION

tel: 01279 870257 **Smiths Green CM22 6NR**
email: enquiries@whitehousestansted.co.uk **web:** www.whitehousestansted.co.uk
dir: *M11 junction 8, B1256 towards Takeley. Through lights at Four Ashes crossroads. 400 yards, corner of B1256 and Smiths Green.*

The White House is a delightful 16th-century property situated close to Stansted Airport – but not under the flight path. The stylish bedrooms feature superb beds, luxurious bathrooms and many thoughtful touches. Traditional breakfasts, served in the farmhouse-style kitchen, are made from local ingredients; evening meals are available at the Lion and Lamb, a nearby pub and restaurant owned by the proprietors, who can usually provide transport to and from The White House.

Rooms: 3 rms (2 en suite) (1 pri facs) (3 fmly) **Facilities:** FTV DVD tea/coffee Dinner available WiFi **Extras:** Robes, speciality toiletries, bottled water, Nespresso coffee machine **Conf:** Max 25 **Parking:** 6 **Notes:** Closed 24–25, 31 December and 1 January

THAXTED   Map 12 TL63

The Farmhouse Inn

★★★ INN

tel: 01371 830864 **Monk Street CM6 2NR**
email: info@farmhouseinn.org **web:** www.farmhouseinn.org
dir: *M11 to A120 to B184, 1 mile from Thaxted, between Thaxted and Great Dunmow.*

This 16th-century inn overlooks the Chelmer Valley, and is surrounded by open countryside. The property is ideally situated in the quiet hamlet of Monk Street about two miles from the historic town of Thaxted. Bedrooms are pleasantly decorated and equipped with modern facilities. Public rooms include a cosy lounge bar and a large, smartly appointed restaurant.

Rooms: 11 annexe en suite **Facilities:** FTV tea/coffee Dinner available WiFi **Conf:** Max 80 Thtr 80 Class 60 Board 50 **Parking:** 35

THORPE BAY
See Southend-on-Sea

TOPPESFIELD
Map 12 TL73

Ollivers Farm
★★★ BED AND BREAKFAST

tel: 01787 237642 **CO9 4LS**
web: www.essex-bed-breakfast.co.uk
dir: *500 yards southeast of village centre. Exit A1017 in Great Yeldham to Toppesfield, farm 1 mile on left before T-junction to village.*

Full of charm and character, this impressive 16th-century farmhouse is set amid pretty landscaped gardens in a peaceful rural location. Bedrooms are pleasantly decorated and thoughtfully equipped. Public rooms have a wealth of original features including exposed beams and there is a huge open fireplace in the reception hall.

Rooms: 3 rms (1 en suite) (1 pri facs) **S** fr £50 **D** fr £100* **Facilities:** FTV Lounge tea/coffee WiFi 🚲 Shed for bikes **Parking:** 4 **Notes:** No children 10 years Closed 23 December to 1 January

WIX
Map 13 TM12

Premier Collection

Dairy House Farm
★★★★★ FARMHOUSE

tel: 01255 870322 & 07749 073974 **Bradfield Road CO11 2SR**
email: bridgetwhitworth353@gmail.com **web:** www.dairyhousefarm.info
dir: *Exit A120 into Wix, turn at crossroads to Bradfield, farm 1 mile on left.*

This Georgian house stands amid 550 acres of arable land and is blessed with stunning views of the countryside. Appointed in the Victorian style, the house has original decorative tiled floors, moulded cornices and marble fireplaces. The spacious bedrooms are carefully furnished and equipped with many thoughtful touches. Breakfast is served in the elegant antique-furnished dining room and there is a cosy lounge.

Rooms: 3 en suite **S** fr £58 **D** fr £80* **Facilities:** FTV DVD TVL tea/coffee WiFi 🚲 Farm reservoir fishing **Extras:** Home-made cake – complimentary **Parking:** 8 **Notes:** No children 12 years 550 acres arable

GLOUCESTERSHIRE

ALDERTON
Map 10 SP03

Tally Ho Bed & Breakfast
★★★★ BED AND BREAKFAST

tel: 01242 621482 & 07966 593169 **20 Beckford Road GL20 8NL**
email: tallyhobb@aol.com **web:** www.cotswolds-bedandbreakfast.co.uk
dir: *M5 junction 9, A46 signed Evesham, through Ashchurch. Take B4077 signed Stow-on-the-Wold and Alderton. Left in 1.5 miles opposite garage signed Alderton. Into village, pass Gardeners pub on right, Tally Ho on left.*

Convenient for the M5, this friendly establishment stands in a delightful, quiet village. Bedrooms, including two on the ground floor, offer modern comforts and attractive co-ordinated furnishings. Breakfast is served in the stylish dining room, and for dinner, the village pub is just a stroll away.

Rooms: 3 en suite (1 fmly) (2 GF) **S** fr £65 **D** fr £80* **Facilities:** FTV DVD tea/coffee WiFi **Extras:** Bottled water, speciality toiletries **Parking:** 3 **Notes:** No children 2 years

AMBERLEY
Map 4 SO80

The Amberley Inn
★★★★ INN

tel: 01453 872565 **Culver Hill GL5 5AF**
email: enquiries@theamberleyinn.co.uk **web:** www.theamberleyinn.co.uk
dir: *From A46 follow signs for Amberley, up Culver Hill, in village centre on left.*

This delightful inn is just outside Stroud, with walks from the door in all directions across the Woodchester Valley and commons. Pets are especially welcome here. The bedrooms come in a range of sizes – some are located above the main building while others are in the separate Garden House. A range of real ales and wines is available in the traditional, welcoming bar and a selection of delicious bar and restaurant meals make good use of fine quality local produce.

Rooms: 8 en suite 5 annexe en suite (2 fmly) (1 GF) **Facilities:** FTV Lounge tea/coffee Dinner available Direct dial WiFi 🚲 **Extras:** Speciality toiletries, robes **Conf:** Max 30 **Parking:** 7 **Notes:** LB Civ wed 35

ARLINGHAM
Map 4 SO71

The Old Passage Inn
★★★★ ◎◎ ⚲ RESTAURANT WITH ROOMS

tel: 01452 740547 **Passage Road GL2 7JR**
email: oldpassage@btconnect.com **web:** www.theoldpassage.com
dir: *A38 onto B4071 through Frampton on Severn. 4 miles to Arlingham, through village to river.*

Delightfully located on the very edge of the River Severn, this relaxing restaurant with rooms combines high quality food with an air of tranquillity. Bedrooms and bathrooms are decorated in a modern style, and have a collection of welcome extras including a well-stocked mini-bar. The menu offers a wide range of seafood and shellfish dishes including crab, oysters and lobsters from Cornwall, kept alive in seawater tanks. An outdoor terrace is available in warmer months. No children under 10 at dinner please.

Rooms: 2 en suite **S** fr £80 **D** fr £120* **Facilities:** FTV DVD Lounge tea/coffee Dinner available WiFi 🚲 **Extras:** Mini-bar – chargeable **Parking:** 30 **Notes:** Closed 25–26 December RS January to February closed for dinner Tuesday and Wednesday

BARNSLEY   Map 5 SP00

Premier Collection

The Village Pub

★★★★★ 🍷 🍴 INN

tel: 01285 740000 & 740241 **GL7 5EF**
email: reservations@barnsleyhouse.com **web**: www.thevillagepub.co.uk
dir: *On B4425 in centre of village.*

With a village location as its name suggests, this delightful establishment provides high quality accommodation and an efficient but relaxed style of hospitality and service. Owned by the same company as Barnsley House Hotel (across the road), guests here can enjoy an informal stay with high standards. The bar-dining room serves an excellent choice of top quality, seasonal produce and a varied choice of wines and ales. The bedrooms and bathrooms come in a range of sizes and all are comfortably furnished and equipped.

Rooms: 6 en suite (1 fmly) **S** fr £99 **D** fr £109* **Facilities:** STV FTV DVD iPod docking station tea/coffee Dinner available Direct dial WiFi 🐾 🦢 ♞ Riding **Parking:** 20 **Notes:** LB

BERKELEY   Map 4 ST69

The Malt House

★★★ INN

tel: 01453 511177 **22 Marybrook Street GL13 9BA**
email: the-malthouse@btconnect.com **web**: www.themalthouse.uk.com
dir: *A38 into Berkeley, at town hall follow road to right, premises on right past hospital and opposite school.*

Conveniently located for business and leisure guests, this family-run inn has a convivial atmosphere. The bedrooms are soundly appointed while public areas include a choice of bars, a skittle alley and an attractive restaurant area. Local attractions include Berkeley Castle and the Wildfowl & Wetlands Trust at Slimbridge.

Rooms: 9 en suite (2 fmly) **Facilities:** FTV tea/coffee Dinner available WiFi Skittle alley **Parking:** 30 **Notes:** LB

BIBURY — Map 5 SP10

The Catherine Wheel

★★★★ ⌂ INN

tel: 01285 740250 **Arlington GL7 5ND**
email: rooms@catherinewheel-bibury.co.uk **web:** www.catherinewheel-bibury.co.uk
dir: *On B4425 between Burford and Cirencester.*

This family-run inn provides a pleasant welcome and traditional country pub atmosphere. A range of seating is available in the cosy bar or in the more formal dining room where a selection of carefully-prepared dishes is offered throughout the day and evening. Bedrooms are in an adjacent building and include smaller standard rooms and larger superior rooms – all are comfortably furnished and include welcome extras.

Rooms: 4 annexe en suite (4 GF) **Facilities:** FTV DVD TVL tea/coffee Dinner available Direct dial WiFi ⚓ **Parking:** 23

CHELTENHAM — Map 10 SO92

Premier Collection

The Battledown Bed and Breakfast

★★★★★ ⌂ BED AND BREAKFAST

tel: 01242 233881 & 07807 142069 **125 Hales Road GL52 6ST**
email: info@thebattledown.co.uk **web:** www.thebattledown.co.uk
dir: *0.5 mile east of town centre. A40 onto B4075, 0.5 mile on right.*

The Battledown is a handsome Grade II listed Georgian house on the east side of Cheltenham; it is in a convenient location for the town centre, the racecourse and the surrounding Cotswold countryside. The seven en suite bedrooms have comfortable beds with Egyptian cotton bed linen, Freeview TVs, DVD players and tea- and coffee-making facilities. Guests are welcome to use the garden that has patio areas for relaxation. Locally sourced produce is used for the breakfasts. Free WiFi is available.

Rooms: 7 en suite (1 fmly) **S** fr £65 **D** fr £85* **Facilities:** FTV DVD Lounge tea/coffee WiFi ⚓ **Parking:** 7 **Notes:** LB

Premier Collection

The Bradley

★★★★★ ⌂ GUEST ACCOMMODATION

tel: 01242 519077 & 07502 225031 **19 Royal Parade, Bayshill Road GL50 3AY**
email: enquiries@thebradleyhotel.co.uk **web:** www.thebradleyhotel.co.uk
dir: *Phone for directions.*

The Bradley is a boutique townhouse in the centre of Regency Cheltenham, just a few minutes' stroll from the local shops and the town centre. Bedrooms and bathrooms offer plenty of quality and comfort, and come in a range of shapes and sizes. Breakfast utilises the best quality produce, and is served in the elegant dining room. Parking permits can generally be arranged if booked in advance.

Rooms: 8 en suite 2 annexe en suite (1 fmly) (1 GF) **S** fr £90 **D** fr £100* **Facilities:** FTV Lounge tea/coffee Licensed WiFi ⚓ **Extras:** Coffee machine, fridge, fresh milk

Clarence Court

★★★★ ⌂ GUEST ACCOMMODATION

tel: 01242 580411 **Clarence Square GL50 4JR**
email: enquiries@clarencecourthotel.com **web:** www.clarencecourthotel.com
dir: *Phone for directions.*

Situated in an attractive, tree-lined Georgian square, this property was once owned by the Duke of Wellington. The building is charming and its elegant public rooms reflect the grace of a bygone age. Spacious bedrooms offer ample comfort and quality, and have many original features. The convenience of the peaceful location is a great asset, only a five-minute stroll from the town centre. A varied range of carefully prepared dishes is offered in the café-restaurant from noon to 9pm.

Rooms: 20 en suite (3 fmly) (7 GF) **Facilities:** FTV DVD TVL tea/coffee Dinner available Direct dial Licensed WiFi Free use of Fitness First Leisure Club (adults) **Parking:** 21

Malvern View

★★★★ GUEST ACCOMMODATION

tel: 01242 672017 & 07917 714929 **Cleeve Hill GL52 3PR**
email: info@malvernview.com **web:** www.malvernview.com
dir: *B4632 from Cheltenham towards Winchcombe and Stratford-upon-Avon. Through Southam and Cleeve Hill, Malvern View on right.*

Located just outside Cheltenham, most rooms in this comfortable accommodation have delightful views over the countryside towards the Malvern Hills and beyond. Bedrooms and bathrooms here are comfortably furnished and include some welcome extras. Breakfast is made to order and offers a range of well-presented options. Off-street parking is available.

Rooms: 7 rms (6 en suite) (1 pri facs) (1 fmly) **S** fr £80 **D** fr £100* **Facilities:** FTV iPod docking station Lounge tea/coffee Licensed WiFi ⚓ **Extras:** Honesty bar – chargeable **Conf:** Max 30 Thtr 18 Class 30 Board 18 **Parking:** 12 **Notes:** LB Closed 4–29 January RS weekends (October to March); minimum 2 night stay all year

CHIPPING CAMPDEN — Map 10 SP13

The Kings

★★★★ ◎◎◎ ⌂ RESTAURANT WITH ROOMS

tel: 01386 840256 & 841056 **The Square, High Street GL55 6AW**
email: info@kingscampden.co.uk **web:** www.kingscampden.co.uk
dir: *In centre of town square.*

Located in the centre of this delightful Cotswold town, The Kings effortlessly blends a relaxed and friendly welcome with efficient service. Bedrooms and bathrooms come in a range of shapes and sizes and all are appointed to a high level of quality and comfort. Dining options, whether in the main Jackrabbit Restaurant or the comfortable bar area, serve a tempting menu to suit all tastes, from light salads and pasta, to meat and fish dishes.

Rooms: 13 en suite 5 annexe en suite (3 fmly) (3 GF) **Facilities:** FTV tea/coffee Dinner available Direct dial WiFi **Parking:** 14 **Notes:** LB Civ wed 60

CHIPPING CAMPDEN *continued*

Lygon Arms

★★★★ 🛏 🍴 INN

tel: 01386 840318 & 840089 **High Street GL55 6HB**
email: sandra@lygonarms.co.uk **web:** www.lygonarms.co.uk
dir: *In town centre near church.*

This charming and welcoming inn sits on Chipping Campden's high street – a tranquil location with lots of tempting antique shops. Well managed by a friendly team, the inn has a cosy bar with open log fires and oak beams. Spacious and very well-appointed accommodation is provided in the main building and in mews houses. Both breakfast and dinner are hearty and should not be missed.

Rooms: 10 en suite (3 fmly) (1 GF) **Facilities:** FTV DVD tea/coffee Dinner available WiFi 🛁 **Extras:** Mini-fridge with fruit and water, robes **Parking:** 12 **Notes:** LB

The Seagrave Arms

★★★★ ◉◉ INN

tel: 01386 840192 **Friday Street, Weston-sub-Edge GL55 6QH**
email: enquiries@theseagravearms.com **web:** www.seagravearms.com
dir: *From Moreton-in-Marsh take A44 towards Evesham. Approximately 7 miles right onto B4081 signed Chipping Campden. Becomes Sheep Street. At junction with High Street, left into Dyers Lane. 0.5 mile over Dovers Hill, into Weston-sub-Edge, becomes Church Street. Inn on left.*

Part of The Epicurean Collection, this Grade II listed, 400-year-old house is set in the heart of the Cotswolds. It offers modern accommodation in the main house and also rooms around the courtyard. The inn is full of character, serving award-winning seasonal food every day of the week, with occasional specialist nights. Staff are warm and friendly, and the bar offers local ales and good wines. There is ample parking and attractive gardens.

Rooms: 5 en suite 3 annexe en suite (3 GF) **Facilities:** FTV tea/coffee Dinner available WiFi **Notes:** LB

The Noel Arms

★★★★ 🛏 🍴 INN

tel: 01386 840317 **High Street GL55 6AT**
email: hotelmanager@noelarmshotel.com **web:** www.bespokehotels.com/noelarmshotel
dir: *In the town centre.*

At the heart of the picturesque Cotswold market town of Chipping Campden, The Noel Arms has been welcoming guests, including royalty, for hundreds of years; Charles II is said to have rested there after his defeat to Cromwell in 1651. Needless to say the property has a wealth of period features which are complemented by modern comforts. Public areas include a busy coffee shop and the well-stocked Drovers Bar. Whether dining in the conservatory, restaurant or bar, head chef Indunil Upatissa's award-winning curries are a must. The elegant, well-equipped bedrooms vary in shape and size and include four-poster rooms. Spa treatments can be arranged at the inn's sister property, Cotswold House Hotel & Spa, just across the road.

Rooms: 27 en suite (7 GF) **Facilities:** tea/coffee Dinner available WiFi **Parking:** 27

▌ CHIPPING SODBURY   Map 4 ST78

The Moda House

★★★★ GUEST ACCOMMODATION

tel: 01454 312135 **1 High Street BS37 6BA**
email: enquiries@modahouse.co.uk **web:** www.modahouse.co.uk
dir: *In town centre.*

This popular, Grade II listed Georgian house has an imposing position at the top of the High Street. It has been appointed to provide modern bedrooms of varying shapes and sizes, and has comfortable public areas that have retained many original features. Room facilities include satellite TV and phones.

Rooms: 8 en suite 3 annexe en suite (3 GF) **Facilities:** STV FTV tea/coffee Licensed WiFi **Notes:** No children 16 years

▌ CIRENCESTER   Map 5 SP00

Premier Collection

The Fleece at Cirencester

★★★★★ 🍴 INN

tel: 01285 658507 **Market Place GL7 2NZ**
email: relax@thefleececirencester.co.uk **web:** www.thefleececirencester.co.uk
dir: *Phone for directions.*

Located in the heart of the market town of Cirencester, this country inn has been finished to a high standard with guests and comfort in mind. Bedrooms are sumptuous, and many thoughtful touches add to any stay. Public areas include a traditional bar featuring Thwaites cask ales, a cosy lounge and a popular restaurant.

Rooms: 28 en suite (1 fmly) **Facilities:** FTV Lounge tea/coffee Dinner available WiFi **Parking:** 8

Greensleeves

★★★★ BED AND BREAKFAST

tel: 01285 642516 & 07971 929259 **Baunton Lane, Stratton GL7 2LN**
email: johnps1@tesco.net **web:** www.greensleeves4u.co.uk
dir: *From Cirencester, follow signs for Stratton. Right into Baunton Lane.*

Guests are ensured of a warm and friendly welcome from proprietor John, at this delightful property, just a short drive from Cirencester. The smart en suite accommodation is well equipped with a host of facilities to ensure both leisure and corporate guests feel at home. Delicious breakfasts feature home-baked bread. Off-street parking is provided.

Rooms: 3 en suite **Facilities:** FTV DVD tea/coffee WiFi ⚓ 🔒 **Parking:** 5

COLEFORD   Map 4 SO51

The Miners Country Inn

★★★ ◉◉ INN

tel: 01594 836632 **Chepstow Road, Sling GL16 8LH**
email: info@theminerssling.co.uk **web:** www.theminerssling.co.uk
dir: *1 mile from Coleford town centre.*

The Miners Country Inn is a real family affair, set in the heart of the Forest of Dean. First impressions are of a quintessential pub with beamed ceilings, stone floors and a bar offering an array of local ales. A strong local trade makes for a bustling atmosphere, but really it's the food that's the focus. The chef-patron uses locally sourced ingredients, and suppliers are championed on blackboards and menus, with most supplying the inn exclusively. Dishes are well conceived and offer classic hearty fare with a modern twist. Bedrooms are light and airy, with modern en suite bathrooms.

Rooms: 4 en suite **Facilities:** FTV tea/coffee Dinner available

COWLEY   Map 10 SO91

The Green Dragon Inn

★★★★ INN

tel: 01242 870271 **Cockleford GL53 9NW**
email: green-dragon@buccaneer.co.uk **web:** www.green-dragon-inn.co.uk
dir: *Phone for directions.*

The Green Dragon offers all the charm and character of an English country pub combined with a relaxed atmosphere and carefully prepared food made with local produce; dinner is particularly recommended. Bedrooms, some at ground floor level, are individually furnished and vary in size. There is a terrace at the front where guests may enjoy a drink on warmer days.

Rooms: 9 annexe en suite (1 fmly) (4 GF) **S** fr £80 **D** fr £105* **Facilities:** STV tea/coffee Dinner available WiFi **Extras:** Fresh milk, fruit **Conf:** Max 100 Thtr 100 Class 65 Board 65 **Parking:** 40 **Notes:** LB Closed evenings of 25 December, 26 December and 1 January

DIDMARTON   Map 4 ST88

The Kings Arms

★★★★ ⌂ INN

tel: 01454 238245 **The Street GL9 1DT**
email: enquiries@kingsarmsdidmarton.co.uk **web:** www.kingsarmsdidmarton.co.uk
dir: *M4 junction 18, A46 towards Stroud. 6 miles, right onto A433. 3 miles to Didmarton. Kings Arms on left.*

Part of The Epicurean Collection, The Kings Arms is a real gem. Bedrooms, converted from the old stables, are extremely comfortable, and are named after hounds that once ran with the local hunt. Locally sourced produce is cooked with passion and presented with flair. The inn retains its stone-flagged floors, heavy wooden tables, rustic walls and simple decoration. Real ales are also a feature here. Outside, the garden provides a great space in the summer.

Rooms: 6 en suite (1 GF) **Facilities:** FTV tea/coffee Dinner available WiFi
Conf: Max 30 Thtr 30 Board 18 **Parking:** 29

EBRINGTON   Map 10 SP14

The Ebrington Arms

★★★★★ ◉◉ ⌂ INN

tel: 01386 593223 **GL55 6NH**
email: reservations@theebringtonarms.co.uk **web:** www.theebringtonarms.co.uk
dir: *From Chipping Campden take B4035 towards Shipston on Stour, left to Ebrington.*

Located in the quiet, unspoilt village of Ebrington, just a couple of miles from Chipping Campden, this 17th-century inn offers an excellent selection of real ales, fine wines and really enjoyable award-winning cuisine utilising the finest of produce. Food is served in the friendly bar or in the cosy dining room where the open fire roars on chilly days. Bedrooms are full of character and include some welcome extras. A large beer garden and car park are also available.

Rooms: 5 en suite **Facilities:** FTV tea/coffee Dinner available WiFi **Extras:** Home-made cookies, sherry – complimentary **Conf:** Max 32 Thtr 32 Class 32 Board 25 **Parking:** 10 **Notes:** LB

FRAMPTON MANSELL   Map 4 SO90

The Crown Inn

★★★★ ⌂ INN

tel: 01285 760601 **GL6 8JG**
email: enquiries@thecrowninn-cotswolds.co.uk **web:** www.thecrowninn-cotswolds.co.uk
dir: *Exit A419 signed Frampton Mansell, 0.75 mile, inn at village centre.*

This establishment was a cider house in the 17th century, and guests today will find that roaring log fires, locally brewed ales and traditional, home-cooked food are all on offer. The comfortable, well-equipped bedrooms are in an annexe, and ample parking is available.

Rooms: 12 annexe en suite (1 fmly) (4 GF) **S** fr £70 **D** fr £95* **Facilities:** tea/coffee Dinner available WiFi **Conf:** Max 40 **Parking:** 35 **Notes:** LB

The Wharf House Restaurant with Rooms

★★★★ ◉ RESTAURANT WITH ROOMS

tel: 01452 332900 **Over GL2 8DB**
email: enquiries@thewharfhouse.co.uk **web:** www.thewharfhouse.co.uk
dir: *From A40 between Gloucester and Highnam exit at lights for Over. Establishment signed.*

The Wharf House was built to replace the old lock cottage and it's located at the very edge of the river; it has pleasant views and an outdoor terrace. The bedrooms and bathrooms have been appointed to a high standard, and there are plenty of guest extras. Seasonal, local produce can be enjoyed both at breakfast and dinner in the delightful AA Rosette-awarded restaurant. Dogs are allowed in the ground-floor room and on the terrace, and there is 20-minute rapid car charger and a slow charger. The Wharf House is owned and run by the Herefordshire & Gloucestershire Canal Trust – all profits go towards the promotion and restoration of the canal.

Rooms: 7 en suite (1 fmly) (1 GF) **Facilities:** STV FTV DVD Lounge tea/coffee Dinner available WiFi Fishing ☖ **Extras:** Speciality toiletries – complimentary; Mini-bar – chargeable **Parking:** 37 **Notes:** Closed 22 December to 8 January RS Sunday to Monday check in before 6pm/restaurant closed evening

See advert opposite

The Little Thatch Inn

Ⓤ

tel: 01452 720687 **141 Bristol Road, Quedgeley GL2 4PQ**
email: contact@thelittlethatch.co.uk **web:** www.thelittlethatch.co.uk
dir: *Phone for directions.*

Currently the rating for this establishment is not confirmed. This may be due to a change of ownership or because it has only recently joined the AA rating scheme.

Rooms: 22 en suite **Facilities:** FTV tea/coffee WiFi

Guiting Guest House

★★★★ BED AND BREAKFAST

tel: 01451 850470 **Post Office Lane GL54 5TZ**
email: info@guitingguesthouse.com **web:** www.guitingguesthouse.com
dir: *Phone for directions.*

Guiting Power is a quintessential, beautiful and peaceful Cotswold village surrounded by stunning countryside. Guiting Guest House is very close to the village shop, post office, the church and two excellent pubs. A 16th-century Cotswold-stone farmhouse with warming log fires in the winter, and a delightful garden, it offers comfortable rooms, breakfasts with local produce and home-made bread, and a friendly, peaceful atmosphere; all of which have made it a favourite with guests from all over the world. Some bedrooms have four-poster beds, and baskets of fresh fruit and flowers provide a personal touch. Hairdryer, bathrobes and toiletries are provided for extra comfort. There are lots of walks right from the garden gate.

Rooms: 5 rms (4 en suite) (1 pri facs) (2 GF) **S** fr £85 **D** fr £85* **Facilities:** FTV Lounge tea/coffee WiFi ☖ **Extras:** Fresh fruit, flowers, robes – complimentary **Notes:** No children 18 years Closed 25–26 December

The Ragged Cot

★★★★ INN

tel: 01453 884643 & 07976 011198 **Cirencester Road GL6 8PE**
email: info@theraggedcot.co.uk **web:** www.theraggedcot.co.uk
dir: *M5 junction 13 onto A419 signed Stroud/Cirencester. At Ashton Down Airfield roundabout, right signed Minchinhampton. 2 miles on left.*

Originally a coaching inn in the 17th century, this property has been extended over the years to offer a modern, large, airy bar and restaurant together with a variety of good quality bedrooms equipped for the modern guest. An extensive collection of ever-changing artwork is an interesting feature. This friendly inn serves a wide selection of real ales and a menu focusing on locally-sourced ingredients.

Rooms: 9 en suite (4 GF) **Facilities:** FTV DVD tea/coffee Dinner available WiFi ☖ **Extras:** Speciality toiletries **Parking:** 30

THE WHARF HOUSE

AWARD-WINNING WATERSIDE RESTAURANT WITH ROOMS

MODERN BRITISH AND EUROPEAN CUISINE WITH A TWIST

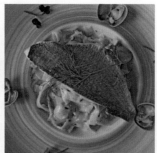

Tasting Menu at The Wharf House Six Courses only £39.99 per person.

Lighter lunches including paninis from £4.50 and deli boards from £13 now available.

Luxury accommodation with stunning riverside views.

01452 332 900
www.thewharfhouse.co.uk

Over, Gloucester, GL2 8DB
enquiries@thewharfhouse.co.uk
Directions: Turn off the A40 at traffic lights
250 yds west of Over Roundabout
(junction A40/A417). GR SO 816197

All profits from ᵀʰᵉ Wharf House will be used for the promotion and restoration of the Hereford & Gloucester Canal.

LECHLADE ON THAMES
Map 5 SU29

The Bell Inn
★★★★ ⊚ INN

tel: 01367 860249 **The Bell, Langford GL7 3LF**
email: info@thebelllangford.com **web:** www.thebelllangford.com
dir: *Phone for directions.*

Newly restored and refurbished throughout, this delightful village inn has been transformed to offer modern comforts yet retains a proper country inn atmosphere. The bedrooms and bathrooms come in a range of shapes and sizes – some are located above the inn and others in the adjacent courtyard. Food here is a highlight with a tempting selection of carefully-prepared dishes using top-quality ingredients. Advance reservations are always recommended for the popular meals as the cosy dining area and bar are quite small.

Rooms: 8 en suite **Facilities:** Dinner available **Extras:** Speciality toiletries

The Riverside
★★★ INN

tel: 01367 252534 **Park End Wharf GL7 3AQ**
email: riverside@arkells.com **web:** www.riverside-lechlade.com
dir: *Phone for directions.*

Located on the banks of the Thames, with an unrivalled position in Lechlade, this traditional inn is within easy reach of Swindon, Cirencester and the Cotswolds. Comfortable accommodation is located adjacent to the inn with its own entrance; all rooms are en suite and some are suitable for families. Owned by the Arkell's family brewers, a great range of traditionally brewed beers is available.

Rooms: 6 en suite

LOWER SLAUGHTER
Map 10 SP12

Premier Collection

The Slaughters Country Inn
★★★★★ ⊚⊚ INN

tel: 01451 822143 **GL54 2HS**
email: info@theslaughtersinn.co.uk **web:** www.theslaughtersinn.co.uk
dir: *Exit A429 at 'The Slaughters' sign, between Stow-on-the-Wold and Bourton-on-the-Water. In village centre.*

This attractive 17th-century inn is set in beautiful grounds beside the River Eye. Inside, contemporary high-quality bedrooms, all with modern bathrooms, are in keeping with the more traditional bar area with its beamed ceilings, open fires, and flagstone floors. The Eton Restaurant is an attractive setting for enjoying modern British and classical dishes; there's a comfortable lounge in which to relax. Parking is a bonus.

Rooms: 19 en suite 12 annexe en suite (3 fmly) (6 GF) **S** fr £110 **D** fr £120*
Facilities: FTV Lounge tea/coffee Dinner available Direct dial WiFi
🔒 **Extras:** Bottled water – complimentary **Parking:** 45 **Notes:** Civ wed 80

MARSHFIELD
Map 4 ST77

The Lord Nelson Inn
★★★ INN

tel: 01225 891820 **1 & 2 High Street SN14 8LP**
email: enquiries@lordnelsonatmarshfield.com **web:** www.lordnelsonatmarshfield.com
dir: *Phone for directions.*

A popular and traditional-style village inn with a good local following and a range of home-cooked meals and ales available in the relaxing bar. The bedrooms and bathrooms come in a range of shapes and sizes and are all located upstairs. Parking is usually possible on the main street right outside the inn.

Rooms: 3 en suite

MORETON-IN-MARSH
Map 10 SP23

Horse and Groom
★★★★ ⚐ ⌣ INN

tel: 01386 700413 **Bourton-on-the-Hill GL56 9AQ**
email: info@horseandgroom.info **web:** www.horseandgroom.info
dir: *Phone for directions.*

Located on the hill at Bourton-on-the-Hill, this relaxing inn offers an ideal base for exploring many famous Cotswold villages and attractions. Bedrooms and bathrooms are very well decorated and furnished, and a good selection of real ales is offered in the bar. Both dinner and breakfast are highlights here and offer a range of delicious dishes made from local quality produce. Dinner is by way of blackboard specials to reflect the freshest produce available. A car park and rear garden with seating are both welcome extras.

Rooms: 5 en suite **Facilities:** Dinner available

NAILSWORTH
Map 4 ST89

Wild Garlic Restaurant and Rooms
★★★★ ⊚⊚ ⚐ RESTAURANT WITH ROOMS

tel: 01453 832615 **3 Cossack Square GL6 0DB**
email: info@wild-garlic.co.uk **web:** www.wild-garlic.co.uk
dir: *M4 junction 18, A46 towards Stroud. Enter Nailsworth, left at roundabout, immediately left. Establishment opposite Britannia pub.*

Situated in a quiet corner of charming Nailsworth, this restaurant with rooms offers a delightful combination of welcoming, relaxed hospitality and serious cuisine. The spacious and well-equipped bedrooms are situated above the award-winning restaurant. The small and friendly team of staff ensure guests are very well looked after throughout their stay.

Rooms: 5 en suite (2 fmly) **Facilities:** STV FTV DVD tea/coffee Dinner available WiFi ⚓ Fishing Riding Shooting Hot air ballooning **Extras:** Speciality toiletries, spring water – complimentary; mini-bar – chargeable **Conf:** Max 6 Thtr 6 Class 6 Board 6

NAUNTON
Map 10 SP12

Mill View Guest House
★★★★ GUEST HOUSE

tel: 01451 850586 & 07887 553571 **2 Mill View GL54 3AF**
email: patricia@millview.myzen.co.uk **web:** www.millviewguesthousecotswolds.com
dir: *Exit B4068 to east end of village.*

Mill View Guest House takes its name from the historic watermill opposite, and the owners of this former family home aim to provide every comfort. A warm welcome and attentive care is assured in this non-smoking house, which has one ground-floor bedroom equipped for easier access. This establishment provides a good base for walkers or for those touring Gloucestershire.

Rooms: 3 en suite (1 GF) **S** fr £45 **D** fr £65* **Facilities:** FTV DVD iPod docking station TVL tea/coffee Dinner available WiFi ⚓ **Extras:** Snacks, sherry – complimentary **Parking:** 4 **Notes:** LB

NEWENT
Map 10 SO72

Kilcot Inn
★★★★ ⊜ INN

tel: 01989 720707 **Ross Road GL18 1NA**
email: info@kilcotinn.com **web:** www.kilcotinn.com
dir: *Phone for directions.*

The inviting Kilcot Inn offers the best traditions of hospitality, food and drink. From the selection of real ales and local ciders on tap, to the high-quality produce used in the delicious dishes in the bar/restaurant, there is something for everyone. The bedrooms and bathrooms above the inn provide top quality and comfort. Outdoor seating is also available, including a pleasant garden area to the rear of the property.

Rooms: 4 en suite **Facilities:** FTV Lounge tea/coffee Dinner available WiFi ⚓ **Parking:** 40

OLD SODBURY
Map 4 ST78

The Sodbury House
★★★★ GUEST HOUSE

tel: 01454 312847 **Badminton Road BS37 6LU**
email: info@sodburyhouse.co.uk **web:** www.sodburyhouse.co.uk
dir: *M4 junction 18, A46 north, 2 miles left onto A432 to Chipping Sodbury, house 1 mile on left.*

This comfortably furnished, 19th-century farmhouse stands in six acres of grounds. The bedrooms, some located on the ground floor and some in buildings adjacent to the main house, have many extra facilities. Breakfast offers a varied choice and is served in the spacious breakfast room.

Rooms: 6 en suite 3 annexe en suite (1 fmly) (2 GF) **Facilities:** FTV Lounge TVL tea/coffee WiFi 🐾 ⚓ **Parking:** 30 **Notes:** Closed 24 December to 3 January

PAINSWICK
Map 4 SO80

The Falcon
★★★★ ☕ ⊜ INN

tel: 01452 814222 **New Street GL6 6UN**
email: info@falconpainswick.co.uk **web:** www.falconpainswick.co.uk
dir: *On A46 in centre of Painswick.*

The Falcon is an imposing Cotswold-stone building that dates back to 1554 and sits on the main street of this attractive Cotswold village. Overlooking St Mary's church with its famous clipped yews, it's also within easy driving distance of Cheltenham Racecourse. Bedrooms are individually designed and well equipped with comfortable beds, crisp white linen and very good quality toiletries. With an eclectic mix of furnishings and chalky white and muted duck egg blue walls, this popular place has a charming atmosphere where locals and tourists mingle. The kitchen serves an accomplished bistro-style menu based on locally-sourced, seasonal ingredients.

Rooms: 8 en suite 3 annexe en suite (1 fmly) (1 GF) **Facilities:** FTV tea/coffee Dinner available WiFi ♿ ⚓ **Extras:** Speciality toiletries **Conf:** Max 30 Thtr 30 Class 20 Board 20 **Parking:** 20

PUCKLECHURCH   Map 4 ST77

Orchard Cottage Bed & Breakfast

AA ADVERTISED

tel: 0117 937 3284 **18 Homefield Road BS16 9QD**
email: davidmstacey@gmail.com web: www.orchardcottagebandb.co.uk
dir: *Contact for directions.*

Orchard Cottage is adjacent to Pucklechurch conservation area, and is a completely private duplex apartment with its own entrance and free parking, available for B&B or self-catering. The apartment includes a lounge with designer furniture, LCD TV, WiFi, iPod dock, fridge and tea/coffee making facilities. The bedroom has a round window with a lovely view of the conservation area barn. The apartment is suitable for adults only.

Rooms: 1 en suite **S** fr £69 **D** fr £79* **Facilities:** STV FTV DVD iPod docking station TVL tea/coffee WiFi ⚿ **Parking:** 4 **Notes:** No children 18 years

SELSLEY   Map 4 SO80

The Bell Inn

★★★★ ◎◎ INN

tel: 01453 753801 **Bell Lane GL5 5JY**
email: info@thebellinnselsley.com web: www.thebellinnselsley.com
dir: *M5 junction 13 take A419 Stroud. At Sainsburys roundabout take 3rd exit Selsley Hill. The Bell 0.5 mile on left.*

This traditional 16th-century Grade II listed country inn has been appointed to provide quality and comfort throughout. Guests can choose from a selection of real ales in the bar or enjoy the countryside views from the seats in the pleasant garden. A separate gin bar stocks around 30 gins. The food here should not be missed, with a range of carefully selected and locally sourced produce on the menus.

Rooms: 2 en suite **S** fr £70 **D** fr £90 (room only)* **Facilities:** FTV Dinner available WiFi **Extras:** Nespresso machines, specialist toiletries, Bose sound system **Parking:** 12 **Notes:** No children RS winter closed 3–5pm

STOW-ON-THE-WOLD   Map 10 SP12

Premier Collection

Old Stocks Inn

★★★★★ ◎ ⬥ RESTAURANT WITH ROOMS

tel: 01451 830666 **The Square GL54 1AP**
email: info@oldstocksinn.com web: www.oldstocksinn.com
dir: *From A429 turn into Market Square, located opposite Town Hall.*

Old Stocks Inn has been lovingly restored and offers a mix of modern facilities and 17th-century charm. Stylish bedrooms are well designed and make good use of space; there are some unique features in the 'Amazing Great Rooms'. Cuisine is very much at the heart of the operation with a café, restaurant and bar making up the impressive ground floor. Not only are the breakfasts award-winning, but so is the food served at lunch and dinner.

Rooms: 13 en suite 3 annexe en suite (4 fmly) (3 GF) **Facilities:** FTV iPod docking station Lounge tea/coffee Dinner available Direct dial WiFi ⚿ **Extras:** Mini-bar, Nespresso machine **Conf:** Max 16 Thtr 10 Board 16 **Parking:** 10 **Notes:** Closed 25 December RS 24 December no accommodation

Premier Collection

The Porch House

★★★★★ ◎ ⬥ INN

tel: 01451 870048 **Digbeth Street GL54 1BN**
email: book@porch-house.co.uk web: www.porch-house.co.uk/home
dir: *Short walk from main square, on left.*

Originally built in 975 AD, The Porch House is reputed to be England's oldest inn, and many of the original features can be seen today in the beautifully presented public areas. The inn has 13 individually styled bedrooms, all equipped to a high standard, with WiFi available throughout. Guests have a choice of cosy authentic bars — with exposed stone walls and log fires — for casual dining. The award-winning restaurant is worth visiting and the unmissable breakfast features lots of local produce.

Rooms: 13 en suite (2 fmly) (2 GF) **Facilities:** STV FTV Lounge TVL tea/coffee Dinner available WiFi ⚿ **Conf:** Max 12 **Parking:** 4

Woodlands Guest House

★★★★ ⬥ GUEST ACCOMMODATION

tel: 01451 832346 **Upper Swell GL54 1EW**
email: amandak247@talktalk.net web: www.woodlands-guest-house.co.uk
dir: *Upper Swell 1 mile from Stow-on-the-Wold, take B4077 (Tewkesbury Road).*

Situated in the small hamlet of Upper Swell, Woodlands Guest House provides an ideal base for exploring the many charming nearby villages. This establishment enjoys delightful rural views and has comfortably appointed bedrooms with a good range of extra accessories. Breakfast is served in the welcoming dining room around the communal dining table. Off-road parking is available.

Rooms: 4 en suite (2 GF) **Facilities:** FTV tea/coffee WiFi **Parking:** 8 **Notes:** LB

Sheep on Sheep Street

★★★★ INN

tel: 01451 830344 **Sheep Street GL54 1AG**
email: info@thesheepstow.co.uk **web:** www.thesheepstow.co.uk
dir: *From A429 onto A436 (Sheep Street).*

Several attractive 17th-century buildings make up the Sheep on Sheep Street that offers well-appointed and attractively furnished accommodation. All bedrooms have modern en suite facilities that include luxurious toiletries. On the ground floor, the bar and dining area provide a relaxed and casual atmosphere – a wood-fired oven is used for a wide range of speciality pizzas alongside à la carte dishes. Parking is at the rear of the building and complimentary WiFi is available throughout.

Rooms: 22 en suite (1 fmly) (3 GF) **Facilities:** Lounge tea/coffee Dinner available Direct dial WiFi **Extras:** Speciality toiletries **Parking:** 22 **Notes:** LB

Corsham Field Farmhouse

★★★★ FARMHOUSE

tel: 01451 831750 **Bledington Road GL54 1JH**
email: farmhouse@corshamfield.co.uk **web:** www.corshamfield.co.uk
dir: *A436 from Stow-on-the-Wold towards Chipping Norton. After 1 mile bear right onto B4450 (Bledington Road), 1st farm on right in 0.5 mile, opposite Oddington turn.*

This charming farmhouse offers superb views over the peaceful Cotswold countryside and has comfortable, well-furnished bedrooms located in the main house and in an adjoining cottage. The garden, with chairs and tables for relaxing, provides a lovely spot for picnics and observing the wildlife. Freshly-prepared breakfast is served in the spacious dining room/lounge, and the local pub is only five minutes' walk away for dinner.

Rooms: 7 rms (6 en suite) (1 pri facs) (2 fmly) (2 GF) **S** fr £55 **D** fr £75*
Facilities: FTV Lounge tea/coffee WiFi **Extras:** Speciality toiletries, sweets **Parking:** 10 **Notes:** LB No children 5 years 100 acres arable

The Kings Head Inn

★★★★ @ INN

tel: 01608 658365 **The Green, Bledington OX7 6XQ**
email: info@kingsheadinn.net **web:** www.kingsheadinn.net
dir: *4 miles southeast off B4450.*

In prime position on the delightful village green near the river, this 16th-century inn has spacious public areas with open fires, uneven floors, beams and wood furnishings. The comfortable restaurant offers an excellent dining experience and the bedrooms have been creatively decorated and well furnished; some rooms are in a converted annexe.

Rooms: 6 en suite 6 annexe en suite (3 GF) **Facilities:** FTV TVL tea/coffee Dinner available WiFi **Extras:** Speciality toiletries **Parking:** 24 **Notes:** Closed 25–26 December RS weekdays

---

THORNBURY Map 4 ST69

Thornbury Lodge

★★★★ GUEST ACCOMMODATION

tel: 01454 281144 **Bristol Road BS35 3XL**
email: info@thornburygc.co.uk **web:** www.thornburygc.co.uk
dir: *M5 junction 16, A38 towards Thornbury. At lights (Berkeley Vale Motors) turn left, 1 mile on left.*

With good access to both the M4 and M5, this lodge offers a popular retreat for both business and leisure guests, and is surrounded by pleasant scenery including a golf course. Dinner and breakfast can be enjoyed in the clubhouse-style dining area where an abundant choice is offered. Spacious and comfortable bedrooms are located in a lodge adjacent to the main clubhouse. An excellent golf driving range is also available.

Rooms: 7 en suite 4 annexe en suite (11 fmly) (7 GF) **Facilities:** FTV TVL tea/coffee Dinner available Direct dial Licensed WiFi ♿ Driving range, practice putting green **Conf:** Max 150 Thtr 120 Class 50 Board 40 **Parking:** 200 **Notes:** LB Closed 25 December Civ wed 120

UPPER ODDINGTON Map 10 SP22

Horse & Groom

★★★ @ INN

tel: 01451 830 584 **GL56 0XH**
email: info@horseandgroomoddington.com **web:** www.horseandgroomoddington.com
dir: *Phone for directions.*

A traditional, charming Cotswolds inn tucked away in the countryside near Stow-on-the-Wold. A cosy atmosphere awaits with friendly staff and good food. The bedrooms are comfortable, and each is individual in size and shape. Guests can relax in the gardens with a drink or a meal.

Rooms: 5 en suite 2 annexe en suite (1 GF) **S** fr £79 **D** fr £89 (room only)*
Facilities: STV FTV tea/coffee Dinner available WiFi **Parking:** 25 **Notes:** No children

WICK   Map 4 ST77

Blue Lodge Farm

★★★★ FARMHOUSE

tel: 0117 937 2254 & 07748 733740 **Lodge Road, Abson BS30 5TX**
email: info@bluelodgefarm.co.uk **web:** www.bluelodgefarm.co.uk
dir: *Phone for directions.*

Peacefully located and surrounded by countryside, this pleasant farm offers a relaxed environment and yet is only a short drive from Bath or Bristol. The spacious and comfortable bedrooms and bathrooms have their own front door as they are located in a modern, purpose-built annexe. Breakfasts using good quality produce are served in the main building. A garden and car park are both available for guests.

Rooms: 3 annexe en suite (1 fmly) (3 GF) **Facilities:** FTV Lounge WiFi
⚓ **Extras:** Speciality toiletries, fruit – complimentary **Parking:** 6 **Notes:** 52 acres beef

WINCHCOMBE   Map 10 SP02

The Lion Inn

★★★★ ◉ INN

tel: 01242 603300 **37 North Street GL54 5PS**
email: reception@thelionwinchcombe.co.uk **web:** www.thelionwinchcombe.co.uk
dir: *In town centre (parking in Chandos Street).*

This 15th-century inn is situated in the centre of historic Winchcombe, a pretty Cotswold village. There are stylish en suite bedrooms of individual character that beautifully incorporate original features of the property. A seasonal menu is offered in the award-winning restaurant enhanced by daily-changing dishes; there is a small garden with tables and chairs. Parking is available in the pay-and-display car park to the rear of the property. Close by is Sudeley Castle, where Queen Katherine Parr, sixth wife of Henry VIII, is buried, while Cheltenham Racecourse is not far away.

Rooms: 8 en suite (1 fmly) (1 GF) **Facilities:** Dinner available Direct dial WiFi
Extras: Speciality toiletries – complimentary **Conf:** Max 20 Thtr 20 Class 12 Board 20 **Notes:** RS 25 December evening closed

Wesley House

★★★★ ◉◉ ⚑ RESTAURANT WITH ROOMS

tel: 01242 602366 **High Street GL54 5LJ**
email: enquiries@wesleyhouse.co.uk **web:** www.wesleyhouse.co.uk
dir: *In town centre.*

This 15th-century, half-timbered property is named after John Wesley, founder of the Methodist Church, who stayed here while preaching in the town. Bedrooms are small and full of character. In the rear dining room, where the food has been awarded two AA Rosettes, a unique lighting system changes colour to suit the mood required, and also highlights the various floral displays created by a world-renowned flower arranger. A glass atrium covers the outside terrace.

Rooms: 5 en suite **S** fr £75 **D** fr £95* **Facilities:** FTV Lounge tea/coffee Dinner available WiFi ⚓ **Notes:** RS Sunday evening to Monday restaurant closed Civ wed 60

The White Hart

★★★★ ⊜ INN

tel: 01242 602359 **High Street GL54 5LJ**
email: info@whitehartwinchcombe.co.uk **web:** www.whitehartwinchcombe.co.uk
dir: *M5 junction 9 signed Winchcombe.*

Located in the heart of the Cotswolds, amid the honey-coloured stone of Winchcombe, the 16th-century White Hart features a smart eatery and a range of spacious and comfortable rooms. Dinner is not to be missed with innovative seasonal dishes offered alongside pub classics. A hearty breakfast will set guests up for a day exploring the surrounding Area of Outstanding Natural Beauty. For those on a budget, three 'rambler' rooms share a bathroom and can be used as a family suite.

Rooms: 11 rms (9 en suite) **D** fr £55* **Facilities:** FTV Dinner available WiFi
Conf: Max 50 Thtr 50 Class 30 Board 30 **Notes:** LB

GREATER MANCHESTER

ALTRINCHAM   Map 15 SJ78

Ash Farm Country House

★★★★ ⚑ GUEST ACCOMMODATION

tel: 0161 929 9290 **Park Lane, Little Bollington WA14 4TJ**
email: ashfarm@gmail.com **web:** www.ashfarm.co.uk
dir: *M56 junction 7 onto A56 at Lymm Road 1st right into Park Lane, house at bottom of lane on right, just before The Swan with Two Nicks pub.*

A warm welcome is guaranteed at this charming 18th-century National Trust farmhouse which enjoys a peaceful location along a quiet country lane. The bedrooms are attractively presented, and public areas include a book-filled lounge with a crackling log fire and cosy sofas. Free WiFi is available and the house is equally popular with business and leisure guests. Dunham Massey Hall and Deerpark is a short stroll from the house while Manchester Airport is just a 15-minute drive away.

Rooms: 3 rms (2 en suite) (1 pri facs) 1 annexe en suite (1 GF) **S** fr £75 **D** fr £90* **Facilities:** FTV Lounge tea/coffee Licensed WiFi ⚓ **Extras:** Robes, mineral water, chocolates **Conf:** Max 10 Class 10 **Parking:** 12 **Notes:** No children 12 years Closed 22 December to 2 January

ASHTON-UNDER-LYNE — Map 16 SJ99

Broadoak

★★★★ ⊜ INN

tel: 0161 330 2764 **69 Broadoak Road OL6 8QD**
email: broadoakhotel@googlemail.com **web:** www.broadoakhotel.co.uk
dir: M60 junction 23 follow signs to Oldham (A627). Right at lights into Wilshaw Lane. Right at roundabout, Broadoak on right.

This inn is popular with locals, and ideally situated for Manchester, with excellent transport links to the ring road and trams into the city. Hearty meals are served in the pub restaurant by the friendly team. Accommodation is bang up to date; stylish with a range of modern amenities including complimentary WiFi and large TVs; a family suite is available. Functions are also catered for.

Rooms: 7 en suite (1 fmly) **Facilities:** FTV Lounge TVL tea/coffee Dinner available Direct dial WiFi ⊜ **Conf:** Max 100 Thtr 100 Class 50 Board 50 **Parking:** 25 **Notes:** LB

BURY — Map 15 SD81

The Red Lion

★★★★ ⊜ INN

tel: 01204 856600 **81 Ramsbottom Road, Hawkshaw BL8 4JS**
email: redlion.bury@jwlees.co.uk **web:** www.redlionbury.co.uk
dir: Phone for directions.

A great dining and real ale-led inn which sits roadside in the charming village of Hawkshaw, just outside Bury. The style is very much that of a traditional country pub though modern flourishes can be seen. Eight well-equipped and spacious bedrooms are available. The food alone is worth the journey – the hearty and generous dishes are created from fresh produce and handled with care; the signature steak pie especially so. Ample parking is provided on site.

Rooms: 8 en suite **Facilities:** FTV tea/coffee Dinner available WiFi

DELPH — Map 16 SD90

The Old Bell Inn

★★★★ ◉ INN

tel: 01457 870130 **5 Huddersfield Road OL3 5EG**
email: info@theoldbellinn.co.uk **web:** www.theoldbellinn.co.uk
dir: M62 junction 22 onto A672. In Denshaw onto A6052, through Delph to crossroads with A62. Turn left, 100 yards on left.

Formerly a coaching inn dating back to 1835 and situated in a rural village yet close to motorway links, The Old Bell has a quiet ambience allied with refined service. Hospitality is a real strength of the young and enthusiastic team. Bedrooms offer space, quality and comfort. The conservatory lounge is the perfect place to finish the evening after dinner in the modern restaurant.

Rooms: 18 en suite (1 fmly) **S** fr £62.50 **D** fr £105* **Facilities:** FTV TVL tea/coffee Dinner available Direct dial WiFi **Parking:** 20

MANCHESTER — Map 15 SJ89

The Ascott

★★★★ GUEST ACCOMMODATION

tel: 0161 950 2453 **6 Half Edge Lane, Ellesmere Park M30 9GJ**
email: ascotthotelmanchester@yahoo.co.uk **web:** www.ascotthotelmanchester.co.uk
dir: M602 junction 2, left into Wellington Road, 0.25 mile, right into Abbey Grove and left into Half Edge Lane.

Set in a mainly residential area close to major routes, this early Victorian house, once the home of the Mayor of Eccles, provides thoughtfully furnished bedrooms with smart modern bathrooms. A choice of breakfast rooms is available and there is an elegant lounge.

Rooms: 14 en suite (1 fmly) (4 GF) **Facilities:** FTV Lounge TVL tea/coffee Direct dial WiFi **Parking:** 12 **Notes:** Closed 22 December to 2 January RS Sunday and Friday Closed 1–5pm

OLDHAM — Map 16 SD90

The White Hart Inn

★★★★ ◉◉ INN

tel: 01457 872566 **51 Stockport Road, Lydgate OL4 4JJ**
email: bookings@thewhitehart.co.uk **web:** www.thewhitehart.co.uk
dir: Phone for directions.

Located on the edge of the Pennines in the small village of Lydgate, this inn is the perfect combination of modern style and old-world tradition. A choice of dining options is provided – The Brasserie serving good quality home cooking and The Dining Room, awarded two AA Rosettes, provides a more contemporary, refined approach. The extremely stylish bedrooms are comfortable and well-appointed with amenities such as TV, complimentary WiFi and well-stocked hospitality trays. Weddings and events are catered for in The Library or in the stunning, purpose-built Oak Room suite and Pavilion.

Rooms: 12 en suite 4 annexe en suite (5 fmly) (2 GF) **Facilities:** FTV DVD Lounge TVL tea/coffee Dinner available Direct dial WiFi **Extras:** Speciality toiletries, home-made biscuits **Conf:** Max 220 Thtr 220 Class 120 Board 60 **Parking:** 65
Notes: Closed 24–26 December, 1 January Civ wed 220

SALE
Map 15 SJ79

Belmore
★★★★ INN

tel: 0161 973 2538 **143 Brooklands Road M33 3QN**
email: belmore@jwlees.co.uk **web:** www.belmoreatsale.co.uk
dir: *Phone for directions.*

A warm welcome awaits you at the Belmore whether you're staying on business or for leisure. Good transport links to the city, airport and Trafford Centre make this an ideal base for exploring Manchester. The comfortable and well-equipped bedrooms include two suites and family rooms. Traditional British pub food is available throughout the day and served in the stylish restaurant or on the terrace.

Rooms: 20 en suite

STOCKPORT
Map 16 SJ89

Innkeeper's Lodge Stockport
★★★ INN

tel: 03451 551551 **271 Wellington Road, North Heaton Chapel SK4 5BP**
email: info@innkeeperslodge.com **web:** www.innkeeperslodge.com
dir: *Phone for directions.*

This Innkeeper's Lodge in Heaton Chapel is just north of Stockport town centre on the road towards Manchester. The en suite bedrooms, in different shapes and sizes, come with TVs, desks and free WiFi as standard; a family room is available. The welcoming interior is traditional in design with bold colours and a wide-ranging choice of dishes is offered on the seasonal menus. There's a beer garden for warmer weather and free parking is provided.

Rooms: 22 en suite (1 fmly) (1 GF) **Facilities:** FTV tea/coffee Dinner available WiFi

HAMPSHIRE

ALTON
Map 5 SU73

The Anchor Inn
★★★★ ◎◎ INN

tel: 01420 23261 **Lower Froyle GU34 4NA**
email: info@anchorinnatlowerfroyle.co.uk **web:** www.anchorinnatlowerfroyle.co.uk
dir: *From A3 follow Bentley signs and inn signs.*

The Anchor Inn is located in the tranquil village of Lower Froyle and offers luxury rooms designed to reflect the traditional English inn style with charming decor, pictures and a selection of books. The restaurant welcomes both residents and non-residents with its classic pub cooking which has been awarded two AA Rosettes; food is served in impressive surroundings of the bar and restaurant which feature wooden floors and period furnishings. The garden overlooks open countryside.

Rooms: 5 en suite **Facilities:** FTV DVD tea/coffee Dinner available Direct dial WiFi
Extras: Mini-fridge **Conf:** Max 40 Thtr 40 Class 30 Board 24 **Parking:** 30
Notes: RS 25–26 December, 31 December to 1 January Civ wed 45

ANDOVER
Map 5 SU34

The George and Dragon
★★★★ ◎ INN

tel: 01264 736277 **The Square, Hurstbourne Tarrant SP11 0AA**
email: info@georgeanddragon.com **web:** www.georgeanddragon.com
dir: *North of Andover on A343, in village centre.*

With a history dating back to the 16th century, this former coaching inn offers wonderfully comfortable beds, stylish decor and contemporary bathrooms. The bar is the focus downstairs, where a pre-dinner drink can be enjoyed before sampling the very enjoyable output from the kitchen. Crackling fires and low beams add to the charm of this village local.

Rooms: 8 en suite (1 fmly) **Facilities:** FTV tea/coffee Dinner available WiFi
🔒 **Conf:** Max 22 Board 22 **Parking:** 17

The Hatchet Inn
★★★ INN

tel: 01264 730229 **Lower Chute SP11 9DX**
email: info@thehatchetinn.co.uk **web:** www.thehatchetinn.co.uk
dir: *A303 exit signed Weyhill/Monxton onto A343. Follow signs for The Chutes.*

Dating back to the 13th century, this picturesque thatched inn is very much the traditional village local, providing a warm welcome to all. Bedrooms offer good levels of comfort with all the essentials for a relaxing and rewarding stay. A good choice is offered at dinner, while breakfast provides a tasty start to the day. Many original features remain in the bar and public areas, all adding to the unique charm of this popular hostelry. Additional facilities include gun cabinets for those shooting in the area.

Rooms: 7 annexe en suite (2 fmly) (3 GF) **S** fr £75 **D** fr £85* **Facilities:** FTV TVL tea/coffee Dinner available WiFi 🔒 **Conf:** Max 20 Board 20 **Parking:** 50 **Notes:** LB

ASHURST
Map 5 SU31

Forest Gate Lodge
★★★★ BED AND BREAKFAST

tel: 023 8029 3026 **161 Lyndhurst Road SO40 7AW**
email: forestgatelodge161@hotmail.co.uk **web:** www.forestgatelodge.co.uk
dir: *From M27 follow A35 to Ashurst. On Lyndhurst Road.*

Forest Gate Lodge is located in Ashurst, just a short drive from all that the New Forest has to offer. Bedrooms have modern decor and furnishings and come equipped with digital TV, DVD and free WiFi. There is a guest lounge on the ground floor and a cooked or continental breakfast is served in the dining room. Off-road parking is available, and there are restaurants and pubs within a short walking distance of the property.

Rooms: 5 en suite **D** fr £70* **Facilities:** FTV DVD iPod docking station TVL tea/coffee WiFi Riding 🔒 **Parking:** 6 **Notes:** LB No children 5 years Closed November to December

BARTON-ON-SEA
Map 5 SZ29

Premier Collection

Pebble Beach
★★★★★ ◎ ⌂ RESTAURANT WITH ROOMS

tel: 01425 627777 **Marine Drive BH25 7DZ**
email: mail@pebblebeach-uk.com **web:** www.pebblebeach-uk.com
dir: A35 from Southampton onto A337 to New Milton, left into Barton Court Avenue to clifftop.

Situated on the clifftop, the restaurant at Pebble Beach boasts stunning views towards The Needles. Bedrooms and bathrooms (situated above the restaurant) are well equipped and provide a range of accessories. A freshly cooked breakfast is served in the main restaurant or outside on the wonderful terrace. Next door, Petit Pebbles delicatessen is well worth a visit.

Rooms: 4 rms (3 en suite) (1 pri facs) **S** fr £69.95 **D** fr £69.95* **Facilities:** FTV tea/coffee Dinner available Direct dial WiFi **Extras:** Speciality toiletries **Conf:** Max 16 Thtr 16 Class 16 Board 16 **Parking:** 20 **Notes:** RS 25 December and 1 January dinner not available

BASINGSTOKE
Map 5 SU65

Innkeeper's Lodge Basingstoke
★★★ INN

tel: 03451 551551 **Andover Road, Clerken Green RG23 7EP**
email: info@innkeeperslodge.com **web:** www.innkeeperslodge.com
dir: Phone for directions.

Located near Oakley just outside Basingstoke, this Innkeeper's Lodge (The Beach Arms) provides a good level of comfort and quality through the accommodation and public areas. The en suite, modern bedrooms come in different shapes and sizes and have TVs, desks, free WiFi, tea- and coffee-making facilities as standard; family rooms are available. A wide choice on the menu is sure to suit any appetite and all tastes. There's outdoor space for eating and drinking in warmer weather and on-site parking is provided.

Rooms: 22 en suite (4 fmly) (22 GF) **Facilities:** FTV tea/coffee Dinner available Direct dial WiFi **Parking:** 45

BRANSGORE
Map 5 SZ19

Tothill House
★★★★ BED AND BREAKFAST

tel: 01425 674414 **Black Lane, off Forest Road BH23 8EA**
email: enquiries@tothillhouse.com **web:** www.tothillhouse.com
dir: M27 onto A31 or A35, between Burley and Bransgore.

Built for an admiral in 1908, Tothill House is located in the southern part of the New Forest. The garden backs onto the forest and is frequently visited by deer, ponies and other wildlife. The spacious bedrooms are furnished to a high standard that reflects the character of the house. There is an elegant library, and a generous breakfast is served in the dining room.

Rooms: 3 rms (2 en suite) (1 pri facs) **D** fr £85* **Facilities:** Lounge tea/coffee WiFi **Parking:** 6 **Notes:** No children 16 years Closed November to February

BROCKENHURST
Map 5 SU30

The Filly Inn
★★★★ INN

tel: 01590 623449 **Lymington Road SO42 7UF**
email: info@thefillyinn.co.uk **web:** www.thefillyinn.co.uk
dir: Phone for directions.

Conveniently located in the New Forest, this traditional inn has a restaurant and bar with lots of character with many original features. All the bedrooms are en suite with stylish decor and very comfortable furnishings. There is plenty of parking on site and a large garden for guests to enjoy. Both cooked and continental breakfasts are served in the main restaurant.

Rooms: 5 en suite **Facilities:** FTV Dinner available

BROOK
Map 5 SU21

The Bell Inn
★★★★ ◎ INN

tel: 023 8081 2214 **SO43 7HE**
email: bell@bramshaw.co.uk **web:** www.bellinnbramshaw.co.uk
dir: M27 junction 1 onto B3079, 1.5 miles on right.

This delightful inn is part of the Bramshaw Golf Club and makes an ideal base for visiting the New Forest. Bedrooms are spacious and have been appointed to a high standard. Public areas are full of character and there is a welcoming bar, a popular restaurant and a comfortable lounge.

Rooms: 26 en suite 2 annexe en suite (2 fmly) (8 GF) **Facilities:** TVL tea/coffee Dinner available Direct dial WiFi ⌂ Boules, garden chess **Conf:** Max 40 Thtr 40 Class 16 Board 24 **Parking:** 150 **Notes:** LB Civ wed 50

BURGHCLERE
Map 5 SU46

Carpenters Arms
★★★ INN

tel: 01635 278251 **Harts Lane RG20 9JY**
email: thecarpenters.burghclere@arkells.com
web: www.carpentersarms-burghclere.co.uk
dir: A34 Newbury Tothill Services, at roundabout take 2nd exit signed Burghclere. At end of road, turn left, 200 metres on right.

Located in a tranquil setting just a couple of miles outside Newbury, this traditional inn offers comfortably appointed, annexe bedrooms boasting some traditional features and modern furnishings. There's plenty of on-site parking and guests can enjoy breakfast, lunch or dinner with a range of traditional pub dishes in the conservatory restaurant or bar.

Rooms: 4 annexe en suite (1 fmly) **Facilities:** FTV tea/coffee Dinner available **Parking:** 18

COSHAM
Map 5 SU60

Innkeeper's Lodge Portsmouth, Cosham

★★★★ GUEST ACCOMMODATION

tel: 03451 551551 **The Red Lion, London Road PO6 3EE**
email: info@innkeeperslodge.com **web:** www.innkeeperslodge.com
dir: *From A27 follow signs for Cosham (A397 Northern Road) to London Road.*

This lodge is an ideal venue for business meetings or a base for exploring local attractions. Convenient for the M3 and M27, Cosham and Portsmouth and Southsea railway stations. It has fresh and contemporary, comfortable, en suite bedrooms, attractive public areas and friendly, welcoming staff. The Red Lion offers a variety of drinks and a menu that includes hand-made stone-baked pizzas. Free WiFi and on-site parking are a plus.

Rooms: 16 en suite **Facilities:** FTV Lounge TVL tea/coffee Dinner available Licensed WiFi **Parking:** 16

DUMMER
Map 5 SU54

Tower Hill House

★★★ BED AND BREAKFAST

tel: 01256 398340 **Tower Hill, Winchester Road RG25 2AL**
email: martin.hyndman@virgin.net **web:** www.accommodationinbasingstoke.co.uk
dir: *In village. M3 junction 7, A30 towards Winchester, 2nd left, opposite sign for North Waltham.*

Ideally situated for access to the M3 and A30 and overlooking fields, this family-run bed and breakfast is in the pretty village of Dummer, just a 10-minute drive from the centre of Basingstoke. The bedrooms are simply but comfortably furnished, and a well-prepared breakfast is served in the cheerful dining room.

Rooms: 4 en suite **Facilities:** tea/coffee WiFi **Parking:** 6

EMSWORTH
Map 5 SU70

36 on the Quay

★★★★ ◉◉◉ RESTAURANT WITH ROOMS

tel: 01243 375592 & 372257 **47 South Street PO10 7EG**
email: info@36onthequay.co.uk **web:** www.36onthequay.co.uk
dir: *Last building on right in South Street, which runs from square in centre of Emsworth.*

Occupying a prime position with far-reaching views over the estuary, this 16th-century house is the scene for accomplished and exciting cuisine. The elegant restaurant occupies centre stage with peaceful pastel shades, local art and crisp napery together with glimpses of the bustling harbour outside. The contemporary bedrooms offer style, comfort and thoughtful extras.

Rooms: 4 en suite **Facilities:** FTV iPod docking station tea/coffee Dinner available WiFi **Parking:** 6 **Notes:** LB Closed 3 weeks January, 1 week late May

The Jingles

★★★★ ⚇ GUEST ACCOMMODATION

tel: 01243 373755 **77 Horndean Road PO10 7PU**
email: info@thejingles.co.uk **web:** www.thejingles.co.uk
dir: *A3 (M) junction 2, follow signs for Emsworth, 4 miles, 1st building in Emsworth on right.*

The Jingles is a family-run business, located in the charming maritime village of Emsworth. Situated adjacent to open farmland, it's a great location for exploring both Portsmouth and Chichester. All bedrooms are en suite and decorated to a high standard. The dining room is the setting for a cooked English breakfast, and a drawing room is available for relaxing in. WiFi is available.

Rooms: 28 en suite (2 fmly) (7 GF) **Facilities:** FTV Lounge tea/coffee Licensed WiFi ⚓ **Extras:** Bottled water – complimentary **Parking:** 35 **Notes:** LB Closed 24 December to 2 January

The Crown

★★★ INN

tel: 01243 372806 **High Street PO10 7AW**
email: thecrownofemsworth@gmail.com **web:** www.thecrownemsworth.com
dir: *Phone for directions.*

This is a historic property conveniently located in the centre of town with ample parking at the back. Long, winding stairs and uneven corridors lead to well-appointed bedrooms which offer a range of amenities such as TVs and WiFi. Freshly prepared food is served in the well-stocked bar and the restaurant.

Rooms: 9 rms (7 en suite) (2 pri facs) (2 fmly) **Facilities:** FTV tea/coffee Dinner available WiFi ♿ **Conf:** Max 48 Thtr 48 Class 36 Board 24 **Parking:** 16

FARNBOROUGH
Map 5 SU85

The Alexandra Pub

★★★ INN

tel: 01252 519964 **74 Victoria Road GU14 7PH**
email: thealex@alexandrapub.co.uk **web:** www.alexandrapub.co.uk
dir: *M3 junction 4 onto A331 (Farnborough), at 1st roundabout take 2nd exit. Follow signs for A331 Hawley/Farnborough, at next roundabout 3rd exit. At next roundabout 1st exit onto Farnborough Road (A325). 3rd exit at next roundabout into Victoria Road.*

Named after a young Danish princess who became a much loved queen, The Alexandra Pub remains at the heart of the local community. The inn has been appointed to a good standard and conveys a warm and welcoming atmosphere. There are three well-equipped, en suite rooms offering comfortable accommodation. The bar is well stocked and secure parking is provided at the rear of the inn, as well as a dedicated smoking area.

Rooms: 3 en suite **S** fr £50 **D** fr £50* **Facilities:** STV FTV DVD TVL tea/coffee WiFi **Extras:** Snacks **Parking:** 16 **Notes:** Closed 24–25 December RS Christmas

HAWKLEY
Map 5 SU72

The Hawkley Inn
★★★★ ⌂ INN

tel: 01730 827205 **Pococks Lane GU33 6NE**
email: info@hawkleyinn.co.uk **web:** www.hawkleyinn.co.uk
dir: *A3 Liss roundabout towards Liss B3006. Right at Spread Eagle, follow brown tourist signs. After 3 miles, left to village centre.*

The Hawkley Inn captures all that is expected of a traditional inn, and then more. Beautifully appointed double rooms, offer all the comforts required by discerning guests. The bar is well stocked and includes a range of real ales, while the chef-proprietor is passionate about local produce and prepares excellent dishes. The rear garden is a haven of tranquillity.

Rooms: 6 en suite (1 fmly) **Facilities:** STV FTV tea/coffee Dinner available WiFi ⅃ **Extras:** Speciality teas **Parking:** 4

HAYLING ISLAND
Map 5 SU70

Ravensdale
★★★★ BED AND BREAKFAST

tel: 023 9246 3203 & 07802 188259 **19 St Catherines Road PO11 0HF**
email: phil.taylor@tayloredprint.co.uk **web:** www.ravensdale-hayling.co.uk
dir: *A27 onto A3023 at Langstone, cross Hayling Bridge, 3 miles to mini roundabout, right into Manor Road, 1 mile. Right by Barley Mow into Station Road, 3rd left into St Catherines Road.*

A warm welcome awaits at this comfortable home, quietly situated near the beach and golf course. Bedrooms are attractive, very comfortable and enhanced with numerous thoughtful extras; one room is a triple and has its own separate facilities. Home cooking can be enjoyed at breakfast in the dining room, and there is also a lounge area.

Rooms: 3 rms (2 en suite) (1 pri facs) (1 fmly) **S** fr £55 **D** fr £85* **Facilities:** FTV DVD tea/coffee WiFi **Extras:** Flowers, chocolates – complimentary **Parking:** 4 **Notes:** No children 8 years Closed last 2 weeks December and 1st 2 weeks January

HIGHCLERE
Map 5 SU45

The Yew Tree
★★★★ ◉◉ RESTAURANT WITH ROOMS

tel: 01635 253360 **Hollington Cross RG20 9SE**
email: info@theyewtree.co.uk **web:** www.theyewtree.co.uk
dir: *1 mile south of Highclere village.*

Part of The Epicurean Collection, this attractive 17th-century country inn has comfortable bedrooms decorated with William Morris print wallpaper and traditional features have been retained which creates a cosy atmosphere. Great British cooking can be enjoyed in the attractively decorated restaurant, where good use is made of high-quality produce and fresh ingredients. The garden, with its own bar and dining areas, is a real bonus.

Rooms: 6 en suite 2 annexe en suite (2 GF) **S** fr £110 **D** fr £110* **Facilities:** FTV Lounge tea/coffee Dinner available WiFi ⌂ **Extras:** Speciality toiletries **Parking:** 35

HOOK
Map 5 SU75

Innkeeper's Lodge Hook
★★★★ INN

tel: 03451 551551 **The White Hart, London Road RG27 9DZ**
email: info@innkeeperslodge.com **web:** www.innkeeperslodge.com
dir: *M3 junction 5, follow signs for Hook (B3349). At next roundabout, 1st exit into Station Road. Next roundabout 3rd exit into London Road (A30), on right.*

This inn is located in the centre of Hook, between Basingstoke and Fleet. Bedrooms are modern in style and very comfortably appointed, ideal for both leisure and corporate guests alike. All rooms are well equipped with Hypnos beds, digital TVs and free WiFi throughout. A cooked or continental breakfast is served in the restaurant where guests can also relax in the evening for dinner.

Rooms: 21 en suite (4 fmly) (21 GF) **Facilities:** FTV Lounge tea/coffee Dinner available WiFi **Parking:** 21 **Notes:** LB

HURSLEY
Map 5 SU42

The Kings Head
★★★★ ◉ INN

tel: 01962 775208 **Main Road SO21 2JW**
email: enquiries@kingsheadhursley.co.uk **web:** www.kingsheadhursley.co.uk
dir: *M3 junction 11, follow signs for A3090 and Hursley.*

Part of The Epicurean Collection, The Kings Head is a traditional inn a short drive from Winchester in an idyllic quiet village. The bar and restaurant areas are smart yet cosy, and quality food is available. Rooms are exceptionally well presented with comfortable beds and a host of extras to make your stay even more enjoyable. A full English breakfast can be enjoyed each morning in the Snug.

Rooms: 7 en suite 1 annexe en suite **Facilities:** FTV Lounge tea/coffee Dinner available WiFi Skittle alley **Conf:** Max 50 **Parking:** 30

LEE-ON-THE-SOLENT
Map 5 SU50

West Wind Guest House
★★★★ GUEST ACCOMMODATION

tel: 023 9255 2550 & 07748 010102 **197 Portsmouth Road PO13 9AA**
email: info@west-wind.co.uk **web:** www.west-wind.co.uk
dir: *M27 junction 11 follow Gosport and Fareham signs, B3385 for Lee-on-the-Solent. At seafront left along Marine Parade, 600 metres left into Portsmouth Road. West Wind on right.*

This family-run property is found in a quiet, residential area within walking distance of the beach and town centre. The bedrooms are comfortable and nicely appointed, some with TV and all with free WiFi. There is an attractive breakfast room and off-street parking.

Rooms: 6 en suite (1 GF) **Facilities:** FTV DVD iPod docking station tea/coffee WiFi **Parking:** 6 **Notes:** No children 8 years

LISS
Map 5 SU72

The Jolly Drover

★★★★ ➡ INN

tel: 01730 893137 **London Road, Hillbrow GU33 7QL**
email: thejollydrover@googlemail.com **web:** www.thejollydrover.co.uk
dir: *From Liss on B3006, at junction with B2070.*

Situated on the West Sussex–Hampshire border, this traditional inn prides itself on local ales, good home-cooked food and a warm welcome. It is popular with both business and leisure guests due to its close proximity to Petersfield and transport links. The bedrooms are situated in traditional outbuildings and have been appointed in a comfortable, modern style with all expected guest amenities. Free WiFi is available. A large beer garden to the rear of the inn is the perfect place to enjoy a summer's day, and ample parking is provided.

Rooms: 6 annexe rms (6 pri facs) (1 fmly) (6 GF) **Facilities:** FTV tea/coffee Dinner available WiFi **Extras:** Bottled water **Parking:** 48 **Notes:** LB Closed 25–26 December and 1 January

LYMINGTON
Map 5 SZ39

Britannia House

★★★★ ⌂ BED AND BREAKFAST

tel: 01590 672091 & 07808 792639 **Station Street SO41 3BA**
email: enquiries@britannia-house.com **web:** www.britannia-house.com
dir: *Follow signs to railway station, at corner of Station Street and Mill Lane.*

Built in 1865 as the Britannia Commercial Hotel, Britannia House occupies a quiet location only two minutes' walk from the quay, waterfront and the High Street with its many shops, pubs and restaurants. Rooms are elegant with a refined air, there is a charming lounge and breakfast is taken in the homely kitchen.

Rooms: 3 en suite 2 annexe en suite (2 GF) **S** fr £85 **D** fr £99* **Facilities:** FTV Lounge tea/coffee WiFi ⌂ **Parking:** 4 **Notes:** LB No children 8 years

The Mayflower

★★★★★ ◎ INN

tel: 01590 672160 **King's Saltern Road SO41 3QD**
email: info@themayflowerlymington.co.uk **web:** www.themayflowerlymington.co.uk
dir: *Phone for directions.*

Set just behind the Royal Lymington Yacht Club and a 10-minute walk from the centre of Lymington, The Mayflower offers impressive levels of quality and comfort in a bustling pub environment. There are six beautifully styled, nautically-themed, en suite bedrooms, all with Egyptian linen bedding and thoughtful extras; some have feature baths set in the bedroom. The bar and dining areas have open fires and there is an extensive garden to enjoy in the warmer months. The Mayflower is also dog friendly.

Rooms: 6 en suite **Facilities:** Dinner available

The Elderflower Restaurant

★★★★ ◎◎◎ RESTAURANT WITH ROOMS

tel: 01590 676908 **4–5 Quay Street SO41 3AS**
email: reservations@elderflowerrestaurant.co.uk **web:** www.elderflowerrestaurant.co.uk
dir: *Phone for directions.*

Situated on the cobbled streets in the heart of Lymington, just moments from the quay and a short drive into the New Forest National Park. Owned and run by a husband and wife team, The Elderflower is the realisation of a lifelong dream. Bedrooms and bathrooms are well appointed and situated above the restaurant.

Cuisine is a real treat, with the team preparing modern British food with French influences using only the very best locally sourced, sustainable produce. Parking is available nearby in the town's many car parks.

Rooms: 2 en suite **Facilities:** FTV tea/coffee Dinner available WiFi **Notes:** No children 12 years (weekend only) Closed 26 December

LYNDHURST
Map 5 SU30

The Rufus House

★★★★ ⌂ GUEST ACCOMMODATION

tel: 023 8028 2930 **Southampton Road SO43 7BQ**
email: stay@rufushouse.co.uk **web:** www.rufushouse.co.uk
dir: *From Lyndhurst centre onto A35 (Southampton Road), 300 yards on left.*

Located on the edge of town, this delightful family-run Victorian property is well situated for exploring the New Forest. The brightly decorated bedrooms are appointed to a high standard, while the turret lounge and the garden terrace are great spots for relaxing.

Rooms: 10 en suite (1 fmly) (2 GF) **Facilities:** FTV tea/coffee WiFi ⌂ ⌂ **Parking:** 12 **Notes:** LB No children 5 years

NORTHINGTON
Map 5 SU53

The Woolpack Inn

★★★★ ◎ INN

tel: 01962 734184 **Totford SO24 9TJ**
email: info@thewoolpackinn.co.uk **web:** www.thewoolpackinn.co.uk
dir: *On B3046 south of Basingstoke.*

Part of The Epicurean Collection, this attractive country inn, tucked away in Hampshire's Candover Valley, offers a traditional atmosphere with lots of character. The flint and brick building dates back to 1880 and many original features can be seen throughout. The inviting bar has flagstone floors, leather armchairs and open fires, while the dining room features smart fabrics, candle-lit tables and the same relaxed, friendly ambiance. There is also a wood-fired, pizza oven (in summer) and a small private dining room. Bedrooms, each named after a game bird, are richly furnished and very well equipped; each has a contemporary en suite bath or shower room.

Rooms: 7 en suite (1 fmly) (4 GF) **Facilities:** FTV tea/coffee Dinner available Direct dial WiFi ⌂ Fishing Riding **Conf:** Max 15 Thtr 15 Class 12 Board 12 **Parking:** 50

RINGWOOD
Map 5 SU10

Moortown Lodge

★★★★ GUEST ACCOMMODATION

tel: 01425 471404 **244 Christchurch Road BH24 3AS**
email: enquiries@moortownlodge.co.uk **web:** www.moortownlodge.co.uk
dir: *1 mile south of Ringwood. Exit A31 at Ringwood onto B3347, follow signs to Sopley. Lodge adjacent to David Lloyd Leisure Club.*

Moortown Lodge was originally a Georgian hunting lodge and is conveniently located 10 miles from the Dorset coast, not far from Christchurch, and just five minutes south of Ringwood. A warm welcome is assured, with every effort made to ensure a relaxed and rewarding stay. Bedrooms offer impressive levels of comfort combined with individual styling and a host of additional facilities. The elegant dining room is the venue for satisfying breakfasts which make use of local New Forest produce. Moortown Lodge is a very convenient base for exploring this delightful area.

Rooms: 7 en suite (1 fmly) (2 GF) **Facilities:** FTV DVD Lounge tea/coffee Direct dial WiFi Reduced rates at local David Lloyds Leisure Club **Extras:** Speciality toiletries, robes, bottled water, Netflix **Parking:** 7 **Notes:** No children 5 years

ST MARY BOURNE · Map 5 SU45

Bourne Valley Inn
★★★★ INN

tel: 01264 738361 **SP11 6BT**
email: enquiries@bournevalleyinn.com **web:** www.bournevalleyinn.com
dir: *South of St Mary Bourne on B3048.*

Part of The Epicurean Collection, Bourne Valley Inn is located in the village of St Mary Bourne. Ample customer parking and a large riverside beer garden are real assets. The inn is both child- and dog-friendly, and the style of the en suite accommodation, including three dog-friendly rooms, is in keeping with the character of this rustic building. Food is a highlight and locally sourced produce is featured on the menus; Sunday lunch is a real treat. The barn is the perfect setting for private events. The hospitality from the young and enthusiastic management and team is excellent.

Rooms: 9 en suite (3 GF) **Facilities:** FTV Lounge tea/coffee Dinner available WiFi Fishing **Conf:** Max 80 **Notes:** LB

SOUTHAMPTON · Map 5 SU41

Premier Collection

Ennio's Restaurant & Boutique Rooms
★★★★★ RESTAURANT WITH ROOMS

tel: 023 8022 1159 & 07748 966113 **Town Quay Road SO14 3AS**
email: info@ennios.co.uk **web:** www.ennios.co.uk
dir: *Opposite Red Funnel Ferry terminal.*

This fine property, lovingly converted from a former Victorian warehouse, offers luxurious accommodation on Southampton's waterfront. All bedrooms are en suite and are furnished to a very high standard, including mini-bars and over-sized showers. Downstairs, the popular Ennio's Restaurant and bar is the ideal setting in which to dine, offering an authentic Italian atmosphere and a wonderful selection of dishes. There is limited parking to the rear of the building.

Rooms: 10 en suite **Facilities:** FTV iPod docking station Lounge tea/coffee Dinner available WiFi **Extras:** Speciality toiletries, mini-bar, trouser press **Parking:** 6 **Notes:** LB Closed 24–26 December

Premier Collection

THE PIG in the Wall
★★★★★ INN

tel: 023 8063 6900 **8 Western Esplanade SO14 2AZ**
email: reception@thepiginthewall.com **web:** www.thepighotel.com
dir: *Phone for directions.*

Located close to the city centre, this beautifully restored property has high quality bedrooms in all shapes and sizes – some with roll-top baths and all with air conditioning, a larder of goodies and a Nespresso machine. There is secure parking and the deli-bar showcases local produce. The style here is homely, relaxed and shabby-chic. An extensive continental breakfast is available to guests each morning.

Rooms: 12 en suite (2 GF) **S** fr £135 **D** fr £135 (room only)* **Facilities:** FTV DVD Lounge tea/coffee Dinner available Direct dial WiFi **Extras:** Nespresso – complimentary; stocked larder – chargeable **Parking:** 12

Prince Consort
★★★ INN

tel: 023 8045 2676 & 07419 999370 **Victoria Road, Netley SO31 5DQ**
email: info@theprinceconsortpub.co.uk **web:** www.theprinceconsortpub.co.uk
dir: *Situated next to main entrance of Royal Victoria Country Park.*

The Prince Consort is situated just five minutes' walk from the seafront, and enjoys a friendly atmosphere. Food is available every evening in the spacious bar and restaurant. Bedrooms are contemporary and well presented, with smart, fully tiled en suites. Outdoor seating is a real bonus, as is the on-site parking.

Rooms: 7 annexe en suite (1 fmly) (5 GF) **S** fr £52.50 **D** fr £67.50* **Facilities:** STV FTV tea/coffee Dinner available WiFi **Conf:** Max 40 Class 40 Board 20 **Parking:** 25

The Brimar Guest House
★★ GUEST ACCOMMODATION

tel: 023 8086 2950 **10-14 High Street, Totton SO40 9HN**
email: info@brimar-guesthouse.co.uk **web:** www.brimar-guesthouse.co.uk
dir: *3 miles west of city centre, exit A35 (Totton bypass) into Totton High Street.*

This property offers practical, comfortable accommodation at reasonable prices. Not all rooms are en suite but bathrooms are well located. Breakfast is served in the dining room or as a take-away option. The Brimar is conveniently situated for the M27 and Southampton docks, and off-road parking is available.

Rooms: 21 rms (8 en suite) (7 pri facs) (2 fmly) (8 GF) **Facilities:** FTV WiFi **Parking:** 20

STOCKBRIDGE · Map 5 SU33

The Greyhound on the Test
★★★★ RESTAURANT WITH ROOMS

tel: 01264 810833 **31 High Street SO20 6EY**
email: info@thegreyhoundonthetest.co.uk **web:** www.thegreyhoundonthetest.co.uk
dir: *9 miles northwest of Winchester, 8 miles south of Andover. Off A303.*

The River Test, famous worldwide for its fishing, flows at the back of this restaurant with rooms. The luxury bedrooms are generally spacious, beautifully styled and come with a host of extras (one is on the ground-floor); most of the modern bathrooms have walk-in showers. The inn holds two AA Rosettes for its modern cuisine that's based on local ingredients; the food is a real draw. There is also ample parking and well-kept grounds.

Rooms: 10 en suite (1 GF) **Facilities:** FTV DVD Lounge tea/coffee Dinner available WiFi Fishing Riding **Extras:** Speciality toiletries – complimentary; honesty bar **Conf:** Max 12 Board 12 **Parking:** 28 **Notes:** Closed 24–25 December

The Three Cups Inn
★★★★ INN

tel: 01264 810527 **High Street SO20 6HB**
email: manager@the3cups.co.uk **web:** www.the3cups.co.uk
dir: *Phone for directions.*

Standing on Stockbridge high street, The Three Cups Inn dates from the 15th century. A former coaching inn, it has bags of charm and character and there are many cask ales to try in the cosy bar. The bedrooms are individually furnished, comfortable and equipped to a high standard. Excellent food is available every evening, served in both the cosy, snug-like dining room and the Orangery overlooking the garden.

Rooms: 8 en suite (3 fmly) **Facilities:** FTV tea/coffee Dinner available WiFi Fishing **Extras:** Speciality toiletries, fresh milk **Parking:** 15

STOCKBRIDGE *continued*

The Peat Spade Inn

★★★★ INN

tel: 01264 810612 **Village Street, Longstock SO20 6DR**
email: info@peatspadeinn.co.uk **web:** www.peatspadeinn.co.uk
dir: *M3 junction 8, A303 west approximately 15 miles, then take A3057 Stockbridge/Andover.*

In a delightfully tranquil setting between the historic cities of Winchester and Salisbury, Longstock is just north of Stockbridge, in the heart of the Test Valley, known for its fly fishing and picture-postcard villages. The inn has lots of character, with bedrooms located in the main building and the adjacent former peat house. All are comfortable and furnished in a modern style yet in keeping with the date of the original building. The inn is popular for both dining and drinking; the modern British menus are well balanced and use seasonal ingredients sourced from the local area.

Rooms: 3 rms (3 pri facs) 5 annexe rms (5 pri facs) (3 GF) **Facilities:** FTV tea/coffee Dinner available Direct dial WiFi ⌴ Fishing Riding ⚬ Shooting **Extras:** Bottled water, mini-fridge, speciality toiletries **Conf:** Max 16 Board 16 **Parking:** 19

WARNFORD — Map 5 SU62

George & Falcon

★★★★ ◡ INN

tel: 01730 829623 **Warnford Road SO32 3LB**
email: reservations@georgeandfalcon.com **web:** www.georgeandfalcon.com
dir: *Adjacent to A32 in village.*

Set in the picturesque village of Warnford, close to major transport links to Winchester, Portsmouth and Southampton, the George & Falcon offers tastefully appointed bedrooms that retain the charm and character of a coaching inn yet provide modern facilities. Traditional fare is served in the popular restaurant and bar, and there is a large decking area which proves a useful addition in summer months.

Rooms: 6 en suite (1 fmly) **S** fr £65 **D** fr £70 (room only)* **Facilities:** FTV Lounge tea/coffee Dinner available WiFi ⌴ Fishing Riding ⚬ **Extras:** Speciality toiletries, mineral water **Conf:** Max 30 Thtr 30 Class 15 Board 15 **Parking:** 47 **Notes:** LB Civ wed 135

WHITCHURCH — Map 5 SU44

White Hart Whitchurch

★★★ INN

tel: 01256 892900 **The Square RG28 7DN**
email: thewhitehart.whitchurch@arkells.com **web:** www.whitehartotelwhitchurch.co.uk
dir: *Phone for directions.*

Located in the centre of Whitchurch, the White Hart is steeped in history and has served the local community for over 500 years. En suite bedrooms are well equipped – some are located in an adjacent building. The inn is very popular with locals and guests alike. A very warm welcome from the friendly team is assured. Owned by Arkell's family brewers, a great range of traditionally brewed beers is available.

Rooms: 10 en suite (3 fmly) **Facilities:** FTV tea/coffee Dinner available WiFi **Parking:** 12

WINCHESTER — Map 5 SU42

Giffard House

★★★★★ GUEST HOUSE

tel: 01962 852628 **50 Christchurch Road SO23 9SU**
email: giffardhotel@aol.com **web:** www.giffardhotel.co.uk
dir: *M3 junction 11, at roundabout 3rd exit onto A333 (St Cross road) for 1 mile. Pass BP garage on right, next left, 2nd right. 150 metres on left.*

Expect a warm welcome at Giffard House, a stunning Victorian property, close to the university. The accommodation is luxurious, comfortable and well equipped for both the business and leisure traveller. Beds are made up with crisp linen, and breakfast is served in the dining room. There is also a fully licensed bar in the elegant conservatory. Parking is a real bonus.

Rooms: 13 en suite (1 fmly) (4 GF) **Facilities:** STV FTV Lounge tea/coffee Direct dial Licensed WiFi ⚬ **Extras:** Speciality toiletries **Conf:** Max 15 Thtr 15 Class 15 Board 13 **Parking:** 13 **Notes:** Closed 24 December to 2 January

The Old Vine

★★★★ INN

tel: 01962 854616 **8 Great Minster St SO23 9HA**
email: reservations@oldvinewinchester.com **web:** www.oldvinewinchester.com
dir: *M3 junction 11 towards St Cross, right at Green Man Pub, left into Symonds Street, left into Little Minster Street.*

Overlooking the cathedral, this Grade II listed 18th-century inn mixes the elegance of days gone by with chic, modern comfort. The beautifully appointed bedrooms are named after designers and blend antique with contemporary; the attractive dining room serves quality fare using local produce. Permit parking is available.

Rooms: 5 en suite 1 annexe en suite (2 fmly) **Facilities:** FTV tea/coffee Dinner available WiFi ⚬ **Extras:** Speciality toiletries, water, fruit juices – complimentary

The Wykeham Arms

★★★★ ◉◉ ◡ INN

tel: 01962 853834 **75 Kingsgate Street SO23 9PE**
web: www.wykehamarmswinchester.co.uk
dir: *Immediately south of cathedral, by Kingsgate and opposite Winchester College.*

This is one of the oldest and best-loved public houses in Hampshire and is situated just south of the ancient cathedral. All areas are furnished to a high standard with excellent facilities. Dining in the restaurant or bar is recommended – walls are adorned from top to bottom with every kind of bijouterie imaginable and the regularly changing menu uses fresh ingredients.

Rooms: 14 en suite **Facilities:** FTV Lounge tea/coffee Dinner available Direct dial WiFi ⌴ ⚬ **Extras:** Mineral water – complimentary; robes in some rooms **Conf:** Max 20 Thtr 20 Class 20 Board 20 **Parking:** 10 **Notes:** No children 14 years

Running Horse Inn

★★★★ ◉◉ INN

tel: 01962 880218 **88 Main Road, Littleton SO22 6QS**
email: info@runninghorseinn.co.uk **web:** www.runninghorseinn.co.uk
dir: *B3049 from Winchester 1.5 miles, turn right into Littleton after 1 mile, Running Horse on right.*

Situated in a pretty, rural location, yet with easy access to the M3, this is a great location for business and leisure guests visiting Hampshire. Offering quality accommodation, Running Horse Inn is minimalist in its design, and provides comfortable beds plus a small workstation area. Highlights of a stay here are the meals in the smart restaurant or a drink in the bar.

Rooms: 15 annexe en suite (1 fmly) (15 GF) **D** fr £95* **Facilities:** FTV tea/coffee Dinner available WiFi **Parking:** 40

The Westgate

★★★★ GUEST ACCOMMODATION

tel: 01962 820222 & 07710 545999 **The Westgate SO23 8TP**
email: info@westgatewinchester.com **web:** www.westgatewinchester.com
dir: *At the top of Winchester High Street by Romsey Road roundabout. Next to The Westgate and The Great Hall.*

The Westgate sits in a commanding position at the top of historic Winchester's high street and a short stroll from the fortified medieval gateway after which it was named. The 'real' Westgate served as a debtors' prison for 150 years – you can still read some of the prisoners' graffiti. Good quality, interesting dishes are served at breakfast, lunch and dinner in the warm and welcoming bar. The Westgate offers light, airy and elegant bedrooms with wonderful views of this beautiful city.

Rooms: 10 en suite (3 fmly) **Facilities:** FTV tea/coffee Dinner available Licensed WiFi

HEREFORDSHIRE

| AYMESTREY | Map 9 SO46 |

The Riverside at Aymestrey

★★★★ ◉◉ INN

tel: 01568 708440 **HR6 9ST**
email: enquiries@riversideaymestrey.co.uk **web:** www.riversideaymestrey.co.uk
dir: *On A4110, just before arched bridge.*

The Riverside Inn sits alongside the River Lugg in a rural part of Herefordshire, offering peace and tranquillity for guests. This 16th-century black-and-white inn offers a range of comfortable bedrooms including suites, which successfully bring together traditional features with a more contemporary feel. Dinner is a labour of love for chef patron Andy Link, and is not to be missed. Local sourcing and home-grown produce are key to the ethos here, with a large kitchen garden providing most of the fruit, vegetables and herbs. The larger centres of Ludlow, Leominster and Hereford are easily accessed by car.

Rooms: 4 en suite 2 annexe en suite (2 fmly) (1 GF) **S** fr £80 **D** fr £90*
Facilities: FTV Dinner available WiFi Fishing **Extras:** Speciality toiletries, robes, mini-bar, fresh coffee and milk **Conf:** Max 40 Thtr 40 Class 25 Board 25 **Parking:** 30
Notes: RS Monday closed for lunch

| BODENHAM | Map 10 SO55 |

The Coach House at England's Gate Inn

★★★★ ◠ INN

tel: 01568 797286 **HR1 3HU**
email: englandsgate@btconnect.com **web:** www.englandsgate.co.uk
dir: *Just off A417.*

This fine black-and-white, 16th-century inn is run by the McNeil family who pride themselves on quality service. It is set in attractive gardens which are ideal for alfresco dining on warmer days. The detached coach house has comfortable bedrooms with modern en suite facilities; the views are spectacular from the upstairs rooms. Continental breakfast is served in the coach house dining area on weekdays, and a fully cooked breakfast is available at weekends.

Rooms: 7 en suite (2 fmly) (4 GF) **Facilities:** FTV DVD tea/coffee Dinner available Direct dial WiFi ◍ **Extras:** Bottled water **Conf:** Max 12 Board 12 **Parking:** 30

| BOLSTONE | Map 10 SO53 |

Premier Collection

Prickett's Place

★★★★★ ◍ BED AND BREAKFAST

tel: 01432 870221 **HR2 6LZ**
email: prickettsplace@btinternet.com **web:** www.prickettsplace.com
dir: *M50 junction 4 onto A49, right towards Hoarwithy. Follow signs for Cottage of Content public house, turn left then turn right, Prickett's Place on left.*

Surrounded by magnificent countryside in the beautiful Wye Valley, Prickett's Place is peacefully located just seven miles from Hereford and nine miles from Ross-on-Wye. The bedrooms are very well furnished and equipped with welcome extras. Guests can enjoy tea in the garden upon arrival and also have use of a comfortable lounge. An excellent selection of high-quality ingredients is offered at breakfast.

Rooms: 1 en suite 1 annexe en suite (1 fmly) **S** fr £55 **D** fr £74* **Facilities:** FTV DVD TVL tea/coffee WiFi ◍ **Extras:** Speciality toiletries, fruit, fridge in annexe **Parking:** 6 **Notes:** No children 7 years Closed Christmas and New Year

| BREDWARDINE | Map 9 SO34 |

Red Lion

★★★ INN

tel: 01981 500303 **HR3 6BU**
email: info@redlion-hotel.com **web:** www.redlion-hotel.com
dir: *Off A438 (Hereford to Brecon road).*

This traditionally styled inn is set in a pleasant village and provides an ideal base for exploring the local countryside and enjoying river walks. Popular with anglers, the inn has a fishing theme running throughout the public areas. Bedrooms come in a range of shapes and sizes and are located either above the inn or in an adjacent annexe. Home-cooked meals are served at both lunch and dinner.

Rooms: 7 en suite 3 annexe en suite (1 fmly) (2 GF) **Facilities:** FTV TVL tea/coffee Dinner available WiFi Fishing ◍ **Parking:** 20 **Notes:** LB Closed December to 1 March RS March to May closed Sunday evening to Wednesday morning

AA FRIENDLIEST B&B
OF THE YEAR 2018–19

The Temple Bar Inn

★★★★ ●● ⬤ INN

tel: 01981 240423 **HR2 0EU**
email: phillytemplebar@btinternet.com **web:** www.thetemplebarinn.co.uk
dir: *From Pontrilas (A465) onto B4347 signed Ewyas Harold. After 1 mile left into village. On right in 0.1 mile.*

Standing in the centre of the village, The Temple Bar Inn was lovingly brought back to life by the current owners, with the help of local craftsmen, to make it the hub of this community. The smart bedrooms are well equipped and complemented by modern en suite bathrooms. There is a bustling bar area with a separate games room and a small dining room serving high quality, locally sourced seasonal dishes.

Rooms: 3 en suite (1 fmly) **S** fr £65 **D** fr £90* **Facilities:** FTV tea/coffee Dinner available WiFi **Extras:** Speciality toiletries, fresh milk – complimentary; hairdryer, iron **Conf:** Max 45 Thtr 45 Class 24 Board 16 **Parking:** 10 **Notes:** Closed 1 week November, 25 December and 1 week January/February RS Sunday to Tuesday No evening meals

No 21

★★★★ GUEST ACCOMMODATION

tel: 01432 279897 & 07967 525403 **21 Aylestone Hill HR1 1HR**
email: jane@21aylestonehill.co.uk **web:** www.21aylestonehill.co.uk
dir: *On A4103 from Worcester to roundabout at approach to Hereford. Take 1st exit to town centre (A465).*

A warm welcome awaits visitors to this peaceful detached property, not far from the train station and the centre of Hereford. The spacious bedrooms, that offer many extras, and smart modern bathrooms are appointed to a high standard; one ground-floor room, with a wet room, is ideal for guests that have difficulty with stairs. Breakfast is served in the spacious dining room at the front of the property, and there is ample, secure parking.

Rooms: 4 en suite (1 fmly) (1 GF) **Facilities:** FTV TVL tea/coffee WiFi
🔒 **Extras:** Orange juice, bottled water, fresh milk – complimentary **Parking:** 8

Sink Green Farm

★★★★ FARMHOUSE

tel: 01432 870223 **Rotherwas HR2 6LE**
email: enquiries@sinkgreenfarm.co.uk **web:** www.sinkgreenfarm.co.uk
dir: *3 miles southeast of city centre. Exit A49 onto B4399 for 2 miles.*

This charming 16th-century farmhouse stands in attractive countryside and has many original features, including flagstone floors, exposed beams and open fireplaces. Bedrooms are traditionally furnished and one has a four-poster bed. The pleasant garden has a comfortable summer house, hot tub and barbecue.

Rooms: 3 en suite **S** fr £50 **D** fr £80 **Facilities:** FTV iPod docking station Lounge TVL tea/coffee WiFi 🔒 Hot tub **Extras:** Home-made biscuits **Parking:** 10 **Notes:** LB 180 acres beef

The Bay Horse Inn

★★★★ INN

tel: 01432 273351 **236 Kings Acre Road HR4 0SD**
email: info@bayhorseinnhereford.co.uk **web:** www.bayhorseinnhereford.co.uk
dir: *On A438, pass Wyevale garden centre, 100 yards on left.*

Located just outside the city centre, The Bay Horse Inn combines comfortable bedrooms and bathrooms with an excellent range of food available during the day and evening. There is a relaxed atmosphere and welcoming service throughout. Guests can use the outdoor seating in warmer weather and there is a car park. A good selection of real ales, wine and bottled ciders is available.

Rooms: 8 annexe en suite (3 fmly) (4 GF) **Facilities:** STV FTV TVL tea/coffee Dinner available WiFi **Conf:** Max 60 Thtr 35 Class 60 Board 20 **Parking:** 56 **Notes:** Closed 26 December

Heron House

★★★ 🅰 BED AND BREAKFAST

tel: 01432 761111 **Canon Pyon Road, Portway HR4 8NG**
email: info@theheronhouse.com **web:** www.theheronhouse.com
dir: *A4103 onto A4110 to Portway crossroads, Heron House 200 yards on left.*

Dating from the 18th century when it was just a cottage, Heron House was considerably extended about 30 years ago. It is quietly located at Burghill, some four miles north of Hereford. The accommodation consists of one twin and one double room, both with modern furnishings and equipment. Separate tables are provided in the breakfast room.

Rooms: 2 rms (1 en suite) **S** fr £34 **D** fr £72* **Facilities:** DVD tea/coffee **Parking:** 5 **Notes:** No children 10 years

Grove Farm B&B

★★★ FARMHOUSE

tel: 01568 613425 & 07890 471314 **Grove Farm HR6 0HE**
email: fiona@grovefarmdirect.co.uk **web:** www.grovefarmdirect.co.uk
dir: *A49 north of Leominster onto A4112, signed Leysters. Into Kimbolton, turn left at pub, 500 metres on left.*

Located in the Herefordshire countryside, this working farm offers a proper farmhouse atmosphere with a friendly welcome, tea and cake on arrival and plenty of animals around. The bedrooms come in a range of shapes and sizes including one on the ground floor. Breakfast includes home-produced sausages and bacon in addition to apple juice from a nearby farm. For dinner, the local pub is just a few minutes' stroll along the lane, or you could prepare something yourself in the well-equipped guest kitchen which has a microwave and a fridge-freezer. Dogs are welcome here.

Rooms: 3 en suite (1 fmly) (1 GF) **Facilities:** FTV Lounge tea/coffee Dinner available WiFi 🔒 🔒 Table tennis **Extras:** Fresh milk, home-made cake **Conf:** Max 20 Thtr 20 Class 20 Board 20 **Parking:** 6 **Notes:** LB 40 acres pigs/sheep/orchard

LEINTWARDINE	Map 9 SO47

Premier Collection

The Lion

★★★★★ ⓘ 🍴 RESTAURANT WITH ROOMS

tel: 01547 540203 & 540747 **High Street SY7 0JZ**
email: enquiries@thelionleintwardine.co.uk **web:** www.thelionleintwardine.co.uk
dir: *Beside bridge on A4113 (Ludlow to Knighton road) in Leintwardine.*

This quiet country restaurant with rooms in the picturesque village of Leintwardine, set beside the River Teme, is just a short distance from Ludlow and Craven Arms. The interior is stylish and all the contemporary bedrooms are en suite. Eating is taken seriously here and the modern, imaginative food uses the freshest local ingredients. The well-stocked bar offers a selection of real ales and lagers, and there is a separate drinkers' bar too. The Lion is particularly popular with families as the garden has a secure children's play area, and in warmer months guests can eat alfresco. The friendly staff help to make a visit memorable.

Rooms: 8 en suite (1 fmly) **Facilities:** FTV Lounge tea/coffee Dinner available WiFi Fishing 🛁 **Extras:** Home-made shortbread — complimentary **Conf:** Max 25 Class 25 Board 25 **Parking:** 25 **Notes:** Closed 25 December

LEOMINSTER	Map 10 SO45

Premier Collection

Hills Farm

★★★★★ 🍴 FARMHOUSE

tel: 01568 750205 **Leysters HR6 0HP**
email: thehillsfarmleysters@gmail.com **web:** www.thehillsfarm.co.uk
dir: *Off A4112 (Leominster to Tenbury Wells), on outskirts of Leysters.*

Set in a peaceful location with views over the countryside, this property dates in part from the 16th century. The friendly, attentive proprietors provide a relaxing and homely atmosphere. The attractive bedrooms, in the converted barns, are spacious and comfortable. Breakfasts, served in the dining room and conservatory, feature fresh local produce.

Rooms: 3 annexe en suite (1 GF) **D** fr £97 **Facilities:** FTV iPod docking station Lounge tea/coffee WiFi 🛁 **Extras:** Fridge, microwave, crockery, cutlery **Parking:** 8 **Notes:** No children 12 years Closed November to March 120 acres arable

ROSS-ON-WYE	Map 10 SO52

Premier Collection

Wilton Court Restaurant with Rooms

★★★★★ ⓘⓘ 🍴 RESTAURANT WITH ROOMS

tel: 01989 562569 **Wilton Lane HR9 6AQ**
email: info@wiltoncourthotel.com **web:** www.wiltoncourthotel.com
dir: *M50 junction 4, A40 towards Monmouth at 3rd roundabout left signed Ross-on-Wye, 1st right, on right.*

Dating back to the 16th century, Wilton Court has great charm and a wealth of character. It stands on the banks of the River Wye, just a short walk from the town centre, and a genuinely relaxed, friendly and unhurried atmosphere is created by hosts Roger and Helen Wynn and their reliable team. The bedrooms are tastefully furnished and well equipped, while public areas include a comfortable lounge, traditional bar and pleasant restaurant with a conservatory extension overlooking the garden. High standard food, using fresh, locally sourced ingredients, is offered.

Rooms: 11 en suite (1 fmly) (1 GF) **S** fr £100 **D** fr £135* **Facilities:** FTV DVD Lounge tea/coffee Dinner available Direct dial WiFi ⚓ ⚷ Fishing 🛁 **Extras:** Kimonos, bottled water **Parking:** 20 **Notes:** LB Closed 3–15 January

Lea House

★★★★ 🍴 GUEST ACCOMMODATION

tel: 01989 750652 & 07495 713603 **Lea HR9 7JZ**
email: enquiries@leahouse.co.uk **web:** www.leahouse.co.uk
dir: *4 miles southeast of Ross on A40 towards Gloucester, in Lea.*

This former coaching inn, near Ross-on-Wye, has a relaxed atmosphere and makes a good base for exploring the Forest of Dean and the Wye Valley. The individually furnished bedrooms are thoughtfully equipped and very homely. Breakfast in the oak-beamed dining room offers home-made breads, freshly squeezed juice, fresh fruit platters, local sausages and fish choices.

Rooms: 3 en suite (1 fmly) **S** fr £49.30 **D** fr £69.70* **Facilities:** FTV DVD TVL tea/coffee WiFi 🛁 **Extras:** Speciality toiletries, chocolate, fresh milk **Parking:** 4 **Notes:** LB

Thatch Close

★★★★ GUEST ACCOMMODATION

tel: 01989 770300 **Llangrove HR9 6EL**
email: info@thatchclose.co.uk **web:** www.thatchclose.co.uk
dir: *Exit A40 at Symonds Yat West/Whitchurch junct to Llangrove, right at crossroads after Post Office and before school. Thatch Close 0.5 mile on left.*

Standing in 13 acres, this sturdy 18th-century farmhouse is full of character. Expect a wonderfully warm atmosphere with a genuine welcome from your hosts. The homely bedrooms are equipped for comfort with many thoughtful extras. Breakfast is served in the elegant dining room and a lounge is available. The extensive patios and gardens are popular in summer — providing plenty of space to find a quiet corner and relax with a good book.

Rooms: 3 en suite **Facilities:** FTV TVL tea/coffee WiFi 🛁 **Extras:** Snacks — complimentary **Parking:** 8 **Notes:** LB Closed 21–29 December

SYMONDS YAT [EAST]   Map 10 SO51

See also Coleford (Gloucestershire)

The Royal Lodge

★★★★ GUEST ACCOMMODATION

tel: 01600 890238 **HR9 6JL**
email: info@rhhotels.co.uk **web:** www.rhhotels.co.uk
dir: *Midway between Ross and Monmouth exit A40 at signs for Goodrich and B4229 to Symonds Yat East.*

The Royal Lodge stands at the top end of the village overlooking the River Wye. Bedrooms are spacious and comfortable, and come complete with TVs and many guest extras; the bathrooms offer modern facilities. There is a cosy lounge with an open fireplace and two bars are available. Meals are offered in the welcoming restaurant, which provides carefully prepared meals using fresh and local ingredients. Staff are pleasant and friendly.

Rooms: 24 en suite (5 fmly) **Facilities:** FTV DVD TVL tea/coffee Dinner available Direct dial Licensed WiFi Fishing **Extras:** Mineral water **Conf:** Max 120 Thtr 120 Class 80 Board 80 **Parking:** 150 **Notes:** LB Civ wed 150

Saracens Head Inn

★★★★ INN

tel: 01600 890435 **HR9 6JL**
email: contact@saracensheadinn.co.uk **web:** www.saracensheadinn.co.uk
dir: *Exit A40 at South Herefordshire Motorcaravan Centre, signed Symonds Yat East, 2 miles.*

Dating from the 16th century, the friendly, family-run Saracens Head faces the River Wye and has wonderful views. The well-equipped bedrooms are decorated in a cottage style, and there is a cosy lounge, an attractive dining room and a popular public bar that leads onto a riverside patio. All meals are offered from a regularly-changing and comprehensive menu that includes locally sourced produce.

Saracens Head Inn

Rooms: 7 en suite 2 annexe en suite (1 GF) **S** fr £65 **D** fr £95* **Facilities:** FTV TVL tea/coffee Dinner available Direct dial WiFi Fishing **Conf:** Max 25 Thtr 25 Class 25 Board 25 **Parking:** 35 **Notes:** No children 12 years RS Christmas only open at lunch

See advert opposite

UPPER SAPEY   Map 10 SO66

The Baiting House

★★★★ INN

tel: 01886 853201 & 07825 232843 **Stourport Road WR6 6XT**
email: info@baitinghouse.co.uk **web:** www.baitinghouse.co.uk
dir: *On B4203 between Bromyard and Great Witley.*

Dating back to the 1800s, The Baiting House is a quintessential country inn brought right up to date. Purchased by a local couple to save it from redevelopment, this inn has become a popular place where locals and visitors alike are welcomed by the friendly team. Local sourcing is very important here, not only concerning the food but also the cask ales and ciders. A separate 'clubhouse' with traditional pub games can also be used for private dining. Dinner should not be missed, with a constantly changing menu of exciting dishes showcasing the best the area has to offer. Three bedrooms are located in the main building plus three ground-floor rooms in the annexe. A spacious terrace affords stunning views over the countryside – the perfect spot for an alfresco dinner.

Rooms: 6 en suite (1 fmly) (3 GF) **D** fr £60* **Facilities:** FTV tea/coffee Dinner available WiFi **Extras:** Home-made muffins on arrival, coffee machine **Conf:** Max 20 Class 20 Board 20 **Parking:** 60 **Notes:** LB

WHITCHURCH
Map 10 SO51

Norton House
★★★★ ⚜ BED AND BREAKFAST

tel: 01600 890046 & 07948 079660 **Old Monmouth Road HR9 6DJ**
email: lynda.mwhittle@gmail.com **web:** www.norton-house.com
dir: *Phone for directions.*

Built as a farmhouse, Norton House dates back some 300 years and has retained a lot of character, with flagstone floors and beamed ceilings. A warm and friendly welcome awaits all guests from hosts Lynda and David. The bedrooms, including a four-poster room, are individually styled and furnished for maximum comfort. Charming public areas include a snug with a wood-burning stove and comfortable lounge, a perfect location to enjoy the home-baked cakes on arrival. Excellent local produce is used to create an imaginative range of breakfast dishes. Parking is off-road, and self-catering cottages are also available.

Rooms: 3 en suite **S** fr £60 **D** fr £80* **Facilities:** FTV iPod docking station Lounge TVL tea/coffee WiFi ⚒ **Extras:** Fruit, biscuits **Parking:** 5 **Notes:** LB No children 13 years

WHITNEY-ON-WYE
Map 9 2024

Rhydspence Inn
★★★★ ⚌ INN

tel: 01497 831262 **HR3 6EU**
email: info@rhydspence.com **web:** www.rhydspence.com
dir: *On A438 between Hereford and Brecon, on right at England/Wales border.*

The Rhydspence Inn is full of character and history. Spanning the Wales–England border, this popular property is ideally located for Hay-on-Wye and Hereford. Parts of the building date from 1380 and extensions were added in the 17th to 20th centuries. A friendly welcome and relaxing atmosphere are found in both the bar and the dining room where locals and guests mingle. Bedrooms, located above the inn, come in a variety of shapes and sizes. Both dinner and breakfast offer a good selection of home-made, carefully-prepared dishes.

Rooms: 8 en suite **Facilities:** FTV Lounge TVL tea/coffee Dinner available WiFi Fishing **Extras:** Speciality toiletries **Conf:** Max 30 Thtr 30 Class 30 Board 30 **Parking:** 30 **Notes:** LB

YARKHILL
Map 10 SO64

Garford Farm
★★★★ FARMHOUSE

tel: 01432 890226 **HR1 3ST**
email: garfordfarm@btconnect.com
dir: *Exit A417 at Newtown crossroads onto A4103 for Hereford, farm 1.5 miles on left.*

This black-and-white, timber-framed farmhouse, set on a large arable holding, dates from the 17th century. Its character is enhanced by period furnishings, and fires burn in the comfortable lounge during colder weather. The traditionally furnished bedrooms, including a family room, have modern facilities.

Rooms: 2 en suite (1 fmly) **S** fr £50 **D** fr £70* **Facilities:** FTV Lounge tea/coffee WiFi ⚒ ⚒ **Parking:** 6 **Notes:** No children 2 years Closed 25–26 December 200 acres arable

HERTFORDSHIRE

BISHOP'S STORTFORD
Map 6 TL42

The PitStop
★★★★ GUEST ACCOMMODATION

tel: 01279 725725 & 725007 **The Morgan Garage, Little Hallingbury CM22 7RA**
email: mr@melvyn-rutter.net **web:** www.the-pitstop.net
dir: *3 miles south of Bishop's Stortford, signed Melvyn Rutter Ltd – Morgan Garage.*

The PitStop offers four individually styled en suite rooms. Located above The Morgan Garage, guests can enjoy a good night's sleep and hire a modern classic Morgan car for the day. All bedrooms are very well equipped and meet the needs of a varied clientele. Self-service continental breakfast can be taken in the American-style diner.

Rooms: 4 en suite (1 fmly) **S** fr £95 **D** fr £89* **Facilities:** FTV iPod docking station TVL Lift WiFi Hire of Morgan sports cars **Extras:** Fruit, snacks – complimentary **Parking:** 30

The Saracens Head Inn

For centuries the *Saracens Head Inn* has occupied its spectacular position on the east bank of the River Wye, where the river flows into a steep wooded gorge. The Inn's own ferry across the river still operates by hand, just as it has for the past 200 years.

There's a relaxed atmosphere throughout the Inn, from the flagstoned bar to the cosy lounge and dining room. The riverside terraces are a great place to watch the world go by.

The Inn has a reputation for high quality food, using fresh local ingredients where possible, with a regularly changing menu and daily specials – not to mention a tempting choice of 6 real ales (featuring local breweries), and freshly-ground coffee.

Symonds Yat East is situated in an Area of Outstanding Natural Beauty on the edge of the Forest of Dean, so a stay in one of the guest bedrooms is a must for exploring the unspoilt local countryside.

The Wye Valley Walk passes the Inn, as does the Peregrine cycle trail. Walking, cycling, mountain biking, river cruises, canoeing, kayaking, climbing and fishing are all available nearby.

Symonds Yat East
Ross on Wye
Herefordshire
HR9 6JL

Tel: 01600 890435

E: contact@saracensheadinn.co.uk

Web: www.saracensheadinn.co.uk

BISHOP'S STORTFORD *continued*

Bonningtons Guest House

★★★ GUEST HOUSE

tel: 01279 507472 & 07815 704830 **George Green, Little Hallingbury CM22 7SP**
email: info@bonningtons.net **web:** www.bonningtons.net
dir: *M11 junction 8 onto A120 towards Bishop's Stortford. Left at next roundabout, at lights left onto A1060 towards Hatfield Heath. In centre of Little Hallingbury, turn right opposite The George pub.*

Set in its own grounds, Bonningtons is a stylish guest house with a range of individually designed, modern, well-equipped bedrooms. Continental-style breakfasts offer very good choices. Free WiFi is available along with secure parking. Stansted Airport is a short drive away and daily rates for parking are available. This is an ideal base from which to explore the Cambridgeshire and Essex countryside.

Rooms: 6 annexe en suite (1 fmly) (4 GF) **Facilities:** FTV Lounge tea/coffee WiFi
🍫 **Extras:** Chocolates **Parking:** 20 **Notes:** No children 5 years

BUNTINGFORD
Map 12 TL32

Sword Inn Hand

★★★★ 🍺 INN

tel: 01763 271356 **Westmill SG9 9LQ**
email: theswordinnhandrestaurant@gmail.com **web:** www.theswordinnhand.co.uk
dir: *In Westmill, off A10 south of Buntingford.*

Set in the peaceful village of Westmill amid rolling countryside, this charming 14th-century inn offers excellent accommodation in a friendly and relaxed atmosphere. The purpose-built, ground-floor bedrooms are located just off the rear gardens; all are very well-equipped and carefully appointed and have their own access. Character public rooms offer a choice of restaurant and bar dining options, along with a choice of draught ales.

Rooms: 4 en suite (4 GF) **Facilities:** STV FTV TVL tea/coffee Dinner available
🍫 **Parking:** 25

MUCH HADHAM
Map 6 TL41

High Hedges Bed & Breakfast

★★★★ BED AND BREAKFAST

tel: 01279 842505 **High Hedges, Green Tye SG10 6JP**
email: info@high-hedges.co.uk **web:** www.high-hedges.co.uk
dir: *From B1004 turn off to Green Tye at Prince of Wales pub, turn into private road, 1st on right.*

Expect a warm welcome at High Hedges, a family-run B&B close to Stansted Airport, and convenient for visiting London and Cambridge. Bedrooms are well presented and comfortable, and come with many thoughtful extra touches. A substantial breakfast is served in the pleasant dining room.

Rooms: 3 rms (2 en suite) (1 pri facs) (1 fmly) (1 GF) **Facilities:** FTV tea/coffee WiFi
Parking: 3 **Notes:** Closed 25–26 December and 31 December to 1 January

NUTHAMPSTEAD
Map 12 TL43

The Woodman Inn

★★★ INN

tel: 01763 848328 **SG8 8NB**
email: enquiries@thewoodman-inn.co.uk **web:** www.thewoodman-inn.co.uk
dir: *M11 junction 20, A505 towards Royston, left onto B1368 to Barkway, 1st left past Tally Ho, right in 2 miles. Inn on left. Or from Royston take A505 signed motorway (M11) and Newmarket. Right onto B1368 and then as above.*

This 17th-century inn has many fine features, and is close to the Duxford Imperial War Museum. The practical bedrooms are decorated in a traditional style. The kitchen offers a good range of British meals, plus a generous breakfast.

Rooms: 2 annexe en suite (2 GF) **Facilities:** FTV tea/coffee Dinner available WiFi 🎣 Shooting range by arrangement **Parking:** 30 **Notes:** RS Sunday evening to Monday bar and restaurant closed

ST ALBANS
Map 6 TL10

Innkeeper's Lodge St Albans, London Colney

★★★★ INN

tel: 03451 551551 **Barnet Road, London Colney AL2 1BL**
email: info@innkeeperslodge.com **web:** www.innkeeperslodge.com
dir: *Phone for directions.*

Conveniently located close to the historic town of St Albans and the M25, this Innkeeper's Lodge (The Colney Fox) has a charming, welcoming bar with log fires lit on cooler evenings. It is a very popular dining venue and the extensive menus cater for most tastes. The stylish bedrooms are attractively presented yet still retain many original features. Free WiFi, a beer garden and ample secure parking are provided.

Rooms: 13 en suite **Facilities:** FTV tea/coffee Dinner available WiFi

WELWYN
Map 6 TL21

Premier Collection

The Wellington

★★★★★ ⚜ INN

tel: 01438 714036 **High Street AL6 9LZ**
email: info@wellingtonatwelwyn.co.uk **web:** www.wellingtonatwelwyn.co.uk
dir: *A1(M) junction 6 follow signs to Welwyn. In the High Street opposite St Mary Church.*

Enjoying a prominent position in the heart of the pretty village of Welwyn, The Wellington offers a range of beautifully presented, individually styled bedrooms. The most is made of the eye-catching original features in the charming restaurant, and log fires on colder evenings add to the ambience. There is a cosy bar area along with a sheltered terrace at the rear of the property. Ample secure parking is available along with free WiFi for guests.

Rooms: 6 en suite **Facilities:** FTV DVD iPod docking station tea/coffee Dinner available WiFi **Extras:** Bottled water **Parking:** 34

The White Hart

★★★★ ⊛ INN

tel: 01438 715353 2 Prospect Place AL6 9EN
email: info@whitehartwelwyn.co.uk web: www.whitehartwelwyn.co.uk
dir: *Phone for directions.*

Period charm and character are plentiful throughout this inn, which in parts dates back to the 13th century. The spacious bedrooms are individually decorated and thoughtfully equipped, some in a boutique style and those in the stable block in a more traditional style. Public rooms include a cosy bar, which has a great range of quality wines, ales and gins, and the atmospheric restaurant with inglenook fireplace and flagstone floors. There is also a function room and on-site parking.

Rooms: 9 en suite 4 annexe en suite (4 GF) S fr £95 D fr £105* Facilities: FTV tea/coffee Dinner available Direct dial WiFi Conf: Max 50 Thtr 50 Class 26 Board 20 Parking: 20

ISLE OF WIGHT

BEMBRIDGE   Map 5 SZ68

The Spinnaker

★★★★ ⊜ INN

tel: 01983 873572 & 872840 1 Steyne Road PO35 5UH
email: info@thespinnakeriow.co.uk web: www.thespinnakeriow.co.uk
dir: *From A3055 take B3395 (Sandown Road) towards Bembridge. After roundabout becomes Steyne Road.*

A beautifully restored Edwardian inn, set in the heart of Bembridge, open from 9am daily for breakfast, lunch and dinner. The 14 en suite rooms are appointed with modern amenities, while the decor retains the character and charm of this grand building. The bar has a fabulous snug area, chart room and many other cosy corners. The menu uses local produce and island suppliers where possible. There are two intimate function rooms available to hire. Flexible, tailor-made packages are available and advance booking is recommended.

Rooms: 14 en suite (2 fmly) Facilities: FTV DVD iPod docking station tea/coffee Dinner available WiFi ♪ ⚓ Conf: Max 100 Thtr 100 Class 60 Board 50 Parking: 30 Notes: LB Civ wed 50

CHALE   Map 5 SZ47

The Old House

★★★★ ⊜ BED AND BREAKFAST

tel: 01983 551368 & 07746 453398 Gotten Manor, Gotten Lane PO38 2HQ
email: aa@gottenmanor.co.uk web: www.gottenmanor.co.uk
dir: *1 mile north of Chale. Turn right from B3399 into Gotten Lane (opposite chapel), house at end.*

Located in countryside close to the coast, this 17th-century house has 18th- and 19th-century additions. The charming rustic bedrooms have antique bathtubs. Comprehensive breakfasts using the finest ingredients are served in the cosy dining room, and there is a spacious lounge with an open fire.

Rooms: 2 en suite S fr £80 D fr £95 Facilities: STV FTV iPod docking station Lounge tea/coffee WiFi ♨ ⚓ Parking: 3 Notes: LB No children 12 years

COWES   Map 5 SZ49

Duke of York Inn

★★★ INN

tel: 01983 295171 Mill Hill Road PO31 7BT
email: bookings@dukeofyorkcowes.co.uk web: www.dukeofyorkcowes.co.uk

This family-run inn is situated very close to the centre of Cowes. Comfortable bedrooms are divided between the main building and a separate annexe only seconds away. Home-cooked meals, with a number of fish and seafood dishes, feature on the menu every evening and are served in the bar and dining area; outdoor covered dining is also an option. Parking is a bonus.

Rooms: 8 en suite (1 fmly) (1 GF) Facilities: FTV tea/coffee Dinner available WiFi Parking: 10

FISHBOURNE   Map 5 SZ59

The Fishbourne

★★★★ ⊜ INN

tel: 01983 873572 & 882823 111 Fishbourne Lane PO33 4EU
email: info@thefishbourne.co.uk web: www.thefishbourne.co.uk
dir: *Off A3054 (Newport to Ryde road), next to Wightlink Ferry Terminal.*

The Fishbourne is conveniently located just by the Wightlink ferry terminal. The inn offers five stylishly decorated bedrooms with light and airy decor and modern fixtures including LCD TV and free WiFi. Guests can enjoy breakfast, lunch or dinner in the open-plan bar and restaurant area; on the menu is a wide range of traditional pub dishes made from locally-sourced produce.

Rooms: 5 en suite (2 fmly) Facilities: FTV DVD iPod docking station tea/coffee Dinner available WiFi ♪ Parking: 40 Notes: LB

NEWPORT   Map 5 SZ58

Bank Cottage B&B

★★★★ BED AND BREAKFAST

tel: 01983 822255 & 07796 945019 Dodnor Lane PO30 5TD
email: bankcottagebnb@gmail.com web: www.bankcottagebandb.co.uk

Bank Cottage offers a one-bedroom suite with private facilities and a private terrace on which to relax in warmer months. The suite has been well designed and can be configured in different ways to accommodate guest requirements. In-room breakfast is served at the dining table, and guests can choose from a well-written breakfast menu the night before for a prompt delivery in the morning. The suite also offers all mod cons including free WiFi. Secure parking is available. This is an ideal place for those searching for a quiet location to unwind and recharge their batteries.

Rooms: 1 rm (1 pri facs) (1 fmly) Facilities: FTV TVL tea/coffee WiFi ⚓ Extras: Slippers Parking: 3

NEWPORT *continued*

Castle Lodge

★★★ GUEST ACCOMMODATION

tel: 01983 527862 & 07789 228203 **54 Castle Road PO30 1DP**
email: castlelodge@hotmail.co.uk **web:** www.castlelodgeiow.co.uk
dir: *0.5 mile southwest of town centre. On B3323 towards Carisbrooke Castle.*

Well-presented Castle Lodge is located in a quiet residential area within close walking distance of the famous Carisbrooke Castle. A comfortable stay is assured in attractive and restful bedrooms, together with a bright and airy dining room where a substantial breakfast can be enjoyed.

Rooms: 3 en suite 4 annexe en suite (1 fmly) (4 GF) **D** fr £65* **Facilities:** FTV Lounge tea/coffee WiFi 🔒 **Parking:** 5 **Notes:** Closed Christmas and New Year

SANDOWN
Map 5 SZ58

The Wight

★★★★ GUEST ACCOMMODATION

tel: 01983 403722 **11 Avenue Road PO36 8BN**
email: enquiries@wighthotel.co.uk **web:** www.wighthotel.co.uk
dir: *100 yards after mini roundabout between High Street and Avenue Road.*

A family establishment, set in secluded grounds, only a short walk from Sandown's beach and high street shops. Bedrooms are very welcoming and are either on the ground or first floor. There's a heated swimming pool and a spa facility; there's also evening entertainment in the bar. A plentiful breakfast is served in the colourful dining room.

Rooms: 41 en suite (17 fmly) (18 GF) **Facilities:** FTV Lounge TVL tea/coffee Licensed WiFi ⌖ Snooker Sauna Gym 🔒 Steam room, jacuzzi **Parking:** 36 **Notes:** LB Civ wed 80

SEAVIEW
Map 5 SZ69

The Boathouse

★★★★ ⌂ INN

tel: 01983 873572 & 01938 810616 **Springvale Road PO34 5AW**
email: info@theboathouseiow.co.uk **web:** www.theboathouseiow.co.uk
dir: *From Seaview follow sea road, The Boathouse on corner of Springvale Road and Puckpool Hill.*

This very pleasant inn has a shore-side location and is a relaxing, friendly and comfortable place to stay. Food is a focus here with fresh, local produce and speciality lobster and crab dishes. The inn provides a contemporary style throughout; bedrooms are pleasantly spacious and most have beach views. There is ample parking and a garden, where in warmer times food and drink are served.

Rooms: 4 en suite (1 fmly) **Facilities:** FTV DVD iPod docking station tea/coffee Dinner available WiFi **Parking:** 20 **Notes:** LB

SHANKLIN
Map 5 SZ58

Premier Collection

Haven Hall

★★★★★ GUEST ACCOMMODATION

tel: 07914 796494 **5 Howard Road PO37 6HD**
email: david@havenhall.uk **web:** www.havenhall.uk
dir: *Exit A3055, between Shanklin and Lake, into Howard Road. At end, on right.*

This gabled Victorian house occupies an extraordinary location on top of the cliffs with stunning 180-degree views overlooking Sandown Bay. Situated at the far end of a cul-de-sac, it is surprisingly quiet and tranquil. The grounds have been extensively landscaped to enhance the natural beauty of the view. The house retains original features and is attractively decorated throughout; public areas include a comfortable lounge with a small bar. The homely bedrooms come with a wealth of thoughtful extras, and excellent breakfasts are served in the conservatory. Self-catering flats are also available.

Rooms: 14 en suite (3 GF) **S** fr £147 **D** fr £147 (room only)* **Facilities:** FTV DVD iPod docking station Lounge tea/coffee Direct dial Licensed WiFi ⌖ ♨ ⛱ ⛳ **Extras:** Speciality toiletries **Conf:** Max 45 Thtr 45 Class 45 Board 28 **Parking:** 25 **Notes:** LB No children Civ wed 35

Fernbank

★★★★ ⌂ GUEST ACCOMMODATION

tel: 01983 862790 **6 Highfield Road PO37 6PP**
email: fernbank2010@btconnect.com **web:** www.fernbank-iow.co.uk
dir: *Approaching Shanklin on A3020, right into Highfield Road. 300 yards on left.*

Located in Shanklin Old Village, Fernbank offers modern, comfortable and spacious accommodation. Home-made refreshments are available throughout the afternoon and guests can enjoy a wide range of both cooked and continental breakfasts in the airy dining room. There is an indoor swimming pool and plenty of outside space within the landscaped gardens in which to relax. Free WiFi is available throughout.

Rooms: 17 en suite (1 fmly) (2 GF) **S** fr £53 **D** fr £86* **Facilities:** FTV DVD Lounge tea/coffee Licensed WiFi ⌖ 🔒 Petanque **Parking:** 13 **Notes:** LB No children 12 years Closed November to February

The Belmont

★★★★ ⌂ GUEST ACCOMMODATION

tel: 01983 862864 & 867875 **8 Queens Road PO37 6AN**
email: enquiries@belmont-iow.co.uk **web:** www.belmont-iow.co.uk
dir: *From Sandown (on A3055), half turn left at Fiveways lights signed Ventnor. Belmont 400 metres on right, opposite St Saviour's Church.*

Situated less than a 10-minute walk from Shanklin beach and only five minutes from Shanklin Old Village, The Belmont offers comfortable accommodation and several rooms with stunning sea views. The Belmont is licensed, and drinks and sandwiches are available during the day and evening. Off-road parking is a benefit, and during summer months guests can enjoy the outdoor swimming pool.

Rooms: 12 en suite (2 GF) **Facilities:** FTV TVL tea/coffee Dinner available Licensed WiFi ⌖ Sauna 🔒 **Parking:** 9 **Notes:** LB No children 16 years

The Rowborough

★★★★ GUEST ACCOMMODATION

tel: 01983 866072 **32 Arthurs Hill PO37 6EX**
email: info@rowboroughhotel.com **web:** www.rowboroughhotel.com
dir: *Off A3055 (Sandown Road), on corner of Arthurs Hill and Wilton Park Road.*

A warm welcome is guaranteed at this family-run Victorian house, set in beautifully tended gardens within walking distance of Shanklin Village, Chine and beaches. All nine bedrooms are comfortably furnished, serviced to a high standard, and come equipped with Freeview TV and DVD player. Breakfast and dinner are served in the light and airy dining room, which has doors leading out to the patio and gardens. Guests can enjoy a drink at the well-stocked bar or simply relax in either the guest lounge or modern conservatory. Free WiFi is available throughout. Children over the age of five and small dogs are welcome.

Rooms: 9 en suite (2 fmly) (1 GF) **S** fr £35 **D** fr £70* **Facilities:** FTV DVD Lounge TVL tea/coffee Dinner available Licensed WiFi **Extras:** Speciality toiletries **Parking:** 5 **Notes:** LB No children 5 years Closed November to February

The Grange

★★★★ GUEST ACCOMMODATION

tel: 01983 867644 **9 Eastcliff Road PO37 6AA**
email: info@thegrangebythesea.com **web:** www.thegrangebythesea.com
dir: *Off A3055 (High Street).*

This delightful house specialises in holistic breaks and enjoys a tranquil yet convenient setting among manicured grounds, close to the seafront and village centre. Care has been taken over the beautifully presented bedrooms and spacious public areas. Breakfast is taken en famille (outside in fine weather).

Rooms: 15 en suite (2 fmly) (6 GF) **Facilities:** Lounge TVL tea/coffee Licensed WiFi Sauna Beauty treatments and massage **Extras:** Speciality toiletries **Parking:** 10 **Notes:** LB Civ wed 100

Hayes Barton

★★★★ 🍽 GUEST ACCOMMODATION

tel: 01983 867747 **7 Highfield Road PO37 6PP**
email: enquiries@hayesbarton.co.uk **web:** www.hayesbarton.co.uk
dir: *A3055 onto A3020 (Victoria Avenue), 3rd left.*

Hayes Barton has the relaxed atmosphere of a family home and provides well-equipped bedrooms and a range of comfortable public areas. Dinner is available from a short selection of home-cooked dishes, and there is a cosy bar-lounge. Shanklin Old Village, beach and promenade are all within walking distance.

Hayes Barton

Rooms: 9 en suite (1 fmly) (2 GF) **S** fr £49 **D** fr £86* **Facilities:** FTV DVD TVL tea/coffee Dinner available Licensed WiFi **Extras:** Bottled water **Parking:** 9 **Notes:** LB No children 7 years Closed October to April

---

TOTLAND BAY　　　　　　　　　　　Map 5 SZ38

The Hermitage

★★★ GUEST ACCOMMODATION

tel: 01983 752518 **Cliff Road PO39 0EW**
email: blake_david@btconnect.com **web:** www.thehermitagebnb.co.uk
dir: *From Church Hill (B3322), right into Eden Road, left into Cliff Road, 0.5 mile on right.*

The Hermitage is an extremely pet- and people-friendly establishment which occupies a stunning and unspoilt location near to the cliff top in Totland Bay. Extensive gardens are well maintained and off-road parking is a bonus. Accommodation is comfortable and guests are assured of a genuinely warm welcome here. A range of delicious items at breakfast provide a substantial start to the day.

Rooms: 6 rms (5 en suite) (1 pri facs) (1 fmly) **Facilities:** FTV Lounge TVL tea/coffee Dinner available WiFi 🐾 **Parking:** 6 **Notes:** LB

The Highdown Inn

★★★ INN

tel: 01983 752450 & 07964 322044 **Highdown Lane PO39 0HY**
email: susan@highdowninn.com **web:** www.highdowninn.com
dir: *Phone for directions.*

This traditional country pub and restaurant is located on a quiet crossroads, only a few minutes from nearby beaches, stunning bay views and the iconic Needles. Walkers and cyclists are welcome, as are dogs (in the bar). The bar offers real ales, an open fire and a wide range of dishes including local seafood. There is also a smartly presented dining room and a sunny garden with decking, vegetable plot and a children's play area.

Rooms: 3 en suite **Facilities:** FTV DVD tea/coffee Dinner available WiFi ⚓ Riding 🐾 **Extras:** Robes **Parking:** 30 **Notes:** LB

VENTNOR
Map 5 SZ57

Premier Collection

The Hambrough

★★★★★ 🛏 GUEST ACCOMMODATION

tel: 01983 856333 **Hambrough Road PO38 1SQ**
email: info@thehambrough.com **web:** www.thehambrough.com
dir: *Phone for directions.*

A former Victorian villa set on the hillside above Ventnor and with memorable views out to sea, The Hambrough has a modern, stylish interior with well-equipped and boutique-style accommodation. Afternoon tea is available in the bar from Tuesday to Saturday.

Rooms: 7 en suite (3 fmly) **D** fr £120* **Facilities:** FTV DVD Lounge tea/coffee Direct dial Licensed WiFi 🛁 **Extras:** Speciality toiletries – complimentary; mini-bar – chargeable **Conf:** Max 40 Thtr 40 Class 20 Board 24 **Notes:** LB Civ wed 40

Premier Collection

The Leconfield

★★★★★ 🛏 GUEST ACCOMMODATION

tel: 01983 852196 **85 Leeson Road, Upper Bonchurch PO38 1PU**
email: enquiries@leconfieldhotel.com **web:** www.leconfieldhotel.com
dir: *On A3055, 3 miles from Shanklin Old Village.*

This country house is situated on an elevated position with panoramic sea views over the historic village of Bonchurch. Luxury bedrooms and suites are spacious and individually styled. Public rooms include two lounges and a conservatory, and freshly prepared breakfasts can be enjoyed, using local produce where possible. Additional facilities include the outdoor pool, terrace area and ample off-road parking.

Rooms: 6 en suite 5 annexe en suite (3 GF) **S** fr £70 **D** fr £80* **Facilities:** FTV DVD iPod docking station Lounge tea/coffee Licensed WiFi 🦶 🛁 **Extras:** Bath robes – complimentary **Parking:** 14 **Notes:** LB No children 16 years Closed 24–26 December and 3–27 January

Little Rannoch

★★★★ 🛏 BED AND BREAKFAST

tel: 01983 852263 **1 Steephill Court Road PO38 1UH**
email: littlerannoch@btinternet.com **web:** www.littlerannoch.co.uk
dir: *From Ventnor town centre onto A3055 to St Lawrence. After 1.3 miles turn right after Ventnor Botanic Gardens into Steephill Court Road, Little Rannoch on left.*

Little Rannoch is a south-facing bungalow less than a mile from Ventnor, close to Ventnor Botanic Garden, cricket ground and Steephill Cove. The accommodation comprises one self-contained suite with a double bedroom, dining room/kitchenette, shower room plus a patio with garden and sea views. Breakfast features local and home-made items. Off-street parking is available, and the resorts of Shanklin and Sandown are within eight miles.

Rooms: 1 en suite (1 GF) **S** fr £80 **D** fr £120* **Facilities:** STV FTV tea/coffee WiFi 🛁 **Extras:** Snacks, home-made biscuits – complimentary **Parking:** 1 **Notes:** No children Closed November to 1 March

St Maur

★★★★ GUEST ACCOMMODATION

tel: 01983 852570 & 853645 **Castle Road PO38 1LG**
email: info@stmaur.co.uk **web:** www.stmaur.co.uk
dir: *Exit A3055 at end of Park Avenue into Castle Road, premises 150 yards on left.*

A warm welcome awaits at this Victorian villa, which is pleasantly and quietly located in an elevated position overlooking the bay. The well-equipped bedrooms are traditionally decorated, while public areas include a spacious lounge and cosy residents' bar. The gardens here are a delight.

Rooms: 8 en suite (2 fmly) **Facilities:** STV FTV Lounge tea/coffee Dinner available Licensed WiFi 🛁 **Extras:** Speciality toiletries **Parking:** 8 **Notes:** LB No children 4 years Closed December

The Eversley

★★★ GUEST ACCOMMODATION

tel: 01983 852244 **Park Avenue PO38 1LB**
email: eversleyhotel@yahoo.co.uk **web:** www.eversleyhotel.uk.com
dir: *On A3055 west of Ventnor, next to Ventnor Park.*

Located west of Ventnor, this family-run property enjoys a quiet location and has some rooms with garden and pool views. Bedrooms are generally of a good size and meet the needs of leisure and business travellers alike. The spacious restaurant is sometimes used for local functions, and there is a bar where light meals are served, as well as a TV room, a lounge area and a card room. Further facilities include a jacuzzi and gym.

Rooms: 20 rms (6 fmly) (2 GF) **Facilities:** 🦶 Gym **Notes:** Closed 30 November to 22 December and 2 January to 1 March

KENT

BENENDEN
Map 7 TQ83

Apple Trees B&B

★★★★ BED AND BREAKFAST

tel: 01580 240622 **Goddards Green TN17 4AR**
email: garryblanch@aol.com **web:** www.appletreesbandb.co.uk
dir: *3 miles east of Cranbrook. Exit A262 at Sissinghurst south into Chaple Lane, over crossroads, 2 miles left to Goddards Green, 1 mile on right.*

This spacious cottage is situated in the heart of the Kentish countryside, and is convenient for those visiting Sissinghurst Castle and Great Dixter. Bedrooms are attractively presented and include plenty of thoughtful extras such as TVs and complimentary internet connection. Breakfast is served in the rustic dining room overlooking the garden.

Rooms: 3 rms (1 en suite) (2 pri facs) (3 GF) **S** fr £65 **D** fr £70* **Facilities:** TVL tea/coffee WiFi 🦶 🛁 **Parking:** 6

BOUGHTON STREET
Map 7 TR05

The White Horse Inn

★★★★ INN

tel: 01227 751343 **246 The Street, Boughton-under-Blean ME13 9AL**
email: whitehorseinn@live.co.uk **web:** www.whitehorsecanterbury.co.uk
dir: *M2 junction 7, slip road left towards Channel Tunnel/Canterbury/Dover. At roundabout 4th exit onto A2 then slip road left to Boughton. On left on entering village.*

This traditional inn is located in the picturesque village of Boughton-under-Blean, just a short drive from Canterbury city centre. The White Horse Inn has a spacious pub and restaurant area where lunch, dinner and breakfast are served daily. Bedrooms are modern in style and comfortably appointed and come well equipped with digital TVs and free WiFi.

Rooms: 13 en suite (3 fmly) (2 GF) **Facilities:** FTV Lounge TVL tea/coffee Dinner available Direct dial WiFi ⚓ **Extras:** Speciality toiletries, water – complimentary; slippers **Parking:** 31 **Notes:** LB

BROADSTAIRS
Map 7 TR36

The Victoria Bed and Breakfast

★★★★ BED AND BREAKFAST

tel: 01843 871010 **23 Victoria Parade CT10 1QL**
email: helkemp2@gmail.com **web:** www.thevictoriabroadstairs.co.uk
dir: *A299 into Broadstairs, pass train station and continue on High Street. Turn right into Charlotte Street, 1st left then right into Victoria Parade.*

The Victoria Bed and Breakfast offers very comfortable seaside accommodation in an excellent location. The breakfast room/lounge and top-floor bedroom have stunning sea views and the house is just 30 metres from the beach. All bedrooms are well furnished with en suite bathrooms, Freeview TV and tea- and coffee-making facilities. Breakfast is cooked to order, and a range of options is available with most items locally sourced. Private parking or nearby permit parking is available at no charge.

Rooms: 3 en suite (1 fmly) **S** fr £70 **D** fr £90 **Facilities:** FTV DVD Lounge tea/coffee WiFi ⚓ **Extras:** Fridge, fresh milk, mineral water – complimentary **Parking:** 1 **Notes:** LB RS Christmas

CANTERBURY
Map 7 TR15

Renville Oast

★★★★ BED AND BREAKFAST

tel: 01227 830932 & 07754 243819 **Renville, Bridge CT4 5AD**
email: jamesokeeffe3710@gmail.com **web:** www.renvilleoast.co.uk
dir: *M2 junction 7 onto A2 (Boughton bypass) signed Canterbury/Dover. Take exit signed Bridge (immediately after Canterbury exit). At T-junction, turn right over the bridge; right at next fork; right at T-junction. Fork left (on A2 slip road), 200 yards on left exit into farm road, 2nd property on left.*

This beautiful oast house offers three comfortably appointed bedrooms; all feature modern decor, high-quality soft furnishings, free WiFi, comfortable seating and views of the surrounding countryside. Guest can enjoy a hearty breakfast in the dining room. Renville Oast is located in a quiet and tranquil position, yet just off the A2 and within five minutes of Canterbury's city centre.

Rooms: 3 en suite (3 fmly) **Facilities:** FTV Lounge tea/coffee WiFi **Extras:** Snacks, robes, bottled water **Parking:** 3 **Notes:** No children Closed 22–28 December

Yorke Lodge Bed & Breakfast

★★★★ GUEST ACCOMMODATION

tel: 01227 451243 **50 London Road CT2 8LF**
email: info@yorkelodge.com **web:** www.yorkelodge.com
dir: *M2 junction 7, A2, exit left signed Canterbury. At 1st roundabout turn left into London Road.*

Yorke Lodge stands in a tree-lined road just a 10-minute walk from the town centre and railway station. The spacious bedrooms are thoughtfully equipped and carefully decorated using a calming palette of neutral and pastel shades; some rooms have four-poster beds. The stylish dining room leads to a conservatory which opens onto a superb terrace.

Rooms: 8 en suite (2 fmly) **S** fr £68 **D** fr £90* **Facilities:** FTV Lounge TVL tea/coffee WiFi **Extras:** Speciality toiletries, sweets **Parking:** 5 **Notes:** LB No children 5 years

CANTERBURY *continued*

The Corner House

★★★★ RESTAURANT WITH ROOMS

tel: 01227 780793 & 01843 823000 **1 Dover Street CT1 3HD**
email: matt@cornerhouserestaurants.co.uk **web:** www.cornerhouserestaurants.co.uk
dir: *Phone for directions.*

Located right in the city centre, The Corner House offers three stylishly decorated bedrooms. They are very spacious and appointed to a high standard yet still showcase some of the building's original features. Lunch, dinner and breakfast are available in the restaurant, though dinner is not available on a Monday when the restaurant is closed.

Rooms: 3 en suite **Facilities:** FTV DVD tea/coffee Dinner available WiFi
🔒 **Extras:** Fridge **Conf:** Max 20 Class 20 Board 10

The Duke William

★★★★ 🍽 INN

tel: 01227 721308 **Ickham CT3 1QP**
email: info@thedukewilliamickham.com **web:** www.thedukewilliamickham.com
dir: *A257 (Canterbury to Sandwich) into Littlebourne, left opposite The Anchor into Nargate Street. 0.5 mile, right into Drill Lane, right into The Street.*

Located in the quiet village of Ickham, this village pub is a mix of traditional – exposed beams and roaring wood fires – and modern with up-to-date and stylish touches. Each of the four bedrooms has stylish decor, modern fabrics and contemporary furnishings that offer guests high quality and comfort – king-sized beds, TVs, DAB radios, tea- and coffee-making facilities and complimentary toiletries come as standard. A same daily menu is served in the restaurant 'The Den', the conservatory overlooking the garden and the bar with its warming fire in the winter. From the Duke William, it is just a short drive into Canterbury.

Rooms: 4 en suite **D** fr £60* **Facilities:** FTV tea/coffee Dinner available WiFi
Extras: Speciality toiletries – complimentary

Canterbury Lodge

★★★★ GUEST ACCOMMODATION

tel: 01227 768767 **63 London Road CT2 8JZ**
email: info@canterburylodge.uk **web:** www.canterburylodge.uk
dir: *M2 onto A2, 1st exit signed Canterbury. At 1st roundabout, left into London Road.*

Conveniently located on London Road in the centre of Canterbury, this spacious establishment offers comfortably appointed, en suite accommodation. The well-equipped rooms are modern in style yet still retain many original features. Free WiFi and off-road parking are available. Guests can enjoy a hearty cooked and continental breakfast daily in the dining room on the ground floor.

Rooms: 10 en suite (2 fmly) **S** fr £55 **D** fr £75* **Facilities:** FTV Lounge TVL tea/coffee WiFi 🔒 **Parking:** 9 **Notes:** LB No children 5 years

Peregrine House

★★★★ GUEST ACCOMMODATION

tel: 01227 761897 **18 Hawks Lane CT1 2NU**
email: enquiries@castlehousehotel.co.uk **web:** www.theperegrinehouse.co.uk

Peregrine House is centrally located right in the heart of Canterbury; it is a sister property to Castle House. Guests register at Castle House and then take a short walk to Peregrine House, alternatively a courtesy car is available to help transport guests and their luggage. Bedrooms and bathrooms offer clean, modern comfortable accommodation. Close to the main high street, cathedral, shops and restaurants.

Rooms: 13 rms (11 en suite) (2 pri facs) (5 fmly) (3 GF) **Facilities:** TVL tea/coffee Dinner available Licensed WiFi **Parking:** 14

Cathedral Gate

★★★ GUEST ACCOMMODATION

tel: 01227 464381 **36 Burgate CT1 2HA**
email: cathedralgatehotel@btconnect.com **web:** www.cathgate.co.uk
dir: *In city centre. Next to main gateway into cathedral precincts.*

Dating from 1438, this house has an enviable central location next to the cathedral. Old beams and winding corridors are part of the character of the property. Bedrooms are traditionally furnished, equipped to modern standards and many have cathedral views. Luggage can be unloaded at reception before parking in a nearby car park.

Rooms: 12 rms (2 en suite) 12 rms annexe (10 en suite) (1 fmly) **S** fr £50 **D** fr £84.50* **Facilities:** FTV Lounge tea/coffee Direct dial Licensed WiFi **Notes:** Closed 20–27 December

St Stephens Guest House

★★★ GUEST ACCOMMODATION

tel: 01227 767644 **100 St Stephens Road CT2 7JL**
email: info@ststephensguesthouse.co.uk **web:** www.ststephensguesthouse.co.uk
dir: *A290 from city, Westgate and sharp right into North Lane, 2nd roundabout left into St Stephens Road, right into Market Way, car park on right.*

St Stephens Guest House offers well-appointed and well-equipped accommodation. It is located just a 10-minute walk from Canterbury's town centre and is conveniently located near the University of Kent and Christchurch College. The dining room is traditionally decorated and has views of the garden; guests can enjoy a cooked or continental breakfast.

Rooms: 1 en suite 8 annexe en suite (2 fmly) (3 GF) **S** fr £54 **D** fr £75*
Facilities: FTV tea/coffee WiFi **Parking:** 6 **Notes:** Closed mid December to mid January

Innkeeper's Lodge Canterbury

★★★ INN

tel: 03451 551551 **162 New Dover Road CT1 3EL**
email: info@innkeeperslodge.com **web:** www.innkeeperslodge.com
dir: *Phone for directions.*

Built in the 19th century and with easy access to the A2, this Innkeeper's Lodge (The Old Gate) is located south of Canterbury. The welcoming interior is traditional in design. The en suite bedrooms, in different shapes and sizes, come with TVs, desks and free WiFi as standard; family rooms are available. A wide-ranging choice of dishes is offered on the seasonal menus. Free parking is provided.

Rooms: 9 en suite (1 fmly) **Facilities:** FTV tea/coffee Dinner available WiFi

---

DARTFORD   Map 6 TQ57

The Rising Sun Inn

★★★ ⇔ INN

tel: 01474 872291 **Fawkham Green DA3 8NL**
email: admin@risingsun-fawkham.com **web:** www.risingsun-fawkham.com
dir: *M25 junction 3, A20 Brands Hatch. Turn into Scratchers Lane until sign for Fawkham. Left into Brandshatch Road, inn on left.*

This popular inn overlooks the village green and is just a short drive from Brands Hatch. All the en suite bedrooms are spacious, pleasantly decorated and comfortable. There is a busy character bar, restaurant, and a patio for alfresco dining in warmer weather.

Rooms: 5 en suite (1 fmly) (2 GF) **Facilities:** FTV tea/coffee Dinner available WiFi **Extras:** Bottled water – complimentary **Parking:** 20

DEAL   Map 7 TR35

Premier Collection

Sutherland House

★★★★★ GUEST ACCOMMODATION

tel: 01304 362853 **186 London Road CT14 9PT**
email: sutherlandhousehotel@gmail.com **web:** www.sutherlandhousehotel.co.uk
dir: *0.5 mile west of town centre/seafront on A258.*

This stylish accommodation demonstrates impeccable taste with its charming, well-equipped bedrooms and a comfortable lounge. A fully stocked bar, books, free WiFi, Freeview TV and radio are some of the many amenities offered. The elegant dining room is the venue for a hearty breakfast and dinner is available by prior arrangement.

Rooms: 4 en suite (1 GF) **S** fr £75 **D** fr £85* **Facilities:** FTV DVD iPod docking station Lounge tea/coffee Dinner available Direct dial Licensed WiFi
🛁 **Extras:** Speciality toiletries, honesty bar **Conf:** Max 12 Thtr 12 Class 12 Board 12 **Parking:** 7 **Notes:** LB No children 5 years

---

DOVER   Map 7 TR34

Premier Collection

The Marquis at Alkham

★★★★★ ◉◉ RESTAURANT WITH ROOMS

tel: 01304 873410 & 822945 **Alkham Valley Road, Alkham CT15 7DF**
email: info@themarquisatalkham.co.uk **web:** www.themarquisatalkham.co.uk
dir: *A256 from Dover, at roundabout 1st exit into London Road, left into Alkham Road, Alkham Valley Road. Establishment 1.5 miles after sharp bend.*

Located between Dover and Folkestone, this contemporary restaurant with rooms offers luxury accommodation with modern features – TVs, WiFi, monsoon showers and bathrobes, to mention a few. All the stylish bedrooms are individually designed and have fantastic views of the Kent Downs. The award-winning restaurant, open for lunch, afternoon tea and dinner, specialises in modern British cuisine with a strong emphasis on locally sourced ingredients. Both continental and a choice of cooked breakfasts are offered.

Rooms: 10 en suite (3 fmly) (1 GF) **Facilities:** FTV DVD Lounge tea/coffee Dinner available Direct dial WiFi **Extras:** Speciality toiletries **Conf:** Max 20 Thtr 20 Class 20 Board 16 **Parking:** 22 **Notes:** LB Civ wed 55

Maison Dieu Guest House

★★★★ GUEST ACCOMMODATION

tel: 01304 204033 **89 Maison Dieu Road CT16 1RU**
email: info@maisondieu.co.uk **web:** www.maisondieu.co.uk
dir: *M20/A20 to Dover. Left into York Street, at roundabout 2nd exit. Right at lights into Ladywell, right at next lights, 100 yards on left.*

Maison Dieu offers the perfect stopover en route to and from Dover and mainland Europe; Dover's ferry and cruise terminals and The White Cliffs of Dover are just five minutes away and the Channel Tunnel is 10 minutes by car. Bedrooms are comfortably decorated and come well equipped with WiFi and digital TV. Guests can enjoy a cooked or continental breakfast daily in the dining room.

Rooms: 6 rms (4 en suite) (2 pri facs) (4 fmly) **S** fr £41 **D** fr £60 (room only)*
Facilities: FTV tea/coffee WiFi 🛁 **Parking:** 6 **Notes:** LB No children 4 years Closed 30 December to 15 February

DOVER *continued*

Castle Guest House

★★★★ GUEST HOUSE

tel: 01304 201656 **10 Castle Hill CT16 1QW**
email: info@castle-guesthouse.com **web:** www.castle-guesthouse.co.uk
dir: *A20 Dover, follow signs for Dover Castle. At foot of hill, on right.*

Castle Guest House is located in the centre of Dover just minutes from the town centre, Dover ferry port and Channel Tunnel terminal. Bedrooms are modern and comfortably appointed and include digital TVs and free WiFi. A cooked and continental breakfast is served daily in the dining room. Free off-road parking is available, and there's secure parking for motorbikes or bikes on request.

Rooms: 6 en suite (2 fmly) **S** fr £45 **D** fr £80 **Facilities:** FTV DVD tea/coffee WiFi
🔒 **Notes:** LB Closed Christmas

Bleriot's

★★★ GUEST ACCOMMODATION

tel: 01304 211394 **Belper House, 47 Park Avenue CT16 1HE**
email: info@bleriotsguesthouse.co.uk **web:** www.bleriotsguesthouse.co.uk
dir: *A20 to Dover, left into York Street, right at lights into Ladywell. Left at next lights into Park Avenue.*

This large, family-run Victorian property is convenient for the ferry port and town centre. Guests receive a warm welcome and can enjoy a range of comfortable, spacious en suite bedrooms. The attractive dining room is the venue for a wholesome breakfast to set you up for the day.

Rooms: 8 en suite (2 fmly) **S** fr £38 **D** fr £58 (room only)* **Facilities:** FTV Lounge tea/coffee WiFi 🔒 **Extras:** Bottled water **Parking:** 8 **Notes:** LB

| EGERTON | Map 7 TQ94 |

Premier Collection

Frasers

★★★★★ ◎◎ ♀ GUEST ACCOMMODATION

tel: 01233 756122 **Coldharbour Farm, Barhams Mill Road TN27 9DD**
email: lisa@frasersegerton.co.uk **web:** www.frasersegerton.co.uk
dir: *Phone for directions.*

Frasers is situated at the end of a private drive on a working farm set deep in beautiful Kent countryside halfway between Maidstone and Ashford. The bedrooms are spacious and individual in style with excellent quality furnishings ensuring a comfortable stay. Guests can enjoy an extensive cooked or continental breakfast in the main restaurant; this is also where the AA Rosette-worthy dinners are served.

Rooms: 8 en suite **S** fr £75 **D** fr £130* **Facilities:** FTV tea/coffee Dinner available Licensed ♦ Fishing **Extras:** Speciality toiletries, robes, slippers **Conf:** Max 150 Thtr 150 Class 50 Board 50 **Parking:** 50 **Notes:** LB Civ wed 100

| EYTHORNE | Map 7 TR24 |

Brambles

★★★★ ♀ BED AND BREAKFAST

tel: 01304 832424 & 07801 953556 **Church Hill CT15 4AF**
email: hello@bramblesbreakfast.co.uk **web:** www.bramblesbreakfast.co.uk
dir: *From A2, at lights follow signs for Eythorne and Shepherdswell. Through Shepherdswell to Eythorne, turn left into Church Hill, 100 yards on right.*

A lovely family home in a quiet Kent village, with secure parking and a peaceful rear garden that offers well-appointed rooms and an award-winning breakfast. The 2 bedrooms differ in size but they are well equipped to meet the needs of both the leisure and business traveller. WiFi is provided. Your hosts will welcome you with a warm drink and home-made goodies.

Rooms: 3 en suite **D** fr £90* **Facilities:** TVL tea/coffee WiFi 🔒 **Extras:** Home-made cake, fridge with water and fresh milk **Parking:** 3

FAVERSHAM — Map 7 TR06

Faversham Creek & Red Sails Restaurant

★★★★ ◎◎ RESTAURANT WITH ROOMS

tel: 01795 533535 & 534689 **Conduit Street ME13 7BH**
email: office@favershamcreekhotel.co.uk **web:** www.favershamcreekhotel.co.uk
dir: M2 junction 6 onto A251. At T-junction left then right into The Mall. Pass railway station, continue on B2041. Left into Quay Lane.

Located in the heart of Faversham and adjacent to the creek, this restaurant with rooms offers modern accommodation with its own individual style, and rooms named after characters from the Faversham area. Bedrooms are well equipped and ideal for both business and leisure guests alike. There is a courtyard terrace where guests can enjoy lunch or pre-dinner drinks before dining in the award-winning Red Sails Restaurant. Parking is available on site.

Rooms: 6 en suite (4 fmly) **S** fr £75 **D** fr £85* **Facilities:** STV FTV Lounge tea/coffee Dinner available Direct dial WiFi ⚓ 🅿 **Parking:** 4

FOLKESTONE — Map 7 TR23

Rocksalt Rooms

★★★★ ◎◎ RESTAURANT WITH ROOMS

tel: 01303 212070 **2 Back Street CT19 6NN**
email: info@rocksaltfolkestone.co.uk **web:** www.rocksaltfolkestone.co.uk
dir: M20 junction 13 follow signs to harbour (A259). At harbour left onto Fish Market.

Overlooking the busy harbour, often crowded with small leisure boats, and with wonderful sea views, Rocksalt Rooms enjoys a great location in Folkestone. Bedrooms are stylish, well-appointed with original antique beds and equipped with a host of thoughtful little extras. Continental breakfasts are delivered promptly to the guests' rooms each morning, and dinner is served in the award-winning restaurant, also blessed with panoramic views.

Rooms: 4 en suite (1 fmly) **Facilities:** FTV iPod docking station tea/coffee Dinner available WiFi **Extras:** Nespresso machine, fruit, speciality toiletries

The Relish

★★★★ GUEST ACCOMMODATION

tel: 01303 850952 **4 Augusta Gardens CT20 2RR**
email: reservations@hotelrelish.co.uk **web:** www.hotelrelish.co.uk
dir: M20 junction 13 onto A2034 (0.6 mile), then B2064 (0.6 mile). Right into Earls Avenue, then left into Bouverie Road West, right into Trinity Gardens.

Expect a warm welcome at this impressive Victorian terrace property, which overlooks Augusta Gardens in the fashionable West End of town. The bedrooms feature beautiful, contemporary natural-wood furniture, lovely co-ordinated fabrics and many thoughtful extras such as DVD players and free WiFi. Public rooms include a modern lounge-dining room, and a sun terrace where breakfast is served in the summer.

Rooms: 10 en suite **Facilities:** FTV DVD Lounge tea/coffee Direct dial WiFi **Extras:** Home-made cake, bottled water, glass of wine or a bottle of beer – complimentary **Conf:** Max 12 Thtr 9 Class 9 Board 12 **Notes:** Closed 23–31 December

The Wycliffe Guest House

★★★ GUEST HOUSE

tel: 01303 252186 **63 Bouverie Rd West CT20 2RN**
email: wycliffegh@gmail.com **web:** www.wycliffeguesthouse.co.uk
dir: M20 junction 13 onto A20. 2nd set of lights take middle lane and proceed straight over. After 1 km turn right signed A259 Sandgate/Hastings into Earls Avenue. Then 2nd left into Bouverie Road West, 200 metres on right.

The Wycliffe is located in the heart of Folkestone, just a short walk from the town centre and main promenade. The bedrooms are spacious and traditional in style with modern amenities including digital TV and free WiFi. There is a bar and a large dining room where guests can enjoy breakfast, and evening meals by prior arrangement. A convenient and secure parking area is available on a first-come-first-served basis.

Rooms: 13 rms (9 en suite) (1 pri facs) (3 fmly) **S** fr £35 **D** fr £55 (room only)*
Facilities: FTV DVD TVL tea/coffee Dinner available Licensed WiFi **Parking:** 10
Notes: LB

GOUDHURST — Map 6 TQ73

The Star & Eagle

★★★★ 🍴 INN

tel: 01580 211512 **High Street TN17 1AL**
email: starandeagle@btconnect.com **web:** www.starandeagle.co.uk
dir: Exit A21 onto A262 to Goudhurst, inn at top of village next to church. Car park at rear.

A warm welcome is assured at the 15th-century Star & Eagle, located in the heart of this delightful village. Within easy reach of Royal Tunbridge Wells and the Weald, this is a great base for walkers. Both bedrooms and public areas boast original features and much character. A wide range of delicious home-made dishes is available in the restaurant and bar.

Rooms: 10 rms (8 en suite) (2 pri facs) **S** fr £95 **D** fr £110* **Facilities:** FTV tea/coffee Dinner available Direct dial WiFi 🅿 **Extras:** Speciality toiletries, home-made shortbread **Conf:** Max 30 Thtr 30 Class 15 Board 12 **Parking:** 20 **Notes:** RS 25–26 December evening closed Civ wed 50

GRAFTY GREEN
Map 7 TQ84

Premier Collection

Who'd A Thought It
★★★★★ ⦿⦿ GUEST ACCOMMODATION

tel: 01622 858951 **Headcorn Road ME17 2AR**
email: joe@whodathoughtit.com **web:** www.whodathoughtit.com
dir: *M20 junction 8 onto A20 towards Lenham. After 1 mile take turn signed Grafty Green, follow brown tourism signs for 4-5 miles.*

The unusually named Who'd A Thought It is located in the quiet village of Grafty Green, convenient for both Maidstone and Ashford. Bedrooms and bathrooms are spacious and individually designed, using eclectic furnishings and stylish decor. Bathrooms feature hot tubs or jacuzzi baths, along with speciality toiletries. The restaurant has been awarded two AA Rosettes and offers an intimate and comfortable ambience. Meals are served daily in the restaurant and there is also a bar menu available.

Rooms: 19 annexe en suite (19 GF) **S** fr £80 **D** fr £150* **Facilities:** STV FTV DVD iPod docking station Lounge tea/coffee Dinner available Licensed WiFi ⌕ Fishing **Extras:** Chocolates, champagne, bottled water, robes, speciality toiletries **Conf:** Max 30 Thtr 30 Class 30 Board 20 **Parking:** 40

HALSTEAD
Map 6 TQ46

7 Motel Diner
★★★★ GUEST ACCOMMODATION

tel: 01959 535890 **London Road, Polhill TN14 7AA**
email: reservations@7hoteldiner.co.uk **web:** www. 7hoteldiner.co.uk
dir: *M25 junction 4, 2 miles towards Sevenoaks.*

This guest accommodation is conveniently located off the M25 and is just a short drive from Sevenoaks. The well-equipped bedrooms have been stylishly decorated to offer modern, comfortable accommodation; all have custom-made furniture, TVs and free WiFi. The lounge has a huge 50" TV with BT Sport coverage. There is an American-themed diner complete with authentic jukebox and leather booths, and all-day dining is available from 7am to 9.30pm.

Rooms: 26 en suite (2 fmly) (6 GF) **Facilities:** FTV TVL tea/coffee Dinner available Direct dial Licensed WiFi **Parking:** 50

HAWKHURST
Map 7 TQ73

The Queen's Inn
★★★★ INN

tel: 01580 754233 **Rye Road TN18 4EY**
email: info@queensinn.co.uk **web:** www.thequeensinnhawkhurst.co.uk
dir: *From M25 junction 5 take A21 to Flimwell. Turn left at lights to Hawkhurst.*

Carefully brought back to life after years of decline, The Queen's Inn offers individually styled, smart, en suite bedrooms with deep, comfortable beds and home-made goodies. The restaurant uses local, seasonal produce with many items such as breads, jams and marmalade made on-site by the talented co-owner and head chef. Free WiFi is offered in the public spaces and parking is provided.

Rooms: 7 en suite (2 fmly) **Facilities:** FTV iPod docking station Lounge tea/coffee Dinner available Direct dial WiFi **Extras:** Home-made brownies, fresh milk, robes – complimentary **Conf:** Max 100 Thtr 100 Class 50 Board 50 **Parking:** 30

Applebloom Bed and Breakfast
★★★★ BED AND BREAKFAST

tel: 01580 753347 **White Rose Cottage, Conghurst Lane TN18 5DZ**
email: enquiries@applebloom.co.uk **web:** www.applebloom.co.uk
dir: *A21 onto A268 at Flimwell. Through Hawkhurst, after 1.1 miles turn right at crossroads into Conghurst Lane. 400 metres on right.*

Applebloom Bed and Breakfast is set in its own attractive garden and surrounded by the beautiful Kent countryside. The two bedrooms are individually appointed and offer style, quality and comfort. Guests can relax either in the lounge, or in the garden during the warm months of the year. Breakfast is served at a communal table overlooking the garden; expect home-made and locally sourced items of the highest quality.

Rooms: 2 rms (1 en suite) (1 pri facs) **S** fr £60 **D** fr £70* **Facilities:** FTV Lounge tea/coffee WiFi **Parking:** 2 **Notes:** No children 12 years

HERNE COMMON
Map 7 TR16

Westgrange House B&B

★★★ GUEST ACCOMMODATION

tel: 01227 740663 **42 Bushyfields Road CT6 7LJ**
email: westgrangebandb@ymail.com **web:** www.westgrangehouse.co.uk
dir: *Phone for directions.*

Located in a quiet and tranquil area, this family-run bed and breakfast offers comfortable rooms, all equipped with WiFi and TVs. Off-road parking is available for all guests and a cooked and continental breakfast is served daily in the dining room. Herne Bay with its shops, bars and restaurants, is only a 10-minute drive away.

Rooms: 4 rms **Facilities:** WiFi

LEYSDOWN-ON-SEA
Map 7 TR07

The Ferry House Inn

★★★★ ◉ INN

tel: 01795 510214 **Harty Ferry Road ME12 4BQ**
email: info@theferryhouseinn.co.uk **web:** www.theferryhouseinn.co.uk
dir: *A249 over Sheppey Bridge, follow signs for Leysdown. Past Eastchurch, turn right before Leysdown.*

The Ferry House Inn is on the Isle of Sheppey, and offers spacious and comfortable accommodation as well as some fantastic views. All rooms have modern fixtures, fittings and decor. Guests can enjoy dinner in the main restaurant or in the bar area with lots of local produce sourced from surrounding farms. A cooked or continental breakfast is served daily.

Rooms: 5 en suite **Facilities:** FTV DVD iPod docking station Lounge tea/coffee Dinner available WiFi **Conf:** Max 80 Thtr 80 Class 40 Board 40 **Parking:** 50 **Notes:** LB No children 12 years Closed 24–30 December Civ wed 150

MAIDSTONE
Map 7 TQ75

See also Marden

Premier Collection

Maiden's Tower at Leeds Castle

★★★★★ GUEST ACCOMMODATION

tel: 01622 767823 & 765400 **Leeds Castle Estate ME17 1PL**
email: accommodation@leeds-castle.co.uk **web:** www.leeds-castle.com
dir: *M20 junction 8, follow brown tourist signs. After 3rd sign, continue over roundabout on A20. Pass Park Gate Inn on right, turn next right signed Broomfield.*

The Maiden's Tower was built as an annexe to the castle and used for house parties when the castle was still a private residence. Today, it offers five en suite, beautifully appointed bedrooms – all with stunning views and equipped with modern amenities. The venue can be hired for exclusive use for family parties or intimate ceremonies. Breakfast and dinner are served in the 17th-century, oak-beamed Fairfax Restaurant. Guests are free to explore the castle, grounds and gardens while in residence. Free parking is provided.

Rooms: 5 en suite **D** fr £225* **Facilities:** FTV DVD tea/coffee Dinner available Direct dial Licensed WiFi ⚓ Facilities available within Leeds Castle grounds **Extras:** Speciality toiletries, robes, slippers, coffee machine **Conf:** Max 100 Thtr 100 Class 40 Board 30 **Parking:** 15 **Notes:** Closed 25–26 December Civ wed 100

The Black Horse Inn

★★★★ ☕ INN

tel: 01622 737185 **Pilgrims Way, Thurnham ME14 3LD**
email: info@wellieboot.net **web:** www.wellieboot.net
dir: *M20 junction 7, north A249. Right into Detling, opposite pub into Pilgrims Way for 1 mile.*

This charming inn dates from the 17th century, and the public areas showcase a wealth of oak beams, exposed brickwork and open fireplaces. The stylish bedrooms are in a series of cosy cabins behind the premises; each one is attractively furnished and thoughtfully equipped, and the bathrooms are of an equally high standard.

Rooms: 27 annexe en suite (8 fmly) (27 GF) **Facilities:** FTV tea/coffee Dinner available WiFi ⚓ **Conf:** Max 80 Thtr 80 Class 40 Board 28 **Parking:** 40 **Notes:** LB Closed 24–27 December Civ wed 100

Stable Courtyard at Leeds Castle

★★★★ GUEST ACCOMMODATION

tel: 01622 767823 & 767786 **Leeds Castle Estate ME17 1PL**
email: accommodation@leeds-castle.co.uk **web:** www.leeds-castle.com
dir: *M20 junction 8, follow brown tourist signs. After 3rd sign, continue over roundabout on A20. Pass Park Gate Inn on right, turn next right signed Broomfield.*

Stable Courtyard is located right in the heart of the grounds at Leeds Castle. The stylishly appointed bedrooms are spacious, and many benefit from excellent views of the formal gardens and lake. Guests are welcome to explore the grounds and castle as part of their stay. Dinner and breakfast are served just opposite in The Great British Kitchen Restaurant.

Rooms: 17 annexe en suite (1 fmly) (5 GF) **S** fr £85 **D** fr £100* **Facilities:** FTV DVD tea/coffee Dinner available Direct dial Licensed WiFi ⚓ **Extras:** Robes, slippers **Conf:** Max 90 Thtr 90 Class 40 Board 30 **Parking:** 30 **Notes:** Closed 25–26 December Civ wed 100

Innkeeper's Lodge Maidstone

★★★ INN

tel: 03451 551551 **Sandling Road ME14 2RF**
email: info@innkeeperslodge.com **web:** www.innkeeperslodge.com
dir: *Phone for directions.*

Known as The White Rabbit Sandling, this Innkeeper's Lodge is situated close to the centre of town, and dates back to 1797 when it was built as the officers' quarters of the Invicta Barracks. Lodge bedrooms are modern, spacious and well appointed with a good range of facilities. Public rooms feature plush seating and dining areas where a good choice of food is available.

Rooms: 12 en suite (1 fmly) **Facilities:** FTV tea/coffee Dinner available WiFi

MARDEN
Map 6 TQ74

Premier Collection

Merzie Meadows

★★★★★ BED AND BREAKFAST

tel: 01622 820500 & 07762 713077 **Hunton Road TN12 9SL**
email: pamela@merziemeadows.co.uk **web:** www.merziemeadows.co.uk
dir: A229 onto B2079 for Marden, 1st right into Underlyn Lane, 2.5 miles at large Chainhurst sign, right onto drive signed Merzie Meadows.

Merzie Meadows is a detached property set in 20 acres of mature gardens in the Kent countryside. The generously proportioned bedrooms are housed in two wings which overlook a terrace; each room is carefully decorated, thoughtfully equipped and furnished with well-chosen pieces. The attractive breakfast room has an Italian tiled floor and superb views of the garden.

Rooms: 1 en suite (1 fmly) (1 GF) **S** fr £100 **D** fr £120* **Facilities:** STV FTV TVL tea/coffee WiFi **Extras:** Speciality toiletries, chocolates, magazines – complimentary **Parking:** 4 **Notes:** No children 15 years Closed mid December to mid February

NEW ROMNEY
Map 7 TR02

The Ship

★★★ INN

tel: 01797 362776 **83 High Street TN28 8AZ**
email: theshiphotelandrestaurant@gmail.com **web:** www.the-ship-hotel.co.uk
dir: M20 junction 10 onto A2070 to Brenzett. At roundabout 1st exit onto A259 to New Romney. Next to petrol station on right.

This traditional inn is located in the very centre of Romney Marsh; bedrooms are traditional in style and are located above the main pub area. The restaurant is spacious, seating up to 70 people, and is ideal for events and functions. The main bar area, conservatory and fully-heated patio provide a good choice of seating areas for guests. Breakfast, lunch and dinner are served here daily.

Rooms: 10 en suite (1 fmly) **S** fr £55 **D** fr £85* **Facilities:** FTV DVD tea/coffee Dinner available WiFi ⌁ ⌔ **Conf:** Max 130 Thtr 130 Class 80 Board 40 **Parking:** 20 **Notes:** LB

PEMBURY
Map 6 TQ64

Camden Arms

★★★★ INN

tel: 01892 822012 **1 High Street TN2 4PH**
email: food@camdenarms.co.uk **web:** www.camdenarms.co.uk
dir: Off A21, opposite village green.

Located in a central position and just a couple of minutes' drive from Tunbridge Wells, this inn offers comfortable, well-equipped accommodation with LCD TVs, free WiFi throughout and spacious en suite bathrooms. The large garden has outdoor seating, and the restaurant and bar area serve a large variety of regularly-changing local beers and pub meals seven days a week. Guests can choose a continental breakfast, or, for an extra charge, a hearty traditional English breakfast.

Rooms: 15 annexe en suite (1 fmly) (8 GF) **Facilities:** FTV tea/coffee Dinner available WiFi ⌔ **Extras:** Trouser press **Conf:** Max 50 Thtr 50 Class 24 Board 16 **Parking:** 68

QUEENBOROUGH
Map 7 TQ97

Queen Phillippa B&B

★★★★ GUEST ACCOMMODATION

tel: 01795 228756 **High Street ME11 5AQ**
email: queenphillippabedandbreakfast@gmail.com **web:** www.queenphillippa.com
dir: A249 onto the Isle of Sheppey, follow signs for Queenborough. Located opposite entrance to railway station.

This former pub offers rooms with modern decor, stylish furnishings, free WiFi, digital TV and beverage-making facilities. Breakfast is served daily in the dining area on the ground floor where guests can enjoy a cooked or continental breakfast.

Rooms: 10 en suite 3 annexe en suite (13 fmly) **Facilities:** FTV TVL tea/coffee Licensed WiFi ⌁ **Parking:** 9 **Notes:** LB

SANDWICH
Map 7 TR35

The New Inn

★★★ INN

tel: 01304 612335 **2 Harnet Street CT13 9ES**
email: new.inn@thorleytaverns.com **web:** www.thenewinnsandwich.com
dir: Off A256, one-way system into town centre, inn on right.

The New Inn is situated in the heart of busy Sandwich. The large open-plan lounge bar offers an extensive range of beers and an interesting choice of home-made dishes. Bedrooms are furnished in pine and have many useful extras.

Rooms: 5 en suite (3 fmly) **Facilities:** STV tea/coffee Dinner available Direct dial WiFi ⌔ **Parking:** 17

SITTINGBOURNE
Map 7 TQ96

Sandhurst Farm Forge

★★★★ BED AND BREAKFAST

tel: 01795 886854 **Seed Road, Newnham ME9 0NE**
email: rooms.forge@btinternet.com **web:** www.sandhurstfarmforge.co.uk
dir: Exit A2 into Newnham, into Seed Road by church, establishment 1 mile on right.

A warm welcome is assured at this peaceful location, which also features a working forge. The spacious bedrooms are in a converted stable block and provide smartly furnished accommodation. Breakfast is served in the dining room adjoining the bedrooms. The owner has won an award for green tourism by reducing the impact of the business on the environment.

Rooms: 2 annexe en suite (2 GF) **S** fr £60 **D** fr £85* **Facilities:** STV DVD tea/coffee WiFi ⌔ **Extras:** Snacks, bottled water **Parking:** 6 **Notes:** LB No children 6 months to 12 years Closed 23 December to 2 January

TENTERDEN
Map 7 TQ83

Little Dane Court

★★★★ BED AND BREAKFAST

tel: 01580 763389 & 07776 193399 **1 Ashford Road TN30 6AB**
email: littledanecourt@gmail.com **web:** www.littledanecourt.co.uk
dir: *A28 to Tenterden, after 1 mile pass 2 red telephone boxes. Little Dane 4th house on right.*

Little Dane Court has a long and fascinating history and offers a range of well-appointed bedrooms that meet the needs of discerning travellers. All bedrooms are well equipped, and for something a bit more individual, the Japanese-style cottage offers extra privacy and space. Breakfast is served at the communal table in the dining room or in the courtyard during the warm months of the year. The Japanese-style garden is a pocket of tranquillity.

Rooms: 3 rms (2 en suite) (1 pri facs) 1 annexe en suite **S** fr £50 **D** fr £95*
Facilities: FTV DVD TVL tea/coffee Dinner available WiFi ⚓ **Conf:** Max 10 Thtr 10 Board 10 **Parking:** 6 **Notes:** LB

TUNBRIDGE WELLS (ROYAL)
Map 6 TQ53

Premier Collection

Danehurst House

★★★★★ 🍽 BED AND BREAKFAST

tel: 01892 527739 **41 Lower Green Road, Rusthall TN4 8TW**
email: info@danehurst.net **web:** www.danehurst.net
dir: *1.5 miles west of Tunbridge Wells in Rusthall. Exit A264 into Coach Road and Lower Green Road.*

Situated in pretty gardens in a quiet residential area, this gabled Victorian house is located to the west of the historic spa town. The house retains many original features and is attractively decorated throughout. Public areas include a comfortable lounge with a small bar. The homely bedrooms come with a wealth of thoughtful extras, and excellent breakfasts are served in the conservatory.

Rooms: 4 en suite **Facilities:** FTV DVD iPod docking station TVL tea/coffee Licensed WiFi **Extras:** Speciality toiletries, Nespresso coffee machine **Parking:** 6 **Notes:** No children 12 years Closed Christmas

Salomons

★★★★ GUEST ACCOMMODATION

tel: 01892 515152 **Salomons Estate, Broomhill Road TN3 0TG**
email: reception@salomons-estate.com **web:** www.salomons-estate.com
dir: *M25 junction 5, A21 signed Hastings. Then A26 (Southborough and Tunbridge Wells). In Southborough right at 2nd lights into Speldhurst Road. 2nd left into Broomhill Road, entrance on right.*

Salomons is located on a private, 36-acre estate just a short distance from Royal Tunbridge Wells. The contemporary bedrooms are well equipped and ideal for both business and leisure guests. Breakfast, lunch and dinner are served in the main manor house daily. This is also a very popular wedding venue and a great range of conference rooms is available.

Rooms: 47 annexe en suite (23 GF) **Facilities:** STV FTV tea/coffee Dinner available Direct dial Licensed WiFi Gym **Extras:** Speciality toiletries **Conf:** Max 230 Thtr 230 Class 77 Board 68 **Parking:** 200 **Notes:** Civ wed 200

Innkeeper's Lodge Tunbridge Wells

★★★ INN

tel: 03451 551551 **London Road, Southborough TN4 0QB**
email: info@innkeeperslodge.com **web:** www.innkeeperslodge.com
dir: *Phone for directions.*

This Innkeeper's Lodge, The Hand & Sceptre, is on the A26 overlooking a park; it has a modern interior and the smart en suite bedrooms, in different shapes and sizes, come with TVs, tea- and coffee-making facilities and free WiFi as standard; family rooms are available. The menu of pub favourites will appeal to all tastes and there's a terrace to sit on in warmer weather. A meeting room is also available.

Rooms: 14 en suite (2 fmly) **Facilities:** FTV tea/coffee Dinner available WiFi

WINGHAM
Map 7 TR25

The Dog at Wingham

★★★★ 🌐 RESTAURANT WITH ROOMS

tel: 01227 720339 **Canterbury Road CT3 1BB**
email: marc@thedog.co.uk **web:** www.thedog.co.uk
dir: *On A257, in village of Wingham.*

Located in the village of Wingham, The Dog has undergone a complete make-over – the public areas retain plenty of original character along with stylish new furnishings. Bedrooms and en suite shower rooms are also of high quality throughout with modern designer-decor, Hypnos beds and WiFi. Breakfast, lunch and dinner are served downstairs in the airy, wood-panelled restaurant; the award-winning menus are based on seasonal British ingredients.

Rooms: 8 en suite (1 fmly) (1 GF) **S** fr £60 **D** fr £90* **Facilities:** Lounge tea/coffee Dinner available WiFi ⚘ **Parking:** 13 **Notes:** LB Civ wed 60

WOODCHURCH
Map 7 TQ93

Premier Collection

Brook Farm Bed & Breakfast

★★★★★ BED AND BREAKFAST

tel: 01233 860444 & 07790 906611 **Brook Street TN26 3SR**
email: reservations@brook.farm **web:** www.brook.farm
dir: *M20 junction 9 onto A28 south. After 4 miles turn left signed Woodchurch, 3 miles to village. Through village to T-junction, turn right onto B2067. 0.5 mile on right.*

Brook Farm offers three cottage-style bedrooms with their own private entrances and convenient parking space. All rooms have been very well configured and appointed to the highest standard to ensure a relaxing and enjoyable stay. Freshly prepared breakfasts are served in the attractive breakfast room in the farmhouse.

Rooms: 3 annexe en suite (3 GF) **Facilities:** FTV iPod docking station tea/coffee WiFi ⚘ **Extras:** Nespresso machine, speciality toiletries, slippers **Parking:** 4 **Notes:** LB No children 12 years

WROTHAM
Map 6 TQ65

The Bull

★★★★ ◉◉ INN

tel: 01732 789800 **Bull Lane TN15 7RF**
email: info@thebullhotel.com **web:** www.thebullhotel.com
dir: *M20 junction 2, A20 signed Paddock Wood, Gravesend and Tonbridge. At roundabout take 3rd exit onto A20 signed Wrotham, Tonbridge, Borough Green, M20 and M25. At roundabout take 4th exit into Bull Lane signed Wrotham.*

Dating back to 1385 and first licensed in 1495, The Bull offers modern facilities yet retains many traditional features including original exposed beams. High quality meals can be enjoyed at breakfast, lunch and dinner; the inn sources local produce from nearby farms, south coast landed fish and real ales from the Dark Star micro-brewery. Dinner can be taken in the two AA Rosette à la carte restaurant, while more relaxed fare is offered in the smokehouse bar. The bedrooms, including one four-poster room, are decorated with modern furnishings. The Buttery function room was originally the village bakery.

Rooms: 11 en suite (1 fmly) **S** fr £69 **D** fr £79 (room only) **Facilities:** FTV tea/coffee Dinner available WiFi ♿ **Extras:** Speciality toiletries – complimentary **Conf:** Max 100 Thtr 60 Class 60 Board 40 **Parking:** 30 **Notes:** Closed 1 January Civ wed 60

WYE
Map 7 TR04

Wife of Bath

★★★★ ◉◉ RESTAURANT WITH ROOMS

tel: 01233 812232 **4 Upper Bridge Street TN25 5AF**
email: info@thewifeofbath.com **web:** www.thewifeofbath.com
dir: *M20 junction 10, A2070 signed Kennington. At roundabout right onto A28 (Canterbury Road). Right at crossroads into Harville Road signed Wye. At T-junction (station opposite) right into Bridge Road, becomes Churchfield Way. Right into Church Street. At T-junction left, Wife of Bath on right.*

Located in the heart of this picturesque village of Wye, the Wife of Bath offers stylish en suite bedrooms that are very comfortably appointed and still show

---

THE WIFE OF BATH

Tel: 01233 812232 **Email:** info@thewifeofbath.com
Twitter: @WifeOfBathWye **Instagram:** @wifeofbathwye
Web: thewifeofbath.com

Acquired and refurbished in 2016 by Mark Sargeant, owner and operator of the award-winning Rocksalt in Folkestone and The Duke William pub in Ickham, The Wife of Bath serves Northern Spanish inspired and locally sourced dishes throughout it's A La Carte and Tasting Menus. The restaurant also boasts six beautifully appointed guest rooms, each complete with its own unique identity, and are perfect for a nights stay after dinner or a relaxing short break in the Kent countryside.

Situated in the picturesque village of Wye, in the heart of the Garden of England, The Wife of Bath has long been regarded as one of Kent's premier dining destinations and first opened as a restaurant in 1962. This culinary heritage is continued under the ownership of Mark Sargeant, ex-right hand man to Gordon Ramsay, whilst instilling a new and exciting lease of life through the decor and menus, utilising the best seasonal produce available - both from the surrounding countryside and direct from Spain.

The six guest rooms have been decorated and refurbished to the highest standard, being sympathetic to the period oak beams and vaulted ceilings, whilst incorporating a high end, luxurious finish with meticulous attention to detail. Each room has access to our pantry and honesty bar where guests can help themselves to locally sourced, artisan food and drink.

original features including exposed oak beams. All have Egyptian cotton bedding, TVs, free WiFi, Nespresso machines and complimentary toiletries. The restaurant is open daily for breakfast, lunch and dinner. Menus are influenced by northern Spanish cuisine to create vibrant, award-winning dishes.

Wife of Bath

Rooms: 3 en suite 3 annexe en suite (3 GF) **S** fr £105 **D** fr £105* **Facilities:** FTV tea/coffee Dinner available WiFi **Extras:** Fruit, snacks, robes **Parking:** 10

See advert opposite

LANCASHIRE

ACCRINGTON
Map 18 SD72

Pilkington's Guest House
★★★ GUEST HOUSE

tel: 01254 237032 **135 Blackburn Road BB5 0AA**
email: pilkingtonsaccrington@hotmail.com
web: www.pilkingtonsbedandbreakfast.webs.com
dir: *M65 junction 7 follow signs to Accrington town centre, establishment opposite railway station. M66 onto A56 to Accrington town centre.*

Located close to the railway station, this family-run end-of-terrace property has two comfortable bedrooms in the main house and four further bedrooms in the same terrace just a short way along the street. Home-cooked breakfasts are served in the main house.

Rooms: 6 rms (6 pri facs) (2 GF) **S** fr £30 **D** fr £60 (room only) **Facilities:** FTV DVD Lounge TVL tea/coffee WiFi ⚓ **Extras:** Slippers, robes **Parking:** 2

BARLEY
Map 18 SD84

Barley Mow
★★★★ ⬤ INN

tel: 01282 690868 **BB12 9JX**
email: info@barleymowpendle.co.uk **web:** www.seafoodpubcompany.com
dir: *M65 junction 13, at roundabout exit onto A682. Left into Pasture Lane, right into Ridge Lane, continue on Barley New Road. Turn right.*

This relaxed dining pub is full of stripped back rustic charm. Although managed by the Seafood Pub Company, there is plenty for meat lovers as traditional pub fare with an international twist is also a staple. Six bedrooms upstairs are spacious and equipped with smart TVs, free WiFi and deeply comfortable beds. The rural location offers a peaceful setting but quick motorway links are also on the doorstep.

Rooms: 6 en suite (2 fmly) **Facilities:** FTV tea/coffee Dinner available WiFi **Extras:** Mineral water, fresh milk **Parking:** 10

BLACKBURN
Map 18 SD62

Premier Collection

The Millstone at Mellor
★★★★★ ⬤ INN

tel: 01254 813333 **Church Lane, Mellor BB2 7JR**
email: relax@millstonemellor.co.uk **web:** www.millstonemellor.co.uk
dir: *A677 from Blackburn (or from A59) follow signs to Mellor.*

Once a coaching inn, The Millstone is situated in a village just outside Blackburn. It provides a very high standard of accommodation and professional and friendly service. Bedrooms, some in an adjacent house, are comfortable and generally spacious, and all are very well equipped; a room for less mobile guests is also available. Meals in the AA Rosetted restaurant make excellent use of the highest quality Ribble Valley produce.

Rooms: 17 en suite 6 annexe en suite (5 fmly) (8 GF) **Facilities:** STV Lounge tea/coffee Dinner available Direct dial WiFi **Conf:** Max 10 Board 10 **Parking:** 40

Bluebird Inn
Ⓤ

tel: 01254 813900 **Myerscough Road BB2 7LE**
email: bluebird.inn@jwlees.co.uk **web:** www.bluebirdinn.co.uk
dir: *From M6 junction 31 take A59 towards Blackburn/Clitheroe for 2.5 miles. Bluebird Inn on left.*

Currently the rating for this establishment is not confirmed. This may be due to a change of ownership or because it has only recently joined the AA rating scheme.

Rooms: 20 en suite (4 fmly) (10 GF) **S** fr £75 **D** fr £75* **Facilities:** FTV tea/coffee Dinner available Licensed WiFi **Extras:** Mineral water **Conf:** Max 12 Thtr 12 Class 8 Board 12 **Parking:** 75 **Notes:** LB

BLACKPOOL
Map 18 SD33

The Fylde International
★★★★ GUEST HOUSE

tel: 01253 623735 **93 Palatine Road FY1 4BX**
email: fyldeinternationalblackpool@gmail.com
web: www.familyaccommodationblackpool.com
dir: *A5099 (Central Drive) into town centre, right into Palatine Road. Property on right before lights.*

This family-run guest house has a prime central location, close to all Blackpool's attractions. Accommodation is comfortable and all rooms are equipped with modern facilities. Families are well catered for with a choice of family rooms and suites available. A spacious lounge and a separate dedicated children's area ensure all guests can enjoy the relaxed and welcoming environment. A substantial buffet breakfast is served. Parking is available.

Rooms: 7 en suite (4 fmly) (1 GF) **D** fr £60* **Facilities:** FTV TVL tea/coffee Licensed WiFi ⚓ **Parking:** 6 **Notes:** LB

BLACKPOOL *continued*

Ashley Victoria

★★★★ GUEST ACCOMMODATION

tel: 01253 348787 **17–19 Alexandra Road FY1 6BU**
email: admin@blackpoolfamilyaccommodation.com
web: www.ashleyvictoriablackpool.co.uk
dir: *Phone for directions.*

This modern property has a central location close to the promenade and offers smartly furnished and well-equipped bedrooms suitable for a wide clientele. Families are well catered for with inter-connecting suites available. Satellite TV comes as standard as does fast WiFi. There is a games room, licensed bar and children's facilities. Breakfast is buffet style and generous.

Rooms: 29 en suite

The Bromley

★★★★ BED AND BREAKFAST

tel: 01253 624171 **306 Promenade FY1 2EY**
email: bromleyblackpool@gmail.com **web:** www.thebromleyhotelblackpool.co.uk
dir: *0.1 mile north past Blackpool Tower, on right.*

Located on the North Shore promenade, just a short walk from many of the main attractions, The Bromley offers comfortable, en suite accommodation. There is a licensed bar and lounge on the ground floor. Free WiFi is available in public areas, and off-road parking at the front of the property is a real bonus.

Rooms: 13 en suite (3 fmly) (1 GF) **S** fr £45 **D** fr £70* **Facilities:** FTV DVD TVL tea/coffee Licensed WiFi 🔒 **Parking:** 14

The Craigmore

★★★★ GUEST HOUSE

tel: 01253 355098 **8 Willshaw Road, Gynn Square FY2 9SH**
email: enquiries@thecraigmore.com **web:** www.thecraigmore.com
dir: *1 mile north of Tower. A584 north over Gynn roundabout, 1st right into Willshaw Road. The Craigmore 3rd on left.*

This friendly and welcoming guest house is in an attractive location overlooking Gynn Square gardens, with the Promenade and tram stops just metres away. Three of the smart and modern bedrooms are suitable for families. There is a comfortable lounge, a separate sun lounge and patio to the front, and the dining room has a small bar.

Rooms: 5 en suite (3 fmly) **Facilities:** FTV Lounge TVL tea/coffee WiFi **Notes:** LB No children 5 years Closed November to March

Pelham Lodge

★★★★ GUEST ACCOMMODATION

tel: 01253 625127 & 07717 342897 **7–9 General Street FY1 1RW**
email: info@pelhamlodge.co.uk **web:** www.pelhamlodge.co.uk
dir: *Phone for directions.*

Situated close to attractions such as the Winter Gardens and Blackpool Tower, Pelham Lodge is only a five-minute walk from the train station. Good quality and comfortable accommodation is promised and a friendly welcome on arrival is guaranteed. Limited parking is available to the rear.

Rooms: 15 en suite (2 fmly) (2 GF) **S** fr £38 **D** fr £58* **Facilities:** FTV TVL tea/coffee WiFi **Extras:** Bottled water – complimentary **Parking:** 4 **Notes:** Closed 24–25 December

Bianca Guesthouse

★★★ GUEST HOUSE

tel: 01253 752824 **25 Palatine Road FY1 4BX**
email: enquiries@hotelbianca.co.uk **web:** www.hotelbianca.co.uk
dir: *Phone for directions.*

A warm Blackpool welcome awaits at Bianca Guesthouse, situated centrally, and within easy walking distance of all the town's attractions and amenities. The homely accommodation is decorated with modern floral prints; family rooms are available, as well as a range of cosy doubles fitted with impressively comfortable beds. There is a licensed bar for residents.

Rooms: 10 en suite (2 fmly) **Facilities:** FTV tea/coffee Licensed WiFi **Notes:** Closed 20–27 December

Casablanca

★★★ GUEST HOUSE

tel: 01253 622574 **84 Hornby Road FY1 4QS**
email: jdixon8969@aol.com
dir: *Phone for directions.*

This personally-run and homely guest house is perfectly situated within easy reach of all of Blackpool's central attractions. Accommodation is fully en suite and features modern accessories and a choice of room types. There is a comfortable lounge, breakfasts are generous and limited parking is available.

Rooms: 9 en suite (2 fmly) **Facilities:** FTV TVL tea/coffee 🔒 **Parking:** 2 **Notes:** LB Closed 20 December to 4 January

The Derby

★★★ 🍷 GUEST ACCOMMODATION

tel: 01253 623708 & 07809 143248 **2 Derby Road FY1 2JF**
email: tj52way@yahoo.com **web:** www.thederbyhotel.co.uk
dir: *From promenade, pass North Pier, heading north. Turn right next to Hilton Hotel into Derby Road, The Derby on right.*

The Derby is a family-friendly establishment offering good value, modern accommodation in a variety of sizes. Dinner is available and guests have the use of a comfortable lounge and a separate bar. Breakfast is the highlight of any stay with quality cooking and hearty portions to be expected.

Rooms: 9 rms (5 en suite) (4 pri facs) (3 fmly) **S** fr £25 **D** fr £50 **Facilities:** FTV TVL tea/coffee Dinner available Licensed WiFi 🔒 **Parking:** 5 **Notes:** LB

BURNLEY
Map 18 SD83

Premier Collection

Crow Wood
★★★★★ ◉◉ GUEST ACCOMMODATION

tel: 01282 471913 **Royle Lane BB12 0RT**
email: info@thewoodlandspa.com **web:** www.crowwood.com
dir: *M65 junction 11 (Westbound, no exit Eastbound), take 3rd exit at roundabout signed Crow Wood and The Woodland Spa.*

Crow Wood is situated in 100 acres of woodland and offers modern bedrooms, attractively appointed and well equipped for both leisure and business guests. A good range of accessories are in place including complimentary WiFi and fluffy bathrobes; some rooms have air conditioning. Award-winning meals can be enjoyed in Bertram's Restaurant as well as more relaxed meals and snacks in the lounge. Tapas is also available in the spa areas. Extensive leisure and spa facilities are provided at The Woodland Spa. Free on-site parking is provided.

Rooms: 10 en suite (1 fmly) (6 GF) **Facilities:** FTV Lounge Dinner available Direct dial Licensed WiFi 🚫 Sauna Gym **Extras:** Speciality toiletries **Conf:** Max 56 Thtr 40 Board 26 **Parking:** 100 **Notes:** No children

CHORLEY
See Eccleston

CLITHEROE
Map 18 SD74

Premier Collection

The Assheton Arms
★★★★★ ◉ RESTAURANT WITH ROOMS

tel: 01200 441227 **Downham BB7 4BJ**
email: info@asshetonarms.com **web:** www.seafoodpubcompany.com
dir: *A59 to Chatburn, then follow Downham signs.*

This historic Grade II listed building is located in the conservation village of Downham, with stunning views of Pendle Hill. The inn is owned by the Seafood Pub Company which means you can expect outstanding seafood. The smart bedrooms are spacious with a combination of traditional and contemporary decor; some rooms are dog-friendly. The team here are young, friendly and guarantee a warm welcome.

Rooms: 1 en suite 11 annexe en suite (4 fmly) (6 GF) **S** fr £70 **D** fr £80*
Facilities: FTV Lounge tea/coffee Dinner available WiFi ⚓ 🐾 **Extras:** Mineral water, fresh milk **Conf:** Max 20 **Parking:** 18

COWAN BRIDGE
Map 18 SD67

Premier Collection

Hipping Hall
★★★★★ ◉◉◉ 🍴 RESTAURANT WITH ROOMS

tel: 015242 71187 **LA6 2JJ**
email: info@hippinghall.com **web:** www.hippinghall.com
dir: *M6 junction 36, A65 through Kirkby Lonsdale towards Skipton. On right after Cowan Bridge.*

Close to the market town of Kirkby Lonsdale, Hipping Hall offers spacious bedrooms, designed using soft shades with sumptuous textures and fabrics; the bathrooms use natural stone, slate and limestone to great effect. There are also three spacious cottage suites that create a real hideaway experience. The sitting room, with large, comfortable sofas has a traditional feel. The three AA Rosette-worthy restaurant is a 15th-century hall with tapestries and a minstrels' gallery that is as impressive as it is intimate.

Rooms: 7 en suite 8 annexe en suite (7 GF) **Facilities:** FTV Lounge Dinner available Direct dial WiFi 🐾 **Extras:** Speciality toiletries, fruit **Conf:** Max 12 Board 12 **Parking:** 30 **Notes:** No children 12 years Civ wed 42

ECCLESTON
Map 15 SD51

Parr Hall Farm
★★★★ GUEST ACCOMMODATION

tel: 01257 451917 **8 Parr Lane PR7 5SL**
email: enquiries@parrhallfarm.com **web:** www.parrhallfarm.com
dir: *M6 junction 27, B5250 north for 5 miles to Parr Lane on right. 1st property on left.*

This attractive, well-maintained farmhouse and sometime wedding venue is located in a quiet corner of the village yet close to the M6. Dating back to the 18th century, the majority of bedrooms are located in a sympathetic barn conversion and include luxury en suite bathrooms and lots of thoughtful extras. A comprehensive continental breakfast is included in the room price.

Rooms: 10 annexe en suite (1 fmly) (5 GF) **S** fr £60 **D** fr £80* **Facilities:** FTV tea/coffee WiFi ⚓ 🚲 Guided walks **Extras:** Sweets – complimentary **Conf:** Max 15 Class 15 Board 15 **Parking:** 20

FENCE
Map 18 SD83

The Forest
★★★★ INN

tel: 01282 692228 **Cuckstool Lane BB12 9PA**
email: info@forestfence.co.uk
web: www.seafoodpubcompany.com/venue-promotions/forest-fence/
dir: *Phone for directions.*

Owned by Seafood Pub Company, this modern dining pub has much to offer. Food has an eclectic Mediterranean focus with local produce and grills cooked over burning coals; outdoor dining is a big draw in the summer months. The accommodation is contemporary and well equipped. Ample on-site parking is provided.

Rooms: 8 en suite **Facilities:** Dinner available **Notes:** No children

GREAT ECCLESTON — Map 18 SD44

Premier Collection

The Cartford Inn

★★★★★ INN

tel: 01253 670166 **Cartford Lane, Little Eccleston PR3 0YP**
email: info@thecartfordinn.co.uk **web:** www.thecartfordinn.co.uk
dir: *North of A586 (west of Great Eccleston).*

This 17th-century, family-run inn enjoys extensive views towards the Lake District and offers stylish and chic accommodation together with award-winning food. The double and twin bedrooms, with impressive en suites, have Juliet balconies with views of the river. There's also a top-floor penthouse suite and newly built are two luxury studio cabins. Dining is a must here, with the kitchen team using local produce which they also sell in the on-site deli, Toti (short for Taste of the Inn). Eating on the terrace is possible in warmer weather and a private function room is available for small parties.

Rooms: 17 en suite (1 fmly) (3 GF) **S** fr £80 **D** fr £110* **Facilities:** FTV tea/coffee Dinner available WiFi ⚓ **Conf:** Max 35 Thtr 35 Class 14 Board 16 **Parking:** 50 **Notes:** Closed 25 December

HEYSHAM — Map 18 SD46

The Royal

★★★★ INN

tel: 01524 859298 **Main Street LA3 2RN**
email: paulturner@theroyalheysham.co.uk **web:** www.theroyalheysham.co.uk
dir: *A589 follow signs for Heysham Village, then brown tourist signs for St Peter's Church. The Royal is next to church.*

This 16th-century former grain store became a pub around 100 years ago. Today, the inn has been lovingly restored to provide 11 en suite rooms and has retained many original features. Part of the pub is the former cottage which was famed for producing nettle beer, but things have changed and now guests can choose from a range of hand-pulled ales and traditional pub food including home-made, hand-raised pies and Morecambe Bay shrimps.

Rooms: 4 en suite 7 annexe en suite (3 GF) **Facilities:** tea/coffee Dinner available WiFi **Parking:** 30

LANCASTER — Map 18 SD46

The Fenwick Steak & Seafood Pub

★★★★ ⬕ INN

tel: 015242 21157 **Lancaster Road, Claughton LA2 9LA**
email: info@fenwickarms.co.uk **web:** www.fenwickarms.co.uk
dir: *Phone for directions.*

Part of the Seafood Pub Company group, this charming roadside, dining pub has been stylishly appointed to provide smart, comfortable bedrooms and suites with TV and free WiFi. The property is over 250 years old so it is full of character and charm – low ceilings, stone floors and blazing wood-burning fires set the scene. The public bar and restaurant areas are the setting for the fish and grill menu and a great choice of real ales and wines.

Rooms: 9 en suite **Facilities:** Dinner available WiFi

Toll House Inn

★★★★ INN

tel: 01524 599900 **Penny Street LA1 1XT**
email: relax@tollhouseinnlancaster.co.uk **web:** www.tollhouseinnlancaster.co.uk

Ideally situated in the heart of the city, Toll House Inn has been transformed from a typical Victorian property to one that is fresh and contemporary, yet retains all the elegance of its original era. Bedrooms are modern and very well equipped. The stylish bar and brasserie are popular with both guests and local residents, serving meals and light bites throughout the day.

Rooms: 28 en suite (2 fmly) (2 GF) **Facilities:** FTV tea/coffee Dinner available Lift WiFi ⚓ **Conf:** Max 20 Thtr 20 Board 20 **Parking:** 3 **Notes:** LB

LANESHAW BRIDGE — Map 18 SD94

The Alma Inn

★★★★ INN

tel: 01282 857830 **Emmott Lane BB8 7EG**
email: reception@thealmainn.com **web:** www.thealmainn.com
dir: *At end of M65 onto A6068 (Vivary Way) towards Skipton. At 3rd roundabout, 1st exit into Skipton Old Road, after 0.5 mile right into Hill Lane. 0.5 mile on right.*

Part of the Seafood Pub Company, The Alma Inn is a longstanding gem in the magnificent Pendle countryside. Dating back to 1725, it is a rural coaching inn that features open fires, stone floors and oak beams. Guests can dine well in the lounge-style bars or the more lavishly appointed restaurant. The stylish rooms come in a variety of sizes, but all are thoroughly equipped with Nespresso machines, DAB radio and safes. Function facilities, ample parking and even a helicopter landing pad are available.

Rooms: 9 en suite (8 fmly) **Facilities:** FTV iPod docking station Lounge tea/coffee Dinner available Direct dial WiFi ⚓ **Extras:** Speciality toiletries, Nespresso coffee machine **Conf:** Max 150 Thtr 100 Class 50 Board 40 **Parking:** 45 **Notes:** LB Civ wed 200

Rye Flatt Bed & Breakfast

★★★★ BED AND BREAKFAST

tel: 01282 871565 **20 School Lane BB8 7JB**
email: info@rye-flatt.co.uk **web:** www.rye-flatt.co.uk
dir: *M65 onto A6068 towards Keighley. Turn right at Emmott Arms, park on left, immediately after bridge.*

Situated on the Lancashire and Yorkshire border with great transport links, this B&B operates from a 17th-century farmhouse which has some fantastic original features. Ideally located for business or leisure, the house features cosy bedrooms and well-equipped bathrooms. Warm hospitality and a memorable breakfast are highlights of any stay here. There is also a garden for sunnier days.

Rooms: 2 en suite **S** fr £50 **D** fr £80* **Facilities:** FTV Lounge tea/coffee WiFi ⚓ **Parking:** 2

LONGRIDGE — Map 18 SD63

Derby Arms
★★★★ INN

tel: 01772 782370 **Chipping Road PR3 2NB**
email: info@derbyarmslongridge.co.uk web: www.derbyarmslongridge.co.uk
dir: *Phone for directions.*

This relaxed dining pub is managed by the Seafood Pub Company so although classic British pub fare is to be expected, the emphasis is on locally landed fish. The stylish accommodation upstairs is spacious and equipped with smart TVs and free WiFi; the little luxury extras such as quality toiletries are noteworthy, and a deeply comfortable bed is guaranteed. The inn is situated in a peaceful, rural location but nearby motorway links are also a boon.

Rooms: 6 en suite (1 fmly) **Facilities:** FTV tea/coffee Dinner available ⅃
Conf: Max 15 Thtr 15 Class 15 Board 15 **Parking:** 50

LYTHAM ST ANNES — Map 18 SD32

Innkeeper's Lodge Lytham St Annes
★★★★ INN

tel: 03451 551551 **The County Hotel, Church Road FY8 5LH**
email: info@innkeeperslodge.com web: www.innkeeperslodge.com
dir: *M55 junction 4, A5239 (Progress Way) leads onto A5230 (Squires Gate Lane). At end of road at Starr Gate turn left onto A584 (Clifton Drive North). Follow Kilgrimol Garden signs on A584, left into Beach Street, right into Henry Street. Next left into Church Road. Lodge on left.*

The Innkeeper's Lodge Lytham St Annes is ideally situated in the heart of the town between the golf courses and just off the west beach promenade. This busy dining pub offers fresh and contemporary bedrooms which are well equipped for the modern traveller. The stylish bar and pizza kitchen are popular with both guests and local residents, serving meals and light bites throughout the day.

Rooms: 21 en suite (3 fmly) **Facilities:** FTV Lounge tea/coffee Dinner available WiFi **Parking:** 5 **Notes:** LB

Strathmore
★★★ GUEST ACCOMMODATION

tel: 01253 725478 **305 Clifton Drive South FY8 1HN**
dir: *In centre of St Annes opposite Post Office.*

The long-established, family-run Strathmore has a central location close to the promenade, and offers smartly furnished and well-equipped bedrooms. There is an elegant lounge and a smart dining room.

Rooms: 4 en suite **S** fr £33 **D** fr £66* **Facilities:** FTV Lounge tea/coffee WiFi
Parking: 5 **Notes:** LB No children 9 years

MORECAMBE — Map 18 SD46

The Morecambe Hotel
★★★★ INN

tel: 01524 415239 & 415515 **25 Lord Street, Poulton LA4 5HX**
email: hello@themorecambehotel.co.uk web: www.themorecambehotel.co.uk
dir: *M6 junction 34 onto A683 to Morecambe. Follow signs for town centre (Lancaster Road). At roundabout 2nd exit into Thornton Road, The Morecambe is opposite St Mary's Church.*

This 18th-century, former coaching inn has been lovingly appointed to a high standard and provides several en suite bedrooms, a small function room for up to 30 people and an extensive dining area. A large garden to the rear has a children's play area and a terrace for alfresco dining.

Rooms: 7 en suite **Facilities:** FTV DVD iPod docking station Lounge TVL tea/coffee Dinner available WiFi **Extras:** Speciality toiletries, slippers, robes – complimentary **Conf:** Max 24 Thtr 24 Class 24 Board 24 **Parking:** 10 **Notes:** LB

Yacht Bay View
★★★★ GUEST HOUSE

tel: 01524 414481 **359 Marine Road East LA4 5AQ**
email: yachtbayview@hotmail.com web: www.yachtbay.co.uk
dir: *0.5 mile northeast of town centre on seafront promenade.*

This comfortable seafront guest house is situated in pride of place on Morecambe's promenade. Seven guest rooms are available in a range of sizes, all smartly appointed and well equipped. Front-facing rooms have splendid views across the sands to the Cumbrian mountains. The welcome is always warm and generous, and breakfast is a highlight of any stay.

Rooms: 7 en suite (1 fmly) **S** fr £45 **D** fr £70* **Facilities:** FTV DVD TVL tea/coffee WiFi **Extras:** Bottled water, fresh milk

Beach Mount
★★★ GUEST ACCOMMODATION

tel: 01524 420753 **395 Marine Road East LA4 5AN**
email: beachmounthotel@aol.com web: www.beachmounthotelmorecambe.co.uk
dir: *M6 junction 34/35, follow signs to Morecambe. Beach Mount 0.5 mile from town centre on East Promenade.*

This spacious property overlooks the bay and features a range of room styles that includes a junior suite. Guests have use of a comfortable lounge with fully licensed bar, and breakfasts are served in a pleasant, separate dining room.

Rooms: 10 en suite (1 GF) **S** fr £29.25 **D** fr £58.50* **Facilities:** FTV DVD Lounge tea/coffee Licensed WiFi **Notes:** LB Closed November to March

MORECAMBE *continued*

Silverwell

★★★ GUEST HOUSE

tel: 01524 410532 **20 West End Road LA4 4DL**
email: slverwlll@gmail.com **web:** www.silverwellhotel.co.uk
dir: *Follow signs to West End, turn right at promenade, take 3rd on right, Silverwell on left.*

Silverwell offers comfortable accommodation in a quiet residential street, with bedrooms in a range of sizes with singles and families catered for. There is a licensed bar and lounge for guest use. Evening meals are available by prior arrangement.

Silverwell

Rooms: 14 rms (8 en suite) (6 pri facs) (3 fmly) (4 GF) **S** fr £28 **D** fr £56*
Facilities: FTV TVL tea/coffee Dinner available Licensed WiFi 🛁 **Conf:** Max 20 Thtr 15 Class 20 Board 12

See advert below

ORMSKIRK
Map 15 SD40

Premier Collection

Moor Hall Restaurant with Rooms

★★★★★ ◎◎◎◎◎ ⊚ RESTAURANT WITH ROOMS

tel: 01695 572511 **Prescot Road, Aughton L39 6RT**
email: enquiry@moorhall.com web: www.moorhall.com
dir: *From M58 junction 1, take first exit at roundabout then first left. Continue for 1.7 miles. Moor Hall is signed on right.*

Located within west Lancashire in five-acre gardens with stunning views over a beautiful lake, said to be the remains of a medieval moat. This Grade II listed house has been transformed with care and attention to detail into a true destination restaurant with rooms. Bedrooms are stunning, with many showcasing original features paired with exciting modern styling. Mark Birchall is at the helm here and has created a refined dining experience in relaxed surroundings. Local provenance is at the forefront of this modern British cuisine; produce grown on the five-acre Moor Hall site or by local suppliers is used whenever possible. The Barn offers a more casual dining experience with the same strong ethos. Throughout the establishment, the knowledgeable and friendly team are passionate about what they do. Please note, children under 12 are welcome at lunch only.

Moor Hall Restaurant with Rooms

Rooms: 5 en suite 2 annexe en suite (2 fmly) (2 GF) **S** fr £195 **D** fr £195*
Facilities: FTV Lounge tea/coffee Dinner available WiFi **Extras:** Fruit, snacks, mini-bar **Parking:** 40 **Notes:** Closed 3 January for 2 weeks and 31 July for 2 weeks

See advert below

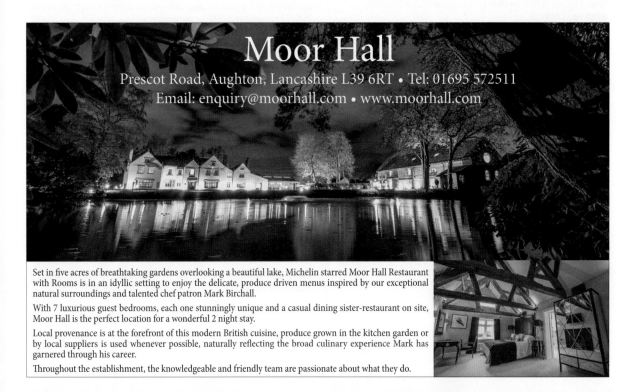

ORMSKIRK *continued*

Innkeeper's Lodge Ormskirk

★★★★ INN

tel: 03451 551551 **Springfield Road, Aughton L39 6ST**
email: info@innkeeperslodge.com **web:** www.innkeeperslodge.com
dir: *Phone for directions.*

This Innkeeper's Lodge (The Miller & Carter) is on the edge of the pretty village of Aughton and provides smart yet affordable accommodation; it makes a good base for a country escape, away from the hectic pace of life in Liverpool or Southport. The en suite bedrooms include desks, TVs, free WiFi and tea- and coffee-making facilities as standard; a family room is available. The Miller & Carter Steakhouse is popular for its good selection of 30-day British and Irish steaks alongside other pub-favourite dishes. The property is within easy reach of attractions such as Knowsley Safari Park, Chester Zoo, Formby Golf Club and Aintree Racecourse.

Rooms: 12 en suite (1 fmly) **Facilities:** FTV tea/coffee Dinner available Lift WiFi

▌ PRESTON   Map 18 SD52

Birch Croft Bed & Breakfast

★★★ BED AND BREAKFAST

tel: 01772 613174 & 07761 817187 **Gill Lane, Longton PR4 4SS**
email: johnsuts@btinternet.com **web:** www.birchcroftbandb.co.uk
dir: *From A59 right at roundabout to Midge Hall. Premises 4th on left.*

Situated only 10 minutes from major motorway links (M6, M65, M61), Birch Croft is on the doorstep of many attractions and close to Southport, Preston and Blackpool. This is a friendly, family-run business which offers comfortable accommodation in a very peaceful location.

Rooms: 3 en suite (1 fmly) **Facilities:** FTV DVD Lounge TVL tea/coffee WiFi
🔒 **Parking:** 11 **Notes:** LB

▌ RILEY GREEN   Map 18 SD62

Grill & Grain at the Boatyard

[U]

tel: 01254 209841 **Bolton Road PR5 0SP**
email: markmckeown@grillandgrainboatyard.co.uk
web: www.grillandgrainboatyard.co.uk
dir: *M65 junction 3 onto A675 signed Hoghton Tower. 500 metres on right.*

Currently the rating for this establishment is not confirmed. This may be due to a change of ownership or because it has only recently joined the AA rating scheme.

Rooms: 6 annexe en suite (6 GF) **Facilities:** FTV tea/coffee Dinner available Licensed WiFi **Extras:** Bottled water, fresh milk – complimentary **Parking:** 72

▌ SAMLESBURY   Map 18 SD53

Samlesbury Hall Lodge

★★★★ GUEST ACCOMMODATION

tel: 01254 812010 **Preston New Road PR5 0UP**
email: info@samlesburyhall.co.uk **web:** www.samlesburyhall.co.uk
dir: *M6 junction 31 onto A59 then A677 signed Blackburn.*

The gate lodge of Samlesbury Hall provides a cosy getaway for small groups, or couples looking for a romantic retreat. Accommodation comprises a large suite with two sitting rooms on one level, making it accessible for guests with less mobility. The sitting rooms can be converted to allow six guests to stay. Breakfasts are served either in the Hall itself or in the suite by prior arrangement. Samlesbury Hall serves hearty lunches and has art exhibitions, guided tours, a bee and heritage centre and gardens to explore.

Rooms: 3 en suite (3 fmly) (3 GF) **S** fr £90 **D** fr £120 (room only)* **Facilities:** FTV DVD Lounge TVL tea/coffee Licensed WiFi 🔒 Historic house, golf driving range, play trail, mayflower playground **Conf:** Max 150 Thtr 150 Class 150 Board 150 **Parking:** 4 **Notes:** Civ wed 120

▌ WARTON   Map 18 SD42

The Birley Arms

★★★★ ☕ INN

tel: 01772 679988 **Bryning Lane PR4 1TN**
email: birley@thebirleyarmshotel.co.uk **web:** www.thebirleyarmshotel.co.uk
dir: *M55 junction 3 (Kirkham), 1st left, then over 3 roundabouts. Straight on at mini roundabout, at next roundabout left signed Warton. 2 miles on left.*

The Birley Arms is a smartly appointed inn situated in the charming village of Warton, between Lytham St Annes and Preston. The bedrooms are neatly presented and equipped with modern facilities. Open-plan public areas are light and airy, and feature a conservatory, lounge bar and a restaurant.

Rooms: 16 en suite (1 fmly) (8 GF) **Facilities:** FTV DVD tea/coffee Dinner available WiFi 🔒 **Extras:** Speciality toiletries – complimentary **Conf:** Max 30 Board 30 **Parking:** 60

LEICESTERSHIRE

▌ LONG WHATTON   Map 11 SK42

The Royal Oak

★★★★★ ◎ ☕ INN

tel: 01509 843694 **26 The Green LE12 5DB**
email: enquiries@theroyaloaklongwhatton.co.uk **web:** www.theroyaloaklongwhatton.co.uk
dir: *Phone for directions.*

The Royal Oak is a popular gastro pub with rooms, located in a small village just four miles from East Midlands Airport. Members of the young team offer a warm welcome and service is attentive. The spacious en suite bedrooms are to the rear of the property and have been designed with comfort and style in mind. There is plenty of parking available and a small garden for the warmer months.

Rooms: 12 en suite (12 GF) **S** fr £89 **D** fr £104* **Facilities:** FTV tea/coffee Dinner available WiFi **Extras:** Speciality toiletries, mineral water **Parking:** 36

MARKET BOSWORTH · Map 11 SK40

Softleys

★★★ 🛏 GUEST ACCOMMODATION

tel: 01455 290464 **2 Market Place CV13 0LE**
email: softleysrestaurant@gmail.com **web:** www.softleys.com
dir: On B585 in Market Place.

Softleys is a Grade II listed building dating back to 1794. The bedrooms are en suite and set on the third floor offering picturesque views over Market Bosworth. Quality food, using locally-sourced ingredients, is offered.

Rooms: 3 en suite (1 fmly) **S** fr £69 **D** fr £99* **Facilities:** FTV tea/coffee Dinner available Direct dial Licensed WiFi **Conf:** Max 26 Thtr 26 Class 26 Board 26
Notes: RS Sunday evening and Monday no food available

LINCOLNSHIRE

CLEETHORPES · Map 17 TA30

The Comat

★★★★ GUEST ACCOMMODATION

tel: 01472 694791 & 591861 **26 Yarra Road DN35 8LS**
email: comat-hotel@ntlworld.com **web:** www.comat-hotel.co.uk
dir: Exit A1098 (Alexandra Road), left of library.

A short walk from the shops and seafront, the welcoming Comat offers cosy, well-equipped bedrooms which includes ground-floor rooms and a family suite; all featuring smart, modern en suite bath or shower rooms. Tasty English breakfasts are served in the bright dining room and an attractive lounge is also available.

Rooms: 5 en suite (2 fmly) (1 GF) **Facilities:** FTV DVD TVL tea/coffee WiFi **Notes:** LB Closed Christmas

Ginnie's Guest House

★★★ 🅐 GUEST HOUSE

tel: 01472 694997 **27 Queens Parade DN35 0DF**
email: enquiries@ginnies.co.uk **web:** www.ginnies.co.uk
dir: From Kingsway (seafront) into Queens Parade (A1098).

Ginnie's Guest House is a Victorian terraced house situated in a quiet location close to the Winter Gardens, Playtower and many other amenities. The house is well maintained by the resident proprietor who takes pride in the fact that many guests return for further visits.

Rooms: 7 rms (5 en suite) (2 pri facs) (3 fmly) (1 GF) **S** fr £35 **D** fr £55*
Facilities: FTV DVD iPod docking station TVL tea/coffee WiFi **Extras:** Speciality toiletries – complimentary **Parking:** 4 **Notes:** LB RS 24–25 and 31 December room only

GREAT LIMBER · Map 17 TA10

The New Inn

★★★★ 🏵🏵 INN

tel: 01469 569998 **2 High Street DN37 8JL**
email: enquiries@thenewinngreatlimber.co.uk **web:** www.thenewinngreatlimber.co.uk
dir: 2 miles from Humberside Airport on A18.

The Grade II New Inn sits on the Brocklesby Estate and has close links to nearby areas of Grimsby and Hull. Appointed to a modern standard throughout, the inn offers stylish bedrooms in muted colours schemes with smart TVs, quality bed linen and good WiFi connectivity. Dinners served in the award-winning restaurant are the highlight of any stay – expect an interesting choice of vibrant dishes based on home-grown estate produce and fish from Grimsby; meals can also be enjoyed in the more relaxed bar area. Parking is available on site.

Rooms: 10 en suite (1 fmly) (3 GF) **Facilities:** FTV Lounge Dinner available WiFi **Extras:** Speciality toiletries – complimentary **Conf:** Max 18 Thtr 18 Class 18 Board 18 **Parking:** 15

HEMSWELL · Map 17 SK99

Premier Collection

Hemswell Court

★★★★★ 🍴 🛏 GUEST ACCOMMODATION

tel: 01427 668508 **Lancaster Green, Hemswell Cliff DN21 5TQ**
email: function@hemswellcourt.com **web:** www.hemswellcourt.com
dir: 1.5 miles southeast of Hemswell on A631 in Hemswell Cliff.

Originally an officers' mess, Hemswell Court is a popular venue for conferences, weddings or private gatherings. The modern bedrooms and many suites are ideal for families or groups of friends, and all rooms are well equipped. The lounges and dining rooms are enhanced by many antique pieces.

Rooms: 25 en suite (3 fmly) (6 GF) **S** fr £95 **D** fr £120* **Facilities:** Lounge TVL tea/coffee Dinner available Licensed WiFi 🛎 **Extras:** Slippers, robes **Conf:** Max 200 Thtr 200 Class 150 Board 150 **Parking:** 150
Notes: Closed Christmas and New Year Civ wed 200

HORNCASTLE · Map 17 TF26

Premier Collection

Magpies Restaurant with Rooms

★★★★★ 🏵🏵 RESTAURANT WITH ROOMS

tel: 01507 527004 **71–73 East Street LN9 6AA**
email: info@magpiesrestaurant.co.uk **web:** www.magpiesrestaurant.co.uk
dir: A158 into Horncastle, continue at lights. On left opposite Trinity Centre.

This quaint and charming property is situated in the popular market town of Horncastle. The spacious en suite accommodation features three individually appointed rooms; all provide TVs, complimentary WiFi, home-made biscuits, mini-bar and luxurious bathrooms. There is a cosy lounge area with a wood-burning stove which is perfect for chilly winter evenings. The two AA Rosette award-winning restaurant provides a good choice of imaginative dishes at both lunch and dinner, and afternoon tea is also served. On-street parking is available nearby.

Rooms: 3 en suite **S** fr £70 **D** fr £110* **Facilities:** FTV iPod docking station Lounge tea/coffee Dinner available WiFi **Extras:** Bottled water, home-made biscuits and jam, mini-bar **Notes:** No children Closed 26–30 December and 1–7 January RS Monday to Tuesday closed

| HOUGH-ON-THE-HILL | Map 11 SK94 |

Premier Collection

The Brownlow Arms

★★★★★ INN

tel: 01400 250234 **High Road NG32 2AZ**
email: armsinn@yahoo.co.uk **web:** www.thebrownlowarms.com
dir: Take A607 (Grantham to Sleaford road). Hough-on-the-Hill signed from Barkston.

The Brownlow Arms is a beautiful 16th-century property that enjoys a peaceful location in this picturesque village, located between Newark and Grantham. Tastefully appointed and spacious public areas have many original features, and include a choice of luxurious lounges and an elegant restaurant offering imaginative cuisine. The bedrooms are stylish, comfortable and particularly well equipped.

Rooms: 4 en suite 1 annexe en suite (1 GF) **Facilities:** FTV DVD tea/coffee Dinner available Direct dial WiFi 🔒 **Parking:** 20 **Notes:** No children 8 years Closed 25–27 December and 31 December to 1 January

| LINCOLN | Map 17 SK97 |

See also Horncastle & Marton (village)

Eagles Guest House

★★★★ GUEST ACCOMMODATION

tel: 01522 686346 **552A Newark Road, North Hykeham LN6 9NG**
email: eaglesguesthouse@yahoo.co.uk **web:** www.eaglesguesthouse.co.uk
dir: A46 onto A1434, signed Lincoln South, North Hykeham and South Hykeham. 0.5 mile on right opposite Cornflower Way.

This large, modern detached house is situated within easy access of the A46 and the historic city of Lincoln. The smartly appointed, thoughtfully equipped bedrooms are bright and fresh in appearance. A substantial breakfast is served in the pleasant dining room. There's free WiFi throughout the property and an electric car charging point outside.

Rooms: 6 en suite (2 fmly) (2 GF) **S** fr £48 **D** fr £65* **Facilities:** FTV tea/coffee WiFi **Extras:** USB socket **Parking:** 6 **Notes:** No children 9 years

The Loudor

★★★★ GUEST ACCOMMODATION

tel: 01522 680333 **37 Newark Road, North Hykeham LN6 8RB**
email: info@loudorhotel.co.uk **web:** www.loudorhotel.co.uk
dir: 3 miles from city centre. A46 onto A1434 for 2 miles, on left opposite shopping centre.

The Loudor can be found opposite The Forum shopping centre and a short walk from the sports centre. This friendly place offers well-equipped bedrooms, and breakfast is served at individual tables in the spacious dining room. There is some on-site parking.

Rooms: 9 en suite (1 fmly) (2 GF) **S** fr £42 **D** fr £63* **Facilities:** FTV Lounge tea/coffee WiFi 🔒 **Extras:** Home-made biscuits **Conf:** Max 30 **Parking:** 8

The Old Bakery

★★★★ ◎◎ RESTAURANT WITH ROOMS

tel: 01522 576057 & 07772 667606 **26-28 Burton Road LN1 3LB**
email: enquiries@theold-bakery.co.uk **web:** www.theold-bakery.co.uk
dir: Exit A46 at Lincoln North follow signs for cathedral. 3rd exit at 1st roundabout, 1st exit at next roundabout.

Situated close to the castle at the top of the town, this converted bakery offers well-equipped bedrooms and a delightful dining operation. The cooking has gained two AA Rosettes, and uses much local produce. Expect good friendly service from the dedicated staff.

Rooms: 3 rms (2 en suite) (1 pri facs) (1 fmly) **Facilities:** FTV tea/coffee Dinner available WiFi 🔒 **Extras:** Bottled water, home-made cookies – complimentary **Notes:** Closed 25–26 December, 1–16 January, 1–12 August RS Sunday to Monday closed

| LOUTH | Map 17 TF38 |

The Manse B&B

★★★ BED AND BREAKFAST

tel: 01507 327495 **Middlesykes Lane, Grimoldby LN11 8TE**
email: knowles578@btinternet.com **web:** www.themansebb.co.uk
dir: Grimoldby 4 miles from Louth on B1200. Into Tinkle Street, right into Middlesykes Lane.

Located on a quiet country lane, this pleasantly appointed house offers comfortable accommodation and a friendly, warm welcome. The proprietors are enthusiastic and helpful, ensuring guests will enjoy their stay. Bedrooms offer a range of homely extras, and freshly cooked evening meals are available by prior arrangement. The Manse is an ideal location for exploring the delights of the Wolds.

Rooms: 4 rms (3 en suite) (1 pri facs) (1 fmly) (1 GF) **S** fr £55 **D** fr £80* **Facilities:** FTV TVL tea/coffee Dinner available WiFi **Parking:** 5 **Notes:** LB No children 5 years Closed 25 December

| MARKET RASEN | Map 17 TF18 |

Premier Collection

The Advocate Arms

★★★★★ ◎◎ RESTAURANT WITH ROOMS

tel: 01673 842364 **2 Queen Street LN8 3EH**
email: info@advocatearms.co.uk **web:** www.advocatearms.co.uk
dir: In town centre.

Appointed to a high standard, this 18th-century property is located in the heart of Market Rasen and combines historic character with contemporary design. The operation centres around the stylish restaurant where service is friendly yet professional and the food is a highlight. The attractive bedrooms are very well equipped and feature luxury bathrooms.

Rooms: 10 en suite (2 fmly) **Facilities:** FTV tea/coffee Dinner available WiFi ♿ 🔒 **Conf:** Max 22 Thtr 18 Class 22 Board 18 **Parking:** 6

Wold View House B&B

★★★ ♨ BED AND BREAKFAST

tel: 01673 838226 & 07976 563473 Bully Hill Top, Tealby LN8 6JA
email: enquiries@woldviewhouse.co.uk web: www.woldviewhouse.co.uk
dir: A46 onto B1225 towards Horncastle, after 7 miles Wold View House at crossroads.

Situated at the top of Bully Hill with expansive views across The Wold, this smart bed and breakfast offers modern bedrooms and warm hospitality. Ideal for walking, riding or touring the charming nearby villages and coastline, Wold View House is just a short drive from Lincoln.

Rooms: 3 rms (2 en suite) (1 pri facs) (1 fmly) S fr £60 D fr £80* Facilities: FTV Lounge TVL tea/coffee Dinner available Licensed WiFi ⋒ Parking: 15 Notes: LB

MARTON (VILLAGE)　　　　Map 17 SK88

Black Swan Guest House

★★★★ GUEST ACCOMMODATION

tel: 01427 718878 21 High Street DN21 5AH
email: info@blackswanguesthouse.co.uk web: www.blackswanguesthouse.co.uk
dir: On A156 in village centre at junction with A1500.

Centrally located in the village, this 18th-century former coaching inn retains many original features and offers good hospitality and homely bedrooms with modern facilities. Tasty breakfasts are served in the cosy dining room and a comfortable lounge where WiFi is available. Transport to nearby pubs and restaurants can be provided.

Rooms: 6 en suite 4 annexe en suite (2 fmly) (4 GF) Facilities: FTV tea/coffee Licensed WiFi ⋒ Parking: 10 Notes: LB

SAXILBY　　　　Map 17 SK87

Orchard Cottage

★★★★ ♨ BED AND BREAKFAST

tel: 01522 703192 3 Orchard Lane LN1 2HT
email: margaretallen@orchardcottage.org.uk web: www.orchardcottagesaxilby.co.uk
dir: From A57 onto B1241 signed Saxilby village. Turn immediately left into Queensway Pass The Anglers and village hall, turn next right into Highfield Road, then left into Orchard Lane. 4th property on the right.

A friendly and peaceful owner-run B&B situated in a quiet residential village a short driving distance from the centre of Lincoln. There is a choice of two guest bedrooms, one in the main house and one that is annexed. They are full of traditional charm and provide a good range of modern accessories including complimentary WiFi. A well cared for garden sits to the rear and can be enjoyed by guests in the warmer months. Breakfasts are served with excellent quality produce and a number of home made items such as toast and preserves. On-site car parking is available.

Rooms: 1 en suite 1 annexe en suite S fr £70 D fr £80* Facilities: FTV TVL tea/coffee WiFi ⋑ ⋒ Extras: Speciality toiletries Parking: 2

SCOTTER　　　　Map 17 SE80

The White Swan

★★★★ ◎ INN

tel: 01724 763061 9 The Green DN21 3UD
email: info@whiteswanscotter.com web: www.whiteswanscotter.com
dir: Phone for directions.

This smartly-presented property provides stylish, contemporary accommodation in a peaceful village location. Guests can eat in the modern, split-level restaurant

which has vaulted ceilings or in the traditional pub, The Mucky Duck. A lounge bar and impressive garden add to the range of places where guests can relax. Accommodation rates include a continental breakfast, but other breakfast options are available. Weddings and other special events are well catered for.

Rooms: 11 en suite 18 annexe en suite Facilities: FTV tea/coffee Dinner available WiFi Conf: Max 50 Thtr 50 Class 35 Board 35 Parking: 35 Notes: Civ wed 110

SCUNTHORPE　　　　Map 17 SE81

San Pietro Restaurant Rooms

★★★★ ◎◎ RESTAURANT WITH ROOMS

tel: 01724 277774 11 High Street East DN15 6UH
email: info@sanpietro.uk.com web: www.sanpietro.uk.com
dir: 3 miles from M180, follow signs for Scunthorpe town centre and railway station, left into Brigg Road/Station Road. Near windmill.

This family-run restaurant with rooms was purpose-built and offers comfortable, modern and stylish accommodation. Bedrooms and bathrooms provide a range of additional extras such as smart TVs, mini bars, home-made cakes and complimentary WiFi. Meals are served in the annexed Ristorante. Dinner menus reveal the chef's Italian heritage, and guests have plenty of choice including a chef's tasting menu as well as a full à la carte. Continental breakfasts are included but guests can upgrade to a hearty, cooked breakfast.

Rooms: 14 en suite (5 GF) Facilities: STV FTV iPod docking station tea/coffee Dinner available Direct dial Lift WiFi ⋑ ⋒ Cooking masterclasses Extras: Speciality toiletries, home-made cake, mini-bar, complimentary mineral water Conf: Max 100 Thtr 100 Class 50 Board 24 Parking: 25 Notes: Closed 1–7 January, Bank holiday Monday RS 8–10 January at 6pm, Sunday pm restaurant closed Civ wed 100

SKILLINGTON
Map 11 SK82

The Cross Swords Inn

★★★ 🍺 INN

tel: 01476 861132 **The Square NG33 5HB**
email: harold@thecross-swordsinn.co.uk **web:** www.thecross-swordsinn.co.uk
dir: *Exit A1 at Colsterworth junction between Grantham and Stamford.*

Very popular with the local community, this traditional inn offers three modern, well-equipped bedrooms, housed in an attractive cottage at the top of the courtyard, and named in keeping with the history of the village. All are very comfortable and coupled with smart modern bathrooms. The inn provides imaginative food and a range of real ales in a rustic period setting.

Rooms: 3 annexe en suite (3 GF) **Facilities:** FTV tea/coffee Dinner available WiFi **Parking:** 12 **Notes:** No children 10 years RS Sunday evening and Monday lunch bar and restaurant closed

SOUTH FERRIBY
Map 17 SE92

The Hope and Anchor Pub

★★★★ ◉◉ RESTAURANT WITH ROOMS

tel: 01652 635334 **Sluice Road DN18 6JQ**
email: info@thehopeandanchorpub.co.uk **web:** www.thehopeandanchorpub.co.uk
dir: *Phone for directions.*

This pub dates back to the 19th century and is perfectly situated in the town of South Ferriby with stunning views of the Humber Bridge. The bedrooms are modern and furnished to a high standard with exceptionally comfortable beds plus amenities such as Nespresso machines, TVs and complimentary WiFi. Dinner in the award-winning restaurant will surely be a highlight of any stay as are the hearty breakfasts. The staff are friendly and welcoming and a relaxed atmosphere is guaranteed. Complimentary on-site parking is provided.

Rooms: 5 en suite **Facilities:** iPod docking station Lounge Dinner available WiFi **Extras:** Nespresso machine, speciality toiletries **Notes:** RS Sunday to Monday closed

SPALDING
Map 12 TF22

The Cley Hall

★★★★ GUEST ACCOMMODATION

tel: 01775 725157 **22 High Street PE11 1TX**
email: reception@cleyhall.com **web:** www.cleyhall.com

This lovely Georgian property is situated a short walk from the town centre. The individually decorated bedrooms are well appointed and have a good range of additional facilities that include large TVs and WiFi. The public areas include a smart lounge bar and a well presented dining room with individual tables. Guests have access to an adjacent gym and a pretty landscaped garden.

Rooms: 10 en suite 11 annexe en suite (2 fmly) (5 GF) **S** fr £55 **D** fr £99* **Facilities:** FTV iPod docking station Lounge TVL tea/coffee Licensed WiFi Gym 🛁 **Extras:** Mini bar in some rooms **Conf:** Max 30 Thtr 30 Class 30 Board 30 **Parking:** 17

STAMFORD
Map 11 TF00

Premier Collection

Meadow View

★★★★★ 🍽 BED AND BREAKFAST

tel: 01780 762133 & 07833 972577 **Wothorpe Road PE9 2JR**
email: bookings@bedandbreakfast-stamford.co.uk
web: www.bedandbreakfast-stamford.co.uk
dir: *Off A1 signed Stamford, follow road past entrance to Burley House, bottom of hill, left at lights. Follow road round, 1st house on left.*

Meadow View is a stylish property situated just a short walk from the town centre and Burghley House. The tastefully appointed bedrooms are contemporary in style with lovely co-ordinated soft furnishings and many thoughtful touches. Breakfast is served at a large communal table in the open-plan kitchen/dining room, and guests have the use of a smartly appointed lounge with plush sofas.

Rooms: 3 en suite **Facilities:** FTV iPod docking station TVL tea/coffee WiFi 🛁 **Extras:** Chocolates, sherry, still/sparkling water **Notes:** LB

The Bull & Swan at Burghley

★★★★ ◉ 🍽 INN

tel: 01780 766412 **High Street, St Martins PE9 2LJ**
email: enquiries@thebullandswan.co.uk **web:** www.thebullandswan.co.uk
dir: *A1 onto Old Great North Road, left onto B1081, follow Stamford signs.*

This delightful inn dates back to the 16th century when it is said to have been a gentlemen's drinking club. The public rooms include a large bar with a range of ales. There is also a separate restaurant serving AA Rosette award-winning food. The stylish bedrooms are extremely well appointed with lovely soft furnishings and a range of thoughtful touches.

Rooms: 9 en suite (2 fmly) **Facilities:** FTV iPod docking station tea/coffee Dinner available WiFi 🛁 **Extras:** Organic vodka **Parking:** 7 **Notes:** LB

Candlesticks

★★★ RESTAURANT WITH ROOMS

tel: 01780 764033 **1 Church Lane PE9 2JU**
email: info@candlestickshotel.co.uk **web:** www.candlestickshotel.co.uk
dir: *B1081 into Stamford. Left onto A43. Right into Worthorpe Road, right into Church Lane.*

Candlesticks is a 17th-century property situated in a quiet lane in the oldest part of Stamford, just a short walk from the centre of town. The bedrooms are pleasantly decorated and equipped with a good range of useful extras. Public rooms include Candlesticks restaurant and a cosy bar.

Rooms: 8 en suite **Facilities:** STV FTV Lounge tea/coffee Dinner available Direct dial WiFi 🔒 **Parking:** 8 **Notes:** LB RS Monday no restaurant or bar service

WINTERINGHAM   Map 17 SE92

Premier Collection

Winteringham Fields

★★★★★ ◉◉◉◉ RESTAURANT WITH ROOMS

tel: 01724 733096 **1 Silver Street DN15 9ND**
email: reception@winteringhamfields.co.uk **web:** www.winteringhamfields.co.uk
dir: *In village centre at crossroads.*

This highly regarded restaurant with rooms, located deep in the countryside in Winteringham village, is six miles west of the Humber Bridge. Public rooms and bedrooms, some of which are housed in renovated barns and cottages, are delightfully luxurious. There is an abundance of charm, and period features are combined with rich furnishings and fabrics. The award-winning food is a highlight of any stay and guests can expect highly skilled dishes, excellent quality and stunning presentation.

Rooms: 4 en suite 11 annexe en suite (6 fmly) (3 GF) **Facilities:** iPod docking station tea/coffee Dinner available Direct dial WiFi 🔒 **Conf:** Max 50 Thtr 50 Class 50 Board 50 **Parking:** 14 **Notes:** LB Closed 25 December for 2 weeks, last week October, 2 weeks August Civ wed 60

WOODHALL SPA   Map 17 TF16

Oglee Guest House

★★★★ 🛏 GUEST HOUSE

tel: 01526 353512 **16 Stanhope Avenue LN10 6SP**
email: ogleeguesthouse@gmail.com **web:** www.oglee.co.uk
dir: *Close to junction of B1191 and B1192.*

This Edwardian family home is ideally situated for exploring Lincolnshire. It is also within easy reach of several RAF bases and the well-regarded Hotchkin Course at the National Golf Centre. The spacious bedrooms offer a high level of comfort and have modern amenities. Hearty breakfasts use local produce and feature hand-made jams and additional special dishes; evening meals are available by prior arrangement.

Rooms: 3 en suite (1 fmly) **S** fr £56 **D** fr £84* **Facilities:** FTV DVD TVL tea/coffee Dinner available WiFi 🔒 **Extras:** Fruit, bottled water, speciality teas – complimentary **Parking:** 4 **Notes:** LB

WOOLSTHORPE   Map 11 SK83

Chequers Inn

★★★★ ◉ INN

tel: 01476 870701 **Main Street NG32 1LU**
email: justinnabar@yahoo.co.uk **web:** www.chequersinn.net
dir: *From Melton Mowbray on A607 towards Grantham, follow brown heritage signs to Belvoir Castle. Turn left at crossroads and follow signs.*

Situated in the picturesque village of Woolsthorpe in the unspoilt Vale of Belvoir, the Chequers Inn is a quintessentially English hostelry dating from the 17th century. It has roaring fires in the winter and a well-maintained garden for alfresco dining in the summer. The snug and bar were once the village bakery. The bedrooms are situated in the adjacent stables and are tastefully decorated. Good food is served in the bar and in the restaurant.

Rooms: 4 annexe en suite (1 fmly) (3 GF) **Facilities:** FTV DVD tea/coffee Dinner available ⛴ 🔒 **Conf:** Max 80 Thtr 80 Class 80 Board 30 **Parking:** 40 **Notes:** Closed 25 December evening, 26 December evening and 1 January evening Civ wed 80

LONDON

E1

The Culpeper   PLAN 1 G4

★★★★ ◉ RESTAURANT WITH ROOMS

tel: 020 7247 5371 **40 Commercial Street E1 6LP**
email: bookings@theculpeper.com **web:** www.theculpeper.com
dir: *From Aldgate East tube station left into Commercial Street, The Culpeper on right.*

Located on Commercial Street and just a stone's throw from Spitalfields Market and Brick Lane, The Culpeper offers comfortably appointed en suite bedrooms. All showcase stripped-back decor and original features yet still include modern furnishings and fixtures. There is a busy pub on the ground floor, a roof-top terrace and conservatory which serves barbecue tapas, and a main restaurant on the second floor which is open for breakfast, lunch and dinner. This is a real gem in the heart of East London, ideal for leisure and business guests alike.

Rooms: 5 en suite **D** fr £120* **Facilities:** FTV tea/coffee Dinner available WiFi **Extras:** Home-made cookies **Notes:** Closed 24–30 December

N4

Best Western London Highbury   PLAN 2 F5

★★★ GUEST ACCOMMODATION

tel: 020 8802 6551 **372–374 Seven Sisters Road N4 2PG**
email: reservations@highbury.com **web:** www.bwhighbury.com
dir: *0.5 mile from Finsbury Park Station.*

Opposite Finsbury Park and only a short tube ride from the centre of London, this establishment offers a range of well-appointed and well-equipped accommodation. There is ample and secure parking and a well-stocked bar. Hot and cold breakfasts are served in the lower-ground floor breakfast room.

Rooms: 45 en suite (6 fmly) (7 GF) **S** fr £105 **D** fr £125 (room only)* **Facilities:** STV FTV TVL tea/coffee Direct dial Lift Licensed WiFi 🔒 **Extras:** Chocolates **Parking:** 20

NW1

TheWesley
PLAN 1 C5

★★★★ GUEST ACCOMMODATION

tel: 020 7380 0001 **81–103 Euston Street NW1 2EZ**
email: reservations@thewesley.co.uk **web:** www.thewesley.co.uk
dir: *Euston Road left at lights into Melton Street, 1st left into Euston Street, 100 yards on left.*

Located within walking distance of Euston station, this smart property is convenient for central London. Stylish air-conditioned bedrooms are thoughtfully equipped for business and leisure. The airy Atrium Bar and Restaurant offers drinks, light snacks and an evening menu. Extensive conference and meeting facilities are available.

Rooms: 100 en suite (5 fmly) (7 GF) **Facilities:** STV FTV TVL tea/coffee Dinner available Direct dial Lift Licensed WiFi **Extras:** Speciality toiletries, safe **Conf:** Max 150 Thtr 150 Class 50 Board 45 **Notes:** LB Civ wed

NW3

The Langorf
PLAN 2 E4

★★★★ GUEST ACCOMMODATION

tel: 020 7794 4483 **20 Frognal, Hampstead NW3 6AG**
email: info@langorfhotel.com **web:** www.langorfhotel.com
dir: *Off A41 (Finchley Road), near Finchley Road tube station.*

Located on a leafy and mainly residential avenue within easy walking distance of shops and restaurants, this elegant Edwardian property has been appointed to provide high standards of comfort and facilities. Bedrooms are furnished with flair and a warm welcome is assured.

Rooms: 31 en suite (4 fmly) (3 GF) **Facilities:** STV Lounge TVL tea/coffee Direct dial Lift Licensed WiFi **Conf:** Max 30 Thtr 30 Class 20 Board 15 **Notes:** LB

La Gaffe
PLAN 2 E5

★★★ GUEST ACCOMMODATION

tel: 020 7435 8965 & 7435 4941 **107–111 Heath Street NW3 6SS**
email: info@lagaffe.co.uk **web:** www.lagaffe.co.uk
dir: *On A502, 250 yards north of Hampstead tube station.*

This family-owned and -run guest accommodation, just north of Hampstead High Street, offers charm and warm hospitality. The Italian restaurant, which is open most lunchtimes and for dinner, is popular with locals. Bedrooms are compact, but all are en suite.

Rooms: 11 en suite 7 annexe en suite (2 fmly) (2 GF) **Facilities:** FTV tea/coffee Dinner available Direct dial Licensed WiFi **Conf:** Max 10 Board 10 **Notes:** RS 25–26 December (Restaurant closed 25 December evening and 26 December).

NW11

Martel Guest House
PLAN 2 D5

★★★ GUEST HOUSE

tel: 020 8455 1802 & 07587 655181 **27 The Ridgeway NW11 8QP**
email: reservations@bedbreakfastlondon.co.uk **web:** www.bedbreakfastlondon.co.uk
dir: *Phone for directions.*

Martel Guest House is in a quiet residential area of north London, just a 15-minute underground journey from central London, and only five minutes from the M1. Restaurants and convenience stores are just a short walk away. The accommodation is nicely appointed and offers all modern comforts including air conditioning and free WiFi. A self-service, continental breakfast or a freshly-cooked English breakfast are served in the family-style breakfast room overlooking the rear garden. Secure parking is offered.

Rooms: 9 en suite (2 fmly) (3 GF) **Facilities:** FTV tea/coffee Direct dial WiFi **Extras:** Fridge, bottled water, canned drinks **Parking:** 7

SE10

Innkeeper's Lodge London, Greenwich
PLAN 2 G3

★★★★ INN

tel: 03451 551551 **291 Greenwich High Road, Greenwich SE10 8NA**
email: info@innkeeperslodge.com **web:** www.innkeeperslodge.com
dir: *Phone for directions.*

This Innkeeper's Lodge, The Mitre, is south of the River Thames in Greenwich (a UNESCO World Heritage Site) and a five-minute walk from *The Cutty Sark*. The en suite bedrooms, in different shapes and sizes, come with TVs, desks and free WiFi as standard; family rooms are available. The welcoming interior is traditional in design and the menus of pub dishes prove very popular. The Mitre has a lift and there's an enclosed area for alfresco eating and drinking in good weather.

Rooms: 24 en suite (3 fmly) **Facilities:** FTV tea/coffee Dinner available Lift WiFi

SW1

Premier Collection

Georgian House
PLAN 1 C1

★★★★★ GUEST ACCOMMODATION

tel: 0207 834 1438 **35–39 St George's Drive SW1V 4DG**
email: adam@georgianhousehotel.co.uk **web:** www.georgianhousehotel.co.uk
dir: *Phone for directions.*

Located just a couple of minutes walk from Victoria Station, this grand property has been renovated and offers guests excellent comfort and style. The rooms are stylish and contemporary and the building retains many of its original features. The Wizard Chamber and the Enchanted Chamber on the lower ground provide something a little different and a touch of magical charm. The Pimlico Pantry offers a great variety at breakfast and also snacks and drinks throughout the day and evening.

Rooms: 45 en suite 14 annexe en suite (11 fmly) (9 GF) **Facilities:** FTV DVD tea/coffee Direct dial Licensed WiFi Cinema **Extras:** Robes, speciality toiletries **Conf:** Max 14 Board 14

The Windermere
PLAN 1 C1

★★★★ ⚄ 🍽 GUEST ACCOMMODATION

tel: 020 7834 5163 **142–144 Warwick Way, Victoria SW1V 4JE**
email: reservations@windermere-hotel.co.uk **web:** www.windermere-hotel.co.uk
dir: *B324 off Buckingham Palace Road, on Warwick Way, at junction with Alderney Street.*

The Windermere is a relaxed, informal and family-run establishment within easy reach of Victoria Station and many of the capital's attractions. Bedrooms, although varying in size, are stylish, comfortable and well equipped. The Windermere Brasserie serves good quality evening meals and hearty, cooked breakfasts.

Rooms: 19 en suite (3 fmly) (3 GF) **S** fr £155 **D** fr £185* **Facilities:** FTV Lounge TVL tea/coffee Dinner available Direct dial Lift Licensed WiFi **Extras:** Speciality toiletries
Notes: No children 5 years

Best Western Corona
PLAN 1 C1

★★★★ GUEST ACCOMMODATION

tel: 020 7828 9279 & 7487 0673 **87–89 Belgrave Road SW1V 2BQ**
email: info@coronahotel.co.uk **web:** www.coronahotel.co.uk
dir: *From Pimlico Station into Tachbrook Street. 1st left into Moreton Street, 1st right into Belgrave Road.*

This elegant Victorian property is located within walking distance of Victoria railway station and a number of London landmarks. The smart, well-equipped bedrooms offer comfortable, modern accommodation. A choice of breakfasts is served in the lower ground–floor dining room, and room service is also available. In addition, a range of restaurants is only a few steps away. There is a small lounge in which to relax and the team is very knowledgeable and helpful.

Rooms: 51 en suite (13 fmly) (7 GF) **Facilities:** FTV Lounge tea/coffee Direct dial Lift WiFi

The Lidos
PLAN 1 C1

★★★ GUEST ACCOMMODATION

tel: 020 7828 1164 **43–45 Belgrave Road, Victoria SW1V 2BB**
email: reservations@lidoshotel.com **web:** www.lidoshotel.com
dir: *From Victoria railway station exit to Wilton Road. After 2nd set of lights into Denbigh Street. Left at next lights into Belgrave Road. On left.*

The Lidos offers affordable accommodation within walking distance of Victoria Station and the tube. In addition, there's a bus stop right in front of the main entrance making access easy to all major sites. All bedrooms have en suite facilities and are equipped with modern amenities. An inclusive continental breakfast is offered to all guests, and a range of restaurants and pubs can be found nearby.

Rooms: 39 en suite (2 fmly) (4 GF) **Facilities:** FTV tea/coffee Lift WiFi
Notes: Closed 24–26 December

Best Western Victoria Palace
PLAN 1 C1

★★★ GUEST ACCOMMODATION

tel: 020 7821 7113 **60–64 Warwick Way SW1V 1SA**
email: info@bestwesternvictoriapalace.co.uk **web:** www.bestwesternvictoriapalace.co.uk
dir: *Phone for directions.*

An elegant, 19th-century building located in the heart of London, near to Belgravia and a five-minute walk from Victoria rail, underground and coach stations. The bedrooms have en suite shower rooms. A buffet-style breakfast is served in the basement dining room.

Rooms: 43 en suite 44 annexe en suite (4 fmly) (4 GF) **Facilities:** FTV Lounge tea/coffee Direct dial Lift WiFi

Comfort Inn Buckingham Palace Road
PLAN 1 C1

★★★ GUEST ACCOMMODATION

tel: 020 7834 2988 **8–12 St George's Drive SW1V 4BJ**
email: info@comfortinnbuckinghampalacerd.co.uk
web: www.comfortinnbuckinghampalacerd.co.uk
dir: *From Buckingham Palace Road into St George's Drive. Comfort Inn on left.*

Located just a short walk south from Victoria Station, this establishment is a good base for visiting the capital's attractions. All bedrooms and public areas are smartly appointed and offer very good levels of comfort. An extensive continental breakfast is served.

Rooms: 81 en suite (13 fmly) (15 GF) **Facilities:** STV TVL tea/coffee Direct dial Lift WiFi **Conf:** Max 20 Thtr 20 Class 20 Board 20

Comfort Inn London Westminster
PLAN 1 C1

★★★ GUEST ACCOMMODATION

tel: 020 7834 8036 **39 Belgrave Road SW1V 2BB**
email: stay@comfortinnwestminster.co.uk **web:** www.comfortinnwestminster.co.uk
dir: *Near Victoria Station.*

Located a short walk from Victoria Station, the Comfort Inn London Westminster offers affordable accommodation. Bedroom sizes vary, but each room is suitably appointed and has an en suite, compact shower room. A contemporary lobby is equipped with a large TV and computer desk. A self-service continental breakfast is offered in the dining room on the lower-ground floor.

Rooms: 54 en suite (4 fmly) (7GF) **Facilities:** FTV TVL tea/coffee Direct dial Lift WiFi
Notes: LB

Comfort Inn Victoria
PLAN 1 C1

★★★ GUEST ACCOMMODATION

tel: 020 7233 6636 **18–24 Belgrave Road, Victoria SW1V 1QF**
email: stay@comfortinnvictoria.co.uk **web:** www.comfortinnvictoria.co.uk
dir: *Phone for directions.*

With a prime location close to Victoria Station, this property offers brightly appointed en suite accommodation that is thoughtfully equipped for business and leisure guests. A continental breakfast is offered in the basement dining room.

Rooms: 50 rms (48 en suite) (16 fmly) (9 GF) **Facilities:** STV FTV TVL tea/coffee Direct dial Lift WiFi

SW1 *continued*

The Victoria Inn
PLAN 1 C1

★★★ GUEST HOUSE

tel: 020 7834 6721 **65–67 Belgrave Road, Victoria SW1V 2BG**
email: welcome@victoriainn.co.uk **web:** www.victoriainn.co.uk
dir: *On A3213, 0.4 mile southeast of Victoria Station, near Pimlico tube station.*

A short walk from London Victoria Station, this Victorian property offers modern, well-equipped accommodation for business and leisure guests. There is a comfortable reception lounge, and a limited self-service buffet breakfast is available in the basement breakfast room.

Rooms: 43 en suite (7 fmly) **Facilities:** FTV TVL tea/coffee Direct dial Lift WiFi
Notes: LB

Stanley House
PLAN 1 C1

★★ ⬛ BED AND BREAKFAST

tel: 020 7834 5042 & 7834 7292 **19–21 Belgrave Road, Victoria SW1V 1RB**
email: cmahotel@aol.com **web:** www.londonbudgethotels.co.uk
dir: *Near Victoria Station.*

Stanley House is conveniently situated close to Victoria Station and has easy access to the West End. Plain, soundly appointed bedrooms of varying sizes are offered, with breakfasts served in the lower ground-floor dining room; guests also have use of a ground-floor TV lounge area.

Rooms: 44 rms (41 en suite) (7 fmly) (8 GF) **Facilities:** FTV TVL Direct dial WiFi
Notes: LB No children 5 years

SW3

Premier Collection

San Domenico House
PLAN 1 B1

★★★★★ 🏆 GUEST ACCOMMODATION

tel: 020 7581 5757 **29–31 Draycott Place SW3 2SH**
email: info@sandomenicohouse.com **web:** www.sandomenicohouse.com

This stunning property in the heart of Chelsea offers beautiful, individually styled bedrooms, all with antique and period pieces, and well-appointed en suites complete with Italian Spa toiletries. A sumptuous drawing room with wonderful works of art is available for guests to relax in or maybe to enjoy afternoon tea. Breakfast is served either in guests' bedrooms or in the elegant lower ground-floor dining room. Staff are friendly and attentive.

Rooms: 17 en suite (4 fmly) (1 GF) **Facilities:** STV Lounge Dinner available Direct dial Lift Licensed

Premier Collection

Sydney House Chelsea
PLAN 1 A1

★★★★★ 🏆 GUEST ACCOMMODATION

tel: 020 7376 7711 & 7376 6900 **9–11 Sydney Street, Chelsea SW3 6PU**
email: info@sydneyhousechelsea.co.uk **web:** www.sydneyhousechelsea.co.uk
dir: *A4 (Cromwell Road), pass Natural History Museum on left, turn next right. Sydney Street on left.*

Located in the heart of Chelsea, this smart Grade II listed Georgian townhouse offers stylish and very comfortable accommodation, well equipped for both corporate and leisure guests. There is a small bar and drawing room and room service is also available. Staff are attentive and are always on hand to ensure guests feel at home. Breakfast is a particular highlight.

Rooms: 21 en suite **S** fr £129 **D** fr £129 (room only)* **Facilities:** STV FTV DVD Lounge tea/coffee Dinner available Direct dial Lift Licensed WiFi **Extras:** Still mineral water

SW5

Best Western The Boltons
PLAN 2 E3

★★★★ GUEST ACCOMMODATION

tel: 020 7373 3900 **19–21 Penywern Road, Earl's Court SW5 9TT**
email: london@theboltonshotel.co.uk **web:** www.theboltonshotel.co.uk
dir: *A3220 from Cromwell Road, follow road past Earl's Court station, 1st right into Penywern Road. Located on left.*

Located right in the heart of Earl's Court, and just around the corner from Earl's Court underground station, The Boltons offers modern and comfortably appointed rooms, all with en suite facilities, digital TVs, beverage-making facilities, and free WiFi throughout. There is a cosy dining room on the ground floor where breakfast is served, and a wide range of restaurants, cafés and bars is within a short walking distance.

Rooms: 56 en suite (4 fmly) (4 GF) **Facilities:** FTV iPod docking station Lounge tea/coffee Direct dial Lift WiFi **Notes:** No children 18 years

The Park Grand London Kensington
PLAN 2 E3

★★★★ GUEST ACCOMMODATION

tel: 020 7370 6831 **33–37 Hogarth Road SW5 0QQ**
email: info@parkgrandkensington.co.uk **web:** www.parkgrandkensington.co.uk
dir: *Phone for directions.*

Well appointed to a high standard, this property has a smart modern feel and is conveniently located for the West End and local transport links. Bedrooms are furnished and decorated to a very high standard, offering guests a comprehensive range of modern facilities and amenities.

Rooms: 132 en suite (7 GF) **Facilities:** STV FTV iPod docking station tea/coffee Dinner available Direct dial Lift Licensed WiFi Gym Fitness centre **Conf:** Max 15 Board 15

SW7

Premier Collection

The Exhibitionist
PLAN 1 A2

★★★★★ GUEST ACCOMMODATION

tel: 020 7915 0000 **8–10 Queensberry Place, South Kensington SW7 2EA**
email: info@theexhibitionisthotel.com **web:** www.theexhibitionisthotel.com
dir: Exit A4 (Cromwell Road) opposite Natural History Museum, near South Kensington tube station.

The Exhibitionist can be found close to Kensington and Knightsbridge and offers friendly hospitality, attentive service and sumptuously furnished bedrooms; some have a private terrace. Public areas include a choice of lounges (one with internet access) and an elegant bar. There is an option of English or continental breakfast, and 24-hour room service is available.

Rooms: 37 en suite **Facilities:** STV FTV iPod docking station Lounge tea/coffee Dinner available Direct dial Lift Licensed WiFi **Extras:** Speciality toiletries, mineral water **Conf:** Max 40 Thtr 40 Class 35 Board 30

The Gainsborough
PLAN 1 A2

★★★★ GUEST ACCOMMODATION

tel: 020 7957 0000 **7–11 Queensberry Place, South Kensington SW7 2DL**
email: reservations@thegainsboroughhotel.com **web:** www.thegainsboroughhotel.com
dir: Off A4 (Cromwell Road) opposite Natural History Museum, near South Kensington tube station.

This smart Georgian house is in a quiet street near South Kensington's museums. Bedrooms are individually designed with fine fabrics and quality furnishings in co-ordinated colours. A choice of breakfasts is offered in the attractive dining room. There is also a delightful lobby lounge, and 24-hour room service is available.

Rooms: 48 en suite (5 fmly) (4 GF) **Facilities:** STV Lounge tea/coffee Dinner available Direct dial Lift Licensed WiFi **Conf:** Max 40 Class 40 Board 30

W1

Premier Collection

The Marble Arch by Montcalm
PLAN 1 B4

★★★★★ GUEST ACCOMMODATION

tel: 020 7258 0777 **31 Great Cumberland Place W1H 7TA**
email: info@marblearchbymontcalm.co.uk **web:** www.themarblearchlondon.co.uk
dir: Phone for directions.

Located just a short walk from Marble Arch, this luxury boutique townhouse property offers elegant, stylish and comfortable accommodation. Bedrooms are well equipped for the modern guest – all rooms offer a media hub, WiFi and mini-bar.

Rooms: 43 en suite (1 fmly) **Facilities:** STV FTV TVL tea/coffee Lift Licensed WiFi

Premier Collection

The Piccadilly London West End
PLAN 1 D3

★★★★★ GUEST ACCOMMODATION

tel: 020 7871 6000 **65–73 Shaftesbury Avenue W1D 6EX**
email: reservations@thepiccadillywestend.co.uk
web: www.thepiccadillywestend.co.uk
dir: From Piccadilly Circus 300 yards up Shaftesbury Avenue, at junction with Dean Street.

In the centre of the West End, this boutique property offers plenty of warm, traditional hospitality. It's located close to two major underground stations and has a comfortable club lounge, a popular Japanese bar/restaurant, a fitness room and a small spa. The high quality bedrooms and bathrooms come in a variety of sizes, but all are well-equipped and smartly presented.

Rooms: 67 en suite (6 fmly) **Facilities:** FTV iPod docking station TVL tea/coffee Dinner available Direct dial Lift Licensed WiFi Sauna Gym Steam room, Treatment rooms **Extras:** Fruit – complimentary; Mini-bar – chargeable **Notes:** LB

The Sumner
PLAN 1 B4

★★★★ GUEST ACCOMMODATION

tel: 020 7723 2244 **54 Upper Berkeley Street, Marble Arch W1H 7QR**
email: hotel@thesumner.com **web:** www.thesumner.com
dir: Phone for directions.

Centrally located and just five minutes' walk from Marble Arch, The Sumner is part of a Georgian terrace. Appointed throughout to a very high standard, this delightful property combines much of the original character of the building with modern comfort. The air-conditioned bedrooms are designer-decorated and feature wide-screen LCD TVs as well as a range of traditional amenities. The breakfast buffet is included in the room rate.

Rooms: 20 en suite **Facilities:** FTV Lounge Direct dial Lift Licensed WiFi
Notes: No children 5 years

W2

Premier Collection

Park Grand London Lancaster Gate
PLAN 1 A3

★★★★★ GUEST ACCOMMODATION

tel: 020 7262 0111 **14–16 Craven Hill Road, Paddington W2 3DU**
email: info@parkgrandlancastergate.co.uk **web:** www.parkgrandlancastergate.co.uk
dir: Phone for directions.

Close to both Lancaster Gate and Paddington tube stations, this boutique property has a lot to offer. A warm welcome is assured, and the team of dedicated staff deliver attentive service. There is a small comfortable club lounge and all-day dining is available in the restaurant. In warmer months, drinks and snacks can also be enjoyed outside. High quality bedrooms and bathrooms come in a variety of sizes – all are well-equipped and smartly presented. WiFi and the high standard of amenities come as standard.

Rooms: 64 en suite **Facilities:** WiFi

W2 *continued*

Best Western Mornington

★★★★ GUEST ACCOMMODATION

tel: 020 7262 7361 **12 Lancaster Gate W2 3LG**
email: london@mornington.co.uk **web:** www.morningtonhotel.co.uk
dir: *North of Hyde Park, off A402 (Bayswater Road).*

This fine Victorian building is located in a quiet road and close to Lancaster Gate station for easy access to the West End. The bedrooms have been appointed to provide comfortable, stylish accommodation. There is a lounge bar and an attractive dining room where an extensive Scandinavian-style breakfast is served.

Rooms: 70 en suite (10 fmly) (4 GF) **Facilities:** STV FTV tea/coffee Direct dial Lift Licensed WiFi **Extras:** Mini-bar **Conf:** Max 14 Thtr 14 Class 14 Board 14

PLAN 1 A3

Park Grand London Paddington

★★★★ GUEST ACCOMMODATION

tel: 020 7298 9800 **1–2 Queens Gardens W2 3BA**
email: info@parkgrandlondon.co.uk **web:** www.parkgrandlondon.co.uk
dir: *Exit Paddington station via Praed Street, turn right. After 3 sets of lights right into Devonshire Terrace. 100 metres to Park Grand London Paddington.*

Park Grand London Paddington enjoys a central location just a moments' walk from Paddington station and Hyde Park, not to mention the city's main shopping districts and attractions. Bedrooms vary in size and are appointed to a very high standard; several stylish suites are also available. The Atlantic bar serves a range of light snacks throughout the day and evening. Additional facilities include state-of-the-art technology with free internet access, TV and fridges.

Rooms: 157 en suite (11 fmly) (23 GF) **Facilities:** FTV TVL tea/coffee Dinner available Direct dial Lift Licensed WiFi Fitness room

PLAN 1 A4

The Chilworth London Paddington

★★★★ GUEST ACCOMMODATION

tel: 020 7723 3434 **55–61 Westbourne Terrace W2 6QA**
email: reservations@thechilworth.co.uk **web:** www.thechilworth.co.uk
dir: *Exit A40 into Lancaster Terrace*

This newly refurbished property is located within a couple of minutes of London Paddington Station, Hyde Park and Lancaster Gate. The bedrooms are stylish and modern with high quality furnishings ideal for both business and leisure guests. There is a new bar and restaurant on the ground floor and spa facilities on the lower-ground floor.

Rooms: 118 en suite (7 fmly) (20 GF) **Facilities:** STV TVL tea/coffee Dinner available Direct dial Lift Licensed WiFi **Parking:** 12

PLAN 1 A4

Grand Royale London Hyde Park

★★★★ GUEST ACCOMMODATION

tel: 020 7313 7900 **1 Inverness Terrace W2 3JP**
email: info@shaftesburyhotels.com **web:** www.shaftesburyhotels.com
dir: *On A40 (Bayswater Road).*

Located adjacent to Hyde Park, fashionable Notting Hill and within easy reach of the West End, the Grand Royale combines its rich heritage with the requirements of the modern guest. The accommodation is contemporary in style and very well equipped. Breakfast is served in the restaurant, a former state room.

Rooms: 188 en suite (2 GF) **Facilities:** tea/coffee Direct dial Lift Licensed WiFi **Conf:** Max 20 Thtr 20 Class 20 Board 20

PLAN 2 E3

Hyde Park Radnor

★★★★ GUEST ACCOMMODATION

tel: 020 7723 5969 **7–9 Sussex Place, Hyde Park W2 2SX**
email: hydeparkradnor@btconnect.com **web:** www.hydeparkradnor.com
dir: *A402 (Bayswater Road) into Lancaster Terrace and Sussex Gardens, right into Sussex Place.*

This family-run property is within walking distance of Paddington Station, Lancaster Gate underground station, and handy for all London's central attractions. There is a choice of well-appointed bedrooms with modern en suites to meet the needs of a varied clientele; all are well equipped with a range of useful amenities including free WiFi. The dining room is located on the lower-ground floor where both a continental buffet and a freshly-cooked breakfast are served daily.

Rooms: 36 en suite (10 fmly) (5 GF) **Facilities:** STV FTV TVL tea/coffee Direct dial Lift WiFi **Notes:** LB

PLAN 1 A4

Mercure London Paddington

★★★★ GUEST ACCOMMODATION

tel: 020 7835 2000 **144 Praed Street, Paddington W2 1HU**
email: stay@mercurepaddington.com **web:** www.mercurepaddington.com
dir: *Phone for directions.*

Contemporary and stylish, Mercure London Paddington enjoys a central location, adjacent to Paddington Station. Bedrooms and en suites vary in size but all are smartly appointed and boast a host of extra facilities including CD players, TVs, room safes and internet access. A small gym, stylish lounge and meeting rooms are also available.

Rooms: 86 en suite (12 fmly) **Facilities:** STV TVL tea/coffee Dinner available Direct dial Lift Licensed WiFi Gym **Conf:** Max 22 Thtr 22 Class 20 Board 22

PLAN 1 A4

Park Grand London Hyde Park

★★★★ GUEST ACCOMMODATION

tel: 020 7262 4521 **78–82 Westbourne Terrace W2 6QA**
email: reservations@londonpremierhotels.co.uk **web:** www.parkgrandhydepark.co.uk
dir: *A40 into Lancaster Terrace, at crossing left onto slip road.*

This attractive property enjoys a convenient location and within easy reach of central London shops and attractions. The en suite bedrooms and public areas have a smart, contemporary feel. Although bedrooms vary in size, all boast many useful facilities such as complimentary broadband, plasma TVs, mini-fridges and irons.

Rooms: 119 en suite (10 fmly) (19 GF) **Facilities:** FTV Lounge tea/coffee Direct dial Lift Licensed WiFi **Parking:** 11

PLAN 1 A4

Park Grand Paddington Court London

★★★★ GUEST ACCOMMODATION

tel: 020 7745 1200 **27 Devonshire Terrace W2 3DP**
email: info@parkgrandpaddingtoncourt.co.uk **web:** www.parkgrandpaddingtoncourt.co.uk
dir: *From A40 take exit before Paddington flyover, follow Paddington Station signs. Devonshire Terrace is off Craven Road.*

This establishment benefits from its convenient location, close to Paddington Station, which has links to the tube and the Heathrow Express terminal. Situated next to Hyde Park and Kensington Palace Gardens, this property comprises smart and comfortable bedrooms, and a substantial breakfast is offered. Club Rooms are also available with additional extras including the exclusive use of the Club Lounge. A room is available for small meetings by prior arrangement.

Rooms: 175 en suite 35 annexe en suite (43 fmly) (45 GF) **Facilities:** STV FTV TVL tea/coffee Dinner available Direct dial Lift Licensed **Notes:** No children

PLAN 1 A4

The Premier Notting Hill
PLAN 2 E3

★★★★ GUEST ACCOMMODATION

tel: 020 7792 1414 & 07931 623158 **5–7 Princes Square, Bayswater W2 4NP**
email: aparna@premiernottinghill.com **web:** www.premiernottinghill.com
dir: *Nearest tube: Bayswater.*

Situated on the quiet Princes Square and close to Bayswater, Notting Hill Gate and Queensway tube stations, is this attractive property. The service here is both friendly and professional. The bedrooms are smartly presented and well equipped and there's WiFi access throughout. Breakfast is served in the basement restaurant where both continental and cooked options are available.

Rooms: 68 en suite (10 GF) **S** fr £60 **D** fr £80 (room only)* **Facilities:** FTV Lounge TVL tea/coffee Direct dial Lift WiFi

Princes Square
PLAN 2 E3

★★★★ GUEST ACCOMMODATION

tel: 020 7229 9876 **23–25 Princes Square, off Ilchester Gardens W2 4NJ**
email: info@princessquarehotel.co.uk **web:** www.princessquarehotel.co.uk
dir: *From Bayswater 1st left into Moscow Road, 3rd right into Ilchester Gardens.*

This fine building is in a quiet road close to a number of tube stations, with easy access to the West End. The comfortable bedrooms provide stylish accommodation, and are equipped with a range of useful amenities. A continental breakfast is served in the attractive dining room.

Rooms: 50 en suite (3 fmly) (6 GF) **Facilities:** STV FTV tea/coffee Direct dial Lift WiFi
Notes: LB

Shaftesbury Hyde Park International
PLAN 2 E3

★★★★ GUEST ACCOMMODATION

tel: 020 7985 8300 **52–55 Inverness Terrace W2 3LB**
email: info@shaftesburyhotels.com **web:** www.shaftesburyhotels.com
dir: *Off A402 (Bayswater Road).*

A smart, modern establishment near to Bayswater, Queensway and Paddington underground stations, the Shaftesbury Hyde Park International is also within walking distance of a myriad of dining options. Bedrooms and bathrooms are decorated to a very high standard with a good range of in-room facilities including TV, iron and ironing board and complimentary internet or WiFi access. Continental and cooked buffet breakfasts are served daily. There is a limited number of off-road parking spaces.

Rooms: 70 en suite (2 GF) **Facilities:** STV TVL tea/coffee Direct dial Lift Licensed WiFi **Extras:** Mini-bar, fruit, snacks **Conf:** Max 12 Thtr 12 Class 8 Board 8 **Parking:** 3

Shaftesbury Metropolis London Hyde Park
PLAN 1 A4

★★★★ GUEST ACCOMMODATION

tel: 020 7723 7723 **78–84 Sussex Gardens, Hyde Park W2 1UH**
email: dm@shaftesburymetropolitan.com **web:** www.shaftesburyhotels.com

This establishment is in an ideal location close to Paddington Station with express links to Heathrow Airport. Smartly decorated bedrooms with highly comfortable beds are available in a range of sizes, all with stylish en suite provision. On-site facilities include complimentary internet or WiFi, and continental and full English breakfasts are served every day. The reception is staffed 24 hours a day.

Rooms: 90 en suite (14 GF) **Facilities:** STV FTV TVL tea/coffee Direct dial Lift Licensed WiFi Small fitness centre

Number 63
PLAN 1 A3

★★★ GUEST ACCOMMODATION

tel: 020 7723 8575 **63 Bayswater Road W2 3PH**
email: info@number63.co.uk **web:** www.number63.co.uk
dir: *Phone for directions.*

Number 63 offers a surprisingly tranquil environment just a minute's walk from Lancaster Gate tube and directly opposite Hyde Park. All bedrooms are comfortable with en suite facilities and consist of a range of singles and twins; there is also a triple room. Hot snacks are available throughout the afternoon and evening (by prior arrangement) and a good continental or cooked breakfast is served each morning. A meeting/function room is available. Parking can be arranged.

Rooms: 16 en suite (1 fmly) **Facilities:** FTV Lounge TVL tea/coffee Dinner available Direct dial Lift Licensed WiFi **Conf:** Max 32 Thtr 32 Board 24 **Notes:** No children 5 years Closed 22–27 December

Griffin House
PLAN 1 B4

★★★ GUEST ACCOMMODATION

tel: 020 7723 6532 & 7491 0683 **10 Connaught Street, Marble Arch W2 2AH**
email: info@griffinhousehotel.co.uk **web:** www.griffinhousehotel.co.uk
dir: *Phone for directions.*

A compact establishment, strategically located in the heart of central London, very well connected to the public transport network and with many landmarks just a stone's throw away. Bedrooms are comfortable and have practical amenities. A substantial continental breakfast is served in the lower-ground floor breakfast room, overseen by attentive staff.

Rooms: 15 rms **Facilities:** STV Direct dial WiFi 🔒 **Extras:** Mini-bar

Kingsway Park Guest Accommodation
PLAN 1 A4

★★★ GUEST ACCOMMODATION

tel: 020 7723 5677 & 7724 9346 **139 Sussex Gardens W2 2RX**
email: info@kingswaypark-hotel.com **web:** www.kingswaypark-hotel.com
dir: *A40 eastbound junction for Paddington, through to Sussex Gardens.*

This Victorian property has a central location within walking distance of Marble Arch, Hyde Park and Paddington. Bedrooms offer well-equipped, good value accommodation. Public areas include a reception lounge and a basement breakfast room adorned with interesting artwork. A limited number of parking spaces is available.

Rooms: 22 en suite (5 fmly) (2 GF) **Facilities:** STV FTV Lounge TVL tea/coffee Direct dial Licensed **Conf:** Max 30 **Parking:** 3 **Notes:** LB

W6

Best Western Plus Seraphine
PLAN 2 D3

★★★★ GUEST ACCOMMODATION

tel: 020 8600 0555 & 8741 6464 **84 King Street W6 0QW**
email: hammersmith@seraphinehotel.co.uk **web:** www.seraphinehotel.co.uk
dir: *A4 exit into Hammersmith Bridge Road before Hammersmith flyover. Left into King Street.*

Located just a short walk from Hammersmith tube station, this establishment is a good base for visiting the capital's attractions. All bedrooms and public areas are smartly appointed and offer very good levels of comfort. Continental and cooked breakfasts are served in the open-plan breakfast room. The bar offers a suitable range of drinks and snacks.

Rooms: 62 en suite (14 fmly) **S** fr £99 **D** fr £129 **Facilities:** STV FTV Lounge TVL tea/coffee Direct dial Lift Licensed WiFi **Extras:** Bottled water on arrival **Notes:** LB

W8

Best Western Seraphine Kensington Olympia
PLAN 2 E3

★★★★ GUEST ACCOMMODATION

tel: 020 7938 5911 **225 Kensington High Street W8 6SA**
email: olympia@seraphinehotel.co.uk **web:** www.seraphinehotel.co.uk
dir: *A4 left onto A330, then right onto A315. On corner of Kensington High Street and Abingdon Road.*

This chic and intimate property enjoys a prime location in High Street Kensington, and is ideally positioned for Holland Park, local attractions, shops and museums. Bedrooms vary in size but all are well equipped with interactive TV, iPod docking stations, laptop safes and free WiFi; the en suites are modern with powerful showers. An extensive, continental breakfast is included and fully-cooked breakfasts can be requested.

Rooms: 40 en suite (40 fmly) **S** fr £99 **D** fr £129 **Facilities:** STV FTV TVL tea/coffee Direct dial Lift Licensed WiFi **Extras:** Bottled water

Mercure London Kensington
PLAN 2 E3

★★★★ GUEST ACCOMMODATION

tel: 020 7244 2400 **1a Lexham Gardens, Kensington W8 5JJ**
email: stay@mercurekensington.com **web:** www.mercurekensington.com
dir: *Phone for directions.*

Mercure London Kensington enjoys a prime location adjacent to the famous Cromwell Road Hospital, and is within easy reach of the V&A and the chic shops of Knightsbridge and South Kensington. Bedrooms are extremely well equipped and, along with the comfortable public areas, have a stylish, contemporary feel. The smart and popular bar is a feature.

Rooms: 82 en suite **Facilities:** STV TVL tea/coffee Dinner available Direct dial Lift Licensed

W12

W12 Rooms
PLAN 2 D3

★★★★ GUEST ACCOMMODATION

tel: 0203 6758 551 **54 Uxbridge Road, Shepherd's Bush W12 8LP**
email: info@w12rooms.co.uk **web:** www.w12rooms.co.uk
dir: *Phone for directions.*

W12 Rooms offers smart accommodation in a very convenient location for a reasonable price. The comfortable, contemporary bedrooms are offered on a room-only basis – there are various cafés and eateries a short walk away. All rooms have air conditioning, free high-speed internet access and a mini fridge. Westfield Shopping Centre is just minutes away, and Portobello Market, Holland Park and famous music and sports venues are close by. Most of London's major tourist attractions, including the London Eye, Buckingham Palace and the Shard are also easily accessible.

Rooms: 19 en suite (1 fmly) **Facilities:** FTV TVL tea/coffee WiFi **Notes:** No children 2 years

W13

Best Western Maitrise Suites
PLAN 2 C3

★★★★ GUEST ACCOMMODATION

tel: 020 8799 3850 **50–54 The Broadway, West Ealing W13 0SU**
email: info@maitrisesuites.com **web:** www.maitrisesuites.com
dir: *Phone for directions.*

This establishment offers fully serviced accommodation. The rooms comprise stylish one- and two-bedroom apartments and a studio – all have kitchens and lounge areas and come fully equipped with all modern amenities including digital TV and free WiFi. A continental room-service breakfast can be enjoyed daily. This property has parking available and is just 10 minutes from Ealing Broadway tube station.

Rooms: 17 en suite (17 fmly) **Facilities:** FTV iPod docking station Lounge tea/coffee Direct dial Lift WiFi **Parking:** 8

WC1

The George
PLAN 1 D5

★★★ GUEST ACCOMMODATION

tel: 020 7387 8777 **58–60 Cartwright Gardens WC1H 9EL**
email: reception@georgehotels.co.uk **web:** www.georgehotel.com
dir: *From St Pancras 2nd left into Marchmont Street and 1st left into Cartwright Gardens.*

The George is within walking distance of Russell Square and the tube, and convenient for London's central attractions. The brightly appointed bedrooms vary in size, and some have en suites. A substantial breakfast is served in the attractive ground-floor dining room.

Rooms: 41 rms (31 en suite) (10 pri facs) (5 GF) **Facilities:** FTV Lounge TVL tea/coffee Direct dial WiFi

GREATER LONDON

BARNET
Map 6 TQ29

Savoro Restaurant with Rooms
★★★★ ◎ RESTAURANT WITH ROOMS

tel: 020 8449 9888 **206 High Street EN5 5SZ**
email: savoro@savoro.co.uk **web:** www.savoro.co.uk
dir: *M25 junction 23, A1000. Establishment in crescent behind Hadley Green Jaguar Garage.*

Set back from the main high street, the traditional frontage of this establishment belies the stylishly contemporary bedrooms within. Several have modern four-poster beds, and all have well designed bathrooms. The award-winning restaurant is an additional bonus, serving food that is freshly prepared in-house – from the breads to the ice creams.

Rooms: 11 rms (9 en suite) (2 pri facs) (2 fmly) (3 GF) **Facilities:** FTV tea/coffee Dinner available WiFi **Extras:** Bottled water – complimentary **Conf:** Max 20 Class 20 Board 20 **Parking:** 9 **Notes:** LB

BECKENHAM

Innkeeper's Lodge Beckenham
PLAN 2 G1
★★★ INN

tel: 03451 551551 **422 Upper Elmers End Road BR3 3HQ**
email: info@innkeeperslodge.com **web:** www.innkeeperslodge.com
dir: *Phone for directions.*

Just 12 miles from central London, this Innkeeper's Lodge offers bedrooms with TVs, desks, tea-and-coffee making facilities and free WiFi as standard; family rooms are available. The on-site Toby Carvery meals are popular. There is a beer garden for the summer months and parking is provided.

Rooms: 24 en suite (1 fmly) (8 GF) **Facilities:** FTV tea/coffee Dinner available Direct dial WiFi **Parking:** 40

CRANFORD
See Heathrow Airport

CROYDON
Map 6 TQ36

Best Western Plus London Croydon Aparthotel
★★★★ GUEST ACCOMMODATION

tel: 020 8903 4349 **2 Dunheved Road South, Thornton Heath CR7 6AD**
web: www.lcah.co.uk
dir: *Phone for directions.*

Located not far from West Croydon Station is this newly-built property which offers stylish and contemporary accommodation. All rooms are well equipped and have air conditioning, smart TVs, WiFi, sinks, fridges and microwaves. Ground-floor public areas feature a small bar and the Restaurant Pizzapolli which serves a popular range of dishes. There's also a convenient underground car park on-site.

Rooms: 105 en suite **Facilities:** Dinner available Lift Licensed WiFi **Parking:** 35

Kirkdale
★★★ GUEST HOUSE

tel: 020 8688 5898 **22 St Peters Road CR0 1HD**
email: reservations@kirkdalehotel.co.uk **web:** www.kirkdalehotel.co.uk
dir: *A23 onto A232 west and A212 (Lower Coombe Street), 500 yards right.*

Close to the town centre, this Victorian property retains many original features. Public areas include a small lounge bar and an attractive breakfast room, and the bedrooms have good facilities. There is a sheltered patio for use in the summer.

Rooms: 16 en suite (5 GF) **Facilities:** FTV TVL tea/coffee Direct dial Licensed WiFi **Parking:** 12

HARROW ON THE HILL

Old Etonian
PLAN 2 B5

★★★ ☕ GUEST ACCOMMODATION

----

tel: 020 8423 3854 & 8422 8482 **36–38 High Street HA1 3LL**
email: info@oldetonian.com **web:** www.oldetonian.com
dir: *In town centre. On B458 opposite Harrow School.*

In the heart of this historic part of London and opposite the prestigious school, this friendly guest accommodation is a delight. Bedrooms are attractive, well appointed and comfortable. A continental breakfast is served in the dining room, which in the evening becomes a lively restaurant. Roadside parking is available.

Rooms: 9 en suite (1 GF) **Facilities:** FTV tea/coffee Dinner available Direct dial Licensed WiFi 🔒 **Extras:** Snacks – complimentary **Conf:** Max 30 Thtr 20 Class 20 Board 20 **Parking:** 3

HEATHROW AIRPORT

The Cottage
PLAN 2 B3

★★★★ GUEST ACCOMMODATION

----

tel: 020 8897 1815 **150–152 High Street TW5 9WB**
email: info@the-cottage.eu **web:** www.the-cottage.eu
dir: *M4 junction 3, A312 towards Feltham, left at lights, left after 1st pub on left.*

This beautiful property is a peacefully situated, family-run oasis, within five minutes of Heathrow Airport. It offers comfortable and spacious accommodation, in the tastefully decorated main house and six bedrooms located at the rear of the garden, connected to the main building by a covered walkway overlooking the stunning courtyard.

Rooms: 14 en suite 6 annexe en suite (4 fmly) (12 GF) **Facilities:** FTV tea/coffee WiFi **Parking:** 16 **Notes:** Closed 24–26 December and 31 December to 1 January

Crompton Guest House
PLAN 2 B2

★★★★ GUEST HOUSE

tel: 020 8570 7090 **49 Lampton Road TW3 1JG**
email: cromptonguesthouse@btconnect.com **web:** www.cromptonguesthouse.co.uk
dir: *M4 junction 3, follow signs for Hounslow. Into Bath Road (A3005), left at Yates pub. 200 yards on right just before bridge.*

Located just a moment's walk away from Hounslow underground station, this guest house is popular with both business and leisure guests. The comfortable bedrooms and bathrooms are well equipped with good facilities including air conditioning.

Breakfast is served in the intimate dining room where a freshly-prepared dishes are served. Parking is a bonus and is free for up to 15 days.

Crompton Guest House

Rooms: 11 en suite (7 fmly) (2 GF) **S** fr £90 **D** fr £100* **Facilities:** STV FTV DVD iPod docking station tea/coffee Dinner available Direct dial WiFi 🔒 **Extras:** Speciality toiletries, safe, mini-bar **Parking:** 12 **Notes:** LB

HORNCHURCH
Map 6 TQ58

Innkeeper's Lodge Hornchurch

★★★ INN

----

tel: 03451 551551 **Station Lane RM12 6SB**
email: info@innkeeperslodge.com **web:** www.innkeeperslodge.com
dir: *Phone for directions.*

This Innkeeper's Lodge, The Railway, is convenient for access into London and also for delegates visiting the CEME Conference Centre in Rainham. The en suite bedrooms, in different shapes and sizes, come with TVs, desks and free WiFi as standard; family rooms are available. The welcoming interior is traditional in design and seasonal menus prove very popular. There's a meeting room, and free parking is provided.

Rooms: 12 en suite (1 fmly) **Facilities:** FTV tea/coffee Dinner available WiFi **Conf:** Max 60 **Parking:** 40

HOUNSLOW

See Heathrow Airport

ILFORD

Best Western Greater London
PLAN 2 H5

★★★★ GUEST ACCOMMODATION

----

tel: 020 8514 0444 **60 Cranbrook Road IG1 4NH**
email: info@bestwesterngreaterlondon.com **web:** www.bestwesterngreaterlondon.com
dir: *Phone for directions.*

The Best Western Greater London is an ideal base from which to explore the capital. This stylish modern property enjoys a prominent position on the high street in Ilford, and secure parking can be arranged in advance at reception. There is a comfortable lounge area and breakfast room that can be also used for private events. Comfortable, modern bedrooms are finished to a high standard and free WiFi is available.

Rooms: 22 en suite **Facilities:** tea/coffee WiFi

Best Western Ilford
PLAN 2 H5

★★★★ GUEST ACCOMMODATION

tel: 020 8911 6083 **3–5 Argyle Road IG1 3BH**
email: manager@expresslodging.co.uk **web:** www.expresslodging.co.uk
dir: *From A406 east towards Ilford, then A118 and 1st left after Ilford Station.*

This establishment is conveniently located for easy access to central London and all the major landmarks. The accommodation, housed in two well-presented buildings, is very comfortable and offers a range of amenities such as free internet access and a state-of-the-art media hub. Breakfast offers an ample choice to meet the needs of a varied clientele. 24-hour room service and limited parking are also provided.

Rooms: 34 en suite 26 annexe en suite (9 fmly) (15 GF) **Facilities:** FTV Lounge TVL tea/coffee Dinner available Direct dial WiFi 🔒 **Conf:** Max 30 Thtr 30 Class 30 Board 30 **Parking:** 12 **Notes:** LB

Lucky 8
PLAN 2 H5

★★★ GUEST ACCOMMODATION

tel: 020 8514 5050 & 07450 288336 **21–25 York Road IG1 3AD**
email: info@lucky8hotels.com **web:** www.lucky8hotels.com
dir: *Phone for directions.*

This property is conveniently located just a short walk from the overground station into central London and provides a range of bedrooms to suit all budgets. Lucky 8 offers cosy rooms with comfortable beds, free WiFi and coffee-making facilities. Breakfast is included in the room price. Various restaurants and convenience stores are within walking distance. Limited parking is available.

Rooms: 38 en suite (4 fmly) (15 GF) **Facilities:** FTV TVL tea/coffee Direct dial WiFi 🔒 **Parking:** 15 **Notes:** LB

MERSEYSIDE

BIRKENHEAD
Map 15 SJ38

Shrewsbury Lodge

★★★ GUEST HOUSE

tel: 0151 652 4029 & 07912 846197 **31 Shrewsbury Road, Oxton CH43 2JB**
email: info@shrewsbury-hotel.com **web:** www.shrewsbury-hotel.com
dir: *Phone for directions.*

This guest house is situated in a quiet residential area yet is close to travel links and within easy walking distance of local amenities. Family-run, it provides well-equipped, modern bedrooms, and good breakfasts are served in the pleasant dining room. The friendly and attentive service is noteworthy here.

Rooms: 15 rms (12 en suite) (3 pri facs) (3 fmly) (4 GF) **S** fr £55 **D** fr £68 (room only)* **Facilities:** FTV Lounge TVL tea/coffee Licensed WiFi 🏊 🎣 Fishing Riding **Extras:** Bottled water **Conf:** Max 20 Thtr 20 Class 20 Board 20 **Parking:** 12 **Notes:** LB

BOOTLE
Map 15 SJ39

Breeze Guest House

★★★ GUEST HOUSE

tel: 0151 933 2576 **237 Hawthorne Road L20 3AW**
email: breezegh@gmail.com **web:** www.breezeguesthouse.co.uk
dir: *Phone for directions.*

This pleasant family-run guest house provides a friendly place to stay. With secure parking and great transport links, it is ideally located for Anfield and Goodison Park as well as being convenient for Aintree. Dinner is available and there is a pleasant bar too. Bedrooms are spacious and comfortable.

Rooms: 10 en suite (1 fmly) (1 GF) **S** fr £45 **D** fr £80* **Facilities:** FTV DVD TVL tea/coffee Licensed WiFi **Extras:** Bottled water **Parking:** 8 **Notes:** LB Closed 20 December to 5 January

BROMBOROUGH
Map 15 SJ38

Pesto at the Dibbinsdale Inn

★★★★ 🍽 INN

tel: 0151 334 9818 **Dibbinsdale Road CH63 0HJ**
email: pestodibbinsdale@hotmail.com **web:** www.pestorestaurants.co.uk
dir: *M53 junction 5 onto A41 towards Birkenhead. After 2 miles left towards railway station, through 2 sets of lights, 2nd right into Dibbinsdale Road. 600 yards on right.*

Pesto at the Dibbinsdale Inn offers plenty of those little luxuries you'd expect from a larger establishment, combined with the relaxed comfort of an independently-run inn, all in a peaceful setting. With high standards of comfort and facilities, the stylish en suite bedrooms are equipped for both leisure and business guests. With real ales on tap and open fires, the restaurant also offers Pesto's informal Italian dining experience with its piattini menu of small plates. A special party menu is available for group bookings.

Rooms: 12 en suite (1 fmly) **S** fr £59 **D** fr £75* **Facilities:** FTV Lounge tea/coffee Dinner available WiFi ♿ **Parking:** 25 **Notes:** LB RS 25 December restaurant closed

IRBY
Map 15 SJ28

Manor Garden Lodge

★★★★ BED AND BREAKFAST

tel: 0151 648 7212 & 07855 512008 **5 Manor Road CH61 4UA**
email: markwhite7212@gmail.com **web:** www.manorgardenlodge.co.uk
dir: *M53 junction 3 onto A552 towards Heswall. Left into Arrowe Park Road, then right into Thingwall Road East. After 1 mile at T-junction turn right, then 1st right.*

This is a B&B with a difference – it is located in the heart of the Wirral, and handy for many venues and golf courses as well as easy transport links into Liverpool and Chester. The wooden lodge at the secluded end of the neat garden is split into two spacious and well-equipped bedrooms that have modern facilities and thoughtful extras. Breakfast is taken in the main house. A warm and personal welcome and good service are guaranteed.

Rooms: 2 annexe en suite (2 GF) **D** fr £75* **Facilities:** FTV iPod docking station tea/coffee WiFi ♿ **Parking:** 2 **Notes:** LB

LIVERPOOL   Map 15 SJ39

Liverpool Gateway B&B

★★★ GUEST ACCOMMODATION

tel: 0151 298 2288 & 07714 090842 **95 Saint Oswald's Street L13 5SB**
email: info@liverpoolgateway.co.uk **web:** www.liverpoolgateway.co.uk
dir: *End of M62 through 2 pedestrian lights, through next lights, on right.*

Ideally situated for the M62 and with easy access to the city centre and its
attractions, Liverpool Gateway B&B provides comfortable accommodation, good
facilities and thoughtful extras. Continental breakfasts are served in a communal
kitchen; secure off-road parking is provided.

Rooms: 10 rms (4 GF) **Facilities:** FTV WiFi 🔒 **Parking:** 15 **Notes:** No children 10 years

SOUTHPORT   Map 15 SD31

Bay Tree House B&B

★★★★ ⌢ GUEST ACCOMMODATION

tel: 01704 510555 **1 Irving Street, Marine Gate PR9 0HD**
email: info@baytreehousesouthport.co.uk **web:** www.baytreehousesouthport.co.uk
dir: *From roundabout on Lord Street (A565) into Leicester Street (B5245). 3rd right into
Irving Street.*

A warm welcome is assured at this immaculately maintained house, located a short
walk from the promenade and central attractions. Bedrooms are equipped with a
wealth of thoughtful extras, and delicious imaginative breakfasts are served in an
attractive dining room overlooking the pretty front patio garden.

Rooms: 6 en suite **Facilities:** FTV DVD iPod docking station Lounge tea/coffee
Licensed WiFi ⌁ Discounts available for local swimming baths and gym
Extras: Speciality toiletries, mini-bar, snacks, robes, slippers **Parking:** 2
Notes: Closed 15 November to January

The Leicester

★★★★ ⌢ GUEST HOUSE

tel: 01704 501703 **24 Leicester Street PR9 0EZ**
email: relax@theleicester.com **web:** www.theleicester.com
dir: *Phone for directions.*

Jayne and Cliff run this comfortable and welcoming Southport guest house that is
situated handily for the attractions and eateries of Lord Street andt also the
promenade. The 10 guest rooms are available in a range of sizes but all are smartly
appointed and very well equipped. Breakfast is the highlight of any stay, the
generous portions and superb local produce are noteworthy.

Rooms: 10 en suite

NORFOLK

BAWBURGH
Map 13 TG10

The Kings Head Bawburgh

★★★★ ◉◉ INN

tel: 01603 744977 **Harts Lane NR9 3LS**
email: anton@kingsheadbawburgh.co.uk **web:** www.kingshead-bawburgh.co.uk
dir: *Exit A47 signed, university and hospital, onto B1108 (Whatton). 500 yards right into Stocks Hill. Into centre of Bawburgh, opposite river.*

Built in 1602, The Kings Head Bawburgh is Grade II listed and situated in the picturesque village of Bawburgh, opposite the river and only a 10-minute drive from the centre of Norwich. The pub boasts six boutique-style bedrooms with modern bathrooms and high-quality fixtures and fittings throughout. The gastro pub below offers award-winning food in a traditional dining area complete with oak beams, inglenook fireplace and wood-burners. There is also a lovely outdoor patio for alfresco dining in the summer; a good range of real ales is available. Nothing is too much trouble for the owners who will ensure all guests feel welcomed.

Rooms: 6 en suite (1 fmly) **S** fr £90* **Facilities:** FTV iPod docking station tea/coffee Dinner available WiFi ⅃ **Extras:** Speciality toiletries, home-made biscuits
Conf: Max 20 Thtr 20 Class 20 Board 12 **Parking:** 51 **Notes:** LB

BLAKENEY
Map 13 TG04

The White Horse

★★★★ ⚓ INN

tel: 01263 740574 **4 High Street NR25 7AL**
email: thewhitehorse@adnams.co.uk **web:** www.whitehorseblakeney.co.uk
dir: *Phone for directions.*

Situated on the High Street just a short walk from Blakeney Harbour and a selection of shops, the bedrooms at the White Horse are tastefully appointed and equipped with modern facilities. Some rooms have views of the marshes. The public rooms offer a wide choice of areas in which to relax and include a conservatory, dining room, large open plan bar and a great outside terrace.

Rooms: 10 en suite **Facilities:** tea/coffee Dinner available

BROOKE
Map 13 TM29

The Old Vicarage

★★★★ BED AND BREAKFAST

tel: 01508 558329 **48 The Street NR15 1JU**
web: www.bedandbreakfastdirect.co.uk
dir: *From Norwich on B1332, turn left after Kings Head pub. 1st left at fork in road to village. Immediately before church on right.*

Set in mature gardens in a peaceful village, this charming house is within easy driving distance of Norwich. The individually decorated bedrooms are thoughtfully furnished and equipped, and one room has a lovely four-poster bed. There is an elegant dining room and a cosy lounge, and dinner is available by arrangement. Service is genuinely helpful, and provided in a relaxed and friendly manner.

Rooms: 2 en suite **S** fr £40 **D** fr £75* **Facilities:** TVL tea/coffee Dinner available
Parking: 4 **Notes:** LB No children 18 years

BURNHAM MARKET   Map 13 TF84

The Nelson Country Inn
★★★★ 🛌 INN

tel: 01328 738321 **4 Creake Road PE31 8EN**
email: stay@the-nelson.com **web:** www.the-nelson.com
dir: *From Market Place onto Front Street (at lower end). 200 yards, on Creake Road.*

This country inn is set in the pretty north Norfolk village of Burnham Market, within easy reach of King's Lynn, Norwich, Hunstanton and Cromer. The bedrooms are individually styled and comfortable. Hearty meals are served daily, making good use of local and seasonal produce whenever possible.

Rooms: 5 en suite 2 annexe en suite (2 GF) **Facilities:** FTV tea/coffee Dinner available WiFi 🔒 **Extras:** Sweets **Conf:** Max 18 Thtr 12 Class 18 Board 14 **Parking:** 20

CASTLE ACRE   Map 13 TF81

Ostrich Inn
★★★★ 🛌 INN

tel: 01760 755398 **Stocks Green PE32 2AE**
email: info@ostrichcastleacre.com **web:** www.ostrichcastleacre.com
dir: *0.3 mile on right of Castle Acre Priory.*

The 15th-century Ostrich Inn is situated adjacent to the village green in the centre of Castle Acre. The warm and inviting public areas have a wealth of original features such as exposed brickwork, oak beams and open fires. The spacious bedrooms are in an adjacent building; each room is equipped with modern facilities.

Rooms: 6 en suite (1 fmly) (1 GF) **Facilities:** FTV Lounge tea/coffee Dinner available Direct dial WiFi 🔒 **Conf:** Max 25 Thtr 25 Class 25 Board 25 **Parking:** 30 **Notes:** LB

CLEY NEXT THE SEA   Map 13 TG04

Premier Collection

Old Town Hall House
★★★★★ 🛌 GUEST HOUSE

tel: 01263 741439 & 07813 335236 **High Street NR25 7RB**
email: bookings@oldtownhallhouse.com **web:** www.oldtownhallhouse.com
dir: *On A149 in centre of Cley. On High Street, opposite old red phone box.*

Old Town Hall House is located in the popular little village of Cley next the Sea in an Area of Outstanding Natural Beauty which has a superb bird-watching reserve on its outskirts. The tastefully appointed bedrooms offer luxurious fabrics and retro accessories with a modern touch. Dinner is available on certain nights and guests can enjoy a pre-dinner drink in the lounge beforehand. Chef-patron James has worked in some of the finest restaurants in Europe and only high-quality ingredients will be on the menu. Breakfast is equally enjoyable.

Rooms: 4 en suite (1 fmly) **D** fr £95* **Facilities:** Lounge tea/coffee Dinner available Licensed WiFi ⚓ 🔒 **Extras:** Speciality toiletries, fresh milk — complimentary **Notes:** LB

The George
★★★★ 🛌 INN

tel: 01263 740652 **The High Street NR25 7RN**
email: info@thegeorgehotelatcley.co.uk **web:** www.thegeorgehotelatcley.co.uk
dir: *On A149 (coast road).*

The George is located in Cley next the Sea, within easy reach of Blakeney and Holt. This is a great spot for bird watchers, and The George overlooks the Cley Marshes and bird reserve, looking out towards Blakeney Harbour. This is a quiet little village, without street lights, that retains its original charm, complete with a red phone box. The bedrooms provide modern amenities, and each is attractively decorated; most overlook the marshes. Guests can enjoy a range of freshly prepared dishes in the restaurant (where food is served all day in the summer), including a fantastic breakfast.

Rooms: 10 en suite (1 fmly) **Facilities:** FTV DVD tea/coffee Dinner available WiFi **Extras:** Bottled water — complimentary **Parking:** 10

CROMER   Map 13 TG24

See also Sheringham

The Grove Cromer
★★★★ ◉◉ GUEST ACCOMMODATION

tel: 01263 512412 **95 Overstrand Road NR27 0DJ**
email: enquiries@thegrovecromer.co.uk **web:** www.thegrovecromer.co.uk
dir: *Into Cromer on A149, right at 1st mini roundabout into Cromwell Road. At double mini roundabout straight over into Overstrand Road, 200 metres on left.*

A charming Georgian house, The Grove Cromer sits amid several acres of landscaped gardens and is just a short walk from Cromer town centre, cliff walks and the beach. There are several bedroom styles to choose from — the well-appointed, comfortable bedrooms in the main house and the stylish garden rooms. There is an indoor, heated swimming pool available for guests along with a children's play area in the woodland walk. Delicious dinners are served in the restaurant and guests are guaranteed a warm welcome at this fine property.

Rooms: 11 en suite 5 annexe en suite (4 fmly) (5 GF) **S** fr £55 **D** fr £100*
Facilities: FTV DVD Lounge TVL tea/coffee Dinner available Direct dial Licensed WiFi
🕒 ⚓ 🔒 **Conf:** Max 24 Thtr 24 Class 24 Board 18 **Parking:** 25 **Notes:** LB
Closed 2–23 January Civ wed 25

The Red Lion Food and Rooms
★★★★ 🛌 INN

tel: 01263 514964 **Brook Street NR27 9HD**
email: info@redlion-cromer.co.uk **web:** www.redlion-cromer.co.uk
dir: *Follow one-way system, pass church on left and take next left into Brook Street.*

The Red Lion is a charming Victorian inn in an elevated position at the heart of the town centre, overlooking the beach and the sea. The open-plan public areas include a lounge bar, a popular restaurant and sunny conservatory. The spacious bedrooms are tastefully decorated with co-ordinated soft furnishings and include many thoughtful touches.

Rooms: 14 en suite (3 fmly) **Facilities:** FTV DVD iPod docking station tea/coffee Dinner available WiFi 🔒 **Extras:** Honesty box including chocolate, wine, snacks **Parking:** 20 **Notes:** LB

Shrublands Farm

★★★★ ☺ FARMHOUSE

tel: 01263 579297 **Church Street, Northrepps NR27 0AA**
email: youngman@farming.co.uk **web:** www.shrublandsfarm.com
dir: *Exit A149 to Northrepps, through village, past Foundry Arms, cream house 50 yards on left.*

Expect a warm welcome from the caring host at this delightful 18th-century farmhouse, set in landscaped grounds and surrounded by 300 acres of arable farmland. Public areas include a cosy lounge with a wood-burning stove, and breakfast is served at a communal table in the elegant dining room.

Rooms: 2 rms (1 en suite) (1 pri facs) **S** fr £65 **D** fr £85* **Facilities:** FTV DVD TVL tea/coffee WiFi 🔒 **Extras:** Speciality toiletries, snacks, confectionery – complimentary **Parking:** 5 **Notes:** LB No children 12 years Closed 25–26 December 300 acres arable

The White Horse Overstrand

★★★★ ☺☺ INN

tel: 01263 579237 **34 High Street, Overstrand NR27 0AB**
email: reservations@whitehorseoverstrand.co.uk **web:** www.whitehorseoverstrand.co.uk
dir: *From A140, before Cromer, turn right into Mill Road. At bottom, right into Station Road. After 2 miles, bear left into High Street, White Horse on left.*

The White Horse Overstrand is a smartly appointed inn ideally situated in the heart of this popular village on the north Norfolk coast. The modern bedrooms are tastefully appointed and equipped with a good range of useful extras. Public rooms include a large open-plan lounge bar with comfortable seating and a relaxed dining area. Cooking is taken seriously here as is reflected in its award of two AA Rosettes.

Rooms: 10 en suite (2 fmly) **Facilities:** STV TVL tea/coffee Dinner available WiFi **Parking:** 6 **Notes:** LB

Homefield Guest House

★★★★ GUEST HOUSE

tel: 01263 837337 **48 Cromer Road, West Runton NR27 9AD**
email: homefield@hotmail.co.uk **web:** www.homefieldguesthouse.co.uk
dir: *On A149 (coast road) between Sheringham and Cromer.*

This large Victorian house was previously owned by the Canon of Cromer and is situated in the peaceful village of West Runton between Cromer and Sheringham. The pleasantly co-ordinated bedrooms have many useful extras. Breakfast, which includes locally sourced produce, is served at individual tables in the smart dining room.

Rooms: 6 en suite **Facilities:** STV tea/coffee WiFi 🔒 **Parking:** 8 **Notes:** LB No children 14 years

The Sandcliff Guest House

★★★ GUEST HOUSE

tel: 01263 512888 **Runton Road NR27 9AS**
email: bookings@sandcliffcromer.co.uk **web:** www.sandcliffcromer.co.uk
dir: *500 yards west of town centre on A149.*

Ideally situated on the seafront just a short walk from the town centre, this guest house offers a large lounge with comfortable seating and a spacious dining room where breakfast is served. The bedrooms are pleasantly decorated, thoughtfully equipped and some have superb sea views.

Rooms: 23 rms (17 en suite) (6 pri facs) (10 fmly) (3 GF) **S** fr £52 **D** fr £52 (room only)* **Facilities:** FTV TVL tea/coffee WiFi 🔒 **Parking:** 10

Orchard Cottage

★★★★ BED AND BREAKFAST

tel: 01362 860265 **The Drift, Gressenhall NR20 4EH**
email: walkers.norfolk@btinternet.com **web:** www.walkers-norfolk.co.uk
dir: *2 miles northeast of Dereham. Exit B1146 in Beetley to Gressenhall, right at crossroads into Bittering Street, right at crossroads, 2nd right.*

Orchard Cottage is an attractive Norfolk flint building situated in the historic village of Gressenhall near Dereham. The comfortable, country-style bedrooms are smartly decorated and situated on the ground floor; one of the rooms has a superb wet room. Public rooms include a lounge, a dining room and a study. Dinner is available by arrangement.

Rooms: 2 en suite (2 GF) **S** fr £58 **D** fr £82* **Facilities:** FTV Lounge TVL tea/coffee Dinner available WiFi 🔒 **Parking:** 2 **Notes:** LB

Aldercarr Hall

★★★★ GUEST ACCOMMODATION

tel: 01953 455766 & 07710 752213 **Attleborough Road NR17 1LQ**
email: bedandbreakfast@aldercarr-limited.co.uk **web:** www.aldercarrhall.co.uk
dir: *On B1077, 500 yards southeast of village.*

Aldercarr Hall is set in extensive grounds and surrounded by open countryside on the edge of Great Ellingham. Public rooms include a comfortably appointed conservatory and a delightful dining room where breakfast is served around a large table. The excellent facilities include a health, beauty and hairdressing studio, an indoor swimming pool, a jacuzzi and a large function suite.

Rooms: 3 annexe en suite (1 fmly) (3 GF) **Facilities:** FTV TVL tea/coffee WiFi ⏱ ⚓ Fishing Riding Sauna 🔒 **Parking:** 200 **Notes:** LB

South Norfolk Guest House

★★★★ GUEST HOUSE

tel: 01379 677359 & 07796 448106 **Frith Way NR15 2HE**
email: info@sngh.co.uk **web:** www.southnorfolkguesthouse.co.uk
dir: *From A140 (north), in Long Stratton turn left at 1st set of lights. Through Wacton, pass sign to Coronation Hall on right. 1st property on right in Great Moulton, past house, turn right and right again.*

This former village school enjoys a peaceful rural location yet is only a short drive from Norwich. A warm welcome is guaranteed from the friendly proprietors and bedrooms are very comfortable. Ample secure parking is available for guests along with free WiFi. Delicious hot breakfasts are served in the conservatory breakfast room.

Rooms: 9 rms (8 en suite) (1 pri facs) (1 fmly) (4 GF) **Facilities:** FTV DVD TVL tea/coffee WiFi 🔒 **Parking:** 14 **Notes:** LB

GREAT RYBURGH
Map 13 TF92

The Blue Boar Inn

★★★ 🖴 INN

tel: 01328 829212 **5 Station Road NR21 0DX**
email: blueboarinnryburgh@gmail.com **web:** www.blueboar-norfolk.co.uk
dir: *1 mile from A1067 (Norwich to Fakenham road).*

Built in 1635, The Blue Boar Inn has been at the heart of village life in Great
Ryburgh for over three centuries. The cosy wood-beamed bar has an original
inglenook fireplace and guests are guaranteed a warm welcome. Bedrooms are
comfortable, attractively presented and well equipped. The restaurant serves an
extensive choice of imaginative dishes using the best local produce; hearty
breakfasts are cooked to order. Secure parking and free WiFi are available for
guests.

Rooms: 6 en suite **Facilities:** FTV tea/coffee Dinner available WiFi **Parking:** 40

GREAT YARMOUTH
Map 13 TG50

Barnard House

★★★★ 🍴 GUEST ACCOMMODATION

tel: 01493 855139 **2 Barnard Crescent NR30 4DR**
email: jill@barnardhouse.com **web:** www.barnardhouse.com

A 1920s-style detached house in a leafy crescent in a peaceful part of town. The
property sits in an attractive garden with plenty of mature shrubs and well-
manicured lawns. It has three bedrooms, all with en suite facilities, and there is
also a self-catering cottage to the rear.

Rooms: 3 en suite **S** fr £55 **D** fr £75 **Facilities:** FTV DVD tea/coffee WiFi
Notes: No children Closed Christmas and New Year

The Classic Lodge

★★★★ BED AND BREAKFAST

tel: 01493 852851 **13 Euston Road NR30 1DY**
email: classiclodge@uwclub.net **web:** www.classiclodge.com
dir: *A12 to A47, follow signs for seafront. Turn left at Sainsbury's, ahead at lights
200 metres on right, 100 metres from seafront.*

The Classic Lodge is an impressive Victorian villa situated just a short stroll from
the seafront and town centre. Breakfast is served at individual tables in the large
lounge-dining room, and the spacious bedrooms are carefully furnished and
equipped with a good range of facilities. Secure parking is provided at the rear of
the property.

Rooms: 3 en suite **Facilities:** FTV TVL tea/coffee WiFi **Parking:** 5 **Notes:** LB
No children 18 years Closed November to March

Marine Lodge

★★★★ 🖴 GUEST ACCOMMODATION

tel: 01493 331120 **19–20 Euston Road NR30 1DY**
email: res@marinelodge.co.uk **web:** www.marinelodge.co.uk
dir: *Follow signs for seafront, 300 metres north of Britannia Pier.*

This establishment's enviable seafront position offers panoramic views of the
bowling greens and beach, and is within easy walking distance of Britannia Pier.
Bright, modern bedrooms are complemented by smart public spaces that include a
bar area where light snacks are available during the evening. Guests also have
complimentary use of the indoor swimming pool at the sister Palm Court Hotel.

Rooms: 40 en suite (5 fmly) (5 GF) **Facilities:** FTV TVL tea/coffee Dinner available Lift
Licensed WiFi **Parking:** 38 **Notes:** LB

Swiss Cottage Bed and Breakfast

★★★★ GUEST ACCOMMODATION

tel: 01493 855742 & 07986 399857 **31 North Drive NR30 4EW**
email: info@swiss-cottage.info **web:** www.swisscottagebedandbreakfast.co.uk
dir: *0.5 mile north of town centre. Exit A47 or A12 to seafront, 750 yards north of pier.
Left at Britannia Pier. Swiss Cottage on left opposite Water Gardens.*

Swiss Cottage Bed and Breakfast is a charming property situated in a peaceful part
of town overlooking the Venetian waterways and the sea beyond. The comfortable
bedrooms are pleasantly decorated with co-ordinated fabrics and have many useful
extras. Breakfast is served in the smart dining room and guests have use of an
open-plan lounge area.

Rooms: 8 en suite 1 annexe en suite (2 GF) **S** fr £49 **D** fr £70* **Facilities:** FTV
Lounge tea/coffee WiFi 🛁 **Extras:** Speciality toiletries **Parking:** 9 **Notes:** LB
No children 16 years Closed November to February

The Chequers

★★★★ GUEST HOUSE

tel: 01493 853091 **27 Nelson Road South NR30 3JA**
email: mitchellsatchequers@hotmail.co.uk **web:** www.thechequersguesthouse.co.uk
dir: *Exit A47 signed seafront, right into Marine Parade and Kings Rd, 1st right.*

Guests will receive a warm welcome from the caring hosts at this privately-run
establishment, situated just a short walk from Wellington Pier and the beach.
Public rooms include a cosy bar, residents' lounge and a smart dining room.
Bedrooms are cheerfully decorated and have many thoughtful touches.

Rooms: 8 rms (7 en suite) (1 pri facs) (2 fmly) **Facilities:** FTV TVL tea/coffee Dinner
available Licensed WiFi **Notes:** LB

The Hamilton

★★★★ GUEST HOUSE

tel: 01493 844662 **23–24 North Drive NR30 4EW**
email: enquiries@hamilton-hotel.co.uk **web:** www.hamilton-hotel.co.uk
dir: *Phone for directions.*

Overlooking the beach with fantastic views of the sea, this property is ideally
situated for the theatre, tourist attractions, town centre and Yarmouth Racecourse.
Public rooms include a smart lounge bar with plush leather seating, a breakfast
room and a residents' lounge with comfy sofas. Bedrooms are bright and airy with
many thoughtful touches; most rooms have lovely sea views.

Rooms: 21 en suite (4 fmly) (2 GF) **Facilities:** FTV TVL tea/coffee Dinner available
Licensed WiFi 🎵 **Conf:** Max 40 Thtr 40 Class 26 Board 26 **Parking:** 20 **Notes:** LB

The Winchester

★★★★ 🖴 GUEST ACCOMMODATION

tel: 01493 843950 & 07807 733161 **12 Euston Road NR30 1DY**
email: webenquiry@winchesterprivatehotel.com **web:** www.winchesterprivatehotel.com
dir: *A12 onto A47, signs for seafront, left at Sainsbury's, over lights, premises 400 yards
on right.*

A warm welcome is assured from the friendly hosts at The Winchester, just off the
seafront. The pleasant bedrooms vary in size and style and are thoughtfully
equipped. Public rooms include a large lower ground-floor dining room, a small
conservatory and a foyer with comfortable sofas.

Rooms: 14 en suite (2 fmly) (5 GF) **S** fr £30 **D** fr £60* **Facilities:** FTV TVL tea/coffee
Dinner available WiFi 🛁 **Parking:** 10 **Notes:** LB No children 12 years
Closed December to January RS October to Easter no evening meals

Silverstone House

★★★ GUEST ACCOMMODATION

tel: 01493 844862 **29 Wellesley Road NR30 1EY**
email: silverstonehouse@yahoo.co.uk **web:** www.silverstone-house.co.uk
dir: A47 into Great Yarmouth. Over 2 roundabouts, left at lights signed seafront. Over next lights, turn left.

A warm welcome is guaranteed at this family-run property. Silverstone House is conveniently located close to the seafront and a short walk to the main shopping district. This four-storey Victorian terraced house has nine well-appointed, comfortable bedrooms. Freshly prepared hot breakfasts are served to individual tables in the charming breakfast room.

Rooms: 9 en suite (4 fmly) (1 GF) **S** fr £25 **D** fr £45* **Facilities:** FTV tea/coffee WiFi **Extras:** Mini-fridge – complimentary **Notes:** LB

HINDOLVESTON   Map 13 TG02

The Old Bakery B&B

★★★★ 🛏 🍴 BED AND BREAKFAST

tel: 01263 862802 & 07771 391967 **34 The Street NR20 5DF**
email: mike@theoldbakerynorfolk.co.uk **web:** www.theoldbakerynorfolk.co.uk
dir: From A148 exit at Little Snoring signed Fulmodeston, follow signs to Hindolveston. At next junction continue for 1.3 miles, house on corner of turn to Foulsham.

The Old Bakery B&B is a delightful property which was originally the village bakery and dates back to the 17th century. Guests will be welcomed into the property by Mike and Alison, previous winners of an AA B&B award. The spacious bedrooms are well equipped and include many thoughtful touches. Breakfast and dinner are served at a large communal table in the smart dining room, and good use is made of fresh seasonal ingredients.

Rooms: 2 en suite **S** fr £70 **D** fr £80* **Facilities:** FTV DVD iPod docking station tea/coffee Dinner available WiFi 🛁 🐾 **Extras:** Cakes on arrival – complimentary; fridge **Parking:** 4 **Notes:** LB No children

---

HOLT   Map 13 TG03

The Lawns

★★★★ 🏵 RESTAURANT WITH ROOMS

tel: 01263 713390 **26 Station Road NR25 6BS**
email: info@lawnshotelholt.co.uk **web:** www.lawnshotelholt.co.uk
dir: A148 (Cromer road). 0.25 mile from Holt roundabout, turn left, 400 yards along Station Road, on left.

The Lawns is a superb Georgian house situated in the centre of this delightful north Norfolk market town. The open-plan public areas include a large wine bar, a conservatory and a smart restaurant. The spacious bedrooms are tastefully appointed with co-ordinated soft furnishings and have many thoughtful touches.

Rooms: 8 en suite 2 annexe en suite (2 GF) **S** fr £95 **D** fr £105* **Facilities:** FTV DVD TVL tea/coffee Dinner available WiFi **Extras:** Speciality toiletries **Conf:** Max 20 Thtr 20 Class 12 **Parking:** 18

The Feathers

★★★★ INN

tel: 01263 712318 **6 Market Place NR25 6BW**
email: enquiries@thefeathershotel.com **web:** www.thefeathershotel.com

This former coaching inn enjoys a prominent position in the heart of the pretty village of Holt. Bedrooms vary in size but all are well equipped and comfortable. The bar, with its real fire, is extremely popular with locals and the dinner menu offers an extensive choice.

Rooms: 13 en suite (3 fmly) **S** fr £90 **D** fr £115* **Facilities:** FTV Lounge tea/coffee Dinner available Direct dial WiFi 🛁 🐾 **Conf:** Max 100 Thtr 100 Class 80 Board 80 **Parking:** 15

Holm Oaks

★★★★ GUEST HOUSE

tel: 01263 711061 & 07778 600600 **83a Cromer Road NR25 6DY**
email: holmoaks@btinternet.com **web:** www.holmoaksatholt.co.uk
dir: Phone for directions.

Holm Oaks enjoys a very convenient location on the outskirts of the Georgian town of Holt. The four bedrooms are attractively presented and free WiFi is available throughout the house. Breakfast is served at individual tables in the conservatory which overlooks the landscaped gardens. Secure parking is available. This makes an ideal base from which to explore beautiful north Norfolk.

Rooms: 4 en suite (4 GF) **S** fr £65 **D** fr £85 **Facilities:** FTV DVD Lounge tea/coffee WiFi **Parking:** 5 **Notes:** LB No children

HORNING   Map 13 TG31

Innkeeper's Lodge Norfolk Broads, Horning

★★★ INN

tel: 03451 551551 10 Lower Street NR12 8AA
email: info@innkeeperslodge.com web: www.innkeeperslodge.com
dir: Phone for directions.

An attractive timber and brick building dating back as far as 1696, this Innkeeeper's Lodge (The Swan Inn) sits right beside the River Bure in the ever-popular Norfolk Broads. The en suite bedrooms, in different shapes and sizes, are smart and come with TVs, tea- and coffee-making facilities and free WiFi as standard. Tables and chairs are provided outside beside the water – an ideal spot to watch the boats go by on a summer's day. The seasonal menus will appeal to all tastes.

Rooms: 8 en suite (3 fmly) Facilities: FTV tea/coffee Dinner available WiFi

HUNSTANTON   Map 12 TF64

Premier Collection

The Neptune Restaurant with Rooms

★★★★★ ⊛⊛⊛ RESTAURANT WITH ROOMS

tel: 01485 532122 85 Old Hunstanton Road, Old Hunstanton PE36 6HZ
email: reservations@theneptune.co.uk web: www.theneptune.co.uk
dir: On A149, past Hunstanton, 200 metres on left after post office.

This charming 18th-century coaching inn, now a restaurant with rooms, is ideally situated for touring the Norfolk coastline. The smartly appointed bedrooms are brightly finished with co-ordinated fabrics and hand-made New England furniture. Public rooms feature white clapboard walls, polished dark wood floors, fresh flowers and Lloyd Loom furniture. Obviously, the food is very much a draw here – the carefully prepared, award-winning cuisine uses excellent local produce such as oysters and mussels from Thornham and quinces grown on a neighbouring farm.

Rooms: 5 en suite S fr £160 D fr £280* Facilities: FTV tea/coffee Dinner available Direct dial WiFi ⓟ Parking: 6 Notes: No children 10 years Closed 1 week November, 3 weeks January, 1 week May RS October to April closed Monday

Gemini Lodge Guest House

★★★★ GUEST ACCOMMODATION

tel: 01485 533902 5 Alexandra Road PE36 5BT
web: www.geminilodgehunstanton.co.uk
dir: Phone for directions.

Gemini Lodge Guest House is in an elevated position close to the centre of town and seafront. The bedrooms are smartly decorated in neutral colours with lovely co-ordinated soft furnishings and fabrics; some rooms have lovely views of the sea. Public rooms include a smart lounge with plush sofas, and breakfast is served at a large communal table in the contemporary dining room.

Rooms: 3 en suite Facilities: FTV TVL tea/coffee Parking: 3 Notes: LB

The King William IV Country Inn & Restaurant

★★★★ ⊜ INN

tel: 01485 571765 Heacham Road, Sedgeford PE36 5LU
email: info@thekingwilliamsedgeford.co.uk web: www.thekingwilliamsedgeford.co.uk
dir: A149 to Hunstanton, right at Norfolk Lavender in Heacham onto B1454, signed Docking. 2 miles to Sedgeford.

Tucked away in the village of Sedgeford, close to Norfolk's beautiful coast line, The King William IV Country Inn & Restaurant is a family-run inn that has been welcoming travellers and locals since 1836. The menu offers classic dishes, complemented by daily specials and seasonal offerings, and guests can enjoy a drink outside in summer months. Bedrooms are full of character and offer a comfortable stay.

Rooms: 9 en suite (4 fmly) S fr £80 D fr £105 Facilities: Lounge tea/coffee Dinner available WiFi ⓟ ⓠ Extras: Speciality toiletries Parking: 60 Notes: LB

The White Cottage

★★★ GUEST ACCOMMODATION

tel: 01485 532380 19 Wodehouse Road PE36 6JW
dir: Phone for directions.

A charming cottage situated in a quiet side road in Old Hunstanton, The White Cottage has been owned and run by Mrs Burton for 30 years. The spacious bedrooms are attractively decorated, and some have lovely sea views. There is a cosy sitting room with a TV.

Rooms: 3 rms (1 en suite) (1 pri facs) S fr £40 D fr £78* Facilities: TVL tea/coffee WiFi ⓠ Parking: 4 Notes: LB No children 10 years

Old Marine Inn

★★★ INN

tel: 01485 533310 10 St Edmunds Terrace PE36 5EH
email: administrator@marinebar.demon.co.uk web: www.marinehotelhunstanton.com
dir: Phone for directions.

Situated in the centre of Hunstanton, some bedrooms at the Old Marine Inn benefit from sea views – all provide good levels of comfort. A range of dining options is available with either a bar meal in the Marine bar below or for something more special in the Steak and Stilton Restaurant which offers a good range of à la carte dishes.

Rooms: 10 rms Facilities: FTV tea/coffee Dinner available WiFi ⓟ Parking: 10

KING'S LYNN   Map 12 TF62

Linden Bed & Breakfast

★★★★ ⓠ BED AND BREAKFAST

tel: 01485 609198 & 07867 686216 Station Road PE31 6DE
email: info@lindenbedandbreakfast.co.uk web: www.lindenbedandbreakfast.co.uk
dir: From A148 onto B1153 signed Congham, 200 metres on left before St Mary's church.

A modern house, Linden Bed & Breakfast offers three individual, well-appointed en suite bedrooms along with a spacious guest lounge, a pretty garden overlooking the Norfolk countryside and a family-style breakfast/dining room. In the warmer months, cream teas are available and light suppers can also be arranged with prior notice.

Rooms: 3 en suite S fr £58 D fr £73* Facilities: FTV iPod docking station TVL tea/coffee WiFi ⓠ Extras: Speciality toiletries – complimentary Parking: 5 Notes: No children 12 years

LITCHAM
Map 13 TF81

Bramley

★★★★ BED AND BREAKFAST

tel: 01328 701592 & 07778 783412 **Weasenham Road PE32 2QT**
email: bramleybandb@hotmail.co.uk **web:** www.bramley-litcham.co.uk
dir: A1065 onto B1145. Left at crossroads, left at school, 4th house on left.

A warm welcome awaits at Bramley, a delightful detached house, set in a peaceful location on the fringe of the village, with ample safe parking in the generous grounds. The mostly spacious bedrooms are thoughtfully furnished to ensure guest comfort and have smartly appointed en suite shower rooms. A hearty, freshly-cooked breakfast is served at individual tables in the separate, elegant dining room.

Rooms: 4 en suite (1 fmly) **S** fr £45 **D** fr £75* **Facilities:** FTV tea/coffee WiFi
🌙 **Parking:** 4 **Notes:** LB

LITTLE PLUMSTEAD
Map 13 TG31

Wayside B&B

★★★★ BED AND BREAKFAST

tel: 01603 721827 & 07769 655682 **Honeycombe Road NR13 5HY**
email: info@littleplumsteadbedandbreakfast.com
web: www.littleplumsteadbedandbreakfast.com
dir: From A47 follow signs for Little Plumstead and Witton. At crossroads in Little Plumstead into Honeycombe Road, immediately on left.

Wayside B&B is a charming house in the pretty village of Little Plumstead and is conveniently located close to Norwich and the Norfolk Broads. The bedrooms are comfortable and very well equipped. Guests can relax on the terrace, and the continental breakfast offers a very good choice. Free WiFi is available along with secure parking.

Rooms: 3 en suite 3 annexe en suite (2 fmly) (4 GF) **Facilities:** FTV TVL tea/coffee WiFi 🌙 **Conf:** Max 8 Board 8 **Parking:** 6

LODDON
Map 13 TM39

The Loddon Swan

★★★★ ◉◉ INN

tel: 01508 528039 **23 Church Plain NR14 6LX**
email: info@theloddonswan.co.uk **web:** www.theloddonswan.co.uk
dir: A146 exit signed High Bungay Road. Follow road into Loddon High Street.

The Loddon Swan is situated in the centre of Loddon, just a minute's walk from the River Chet. This popular 18th-century inn offers modern accommodation. Dinner is available in the attractive restaurant overlooking a patio garden, and guests can enjoy viewing the gallery of original artwork. Good use is made of seasonal and local produce in some innovative and enjoyable dishes.

The Loddon Swan

Rooms: 7 annexe en suite (5 GF) **Facilities:** FTV tea/coffee Dinner available WiFi **Conf:** Max 30 Thtr 30 Class 20 Board 20 **Parking:** 20

NORWICH
Map 13 TG20

Brasteds

★★★★★ ◉◉ 🍴 RESTAURANT WITH ROOMS

tel: 01508 491112 **Manor Farm Barns, Fox Road NR14 7PZ**
email: enquiries@brasteds.co.uk **web:** www.brasteds.co.uk
dir: A11 onto A47 towards Great Yarmouth, then A146. 0.5 mile, right into Fox Road, 0.5 mile on left.

Brasteds is a lovely detached property set in 20 acres of mature, landscaped parkland on the outskirts of Norwich. The tastefully appointed bedrooms have beautiful soft furnishings and fabrics along with comfortable seating and many thoughtful touches. Public rooms include a cosy snug with plush sofas, and a smart dining room where breakfast is served. Dinner is available in Brasteds Restaurant, which can be found in an adjacent building.

Rooms: 6 en suite (1 fmly) (3 GF) **Facilities:** FTV DVD iPod docking station TVL tea/coffee Dinner available Direct dial WiFi 🌙 **Extras:** Mini-bar **Conf:** Max 120 Thtr 120 Class 100 Board 40 **Parking:** 50 **Notes:** LB Civ wed 160

38 St Giles

★★★★★ 🍴 GUEST ACCOMMODATION

tel: 01603 662944 & 07492 050098 **38 Saint Giles Street NR2 1LL**
email: booking@38stgiles.co.uk **web:** www.38stgiles.co.uk

38 St Giles is a stunning Georgian, Grade II listed building situated in the centre of Norwich that offers boutique accommodation. All the en suite bedrooms offer high quality furnishings, including Bang and Olufsen TVs and free WiFi. Guests are welcomed with home-made cake on arrival, and breakfast offers a wide selection of locally sourced and organic products.

Rooms: 8 en suite (1 fmly) (1 GF) **S** fr £95 **D** fr £140* **Facilities:** FTV Lounge tea/coffee WiFi **Extras:** Speciality toiletries, home-made cakes, flowers

NORWICH *continued*

Gothic House Bed & Breakfast

★★★★ 🛏 BED AND BREAKFAST

tel: 01603 631879 **King's Head Yard, Magdalen Street NR3 1JE**
email: charvey649@aol.com **web:** www.gothic-house-norwich.com
dir: *Follow signs for A147, exit at roundabout past flyover into Whitefriars. Right into Fishergate, at end, right into Magdalen Street.*

Gothic House Bed & Breakfast is an elegant Grade II listed Regency townhouse set in a quiet courtyard in the heart of Norwich. The property retains much original character and the spacious bedrooms are individually decorated and have many thoughtful touches. Breakfast, which includes locally sourced produce, is served in the elegant dining room.

Rooms: 2 rms (2 pri facs) **S** fr £65 **D** fr £95* **Facilities:** STV FTV tea/coffee WiFi
🛡 **Extras:** Speciality toiletries **Parking:** 2 **Notes:** No children 18 years Closed February

The Old Rectory

★★★★ @@ RESTAURANT WITH ROOMS

tel: 01603 700772 **103 Yarmouth Road, Thorpe St Andrew NR7 0HF**
email: enquiries@oldrectorynorwich.com **web:** www.oldrectorynorwich.com
dir: *From A47 southern bypass onto A1042 towards Norwich north and east. Left at slip road onto A1042. Follow signs to "All routes" and Thorpe St Andrew, at mini roundabout left onto A1242. Straight on at lights, entrance on right.*

This delightful Grade II listed Georgian property is ideally located in a peaceful area overlooking the River Yare, just a few minutes' drive from the city centre. Spacious bedrooms are individually designed with carefully chosen soft fabrics, plush furniture and many thoughtful touches; many of the rooms overlook the swimming pool and landscaped gardens. Accomplished cooking is offered via an interesting daily-changing menu, which features skilfully prepared local produce.

Rooms: 5 en suite 3 annexe en suite **Facilities:** FTV iPod docking station Lounge tea/coffee Dinner available Direct dial WiFi ↘ 🛡 **Extras:** Robes, speciality toiletries **Conf:** Max 14 Thtr 14 Class 10 Board 14 **Parking:** 12 **Notes:** LB Closed 22 December to 3 January RS Sunday to Monday no dinner served

Old Thorn Barn

★★★★ GUEST ACCOMMODATION

tel: 01953 607785 & 07894 203208 **Corporation Farm, Wymondham Road NR14 8EU**
email: danny@oldthornbarn.co.uk **web:** www.oldthornbarn.co.uk
dir: *6 miles southwest of Norwich. Follow signs for Lotus Cars from A11 or B1113, on Wymondham Road.*

This is a delightful Grade II listed barn situated in a peaceful rural location just a short drive from the city centre. The property has stylish, thoughtfully-equipped

bedrooms with polished wood floors and antique pine furniture. Breakfast is served in an open-plan area which has a wood-burning stove and there's also a cosy lounge.

Rooms: 5 en suite 2 annexe en suite (7 GF) **Facilities:** FTV TVL tea/coffee WiFi
🛡 **Parking:** 14

Cringleford Guest House

★★★★ GUEST HOUSE

tel: 01603 451349 & 07775 725933 **1 Gurney Lane, Cringleford NR4 7SB**
email: robandkate@cringlefordguesthouse.co.uk **web:** www.cringlefordguesthouse.co.uk
dir: *From A11 and A47 Thickthorn roundabout follow signs to Norwich, 0.25 mile slip road to Cringleford, left at junction into Colney Lane. Gurney Lane 5th on right.*

Cringleford Guest House is a delightful property, situated just a short drive from the hospital, University of East Anglia and major roads. The pleasant, well-equipped bedrooms have co-ordinated fabrics and pine furniture. Breakfast is served at individual tables in the smart dining room.

Rooms: 5 en suite 1 annexe en suite (3 fmly) (1 GF) **S** fr £80 **D** fr £100*
Facilities: FTV DVD TVL tea/coffee WiFi 🛡 **Conf:** Max 10 Thtr 10 Class 10 Board 10
Parking: 6 **Notes:** LB

Church Farm

★★★★ GUEST ACCOMMODATION

tel: 01603 898020 & 898582 **Church Street, Horsford NR10 3DB**
email: churchfarmgh@aol.com **web:** www.churchfarmgh.co.uk
dir: *5 miles northwest of city centre. A140 onto B1149, right at crossroads.*

Church Farm is set in a peaceful rural location just a short drive from Norwich airport and the city centre. The spacious bedrooms are smartly decorated, pleasantly furnished and have many considerate extras. Breakfast is served at individual tables in the conservatory-style lounge-dining room which overlooks the garden and sun terrace.

Rooms: 10 en suite (1 fmly) (3 GF) **Facilities:** FTV TVL tea/coffee WiFi **Parking:** 20

Salhouse Lodge Inn

★★★★ INN

tel: 01603 782828 **Vicarage Road, Salhouse NR13 6HD**
email: thelodgeinn@hotmail.co.uk **web:** www.salhouselodge.co.uk
dir: *From A1042 (ring road), northeast of Norwich centre, exit at lights into Salhouse Road signed New Rackheath. Through New Rackheath to Salhouse. Left onto B1140 signed Wroxham. Right in Vicarage Road at sign for inn.*

Situated on the outskirts of Norwich, this former rectory has extensive gardens and enjoys a peaceful rural location close to the Norfolk Broads. All the bedrooms are of a high standard and are very well equipped. Evening meals are available, and the log fire really comes into its own on cooler evenings.

Rooms: 7 en suite (2 fmly) **Facilities:** FTV tea/coffee Dinner available WiFi ♿
🛡 **Parking:** 50 **Notes:** LB

Stower Grange

★★★★ @ RESTAURANT WITH ROOMS

tel: 01603 860210 **40 School Road, Drayton NR8 6EF**
email: enquiries@stowergrange.co.uk **web:** www.stowergrange.co.uk
dir: *Norwich ring road north to Asda supermarket. Take A1067 (Fakenham Road) at Drayton, right at lights into School Road. Stower Grange 150 yards on right.*

Expect a warm welcome at this 17th-century, ivy-clad property situated in a peaceful residential area close to the city centre and airport. The individually decorated bedrooms are generally quite spacious; each is tastefully furnished and equipped with many thoughtful touches. Public rooms include a smart open-plan lounge bar and an elegant restaurant.

Rooms: 11 en suite (1 fmly) **Facilities:** ⟲ **Notes:** Civ wed 100

Innkeeper's Lodge Norwich

★★★ INN

tel: 03451 551551 **18–22 Yarmouth Road NR7 0EF**
email: info@innkeeperslodge.com **web:** www.innkeeperslodge.com
dir: *Phone for directions.*

Ideally located close to the beautiful city of Norwich, with its medieval architecture, and the Norfolk Broads, this Innkeeper's Lodge (The Town House) has 14 well-appointed, en suite bedrooms; each has a TV, a desk, free WiFi and tea- and coffee-making facilities; family rooms are available. Set beside the banks of the River Yare, the large garden is a pleasant place to relax in the warmer months. There is a very popular restaurant and the lounge is spacious and comfortable.

Rooms: 14 en suite (5 fmly) **Facilities:** FTV tea/coffee Dinner available WiFi **Parking:** 16

SHERINGHAM   Map 13 TG14

See also Cromer

Premier Collection

The Eiders Bed & Breakfast

★★★★★ BED AND BREAKFAST

tel: 01263 837280 **Holt Road, Aylmerton NR11 8QA**
email: enquiries@eiders.co.uk **web:** www.eiders.co.uk
dir: *From Cromer on A148, enter Aylmerton, pass garage on left. After crossroads, 2nd entrance on right.*

The Eiders Bed & Breakfast is just a short drive from the centre of Sheringham and is ideally placed for touring the north Norfolk coast. The tastefully appointed bedrooms have lovely co-ordinated fabrics and many extras. Breakfast is served at individual tables in the conservatory which overlooks the gardens and a duck pond. Guests have the use of a heated swimming pool which is open from May to September.

Rooms: 6 en suite (1 fmly) (6 GF) **S** fr £85 **D** fr £115* **Facilities:** FTV DVD iPod docking station TVL tea/coffee WiFi ⚐ **Extras:** Bottled water – complimentary; mini-bar, snacks – chargeable **Parking:** 7 **Notes:** LB

Roman Camp Inn

★★★★ INN

tel: 01263 838291 **Holt Road, Aylmerton NR11 8QD**
email: enquiries@romancampinn.co.uk **web:** www.romancampinn.co.uk
dir: *On A148 between Sheringham and Cromer, approximately 1.5 miles from Cromer.*

Roman Camp Inn provides spacious, tastefully appointed bedrooms with a good range of useful facilities including hairdryers. Five rooms are presented as deluxe, and two are suitable for less able guests. Public rooms include a smart conservatory-style restaurant, a comfortable open-plan lounge/bar and a dining area. Room service is available, guests have complimentary use of local leisure facilities, and there is ample, free parking.

Rooms: 15 en suite (1 fmly) (10 GF) **S** fr £75 **D** fr £120* **Facilities:** FTV DVD Lounge TVL tea/coffee Dinner available Direct dial WiFi Fishing Free use of nearby leisure complex and pool **Extras:** Home-made biscuits, speciality toiletries **Conf:** Max 20 Thtr 20 Class 20 Board 20 **Parking:** 50 **Notes:** LB Closed 25–26 December

Bay Leaf Guest House

★★★ GUEST HOUSE

tel: 01263 823779 **10 St Peters Road NR26 8QY**
email: bayleafgh@aol.com **web:** www.bayleafbandb.co.uk
dir: *A149 (Cromer road) into Station Road. 1st left into Station Approach, 2nd right into St Peters Road.*

This lovely Victorian property is ideally situated just a short walk from the golf course, steam railway and town centre. There is a smart lounge bar, and breakfast is served in the conservatory dining room which overlooks the patio. Bedrooms vary in size and style, all are comfortable.

Rooms: 7 en suite (2 fmly) (2 GF) **S** fr £55 **D** fr £74* **Facilities:** FTV tea/coffee Licensed WiFi **Parking:** 5 **Notes:** LB No children 8 years

The Lobster Inn

★★★ GUEST ACCOMMODATION

tel: 01263 822716 & 07944 842832 **13 High Street NR26 8JP**
email: grahamdeans1@googlemail.com **web:** www.thelobsterinn.co.uk
dir: *From A148 onto A1082. At roundabout straight over, turn right at end of Station Road. On right.*

A traditional fisherman's style inn set in the heart of Sheringham and just a stone's throw from the beach. The public areas have wooden panelling, open fire places and are adorned with nautically themed memorabilia. The accommodation is set in different places – the main building, across the courtyard in The Stables, and a very short walk round the corner in the Smugglers.

Rooms: 5 rms (4 en suite) (1 pri facs) 12 annexe en suite (3 fmly) (5 GF) **Facilities:** FTV tea/coffee Dinner available Licensed WiFi ⚐ **Extras:** Mini-fridges **Parking:** 4

SNETTISHAM   Map 12 TF63

The Rose & Crown

★★★★ ◉ INN

tel: 01485 541382 **Old Church Road PE31 7LX**
email: info@roseandcrownsnettisham.co.uk **web:** www.roseandcrownsnettisham.co.uk
dir: *A149 towards Hunstanton. In village centre into Old Church Road, 100 yards on left.*

This lovely village inn provides comfortable, well-equipped bedrooms. A range of quality meals is served in the many dining areas, complemented by a good variety of real ales and wines. Service is friendly and a delightful atmosphere prevails. A walled garden is available on sunny days, as is a children's play area.

Rooms: 16 en suite (4 fmly) (2 GF) **Facilities:** FTV Lounge tea/coffee Dinner available WiFi ⚐ **Extras:** Speciality toiletries, milk, home-made biscuits **Conf:** Max 80 **Parking:** 60 **Notes:** LB

THORPE MARKET
Map 13 TG23

Premier Collection

The Green House B&B

★★★★★ 🛏 GUEST ACCOMMODATION

tel: 01263 834701 & 07786 195213 **Cromer Road NR11 8TH**
email: greenhouse.norfolk@btinternet.com **web:** www.greenhousenorfolk.co.uk
dir: *A140 in village of Roughton, right at mini roundabout into Thorpe Market Road. After 1.5 miles turn right at crossroads, 200 yards on left.*

The Green House B&B is situated only four miles from both Cromer and the beach, and a very warm welcome is offered by Rosanna and Simon who have both worked at several top hotels in London. This 16th-century property has been carefully modernised throughout, offering high quality and comfort; plenty of care has been taken to retain period features. Dinner can be pre-arranged and there is a comfortable lounge and bar area; the attractive garden will appeal to guests in the summer months.

Rooms: 5 en suite **S** fr £90 **D** fr £90* **Facilities:** FTV DVD iPod docking station Lounge tea/coffee Licensed WiFi 🛝 🛁 **Extras:** Speciality toiletries, sweets – complimentary **Parking:** 6 **Notes:** No children 14 years

The Barns at Thorpe Market

★★★★ 🛏 GUEST ACCOMMODATION

tel: 01263 833033 **Common Lane NR11 8TP**
email: info@bedbreakfastnorfolk.com **web:** www.bedbreakfastnorfolk.com
dir: *A140 at Roughton onto B1436. At end turn right onto A149, onto slip road just past bus stop.*

This charming 18th-century converted barn offers a range of beautifully presented bedrooms overlooking a central courtyard. The bedrooms are spacious and very comfortable, and original flint walls are a real feature of the property. Thorpe Market is a short drive from Norwich and is close to the Norfolk Broads as well as a number of National Trust properties. Breakfast is served in the vaulted breakfast room, and features the best local produce. WiFi is available for guests along with secure bike storage.

Rooms: 3 en suite (3 GF) **S** fr £80 **D** fr £85 **Facilities:** FTV tea/coffee WiFi 🛁 **Extras:** Fridge **Parking:** 3 **Notes:** No children 14 years

TIVETSHALL ST MARGARET
Map 13 TM18

Red House Farm Bed & Breakfast

★★★★ BED AND BREAKFAST

tel: 01379 676566 & 07719 437007 **Station Road NR15 2DJ**
email: office@redhousefarm.info **web:** www.redhousefarm.info
dir: *500 metres from Pulham roundabout, A140.*

A warm welcome is assured at this delightful 17th-century barn conversion, situated on a small working farm in a peaceful rural location. The tastefully appointed bedrooms have modern furniture and lovely countryside views. Breakfast, which includes home-grown produce, is served at a large communal table in the smart kitchen.

Rooms: 1 en suite 2 annexe en suite (3 GF) **Facilities:** FTV tea/coffee WiFi **Parking:** 4

WIVETON
Map 13 TG04

Wiveton Bell

★★★★ ◉◉ INN

tel: 01263 740101 **The Green, Blakeney Road NR25 7TL**
email: wivetonbell@me.com **web:** www.wivetonbell.com
dir: *1 mile from Blakeney.*

Wiveton Bell is situated in a quiet and scenic part of Norfolk. The luxurious bedrooms, with outside seating, come complete with a whole host of accessories including TVs, Blu-ray/DVD players, complimentary Prosecco, REN toiletries, Egyptian cotton linen and duck- and goose-down bedding. Hampers containing continental breakfasts are delivered to the rooms and include fresh pastries from the local baker. Dinner can be taken in the AA Rosette award-winning restaurant and good use is made of fresh and local ingredients.

Rooms: 6 en suite (2 GF) **Facilities:** FTV DVD tea/coffee Dinner available WiFi 🛝 **Extras:** Prosecco, speciality toiletries – complimentary **Parking:** 60 **Notes:** Closed 25 December

WRENINGHAM
Map 13 TM19

The Bird In Hand

★★★★ 🅰 INN

tel: 01508 489438 **Church Road NR16 1BJ**
email: mail@davidbrake.com **web:** www.birdinhandwreningham.com
dir: *South of Norwich on B1113.*

The Bird In Hand is a family-run free house and restaurant combining all the atmosphere of a traditional British pub with quality food and drink and comfortable surroundings. You are guaranteed a friendly welcome from the whole team who always work hard to ensure your experience is an enjoyable one. There is a large parking area, indoor and outdoor seating areas, restaurant, bar area and above all, a friendly atmosphere.

Rooms: 8 annexe en suite (8 GF) **S** fr £80 **D** fr £80 (room only)* **Facilities:** FTV tea/coffee Dinner available WiFi **Extras:** Speciality toiletries, mineral water **Conf:** Max 60 Thtr 60 Class 60 Board 30 **Parking:** 90

WROXHAM
Map 13 TG31

Delaware

★★★★ BED AND BREAKFAST

tel: 01603 781947 & 07805 023249 **Tunstead Road, Hoveton NR12 8QN**
email: eilidh-villa@hotmail.co.uk **web:** www.delawarewroxham.co.uk
dir: *Into Wroxham on A1151, turn left into Horning Road, then right into Tunstead Road.*

A charming, family-run B&B that is conveniently located close to the centre of Wroxham and the splendid Norfolk Broads. Norwich is a short drive away and Delaware makes an ideal base from which to explore the lovely county of Norfolk. Bedrooms are comfortable, and freshly cooked breakfasts are served at individual tables. Parking is available, along with free WiFi for guests.

Rooms: 3 rms (2 en suite) (1 pri facs) (1 GF) **Facilities:** FTV tea/coffee WiFi 🛁 **Parking:** 4 **Notes:** LB No children 14 years Closed November to beginning of March

NORTHAMPTONSHIRE

ASHBY ST LEDGERS
Map 11 SP56

Olde Coach House
★★★★ 🛏 INN

tel: 01788 890349 **Main Street CV23 8UN**
email: info@oldecoachhouse.co.uk **web:** www.oldecoachhouse.co.uk
dir: M1 junction 18 onto A428. Follow signs for Daventry (A361), Ashby St Ledgers signed on left.

The Olde Coach House is a delightful old building offering stylish public areas in keeping with the age of the building. There is a large bar and a spacious, raised dining area, with open fires and exposed beams. The accommodation is smartly presented; rooms vary in size but all are equipped to the same high standard with TVs, iPod docking stations and wonderfully comfortable beds. The property benefits from excellent parking and outside areas for dining and drinking.

Rooms: 4 en suite 11 annexe en suite (6 GF) **Facilities:** FTV iPod docking station Lounge tea/coffee Dinner available Direct dial WiFi ⚓ **Extras:** Robes, speciality toiletries, snacks **Parking:** 30

DESBOROUGH
Map 11 SP88

The R Inn
★★★ INN

tel: 01536 648050 & 763510 **11–15 Station Road NN14 2RL**
email: enquiries@ketteringvenues.co.uk **web:** www.desboroughhotel.co.uk
dir: Phone for directions.

The R Inn enjoys a prominent position in the peaceful village of Desborough which is located in the heart of the lovely Ise Valley. There is a popular tapas bar along with well-equipped conference facilities, and a selection of stylish bedrooms that have been appointed to a high standard. Secure parking is available along with free WiFi for guests.

Rooms: 25 en suite (2 fmly) (1 GF) **S** fr £35 **D** fr £40 (room only)* **Facilities:** FTV tea/coffee Dinner available WiFi ⚓ **Conf:** Max 600 Thtr 400 Class 300 Board 50 **Parking:** 40 **Notes:** Civ wed 600

NASSINGTON
Map 12 TL09

The Queens Head Inn
★★★★ ◎ INN

tel: 01780 784006 **54 Station Road PE8 6QB**
email: info@queensheadnassington.co.uk **web:** www.queensheadnassington.co.uk
dir: A1 northbound exit junction 17, follow signs for Yarwell, then Nassington. Queens Head on left on entering the village.

The Queens Head Inn, on the banks of the River Nene in the picturesque village of Nassington, offers a friendly atmosphere and a warm welcome. The adjacent bedrooms are constructed from local stone; each one is smartly appointed and well equipped. Public rooms include a smart lounge bar, a restaurant and a light-filled conservatory dining room.

Rooms: 10 en suite (2 fmly) (10 GF) **Facilities:** FTV tea/coffee Dinner available Direct dial WiFi Fishing ⚓ **Extras:** Home-made biscuits **Conf:** Max 50 Thtr 50 Class 20 Board 20 **Parking:** 45 **Notes:** LB Civ wed 70

NORTHAMPTON
Map 11 SP76

The Hopping Hare
★★★★ ◎◎ INN

tel: 01604 580090 **18 Hopping Hill Gardens, Duston NN5 6PF**
email: info@hoppinghare.com **web:** www.hoppinghare.com
dir: Off A428, 2 miles from centre of Northampton.

Situated in a quiet location just two miles from Northampton city centre, this inn provides luxury accommodation that meets the needs of holidaymakers and business guests alike. Bedrooms have been attractively decorated with high quality soft furnishings, TVs and free WiFi. Dinner can be enjoyed in the restaurant where the food has been awarded two AA Rosettes. A very good selection of dishes is available, with good use made of fresh quality ingredients sourced from local suppliers.

Rooms: 20 en suite (8 fmly) (1 GF) **Facilities:** FTV tea/coffee Dinner available Direct dial WiFi **Parking:** 40

WEEDON BEC
Map 11 SP65

Narrow Boat at Weedon
★★★★ ◎◎ INN

tel: 01327 340333 **Stowe Hill, A5 Watling Street NN7 4RZ**
email: info@narrowboatatweedon.co.uk **web:** www.narrowboatatweedon.co.uk
dir: M1 junction 16 follow signs to Flore and Weedon. In Weedon at crossroads turn left up hill, on left.

The Narrow Boat at Weedon has a superb location beside the Grand Union Canal, just off the A5. Close to both Milton Keynes and Northampton, it makes an ideal location for those wishing to visit Silverstone and the Althorp Estate. There are seven very comfortable en suite bedrooms at the rear of the property, each with external access. Modern British cuisine and traditional pub classics can be enjoyed in both the bar and the restaurant, which has been awarded two AA Rosettes, or out on the heated decking area in the garden by the canal, weather permitting of course.

Rooms: 7 annexe en suite (7 GF) **Facilities:** FTV DVD tea/coffee Dinner available WiFi **Conf:** Max 30 Class 30 Board 30 **Parking:** 40

NORTHUMBERLAND

ALNWICK
Map 21 NU11

The Hogs Head Inn

★★★ ⌂ INN

tel: 01665 606576 & 0191 580 3610 **Hawfinch Drive, Cawledge NE66 2BF**
email: info@hogsheadinnalnwick.co.uk **web:** www.hogsheadinnalnwick.co.uk
dir: *A1 to Alnwick, follow signs for Cawledge Park.*

Purpose built, The Hogs Head Inn took its name from the hostelry featured in the Harry Potter books as it is near Alnwick Castle where much filming took place. Ideally located just off the A1 on the edge of Alnwick, it is a good place to stay if visiting the castle and gardens. It offers comfortable, spacious and well-equipped bedrooms, and WiFi is available throughout the property. The bar and restaurant serve tasty dishes in comfortable, informal surroundings. There is outside seating for alfresco dining.

Rooms: 53 en suite (9 fmly) (25 GF) **Facilities:** FTV Lounge TVL tea/coffee Dinner available Lift WiFi ⛷ **Parking:** 125

AMBLE
Map 21 NU20

The Amble Inn

[U]

tel: 0191 580 3610 **Coquet Enterprise Park, Quay Road NE65 0PE**
email: enquiries@theambleinn.co.uk **web:** www.theambleinnamble.co.uk
dir: *Phone for directions.*

Due to open in late Autumn 2018. The Amble Inn will be a purpose-built modern inn with 30 contemporary-styled bedrooms, situated in the picturesque Northumbrian coastal town of Amble. It is part of The Inn Collection Group who pride themselves on quality food, ales and hospitality.

Rooms: 30 en suite **Facilities:** FTV tea/coffee Dinner available Lift Licensed WiFi

BEADNELL
Map 21 NU23

The Craster Arms

★★★★ ⌂ INN

tel: 01665 720272 & 07958 678280 **The Wynding NE67 5AX**
email: michael@crasterarms.co.uk **web:** www.crasterarms.co.uk
dir: *From A1 junction at Brownieside Head East, through Preston and Chathill to Beadnell.*

Parts of The Craster Arms date back to the 15th century. The property has it all – an open fire, beer garden and spacious well-appointed, comfortable bedrooms. The bar serves real ales along with good quality food using local produce and offers generous portion sizes. Well located in the peaceful village of Beadnell and just a short drive to the beach, Seahouses and Bamburgh with world famous Craster kippers available for breakfast.

Rooms: 3 en suite (2 fmly) (1 GF) **Facilities:** FTV TVL tea/coffee Dinner available WiFi ⛷ Riding **Parking:** 20

BELFORD
Map 21 NU13

Premier Collection

Market Cross Guest House

★★★★★ ⌂ GUEST HOUSE

tel: 01668 213013 & 07595 453208 **1 Church Street NE70 7LS**
email: info@marketcrossbelford.co.uk **web:** www.marketcrossbelford.co.uk
dir: *Exit A1 into village, opposite church.*

Market Cross Guest House goes from strength to strength; the owners have added their own personal slant to the property. Comfortable bedrooms have a whole array of personal touches including Nespresso machines, home baking and mini-fridges.

Rooms: 4 en suite **Facilities:** FTV iPod docking station tea/coffee WiFi ⛷ **Extras:** Home-made snacks, Nespresso machine, mini-fridge, robes, speciality toiletries **Parking:** 4 **Notes:** No children 10 years Closed 23–28 December

Post Office House Bed & Breakfast

★★★★ ⌂ BED AND BREAKFAST

tel: 01668 219622 **2 Church Street NE70 7LS**
email: enquiries@postofficehouse.com **web:** www.postofficehouse.com
dir: *From A1 follow signs for Belford, into village centre, opposite St Marys Church. Parking at rear of property.*

This property was built in 1893 as a dedicated post office with its own sorting room and telegraph facilities, then many years later it was lovingly restored and made into a B&B. Inside are high quality fixtures, fittings and many thoughtful extras. The hospitality is excellent and enhanced with home-baking as well as the offer of a glass of the famous Lindisfarne Mead. Breakfast is a highlight of a stay. This is a wonderful location, close to the coastal areas of Bamburgh and Seahouses but just a few minutes' drive from the A1. The Cheviots are also in easy striking distance.

Rooms: 3 en suite (1 GF) **S** fr £79 **D** fr £89* **Facilities:** FTV tea/coffee WiFi ⛷ **Extras:** Nespresso machine, chocolates, speciality toiletries, robes, slippers **Parking:** 3 **Notes:** No children 15 years Closed 24–26 December

BERWICK-UPON-TWEED
Map 21 NT95

Premier Collection

The Captain's Quarters

★★★★★ GUEST ACCOMMODATION

tel: 01289 763209 & 07591 598574 **1 Sallyport, Off Bridge Street TD15 1EZ**
email: info@sallyport.co.uk **web:** www.thecaptainsquartersberwick.co.uk
dir: *Phone for directions.*

The Captain's Quarters, a Grade II listed townhouse dating back to the 17th century, is centrally located in the heart of the old town area. All bedrooms are individually designed and presented to a high standard; stairs have to be negotiated to all bedrooms and the rooms at the top of the property have sloping roofs. Very good extras are provided as standard along with high-quality decor, fittings, artwork and objets d'art. Accommodation is sold on a room-only basis with breakfast as an extra and delivered to your room. Warm and genuine hospitality is a given here.

Rooms: 5 en suite **D** fr £95 (room only)* **Facilities:** STV DVD tea/coffee WiFi ⛷

Rob Roy Bed & Breakfast

★★★★ BED AND BREAKFAST

tel: 01289 306428 **Dock Road, Tweedmouth TD15 2BE**
email: therobroy@hotmail.co.uk **web:** www.robroyberwick.co.uk
dir: *Phone for directions.*

The Rob Roy Bed & Breakfast enjoys views over the Tweed estuary and across to the historical border town of Berwick-upon-Tweed. This family-run business delivers high standards of accommodation. Breakfast offers good quality food and a great start to the day. The town centre is only a five-minute walk away whilst Spittle Beach and promenade is just 10 minutes in the opposite direction.

Rooms: 5 en suite (1 fmly) **Facilities:** tea/coffee Licensed WiFi 🔒 **Notes:** No children Closed 25 December

Lindisfarne Inn

★★★ INN

tel: 01289 381223 **Beal TD15 2PD**
email: enquiries@lindisfarneinn.co.uk **web:** www.lindisfarneinn.co.uk
dir: *Exit A1 for Holy Island.*

The Lindisfarne Inn stands on the site of the old Plough Hotel at Beal, on the road leading to Holy Island. The inn has a traditional bar, rustic-style restaurant and comfortably equipped, courtyard bedrooms in the adjacent wing. Food is available all day.

Rooms: 23 annexe en suite (20 fmly) (11 GF) **Facilities:** FTV TVL tea/coffee Dinner available WiFi 🔒 **Parking:** 25

BLYTH · Map 21 NZ38

The Commissioners Quay Inn

★★★ INN

tel: 01670 335060 **Quay Road NE24 3AF**
email: enquiries@cqi-blyth.co.uk **web:** www.commissionersquayinn.com

The Commissioners Quay Inn is part of The Inn Collection group. It is a purpose-built inn that offers high levels of comfort and quality along with wonderful hospitality and customer care. The spacious, modern bedrooms are well appointed, and some rooms that face the sea have their own private balcony with seating. The large bar and restaurant area serves food all day plus a great selection of real ales and cocktails. There is ample parking including a charging point for an electric car.

Rooms: 40 en suite (8 fmly) **Facilities:** FTV tea/coffee Dinner available Lift WiFi 🔒 **Parking:** 90

CHATTON · Map 21 NU02

Percy Arms

★★★★ 🍴 🍷 INN

tel: 01668 215244 **Main Street NE66 5PS**
email: percyarmschatton@gmail.com **web:** www.percyarmschatton.co.uk
dir: *From A1 onto B6348 signed Chatton, in village centre.*

The Percy Arms is ideally located in the tranquil village of Chatton just a short drive from the A1. Alnwick, Seahouses, Bamburgh and Holy Island are all easily accessible, as are some wonderful beaches on the Northumbrian coastline. Appointed to a very high standard, bedrooms and their en suites are luxurious and

comfortable. The pub boasts a number of local real ales and offers a warm welcome. The decor is sympathetic to the age and style of the building. The food is good, with the relaxed menu making the best of what local suppliers have to offer.

Rooms: 5 en suite (3 fmly) **Facilities:** FTV tea/coffee Dinner available WiFi 🔒 **Extras:** Robes **Conf:** Max 40 Thtr 40 Class 40 Board 40 **Parking:** 30 **Notes:** LB Civ wed 60

CRAMLINGTON · Map 21 NZ27

Innkeeper's Lodge Cramlington

★★★ INN

tel: 03451 551551 **Blagdon Lane NE23 8AU**
email: info@innkeeperslodge.com **web:** www.innkeeperslodge.com
dir: *Phone for directions.*

Just off the A1, this Innkeeper's Lodge, The Snowy Owl, overlooks open countryside and has a beer garden to enjoy in summer plus plenty of parking. The comfortable, updated bedrooms have Hypnos beds, digital TVs, desks, tea- and coffee-making facilities, power showers and free WiFi as standard; family rooms are available. In the stylish eating areas, guests can choose from wide-ranging, seasonal menus.

Rooms: 18 en suite (4 fmly) (10 GF) **Facilities:** FTV tea/coffee Dinner available Direct dial WiFi **Parking:** 50

FALSTONE · Map 21 NY78

Pheasant Inn

★★★★ 🍴 🍷 INN

tel: 01434 240382 **Stannersburn NE48 1DD**
email: stay@thepheasantinn.com **web:** www.thepheasantinn.com
dir: *From A69 (north of Hexham) take A6079 signed Otterburn and Bellingham. Left onto B6320 signed Bellingham. Before Bellingham follow Hesleyside sign, then signs for Kielder and Stannersburn.*

Pheasant Inn is a traditional, charming country inn; it has character, good food and warm hospitality. Bright modern bedrooms, some with their own entrances, can be found in stone buildings adjoining the inn. Delicious home-cooked meals are served in the bar with its low-beamed ceilings and exposed stone walls, or in the attractive dining room. Dogs are welcome by arrangement.

Rooms: 8 annexe en suite (1 fmly) (5 GF) **Facilities:** tea/coffee Dinner available WiFi 🔒 **Extras:** Speciality toiletries **Parking:** 40 **Notes:** LB Closed 4 days Christmas RS November to March closed Monday and Tuesday

FELTON · Map 21 NU10

Birchwood House

★★★★ 🍴 GUEST ACCOMMODATION

tel: 01670 787828 **Kitswell Dene NE65 9NZ**
email: gbblewitt@btinternet.com **web:** www.birchwood-house.co.uk
dir: *Just off A1. Take 2nd Swarland exit, bear left, left again.*

Ideally located for the A1, this spacious house combines very high standards of accommodation with warmth and great hospitality. The modern bedrooms and en suites cater well for guests, and a fantastic large lounge is also made available. A well-cooked breakfast will set you up for your day.

Rooms: 3 en suite (3 GF) **Facilities:** FTV iPod docking station TVL tea/coffee WiFi **Parking:** 20 **Notes:** No children 14 years

FELTON *continued*

The Northumberland Arms

★★★★ 🚐 INN

tel: 01670 787370 **The Peth, West Thirston NE65 9EE**
email: thenorthumberlandarmsfelton@gmail.com
web: www.northumberlandarms-felton.co.uk
dir: *From A1, follow signs for coastal route/Felton.*

The Northumberland Arms enjoys a wonderful location just a mile away from the A1. Built back in the 1820s by the 3rd Duke of Northumberland as a coaching inn, it overlooks the River Coquet. The standards are high in all areas from the warm and welcoming bar to the conservatory and main restaurant. Bedrooms are very well appointed, combining the age and character of the building with quality furniture, fixtures and fittings. Finishing touches are provided with an array of luxurious extras which are the icing on the cake. Look for real ales and excellent food which uses the best that Northumbria's larder has to offer.

Rooms: 6 en suite (1 fmly) **S** fr £133 **D** fr £160* **Facilities:** FTV tea/coffee Dinner available Direct dial WiFi ⅃ **Extras:** Speciality toiletries **Conf:** Max 35 Thtr 35 Class 35 Board 35 **Parking:** 20 **Notes:** LB Civ wed 40

FORD
Map 21 NT93

The Estate House

★★★★ GUEST HOUSE

tel: 01890 820668 & 07436 266951 **TD15 2PX**
email: admin@theestatehouse.info **web:** www.theestatehouse.info
dir: *1 mile from A697, follow signs to Ford on B6354.*

Located in the heart of peaceful Ford village, this Edwardian house is set in its own mature gardens. A pet-friendly house that offers spacious, well-appointed accommodation with well-dressed and comfortable beds. A guests' lounge is available, and during the day the property runs a popular tea room. This makes a wonderful base from which to tour this area of Northumberland.

Rooms: 4 rms (3 en suite) (1 pri facs) (1 fmly) **Facilities:** FTV DVD iPod docking station TVL tea/coffee Dinner available Licensed WiFi ⤳ Fishing 🔒 **Extras:** Bottled water – complimentary

HAYDON BRIDGE
Map 21 NY86

Old Repeater Station

★★★★ BED AND BREAKFAST

tel: 01434 688668 & 07941 238641 **Military Road, Grindon NE47 6NQ**
email: les.gibson@tiscali.co.uk **web:** www.hadrians-wall-bedandbreakfast.co.uk
dir: *Phone for directions.*

Old Repeater Station started life as one of a number of buildings used as repeater stations on the Newcastle to Carlisle line. Now converted into a bed and breakfast, it enjoys an enviable location roughly half way along the world-famous Hadrian's Wall. This B&B offers simple, practical accommodation which makes it an ideal stop-off point for anyone walking the wall or for guests looking to explore this historic area. Dinner, by prior arrangement, is offered, and for walkers and cyclists there are drying-room facilities. Family-style breakfasts use quality, locally sourced produce. Guest have use of a comfortable lounge as well as seating in the garden overlooking Sewingshield Crags.

Rooms: 4 en suite (1 fmly) (2 GF) **Facilities:** FTV TVL tea/coffee Dinner available Licensed WiFi 🔒 **Parking:** 4 **Notes:** Closed November to February

HEXHAM
Map 21 NY96

The Barrasford Arms

★★★★ 🏵 INN

tel: 01434 681237 **Barrasford NE48 4AA**
email: barrasfordarms@outlook.com **web:** www.barrasfordarms.co.uk
dir: *Phone for directions.*

This ivy-clad country inn is located in the peaceful village of Barrasford, close to Hadrian's Wall, and is surrounded by the undulating grandeur of the Northumberland hills. Bedrooms differ in size but all offer comfort along with some thoughtful extras. Public areas have benefited from a refurbishment; the three dining rooms are kitted out with rustic furniture and the walls hung with pictures of the inn in bygone days. Owner and chef, Michael Eames works to a modern English template, the emphasis firmly placed on produce from local estates and punchy flavours for his award-winning restaurant. Salmon fishing on the North Tyne River with a ghillie can be arranged.

Rooms: 7 en suite (1 fmly) **S** fr £65 **D** fr £95* **Facilities:** STV FTV tea/coffee Dinner available WiFi 🔒 **Parking:** 30 **Notes:** LB

LONGFRAMLINGTON
Map 21 NU10

The Granby Inn

★★★★ 🚐 INN

tel: 01665 570228 & 570362 **Front Street NE65 8DP**
email: info@thegranbyinn.co.uk **web:** www.thegranbyinn.co.uk
dir: *Exit A1 onto A697 signed Coldstream. On right in Longframlington.*

The Granby Inn is a traditional, family-run coaching inn dating back over 250 years, situated in the heart of the village. Bedrooms are comfortable and some have wonderful, far-reaching views to the coast. Food is a real highlight here and the team take great pride in their locally sourced produce. The bar is welcoming and reservations to eat are always recommended.

Rooms: 5 en suite **S** fr £45 **D** fr £55* **Facilities:** FTV DVD tea/coffee Dinner available Direct dial WiFi 🔒 **Parking:** 24 **Notes:** LB Closed 25–26 December, 1 January

NEWTON-ON-THE-MOOR
Map 21 NU10

The Cook and Barker Inn

★★★★ 🏵 INN

tel: 01665 575234 **NE65 9JY**
email: info@cookandbarkerinn.co.uk **web:** www.cookandbarkerinn.co.uk
dir: *North on A1, pass Morpeth. A1 becomes single carriageway for 8 miles, then dual carriageway. Up slight incline 3 miles, follow signs on left to Newton-on-the-Moor.*

Set in the heart of a quiet village, this inn is popular with visitors and locals alike. The emphasis is on food here with interesting home-made dishes offered in the restaurant and bar areas. The bedrooms are smartly furnished and well equipped, and are split between the main house and the adjacent annexe.

Rooms: 1 en suite 15 annexe en suite (2 fmly) (7 GF) **S** fr £89 **D** fr £109 (room only)* **Facilities:** FTV tea/coffee Dinner available Direct dial WiFi **Conf:** Max 50 Thtr 50 Class 50 Board 25 **Parking:** 64 **Notes:** LB

SEAHOUSES   Map 21 NU23

The Olde Ship Inn
★★★★ ⚬ INN

tel: 01665 720200 **NE68 7RD**
email: theoldeship@seahouses.co.uk **web:** www.seahouses.co.uk
dir: *Lower end of main street above harbour.*

Under the same ownership since 1910, this friendly inn overlooks the harbour and is full of character. Lovingly maintained, its sense of history is evident in the amount of nautical memorabilia on display. Public areas include a character bar, a cosy snug, a restaurant and a guests' lounge. The individual bedrooms are smartly presented. Two separate buildings contain executive apartments, all with sea views.

Rooms: 12 en suite 6 annexe en suite (4 GF) **S** fr £50 **D** fr £100* **Facilities:** FTV Lounge TVL tea/coffee Dinner available Direct dial WiFi 🔒 **Parking:** 18 **Notes:** LB No children 10 years Closed December to January

Bamburgh Castle Inn
★★★ INN

tel: 01665 720283 **NE68 7SQ**
email: enquiries@bamburghcastleinn.co.uk **web:** www.bamburghcastleinn.co.uk
dir: *A1 onto B1341 to Bamburgh, B1340 to Seahouses, follow signs to harbour.*

Situated in a prime location on the quayside, this establishment has arguably the best view along the coast. Dating back to the 18th century, the inn has superb dining and bar areas, with outside seating available in warmer weather. There are smart, comfortable bedrooms, many with views of the Farne Islands and the inn's famous namesake, Bamburgh Castle.

Rooms: 31 rms (3 en suite) 15 annexe en suite (7 fmly) (14 GF) **Facilities:** FTV TVL tea/coffee Dinner available WiFi 🔒 🔒 Complimentary use of Seafield Ocean Club **Parking:** 35 **Notes:** LB

STOCKSFIELD   Map 21 NZ06

Premier Collection

The Duke of Wellington Inn
★★★★★ ◎ 🍽 INN

tel: 01661 844446 **Newton NE43 7UL**
email: info@thedukeofwellingtoninn.co.uk **web:** www.thedukeofwellingtoninn.co.uk
dir: *Off A69, follow signs to Newton, 3 miles from Corbridge.*

Set in the peaceful village of Newton, in the Tyne Valley, The Duke of Wellington Inn is reputedly one of Northumberland's oldest pubs. Located close to Corbridge, in Hadrian's Wall country, not far from Newcastle and just minutes from the A69, the inn offers high standards of accommodation, food and hospitality. Generous sized bedrooms have quality beds, bedding and branded toiletries, with every small detail taken care of. The busy bar and restaurant make great use of the best local produce. Terraces outside allow guests to make the best of the fine weather.

Rooms: 7 en suite **Facilities:** FTV DVD iPod docking station tea/coffee Dinner available Direct dial WiFi 🔒 🔒 **Extras:** Speciality toiletries **Parking:** 30

THROPTON   Map 21 NU00

The Three Wheat Heads
★★★★ ⚬ INN

tel: 01669 620262 **NE65 7LR**
email: info@threewheatheads.co.uk **web:** www.threewheatheads.co.uk
dir: *On B6341, 2 miles north of Rothbury.*

The Three Wheat Heads is located on the edge of the Northumberland National Park just a few miles from Rothbury. All bedrooms are decorated to a high standard, and most offer picture-postcard, countryside views. Good food is served in a choice of areas and there's a beer garden to the rear of the property.

Rooms: 5 en suite (1 fmly) **Facilities:** FTV tea/coffee Dinner available WiFi 🔒 Fishing 🔒 **Parking:** 14 **Notes:** LB

NOTTINGHAMSHIRE

BLIDWORTH
Map 16 SK55

The Black Bull

★★★★ ◎◎ INN

tel: 01623 490222 **Main Street NG21 0QH**
email: info@blackbullblidworth.co.uk **web:** www.blackbullblidworth.co.uk
dir: *M1 junction 27, A608 east, left at Derby roundabout, right onto B6020. Into Blidworth, 1st right after St Marys Church.*

The Black Bull in the village of Blidworth can trace its history as an ale house back to the 17th century. It is appointed to a high standard in a contemporary manner, but still retains many traditional features. The inn provides a comfortable and friendly environment in which to have a drink; the restaurant provides a wide range of well-cooked, good quality, locally-sourced dishes, and the bedrooms are spacious and encourage a good night's sleep.

Rooms: 4 en suite (1 fmly) **S** fr £75 **D** fr £75* **Facilities:** FTV iPod docking station tea/coffee Dinner available WiFi ⌖ ♨ Local cycle hire with discount **Extras:** Bottled water, biscuits **Parking:** 6 **Notes:** Closed 24–26 December, 31 December

COTGRAVE
Map 11 SK63

Jerico Farm

★★★★ ♨ FARMHOUSE

tel: 01949 81733 **Fosse Way NG12 3HG**
email: info@jericofarm.co.uk **web:** www.jericofarm.co.uk
dir: *Off A46, signed Kinoulton. North of junction with A606.*

A friendly relaxed atmosphere is offered at Jerico Farm, an attractive building, which stands in the beautiful Nottinghamshire countryside just off the A46, close to Nottingham, Trent Bridge and the National Water Sports Centre. Day rooms include a comfortable lounge, and a separate dining room in which substantial, tasty breakfasts are served overlooking the gardens. Spacious bedrooms are individually appointed and thoughtfully equipped.

Rooms: 3 en suite (1 fmly) **Facilities:** FTV TVL tea/coffee WiFi Fishing
Extras: Speciality toiletries **Parking:** 4 **Notes:** No children 10 years Closed 24 December to 2 January 150 acres mixed

EDWINSTOWE
Map 16 SK66

The Forest Lodge

★★★★ INN

tel: 01623 824443 **Church Street NG21 9QA**
email: reception@forestlodgehotel.co.uk **web:** www.forestlodgehotel.co.uk
dir: *A614 into Edwinstowe. On B6034, opposite St Mary's church.*

Situated in the heart of Sherwood Forest, The Forest Lodge is a 17th-century coaching inn that provides the visitor with a warm and homely base from which to explore this fascinating and historic area. The bedrooms have been tastefully finished and the bar provides home comforts and good company. Food is served in the bar and in the restaurant.

Rooms: 8 en suite 5 annexe en suite (2 fmly) (5 GF) **S** fr £75 **D** fr £80*
Facilities: FTV tea/coffee Dinner available WiFi ⌖ ♨ **Extras:** Speciality toiletries – complimentary **Conf:** Max 75 Thtr 75 Class 45 Board 50 **Parking:** 37

ELTON
Map 11 SK73

Premier Collection

The Grange

★★★★★ BED AND BREAKFAST

tel: 07887 952181 **Sutton Lane NG13 9LA**
email: d.bmasson@btinternet.com **web:** www.thegrangebedandbreakfastnotts.co.uk
dir: *From Grantham A1 onto A52 to Elton crossroads, left 200 yards, The Grange on right.*

Parts of this lovely house date back to the early 17th century and the rooms command fine views across the gardens and rolling open countryside. Bedrooms contain many thoughtful extras and fine hospitality is assured from the proprietors. There is also a lounge as well as a reading room for residents' use, both furnished in warm tones with welcoming soft sofas and wood-burning stoves.

Rooms: 3 en suite **S** fr £55 **D** fr £85* **Facilities:** FTV DVD Lounge TVL tea/coffee WiFi ♨ **Extras:** Chocolate, snacks, orange juice, water – complimentary **Parking:** 8

MANSFIELD
Map 16 SK56

Bridleways Guest House & Holiday Homes

★★★★ GUEST HOUSE

tel: 01623 635725 **Newlands Road, Forest Town NG19 0HU**
email: bridleways@outlook.com **web:** www.stayatbridleways.co.uk
dir: *From Mansfield take B6030 towards New Clipstone. Right at roundabout, follow Crown Farm Industrial Park sign. 1st left into Newlands Road. Guest house on left.*

Beside a quiet bridleway that leads to Vicar Water Country Park and Sherwood Pines Forest Park, this friendly guest house is a good touring base for walking, cycling or sightseeing. The double, twin and family bedrooms are particularly spacious and all are en suite. Lovely breakfasts are served in a cottage-style dining room.

Rooms: 9 en suite (1 fmly) (2 GF) **S** fr £49 **D** fr £82.50* **Facilities:** FTV tea/coffee WiFi ♨ **Parking:** 14

NEWARK-ON-TRENT
Map 17 SK75

The Hollies

★★★★ BED AND BREAKFAST

tel: 01636 707486 & 07880 722323 **41 Victoria Street NG24 4UU**
email: caroline@theholliesnewark.co.uk **web:** www.theholliesnewark.co.uk
dir: *2.4 miles to A1, 1 mile from A46.*

The Hollies, in the historic town of Newark, is a beautiful Georgian townhouse that has now been refurbished to offer three attractive, boutique-style bedrooms, each with its own private bathroom or en suite. A wonderful breakfast is offered every morning. The attractive drawing room is an ideal venue for weddings, and owner Caroline offers bespoke bridal packages on request.

Rooms: 3 rms (2 en suite) (1 pri facs) **Facilities:** FTV Lounge tea/coffee WiFi
Extras: Snack machine

NOTTINGHAM
Map 11 SK53

See also Cotgrave

Premier Collection

Restaurant Sat Bains with Rooms

★★★★★ @@@@@ RESTAURANT WITH ROOMS

tel: 0115 986 6566 **Lenton Lane, Trentside NG7 2SA**
email: info@restaurantsatbains.net **web:** www.restaurantsatbains.com
dir: *M1 junction 24, A453 Nottingham south. Over River Trent into central lane to roundabout. Left, left again towards river. Establishment on left after bend.*

This charming restaurant with rooms, a stylish conversion of Victorian farm buildings, is situated on the river and close to the industrial area of Nottingham. The bedrooms create a warm atmosphere by using quality soft furnishings together with antique and period furniture; suites and four-poster rooms are available. Public areas are chic and cosy, and the delightful restaurant complements the truly outstanding, world-famous cuisine.

Rooms: 7 en suite **Facilities:** STV tea/coffee Dinner available **Parking:** 22
Notes: No children 8 years Closed 1st week January and 2 weeks mid August

The Yellow House

★★★★ BED AND BREAKFAST

tel: 0115 926 2280 **7 Littlegreen Road, Woodthorpe NG5 4LE**
email: suzanne.prewsmith1@gmail.com **web:** www.bandb-nottingham.co.uk
dir: *Exit A60 (Mansfield Road) north from city centre into Thackeray's Lane, over roundabout, right into Whernside Road to crossroads, left into Littlegreen Road, house on left.*

This semi-detached private house is in an easily-accessible and quiet residential suburb to the northeast of the city. The one purpose-built bedroom contains many thoughtful extras. A warm welcome is assured here and the proprietors' pet dog is also very friendly.

Rooms: 1 en suite **S** fr £55 **D** fr £75* **Facilities:** FTV tea/coffee WiFi **Parking:** 1
Notes: No children Closed 24–26 and 31 December, 1 January

Innkeeper's Lodge Nottingham, Lowdham

★★★ INN

tel: 03451 551551 **Old Epperstone Road, Lowdham NG14 7BZ**
email: info@innkeeperslodge.com **web:** www.innkeeperslodge.com
dir: *From city centre follow A612, signed Southwell onto A6097 (Epperstone bypass). Through Lowdham, left into Old Epperstone Road.*

A very well-presented building that has been styled to have a fresh and contemporary look. The inn provides somewhere to eat, drink and stay for locals and guests alike in a comfortable and friendly environment. There is a range of comfortable seating for relaxing or dining. The menu offers a good range of pub staples and more refined dishes.

Rooms: 11 en suite (1 fmly) **Facilities:** FTV tea/coffee Dinner available WiFi
Parking: 30 **Notes:** LB

RETFORD
Map 17 SK78

Premier Collection

Blacksmiths

★★★★★ @ RESTAURANT WITH ROOMS

tel: 01777 818171 **Town Street, Clayworth DN22 9AD**
email: enquiries@blacksmithsclayworth.com **web:** www.blacksmithsclayworth.com
dir: *From A631, 2.4 miles to Clayworth.*

Blacksmiths is a modern restaurant with annexed accommodation, situated in the quiet village of Clayworth, which is a short drive from Retford. Meals in the restaurant are one of the many highlights of a stay here – the hearty breakfasts can be delivered as room service. Bedrooms have been finished to an excellent standard and include many gadgets and accessories such as climate control, large wide-screen TVs, WiFi, fluffy bathrobes and luxurious toiletries. A warm welcome is guaranteed at this owner-run establishment.

Rooms: 4 en suite (2 fmly) (2 GF) **S** fr £108 **D** fr £120 **Facilities:** FTV iPod docking station tea/coffee Dinner available WiFi **Conf:** Max 120 Thtr 70 Class 20 Board 20 **Parking:** 31 **Notes:** Civ wed 70

WORKSOP
Map 16 SK57

Acorn Lodge

★★★★ GUEST ACCOMMODATION

tel: 01909 478383 **85 Potter Street S80 2HL**
email: info@acornlodgeworksop.co.uk **web:** www.acornlodgeworksop.co.uk
dir: *A1 onto A57. Take B6040 (town centre) through Manton. Lodge on right, 100 metres past Priory.*

Originally part of the community house of the Priory Church, this property has been modernised to offer comfortable, well-appointed accommodation. Good breakfasts are served in the pleasant breakfast room and ample private parking is available at the rear.

Rooms: 7 en suite (2 fmly) **Facilities:** FTV tea/coffee WiFi **Parking:** 15 **Notes:** LB

OXFORDSHIRE

ABINGDON-ON-THAMES
Map 5 SU49

Premier Collection

B&B Rafters

★★★★★ BED AND BREAKFAST

tel: 01865 391298 & 07824 378720 **Abingdon Road, Marcham OX13 6NU**
email: enquiries@bnb-rafters.co.uk **web:** www.bnb-rafters.co.uk
dir: *A34 onto A415 towards Witney. Rafters on A415 in Marcham adjacent to pedestrian crossing, on right.*

Set amid immaculate gardens, this modern house is built in a half-timbered style and offers spacious accommodation together with a warm welcome. Bedrooms are stylishly furnished and equipped in a boutique style with a range of homely extras. Comprehensive breakfasts feature local and organic produce whenever possible.

Rooms: 4 en suite **S** fr £60 **D** fr £119* **Facilities:** FTV DVD iPod docking station Lounge tea/coffee WiFi **Extras:** Speciality toiletries, bottled water – complimentary **Parking:** 4 **Notes:** No children 12 years

ABINGDON-ON-THAMES *continued*

Abbey Guest House

★★★★ BED AND BREAKFAST

tel: 01235 537020 & 07976 627252 **136 Oxford Road OX14 2AG**
email: info@abbeyguest.uk **web:** www.abbeyguest.uk
dir: *1 mile from A34 southbound, exit at North Abingdon.*

A warm welcome is assured at Abbey Guest House. This well maintained property offers very comfortable, modern bedrooms with many useful extras and a relaxed atmosphere. Terry's business ethos is firmly focused on inclusivity, and the guest house's website offers comprehensive information on the facilities available for guests with different forms of disability. There are a couple of local pubs nearby as well as very good bus links to Oxford from just outside the property. Freshly prepared breakfasts are served in the airy dining room overlooking the garden. Free WiFi is available throughout the house and off-road parking is provided.

Rooms: 7 en suite (2 fmly) (1 GF) **S** fr £55 **D** fr £90* **Facilities:** FTV DVD Lounge tea/coffee Lift WiFi ⚓ **Extras:** Use of fridge and microwave, guest PC **Parking:** 7

BANBURY　　　　　　　　　　　　　　　Map 11 SP44

The Three Pigeons Inn

★★★★ ⓜ INN

tel: 01295 275220 **3 Southam Road OX16 2ED**
email: manager@thethreepigeons.com **web:** www.thethreepigeons.com
dir: *M40 junction 11 onto A422 signed Banbury. Left at Southam Road roundabout onto A361. Inn on left at lights.*

Located in the centre of Banbury, this 17th-century coaching inn offers high levels of quality and comfort. The individually styled bedrooms with well-equipped bathrooms overlook the attractive courtyard garden. Low beams and uneven floors add to the inn's charm. Guests can enjoy a drink in the comfortable bar and should not miss the carefully prepared dishes at dinner. Free WiFi and on-site parking are available.

Rooms: 3 en suite (1 fmly) **Facilities:** STV FTV tea/coffee Dinner available Direct dial WiFi **Conf:** Max 20 Thtr 20 Class 20 Board 20 **Parking:** 11

Ashlea Guest House

★★★★ GUEST HOUSE

tel: 01295 250539 & 07818 431429 **58 Oxford Road OX16 9AN**
email: enquiry@ashleaguesthouse.co.uk **web:** www.ashleaguesthouse.co.uk
dir: *M40 junction 11, follow signs to Banbury. At 2nd roundabout take 1st exit (Concord Avenue), next roundabout 1st exit. Through 3 sets of lights, into right lane at 4th set of lights, opposite junction.*

Ashlea Guest House is a family-run establishment where the husband and wife team ensure their guests are warmly welcomed and made to feel at home. There is a choice of well-presented rooms to match all budgets. The guest house is the perfect base to explore the historic town of Banbury or the beautiful Cotswold countryside.

Rooms: 6 rms (5 en suite) (1 pri facs) 6 annexe en suite (1 fmly) (5 GF) **Facilities:** FTV DVD tea/coffee WiFi ⚓ **Parking:** 13 **Notes:** LB

Horse & Groom Inn

★★★★ ⌂ INN

tel: 01295 722142 & 07774 210943 **Milcombe OX15 4RS**
email: horseandgroominn@gmail.com **web:** www.thehorseandgroominn.co.uk
dir: *M40 junction 11, A422 towards Banbury. Onto A361 signed Chipping Norton, past Bloxham turn right signed Milcombe. At end of village.*

This 17th-century coaching house is a traditional village pub with a good atmosphere, friendly service and comfortable, well-appointed bedrooms. The restaurant offers a good choice of well-prepared and tasty dishes. The establishment is convenient for Banbury, Stratford-upon-Avon and the Cotswolds.

Rooms: 4 en suite (1 fmly) **Facilities:** FTV DVD iPod docking station tea/coffee Dinner available WiFi ⚓ Fishing ⚓ **Conf:** Max 40 Thtr 40 Class 30 Board 20 **Parking:** 20

BURFORD

Map 5 SP21

The Angel at Burford

★★★★ ◉ INN

tel: 01993 822714 **14 Witney Street OX18 4SN**
email: enquiries@theangelatburford.co.uk **web:** www.theangelatburford.co.uk
dir: *Phone for directions.*

Just off the high street in the picturesque market town of Burford, this 16th-century coaching inn features beamed ceilings and open fires. Guests can dine well in the restaurant, and the character bedrooms are thoughtfully equipped. Service is friendly here and families, children and dogs are all welcome.

Rooms: 3 en suite **D** fr £110* **Facilities:** FTV DVD iPod docking station Lounge tea/coffee Dinner available WiFi ♨ **Extras:** Refreshments – complimentary **Notes:** LB

The Maytime Inn

★★★★ ⬟ ⬭ INN

tel: 01993 822068 **Asthall OX18 4HW**
email: info@themaytime.com **web:** www.themaytime.com
dir: *Phone for directions.*

This 17th-century inn has retained its country charm albeit with some modern enhancement, and is located just a few miles outside Burford, known as 'The

gateway to the Cotswolds'. The six en suite bedrooms are individual in design and offer a very comfortable stay. Food is available every day and alfresco dining is possible in the delightful garden which overlooks the countryside.

The Maytime Inn

Rooms: 2 en suite 4 annexe en suite (6 GF) **S** fr £95 **D** fr £95* **Facilities:** FTV iPod docking station tea/coffee Dinner available Direct dial WiFi ♨ Petanque **Extras:** Speciality toiletries **Conf:** Max 22 Thtr 15 Class 15 Board 22 **Parking:** 30 **Notes:** LB

See advert below

The Highway Inn

★★★★ ⬭ INN

tel: 01993 823661 & 07725 146006 **117 High Street OX18 4RG**
email: scott.williamson@thehighwayinn.co.uk **web:** www.thehighwayinn.co.uk
dir: *Phone for directions.*

Built in 1480, The Highway Inn has had many guises over the years and first welcomed overnight travellers in the early 1920s. Following a refurbishment, it now provides guests with modern day comfort, yet retains many of its period features including an original fireplace in the bar area and the beautiful Oriel windows. Rooms vary in size and shape, with each individually decorated. A warm welcome is assured.

Rooms: 11 rms (10 en suite) (1 pri facs) **Facilities:** FTV tea/coffee Dinner available WiFi **Extras:** Speciality toiletries **Conf:** Max 20 Thtr 20 Class 20 Board 20

BURFORD *continued*

The Bull at Burford

★★★★ INN

tel: 01993 822220 **105 High Street OX18 4RG**
email: info@bullatburford.co.uk **web:** www.bullatburford.co.uk
dir: *In town centre, on the High Street.*

Situated in the heart of a pretty Cotswold town, The Bull was originally built in 1475 as a rest house for the local priory. It now has stylish, attractively presented bedrooms that reflect plenty of charm and character. Dinner is a must and the award-winning restaurant has an imaginative menu along with an excellent choice of wines. Lunch is served daily and afternoon tea is popular. There is a residents' lounge, and free WiFi is available.

Rooms: 15 en suite 3 annexe en suite (1 fmly) (3 GF) **Facilities:** STV FTV Lounge tea/coffee Dinner available WiFi **Parking:** 6 **Notes:** LB

The Golden Pheasant Inn

★★★★ INN

tel: 01993 823223 **91 High Street OX18 4QA**
email: bournehospitality@hotmail.co.uk **web:** www.goldenpheasantburford.com
dir: *Phone for directions.*

This attractive inn is set on Burford's main street and dates, in part, back to the 16th century. Bedrooms vary in size but are well furnished with attractive fabrics and some period furniture. The bar and open-plan restaurant is full of character, and lunch and dinner are served here daily.

Rooms: 12 rms (11 en suite) (1 pri facs) 6 annexe en suite (5 GF) **S** fr £65 **D** fr £65* **Facilities:** FTV TVL tea/coffee Dinner available WiFi **Parking:** 8 **Notes:** Closed 24 December RS 25 December no accommodation, bar open

CULHAM
Map 5 SU59

The Railway Inn

★★★ INN

tel: 01235 528046 **Station Road OX14 3BT**
email: info@railwayinnculham.co.uk **web:** www.railwayinnculham.co.uk
dir: *2.5 miles southeast of Abingdon-on-Thames on A415. Turn left signed Culham railway station.*

The Railway Inn is located beside Culham railway station and is the perfect base to explore Abingdon-on-Thames, Didcot and Oxford. The inn offers a choice of comfortable and affordable rooms, a selection of real ales and home-cooked food. In addition, there is a permanent marquee in the garden, which is suitable for all types of occasions.

Rooms: 6 rms (5 en suite) (1 pri facs) 4 annexe en suite (2 fmly) (1 GF) **S** fr £65 **D** fr £83* **Facilities:** FTV Lounge TVL tea/coffee Dinner available WiFi **Extras:** Coffee machine **Parking:** 30 **Notes:** Closed 24 December to 2 January

CUMNOR
Map 5 SP40

Bear and Ragged Staff

★★★★ ◎ INN

tel: 01865 862329 **28 Appleton Road OX2 9QH**
email: enquiries@bearandraggedstaff.com **web:** www.bearandraggedstaff.com
dir: *Phone for directions.*

On the outskirts of Oxford, this country inn offers a range of dining options along with well-appointed accommodation suitable for both business or leisure guests. The friendly pub has much old-world charm – flagstone floors, mullioned windows, roughcast stone walls and large fireplaces – but has added a contemporary twist. The smart restaurant offers forward-thinking menus of trend-conscious British food; the dinner menu, coupled with daily specials, makes good use of local produce. Of the nine bedrooms, four are in converted cottages and five above the inn, which due to the age of this Grade II listed property are of varying shapes and sizes.

Rooms: 9 en suite

FARINGDON
Map 5 SU29

Premier Collection

Buscot Manor B&B

★★★★★ BED AND BREAKFAST

tel: 01367 252225 & 07973 831690 **SN7 8DA**
email: romneypargeter@hotmail.co.uk **web:** www.buscotmanor.co.uk
dir: *Phone for directions.*

Delightfully located in a peaceful village, Buscot Manor dates from 1692 and is full of character and quality. Guests are welcome to use the two comfortable lounges in addition to the pleasant gardens, where tea may be enjoyed in the summer months. The two upper-floor bedrooms have traditional four-poster beds. A more contemporary room is located on the ground floor. Breakfast is taken around one large table in the elegant dining room.

Rooms: 2 en suite 1 annexe en suite (3 fmly) (1 GF) **Facilities:** FTV DVD Lounge TVL tea/coffee WiFi ⚓ Fishing Riding Sauna Gym ⚓ Watersports weekends available **Extras:** Speciality toiletries, fruit, snacks **Conf:** Max 12 Board 12 **Parking:** 30

The Trout Inn

★★★★ ◎ INN

tel: 01367 870382 **Buckland Marsh SN7 8RF**
email: info@troutinn.co.uk **web:** www.troutinn.co.uk
dir: *A420 (Swindon to Oxford road), turn signed Bampton. Inn 2 miles on right.*

Located in a tranquil location just a couple of miles from the village of Bampton and within a short distance of the Cotswolds, this inn offers stylish and comfortably appointed accommodation. The inn boasts many original features including flagstone flooring and exposed beams yet is tastefully appointed with modern furnishings and roaring log-burners. The inn is located right on the River Thames with a large beer garden. A hearty breakfast is served daily in the restaurant and lunch and dinner is available throughout the week.

Rooms: 6 en suite (1 fmly) (4 GF) **Facilities:** STV tea/coffee Dinner available Direct dial WiFi **Extras:** Speciality toiletries **Conf:** Max 20 Thtr 20 Class 20 Board 20 **Parking:** 25 **Notes:** Civ wed

| GORING | Map 5 SU68 |

The Miller of Mansfield

★★★★ ◉◉ RESTAURANT WITH ROOMS

tel: 01491 872829 & 07702 853413 **High Street RG8 9AW**
email: reservations@millerofmansfield.com **web:** www.millerofmansfield.com
dir: M4 junction 12, south on A4 towards Newbury. 3rd roundabout onto A340 to Pangbourne. A329 to Streatley, right at lights onto B4009 into Goring.

The frontage of this former coaching inn hides sumptuous rooms furnished in a distinctive and individual style. The two AA Rosette restaurant serves appealing dishes using locally sourced ingredients, and there is a comfortable bar, which serves real ales, fine wines and afternoon tea; a bar menu provides quick bites to eat.

Rooms: 13 en suite (2 fmly) **S** fr £79 **D** fr £99* **Facilities:** FTV Lounge tea/coffee Dinner available WiFi ⥮ Boat hire and beauty therapies can be arranged
Extras: Speciality toiletries, home-made biscuits **Conf:** Max 12 Board 12 **Parking:** 2
Notes: LB Closed 27–28 December

| HENLEY-ON-THAMES | Map 5 SU78 |

Phyllis Court Club

★★★★ ⌂ GUEST ACCOMMODATION

tel: 01491 570500 **Marlow Road RG9 2HT**
email: enquiries@phylliscourt.co.uk **web:** www.phylliscourt.co.uk
dir: A404 onto A4130 into town centre. Follow A4155, 150 metres on right.

Phyllis Court was founded in 1906 as a private members' club and has welcomed many distinguished visitors over the years. Set in 18 acres, with lawns sweeping down to the Thames, it offers a unique blend of traditional elegance and modern comforts. The club takes centre stage during Henley Royal Regatta week, being positioned opposite the finishing line. The individually styled bedrooms are well appointed and very comfortable. There is restricted meal service two days before and after the regattas in June and July. An excellent range of function venues is available, and the Grade II listed Grandstand Pavilion is perfect for weddings.

Rooms: 17 en suite **D** fr £145* **Facilities:** FTV Lounge TVL tea/coffee Dinner available Direct dial Lift Licensed WiFi ⌚ **Extras:** Speciality toiletries, trouser press, magazines **Conf:** Max 250 Thtr 250 Class 100 Board 30 **Parking:** 200
Notes: RS 26–28 December, 2–3 January, regattas June to July limited menu Civ wed 250

Leander Club

★★★★ ⌂ GUEST ACCOMMODATION

tel: 01491 575782 **Leander Way RG9 2LP**
email: events@leander.co.uk **web:** www.leander.co.uk
dir: M4 junction 8/9 follow signs for Henley (A404(M) and A4130). Turn right immediately before Henley Bridge to Club and car park.

This historic rowing club's location on the River Thames is breathtaking, particularly in the morning when the rowers can be seen setting out. Each bedroom is named after colleges and universities and display interesting photos and memorabilia linking them with the Leander Club. The en suite rooms, some overlooking the river, have Hypnos beds, TVs, free WiFi, USB charging points and a complimentary glass of Leander Pink bubbly. Public areas also feature lots of trophies, pictures and artefacts – it all makes for a most interesting and unusual place to stay.

Rooms: 11 en suite (1 fmly) **Facilities:** STV FTV Lounge TVL tea/coffee Dinner available Direct dial Lift Licensed WiFi **Extras:** Snacks – complimentary
Conf: Max 120 Thtr 120 Class 40 Board 20 **Parking:** 60 **Notes:** No children 10 years Closed Christmas to New Year RS 1st week July Henley Royal Regatta Civ wed 120

HENLEY-ON-THAMES *continued*

Badgemore Park Golf Club

★★★★ GUEST ACCOMMODATION

tel: 01491 637300 **Badgemore Park, Badgemore RG9 4NR**
email: info@badgemorepark.com **web:** www.badgemorepark.com
dir: *Phone for directions.*

Located close to Henley-on-Thames, this property offers comfortable guest accommodation in quiet surroundings within the secluded and private walled gardens, situated just 100 metres away from the main clubhouse. In summer months, dinner and a bar are available until 6pm. The venue also caters well for business meetings and comes complete with its own lounge and kitchen. Free WiFi is available.

Rooms: 8 rms annexe (7 en suite) (1 pri facs annexe) (3 fmly) (3 GF) **Facilities:** FTV TVL tea/coffee Licensed WiFi ⚘ **Extras:** Bottled water **Conf:** Max 120 Thtr 120 Class 60 Board 45 **Parking:** 120 **Notes:** Closed 25 December Civ wed 120

The Baskerville

★★★★ ⚜ INN

tel: 0118 940 3332 **Station Road, Lower Shiplake RG9 3NY**
email: enquiries@thebaskerville.com **web:** www.thebaskerville.com
dir: *2 miles south of Henley in Lower Shiplake. Exit A4155 into Station Road, inn signed.*

Located close to Shiplake station and just a short drive from Henley, this smart pub is perfect for a business visit or leisure break. The accommodation is well equipped and it's a good base for exploring the Oxfordshire countryside and surrounding areas. The award-winning dinner menu, coupled with daily specials, makes good use of local produce.

Rooms: 4 en suite (1 fmly) **S** fr £79 **D** fr £89* **Facilities:** FTV tea/coffee Dinner available WiFi ⚘ **Extras:** Bottled water, sweets, speciality toiletries – complimentary **Conf:** Max 15 Thtr 15 Class 15 Board 15 **Parking:** 15 **Notes:** Closed 1 January RS Sunday restaurant closed in evening

HORNTON
Map 11 SP34

Hornton Grounds Country House

★★★★ ⬚ FARMHOUSE

tel: 01295 678318 **OX15 6HH**
email: catherine@horntongrounds.com **web:** www.horntongrounds.co.uk
dir: *From Banbury onto A422 signed Stratford. Through Wroxton, pass Indian Queen pub, next right and follow long drive.*

A very warm welcome waits at Hornton Grounds Country House, an impressive retreat set on a busy working farm. It's an ideal setting for those wishing to explore the north Cotswold countryside. Guests are encouraged to enjoy the extensive grounds on foot, or you can even bring your own horse (stabling available). Evening meals are available by prior arrangement.

Rooms: 4 rms (2 en suite) (2 pri facs) **Facilities:** TVL tea/coffee Dinner available WiFi ⬚ ⬚ Riding ⬚ Stabling for guests' horses **Parking:** 8 **Notes:** 200 acres pigs/beef/sheep

KINGHAM
Map 10 SP22

Premier Collection

The Wild Rabbit

★★★★★ ◉◉◉ ⬚ RESTAURANT WITH ROOMS

tel: 01608 658389 **Church Street OX7 6YA**
email: theteam@thewildrabbit.co.uk **web:** www.thewildrabbit.co.uk
dir: *Phone for directions.*

Situated in the idyllic Cotswold village of Kingham, this Grade II listed Georgian building has been lovingly restored to create a thoroughly modern restaurant with rooms. The very stylish bedrooms, in muted colours, feature exposed brick walls and old beams, and include smart TVs, DAB radios, iPod docks, free WiFi, and luxury toiletries in the stunning en suites. The public spaces are equally noteworthy with a large bar, open-plan restaurant-kitchen and an outside dining area. The food is exceptional, with many French influences evident in the cooking. Service is informal yet professional and very friendly. Ample parking is provided.

Rooms: 11 en suite 1 annexe en suite (1 fmly) (4 GF) **Facilities:** FTV DVD iPod docking station Lounge tea/coffee Dinner available WiFi ⬚ Spa, cookery and floristry classes available at Daylesford Organic Farm **Extras:** Mini-bar — chargeable **Conf:** Max 20 Thtr 20 Board 20 **Parking:** 15

The Kingham Plough

★★★★ ◉◉ ⬚ INN

tel: 01608 658327 **The Green OX7 6YD**
email: book@thekinghamplough.co.uk **web:** www.thekinghamplough.co.uk
dir: *From Chipping Norton, take B4450 to Churchill. Take 2nd right to Kingham, left at T-junction in Kingham. Pub on right.*

The Kingham Plough is a quintessential Cotswold inn set in the pretty village of Kingham, just minutes from the well-known Daylesford Organic Estate. The en suite bedrooms have Cotswold character and offer impressive quality and comfort throughout. The food here is a real draw and has been recognised with two AA Rosettes; the team deliver excellent results using locally sourced produce.

Rooms: 4 en suite 2 annexe en suite (2 fmly) **S** fr £110 **D** fr £145* **Facilities:** FTV DVD iPod docking station Lounge tea/coffee Dinner available WiFi ⬚ ⬚ Discounted rates at local spa **Extras:** Speciality toiletries, home-made biscuits, robes — complimentary; mini-bar chargeable **Parking:** 25 **Notes:** Closed 25 December

MARSTON
Map 5 SP50

Hill Farm

★★★★ BED AND BREAKFAST

tel: 07976 288329 **Mill Lane OX3 0QF**
email: laura@cherbridgecottages.co.uk **web:** www.cherbridgecottages.co.uk
dir: *Phone for directions.*

Hill Farm is set in its own extensive grounds yet is conveniently close to Oxford city centre. This 18th-century cottage has many original features and is most comfortable. Bedrooms are very well appointed and there is a four-poster bed in the larger bedroom. Surrounded by open countryside, there is a pretty walk to the rear of the property along with a show-jumping ground and working stables. Freshly cooked breakfasts feature the best local produce and free WiFi is available throughout the house.

Rooms: 2 rms (1 en suite) (1 pri facs) **Facilities:** FTV Lounge TVL tea/coffee WiFi ⬚ **Conf:** Max 80 Thtr 70 Class 60 Board 50 **Notes:** LB Closed 19 December to 4 January

OXFORD
Map 5 SP50

Premier Collection

Burlington House

★★★★★ ⬚ GUEST ACCOMMODATION

tel: 01865 513513 **374 Banbury Road, Summertown OX2 7PP**
email: stay@burlington-house.co.uk **web:** www.burlington-house.co.uk
dir: *Opposite Oxford Conference Centre on A4165 on corner of Hernes Road and Banbury Road.*

Guests are assured of a warm welcome and attentive service at this smart, beautifully maintained Victorian house, which is within walking distance of Summertown's fashionable restaurants. Elegant, contemporary bedrooms are filled with a wealth of thoughtful extras, and some open onto a pretty patio garden. Memorable breakfasts, served in the delightful dining room, include home-made preserves, fruit breads, granola and excellent coffee.

Rooms: 13 en suite 3 annexe en suite (4 GF) **Facilities:** FTV tea/coffee Direct dial WiFi ⬚ **Parking:** 5 **Notes:** No children 12 years Closed 24 December to 2 January

Galaxie

★★★★ GUEST ACCOMMODATION

tel: 01865 515688 **180 Banbury Road OX2 7BT**
email: info@galaxie.co.uk **web:** www.galaxie.co.uk
dir: *1 mile north of Oxford centre, on right before shops in Summertown.*

In the popular Summertown area of the city, Galaxie has a welcoming atmosphere and good quality accommodation. All the well-equipped bedrooms are very comfortable and come with a range of extra facilities. The attractive conservatory dining room looks over the garden that features sculptures by a local artist.

Rooms: 32 rms (28 en suite) (3 fmly) **Facilities:** TVL tea/coffee Direct dial Lift WiFi **Parking:** 30

OXFORD *continued*

The Oxford Townhouse

★★★★ GUEST ACCOMMODATION

tel: 01865 511122 **88-90 Abingdon Road OX1 4PX**
email: stay@theoxfordtownhouse.co.uk **web:** www.theoxfordtownhouse.co.uk
dir: *Phone for directions.*

The Oxford Townhouse overlooks The Queen's College playing fields and is an ideal base for exploring the city. Spread over two Victorian townhouses, it offers a range of modern, spacious bedrooms. Freshly prepared breakfasts are served at individual tables and service is friendly and attentive. WiFi is available throughout the house and there is secure parking.

Rooms: 15 en suite **S** fr £90 **D** fr £110* **Facilities:** FTV Lounge tea/coffee WiFi **Extras:** Bottled water, soft drinks – complimentary **Parking:** 9
Notes: No children 10 years Closed 24–26 December

Parklands

★★★★ GUEST ACCOMMODATION

tel: 01865 554374 **100 Banbury Road OX2 6JU**
email: stay@parklandsoxford.co.uk **web:** www.parklandsoxford.co.uk
dir: *Phone for directions.*

Parklands, once the home of an Oxford don, enjoys a prominent position along the tree-lined Banbury road and is only a short walk from the city centre. This beautiful Victorian building has a range of individually designed, spacious bedrooms. The walled garden is a peaceful retreat and the residents' lounge is very well appointed. Secure parking is available and free WiFi is provided.

Rooms: 13 en suite **S** fr £70 **D** fr £100* **Facilities:** FTV Lounge tea/coffee Direct dial Licensed WiFi **Extras:** Bottled water – complimentary **Parking:** 14
Notes: No children 18 years Closed 24–26 December

Red Mullions Guest House

★★★★ 🍴 GUEST HOUSE

tel: 01865 742741 **23 London Road, Headington OX3 7RE**
email: stay@redmullions.co.uk **web:** www.redmullions.co.uk
dir: *M40 junction 8, A40. At Headington roundabout, 2nd exit signed Headington into London Road.*

Red Mullions Guest House takes its name from the brick columns between the windows of the building, and is located within easy reach of motorway networks and Oxford city centre. Modern bedrooms offer comfortable accommodation and the hearty breakfasts provide a good start to any day.

Rooms: 16 rms (15 en suite) (1 pri facs) (3 fmly) (7 GF) **S** fr £95 **D** fr £110*
Facilities: STV FTV tea/coffee WiFi **Extras:** Bottled water – complimentary **Parking:** 11

Remont Oxford

★★★★ GUEST ACCOMMODATION

tel: 01865 311020 **367 Banbury Road OX2 7PL**
email: info@remont-oxford.co.uk **web:** www.remont-oxford.co.uk
dir: *Phone for directions.*

Remont Oxford is in the popular Summertown area, some two miles from the city centre. The well-equipped bedrooms and bathrooms are modern and stylish and come with TVs, complimentary WiFi and well-stocked beverage trays; all rooms offer high quality and comfort. Parking is available and there is a delightful garden for guests to enjoy. Cooked and continental buffet breakfasts are served in the light and airy dining room.

Rooms: 18 en suite 7 annexe en suite (2 fmly) (8 GF) **Facilities:** FTV Lounge tea/coffee Lift WiFi **Parking:** 18

The Black Boy

★★★★ INN

tel: 01865 741137 **91 Old High Street, Headington OX3 9HT**
email: abi@theblackboy.uk.com **web:** www.theblackboy.uk.com
dir: *Phone for directions.*

Located in the pretty village of Old Headington, The Black Boy was built in the 1930s and stands in the grounds of a 17th-century inn. It offers guests modern and deeply comfortable rooms each featuring local artwork and designer pieces. Dinner is not to be missed, nor should the well-stocked bar complete with local gins and ales be overlooked. A small number of on-site parking spaces are available. And it's all within a 10-minute drive of Oxford city centre.

Rooms: 5 en suite **S** fr £125 **D** fr £125* **Facilities:** Dinner available

Conifers Guest House

★★★★ GUEST ACCOMMODATION

tel: 01865 763055 **116 The Slade, Headington OX3 7DX**
email: stay@conifersguesthouse.co.uk **web:** www.conifersguesthouse.co.uk
dir: *Exit ring road onto A420 towards city centre. Left onto B4495 (Windmill Road), straight over at lights, house on left past Nuffield Orthopaedic Centre.*

Situated in the Headington area, Conifers is within walking distance of the Headington Hospitals, the Mini plant, Cowley Business Park and Oxford Brookes University, as well as Shotover Country Park. It is an impressive Edwardian house that provides comfortable accommodation in pine-furnished bedrooms. Breakfast is served in a smart, front-facing dining room. The private car park and a large rear garden are bonuses.

Rooms: 12 en suite (4 fmly) **Facilities:** FTV tea/coffee WiFi **Parking:** 8

Cotswold House

★★★★ GUEST ACCOMMODATION

tel: 01865 310558 **363 Banbury Road OX2 7PL**
email: d.r.walker@talk21.com **web:** www.cotswoldhouse.co.uk
dir: *A40 onto A423 into city centre, follow signs to Summertown, house 0.5 mile on right.*

Situated in a leafy avenue close to the northern ring road and Summertown, this well-maintained house offers comfortable, well-equipped bedrooms and a relaxed atmosphere. Enjoy a traditional, hearty breakfast with vegetarian choices, including home-made muesli and fresh fruit, served in the bright attractive dining room.

Rooms: 7 en suite (2 fmly) (1 GF) **S** fr £76 **D** fr £125 **Facilities:** FTV Lounge tea/coffee WiFi ♨ **Parking:** 6 **Notes:** Closed 28 December to 10 January

Manor House

★★★★ GUEST ACCOMMODATION

tel: 01865 727627 **250 Iffley Road OX4 1SE**
email: manorhousehotel@hotmail.com **web:** www.manorhouseoxford.com
dir: *On A4158, 1 mile from city centre.*

This family-run establishment is easily accessible from the city centre and all major road links. The hotel provides informal, friendly and attentive service. The comfortably furnished bedrooms are well equipped. The hotel has a bar but there is a selection of restaurants and popular pubs within easy walking distance. Limited private parking is available.

Rooms: (2 fmly) **S** fr £89 **D** fr £120* **Notes:** Closed 20 December to 20 January

Green Gables

★★★ GUEST ACCOMMODATION

tel: 01865 725870 **326 Abingdon Road OX1 4TE**
email: enquiries@greengables.uk.com **web:** www.greengables.uk.com
dir: *Exit ring road onto A4144 towards city centre, Green Gables 0.5 mile on left.*

A warm welcome is assured at Green Gables, located within easy walking distance of the city centre. Bedrooms are equipped with a range of practical and homely extras, and a comprehensive breakfast is served in the cosy dining room. Guests have free access to the internet in the smart conservatory-lounge, and some private parking is available.

Rooms: 11 en suite (2 fmly) (4 GF) **S** fr £50 **D** fr £85 (room only)* **Facilities:** FTV Lounge tea/coffee WiFi **Parking:** 9 **Notes:** No children 5 years Closed 23-31 December

Oxford Guest House

★★★ GUEST HOUSE

tel: 01865 308833 & 07855 737373 **228 London Road, Headington OX3 9EG**
email: oxfordguesthouse@gmail.com **web:** www.theoxfordguesthouse.co.uk
dir: *M40 junction 8 onto A40 towards Oxford. At Headington roundabout take 2nd exit signed Headington into London Road (A420). On left after 2nd set of lights.*

The purpose-built Oxford Guest House is located in a quiet residential area and offers well-configured bedrooms finished to a very good standard; all have TVs and free WiFi. A choice of breakfasts is served daily in the well-appointed breakfast room. Off-street parking is provided.

Rooms: 6 en suite (1 fmly) (2 GF) **Facilities:** STV FTV tea/coffee WiFi **Parking:** 6 **Notes:** LB

Sports View Guest House

★★★ GUEST HOUSE

tel: 01865 244268 **106–110 Abingdon Road OX1 4PX**
email: stay@sportsviewguesthouse.co.uk **web:** www.sportsviewguesthouse.co.uk
dir: *Exit Oxford south at Kennington roundabout towards city centre, 1.25 miles on left.*

This family-run Victorian property overlooks The Queen's College sports ground, south of the city – it is within walking distance of the centre. The comfortable bedrooms have Freeview TVs, and full English, continental and vegetarian breakfasts are offered. The property benefits from off-road parking on a first-come-first served basis.

Rooms: 20 rms (19 en suite) (1 pri facs) (4 fmly) (5 GF) **Facilities:** FTV Lounge tea/coffee WiFi **Parking:** 7 **Notes:** No children 3 years Closed 25–26 December and 1 January

---

SHIPTON-UNDER-WYCHWOOD · Map 10 SP21

The Wychwood Inn

★★★★ INN

tel: 01993 831185 **High Street OX7 6BA**
email: mail@thewychwoodinn.com **web:** www.thewychwoodinn.com
dir: *Phone for directions.*

A traditional Cotswolds village pub that has been lovingly refurbished by its owners to provide a modern country atmosphere with seasonal influences in the public areas. A warm and friendly welcome awaits, with well decorated, comfortable rooms as well as good food and drink.

Rooms: 5 en suite **S** fr £89 **D** fr £99* **Facilities:** Lounge tea/coffee Dinner available WiFi **Parking:** 20 **Notes:** Closed 2–15 January

---

SHRIVENHAM · Map 5 SU28

The White Horse View

★★★★ BED AND BREAKFAST

tel: 01793 780301 & 07967 497926 **Cherry Bungalow, Station Road SN6 8JL**
email: colin@thewhitehorseview.com **web:** www.thewhitehorseview.com
dir: *Phone for directions.*

Located in the pretty village of Shrivenham, this bed and breakfast offers modern en suite bedrooms set away from the main house, each with their own outdoor seating and spectacular countryside views. Breakfasts are served in the conservatory and feature local produce. This is a good location for those wanting to walk the Ridgeway or take in the sights of historic Marlborough.

Rooms: 4 en suite (1 fmly) (4 GF) **Facilities:** FTV TVL tea/coffee WiFi **Parking:** 3

| **SOUTH LEIGH** | Map 5 SP30 |

Premier Collection

Artist Residence Oxfordshire

★★★★★ ◎◎ INN

tel: 01993 656238 **Station Road OX29 6XN**
email: sayhello@hanburydiningroom.co.uk **web:** www.hanburysmasonarms.co.uk
dir: *A40 north of Oxford, follow signs for Cheltenham. Continue past Eynsham, exit A40 onto B4022 (signed Witney East), next left to South Leigh. On right.*

A beautiful old English inn tucked away in the countryside just outside Oxford that has been renovated to provide stylish, quirky, high-end, extremely comfortable bedrooms and suites as well as a friendly, cosy pub and restaurant, Mr Hanbury's Masons Arms. Adding to the accommodation options, there is also a new shepherd's hut, for two, in the garden. A noteable feature is all the local artwork on display which is part of the story of the business. Award-winning food, based on local and fresh produce, is offered on daily-changing menus.

Rooms: 5 en suite 4 annexe en suite **D** fr £120 (room only)* **Facilities:** FTV Lounge tea/coffee Dinner available Direct dial WiFi **Extras:** Freshly baked cookies, Nespresso machine, speciality toiletries, mini-bar **Parking:** 27

| **STADHAMPTON** | Map 5 SU69 |

Premier Collection

The Crazy Bear

★★★★★ ◎◎ 🍷 INN

tel: 01865 890714 **Bear Lane OX44 7UR**
email: enquiries@crazybear-stadhampton.co.uk **web:** www.crazybeargroup.co.uk
dir: *M40 junction 7, A329. In 4 miles left after petrol station, left into Bear Lane.*

This popular and attractive inn successfully combines modern chic with old world character. Cuisine is extensive and varied, with award-winning Thai and English restaurants under the same roof (both with AA Rosettes). Those choosing to make a night of it can enjoy staying in one of the concept bedrooms, all presented to a very high standard and styled with exciting themes; the 'infinity suites' have state-of-the-art facilities.

Rooms: 4 en suite 12 annexe en suite (3 fmly) (4 GF) **Facilities:** STV FTV Dinner available Direct dial WiFi 🏊 **Conf:** Max 40 Thtr 30 Class 30 Board 30 **Parking:** 100 **Notes:** Civ wed 200

| **SWINBROOK** | Map 5 SP21 |

The Swan Inn

★★★★ ◎ INN

tel: 01993 823339 **OX18 4DY**
email: info@theswanswinbrook.co.uk **web:** www.theswanswinbrook.co.uk
dir: *1 mile from A40, 2 miles east of Burford.*

The idyllic location and award-winning food are only two of the reasons why this is the perfect place for a comfortable business visit or a relaxed weekend. The bar offers real ales, local lagers and an appealing wine list. The accommodation is sumptuous and combines modern facilities with traditional comfort.

Rooms: 6 en suite (1 fmly) (4 GF) **Facilities:** FTV tea/coffee Dinner available WiFi ♿ Riding **Parking:** 20 **Notes:** Closed 25 December

| **UFFINGTON** | Map 5 SU38 |

The Fox and Hounds

★★★★ INN

tel: 01367 820680 **High Street SN7 7RP**
email: enquiries@uffingtonpub.co.uk **web:** www.uffingtonpub.co.uk
dir: *From A420 (south of Faringdon) follow Fernham or Uffington signs. From M4 junction 14 via Lambourn and Kingston Lisle.*

The Fox and Hounds is a traditional pub located in the charming village of Uffington and an ideal base to explore this delightful area. The two cottage-style bedrooms are well appointed and offer a range of amenities. The beamed bar is well stocked and includes a selection of real ales, while the restaurant offers a daily menu with an oriental twist.

Rooms: 4 annexe en suite (3 fmly) (4 GF) **S** fr £85 **D** fr £85 (room only)*
Facilities: FTV DVD tea/coffee Dinner available WiFi ♿ **Parking:** 14

| **WANTAGE** | Map 5 SU38 |

The Star Inn

★★★★ ◎◎ INN

tel: 01235 751873 **Watery Lane, Sparsholt OX12 9PL**
email: info@thestarsparsholt.co.uk **web:** www.thestarsparsholt.co.uk
dir: *From B4507, 4 miles west of Wantage turn right to Sparsholt. The Star Inn is signposted.*

Located in the picturesque village of Sparsholt, at the foot of the famous Ridgeway. At the heart of the community for over 300 years, The Star Inn offers bedrooms that are peacefully situated in a converted barn at the rear of the property, each providing a very good level of comfort. The two AA Rosette-worthy food is a highlight of any stay; excellent quality ingredients are skilfully prepared and carefully presented.

Rooms: 8 en suite (1 fmly) (5 GF) **Facilities:** FTV DVD tea/coffee Dinner available WiFi ♿ **Extras:** Speciality toiletries **Conf:** Max 30 Board 30 **Parking:** 15

La Fontana Restaurant with Accommodation

★★★★ 🍴 RESTAURANT WITH ROOMS

tel: 01235 868287 & 07836 730048 **Oxford Road, East Hanney OX12 0HP**
email: anna@la-fontana.co.uk **web:** www.la-fontana.co.uk
dir: *A338 from Wantage towards Oxford. Restaurant on right in East Hanney.*

Guests are guaranteed a warm welcome at this family-run Italian restaurant located on the outskirts of the busy town of Wantage. The stylish bedrooms are individually designed, well equipped and very comfortable. Dinner should not be missed – the menu features a wide range of regional Italian specialities.

Rooms: 12 en suite 3 annexe en suite (1 fmly) (4 GF) **S** fr £67.50 **D** fr £87.50*
Facilities: FTV Lounge tea/coffee Dinner available Direct dial WiFi **Parking:** 30
Notes: Civ wed 120

WATLINGTON
Map 5 SU69

The Fat Fox Inn

★★★★ INN

tel: 01491 613040 **13 Shirburn Street OX49 5BU**
email: info@thefatfoxinn.co.uk **web:** www.thefatfoxinn.co.uk
dir: M40 junction 6 onto B4009 south for 2.5 miles. On right in village.

Just 20 minutes from the city of Oxford, this inn is conveniently located for both leisure guests – especially walkers of the nearby Ridgeway – and business visitors looking for a quiet location. Guests can enjoy lunch and dinner in the relaxed bar or in the restaurant, where well-sourced, seasonal food is offered. Some of the en suite bedrooms are in the converted barn and have hand-made sleigh beds and exposed beams, others are located in the main house.

Rooms: 7 en suite (1 fmly) (4 GF) **S** fr £79 **D** fr £110* **Facilities:** FTV tea/coffee Dinner available WiFi **Parking:** 20

WHEATLEY
Map 5 SP50

Gidleigh House

★★★★ BED AND BREAKFAST

tel: 01865 875150 & 07733 026882 **27 Old London Road OX33 1YW**
web: www.gidleighhousebb.co.uk
dir: M40 junction 8 follow signs to Wheatley. Pass Asda on left and right turn to Hotton/Waterperry. Next right, marked private road.

You are assured of a warm, personal welcome at this modern home which is located on a private road in a quiet village just 10 minutes from Oxford city centre and has easy access to the M40. The two en suite rooms are spacious, very comfortable and equipped with thoughtful extras. Relax over a newspaper in the conservatory at the family-style table while your breakfast is freshly prepared.

Rooms: 2 en suite (2 fmly) **Facilities:** TVL tea/coffee **Extras:** Fruit, chocolates **Parking:** 4 **Notes:** No children 10 years Closed 18 December to 5 January

WITNEY
Map 5 SP31

Premier Collection

Old Swan & Minster Mill

★★★★★   INN

tel: 01993 774441 **Old Minster OX29 0RN**
email: enquiries@oldswanandminstermill.com **web:** www.oldswanandminstermill.com
dir: Exit A40 signed Minster Lovell, through village right at T-junction, 2nd left.

Located within its own stunning grounds and gardens including a private stretch of the River Windrush, the Old Swan & Minster Mill comprise two distinct accommodation areas – both offering quality and individuality. Check-in is at the Minster Mill, where guests are welcomed and escorted to their room or suite. The Old Swan rooms are traditional, with old oak beams and fireplaces in some rooms, while Mill rooms are more contemporary in style – many feature great views of the river and grounds. Award-winning cuisine is served in the dining room. There is a two-night minimum stay at weekends.

Rooms: 60 rms (52 en suite) (4 fmly) (19 GF) **Facilities:** FTV Lounge tea/coffee Dinner available Direct dial WiFi Fishing Riding Gym Petanque **Extras:** Speciality toiletries, decanter of sloe gin **Conf:** Max 55 Thtr 55 Class 22 Board 24 **Parking:** 70 **Notes:** LB Civ wed 50

Corncroft Guest House

★★★★ GUEST HOUSE

tel: 01993 773298 **69-71 Corn Street OX28 6AS**
web: www.corncroftguesthouse.com
dir: A40 to town centre, from Market Square into Corn Street, 400 metres on left.

Located in the quieter end of town, yet close to the centre, Corncroft Guest House offers comfortable well-equipped accommodation in a friendly atmosphere. Substantial breakfasts featuring local produce are served in the attractive dining room.

Rooms: 11 en suite (1 fmly) (2 GF) **Facilities:** FTV DVD TVL tea/coffee WiFi **Extras:** Sweets – complimentary **Notes:** Closed 24–26 December

WOODSTOCK
Map 11 SP41

Premier Collection

The Glove House

★★★★★ BED AND BREAKFAST

tel: 01993 813475 & 07447 012832 **24 Oxford Street OX20 1TS**
email: info@theglovehouse.co.uk **web:** www.theglovehouse.co.uk
dir: M40 junction 8 onto A40, then A44 signed to Evesham/Woodstock. The Glove House on right.

The Glove House is a 17th-century, Grade II listed property which has been sympathetically renovated and enjoys a prime location; Blenheim Palace is within walking distance. The en suite bedrooms are very well appointed and ooze style, quality and comfort. Breakfast can be served in the walled garden during the summer.

Rooms: 2 en suite (2 fmly) **S** fr £155 **D** fr £170* **Facilities:** FTV DVD iPod docking station Lounge tea/coffee WiFi **Extras:** Speciality toiletries, mini-bar, snacks **Notes:** No children 10 years

Duke of Marlborough Country Inn

★★★★ INN

tel: 01993 811460 **Woodleys OX20 1HT**
email: sales@dukeofmarlborough.co.uk **web:** www.dukeofmarlborough.co.uk
dir: 1 mile north of Woodstock on A44 crossroads.

The Duke of Marlborough is just outside the popular town of Woodstock, convenient for local attractions including Blenheim Palace. Bedrooms and bathrooms are in an adjacent lodge-style building and offer high standards of quality and comfort. Dinner includes many tempting home-cooked dishes, complemented by a good selection of ales and wines.

Rooms: 13 annexe en suite (2 fmly) (7 GF) **Facilities:** FTV tea/coffee Dinner available Direct dial WiFi **Extras:** Snacks **Conf:** Max 20 Thtr 20 Class 16 Board 12 **Parking:** 42 **Notes:** LB

WOODSTOCK *continued*

The Woodstock Arms

★★★ ◉ INN

tel: 01993 811251 **6–8 Market Street OX20 1SX**
email: info@thewoodstockarms.com **web:** www.thewoodstockarms.com
dir: *Phone for directions.*

Set in a charming and popular town, The Woodstock Arms is a well-presented and comfortable property; it makes an ideal base for visiting Blenheim Palace, Oxford or the Cotswolds. Expect a warm welcome, individually designed, smart bedrooms alongside tasty British dishes using quality, seasonal ingredients. The bedrooms have Hypnos beds, smart TVs, Egyptian cotton sheets, digital radios and docks and WiFi among their many facilities. Completing the picture are roaring fires in winter and a lovely courtyard in summer.

Rooms: 5 en suite **Facilities:** FTV tea/coffee Dinner available WiFi

The Townhouse

★★★ GUEST ACCOMMODATION

tel: 01993 810843 **15 High Street OX20 1TE**
email: townhousewoodstock@hotmail.co.uk **web:** www.woodstock-townhouse.com
dir: *Off A44 into High Street.*

This early 18th-century stone town house is full of character and offers five individually styled, cosy en suite bedrooms. Situated in the heart of the town just a short walk from Blenheim Palace, it is an ideal base for exploring many famous Cotswold locations. Breakfasts are cooked to order and served in the small conservatory room overlooking the walled garden.

Rooms: 5 en suite (1 fmly) **Facilities:** FTV TVL tea/coffee WiFi

WOOTTON   Map 11 SP41

The Killingworth Castle

★★★★ ◉◉ INN

tel: 01993 811401 & 832849 **Glympton Road OX20 1EJ**
email: reservations@thekillingworthcastle.com **web:** www.thekillingworthcastle.com
dir: *Phone for directions.*

This 17th-century, roadside country inn, located just a few miles from Woodstock and Blenheim Palace, retains its country charm with many modern creature comforts added. There are eight comfortable, en suite bedrooms all within a converted Cotswold-stone barn less than a stone's throw from the inn – they offer a very comfortable stay in a peaceful setting. A warm welcome is guaranteed and dinner should not be missed.

Rooms: 8 annexe en suite (4 GF) **Facilities:** FTV tea/coffee Dinner available WiFi
Extras: Sherry **Parking:** 40 **Notes:** No children 16 years

RUTLAND

CLIPSHAM   Map 11 SK91

Beech House

★★★★★ ◉◉ ⬚ INN

tel: 01780 410355 **Main Street LE15 7SH**
email: info@theolivebranchpub.com **web:** www.theolivebranchpub.com
dir: *From A1 take B668 signed Stretton and Clipsham.*

Beech House stands over the road from The Olive Branch restaurant. Its bedrooms are furnished with style and finesse, combining crisp linens, natural wood and retro-style accessories with traditional and modern furniture. Breakfasts are served in The Olive Branch and should not be missed. Excellent, award-winning lunches and dinners are also available.

Rooms: 5 en suite 1 annexe en suite (2 fmly) (3 GF) **S** fr £97.50 **D** fr £115*
Facilities: FTV DVD tea/coffee Dinner available Direct dial WiFi ⅃
🍎 **Extras:** Speciality toiletries – complimentary; fruit – chargeable **Conf:** Max 20 Thtr 20 Class 12 Board 16 **Parking:** 10 **Notes:** LB

LYDDINGTON   Map 11 SP89

The Marquess of Exeter

★★★★★ ◉ INN

tel: 01572 822477 **52 Main Street LE15 9LT**
email: info@marquessexeter.co.uk **web:** www.marquessexeter.co.uk
dir: *M1 junction 19, A14 to Kettering, then A6003 to Caldecott. Right into Lyddington Road, 2 miles to village.*

Situated in the picturesque Rutland countryside, the inn is appointed with contemporary touches while retaining many original features such as timber beam ceilings, log fires and flagstone floors. The stylish bedrooms, situated across a courtyard, are individually decorated and comfortable. The food is imaginative with the chef's 'sharing dishes' being particularly noteworthy.

Rooms: 17 rms (16 en suite) (1 pri facs) (3 fmly) (10 GF) **Facilities:** FTV Lounge tea/coffee Dinner available Direct dial WiFi **Conf:** Max 50 Thtr 50 Class 40 Board 40 **Parking:** 60 **Notes:** Closed 25 December

OAKHAM   Map 11 SK80

Fox & Hounds

★★★★★ ◉◉ INN

tel: 01572 812403 **19 The Green, Exton LE15 8AP**
email: info@afoxinexton.co.uk **web:** www.afoxinexton.co.uk
dir: *From A1, follow signs to Rutland Water on A606. Turn right at Barnsdale Avenue then right towards Exton. On The Green.*

This 17th-century coaching inn overlooks the green in the picturesque Rutland village of Exton; the property offers individually designer-led bedrooms with co-ordinated furnishings, king-size beds, Egyptian cotton bedding, TVs with Netflix and feature interesting objects from around the world. The public spaces include a lounge bar, restaurant and library; the building has a wealth of original features. The award-winning food is thoroughly contemporary. Warming fires in winter and landscape gardens to enjoy in the summer complete the picture.

Rooms: 4 en suite (1 fmly) (1 GF) **Facilities:** STV FTV DVD Lounge tea/coffee Dinner available WiFi ⅃ Fishing Riding 🍎 **Extras:** Speciality toiletries **Conf:** Max 20 Thtr 14 Class 16 Board 20 **Parking:** 20

UPPINGHAM
Map 11 SP89

The Lake Isle
★★★★ @@ ⬖ RESTAURANT WITH ROOMS

tel: 01572 822951 **16 High Street East LE15 9PZ**
email: info@lakeisle.co.uk **web:** www.lakeisle.co.uk
dir: *From A47, turn left at 2nd lights, 100 yards on right.*

This attractive townhouse centres around a delightful restaurant and small elegant bar. There is also an inviting first-floor guest lounge, and the bedrooms are extremely well appointed and thoughtfully equipped; spacious split-level cottage suites situated in a quiet courtyard are also available. The imaginative cooking and an extremely impressive wine list are highlights here.

Rooms: 9 en suite 3 annexe rms (3 pri facs) (1 fmly) (1 GF) **S** fr £70 **D** fr £90*
Facilities: FTV Lounge tea/coffee Dinner available Direct dial WiFi ⬖ **Extras:** Home-made biscuits – complimentary **Conf:** Max 16 Board 16 **Parking:** 7 **Notes:** Closed 1 January and bank holidays RS Sunday evening and Monday lunch closed

The Crown
★★★ INN

tel: 01572 822302 **19 High Street, East Uppingham LE15 9PY**
email: info@thecrownrutland.co.uk **web:** www.thecrownrutland.co.uk
dir: *Phone for directions.*

Located on the high street in the centre of Uppingham, this traditional inn dates back to 1739, and with some modernisation to the bedrooms, now offers comfortable accommodation. Guests can enjoy a range of real ales and a selection of bar meals. There is parking to the rear, and free WiFi is available.

Rooms: 7 en suite (1 fmly) **Facilities:** FTV TVL tea/coffee Dinner available WiFi ⬖ **Conf:** Max 25 Thtr 25 Class 25 Board 25 **Parking:** 10

WING
Map 11 SK80

Kings Arms Inn & Restaurant
★★★★ @@ ⬖ INN

tel: 01572 737634 **13 Top Street LE15 8SE**
email: info@thekingsarms-wing.co.uk **web:** www.thekingsarms-wing.co.uk
dir: *1.5 miles off A6003 in village centre.*

This traditional village inn, with its open fires, flagstone floors and low beams, dates from the 17th century. The restaurant is more contemporary and offers a wide range of interesting, freshly produced dishes. Service is attentive and friendly. The spacious, well-equipped bedrooms are in The Old Bake House and Granny's Cottage, in the nearby courtyard.

Rooms: 8 en suite (4 GF) **S** fr £65 **D** fr £75 (room only) **Facilities:** FTV tea/coffee Dinner available WiFi **Extras:** Speciality toiletries **Parking:** 30

SHROPSHIRE

BISHOP'S CASTLE
Map 15 SO38

The Castle
★★★★ ⬖ INN

tel: 01588 638403 **Market Square SY9 5BN**
email: stay@thecastlehotelbishopscastle.co.uk
web: www.thecastlehotelbishopscastle.co.uk
dir: *Exit A488 into Bishop's Castle, at top of High Street on left.*

Overlooking this medieval town, with its mixed architecture and unusually painted houses, sits the remains of a castle. In 1719, much of the stone from this castle was used to create The Castle Hotel, built on the old baille (or enclosed courtyard) on the instruction of a wealthy landowner. Nearly 300 years on and The Castle continues to welcome guests from far and wide. Many of the comfortably furnished rooms have stunning views across the Welsh Marches. Hearty meals are served in the bar, dining room and on sunny days, on the garden terrace. Bishop's Castle is famed for its ale and is home to the oldest working brewery in the country. Offa's Dyke, The Shropshire Way and Kerry Ridgeway are all within easy striking distance.

Rooms: 12 en suite 1 annexe en suite (2 fmly) **S** fr £85 **D** fr £95* **Facilities:** FTV TVL tea/coffee Dinner available WiFi ⬖ **Conf:** Max 24 **Parking:** 25 **Notes:** LB Closed 25 December

The Coach House
★★★★★ @@ ⬖ RESTAURANT WITH ROOMS

tel: 01588 650846 & 07930 694516 **Norbury SY9 5DX**
email: info@coachhousenorbury.com **web:** www.coachhousenorbury.com
dir: *3 miles northeast of Bishop's Castle. Exit A488/A489 into Norbury.*

Located in an Area of Outstanding Natural Beauty, this quaint, fully refurbished property in the centre of a pretty Shropshire village has been welcoming travellers since the 1700s. A warm welcome is assured by the current owners. Bedrooms offer comfortable accommodation and are located either in the main building or the attached coach house annexe which is dog friendly. Cosy lounges with log-burning fires are an ideal place to enjoy a locally-produced beer or one of the quality wines on offer. Award-winning dinners and breakfasts offer innovative menus showcasing the best local produce.

Rooms: 4 rms (3 en suite) (1 pri facs) 3 annexe en suite (1 fmly) (1 GF) **Facilities:** FTV DVD Lounge tea/coffee Dinner available WiFi ⬖ **Extras:** Speciality toiletries, home-made biscuits **Conf:** Max 18 Thtr 18 Class 18 Board 18 **Parking:** 8 **Notes:** LB No children 5 years Closed 2–31 January

Boars Head
★★★★ INN

tel: 01588 638521 **Church Street SY9 5AE**
email: info@boarsheadhotel.co.uk **web:** www.boarsheadhotel.co.uk
dir: *Phone for directions.*

The Boars Head is situated in the centre of Bishop's Castle, and is a traditional inn with comfortable and spacious bedrooms in a separate annexe. The inn incorporates a post office with a cash machine and phone top-up facilities. Food is on offer all day. Parking is available to the rear of the inn.

Rooms: 4 annexe en suite (1 fmly) (3 GF) **Facilities:** FTV DVD iPod docking station Lounge tea/coffee Dinner available WiFi **Extras:** Fridge, digital safe, mineral water **Parking:** 60

BRIDGNORTH · Map 10 SO79

The Halfway House Inn
★★★ INN

tel: 01746 762670 **Cleobury Road WV16 5LS**
email: info@halfwayhouseinn.co.uk **web:** www.halfwayhouseinn.co.uk
dir: *1.5 miles from town centre on B4363 to Cleobury Mortimer.*

Located in a rural area, this family-owned, 16th-century inn provides good standards of comfort, while retaining its original character. The bedrooms, some in converted stables and cottages, are especially suitable for families and groups.

Rooms: 10 en suite (10 fmly) (6 GF) **S** fr £69 **D** fr £85 **Facilities:** FTV TVL tea/coffee Dinner available WiFi ⚓ Fishing ⚓ **Conf:** Max 30 Thtr 30 Class 24 Board 20 **Parking:** 30 **Notes:** LB Closed 25–26 December RS Winter Sunday evening (excluding bank holidays) from 4pm

CHURCH STRETTON · Map 15 SO49

Court Farm
★★★★ FARMHOUSE

tel: 01694 771219 **Gretton SY6 7HU**
email: alison@courtfarm.eu **web:** www.courtfarm.eu
dir: *Exit B4371 at Longville, left at crossroads, 1st on left.*

Located in the village of Gretton, this Grade II listed stone-built Georgian house is on a 330-acre working farm, and its bedrooms overlook the pretty gardens. Home to the Norris family since 1898, over the years they have sympathetically restored and modernised the building. Comprehensive breakfasts are served in an elegant dining room, and a comfortable guest lounge is also available. Court Farm is an ideal base for exploring Shropshire and surrounding areas.

Rooms: 2 en suite **S** fr £60 **D** fr £80* **Facilities:** FTV TVL tea/coffee WiFi ⚓ **Parking:** 4 **Notes:** No children 12 years 330 acres mixed

Belvedere Guest House
★★★★ GUEST HOUSE

tel: 01694 722232 **Burway Road SY6 6DP**
email: info@belvedereguesthouse.co.uk **web:** www.belvedereguesthouse.co.uk
dir: *Exit A49 into town centre, over crossroads into Burway Road.*

Popular with walkers and cyclists and peacefully located on the lower slopes of the Long Mynd, this impressive, well-proportioned Edwardian house has a range of homely bedrooms, equipped with practical extras and complemented by modern bathrooms. Ground-floor areas include a cottage-style dining room overlooking the pretty garden and large lounge complete with TV, a large selection of reading material and board games.

Rooms: 7 rms (6 en suite) (2 fmly) **S** fr £35 **D** fr £60* **Facilities:** TVL tea/coffee WiFi ⚓ **Extras:** Mini-fridge, snacks, bottled water – chargeable **Parking:** 9 **Notes:** LB Closed Christmas and January

DORRINGTON · Map 15 SJ40

Upper Shadymoor Farm
★★★★ FARMHOUSE

tel: 01743 718670 **Stapleton SY5 7AL**
email: kevan@shadymoor.co.uk **web:** www.shadymoor.co.uk
dir: *Phone for directions.*

Upper Shadymoor Farm has it all really – a family atmosphere, a tranquil location, smart bedrooms, a formal dining room, farm animals, a deer park and much more. Expect a warm welcome from the Fox family and a truly enjoyable stay. The bedrooms (a twin, a double and a family room) have TVs and hot drinks-making facilities as standard. Produce from the farm is used at dinner and breakfast.

Rooms: 3 en suite (1 fmly) **S** fr £60 **D** fr £85* **Facilities:** Lounge tea/coffee Dinner available WiFi Fishing ⚓ **Parking:** 20 **Notes:** 200 acres beef/mixed/sheep

IRONBRIDGE · Map 10 SJ60

Broseley House
★★★★ GUEST HOUSE

tel: 01952 882043 & 07790 732723 **1 The Square, Broseley TF12 5EW**
email: info@broseleyhouse.co.uk **web:** www.broseleyhouse.co.uk
dir: *1 mile south of Ironbridge in Broseley town centre.*

A warm welcome is assured at this impressive Georgian house in the centre of Broseley. Quality, individual decor and soft furnishings highlight the many original features, and the thoughtfully furnished bedrooms are equipped with a wealth of homely extras. Comprehensive breakfasts are taken in an elegant dining room; a stylish apartment is also available.

Rooms: 6 en suite (2 fmly) (1 GF) **S** fr £50 **D** fr £80 **Facilities:** FTV DVD iPod docking station tea/coffee WiFi ⚓ **Extras:** Fridge, robes, slippers **Notes:** LB No children 5 years

White Hart
★★★★ ⚜ INN

tel: 01952 432901 **The Wharfage TF8 7AW**
email: info@whitehartironbridge.com **web:** www.whitehartironbridge.com
dir: *In centre of Ironbridge, 200 yards from Bridge.*

The White Hart is located in what is often referred to as the birthplace of the industrial revolution, Ironbridge holds UNESCO World Heritage Site status. Dating back to the 18th century, this inn is steeped in history and offers a host of period features carefully blended with modern comforts. Each of the en suite rooms differs in size due to nature of the building but all are smartly appointed and provide very good levels of comfort.

Rooms: 5 en suite (1 fmly) **S** fr £69 **D** fr £89* **Facilities:** FTV tea/coffee Dinner available WiFi

LUDLOW   Map 10 SO57

Old Downton Lodge

★★★★★ ◉◉◉ ⏚ RESTAURANT WITH ROOMS

tel: 01568 771826 & 07977 475881 **Downton on the Rock SY8 2HU**
email: bookings@olddowntonlodge.com **web:** www.olddowntonlodge.com
dir: *From Ludlow onto A49 towards Shrewsbury, 1st left onto A4113. After 1.9 miles turn left signed Downton, 3 miles on single track road. Turn right, signed.*

Peacefully situated, Old Downton Lodge is within easy reach of Ludlow's many attractions and has good parking, pleasant grounds, and is ideal for walks and country pursuits. Originally a farmhouse, this high-end establishment has bags of character and style. Bedrooms are spacious and very well appointed with comfortable beds and luxurious bathrooms. There is an honesty bar and excellent wine list. Breakfast should not be missed, and the three AA Rosette-worthy dinner is a highlight; offered every Tuesday to Saturday evening, the imaginative five- or seven-course tasting menus use local, seasonal and foraged produce.

Rooms: 10 en suite (5 GF) **S** fr £145 **D** fr £145* **Facilities:** FTV DVD Lounge tea/coffee Dinner available Direct dial WiFi **Extras:** Speciality toiletries, home-made biscuits **Conf:** Max 40 Thtr 40 Class 40 Board 40 **Parking:** 20 **Notes:** LB No children 13 years Closed 24–26 December Civ wed 60

The Charlton Arms

★★★★★ ◉ INN

tel: 01584 872813 **Ludford Bridge SY8 1PJ**
email: reservations@thecharltonarms.co.uk **web:** www.thecharltonarms.co.uk
dir: *Phone for directions.*

The accommodation at this riverside inn reflects the character of the historic building which offers all modern comforts. Diners can enjoy fresh, locally-sourced ingredients in the award-winning dishes they choose and a panoramic view across the River Teme. As a free house, it also offers a fine selection of local beers plus there's a tiered decking area overlooking the river to enjoy drinks or a meal on warmer days. Of the nine stylish en suite bedrooms, there is one suite with a private terrace and hot tub.

Rooms: 9 en suite (1 fmly) **S** fr £95 **D** fr £100* **Facilities:** FTV tea/coffee Dinner available WiFi **Conf:** Max 100 Thtr 100 Class 80 Board 70 **Parking:** 30

The Clive Bar & Restaurant with Rooms

★★★★★ ◉ ⏚ RESTAURANT WITH ROOMS

tel: 01584 856565 & 856665 **Bromfield SY8 2JR**
email: info@theclive.co.uk **web:** www.theclive.co.uk
dir: *2 miles north of Ludlow on A49 in Bromfield.*

The Clive is just two miles from the busy town of Ludlow and is a convenient base for guests visiting the local attractions or for those on business. Based at the Ludlow Food Centre, good use is made of food made on site or from the company farms, ensuring local, seasonal produce at every meal. The bedrooms, located in an annexe, are spacious and well equipped; one is suitable for families and many are on the ground-floor level. Meals are available in the well-known Clive Restaurant or in the bar areas. The property also has a small meeting room.

Rooms: 14 annexe en suite (1 fmly) (10 GF) **Facilities:** FTV tea/coffee Dinner available Direct dial WiFi **Extras:** Mini-bar with local produce **Conf:** Max 40 Thtr 40 Class 40 Board 24 **Parking:** 80 **Notes:** LB Closed 25–26 December

The Cliffe at Dinham

★★★★ ◉◉ ⏚ RESTAURANT WITH ROOMS

tel: 01584 872063 & 876975 **Halton Lane, Dinham SY8 2JE**
email: info@thecliffeatdinham.co.uk **web:** www.thecliffeatdinham.co.uk
dir: *Phone for directions.*

This former gentleman's residence is a short stroll from the River Teme, with magnificent views of Ludlow Castle and just a short walk from the vibrant centre of Ludlow. The Cliffe is a successful blend of the Victorian features and more contemporary style. The bedrooms are comfortable and well equipped. Relaxed dining and modern British dishes are offered in the attractive dining room, and there is a pleasant terraced area overlooking the gardens.

Rooms: 11 en suite 2 annexe en suite (3 fmly) (2 GF) **S** fr £65 **D** fr £80* **Facilities:** FTV tea/coffee Dinner available Direct dial WiFi **Parking:** 30 **Notes:** LB Closed 26 December and 1–15 January

Angel House Bed and Breakfast

★★★★ BED AND BREAKFAST

tel: 01584 891377 & 07568 142626 **Angel Bank, Bitterley SY8 3HT**
email: angelhouse48@gmail.com **web:** www.angelhousecleehill.co.uk
dir: *On A4117 towards Kidderminster.*

Angel House has an excellent location, set just outside the busy hustle and bustle of Ludlow. The friendly proprietors are very attentive and provide a comfortable place to stay. The bedrooms are very well appointed with lots of thoughtful extras. The gardens are spacious and home to the chickens that provide the breakfast eggs. The house has plentiful parking and super views.

Rooms: 2 en suite (1 fmly) **S** fr £75 **D** fr £85* **Facilities:** FTV DVD Lounge tea/coffee Dinner available WiFi **Extras:** Speciality toiletries **Parking:** 3 **Notes:** No children 7 years

LUDLOW *continued*

Dinham Hall

★★★★ RESTAURANT WITH ROOMS

tel: 01584 876464 **By The Castle SY8 1EJ**
email: info@dinhamhall.com **web:** www.dinhamhall.com
dir: *In town centre, opposite castle.*

Built in 1792, this lovely house stands in attractive gardens immediately opposite Ludlow Castle, and it has a well-deserved reputation for warm hospitality. The well-equipped bedrooms include two in a converted cottage, and some rooms have four-poster beds. The comfortable public rooms are elegantly appointed. Dishes served in the brasserie-style restaurant are based on good, seasonal produce.

Rooms: 11 en suite 2 annexe en suite (2 fmly) (2 GF) **S** fr £99 **D** fr £119*
Facilities: Lounge tea/coffee Dinner available WiFi **Parking:** 13
Notes: No children 7 years

130 Corve Street B&B

★★★★ BED AND BREAKFAST

tel: 01584 875548 **130 Corve Street SY8 2PG**
email: info@130corvestreet.co.uk **web:** www.130corvestreet.co.uk
dir: *North side of town on B4361, adjacent to Tesco supermarket.*

Expect a warm welcome at this Grade II listed building, situated within easy access of the town's many amenities and restaurants. The attractive bedrooms, situated on the ground floor at the rear, are comfortable and have independent entrances. Hearty breakfasts are served in the first-floor dining room. There is secure off-road parking next to the property.

Rooms: 3 en suite (3 GF) **S** fr £59 **D** fr £79* **Facilities:** FTV tea/coffee WiFi
Parking: 3 **Notes:** No children 12 years

The Graig B&B Ludlow

[U]

tel: 01584 890204 **Office Lane, Angel Bank SY8 3PG**
email: info@thegraigludlow.co.uk **web:** www.thegraigludlow.co.uk
dir: *Phone for directions.*

Currently the rating for this establishment is not confirmed. This may be due to a change of ownership or because it has only recently joined the AA rating scheme.

Rooms: 5 en suite (5 GF) **Facilities:** tea/coffee WiFi **Notes:** No children 12 years

---

MARKET DRAYTON   **Map 15 SJ63**

Premier Collection

Ternhill Farm House

★★★★★ ☗ GUEST ACCOMMODATION

tel: 01630 638984 **Ternhill TF9 3PX**
email: info@ternhillfarm.co.uk **web:** www.ternhillfarm.co.uk
dir: *On junction A53 and A41, archway off A53 to back of property.*

This elegant Grade II listed Georgian property, once a farmhouse, has been lovingly converted into friendly, family-run guest accommodation. Bedrooms are individually designed and offer high levels of comfort. A choice of cosy lounges is available, and the large garden is a pleasant feature. The Cottage Restaurant is small and contemporary. Dinner must be reserved when the room reservation is made, and menu choices are required a minimum of 24 working hours prior to arrival. In addition, The Cottage Restaurant and/or Dining Room may be reserved for pre-booked, non-resident parties of between 10 and 24 people.

Rooms: 8 rms (7 en suite) (1 pri facs) **S** fr £55 **D** fr £75* **Facilities:** FTV DVD Lounge tea/coffee Licensed WiFi **Extras:** Speciality toiletries, mineral water, honesty bar **Parking:** 16 **Notes:** LB No children 14 years

---

MUNSLOW   **Map 10 SO58**

Crown Country Inn

★★★★ ☺☺ ☗ INN

tel: 01584 841205 **SY7 9ET**
email: info@crowncountryinn.co.uk **web:** www.crowncountryinn.co.uk
dir: *Exit B4368 into village.*

Located between Much Wenlock and Craven Arms, this impressive pastel-coloured and half-timbered Tudor inn is full of character and charm with stone floors, exposed beams and blazing log fires during winter. The smart pine-furnished bedrooms are in a converted stable block, and the spacious public areas include two dining rooms.

Rooms: 3 en suite (1 GF) **S** fr £68 **D** fr £99* **Facilities:** FTV DVD tea/coffee Dinner available WiFi ⅃ ☗ **Conf:** Max 30 Thtr 30 Class 30 Board 20 **Parking:** 20 **Notes:** LB No children 12 years Closed 25 December RS Closed Sunday evening and Monday for food and drink

NORTON
Map 10 SJ70

The Hundred House

★★★★ ◉ INN

tel: 01952 580240 & 0845 644 6100 *(Calls cost 7p per minute plus your phone company's access charge)* **Bridgnorth Road TF11 9EE**
email: reservations@hundredhouse.co.uk **web:** www.hundredhouse.co.uk
dir: *M54 junction 5, follow signs for Bridgnorth (A442), midway between Bridgnorth and Telford.*

This interesting property has a genuine atmosphere of rural charm, setting it apart from the modern style of country 'food destination' pubs. With a rabbit warren of public bars and restaurants, it provides respite for weary travellers and locals alike, many of whom come for the excellent meals. The well-equipped bedrooms are individually designed, with quirky furnishings and decor. The large beer garden is just the place in good weather, with well-stocked herb and flower gardens to encourage a wander.

Rooms: 9 en suite (4 fmly) **S** fr £70 **D** fr £75* **Facilities:** FTV tea/coffee Dinner available Direct dial WiFi ⚷ ⚘ **Extras:** Bottled water, sweets **Conf:** Max 100 Thtr 80 Class 30 Board 35 **Parking:** 50 **Notes:** LB RS 25 December restaurant closed pm Civ wed 120

OSWESTRY
Map 15 SJ22

Sebastians

★★★★ ◉◉ ⚑ RESTAURANT WITH ROOMS

tel: 01691 655444 **45 Willow Street SY11 1AQ**
email: info@sebastians-hotel.com **web:** www.sebastians-hotel.com
dir: *From town centre, take turn signed Selattyn into Willow Street. 400 yards from junction on left opposite Willow Street Gallery.*

Sebastians is an intrinsic part of the leisure scene in Oswestry and has built up a loyal local following. The meals feature French influences, with a monthly-changing, three-course menu with complimentary appetiser and sorbet before main courses. Bedrooms are set around a pretty terrace courtyard and provide very comfortable accommodation with all the comforts of home.

Rooms: 2 en suite 4 annexe en suite (2 fmly) (2 GF) **S** fr £75 **D** fr £85 (room only)*
Facilities: iPod docking station Lounge tea/coffee Dinner available WiFi
Extras: Speciality toiletries, fruit, sweets – complimentary **Parking:** 6
Notes: Closed Christmas/New Year and bank holidays

SHREWSBURY
Map 15 SJ41

See also Criggion (Powys) and Wem

Premier Collection

Darwin's Townhouse

★★★★★ ⚑ BED AND BREAKFAST

tel: 01743 343829 & 07576 076376 **37 St Julians Friars SY1 1XL**
email: info@darwinstownhouse.com **web:** www.darwinstownhouse.com
dir: *Cross English Bridge, bear left (over pedestrian crossing) into Beeches Lane. 1st left into Williams Way, turn 1st left after car park, on left.*

Darwin's Townhouse is a beautifully restored Georgian property. Although situated in the centre of Shrewsbury, within walking distance of the many shops and restaurants, it sits on a peaceful street near the river. The bedrooms of various sizes are stylish and comfortable and are located either in the main house or in the garden rooms to the rear of the property. Breakfast is served in the conservatory by the friendly team, using the finest local, seasonal produce. There is an honesty bar.

Rooms: 12 en suite 8 annexe en suite (1 fmly) (4 GF) **Facilities:** FTV iPod docking station Lounge TVL tea/coffee Licensed WiFi ⚘ **Extras:** Speciality toiletries, robes, slippers; Honesty bar and snacks – chargeable **Conf:** Max 50 Thtr 50 Class 40 Board 30 **Notes:** LB

Darwin's Kitchen

★★★★ ⚑ RESTAURANT WITH ROOMS

tel: 01743 358870 & 761220 **15 Saint Mary's Street SY1 1EQ**
email: hello@darwinskitchen.co.uk **web:** www.darwinskitchen.co.uk
dir: *Follow one-way system around town, opposite St Mary's church.*

Situated in the heart of the town, this establishment offers four individually designed bedrooms, including a suite, that are very comfortable and have spacious and contemporary bathrooms. Food, based on locally sourced ingredients, is the focal point of the operation and can be enjoyed in the smart restaurant or conservatory area. Continental breakfasts are delivered to the bedrooms, or if a cooked breakfast is required then they are served at Darwin's Townhouse or The Loopy Shrew (both in the same company) a couple of minutes' walk away. Secure parking is available in a nearby public car park.

Rooms: 4 en suite (1 fmly) **Facilities:** FTV tea/coffee Dinner available WiFi
Extras: Speciality toiletries, robes, chef's complimentary treats **Notes:** LB
Closed 25–26 December and 1 January RS Christmas and New Year

SHREWSBURY *continued*

The Loopy Shrew

★★★★ INN

tel: 01743 366505 **15–17 Bellstone SY1 1HU**
email: hello@loopyshrew.com web: www.loopyshrew.com
dir: *In centre of town, follow one-way system.*

Sister property to Darwin's Kitchen, The Loopy Shrew offers 12 comfortably furnished en suite rooms in the heart of historic Shrewsbury. The open-plan, ground floor includes a well-stocked bar, coffee lounge and split-level restaurant. Long stay parking is available within a few minutes' walk.

Rooms: 12 en suite **Facilities:** FTV tea/coffee Dinner available WiFi **Extras:** Speciality toiletries – complimentary **Notes:** LB Closed 25–26 December and 1 January

The Mytton and Mermaid

★★★★ ◉ INN

tel: 01743 761220 **Atcham SY5 6QG**
email: reception@myttonandmermaid.co.uk web: www.myttonandmermaid.co.uk
dir: *Phone for directions.*

Adjacent to the main gates of Attingham Park, The Mytton and Mermaid resides on the southern bank of the winding River Severn. The inn has been welcoming guests for nearly 300 years. Split between the main inn and the courtyard, the rooms are comfortable and well equipped for the modern day traveller and most contain a nod to the property's history in the form of period features.

Rooms: 19 en suite (6 GF) **Facilities:** FTV tea/coffee Dinner available Direct dial WiFi Fishing **Conf:** Max 80 Thtr 80 Class 50 Board 40 **Parking:** 60 **Notes:** Civ wed 100

The Old Station

★★★★ BED AND BREAKFAST

tel: 01939 290905 & 07714 068305 **Leaton, Bomere Heath SY4 3AP**
email: enquiries@theoldstationshropshire.co.uk web: www.theoldstationshropshire.co.uk
dir: *M54 junction 7 onto A5 then A49 north. At Battlefield (A5124) over roundabout into Huffley Lane, left by cricket field, 100 metres on right.*

This former railway station, built in 1847, is set in the heart of the Shropshire countryside yet just four miles from Shrewsbury. The railway theme runs throughout the bedrooms which come in a range of shapes and sizes. Stained-glass windows are a feature throughout the house. Breakfast is served in the well-furnished dining room – some tables are located on what was previously the station platform. A garden and a small lounge are provided and there is ample parking.

Rooms: 6 en suite (4 fmly) (1 GF) **Facilities:** FTV TVL tea/coffee Dinner available WiFi 🔒 **Extras:** Fridge in 2 bedrooms **Parking:** 11 **Notes:** LB Closed December to February

TELFORD   Map 10 SJ60

The Old Rectory of St James

★★★★ ⬦ GUEST HOUSE

tel: 01952 598519 & 07747 058512 **Stirchley Village TF3 1DY**
email: enquiries@theoldrectoryofstjames.co.uk web: www.theoldrectoryofstjames.co.uk
dir: *Follow signs for Stirchley, into Stirchley Road, pass Rose and Crown pub and follow brown signs for Street James Church.*

A warm welcome is assured from Adrian and Rosemary at The Old Rectory of St James. Located in a quiet area of Telford, the property is ideally located for the town centre and just a short drive from Ironbridge, Shrewsbury and Bridgnorth. The gardens are a feature here, and produce from the vegetable patch is used at breakfast and dinner. The afternoon teas are noteworthy with home-made cakes

and tea served on arrival in the guest lounge. The award-winning breakfast sees local sourcing of sausages and bacon, home-made breads and jams and eggs supplied by the family chickens.

Rooms: 4 rms (3 en suite) (1 pri facs) **S** fr £75 **D** fr £90 **Facilities:** FTV DVD Lounge tea/coffee Dinner available WiFi 🔒 **Extras:** Home-made biscuits, bottled water – complimentary **Parking:** 4 **Notes:** No children 16 years

UPTON MAGNA   Map 10 SJ51

The Haughmond

★★★★ ◉◉ ⬦ INN

tel: 01743 709918 **Pelham Road SY4 4TZ**
email: contact@thehaughmond.co.uk web: www.thehaughmond.co.uk
dir: *Phone for directions.*

This delightful village inn provides a contemporary dining area and bar with a range of comfortable bedrooms above. All rooms offer welcome extras and WiFi, with large rain showers in the bathrooms. Carefully prepared dishes, making good use of quality, local produce, are served for breakfast, lunch, afternoon tea and dinner. Parking, a garden with seating and even the village shop/café are on site.

Rooms: 5 en suite (1 fmly) **Facilities:** STV FTV iPod docking station Lounge tea/coffee Dinner available WiFi 🔒 **Extras:** Smart TVs with Netflix **Conf:** Max 60 Thtr 40 Class 60 Board 30 **Parking:** 30

WELLINGTON   Map 10 SJ61

The Lord Nelson

★★ GUEST ACCOMMODATION

tel: 01952 240055 **11–13 Park Street TF1 3AE**
web: www.hotelintelford.com
dir: *Contact The Lord Nelson for detailed directions.*

This Grade II listed property is located in a quiet residential area close to town. Inside, there are a number of eating options, as well as comfortably appointed bedrooms in a range of sizes. There is a large car park to the rear and free WiFi is available throughout.

Rooms: 12 en suite **Facilities:** FTV tea/coffee Licensed WiFi **Parking:** 12 **Notes:** Closed 16 December to 6 January

WEM   Map 15 SJ52

Aston Lodge Guest House

★★★★ BED AND BREAKFAST

tel: 01939 232577 **Soulton Road SY4 5BG**
email: astonlodge@btconnect.com web: www.aston-lodge.co.uk
dir: *On B5065, close to Wem railway station.*

Aston Lodge is an elegant Georgian house situated in a quiet, convenient position close to the train station in the heart of Wem. Some bedrooms are in the main house while the others are found in the adjoining coach house. Of the latter, two are on the ground floor and the other has its own lounge. All rooms are of a high standard and have free WiFi and high-quality bathrooms. Breakfast is served in the spacious dining room using fine quality and, whenever possible, locally-sourced produce. A comfortable lounge is available for guest use. There is ample off-road parking and a pleasant, good-sized garden.

Rooms: 3 rms (2 en suite) (1 pri facs) 3 annexe en suite (1 fmly) (2 GF) **S** fr £54 **D** fr £74* **Facilities:** FTV DVD TVL tea/coffee WiFi **Extras:** Speciality toiletries **Parking:** 6 **Notes:** No children 10 years RS 25–26 December and 31 December to 1 January room only

SOMERSET

AXBRIDGE
Map 4 ST45

The Oak House
★★★★★ ◉◉ ☺ RESTAURANT WITH ROOMS

tel: 01934 732444 **The Square BS26 2AP**
email: info@theoakhousesomerset.com **web:** www.theoakhousesomerset.com
dir: *M5 junction 22, A38 north, turn right towards Axbridge and Cheddar.*

This impressive restaurant with rooms is located in the middle of the village and provides a relaxed, high quality experience, whether guests are coming to enjoy the restaurant or to stay in one of the nine bedrooms above. Hospitality and service are delivered in an efficient and helpful manner by a young and enthusiastic team. The kitchen has a serious approach and delivers delightful dishes full of flavour, utilising the best quality produce.

Rooms: 9 en suite (2 fmly) **Facilities:** FTV DVD Lounge tea/coffee Dinner available WiFi **Notes:** Closed 2–5 January RS Sunday evening and Monday evening restaurant closed

Old Manor House B&B
★★★★ BED AND BREAKFAST

tel: 01934 709542 **Cross Lane, Cross BS26 2ED**
email: graham@oldmanorhouse.net **web:** www.oldmanorhouse.net
dir: *M5 junction 22, 3rd exit at roundabout (A38 Bristol). On A38 at 40mph sign turn right signed Wells. Entrance to parking on left at the end of cream building.*

Located at the foot of the Mendip Hills, this beautifully restored manor house is around 400 years old and is an ideal base from which to explore the nearby attractions of Cheddar, Wells and Bath – all a short drive away. The building is full of character and charm and offers well-equipped rooms of various sizes including some on the ground floor. Breakfast is served in the well-furnished dining room and includes home-made breads and jams. A guest lounge and off-street parking are also provided.

Rooms: 7 rms (6 en suite) (1 pri facs) (2 fmly) (2 GF) **D** fr £79* **Facilities:** FTV DVD TVL tea/coffee WiFi **Parking:** 7

BABCARY
Map 4 ST52

The Red Lion Inn
★★★★ ☺ INN

tel: 01458 223230 **Main Street TA11 7ED**
email: info@redlionbabcary.com **web:** www.redlionbabcary.co.uk
dir: *Off A303 and A37.*

Tucked away in a sleepy village, this engaging country pub has so much to offer and provides an appealing blend of traditional and contemporary styles. The thatched roof, flagstone floors and crackling log fires all set the tone alongside a committed team dedicated to ensuring guests are properly looked after. Bedrooms are located in the adjacent barn and provide impressive levels of comfort and quality, with all the necessities for a thoroughly relaxing stay. Food is not to be missed, as a skilled kitchen team make excellent use of the best the area has to offer. An alternative option in spring and summer is The Den, a stylish function room in the gardens which houses a wood-fired pizza oven.

Rooms: 6 annexe en suite (2 fmly) (4 GF) **Facilities:** DVD tea/coffee Dinner available Direct dial WiFi **Extras:** Speciality toiletries, snacks **Parking:** 35

BACKWELL
Map 4 ST46

The Rising Sun
★★★★★ ☺ INN

tel: 01275 462215 **91 West Town Road BS48 3BH**
email: therisingsun@ohhcompany.co.uk **web:** www.ohhpubs.co.uk
dir: *Phone for directions.*

The Rising Sun has been transformed by the current owners and delivers high-quality bedrooms and bathrooms together with excellent hospitality and service. Bedrooms come in a range of shapes and sizes but all are appointed to very comfortable standards. A good selection of real ales and wines is available to accompany the range of tempting dishes on the regularly-changing dinner menu. Breakfast also offers a good selection and features high quality produce. A car park and rear garden with seating are also available.

Rooms: 6 en suite **Facilities:** Dinner available

BALTONSBOROUGH
Map 4 ST53

Lower Farm
★★★★ FARMHOUSE

tel: 01458 850206 & 07773 497188 **Lottisham BA6 8PF**
email: dboard51@btinternet.com **web:** www.lowerfarmbandb.co.uk
dir: *From Shepton Mallet take A37 over Wraxall Hill past Queens Arms. Take 3rd turning on right to Lottisham, 1st on right.*

A working farm peacefully located and surrounded by pleasant countryside, where the proprietors offer a genuine welcome and traditional farmhouse hospitality. The one en suite bedroom is spacious and well equipped, and is located on the ground floor at one end of the main building. Breakfast is taken in the comfortable dining room where a wood-burning fire adds to the ambience during the winter.

Rooms: 1 en suite (1 GF) **Facilities:** FTV TVL tea/coffee ⚹ **Notes:** beef/sheep farm

BATH
Map 4 ST76

See also Box (Wiltshire), Bradford-on-Avon (Wiltshire) and Frome

Apple Tree Guest House
★★★★★ ☺ GUEST HOUSE

tel: 01225 337642 **7 Pulteney Gardens BA2 4HG**
email: enquiries@appletreebath.com **web:** www.appletreeguesthouse.com
dir: *A4 onto A36 into Pulteney Road. Under railway bridge, take 2nd left into Pulteney Gardens.*

This charming house is quietly located, and offers a tranquil setting. Some parking is available, and the location is within walking distance of Bath's many attractions. Excellent breakfasts are served in the cosy breakfast lounge. Bedrooms are thoughtfully appointed, and beds are particularly comfortable.

Rooms: 4 en suite **Facilities:** FTV tea/coffee WiFi Massage and beauty treatments **Extras:** Speciality toiletries – complimentary **Parking:** 2 **Notes:** No children 11 years Closed 14 December to 9 January

BATH *continued*

Apsley House

★★★★★ 🛏 BED AND BREAKFAST

tel: 01225 336966 **Newbridge Hill BA1 3PT**
email: info@apsley-house.co.uk **web:** www.apsley-house.co.uk
dir: *1.3 miles west of city centre on A431.*

Built in 1830 by the Duke of Wellington, Apsley House is within walking distance (allow around half an hour) of the city centre. The house is extremely elegant, and the spacious bedrooms have pleasant views. Some rooms have four-poster beds, and there are two family rooms. A smart breakfast room and a delightful lounge are available.

Rooms: 11 en suite (2 fmly) (1 GF) **S** fr £90 **D** fr £140* **Facilities:** STV FTV DVD iPod docking station Lounge tea/coffee Direct dial Licensed WiFi
Extras: Speciality toiletries, bottled water, mini-bar **Parking:** 12 **Notes:** LB Closed 3 days Christmas

River House and Friary Coach House

★★★★★ GUEST ACCOMMODATION

tel: 01225 722252 & 07712 437478 **Friary, Freshford BA2 7UE**
email: info@riverhousebath.com **web:** www.riverhousebath.com
dir: *A36 south of Bath, pass signs for Freshford on left, left at crossroads sign, down narrow lane signed "No through road".*

Set in eleven acres of delightfully peaceful former monastery grounds, River House offers views over the beautiful gardens, and is just five miles from Bath. Accommodation consists of comfortable bedrooms in the main house with lounges and relaxing areas for guests to enjoy, and the separate Friary Coach House – a luxurious, self-contained building adjacent to the main house. Guests in the Coach House have the option of breakfast being delivered to their own dining room. Attentive service and a genuine welcome are assured.

Rooms: 5 rms (4 en suite) 1 annexe en suite (2 fmly) (2 GF) **Facilities:** STV FTV DVD iPod docking station Lounge TVL tea/coffee Dinner available Direct dial Licensed WiFi 🏊 🚴 Fishing Riding 🛁 Hot tub, badminton, art, nature trail, clock golf **Extras:** Chocolates, fridge, speciality toiletries, fresh fruit, flowers – complimentary **Parking:** 10 **Notes:** LB

Chestnuts House

★★★★★ 🛏 GUEST ACCOMMODATION

tel: 01225 334279 **16 Henrietta Road BA2 6LY**
email: reservations@chestnutshouse.co.uk **web:** www.chestnutshouse.co.uk
dir: *Enter Bath on A46, under flyover, right at roundabout. Follow signs for A36 Warminster, over Cleveland Bridge and turn right. 50 metres on left.*

Located just a few minutes' walk from the city centre and appointed using light shades and oak, the accommodation at Chestnut House is fresh and airy. Bedrooms are attractively co-ordinated, well equipped and comfortable; free WiFi in the rooms is available. Breakfast, which features quite an extensive buffet and daily specials, is served in the dining room that opens onto the pretty rear garden. There is a cosy lounge, and the small car park is a bonus.

Rooms: 5 en suite (1 fmly) (2 GF) **Facilities:** STV FTV DVD TVL tea/coffee WiFi Riding **Extras:** Speciality toiletries **Parking:** 5

Dorian House

★★★★★ 🛏 GUEST ACCOMMODATION

tel: 01225 426336 **1 Upper Oldfield Park BA2 3JX**
email: info@dorianhousebath.co.uk **web:** www.dorianhouse.co.uk
dir: *Phone for directions.*

This elegant, imposing Victorian property in an elevated location has delightful views over the city of Bath from many of the stylish bedrooms. All rooms are very comfortably furnished and include TVs, power showers, bathrobes and luxury toiletries; four rooms have four-poster beds. A guest lounge and a small honesty bar are available; carefully prepared breakfasts are served in the orangery overlooking the terraced, Japanese-inspired garden to the rear of the property. A very pleasant welcome and attentive service are offered throughout the stay. Free parking and WiFi are provided.

Rooms: 13 en suite (2 GF) **Facilities:** FTV Lounge tea/coffee Direct dial Licensed WiFi **Parking:** 13 **Notes:** Closed 24–25 December

Haringtons

★★★★★ GUEST ACCOMMODATION

tel: 01225 461728 **8–10 Queen Street BA1 1HE**
email: post@haringtonshotel.co.uk **web:** www.haringtonshotel.co.uk
dir: *A4 into George Street, into Milsom Street. 1st right into Quiet Street, 1st left into Queen Street.*

This delightful accommodation could hardly be more central to the middle of Bath and provides a range of very well decorated bedrooms and bathrooms in a selection of shapes and sizes. All rooms include very comfortable beds and quality bedding and some welcome extras to add to guests' comfort. A bar and lounge area is available during the day plus light snacks in the evening. Breakfast provides a very good range of well-cooked and well-presented hot and cold options. A permit is available for reduced-rate, overnight parking at a nearby car park.

Rooms: 13 en suite (3 fmly) **S** fr £80 **D** fr £85 **Facilities:** Licensed WiFi
Extras: Nespresso machine, speciality toiletries

Waterhouse

★★★★★ 🛏 GUEST ACCOMMODATION

tel: 01225 721999 **Waterhouse Lane, Monkton Combe BA2 7JB**
email: waterhouse@wilsher-group.com **web:** www.waterhousebath.co.uk
dir: *From Bath on A36 to Monkton Combe, over viaduct, turn right into Waterhouse Lane. From south on A36 turn left into Waterhouse Lane, at bottom of the hill.*

This 18th-century manor house is in a peaceful location just a couple of miles from Bath. It offers modern bedrooms and bathrooms with plenty of welcome guest extras, and a range of relaxing lounges. Guests can enjoy the garden, and country walks start straight from the front door. Breakfast is served in the contemporary dining room, and meeting rooms are also available.

Rooms: 13 en suite (4 fmly) **Facilities:** FTV Lounge TVL tea/coffee Direct dial Lift Licensed WiFi Fishing 🛁 **Extras:** Fresh milk, bottled water – complimentary; fridge **Conf:** Max 40 Thtr 40 Class 20 Board 16 **Parking:** 45 **Notes:** LB

The Windsor Townhouse

★★★★★ GUEST HOUSE

tel: 01225 422100 **69 Great Pulteney Street BA2 4DL**
email: sales@bathwindsorguesthouse.com **web:** www.bathwindsorguesthouse.com
dir: *Phone for directions.*

An easy two-minute walk from the city centre, shops, restaurants and attractions, The Windsor is a Grade I listed Georgian townhouse on Great Pulteney Street, one of the finest boulevards in Europe. Inside are 15 individually-styled, en suite bedrooms. Period features, free WiFi, air conditioning, TVs, tea- and coffee-making facilities, hairdryers, mini-safes and ironing boards come as standard. The addition of thick, soft fluffy towels, cosy Dorma duvets, pillows and luxury toiletries complete the package. Breakfast offers a good selection of well-prepared, hot and cold dishes, and staff are very friendly and willing to help. Parking permits can be purchased for the street outside.

Rooms: 15 en suite (1 fmly) **Facilities:** STV FTV DVD iPod docking station tea/coffee Direct dial Licensed WiFi **Extras:** Speciality toiletries, mini-bar, mini-safe **Parking:** 4

Astor House

★★★★ BED AND BREAKFAST

tel: 01225 429134 & 07921 139558 **14 Oldfield Road BA2 3ND**
email: astorhouse.visitus@virgin.net **web:** www.astorhouse-bath.co.uk
dir: *A4 into Bath to lights, follow A36 (avoiding city centre). Onto A367, 2nd right.*

Astor House offers very comfortable accommodation and personal, friendly service. The bedrooms are understately elegant and equipped with a wealth of extras for the modern guest. Hearty breakfasts are served in the light dining room. The location, in a quiet street, is within easy distance of all central attractions, making it an ideal base from which to explore the city.

Rooms: 7 en suite (2 fmly) **S** fr £60 **D** fr £90 **Facilities:** FTV Lounge TVL tea/coffee Direct dial WiFi ♨ ⚓ **Parking:** 5

The Bailbrook Lodge

★★★★ 🏅 GUEST HOUSE

tel: 01225 859090 **35–37 London Road West BA1 7HZ**
email: hotel@bailbrooklodge.co.uk **web:** www.bailbrooklodge.co.uk
dir: *M4 junction 18, A46 south to A4 junction, left signed Batheaston. Lodge 1st on left.*

Set in extensive gardens on the eastern edge of the city, this imposing Georgian building provides smart accommodation. The well-equipped bedrooms include some with four-poster beds and period furniture, and service is professional and efficient. The inviting lounge has a small bar, and light snacks are available from noon until evening. Breakfast is served in the elegant dining room.

Rooms: 15 en suite (1 fmly) (1 GF) **Facilities:** FTV DVD iPod docking station Lounge tea/coffee Licensed WiFi ⚓ **Extras:** Mineral water, bath robes in some rooms **Parking:** 15 **Notes:** LB

Villa Claudia

★★★★ BED AND BREAKFAST

tel: 01225 329670 **19 Forester Road, Bathwick BA2 6QE**
email: claudiaamato77@aol.com **web:** www.villaclaudia.co.uk
dir: *From A4 into Cleveland Place East (A36), at next roundabout 1st exit into Beckford Road, left into Forester Road.*

Villa Claudia is a beautiful Victorian property located on a quiet, tree-lined residential street within easy walking distance of the city centre's attractions and restaurants. The Italian owners provide attentive and personal service. Bedrooms and bathrooms are beautifully decorated and very comfortable; a four-poster room is available. Delicious breakfasts are served in the charming dining room at a communal table.

Rooms: 3 rms (1 en suite) (2 pri facs) (1 fmly) **Facilities:** FTV DVD tea/coffee WiFi **Extras:** Mineral water – complimentary **Parking:** 4 **Notes:** No children 5 years Closed 21 December to 1 January

The Hollies

★★★★ GUEST ACCOMMODATION

tel: 01225 313366 **Hatfield Road BA2 2BD**
email: davcartwright@lineone.net **web:** www.theholliesbath.co.uk
dir: *A36 onto A367 Wells Road and Wellsway, 0.7 mile, opposite Devonshire Arms.*

This delightful house stands in impressive gardens overlooking a magnificent church, and is within easy reach of the city centre. The individually decorated, themed bedrooms are appointed to provide excellent levels of comfort and have good facilities. Breakfast served in the elegant dining room is an enjoyable start to the day.

Rooms: 3 rms (2 en suite) (1 pri facs) **D** fr £120 **Facilities:** FTV Lounge tea/coffee WiFi ⚓ **Extras:** Sweets **Parking:** 3 **Notes:** No children 16 years Closed 15 December to 15 January

Poplar House

★★★★ BED AND BREAKFAST

tel: 01225 852629 **9 The Batch BA1 7DR**
email: poplarhousebath@gmail.com **web:** www.poplarhousebath.co.uk
dir: *M4 junction 18 onto A46 (London Road). Left at roundabout, house on left.*

Located a short drive from the centre of Bath, Poplar House is a very well-maintained property that offers comfortable accommodation in a peaceful setting. Bedrooms come in a range of shapes and sizes, and guests are also welcome to use the comfortable lounge and outdoor seating terrace. Breakfast utilises good quality produce and is served around one large table in the very pleasant dining room.

Rooms: 3 en suite **Facilities:** FTV TVL tea/coffee WiFi ⚓ **Extras:** Robes, sweets – complimentary **Parking:** 6

Brocks Guest House

★★★★ GUEST ACCOMMODATION

tel: 01225 338374 **32 Brock Street BA1 2LN**
email: brocks@brocksguesthouse.co.uk **web:** www.brocksguesthouse.co.uk
dir: *Just off A4 between Circus and Royal Crescent.*

A warm welcome is extended at this delightful Georgian property, located in the heart of the city just a few hundred yards from Royal Crescent. All rooms reflect the comfortable elegance of the Georgian era. A traditional breakfast is served in the charming dining room, which also offers a lounge area with comfortable seating.

Rooms: 6 en suite (2 fmly) **Facilities:** FTV Lounge tea/coffee WiFi ⚓ **Notes:** Closed 24 December to 1 January

BATH *continued*

Milton House Bed & Breakfast

★★★★ BED AND BREAKFAST

tel: 01225 335632 & 07875 319567 **75 Wellsway BA2 4RU**
email: info@milton-house.co.uk **web:** www.milton-house.co.uk
dir: *A36 (inner ring road) onto A367 (Wells Road). After 0.5 mile, sharp right, Milton House 150 yards on left.*

Located in a residential area just 15 minutes' walk from the centre of Bath, this comfortable establishment is run by Gibson and Blessing Mutandwa, who offer a very warm welcome to all guests. Bedrooms come in a range of shapes and sizes but are all well furnished and well equipped. A carefully prepared breakfast is provided in the comfortable dining room. Parking is available on the side streets nearby, or on the main road outside.

Rooms: 4 en suite (1 fmly) **Facilities:** FTV tea/coffee WiFi ⚓
Notes: No children 8 years

Pulteney House

★★★★ GUEST ACCOMMODATION

tel: 01225 460991 **14 Pulteney Road BA2 4HA**
email: pulteneyhouse@gmail.com **web:** www.pulteneyhotel.co.uk
dir: *On A36.*

This large detached property situated in a well-tended garden is within walking distance of the city centre. The bedrooms vary in size and include some annexe rooms; all are well equipped with useful facilities. Full English breakfasts are served in the dining room at individual tables. A guest lounge and car park are both welcome features.

Pulteney House

Rooms: 12 rms (11 en suite) (1 pri facs) 5 annexe en suite (3 fmly) (2 GF) **S** fr £70 **D** fr £95 **Facilities:** STV FTV TVL tea/coffee WiFi ⚓ **Parking:** 18 **Notes:** LB Closed 24–26 December

See advert below

Wentworth House

★★★★ GUEST ACCOMMODATION

tel: 01225 339193 **106 Bloomfield Road BA2 2AP**
email: stay@wentworthhouse.co.uk **web:** www.wentworthhouse.co.uk
dir: *From city centre on A367 (signed Shepton Mallet), right into Bloomfield Road.*

Set in an elevated position above Bath with views over the city, Wentworth House is a comfortable establishment that includes a relaxing guest lounge, bar and garden with pool and hot tub in the summer. Bedrooms come in a range of shapes and sizes – some have four-posters. Breakfast is served in the spacious dining room overlooking the garden.

Rooms: 19 rms (18 en suite) (1 pri facs) 1 annexe en suite (3 fmly) (9 GF) **Facilities:** FTV TVL tea/coffee Direct dial Licensed WiFi ↘ Hot tub **Conf:** Max 15 Class 15 Board 15 **Parking:** 15 **Notes:** LB

The Rising Sun Inn

★★★ INN

tel: 01225 425918 & 07815 741764 **3–4 Grove Street BA2 6PJ**
email: therisingsunbath@gmail.com **web:** www.therisingsunbath.co.uk
dir: *From A46 into Bath. Left at lights, over Cleveland Bridge, 1st right into St John's Road, leads into Grove Street.*

This inn has an excellent location, just a few minutes' stroll from central Bath and all its attractions. Bedrooms are comfortably furnished and come in a range of shapes and sizes. A good selection of real ales is offered at the bar along with traditional dishes and home-cooked specials.

Rooms: 8 en suite (3 fmly) **S** fr £76.50 **D** fr £84.15* **Facilities:** FTV tea/coffee Dinner available WiFi **Notes:** Closed 24–26 December, 31 December to 2 Janaury

Waltons Guest House

★★★ GUEST HOUSE

tel: 01225 426528 **17 Crescent Gardens, Upper Bristol Road BA1 2NA**
email: rose@waltonsguesthouse.co.uk **web:** www.bathguesthouse.com
dir: *On A4 350 yards west of city centre.*

There is a warm welcome at Waltons Guest House, situated within strolling distance of the centre of Bath. The cosy bedrooms come with useful extra facilities, and a traditional English breakfast is served at individual tables in the dining room.

Waltons Guest House

Rooms: 7 en suite (1 fmly) **S** fr £55 **D** fr £90* **Facilities:** FTV tea/coffee WiFi

See advert below

BRIDGWATER   Map 4 ST23

Blackmore Farm

★★★★ FARMHOUSE

tel: 01278 653442 **Blackmore Lane, Cannington TA5 2NE**
email: dyerfarm@aol.com **web:** www.blackmorefarm.co.uk
dir: *3 miles west of Bridgwater. Follow brown tourist signs on A39, before Cannington.*

Dating back to the 15th century, this Grade I listed manor house is truly unique; it has a wealth of original features such as oak beams, huge open fireplaces, stone archways and even a chapel. Bedrooms located in the main house are individual in style and one has a wonderful four-poster and a lofty, oak-beamed ceiling. Additionally, some bedrooms are located in a separate area that offers flexible accommodation with wonderful views across the rolling countryside. Breakfast is taken in the grandeur of the dining room around one incredibly long table – a truly memorable experience.

Rooms: 3 en suite 6 annexe en suite (1 fmly) (6 GF) **Facilities:** FTV TVL tea/coffee Licensed WiFi ⬇ ⚓ Fishing 🔔 Farm shop café **Extras:** Fruit, bath robes in some rooms – complimentary **Conf:** Max 30 Board 30 **Parking:** 10 **Notes:** LB 900 acres dairy/arable

BRIDGWATER *continued*

Ash-Wembdon Farm

★★★★ FARMHOUSE

tel: 01278 453097 **Hollow Lane, Wembdon TA5 2BD**
email: mary.rowe@btinternet.com **web:** www.farmaccommodation.co.uk
dir: *M5, A38, A39 to Minehead, at roundabout 3rd exit into Homeburg Way, at lights take B3339, right into Hollow Lane.*

Near the Quantock Hills, this is a 17th-century farmhouse on a working beef and arable farm, offering homely and comfortable accommodation. All rooms have en suite showers or private bathrooms, and English or continental breakfasts are served in the guest dining room. Guests also have use of a lounge and landscaped garden.

Rooms: 3 rms (2 en suite) (1 pri facs) **S** fr £45 **D** fr £65 **Facilities:** FTV Lounge tea/coffee WiFi 🍷 **Parking:** 3 **Notes:** LB No children 12 years Closed 22 December to 3 January 340 acres arable/beef

---

BROMPTON REGIS	Map 3 SS93

Holworthy Farm

★★★★ 🍴 FARMHOUSE

tel: 01398 371244 **TA22 9NY**
email: holworthyfarm@aol.com **web:** www.holworthyfarm.co.uk
dir: *2 miles east of Brompton Regis. Exit A396 on east side of Wimbleball Lake.*

Set in the south-east corner of Exmoor, this working livestock farm has spectacular views over Wimbleball Lake. The bedrooms are traditionally furnished and well equipped. The dining room, overlooking the garden, is an attractive setting for breakfast. Dinner is available by arrangement.

Rooms: 5 rms (3 en suite) (2 pri facs) (2 fmly) (1 GF) **Facilities:** FTV DVD Lounge TVL tea/coffee Dinner available WiFi 🍷 **Extras:** Bottled water – complimentary **Conf:** Max 20 Class 20 Board 20 **Parking:** 8 **Notes:** LB 200 acres beef/sheep

---

CANNINGTON	Map 4 ST23

The Malt Shovel Inn

[U]

tel: 01278 653432 **Blackmore Lane TA5 2NE**
email: themaltshovelcannington@gmail.com **web:** www.themaltshovelcannington.com
dir: *Phone for directions.*

Currently the rating for this establishment is not confirmed. This may be due to a change of ownership or because it has only recently joined the AA rating scheme.

Rooms: 8 en suite (1 fmly) (8 GF) **S** fr £50 **D** fr £60* **Facilities:** FTV tea/coffee Dinner available WiFi **Parking:** 20 **Notes:** LB

CASTLE CARY	Map 4 ST63

The Pilgrims

★★★★★ ◉◉ 🍷 RESTAURANT WITH ROOMS

tel: 01963 240600 **Lovington BA7 7PT**
email: jools@thepilgrimsatlovington.co.uk **web:** www.thepilgrimsatlovington.co.uk
dir: *On B3153, 1.5 miles east of lights on A37 at Lydford.*

The Pilgrims describes itself as 'the pub that thinks it's a restaurant', which is pretty accurate. With a real emphasis on fresh, local and carefully prepared produce, both dinner and breakfast are the focus of any stay here. In addition, the resident family proprietors provide a friendly and relaxed atmosphere. Comfortable and well-equipped bedrooms are available in the adjacent converted cider barn.

Rooms: 5 annexe en suite (5 GF) **Facilities:** FTV Lounge tea/coffee Dinner available WiFi **Extras:** Speciality toiletries **Parking:** 5 **Notes:** LB No children 14 years RS Sunday lunch to Tuesday lunch Restaurant and bar closed to non-residents

---

CHARD	Map 4 ST30

Hornsbury Mill

★★★★ 🍴 GUEST ACCOMMODATION

tel: 01460 63317 **Eleighwater TA20 3AQ**
email: info@hornsburymill.co.uk **web:** www.hornsburymill.co.uk
dir: *Off A358.*

Hornsbury Mill is a charming example of an early 19th-century corn mill, built of local flint with hamstone mullion windows. The waterwheel has been lovingly restored and turns during daylight hours; and there are four acres of beautiful gardens, making this a popular wedding venue. Bedrooms include a ground-floor room with good disabled access and facilities, and the delightful Crown Wheel Suite with four-poster bed and separate sitting room.

Rooms: 10 en suite (2 fmly) (1 GF) **S** fr £85 **D** fr £110* **Facilities:** FTV DVD Lounge tea/coffee Dinner available Direct dial Licensed WiFi 🍷 **Extras:** Speciality toiletries – complimentary **Conf:** Max 150 Thtr 150 Class 50 Board 50 **Parking:** 80 **Notes:** Closed 24 December to 7 January Civ wed 130

CHEDDAR	Map 4 ST45

The Bath Arms

★★★★★ ◉◉ INN

tel: 01934 742425 **Bath Street BS27 3AA**
email: info@batharms.com **web:** www.batharms.com
dir: *Phone for directions.*

This delightful inn has undergone much refurbishment to offer high quality and comfort in the bedrooms, bathrooms and public spaces. An excellent mix of traditional inn hospitality along with helpful and efficient service can be expected. Guests can choose from the more relaxed bar setting and menu or the superb dishes utilising high quality produce in the comfortable restaurant. A large car park and outdoor seating both to the front and rear of the inn are welcome additions. Cheddar Village is a couple of minutes' stroll from the front door.

Rooms: 6 en suite **Facilities:** FTV tea/coffee Dinner available WiFi **Extras:** Speciality toiletries, bottled water, snacks – complimentary **Parking:** 60 **Notes:** LB No children 18 years

CHEW MAGNA	Map 4 ST56

The Bear & Swan

★★★★★ ⏺ INN

tel: 01275 331100 **13 South Parade BS40 8PR**
email: thebearandswan@ohhcompany.co.uk **web:** www.ohhpubs.co.uk
dir: *Chew Magna signed from A37 and A38, in centre of village.*

Part of a small and impressive collection of fine quality inns, this delightful village pub offers the best traditional hospitality with an impressive range of dishes served throughout the day and evening. The bedrooms and bathrooms provide plenty of quality and comfort with sumptuous beds and bedding, and modern, spacious showers. All this, along with a well-chosen selection of ales and wines, will ensure a very relaxing stay.

Rooms: 4 en suite (1 fmly) **Facilities:** FTV tea/coffee Dinner available Direct dial WiFi ⏺ **Extras:** Slippers **Parking:** 6 **Notes:** LB

CLUTTON	Map 4 ST65

The Hunters Rest

★★★★ ⏺ INN

tel: 01761 452303 **King Lane, Clutton Hill BS39 5QL**
email: paul@huntersrest.co.uk **web:** www.huntersrest.co.uk
dir: *Exit A37 onto A368 towards Bath, 100 yards right into lane, left at T-junction, inn 0.25 mile on left.*

The Hunters Rest was originally built around 1750 as a hunting lodge for the Earl of Warwick. Set in delightful countryside, it is ideally located for Bath, Bristol and Wells. Bedrooms and bathrooms are furnished and equipped to excellent standards, and the ground floor combines the character of a real country inn with an excellent range of home-cooked meals.

Rooms: 5 en suite (2 fmly) **Facilities:** FTV iPod docking station tea/coffee Dinner available Direct dial WiFi ⏺ Fishing Riding ⏺ **Conf:** Max 40 Thtr 40 Class 25 Board 25 **Parking:** 90 **Notes:** LB

COMPTON MARTIN	Map 4 ST55

Ring O Bells

★★★★ ⏺ INN

tel: 01761 221284 **BS40 6JE**
email: ring_o_bells@btconnect.com **web:** www.ringobellscomptonmartin.co.uk
dir: *On A368 between Blagdon and Chew Valley.*

The Ring O Bells is a delightful village inn that offers a rare combination of traditional character and hospitality with some more modern, quirky additions. The bar and dining areas are full of interest, and along with a good selection of real ales, a range of excellent dishes is offered. Bedrooms include very comfortable king-sized beds and quality showers in the bathrooms. Outdoor seating in the rear garden and on-site parking are both welcome features.

Rooms: 1 en suite 1 annexe en suite (2 GF) **Facilities:** FTV iPod docking station Lounge tea/coffee Dinner available WiFi ⏺ ⏺ **Parking:** 60 **Notes:** LB RS Monday to Wednesday closed 3–6pm

CORTON DENHAM	Map 4 ST62

The Queens Arms

★★★★★ ◉◉ ⏺ INN

tel: 01963 220317 **Corton Denham DT9 4LR**
email: relax@thequeensarms.com **web:** www.thequeensarms.com
dir: *A303 exit Chapel Cross signed South Cadbury and Corton Denham. Follow signs to South Cadbury. Through village, after 0.25 mile turn left up hill signed Sherborne and Corton Denham. Left at top of hill, pub at end of village on right.*

This is a proper inn located in peaceful countryside. Staff are friendly and welcoming, and the pub dog can usually be found in front of the roaring log fire in the bar. Bedrooms and bathrooms offer impressive levels of comfort, style and quality. In addition to a very good selection of real ales, this is a paradise for bottled beer lovers with a great choice from around the world. Excellent quality local produce can be found in the choice of delicious dinners which may be enjoyed in the traditional bar or character restaurant.

Rooms: 5 en suite 3 annexe en suite (1 GF) **S** fr £80 **D** fr £99* **Facilities:** FTV DVD iPod docking station Lounge tea/coffee Dinner available Direct dial WiFi ⏺ **Extras:** Nespresso coffee, speciality toiletries, robes/slippers **Conf:** Max 35 Thtr 35 Class 25 Board 30 **Parking:** 20 **Notes:** LB

See advert on page 222

EAST LYDFORD

Map 4 ST53

Cross Keys Inn

★★★★ INN

tel: 01963 240473 **TA11 7HA**
email: enquiries@crosskeysinn.info **web:** www.crosskeysinn.info
dir: *From A303 take A37 at Podimore roundabout. Approximately 5 miles to crossroads turn right, pub immediately on right. From Shepton Mallet take A37 to Lydford-on-Fosse. Left at crossroads, pub on right.*

Cross Keys Inn is a warm and welcoming establishment with a very relaxed and engaging atmosphere. There is plenty to admire with stone-flagged floors, original beams and a genuine sense of hospitality. Bedrooms offer contemporary comforts and quality bathrooms. The food is honest and tasty and real ale lovers are very well looked after. There is also a lovely garden in which to sit, unwind and enjoy the delights of this popular inn.

Rooms: 6 en suite (1 fmly) **Facilities:** FTV tea/coffee Dinner available WiFi
Camping site, skittle alley **Extras:** Speciality toiletries, bottled water –
complimentary **Conf:** Max 100 Thtr 100 Class 75 Board 50 **Parking:** 50

EXFORD

Map 3 SS83

Stockleigh Lodge

★★★★ BED AND BREAKFAST

tel: 01643 831500 **TA24 7PZ**
email: stay@stockleighexford.co.uk **web:** www.stockleighexford.co.uk
dir: *On B3224 through Wheddon Cross to Exford. Over river bridge into Simonsbath Road, up hill on right.*

Situated at the very heart of Exmoor, Stockleigh Lodge dates from around 1900 and provides a perfect base from which to discovery this spectacular area. Whether

exploration is by car or cycle, on foot or on horseback, your hosts will be only too pleased to help with local information. The bedrooms are very comfortable and enjoy lovely views, while public areas include a spacious guest lounge warmed by a crackling fire in cooler months. Aga-cooked breakfasts will get the day off to a satisfying start. Stabling is also available for those wishing to bring their horses with them on holiday.

Rooms: 9 en suite (2 fmly) **S** fr £40 **D** fr £80* **Facilities:** TVL tea/coffee WiFi Riding
Stabling for guests horses **Parking:** 10

FIVEHEAD

Map 4 ST32

Premier Collection

Langford Fivehead

★★★★★ ◎◎ 🍽 RESTAURANT WITH ROOMS

tel: 01460 282020 **Lower Swell TA3 6PH**
email: rebecca@thelangford.co.uk **web:** www.langfordfivehead.co.uk
dir: *Phone for directions.*

Documents indicate that there has been a house on this site since 1255 and the current property retains a significant proportion of a 15th-century hall house. In keeping with the grand character found throughout the building, guests can be assured of the most pleasant of welcomes and helpful, relaxing hospitality and service. Bedrooms come in a range of shapes and styles, but all are decorated and equipped to very high standards (although deliberately, there are no TVs in the bedrooms). The restaurant is a delight of home-grown and local produce, providing delicious dishes at both dinner and breakfast.

Rooms: 6 en suite **Facilities:** Dinner available **Notes:** Closed 25 July to 7 August, 2–15 January

The Queens Arms

Corton Denham, Sherborne, Somerset DT9 4LR • Tel: 01963 220317
Website: www.thequeensarms.com • Email: relax@thequeensarms.com
Facebook: www.facebook.com/thequeensarms • Twitter: @queensarmspub

Taste Of The West Gold Winner 2016, Double Silver Winners, Best Tourism Pub and Best B&B Accommodation – South West Tourism Excellence Awards 2014–15. Taste of Somerset Best Pub 2013, Best National Freehouse 2012 and former AA Pub of the Year 2008–9. Quintessentially English Georgian Inn, in a gloriously rural setting, with the gently rolling landscape on the Dorset/Somerset Hills. A pilgrimage for Foodies – note their own smallholding (Pigs, Cows and Hens). Snuggle up in front of the roaring open fire with newspapers, a pint and a homemade pork pie – oodles of rustic charm. Their eight en-suite rooms live up to the surroundings and wonderful views, and are all decorated with understated opulence.

AA
★★★★★
Bed & Breakfast
2018
Silver Award

FLAX BOURTON — Map 4 ST56

Premier Collection

Backwell House

★★★★★ ◎◎ RESTAURANT WITH ROOMS

tel: 0117 325 1110 **Farleigh Road BS48 3QA**
email: guy@backwellhouse.co.uk **web:** www.backwellhouse.co.uk
dir: Phone for directions.

Located in a peaceful countryside setting with delightful views, this stylish property is surprisingly only a 10-minute drive from Bristol's city centre. The luxurious bedrooms and bathrooms come in a range of shapes and sizes but all include very comfortable beds plus some welcome extras. Breakfast includes a range of high quality hot and cold dishes while dinner is available on Wednesday to Saturday evenings and has an emphasis on local, seasonal and organic produce – much is provided by Backwell House's own garden.

Rooms: 9 en suite **Facilities:** Dinner available **Notes:** Closed 24–27 December

FROME — Map 4 ST74

Premier Collection

Lullington House

★★★★★ BED AND BREAKFAST

tel: 01373 831406 & 07979 290146 **Lullington BA11 2PG**
email: info@lullingtonhouse.co.uk **web:** www.lullingtonhouse.co.uk
dir: 2.5 miles north of Frome. Exit A36 into Lullington.

Built in 1866 as a rectory, this quintessentially English, stone-built country house stands in extensive grounds and gardens, which convey an air of peace, quiet and tranquillity. The luxurious large bedrooms, some with four-poster beds, are decorated to high standards using beautiful fabrics, fine antique furniture and many extras such as WiFi, decanters of sherry, fresh flowers and well-stocked beverage trays. Breakfast is served in the impressive dining room with an excellent selection of dishes available.

Rooms: 3 en suite **Facilities:** FTV tea/coffee WiFi ⅃ 🐾 **Parking:** 4 **Notes:** Closed Christmas and New Year

Archangel

★★★★ 🏠 INN

tel: 01373 456111 **1 King Street BA11 1BH**
email: hello@archangelfrome.com **web:** www.archangelfrome.com
dir: B3090 into Frome, into King Street, just off market place.

With a history dating back many centuries, this fascinating and vibrant establishment is situated in the heart of the bustling town of Frome. The style here is an engaging blend of old and new, a fusion which has broad appeal for those visiting for business or leisure. The stylish bedrooms are located in the main building and in the courtyard, the former boasting roll-top zinc baths and wall murals. The bar offers a range of cocktails in addition to real ales and an extensive wine list. Food should not be missed – the menu features flavoursome, well-crafted dishes.

Rooms: 6 en suite 4 annexe en suite (1 fmly) (2 GF) **Facilities:** FTV DVD Lounge tea/coffee Dinner available Direct dial WiFi **Extras:** Bottled water **Conf:** Max 25 Thtr 25 Class 25 Board 16 **Notes:** LB

Orchardleigh House

★★★★ GUEST ACCOMMODATION

tel: 01373 472550 & 07887 512450 **Orchardleigh BA11 2PH**
email: info@orchardleigh.net **web:** www.orchardleigh.net
dir: Phone for directions.

Popular as a wedding venue, Orchardleigh House is a large imposing manor with a wealth of history and character. Guests can choose from a wide range of bedrooms and bathrooms, ranging from very large suites to more compact rooms, some including a bath or shower in the bedroom. Public areas are grand and include a formal dining room, billiard room and well furnished breakfast room. Delightful grounds surround the building including an 18-hole golf course. The property can be hired for exclusive use, although regular bed and breakfast guests are also welcome.

Rooms: 43 rms (41 en suite) (7 fmly) (1 GF) **Facilities:** FTV Lounge TVL tea/coffee Licensed WiFi 🐾 ⅃ Fishing Riding Snooker 🐾 **Conf:** Max 165 **Parking:** 85 **Notes:** LB Civ wed 144

GLASTONBURY — Map 4 ST53

See also Somerton

The Glastonbury Town House

★★★★ BED AND BREAKFAST

tel: 01458 831040 & 07557 340247 **Hillclose, Street Road BA6 9EG**
email: stay@glastonburytownhouse.co.uk **web:** www.glastonburytownhouse.co.uk
dir: M5 junction 23 towards Glastonbury. Continue on A39, at B&Q roundabout 3rd exit, 200 yards on right.

A very warm welcome is guaranteed at The Glastonbury Town House where guests can expect to enjoy a comfortable night's rest followed by a hearty breakfast. The helpful owners offer comfortable bedrooms and bathrooms that are comfortable and well equipped including free WiFi. Centrally located with off-street parking, the house is well placed for exploring Glastonbury Tor and the Chalice Well.

Rooms: 3 en suite **Facilities:** FTV Lounge tea/coffee Dinner available WiFi 🐾 **Extras:** Speciality toiletries, bottled water, fresh milk **Parking:** 3 **Notes:** No children 5 years

HATCH BEAUCHAMP
Map 4 ST32

Frog Street Farmhouse
★★★★★ 🥂 BED AND BREAKFAST

tel: 01823 481883 **Hatch Beauchamp TA3 6AF**
email: frogstreet@hotmail.com **web:** www.frogstreet.co.uk
dir: *From A358, follow signs for Beercrocombe/Stewley. At T-junction (Elm Bridge Cottages) turn right, over bridge, driveway on right signed Frog Street Farmhouse.*

Peacefully located on the edges of this pleasant village, this traditional Somerset longhouse is full of character with parts of the building dating back over 600 years. The relaxing bedrooms are well decorated and stylish and have especially comfortable beds. Guests are welcome to use the large, comfortable lounge with a fireplace or sit in the pleasant gardens. Breakfast is a treat with high quality, mainly local produce, all cooked to order.

Rooms: 4 en suite (1 fmly) **D** fr £100 **Facilities:** STV TVL tea/coffee WiFi **Extras:** Speciality toiletries – complimentary **Parking:** 4 **Notes:** Closed December to February

---

The Hatch Inn
★★★★ 🍽 INN

tel: 01823 480245 **Village Road TA3 6SG**
email: info@thehatchinn.co.uk

Located in the historical village of Hatch Beauchamp, this popular inn welcomes guests and locals alike with friendly hospitality and a relaxed traditional inn ambience. Bedrooms and bathrooms are located in the main building and come in a range of shapes and sizes – all are comfortable and well equipped with plenty of welcome extras. Both dinner and breakfast utilise local, quality produce and can be enjoyed in the character dining room.

Rooms: 5 en suite (2 fmly) **D** fr £65 (room only)* **Facilities:** FTV tea/coffee Dinner available WiFi **Parking:** 10 **Notes:** Closed Sunday evening and Monday

HOLCOMBE
Map 4 ST64

The Holcombe Inn
★★★★★ 🏵🏵 🥂 INN

tel: 01761 232478 **Stratton Road BA3 5EB**
email: bookings@holcombeinn.co.uk **web:** www.holcombeinn.co.uk
dir: *From Bath or Shepton Mallet take A367 (Fosse Way) to Stratton. Follow inn signs.*

Dating back to the 16th century, this inn has views towards Downside Abbey in the distance. The attentive owners and pleasant staff create a friendly and relaxed atmosphere. Bedrooms are individually furnished and very comfortable. Real ales are served in the open-plan bar which has an attractive split-level restaurant.

Rooms: 8 en suite 2 annexe en suite (5 fmly) (2 GF) **Facilities:** FTV DVD Lounge tea/coffee Dinner available Direct dial WiFi **Extras:** Speciality toiletries – complimentary **Parking:** 40 **Notes:** LB

ILCHESTER
Map 4 ST52

Liongate House
★★★★ 🥂 BED AND BREAKFAST

tel: 01935 841741 & 07951 538692 **Northover BA22 8NG**
email: info@liongatehouse.com **web:** www.liongatehouse.com
dir: *On B3151 opposite Texaco petrol station.*

Located in the centre of this pleasant village and a short stroll from a choice of inns and restaurants, this very comfortable B&B demonstrates high quality throughout the bedrooms and bathrooms. The proprietors offer a genuine welcome and are very focused on customer care. Breakfast offers a range of top local produce and includes home-made bread alongside jams made from the garden's fruit.

Rooms: 3 en suite (1 fmly) (1 GF) **Facilities:** FTV DVD tea/coffee WiFi 🛁 **Extras:** Fridge stocked with refreshments – complimentary **Parking:** 4 **Notes:** LB

ILMINSTER
Map 4 ST31

The New Inn
★★★★ 🍽 INN

tel: 01460 52413 **Dowlish Wake TA19 0NZ**
email: newinn-ilminster@btconnect.com **web:** www.newinn-ilminster.com
dir: *A358 or A303, follow signs for Perry's Cider, well-signed in village.*

Situated in the tranquil and unspoilt village of Dowlish Wake, The New Inn is a proper local pub with a friendly welcome. All the bedrooms are on the ground floor; they are contemporary in style and located to the rear overlooking the garden. The menu offers a range of enduring favourites and daily specials, with good local produce used whenever possible. Breakfast is a substantial offering, just right for healthy appetites.

Rooms: 4 annexe en suite (4 GF) **S** fr £60 **D** fr £70 **Facilities:** FTV tea/coffee Dinner available WiFi **Parking:** 20 **Notes:** LB

KEYNSHAM — Map 4 ST66

Grasmere Court

★★★★ GUEST ACCOMMODATION

tel: 0117 986 2662 **22–24 Bath Road BS31 1SN**
email: reception@grasmerecourt.co.uk **web:** www.grasmerecourt.com
dir: On B3116 just off A4 between Bath and Bristol.

This very friendly establishment is located between Bath and Bristol. Bedrooms vary in size, with one room boasting a four-poster bed. A comfortable lounge and a well-stocked bar are available, and good value, freshly-prepared food is served in the attractive dining room overlooking the garden. Functions are also catered for.

Rooms: 16 en suite (1 fmly) (4 GF) **Facilities:** FTV DVD TVL tea/coffee Dinner available Direct dial Licensed WiFi 🅿 **Extras:** Bottled water, hot chocolate **Conf:** Max 30 **Parking:** 13

LOWER GODNEY — Map 4 ST74

The Sheppey

★★★★ 🅰 INN

tel: 01458 831594 **BA5 1RZ**
email: hi@thesheppey.co.uk **web:** www.thesheppey.co.uk
dir: Phone for directions.

With a rural location, surrounded by peat moors and wildlife reserves, this inn is an unexpected treat. Three bedrooms are located upstairs (one with its own balcony) and all are decorated in the eclectic and quirky style for which the inn has become known. Continental breakfast-hampers are provided in the bedrooms. An excellent range of real ales and proper ciders is offered in addition to an interesting wine selection. Dinner shouldn't be missed – the fine selection of quality dishes has been awarded a well-deserved AA Rosette. Regular themed nights with food and wine pairings are also offered.

Rooms: 3 en suite **Facilities:** Dinner available

MILVERTON — Map 3 ST12

The Globe

★★★ 🅰 INN

tel: 01823 400534 **Fore Street TA4 1JX**
email: adele@theglobemilverton.co.uk **web:** www.theglobemilverton.co.uk
dir: M5 junction 27 follow B3277 to Milverton. In village centre.

This popular village local was once a coaching inn, and even though it has been given contemporary styling it still retains much traditional charm. The welcome is warm and genuine with a convivial atmosphere always guaranteed. Bedrooms are appointed in a similar modern style and have comfy beds. The hard-working kitchen is committed to quality, with excellent locally-sourced produce used in impressive dishes. Continental breakfast is served.

Rooms: 3 en suite (1 fmly) **Facilities:** tea/coffee Dinner available WiFi **Parking:** 4 **Notes:** LB Closed 20 December to 2 January

MINEHEAD — Map 3 SS94

Alcombe House

★★★★ GUEST ACCOMMODATION

tel: 01643 705130 & 07549 887456 **Bircham Road, Alcombe TA24 6BG**
email: info@alcombehouse.co.uk **web:** www.alcombehouse.co.uk
dir: A39, pass junction for Dunster, straight over at floral roundabout. Alcombe House on left.

This elegant period house is a perfect base from which to explore the many and varied delights of the area. The welcome is warm and genuine with plenty of attentive service. Bedrooms provide impressive levels of quality and comfort with ample space to relax and unwind. Public areas combine contemporary and traditional styling, and include a wonderful lounge where indulgent afternoon teas can be sampled. The attractive dining room is the venue for breakfast, and dinner (by prior arrangement).

Rooms: 7 en suite **Facilities:** FTV DVD Lounge TVL tea/coffee Dinner available Licensed WiFi ♿ 🅿 **Parking:** 8 **Notes:** LB No children

Kenella House

★★★★ GUEST ACCOMMODATION

tel: 01643 703128 & 07710 889079 **7 Tregonwell Road TA24 5DT**
email: kenellahouse7@gmail.com **web:** www.kenellahouse.co.uk
dir: Exit A39 into Townsend Road, right into Ponsford Road and Tregonwell Road.

A warm welcome and a relaxed atmosphere are found at Kenella House, located close to the town centre, and also convenient for a visit to the steam railway. Walkers are welcomed and a heated boot cupboard is available for drying purposes. The well-maintained bedrooms are very comfortable and have many extras. Hearty breakfasts are served in the smart dining room.

Rooms: 6 en suite (1 GF) **S** fr £60 **D** fr £70* **Facilities:** FTV tea/coffee WiFi 🅿 **Parking:** 8 **Notes:** LB No children 14 years Closed November to February

MONKSILVER — Map 3 ST03

The Notley Arms Inn

★★★★ 🅰 🍽 INN

tel: 01984 656095 **Front Street TA4 4JB**
email: uksi@hotmail.com **web:** www.notleyarmsinn.co.uk
dir: From A358 at Bishop's Lydeard, onto B3224. After 5 miles right onto B3188 to Monksilver.

The Notley Arms was re-built around 1870 and is a warm, friendly and inviting village inn. Crackling log fires, comfy sofas and attentive service all contribute to a relaxing atmosphere. Bedrooms are located in the adjacent coach house and all provide impressive levels of quality, comfort and sophistication. The bar comes well stocked with local ales; likewise the menu focuses on sourcing the best the region has to offer, with a range of flavoursome and thoroughly enjoyable dishes. A garden is also available.

Rooms: 6 en suite (2 fmly) (3 GF) **Facilities:** FTV Lounge tea/coffee Dinner available WiFi 🅿 Petanque court **Extras:** Speciality toiletries, home-made biscuits – complimentary **Parking:** 20 **Notes:** LB

NORTH WOOTTON   Map 4 ST54

Premier Collection

Crossways Inn
★★★★★ INN

tel: 01749 899000 **Stocks Lane BA4 4EU**
email: enquiries@thecrossways.co.uk **web:** www.thecrossways.co.uk
dir: *Exit M5 junction 22 towards Shepton Mallet, 0.2 mile from Pilton.*

This family-run establishment is tucked away down a quiet lane, within easy reach of Wells and Glastonbury. The bedrooms and bathrooms are spacious, and provide high levels of quality and comfort. There is a large bar-restaurant and a smaller dining room where breakfast is served. The extensive menu (served Wednesday to Sunday) features high quality produce with a choice of traditional pub classics or an à la carte option.

Rooms: 22 en suite (8 fmly) **S** fr £49 **D** fr £69* **Facilities:** FTV Lounge TVL tea/coffee Dinner available WiFi 🍺 Skittle alley **Conf:** Max 150 Thtr 120 Class 60 Board 25 **Parking:** 100 **Notes:** LB Civ wed 150

OAKHILL   Map 4 ST64

The Oakhill Inn
★★★★ INN

tel: 01749 840442 **Fosse Road BA3 5HU**
email: info@theoakhillinn.com **web:** www.theoakhillinn.com
dir: *On A367 between Stratton-on-the-Fosse and Shepton Mallet.*

A welcoming country inn, offering warm hospitality, locally sourced food and a wide selection of fine ales from local microbreweries. The comfortable bedrooms include luxuries such as Egyptian cotton sheets and DVD players. In addition to lighter bar snacks, a full range of high-quality AA Rosette award-winning dishes, made with fresh local produce, is also available.

Rooms: 5 en suite (1 fmly) **Facilities:** FTV DVD Lounge tea/coffee Dinner available WiFi ⚓ 🍺 **Extras:** Mineral water – complimentary **Conf:** Max 30 Thtr 30 Class 30 Board 30 **Parking:** 12 **Notes:** LB RS 25 December no food, 26 December no dinner service

PORLOCK   Map 3 SS84

Tudor Cottage
★★★★ GUEST ACCOMMODATION

tel: 01643 862255 & 07703 464909 **Bossington TA24 8HQ**
email: tudorcottagebossington@btinternet.com
dir: *From Porlock on A39, bear left signed Bossington. Continue to village centre, on left.*

Located in the centre of this delightful village, Tudor Cottage is full of character and charm. Bedrooms and bathrooms have been designed in keeping with the age and character of the building, while delicious breakfasts are cooked to order and served in the relaxing dining room. Guests are served tea on arrival in a cosy lounge or in the pleasant gardens during warmer months. Home-cooked dinners are available by prior arrangement.

Rooms: 3 rms (1 en suite) (2 pri facs) **Facilities:** FTV DVD TVL tea/coffee Dinner available Licensed WiFi 🍺 **Extras:** Mini-bar **Parking:** 3 **Notes:** No children 10 years

RADSTOCK   Map 4 ST65

The Redan Inn
★★★★ ⑱⑱ INN

tel: 01761 258560 **Fry's Well, Chilcompton BA3 4HA**
email: info@theredaninn.co.uk **web:** www.theredaninn.co.uk
dir: *From Radstock on A367, at roundabout exit signed Wells and Chilcompton (B3139). In village of Chilcompton, right into Frys Well, inn on right.*

Located just off the main road and an easy drive to Bath, this delightful property was originally a coaching inn but has been newly upgraded throughout to provide high quality contemporary bedrooms and bathrooms in various shapes and sizes. Carefully prepared dishes are available at lunch and dinner, where the kitchen shows a serious approach to utilising the finest quality produce. A pleasant garden with outdoor seating terrace, and a small car park are also available to guests.

Rooms: 7 en suite (1 fmly) **Facilities:** FTV tea/coffee Dinner available WiFi **Extras:** Speciality toiletries **Conf:** Max 12 Board 12 **Parking:** 15

SHEPTON MALLET   Map 4 ST64

Longbridge House Bed & Breakfast
★★★★ BED AND BREAKFAST

tel: 01749 572311 & 07809 437325 **78 Cowl Street BA4 5EP**
email: longbridgehouse@gmail.com **web:** www.longbridgehouse.co.uk
dir: *Phone for directions.*

Guests who enjoy staying in a place with plenty of interesting history will love this building – it is where the Duke of Monmouth is reputed to have stayed in 1685, before and after the Battle of Sedgemoor. The three individually designed bedrooms offer king-size beds with either en suite shower rooms or an en suite bathroom with a roll-top bath. Thoughtful extras include fluffy robes, safes in each room and ironing boards. Breakfast is a leisurely affair as you watch your host prepare your food on the red Aga, which is then served at either at the large table in the comfortable kitchen, or in the courtyard, weather permitting.

Rooms: 3 en suite **D** fr £79* **Facilities:** FTV tea/coffee WiFi 🍺 **Extras:** Bottled water, fluffy robes, ironing boards **Notes:** No children

The Natterjack Inn
★★★★ 🛏 INN

tel: 01749 860253 **Evercreech Junction BA4 6NA**
email: natterjack@btconnect.com **web:** www.thenatterjackinn.co.uk
dir: *On A371 between Bath and Castle Cary, 2 miles past Bath and West Showground heading towards Castle Cary.*

The Natterjack Inn offers plenty of traditional character and hospitality with a log fire, cosy seating and an excellent range of real ales and ciders. Dinner is a highlight with a varied menu to suit all tastes. Bedrooms are located in the adjacent converted cider bar; they come in a range of shapes and sizes but all have very good quality bathrooms and showers. Breakfast is served in the pleasant dining room overlooking the large garden.

Rooms: 9 annexe en suite (2 fmly) (4 GF) **S** fr £70 **D** fr £90* **Facilities:** FTV DVD tea/coffee Dinner available WiFi ⚓ Fishing **Extras:** Speciality toiletries, home-made biscuits – complimentary **Parking:** 20 **Notes:** LB

SOMERTON
Map 4 ST42

Premier Collection

Cartways Bed and Breakfast

★★★★★ 🍴 BED AND BREAKFAST

tel: 01458 223104 & 07704 776748 **High Street, Keinton Mandeville TA11 6EF**
email: cartways@outlook.com **web:** www.cartwaysbandb.co.uk
dir: *From Somerton east on B3151, through Kingweston into Keinton Mandeville. 3rd house on left on entering village.*

Situated on the edge of Keinton Mandeville, this grand house has much to offer, not least being the warmth of the welcome from hosts, Judy and Tony. Given its location, with easy access to the A303 and M5, this is a perfect choice for those looking to break their journey, perhaps en route to Cornwall. The bedrooms offer comfort and quality with a host of thoughtful extras, whilst bathrooms come complete with cosseting bath sheets, robes, slippers and pampering toiletries. Guests can use the wonderful drawing room with its comfy sofas and wood-burner, and there's also a snooker room with a full-size table. Breakfasts, served either in the dining room or the more informal breakfast room, are generous and tasty, with eggs provided by the resident hens.

Rooms: 3 en suite **Facilities:** FTV Lounge tea/coffee WiFi 🛏 ⚘ Riding Snooker ⚓ **Extras:** Speciality toiletries, bottled water, robes, slippers, fresh milk – complimentary **Parking:** 8 **Notes:** No children 10 years

The Devonshire Arms

★★★★ ◉ INN

tel: 01458 241271 **Long Sutton TA10 9LP**
email: mail@thedevonshirearms.com **web:** www.thedevonshirearms.com
dir: *A303 onto A372 at Podimore roundabout. After 4 miles left onto B3165, signed Martock and Long Sutton.*

This popular village inn offers an appealing blend of traditional and contemporary styling throughout. The bedrooms are individually designed and provide impressive levels of comfort and quality. Public areas include a convivial bar and an elegant restaurant where excellent use is made of local produce in skilfully executed dishes.

Rooms: 7 en suite 2 annexe en suite (1 fmly) (2 GF) **Facilities:** FTV tea/coffee Dinner available WiFi 🛏 ⚘ ⚓ **Conf:** Max 14 Board 14 **Parking:** 6 **Notes:** LB Closed 25–26 December

Somerton Court Country House

★★★★ GUEST ACCOMMODATION

tel: 01458 274694 **TA11 7AH**
email: enquiries@somertoncourt.com **web:** www.somertoncourt.com
dir: *From A303 onto A372 at Podimore roundabout. In 3 miles right onto B3151 to Somerton and follow signs.*

Dating back to the 17th century and set in extensive gardens and grounds, this house provides a tranquil haven away from the pressures of modern life. The comfortable bedrooms have lovely views, and breakfast is served in a delightful dining room that overlooks the gardens.

Rooms: 4 en suite 2 annexe en suite (1 fmly) (2 GF) **Facilities:** Lounge tea/coffee WiFi Riding ⚓ **Parking:** 30 **Notes:** LB Closed Christmas and New Year

STOGUMBER
Map 3 ST03

Wick House

★★★★ GUEST ACCOMMODATION

tel: 01984 656422 **Brook Street TA4 3SZ**
email: sheila@wickhouse.co.uk **web:** www.wickhouse.co.uk
dir: *Exit A358 into village, left at crossroads, Wick House 3rd on left.*

Wick House offers homely accommodation in a pretty village on the edge of Exmoor National Park. There is a cosy lounge with a wood-burning stove, a TV room and a pleasant dining room overlooking the garden. One bedroom is designed for easier access.

Rooms: 9 en suite (1 GF) **S** fr £50 **D** fr £80 **Facilities:** FTV Lounge TVL tea/coffee Licensed WiFi ⚓ **Extras:** Sweets – complimentary **Parking:** 6 **Notes:** LB

TAUNTON
Map 4 ST22

Lower Marsh Farm
★★★★ FARMHOUSE

tel: 01823 451331 **Kingston St Mary TA2 8AB**
email: info@lowermarshfarm.co.uk **web:** www.lowermarshfarm.co.uk
dir: *M5 junction 25. Lower Marsh Farm between Taunton and Kingston St Mary just past King's Hall School on right.*

Located at the foot of the Quantock Hills, this delightful family-run farm warmly welcomes guests with a pot of tea and a slice of cake ready and waiting. Bedrooms are individually styled and reflect the traditional charm of the house; an impressive level of quality is complemented by numerous thoughtful extras. The Aga-cooked breakfast is a real treat, served in the dining room around one grand table. There is a spacious lounge warmed by a crackling log fire in winter.

Rooms: 4 en suite (2 fmly) **Facilities:** TVL tea/coffee Dinner available WiFi
Parking: 6 **Notes:** 300 acres arable/sheep

TINTINHULL
Map 4 ST41

Crown & Victoria
★★★★ ◉ INN

tel: 01935 823341 **Farm Street BA22 8PZ**
email: info@thecrownandvictoria.co.uk **web:** www.thecrownandvictoria-yeovil.co.uk
dir: *Off A303, follow signs for Tintinhull Gardens.*

Appointed to a high standard, this light and airy property has very well-equipped bedrooms. The staff ensure guests are well cared for, and the contemporary bar and restaurant provide a good selection of carefully prepared dishes. The food here has been awarded an AA Rosette.

Rooms: 5 en suite **Facilities:** FTV DVD tea/coffee Dinner available WiFi
Extras: Bottled water **Parking:** 60

WATCHET
Map 3 ST04

The Georgian House

★★★★ GUEST HOUSE

tel: 01984 639279 **28 Swain Street TA23 0AD**
email: bookings@georgianhouse.info **web:** www.georgian-house.info
dir: *From A39 over railway bridge into main street.*

This elegant Georgian property is situated in the heart of the increasingly popular coastal resort, and is within a short walk of the impressive marina. The comfortable bedrooms combine quality and individuality. Breakfast (and dinner by arrangement) is served in the well-appointed dining room. Additional facilities for guests include a lounge and the use of the garden.

Rooms: 3 en suite **Facilities:** Dinner available **Parking:** 2 **Notes:** LB

WEDMORE
Map 4 ST44

The George

★★★★ INN

tel: 01934 712124 **Church Street BS28 4AB**
email: info@thegeorgewedmore.co.uk **web:** www.thegeorgewedmore.co.uk
dir: *M5 junction 22, follow Bristol/Cheddar signs (A38). From dual carriageway right, follow signs for Mark, then Wedmore. In village centre.*

The George is a traditional inn offering plenty of character, log fires and a fine selection of ales. Bedrooms come in a variety of shapes and sizes and are located on the first floor above the inn. A range of dishes is offered at lunch and dinner to suit all tastes and may be taken in the cosy bar or more formal dining areas. Outdoor seating and parking are also available.

Rooms: 4 en suite **Facilities:** FTV DVD iPod docking station Lounge tea/coffee Dinner available WiFi **Extras:** Speciality toiletries **Conf:** Max 60 Thtr 30 Class 30 Board 30 **Parking:** 30 **Notes:** Civ wed 100

WELLINGTON
Map 3 ST12

The Cleve Spa

★★★★ GUEST ACCOMMODATION

tel: 01823 662033 **Mantle Street TA21 8SN**
email: reception@clevehotel.com **web:** www.clevehotel.com
dir: *M5 junction 26 follow signs to Wellington town centre. Continue for 600 metres, entrance on left.*

This elegant Victorian country house is situated in an elevated position with commanding views. Bedrooms provide high levels of comfort and quality, with well appointed and stylish bathrooms. Dinner and breakfast are served in the attractive restaurant, after which a stroll around the extensive grounds is pleasant. An impressive array of leisure facilities is also offered, including indoor pool, spa bath, steam room and fully-equipped fitness studio.

Rooms: 21 en suite (3 GF) **Facilities:** FTV Lounge tea/coffee Dinner available Direct dial Licensed WiFi Sauna Gym Spa beauty treatments **Conf:** Max 250 Thtr 250 Class 100 Board 60 **Parking:** 100 **Notes:** LB No children 16 years Closed 25 December to 2 January Civ wed 200

WELLS
Map 4 ST54

Double-Gate Farm

★★★★ FARMHOUSE

tel: 01458 832217 & 07843 924079 **Godney BA5 1RZ**
email: doublegatefarm@aol.com **web:** www.doublegatefarm.com
dir: *A39 from Wells towards Glastonbury, at Polsham right signed Godney/Polsham. 2 miles to crossroads, continue to farmhouse on left after inn.*

Expect a warm welcome not only from the owners, but also their friendly tabby cat. Set on the banks of the River Sheppey in the Somerset Levels, this comfortable farmhouse is well known for its attractive summer flower garden. Guests have use of a games room and free internet access is available throughout the property. Both afternoon tea and baby-sitting are available if pre-arranged.

Rooms: 1 en suite 7 annexe en suite (4 fmly) (5 GF) **S** fr £60 **D** fr £80*
Facilities: FTV DVD TVL tea/coffee Direct dial Licensed WiFi Fishing Snooker Table tennis **Extras:** Mini-fridges in some rooms, speciality toiletries **Parking:** 9 **Notes:** LB RS 2 weeks Christmas accommodation only 8 acres non-working

See advert on page 230

WELLS *continued*

The Crown at Wells

★★★★ ⬤ INN

tel: 01749 673457 **Market Place BA5 2RP**
email: stay@crownatwells.co.uk **web:** www.crownatwells.co.uk
dir: *On entering Wells follow signs for Hotels and Deliveries, in Market Place, car park at rear.*

Retaining its original features and 15th-century period charm, this historic inn is situated in the heart of the city. The building has featured in films and TV productions including *Hot Fuzz* and *Poldark*. Bedrooms are in-keeping with the property's character, varying in size and style. Egyptian cotton sheets and full-size bath towels are standard. The Crown has a popular eatery, Anton's Bistrot, which is a light, airy environment and has a relaxed atmosphere; lunch, dinner and afternoon teas are served daily. The Penn Bar serves food all day from midday 'til late and offers a variety of real ales and cider. A warm welcome and friendly service are guaranteed.

Rooms: 15 en suite (2 fmly) **Facilities:** FTV Lounge TVL tea/coffee Dinner available WiFi ⬤ **Extras:** Speciality toiletries, filtered water – complimentary **Parking:** 10 **Notes:** LB

Highfield

★★★★ BED AND BREAKFAST

tel: 01749 675330 **93 Portway BA5 2BR**
email: steph@wellsbandb.com **web:** www.wellsbandb.com
dir: *Enter Wells and follow signs for A371 Cheddar. Highfield on Portway after last lights at top of hill.*

Within walking distance of the city and cathedral, this delightful home maintains Edwardian style and provides comfortable accommodation. There are pleasant views of the countryside and some bedrooms have balconies. A carefully prepared breakfast is served around one large table in the well furnished breakfast room. Welcome extra features include the well-tended garden and off-street parking.

Rooms: 3 en suite **Facilities:** FTV tea/coffee WiFi **Parking:** 7 **Notes:** LB
No children 2 years Closed 23 December to 1 January

The White Hart

[U]

tel: 01749 672056 **19–21 Sadler Street BA5 2RR**
email: reservations@whitehartwells.com **web:** www.@whitehartwells.com
dir: *Phone for directions.*

Currently the rating for this establishment is not confirmed. This may be due to a change of ownership or because it has only recently joined the AA rating scheme.

Rooms: 15

WEST HUNTSPILL	Map 4 ST34

Crossways Inn

★★★★ INN

tel: 01278 782500 **Withy Road TA9 3RA**
email: accommodation@crosswaysinn.com **web:** www.crosswaysinn.com
dir: *On A38 between M5 junction 22 and 23.*

Crossways is a traditional inn serving good food and offering a very high standard of accommodation, accompanied by warm friendly service. The bedrooms are very comfortable and have a host of extras including iPod docks and WiFi.

Rooms: 8 en suite (1 fmly) (2 GF) **Facilities:** FTV iPod docking station tea/coffee Dinner available Lift WiFi **Parking:** 72

WESTON-SUPER-MARE
Map 4 ST36

Premier Collection

The Park B&B

★★★★★ ⚲ GUEST ACCOMMODATION

tel: 01934 4147560 **2 Clarence Road East BS23 4BT**
email: info@theparkbandb.co.uk **web:** www.theparkbandb.co.uk
dir: *Phone for directions.*

A touch of New England has arrived has arrived in Weston-super-Mare! This newly completed, luxurious bed and breakfast is located in a quiet residential part of the town overlooking the park yet is only a few minutes' stroll from the seafront. The two bedrooms and bathrooms are decorated and furnished to the highest standards and include some welcome extras to add to guests' comfort. Breakfast includes freshly prepared fruits, home-made bread and jams in addition to a selection of top quality cooked items.

Rooms: 2 en suite **S** fr £80 **D** fr £95* **Facilities:** FTV tea/coffee WiFi
Extras: Speciality toiletries – complimentary **Parking:** 2 **Notes:** No children

Premier Collection

Church House

★★★★★ BED AND BREAKFAST

tel: 01934 633185 **27 Kewstoke Road, Kewstoke BS22 9YD**
email: info@churchhousekewstoke.co.uk **web:** www.churchhousekewstoke.co.uk
dir: *From M5 junction 21 follow signs for Kewstoke 2.5 miles, next to Kewstoke Church.*

In a peaceful location at the foot of Monk's Hill, Church House is a delightful property that enjoys wonderful views of the Bristol Channel and as far as Wales on clear days. The bedrooms are stylish and spacious, with lots of thoughtful extras and well-appointed en suites. Public areas include a pleasant conservatory and an elegant dining room where impressive breakfasts are served.

Rooms: 5 en suite **S** fr £95 **D** fr £110* **Facilities:** FTV DVD iPod docking station Lounge tea/coffee WiFi ⏱ ⚴ Mobile spa offered in rooms **Extras:** Home-made cake, sweets – complimentary **Parking:** 6

Oakover Guest House

★★★★ GUEST HOUSE

tel: 01934 620125 & 07557 417208 **25 Clevedon Road BS23 1DA**
email: info@oakover.co.uk **web:** www.oakover.co.uk
dir: *M5 junction 21 onto A370 (Beach Road), at 6th roundabout left onto A3033. 2nd right into Brighton Road. Over lights into Clevedon Road.*

Located just a short walk from the seafront, this well-established quality accommodation is run by enthusiastic and welcoming proprietors. Bedrooms and bathrooms are decorated and maintained to high standards and provide guests with plenty of quality and comfort throughout. A good range of breakfast dishes is offered and served in the stylish breakfast room. Parking is available to the rear via a fairly narrow entrance.

Rooms: 6 en suite (2 GF) **S** fr £65 **D** fr £70 **Facilities:** FTV DVD tea/coffee WiFi
Parking: 6 **Notes:** No children 10 years

Camellia Lodge

★★★★ BED AND BREAKFAST

tel: 01934 613534 **76 Walliscote Road BS23 1ED**
email: dachefs@aol.com **web:** www.camellialodge.net
dir: *200 yards from seafront.*

Guests return regularly for the warm welcome at Camellia Lodge, an immaculate Victorian family home which is just off the seafront and within walking distance of the town centre. Bedrooms have a range of thoughtful touches, and carefully prepared breakfasts are served in the relaxing dining room.

Rooms: 5 en suite (1 fmly) **S** fr £37.50 **D** fr £75* **Facilities:** FTV tea/coffee WiFi

Linden Lodge Guest House

★★★★ ⚲ GUEST ACCOMMODATION

tel: 01934 645797 **27 Clevedon Road BS23 1DA**
email: info@lindenlodge.com **web:** www.lindenlodge.com
dir: *Follow signs to seafront. 0.5 mile south of grand pier turn into Clevedon Road.*

Just a short walk from the town centre and the seafront, Linden Lodge offers welcoming hospitality and guest care in a traditional style. Bedrooms come in a range of shapes and sizes, but all are well decorated and equipped. A good selection is offered at breakfast including home-made bread and yogurt, all served in the pleasant conservatory.

Rooms: 5 en suite **Facilities:** FTV tea/coffee WiFi **Parking:** 3 **Notes:** LB
No children 18 years

Goodrington Guest House

★★★ GUEST HOUSE

tel: 01934 623229 **23 Charlton Road BS23 4HB**
email: vera.bishop@talk21.com **web:** www.goodrington.info
dir: *A370 (Beach Road) south into Uphill Road, left into Charlton Road.*

The owners of Goodrington Guest House make every effort to ensure that their guests enjoy staying at their charming Victorian house tucked away in a quiet residential area. The bedrooms are comfortably furnished and there is an attractive lounge. Families are especially welcome and this makes a good holiday base.

Rooms: 3 rms (2 en suite) (1 pri facs) (1 fmly) (1 GF) **S** fr £45 **D** fr £65*
Facilities: FTV DVD TVL tea/coffee WiFi **Notes:** LB Closed October to Easter

Corbiere Guest House

★★★ GUEST HOUSE

tel: 01934 629607 & 429866 **24 Upper Church Road BS23 2DX**
email: corbierehotel@btinternet.com **web:** www.corbiereguesthouse.com
dir: *M5 junction 21, take 2nd exit to seafront.*

Located on a residential street just a few minutes' walk from the seafront, this relaxed and welcoming guest house offers bedrooms in a range of shapes and sizes; all are well furnished and have comfortable beds and bedding. Breakfast is served in the lower-ground floor dining room and offers a good selection of hot and cold dishes.

Rooms: 10 en suite (4 fmly) (2 GF) **Facilities:** FTV DVD Lounge TVL tea/coffee Dinner available **Notes:** LB

WHEDDON CROSS
Map 3 SS93

The Rest and Be Thankful Inn
★★★★ INN

tel: 01643 841222 **TA24 7DR**
email: stay@restandbethankful.co.uk web: www.restandbethankful.co.uk
dir: *M5 junction 25, A358 to Minehead, left onto B3224 at Wheddon Cross sign.*

The Rest and Be Thankful Inn is situated in the highest village on Exmoor, overlooking Dunkery Beacon. The comfortable bedrooms are extremely well equipped, with extras such as mini-bars, safe boxes and tea-and coffee-making facilities. The convivial bar, complete with crackling log fires, is a popular meeting point for locals and visitors alike. A range of wholesome dishes is offered in the bar, the restaurant or outside on the patio which enjoys lovely countryside views.

Rooms: 8 en suite (1 fmly) **Facilities:** FTV tea/coffee Dinner available Direct dial WiFi Skittle alley, table tennis **Extras:** Mini-bar — chargeable **Conf:** Max 50 Class 50 Board 50 **Parking:** 10 **Notes:** Closed 25 December

WILLITON
Map 3 ST04

The White House
★★★★ GUEST ACCOMMODATION

tel: 01984 632306 **11 Long Street TA4 4QW**
email: whitehouselive@btconnect.com web: www.whitehousewilliton.co.uk
dir: *A39 (Bridgwater to Minehead), in Williton on right prior to Watchet turning.*

This Grade II listed Georgian house is in the perfect location for guests wishing to explore the beautiful Somerset countryside and coast. Many original features have been retained and add to the character of the house. Bedrooms are well equipped, and guests can choose whether to stay in the main house or in a courtyard room. Additional facilities include a bar and lounge.

Rooms: 8 rms (7 en suite) (1 pri facs) 6 annexe en suite (2 fmly) (6 GF) **S** fr £55 **D** fr £85* **Facilities:** FTV TVL tea/coffee Licensed WiFi Parking: 12

WINSFORD
Map 3 SS93

The Royal Oak Exmoor
★★★★ INN

tel: 01643 851455 **Halse Lane TA24 7JE**
email: enquiries@royaloakexmoor.co.uk web: www.royaloakexmoor.co.uk
dir: *Phone for directions.*

Originally part of a farm and dating back to the 12th century, this thatched pub is very much at the heart of this picturesque Exmoor village. Character abounds throughout public areas with lots of cosy areas to sit and sup a pint and enjoy the warm and convivial atmosphere. A range of skilfully-prepared dishes make use of local, seasonal produce. Bedrooms provide impressive levels of comfort, with quality linen and wonderful beds. Breakfast is the perfect start to a day before exploring this stunning area.

Rooms: 10 en suite 4 annexe en suite (2 GF) **Facilities:** STV Lounge tea/coffee Dinner available Direct dial WiFi **Conf:** Max 40 Thtr 40 Class 24 Board 12 **Parking:** 14

WITHYPOOL
Map 3 SS83

Premier Collection

Kings Farm
★★★★★ BED AND BREAKFAST

tel: 01643 831381 **TA24 7RE**
email: info@kingsfarmexmoor.co.uk web: www.kingsfarmexmoor.co.uk
dir: *Exit B3223 to Withypool, over bridge and sharp left to farm.*

This delightful farmhouse is set in over two acres of landscaped gardens in an idyllic valley beside the River Barle. It combines the character and charm of its 19th-century origins with modern comforts. From the carefully planned bedrooms to the sumptuously furnished sitting room, delicious home-cooked breakfasts and the warmest of welcomes, top quality is most definitely the hallmark of Kings Farm. Both stabling and fishing are available.

Rooms: 2 rms (1 en suite) (1 pri facs) **S** fr £80 **D** fr £105* **Facilities:** STV FTV Lounge tea/coffee WiFi Fishing **Extras:** Speciality toiletries, fruit, chocolates — complimentary **Parking:** 3 **Notes:** No children 14 years

WRAXALL
Map 4 ST47

The Battleaxes
★★★★ INN

tel: 01275 857473 **Bristol Road BS48 1LQ**
email: thebattleaxes@flatcappers.co.uk web: www.flatcappers.co.uk
dir: *From Bristol, A370 to Weston-super-Mare, take Clevedon exit then follow signs for Nailsea. From M5 junction 19 to Portbury, then follow signs for Nailsea.*

Part of the small local Flatcappers Group, this delightful inn offers a pleasing mix of traditional comfort and hospitality with some more contemporary features. Bedrooms are spacious and well equipped and free WiFi is included. Carefully prepared dishes are available throughout the day whether at breakfast, lunch or dinner. A good selection of real ales and wines by the glass adds to the relaxing ambience created throughout the bar and dining areas. A large car park is also available.

Rooms: 6 en suite **Facilities:** FTV iPod docking station Lounge tea/coffee Dinner available WiFi **Conf:** Max 30 Thtr 30 Class 30 Board 30 **Parking:** 50 **Notes:** Civ wed 90

YEOVIL | Map 4 ST51

Premier Collection

Little Barwick House

★★★★★ ⊛⊛⊛ ⌢ RESTAURANT WITH ROOMS

tel: 01935 423902 **Barwick BA22 9TD**
email: info@littlebarwick.co.uk **web:** www.littlebarwickhouse.co.uk
dir: From Yeovil A37 towards Dorchester, left at 1st roundabout, 1st left, 0.25 mile on left.

Situated in a quiet hamlet in three and half acres of gardens and grounds, this listed Georgian dower house is an ideal retreat for those seeking peaceful surroundings and good food. Just one of the highlights of a stay here is a meal in the restaurant, where good use is made of local ingredients. Each of the bedrooms has its own character, and a range of thoughtful extras such as fresh flowers, bottled water and magazines is provided.

Rooms: 6 en suite **Facilities:** FTV iPod docking station tea/coffee Dinner available Direct dial WiFi 🔒 **Parking:** 30 **Notes:** LB No children 5 years RS Sunday evening and Monday closed

The Masons Arms

★★★★ ⌢ ⌢ INN

tel: 01935 862591 **41 Lower Odcombe BA22 8TX**
email: info@masonsarmsodcombe.co.uk **web:** www.masonsarmsodcombe.co.uk
dir: From A303 take A3088 to Yeovil, follow signs to Montacute after village, 3rd turning on right.

Dating back to the 16th century, The Masons Arms claims to be the oldest building in this small village on the outskirts of Yeovil. The spacious bedrooms are contemporary in style, with clean lines, a high level of comfort and a wide range of considerate extras. The friendly hosts run their own microbrewery, and their ales are available at the bar along with other brews. Public areas include a bar-restaurant, which offers a full menu of freshly prepared dishes, along with a choice of lighter snacks.

Rooms: 6 en suite (1 fmly) (6 GF) **Facilities:** FTV tea/coffee Dinner available Direct dial WiFi 🔒 **Extras:** Mineral water/beer in room fridge **Conf:** Max 15 Class 15 Board 15 **Parking:** 35

The Halfway House Inn Country Lodge

★★★ INN

tel: 01935 840350 & 849005 **Ilchester Road BA22 8RE**
email: paul@halfwayhouseinn.com **web:** www.halfwayhotelyeovil.com
dir: A303 onto A37 (Yeovil road) at Ilchester, inn 2 miles on left.

This roadside inn offers comfortable accommodation, which consists of bedrooms in the main house, in addition to contemporary annexe rooms, each with its own front door; all bedrooms are bright and well equipped. Meals are available in the cosy restaurant and bar, where friendly staff ensure a warm welcome.

Rooms: 10 en suite 9 annexe en suite (7 fmly) (8 GF) **Facilities:** FTV TVL tea/coffee Dinner available WiFi Fishing **Conf:** Max 90 Thtr 90 Class 60 Board 60 **Parking:** 49 **Notes:** LB

At Your Service B&B

★★★ BED AND BREAKFAST

tel: 01935 706932 & 07957 473407 **102 West Coker Road BA20 2JG**
email: atyourserviceuk@gmail.com **web:** www.atyourserviceuk.wordpress.com
dir: Phone for directions.

Conveniently located on the main through road, this relaxed bed and breakfast makes an ideal base from which to explore the various nearby attractions. Bedrooms come in a range of shapes and all are on the ground floor. There is a car park to the rear of the property.

Rooms: 4 en suite (4 GF) **S** fr £40 **D** fr £65 **Facilities:** FTV tea/coffee WiFi 🔒 **Extras:** Bottled water – complimentary **Parking:** 10

The Half Moon Inn

★★★ INN

tel: 01935 850289 **Main Street, Mudford BA21 5TF**
email: enquiries@thehalfmooninn.co.uk **web:** www.thehalfmooninn.co.uk
dir: A303 at Sparkford onto A359 to Yeovil, 3.5 miles on left.

Situated north of Yeovil, this delightful village inn dates from the 17th century. It has a wealth of character including exposed beams and flagstone floors. The inn proves very popular for its extensive range of wholesome food, and there is a choice of bar and dining areas. Most of the spacious, well-equipped bedrooms are on the ground floor and are situated in an adjacent building.

Rooms: 14 en suite (4 fmly) (9 GF) **Facilities:** STV FTV tea/coffee Dinner available WiFi 🔒 **Parking:** 36 **Notes:** Closed 25–26 December

STAFFORDSHIRE

BARTON-UNDER-NEEDWOOD | Map 10 SK11

The Three Horseshoes

★★★★ ⌢ INN

tel: 01283 716268 **2 Station Road DE13 8DR**
email: enquiries@3horseshoesbarton.co.uk **web:** www.3horseshoesbarton.co.uk
dir: Phone for directions.

This popular inn, south-west of Burton upon Trent, retains traditional hospitality values and offers modern, individually-styled accommodation. The Bit 'n' Cherry restaurant, located in a converted cobbler's workshop, offers a wide selection of imaginative meals.

Rooms: 3 en suite **Facilities:** FTV tea/coffee Dinner available WiFi **Parking:** 14

ECCLESHALL | Map 15 SJ82

Slindon House Farm

★★★★ ⌢ FARMHOUSE

tel: 01782 791237 **Slindon ST21 6LX**
email: helenbonsall13@gmail.com **web:** www.slindonhousefarm.co.uk
dir: 2 miles north of Eccleshall on A519.

This large, charming, Victorian farmhouse is fronted by a lovely garden and situated on a dairy, arable and livestock farm in the village of Slindon, some two miles from Eccleshall. It has one twin and one double room, both of which are thoughtfully equipped. Breakfast is served at individual tables in the traditionally furnished combined breakfast room and lounge.

Rooms: 2 rms (1 en suite) (1 pri facs) **Facilities:** FTV DVD TVL tea/coffee WiFi **Parking:** 4 **Notes:** Closed 23 December to 3 January and 1–25 April 175 acres arable/dairy/sheep/beef

FROGHALL
Map 10 SK04

Hermitage Working Farm

★★★ FARMHOUSE

tel: 01538 266515 **ST10 2HQ**
email: jeff@hermitagefarm.co.uk **web:** www.hermitagefarm.co.uk
dir: *Phone for directions.*

This family-run farm, peacefully located overlooking the picturesque Churnet Valley, offers a warm welcome. Traditionally furnished and well-equipped, the accommodation is split between the main house and converted farm buildings; the stone barn conversions offer greater privacy and cooking facilities for the more independent guest. Full English breakfasts are served in the family dining room.

Rooms: 3 en suite 6 annexe en suite **Facilities:** FTV tea/coffee WiFi 🔒 **Parking:** 10 **Notes:** LB 105 acres beef/poultry

KINGSLEY
Map 10 SK04

The Church Farm

★★★★ FARMHOUSE

tel: 01538 754759 **Holt Lane ST10 2BA**
email: thechurchfarm@yahoo.co.uk
dir: *From A52 in Kingsley into Holt Lane, 150 metres on right opposite school drive.*

A warm welcome is assured at this charming farmhouse situated in the village of Kingsley. Thoughtfully equipped bedrooms with stylish furnishings are available in the main house. A hearty breakfast is served at individual tables overlooking the cottage gardens.

Rooms: 2 en suite **S** fr £60 **D** fr £80* **Facilities:** FTV DVD Lounge tea/coffee WiFi **Extras:** Speciality toiletries, fruit tea – complimentary **Parking:** 6 **Notes:** LB Closed 23 December to 2 January 100 acres mixed

LEEK
Map 16 SJ95

Three Horseshoes Country Inn & Spa

★★★★ ◉◉ INN

tel: 01538 300296 **Buxton Road, Blackshaw Moor ST13 8TW**
email: enquiries@threeshoesinn.co.uk **web:** www.threeshoesinn.co.uk
dir: *2 miles north of Leek on A53.*

This traditional, family-owned hostelry provides stylish, individually designed, modern bedrooms, including several 'Garden rooms' with hot tubs. The smart brasserie, with an open kitchen and countryside views, offers modern English dishes using the best of seasonal ingredients. There is also a busy carvery, and the award-winning gardens and grounds are ideal for alfresco dining. The team are attentive and friendly. Spa facilities are available by prior arrangement.

Rooms: 26 en suite (2 fmly) (10 GF) **D** fr £110* **Facilities:** FTV tea/coffee Dinner available Lift WiFi Skittles **Parking:** 80 **Notes:** Closed 24 December to 1 January Civ wed 220

LICHFIELD
Map 10 SK10

Innkeeper's Lodge Lichfield

★★★ INN

tel: 03451 551551 **Stafford Road WS13 8JB**
email: info@innkeeperslodge.com **web:** www.innkeeperslodge.com
dir: *Phone for directions.*

Conveniently located close to the M6 Toll, M42 and Birmingham, and ideal for both business and leisure guests, this 18th-century property has been beautifully restored. Bedrooms are attractively presented and well equipped – free WiFi is available. There is a very popular restaurant together with large gardens suitable for alfresco dining.

Rooms: 9 en suite (1 fmly) **Facilities:** FTV tea/coffee Dinner available WiFi

STAFFORD
Map 10 SJ92

Rooks Nest

★★★★ FARMHOUSE

tel: 01889 270624 & 07966 732953 **Rooks Nest Farm, Weston ST18 0BA**
email: info@rooksnest.co.uk **web:** www.rooksnest.co.uk
dir: *From Stafford on A518 towards Weston. Left to Rooks Nest Farm, 1st property.*

Rooks Nest is in a peaceful location with panoramic views over the Trent Valley and countryside. This modern farmhouse has comfortable bedrooms with homely extras. The establishment is handy for visiting the County Showground and Stafford University, with easy access to all Staffordshire's attractions.

Rooms: 2 en suite (1 fmly) **S** fr £39.50 **D** fr £68* **Facilities:** FTV DVD tea/coffee WiFi **Parking:** 4 **Notes:** 220 acres arable/beef

STONE
Map 10 SJ93

Field House
★★★ BED AND BREAKFAST

tel: 01785 605712 **59 Stafford Road ST15 0HE**
email: info@fieldhousehotel.co.uk **web:** www.fieldhousehotel.co.uk
dir: *From A34, northwest into town centre, right into Stafford Road, opposite Walton Grange.*

This family home stands in secluded, pretty gardens close to the town centre. The Georgian house has traditionally furnished bedrooms, some with family pieces. Guests breakfast together in the lounge-dining room, and hospitality is very welcoming.

Rooms: 2 rms (1 en suite) (1 pri facs) **Facilities:** STV FTV TVL tea/coffee WiFi Art tuition on request **Parking:** 4 **Notes:** LB Closed Christmas

TAMWORTH
Map 10 SK20

Oak Tree Farm
★★★★ GUEST ACCOMMODATION

tel: 01827 56807 **Hints Road, Hopwas B78 3AA**
email: oaktreefarm1@aol.com **web:** www.oaktreefarmhotel.co.uk
dir: *2 miles northwest of Tamworth. Off A51 in Hopwas.*

A warm welcome is assured at this well-loved farmhouse, located in peaceful rural surroundings yet only a short drive from the NEC. Spacious bedrooms are filled with homely extras. The elegant dining room, adorned with Oriental artefacts, is the setting for breakfast.

Rooms: 4 en suite 10 annexe en suite (4 fmly) (7 GF) **Facilities:** FTV TVL tea/coffee WiFi ⊗ **Parking:** 20 **Notes:** No children 16 years

Globe Inn
★★★ INN

tel: 01827 60455 **Lower Gungate B79 7AW**
email: info@theglobetamworth.com **web:** www.theglobetamworth.com

Located in the centre of Tamworth, this popular inn provides well-equipped and pleasantly decorated accommodation. The public areas include a spacious lounge bar and a relaxed dining area where a varied selection of dishes is available. There is also a function room and adjacent parking.

Rooms: 18 en suite (2 fmly) **S** fr £35 **D** fr £55* **Facilities:** STV FTV tea/coffee Dinner available WiFi ⅃ **Parking:** 30 **Notes:** Closed 25 December, 1 January

SUFFOLK

BURY ST EDMUNDS
Map 13 TL86

Premier Collection

The Northgate
★★★★★ RESTAURANT WITH ROOMS

tel: 01284 339604 **13–14 Northgate Street IP33 1HP**
email: info@thenorthgate.com **web:** www.thenorthgate.com
dir: *A14 junction 43 onto A1101 towards town centre. 1st exit at roundabout into Northgate Street.*

This historic house is situated a short stroll from the town centre and the Abbey with its beautiful grounds. The individually styled bedrooms are tastefully appointed and equipped with modern facilities (TVs and Nespresso coffee machines). The smartly presented public areas include a contemporary cocktail bar, conservatory, open-plan restaurant and a separate chef's table in the heart of the kitchen; there is a heated outside terrace for alfresco dining too.

Rooms: 9 en suite (1 fmly) **S** fr £115 **D** fr £120* **Facilities:** FTV tea/coffee Dinner available WiFi **Extras:** Nespresso coffee machine **Conf:** Max 25 Thtr 15 Class 18 Board 25 **Parking:** 10

The Chantry
★★★★ GUEST ACCOMMODATION

tel: 01284 767427 **8 Sparhawk Street IP33 1RY**
email: chantryhotel1@aol.com **web:** www.chantryhotel.com
dir: *From cathedral south into Crown Street, left into Honey Hill then right into Sparhawk Street.*

The Chantry is an attractive Georgian property, just a short walk from the town centre. The individually decorated bedrooms are furnished with well-chosen pieces and have many extra thoughtful touches. Breakfast is served in the smart restaurant, and there is a cosy lounge-bar.

Rooms: 11 en suite 3 annexe en suite (1 fmly) (1 GF) **S** fr £89 **D** fr £126*
Facilities: FTV Lounge tea/coffee Direct dial Licensed WiFi ⚓ **Parking:** 14 **Notes:** LB

BURY ST EDMUNDS *continued*

The Abbey

★★★★ GUEST ACCOMMODATION

tel: 01284 762020 **35 Southgate Street IP33 2AZ**
email: reception@abbeyhotel.co.uk **web:** www.abbeyhotel.co.uk
dir: *A14 junction 44, A1302 to town centre, into Southgate Street, premises 400 yards.*

The Abbey is well placed for visiting the historic town centre. The property is split between several old buildings, the main core dating from the 15th century. The public rooms in the Tudor inn section feature a comfortable lounge and an informal dining area. Bedrooms vary in size and style, but all are comfortably furnished and well equipped.

Rooms: 12 en suite (1 GF) **Facilities:** FTV Lounge tea/coffee WiFi 🔒 **Parking:** 12 **Notes:** LB No children 10 years

The Six Bells at Bardwell

★★★★ 🛏 INN

tel: 01359 250820 **The Green, Bardwell IP31 1AW**
email: sixbellsbardwell@aol.com **web:** www.sixbellsbardwell.co.uk
dir: *8 miles northeast, off A143 on edge of village. Follow brown signs from A143.*

This 16th-century inn lies in the peaceful village of Bardwell. The bedrooms, in a converted stable block next to the main building, are furnished in a country style and thoughtfully equipped. Public rooms have original character and provide a choice of areas in which to relax.

Rooms: 10 annexe en suite (1 fmly) (10 GF) **S** fr £65 **D** fr £80* **Facilities:** FTV Lounge tea/coffee Dinner available WiFi 🔒 **Parking:** 50 **Notes:** LB Closed 25 December to 3 January

Hamilton House

★★★ BED AND BREAKFAST

tel: 01284 703022 & 07787 146553 **4 Nelson Road IP33 3AG**
email: hamiltonhouse@hotmail.co.uk **web:** www.hamiltonhousebse.co.uk
dir: *A14 junction 42, follow A1302 across roundabout, then 1st right.*

A warm welcome awaits at Hamilton House, a relaxing Edwardian villa, situated in a quiet side road just a short walk from the town centre. The bedrooms are brightly decorated with co-ordinated fabrics and have a good range of facilities. Breakfast is served at a large communal table in the dining room.

Rooms: 4 rms (2 en suite) (1 fmly) **S** fr £32 **D** fr £65* **Facilities:** FTV DVD tea/coffee WiFi 🔒 **Extras:** Fridge in en suite rooms

The Old Cannon Brewery

★★★ 🛏 INN

tel: 01284 768769 **86 Cannon Street IP33 1JR**
email: info@oldcannonbrewery.co.uk **web:** www.oldcannonbrewery.co.uk
dir: *A14 junction 43, A134 towards town centre. At roundabout after Tesco left then sharp right into Cadney Lane, left into Cannon Street, on left.*

Originally a beer house and brewery, this delightful Victorian property is sure to please; the brewery's output can be sampled in the bar. The open-plan bar and dining area features the polished stainless steel mash tun and kettle. The well-equipped bedrooms are located in an adjacent building, and every visitor will find a bottle of beer waiting for them after they check in.

Rooms: 7 annexe en suite (3 GF) **S** fr £95 **D** fr £110 (room only)* **Facilities:** STV tea/coffee Dinner available WiFi 🔒 **Parking:** 7 **Notes:** No children 10 years

6 Orchard Street

★★★ BED AND BREAKFAST

tel: 07946 590265 **IP33 1EH**
email: mariellascarlett@me.com **web:** www.number6orchardstreet.co.uk
dir: *In town centre near St John's Church on one-way system; Northgate Street turn right into Looms Lane, 2nd right into Well Street, straight on into Orchard Street.*

Expect a warm welcome from the caring hosts at this terrace property, situated just a short walk from the town centre. The pleasant bedrooms are comfortably appointed and have a good range of useful extras. Breakfast is served at a large communal table in the cosy dining room.

Rooms: 3 rms (2 en suite) (1 pri facs) **S** fr £35 **D** fr £60* **Facilities:** FTV tea/coffee WiFi 🔒 **Notes:** No children 6 years

The Black Boy

★★★ INN

tel: 01284 752723 **69 Guildhall Street IP33 1QD**
email: enquiries@theblackboypublichouse.co.uk **web:** www.theblackboypublichouse.co.uk
dir: *Exit A14 to town centre.*

The Black Boy is a popular inn situated in the centre of this historic town. The spacious bedrooms have co-ordinated fabrics, pine furniture and many thoughtful touches. Public areas feature a large open-plan bar with a good selection of ales. There is a wide variety of pubs and restaurants within a short walk. Breakfast is served daily in the bar.

Rooms: 5 en suite **S** fr £47.50 **D** fr £85* **Facilities:** FTV tea/coffee Dinner available WiFi **Parking:** 6 **Notes:** No children 5 years

| CAVENDISH | Map 13 TL84 |

The George

★★★★ ◉◉ 🍷 RESTAURANT WITH ROOMS

tel: 01787 280248 **The Green CO10 8BA**
email: thegeorgecavendish@gmail.com **web:** www.thecavendishgeorge.co.uk
dir: *A1092 into Cavendish, The George next to village green.*

The George is situated in the heart of the pretty village of Cavendish and has stylish bedrooms which have retained many of their original features, as well as being comfortable and spacious. The front-facing rooms overlook the village. The award-winning restaurant is very well appointed and dinner should not be missed. Guests are guaranteed to receive a warm welcome, attentive friendly service and great food.

Rooms: 4 en suite (1 fmly) **S** fr £60 **D** fr £85* **Facilities:** FTV DVD tea/coffee Dinner available WiFi 🔒 **Extras:** Speciality toiletries, mineral water, sweets **Notes:** Closed 25 December and 1 January

DUNWICH
Map 13 TM47

The Ship at Dunwich

★★★★ INN

tel: 01728 648219 **St James Street IP17 3DT**
email: info@shipatdunwich.co.uk **web:** www.shipatdunwich.co.uk
dir: *From north: A12, exit at Blythburgh onto B1125, then left to village. Inn at end of road. From south: A12, turn right to Westleton. Follow signs for Dunwich.*

The Ship is a delightful inn situated in the heart of this quiet village, surrounded by nature reserves and heathland, and just a short walk from the beach. Public rooms feature a smart lounge bar with an open fire and real ales on tap. The comfortable bedrooms are traditionally furnished; some rooms have lovely views across the sea or marshes.

Rooms: 11 en suite 5 annexe en suite (4 fmly) (5 GF) **Facilities:** FTV tea/coffee Dinner available WiFi **Extras:** Speciality toiletries **Parking:** 10 **Notes:** LB

ELVEDEN
Map 13 TL88

Premier Collection

The Elveden Inn

★★★★★ ⇔ INN

tel: 01842 890876 **Brandon Road IP24 3TP**
email: enquiries@elvedeninn.com **web:** www.elvedeninn.com
dir: *A11 (dual carriageway) onto B1106 (Brandon Road) towards Bury St Edmunds.*

This charming country inn offers a range of beautifully presented bedrooms and sleek modern bathrooms. Enjoying a peaceful location in the heart of East Anglia, the inn is part of the Guinness family-owned Elveden Estate. The bar is full of character and the terrace is a popular dining venue on warmer days. The Elveden courtyard shops are nearby and the café is very popular. The inn holds an AA Dinner Award for the very special meals that have an emphasis on freshly-prepared, local ingredients.

Rooms: 6 en suite (2 fmly) **Facilities:** FTV tea/coffee Dinner available Direct dial WiFi **Extras:** Speciality toiletries, fruit, bottled water – complimentary **Parking:** 100 **Notes:** LB

EYE
Map 13 TM17

The White Horse Inn

★★★★ INN

tel: 01379 678222 **Stoke Ash IP23 7ET**
email: mail@whitehorse-suffolk.co.uk **web:** www.whitehorse-suffolk.co.uk
dir: *On A140 halfway between Ipswich and Norwich.*

The White Horse Inn is a 17th-century coaching inn on the A140, midway between Norwich and Ipswich. It has been run by the same family for over a decade, offering home-made, good quality food in a friendly and comfortable environment; all complemented by well-kept local ales and cider. Comfortable bedrooms are found in the modern, purpose-built motel-style annexe; some have air conditioning, all are well equipped. Complimentary WiFi is available in the public areas and bedrooms.

Rooms: 11 annexe en suite (1 fmly) (9 GF) **Facilities:** FTV tea/coffee Dinner available Direct dial WiFi **Conf:** Max 50 Thtr 50 Class 50 Board 20 **Parking:** 60 **Notes:** LB

FRAMLINGHAM
Map 13 TM26

Colston Hall

★★★★ ⚘ FARMHOUSE

tel: 01728 638375 **Badingham IP13 8LB**
email: liz@colstonhall.com **web:** www.colstonhall.com
dir: *On A1120 between Badingham and Peasenhall.*

Set in a peaceful rural location, Colston Hall offers a range of individually designed spacious bedrooms. This Elizabethan farmhouse has many original features including brick floors and oak beams. Bedrooms have lovely countryside views, overlooking the lakes and the pretty kitchen garden. The hearty breakfasts are not to be missed and the home-made marmalade is rather special.

Rooms: 3 en suite 3 rms annexe (2 en suite) (1 pri facs annexe) (3 GF) **Facilities:** FTV DVD Lounge TVL tea/coffee WiFi Fishing Snooker ⚘ **Conf:** Max 50 Thtr 50 Class 50 Board 50 **Parking:** 22 **Notes:** LB 27 acres sheep

INGHAM
Map 13 TL87

The Cadogan Arms
★★★★ ⬥ INN

tel: 01284 728443 **The Street IP31 1NG**
email: info@thecadogan.co.uk **web:** www.thecadogan.co.uk
dir: *4 miles from Bury St Edmunds, follow A134 towards Thetford.*

The Cadogan Arms is a popular inn situated four miles from the centre of Bury St Edmunds. The smartly appointed bedrooms have been thoughtfully designed and have many useful extras. The open-plan public rooms are contemporary in style and they include a range of seating areas with plush leather sofas and a smart restaurant.

Rooms: 7 en suite (7 fmly) **S** fr £90 **D** fr £110* **Facilities:** FTV tea/coffee Dinner available WiFi **Extras:** Bottled water **Parking:** 30 **Notes:** LB

LEISTON
Map 13 TM46

Field End
★★★★ GUEST HOUSE

tel: 01728 833527 & 07946 287451 **1 Kings Road IP16 4DA**
email: herbert@herbertwood.wanadoo.co.uk **web:** www.fieldendguesthouse.co.uk
dir: *In town centre off B1122.*

This Edwardian house has been appointed to a high standard and is impeccably maintained by the present owners. Bedrooms have co-ordinated soft furnishings and many thoughtful touches. Breakfast is served in an attractive dining room, which has a large sofa and a range of puzzles and games.

Rooms: 5 rms (2 en suite) (1 pri facs) (1 fmly) (1 GF) **Facilities:** FTV DVD TVL tea/coffee WiFi **Extras:** Fridges **Parking:** 5 **Notes:** No children 6 months

LONG MELFORD
Map 13 TL84

AA RESTAURANT WITH ROOMS OF THE YEAR 2018–19

Premier Collection

Long Melford Swan
★★★★★ ⬥⬥ RESTAURANT WITH ROOMS

tel: 01787 464545 **Hall Street CO10 9JQ**
email: info@longmelfordswan.co.uk **web:** www.longmelfordswan.co.uk
dir: *From A134 into Long Melford, on main road through village.*

Located in the very heart of Long Melford, the Swan offers home-made refreshments on arrival, bedrooms with stylish decor and modern fixtures, feature bathrooms and a turn-down service. All the bedrooms are located just next door in Melford House, adjacent to the main bar and restaurant. This family-run business offers an excellent restaurant with attentive service and a large alfresco dining area in the walled garden. Lunch and dinner are served daily, and a range of cooked and continental dishes are offered for breakfast in the restaurant.

Rooms: 3 en suite 4 annexe en suite (1 fmly) (2 GF) **Facilities:** FTV DVD iPod docking station tea/coffee Dinner available Direct dial WiFi ⅃ Spa treatments by arrangement **Extras:** Speciality toiletries, fruit **Notes:** LB

MILDENHALL
Map 12 TL77

Premier Collection

The Bull Inn
★★★★★ ⬥ INN

tel: 01638 711001 **The Street, Barton Mills IP28 6AA**
email: reception@bullinn-bartonmills.com **web:** www.bullinn-bartonmills.com
dir: *A11 between Newmarket and Mildenhall, signed Barton Mills. Inn by Five Ways roundabout.*

This delightful 16th-century coaching inn is lovingly cared for by the owners. Public rooms offer a choice of bars, a brasserie-style restaurant and a further lounge area. The contemporary bedrooms are tastefully appointed with co-ordinated soft furnishings and many thoughtful touches. All are individually styled with designer wallpaper, bespoke glass walls and many other unique features.

Rooms: 13 en suite 2 annexe en suite (1 fmly) (2 GF) **Facilities:** FTV Lounge tea/coffee Dinner available Direct dial WiFi ⚓ **Extras:** Speciality toiletries **Conf:** Max 30 Thtr 30 Class 20 Board 20 **Parking:** 50 **Notes:** Closed 24–26 December

NEWMARKET
Map 12 TL66

Premier Collection

The Packhorse Inn
★★★★★ ⬥⬥ INN

tel: 01638 751818 **Bridge Street, Moulton CB8 8SP**
email: info@thepackhorseinn.com **web:** www.thepackhorseinn.com
dir: *A14 junction 39 onto B1506. After 1.5 miles turn left at crossroads onto B1085 (Moulton Road). In Moulton, left into Bridge Street.*

The Packhorse Inn is situated just a short drive from Newmarket in the heart of a village close to the River Kennet. The property has eight individually designed, tastefully appointed bedrooms, all with many thoughtful touches and views of the surrounding hills, after which the rooms are named. The open-plan public spaces include a choice of seating and dining areas with an eclectic collection of furniture.

Rooms: 4 en suite 4 annexe en suite (2 fmly) (4 GF) **S** fr £85 **D** fr £95 **Facilities:** FTV Lounge TVL tea/coffee Dinner available WiFi ⅃ ⚓ **Extras:** Speciality toiletries, mineral water, biscuits **Conf:** Max 30 Thtr 30 Class 20 Board 30 **Parking:** 30

ORFORD
Map 13 TM45

Premier Collection

The Crown & Castle
★★★★★ ⬥⬥ RESTAURANT WITH ROOMS

tel: 01394 450205 **IP12 2LJ**
email: info@crownandcastle.co.uk **web:** www.crownandcastle.co.uk
dir: *Turn right from B1084 on entering village, towards castle.*

The Crown & Castle is a delightful property situated adjacent to the Norman castle keep. Contemporary bedrooms are spilt between the main house and the garden wing; the latter are more spacious and have patios with access to the garden. The restaurant has an informal atmosphere with polished tables and local artwork, and a menu that features quality, locally sourced produce.

Rooms: 7 en suite 14 annexe en suite (2 fmly) (13 GF) **D** fr £140* **Facilities:** FTV DVD tea/coffee Dinner available Direct dial WiFi ♿ **Extras:** Speciality toiletries, fresh milk **Parking:** 17 **Notes:** LB No children 8 years

Sibton White Horse Inn

★★★★   INN

tel: 01728 660337 **Halesworth Road IP17 2JJ**
email: info@sibtonwhitehorseinn.co.uk **web:** www.sibtonwhitehorseinn.co.uk
dir: *From A12 in Yoxford take A1120 signed Sibton and Peasenhall. 3 miles, in Peasenhall right opposite butcher's shop. White Horse 600 metres.*

Sibton White Horse Inn is a delightful Grade II listed, 16th-century Tudor property set in open countryside, a few miles from the Suffolk coast. Public rooms include a traditional beamed bar with exposed brick fireplaces and a choice of dining areas. The attractive bedrooms are situated in a converted building adjacent to the inn.

Rooms: 6 annexe en suite (2 fmly) (3 GF) **Facilities:** FTV DVD tea/coffee Dinner available WiFi 🛁 **Extras:** Bottled water, speciality toiletries, cafetières **Parking:** 50 **Notes:** LB No children 12 years Closed 26–27 December

Premier Collection

Sutherland House

★★★★★ ◉◉ RESTAURANT WITH ROOMS

tel: 01502 724544 **56 High Street IP18 6DN**
email: enquiries@sutherlandhouse.co.uk **web:** www.sutherlandhouse.co.uk
dir: *A1095 into Southwold, on High Street on left after Victoria Street.*

Situated in the heart of the bustling town centre, this delightful 16th-century house has a wealth of character – oak beams, exposed brickwork, open fireplaces and two superb ornate plasterwork ceilings. The stylish bedrooms are tastefully decorated using co-ordinated fabrics and include many thoughtful touches. Public rooms feature a large open-plan contemporary restaurant, which has been awarded two AA Rosettes. There's a modern British menu created with care, and the food miles are listed alongside each dish.

Rooms: 5 en suite (1 fmly) **D** fr £100* **Facilities:** FTV DVD tea/coffee Dinner available WiFi **Notes:** No children 10 years RS Monday restaurant closed

The Bell Inn

★★★ 🛏 INN

tel: 01502 723109 **Ferry Road, Walberswick IP18 6TN**
email: bellwalberswick@adnams.co.uk **web:** www.bellinnwalberswick.co.uk
dir: *Phone for directions.*

The Bell Inn is ideally situated adjacent to the village green, in the heart of Walberswick. Just a short walk from the beach, the property is 600 years old and the public areas retain much original charm and character that include hidden alcoves. The bedrooms are well equipped with a good range of facilities.

Rooms: 6 en suite **Facilities:** Dinner available

The Crown

Ⓤ

tel: 01502 722275 **90 High Street IP18 6DP**
email: thecrown@adnams.co.uk **web:** www.thecrownsouthwold.co.uk

Currently the rating for this establishment is not confirmed. This may be due to a change of ownership or because it has only recently joined the AA rating scheme.

Rooms: 14 en suite **Facilities:** tea/coffee Dinner available Licensed WiFi **Extras:** Speciality toiletries

STOKE-BY-NAYLAND   Map 13 TL93

Premier Collection

The Angel Inn

★★★★★ INN

tel: 01206 263245 & 07748 484619 **Polstead Street CO6 4SA**
email: info@angelinnsuffolk.co.uk **web:** www.angelinnsuffolk.co.uk
dir: From A134 onto Bear Street (B1087), 2 miles on right in Stoke-by-Nayland.

This charming inn has welcomed guests since the 16th century. Still popular with the locals, it's well known for its food and ambience. Public areas have a wealth of character and offer a choice of dining rooms that include a smart restaurant with an original well. Bedrooms are pleasantly decorated and thoughtfully equipped.

Rooms: 6 en suite **Facilities:** FTV Lounge tea/coffee Dinner available WiFi
🔒 **Conf:** Max 25 Thtr 15 Class 18 Board 18 **Parking:** 12 **Notes:** LB

SUDBURY   Map 13 TL84

Premier Collection

The Black Lion

★★★★★ ◎◎ INN

tel: 01787 312356 **The Green, Long Melford CO10 9DN**
email: info@theblacklionhotel.com **web:** www.theblacklionhotel.com
dir: Phone for directions.

After a long renovation, The Black Lion has emerged as a very inviting establishment. Roaring log fires in winter, a cosy drawing room and a new conservatory leading out onto an alfresco dining terrace set the scene. The 10 stylish bedrooms range from snug to family rooms; some overlook the green and others the cathedral. All have TVs, tea- and coffee-making facilities, free fast WiFi and luxury toiletries as standard. The skilfully created and beautifully presented food has been awarded two AA Rosettes.

Rooms: 10 en suite **S** fr £90 **D** fr £100* **Facilities:** tea/coffee Dinner available WiFi **Extras:** Speciality toiletries

The Case Restaurant with Rooms

★★★★ ◎ RESTAURANT WITH ROOMS

tel: 01787 210483 **Further Street, Assington CO10 5LD**
email: restaurant@thecaserestaurantwithrooms.co.uk
web: www.thecaserestaurantwithrooms.co.uk
dir: Exit A12 at Colchester onto A134 to Sudbury. 7 miles, establishment on left.

The Case Restaurant with Rooms offers dining in comfortable surroundings, along with luxurious accommodation in bedrooms that all enjoy independent access. Some bathrooms come complete with a corner jacuzzi, while internet access comes as standard. In the restaurant, local produce is used in all dishes and bread and delicious desserts are made fresh every day.

Rooms: 7 en suite (2 fmly) (7 GF) **S** fr £59 **D** fr £79* **Facilities:** FTV Lounge tea/coffee Dinner available WiFi **Extras:** Speciality toiletries – complimentary; snacks – chargeable **Parking:** 25 **Notes:** LB

THORNHAM MAGNA   Map 13 TM17

Premier Collection

Thornham Hall

★★★★★ GUEST ACCOMMODATION

tel: 01379 783314 **IP23 8HA**
email: info@thornhamhall.com **web:** www.thornhamhall.com
dir: Exit A140 at Stoke Ash White Horse pub. After 350 metres right before Four Horseshoes pub. Through village, pass church and into drive signed Thornham Hall.

Set in a formal park, Thornham Hall enjoys a picturesque setting and the comfortable, individually styled bedrooms overlook the extensive gardens. There is a choice of reception rooms in which to relax and the Thornham Estate offers guests over 10 miles of walks through ancient woodland and farmland. The walled garden contains many rare apple trees. The charming town of Eye is nearby and Framlingham is a short drive away.

Rooms: 3 en suite **Facilities:** Lounge TVL tea/coffee Licensed WiFi ⚓ 🎣 Fishing 🔒 **Parking:** 10

WANGFORD   Map 13 TM47

The Plough Inn

[U]

tel: 01502 578239 **London Road NR34 8AZ**
email: thewangfordplough@adnams.co.uk **web:** www.wangfordplough.co.uk
dir: Phone for directions.

Currently the rating for this establishment is not confirmed. This may be due to a change of ownership or because it has only recently joined the AA rating scheme.

Rooms: 5 en suite

WINGFIELD   Map 13 TM27

Holly Tree House

★★★★  BED AND BREAKFAST

tel: 01379 384854 **Bleach Green IP21 5RG**
email: sharon@hollytreehousebandb.co.uk **web:** www.hollytreehousebandb.co.uk

This beautiful, 16th-century, timber-framed house enjoys a peaceful rural location on the Suffolk–Norfolk border. Guests are served refreshment on arrival either in the garden or in the cosy lounge, depending on the weather. The bedrooms are beautifully presented and are very well equipped. The house has been sympathetically restored in recent years and boasts many eye-catching original features as well as lovely gardens.

Rooms: 2 en suite **D** fr £95* **Facilities:** FTV DVD iPod docking station Lounge tea/coffee WiFi 🔒 **Extras:** Speciality toiletries, snacks **Parking:** 4

WOODBRIDGE — Map 13 TM24

Cherry Tree Inn
★★★★ INN

tel: 01394 384627 & 385213 **73 Cumberland Street IP12 4AG**
email: info@thecherrytreepub.co.uk **web:** www.thecherrytreepub.co.uk
dir: *Phone for directions.*

Cherry Tree Inn is a charming 17th-century property located close to the town of Woodbridge. This authentic inn has many original features including oak beams, low ceilings and log fires. There is a great atmosphere in the bar with its good choice of cask ales, and evening meals feature an extensive choice of freshly prepared, traditional dishes. The bedrooms, in a separate converted barn, are spacious and very comfortable – two are on the ground floor.

Rooms: 3 annexe en suite (1 fmly) (2 GF) **Facilities:** STV FTV DVD tea/coffee Dinner available Direct dial WiFi 🛁 **Extras:** Home-made biscuits, still/sparkling water **Parking:** 30

YAXLEY — Map 13 TM17

Premier Collection

The Auberge
★★★★★ RESTAURANT WITH ROOMS

tel: 01379 783604 **Ipswich Road IP23 8BZ**
email: aubmail@the-auberge.co.uk **web:** www.the-auberge.co.uk
dir: *On A140 between Norwich and Ipswich at crossroads with B1117.*

A warm welcome awaits at The Auberge, a charming 15th-century property, which was once a rural pub but is now a smart restaurant with rooms. The restaurant has gained two AA Rosettes for the good use of fresh, quality produce in well-crafted dishes. The public areas have a wealth of character, such as exposed brickwork and beams, and the grounds are particularly well kept and attractive. The spacious bedrooms are tastefully appointed and have many thoughtful touches; one bedroom has a four-poster.

Rooms: 11 annexe en suite (2 fmly) (6 GF) **Facilities:** FTV tea/coffee Dinner available Direct dial WiFi 🛁 **Conf:** Max 30 Thtr 30 Class 20 Board 12 **Parking:** 40 **Notes:** LB

SURREY

ALBURY — Map 6 TQ04

The Drummond at Albury
★★★ INN

tel: 01483 202039 **High Street GU5 9AG**
web: www.thedrummondarms.co.uk
dir: *Phone for directions.*

The Drummond is centrally located in this picturesque village, with attractive gardens running down to a small river at the rear of the property. The bedrooms are individually appointed and offer all the modern comforts. Breakfast is served in the light and airy conservatory while the restaurant offers mouth-watering dishes.

Rooms: 9 en suite **Facilities:** Dinner available **Conf:** Max 40 Thtr 40 Class 40

CAMBERLEY — Map 6 SU86

Hatsue Guest House
★★★★ GUEST ACCOMMODATION

tel: 01276 22160 & 07791 267620 **17 Southwell Park Road GU15 3PU**
email: welcome@hatsueguesthouse.com **web:** www.hatsueguesthouse.com
dir: *M3 junction 4, A331 north, A30 east, at Arena sports centre turn right. At T-junction, turn right, 2nd house on left before church.*

Hatsue Guest House offers comfortable, well-appointed accommodation in a period house which has been sympathetically updated to meet the needs of today's guest. TV and free WiFi are examples of the amenities provided. The breakfast room overlooks the quiet rear garden. Ample parking is available.

Rooms: 5 en suite **Facilities:** FTV tea/coffee WiFi **Parking:** 5

CHIDDINGFOLD — Map 6 SU93

Premier Collection

The Crown Inn
★★★★★ INN

tel: 01428 682255 **The Green, Petworth Road GU8 4TX**
email: enquiries@thecrownchiddingfold.com **web:** www.thecrownchiddingfold.com
dir: *Phone for directions.*

Set in a tranquil location in a picturesque village, the inn dates back to the early 13th century. This charming property offers stylish, modern accommodation that has been tastefully finished without the loss of any period features. Breakfast and dinner can be enjoyed in the oak-panelled dining room, and there is a spacious bar, outside seating and small courtyard.

Rooms: 8 en suite (4 fmly) **Facilities:** STV FTV Lounge tea/coffee Dinner available Direct dial WiFi 🛁 **Extras:** Speciality toiletries **Conf:** Max 40 Thtr 40 Class 25 Board 28 **Parking:** 15

CRANLEIGH — Map 6 TQ03

The Cranley
★★★ INN

tel: 01483 272827 **The Common GU6 8SQ**
email: thecranleyhotel@gmail.com **web:** www.thecranleyhotel.co.uk
dir: *From Guildford on A281 left to Cranleigh.*

This traditional pub, located in the picturesque village of Cranleigh, offers freshly prepared food, at both lunch and dinner, using local produce. Regular entertainment is provided, and the rear garden is popular with families. The comfortable bedrooms have TVs and tea- and coffee-making facilities.

Rooms: 7 en suite **Facilities:** TVL tea/coffee Dinner available WiFi **Parking:** 50

DORKING
Map 6 TQ14

Denbies Farmhouse B&B

★★★★ FARMHOUSE

tel: 01306 876777 **London Road RH5 6AA**
email: bandb@denbiesvineyard.co.uk web: www.denbies.co.uk
dir: *Off A24.*

Denbies Farmhouse enjoys a wonderful location in the heart of England's largest vineyard and is a short walk to the historic market town of Dorking. Very popular with ramblers as there are many beautiful walks nearby. Bedrooms are comfortable and breakfasts are served in the conservatory with its wonderful views of the vineyard.

Rooms: 7 en suite (2 fmly) (2 GF) **Facilities:** STV FTV tea/coffee Licensed WiFi
🔒 **Extras:** Speciality toiletries – complimentary **Parking:** 14 **Notes:** LB
650 acres wine

EFFINGHAM
Map 6 TQ15

Sir Douglas Haig

★★★ INN

tel: 01372 456886 **The Street KT24 5LU**
email: sirdouglashaig@hotmail.com web: www.sirdouglashaig.co.uk
dir: *M25 junction 9, A243 then A24, at roundabout take 2nd exit onto A246. Through Bookham, at lights with golf club on left, turn right. Pub on right.*

A traditional public house located in the village centre, the Sir Douglas Haig retains a country atmosphere and offers comfortable accommodation. The bar is well stocked and provides regular entertainment while the restaurant serves a choice of traditional dishes. Ample parking is available.

Rooms: 7 en suite (1 fmly) **Facilities:** FTV DVD tea/coffee Dinner available WiFi
🔒 **Parking:** 15 **Notes:** LB

GODALMING
Map 6 SU94

Innkeeper's Lodge Godalming

★★★★ INN

tel: 03451 551551 **Ockford Road GU7 1RH**
email: info@innkeeperslodge.com web: www.innkeeperslodge.com
dir: *Phone for directions.*

This Innkeeper's Lodge, The Inn on the Lake, is located in Godalming and offers bedrooms with lake views. The welcoming interior is contemporary in design and a wide-ranging choice of dishes is offered on the seasonal menus. The en suite bedrooms, in different shapes and sizes, come with TVs, desks and free WiFi as standard; family rooms are available. A meeting room and a beer garden are available and free parking is provided.

Rooms: 14 en suite (4 fmly) **Facilities:** FTV tea/coffee Dinner available Direct dial WiFi **Conf:** Max 28

GUILDFORD
Map 6 SU94

The Angel

★★★★ GUEST ACCOMMODATION

tel: 01483 564555 **91 High Street GU1 3DP**
email: reservations@angelpostinghouse.com web: www.angelpostinghouse.com
dir: *From A281 (Horsham Road), turn left into High Street. 200 yards on left.*

On the high street, in the heart of Guildford and within the popular Angel Gate area with its shops and restaurants, this historic property features a range of rooms including spacious suites and traditional doubles. All have TVs, free WiFi and high-

quality bathrooms with power showers; some with separate baths. Rates are room-only; breakfast is available in the adjacent Bill's Guildford restaurant, which is also open for lunch and dinner.

Rooms: 24 en suite **Facilities:** STV FTV Lounge tea/coffee Dinner available Licensed WiFi 🌿 🔒 **Conf:** Max 60 Thtr 60 Class 30 Board 30 **Notes:** Civ wed 50

HASLEMERE
Map 6 SU93

The Wheatsheaf Inn

★★★ 🍴 INN

tel: 01428 644440 **Grayswood Road, Grayswood GU27 2DE**
email: ken@thewheatsheafgrayswood.co.uk web: www.thewheatsheafgrayswood.co.uk
dir: *1 mile north of Haslemere on A286 in Grayswood.*

Situated in a small village just outside Haslemere, this well-presented inn has a friendly atmosphere. The smart conservatory restaurant complements the attractive dining area and popular bar. Bedrooms are furnished to a good standard; all but one are on the ground floor.

Rooms: 7 en suite (6 GF) **S** fr £59 **D** fr £79* **Facilities:** FTV tea/coffee Dinner available Direct dial WiFi **Parking:** 21

HORLEY
See Gatwick Airport (West Sussex)

MICKLEHAM
Map 6 TQ15

Running Horses

★★★★ ⚜ INN

tel: 01372 372279 **Old London Road RH5 6DU**
email: gm@therunninghorses.co.uk web: www.therunninghorses.co.uk
dir: *M25 junction 9 follow signs for Dorking, southbound on A24. Left signed Mickleham, 200 metres on right.*

Located in the tranquil village of Mickleham, this renovated village pub offers modern and very comfortable accommodation, well equipped with up-to-date amenities ideal for both the leisure and corporate guest. The location is quiet yet with easy access to Dorking, Gatwick and the M25. The restaurant offers an excellent range of dishes and is open for breakfast, lunch and dinner.

Rooms: 5 en suite 1 annexe en suite (1 GF) **Facilities:** FTV tea/coffee Dinner available WiFi 🔒

RIPLEY
Map 6 TQ05

The Talbot

★★★★ INN

tel: 01483 225188 **High Street GU23 6BB**
email: manager@thetalbotripley.com web: www.bespokehotels.com/talbotinn
dir: *M25 junction 10 onto A3 (south), follow signs for Ripley. On left in High Street.*

The Talbot has lots of charm and character and has retained many of its original features. Public areas are very comfortable, with real ales and delicious, seasonal food on offer; alfresco dining is possible in the summer months. The Classic Rooms in the Ripley Wing are contemporary in design, and there are nine bedrooms in the main building. The inn also offers a number of rooms for meetings, private parties and weddings. The Wisley Suite accommodates up to 120 guests and comes equipped with the latest technology.

Rooms: 9 en suite 34 annexe en suite (15 GF) **Facilities:** FTV TVL tea/coffee Dinner available Direct dial WiFi 🌿 🔒 **Conf:** Max 100 Thtr 100 Class 60 Board 60
Parking: 43 **Notes:** LB Civ wed 100

WEST END
Map 6 SU96

The Inn West End
★★★★ ⊛ INN

tel: 01276 858652 & 485842 **GU24 9PW**
email: rooms@the-inn.co.uk **web:** www.the-inn.co.uk
dir: M3 junction 3, 3 miles on A322.

A convenient location, attentive service, a traditional pub, a wine shop, a restaurant and 12 individually appointed and comfortable bedrooms are found at The Inn West End. The cottage-style bedrooms offer sumptuous beds, powerful showers and all the amenities expected by the modern traveller. The menu offers a range of dishes to meet the needs of a varied clientele with the focus on fresh and seasonal produce, locally sourced where possible. There is also a relaxing garden, ideal for barbecues during the summer months, and secure parking.

Rooms: 12 annexe en suite (12 GF) **D** fr £130* **Facilities:** FTV tea/coffee Dinner available WiFi ⅃ **Parking:** 35 **Notes:** LB No children 10 years

WEYBRIDGE
Map 6 TQ06

Innkeeper's Lodge Weybridge
★★★★ INN

tel: 03451 551551 **25 Oatlands Chase KT13 9RW**
email: info@innkeeperslodge.com **web:** www.innkeeperslodge.com
dir: Phone for directions.

This Innkeeper's Lodge, The Oakland Chaser, was built on the site of one of Henry VIII's favourite hunting grounds – Ashley Park. Set back from the road, it has lots of space for eating and drinking on the grass area at the front and stylish dining areas inside. The wide-ranging menus feature something for everyone from light bites to traditional Sunday roasts. The en suite bedrooms come with TVs, tea- and coffee-making facilities and free WiFi as standard; family rooms are available. Parking is provided.

Rooms: 19 en suite (5 fmly) (2 GF) **Facilities:** FTV tea/coffee Dinner available WiFi

WOKING
Map 6 TQ05

Innkeeper's Lodge Woking
★★★ INN

tel: 03451 551551 **Chobham Road, Horsell GU21 4AL**
email: info@innkeeperslodge.com **web:** www.innkeeperslodge.com
dir: Phone for directions.

Just a short walk from Woking Station and a 25-minute commute from central London, this Innkeeper's Lodge, The Wheatsheaf, is ideal for both business or leisure guests. The en suite, modern bedrooms come in different shapes and sizes and have TVs, desks, free WiFi, tea- and coffee-making facilities as standard; family rooms are available. The attractive public areas have cosy open fires and friendly, welcoming staff. The seasonal menu choices prove popular and the free on-site parking is a plus.

Rooms: 33 en suite (3 fmly) (13 GF) **Facilities:** FTV tea/coffee Dinner available WiFi **Parking:** 28

Made In Sud
★★★ GUEST ACCOMMODATION

tel: 01483 723080 **14 The Broadway GU21 5AP**
email: madeinsud.woking@gmail.com **web:** www.madeinsudwoking.co.uk
dir: Phone for directions.

A warm welcome is guaranteed at Made in Sud which is within walking distance of Woking train station. All bedrooms are comfortably furnished and come equipped with a range of accessories. Breakfast is served in the light and airy café below. Free WiFi is accessible throughout.

Rooms: 8 en suite **Facilities:** WiFi

EAST SUSSEX

BOREHAM STREET
Map 6 TQ61

Premier Collection

Boreham House
★★★★★ ⊜ BED AND BREAKFAST

tel: 01323 833719 **Boreham Hill BN27 4SF**
email: enquiries@borehamhouse.com **web:** www.borehamhouse.com
dir: On A271 between Herstmonceux and Battle, 100 metres from Bull's Head pub.

This delightful Georgian manor is in a quiet location just a short drive from Bodiam Castle, Hastings and Pevensey Bay. Both sides of the property enjoy excellent views of either the High Wield or across the Pevensey Marshes to the sea. The bedrooms and bathrooms are contemporary in style yet retain many original features. There is a guest lounge and hearty cooked or continental breakfasts are served in the dining room – all ingredients are locally sourced. There is an excellent pub situated within 100 metres.

Rooms: 3 en suite (1 fmly) **Facilities:** FTV Lounge tea/coffee WiFi ⊜ **Parking:** 3

New Steine

★★★★ ⚜ 🍽 GUEST ACCOMMODATION

tel: 01273 681546 **10–11 New Steine BN2 1PB**
email: reservation@newsteinehotel.com **web:** www.newsteinehotel.com
dir: *A23 to Brighton Pier, left into Marine Parade, New Steine on left after Wentworth Street.*

Close to the seafront, off the Esplanade, the New Steine provides spacious and well-appointed accommodation. The Bistro offers simple yet appealing dishes with a French and British influence; produce from farms in Sussex is used for the breakfasts. There are two meeting rooms suitable for a variety of occasions. Street parking can be arranged.

Rooms: 20 rms (16 en suite) (4 pri facs) (4 fmly) (2 GF) **S** fr £34.50 **D** fr £59*
Facilities: FTV Lounge tea/coffee Dinner available Direct dial Licensed WiFi
🔒 **Extras:** Speciality toiletries **Conf:** Max 50 Thtr 50 Class 20 Board 26 **Notes:** LB
No children 4 years

Snooze

★★★★ GUEST ACCOMMODATION

tel: 01273 605797 **25 St George's Terrace BN2 1JJ**
email: info@snoozebrighton.com **web:** www.snoozebrighton.com
dir: *Follow A23 to seafront/pier. Turn left at mini roundabout opposite pier, then left into Bedford Street, 2nd right into St George's Terrace.*

This splendid Victorian terraced property is close to the beach and the popular Kemp Town bars and restaurants. Bedrooms have a distinctly 'retro' feel and all are comfortably appointed. The spacious dining room with its large bay windows is the setting for a choice of hearty breakfasts.

Rooms: 8 en suite (2 GF) **Facilities:** FTV DVD iPod docking station tea/coffee WiFi
Extras: Speciality toiletries

Brighton House

★★★★ ⚜ GUEST ACCOMMODATION

tel: 01273 323282 **52 Regency Square BN1 2FF**
email: info@brighton-house.co.uk **web:** www.brighton-house.co.uk
dir: *Opposite West Pier.*

Situated close to the seafront is the elegant and environmentally-friendly Brighton House. Comfortably appointed bedrooms and bathrooms come in a variety of sizes and are located on four floors. An impressively abundant, organic continental breakfast is served in the spacious and elegant dining room. Parking is in the nearby underground car park.

Rooms: 16 en suite (2 fmly) **Facilities:** FTV tea/coffee Licensed WiFi
Notes: No children 12 years

Gullivers

★★★★ GUEST ACCOMMODATION

tel: 01273 681546 & 695415 **12a New Steine BN2 1PB**
email: reservation@gullivershotel.com **web:** www.gullivershotel.com
dir: *A23 to Brighton Pier, left into Marine Parade, premises 300 yards on left.*

Situated in an impressive Regency square close to the town and seafront, Gullivers has much to offer. Compact rooms use clever design and contemporary colours to ensure comfort, and some have quality shower rooms en suite. The lounge and brasserie, decorated with fine art, are super areas in which to relax and dine.

Rooms: 12 rms (9 en suite) (3 pri facs) (2 GF) **S** fr £29 **D** fr £54.50* **Facilities:** FTV Lounge tea/coffee Dinner available Direct dial Licensed WiFi 🔒 **Extras:** Speciality toiletries – complimentary **Conf:** Max 30 Thtr 30 Class 10 Board 20 **Notes:** LB No children 4 years

Innkeeper's Lodge Brighton, Patcham

★★★★ INN

tel: 03451 551551 **Miller & Carter Brighton, London Road BN1 8YQ**
email: info@innkeeperslodge.com **web:** www.innkeeperslodge.com
dir: *Phone for directions.*

This Innkeeper's Lodge, The Miller & Carter, is located just off the A27 on the northern limits of Brighton. The en suite bedrooms, in different shapes and sizes, come with TVs, desks and free WiFi as standard; family rooms are available. The welcoming interior is a mix traditional and contemporary in design and the Steakhouse menus prove very popular. There's a meeting room, and free parking is provided.

Rooms: 17 en suite (6 fmly) (1 GF) **Facilities:** FTV tea/coffee Dinner available Direct dial WiFi

Marine View

★★★★ GUEST ACCOMMODATION

tel: 01273 603870 **24 New Steine BN2 1PD**
email: info@mvbrighton.co.uk **web:** www.mvbrighton.co.uk
dir: *From A23, left into Marine Parade, left into New Steine, 300 metres.*

Overlooking the elegant Steine Square with the sea just a glance away, this 18th-century property offers comfortable, well-designed accommodation. Plenty of accessories are provided, including free WiFi. A hearty breakfast is available in the bright lounge-dining room.

Rooms: 11 rms (8 en suite) (1 pri facs) (2 fmly) (2 GF) **Facilities:** Lounge tea/coffee WiFi **Notes:** LB

THE BULL
─── DITCHLING ───

This 16th century award winning inn lies at the foot of the South Downs National Park and has recently just completed a sympathetic conversion and extension, offering further bedrooms and additional dining spaces. A proper pub, The Bull is very much at the heart of the village with scrubbed tables and plenty of ales on the bar, including those from their own "Bedlam Brewery". From the newly built kitchen the team are influenced by both the day's market and seasonal local and home grown produce. The bespoke bedrooms are designed for a comfy getaway with huge beds, crisp Egyptian cotton, beautiful bathrooms and organic cowshed products.

Outside there is a vast south facing garden. At night the space comes into its own as the fire pits are lit, blankets are offered and the festoon lighting twinkles. The garden also has its own kitchen, where wood fired ovens allow you to watch your food being prepared and cooked. Parking on site is plentiful and makes for easy access.

Bring your walking boots and bike and pick up a copy of the recommended trail, from behind the bar. All of this and yet only 15 minutes drive from the fun of Brighton and its beach, or an hour from central London.

www.thebullditchling.com

T 01273 843147
E info@thebullditchling.com

The Bull, High Street, Ditchling, East Sussex BN6 8TA

BRIGHTON & HOVE *continued*

Regency Lansdowne Guest House

★★★ GUEST ACCOMMODATION

tel: 01273 321830 **45 Landsdowne Place BN3 1HF**
email: rlgh@btconnect.com **web:** www.regencylansdowne.co.uk
dir: *A23 to Brighton Pier, right onto A259, 1 mile right into Lansdowne Place, house on left before Western Road.*

A warm welcome is guaranteed at this Regency house, located only minutes from the seafront. Comfortable bedrooms are functionally equipped with a good range of facilities, and an extensive continental breakfast is served each day at a communal table overlooking attractive gardens. On-road parking is a short walk away.

Rooms: 7 rms (5 en suite) (2 pri facs) **Facilities:** FTV tea/coffee Lift WiFi
Notes: Closed 20–27 December

Motel Schmotel

★★★ ☕ GUEST ACCOMMODATION

tel: 01273 326129 **37 Russel Square BN1 2EF**
email: info@motelschmotel.co.uk **web:** www.motelschmotel.co.uk

The quirkily named Motel Schmotel is a charming establishment situated in a quiet square just minutes from the beach and the shops. The bedrooms are brightly styled and include thoughtful amenities such as free WiFi and Freeview TV; most have compact shower rooms. The substantial breakfast menu uses fresh, local produce and is served in the comfort of the guest's own room or in the breakfast room.

Rooms: 10 rms (9 en suite) (1 pri facs) **S** fr £50 **D** fr £60*

BURWASH   Map 6 TQ62

The Bear Inn & Burwash Motel

★★★ INN

tel: 01435 882540 **High Street TN19 7ET**
email: enquiries@bear-inn-hotel-burwash.co.uk **web:** www.bear-inn-hotel-burwash.co.uk
dir: *Phone for directions.*

Located in the village of Burwash, this country inn offers en suite bedrooms with external access. The inn is traditional in style and benefits from uninterrupted views of the Sussex countryside. Traditional bar meals are available daily and guests can enjoy a cooked or continental breakfast in the restaurant.

Rooms: 8 en suite (8 GF) **Facilities:** FTV DVD TVL tea/coffee Dinner available WiFi ☃ ♨ Fishing ♨ **Conf:** Max 50 Thtr 50 Class 35 Board 35 **Parking:** 8

CAMBER   Map 7 TQ91

The Gallivant

★★★★ ◎◎ ☕ RESTAURANT WITH ROOMS

tel: 01797 225057 **New Lydd Road TN31 7RB**
email: enquiries@thegallivant.co.uk **web:** www.thegallivant.co.uk
dir: *Phone for directions.*

The Gallivant is located right on the edge of Camber Sands, just a short drive from the historic town of Rye. The inn offers modern, well-equipped, coastal-themed accommodation with light, airy decor and reconditioned driftwood furniture. There's a bar and an award-winning restaurant that opens out onto a secluded decking area serving food daily. The large function suite is open all year round and is

perfect for parties or weddings. The sand dunes and beach are just across the road in front of the inn.

Rooms: 16 en suite 4 annexe en suite (4 fmly) (20 GF) **Facilities:** FTV DVD Lounge tea/coffee Dinner available Direct dial WiFi ♨ ♨ **Extras:** Speciality toiletries **Conf:** Max 120 Thtr 120 Class 60 Board 40 **Parking:** 25 **Notes:** Civ wed 150

DITCHLING   Map 6 TQ31

The Bull

★★★★★ ◎ INN

tel: 01273 843147 **2 High Street BN6 8TA**
email: info@thebullditchling.com **web:** www.thebullditchling.com
dir: *Exit A23 signed Pyecombe, left onto A273 signed Hassocks. Up hill, pass Pyecombe Golf Club on right, 2nd right into New Road (B2112) to Ditchling. Right at mini roundabout, next left into car park.*

Dating back to 1563, The Bull is one of the oldest buildings in this famously pretty Sussex village. First used as an overnight resting place for travelling monks, the inn has also served as a courthouse and a staging post for the London-Brighton coach. Accomplished dishes, using local produce together with local ales are available in the award-winning restaurant. There is a landscaped garden with seating that enjoys stunning views over the South Downs. Bedrooms are very comfortable, offering many stylish features and a range of amenities. An extensive cooked and continental breakfast is served daily in the restaurant.

Rooms: 6 en suite **D** fr £100 (room only)* **Facilities:** FTV DVD iPod docking station tea/coffee Dinner available WiFi ♨ ♨ **Extras:** Speciality toiletries, mineral water, mini-bar **Parking:** 30 **Notes:** LB

See advert on page 245

Premier Collection

Ocklynge Manor

★★★★★   BED AND BREAKFAST

tel: 01323 734121 & 07979 627172 **Mill Road BN21 2PG**
email: ocklyngemanor@hotmail.com **web:** www.ocklyngemanor.co.uk
dir: *From Eastbourne Hospital follow town centre/seafront sign, 1st right into Kings Avenue, Ocklynge Manor at top of road.*

This charming home has seen a variety of uses since serving as a commanderie for the Knights of St John in the 12th century. An air of peace and relaxation is evident in the delightful public rooms, well-tended gardens and the spacious, comfortable bedrooms that come filled with thoughtful extras, including free WiFi. The hospitality is noteworthy, and home-baked bread is just one of the delights at breakfast.

Rooms: 3 rms (2 en suite) (1 pri facs) **S** fr £60 **D** fr £100 **Facilities:** FTV DVD Lounge tea/coffee WiFi 🍴 **Extras:** Snacks – complimentary **Parking:** 3
Notes: No children 18 years

The Mowbray

★★★★ 🍷 GUEST ACCOMMODATION

tel: 01323 720012 **2 Lascelles Terrace BN21 4BJ**
email: info@themowbray.com **web:** www.themowbray.com
dir: *Opposite Devonshire Park Theatre.*

The Mowbray is an elegant townhouse located opposite The Devonshire Park Theatre and a few minutes' walk from the seafront. Bedrooms on all floors are accessible by a lift and vary in size, but all are attractively furnished and comfortable. Public areas include a spacious, well-presented lounge, small, modern bar and a stylish dining room. Breakfast is home-cooked, as are evening meals, available by prior arrangement.

Rooms: 12 en suite (3 fmly) (1 GF) **Facilities:** FTV DVD iPod docking station Lounge TVL tea/coffee Dinner available Lift Licensed WiFi 🍴 **Extras:** Superior rooms – fruit, bottled water, slippers **Conf:** Max 20 Thtr 20 Class 10 Board 10 **Notes:** LB

Bella Vista

★★★★ GUEST ACCOMMODATION

tel: 01323 724222 **30 Redoubt Road BN22 7DH**
email: stay@thebellavista.com **web:** www.thebellavista.com
dir: *500 yards northeast of town centre. Off A259 (Seaside Road).*

Situated on the east side of town, just off the seafront, this is an attractive flint house with the bonus of a car park. Bedrooms are generally spacious, comfortable and neatly appointed with modern facilities including free WiFi. There is a large lounge and a dining room where both dinner and breakfast are served.

Rooms: 9 en suite (3 GF) **Facilities:** FTV TVL tea/coffee Dinner available WiFi **Parking:** 10 **Notes:** LB

The Royal

★★★★ GUEST ACCOMMODATION

tel: 01323 649222 **8–9 Marine Parade BN21 3DX**
email: info@royaleastbourne.org.uk **web:** www.royaleastbourne.org.uk
dir: *On seafront, 100 metres east of pier.*

The Royal enjoys a central seafront location close to the pier and within easy walking distance of the town centre. Spectacular uninterrupted sea views are guaranteed. This eco-friendly property has comfortable, modern bedrooms with TVs and free WiFi; a substantial continental breakfast is served. The Royal offers a full pet-sitting service, and dogs stay free of charge.

Rooms: 9 en suite (1 fmly) (1 GF) **Facilities:** STV FTV DVD tea/coffee WiFi 🛆 🍴 **Extras:** Speciality toiletries – complimentary **Notes:** LB No children 12 years

The Sherwood

★★★★ GUEST HOUSE

tel: 01323 724002 & 07851 716706 **7 Lascelles Terrace BN21 4BJ**
email: info@thesherwood.net **web:** www.thesherwood.net
dir: *Follow signs to seafront. At pier turn into Grand Parade (towards Beachy Head). Right into Lascelles Terrace.*

The Sherwood is an attractive Victorian property just a minute's walk from the seafront, offering well-appointed bedrooms with comfortable, co-ordinated furnishings. The cosy lounge is great to relax in, and the attractive dining room serves a robust breakfast.

Rooms: 11 en suite (1 fmly) (1 GF) **Facilities:** FTV DVD Lounge tea/coffee Licensed WiFi 🍴 **Extras:** Bottled water **Notes:** No children 8 years

Beachy Rise Guest House

★★★ GUEST HOUSE

tel: 01323 639171 **5 Beachy Head Road BN20 7QN**
email: susanne234@hotmail.co.uk **web:** www.beachyrise.com
dir: *1 mile southwest of town centre. Off B2103 Upper Dukes Road.*

This friendly, family-run guest house has a quiet residential location close to Meads. Bedrooms are individually styled with co-ordinated soft furnishings and feature some useful extras. Breakfast is served in the light and airy dining room overlooking the garden, where guests are free to wander.

Rooms: 4 en suite (1 fmly) **S** fr £45 **D** fr £65 **Facilities:** FTV tea/coffee WiFi **Notes:** LB

HALLAND
Map 6 TQ41

The BlackSmiths Arms
★★★ INN

tel: 01825 840304 **Lewes Road BN8 6PN**
email: nigel.fright@btconnect.com **web:** www.theblacklioninn-halland.co.uk
dir: *Phone for directions.*

This traditional inn is located on the A22 between Eastbourne and Uckfield. There is a cosy restaurant and bar area with many original features and an open fireplace; traditional pub food is served daily. Bedrooms are modern and very comfortable with digital TVs, and free WiFi is available throughout. A cooked and continental breakfast is served in the bar area.

Rooms: 7 en suite **Facilities:** Dinner available WiFi

HASTINGS & ST LEONARDS
Map 7 TQ80

Premier Collection

Stream House
★★★★★ BED AND BREAKFAST

tel: 01424 814916 & 07941 911378 **Pett Level Road, Fairlight TN35 4ED**
email: info@stream-house.co.uk **web:** www.stream-house.co.uk
dir: *4 miles northeast of Hastings. Exit A259 onto unclassified road between Fairlight and Cliff End.*

Lovingly converted from three cottages, the Stream House stands in three acres of tranquil grounds, just one mile from Winchelsea Beach. If you arrive before 6pm, you will be greeted with a complimentary cup of tea and slice of Sandra's home-made cake. The well-appointed bedrooms are beautifully decorated, and among the delightful extras are sherry and chocolates along with speciality toiletries in the bathrooms. Delicious breakfasts are served in the lounge-dining room which has an original inglenook fireplace, and during warmer months you can enjoy the extensive garden with its rippling stream and Koi pond.

Rooms: 3 en suite (1 fmly) **S** fr £70 **D** fr £90* **Facilities:** STV Lounge tea/coffee WiFi ♨ **Extras:** Speciality toiletries, chocolates **Parking:** 4 **Notes:** LB No children 8 years Closed November to February

Premier Collection

The Cloudesley
★★★★★ GUEST ACCOMMODATION

tel: 01424 722759 & 07507 000148 **7 Cloudesley Road TN37 6JN**
email: info@thecloudesley.co.uk **web:** www.thecloudesley.co.uk
dir: *A21 (London Road) onto A2102, left into Tower Road. Right into Cloudesley Road, house on left.*

The Cloudesley is located just minutes from Hastings in the quiet residential area of St Leonards, and offers high standards of quality and comfort. The bedrooms have been environmentally designed – the walls have been eco-limewashed, the hand-made beds have Siberian goosedown pillows, and the shampoos are free of parabens and sodiam lauryl sulphate. There is a treatment room for holistic therapies. The two guest lounges are stylish and decorated with photographs taken by the proprietor. An extensive selection of cooked and continental dishes is available for breakfast, which includes locally sourced, organic ingredients.

Rooms: 5 en suite **S** fr £70 **D** fr £75 **Facilities:** iPod docking station Lounge tea/coffee WiFi Holistic therapies and massage **Extras:** Speciality toiletries, mini-fridge **Notes:** LB

Eagle House

★★★ GUEST ACCOMMODATION

tel: 01424 430535 **Pevensey Road TN38 0JZ**
email: info@eaglehousehotel.co.uk **web:** www.eaglehousehotel.co.uk
dir: *Exit seafront (A259) into London Road, 5th left into Pevensey Road. 150 metres on right.*

Eagle House is a Victorian property situated in a peaceful residential area within easy walking distance of the shops, college and seafront. Public areas are sumptuously decorated in a traditional style and the spacious 'retro' bedrooms are simply furnished. A hearty breakfast can be enjoyed in the dining room which overlooks the gardens.

Rooms: 22 rms (19 en suite) (3 fmly) (3 GF) **Facilities:** FTV TVL tea/coffee Dinner available Licensed WiFi **Parking:** 9

HOVE

See Brighton & Hove

LEWES

Map 6 TQ41

Premier Collection

Broadacres

★★★★★ 🍴 🍽 BED AND BREAKFAST

tel: 07568 083616 **Lewes Road, Whitesmith BN8 6JG**
email: joannawild@hotmail.co.uk **web:** www.broadacres-bandb.co.uk
dir: *A22 towards Eastbourne, right onto B2124 just before Golden Cross. 1 mile on left behind black metal gates.*

This beautiful property located very near Lewes, has a single, spacious, self-contained suite for guest use. The richly decorated suite is well equipped – the bedroom features a large TV, super king-size sleigh bed and its own sitting area; there is also generous storage space. The well-equipped and luxurious bathroom has a rolltop bath and separate shower. Breakfast, delivered to the suite's dining room, is a real treat; dinner is also available on request. There's also well-kept extensive grounds to enjoy, WiFi and parking.

Rooms: 1 en suite (1 GF) **Facilities:** FTV tea/coffee Dinner available WiFi Riding 🛁 **Extras:** Speciality toiletries, home-made biscuits **Parking:** 5 **Notes:** LB No children 12 years Closed 24–28 December

NORTHIAM

Map 7 TQ82

Premier Collection

Knelle Dower B&B

★★★★★ 🍴 GUEST ACCOMMODATION

tel: 01797 253163 **Rye Road TN31 6NJ**
email: knelledower@btconnect.com **web:** www.knelledower.co.uk
dir: *A21 to Flimwell onto A268, then A28. In Northiam onto B2088 opposite primary school, on left between Talisman and Boundary House.*

Located in a rural location close to both Rye and the village of Northiam, this converted barn is in a prime location with uninterrupted countryside views. The accommodation is spacious with high-quality decor and furnishings, and there is a private terrace leading from the main living area for guests to enjoy during summer months. Breakfast can be taken here or in the main house.

Rooms: 1 annexe en suite (1 GF) **S** fr £110 **D** fr £130* **Facilities:** FTV DVD iPod docking station tea/coffee WiFi 🛁 🛝 🔒 **Parking:** 2 **Notes:** No children 3 years Closed 21–28 December

RYE

Map 7 TQ92

See also Hastings & St Leonards

Premier Collection

Jeake's House

★★★★★ 🍴 GUEST ACCOMMODATION

tel: 01797 222828 **Mermaid Street TN31 7ET**
email: stay@jeakeshouse.com **web:** www.jeakeshouse.com
dir: *Approach from High Street or The Strand.*

Previously a wool store in the 16th century and then a Baptist school in the 19th, this delightful house stands on a cobbled street in one of the most beautiful parts of this small, bustling town. The individually decorated bedrooms combine elegance and comfort with modern facilities. Breakfast is served at separate tables in the galleried dining room, and there is an oak-beamed lounge as well as a stylish, book-lined bar complete with old pews.

Rooms: 11 rms (10 en suite) (1 pri facs) (2 fmly) **S** fr £95 **D** fr £120* **Facilities:** FTV iPod docking station Lounge tea/coffee Licensed WiFi **Parking:** 20 **Notes:** LB No children 5 years

See advert on page 250

RYE *continued*

Premier Collection

Manor Farm Oast

★★★★★ ≗ BED AND BREAKFAST

tel: 01424 813787 & 07866 818952 **Windmill Lane TN36 4WL**
email: manorfarmoast@outlook.com **web:** www.manorfarmoast.co.uk
dir: *4 miles southwest of Rye. A259 west past Icklesham church, left at crossroads into Windmill Lane, after sharp left bend, left (follow sign) into farmland.*

Manor Farm Oast is a charming 19th-century, environmentally-friendly oast house peacefully located amid orchards in open countryside. The spacious bedrooms are individually styled and include numerous thoughtful extras including free WiFi. A choice of lounges is available, one heated by a roaring log fire during the winter.

Rooms: 3 rms (2 en suite) (1 pri facs) (1 fmly) **S** fr £100 **D** fr £120 **Facilities:** FTV Lounge tea/coffee Licensed WiFi 🛁 **Extras:** Speciality toiletries, fruit, chocolates **Conf:** Max 20 Thtr 20 Board 12 **Parking:** 8 **Notes:** LB No children 11 years Closed 23–26 and 31 December

Strand House

★★★★ ≗ GUEST ACCOMMODATION

tel: 01797 226276 **Tanyards Lane, Winchelsea TN36 4JT**
email: info@thestrandhouse.co.uk **web:** www.thestrandhouse.co.uk
dir: *M20 junction 10, A2070 to Lydd. A259 through Rye to Winchelsea, house in 2 miles.*

This charming 15th-century house is just a few miles from Rye. Traditional character is maintained in comfortably appointed bedrooms and the public areas, while the cottage rooms offer a more contemporary style. Both the main house and the cottage rooms are available for exclusive use. Local produce is a feature of the extensive breakfast menu. Afternoon tea, home-made jams and marmalade, together with honey from the garden and other local produce are offered. Secure parking is available.

Rooms: 10 rms (9 en suite) (1 pri facs) 3 annexe en suite (4 fmly) (3 GF) **S** fr £75 **D** fr £75* **Facilities:** FTV DVD iPod docking station Lounge tea/coffee Licensed WiFi 🛁 **Extras:** Mini-fridge in annexe rooms **Parking:** 15 **Notes:** LB No children 5 years RS weekends (high season) 2 night bookings only Civ wed 30

The Kings Head Inn

★★★★ 🍺 INN

tel: 01797 225962 & 07762 404958 **Rye Hill TN31 7NH**
email: info@kingsheadrye.co.uk **web:** www.kingsheadrye.co.uk
dir: *Phone for directions.*

This inn is located just a couple of miles from the centre of Rye. Bedrooms are stylish and contemporary in style and very comfortable and are split between the main pub and converted annexe rooms with private parking. The bar and restaurant are ideal for relaxing and enjoying a traditional pub lunch or dinner. Breakfast is served in this area daily.

Rooms: 5 en suite 6 annexe en suite (4 fmly) (5 GF) **Facilities:** FTV tea/coffee Dinner available WiFi **Parking:** 40

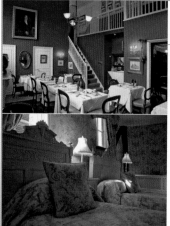

Jeake's House

Mermaid Street, Rye, East Sussex TN31 7ET
Tel: 01797 222828 • Email: stay@jeakeshouse.com
Website: www.jeakeshouse.com

Jeake's House provides outstanding accommodation in Rye. The 16th Century house plays host to the discerning guest who wants to recapture the feel of history while at the same time enjoying a high standard of modern comfort and relaxed hospitality. Rye accommodation is very special and Jeake's House certainly lives up to this reputation. Guests will be invariably welcomed by our flirtatious Tonkinese, Freddie and Monte, cordially complemented by the friendly service of the proprietors, Jenny Hadfield and Richard Martin. Breakfast is served in our galleried dining room and there is a booklined honesty bar to relax in.

Staying at Jeake's House also provides access to the surrounding countryside. There are many historical and beautiful villages and towns nearby. Jenny and Richard are always happy to advise on leisurely trips to historic castles, beautiful gardens and picturesque villages; and can recommend the best local restaurants and friendly inns.

Parking in this small town is notoriously difficult to find and we are happy to be some of the only accommodation in Rye to guarantee guests a space in our private car park. There is a small charge. Our car park is a three minute walk from Jeake's House and we advise that you park on Mermaid Street so that we can assist you with your luggage and provide you with a parking permit.

ST LEONARDS

See Hastings & St Leonards

SEAFORD

Map 6 TV49

Ab Fab Rooms

★★★★ ☕ BED AND BREAKFAST

tel: 01323 895001 & 07713 197915 **11 Station Road, Bishopstone BN25 2RB**
email: stay@abfabrooms.co.uk **web:** www.abfabrooms.co.uk
dir: *Phone for directions.*

Just a short walk from Bishopstone station and sandy beaches, this is a perfect base for visiting local sights and attractions. The three bedrooms are styled in a contemporary fashion and offer superior comfort and amenities – freshly-baked flapjacks are just one of the many baked goods offered. Breakfast, served in the garden conservatory, includes home-made jams and local Sussex produce. There is parking, and a rear garden to enjoy during the warmer months.

Rooms: 3 en suite **Facilities:** STV DVD iPod docking station tea/coffee WiFi **Parking:** 2

TICEHURST

Map 6 TQ63

The Bell in Ticehurst

★★★★ INN

tel: 01580 200300 **TN5 7AS**
email: reservations@thebellinticehurst.com **web:** www.thebellinticehurst.com
dir: *From A21 follow signs for Ticehurst. Pub in village centre.*

Located in the very centre of the picturesque Ticehurst, this transformed inn has plenty of original character in the main pub yet with lots of quirky features. The bedrooms throughout are individual in design, each with its own stylish and funky furnishings. There are also four rustic lodges in the garden which offer spacious and excellent quality, each with cosy outdoor seating area and an integrated log burner. Guests can enjoy a hearty breakfast, lunch or dinner in the main pub.

Rooms: 7 en suite 4 annexe en suite **S** fr £75 **D** fr £75* **Facilities:** FTV tea/coffee WiFi **Extras:** Speciality toiletries **Notes:** Civ wed 80

WADHURST

Map 6 TQ63

Little Tidebrook Farm

★★★★ FARMHOUSE

tel: 01892 782688 & 07970 159988 **Riseden TN5 6NY**
email: info@littletidebrook.co.uk **web:** www.littletidebrook.co.uk
dir: *A267 from Tunbridge Wells to Mark Cross, left onto B2100, 2 miles, right at Best Beech Inn, left after 1 mile into Riseden Road, farm on left.*

This traditional farmhouse has cosy log fires in winter and wonderful garden-dining can be enjoyed in warmer months. The imaginative decor complements the modern amenities (including WiFi) to provide both leisure and business guests with excellent accommodation. It is close to Bewl Water and Royal Tunbridge Wells.

Rooms: 3 rms (2 en suite) (1 pri facs) **Facilities:** FTV DVD TVL tea/coffee WiFi 🅿 **Parking:** 8 **Notes:** No children 12 years 50 acres horses

WILMINGTON

Map 6 TQ50

Crossways

★★★★ ◉◉ RESTAURANT WITH ROOMS

tel: 01323 482455 **Lewes Road BN26 5SG**
email: stay@crosswayshotel.co.uk **web:** www.crosswayshotel.co.uk
dir: *On A27 between Lewes and Polegate, 2 miles east of Alfriston roundabout.*

Proprietors David Stott and Clive James have been welcoming guests to this elegant restaurant with rooms for nearly 30 years. Crossways sits amid stunning gardens and attractively tended grounds. The well-presented bedrooms are tastefully decorated and provide an abundance of thoughtful amenities including free WiFi. Guest comfort is paramount and the warm hospitality ensures guests often return.

Rooms: 7 en suite **S** fr £85 **D** fr £150* **Facilities:** FTV tea/coffee Dinner available Direct dial WiFi 🅿 **Extras:** Speciality toiletries, mini-bar, fresh milk **Parking:** 30 **Notes:** LB No children 12 years Closed 24 December to 23 January

WEST SUSSEX

AMBERLEY
Map 6 TQ01

Woody Banks Cottage

★★★★ BED AND BREAKFAST

tel: 01798 831295 & 07719 916703 **Crossgates BN18 9NR**
email: enquiries@woodybanks.co.uk **web:** www.woodybanks.co.uk
dir: *Exit B2139 into village, right at Black Horse pub, Woody Banks 0.5 mile on left past Sportsman pub.*

Located close to Arundel in an elevated position with stunning views over the Wildbrooks, this immaculately maintained house and gardens is very popular with walkers. It provides two comfortable, homely bedrooms filled with thoughtful extras. Imaginative breakfasts are served in the spacious lounge-dining room.

Rooms: 2 rms (1 pri facs) (1 fmly) **S** fr £55 **D** fr £85* **Facilities:** FTV DVD TVL tea/coffee WiFi 🅟 **Extras:** Fruit teas **Parking:** 2 **Notes:** LB No children 6 years Closed 24–27 December

ANGMERING
Map 6 TQ00

Angmering Manor

★★★★ GUEST ACCOMMODATION

tel: 01903 859849 **High Street BN16 4AG**
email: angmeringmanor@southcoastinns.co.uk
web: www.angmeringmanor.southcoastinns.co.uk
dir: *Follow A27 towards Portsmouth, exit A280, follow signs for Angmering.*

This former manor house in the heart of the village has been stylishly appointed. It offers good food, a bar, an indoor pool and good parking. The staff are friendly and helpful and the bedrooms are very comfortable.

Rooms: 17 en suite (3 fmly) (4 GF) **Facilities:** FTV TVL tea/coffee Dinner available Direct dial Licensed WiFi ⓧ Sauna Gym Beauty salon **Parking:** 25 **Notes:** LB Civ wed 50

ARUNDEL
Map 6 TQ00

See also Amberley

The Town House

★★★★ ◉◉ RESTAURANT WITH ROOMS

tel: 01903 883847 **65 High Street BN18 9AJ**
email: enquiries@thetownhouse.co.uk **web:** www.thetownhouse.co.uk
dir: *A27 to Arundel, into High Street, establishment on left at top of hill.*

This is an elegant, Grade II listed Regency building overlooking Arundel Castle, just a short walk from the shops and centre of the town. Bedrooms and public areas retain the building's unspoilt character. The ceiling in the dining room is particularly spectacular and originated in Florence in the 16th century. The excellent food has been awarded two AA Rosettes.

Rooms: 5 en suite (1 fmly) **S** fr £75 **D** fr £110* **Facilities:** FTV iPod docking station tea/coffee Dinner available WiFi 🅟 **Extras:** Speciality toiletries **Notes:** Closed 2 weeks Easter, 2 weeks October RS Sunday to Monday restaurant closed

White Swan

★★★★ INN

tel: 01903 882677 **16 Chichester Road BN18 0AD**
email: reception@white-swan-arundel.co.uk **web:** www.pebblehotels.com
dir: *From Arundel follow A27 towards Chichester, premises on right at top of hill.*

The White Swan offers very comfortable and stylish accommodation. There is a character bar, a lounge and a restaurant, and informal service is provided by the friendly team. Substantial snacks and meals can be ordered throughout the day and evening. Complimentary WiFi is available in the public areas.

Rooms: 20 en suite (6 GF) **Facilities:** FTV TVL tea/coffee Dinner available Direct dial WiFi **Extras:** Speciality toiletries **Conf:** Max 100 Thtr 100 **Parking:** 100 **Notes:** Civ wed 70

BOGNOR REGIS
Map 6 SZ99

The Old Priory

★★★★ GUEST HOUSE

tel: 01243 863580 & 07484 600297 **80 North Bersted Street PO22 9AQ**
email: bookings@old-priory.com **web:** www.old-priory.com
dir: *1.6 miles northwest of Bognor. Exit A259 (Chichester road) to North Bersted. Old Priory sign on left. Or A29 to roundabout (McDonalds). Turn right into Rowan Way, follow signs.*

Located in the mainly residential area of North Bersted, this 400-year-old property retains many original features. Bedrooms, which are individual in style, are homely, and a couple feature four-poster beds and sunken jacuzzi baths. Rooms are either en suite or have a private bathroom. Delicious breakfasts, featuring home-made jams and cake, as well as excellent cooked dishes, are served at an impressive communal table in the grand dining room. There is also an outdoor pool, hot tub and delightful grounds for guests to enjoy.

Rooms: 3 rms (2 en suite) (1 pri facs) 3 annexe en suite (3 GF) **S** fr £55 **D** fr £87 **Facilities:** STV tea/coffee WiFi 🅟 Hot tub **Parking:** 4

BOLNEY
Map 6 TQ22

8 Bells Bed & Breakfast

★★★★ ⇔ INN

tel: 01444 881396 **The Long House, The Street RH17 5QP**
email: stay@8bellsbandb.com **web:** www.8bellsbandb.com
dir: *A23/A272 junction. Village situated between Ansty and Cowfold on A272.*

This Tudor property is situated in a peaceful village, close to both Gatwick and Brighton. Many original features, including exposed beams, remain, along with high-quality, modern and comfortable accommodation. Guests check in at the pub located directly opposite and it is here that breakfast, lunch and dinner can be enjoyed.

Rooms: 3 en suite (1 fmly) (1 GF) **Facilities:** FTV DVD Lounge tea/coffee Dinner available WiFi **Extras:** Bottled water – complimentary **Parking:** 15 **Notes:** LB

CHARLTON
Map 6 SU81

The Fox Goes Free

★★★★ INN

tel: 01243 811461 **PO18 0HU**
email: enquiries@thefoxgoesfree.com **web:** www.thefoxgoesfree.com
dir: *In village centre.*

This former hunting lodge has retained much original character and is located in lovely countryside at the foot of the South Downs National Park. The bedrooms are well appointed and the pub boasts low ceilings, brick floors and three inglenook fireplaces. The inn serves its own ale and has an inviting, daily-changing menu. During the summer months, guests can take advantage of the rear garden.

Rooms: 3 en suite 2 annexe en suite (3 fmly) (2 GF) **S** fr £73 **D** fr £98*
Facilities: FTV tea/coffee Dinner available WiFi ⬩ **Parking:** 50

CHICHESTER
Map 5 SU80

Premier Collection

Rooks Hill

★★★★★ ⬩ GUEST HOUSE

tel: 01243 528400 & 07802 415639 **Lavant Road, Lavant PO18 0BQ**
email: info@rookshill.co.uk **web:** www.rookshill.co.uk

This beautiful Grade II listed country house is at the foot of the South Downs yet is only a few minutes from Chichester. Goodwood is also close by and a 15-minute drive will take guests to the coast. The house is lovingly maintained with attractive, en suite bedrooms – all balance period features with contemporary style. The oak-beamed breakfast room and lounge is delightful and looks out to the wisteria-clad courtyard. Breakfasts are memorable for their quality, choice and the emphasis on local produce. The hospitality is noteworthy here.

Rooms: 4 en suite (1 GF) **Facilities:** FTV Lounge tea/coffee WiFi ⬩ **Parking:** 4 **Notes:** No children 14 years

Premier Collection

The Royal Oak

★★★★★ ◉ INN

tel: 01243 527434 **Pook Lane, East Lavant PO18 0AX**
email: info@royaloakeastlavant.co.uk **web:** www.royaloakeastlavant.co.uk
dir: *North of Chichester on A286. At mini roundabout take 2nd exit into Pook Lane, signed East Lavant. In centre of village.*

Dating back 200 years, The Royal Oak in East Lavant has an abundance of character and is located at the foot of the South Downs close to the Goodwood Estate and Chichester. This delightful inn has beamed ceilings, timber floors and open fires in the public areas. The rooms are finished to a very high standard with very comfortable beds, power showers, mini fridges, coffee machines, iPod docks and free WiFi. The contemporary, seasonal food in the popular restaurant has been awarded one AA Rosette.

Rooms: 6 en suite 4 annexe en suite (2 GF) **Facilities:** STV FTV DVD iPod docking station tea/coffee Dinner available Direct dial WiFi **Extras:** Espresso machines, mini fridge, robes **Parking:** 28

CHICHESTER *continued*

Blackmill Spinney Boutique B&B

★★★★ GUEST ACCOMMODATION

tel: 01243 543603 **Blackmill Lane, Norton PO18 0JU**
email: info@blackmillspinney.co.uk **web:** www.blackmillspinney.co.uk
dir: *Phone for directions.*

Blackmill Spinney is a spacious, contemporary property situated in three acres between Chichester and Arundel. The comfortable and well-appointed bedrooms are individually designed in a style that blends contemporary with traditional. All rooms have TVs, WiFi, tea- and coffee-making facilities, hairdryers, sweets, robes and a range of toiletries. The freshly-cooked breakfasts are served in the open kitchen-breakfast room that opens out onto the garden during warmer months.

Rooms: 8 rms (7 en suite) (1 pri facs) (2 GF) **S** fr £108 **D** fr £120* **Facilities:** FTV Lounge tea/coffee WiFi ⚓ **Extras:** Sweets, chocolates – complimentary **Parking:** 12 **Notes:** LB No children 14 years Closed 24 December to 2 January

See advert opposite

Musgrove House

★★★★ 🛏 BED AND BREAKFAST

tel: 01243 790179 & 07885 586344 **63 Oving Road PO19 7EN**
email: enquiries@musgrovehouse.co.uk **web:** www.musgrovehouse.co.uk
dir: *From A27 onto B2144 towards city centre, at corner of Oving Road and St James Road.*

Located just outside Chichester city centre, this establishment offers three stylish bedrooms with light, airy decor and modern fixtures and fittings, including free WiFi and digital TVs. Expect a friendly welcome on arrival and a choice of both cooked and continental dishes at breakfast, which makes good use of high-quality and locally sourced produce.

Rooms: 3 en suite **S** fr £75 **D** fr £80* **Facilities:** FTV DVD iPod docking station tea/coffee WiFi ⚓ **Extras:** Speciality toiletries, fresh milk, filtered water **Parking:** 3 **Notes:** No children 12 years

The Bull's Head

★★★★ INN

tel: 01243 839895 **99 Fishbourne Road West PO19 3JP**
email: enquiries@bullsheadfishbourne.net **web:** www.bullsheadfishbourne.net
dir: *A27 onto A259, 0.5 mile on left.*

Located in Fishbourne, yet just a short drive from the centre of Chichester, and within easy access of Portsmouth, The Bull's Head offers comfortably appointed bedrooms in a former coach house. The bedrooms are light and airy with modern decor and furnishings. The pub is traditional in style and offers a wide selection of home-cooked pub classics as well as a good range of cask ales. Breakfast is served in the restaurant. Dogs are allowed in the bar only.

Rooms: 4 annexe en suite (1 fmly) (4 GF) **S** fr £75 **D** fr £110* **Facilities:** FTV DVD tea/coffee Dinner available WiFi ⚓ **Parking:** 35

82 Fishbourne

★★★★ 🛏 🍽 BED AND BREAKFAST

tel: 07854 051013 **82 Fishbourne Road West PO19 3JL**
email: nik@nikwestacott.plus.com **web:** www.theoldgreenhouse.co.uk
dir: *A27 at Chichester roundabout, towards Fishbourne and Bosham on A259. 0.5 mile on right diagonally opposite Woolpack pub.*

Warm and friendly hospitality abounds at 82 Fishbourne, which is just a short drive from historic Chichester. Accommodation is spacious and well equipped. Breakfast provides a substantial start to the day and includes delicious fresh eggs from the free-range hens that live in the back garden. Scheduled activities include 'mushroom hunts', and wine tastings are held throughout the year.

Rooms: 2 en suite (1 GF) **Facilities:** FTV tea/coffee Dinner available Licensed WiFi ⚓ Cookery lessons, fly fishing trips **Parking:** 3 **Notes:** LB

The George & Dragon

★★★ ⬢ INN

tel: 01243 785660 **51 North Street PO19 1NQ**
email: info@georgeanddragoninn.co.uk **web:** www.georgeanddragoninn.co.uk
dir: *At top of North Street, off A286, near Chichester Festival Theatre.*

This inn, located at one end of Chichester's high street, boasts attractively styled rooms and a friendly atmosphere. The bedrooms are comfortable with all the amenities needed for a pleasant night's stay. There is a light and airy dining room set apart from the popular central bar area where dinner and breakfast is served. Regional ales are available.

Rooms: 10 annexe en suite (5 GF) **Facilities:** FTV tea/coffee Dinner available WiFi **Notes:** RS 25–26 December and 1 January no breakfast service and pub closed

CHILGROVE	Map 5 SU81

Premier Collection

The White Horse

★★★★★ ⬡ RESTAURANT WITH ROOMS

tel: 01243 519444 **High Street PO18 9HX**
email: info@thewhitehorse.co.uk **web:** www.thewhitehorse.co.uk
dir: *From Chichester take A286 north, turn left onto B2141 to village.*

Part of The Epicurean Collection, this spacious property offers stylish and relaxed surroundings on the edge of the South Downs. The bar and dining areas have an opulent feel, with lots of quirky touches and interesting features. Guests are welcome to enjoy a pint and relax, or choose dishes from the appealing and wide-ranging menus. The emphasis is on local produce and food is a highlight. Bedrooms offer an attractive blend of traditional and contemporary features, with wooden beams, sheepskin rugs and king-size beds. Most open out onto the private courtyard and feature either copper baths or large rain showers; a couple even have hot tubs.

Rooms: 15 en suite **Facilities:** FTV Lounge tea/coffee Dinner available Direct dial WiFi Fishing **Conf:** Max 20 **Notes:** LB

COMPTON	Map 5 SU71

Apiary Cottage

★★★★ BED AND BREAKFAST

tel: 023 9263 1306 **PO18 9EX**
email: janesmckellar1@hotmail.co.uk **web:** www.apiarycottagebandb.co.uk
dir: *A3 at Horndean into Rowlands Castle Road. Left into Finchdean Road, left onto B1246 to West Marden, then Compton.*

This beautiful cottage near Chichester has two highly individual bedrooms with their own private bathrooms. The richly decorated rooms are well equipped and are ideal for business or leisure use. Public areas include a comfortable lounge and the dining area is a sociable setting for breakfast, which overlooks the gardens. There is also parking available.

Rooms: 2 rms (2 pri facs) **S** fr £65 **D** fr £75* **Facilities:** FTV TVL tea/coffee WiFi **Extras:** Sweets, chocolate **Parking:** 6 **Notes:** LB Closed October to March

GATWICK AIRPORT	Map 6 TQ24

Old House Inn

★★★★ ⬢ INN

tel: 01342 718529 **Effingham Road RH10 3JB**
email: info@theoldhouseinn.co.uk **web:** www.theoldhouseinn.co.uk
dir: *On B2037.*

Part of The Epicurean Collection, and conveniently located just 10 minutes from Gatwick, this stylish inn offers a modern restaurant and bar, and has retained many original features. All the bedrooms are en suite and have stylish decor and very comfortable furnishings. There is plenty of parking on site and a large beer garden for guests to enjoy. Both cooked and continental breakfasts are served daily in the main restaurant.

Rooms: 6 annexe en suite (4 GF) **Facilities:** FTV Lounge tea/coffee Dinner available Direct dial WiFi ⬥ **Parking:** 50 **Notes:** LB

Blackmill Spinney

Blackmill Lane, Norton, Nr Chichester, West Sussex PO18 0JU **Tel:** 01243 543603
Email: info@blackmillspinney.co.uk **Web:** www.blackmillspinney.co.uk

Blackmill Spinney a luxurious and spacious contemporary retreat nestling in 3 Acres between Chichester and Arundel.

Lisa, Mark and Gloria your hosts welcome you to Blackmill Spinney and this beautiful part of the South Downs National Park.

"We pride ourselves on giving you our guests the very best in comfort and service and strive to make your experience of visiting Sussex pleasurable and memorable. Should there be anything in our power to make your stay more enjoyable please let us know"

GATWICK AIRPORT *continued*

Vulcan Lodge Guest House

★★★★ BED AND BREAKFAST

tel: 01293 771522 & 07980 576012 **27 Massetts Road RH6 7DQ**
email: reservations@vulcan-lodge.com **web:** www.vulcan-lodge.com
dir: *M23 junction 9, A23 into Horley, off A23 (Brighton Road).*

A particularly warm and friendly welcome is offered by the hosts of Vulcan Lodge, a charming period house, which sits back from the main road and is convenient for Gatwick Airport. Bedrooms are well equipped and feature many thoughtful extras. A choice of breakfast is offered, including vegetarian, and is served in a delightful dining room.

Rooms: 4 rms (3 en suite) (1 pri facs) (1 fmly) **S** fr £56 **D** fr £80* **Facilities:** FTV TVL tea/coffee WiFi **Extras:** Bottled water **Parking:** 13 **Notes:** Closed 23 December to 2 January

Gainsborough Lodge

★★★ GUEST ACCOMMODATION

tel: 01293 783982 **39 Massetts Road RH6 7DT**
email: enquiries@gainsborough-lodge.co.uk **web:** www.gainsborough-lodge.co.uk
dir: *2 miles northeast of airport off A23 (Brighton Road).*

Close to Gatwick, this fine Edwardian house offers a courtesy service to and from the airport. The bright bedrooms are comfortably appointed, and a varied breakfast, including a vegetarian option is served in the cheerful conservatory-dining room. There is also an attractive lounge.

Rooms: 15 rms (14 en suite) (1 pri facs) 7 annexe en suite (2 fmly) (8 GF) **Facilities:** FTV TVL tea/coffee Licensed WiFi **Parking:** 20

Gatwick White House

★★ GUEST ACCOMMODATION

tel: 01293 402777 & 0800 612 3605 **50–52 Church Road RH6 7EX**
email: hotel@gwhh.com **web:** www.gwhh.com
dir: *In Horley centre off A23 Brighton Road.*

Convenient for the airport and major routes, this establishment offers efficient and functional accommodation. There is a bar and a restaurant that serves good curries as well as traditional dishes. The house has ample parking, and a 24-hour transfer service to Gatwick is available on request.

Rooms: 27 en suite (2 fmly) (10 GF) **Facilities:** FTV TVL tea/coffee Dinner available Direct dial Licensed WiFi **Parking:** 30

| HORSHAM | Map 6 TQ13 |

Springfields

★★★★ GUEST ACCOMMODATION

tel: 01403 246770 **Springfield Park Road RH12 2PW**
email: enquiries@springfieldshotel.co.uk **web:** www.springfieldshotel.co.uk
dir: *Phone for directions.*

This purpose-built guest accommodation is located in the very heart of Horsham; the modern bedrooms are spacious and come equipped with stylish furnishings, free WiFi, digital TV and well-stocked beverage trays. Breakfast is served in the main dining room on the ground floor and ample parking is available on site. There are several restaurants within walking distance including the neighbouring pub that offers traditional dishes.

Rooms: 11 en suite **Facilities:** WiFi

| LITTLEHAMPTON | Map 6 TQ00 |

East Beach Guest House

★★★★ GUEST HOUSE

tel: 01903 714270 **71 South Terrace BN17 5LQ**
email: admin@eastbeachguesthouse.co.uk **web:** www.eastbeachguesthouse.co.uk
dir: *On South Terrace, opposite beach, 200 metres from junction with Pier Road.*

This guest house offers individually styled and comfortable accommodation; all rooms are equipped with a good range of amenities including TVs and WiFi; some bedrooms have sea views. A freshly cooked breakfast, using local produce, is served in the first-floor breakfast room that overlooks the sea.

Rooms: 9 en suite (2 fmly) (2 GF) **Facilities:** FTV DVD TVL tea/coffee WiFi **Extras:** Speciality toiletries — complimentary **Notes:** LB No children 3 years

Leeside

★★★★ GUEST ACCOMMODATION

tel: 01903 723666 & 07791 797131 **Rope Walk BN17 5DE**
email: leeside1@tiscali.co.uk **web:** www.leesidebandb.com
dir: *From A259 into Ferry Road signed Rope Walk and West Beach. 1 mile, turn right into Rope Walk, Leeside on right.*

Leeside is a bright bungalow, close to local sailing clubs, the River Arun and the beach. Visitors will enjoy a warm welcome, and the comfortable, modern bedrooms have TVs and free WiFi. The hearty breakfasts make a good start to the day.

Rooms: 4 en suite (3 GF) **S** fr £45 **D** fr £75* **Facilities:** FTV TVL tea/coffee WiFi **Parking:** 4 **Notes:** No children 14 years

| LODSWORTH | Map 6 SU92 |

Premier Collection

The Halfway Bridge Inn

★★★★★ ◎ ♨ INN

tel: 01798 861281 & 07971 872655 **Halfway Bridge GU28 9BP**
email: enquiries@halfwaybridge.co.uk **web:** www.halfwaybridge.co.uk
dir: *From Petworth on A272 towards Midhurst, 3 miles on right.*

This inn, located between Petworth and Midhurst, has attractively styled rooms in a converted barn setting; the spacious rooms, each with their own contemporary country-style decor, have many thoughtful extras. The popular inn offers warming fires, and intimate dining areas where guests can enjoy award-winning cuisine. The central bar is popular and guest ales feature strongly. The friendly team are key to the business here, making for a memorable stay.

Rooms: 7 en suite (1 fmly) (7 GF) **S** fr £90 **D** fr £145* **Facilities:** FTV DVD iPod docking station tea/coffee Dinner available WiFi **Extras:** Speciality toiletries, fresh milk — complimentary **Parking:** 30

PETWORTH
Map 6 SU92

The Old Railway Station

★★★★ 🛏 GUEST ACCOMMODATION

tel: 01798 342346 & 07941 160180 **Station Road GU28 0JF**
email: info@old-station.co.uk **web:** www.old-station.co.uk
dir: *1.6 miles south of Petworth on A285.*

This building, once the railway station for Petworth, retains much of its railway history and atmosphere. Guest rooms are available in both the Station House and the fully restored Edwardian Pullman railway carriages. The original ticket windows can still be seen in the reception area. Breakfast is served in the 'waiting room' which has a six-metre high vaulted ceiling; weather permitting, breakfast can be taken outside on the platform. Both WiFi and parking are available. The Old Railway Station is an AA Unique B&B of the Year runner up for 2018–19.

Rooms: 2 en suite 8 annexe en suite (1 GF) **S** fr £90 **D** fr £120* **Facilities:** FTV Lounge tea/coffee Licensed WiFi **Extras:** Speciality toiletries **Parking:** 11 **Notes:** LB No children 10 years Closed 23–26 December

The Welldiggers Arms

★★★★ 🍺 INN

tel: 01798 344288 **Low Heath GU28 0HG**
email: enquiries@thewelldiggersarms.co.uk **web:** www.thewelldiggersarms.co.uk
dir: *Phone for directions.*

Situated just outside the historic town of Petworth, this country inn benefits from outstanding views of the South Downs and a quiet location. All bedrooms are stylishly decorated with modern furnishings and offer excellent comfort. Breakfast, lunch and dinner are served daily in the main restaurant. Plenty of parking is available and Chichester is not far away.

Rooms: 14 en suite **Facilities:** Dinner available

The Angel Inn

★★★★ 🍺 INN

tel: 01798 344445 & 342153 **Angel Street GU28 0BG**
email: reception@angelinnpetworth.co.uk **web:** www.angelinnpetworth.co.uk
dir: *Leave one-way system onto A283 east, 100 yards on left.*

Located in the heart of the historic town of Petworth, The Angel Inn has stylish yet traditionally decorated bedrooms and bathrooms. Guests can enjoy breakfast, lunch or dinner in the bar and restaurant area, and there is a large walled garden for alfresco dining during the warmer months. There is parking on site and the inn is just a two-minute walk from the town centre.

Rooms: 7 en suite **S** fr £90 **D** fr £100* **Facilities:** FTV tea/coffee Dinner available WiFi **Parking:** 15

RUSTINGTON
Map 6 TQ00

Rustington Manor

★★★★ 🍺 GUEST ACCOMMODATION

tel: 01903 788782 **12 Broadmark Lane BN16 2HH**
email: enquiries@rustingtonmanor.com **web:** www.rustingtonmanor.co.uk

A warm welcome is assured at family-run Rustington Manor where guests are made to feel at home. Attentive service and excellent food make for a wonderful dining experience. Six comfortable, en suite rooms offer all the amenities that the modern guest requires. The property is just a short walk from the beach.

Rooms: 6 en suite **Facilities:** FTV DVD TVL tea/coffee Dinner available Direct dial Licensed WiFi ♿ **Conf:** Max 40 Thtr 40 Class 40 Board 40 **Parking:** 14 **Notes:** No children 10 years

SIDLESHAM
Map 5 SZ89

Premier Collection

The Crab & Lobster

★★★★★ ◎◎ 🛏 RESTAURANT WITH ROOMS

tel: 01243 641233 **Mill Lane PO20 7NB**
email: enquiries@crab-lobster.co.uk **web:** www.crab-lobster.co.uk
dir: *A27 onto B2145 signed Selsey. 1st left after garage at Sidlesham into Rookery Lane to Crab & Lobster.*

Hidden away on the south coast near Pagham Harbour and only a short drive from Chichester, is this stylish restaurant with rooms. Bedrooms are superbly appointed and bathrooms are a feature, with luxury toiletries and powerful 'raindrop' showers. Guests can enjoy lunch or dinner in the smart restaurant, where the menu offers a range of locally-caught, fresh fish together with other regionally-sourced, seasonal produce.

Rooms: 4 en suite **S** fr £90 **D** fr £185* **Facilities:** FTV DVD iPod docking station tea/coffee Dinner available WiFi **Extras:** Speciality toiletries, fresh milk **Parking:** 12

STEYNING
Map 6 TQ11

The Castle Inn

★★★ INN

tel: 01903 816629 **The Street, Bramber BN44 3WE**
email: steve@castleinnhotel.co.uk **web:** www.castleinnhotel.co.uk
dir: *A283 at roundabout take exit signed Bramber.*

A family-run independent inn located in the quaint village of Bramber, just a stone's throw from the ruined medieval Bramber Castle. The inn has retained many of its original character, yet all bedrooms and public areas have been appointed to meet the needs of modern guests. There is a range of bedrooms to meet all budgets, as well as fine ales and an appealing menu with daily-changing dishes. There is a relaxing beer garden and a convenient car park to the rear of the property.

Rooms: 13 en suite 4 annexe en suite (5 fmly) (1 GF) **S** fr £50 **D** fr £75* **Facilities:** STV tea/coffee Dinner available WiFi ♿ **Extras:** Chocolates **Conf:** Max 40 Thtr 40 Class 30 Board 22 **Parking:** 18

TILLINGTON
Map 6 SU92

The Horse Guards Inn

★★★★ ◎◎ 🛏 INN

tel: 01798 342332 **Upperton Road GU28 9AF**
email: info@thehorseguardsinn.co.uk **web:** www.thehorseguardsinn.co.uk
dir: *Exit A272 to Tillington, up hill opposite All Hallows church.*

This inn is conveniently located close to Petworth and Midhurst in a quiet village setting opposite the quaint church, and is perfect for exploring the beautiful surrounding countryside. The comfortable bedrooms are simply decorated, and delicious breakfasts are prepared to order using the finest local ingredients. The same principles apply to the substantial and flavoursome meals served in the cosy restaurant-bar dining areas.

Rooms: 2 en suite 1 annexe en suite (1 fmly) **S** fr £90 **D** fr £110* **Facilities:** FTV DVD tea/coffee Dinner available WiFi ♿ **Extras:** Speciality toiletries – complimentary **Notes:** Closed 25–26 December

WEST CHILTINGTON — Map 6 TQ01

The Roundabout

★★★★ ◉ GUEST ACCOMMODATION

tel: 01798 817336 **Monkmead Lane RH20 2PF**
email: roundabout@southcoastinns.co.uk **web:** www.southcoastinns.co.uk
dir: *Phone for directions.*

Sculptor, potter and architect Reginald Fairfax Wells sought to build the perfect English village, and The Roundabout was one of his first ventures, and one of the few that remains standing today. It is charming whitewashed property with leaded light windows in a quiet woodland setting in the pretty village of West Chiltington. Stylish and comfortable bedrooms are offered in 'Woodlands', the main house or in one of the cosy cottages. This picturesque setting makes it a popular venue for weddings.

Rooms: 24 en suite **Facilities:** Dinner available

WORTHING — Map 6 TQ10

The Beacons

★★★★ GUEST ACCOMMODATION

tel: 01903 230948 **18 Shelley Road BN11 1TU**
email: thebeacons@btconnect.com **web:** www.beaconsworthing.com
dir: *0.5 mile west of town centre. Exit A259 Richmond Road into Crescent Road, 3rd left.*

This splendid Edwardian property is ideally situated close to the shopping centre, marine garden and pier. Bedrooms are bright, spacious and attractively furnished with many thoughtful amenities, including free WiFi. Guests can enjoy the comfortable lounge with its honesty bar, and breakfast is served in the sunny dining room.

Rooms: 8 en suite (1 fmly) (3 GF) **S** fr £56 **D** fr £82* **Facilities:** FTV Lounge tea/coffee Licensed WiFi **Parking:** 8

The Burlington

★★★★ GUEST ACCOMMODATION

tel: 01903 211222 **Marine Parade BN11 3QL**
email: info@theburlington.net **web:** www.theburlington.net
dir: *On seafront 0.5 mile west of Worthing Pier, at Wordsworth Road junction opposite Heene Terrace.*

This imposing seafront building has a modern contemporary look that appeals to a mainly youthful clientele. The light bar and terrace extends to a night club open at the weekends. Bedrooms are spacious and thoughtfully furnished, with some modern touches. The staff are friendly.

Rooms: 26 en suite (6 fmly) **S** fr £80 **D** fr £105* **Facilities:** FTV Lounge tea/coffee Dinner available Direct dial Licensed WiFi **Conf:** Max 100 Thtr 50 Class 35 Board 40

Merton House

★★★★ GUEST ACCOMMODATION

tel: 01903 238222 & 07767 163059 **96 Broadwater Road BN14 8AW**
email: stay@mertonhouse.co.uk **web:** www.mertonhouse.co.uk
dir: *A24 into Worthing, on left past Manor Green.*

This family-run establishment is located on the A24 that leads into Worthing, just a couple of minutes from the town centre and seafront. There are seven en suite bedrooms, all of a very traditional style yet providing up-to-date facilities including free WiFi and digital TV. A cooked and continental breakfast is served daily in the dining room. Parking is available on site.

Rooms: 7 en suite (2 GF) **S** fr £55 **D** fr £85* **Facilities:** FTV Lounge tea/coffee WiFi **Extras:** Chocolates – complimentary **Parking:** 5 **Notes:** No children 12 years

Moorings

★★★★ GUEST ACCOMMODATION

tel: 01903 208882 **4 Selden Road BN11 2LL**
email: themooringsworthing@hotmail.co.uk **web:** www.mooringsworthing.co.uk
dir: *0.5 mile east of pier off A259 towards Brighton.*

Moorings is a well-presented Victorian house, located in a quiet residential street just a short walk from the seafront and town centre. Bedrooms are attractively co-ordinated with plenty of extras such as WiFi and Freeview TV. Breakfast is served in a homely, traditional dining room and there is a very useful kitchenette with a microwave, fridge and crockery available. The friendly owners also offer secure parking for bikes and motorcycles, but for car owners, on-street parking is available.

Rooms: 6 en suite (1 fmly) **Facilities:** FTV DVD tea/coffee WiFi **Notes:** LB No children 5 years

High Beach Guest House

★★★ GUEST ACCOMMODATION

tel: 01903 236389 **201 Brighton Road BN11 2EX**
email: info@highbeachworthing.com **web:** www.highbeachworthing.com
dir: *On A259, 200 yards past Splashpoint swimming pool.*

High Beach Guest House is situated within a short walk of Worthing town centre, and its seafront location offers uninterrupted sea views from front-facing rooms and the breakfast room. Bedrooms are traditionally decorated and come well equipped. A conservatory with comfortable seating leads onto the front garden where guests can sit during summer months.

Rooms: 7 rms (3 en suite) (1 GF) **Facilities:** FTV Lounge tea/coffee WiFi **Parking:** 3 **Notes:** No children 8 years Closed 23 December to 2 January

TYNE & WEAR

BIRTLEY — Map 19 NZ25

Bowes Incline

★★★★ ⊜ INN

tel: 0191 410 2233 **Northside DH3 1RF**
email: info@thebowesinclinehotel.co.uk **web:** www.thebowesinclinehotel.co.uk
dir: *From roundabout on A1231 northeast of Washington follow Wreckenton sign. Pass lakes on left, approximately 0.5 mile 1st left (signed). Approximately 0.5 mile.*

This inn is located just one mile from the A1 and near the Angel of the North but is surrounded by open countryside. This family-run inn takes its name from the Bowes Incline Railway & Museum that is also close by. Bedrooms are of a good size and very well appointed with modern en suites. The large bar and restaurant offers good food choices which are shown on the large blackboards. The hands-on team are friendly and welcoming, making this inn a perfect base to tour the north-east.

Rooms: 18 en suite (2 fmly) (18 GF) **Facilities:** FTV tea/coffee Dinner available Direct dial WiFi **Parking:** 40 **Notes:** Closed 24 December to 2 January

SOUTH SHIELDS
Map 21 NZ36

Forest Guest House

★★★★ 🖳 GUEST HOUSE

tel: 0191 454 8160 & 07834 690989 **117 Ocean Road NE33 2JL**
email: enquiries@forestguesthouse.com **web:** www.forestguesthouse.com
dir: *Phone for directions.*

Forest Guest House is centrally located, close to both the beach and the town centre. It offers comfortable and modern bedrooms and many thoughtful extras provided as standard. The hospitable owners are always on hand to offer help and recommendations. A well-cooked breakfast is served on individual tables giving a great start to the day.

Rooms: 6 en suite (2 fmly) **S** fr £40 **D** fr £68* **Facilities:** FTV DVD tea/coffee WiFi
🛁 **Extras:** Speciality toiletries, chocolates – complimentary

The Sir William Fox

★★★ GUEST ACCOMMODATION

tel: 0191 456 4554 **5 Westoe Village NE33 3DZ**
email: enquiries@sirwilliamfoxhotel.com **web:** www.sirwilliamfoxhotel.com
dir: *A194 into John Reid Road, then King George Road into Sunderland Road. Over roundabout, turn right and right again.*

Located in the picturesque village of Westoe in the heart of South Shields, The Sir William Fox offers value-for-money accommodation. It benefits from some off-road parking and is within easy walking distance of the Metro and South Tyneside College. Dinner is available and the property is fully licensed.

Rooms: 15 en suite (4 fmly) (2 GF) **Facilities:** FTV DVD TVL tea/coffee Dinner available Direct dial Licensed WiFi 🛁 **Parking:** 10

WHITLEY BAY
Map 21 NZ37

Park Lodge

★★★★ 🖳 GUEST HOUSE

tel: 0191 253 0288 **158-160 Park Avenue NE26 1AU**
email: parklodgewhitleybay@outlook.com **web:** www.parklodgewhitleybay.com
dir: *From south A19 through Tyne Tunnel, right onto A1058 to seafront. Left, after 2 miles left at lights onto A191. On left.*

Set on a leafy avenue overlooking the park and just minutes from the town centre and coastline, you can expect a friendly atmosphere at this Victorian house. Bedrooms are very comfortable, stylishly furnished and feature homely extras. A hearty breakfast is served and free WiFi is available.

Rooms: 5 en suite (1 fmly) (2 GF) **S** fr £70 **D** fr £100* **Facilities:** FTV DVD iPod docking station TVL tea/coffee WiFi 🛁 **Parking:** 2

WARWICKSHIRE

ALDERMINSTER
Map 10 SP24

The Bell at Alderminster

★★★★ 🏵 🖳 INN

tel: 01789 450414 **Shipston Rd CV37 8NY**
email: info@thebellald.co.uk **web:** www.thebellald.co.uk
dir: *Phone for directions.*

This 18th-century former coaching inn is situated in Alderminster just a few miles from Stratford-upon-Avon. It's a warm and friendly place where guests can enjoy a range of AA Rosette-worthy, home-cooked dishes and a good choice of ales and fine wines. The accommodation is smart, stylish and contemporary in design and bedrooms offer a high level of comfort with many thoughtful extras.

Rooms: 4 en suite 5 annexe en suite (2 fmly) (3 GF) **S** fr £75 **D** fr £100*
Facilities: FTV iPod docking station tea/coffee Dinner available Direct dial WiFi
Extras: Speciality toiletries, home-made biscuits, milk **Conf:** Max 12 Thtr 12 Class 12 Board 12 **Parking:** 50

ARMSCOTE
Map 10 SP24

The Fuzzy Duck

★★★★ 🖳 INN

tel: 01608 682635 **Ilmington Road CV37 8DD**
email: info@fuzzyduckarmscote.com **web:** www.fuzzyduckarmscote.com
dir: *Phone for directions.*

The Fuzzy Duck is an English country pub offering boutique bed and breakfast accommodation. The bedrooms are sumptuous, providing guests with lovely accessories such as luxury robes, fluffy socks and slippers. Dinner can be enjoyed in the sophisticated restaurant where the chef uses only the finest quality and fresh ingredients.

Rooms: 4 en suite (2 fmly) **Facilities:** FTV iPod docking station Lounge Dinner available Direct dial WiFi **Extras:** Robes, slippers, speciality toiletries, fruit, snacks, **Conf:** Max 20 **Parking:** 15

BAGINTON   Map 11 SP37

The Oak

★★★ INN

tel: 024 7651 8855 **Coventry Road CV8 3AU**
email: thebagintonoak@aol.com **web:** www.thebagintonoak.co.uk
dir: *Phone for directions.*

Located close to major road links, Coventry Airport and Stoneleigh Park, this popular inn serves a wide range of food throughout the open-plan public areas. Families are especially welcome. Situated in a separate building to the rear of the inn, are the modern and well-equipped bedrooms.

Rooms: 13 annexe en suite (2 fmly) (6 GF) **Facilities:** FTV tea/coffee Dinner available WiFi **Conf:** Max 40 Thtr 40 Class 40 Board 25 **Parking:** 110

COLESHILL   Map 10 SP28

Innkeeper's Lodge Birmingham (NEC) Coleshill

★★★ INN

tel: 03451 551551 **High Street B46 3BL**
email: info@innkeeperslodge.com **web:** www.innkeeperslodge.com
dir: *Phone for directions.*

This Innkeeper's Lodge, The Swan Inn, is located in the centre of Coleshill to the east of Birmingham and has easy access to the M42 and the M6. The en suite bedrooms, in different shapes and sizes, are smart and come with TVs, tea- and coffee-making facilities and free WiFi as standard; family rooms are available. A meeting room and also parking are provided.

Rooms: 33 en suite (7 fmly) (1 GF) **Facilities:** FTV tea/coffee Dinner available Direct dial WiFi **Parking:** 44

EDGEHILL   Map 11 SP34

Castle at Edgehill

★★★★ ◉ RESTAURANT WITH ROOMS

tel: 01295 670255 **Main Street OX15 6DJ**
email: enquiries@castleatedgehill.co.uk **web:** www.castleatedgehill.co.uk
dir: *Phone for directions.*

Built in 1742 to mark the centenary of the Battle of Edgehill (when Charles I raised his standard at the start of the Civil War), this striking castellated property has a unique history. Many original features have can still be seen – the wood-panelling in the restaurant and exposed stone walls and arches really add to the charm of the building. The Tower bedrooms (Rupert and Kings) boast four-poster beds and panoramic views; there is also a room suitable for families and one on the ground

floor – all are stylish. Dinner in the AA Rosette award-winning restaurant should not be missed, and breakfast features the best local produce.

Rooms: 2 en suite 2 annexe en suite (1 fmly) (1 GF) **Facilities:** FTV tea/coffee Dinner available WiFi **Conf:** Max 30 Thtr 24 Class 30 Board 18 **Parking:** 22

FILLONGLEY   Map 10 SP28

Heart of England Conference & Events Centre

★★★★ GUEST ACCOMMODATION

tel: 01676 540333 **Meriden Road CV7 8DX**
email: pa@heartofengland.co.uk **web:** www.heartofengland.co.uk
dir: *Phone for directions.*

The Heart of England Conference & Events Centre is a charming stone-built house that offers attractively presented, well-equipped bedrooms and sleek modern bathrooms. This fine old house has bags of character and the spacious, comfortable lounge has a wood-burning stove, which proves a real bonus on cooler evenings. Delicious hot breakfasts are served at individual tables in the well-appointed breakfast room. The nearby Quicken Tree restaurant serves an extensive choice of imaginative dishes and makes a good choice for evening meals. As the name implies, first-rate conference and business facilities are available on site.

Rooms: 7 en suite 3 rms annexe (1 en suite) (1 GF) **Facilities:** FTV TVL tea/coffee Dinner available Direct dial Licensed WiFi Fishing **Conf:** Max 600 Thtr 600 Class 200 Board 50 **Parking:** 36 **Notes:** LB Civ wed 260

ILMINGTON   Map 10 SP24

Premier Collection

The Howard Arms

★★★★★ ◉ ⬤ INN

tel: 01608 682226 **Lower Green CV36 4LT**
email: info@howardarms.com **web:** www.howardarms.com
dir: *Phone for directions.*

The Howard Arms enjoys a prominent position in the heart of the pretty village of Ilmington. It is a 400-year-old Cotswold-stone, former coaching inn that offers beautifully presented bedrooms. The bar/restaurant includes many original features and real fires burn bright to welcome guests. The inn has a great range of local ales along with an award-winning restaurant.

Rooms: 8 en suite (2 fmly) (1 GF) **S** fr £85 **D** fr £120 **Facilities:** FTV tea/coffee Dinner available Direct dial WiFi **Extras:** Speciality toiletries – complimentary **Parking:** 18

KENILWORTH   Map 10 SP27

Ferndale House

★★★★ GUEST HOUSE

tel: 01926 853214 **45 Priory Road CV8 1LL**
email: info@kenilworth-guesthouse-accommodation.com
web: www.kenilworth-guesthouse-accommodation.com
dir: *From M40 junction 15 onto A46 towards Coventry, then onto A452, Priory Road on right.*

Ferndale House is situated five minutes' walk from Kenilworth, and is on the local bus route close to the university. Each of the bedrooms is attractively designed and modern, and the beds provide a very good night's sleep. Both parking and WiFi are free of charge.

Rooms: 7 en suite (1 GF) **S** fr £42 **D** fr £75* **Facilities:** FTV TVL tea/coffee WiFi **Parking:** 4

Stoneleigh Park Lodge

★★★★ GUEST ACCOMMODATION

tel: 024 7669 0123 **Grandstand Stoneleigh Events, Stoneleigh Park CV8 2LZ**
email: info@stoneleighparklodge.com **web:** www.stoneleighparklodge.com
dir: *2 miles east of Kenilworth in Stoneleigh Park.*

This house lies within the grounds of the National Agricultural Centre and provides modern, well-equipped accommodation. Meals, using local produce, are served in the Park View Restaurant overlooking the showground. Various conference and meeting facilities are available.

Rooms: 58 en suite (4 fmly) (26 GF) **Facilities:** FTV TVL tea/coffee Dinner available Licensed WiFi **Conf:** Max 12 Thtr 12 Class 12 Board 12 **Parking:** 60
Notes: Closed Christmas

LONG COMPTON	Map 10 SP23

The Red Lion

★★★★★ ◉ ♀ INN

tel: 01608 684221 **Main Street CV36 5JS**
email: info@redlion-longcompton.co.uk **web:** www.redlion-longcompton.co.uk
dir: *5 miles south of Shipston on Stour on A3400.*

Located in the pretty rural village of Long Compton, this mid 18th-century posting house retains many original features which are complemented by rustic furniture in the public areas. A good range of ales is offered, and interesting menus capitalise on quality local produce. The bedrooms are well appointed and have a good range of facilities.

Rooms: 5 en suite (1 fmly) **S** fr £65 **D** fr £100* **Facilities:** FTV tea/coffee Dinner available WiFi Children's play area, games room **Extras:** Speciality toiletries, home-made biscuits **Parking:** 60

RUGBY	Map 11 SP57

Innkeeper's Lodge Rugby, Dunchurch

★★★ INN

tel: 03451 551551 **The Green, Dunchurch CV22 6NJ**
email: info@innkeeperslodge.com **web:** www.innkeeperslodge.com
dir: *Phone for directions.*

This Innkeeper's Lodge, The Dun Cow (taking its name from a mythical Warwickshire beast), is in the centre of Dunchurch, south of Rugby. The en suite bedrooms, in different shapes and sizes, are smart and come with TVs, tea-and-coffee making facilities and free WiFi as standard; family rooms are available. The seasonal pub food, served in the inviting eating areas will appeal to all tastes, from the light lunches to the Sunday roasts. A meeting room is available.

Rooms: 16 en suite (2 fmly) (6 GF) **Facilities:** FTV tea/coffee Dinner available WiFi

SHIPSTON ON STOUR	Map 10 SP24

The Bower House

★★★★ GUEST ACCOMMODATION

tel: 01608 663333 **Market Place CV36 4AG**
email: reception@bower.house **web:** www.bower.house
dir: *In market square.*

Situated in Shipston on Stour on the edge of The Cotswolds, The Bower House is a delightfully restored townhouse which was built in the 1700s. Now a listed building, it has five beautifully furnished bedrooms with bathrooms on the first and second floors as well as a charming restaurant and bar on the ground floor. Guests can choose dishes from the fixed price menu or have light snacks, cake, coffee, wine, beer or cocktails. A comfortable stay, friendly staff and tasty food are all to be expected here.

Rooms: 5 en suite (1 fmly) **D** fr £130* **Facilities:** FTV tea/coffee Dinner available Direct dial Licensed WiFi **Notes:** LB Closed 1st 2 weeks of January

STRATFORD-UPON-AVON	Map 10 SP25

Premier Collection

Arden House

★★★★★ ♀ GUEST ACCOMMODATION

tel: 01789 298682 & 206999 **58-59 Rother Street CV37 6LT**
email: info@theardenhotelstratford.com **web:** www.ardenhousestratford.com
dir: *Phone for directions.*

Arden House, set in the heart of this medieval market town, provides an elegant, inviting and relaxed sanctuary. Bedrooms are thoughtfully equipped to the highest standard. The dedicated hosts are on hand to ensure your every need is taken care of – from afternoon tea to evening drinks, you are invited to make yourself at home. There is a welcoming guest lounge and a small outdoor terrace for the warmer months. There are treats in The Pantry, and 5pm is 'Gin o' clock'!

Rooms: 10 en suite (1 fmly) **S** fr £132.50 **D** fr £165* **Facilities:** FTV Lounge TVL Direct dial Licensed WiFi **Extras:** Apple TV, fruit, pantry **Parking:** 8

STRATFORD-UPON-AVON *continued*

Adelphi Guest House

★★★★ ⚲ GUEST ACCOMMODATION

tel: 01789 204469 **39 Grove Road CV37 6PB**
email: info@adelphi-guesthouse.com **web:** www.adelphi-guesthouse.com
dir: *M40 junction 15 onto A46 towards Stratford, then A3400. Straight over at 2 roundabouts, at lights right into Arden Street (A4390). This becomes Grove Road, on right opposite park.*

Based in the centre of Stratford-upon-Avon, the Adelphi is ideally located for those visiting the Royal Shakespeare, Swan or Courtyard Theatres. The bedrooms offer comfort throughout and are all tastefully decorated in period design with many thoughtful extras. All guests will receive a warm and friendly welcome, and breakfast shouldn't be missed with a wide selection of high-quality dishes offered. Free parking and WiFi are also available.

Rooms: 6 rms (5 en suite) (1 pri facs) (1 fmly) (1 GF) **S** fr £50 **D** fr £95*
Facilities: FTV DVD iPod docking station tea/coffee WiFi 🔒 **Parking:** 5 **Notes:** LB No children 10 years

Arden Way Guest House

★★★★ GUEST ACCOMMODATION

tel: 01789 205646 **22 Shipston Road CV37 7LP**
email: info@ardenwayguesthouse.co.uk **web:** www.ardenwayguesthouse.co.uk
dir: *On A3400, south of River Avon, 100 metres on left.*

A warm welcome is assured at this guest house, located within easy walking distance of the butterfly farm and cricket ground. The homely bedrooms are filled with lots of thoughtful extras and an attractive dining room, overlooking the pretty rear garden, is the setting for comprehensive breakfasts.

Rooms: 6 en suite (1 fmly) (2 GF) **S** fr £50 **D** fr £76* **Facilities:** FTV DVD tea/coffee WiFi 🔒 **Parking:** 6 **Notes:** LB

The Townhouse, Stratford

★★★★ GUEST ACCOMMODATION

tel: 01789 262222 **16 Church Street CV37 6HB**
email: book@stratfordtownhouse.co.uk **web:** www.churchst-th.co.uk
dir: *Phone for directions.*

This striking and distinctive 400-year-old, Grade II listed building offers bedrooms that are well-decorated and well-furnished and have a feel of quality to them. All have Nespresso machines, free WiFi and are modern yet sympathetic to the age and style of the property. Downstairs is a bar and dining area that provides a casual and relaxed atmosphere for lunch, dinner or a pre-theatre meal.

Rooms: 12 en suite (1 GF) **Facilities:** TVL tea/coffee Dinner available Licensed WiFi 🔒 **Extras:** Port, home-made biscuits, fresh milk

Twelfth Night

★★★★ GUEST ACCOMMODATION

tel: 01789 414595 **13 Evesham Place CV37 6HT**
email: twelfthnight@gmail.com **web:** www.twelfthnight.co.uk
dir: *In town centre off A4390 (Grove Road).*

This delightful Victorian villa is within easy walking distance of the town centre. Quality decor and furnishings enhance the charming original features, and the elegant dining room is the setting for delicious, imaginative English breakfasts.

Rooms: 7 rms (6 en suite) (1 pri facs) **Facilities:** tea/coffee **Parking:** 6 **Notes:** Closed 11–25 February

Moonraker House

★★★★ GUEST ACCOMMODATION

tel: 01789 268774 **40 Alcester Road CV37 9DB**
email: info@moonrakerhouse.com **web:** www.moonrakerhouse.com
dir: *200 yards from rail station on A422 (Alcester Road).*

Just a short walk from the railway station and the central attractions, this establishment provides a range of comfortable bedrooms. Freshly cooked breakfasts are served in the sitting area. The attractive exterior is enhanced by a magnificent floral display during the summer months.

Rooms: 7 en suite (1 fmly) (2 GF) **S** fr £60 **D** fr £86* **Facilities:** FTV tea/coffee WiFi **Parking:** 7 **Notes:** LB No children 6 years

Salamander Guest House

★★★ 🅰 GUEST HOUSE

tel: 01789 205728 **40 Grove Road CV37 6PB**
email: p.delin@btinternet.com **web:** www.salamanderguesthouse.co.uk
dir: *250 yards west of town centre on A439 (ring road), opposite Firs Garden.*

Ideally located within easy walking distance of central attractions, this well-maintained Edwardian house provides a range of thoughtfully furnished bedrooms most with the benefit of modern and efficient en suite shower rooms. Breakfast is served in an attractive dining room overlooking a pretty park, and private parking is also available.

Rooms: 7 rms (6 en suite) (1 pri facs) (5 fmly) (1 GF) **Facilities:** FTV tea/coffee Dinner available WiFi **Parking:** 12 **Notes:** LB

TEMPLE GRAFTON	Map 10 SP15

The Blue Boar

★★★ INN

tel: 01789 750010 **B49 6NR**
email: info@theblueboar.co.uk **web:** www.theblueboar.co.uk
dir: *From A46 (Stratford-upon-Avon – Alcester), turn left, Blue Boar at 1st crossroads.*

A warm welcome is guaranteed at this country inn. The bedrooms are comfortable and homely, and the dining room and bar menus offer extensive choice, plus additional specials. There is also a beer garden to sit in when the weather allows.

Rooms: 15 en suite (5 fmly) (1 GF) **Facilities:** FTV Dinner available WiFi **Conf:** Max 30 Thtr 30 Class 30 Board 30 **Parking:** 35

WELLESBOURNE   Map 10 SP25

Innkeeper's Lodge Stratford-upon-Avon

★★★ INN

tel: 03451 551551 **Warwick Road CV35 9LX**
email: info@innkeeperslodge.com **web:** www.innkeeperslodge.com
dir: *Phone for directions.*

This Innkeeper's Lodge in Wellesbourne (The Kings Head) is just a 20-minute drive from Stratford; it was a base for RAF air crew in World War II and going back even further, was a hospital in the English Civil War. The en suite bedrooms, in different shapes and sizes, come with TVs, desks and free WiFi as standard; family rooms are available. The welcoming interior is traditional in design and a wide-ranging choice of dishes is offered on the seasonal menus. There's a beer garden for warmer weather and free parking is provided.

Rooms: 9 en suite (2 fmly) **Facilities:** FTV tea/coffee Dinner available WiFi **Parking:** 35

WEST MIDLANDS

BIRMINGHAM   Map 10 SP08

Tri-Star

★★★ GUEST ACCOMMODATION

tel: 0121 782 1010 & 782 6131 **Coventry Road, Elmdon B26 3QR**
email: info@tristarhotel.co.uk **web:** www.tristarhotel.co.uk
dir: *On A45.*

Just a short drive from the airport, Birmingham International station and the NEC, this owner-managed property provides a range of thoughtfully furnished bedrooms with modern bathrooms. The open-plan, ground-floor area includes a bright, attractive dining room and a comfortable lounge and bar. A separate room is available for conferences or functions.

Rooms: 15 en suite (3 fmly) (6 GF) **Facilities:** FTV TVL tea/coffee Dinner available Licensed WiFi Games room **Conf:** Max 20 Thtr 20 Class 10 Board 20 **Parking:** 25

Innkeeper's Lodge Birmingham West (Quinton)

★★★ INN

tel: 03451 551551 **563 Hagley Road West, Quinton B32 1HP**
email: info@innkeeperslodge.com **web:** www.innkeeperslodge.com
dir: *Phone for directions.*

This Innkeeper's Lodge is conveniently located for the International Convension Centre and the Arena Birmingham. The en suite bedrooms, in different shapes and sizes, come with TVs, tea- and coffee-making facilities and free WiFi as standard; family rooms are available. The Toby Carvery menu will appeal to all tastes. A meeting room and parking are provided.

Rooms: 24 en suite (8 fmly) (8 GF) **Facilities:** FTV tea/coffee Dinner available Direct dial WiFi

BIRMINGHAM (NATIONAL EXHIBITION CENTRE)

See Solihull

COVENTRY   Map 10 SP37

Innkeeper's Lodge Birmingham (NEC) Meriden

★★★★ ⬡ INN

tel: 03451 551551 **Main Road, Meriden CV7 7NN**
email: info@innkeeperslodge.com **web:** www.innkeeperslodge.com
dir: *Phone for directions.*

This Innkeeper's Lodge, The Bull's Head, was once a coaching inn in the 17th century and today offers single, twin and double bedrooms with contemporary decor in bright colours. Each room has a TV, desk, tea- and coffee-making facilities and free WiFi as standard; family rooms are available. Guests can sit in the beer garden in warmer weather, and parking is provided.

Rooms: 13 en suite (3 fmly) (4 GF) **Facilities:** FTV tea/coffee Dinner available Direct dial WiFi

SOLIHULL   Map 10 SP17

Premier Collection

Hampton Manor

★★★★★ ◉◉◉◉ 🍴 RESTAURANT WITH ROOMS

tel: 01675 446080 **Shadowbrook Lane, Hampton-in-Arden B92 0EN**
email: info@hamptonmanor.com **web:** www.hamptonmanor.com
dir: *M42 junction 6 follow signs for A45 (Birmingham). At 1st roundabout, 1st exit onto B4438 (Catherine de Barnes Lane). Left into Shadowbrook Lane.*

Beautiful Hampton Manor is set in 45 acres of mature woodland, only minutes from Birmingham's major transport links and the NEC. The manor offers luxurious accommodation with a contemporary and sophisticated style while still maintaining many original features. The bedrooms are beautifully and uniquely designed and boast sumptuous beds. Outstanding fine dining can be enjoyed at Peel's restaurant, which is a fabulous venue for innovative cooking, and will prove the highlight of any stay.

Rooms: 15 en suite (3 fmly) (1 GF) **S** fr £175 **D** fr £190* **Facilities:** FTV DVD iPod docking station Lounge tea/coffee Dinner available Direct dial WiFi Beauty treatments **Extras:** Bottled water, home-made cookies, fresh fruit **Conf:** Max 120 Thtr 120 Class 60 Board 35 **Parking:** 30 **Notes:** LB No children 12 years Civ wed 120

Innkeeper's Lodge Solihull, Knowle

★★★ INN

tel: 03451 551551 **Warwick Road, Knowle B93 0EE**
email: info@innkeeperslodge.com **web:** www.innkeeperslodge.com
dir: *Phone for directions.*

Dating back to 1816, this Innkeeper's Lodge (The Kings Arms) sits on the banks of the Grand Union Canal in Knowle. It has been restored to reflect its original charm. Each room has a TV, desk, tea- and coffee-making facilities and free WiFi as standard; a family room is available. There is a large, attractive eating area with a central wood-burning fire to welcome visitors on chilly days; the seasonal pub food will appeal to all tastes, from light lunches to Sunday roasts. In addition, there's free parking plus a beer garden to enjoy in warmer weather.

Rooms: 11 en suite (1 fmly) **Facilities:** FTV tea/coffee Dinner available WiFi

WILTSHIRE

BOWERCHALKE
Map 5 SU02

Greenbank Bed & Breakfast

★★★★ BED AND BREAKFAST

tel: 01722 780350 **Church Street SP5 5BE**
email: enquiries@greenbank101.com **web:** www.greenbank101.com
dir: *A354 from Salisbury to Coombe Bissett. Right at 1st junction, follow signs for Broad Chalke. Left by public house and follow signs for Bowerchalke.*

Located in the scenic Chalke Valley, a short drive out from Salisbury, Greenbank offers contemporary en suite accommodation. There is ample off-road parking and a warm welcome from your hosts Sue and Paul, who will ensure that your stay is a relaxing and pleasurable experience. Accommodation consists of two en suite double rooms. Guests also have use of a fridge and their own conservatory-lounge where there is access to indoor and outdoor areas, games, magazines and items of local interest.

Rooms: 2 en suite (2 GF) **S** fr £60 **D** fr £80 **Facilities:** FTV Lounge tea/coffee WiFi **Extras:** Fruit, snacks – complimentary **Parking:** 4 **Notes:** No children 18 years

BOX
Map 4 ST86

Premier Collection

The Northey Arms

★★★★★ ◎ INN

tel: 01225 742333 **Bath Road SN13 8AE**
email: thenorthey@ohhcompany.co.uk **web:** www.ohhcompany.co.uk
dir: *Phone for directions.*

This stylish inn combines modern facilities and quality with relaxed and welcoming hospitality. The bedrooms and bathrooms are especially comfortable and well equipped, with large walk-in showers, luxurious towels and toiletries. Food is served throughout the day and utilises high quality produce on a menu which has something for everyone.

Rooms: 5 en suite 5 annexe en suite (1 fmly) (5 GF) **Facilities:** STV tea/coffee Dinner available Direct dial WiFi **Conf:** Max 20 Thtr 20 Class 20 Board 12 **Parking:** 30

BRADFORD-ON-AVON
Map 4 ST86

The George

★★★★ ◎ INN

tel: 01225 865650 & 07511 662784 **67 Woolley Street BA15 1AQ**
email: thegeorgeatwoolley@gmail.com **web:** www.thegeorgebradfordonavon.co.uk
dir: *M4 junction 18 onto A46, A4 then A363 towards Bradford-on-Avon. Onto B3105 at Woolley Green, turn right into Woolley Street.*

This village inn, just outside Bradford-on-Avon offers delightful accommodation, friendly hospitality and quality and character throughout. Two very well-equipped bedrooms with separate kitchen areas are available above the property. A good selection of ales, wines and a menu full of tempting dishes is offered in the very well-appointed and relaxing dining areas.

Rooms: 2 en suite **S** fr £95 **D** fr £120* **Facilities:** FTV tea/coffee Dinner available Direct dial WiFi **Extras:** Fresh fruit, mineral water **Conf:** Max 26 Thtr 26 Class 18 Board 16 **Parking:** 11 **Notes:** LB

Beeches Farmhouse

★★★★ BED AND BREAKFAST

tel: 01225 865170 **Holt Road BA15 1TS**
email: stay@beeches-farmhouse.co.uk **web:** www.beeches-farmhouse.co.uk
dir: *1 mile east of Bradford-on-Avon on B3107, on left just past garden centre.*

Peacefully located and surrounded by delightful countryside, this relaxed and welcoming accommodation offers guest bedrooms in well furnished, converted barns and stables adjacent to the main building. There are various leisure facilities in the grounds including a games room. Breakfast is served in the conservatory of the main farmhouse.

Rooms: 1 en suite 4 annexe en suite (1 fmly) (4 GF) **Facilities:** FTV DVD Lounge tea/coffee WiFi ⅃ ☖ **Extras:** Mineral water, fruit, local biscuits and fudge **Conf:** Max 8 Board 8 **Parking:** 11 **Notes:** LB RS Christmas, New Year room only (no breakfast)

The Tollgate Inn

★★★★ ➣ INN

tel: 01225 782326 **Ham Green, Holt BA14 6PX**
email: laura@tollgateinn.co.uk **web:** www.tollgateinn.co.uk
dir: *A363 Bradford-on-Avon turn left onto B3105, left onto B3107, 100 yards on right at west end of Holt.*

The Tollgate Inn combines the comforts of a traditional hostelry with excellent food, served in delightful surroundings. It stands near the village green in Holt, only a short drive from Bath. The bedrooms, varying in size, are comfortable and thoughtfully equipped with welcome extras. An on-site café, deli and farm shop provide lunches and interesting picnic items.

Rooms: 4 en suite 1 annexe en suite (1 GF) **S** fr £60 **D** fr £70* **Facilities:** FTV DVD tea/coffee Dinner available Direct dial WiFi Boules **Extras:** Fresh fruit, still and sparkling mineral water, home-made biscuits **Parking:** 30 **Notes:** RS Sunday closes at 4pm

---

BURCOMBE	Map 5 SU03

Burcombe Manor B&B

★★★★ BED AND BREAKFAST

tel: 01722 744288 & 07967 594449 **Burcombe Lane SP2 0EJ**
email: enquiries@burcombemanor.co.uk **web:** www.burcombemanor.co.uk
dir: *A30 from Wilton, after 0.75 mile turn left over bridge. At T-junction turn right, 100 metres on left.*

Located in the village of Burcombe, only five miles west of Salisbury, this family home is set at the edge of a 1300-acre farm with views out over the water meadows. Bedrooms, including two en suite rooms, offer comfortable accommodation. Breakfast is served in one of the drawing rooms and there is a spacious lounge for guests to relax in.

Rooms: 3 rms (2 en suite) (1 pri facs) **Facilities:** FTV Lounge tea/coffee WiFi **Parking:** 6

BURTON	Map 4 ST87

Premier Collection

The Old House at Home

★★★★★ ➣ INN

tel: 01454 218227 **SN14 7LT**
email: theoldhouseathome@ohhcompany.co.uk **web:** www.ohhcompany.co.uk
dir: *M4 junction 18, A46, B4040 to Acton Turvill, right onto B4039. 1.5 miles to Burton.*

In a pleasant setting, just a couple of miles from the delightful village of Castle Combe, this well-established country inn is run personally by the resident proprietors and family. Six purpose-built, high-quality bedrooms and bathrooms provide plenty of welcome extras, and are located in a stylish block adjacent to the main building. Dinner here should not be missed, with a varied selection of carefully prepared ingredients used in the dishes, including the daily specials.

Rooms: 6 annexe en suite (6 GF) **Facilities:** FTV tea/coffee Dinner available Direct dial WiFi **Parking:** 20 **Notes:** LB Closed 25 December

---

CALNE	Map 4 ST97

The White Horse

★★★★ 🍴 ➣ INN

tel: 01249 813118 **Compton Bassett SN11 8RG**
email: info@whitehorse-comptonbassett.co.uk
web: www.whitehorse-comptonbassett.co.uk
dir: *M4 junction 16 onto A3102, after Hilmarton turn left to Compton Bassett.*

Located in the Wiltshire countryside, this free house offers a warm welcome and continues to be a hub for the local community. Inside the pub there is a modern, comfortable restaurant where high-quality food is served at breakfast, lunch and dinner. The bedrooms, located separately from the bar and restaurant areas, are individually styled.

Rooms: 8 annexe en suite (3 fmly) (6 GF) **S** fr £85 **D** fr £95* **Facilities:** FTV DVD tea/coffee Dinner available WiFi Boules **Parking:** 40

The Lansdowne

★★★ ◉◉ INN

tel: 01249 812488 **The Strand SN11 0EH**
email: lansdowne@arkells.com **web:** www.lansdownestrand.co.uk
dir: *Phone for directions.*

The Lansdowne has a bright and fresh appearance, with an open-plan bar and dining areas which have stylish contemporary comfort and some delightful pictures tracking the property's changes over the centuries. There is an impressive restaurant here, and chef takes pride in sourcing local products, similarly the lounge and bar offer some traditional and satisfying favourites. The bar has an impressive range of beers, cider and spirits, some especially good gins and a wine list which offers great quality and choice. Bedrooms are pleasantly appointed and include nice touches such as USB ports and high-quality Temple Spa toiletries.

Rooms: 21 en suite 4 annexe en suite (2 fmly) **S** fr £55 **D** fr £80* **Facilities:** FTV tea/coffee Dinner available WiFi 🛎 **Conf:** Max 40 Thtr 40 Class 40 Board 40 **Parking:** 7

CASTLE COMBE   Map 4 ST87

AA B&B STORY OF THE YEAR
2018–19

Fosse Farmhouse B&B

★★★★ ⬤ BED AND BREAKFAST

tel: 01249 782286 **Nettleton Shrub SN14 7NJ**
email: caroncooper@fossefarmhouse.com **web:** www.fossefarmhouse.com
dir: *1.5 miles north from Castle Combe on B4039, left at Gib, 1 mile on right.*

Set in quiet countryside not far from Castle Combe, this bed and breakfast has
well-equipped bedrooms decorated in keeping with its 18th-century origins.
Excellent dinners are served in the farmhouse, and cream teas are served in the
delightful garden throughout the summer months.

Rooms: 2 en suite (1 fmly) **S** fr £95 **D** fr £125* **Facilities:** FTV DVD TVL tea/coffee
Dinner available Licensed WiFi ⚡ 🐾 **Extras:** Speciality toiletries, bottled water,
flowers **Conf:** Max 15 Thtr 10 Class 10 Board 10 **Parking:** 12 **Notes:** LB

COLLINGBOURNE KINGSTON   Map 5 SU25

Manor Farm B&B

★★★★ FARMHOUSE

tel: 01264 850859 **SN8 3SD**
email: stay@manorfm.com **web:** www.manorfm.co.uk
dir: *Opposite church in centre of village.*

An attractive, Grade II listed farmhouse on a working family farm with comfortable
and spacious rooms. This makes an ideal base for exploring the surrounding
countryside – walking and cycling is possible directly from the farm. All bedrooms
have been individually appointed and offer a range of practical amenities.
Sumptuous traditional, vegetarian and special diet breakfasts are served at the
communal table in the dining room.

Rooms: 3 rms (2 en suite) (1 pri facs) (2 fmly) **S** fr £70 **D** fr £80* **Facilities:** FTV
tea/coffee WiFi 🐾 **Extras:** Speciality toiletries, bottled water – complimentary
Parking: 6 **Notes:** LB No children 8 years 550 acres arable

CORSHAM   Map 4 ST87

Premier Collection

The Methuen Arms

★★★★★ ⬤⬤ 🍷 INN

tel: 01249 717060 **2 High Street SN13 0HB**
email: info@themethuenarms.com **web:** www.themethuenarms.com
dir: *M4 junction 17, A350 towards Chippenham, at roundabout take A4 towards Bath.
1 mile after lights, at next roundabout sharp left into Pickwick Road, establishment
0.5 mile on left.*

This well-established inn in the centre of town, provides very high levels of
quality and comfort. Bedrooms are modern and stylish with large comfortable
beds and spacious, well-equipped bathrooms. Guests can enjoy a drink in the
relaxing bar, a light snack in the day or evening, and should not miss the
carefully-prepared, award-winning dishes at dinner.

Rooms: 14 en suite 5 annexe en suite (3 fmly) (3 GF) **S** fr £90 **D** fr £120*
Facilities: FTV Lounge tea/coffee Dinner available WiFi ⚡ 🐾 **Extras:** Speciality
toiletries, digital radios, bottled still and sparkling water **Conf:** Max 60 Thtr 50
Board 14 **Parking:** 40

Pickwick Lodge Farm B&B

★★★★ 🍷 FARMHOUSE

tel: 01249 712207 **Guyers Lane SN13 0PS**
email: bandb@pickwickfarm.co.uk **web:** www.pickwickfarm.co.uk
dir: *Exit A4, Bath side of Corsham, into Guyers Lane, farmhouse at end on right.*

This Grade II listed, 17th-century farmhouse is peacefully located on a 300-acre
beef and arable farm, within easy reach of Bath. The spacious bedrooms are well
equipped with modern facilities and many thoughtful extras. A hearty breakfast,
using the best local produce, is served at a communal table in the dining room.

Rooms: 3 rms (2 en suite) (1 pri facs) **S** fr £57.50 **D** fr £87.50* **Facilities:** FTV TVL
tea/coffee WiFi 🐾 **Extras:** Speciality toiletries, fruit, home-made cake **Parking:** 6
Notes: LB No children 12 years 300 acres arable/beef

CRICKLADE   Map 5 SU09

The Red Lion Inn

★★★★ ⬤ 🍷 INN

tel: 01793 750776 **74 High Street SN6 6DD**
email: info@theredlioncricklade.co.uk **web:** www.theredlioncricklade.co.uk
dir: *Off A419.*

This historic pub is proud to feature real ales from its very own microbrewery on site
along with ciders and other guest ales. A range of menu options is available from
pub classics to modern British dishes. There are five spacious en suite bedrooms,
all designed individually and providing a high level of quality and comfort. Dogs are
welcome in some of the bedrooms.

Rooms: 5 annexe en suite (2 GF) **Facilities:** FTV DVD iPod docking station tea/coffee
Dinner available WiFi 🐾

DEVIZES
Map 4 SU06

Premier Collection

The Peppermill
★★★★★ ◉◉ RESTAURANT WITH ROOMS

tel: 01380 710407 **40 Saint John's Street SN10 1BL**
email: philip@peppermilldevizes.co.uk **web:** www.peppermilldevizes.co.uk
dir: *In market place, town centre.*

Situated in the heart of Devizes, The Peppermill offers seven bedrooms located above the restaurant which is one of the oldest buildings in the town. The en suite bath/shower rooms have underfloor heating, limestone floors and heated mirrors. Hypnos Royal Lansdowne beds, three of which split into twins if needed, have goose-down bedding and Egyptian cotton linen to ensure a good night's sleep. The restaurant serves breakfast, lunch and dinner daily.

Rooms: 7 en suite **D** fr £115* **Facilities:** FTV iPod docking station TVL tea/coffee Dinner available WiFi ⌁ ⚓ **Extras:** Robes **Notes:** LB

Magnolia Tree Bed and Breakfast
★★★★ BED AND BREAKFAST

tel: 01380 738459 **27 Roundway Park SN10 2ED**
email: info@magnoliatreebedandbreakfast.co.uk
web: www.magnoliatreebedandbreakfast.co.uk
dir: *In centre of Devizes onto A361 (signed Swindon), pass Wiltshire Police Headquarters on left. Turn left into Roundway Park.*

Located a short walk from the centre of the market town of Devizes, the Magnolia Tree is within easy reach of the Wessex Ridgeway and the Kennet and Avon Canal's Caen Hill flight of 29 locks. Salisbury, Stonehenge and Bath are also in close proximity. A warm welcome is guaranteed from Candy, Lloyd and their dog Daisy. Bedrooms are comfortably furnished, appointed to a high standard and come equipped with a range of accessories. Breakfast is served in the light and airy dining room. Free WiFi is accessible throughout.

Rooms: 3 en suite **S** fr £50 **D** fr £80* **Facilities:** FTV DVD tea/coffee WiFi ⚓ **Extras:** Home-made biscuits, bottled water **Parking:** 6

EDINGTON
Map 4 ST95

Premier Collection

The Three Daggers
★★★★★ ◉◉ INN

tel: 01380 830940 **Westbury Road BA13 4PG**
email: hello@threedaggers.co.uk **web:** www.threedaggers.co.uk
dir: *A36 towards Warminster, A350 to Westbury, B3098 to Edington.*

Stylishly appointed to offer luxurious standards of quality and comfort throughout, The Three Daggers combines traditional hospitality with contemporary furnishings and decor. The bedrooms and bathrooms come in a range of shapes and sizes, but all are appointed with top-quality Egyptian cotton bedding, large shower heads and a generous range of welcome extras. The bar and dining area menus offer carefully-prepared dishes at both dinner and breakfast. A large lounge with a real fire and comfortable seating is available to guests. Adjoining is a farm shop and brewery.

Rooms: 3 rms (2 en suite) (1 pri facs) (1 fmly) **Facilities:** FTV DVD iPod docking station TVL tea/coffee Dinner available WiFi Riding ⚓ **Extras:** Fruit, speciality toiletries, fresh flowers **Conf:** Max 16 Thtr 16 Class 16 Board 16 **Parking:** 45 **Notes:** LB

FOXHAM
Map 4 ST97

The Foxham Inn
★★★★ ◉ INN

tel: 01249 740665 **SN15 4NQ**
email: info@thefoxhaminn.co.uk **web:** www.thefoxhaminn.co.uk
dir: *Off B4069 between Sutton Benger and Lyneham.*

The Foxham Inn is an unpretentious family-run country pub that serves award-winning food, real ales and fine wines. The two bedrooms are well configured and have been appointed to a very good standard; both offer a range of amenities including free WiFi. The main restaurant is a versatile venue suitable for a range of different occasions.

Rooms: 2 en suite **S** fr £75 **D** fr £90* **Facilities:** FTV Lounge tea/coffee Dinner available WiFi ⌁ Fishing Riding ⚓ **Conf:** Max 40 Thtr 40 Class 40 Board 20 **Parking:** 20 **Notes:** Closed 2–14 January RS Monday, Sunday evening

HORNINGSHAM
Map 4 ST84

The Bath Arms at Longleat
★★★★ ◉ INN

tel: 01985 844308 **Longleat Estate BA12 7LY**
email: enquiries@batharms.co.uk **web:** www.batharms.co.uk
dir: *In Longleat Estate village of Horningsham.*

Peacefully located at the edges of the Longleat Estate, this delightful inn is perhaps best described as offering 'quirky luxury'. The en suite bedrooms come in a variety of shapes and sizes; each has its own style and design; two four-poster rooms are available. High-quality produce is used to prepare delicious, AA Rosette award-winning dinners which are served in the relaxed main restaurant.

Rooms: 9 en suite 8 annexe en suite (8 fmly) (8 GF) **S** fr £55 **D** fr £65* **Facilities:** FTV DVD tea/coffee Dinner available Direct dial WiFi **Conf:** Max 30 Thtr 30 Class 30 Board 20 **Parking:** 6

LACOCK
Map 4 ST96

Sign of the Angel
★★★★ ◎◎ RESTAURANT WITH ROOMS

tel: 01249 730230 **6 Church Street SN15 2LB**
email: info@signoftheangel.co.uk **web:** www.signoftheangel.co.uk
dir: M4 junction 17 onto A350 signed Poole. After 8 mile, left signed Lacock. Left into Church Street.

This delightful 15th-century inn is located in the heart of the National Trust village of Lacock. Packed full of character, rooms vary in size according to the quirks of the building, but all offer very comfortable beds, quality bedding and a welcoming ambience. Guests are welcome to use the cosy bar and outdoor seating in the garden, while the dining room offers top quality British food, carefully sourced from local suppliers. Neither dinner nor breakfast should be missed here.

Rooms: 5 en suite (2 fmly) **S** fr £70 **D** fr £110* **Facilities:** Lounge tea/coffee Dinner available WiFi ⅃ **Extras:** Fudge, home-made cookies **Conf:** Max 16 Board 16 **Notes:** RS Sunday evening and Monday closed

LUDWELL
Map 4 ST92

The Grove Arms
★★★★ INN

tel: 01747 828811 **SP7 9ND**
email: ninabartlett123@gmail.com **web:** www.grovearms-ludwell.co.uk
dir: 2 miles east of Shaftesbury on A30.

This 16th-century, Grade II listed building is located between Salisbury and Shaftesbury, and provides a great base for exploring the Wiltshire and Dorset countryside. The six en suite bedrooms are comfortable and well equipped. Lunch and dinner menus offer a great choice, enhanced with daily specials; traditional ales are also available.

Rooms: 6 en suite (1 fmly) **Facilities:** FTV DVD Lounge tea/coffee Dinner available WiFi ⛗ **Parking:** 35 **Notes:** LB

MALMESBURY
Map 4 ST98

Kings Arms
★★★ INN

tel: 01666 823383 **29 High Street SN16 9AA**
email: thekingsarms.malmesbury@arkells.com **web:** www.thekahotel.co.uk
dir: Phone for directions.

Located on Malmesbury High Street, a stone's throw from the Abbey, this traditional coaching inn is split between either side of the original delivery passage. One side features a cosy bar, the ideal place to enjoy a pint of Arkell's ale; while the more contemporary restaurant is located opposite and is perfect for dining and breakfast. Bedrooms are en suite and located above the main pub building or in the former coach house and stables at the rear. Owned by the Arkell's family brewers, a great range of traditionally brewed beers is available.

Rooms: 12 en suite

PEWSEY
Map 5 SU15

Troutbeck Guest House at the Red Lion Freehouse
★★★★★ ◎◎◎ ⚑ RESTAURANT WITH ROOMS

tel: 01980 671124 **East Chisenbury SN9 6AQ**
email: enquiries@redlionfreehouse.com **web:** www.redlionfreehouse.com
dir: A345 to Upavon, left at T-junction, right signed East Chisenbury.

Troutbeck Guest House at the Red Lion Freehouse offers an interesting blend of sumptuous accommodation and food, yet it retains the informality and laidback atmosphere of a traditional pub. Each of the five rooms have been individually appointed and offers plenty of in-room amenities coupled with beautiful views of the surrounding countryside. The cooking is confident, and a particular flair is brought to the dishes based on seasonal, local ingredients. The pub rears its own pigs and keeps rescue hens. Tucked behind the property is a tranquil tree-shaded beer garden.

Rooms: 5 en suite (1 fmly) (5 GF) **Facilities:** FTV tea/coffee Dinner available WiFi ⅃ Fishing **Extras:** Speciality toiletries, snacks, robes – complimentary; mini-bar – chargeable **Conf:** Max 16 **Parking:** 5 **Notes:** LB

RAMSBURY
Map 5 SU27

The Bell at Ramsbury
★★★★ ◎◎ INN

tel: 01672 520230 **The Square SN8 2PE**
email: thebell@thebellramsbury.com **web:** www.thebellramsbury.com
dir: From Hungerford on B4192 towards Swindon. After 3.5 miles, left into Newton Road. 1 mile on right.

Owned by the local Ramsbury Brewery, this inn offers excellent en suite accommodation either in the main property or in the coach house; Hypnos beds, free WiFi, TVs and luxury toiletries come as standard. Various dining options are available – traditional pub classics served in the bar or garden for a relaxed experience, more formal dining in the restaurant and the Shaker-influenced Café Bella (open daily) offering delicious cakes and much more.

Rooms: 6 en suite 3 annexe en suite **Facilities:** FTV tea/coffee Dinner available WiFi ⅃ ⛗ **Conf:** Max 8 Board 8 **Parking:** 20 **Notes:** Closed 25 December

ROWDE
Map 4 ST96

The George & Dragon
★★★★ ◎◎ RESTAURANT WITH ROOMS

tel: 01380 723053 **High Street SN10 2PN**
email: gm@thegeorgeanddragonrowde.co.uk **web:** www.thegeorgeanddragonrowde.co.uk
dir: 1.5 mile from Devizes on A350 towards Chippenham.

The George & Dragon dates back to the 14th century when it was a meeting house. Exposed beams, wooden floors, antique rugs and open fires create a warm atmosphere in the bar and restaurant. Bedrooms and bathrooms are very well decorated and equipped with some welcome extras. Dining in the bar or restaurant should not be missed, as local produce and fresh fish deliveries from Cornwall are offered on the daily-changing blackboard menu.

Rooms: 3 rms (2 en suite) (1 pri facs) (1 fmly) **S** fr £75 **D** fr £75* **Facilities:** FTV DVD Lounge TVL tea/coffee Dinner available WiFi ⛗ **Extras:** Mini-bar, snacks, robes – complimentary **Parking:** 14

SALISBURY   Map 5 SU12

Websters

★★★★ GUEST HOUSE

tel: 01722 339779 **11 Hartington Road SP2 7LG**
email: enquiries@websters-bed-breakfast.com **web:** www.websters-bed-breakfast.com
dir: From city centre onto A360 (Devizes Road), 1st turn on left.

A warm welcome is assured at Websters, a delightful property, located in a quiet cul-de-sac close to the city centre. The charming, well-presented bedrooms are equipped with numerous extras including broadband. There is one ground-floor room with easier access.

Rooms: 5 en suite (1 GF) **Facilities:** FTV TVL tea/coffee WiFi **Parking:** 5 **Notes:** LB No children 12 years Closed 31 December and 1 January RS Christmas and New Year continental breakfast only at Christmas

STOURTON   Map 4 ST73

Spread Eagle Inn

★★★★ INN

tel: 01747 840587 **Church Lawn BA12 6QE**
email: enquiries@spreadeagleinn.com **web:** www.spreadeagleinn.com
dir: 0.5 mile west off B3092 at entrance to Stourhead Gardens.

Set in the beautiful grounds of Stourhead House with its Palladian temples, lakes and inspiring vistas, the Spread Eagle Inn is an impressive red-brick building with a good reputation for simple, honest and locally-sourced food. In the bedrooms, National Trust antiques sit side by side with modern comforts. The large Georgian windows, low ceilings and uneven floors add to the authentic atmosphere of this delightful country house.

Rooms: 5 en suite **Facilities:** tea/coffee Dinner available Direct dial WiFi **Conf:** Max 30 Thtr 30 Board 20 **Notes:** LB

SWINDON   Map 5 SU18

Sun Inn

★★★★ INN

tel: 01793 523292 **Coate SN3 6AA**
email: sun-inn@arkells.com **web:** www.suninn-swindon.co.uk
dir: M4 junction 15 onto A419, take 1st exit signed Swindon and hospital. 1st exit at roundabout, 1 mile on left.

Located on the outskirts of Swindon, adjacent to the popular Coate Water Country Park, the inn features a large garden and children's play area with a thatched summer house. Accommodation is suitable for both business and leisure guests, offering free WiFi throughout. A regularly-changing blackboard menu offers well-prepared dishes, available throughout the day and evening. The popular Sunday lunch should not be missed. Owned by the Arkell's family brewers, a great range of traditionally brewed beers is available.

Rooms: 10 en suite **D** fr £65* **Facilities:** FTV DVD tea/coffee Dinner available WiFi **Parking:** 80

The Angel

★★★★ ◎ INN

tel: 01793 851161 **47 High Street, Royal Wootton Bassett SN4 7AQ**
email: theangel.wbassett@arkells.com **web:** www.theangelhotelwoottonbassett.co.uk
dir: Phone for directions.

Located directly on the high street of historic Royal Wootton Bassett, The Angel offers everything from morning coffee in the lounge, a drink at the bar to a meal in the popular restaurant. Public areas are intimate and comfortably furnished. Accommodation is located at the rear of the property in a purpose-built wing overlooking the courtyard. The Angel's location makes it ideal for corporate guests and those exploring the local area. The property also includes a boardroom and larger function room.

Rooms: 3 en suite 14 annexe en suite **Facilities:** FTV Lounge tea/coffee Dinner available WiFi **Conf:** Max 100 Thtr 100 Class 36 Board 14 **Notes:** Closed 26 December, 1 January RS 25 December

Ardecca

★★★★ GUEST ACCOMMODATION

tel: 01793 721238 & 07791 120826 **Fieldrise Farm, Kingsdown Lane SN25 5DL**
email: ardecca@gmail.com **web:** www.ardecca-bedandbreakfast.co.uk
dir: A419 onto B4019 to Blunsdon/Highworth, then into Turnpike Road at Cold Harbour pub, left into Kingsdown Lane.

Ardecca is quietly located in 16 acres of pastureland with easy access to Swindon and the Cotswolds. All bedrooms are on the ground floor and are well furnished and equipped. An especially friendly welcome is provided and arts and crafts workshops are available on site.

Rooms: 4 rms (4 pri facs) (1 fmly) (4 GF) **Facilities:** FTV tea/coffee WiFi **Extras:** Bottled water, sweets **Parking:** 5 **Notes:** No children 6 years

The Old Post Office Guest House

★★★★ GUEST HOUSE

tel: 01793 823114 **Thornhill Road, South Marston SN3 4RY**
email: theoldpostofficeguesthouse@yahoo.co.uk
web: www.theoldpostofficeguesthouse.co.uk
dir: M4 junction 15, A419 signed Cirencester/Swindon (East), approximately 3 miles, left onto A420 towards Oxford, at next roundabout 2nd exit into Merlin Way, 0.3 mile, at White Hart roundabout 3rd exit onto A420. At Gablecross roundabout follow South Marston signs.

This attractive property is about two miles from Swindon. Guests are welcomed by the enthusiastic owner, a professional opera singer with a wonderful sense of humour. The comfortable bedrooms vary in size but all are equipped with numerous facilities. An extensive choice is offered at breakfast, which is freshly cooked and uses the best local produce.

Rooms: 5 en suite (1 fmly) **S** fr £50 **D** fr £60 (room only)* **Facilities:** STV tea/coffee WiFi ♨ Use of nearby country club **Extras:** Snacks, chocolate **Parking:** 6 **Notes:** LB

Tawny Owl

★★★★ INN

tel: 01793 706770 **Queen Elizabeth Drive, Taw Hill SN25 1WR**
email: thetawnyowl.swindon@arkells.com **web:** www.arkells.com
dir: 2.5 miles northwest of town centre, signed from A419.

Expect a genuinely friendly welcome from the staff at this modern inn on the northwest outskirts of Swindon. It has comfortable, well-equipped bedrooms and bathrooms. A varied selection of enjoyable home-cooked meals is on offer at both lunch and dinner, together with a range of Arkell's ales and wines. A private function room is available.

Rooms: 5 en suite (2 fmly) **S** fr £50 **D** fr £50 (room only)* **Facilities:** TVL tea/coffee Dinner available WiFi **Conf:** Max 55 Thtr 55 Class 55 Board 55 **Parking:** 75 **Notes:** RS Christmas and New Year

SWINDON *continued*

The White Hart Inn

★★★★ INN

tel: 01793 822272 & 07789 717368 **Oxford Road, Stratton St Margaret SN3 4JD**
email: info@whitehartstratton.co.uk **web:** www.whitehartstratton.co.uk
dir: *On White Hart roundabout, at intersection of A420 and A419.*

Located on the outskirts of Swindon, with good access to the M4 (junction 15 is just a five-minute drive) and close links to Cirencester and the M5. Accommodation has been purpose built and offers comfortable and spacious rooms suitable for both business and leisure guests. The classic pub menu, available throughout the day and evening, features well-prepared dishes; a popular carvery is available on Sundays. Owned by the Arkell's family brewers, a great range of traditionally brewed beers is offered. There's free WiFi, ample free parking and function rooms.

Rooms: 24 en suite (6 fmly) (12 GF) **S** fr £80 **D** fr £80* **Facilities:** FTV Lounge TVL tea/coffee Dinner available WiFi 🛁 **Extras:** Speciality toiletries **Conf:** Max 42 Thtr 42 Class 30 Board 20 **Parking:** 60

Heart in Hand

★★★ INN

tel: 01793 721314 **43 High Street, Blunsdon SN26 7AG**
email: leppardsteve@aol.com **web:** www.heartinhand.co.uk
dir: *Exit A419 into High Street, 200 yards on right.*

Right in the village centre, this family-run inn offers a friendly welcome together with a wide selection of home-cooked food. Bedrooms are spacious, well equipped and offer a number of useful extras. A pleasant patio and rear garden with seating are also available.

Rooms: 4 en suite (1 fmly) **Facilities:** tea/coffee Dinner available **Parking:** 17 **Notes:** LB

Saracens Head

★★ INN

tel: 01793 762284 **High Street, Highworth SN6 7AG**
email: saracenshead@arkells.com **web:** www.arkells.com
dir: *5 miles northeast of Swindon.*

The Saracens Head stands on the main street of a pleasant market town, close to Swindon. It has lots of character, including a popular bar dating from 1828. The fine selection of real ales, and some excellent home-cooked food are highlights. Bedrooms, which vary in size, are generally compact. A rear car park and a patio area are both available.

Rooms: 12 en suite (1 fmly) **Facilities:** tea/coffee Dinner available WiFi **Conf:** Max 10 Thtr 10 Class 10 Board 10 **Parking:** 30 **Notes:** LB

TISBURY Map 4 ST92

Hare Lodge Bed and Breakfast

★★★★ BED AND BREAKFAST

tel: 01747 870582 & 07754 044815 **Monmouth Road, Tuckingmill SP3 6NR**
email: harelodge@btinternet.com **web:** www.hare-lodge.co.uk
dir: *In Tisbury, at The Square, exit signed Semley/Newtown. Pass church on left, over mini-roundabout. Into Tuckingmill, 3rd house on left.*

Located on the edge of the village within an Area of Outstanding Natural Beauty, this Scandinavian-style house is a perfect base for exploring the area. A warm welcome is assured with every effort made to provide a relaxing and rewarding stay. The bedrooms offer generous levels of space and comfort – one room has a balcony, the other is a suite with separate lounge area. Tasty breakfasts are served around the dining table or outside in the summer if preferred. This is a popular area for walkers, and helpful advice is always on offer to help plan routes.

Rooms: 2 en suite (1 fmly) **S** fr £85 **D** fr £95* **Facilities:** FTV DVD tea/coffee WiFi 🛁 **Extras:** Speciality toiletries, fresh milk **Parking:** 3 **Notes:** Closed 23 December to 3 January

---

TOLLARD ROYAL Map 4 ST91

King John Inn

★★★★ ⊛⊛ RESTAURANT WITH ROOMS

tel: 01725 516207 **SP5 5PS**
email: info@kingjohninn.co.uk **web:** www.kingjohninn.co.uk
dir: *From A354 or A350 onto B3081.*

Part of The Epicurean Collection, the King John Inn is a traditional country inn located in a country village. It has a Victorian-style garden pavilion serving seasonal dishes such as chargrilled lobster and pigeon salad. Along with the five bedrooms in the main building, there are three more in The Dove Cottage – all have feature bathrooms. Excellent hospitality and customer care together with good food and wine are real highlights here. Ample parking is provided.

Rooms: 5 en suite 3 annexe en suite (2 GF) **Facilities:** FTV Lounge tea/coffee Dinner available Direct dial WiFi ⚿ **Parking:** 18 **Notes:** LB RS 25 December restaurant closed for dinner

---

WESTBURY Map 4 ST85

The Hollies Inn

★★★★ INN

tel: 01373 864493 **55 Westbury Leigh BA13 3SF**
email: info@theholliesinn.com **web:** www.theholliesinn.com
dir: *Phone for directions.*

This traditional-style inn provides plenty of quality and comfort in both bedrooms and bathrooms, and throughout the public areas. Lighter meals are offered during the day and there is a full menu in the evening along with a good range of ales. Quiz nights and live music are regular features. A car park is provided, together with outdoor seating for the warmer months.

Rooms: 3 en suite **Facilities:** Dinner available

WORCESTERSHIRE

ABBERLEY
Map 10 SO76

Premier Collection

The Manor Arms
★★★★★ INN

tel: 01299 890300 **The Village WR6 6BN**
email: enquiries@themanorarms.co.uk **web:** www.themanorarms.co.uk
dir: *North of Worcester on A443, onto B4202 signed Cleobury Mortimer. Follow brown tourist signs to Manor Arms.*

This charming inn enjoys a prominent position in the heart of the pretty village of Abberley and offers guests a range of high quality, stylish bedrooms; many have views of the rolling countryside. The award-winning restaurant is very popular, and the bar, featuring a wood-burning stove lit in the winter, leads to a patio for the summer months. The Manor Arms is an ideal base from which to explore the historic towns of Worcester and Malvern, both just a short drive away.

Rooms: 6 en suite **S** fr £80 **D** fr £80* **Facilities:** Dinner available WiFi ⅃
Extras: Speciality toiletries, robes, home-made biscuits, fresh milk **Conf:** Max 40 Thtr 40 Class 20 Board 20 **Parking:** 40 **Notes:** Civ wed 70

ALVECHURCH
Map 10 SP07

Alcott Farm
★★★ BED AND BREAKFAST

tel: 01564 824051 & 07736 445188 **Icknield Street, Weatheroak B48 7EH**
email: alcottfarm@btinternet.com **web:** www.alcottfarm.co.uk
dir: *2 miles northeast of Alvechurch. M42 junction 3, A435 for Birmingham, left signed Weatheroak, left at crossroads, down steep hill, left opposite pub, farm 0.5 mile on right up long driveway.*

Hidden away in the leafy Worcestershire countryside is Alcott Farm. A long drive leads to this red-brick farmhouse which is surrounded by well-kept floral displays, making it very easy on the eye in summer months. The house is decorated in keeping with the age and style of the property and has a very homely feel. A warm welcome and hearty breakfast are assured here.

Rooms: 4 en suite 2 annexe en suite (1 GF) **S** fr £55 **D** fr £75* **Facilities:** Lounge TVL tea/coffee WiFi Fishing **Extras:** Snacks **Parking:** 20 **Notes:** LB No children 10 years

ASTWOOD BANK
Map 19 SP06

Corner Cottage
★★★★ BED AND BREAKFAST

tel: 01527 459122 & 07917 582884 **1194 Evesham Road B96 6AA**
email: marilyn_alan1194@hotmail.co.uk **web:** www.corner-cottagebb.co.uk
dir: *A441 through Astwood Bank, Corner Cottage at lights.*

A warm welcome awaits at Corner Cottage, a beautiful Victorian cottage set in a delightful village location that's within walking distance of pubs, shops and restaurants. The bedrooms include WiFi, cable TV, tea-and coffee-making facilities and toiletries. This B&B is convenient for Stratford-upon-Avon, Evesham, Warwick, Birmingham and Worcester.

Rooms: 4 rms (3 en suite) (1 pri facs) **S** fr £45* **Facilities:** FTV TVL tea/coffee WiFi
🔒 **Notes:** LB Closed 1 month at Christmas

BEWDLEY
Map 10 SO77

Premier Collection

Kateshill House
★★★★★ 🍴 GUEST ACCOMMODATION

tel: 01299 401563 **Red Hill DY12 2DR**
email: info@kateshillhouse.co.uk **web:** www.kateshillhouse.co.uk
dir: *A456 onto B4195 signed Bewdley. Bear left over bridge, 1st left into Severnside South. Right into Lax Lane, at T-junction turn left, up hill on right.*

A very warm welcome awaits at Kateshill House, a Georgian manor overlooking Bewdley. Two acres of landscaped gardens provide a dramatic setting for the house, as well as fruit for breakfasts and home-made jams. The elegant bedrooms are individually styled, sumptuously decorated with rich fabrics and period furniture, and equipped with a wealth of amenities for guest use. Small private functions are also catered for.

Rooms: 7 en suite **S** fr £75 **D** fr £90* **Facilities:** FTV Lounge TVL tea/coffee Licensed WiFi 🔒 **Parking:** 10 **Notes:** LB

The Mug House Inn
★★★★ 🍴 INN

tel: 01299 402543 **12 Severnside North DY12 2EE**
email: drew@mughousebewdley.co.uk **web:** www.mughousebewdley.co.uk
dir: *In town centre on riverfront.*

Located on the opposite side of the River Severn to Bewdley Rowing Club, this 18th-century inn combines high standards of comfort and facilities with many original features. Bedrooms are thoughtfully furnished. There is a separate breakfast room and imaginative dinners are served in the restaurant.

Rooms: 4 en suite 3 annexe en suite (1 GF) **S** fr £70 **D** fr £80* **Facilities:** FTV tea/coffee Dinner available WiFi **Notes:** No children 10 years

Royal Forester Country Inn
★★★★ 🍴 🍴 INN

tel: 01299 266286 **Callow Hill DY14 9XW**
email: royalforesterinn@btinternet.com **web:** www.royalforesterinn.co.uk
dir: *Phone for directions.*

Located opposite the Wyre Forest on the town's outskirts, this inn dates back to 1411 and has been sympathetically restored to provide high standards of comfort. Stylish modern bedrooms are complemented by smart bathrooms, and equipped with many thoughtful extras. Decor styles throughout the public areas highlight the many period features, and the restaurant serves imaginative food featuring locally sourced produce.

Rooms: 7 en suite (2 fmly) **S** fr £69 **D** fr £89* **Facilities:** STV FTV TVL tea/coffee Dinner available WiFi **Parking:** 40 **Notes:** LB

BEWDLEY *continued*

Welchgate Guest House

★★★★ GUEST HOUSE

tel: 01299 402655 **1 Welch Gate DY12 2AT**
email: info@welchgate-guesthouse.co.uk **web:** www.welchgate-guesthouse.co.uk
dir: *Phone for directions.*

Welchgate Guest House is a 400-year-old former inn providing modern comfort and good facilities. Bedrooms are equipped with fine furnishings and thoughtful extras, and have smart, modern en suite shower rooms. Hearty breakfasts are taken in a rustic-style café, which is also open to the public during the day.

Rooms: 4 en suite **Facilities:** tea/coffee Licensed WiFi 🔒 **Notes:** LB No children

Bank House

★★★ BED AND BREAKFAST

tel: 01299 402652 **14 Lower Park DY12 2DP**
email: info@bankhousebewdley.co.uk **web:** www.bankhousebewdley.co.uk
dir: *In town centre. Turn into High Street, pass Lax Lane junction, Bank House on left.*

Once a private bank, this Victorian house retains many original features and offers comfortable accommodation. The cosy dining room is the setting for tasty English breakfasts served at one family table. Owner Mrs Nightingale has a comprehensive knowledge of the town and its history.

Rooms: 4 rms **S** fr £38 **D** fr £64* **Facilities:** FTV tea/coffee WiFi 🔒 **Parking:** 2
Notes: Closed 24–26 December

BROADWAY	Map 10 SP03

Premier Collection

Abbots Grange

★★★★★ 🍴 GUEST HOUSE

tel: 020 8133 8698 **Church Street WR12 7AE**
email: rooms@abbotsgrange.com **web:** www.abbotsgrange.com
dir: *M5 junction 9 follow signs to Evesham and Broadway.*

A warm welcome awaits at Abbots Grange, a 14th-century monastic manor house believed to be the oldest dwelling in Broadway. A Grade II listed building, it stands in eight acres of grounds. The bedrooms are luxurious and comprise twin and four-poster suites. Among the thoughtful extras in the rooms are fruit bowls and a selection of alcoholic drinks. The stunning medieval Great Hall is the guests' lounge and makes a romantic setting with its log fire and candles. Tea and cake is offered on arrival, and quality breakfasts are served at the large communal table in the wood-panelled dining room. Abbots Grange has a tennis court and croquet lawn along with a helicopter landing pad.

Rooms: 6 rms (5 en suite) (1 pri facs) **Facilities:** STV FTV DVD iPod docking station Lounge tea/coffee WiFi 🎾 ⛳ 🔒 **Extras:** Port, whisky, sherry, soft drinks, mineral water **Conf:** Max 12 Board 12 **Parking:** 10 **Notes:** No children 6 years

Premier Collection

Russell's

★★★★★ ⚜️⚜️ 🍴 RESTAURANT WITH ROOMS

tel: 01386 853555 **20 High Street WR12 7DT**
email: info@russellsofbroadway.co.uk **web:** www.russellsofbroadway.co.uk
dir: *Opposite village green.*

Situated in the centre of picturesque Broadway, this restaurant with rooms makes a great base for exploring local attractions. The superbly appointed bedrooms, each with its own character, have air conditioning and a wide range of extras. The cuisine is a real draw here with skilful use made of freshly-prepared, local produce.

Rooms: 4 en suite 3 annexe en suite (4 fmly) (2 GF) **Facilities:** FTV DVD tea/coffee Dinner available Direct dial WiFi **Extras:** Honesty bar **Conf:** Max 12 Board 12 **Parking:** 7

CLIFTON UPON TEME	Map 10 SO76

The Lion Inn and Restaurant

★★★★ 🍴 🍺 INN

tel: 01886 812975 **1 The Village WR6 6DH**
email: enquiries@thelioninnclifton.co.uk **web:** www.thelioninnclifton.co.uk
dir: *Phone for directions.*

Clifton upon Teme is a small sleepy village set in the rolling Worcestershire countryside and at its heart is The Lion Inn and Restaurant. Steeped in history, the inn has undergone a sympathetic refurbishment which has carefully blended period features with modern comforts. Each en suite bedroom differs in size due to nature of the building but all are smartly appointed and include Freeview TV and WiFi. Dinner shouldn't be missed, and bookings are recommended. Outdoor seating is available in summer months and there's a small car park to the rear.

Rooms: 3 en suite **Facilities:** FTV Dinner available WiFi

FLYFORD FLAVELL	Map 10 SO95

The Boot Inn

★★★★ 🍺 INN

tel: 01386 462658 **Radford Road WR7 4BS**
email: enquiries@thebootinn.com **web:** www.thebootinn.com
dir: *In village centre, signed from A422.*

An inn has occupied this site since the 13th century, though The Boot itself dates from the Georgian period. Much historic charm remains in the pub, while the bedrooms, furnished in antique pine, are equipped with practical extras and have modern bathrooms. A range of ales, wines and imaginative food is offered in the cosy public areas, which include an attractive conservatory and patio.

The Boot Inn

Rooms: 5 annexe en suite (2 GF) **S** fr £70 **D** fr £80 **Facilities:** FTV DVD iPod docking station Lounge tea/coffee Dinner available WiFi ♨ **Extras:** Bottled still and sparkling water **Parking:** 30 **Notes:** LB

MALVERN   Map 10 SO74

Ashbury Bed & Breakfast

★★★★ ♨ BED AND BREAKFAST

tel: 01684 574225 **Ashbury, Old Hollow WR14 4NP**
email: ashburybandb@btinternet.com **web:** www.ashburybedandbreakfast.co.uk
dir: *A449 onto B4053, 2nd left into Hornyold Road. Right at T-junction into Cowleigh Road, 250 yards on left.*

A warm and friendly welcome awaits you from Karen and Graham at Ashbury Bed & Breakfast. This beautiful and grand Victorian property offers modern, comfortable and stylish bedrooms and the many period features that have been retained add to the overall charm of the house. An enjoyable breakfast made with all fresh ingredients can be enjoyed with views across the Malvern countryside. This is a good location for those wishing to go walking in the Malvern area. Free WiFi is available.

Rooms: 3 en suite (2 GF) **S** fr £65 **D** fr £85 **Facilities:** FTV tea/coffee WiFi
♨ **Extras:** Home-made biscuits, speciality toiletries – complimentary **Conf:** Max 10 Board 10 **Parking:** 4 **Notes:** LB No children 12 years

The Dell House

★★★★ BED AND BREAKFAST

tel: 01684 564448 **2 Green Lane WR14 4HU**
email: stay@thedellhouse.co.uk **web:** www.thedellhouse.co.uk
dir: *Phone for directions.*

This former rectory dates back to the 1820s and is quietly located in its own large garden. Retaining many original features, the rooms are thoughtfully furnished and provide good levels of comfort with suitable extras, and each bedroom benefits from countryside views. The breakfast menu features a number of vegetarian options. This is a good location for those wishing to go walking in the Malverns, or to attend events at the Three Counties Showground.

Rooms: 4 en suite **S** fr £65 **D** fr £85* **Facilities:** Lounge TVL tea/coffee WiFi
♨ **Conf:** Max 10 Thtr 10 Class 8 Board 8 **Parking:** 4 **Notes:** LB

Sidney House

★★★★ BED AND BREAKFAST

tel: 01684 574994 **40 Worcester Road WR14 4AA**
email: info@sidneyhouse.co.uk **web:** www.sidneyhouse.co.uk
dir: *On A449, 200 yards north from town centre.*

Believed to have been purpose-built as a guest house in 1823, this Grade II listed property has a long history of welcoming visitors to Great Malvern. This tradition is continued today by Alexandra and Anthony, whose warm welcome is assured. Situated within easy walking distance of local attractions and restaurants, and within easy reach of the Malvern Hills, the property boasts enviable views across the Severn Vale and beyond. En suite rooms are comfortably furnished with a guest lounge, on-site parking and complimentary WiFi are all provided.

Rooms: 6 en suite **S** fr £60 **D** fr £75* **Facilities:** FTV TVL tea/coffee Licensed WiFi Discounts at local beauty salon **Extras:** Speciality toiletries, home-made brownies, cake, sherry (superior rooms) **Parking:** 8 **Notes:** LB No children 16 years

Wyche Inn

★★★★ INN

tel: 01684 575396 **74 Wyche Road WR14 4EQ**
email: thewycheinn@googlemail.com **web:** www.thewycheinn.co.uk
dir: *1.5 miles south of Malvern. On B4218 towards Malvern and Colwall. Off A449 (Worcester to Ross/Ledbury road).*

Located in an elevated position on the outskirts of Malvern, this inn is popular with locals and visiting walkers. The thoughtfully furnished bedrooms, with stunning countryside views, provide good levels of comfort with suitable guest extras; all bathrooms have a bath and shower. The menus feature home-cooked dishes, including good-value options, and a comprehensive range of real ales is available from the bar.

Rooms: 4 en suite 2 annexe rms (2 pri facs) (1 GF) **Facilities:** FTV DVD tea/coffee Dinner available WiFi **Extras:** Speciality toiletries, bottled mineral water **Parking:** 6 **Notes:** LB Closed 24–25 December RS 25 December no food, bar only 11-3

MARTLEY   Map 10 SO75

The Admiral Rodney at Berrow Green

[U]

tel: 01905 886181 **Berrow Green WR6 6PL**
email: info@admiral-rodney.co.uk **web:** www.admiral-rodney.co.uk
dir: *Phone for directions.*

Currently the rating for this establishment is not confirmed. This may be due to a change of ownership or because it has only recently joined the AA rating scheme.

Rooms: 6 en suite **S** fr £70 **D** fr £70* **Extras:** Nespresso machines, speciality toiletries

UPTON-UPON-SEVERN Map 10 SO84

The Swan

★★★★ INN

tel: 01684 594948 & 07501 223754 **Waterside WR8 0JD**
email: info@theswanhotelupton.co.uk **web:** www.theswanhotelupton.co.uk
dir: *Phone for directions.*

Set in the historic riverside town of Upton-upon-Severn, this 400-year-old inn offers plenty of charm and quirkiness. The modern bedrooms provide good levels of comfort and practicality; some have views of the river. The waterside bar offers good quality meals and cask conditioned ales; a separate restaurant is also available for functions.

Rooms: 6 en suite **Facilities:** FTV tea/coffee Dinner available Direct dial WiFi
🐾 **Extras:** Slippers

The Star Inn

★★★ INN

tel: 01684 593432 & 07721 594001 **3 High Street WR8 0HQ**
email: info@richmondhillbreweries.co.uk **web:** www.thestarinnupton.co.uk
dir: *M5 junction 8 onto M50. Exit after 1 mile at junction 1, signed Malvern (A38). Continue on A38, after 6 miles left signed Upton and follow signs to town centre.*

This charming property is located opposite one of the town's most famous landmarks known locally as 'The Pepperpot'; a copper-clad coppola which is a remnant of a former church that stood on the historic battle site. Run by a husband and wife team, The Star Inn sits back from the riverbank and offers a range of comfortably furnished en suite bedrooms. There is a large sun terrace to the rear which overlooks the River Severn. Evening meals are served in the traditional dining room to the rear of the property.

Rooms: 17 en suite (3 fmly) **Facilities:** FTV DVD TVL tea/coffee Dinner available WiFi

WORCESTER Map 10 SO85

Green Farm Bed & Breakfast

★★★★ 🍴 FARMHOUSE

tel: 01905 381807 **Green Farm, Crowle Green WR7 4AB**
email: thegreenfarm@btinternet.com **web:** www.thegreenfarm.co.uk
dir: *From M5 junction 6 take A4538 towards Evesham. Left at 2nd roundabout, then 1st right towards Crowle. 1st left after 0.75 mile at top of Crowle bank. Green Farm 0.25 mile on right.*

This charming farmhouse is conveniently located just off the M5 yet offers a peaceful and relaxing environment that is a haven for wildlife. Donkeys, ponies, pigs and quails are just some of friends that you can meet here – many have been named by previous guests. Owner Lucy has developed some of the original farm buildings into spacious, comfortable suites, each with its own lounge; one suite has two bedrooms so is ideal for families. The food is noteworthy, from the home-made cake on arrival through to breakfast with home-made jams and bread and honey from their own bees – you could say it's all about 'food steps' not 'food miles'.

Rooms: 2 en suite **S** fr £65 **D** fr £85* **Facilities:** FTV TVL tea/coffee WiFi **Parking:** 16
Notes: 26 acres sheep

Church House Bed & Breakfast

★★★★ FARMHOUSE

tel: 01905 452366 & 07909 968938 **Church House, Claines WR3 7RL**
email: wr37rl@btinternet.com **web:** www.churchhousebandb.co.uk
dir: *M5 junction 6 onto A449, after 3 miles at roundabout take 1st exit. 1st drive on right before Claines church.*

Church House Bed & Breakfast is situated on a working farm in a peaceful area of Worcestershire, within easy reach of the motorway network. This Grade II listed Georgian building offers relaxing and comfortable accommodation; each bedroom is en suite and has WiFi and large-screen TVs. The comfortable beds offer a good night's sleep, and the enjoyable breakfast, with home-made produce from the farm, will provide a good start for the day.

Rooms: 2 en suite **S** fr £60 **D** fr £80* **Facilities:** FTV tea/coffee WiFi
Fishing 🐾 **Extras:** Home-made biscuits – complimentary **Parking:** 10
Notes: No children 12 years 600 acres mixed

EAST RIDING OF YORKSHIRE

BEVERLEY Map 17 TA03

Premier Collection

Newbegin House

★★★★★ 🍴 BED AND BREAKFAST

tel: 01482 888880 **10 Newbegin HU17 8EG**
email: wsweeney@wsweeney.karoo.co.uk **web:** www.newbeginhousebbbeverley.co.uk
dir: *At end of M62 onto B1230 signed North Cave. Through North Cave and Walkington. Left at mini roundabout, 1st left at at next mini roundabout into Admiral Walker Road. 5th right into Newbegin. House on left.*

Newbegin House is a delightful Georgian manor house located on a quiet one-way street in the centre of this historic market town. It is an impressive family home, very spacious and with many original period features and a homely, inviting feel. Excellent breakfasts are served in the grand dining room. The walled garden is also available for guests to enjoy and private parking is provided.

Rooms: 3 en suite (1 fmly) **Facilities:** FTV DVD iPod docking station TVL tea/coffee WiFi 🐾 **Conf:** Max 30 Thtr 30 Class 20 Board 12 **Parking:** 3 **Notes:** LB RS Closed owners' annual holiday

Trinity Guest House

★★★★ GUEST HOUSE

tel: 01482 869537 **Trinity Lane, Station Square HU17 0AR**
email: trinity_house@hotmail.com **web:** www.trinityguesthouse.com
dir: *Opposite railway station.*

This well-presented Victorian townhouse is located next to the train station in the historic town centre – guests simply need to cross the quiet street if they arrive by train. There is a convenient public car park opposite the house or permits are available for on-street parking. The house combines traditional and modern decor with a comfortable lounge also provided. The secluded, walled garden provides additional space for guests to relax in. WiFi is available.

Rooms: 6 en suite (2 fmly) **Facilities:** FTV DVD TVL tea/coffee WiFi 🐾

BRIDLINGTON
Map 17 TA16

Premier Collection

Marton Grange
★★★★★ GUEST ACCOMMODATION

tel: 01262 602034 & 07708 211071
Flamborough Road, Marton cum Sewerby YO15 1DU
email: info@marton-grange.co.uk **web:** www.martongrange.co.uk
dir: 2 miles northeast of Bridlington. On B1255, 600 yards west of Links golf club.

This Grade II listed former farmhouse is set in well-maintained gardens and offers high levels of comfort, service and hospitality. Bedrooms are well appointed with quality fixtures and fittings and public areas offer wonderful views of the gardens. Thoughtful extras, provided as standard, help create a delightful guest experience.

Rooms: 11 en suite (3 GF) **S** fr £65 **D** fr £85* **Facilities:** FTV iPod docking station Lounge tea/coffee Lift Licensed WiFi ⌁ ♨ **Extras:** Home-made shortbread, speciality toiletries, cream tea on arrival — complimentary **Parking:** 11 **Notes:** LB RS January to February restricted opening for refurbishments and staff annual leave

The Royal Bridlington
★★★★ GUEST ACCOMMODATION

tel: 01262 672433 **1 Shaftesbury Road YO15 3NP**
email: info@royalhotelbrid.co.uk **web:** www.royalhotelbrid.co.uk
dir: A615 north to Bridlington (Kingsgate), right into Shaftesbury Road.

Just off the promenade, this immaculate property has a range of thoughtfully furnished bedrooms with smart modern bathrooms. The spacious public areas include a large dining room, conservatory-sitting room, and a cosy TV lounge. Freshly-cooked dinners are a feature and a warm welcome is assured.

Rooms: 14 rms (13 en suite) (1 pri facs) 4 annexe en suite (7 fmly) (4 GF) **S** fr £44 **D** fr £78* **Facilities:** FTV DVD Lounge tea/coffee Dinner available Licensed WiFi ⌁ ♨ **Conf:** Max 85 Thtr 85 Class 20 Board 40 **Parking:** 7 **Notes:** LB No children 16 years

The Brockton
★★★★ GUEST ACCOMMODATION

tel: 01262 673967 & 401771 **4 Shaftesbury Road YO15 3NP**
email: brocktonhotel@yahoo.co.uk **web:** www.brockton-bridlington.co.uk
dir: From A167 (coast road), right at golf course, through lights, 2nd on left.

Located close to the seafront, this family-run property offers comfortable bedrooms, some with sea views, and all with en suite shower rooms. A lounge and bar area is available, and dinner and breakfast are served in the dining room.

Rooms: 10 en suite (2 fmly) (2 GF) **S** fr £41 **D** fr £72* **Facilities:** FTV DVD Lounge TVL tea/coffee Dinner available Licensed WiFi **Conf:** Max 20 **Parking:** 10 **Notes:** LB

HUGGATE
Map 19 SE85

The Wolds Inn
★★★ ⌂ INN

tel: 01377 288217 **Driffield Road YO42 1YH**
email: woldsinn@gmail.com **web:** www.woldsinn.co.uk
dir: Huggate signed from A166 and follow brown signs to Wolds Inn.

At the end of the highest village in the Yorkshire Wolds, midway between York and the coast, this ancient inn is a rural haven beside the Wolds Way walk. Substantial meals are served in the dining room and a good range of well-kept beers is available in the bar. Bedrooms, varying in size, are well equipped and comfortable.

Rooms: 3 en suite **Facilities:** FTV tea/coffee Dinner available WiFi ♨ **Extras:** Bottled water — complimentary **Parking:** 30

SOUTH DALTON
Map 17 SE94

Premier Collection

The Pipe and Glass
★★★★★ ◉◉ ⌂ INN

tel: 01430 810246 **West End HU17 7PN**
email: email@pipeandglass.co.uk **web:** www.pipeandglass.co.uk
dir: Phone for directions.

This former coaching inn stands on the site of the original gatehouse to Dalton Park on the beautiful Dalton Estate; parts of the current building date back to the 17th century. Owners James and Kate have established a fine reputation far and wide and the inn goes from strength to strength. The individually designed and stylish bedrooms are located in the beautifully landscaped garden where, they say, all the plants grown can actually be eaten! Each room has a super king-size bed, large TV, air conditioning, free WiFi, Bluetooth music system and other luxury accessories. James sources top-notch local and seasonal produce for his award-winning, modern British menus. A private dining suite is available.

Rooms: 5 annexe en suite (5 GF) **S** fr £170 **D** fr £195* **Facilities:** FTV DVD iPod docking station Lounge tea/coffee Dinner available Direct dial WiFi **Extras:** Speciality toiletries **Parking:** 60 **Notes:** Closed 2 weeks January RS Monday closed (excluding bank holidays)

WILLERBY
Map 17 TA03

Innkeeper's Lodge Hull, Willerby
★★★ INN

tel: 03451 551551 **Beverley Road HU10 6NT**
email: info@innkeeperslodge.com **web:** www.innkeeperslodge.com
dir: Phone for directions.

Conveniently located five minutes from the city centre and close to the M62 and the Humber Bridge. Bedrooms are modern and offer good space and comfort. There is a Toby Carvery pub on site where guests can enjoy a wide range of drinks and food, including roast dinners. Complimentary WiFi is provided and there is also on-site parking.

Rooms: 32 en suite (12 fmly) (8 GF) **Facilities:** FTV tea/coffee Dinner available WiFi **Parking:** 70

NORTH YORKSHIRE

ALLERSTON — Map 19 SE88

Rains Farm Holidays

★★★★ FARMHOUSE

tel: 01723 859333 **YO18 7PQ**
email: rainsholidays@btconnect.com **web:** www.rains-farm-holidays.co.uk
dir: *1.5 miles south of A170 (Pickering to Scarborough road), through village, 1 mile on right between Allerston and Yedingham.*

A warm welcome awaits at Rains Farm Holidays situated a short drive from the popular town of Pickering. The bedrooms and bathrooms are comfortably appointed, and a lounge area and a modern kitchen are available for guest use. Delicious, hearty, cooked breakfasts are served at a communal dining table. The gardens are an attractive feature with outdoor seating available in the summer months. The parking is generous.

Rooms: 3 en suite (1 GF) **S** fr £70 **D** fr £100 **Facilities:** FTV TVL tea/coffee WiFi **Extras:** Use of kitchen **Parking:** 6 **Notes:** LB No children 12 years Closed Christmas and New Year 7 acres non-working

AMPLEFORTH — Map 19 SE57

Premier Collection

Shallowdale House

★★★★★ GUEST ACCOMMODATION

tel: 01439 788325 **West End YO62 4DY**
email: stay@shallowdalehouse.co.uk **web:** www.shallowdalehouse.co.uk
dir: *Off A170 at west end of village, on turn to Hambleton.*

An outstanding example of an architect-designed 1960s house, Shallowdale lies in two acres of hillside gardens. There are stunning views from every room, and the elegant public rooms include a choice of lounges. Spacious bedrooms blend traditional and 60s style with many home comforts. Expect excellent service and genuine hospitality from Anton and Phillip. The very imaginative, freshly cooked dinners shouldn't be missed.

Rooms: 3 rms (2 en suite) (1 pri facs) **S** fr £110 **D** fr £130* **Facilities:** FTV Lounge tea/coffee Dinner available Licensed WiFi **Extras:** Speciality toiletries – complimentary **Parking:** 3 **Notes:** No children 12 years Closed Christmas and New Year

ARKENGARTHDALE — Map 18 NY90

Charles Bathurst Inn

★★★★ INN

tel: 01748 884567 **DL11 6EN**
email: info@cbinn.co.uk **web:** www.cbinn.co.uk
dir: *B6270 to Reeth, at Buck Hotel turn north to Langthwaite, pass church on right, inn 0.5 mile on right.*

The CB Inn, as it is known by locals, is surrounded by magnificent scenery high in the Dales. Food is the focus of the pub, where a choice of rustic eating areas makes for atmospheric dining. The well-equipped bedrooms blend contemporary and traditional styles, and cosy lounge areas are available. A function suite is also offered.

Rooms: 19 en suite (3 fmly) (5 GF) **Facilities:** Lounge tea/coffee Dinner available Direct dial WiFi Fishing Riding **Extras:** Speciality toiletries, home-made shortbread **Conf:** Max 70 Thtr 70 Class 30 Board 30 **Parking:** 35 **Notes:** LB Closed 25 December Civ wed 70

ASENBY — Map 19 SE37

Premier Collection

Crab Manor

★★★★★ RESTAURANT WITH ROOMS

tel: 01845 577286 **Dishforth Road YO7 3QL**
web: www.crabandlobster.co.uk
dir: *A1(M) junction 49, on outskirts of village.*

This stunning 18th-century, Grade II listed Georgian manor is located in the heart of the North Yorkshire Dales. Each bedroom is themed around the world's most famous hotels and has high-quality furnishings, beautiful wallpapers and thoughtful extras. Scandinavian log cabins are also available in the grounds – each has its own terrace with hot tub. There is a comfortable lounge bar where guests can relax in the manor before enjoying dinner next door in the Crab & Lobster Restaurant which specialises in fresh local seafood. The attractive landscape gardens are noteworthy too.

Rooms: 8 en suite 12 annexe en suite (3 fmly) **Facilities:** FTV iPod docking station Lounge tea/coffee Dinner available Direct dial WiFi Sauna **Conf:** Max 16 Board 16 **Parking:** 90 **Notes:** Civ wed 105

AUSTWICK — Map 18 SD76

Premier Collection

The Traddock

★★★★★ RESTAURANT WITH ROOMS

tel: 015242 51224 **Settle LA2 8BY**
email: info@thetraddock.co.uk **web:** www.thetraddock.co.uk
dir: *From Skipton take A65 towards Kendal, 3 miles after Settle turn right signed Austwick, cross hump back bridge, 100 yards on left.*

Situated within the Yorkshire Dales National Park and a peaceful village environment, this fine Georgian country house with well-tended gardens offers a haven of calm and good hospitality. There are two comfortable lounges with real fires and fine furnishings, as well as a cosy bar and an elegant dining room serving fine cuisine. Bedrooms are individually styled with many homely touches.

Rooms: 12 en suite (2 fmly) (1 GF) **Facilities:** FTV DVD Lounge tea/coffee Dinner available Direct dial WiFi **Extras:** Speciality toiletries, fruit, home-made biscuits, bottled water – complimentary **Conf:** Max 24 Thtr 24 Class 16 Board 16 **Parking:** 20 **Notes:** LB

AYSGARTH
Map 19 SE08

The Aysgarth Falls
★★★★ INN

tel: 01969 663775 **DL8 3SR**
email: info@aysgarthfallshotel.com **web:** www.aysgarthfallshotel.com
dir: *On A684 between Leyburn and Hawes.*

A friendly, high-quality inn, perfectly located for exploring the Yorkshire Dales – the grounds lead down to Aysgarth Falls. Excellent meals are served throughout the bar and dining areas and also on the outdoor terraces in warmer weather. The bedrooms are contemporary and feature comfortable beds, TVs and luxurious en suites. Residents also have use of a drying room for wet-weather gear and boots.

Rooms: 11 en suite 2 annexe en suite (2 fmly) (2 GF) **Facilities:** FTV DVD tea/coffee Dinner available WiFi 🔒 **Conf:** Max 40 Thtr 40 Board 16 **Parking:** 30

BAINBRIDGE
Map 18 SD99

Premier Collection

Yorebridge House
★★★★★ ◎◎◎ 🍽 RESTAURANT WITH ROOMS

tel: 01969 652060 **DL8 3EE**
email: enquiries@yorebridgehouse.co.uk **web:** www.yorebridgehouse.co.uk
dir: *A648 to Bainbridge. Yorebridge House north of centre on right before river.*

Yorebridge House is situated by the river on the edge of Bainbridge, in the heart of the North Yorkshire Dales. In the Victorian era this was a schoolmaster's house and school; the building now offers luxury boutique-style accommodation. Each bedroom is individually designed with high-quality furnishings and thoughtful extras. All rooms have stunning views of the Dales and some have their own terrace with hot tub. There is a comfortable lounge bar where guests can relax before enjoying an excellent, three AA Rosette award-winning dinner in the attractive and elegant dining room.

Rooms: 7 en suite 4 annexe en suite (11 fmly) (5 GF) **Facilities:** STV FTV DVD iPod docking station Lounge tea/coffee Dinner available Direct dial WiFi 🎣 Fishing **Extras:** Speciality toiletries **Conf:** Max 70 Thtr 70 Class 60 Board 30 **Parking:** 30 **Notes:** LB Civ wed 100

BIRSTWITH
Map 19 SE25

The Station Hotel
★★★★ ◎ 🍽 INN

tel: 01423 770254 **Station Road HG3 3AG**
email: admin@station-hotel.net **web:** www.station-hotel.net
dir: *A59 (Harrogate to Skipton road), turn into Chain Bar Lane, signed Hampsthwaite. At T-junction left into Hollins Lane, in 1 mile at next T-junction right into Hampsthwaite High Street. 1.6 miles to Birstwith, right into Wreaks Road. 0.5 mile on left.*

This is a family-owned country inn in the village of Birstwith, on the edge of Nidderdale, which means stunning scenery and great walks are right on the doorstep. There are four bedrooms on the first floor of the main pub building and also a ground-floor room in the annexe. All rooms are appointed with traditional oak furniture and comfortable beds plus useful items such as tea- and coffee-making facilities, alarm clocks, free internet access and Freesat TVs. The restaurant serves food daily, and vegetarians are well catered for; a hearty Yorkshire breakfast is included in the price. On-site parking is provided.

Rooms: 4 en suite 1 annexe en suite (1 fmly) (1 GF) **S** fr £80 **D** fr £100 **Facilities:** STV FTV iPod docking station tea/coffee Dinner available WiFi 🔒 **Parking:** 25

BOLTON ABBEY
Map 19 SE05

Howgill Lodge
★★★★ GUEST ACCOMMODATION

tel: 01756 720655 **Barden BD23 6DJ**
email: info@howgill-lodge.co.uk **web:** www.howgill-lodge.co.uk
dir: *B6160 from Bolton Abbey signed Burnsall, 3 miles right at Barden Tower signed Appletreewick, Howgill Lodge 1.25 miles on right at phone box.*

In an idyllic position high above the valley, this converted stone granary provides a quality get-away. The stylish bedrooms provide a host of thoughtful touches and are designed to feature original stone walls, flagstone floors and timber beams; all boast spectacular, memorable views. Breakfasts make excellent use of fresh local ingredients.

Rooms: 4 en suite (1 fmly) (4 GF) **S** fr £65 **D** fr £85* **Facilities:** FTV tea/coffee **Extras:** Fridge **Parking:** 6 **Notes:** LB Closed November and 24–26 December

BOROUGHBRIDGE
Map 19 SE36

The Crown Inn
★★★★ ◉◉ ♀ RESTAURANT WITH ROOMS

tel: 01423 322300 **Roecliffe** YO51 9LY
email: info@crowninnroecliffe.co.uk **web:** www.crowninnroecliffe.co.uk
dir: A1(M) junction 48, follow signs for Boroughbridge. At roundabout exit towards Roecliffe.

The Crown is a 16th-century coaching inn providing an excellent combination of traditional charm and modern comforts. Service is friendly and professional and food is a highlight of any stay. The kitchen team uses the finest Yorkshire produce from the best local suppliers to create a weekly-changing seasonal menu. Bedrooms are attractively furnished with stylish en suite bathrooms.

Rooms: 4 en suite (1 fmly) **S** fr £85 **D** fr £85* **Facilities:** FTV DVD tea/coffee Dinner available WiFi 🔒 **Extras:** Home-made chocolates and biscuits **Conf:** Max 100 Thtr 100 Class 60 Board 30 **Parking:** 40 **Notes:** Civ wed 120

BURNSALL
Map 19 SE06

The Devonshire Fell
★★★★ ◉ RESTAURANT WITH ROOMS

tel: 01756 729000 & 718111 **BD23 6BT**
email: manager@devonshirefell.co.uk **web:** www.devonshirefell.co.uk
dir: From roundabout on A59 at Bolton Abbey take B6160 to Burnsall. 6 miles.

Located on the edge of the attractive village of Burnsall, The Devonshire Fell is colourful, contemporary and quirky. Originally a gentleman's club, it enjoys what may be one of the finest locations in the country. A brasserie-style menu is served in the light and airy conservatory restaurant, which has original modern artwork and views of the Fells and Dales. Intimate and friendly, The Devonshire Fell is a superb choice for those looking to escape from it all. Expect quality throughout, home comforts and a friendly, warm welcome.

Rooms: 16 en suite (2 fmly) **Facilities:** STV FTV DVD tea/coffee Dinner available Direct dial WiFi ⌛ Fishing 🔒 Free use of spa facilities at sister hotel **Conf:** Max 50 Thtr 50 Class 30 Board 24 **Parking:** 40 **Notes:** LB Civ wed 80

CLAPHAM
Map 18 SD76

Premier Collection

The New Inn
★★★★★ ♀ 🚬 INN

tel: 015242 51203 **The Green LA2 8HH**
email: info@newinn-clapham.co.uk **web:** www.newinn-clapham.co.uk
dir: From Skipton take A65 towards Kendal. Follow Clapham signs.

The New Inn has been in operation since 1745 and is ideally located in the heart of the conservation village of Clapham, beside Clapham Beck in the Yorkshire Dales National Park. The whole property has been appointed to a very high standard and the interior design is in keeping with the character of the building and the environment. The fully en suite bedrooms cater well for visitors to this lovely and peaceful village. There is a small but comfortable lounge on the first floor and the bars are full of charm and character enhanced with a log-burning stove. The restaurant menus show imagination and flair, and an extensive and hearty breakfast is served.

Rooms: 15 en suite 5 annexe en suite (3 fmly) (2 GF) **S** fr £90 **D** fr £110*
Facilities: FTV DVD Lounge TVL tea/coffee Dinner available WiFi ⌛ 🔒 Seasonal game shooting **Extras:** Speciality toiletries, bottled water **Conf:** Max 30 Thtr 30 Class 25 Board 25 **Parking:** 40 **Notes:** LB

Brookhouse Guest House
★★★★ 🚬 GUEST HOUSE

tel: 015242 51580 **Station Road LA2 8ER**
email: admin@brookhouseclapham.co.uk **web:** www.brookhouse-clapham.co.uk
dir: Exit A65 into village.

Beside the river, in the pretty conservation village of Clapham, this personally run guest house provides comfortable accommodation and warm hospitality. Brookhouse also provides an evening bistro, popular with locals, which offers an interesting selection of home-made meals. Secure storage for bikes is also available.

Rooms: 3 rms (2 en suite) (1 pri facs) (1 fmly) **Facilities:** FTV tea/coffee Dinner available Licensed WiFi ⌛ ⌛ **Notes:** LB

CRAYKE
Map 19 SE57

Premier Collection

The Durham Ox
★★★★★ 🅰 RESTAURANT WITH ROOMS

tel: 01347 821506 **Westway YO61 4TE**
email: enquiries@thedurhamox.com **web:** www.thedurhamox.com
dir: A19 to Easingwold. Through market place to Crayke, 1st left up hill.

The Durham Ox is some 300 years old. The owners pride themselves on offering a friendly and efficient service, plus traditional pub food using only the best local ingredients. The pub has a breathtaking outlook over the Vale of York on three sides, and a charming view up the hill to the medieval church on the other. Accommodation is in converted farm cottages and a studio suite in the main building. Crayke is in the heart of 'Herriot Country' and about a 30-minute drive from York city centre.

Rooms: 1 en suite 5 annexe en suite (1 fmly) (3 GF) **Facilities:** FTV DVD iPod docking station tea/coffee Dinner available WiFi 🔒 Shooting, fishing, riding by arrangement **Extras:** Speciality toiletries, honesty bar **Conf:** Max 80 Thtr 80 Class 60 Board 30 **Parking:** 35 **Notes:** LB

EASINGWOLD
Map 19 SE56

George at Easingwold
★★★★ 🚬 INN

tel: 01347 821698 **Market Place YO61 3AD**
email: info@the-george-hotel.co.uk **web:** www.the-george-hotel.co.uk
dir: From A19 follow signs for Easingwold. Into Market Place, on right.

The George has a prominent position in the centre of the village and is only a 30-minute drive into York. The inn is very well managed and run by the owners Kay and Michael. The comfortable bedrooms have modern en suite bathrooms and the public areas are quite spacious. Food is a must here – local produce, good sized portions and all freshly cooked; hand-pulled beers and a good choice of wines are also available. There is limited parking.

Rooms: 15 en suite (2 fmly) (6 GF) **S** fr £69 **D** fr £79* **Facilities:** FTV DVD Lounge tea/coffee Dinner available Direct dial WiFi 🔒 Complimentary use of adjacent gym **Extras:** Bottled water **Conf:** Max 40 Thtr 40 Class 20 Board 20 **Parking:** 8 **Notes:** LB Closed 24–25 December

| ELLERBY | Map 19 NZ71 |

Ellerby Residential Country Inn

★★★★ ⊜ INN

tel: 01947 840342 **12-14 Ryeland Lane TS13 5LP**
email: relax@ellerbyhotel.co.uk **web:** www.ellerbyhotel.co.uk
dir: *From A171 onto B1266, follow signs for Ellerby. Or from A174 (Whitby) follow signs for Ellerby.*

Located in the North York Moors National Park, this friendly, family-run inn is in a quiet country setting just eight miles from Whitby. There is a traditional bar with open fire and real ales, a spacious restaurant, a beautiful, secluded garden and a residents' conservatory lounge. A range of bedrooms is available including ground-floor rooms, family rooms and a disabled accessible room. Complimentary WiFi is provided and there is secure bicycle storage.

Rooms: 10 en suite (4 fmly) (4 GF) **Facilities:** STV FTV Lounge tea/coffee Dinner available Direct dial WiFi ⌖ **Extras:** Fresh milk, fridge, robes **Parking:** 30 **Notes:** LB

| FILEY | Map 17 TA18 |

Premier Collection

All Seasons Guesthouse

★★★★★ ⚲ GUEST HOUSE

tel: 01723 515321 **11 Rutland Street YO14 9JA**
email: joy@allseasonsfiley.co.uk **web:** www.allseasonsfiley.co.uk
dir: *From A165 at roundabout follow signs for Filey. Continue to town centre, right into West Avenue, 2nd left into Rutland Street.*

This immaculately presented, contemporary guest house is a short stroll from the seafront and is also close to the Crescent Gardens and town centre. There is a friendly, welcoming atmosphere and a lovely lounge for guests to relax in. Bedrooms and bathrooms are stylish and very comfortable. They include a luxury suite, a king-size room, family and twin rooms. Breakfast is a highlight of any stay with all produce either locally sourced or home made. Complimentary WiFi is provided.

Rooms: 6 en suite (1 fmly) **S** fr £65 **D** fr £85* **Facilities:** STV FTV TVL tea/coffee WiFi ⌖ ⌖ ⌖ **Extras:** Dressing gowns, slippers – complimentary **Notes:** LB No children 10 years

| FLIXTON | Map 17 TA07 |

Orchard Lodge

★★★★ ⚲ GUEST ACCOMMODATION

tel: 01723 890202 & 07789 228682 **North Street YO11 3UA**
email: orchardlodgescarborough@gmail.com **web:** www.orchard-lodge.com
dir: *Exit A1039 in village centre.*

A warm welcome is guaranteed at this owner-run property situated in the small village of Flixton near the popular seaside resort of Scarborough. Bedrooms are comfortably appointed with modern accessories including complimentary WiFi. Award-winning breakfasts are served in the spacious dining room which also opens as a tearoom throughout the afternoon. A focus on local and home-made produce means eggs are sourced from the resident hens and the fruit used for jams and juices is picked from the on-site orchard. Free parking is also available.

Rooms: 6 en suite **S** fr £85 **D** fr £95* **Facilities:** FTV Lounge tea/coffee Licensed WiFi ⌖ **Extras:** Fridge, speciality toiletries **Conf:** Max 12 **Parking:** 6 **Notes:** LB No children 12 years Closed 8–31 January

| FYLINGTHORPE | Map 19 NZ90 |

Flask Inn

★★★★ ⊜ INN

tel: 01947 880305 & 880592 **YO22 4QH**
email: info@flaskinn.com **web:** www.theflaskinn.co.uk
dir: *On A171 from Whitby, on left.*

This traditional inn offers spacious bar and dining areas along with smart, contemporary bedrooms. The rooms are very well equipped and feature modern en suites. There is a friendly atmosphere, and food is a highlight of any stay with a high standard of cooking and a wide choice on the appealing menus. The inn, set in the beautiful North Yorkshire countryside, is in a very convenient location close to the A171 which is a scenic drive between Whitby and Scarborough.

Rooms: 9 en suite (2 fmly) (3 GF) **Facilities:** FTV tea/coffee Dinner available WiFi ⌖ **Extras:** Bottled water **Parking:** 25 **Notes:** LB Closed 2 January to 7 February

| GILLING EAST | Map 19 SE67 |

The Fairfax Arms

★★★★ ⊚⊚ INN

tel: 01439 788212 & 788819 **Main Street YO62 4JH**
email: info@thefairfaxarms.co.uk **web:** www.thefairfaxarms.co.uk
dir: *From A170 turn right onto B1257, right again onto B1363 to Gilling East, pub on right.*

This independently owned inn, in the quiet village of Gilling East, is within easy driving distance of Helmsley. The owners have struck a perfect balance between providing up-to-date facilities alongside original features such as wooden beams and open fires. Bedrooms are well appointed with comfortable beds that are guaranteed to provide a good night's sleep; thoughtful accessories include iPod docking stations, TVs and luxurious toiletries; PlayStation consoles are also available on request. Award-winning dinners, that focus on excellent quality local produce, can be enjoyed both in the bar and restaurant areas. On-site parking is available.

Rooms: 8 en suite 4 annexe en suite (2 fmly) (3 GF) **S** fr £95 **D** fr £120 **Facilities:** FTV DVD iPod docking station tea/coffee Dinner available Direct dial WiFi ⌖ **Extras:** Speciality toiletries **Parking:** 14 **Notes:** LB

GOLDSBOROUGH   Map 19 SE35

Premier Collection

Goldsborough Hall

★★★★★ ◉◉ ⬚ GUEST ACCOMMODATION

tel: 01423 867321 **Church Street HG5 8NR**
email: info@goldsboroughhall.com **web:** www.goldsboroughhall.com
dir: *A1(M) junction 47, A59 to Knaresborough. 2nd left into Station Road, at T-junction left into Church Street.*

It's not every day that you get the chance to stay in the former residence of a Royal Princess, in this case HRH Princess Mary (1897–1965), who was one of the Queen's aunts. Hospitality at Goldsborough Hall is second to none. The luxury bedrooms are appointed to the highest standards, and the bathrooms have a real 'wow' factor. Some of the main house bedrooms feature hand-made mahogany four-poster beds, chesterfields and 60" TVs. The popular, seasonal afternoon tea is served either in front of the roaring fire in the Jacobean Library or in the Dining Room. Reservations for dinner from non-residents are welcomed. Three Tesla charging stations are also available.

Rooms: 6 en suite 10 annexe en suite (4 fmly) (4 GF) **Facilities:** FTV Lounge tea/coffee Dinner available Direct dial Lift Licensed WiFi ⬚ ⬚ Outdoor hot tub **Extras:** Speciality toiletries, mini-bar – chargeable **Conf:** Max 150 Thtr 150 Class 50 Board 30 **Parking:** 50 **Notes:** LB Closed 24–26 December Civ wed 150

GRASSINGTON   Map 19 SE06

Premier Collection

Grassington House

★★★★★ ◉◉ ⬚ RESTAURANT WITH ROOMS

tel: 01756 752406 **5 The Square BD23 5AQ**
email: bookings@grassingtonhouse.co.uk **web:** www.grassingtonhouse.co.uk
dir: *A59 into Grassington, in town square opposite post office.*

Located in the square of the popular village of Grassington, this beautifully converted Georgian house is personally run by owners John and Sue. Delicious food, individually designed bedrooms and warm hospitality ensure an enjoyable stay. There is a stylish lounge bar looking out to the square and the restaurant is split between two rooms; here guests will find the emphasis is on fresh, local ingredients and attentive, friendly service.

Rooms: 9 en suite (2 fmly) **S** fr £117.50 **D** fr £135* **Facilities:** STV FTV tea/coffee Dinner available Direct dial WiFi ⬚ **Extras:** Speciality toiletries **Parking:** 25 **Notes:** LB Closed 25 December Civ wed 44

HARROGATE   Map 19 SE35

Premier Collection

The Grafton Boutique B&B

★★★★★ ⬚ GUEST ACCOMMODATION

tel: 01423 508491 **1-3 Franklin Mount HG1 5EJ**
email: enquiries@graftonhotel.co.uk **web:** www.graftonhotel.co.uk
dir: *Follow signs to International Centre, into Kings Road (with Centre on left), Franklin Mount 450 yards on right.*

The Grafton is a stylish townhouse, in a quiet location, just a short walk from the conference centre and town. It is a period property but with contemporary interior design throughout and a luxurious feel. There is a beautifully appointed lounge looking out to the garden, and breakfast is served in a spacious and striking dining room. Complimentary WiFi is provided.

Rooms: 13 en suite (1 GF) **D** fr £90* **Facilities:** FTV Lounge tea/coffee Direct dial Licensed WiFi ⬚ ⬚ **Parking:** 1 **Notes:** LB Closed 15 December to 6 January

Innkeeper's Lodge Harrogate (West)

★★★★ INN

tel: 03451 551551 **Beckwith Knowle, Otley Road HG3 1UE**
email: info@innkeeperslodge.com **web:** www.innkeeperslodge.com
dir: *Phone for directions.*

Located close to town in Beckwith Knowle, this period property, The Pine Marten, is ideal for exploring historic and vibrant Harrogate and the Yorkshire Dales National Park. The spacious public areas are stylish and full of character. Seasonally-changing menus feature traditional favourites as well as Mediterranean influenced dishes and the chef's daily specials. The en suite, modern bedrooms come in different shapes and sizes and have TVs, desks, free WiFi, tea- and coffee-making facilities as standard; family rooms are available.

Rooms: 12 en suite (4 fmly) **Facilities:** FTV tea/coffee Dinner available WiFi **Parking:** 60

HELMSLEY   Map 19 SE68

Premier Collection

Shallowdale House

★★★★★ ⬚ ⬚ GUEST ACCOMMODATION

tel: 01439 788325 **West End YO62 4DY**
email: stay@shallowdalehouse.co.uk **web:** www.shallowdalehouse.co.uk

(For full entry see Ampleforth)

Plumpton Court

★★★★ GUEST ACCOMMODATION

tel: 01439 771223 **High Street, Nawton YO62 7TT**
email: mail@plumptoncourt.com **web:** www.plumptoncourt.com
dir: *2.5 miles east of Helmsley. Exit A170 in Nawton, signed.*

Situated in the small village of Nawton between Helmsley and Kirkbymoorside, Plumpton Court has six modern and individually decorated bedrooms. Guests can relax in front of a real fire in the homely lounge with a bottle of wine from the well-stocked bar and enjoy a leisurely breakfast made with locally sourced ingredients. Chris and Jenny are welcoming hosts and take delight in helping guests make the most of their visit to North Yorkshire. To the rear of the house is a private, secure car park and a secluded garden.

Rooms: 6 en suite (1 GF) **S** fr £70 **D** fr £80* **Facilities:** FTV DVD Lounge tea/coffee Licensed WiFi ⅃ ⸙ **Parking:** 7 **Notes:** No children 12 years Closed 22–29 December and 4–31 January

The Feathers

★★★★ INN

tel: 01439 770275 **Market Place YO62 5BH**
email: feathers@innmail.co.uk **web:** www.feathershotelhelmsley.co.uk
dir: *A1(M) junction 49 onto A168 signed Thirsk. Bear left, then take 2nd exit at roundabout onto A170 to Helmsley. In Market Place.*

This fine old property enjoys a prominent position overlooking the busy town square in pretty Helmsley. The bar and lounge areas are full of character and real fires glow on the cooler evenings. There is an extensive dinner menu along with a nightly specials board, which uses the best in local, seasonal produce. Bedrooms have been decorated to a high standard and are most comfortable. Some secure parking is available for guests at the rear of the inn. The Feathers is an ideal base from which to explore the North York Moors National Park, and Helmsley is situated on the Cleveland Way walk.

Rooms: 21 en suite 4 annexe en suite (2 fmly) (2 GF) **Facilities:** FTV Lounge tea/coffee Dinner available WiFi ⅃ ⸙ **Conf:** Max 100 Thtr 100 Class 70 Board 40 **Parking:** 15 **Notes:** LB Civ wed 100

HETTON
Map 18 SD95

Premier Collection

The Angel Inn

★★★★★ ◎◎ ⸙ RESTAURANT WITH ROOMS

tel: 01756 730263 **BD23 6LT**
email: info@angelhetton.co.uk **web:** www.angelhetton.co.uk
dir: *B6265 from Skipton towards Grassington. At Rylstone turn left by pond, follow signs to Hetton.*

This roadside inn, easily recognised by the creeper on the walls and the green canopies, is steeped in history – parts of the building go back more than 500 years. The Angel's restaurant and bar are in the main building, and the food is a highlight of any stay; the kitchen uses excellent ingredients to produce skilfully prepared and carefully presented dishes. The large, stylish bedrooms are across the road in a converted barn which has great views of the Dales. There is private parking and the inn has its own wine cave.

Rooms: 9 en suite (3 GF) **Facilities:** FTV tea/coffee Dinner available Direct dial WiFi ⸙ Wine tasting cave **Conf:** Max 16 Board 14 **Parking:** 40 **Notes:** LB Closed 25 December and 1 week January Civ wed 40

HUNTON
Map 19 SE19

The Countryman's Inn

★★★ INN

tel: 01677 450554 & 07734 556845 **South View DL8 1PY**
email: tony@countrymansinn.co.uk **web:** www.countrymansinn.co.uk
dir: *Exit A1(M) at Leeming Bar onto A684 towards Bedale/Leyburn. Through Patrick Brompton, right at crossroads. After 1.25 miles turn left signed Hunton.*

This traditional country pub offers a friendly atmosphere, cask ales and great food. The bar features a real fire and beamed ceiling and there is a beer garden for warmer weather. A wide choice of freshly prepared meals is served in the smartly presented dining room. Bedrooms and bathrooms are more contemporary with a fresh, bright style; good provision is made for families plus there's a designated 'pet-friendly' room. Other facilities include complimentary WiFi and private parking.

Rooms: 4 en suite (2 fmly) **Facilities:** FTV DVD iPod docking station TVL tea/coffee Dinner available WiFi ⸙ Riding ⸙ **Extras:** Still and sparkling water **Parking:** 8 **Notes:** LB

KETTLEWELL
Map 18 SD97

Belk's Bed & Breakfast

★★★★ BED AND BREAKFAST

tel: 01756 761188 & 07538 566495 **Middle Lane BD23 5QX**
email: davidbelk23@gmail.com **web:** www.zarinaskettlewell.co.uk
dir: *Into Kettlewell on B6160, turn opposite Racehorses Hotel, 200 metres on right.*

Belk's Bed & Breakfast is located in the picturesque village of Kettlewell and is popular with cyclists and walkers. The hosts provide guests with a warm and friendly welcome. Bedrooms are comfortable and well equipped with many thoughtful extras. Memorable breakfasts, served in the pleasantly appointed tea room, feature eggs from the Belk's own chickens as well as home-made preserves. An outside garden seating area is available in warmer weather.

Rooms: 3 en suite **S** fr £49 **D** fr £85* **Facilities:** FTV DVD tea/coffee Licensed WiFi ⸙ **Extras:** Mini-bar **Parking:** 2 **Notes:** LB No children 18 years Closed January

King's Head

★★★★ ◎ INN

tel: 01756 761600 **The Green BD23 5RD**
email: kingsheadkettlewell@outlook.co.uk **web:** www.thekingsheadkettlewell.co.uk
dir: *Phone for directions.*

This owner-run inn is in the peaceful and popular village of Kettlewell – it's the perfect base for leisure guests and keen walkers alike. Award-winning meals can be enjoyed in the cosy bar area beside a roaring open fire, and the hearty breakfasts are noteworthy too for their use of the top local produce. With views of either the village church or the Yorkshire Dales, the smart bedrooms offer en suite shower rooms, Freeview TVs, DVD players, quality toiletries and home-made biscuits along with tea- and coffee-making facilities. On-site parking is not available but there are plenty of public car parks within a short distance.

Rooms: 6 en suite **Facilities:** Dinner available

| KIRKBY FLEETHAM | Map 19 SE29 |

Premier Collection

Black Horse Inn

★★★★★ ⚜ INN

tel: 01609 749010 & 749011 **7 Lumley Lane DL7 0SH**
email: reservations@blackhorseinnkirkbyfleetham.com
web: www.blackhorseinnkirkbyfleetham.com
dir: *A1 onto A648 towards Northallerton. Left into Ham Hall Lane, through Scruton. At T-junction left into Fleetham Lane. Through Great Fencote to Kirkby Fleetham, into Lumley Lane, inn on left past post office.*

The Black Horse Inn is set in the heart of Kirkby Fleetham and offers free parking, free WiFi in public areas, a bar, a garden and a restaurant. Each of the seven bedrooms is decorated in neutral colours and feature antique furniture, a breakfast hamper, TV and a mini-fridge with fresh orange juice, milk and water. The en suite bathrooms have bath and/or power shower with complimentary toiletries; some bedrooms have an in-room roll-top bath. Guests can relax in the bar or garden, and the restaurant serves traditional British dishes. Catterick Racecourse is 10 minutes away and the Yorkshire Dales National Park just 40 minutes.

Rooms: 7 en suite (1 fmly) (2 GF) **Facilities:** FTV tea/coffee Dinner available WiFi ⚓ Fishing Quoits pitch **Extras:** Fridge, fresh milk, orange juice – complimentary **Conf:** Max 40 Thtr 40 Class 30 Board 24 **Parking:** 90 **Notes:** LB

| KIRKBY MALZEARD | Map 19 SE27 |

The Moorhouse

★★★★ ⚜ BED AND BREAKFAST

tel: 01765 658371 **HG4 3RH**
email: enquiries@moorhousebnb.co.uk **web:** www.moorhousebnb.co.uk
dir: *From Ripon on B6265 to Pateley Bridge, turn right to Grantley. Left after pub to T-junction, turn right. On left after 1.5 miles.*

A warm welcome is guaranteed along with afternoon tea, served by the open fire in the guest lounge on colder days. This friendly B&B is situated in the countryside, with popular destinations such as Ripon and Harrogate easily reachable by car. Bedrooms are well appointed and comfortable. Thoughtful extras such as bathrobes, luxurious toiletries and well-stocked hospitality trays are provided. Hearty Yorkshire breakfasts are served in the dining room alongside more healthy options such as fresh fruit smoothies. Plenty of parking is provided.

Rooms: 5 en suite (2 GF) **Facilities:** FTV TVL tea/coffee Licensed WiFi **Parking:** 5 **Notes:** No children 12 years Closed August to March

| KNARESBOROUGH | Map 19 SE35 |

Premier Collection

General Tarleton Inn

★★★★★ ⚛⚛ RESTAURANT WITH ROOMS

tel: 01423 340284 **Boroughbridge Road, Ferrensby HG5 0PZ**
email: gti@generaltarleton.co.uk **web:** www.generaltarleton.co.uk
dir: *A1(M) junction 48 at Boroughbridge, take A6055 to Knaresborough. 4 miles on right.*

This 18th-century coaching inn is both beautiful and stylish. Though the physical aspects are impressive, the emphasis here is on food with high-quality, skilfully prepared dishes served in the smart bar-brasserie and in the Orangery. There is also a richly furnished cocktail lounge with a galleried private dining room above it. Bedrooms are very comfortable and business guests are also well catered for.

Rooms: 13 en suite (7 GF) **S** fr £75 **D** fr £129* **Facilities:** FTV Lounge tea/coffee Dinner available Direct dial WiFi ⚓ **Extras:** Speciality toiletries, home-made biscuits **Conf:** Max 40 Thtr 40 Class 35 Board 20 **Parking:** 40 **Notes:** LB Closed 24–26 December, 1 January

Newton House

★★★★ ⚜ GUEST ACCOMMODATION

tel: 01423 863539 & 07801 557388 **5–7 York Place HG5 0AD**
email: info@newtonhouseyorkshire.com **web:** www.newtonhouseyorkshire.com
dir: *A1(M) junction 47 onto A59 towards Knaresborough. Right at 1st roundabout, continue to town centre, on right before lights.*

This elegant Georgian property is only a short walk from the river, castle and market square; it is entered via an archway into the courtyard. Attractive, very well-equipped bedrooms include some with four-poster beds and others with king-sized doubles. There is a comfortable lounge with honesty bar and memorable breakfasts are served in the attractive dining rooms.

Rooms: 9 rms (8 en suite) (1 pri facs) 3 annexe en suite (2 fmly) (4 GF) **S** fr £60 **D** fr £85* **Facilities:** FTV DVD Lounge tea/coffee Licensed WiFi ⚓ ⚓ Special arrangement for guests to use nearby spa **Extras:** Speciality toiletries, filtered water, mini-bar in most rooms **Conf:** Max 20 Thtr 20 Board 12 **Parking:** 7 **Notes:** LB

Innkeeper's Lodge Harrogate (East)

★★★ INN

tel: 03451 551551 **Wetherby Road, Plompton HG5 8LY**
email: info@innkeeperslodge.com **web:** www.innkeeperslodge.com
dir: *Phone for directions.*

This country pub and lodge is convenient for Harrogate, with its tourist attractions, shops, tearooms and conference centre. It is also well located for visiting picturesque Knaresborough, Ripon and the Yorkshire Dales. The hearty, seasonal food and cask ales are noteworthy, along with real fires and a variety of spaces in which to relax including a lovely beer garden in warmer weather. The bedrooms are comfortable. Complimentary WiFi and on-site parking are provided.

Rooms: 10 en suite (2 fmly) **Facilities:** FTV tea/coffee Dinner available Direct dial WiFi

LEEMING BAR
Map 19 SE28

Premier Collection

Little Holtby

★★★★★ 🍽 BED AND BREAKFAST

tel: 01609 748762 **DL7 9LH**
email: littleholtby@yahoo.co.uk **web:** www.littleholtby.co.uk
dir: *0.5 mile north of A684 (junction with A1), on A6055 north.*

Little Holtby is a charming farmhouse on land which formed part of an estate that is mentioned in the Domesday Book, although the current house dates back to the late 17th century. Ideally placed close to the A1 and convenient for Leeming Bar and Bedale, this is a great location for touring this part of North Yorkshire. A warm welcome awaits along with cakes and a drink. The bedrooms are generous in size and include all necessary facilities including a well-stocked hospitality tray. The gardens and surrounding countryside add to the experience as do the open log fires which keep away the outdoor chill. Award-winning breakfasts get the day off to the right start.

Rooms: 3 rms (2 en suite) (1 pri facs) **S** fr £50 **D** fr £90* **Facilities:** FTV DVD TVL tea/coffee WiFi ⚓ 🚲 **Extras:** Speciality toiletries, fruit, snacks – complimentary **Parking:** 7 **Notes:** LB No children 12 years

LEVISHAM
Map 19 SE89

The Horseshoe Inn

★★★★ 🍺 INN

tel: 01751 460240 **Main Street YO18 7NL**
email: info@horseshoelevisham.co.uk **web:** www.horseshoelevisham.co.uk
dir: *From Pickering on A169, after 4 miles pass Fox & Rabbit Inn on right. 0.5 mile left to Lockton, then follow steep winding road to village.*

The Horseshoe Inn is a charming 19th-century property with a peaceful location in Levisham. The spacious bar and dining area are traditionally furnished, and food is a highlight with a wide choice and generous portions. The attractive bedrooms include seven garden rooms, and most rooms in the main house have lovely views of the village.

Rooms: 11 en suite (7 GF) **D** fr £90* **Facilities:** FTV Lounge tea/coffee Dinner available WiFi **Parking:** 30 **Notes:** LB

LEYBURN
Map 19 SE19

Premier Collection

Braithwaite Hall

★★★★★ 🍽 BED AND BREAKFAST

tel: 01969 640287 **East Witton DL8 4SY**
email: info@braithwaitehall.co.uk **web:** www.braithwaitehall.co.uk
dir: *1.5 miles from East Witton on single track road.*

This impressive 17th-century building is set in open farmland in Coverdale with views over the Pennines bordering Wensleydale. Inside are many period features including antique furnishings and a stunning oak staircase; the drawing room comes complete with oak panelling from the 1660s. The bedrooms are spacious and very comfortable. Delicious breakfasts are served in the elegant dining room and there is a friendly, welcoming atmosphere.

Rooms: 3 rms (2 en suite) (1 pri facs) **S** fr £70 **D** fr £100* **Facilities:** FTV DVD tea/coffee 🎣 Fishing **Extras:** Speciality toiletries, fruit, port **Parking:** 7 **Notes:** No children 12 years Closed November to February

AA GUEST ACCOMMODATION OF THE YEAR FOR ENGLAND 2018–19

Premier Collection

The Old Town Hall

★★★★★ 🍽 GUEST ACCOMMODATION

tel: 01969 625641 **Priory Close, Redmire DL8 4ED**
email: enquiries@theoldtownhall.co.uk **web:** www.theoldtownhall.co.uk

Louise and David run this romantic, luxury property which is set in stunning countryside between Leyburn and Aysgarth Falls. The three bedrooms are charming – simply yet elegantly decorated. All have beamed ceilings and seating areas, and one has a double spa bath and body-jet shower. There are soft towels and bathrobes, luxury Temple Spa toiletries and a well-stocked fridge with fresh milk, water and cordials. On arrival, tea or coffee with home-made cake and biscuits are offered in the guest lounge. Breakfast is cooked to order and features local produce as well as fresh, home-baked bread.

Rooms: 3 rms (2 en suite) (1 pri facs) **S** fr £95 **D** fr £115* **Facilities:** FTV DVD Lounge tea/coffee WiFi 🚲 **Extras:** Speciality toiletries, home-made biscuits, silent fridge, fresh milk, chocolates – complimentary **Parking:** 3 **Notes:** No children 18 years

The Queens Head

★★★★ 🍽 🍺 INN

tel: 01677 450259 **Westmoor Lane, Finghall DL8 5ND**
email: enquiries@queensfinghall.co.uk **web:** www.queensfinghall.co.uk
dir: *From Bedale follow A684 west towards Leyburn, just after pub and caravan park turn left signed to Finghall. Follow road, on left.*

Located in the quiet village of Finghall, this country inn dates back to the 18th century and has original oak beams. A wide choice of freshly prepared meals is served in either the bar or more contemporary restaurant, which has lovely views of the surrounding countryside. Bedrooms are spacious and located in an adjacent annexe.

Rooms: 3 annexe en suite (1 fmly) (3 GF) **Facilities:** FTV DVD tea/coffee Dinner available WiFi 🚲 **Parking:** 40 **Notes:** LB

| **LOW ROW** | **Map 18 SD99** |

The Punch Bowl Inn

★★★★ INN

tel: 03337 000779 **DL11 6PF**
email: info@pbinn.co.uk **web:** www.pbinn.co.uk
dir: *From Scotch Corner take A6108 to Richmond then B6270 to Low Row.*

This friendly inn is appointed in a contemporary style. Real ales and freshly-cooked meals are served in either the spacious bar or dining room. The modern bedrooms are stylish yet simply furnished, with well-equipped bathrooms. Guests also have use of a lounge which has stunning views of the Dales.

Rooms: 9 en suite 2 annexe en suite (1 fmly) (1 GF) **Facilities:** FTV Lounge tea/coffee Dinner available Direct dial WiFi Fishing **Extras:** Speciality toiletries, home-made shortbread **Parking:** 20 **Notes:** LB Closed 25 December

| **MALHAM** | **Map 18 SD96** |

The Lister Arms

★★★★ INN

tel: 01729 830444 **BD23 4DB**
email: relax@listerarms.co.uk **web:** www.listerarms.co.uk
dir: *From A59 into Malham, right in centre of village.*

Located in Malham in the Yorkshire Dales National Park, The Lister Arms is a traditional country inn with wood beams and open fires. It is close to the village green and a babbling stream. The accommodation is comfortable and well equipped, and a wide selection of imaginative dishes, together with real ales and fine wines, are served in the busy bar and restaurant, where the atmosphere is relaxed and comfortable.

Rooms: 15 en suite 8 annexe en suite (3 fmly) (4 GF) **S** fr £94 **D** fr £100*
Facilities: FTV tea/coffee Dinner available WiFi Dog washing facilities and drying room in barn **Extras:** Luxury toiletries, fresh milk flask and home-made biscuits **Conf:** Max 10 **Parking:** 30

| **MIDDLEHAM** | **Map 19 SE18** |

Premier Collection

The Saddle Room

★★★★★ GUEST ACCOMMODATION

tel: 01969 640596 **Tupgill Park, Coverdale DL8 4TJ**
email: info@thesaddleroom.co.uk **web:** www.thesaddleroom.co.uk

The Saddle Room is located in the idyllic Tupgill Park Estate in the heart of the Yorkshire Dales. The high-quality accommodation comes with many thoughtful extras provided as standard. The hands-on team are proactive and show wonderful customer care to their guests and really go that extra mile. The bar and restaurant actively promote quality local produce whenever possible, and the setting of the old stables with its fantastic horseracing objets d'art makes for a really unique space.

Rooms: 9 en suite (3 GF) **D** fr £90* **Facilities:** FTV tea/coffee Dinner available Direct dial Lift Licensed WiFi Fishing **Extras:** Mini-bar, Nespresso machine **Conf:** Max 100 Thtr 100 Class 100 Board 50 **Parking:** 200 **Notes:** Civ wed 100

| **MIDDLETON TYAS** | **Map 19 NZ20** |

Premier Collection

The Coach House

★★★★★ RESTAURANT WITH ROOMS

tel: 01325 377977 **Middleton Lodge DL10 6NJ**
email: info@middletonlodge.co.uk **web:** www.middletonlodge.co.uk
dir: *Phone for directions.*

In a picturesque setting, this former coach house, on a 200-acre estate, is surrounded by tall trees and winding footpaths. There is variety of luxury bedrooms – garden rooms with private terraces, hayloft rooms looking down on the courtyard and the spacious Tack Room suite. Traditional features such as exposed beams and high ceilings are coupled with a wide range of modern accessories such as TV, Nespresso machines and complimentary WiFi. The kitchen takes a modern approach, using seasonal, regional produce for an interesting range of dishes served in both the The Forge Restaurant and Coach House Restaurant. Beauty treatments are offered, and weddings and private functions are held in the main house, Middleton Lodge.

Rooms: 16 en suite 29 annexe en suite (10 fmly) (10 GF) **S** fr £125 **D** fr £150*
Facilities: STV FTV DVD Lounge tea/coffee Dinner available Direct dial WiFi **Extras:** Snacks, juice – complimentary **Parking:** 70 **Notes:** LB Civ wed 120

See advert opposite

NEWTON UNDER ROSEBERRY
Map 19 NZ51

The Kings Head Inn

★★★ ⊜ INN

tel: 01642 722318 **The Green TS9 6QR**
email: info@kingsheadinn.co.uk **web:** www.kingsheadinn.co.uk
dir: *A171 towards Guisborough, at roundabout onto A173 to Newton under Roseberry.*

The Kings Head Inn enjoys a wonderful location with Roseberry Topping providing an iconic back drop and is located at the edge of the North York Moors within easy striking distance of Whitby, York and Newcastle. The comfortable bedrooms are located in adjacent 17th-century cottages. The pub serves good, home-cooked food and the staff are friendly and welcoming.

Rooms: 12 annexe en suite (1 fmly) (6 GF) **Facilities:** tea/coffee Dinner available WiFi **Parking:** 50

NORTHALLERTON
Map 19 SE39

Premier Collection

Woodlands Farm

★★★★★ ⊜ GUEST ACCOMMODATION

tel: 01609 883524 **Thimbleby DL6 3PY**
email: info@woodlandsfarmthimbleby.com **web:** www.woodlandsfarmthimbleby.com
dir: *East of Northallerton. From A19 follow signs for Thimbleby, after 1 mile, Woodlands Farm is 1st house on left after 30mph and village sign.*

Woodlands Farm is a Grade II listed building located in the peaceful hamlet of Thimbleby on the edge of the North Yorkshire Moors. The spacious, en suite bedrooms are accessed from the outside and are part of a stable and outbuilding conversion which uses high-quality furniture, fixtures and fittings from local suppliers; each is well-equipped with many thoughtful modern amenities provided as standard. Quality local produce is a feature, especially in the award-winning breakfasts.

Rooms: 4 en suite (2 fmly) (4 GF) **D** fr £100 (room only)* **Facilities:** FTV DVD iPod docking station tea/coffee Licensed WiFi **Extras:** Speciality toiletries, Home-made biscuits **Parking:** 5 **Notes:** LB

OLDSTEAD
Map 19 SE57

Premier Collection

The Black Swan at Oldstead

★★★★★ ◎◎◎◎ ⊜ RESTAURANT WITH ROOMS

tel: 01347 868387 **YO61 4BL**
email: reception@blackswanoldstead.co.uk **web:** www.blackswanoldstead.co.uk
dir: *Exit A19, 3 miles south Thirsk for Coxwold, left in Coxwold, left at Byland Abbey for Oldstead.*

The Black Swan, run by the Banks family, is set amidst the stunning scenery of the North York Moors National Park, and parts of the building date back to the 16th century. The well-appointed, very comfortable and stylish bedrooms provide the perfect luxury getaway; some are on the ground floor overlooking the kitchen garden, others are in the Georgian House and feature both baths and wet-room showers. These lovely bedrooms, welcoming open fires and a traditional bar all combine with the outstanding, award-winning food of Tommy Banks to make this a 'real little gem' of a property.

Rooms: 4 en suite 5 annexe en suite (6 GF) **S** fr £350 **D** fr £350* **Facilities:** FTV tea/coffee Dinner available WiFi **Extras:** Home-made biscuits, speciality toiletries **Parking:** 20 **Notes:** No children 18 years

The Coach House at Middleton Lodge

Kneeton Lane, Middleton Tyas, Richmond, North Yorkshire DL10 6NJ

Tel: 01325 377 977

Email: info@middletonlodge.co.uk **Web:** www.middletonlodge.co.uk

OSMOTHERLEY
Map 19 SE49

Premier Collection

The Cleveland Tontine

★★★★★ ⍟⍟ ⍨ RESTAURANT WITH ROOMS

tel: 01609 882671 **Staddlebridge DL6 3JB**
email: enquiries@provenanceinns.com **web:** www.theclevelandtontine.co.uk
dir: *Just off A172 junction on A19 northbound.*

This iconic destination restaurant with rooms is a stunning place. Contemporary public areas sit alongside a traditional restaurant with open fires, tiled flooring and great food. Afternoon tea can be taken in the conservatory overlooking the gardens. Bedrooms are individually designed, with modern furniture and feature bathrooms. The service is friendly and relaxed, there is ample parking and major road links are close by.

Rooms: 7 en suite (4 fmly) **Facilities:** FTV Lounge tea/coffee Dinner available Direct dial WiFi **Extras:** Speciality toiletries **Conf:** Max 70 Thtr 56 Class 28 Board 38 **Parking:** 60 **Notes:** Civ wed 56

PICKERING
Map 19 SE78

Premier Collection

17 Burgate

★★★★★ ⍨ GUEST ACCOMMODATION

tel: 01751 473463 **17 Burgate YO18 7AU**
email: info@17burgate.co.uk **web:** www.17burgate.co.uk
dir: *From A170 follow sign to Castle. 17 Burgate on right.*

An elegant house close to the centre of Pickering and the castle, 17 Burgate offers comfortable, individually designed bedrooms with all modern facilities, including free broadband, iPod docks, DVD/CD players and comfy sofas. Public areas include a restful lounge, and breakfast features a wide choice of local, healthy foods. The proprietors make every effort to maintain green and sustainable credentials.

Rooms: 3 en suite **S** fr £90 **D** fr £97* **Facilities:** FTV DVD iPod docking station Lounge tea/coffee WiFi **Extras:** Chocolate, snacks – chargeable **Conf:** Max 12 Thtr 12 Class 12 Board 12 **Parking:** 7 **Notes:** LB No children 10 years Closed 24 October to 15 March RS 15–29 December

Fox & Hounds Country Inn

★★★★ ⍟ INN

tel: 01751 431577 **Main Street, Sinnington YO62 6SQ**
email: fox.houndsinn@btconnect.com **web:** www.thefoxandhoundsinn.co.uk
dir: *3 miles west of Pickering. Off A170 between Pickering and Helmsley.*

An attractive village inn offering smart, well-equipped bedrooms. The public areas include a bar, a cosy lounge and a restaurant which offers an impressive range of well presented and well cooked dishes. Food here has been awarded an AA Rosette.

Rooms: 10 en suite (4 GF) **S** fr £59 **D** fr £80* **Facilities:** FTV Lounge tea/coffee Dinner available Direct dial WiFi **Parking:** 40 **Notes:** LB Closed 25–27 December

Black Swan Inn

★★★★ ⎙ INN

tel: 01751 798209 **18 Birdgate YO18 7AL**
email: office@blackswan.co.uk **web:** www.blackswan-pickering.co.uk
dir: *From Malton at roundabout in Pickering left onto A170. Follow brown signs for car park.*

The Black Swan Inn has a long-established history – it has been trading since 1729 and has welcomed famous visitors including Charles Dickens. The rolling refurbishment programme has achieved great results to date. Bedrooms differ in size but are well appointed for the modern guest. The bar boasts great real ales and a number come from their own brew house. High quality food is served including a wonderful breakfast to start the day. Open at weekends, Whistlers Cocktail Bar serves a wide array of cocktails together with a great collection of gins.

Rooms: 9 en suite (2 fmly) **S** fr £60 **D** fr £80* **Facilities:** FTV tea/coffee Dinner available WiFi ⅃ **Extras:** Bottled water – complimentary **Conf:** Max 30 Class 30 Board 20 **Parking:** 22

Grindale House

★★★★ ⒜ GUEST ACCOMMODATION

tel: 01751 476636 **123 Eastgate YO18 7DW**
email: info@grindalehouse.com **web:** www.grindalehouse.com
dir: *Phone for directions.*

Close to the North York Moors National Park and North Riding Forest Park, Grindale House is a charming stone building with self-catering cottages to the side and behind. The guest accommodation is comfortable and attractive and breakfasts are memorable – much of the produce has come from local farms and suppliers. There is also on-site parking, WiFi and a secure bike lock-up.

Rooms: 6 rms (5 en suite) (1 pri facs) 2 annexe en suite (1 fmly) (2 GF) **S** fr £70 **D** fr £90* **Facilities:** FTV Lounge tea/coffee WiFi **Parking:** 8 **Notes:** LB Closed mid December to March

REETH
Map 19 SE09

Arkleside Guesthouse Bed and Breakfast

★★★ GUEST HOUSE

tel: 01748 884200 **DL11 6SG**
email: enquiries@arklesidereeth.co.uk **web:** www.arklesidereeth.co.uk
dir: *From Richmond on A6108, right onto B6270 signed Reeth. In village bear right at village green.*

Arkleside is located in a quiet courtyard in the peaceful village of Reeth, with stunning views of Swaledale and Fremington Edge. Bedrooms are well appointed and nicely presented, and the high-quality breakfast uses produce from local butchers and farmers, creating a great start to the day. Reeth is an ideal base for touring the Dales, for walking or for cyclists who would like to replicate the 2014 Tour de France stage.

Rooms: 4 en suite **Facilities:** FTV tea/coffee Licensed WiFi **Parking:** 4

RICCALL
Map 16 SE63

White Rose Villa

★★★★ 🅐 BED AND BREAKFAST

tel: 01757 248115 **33 York Road YO19 6QG**
email: whiterosevilla@btinternet.com **web:** www.whiterosevilla.info
dir: *South of York, from A19, signed Riccall, 50 metres on right.*

Expect a warm and friendly welcome from Viv and Steve when visiting White Rose Villa. Conveniently located in the heart of the Yorkshire countryside, the popular village of Riccall is close to both York and Selby. All bedrooms are en suite and well equipped. There is a TV lounge to relax in, complete with a selection of DVDs, CDs, books and board games. Breakfast is served in the sunny dining room, and special diets are catered for by prior arrangement.

Rooms: 3 en suite (2 fmly) **S** fr £40 **D** fr £65* **Facilities:** FTV DVD TVL tea/coffee WiFi **Extras:** Speciality toiletries **Parking:** 4 **Notes:** LB Closed 24–26 and 31 December

RICHMOND
Map 19 NZ10

Whashton Springs Farm

★★★★ FARMHOUSE

tel: 01748 822884 **DL11 7JS**
email: thefarmhouse@whashtonsprings.co.uk **web:** www.whashtonsprings.co.uk
dir: *In Richmond north at lights towards Ravensworth, 3 miles down steep hill. Farm at bottom on left.*

A friendly welcome awaits at Whashton Springs Farm, situated in the heart of the countryside yet convenient for major routes. Bedrooms are split between the courtyard rooms and the main farmhouse. Traditional hearty breakfasts are served that include free range-eggs from the farm's own hens as well as ample amounts of home-made and local produce. The spacious dining room overlooks the beautiful gardens.

Rooms: 3 en suite 5 annexe en suite (2 fmly) (5 GF) **Facilities:** FTV tea/coffee WiFi **Conf:** Max 16 Board 16 **Parking:** 10 **Notes:** LB No children 3 years Closed late December to January 600 acres arable/beef/mixed/sheep

Black Lion

★★★ INN

tel: 01748 826217 **12 Finkle Street DL10 4QB**
email: info@blacklionhotelrichmond.co.uk **web:** www.blacklionhotelrichmond.co.uk
dir: *A1(M) take A1/A66. At roundabout take A6108 to Richmond.*

Situated in the historic market town of Richmond, the Black Lion is a traditional family-run inn which dates back to 1697. The bedrooms are well appointed and comfortable, and the public areas are full of original character and charm with a range of seating areas including a snug. Menus offer a good selection of pub classics. Breakfasts are served in the Shiraz restaurant which is also available to hire as a function room. On-site parking is available to the rear.

Rooms: 14 rms (13 en suite) (1 pri facs) (2 fmly) **Facilities:** FTV TVL tea/coffee Dinner available WiFi ⅃ 🔒 **Conf:** Max 30 Class 30 Board 30 **Parking:** 10

Farmers Arms

★★★ 🔲 INN

tel: 01748 818062 & 07966 984272 **Gatherley Road, Brompton-on-Swale DL10 7HZ**
email: info@farmersarmsyorkshire.com **web:** www.farmersarmsyorkshire.com
dir: *From A1(M) junction 51 take A6136.*

This cosy inn is situated in the small village of Brompton-on-Swale, near Richmond and has easy access to the A1(M). A warm welcome awaits at the Farmers Arms, a family-run inn full of original character and charm that dates back to 1700. The bedrooms are comfortable and well equipped with modern amenities such as large TVs and complimentary WiFi. Evening and lunch menus offer an interesting selection of modern dishes coupled with traditional home-cooked classics. Ample on-site parking is available.

Rooms: 4 en suite (1 fmly) **Facilities:** FTV tea/coffee Dinner available WiFi ⅃ 🔒 **Parking:** 40

RIPON
Map 19 SE37

Premier Collection

Mallard Grange

★★★★★ 🍽 FARMHOUSE

tel: 01765 620242 & 07720 295918 **Aldfield HG4 3BE**
email: maggie@mallardgrange.co.uk **web:** www.mallardgrange.co.uk
dir: *B6265 west from Ripon, Mallard Grange 2.5 miles on right.*

Located near Fountains Abbey, a genuine welcome is always guaranteed at Mallard Grange. The original features of this early 16th-century, Grade II listed farmhouse are highlighted by quality furnishings and decor. Bedrooms, two of which are in a converted smithy, are filled with a wealth of thoughtful extras, and comprehensive breakfasts feature home-reared and local produce.

Rooms: 2 en suite 2 annexe en suite (2 GF) **D** fr £90* **Facilities:** FTV Lounge tea/coffee WiFi **Extras:** Speciality toiletries, home-made biscuits **Parking:** 6 **Notes:** No children 12 years Closed Christmas and New Year 500 acres mixed/beef/sheep/arable

RIPON *continued*

The Old Coach House

★★★★★ ⓐ GUEST ACCOMMODATION

tel: 07912 632296 & 01765 634900 **2 Stable Cottages, North Stainley HG4 3HT**
email: enquiries@oldcoachhouse.info **web:** www.oldcoachhouse.info
dir: *From Ripon take A6108 to Masham. Once in North Stainley, on left opposite Staveley Arms.*

The Old Coach House has been part of the local community for over 20 years, so if you need information on the local area, don't hesitate to ask. This 18th-century building stands in the grounds of North Stainley Hall. All bedrooms are designed to a high specification and are individually decorated; each room is named after a famous Yorkshire landmark or place, and each offers a good range of facilities. All rooms are en suite and some have wet rooms.

Rooms: 8 en suite (4 GF) **S** fr £90 **D** fr £90* **Facilities:** FTV iPod docking station Lounge tea/coffee Direct dial WiFi ⓐ **Extras:** Speciality toiletries – complimentary **Parking:** 8 **Notes:** No children 14 years

St George's Court

★★★★ ⓐ FARMHOUSE

tel: 01765 620618 **Old Home Farm, Grantley HG4 3PJ**
email: info@stgeorgescourt.co.uk **web:** www.stgeorgescourt.co.uk
dir: *B6265 west from Ripon, up hill 1 mile past Risplith sign and next right, 1 mile on right.*

This renovated farmhouse is in a great location, in the delightful countryside close to Fountains Abbey. The attractive, well-equipped, ground-floor bedrooms are located around a central courtyard and provide modern accessories such as in-room fridges and TVs. Imaginative breakfasts are served in the breakfast room, and a guest lounge is available, both have views of the surrounding countryside.

Rooms: 4 en suite (1 fmly) (4 GF) **Facilities:** Lounge tea/coffee WiFi Fishing ⓐ **Conf:** Max 12 **Parking:** 12 **Notes:** LB 20 acres beef/sheep/pigs

RUNSWICK   Map 19 NZ81

The Firs

★★★★ ⓐ GUEST HOUSE

tel: 01947 840433 **26 Hinderwell Lane TS13 5HR**
email: info@the-firs.co.uk **web:** www.the-firs.co.uk
dir: *From Whitby on A174, turn right signed Runswick. At T-junction turn left, 150 yards on right.*

The Firs is a spacious, family-run property located in the picturesque village of Runswick on the stunning North Yorkshire coast. The house is just eight miles north of Whitby and is on the edge of the North York Moors National Park. Free private parking, complimentary WiFi and comfortable bedrooms are offered along with a friendly welcome. The ground-floor rooms are wheelchair accessible and have en suite wet rooms. Please note, credit cards may only be used for online transactions.

Rooms: 9 en suite (3 fmly) (6 GF) **Facilities:** FTV DVD iPod docking station Lounge tea/coffee Direct dial WiFi ⓐ **Extras:** Sweets, filtered water, home-made cake – complimentary **Parking:** 14 **Notes:** LB No children 2 years Closed November to March

SCARBOROUGH   Map 17 TA08

The Plough Scalby

★★★★★ ⓐ INN

tel: 01723 362622 **21–23 High Street, Scalby YO13 0PT**
email: info@theploughscalby.co.uk **web:** www.theploughscalby.co.uk
dir: *Phone for directions.*

A friendly inn situated in the quiet village of Scalby and within a short driving distance of the popular seaside town of Scarborough. The bedrooms are modern and very well appointed, some have four-poster beds. A range of modern accessories is provided such as fully-stocked honesty bars and complimentary WiFi. The bar and restaurant areas are comfortable and inviting. Award-winning, home-cooked meals can be enjoyed both at lunch and at dinner, and hearty Yorkshire breakfasts are served each morning. On-site parking is not provided but free on-street parking is available.

Rooms: 8 en suite (1 fmly) **S** fr £75 **D** fr £90* **Facilities:** STV FTV iPod docking station tea/coffee Dinner available Direct dial WiFi **Extras:** Nespresso machine, mini-bar, still water, fresh milk

Paragon

★★★★ GUEST ACCOMMODATION

tel: 01723 372676 **123 Queens Parade YO12 7HU**
email: lynnandmike@paragonhotel.com **web:** www.paragonhotel.com
dir: *On A64, follow signs for North Bay. Establishment on clifftop.*

This welcoming Victorian terraced house has been carefully renovated to provide stylish, thoughtfully equipped, non-smoking accommodation. Hearty English breakfasts are served in the attractive dining room and there is also a lounge bar with a fabulous sea view.

Rooms: 14 en suite (1 fmly) **S** fr £46 **D** fr £70* **Facilities:** FTV Lounge tea/coffee Licensed WiFi **Parking:** 6 **Notes:** LB No children 5 years Closed 20 November to 24 January

The Whiteley

★★★★ GUEST ACCOMMODATION

tel: 01723 373514 **99–101 Queens Parade YO12 7HY**
email: thewhiteley@gmail.com **web:** www.thewhiteley.co.uk
dir: *A64, A165 to North Bay and Peasholm Park, right into Peasholm Road, 1st left.*

The Whiteley is an immaculately run, sea-facing home-from-home. Bedrooms, though compact, are carefully decorated and have many thoughtful extras. There's a small garden at the rear and a choice of lounges. The establishment has superb views, and the owners provide personal attention and a substantial breakfast.

Rooms: 10 en suite (3 fmly) (1 GF) **S** fr £39.50 **D** fr £67* **Facilities:** Lounge TVL tea/coffee WiFi **Parking:** 8 **Notes:** LB No children 3 years Closed 30 November to January

The Albert

★★★ INN

tel: 01723 447260 **58 North Marine Road YO12 7PE**
email: alberthotel@btinternet.com **web:** www.thealbert-scarborough.co.uk
dir: *From rail station turn left onto Northway. Turn right at lights then straight on. At roundabout turn left, The Albert 100 yards on left.*

Located within a few minutes' walk of Scarborough's North Bay and the town centre, this newly-refurbished, traditional seaside pub offers a selection of locally sourced dishes as well as a wide selection of real ales. The en suite accommodation is comfortable and has a range of modern accessories such as TVs and complimentary WiFi.

Rooms: 3 en suite (2 fmly) **S** fr £55 **D** fr £75* **Facilities:** FTV tea/coffee Dinner available WiFi 🅿 **Extras:** Fruit tea **Parking:** 6 **Notes:** LB

North End Farm Country Guesthouse

★★★ GUEST ACCOMMODATION

tel: 01723 862965 **88 Main Street, Seamer YO12 4RF**
email: northendfarm@tiscali.co.uk **web:** www.northendfarmseamer.co.uk
dir: *A64 north onto B1261 through Seamer, next to roundabout.*

Located in Seamer, a village inland from Scarborough, this 18th-century property offers comfortable, well-equipped en suite bedrooms. Hearty breakfasts are served at individual tables in the smart dining room, and the cosy lounge has a large-screen TV.

Rooms: 3 en suite (1 fmly) **S** fr £45 **D** fr £75* **Facilities:** FTV TVL tea/coffee WiFi 🅿 **Parking:** 6

The Phoenix Guest House

★★★ GUEST HOUSE

tel: 01723 368319 & 07847 102337 **157 Columbus Ravine YO12 7QZ**
email: jnnlms@aol.co.uk **web:** www.phoenixscarborough.wordpress.com
dir: *From railway station at junction of A64 and A165, take A165 signed North Bay. On right, 100 metres from Peasholm Park.*

Located close to Peasholm Park and just a few minutes' walk from the North Bay, this friendly guest house offers smart, comfortable bedrooms. There is a cosy lounge where guests can relax, exchange books or play games at the card table. Complimentary WiFi is provided and packed lunches can also be purchased.

Rooms: 6 en suite (2 fmly) **S** fr £32 **D** fr £44* **Facilities:** FTV DVD TVL tea/coffee WiFi **Notes:** LB

The Sheridan

★★★ 🅰 GUEST ACCOMMODATION

tel: 01723 372094 **108 Columbus Ravine YO12 7QZ**
email: kim@thesheridan.co.uk **web:** www.thesheridanhotel.co.uk
dir: *From railway station left into Northway, over 2 mini roundabouts, establishment 300 yards on left.*

Set on an attractive, tree-lined road close to all North Bay attractions, and only a five-minute walk away from the beach, The Sheridan is a welcoming place to stay. At breakfast, try a full English – special diets are catered for. Traditional Yorkshire cuisine is available in the evening.

Rooms: 9 en suite (2 fmly) (1 GF) **S** fr £48 **D** fr £65* **Facilities:** FTV tea/coffee Dinner available WiFi **Parking:** 5 **Notes:** LB No children 5 years Closed November to January

---

SCOTCH CORNER Map 19 NZ20

The Vintage

★★ 🅰 INN

tel: 01748 824424 **DL10 6NP**
email: thevintagescotchcorner@btinternet.com
dir: *Exit A1 at Scotch Corner onto A66 towards Penrith, premises 200 yards on left.*

A warm welcome and attentive service awaits you at The Vintage, a family-run establishment. Bedrooms come in a variety of styles and sizes and all are well equipped. You can choose either a continental or a cooked breakfast, and a tempting selection of evening meals is available either in the bar or restaurant.

Rooms: 8 rms (5 en suite) **S** fr £35 **D** fr £50 (room only)* **Facilities:** FTV TVL tea/coffee Dinner available WiFi **Extras:** Snacks – complimentary **Conf:** Max 40 Thtr 40 Class 24 Board 20 **Parking:** 40 **Notes:** LB Closed Christmas and New Year

---

SEAMER Map 17 TA08

The Mayfield

★★★ GUEST ACCOMMODATION

tel: 01723 863160 **YO12 4RF**
email: info@themayfieldseamer.co.uk **web:** www.themayfieldseamer.co.uk
dir: *From Thirsk follow A170 to Seamer. From York follow A64 to Staxton roundabout, turn left. At next roundabout turn left into Seamer.*

The Mayfield is set in the quiet village of Seamer near the popular seaside resort of Scarborough. The stylish accommodation boasts many modern extras such as complimentary WiFi, wine fridges and iPod docking stations. The bar is child friendly and has a family room and large soft play area. Menus offer a wide selection of home-made pub classics as well as full carvery choices.

Rooms: 9 en suite 6 annexe en suite (1 fmly) (4 GF) **S** fr £55 **D** fr £70 (room only)* **Facilities:** STV FTV DVD iPod docking station tea/coffee Dinner available Direct dial Licensed WiFi **Extras:** Fridge, safe **Conf:** Max 70 Thtr 70 Class 48 Board 30 **Parking:** 24

SETTLE Map 18 SD86
See also Clapham

The Lion at Settle

★★★★ INN

tel: 01729 822203 **Duke Street BD24 9DU**
email: relax@thelionsettle.co.uk **web:** www.thelionsettle.co.uk
dir: *In town centre opposite Barclays Bank.*

Located in the heart of the market town of Settle, this is a traditional coaching inn with an inglenook fireplace. The accommodation is comfortable and well equipped. A wide selection of imaginative dishes, together with real ales and fine wines, is served in the busy bar, and also the restaurant where the atmosphere is relaxed and comfortable; alfresco dining is possible in the courtyard.

Rooms: 14 en suite (3 fmly) **Facilities:** FTV tea/coffee Dinner available WiFi 🅿 **Notes:** LB

SOUTH STAINLEY
Map 19 SE36

The Inn at South Stainley

★★★★ ⬣ INN

tel: 01423 779060 **HG3 3ND**
email: info@innatstainley.co.uk web: www.innatstainley.co.uk
dir: *Phone for directions.*

The ever-expanding Seafood Pub Company added this roadside Yorkshire inn to its operation in 2017. A complete refurbishment has resulted in a contemporary, luxurious bar and restaurant serving an eclectic pub menu with international scope and a focus on seafood; there's also a wide selection of ales. The smart bedrooms are situated either in the main building or in a lodge in the grounds; all are well equipped and comfortable.

Rooms: 4 en suite 8 annexe en suite **Facilities:** Dinner available

TADCASTER
Map 16 SE44

The Old Presbytery Guest House

★★★ BED AND BREAKFAST

tel: 01937 557708 **London Road, Saxton LS24 9PU**
email: guest@presbytery.plus.com web: www.presbyteryguesthouse.co.uk
dir: *4 miles south of Tadcaster on A162. 100 yards north of Barkston Ash on east side of road.*

Dating from the 18th century, this former dower house has been modernised to provide comfortable accommodation, while retaining many original features. The hall-lounge features a wood-burning stove, and delicious breakfasts are served at an old oak dining table in a cosy breakfast room. The beautiful gardens are a feature in their own right, with an attractive wooden bower providing sheltered outdoor seating space. Secure parking and complimentary WiFi are provided.

Rooms: 4 rms (3 en suite) (1 pri facs) (1 fmly) **S** fr £47 **D** fr £88* **Facilities:** FTV Lounge tea/coffee WiFi ⌖ ⬣ **Parking:** 6 **Notes:** Closed 21 December to 6 January

THIRSK
Map 19 SE48

Newsham Grange Farm Bed and Breakfast

★★★★ BED AND BREAKFAST

tel: 01845 588047 & 07808 903044 **Newsham Grange Farm YO7 4DF**
email: sue@newshamgrangefarm.co.uk web: www.newshamgrangefarm.co.uk
dir: *A1(M) junction with A61, follow signs to Thirsk for 4 miles. Left at roundabout onto A167, 3 miles on left.*

This impressive Georgian farmhouse is set in extensive grounds on the outskirts of Thirsk. It's family run and the friendly owners have appointed the property to a high standard. The four spacious bedrooms feature luxurious touches such as under-floor heating, and they can also be reconfigured to provide family rooms. The grounds are stunning with a decked terrace, outdoor swimming pool and hot tub adding to the idyllic setting overlooking the orchard. Secure parking with CCTV and lockable storage for bikes add to the range of facilities. Complimentary WiFi is also available.

Rooms: 2 en suite 2 annexe rms (2 pri facs) (2 fmly) (4 GF) **Facilities:** FTV tea/coffee Licensed WiFi ⌖ ⌖ Riding ⬣ Hot tub **Extras:** Bath robes, slippers **Parking:** 4 **Notes:** LB No children 7 years

TIMBLE
Map 19 SE15

Premier Collection

The Timble Inn

★★★★★ ◉◉ INN

tel: 01943 880530 **LS21 2NN**
email: info@thetimbleinn.co.uk web: www.thetimbleinn.co.uk
dir: *From A59, west of Harrogate, in Blubberhouses turn left signed Timble and Otley. Turn left signed Timble, continue to village.*

This is a hidden gem (apart from those already in the know of course) as it's off the beaten track near the spa town of Harrogate. This Grade II listed, quintessential Yorkshire village pub has been given a stunning makeover. Charming small spaces, low ceilings, lots of oak, open brickwork and log-burning stoves set the scene. Award-winning food is served in the stylish restaurant. The team here are very friendly, professional and knowledgeable.

Rooms: 5 en suite 4 annexe en suite (1 fmly) (2 GF) **Facilities:** FTV iPod docking station Lounge tea/coffee Dinner available WiFi **Extras:** Home-made biscuits, bottled water, robes, slippers – complimentary **Parking:** 15 **Notes:** LB No children 6 years Monday to Tuesday closed

WASS
Map 19 SE57

The Stapylton Arms

★★★★ GUEST ACCOMMODATION

tel: 01347 868280 **YO61 4BE**
email: info@stapyltonarms.co.uk web: www.stapyltonarms.co.uk
dir: *Phone for directions.*

This owner-run inn is situated within the heart of the peaceful North Yorkshire village of Wass. The accommodation is decorated in a contemporary country style with all the amenities expected by the modern guest. TVs, complimentary WiFi and well-stocked hospitality trays are all included. Dinner menus offer a good level of choice with the addition of daily-changing specials, and hearty breakfasts are also a highlight. On-site parking is provided.

Rooms: 3 en suite **S** fr £100 **D** fr £110* **Facilities:** FTV tea/coffee Dinner available Licensed WiFi **Extras:** Home-made biscuits, fresh milk – complimentary

WEST WITTON · Map 19 SE08

The Wensleydale Heifer

★★★★★ ◉ ≋ RESTAURANT WITH ROOMS

tel: 01969 622322 **Main Street DL8 4LS**
email: info@wensleydaleheifer.co.uk **web:** www.wensleydaleheifer.co.uk
dir: *A1 to Leeming Bar junction, A684 towards Bedale for approximately 10 miles to Leyburn, then towards Hawes 3.5 miles to West Witton.*

Describing itself as 'boutique style', this 17th-century former coaching inn is very much of the 21st century. The bedrooms, with Egyptian cotton linen and Molton Brown toiletries as standard, are each designed with an interesting theme – for example, Malt Whisky, Night at the Movies, James Bond and Shooters, and for chocolate lovers, there's a bedroom where you can eat as much chocolate as you like! The food is very much the focus here in both the informal fish bar and the contemporary restaurant. The kitchen prides itself on sourcing the freshest fish and locally reared meats.

Rooms: 9 en suite 4 annexe en suite (2 fmly) (2 GF) **S** fr £80 **D** fr £120*
Facilities: FTV DVD Lounge tea/coffee Dinner available Direct dial WiFi
Extras: Speciality toiletries, fruit, snacks **Parking:** 30 **Notes:** LB

WESTOW · Map 19 SE76

Woodhouse Farm

★★★★ ≋ FARMHOUSE

tel: 01653 618378 & 07904 293422 **YO60 7LL**
email: stay@wood-house-farm.co.uk **web:** www.wood-house-farm.co.uk
dir: *Exit A64 to Kirkham Priory and Westow. Right at T-junction, farm drive 0.5 mile out of village on right.*

The owners of this house are a young farming family who offer caring hospitality in their rural home. Bedrooms are spacious and there is a comfortable lounge also available for guests. Complimentary WiFi is provided. Home-made bread, preserves and farm produce turn breakfast into a feast, and the views from the house across open fields are splendid.

Rooms: 2 en suite (1 fmly) **S** fr £40 **D** fr £75* **Facilities:** FTV DVD iPod docking station TVL tea/coffee WiFi 🔒 **Extras:** Robes **Parking:** 12 **Notes:** LB Closed Christmas, New Year and mid March to mid April 500 acres arable/sheep/beef

WHITBY · Map 19 NZ81

Abbotsleigh of Whitby

★★★★ ≋ GUEST HOUSE

tel: 01947 606615 & 07866 880707 **5 Argyle Road YO21 3HS**
email: enquiries@abbotsleighofwhitby.co.uk **web:** www.abbotsleighofwhitby.co.uk
dir: *From train station onto Bagdale. At mini roundabout turn right onto Chubb Hill. At next roundabout take 2nd exit and right at next roundabout. Right into Argyle Road.*

Guests can be sure of friendly service at this immaculately presented Victorian house where tea and home-made cake are offered on arrival. The attractively furnished bedrooms and stylish en suite wet rooms have a luxurious feel. Thoughtful accessories such as coffee machines, iPod docking stations and DVD players are provided. Complimentary WiFi is also available.

Rooms: 5 en suite (1 GF) **S** fr £105 **D** fr £105 **Facilities:** STV DVD iPod docking station tea/coffee WiFi **Extras:** Speciality toiletries, home-made biscuits, milk **Parking:** 3 **Notes:** LB No children 12 years

Estbek House

★★★★ ◉◉ ≋ RESTAURANT WITH ROOMS

tel: 01947 893424 **East Row, Sandsend YO21 3SU**
email: info@estbekhouse.co.uk **web:** www.estbekhouse.co.uk
dir: *From Whitby take A174. In Sandsend, left into East Row.*

The speciality seafood restaurant on the first floor is the focus of this listed building in a small coastal village north-west of Whitby. The seasonal menu is based on fresh, local ingredients, and is overseen by Tim the chef, who has guided his team to two AA Rosettes. There is also a small bar and breakfast room, and four individually appointed bedrooms offering high levels of comfort.

Rooms: 4 rms (3 en suite) (1 pri facs) **Facilities:** tea/coffee Dinner available WiFi
Parking: 6 **Notes:** LB No children 14 years

Netherby House

★★★★ ≋ GUEST ACCOMMODATION

tel: 01947 810211 **90 Coach Road, Sleights YO22 5EQ**
email: info@netherby-house.co.uk **web:** www.netherby-house.co.uk
dir: *In village of Sleights, off A169 (Whitby to Pickering road).*

This fine Victorian house offers thoughtfully furnished, individually styled bedrooms together with delightful day rooms. There is a fine conservatory and the grounds are extensive, with exceptional views from the summer house at the bottom of the garden.

Rooms: 6 en suite 5 annexe en suite (1 fmly) (5 GF) **S** fr £45 **D** fr £90*
Facilities: FTV Lounge tea/coffee Licensed WiFi 🔒 **Parking:** 17
Notes: No children 2 years Closed 25–26 December

WHITBY *continued*

Overdale Guest House

★★★★ GUEST HOUSE

tel: 01947 605612 & 07763 339818 **39 Prospect Hill YO21 1QE**
email: jayneoates@hotmail.co.uk **web:** www.overdaleguesthouse.co.uk
dir: *A171 to Whitby, onto A174 signed Town Centre. Guest house on left.*

This fine Victorian terraced house has been appointed to offer guests four
charming, very well-appointed bedrooms. Built originally for a local sea captain,
the house is a short walk from the town centre and Whitby's lovely beaches. Free
WiFi is available throughout the house and parking is available. A warm welcome
is guaranteed, and breakfast is served at individual tables in the light-filled
breakfast room.

Rooms: 4 en suite (1 fmly) **D** fr £95* **Facilities:** FTV Lounge tea/coffee WiFi
⬧ **Parking:** 6 **Notes:** LB No children 12 years Closed 20–30 December

Whitehaven Guest House

★★★★ GUEST ACCOMMODATION

tel: 01947 601569 & 07748 374683 **29 Crescent Avenue YO21 3EW**
email: simon@whitehavenguesthouse.co.uk **web:** www.whitehavenguesthouse.co.uk
dir: *Follow signs to West Cliff, A174 into Crescent Avenue.*

A warm welcome awaits at this attractive, family-run Edwardian house. Occupying
a corner position close to the sports complex and indoor swimming pool,
Whitehaven Guest House is only a short walk from other local attractions. Bedrooms
are modern and co-ordinated with a contemporary twist, and all have TVs with
Freesat channel availability; DVD players are available on request. Freshly prepared
breakfasts are served in the elegant ground-floor dining room. Complimentary WiFi
is available throughout the building and there is free on-street parking.

Rooms: 4 rms (3 en suite) (1 pri facs) (1 fmly) **D** fr £80* **Facilities:** STV FTV DVD
tea/coffee WiFi ⬧ **Extras:** Speciality toiletries **Notes:** LB Closed 23–26 December

Argyle House

★★★★ GUEST ACCOMMODATION

tel: 01947 821877 **18 Hudson Street YO21 3EP**
email: bill@argyle-house.co.uk **web:** www.argyle-house.co.uk
dir: *Follow signs for West Cliff and Whitby Pavilion, with the sea on left, turn into
Royal Crescent and exit through the rear of crescent. Hudson Street is also known as
Abbey Terrace.*

Built originally in the 1850s and enjoying a prominent position in a conservation
area, Argyle House is a short walk from Whitby's town centre, harbour and beaches.
There is a range of comfortable, well-appointed bedrooms on offer. Guests are
guaranteed a warm welcome from the friendly owners, and delicious breakfasts are
served at individual tables in the light-filled breakfast room. Free WiFi is available
throughout.

Rooms: 7 en suite (2 fmly) **Facilities:** STV FTV DVD iPod docking station tea/coffee
WiFi **Extras:** Fruit **Notes:** LB No children 5 years

Boulmer Guest House

★★★★ GUEST HOUSE

tel: 01947 604284 **23 Crescent Avenue YO21 3ED**
email: info@boulmerguesthouse.co.uk **web:** www.boulmerguesthouse.co.uk
dir: *Follow signs for West Cliff, from Royal Crescent into Crescent Avenue, pass church on
right. Road bears to right, 3rd house on left before sorting office.*

This friendly guest house is just a short walk from the beautiful beach and Whitby
Pavilion on the picturesque West Cliff, and is also convenient for shops, cafés and
restaurants. The range of attractively presented bedrooms include family rooms, a
twin, a single, and with prior arrangement, dog-friendly bedrooms. Modern facilities
are provided including complimentary WiFi. Free on-street parking is available.

Rooms: 7 rms (5 en suite) (2 fmly) (1 GF) **S** fr £41 **D** fr £87.50* **Facilities:** FTV DVD
TVL tea/coffee WiFi ⬧ **Notes:** LB

YORK — Map 16 SE65

Premier Collection

The Judge's Lodging

★★★★★ ◉ INN

tel: 01904 638733 **9 Lendal YO1 8AQ**
email: relax@judgeslodgingyork.co.uk **web:** www.judgeslodgingyork.co.uk
dir: *Phone for directions.*

The Judge's Lodging is a Grade I listed Georgian townhouse situated in the heart
of the city centre, just a stone's throw from the Minster. The building has a
wealth of charm and character throughout the public spaces and in the smart,
well-equipped bedrooms. There is an atmospheric cellar bar with original
vaulted ceilings, the Cask Bar on the first floor and a superb 'glass box' where
you can dine inside yet still feel like you're sitting outside. The property also has
sun terraces for alfresco dining.

Rooms: 21 en suite **Facilities:** FTV tea/coffee Dinner available WiFi
Extras: Fresh milk

Ascot House

★★★★ GUEST ACCOMMODATION

tel: 01904 426826 **80 East Parade YO31 7YH**
email: admin@ascothouseyork.com **web:** www.ascothouseyork.com
dir: *0.5 mile northeast of city centre. Exit A1036 (Heworth Green) into Mill Lane, 2nd left.*

Ascot House is situated in a quiet part of the city away from the bustle of the tourist
hotspots but barely a 15-minute walk from York Minster. A Victorian house originally
built as a private residence, it has been lovingly restored to former glory. All
bedrooms have modern en suites and on the first floor, feature four-poster or
antique canopy beds and attractive period furniture, while those on the second floor
have a more contemporary style. The dining room offers a range of breakfast

options including traditional English, vegetarian and continental. The comfortable residents' lounge is the ideal place to enjoy a tea or coffee, or something stronger from the Butler's Pantry.

Ascot House

Rooms: 12 en suite (3 fmly) (2 GF) **S** fr £85 **D** fr £109 **Facilities:** FTV TVL tea/coffee Licensed WiFi 🛁 **Extras:** Bottled water, speciality toiletries **Parking:** 13 **Notes:** LB Closed 21–28 December

Burswood Guest House

★★★★ 🛏 GUEST HOUSE

tel: 01904 702582 **68 Tadcaster Road, Dringhouses YO24 1LR**
email: info@burswoodguesthouse.co.uk **web:** www.burswoodguesthouse.co.uk
dir: *On A1036 (Tadcaster Road).*

Located on the main Tadcaster Road just opposite York racecourse, this well-presented guest house offers very well-equipped bedrooms and bathrooms including some on the ground floor. Breakfast is taken in the comfortable dining room and is freshly cooked to order using good quality ingredients. Off-street parking is a welcome feature and a number of pubs and hotels are within easy walking distance for dinner.

Rooms: 6 en suite (1 fmly) (3 GF) **D** fr £90* **Facilities:** FTV tea/coffee WiFi 🛁 **Extras:** Fresh milk, robes, slippers **Parking:** 6 **Notes:** LB

Guy Fawkes Inn

★★★★ ⚜ INN

tel: 01904 623716 & 466674 **25 High Petergate YO1 7HP**
email: reservations@guyfawkesinnyork.com **web:** www.guyfawkesinnyork.com
dir: *A64 onto A1036 signed York and inner ring road. Over bridge into Duncombe Place, right into High Petergate.*

The Guy Fawkes Inn stands beside York Minster and was the birthplace of the notorious gunpowder plotter, Guido Fawkes. The inn offers stylish rooms furnished with antiques and Italian fabrics and with free WiFi and TVs; the bathrooms have luxury toiletries from Aromatherapy Associates. Many rooms have views of the city or the courtyard. Adding to the atmosphere of this medieval inn are the gas lights and the real log fires. Dine by candlelight in the restaurant which serves traditional food from locally-sourced ingredients. The bar stocks a wide range of real ales and a selection of fruit wines. The world-famous Guy Fawkes Ghost Walk starts every night from just around the corner.

Rooms: 13 en suite (1 fmly) (2 GF) **Facilities:** FTV tea/coffee Dinner available Direct dial WiFi **Extras:** Speciality toiletries – complimentary **Notes:** LB

The Heathers Guest House

★★★★ GUEST ACCOMMODATION

tel: 01904 640989 **54 Shipton Rd, Clifton-Without YO30 5RQ**
email: aabbg@heathers-guest-house.co.uk **web:** www.heathers-guest-house.co.uk
dir: *North of York on A19, halfway between A1237 ring road and York city centre.*

This spacious detached house offers off-street parking and a peaceful setting, only a short drive or walk from the city centre. Each room is individually designed, using quality fabrics. The light, airy breakfast room looks out onto the beautiful large rear garden, which is visited daily by local wildlife. Complimentary WiFi is provided.

Rooms: 4 en suite **D** fr £92 **Facilities:** FTV Lounge tea/coffee WiFi 🛁 **Parking:** 9 **Notes:** No children 12 years Closed Christmas and January

Holmwood House

★★★★ GUEST ACCOMMODATION

tel: 01904 626183 **112/114 Holgate Road YO24 4BB**
email: info@holmwoodhousehotel.co.uk **web:** www.holmwoodhousehotel.co.uk
dir: *Phone for directions.*

A 15-minute walk from Holmwood House takes you into the centre of York. The individually styled bedrooms are richly decorated and smartly furnished with many antiques. There is a comfortable lounge and a substantial breakfast is served in the pleasant basement dining room. Some private parking and complimentary WiFi are also available.

Rooms: 14 en suite 7 annexe en suite (1 fmly) (5 GF) **Facilities:** FTV Lounge tea/coffee WiFi 🛁 **Parking:** 8 **Notes:** LB Closed 24–27 December

YORK *continued*

Ashley Guest House

★★★★ ☕ GUEST HOUSE

tel: 01904 647520 & 07955 250271 **76 Scott Street YO23 1NS**
email: stay@ashleyguesthouse.co.uk **web:** www.ashleyguesthouse.co.uk
dir: *From A64 take York West exit onto A1036 (Tadcaster Road) follow city centre signs. After racecourse (on right) at 2nd lights right into Scarcroft Road. Scott Street 2nd last street before lights.*

Ashley Guest House is a Victorian end of terrace property modernised to create stylish interiors and a distinctive character. Attractively furnished bedrooms and caring hospitality are the hallmarks of this well-located city centre establishment.

Rooms: 5 en suite (1 fmly) **Facilities:** FTV Lounge tea/coffee WiFi
🔒 **Notes:** No children 5 years

City Guest House

★★★★ GUEST ACCOMMODATION

tel: 01904 622483 **68 Monkgate YO31 7PF**
email: info@cityguesthouse.co.uk **web:** www.cityguesthouse.co.uk
dir: *Northeast of city centre on B1036.*

Just a five-minute walk from York Minster and close to the city wall and other sights, this charming Victorian townhouse is well located for business, shopping and sightseeing. Carefully furnished bedrooms are attractively presented and offer a range of thoughtful touches. The traditional and beautifully presented dining room provides a pleasant venue for their hearty breakfasts.

Rooms: 7 rms (6 en suite) (1 pri facs) (1 fmly) (1 GF) **S** fr £46 **D** fr £70*
Facilities: FTV iPod docking station Lounge tea/coffee WiFi ⛷ 🔒 **Parking:** 2
Notes: No children 8 years Closed Christmas and January

Fifth Milestone Cottage

★★★★ GUEST HOUSE

tel: 01904 489361 & 07885 502420 **Hull Road YO19 5LR**
email: mrsmartyn@hotmail.com **web:** www.milestonecottage.co.uk
dir: *From A64 onto A1079 towards Hull. On left after Philip Welch Garage.*

As the name suggests, this spacious cottage is just five miles from York's centre. It is set in large, well-kept grounds with a large decking area where guests can relax in warmer weather. There is a wide range of bedrooms available from doubles, including a four-poster room, twins and a family room. Some rooms also have their own terrace and several offer very good disabled facilities and good access for wheelchair users. Private parking is provided.

Rooms: 3 en suite 3 annexe en suite (1 fmly) (3 GF) **S** fr £58 **D** fr £65 (room only)*
Facilities: FTV DVD tea/coffee WiFi 🔒 Animal farm **Extras:** Hot tub in one room
Parking: 12 **Notes:** RS 25–26 December room only

Lamb & Lion Inn

★★★★ ⊛ INN

tel: 01904 612078 & 654112 **2–4 High Petergate YO1 7EH**
email: reservations@lambandlioninnyork.com **web:** www.lambandlioninnyork.com
dir: *A64 onto A1036. 3.5 miles, at roundabout 3rd exit, continue on A1036. 2 miles, right into High Petergate.*

In the heart of York, just beyond the entrance of Bootham Bar, the Lamb & Lion Inn offers hearty food, real ales and luxurious bedrooms, some with spa baths. The bedrooms are beautifully decorated in earthy colours and all have en suite

bathrooms, free WiFi, and TV and tea- and coffee-making facilities. The restaurant serves authentic, rustic dishes, including a cooked Yorkshire breakfast. A wide range of real ales and lagers is available at the bar. York Minster is close by, while the National Railway Museum is a 15-minute walk, and Harrogate, a 40-minute drive.

Rooms: 12 en suite **S** fr £45 **D** fr £49* **Facilities:** FTV tea/coffee Dinner available WiFi **Conf:** Max 20 Thtr 20 Class 20 Board 20

Greenside

★★★ GUEST HOUSE

tel: 01904 623631 & 07944 665338 **124 Clifton YO30 6BQ**
email: greenside@onebillnet.co.uk **web:** www.greensideguesthouse.co.uk
dir: *A19 north towards city centre, over lights for Greenside, on left opposite Clifton Green.*

Overlooking Clifton Green, this charming detached conservation house is within walking distance of the city centre. Accommodation consists of comfortably furnished bedrooms and the traditional full English breakfast is served in the dining room. Secure parking and WiFi are additional bonuses.

Rooms: 6 rms (3 en suite) 2 annexe rms (2 fmly) (3 GF) **S** fr £35 **D** fr £68*
Facilities: FTV tea/coffee WiFi **Parking:** 6 **Notes:** LB Closed Christmas and New Year

SOUTH YORKSHIRE

DONCASTER
Map 16 SE50

Innkeeper's Lodge Doncaster, Bessacarr

★★★ INN

tel: 03451 551551 **Bawtry Road, Bessacarr DN4 7BS**
email: info@innkeeperslodge.com **web:** www.innkeeperslodge.com
dir: *Phone for directions.*

Comfortable, modern accommodation ideal for Doncaster Racecourse and also convenient for Doncaster Airport. There is a Toby Carvery offering a friendly pub atmosphere and roast dinners every day. There is also a pub menu, free WiFi throughout and Sky Sports is shown in the bar. Ample on-site parking is also available.

Rooms: 25 en suite (3 fmly) (6 GF) **Facilities:** FTV tea/coffee Dinner available Direct dial WiFi

SHEFFIELD
Map 16 SK38

Dog & Partridge

★★★★ ⊜ INN

tel: 01226 763173 **Bord Hill, Flouch S36 4HH**
email: info@dogandpartridgeinn.co.uk **web:** www.dogandpartridgeinn.co.uk
dir: *M1 junction 37 onto A628. At Flouch roundabout, straight over, follow signs for Manchester. 1 mile on left.*

This comfortable family-run inn is located within the Peak District National Park. Bedrooms are situated in the 18th-century barn adjoining the inn; all rooms are comfortably furnished and some superior rooms are available. The beer garden has stunning views of the surrounding moorland and a selection of real ales and imaginative food is served in the public areas.

Rooms: 10 en suite (2 fmly) (7 GF) **Facilities:** FTV tea/coffee Dinner available Direct dial WiFi 🔒 **Conf:** Max 50 Thtr 50 Class 36 Board 20 **Parking:** 70
Notes: Closed 25–27 December Civ wed 80

Innkeeper's Lodge Hathersage, Peak District

★★★ INN

tel: 03451 551551 **Hathersage Road, Longshaw S11 7TY**
email: info@innkeeperslodge.com **web:** www.innkeeperslodge.com
dir: *Phone for directions.*

Dating back to 1773, this Innkeeper's Lodge (The Fox House) has plenty of character and is located on a bend in Longshaw in the Peak District. Both Sheffield and Chesterfield are easily accessible. Each room, some with old beams and exposed brickwork, has a TV, desk, and tea- and coffee-making facilities as standard; family rooms are available. The wide-ranging menus feature something for everyone – the hearty pub favourites prove very popular.

Rooms: 9 en suite (6 fmly) (4 GF) **Facilities:** FTV tea/coffee Dinner available WiFi

WEST YORKSHIRE

HAWORTH   Map 19 SE03

The Old Registry Restaurant and Rooms

★★★★ ⌖ RESTAURANT WITH ROOMS

tel: 01535 646503 **2–6 Main Street BD22 8DA**
email: enquiries@theoldregistryhaworth.co.uk **web:** www.theoldregistryhaworth.co.uk
dir: *Phone for directions.*

A warm welcome is guaranteed at this owner-run establishment in a great location in the West Yorkshire village of Haworth. All rooms, some with four-poster beds, are individually designed and have modern accessories such as complimentary WiFi and TVs. Dinners can be enjoyed in the restaurant, and hearty, cooked breakfasts are provided each morning. On-site parking is not provided but permits are given to guests for a local car park which a short walk away.

Rooms: 8 en suite **S** fr £65 **D** fr £80* **Facilities:** STV FTV DVD Dinner available WiFi

Ashmount Country House

Ⓤ

tel: 01535 645726 **Mytholmes Lane BD22 8EZ**
email: info@ashmounthaworth.co.uk **web:** www.ashmounthaworth.co.uk
dir: *Phone for directions.*

Currently the rating for this establishment is not confirmed. This may be due to a change of ownership or because it has only recently joined the AA rating scheme.

Rooms: 12 en suite **D** fr £99* **Facilities:** tea/coffee Licensed WiFi
Notes: No children 11 years

HOLMFIRTH   Map 16 SE10

The Huntsman Inn

★★★★ INN

tel: 01484 850205 **Greenfield Road HD9 3XF**
email: huntsman@jwlees.co.uk **web:** www.the-huntsman-inn.com
dir: *Phone for directions.*

Only a short distance from the town, this very pleasant inn, owned by JW Lees, has a contemporary style which proves popular with diners, drinkers and residents alike. The individually designed, smart bedrooms come in a range of categories; all are generous in size and attractively appointed. Offered in the very comfortable bar and dining areas is an all-day menu with a great range of well-prepared dishes. There is an extensive outdoor area overlooking the rolling countryside for alfresco eating. Parking is plentiful and easily accessed.

Rooms: 15 en suite (5 fmly) (2 GF) **Facilities:** FTV tea/coffee Dinner available WiFi
Conf: Max 150 Thtr 150 Class 80 Board 40 **Parking:** 60 **Notes:** LB Civ wed 120

Old Bridge Inn & Coffee House

★★★★ INN

tel: 01484 681212 **Market Walk HD9 7DA**
email: oldbridge@innmail.co.uk **web:** www.oldbridgeholmfirth.co.uk
dir: *Phone for directions.*

The Old Bridge Inn & Coffee House is a modern inn in the centre of the popular town of Holmfirth. The bedrooms are more traditional in design and offer good levels of comfort. Cocktails and drinks can be enjoyed in the stylish bar before dinner in the cosy restaurant with its open fire; menus offer an interesting choice of dishes. Home-made cakes can also be enjoyed throughout the day in the coffee shop and bar area. A large car park is provided to all residents, which is certainly an asset.

Rooms: 21 en suite **Facilities:** STV tea/coffee Dinner available WiFi

Rooms at the Nook

★★★★ GUEST ACCOMMODATION

tel: 01484 682373 & 07841 646308 **Victoria Square HD9 2DN**
email: office@thenookbrewhouse.co.uk **web:** www.roomsatthenook.co.uk
dir: *From A6024 in Holmfirth. On A635 (Victoria Street), at bottom of Victoria Street.*

A warm welcome is assured at this centrally-located, 18th-century former inn which offers eight stylish bedrooms. The Nook pub retains many original features and benefits from an on-site microbrewery serving award-winning ales and a good wine selection. An adjacent bar and restaurant, known as The Tap House, specialises in tapas with a Yorkshire twist.

Rooms: 8 en suite (3 fmly) **Facilities:** FTV DVD TVL tea/coffee Dinner available Licensed WiFi ⌖ ⌖

HUDDERSFIELD   Map 16 SE11

Premier Collection

315 Bar and Restaurant

★★★★★ ⌖⌖ RESTAURANT WITH ROOMS

tel: 01484 602613 **315 Wakefield Road, Lepton HD8 0LX**
email: info@315barandrestaurant.co.uk **web:** www.315barandrestaurant.co.uk
dir: *M1 junction 38, A637 towards Huddersfield. At roundabout take A642 towards Huddersfield. Establishment on right in Lepton.*

In a wonderful setting, 315 Bar and Restaurant benefits from countryside views from the well-appointed dining room and conservatory areas. The interior is modern, with open fires that add character and ambiance, while the chef's table gives a real insight into the working of the two AA Rosette, award-winning kitchen. Bedrooms are modern, and most have feature bathrooms; some have air conditioning. Staff are friendly and attentive, and there are excellent parking facilities. There is a fantastic spa facility; treatments and use of the facilities is at an extra charge.

Rooms: 10 en suite 8 annexe en suite (3 fmly) (8 GF) **S** fr £85 **D** fr £95*
Facilities: FTV DVD tea/coffee Dinner available Lift WiFi Sauna **Conf:** Max 150 Thtr 100 Class 75 Board 60 **Parking:** 97 **Notes:** Civ wed 120

HUDDERSFIELD *continued*

Premier Collection

Woodman Inn

★★★★★ ⌐ INN

tel: 01484 605778 **Thunder Bridge Lane HD8 0PX**
email: info@woodman-inn.com web: www.woodman-inn.com

(For full entry see Kirkburton)

Innkeeper's Lodge Huddersfield, Kirkburton

★★★ INN

tel: 03451 551551 **36a Penistone Road, Kirkburton HD8 0PQ**
email: info@innkeeperslodge.com web: www.innkeeperslodge.com
dir: *Phone for directions.*

Situated on Penistone Road beside Foxglove Vintage Inn, this lodge is within easy reach of the National Coal Mining Museum and Huddersfield town centre. Providing modern bedrooms, it is an attractive 19th-century building with real fires and spacious dining areas. A continental buffet breakfast is complimentary for all guests – a cooked option is available at a supplement. Free WiFi is available throughout plus there's ample parking space.

Rooms: 23 en suite (3 fmly) (13 GF) **Facilities:** FTV tea/coffee Dinner available WiFi

Manor House Lindley

[U]

tel: 01484 504000 **1 Lidget Street, Lindley HD3 3JB**
email: hello@manorhouselindley.co.uk web: www.manorhouselindley.co.uk
dir: *Phone for directions.*

Currently the rating for this establishment is not confirmed. This may be due to a change of ownership or because it has only recently joined the AA rating scheme.

Rooms: 11 en suite (1 fmly) (2 GF) **S** fr £119 **D** fr £119* **Facilities:** FTV iPod docking station Lounge TVL tea/coffee Dinner available Direct dial Licensed WiFi Gym ⌂ Studio – personal training, yoga, pilates **Extras:** Mini-bar, safe, robes, slippers, Nespresso machine **Conf:** Max 150 Thtr 150 Class 100 Board 60 **Parking:** 60 **Notes:** LB No children 12 years Civ wed 150

Innkeeper's Lodge Ilkley

★★★ INN

tel: 03451 551551 **Hangingstone Road LS29 8BT**
email: info@innkeeperslodge.com web: www.innkeeperslodge.com
dir: *Phone for directions.*

This Innkeeper's Lodge, The Cow & Calf, is a Victorian property idyllically located in the Yorkshire Dales and has stunning views over Wharfedale. It makes a great base for walkers and for browsing the spa town of Ilkley; it's close to Ben Rhydding golf course and only a short drive from Leeds and Bradford. There is lots of period charm in the inviting public areas where hearty food and cask ales are served. The modern en suite bedrooms have TVs, desks, free WiFi, tea- and coffee-making facilities as standard; family rooms are available. Free parking, a beer garden and a meeting room are provided.

Rooms: 14 en suite (2 fmly) **Facilities:** FTV tea/coffee Dinner available WiFi

Premier Collection

Woodman Inn

★★★★★ ⌐ INN

tel: 01484 605778 **Thunder Bridge Lane HD8 0PX**
email: info@woodman-inn.com web: www.woodman-inn.com
dir: *1 mile southwest of Kirkburton. From A629 into Thunder Bridge Lane.*

The Woodman Inn is extremely popular with locals. The busy bar offers a wide range selection of ales, including Small World Beers brewed only one mile away. Bedrooms are comfortable and comprehensively furnished, making this an ideal place for walking, visiting the Yorkshire Dales, or simply escaping to the country. Weddings and functions are also well catered for.

Rooms: 13 en suite 6 annexe en suite (3 fmly) (6 GF) **Facilities:** FTV Lounge tea/coffee Dinner available Direct dial WiFi ⌂ **Extras:** Speciality toiletries **Conf:** Max 60 Thtr 50 Class 60 Board 30 **Parking:** 60 **Notes:** Civ wed 80

Hinsley Hall

★★★ GUEST ACCOMMODATION

tel: 0113 261 8000 **62 Headingley Lane LS6 2BX**
email: info@hinsley-hall.co.uk web: www.hinsley-hall.co.uk
dir: *On A660 (Leeds to Skipton road), past university and Hyde Park lights. Turn right into Oakfield.*

Set in extensive landscaped gardens, Hinsley Hall enjoys a peaceful setting just a short drive from Leeds city centre and the nearby university. Bedrooms are comfortable, well equipped and well appointed. A lounge is available for guests along with a small bar area. There are large conferencing facilities on site along with a number of meeting rooms. Headingley Stadium is a 10-minute walk away.

Rooms: 50 rms (47 en suite) (3 pri facs) (1 fmly) (4 GF) **S** fr £49.95 **D** fr £65* **Facilities:** FTV Lounge TVL tea/coffee Dinner available Lift Licensed WiFi 🔒 **Conf:** Max 90 Thtr 90 Class 50 Board 36 **Parking:** 100 **Notes:** Closed 24 December to 2 January

Innkeeper's Lodge Leeds Calverley

★★★ INN

tel: 03451 551551 **Calverley Lane, Pudsey LS28 5QQ**
email: info@innkeeperslodge.com **web:** www.innkeeperslodge.com
dir: *Phone for directions.*

The Calverley Arms is a striking Victorian lodge that's peacefully located in the picturesque village of Calverley, yet very convenient for Bradford and Leeds; it's only six miles from Leeds Bradford International Airport. The spacious bar and dining areas are comfortable, with cask ales and a wide choice of food offered. The en suite, modern bedrooms come in different shapes and sizes and have TVs, desks, free WiFi, tea- and coffee-making facilities as standard; family rooms are available. There is a large garden with outside seating.

Rooms: 14 en suite (5 fmly) **Facilities:** FTV tea/coffee Dinner available WiFi

LINTON   Map 16 SE34

The Windmill Inn

★★★★ 🌸 INN

tel: 01937 582209 **Main Street LS22 4HT**
email: enquiries@thewindmillinnlinton.co.uk **web:** www.thewindmillinnlinton.co.uk
dir: *A1(M) junction 45, then 2nd exit at Moore Grange roundabout. Left on A58, right onto A659. Right into Linton Lane, follow road into Main Street.*

The Windmill is a beautiful, traditional country inn tucked away in a charming village. Food is locally sourced and the two bedrooms are in converted outbuildings just across the car park. They are spacious suites with lounge areas, WiFi, TVs and modern bathrooms. There is ample parking and an award-winning beer garden. Families are very welcome.

Rooms: 2 annexe en suite (1 GF) **D** fr £95* **Facilities:** FTV DVD Lounge TVL tea/coffee Dinner available WiFi 🛁 Access to Wood Hall spa and swimming pool **Parking:** 48 **Notes:** Closed 1 January Civ wed 80

MIRFIELD   Map 16 SE21

Mirfield Monastery B&B

★★ GUEST ACCOMMODATION

tel: 01924 483346 & 494318 **Stocks Bank Road WF14 0BN**
email: enquiries@mirfield.org.uk **web:** www.mirfield.org.uk/bed-breakfast/
dir: *M62 junction 25 towards Mirfield. At roundabout, fork left onto A62 (Leeds). 1st right at lights, 0.5 mile.*

This quiet haven is set within the walls of Mirfield Monastery in beautiful gardens tended by the resident monks. Bedrooms are modestly appointed and decorated in calming neutral tones. A continental breakfast is provided on a self-service basis. The emphasis is on peace and quiet, with guests welcome to attend services if they wish. WiFi is available.

Rooms: 8 en suite **S** fr £45 **D** fr £55* **Facilities:** FTV Lounge tea/coffee Licensed WiFi **Conf:** Max 70 Thtr 70 Class 40 Board 25 **Parking:** 10 **Notes:** No children 5 years

NORMANTON   Map 16 SE32

The Grange

★★★★ BED AND BREAKFAST

tel: 01924 892203 & 07970 505157 **2 Snydale Road WF6 1NT**
email: enquiries@thegrangenormanton.co.uk **web:** www.thegrange-normanton.co.uk
dir: *Phone for directions.*

The house has been in Sarah's family for over 100 years and is a well maintained property with gardens that were designed by Chelsea Flower Show winner, Peter Garnett-Orme. The individually styled bedrooms are well appointed and have many thoughtful extras. Guests have use of the lounge with a large-screen TV. Full English breakfasts are served in the dining room.

Rooms: 3 rms (2 en suite) (1 pri facs) (1 fmly) **S** fr £50 **D** fr £70* **Facilities:** FTV TVL tea/coffee Dinner available WiFi 🔒 **Extras:** Fruit juice, bottled water **Parking:** 4 **Notes:** LB No children 2 years

CHANNEL ISLANDS

JERSEY

BEAUMONT   Map 24

Cheffins at the Beaumont Inn

Ⓤ

tel: 01534 722477 **La Route de la Haule JE3 7BA**
email: info@cheffinsbeaumont.com **web:** www.cheffinsbeaumont.com
dir: *Phone for directions.*

Currently the rating for this establishment is not confirmed. This may be due to a change of ownership or because it has only recently joined the AA rating scheme.

Rooms: 5 en suite **D** fr £140 (room only)*

ST AUBIN   Map 24

Premier Collection

The Panorama

★★★★★ 🌸 GUEST ACCOMMODATION

tel: 01534 742429 & 07797 742429 **La Rue du Crocquet JE3 8BZ**
email: info@panoramajersey.com **web:** www.panoramajersey.com
dir: *In village centre.*

Enjoying spectacular views across St Aubin's Bay, The Panorama is a long-established favourite with visitors. The welcome is genuine and many of the well-equipped bedrooms have wonderful views; the bathrooms are finished to a high standard. Public areas also look seaward and have attractive antique fireplaces. Breakfast is excellent and served in two dining areas.

Rooms: 14 en suite (3 GF) **S** fr £50 **D** fr £100* **Facilities:** STV Lounge tea/coffee WiFi 🔒 **Extras:** Robes, slippers, fridge **Notes:** No children 18 years Closed mid October to mid April

Scotland

ABERDEENSHIRE

ABOYNE
Map 23 NO59

The Lodge on the Loch of Aboyne
★★★★ ⬡ GUEST ACCOMMODATION

tel: 013398 86444 **Aboyne Loch Golf Centre AB34 5BR**
email: info@thelodgeontheloch.com web: www.thelodgeontheloch.com
dir: *1 mile east of Aboyne on A93.*

The beautiful location of this lochside property ensures stunning views and a peaceful stay. The wide range of facilities includes a nine-hole golf centre with driving range, osprey viewing deck, fitness centre and a wide choice of treatments offered in the Reflect Spa. Dining options include the restaurant and the bistro bar, with very good function and wedding facilities also available.

Rooms: 14 en suite (2 fmly) (7 GF) **S** fr £90 **D** fr £100 **Facilities:** FTV tea/coffee Dinner available Direct dial Licensed WiFi ⬡ Sauna ⬡ Hot tub, holistic spa treatments **Conf:** Max 80 Thtr 80 Class 40 Board 25 **Parking:** 30 **Notes:** LB Civ wed 120

BALLATER
Map 23 NO39

Deeside Inn
★★★★ INN

tel: 01339 755413 **13–15 Victoria Road AB35 5RA**
email: deeside@crerarhotels.com web: www.crerarhotels.com/the-deeside-inn
dir: *On A93 (Braemar Road).*

Located in the Royal Deeside village of Ballater, in the heart of the Grampian Highlands, Deeside Inn is a great base from which to explore the area. Relax in the stylish bar or public lounge with its large open fires. Comfortable accommodation is provided in the spacious bedrooms.

Rooms: 25 en suite (2 fmly) **Facilities:** STV FTV tea/coffee Dinner available Direct dial WiFi

ELLON
Map 23 NU93

Premier Collection

Aikenshill House
★★★★★ FARMHOUSE

tel: 01358 742990 **Aikenshill, Foveran AB41 6AT**
email: enquiries@aikenshill.co.uk web: www.aikenshill.co.uk
dir: *From Aberdeen north on A90, pass Cock and Bull restaurant and Trump International Golf Links. Turn left signed Aikenshill, 500 metres at end of road.*

This farmhouse enjoys spectacular views from its elevated position overlooking the Trump International Golf Links and the Aberdeenshire coastline beyond. Located close to Aberdeen, the house is well situated for either a peaceful getaway or a city break. Decorated and furnished to an impressive standard, the atmosphere of the modern property is complemented by friendly hospitality from the whole family. Memorable breakfasts include the best ingredients, and dinners by request are also available.

Rooms: 4 en suite **Facilities:** FTV TVL Dinner available WiFi ⬡ ⬡ **Notes:** 300 acres arable

KILDRUMMY
Map 23 NJ41

Kildrummy Inn
★★★★ ⬡⬡ ⬡ INN

tel: 01975 571227 **AB33 8QS**
email: enquiries@kildrummyinn.co.uk web: www.kildrummyinn.co.uk
dir: *On A97, 2 miles from junction with A944 at Mossat in direction of Strathdon and Cairngorms National Park.*

Located in the heart of rural Aberdeenshire, this popular inn is the perfect base for touring the Grampian Mountains and beyond. Personally run and with a unique history, Kildrummy Inn provides four comfortable bedrooms – all are en suite and feature TVs, DVD players and free WiFi. The lounge bar, with a roaring fire and a good selection of beers and whiskies, is a great place in which to while away the time. No visit would be complete without sampling the food on offer, with skilfully created dishes highlighting the best local produce.

Rooms: 4 en suite **D** fr £69 **Facilities:** FTV DVD Lounge tea/coffee Dinner available WiFi Fishing ⬡ **Extras:** Speciality toiletries **Conf:** Max 12 Board 12 **Parking:** 20 **Notes:** Closed January RS Tuesday bar and restaurant closed Civ wed 70

STONEHAVEN
Map 23 NO88

The Ship Inn
★★★ INN

tel: 01569 762617 **5 Shorehead AB39 2JY**
email: enquiries@shipinnstonehaven.com web: www.shipinnstonehaven.com
dir: *From A90 follow signs to Stonehaven, then signs to harbour.*

This popular inn overlooks the harbour in Stonehaven and has been a fixture since 1771. Bedrooms and bathrooms offer good levels of comfort; many have views of the harbour. The Lounge Bar serves a host of whiskies and real ales, while the Captain's Table restaurant specialises in fresh local fish and some spectacular meats. Close to Aberdeen and the A90, the property is in an excellent location for those looking for peace and tranquillity.

Rooms: 11 en suite (2 fmly) **S** fr £80 **D** fr £110* **Facilities:** FTV tea/coffee Dinner available WiFi

TARLAND
Map 23 NJ40

The Commercial
★★★★ INN

tel: 01339 881922 **The Square AB34 4TX**
email: info@thecommercial-hotel.co.uk web: www.thecommerical-hotel.co.uk
dir: *From Aboyne on A93 follow signs for Tarland. In village turn left into The Square, on right by monument.*

This property benefits from a stunning location in the heart of Royal Deeside in the 'Howe O' Cromar'. Near to Aberdeen, the Grampian Mountains and the Cairngorm National Park, The Commercial is ideally located, family-run and offers comfortable accommodation and a range of dining options, including the cosy lounge bar and the more formal Cromar Restaurant.

Rooms: 9 en suite **S** fr £60 **D** fr £90* **Facilities:** FTV DVD iPod docking station Lounge tea/coffee Dinner available WiFi ⬡ **Extras:** Bottled water – complimentary **Parking:** 17 **Notes:** LB

ANGUS

INVERKEILOR
Map 23 NO64

Premier Collection

Gordon's

★★★★★ ⊚⊚⊚ ☕ RESTAURANT WITH ROOMS

tel: 01241 830364 **Main Road DD11 5RN**
email: gordonsrest@aol.com **web:** www.gordonsrestaurant.co.uk
dir: *Exit A92 between Arbroath and Montrose into Inverkeilor.*

It's worth a detour off the main road to this family-run restaurant with rooms set in the centre of the village. The food in the restaurant has been awarded three AA Rosettes, and the excellent breakfasts are equally memorable. A huge fire dominates the restaurant on cooler evenings. Individually designed rooms all come with contemporary Wenge furniture, oversized headboards, chandeliers, decorative cornicing and designer wallpaper. The showcase Thistle Suite is in purple, stone and lavender and has an en suite bathroom with roll-top bath and monsoon shower.

Rooms: 4 en suite 1 annexe en suite (1 GF) **S** fr £110 **D** fr £110* **Facilities:** tea/coffee Dinner available WiFi 🛁 **Extras:** Speciality toiletries – complimentary **Parking:** 6 **Notes:** No children 12 years Closed January

MONTROSE
Map 23 NO75

Oaklands Guest House

★★★ GUEST HOUSE

tel: 01674 672018 **10 Rossie Island Road DD10 9NN**
email: guest.house@oaklandsmontrose.com **web:** www.oaklandsmontrose.com
dir: *On A92 at south end of town.*

A genuine welcome and attentive service are assured at the dog-friendly Oaklands Guest House, a smart, detached house situated on the south side of the town. Bedrooms come in a variety of sizes and are neatly presented. There is a light and airy dining room where hearty breakfasts are served – quality produce is paramount.

Rooms: 7 en suite (1 fmly) (1 GF) **S** fr £40 **D** fr £80* **Facilities:** FTV tea/coffee WiFi 🛁 **Parking:** 5

ARGYLL & BUTE

BARCALDINE
Map 20 NM94

Premier Collection

Ardtorna

★★★★★ ☕ BED AND BREAKFAST

tel: 01631 720125 & 07867 785524 **Mill Farm PA37 1SE**
email: info@ardtorna.co.uk **web:** www.ardtorna.co.uk
dir: *North from Connel on A828, 0.5 mile from Scottish Sea Life Sanctuary.*

Purpose-built as a luxury bed and breakfast, eco-friendly Ardtorna enjoys a commanding position overlooking the Firth of Lorn near Oban. Warm hospitality can always be found here. Floor-to-ceiling windows in the bedrooms let you watch the glorious sunsets in comfort, and the excellent king-size beds will provide a great night's sleep. Bathrooms have luxury toiletries and huge towels. Breakfast will leave you spoilt for choice. 'Butler', 'romantic' and golf, spa and archery packages are available.

Rooms: 4 en suite (4 GF) **Facilities:** FTV DVD iPod docking station tea/coffee WiFi 🛁 🎿 🛁 Leisure facilities available at nearby hotel **Extras:** Fresh fruit, flowers, malt whisky, Baileys **Parking:** 10 **Notes:** LB No children 12 years

CAIRNDOW
Map 20 NN11

Cairndow Stagecoach Inn

★★★ INN

tel: 01499 600286 & 600252 **PA26 8BN**
email: enq@cairndowinn.com **web:** www.cairndowinn.com
dir: *From north take either A82 to Tarbet, A83 to Cairndow, or A85 to Dalmally, A819 to Inveraray and A83 to Cairndow.*

A relaxed, friendly atmosphere prevails at the 18th-century Cairndow Stagecoach Inn overlooking the beautiful Loch Fyne. Bedrooms offer individual decor and thoughtful extras. Traditional public areas include a comfortable beamed lounge, a well-stocked bar where food is served all day, and a spacious restaurant with conservatory extension. Deluxe bedrooms offer more space and luxury.

Rooms: 13 en suite 5 annexe en suite (2 fmly) (5 GF) **Facilities:** STV FTV Lounge tea/coffee Dinner available Direct dial WiFi 🎿 Sauna 🛁 **Conf:** Max 30 Thtr 30 Class 30 Board 30 **Parking:** 30 **Notes:** LB

LOCHGOILHEAD   Map 20 NN10

Premier Collection

The Lodge on Loch Goil

★★★★★ ⊚⊚ ☃ RESTAURANT WITH ROOMS

tel: 01301 703193 **Loch Goil PA24 8AE**
email: dining@thelodge-scotland.com **web:** www.thelodge-scotland.com
dir: *Phone for directions.*

Very accessible from nearby main routes (and by boat), though tucked away near
the head of a sea loch, this peaceful retreat is now a restaurant with rooms. The
lodge is superbly appointed, and its restoration has been a labour of love for the
current owners. In addition to the seven luxury rooms in the main house, there's
the summerhouse right on the loch's edge from where guests can also relax and
enjoy the spectacular scenery. Food is taken seriously here, with imaginative,
award-winning cuisine served at dinner plus superb breakfasts each morning.
Hospitality is generously given, ensuring the warmest of Scottish welcomes.

Rooms: 7 en suite **S** fr £225 **D** fr £250* **Facilities:** Dinner available

LUSS   Map 20 NS39

The Inn on Loch Lomond

★★★★ ⊖ INN

tel: 01436 860678 **Inverbeg G83 8PD**
email: res@innonlochlomond.co.uk **web:** www.innonlochlomond.co.uk
dir: *On A82, north of Balloch.*

Dating back to the 18th century, this inn offers very stylish, comfortable en suite
bedrooms (many with stunning views), and equally attractive public areas that
boast open fires and cow-hide sofas. Food is as much of a feature as the property
itself, with a varied menu offered. The inn has its own chip shop fryer which proves
very popular. The Beach House accommodation, just a short walk from the inn, is a
real treat for those looking for a little more privacy.

Rooms: 25 en suite 8 annexe en suite (1 fmly) (6 GF) **Facilities:** TVL tea/coffee
Dinner available WiFi ☖ **Parking:** 60 **Notes:** LB Civ wed 60

OBAN   Map 20 NM82

Premier Collection

Blarcreen House

★★★★★ GUEST HOUSE

tel: 01631 750272 & 07557 977225 **Ardchattan, Connel PA37 1RG**
email: info@blarcreenhouse.com **web:** www.blarcreenhouse.com
dir: *North over Connel Bridge, turn right signed Bonawe, 6.7 miles to Blarcreen.*

This elegant Victorian mansion house on the side of Loch Etive is the ideal base
for exploring the Highlands. Warm hospitality and log fires await guests arriving
at this property, where they can relax and enjoy comfortable bedrooms and
fantastic views. Evening meals are also available by prior arrangement.

Rooms: 3 en suite **D** fr £120 **Facilities:** FTV DVD iPod docking station TVL tea/
coffee Dinner available Licensed WiFi ☖ **Extras:** Speciality toiletries, chocolates
– complimentary **Parking:** 5 **Notes:** No children 16 years Closed December to
January

MacKay's Guest House

★★★★ ☃ GUEST HOUSE

tel: 01631 563121 & 566356 **Corran Esplanade PA34 5AQ**
email: info@mackaysguesthouse.co.uk **web:** www.mackaysguesthouse.co.uk
dir: *A85 into town, at roundabout 2nd exit to seafront (Corran Esplanade). Pass
Cathedral, 300 yards on right.*

Boasting fantastic views across Oban Bay, this property offers comfort and quality
as well as warm traditional hospitality. All the bedrooms are front-facing and are
spacious and very well appointed. Award-winning breakfasts are served in the
bright conservatory and breakfast room. Dedicated off-road parking and outdoor
seating overlooking the bay add to this wonderful guest experience.

Rooms: 8 en suite (2 GF) **Facilities:** FTV DVD iPod docking station tea/coffee WiFi
Extras: Robes, snacks, water, sherry – complimentary **Parking:** 10
Notes: No children 15 years Closed 13 November to 21 March

Barriemore Guest House

★★★★ GUEST HOUSE

tel: 01631 566356 **Corran Esplanade PA34 5AQ**
email: info@barriemore.co.uk **web:** www.barriemore.co.uk
dir: *A85 into Oban, 1st roundabout exit towards sea. Right at 2nd roundabout, continue
with sea on left, last guest house on right.*

This splendid three-storey Victorian townhouse is in a fantastic location on Oban's
seafront and enjoys great views over Oban Bay. Friendly service and spacious rooms
with modern decor are offered at this family-run property. A hearty Scottish
breakfast will set guests up for the day ahead.

Rooms: 15 en suite (2 fmly) (2 GF) **Facilities:** FTV DVD iPod docking station Lounge
tea/coffee WiFi **Extras:** Fruit, bottled water, sherry, robes, slippers, speciality
toiletries **Parking:** 14 **Notes:** Closed November to April

Glenrigh Guest House

★★★★ GUEST HOUSE

tel: 01631 562991 **Corran Esplanade PA34 5AQ**
email: info@glenrigh.co.uk **web:** www.glenrigh.co.uk
dir: *Down hill into Oban, turn right (with sea on left), along esplanade.*

This former Victorian mansion has fantastic views of Oban Bay and the islands, and has the added bonus of on-site parking. Close to the heart of Oban town centre, it is also within walking distance of local amenities. Glenrigh offers comfortable bedrooms, impressive bathrooms and a hearty breakfast. The friendly team ensure your stay will be memorable.

Rooms: 15 en suite (1 fmly) (5 GF) **Facilities:** FTV DVD iPod docking station TVL tea/coffee WiFi 🔒 **Extras:** Snacks, drinks **Parking:** 20 **Notes:** No children 13 years Closed November to February

NORTH AYRSHIRE

WEST KILBRIDE	Map 20 NS24

Carlton Seamill B&B

AA ADVERTISED

tel: 01294 822075 & 07887 611738 **53 Ardrossan Road, Seamill KA23 9NE**
email: stay@carlton-seamill.co.uk **web:** www.carlton-seamill.co.uk
dir: *On A78 (coastal road).*

Carlton Seamill is an impressive, stone-built Victorian house, set in an ideal location at Seamill on the Ayrshire coast; it enjoys commanding views to the Firth of Clyde and the Isle of Arran. The Rennie family have been at Carlton for over 60 years and provide a relaxing atmosphere. On the ground floor, the handsome reception room has magnificent views over the rose garden and croquet lawn; and the elegant Victorian staircase leads up to the comfortable, first-floor accommodation. Carlton's garden gate leads to the sandy beach, so guests can enjoy a walk before heading to a local hostelry for dinner.

Rooms: 3 rms **Facilities:** FTV DVD tea/coffee WiFi 🔒 **Extras:** Mini fridge **Parking:** 6

DUMFRIES & GALLOWAY

CASTLE DOUGLAS	Map 21 NX76

Craigadam

★★★★ 🍴 🛏 GUEST HOUSE

tel: 01556 650233 & 650100 **Kirkpatrick Durham DG7 3HU**
email: celia@craigadam.com **web:** www.craigadam.com
dir: *From Castle Douglas east on A75 to Crocketford. In Crocketford turn left on A712 for 2 miles. House on hill.*

Set on a farm, this elegant country house offers gracious living in a relaxed environment. The large bedrooms, most set around a courtyard, are strikingly individual in style. Public areas include a billiard room, and the panelled dining room which features a magnificent 15-seater table, is the setting for Celia Pickup's delightful meals.

Rooms: 10 en suite (2 fmly) (7 GF) **Facilities:** FTV DVD Lounge tea/coffee Dinner available Licensed WiFi 🎣 Fishing Snooker 🔒 Shooting, deer stalking, birdwatching, billiards **Extras:** Speciality toiletries **Conf:** Max 22 **Parking:** 12 **Notes:** LB Closed Christmas and New Year Civ wed 180

DUMFRIES	Map 21 NX97

Southpark House

★★★★ GUEST ACCOMMODATION

tel: 01387 711188 **Quarry Road, Locharbriggs DG1 1FA**
email: info@southparkhouse.co.uk **web:** www.southparkhouse.co.uk
dir: *3.5 miles northeast of Dumfries. Exit A701 in Locharbriggs into Quarry Road, last house on left.*

Situated in a quiet residential yet edge-of-town location, this modern property in Dumfries offers thoughtfully decorated, comfortable bedrooms and well appointed en suite bathrooms. There is a relaxing guest lounge and an inviting conservatory dining room where traditional Scottish breakfasts are served overlooking the spectacular valley views. The strength here lies with the host who goes out of his way to ensure guests enjoy their stay.

Rooms: 6 en suite (1 fmly) **S** fr £49 **D** fr £69* **Facilities:** STV FTV Lounge TVL tea/coffee WiFi 2 acres of garden **Parking:** 13 **Notes:** LB

DUMFRIES *continued*

Rivendell

★★★★ GUEST HOUSE

tel: 01387 252251 **105 Edinburgh Road DG1 1JX**
email: info@rivendellbnb.co.uk **web:** www.rivendellbnb.co.uk
dir: *On A701 (Edinburgh Road), 400 yards south of A75 junction.*

Situated just north of the town and close to the bypass, this lovely Charles Rennie Mackintosh inspired 1920s house, standing in extensive landscaped gardens, has been restored to reflect the period style of the property. Bedrooms are thoughtfully equipped, many are spacious and all offer modern facilities. Traditional breakfasts are served in the elegant dining room.

Rooms: 7 rms (6 en suite) (1 pri facs) 3 annexe en suite (2 fmly) (5 GF)
Facilities: FTV iPod docking station tea/coffee WiFi **Parking:** 12 **Notes:** LB

GRETNA (WITH GRETNA GREEN)　Map 21 NY36

Surrone House

★★★★ GUEST ACCOMMODATION

tel: 01461 338341 **Annan Road DG16 5DL**
email: enquiries@surronehouse.co.uk **web:** www. surronehouse.co.uk
dir: *In town centre on B721.*

Guests are assured of a warm welcome at this well-maintained property in attractive gardens set back from the road. Bedrooms are sensibly furnished and include a delightful honeymoon suite. The property is located only 500 yards from the centre of Gretna. Complimentary parking is available on site.

Rooms: 6 en suite (3 fmly) (1 GF) **S** fr £45 **D** fr £65* **Facilities:** FTV TVL tea/coffee WiFi **Extras:** Speciality toiletries – complimentary **Parking:** 10

MOFFAT　Map 21 NT00

Bridge House Moffat

★★★★ GUEST HOUSE

tel: 01683 220558 **Well Road DG10 9JT**
email: bookings@bridgehousemoffat.scot **web:** www.bridgehousemoffat.scot
dir: *Exit A708 (The Holm) into Burnside, bear right into Well Road, house opposite Ballplay Road.*

This luxury Victorian guest house is situated on the outskirts of Moffat, within a short walk of the town centre. It enjoys views of the Moffat Hills and has easy access to a network of walking and cycling routes. All rooms feature complimentary toiletries, Freeview TV and a refreshment tray. Four-poster and superior rooms also have fluffy bathrobes and Egyptian cotton bedding. Well-behaved dogs are welcome and doggy day-care and boarding is available. The bar has a fine selection of Scottish whiskies and gins.

Rooms: 7 en suite (1 fmly) **Facilities:** FTV Lounge tea/coffee Licensed WiFi
Parking: 7 **Notes:** LB

PORTPATRICK　Map 20 NW95

Premier Collection

Knockinaam Lodge

★★★★★ ◎◎◎ RESTAURANT WITH ROOMS

tel: 01776 810471 **DG9 9AD**
email: reservations@knockinaamlodge.com **web:** www.knockinaamlodge.com
dir: *From A77 or A75 follow signs to Portpatrick. Through Lochans. After 2 miles left at signs for lodge.*

Any tour of Dumfries & Galloway wouldn't be complete without a stay at this haven of tranquillity and relaxation. Knockinaam Lodge is an extended Victorian house set in an idyllic cove with its own pebble beach (ideal for a private swim in the summer) and sheltered by majestic cliffs and woodlands. Surrounded by 30 acres of delightful grounds, the lodge was the location for a meeting between Churchill and General Eisenhower in World War II. Today, a warm welcome is assured from the proprietors and their committed team, and much emphasis is placed on providing a sophisticated but intimate home-from-home experience. There are just 10 suites – each individually designed and all with TVs with DVD players, luxury toiletries and complimentary bottled water. The cooking is a real treat and showcases prime Scottish produce on the daily-changing, four-course set menus; guests can always discuss the choices in advance if they wish.

Rooms: 10 en suite (1 fmly) **Facilities:** Dinner available ◄ Fishing Shooting, walking, sea fishing, clay pigeon shooting **Notes:** Civ wed 40

SANQUHAR　Map 21 NS70

Blackaddie House

★★★★ ◎◎ RESTAURANT WITH ROOMS

tel: 01659 50270 **Blackaddie Road DG4 6JJ**
email: ian@blackaddiehotel.co.uk **web:** www.blackaddiehotel.co.uk
dir: *300 yards from A76 on north side of Sanquhar.*

Overlooking the River Nith, in two acres of secluded gardens, this family-run country house offers friendly and attentive hands-on service. The bedrooms and suites, including family accommodation, are all well presented and comfortable, with many useful extras provided as standard. The award-winning food, served in the restaurant, with its lovely garden views, is based on prime Scottish ingredients.

Rooms: 6 en suite 1 annexe en suite (1 GF) **Facilities:** FTV DVD Lounge tea/coffee Dinner available Direct dial WiFi ≿ Chef for a Day experience **Extras:** Speciality toiletries, mineral water, home-made shortbread, home-made scottish tablet, robes, slippers **Conf:** Max 16 Thtr 16 Class 16 Board 12 **Parking:** 20 **Notes:** LB Civ wed 25

WEST DUNBARTONSHIRE

BALLOCH — Map 20 NS38

Innkeeper's Lodge Loch Lomond

★★★ INN

tel: 03451 551551 **Balloch Road G83 8LQ**
email: info@innkeeperslodge.com **web:** www.innkeeperslodge.com
dir: *Phone for directions.*

This property enjoys an excellent location, a stone's throw from Loch Lomond and the nearby Balloch Castle Country Park. The historic lodge provides modern, spacious accommodation. The cosy and welcoming lounge bar is a popular place to dine below the exposed wooden beams. Enjoy a cask ale by the open fire or a dish from their vast and varying menu. Parking is available on site.

Rooms: 11 en suite (3 fmly) **Facilities:** FTV tea/coffee Dinner available WiFi
Parking: 52

EDINBURGH

EDINBURGH — Map 21 NT27

See also Livingston (West Lothian)

Kew House

★★★★★ ☕ GUEST ACCOMMODATION

tel: 0131 313 0700 **1 Kew Terrace, Murrayfield EH12 5JE**
email: info@kewhouse.com **web:** www.kewhouse.com
dir: *1 mile west of Princes Street.*

Forming part of a listed Victorian terrace, Kew House lies within walking distance of the city centre, and is convenient for Murrayfield Stadium and tourist attractions. Meticulously maintained in contemporary style throughout, it offers attractive bedrooms in a variety of sizes, all thoughtfully equipped to suit business and leisure guests. There is a comfortable lounge. Both parking and WiFi are complimentary.

Rooms: 6 en suite (1 fmly) (2 GF) **S** fr £92 **D** fr £109* **Facilities:** FTV Lounge tea/coffee Direct dial WiFi ⛱ **Extras:** Speciality toiletries, sherry, chocolates, fridge **Parking:** 6 **Notes:** LB Closed approximately 5–31 January

21212

★★★★★ ❀❀❀❀ RESTAURANT WITH ROOMS

tel: 0131 523 1030 **3 Royal Terrace EH7 5AB**
email: reservations@21212restaurant.co.uk **web:** www.21212restaurant.co.uk
dir: *Calton Hill, city centre.*

A real jewel in Edinburgh's crown, this establishment takes its name from the number of choices at each course on the five-course dinner menu. Located on the prestigious Royal Terrace, this light and airy, renovated Georgian townhouse stretches over four floors. The four individually-designed bedrooms epitomise luxury living and the bathrooms certainly have the wow factor. At the heart of this restaurant with rooms is the creative and impressive four AA Rosette award-winning cooking of Paul Kitching. Service throughout is friendly and very attentive.

Rooms: 4 en suite **S** fr £150 **D** fr £150 **Facilities:** STV FTV iPod docking station Lounge Dinner available WiFi **Extras:** Speciality toiletries, mineral water, sloe gin **Notes:** No children 5 years Closed 1 week January, 1 week Autumn RS Sunday to Monday restaurant closed

The Witchery by the Castle

★★★★★ ❀ ☕ RESTAURANT WITH ROOMS

tel: 0131 225 5613 **Castlehill, The Royal Mile EH1 2NF**
email: mail@thewitchery.com **web:** www.thewitchery.com
dir: *Top of Royal Mile at gates of Edinburgh Castle.*

Originally built in 1595, The Witchery by the Castle is situated in a historic building at the gates of Edinburgh Castle. The two luxurious and theatrically decorated suites, known as the Inner Sanctum and the Old Rectory, are located above the restaurant and are reached via a winding stone staircase. Filled with antiques, opulently draped beds, large roll-top baths and a plethora of memorabilia, this ancient and exciting establishment is often described as one of the country's most romantic destinations.

Rooms: 4 en suite 5 annexe en suite (1 GF) **Facilities:** STV FTV DVD tea/coffee Dinner available Direct dial WiFi **Extras:** Bottled water – complimentary **Notes:** No children 12 years Closed 25–26 December

Bonnington Guest House

★★★★ GUEST HOUSE

tel: 0131 554 7610 & 07880 312820 **202 Ferry Road EH6 4NW**
email: booking@thebonningtonguesthouse.com **web:** www.thebonningtonguesthouse.com
dir: *On A902, near corner of Ferry Road and Newhaven Road.*

This delightful Georgian house offers individually furnished bedrooms on two floors that retain many of their original features. A family room is also available. A substantial and freshly prepared breakfast is served in the dining room. Off-street parking is an added bonus.

Rooms: 5 rms (4 en suite) (1 pri facs) (1 fmly) **Facilities:** FTV tea/coffee WiFi **Extras:** Speciality toiletries, sherry – complimentary; robes **Parking:** 9 **Notes:** Closed November to March RS 27 December to 2 January; Open for New Year and some weekends November to March

EDINBURGH *continued*

Fraoch House

★★★★ ☺ GUEST ACCOMMODATION

tel: 0131 554 1353 **66 Pilrig Street EH6 5AS**
email: info@fraochhouse.com **web:** www.fraochhouse.com
dir: *1 mile from Princes Street.*

Situated within walking distance of the city centre and convenient for many attractions, Fraoch House, which dates from the 1900s, has been appointed to offer well-equipped and thoughtfully furnished bedrooms. Delicious, freshly cooked breakfasts are served in the charming dining room on the ground floor.

Rooms: 9 rms (7 en suite) (2 pri facs) (1 fmly) (1 GF) **Facilities:** FTV tea/coffee WiFi Free use of DVDs and CDs and internet access

Kingsway Guest House

★★★★ ☺ GUEST HOUSE

tel: 0131 667 5029 **5 East Mayfield EH9 1SD**
email: booking@kingswayguesthouse.com **web:** www.edinburgh-guesthouse.com
dir: *A701 to city centre, after 4 miles road name changes to Mayfield Gardens. Right at lights into East Mayfield.*

Well situated for the city centre and with off-road parking, this well-presented Victorian building retains a number of original features, and genuine and warm hospitality is assured. All the bedrooms are comfortable, and the quality Scottish breakfasts make an excellent start to the day.

Rooms: 7 rms (6 en suite) (1 pri facs) (2 fmly) **D** fr £75* **Facilities:** FTV DVD iPod docking station tea/coffee WiFi ♨ **Extras:** Speciality toiletries – complimentary **Parking:** 4

Sherwood Guest House

★★★★ GUEST HOUSE

tel: 0131 667 1200 **42 Minto Street EH9 2BR**
email: vivienne@sherwood-edinburgh.com **web:** www.sherwood-edinburgh.com
dir: *On A701, south of city centre.*

Sherwood Guest House is located on the south side of the city and is well served by buses. Bedrooms vary in size, and the smaller ones are thoughtfully appointed to make the best use of space. Many thoughtful extras are provided, and a continental breakfast is served in the bright and welcoming dining room. The property has limited parking space on a first-come-first-served basis.

Rooms: 6 rms (5 en suite) (1 pri facs) (2 fmly) (1 GF) **S** fr £80 **D** fr £90* **Facilities:** FTV iPod docking station tea/coffee WiFi **Extras:** Fridge, microwave **Parking:** 3 **Notes:** Closed January

Arden Guest House

★★★ GUEST HOUSE

tel: 0131 664 3985 **126 Old Dalkeith Road EH16 4SD**
email: ardenguesthouse@btinternet.com **web:** www.ardenedinburgh.co.uk
dir: *2 miles southeast of city centre near Craigmillar Castle. On A7, 200 yards west of hospital.*

Arden Guest House is well situated on the southeast side of the city, close to the hospital, and benefits from off-road parking. Many thoughtful extras are provided as standard, including WiFi. Attentive and friendly service enhances the guest experience.

Rooms: 8 en suite (2 fmly) (3 GF) **Facilities:** FTV DVD tea/coffee WiFi ♨ **Parking:** 8

Elder York Guest House

★★★ GUEST HOUSE

tel: 0131 556 1926 **38 Elder Street EH1 3DX**
email: reception@elderyork.co.uk **web:** www.elderyork.co.uk
dir: *Close to Princes Street, next to bus station.*

Elder York Guest House is centrally located just minutes from the bus station, Harvey Nichols and the Royal Botanic Gardens. Accommodation is situated up flights of stairs and all bedrooms are well appointed with many thoughtful extras including WiFi. Quality breakfasts are served at individual tables overlooking Queen Street.

Rooms: 12 rms (11 en suite) (1 pri facs) (1 fmly) **Facilities:** FTV tea/coffee WiFi

Innkeeper's Lodge Edinburgh, Corstorphine

★★★ INN

tel: 03451 551551 **St Johns Road, Corstorphine EH12 8AX**
email: info@innkeeperslodge.com **web:** www.innkeeperslodge.com
dir: *Phone for directions.*

On the east side of Edinburgh and convenient for the M8 and also The Edinburgh ICC (a 15-minute drive), this Innkeeper's Lodge offers bedrooms with TVs, desks, tea-and-coffee making facilities and free WiFi as standard; family rooms are available. The on-site Toby Carvery meals are popular. Parking is provided.

Rooms: 28 en suite (4 fmly) (6 GF) **Facilities:** FTV tea/coffee Dinner available Direct dial WiFi **Parking:** 46

Averon Guest House

★★★ GUEST HOUSE

tel: 0131 229 9932 **44 Gilmore Place EH3 9NQ**
email: info@averon.co.uk **web:** www.averon.co.uk
dir: *From west end of Princes Street onto A702, right at Kings Theatre.*

Situated within walking distance of the west end of the city and close to the Kings Theatre, Averon Guest House offers comfortable, good-value accommodation, with a secure car park to the rear.

Rooms: 10 rms (6 en suite) (1 pri facs) (3 fmly) (5 GF) **Facilities:** tea/coffee **Parking:** 19

Halcyon House

★★★ GUEST HOUSE

tel: 0131 556 1033 & 556 1032 **8 Royal Terrace EH7 5AB**
email: patricia@halcyon-hotel.com **web:** www.halcyon-hotel.com
dir: *Phone for directions.*

Halcyon House, within easy walking distance of the theatre and the centre of Edinburgh, benefits from a fantastic location and has retained many of its original Georgian features. The bedrooms are split over three floors, come in a variety of sizes and are decorated in a basic but comfortable fashion. Front or back rooms offer either wonderful views of the gardens or views across to the Forth.

Rooms: 14 rms (11 en suite) (1 pri facs) (7 fmly) (2 GF) **Facilities:** TVL tea/coffee WiFi **Notes:** LB

RATHO
Map 21 NT17

The Bridge Inn at Ratho

★★★★ ◎ 🍷 INN

tel: 0131 333 1320 **27 Baird Road EH28 8RA**
email: info@bridgeinn.com **web:** www.bridgeinn.com

Located beside the Union Canal and in use as a hostelry since the 19th century, this inn offers modern, spacious and well-furnished bedrooms with views of the canal. The busy bistro's kitchen uses home-grown produce to create award-winning food. Outdoor seating is an added bonus as are the two restaurant barges that serve lunch, afternoon tea and dinner.

Rooms: 4 en suite **S** fr £70 **D** fr £80* **Facilities:** FTV iPod docking station tea/coffee Dinner available WiFi 🍷 **Extras:** Speciality toiletries – complimentary **Parking:** 40 **Notes:** Closed 25 December Civ wed 80

SOUTH QUEENSFERRY
Map 21 NT17

Innkeeper's Lodge Edinburgh South Queensferry

★★★ INN

tel: 03451 551551 **7 Newhalls Road EH30 9TA**
email: info@innkeeperslodge.com **web:** www.innkeeperslodge.com
dir: *Phone for directions.*

The Hawes Inn, an Innkeeper's Lodge, is where Robert Louis Stevenson is said to written part of his famous novel *Kidnapped*, and is located almost under the Forth Road Bridge. The traditionally-styled bedrooms of varying shapes and sizes have views of the Firth of Forth; each room has a TV, desk, tea-and-coffee making facilities and free WiFi as standard; family rooms are available. Seasonal pub dishes are offered, and guests can eat outside when the Scottish weather allows.

Rooms: 14 en suite (5 fmly) (3 GF) **Facilities:** FTV tea/coffee Dinner available Direct dial WiFi **Parking:** 40

FALKIRK

BANKNOCK
Map 21 NS77

Premier Collection

Glenskirlie House & Castle

★★★★★ ◎◎ GUEST ACCOMMODATION

tel: 01324 840201 **Kilsyth Road FK4 1UF**
email: macaloneys@glenskirliehouse.com **web:** www.glenskirliehouse.com
dir: *Phone for directions.*

Set in the leafy suburbs north of Glasgow, Glenskirlie consists of the original house containing the Grill restaurant and the more imposing castle-style building housing boutique-style accommodation in a range of room sizes. There are five suites to choose between – all deeply comfortable and well equipped. Dinner is in the Grill with generous Scottish breakfasts served within the castle.

Rooms: 15 en suite **S** fr £99 **D** fr £99 (room only)* **Facilities:** Dinner available Licensed

FIFE

ANSTRUTHER
Map 21 NO50

The Spindrift

★★★★ 🍷 🍽 GUEST HOUSE

tel: 01333 310573 & 07713 597996 **Pittenweem Road KY10 3DT**
email: info@thespindrift.co.uk **web:** www.thespindrift.co.uk
dir: *Enter town from west on A917, 1st building on left.*

This immaculate Victorian villa stands on the western edge of the village. The attractive bedrooms offer a wide range of extra touches; the Captain's Room, a replica of a wood-panelled cabin, is a particular feature. The inviting lounge has an honesty bar, while imaginative breakfasts are served in the cheerful dining room. This is also the venue, by arrangement, for dinners that use the best in fresh local produce. Free WiFi is available throughout.

Rooms: 8 rms (7 en suite) (1 pri facs) (2 fmly) **S** fr £50 **D** fr £66* **Facilities:** FTV DVD iPod docking station TVL tea/coffee Dinner available Direct dial Licensed WiFi 🛝 🍷 **Extras:** Speciality toiletries, shortbread, chocolates – complimentary **Parking:** 9 **Notes:** LB Closed Christmas to late January

ANSTRUTHER *continued*

The Bank

★★★★ INN

tel: 01333 310189 **23–25 High Street East KY10 3DQ**
email: enquiries@thebank-anstruther.co.uk **web:** www.thebank-anstruther.co.uk
dir: *From St Andrews, in Anstruther turn right towards Pittenweem. 50 metres on left.*

Located in the heart of Anstruther where the Dreel Burn meets the Forth, this friendly inn serves real ales and great pub food; there is a separate building next door for the accommodation. Modern, high quality, en suite bedrooms cater well for guests' needs and some offer great views. The beer garden is a real suntrap and has a children's play area.

Rooms: 13 en suite (1 fmly) (1 GF) **Facilities:** STV FTV iPod docking station tea/coffee Dinner available Direct dial WiFi ⚡ 🅰 **Extras:** Bottled water – complimentary; fridge, safe **Parking:** 3 **Notes:** LB

The Waterfront

★★★★ 🍽 RESTAURANT WITH ROOMS

tel: 01333 312200 **18–20 Shore Street KY10 3EA**
email: info@anstruther-waterfront.co.uk **web:** www.anstruther-waterfront.co.uk
dir: *Off A917, opposite marina.*

Situated overlooking the harbour, The Waterfront offers spacious, stylish, contemporary accommodation, with bedrooms located in lovingly restored buildings in a courtyard behind the restaurant. There is a comfortable lounge with a smartly fitted kitchen and dining room, and laundry facilities are available in the granary. Dinner and breakfast are served in the attractive restaurant that offers a comprehensive menu featuring the best local produce.

Rooms: 10 en suite (3 fmly) (2 GF) **Facilities:** FTV DVD Lounge tea/coffee Dinner available WiFi ⚡ 🅰 **Extras:** Mineral water **Notes:** LB

ELIE · Map 21 NO40

The Ship Inn

★★★★ 🍽 INN

tel: 01333 330246 **The Toft KY9 1DT**
email: info@shipinn.scot **web:** www.shipinn.scot

You'd have to travel a long way to find views better than the ones from this inn. Overlooking the harbour in Elie, The Ship Inn has a beer garden and views over the wide sandy beach to the sea. It is the only pub in Britain to organise cricket matches on a beach, when the weather and tides allow, of course. A comfortable lounge bar and expansive dining space enjoy the views and stunning sunsets. In keeping with rest of the inn, the bedrooms and bathrooms are equally stylish, with Egyptian linens, Nespresso machines, Bose sound systems and beautiful toiletries; two rooms are dog-friendly. No visit would be complete without sampling the food or trying one of the cask ales.

Rooms: 6 en suite (1 GF) **Facilities:** FTV iPod docking station tea/coffee Dinner available WiFi ⚡ 🅰 **Extras:** Nespresso coffee machine

INVERKEITHING · Map 21 NT18

The Roods

★★★★ BED AND BREAKFAST

tel: 01383 415049 **16 Bannerman Avenue KY11 1NG**
email: isobelmarley@hotmail.com **web:** www.the-roods.co.uk
dir: *North of town centre off B981(Church Street/Chapel Place).*

This charming house stands in secluded, well-tended gardens close to the train station. Bedrooms are individually styled and have state-of-the-art bathrooms. There is an inviting lounge, and breakfast is served at a large shared table in an attractive conservatory.

Rooms: 3 en suite (2 GF) **S** fr £45 **D** fr £90* **Facilities:** FTV DVD iPod docking station TVL tea/coffee Direct dial WiFi 🅰 **Parking:** 4 **Notes:** LB

NEWPORT-ON-TAY · Map 21 NO42

The Newport Restaurant

★★★★ ◉◉ RESTAURANT WITH ROOMS

tel: 01382 541449 **1 High Street DD6 8AB**
email: info@thenewportrestaurant.co.uk **web:** www.thenewportrestaurant.co.uk
dir: *Phone for directions.*

Jamie Scott's restaurant with rooms is situated on the shore in Newport looking out over the Tay to Dundee. The style here is modern with a nod to the local maritime and fishing history. The modern restaurant is set over two floors, both enjoying panoramic views. The four bedrooms are spacious and well equipped with comfortable beds and added luxuries.

Rooms: 4 en suite (2 fmly) **Facilities:** FTV iPod docking station Dinner available WiFi **Parking:** 10 **Notes:** Closed 24 December to 9 January

PEAT INN · Map 21 NO40

Premier Collection

The Peat Inn

★★★★★ ◉◉◉ RESTAURANT WITH ROOMS

tel: 01334 840206 **KY15 5LH**
email: stay@thepeatinn.co.uk **web:** www.thepeatinn.co.uk
dir: *At junction of B940 and B941, 5 miles southwest of St Andrews.*

This 300-year-old former coaching inn enjoys a rural location and is close to St Andrews. The Peat Inn is spacious, very well appointed, and offers rooms that all have lounge areas. The inn is steeped in history and for years has proved a real haven for food lovers – the three dining areas create a romantic setting, and chef/owner Geoffrey Smeddle produces excellent, award-winning dishes (please note, no children under 7 years at dinner). Expect welcoming open fires and a relaxed ambiance. An extensive continental breakfast selection is served to guests in their bedrooms each morning.

Rooms: 8 annexe en suite (3 fmly) (8 GF) **S** fr £205 **D** fr £225* **Facilities:** FTV Lounge tea/coffee Dinner available Direct dial WiFi 🅰 **Extras:** Speciality toiletries, home-made brownies, fruit, sherry – complimentary **Parking:** 24 **Notes:** LB Closed 25–26 December, 2 weeks January RS Sunday to Monday closed

GLASGOW

GLASGOW   Map 20 NS56

Georgian House

★★ GUEST HOUSE

tel: 0141 339 0008 & 07973 971563
29 Buckingham Terrace, Great Western Road G12 8ED
email: thegeorgianhouse@yahoo.com web: www.thegeorgianhousehotel.com
dir: *M8 junction 17 towards Dumbarton, through 4 sets of lights and right into Queen Margaret Drive, then right into Buckingham Terrace.*

Georgian House offers good-value accommodation and is situated at the west end of the city in a peaceful tree-lined Victorian terrace near the Botanic Gardens. Bedrooms vary in size and are furnished in a modern style. A continental style breakfast is served in the first-floor lounge-dining room.

Rooms: 11 rms (10 en suite) (1 pri facs) (4 fmly) (3 GF) **Facilities:** FTV tea/coffee WiFi **Parking:** 6 **Notes:** LB

HIGHLAND

ACHARACLE   Map 22 NM66

Mingarry Park

★★★★ ◉◉ RESTAURANT WITH ROOMS

tel: 01967 431202 & 07791 115467 **Mingarry PH36 4JX**
email: info@mingarryparkhouse.co.uk web: www.mingarryparkhouse.co.uk
dir: *From Fort William at roundabout take A82 (Inverness road). At Lochy Bridge junction left onto A830 (Mallaig Road). 26 miles to Lochailort. Left onto A861 (Acharacle/Salen Road). 16 miles to Mingarry. Mingarry Park 1st on left, pass village hall, follow signs.*

Set in breathtaking scenery, Mingarry Park offers individually designed, contemporary bedrooms; each has great views across the deer park and surrounding countryside. Some rooms have balconies and decked areas for relaxation. Diners are treated to the best local produce in creative dishes, with a roaring log-burner as the centrepiece of the restaurant. Afternoon tea is served every other Sunday.

Rooms: 6 en suite (3 GF) **Facilities:** FTV iPod docking station tea/coffee Dinner available WiFi 🛇 **Notes:** Closed February to March

AVIEMORE   Map 23 NH81

Eriskay Bed & Breakfast

★★★ BED AND BREAKFAST

tel: 01479 810717 & 07702 009614 **Craig Na Gower Avenue PH22 1RW**
email: enquiries@eriskay-aviemore.co.uk web: www.eriskay-aviemore.co.uk
dir: *From south turn left into Craig Na Gower Avenue, follow signs to Aviemore dental practice. At end of lane next to dentist.*

This family-run B&B enjoys a quiet location close to the centre of Aviemore and is a great base for exploring the Cairngorms National Park and further afield. All bedrooms have en suite facilities and provide comfortable accommodation. Warm hospitality and good breakfasts are major aspects of any stay here. Self-contained eco-pods in the grounds of the property are an alternative to the main accommodation.

Rooms: 3 en suite (1 fmly) (3 GF) **Facilities:** FTV tea/coffee WiFi **Parking:** 3 **Notes:** LB

BRACHLA   Map 23 NH53

Loch Ness Lodge

★★★★★ 🛇 GUEST ACCOMMODATION

tel: 01456 459469 **Loch Ness-Side IV3 8AU**
email: escape@loch-ness-lodge.com web: www.loch-ness-lodge.com
dir: *A9 from Inverness onto A82 signed Fort William, 9 miles, at 30mph sign. Lodge on right immediately after Clansman Hotel.*

This house enjoys a prominent position overlooking Loch Ness, and each of the individually designed bedrooms enjoys views of the loch. The bedrooms are of the highest standard, and are beautifully presented with a mix of traditional luxury and up-to-date technology, including WiFi. There is a spa with a hot tub, sauna and a therapy room offering a variety of treatments. Guests have a choice of attractive lounges which feature real fires in the colder months and where decadent afternoon teas are served.

Rooms: 7 en suite (1 GF) **Facilities:** FTV DVD Lounge Direct dial Licensed WiFi ♨ Fishing Sauna Hot tub, Therapy room **Extras:** Speciality toiletries **Conf:** Max 14 Thtr 14 Class 10 Board 14 **Parking:** 10 **Notes:** LB No children 10 years Closed 2 November to 27 March (dates may vary) Civ wed 14

CARRBRIDGE   Map 23 NH92

Cairn

★★★ INN

tel: 01479 841212 **Main Road PH23 3AS**
email: info@cairnhotel.co.uk web: www.cairnhotel.co.uk
dir: *Phone for directions.*

Conveniently located in the centre of the Cairngorms National Park, this property is the hub of the local community. The traditional bar and restaurant are complemented by a range of cosy bedrooms featuring modern touches. Guests can relax in front of the log fire with a cask ale or local malt whisky. The inn is an ideal base from which to participate in a number of outdoor activities with activity breaks and packages available to book.

Rooms: 7 rms

CROMARTY   Map 23 NH76

The Factor's House

★★★★★ ◉ 🛇 GUEST ACCOMMODATION

tel: 01381 600394 & 07917 799143 **Denny Road IV11 8YT**
email: info@thefactorshouse.com web: www.thefactorshouse.com
dir: *From Fortrose take A832 towards Cromarty. House on left.*

Situated overlooking the historic town of Cromarty and only a short drive from Inverness, this house provides luxury accommodation in a secluded and peaceful setting. Spacious bedrooms feature Egyptian linens, a host of thoughtful touches and even home-made soaps to complement an impressive range of toiletries. Award-winning dinners and breakfasts are available; both make good use of the best of local produce, including fruit from the garden and eggs from the resident hens. Dinner must be booked 24 hours in advance.

Rooms: 3 en suite (1 GF) **S** fr £115 **D** fr £135* **Facilities:** FTV DVD iPod docking station Lounge tea/coffee Dinner available Licensed WiFi ♨ **Extras:** Speciality toiletries, home-made soap, fresh fruit **Parking:** 3 **Notes:** LB No children 5 years Closed 20 December to 5 January

DORNOCH
Map 23 NH78

Premier Collection

Links House at Royal Dornoch

★★★★★ @@ ⬥ GUEST ACCOMMODATION

tel: 01862 810279 **Golf Road IV25 3LW**
email: info@linkshousedornoch.com **web:** www.linkshousedornoch.com
dir: *From A9 onto A949 into Dornoch. From Castle Street, right into Church Street then left into Golf Road. House at junction of Golf Road and Kennedy Avenue.*

This beautifully restored former manse house enjoys a stunning setting overlooking the famous Royal Dornoch Golf Course. The property provides an exceptional level of accommodation with stunning bedrooms and bathrooms, as well as delightful public areas including a wood-panelled library and a drawing room – both have open fires; outside there's a patio with a fire. The small dining room has a peat fire and is the setting for memorable service, whether guests are enjoying an elaborate evening meal or a sumptuous breakfast. Afternoon teas are also available by prior booking. The property is not just a great base for golfers but also for shooting, fishing, stalking and a host of other activities in this beautiful part of the Highlands.

Rooms: 5 en suite 9 annexe en suite (4 GF) **Facilities:** STV Lounge TVL Dinner available Licensed WiFi ♨ ♿ Leisure activities can be booked in advance **Extras:** Speciality toiletries, fruit – complimentary **Conf:** Max 12 Thtr 12 Class 12 Board 12 **Parking:** 12 **Notes:** Closed 25–27 December and 4 January to 18 March

Premier Collection

2 Quail

★★★★★ ⬥ ⬛ GUEST ACCOMMODATION

tel: 01862 811811 **Castle Street IV25 3SN**
email: theaa@2quail.com **web:** www.2quail.com
dir: *On main street, 200 yards from cathedral.*

The saying 'small is beautiful' applies to this property set in the main street. The cosy public rooms are ideal for conversation, but there are masses of books for those just wishing to relax. The stylish, individual bedrooms match the character of the house and are thoughtfully equipped with a number of useful touches. Dinners and breakfasts are both worth sampling.

Rooms: 3 en suite **S** fr £80 **D** fr £90 **Facilities:** FTV DVD Lounge tea/coffee Dinner available Direct dial Licensed WiFi ♨ **Extras:** Speciality toiletries **Notes:** No children 8 years Closed Christmas and 2 weeks February/March RS November to March winter hours – check when booking

FORT WILLIAM
Map 22 NN17

See also Spean Bridge

Mansefield Guest House

★★★★ GUEST HOUSE

tel: 01397 772262 **Corpach PH33 7LT**
email: mansefield@btinternet.com **web:** www.fortwilliamaccommodation.com
dir: *2 miles north of Fort William. A82 onto A830, house 2 miles on A830 in Corpach.*

Peacefully set in its own well-tended garden, this friendly, family-run guest house provides comfortable, attractively decorated and well-equipped accommodation.

There is a cosy lounge, where a roaring coal fire burns on cold evenings, and an attractive dining room where delicious, home-cooked evening meals and breakfasts are served at individual tables.

Rooms: 6 en suite (1 GF) **Facilities:** FTV DVD TVL tea/coffee Dinner available WiFi ♨ ♿ **Parking:** 7 **Notes:** LB No children 12 years

FOYERS
Map 23 NH42

The Craigdarroch Inn

★★★★ INN

tel: 01456 486400 **IV2 6XU**
email: info@hotel-loch-ness.co.uk **web:** www.thecraigdarrochinn.co.uk
dir: *Take B862 from either end of loch, then B852 signed Foyers.*

Craigdarroch Inn is located in an elevated position, high above Loch Ness on the south side. Bedrooms vary in style and size but all are comfortable and well equipped; those that are front-facing have wonderful views. This friendly inn offers relaxed dining, many tables have loch views, and the staff are friendly and welcoming.

Rooms: 8 en suite (1 fmly) **S** fr £70 **D** fr £80 (room only)* **Facilities:** FTV Lounge TVL tea/coffee Dinner available WiFi ♿ **Conf:** Max 30 Thtr 30 Class 30 Board 30 **Parking:** 24

Foyers Bay Country House

★★★ GUEST HOUSE

tel: 01456 486624 **Lower Foyers, Lochness IV2 6YB**
email: info@foyersbay.co.uk **web:** www.foyersbay.co.uk
dir: *Exit B852 into Lower Foyers.*

Situated in sloping grounds with pines and abundant colourful rhododendrons, this delightful Victorian villa has stunning views of Loch Ness. The attractive bedrooms vary in size and are well equipped. There is a comfortable lounge next to the plant-filled conservatory-café, where traditional breakfasts are served.

Rooms: 7 en suite (1 GF) **Facilities:** FTV TVL tea/coffee Licensed WiFi ♿ **Parking:** 7 **Notes:** No children 16 years

GLENCOE
Map 22 NN15

The Glencoe Inn

★★★★ INN

tel: 01855 811245 & 811625 **Tyndrum Road PH49 4HP**
email: glencoe@crerarhotels.com **web:** www.crerarhotels.com/theglencoe-inn
dir: *Phone for directions.*

This welcoming inn has a stunning location in the shadow of the Pap of Glencoe overlooking Loch Leven. The Glencoe Inn is all about traditional Scottish hospitality, complemented by the nature and adventure that awaits outdoors. The rustic public areas are comfy and very dog-friendly. This is an ideal base for those who want to explore Glencoe, walk the West Highland Way or climb the remote Munros of 'Meall a' Bhùiridh' and 'Bidean Nam-Bain'. After a hard day exploring visit the Glencoe Gathering, a retro fish and chip bar located next door.

Rooms: 15 en suite (2 fmly) **Facilities:** STV FTV Lounge tea/coffee Dinner available WiFi ♿ **Extras:** Speciality toiletries **Parking:** 40

| GLENUIG | Map 22 NM67 |

Glenuig Inn

★★★ Ⓐ INN

tel: 01687 470219 **PH38 4NG**
email: stay@glenuig.com
dir: *From Fort William take A830 to Lochaillort. Exit onto A861, continue 8 miles south.*

The Glenuig Inn is not only renowned for its green credentials – it runs on 100% renewable energy – but it is located amidst some the west coast's most stunning scenery. Right by the beach on the Sound of Arisaig, the inn offers seasonal menus with gluten free and vegetarian options, real ales and organic wines. The accommodation includes rooms suitable for families and groups, and it is dog friendly throughout.

Rooms: 6 en suite (6 fmly) (6 GF) **S** fr £80 **D** fr £80* **Facilities:** FTV Lounge TVL tea/coffee Dinner available WiFi ⚓ **Parking:** 30 **Notes:** LB

| GRANTOWN-ON-SPEY | Map 23 NJ02 |

The Dulaig

★★★★★ ☒ BED AND BREAKFAST

tel: 01479 872065 **Seafield Avenue, Aviemore PH26 3JF**
email: enquiries@thedulaig.com **web:** www.thedulaig.com
dir: *A9 onto A95 to B9102. Into High Street, left into Seafield Avenue for 200 metres, past Rhuarden Court, The Dulaig on left.*

Presented to an exceptional standard, this bed and breakfast benefits from a tranquil setting in 1.5 acres of stunning gardens yet is only a short walk from the town centre. Featuring a summer house, duck pond and plenty of wildlife, the grounds provide a relaxing setting for the house. On offer are luxurious, spacious bedrooms with Arts and Crafts antique furniture and immaculately presented bathrooms with luxury toiletries. Memorable breakfasts, using the best local produce and eggs from their own hens, are served around a large, shared table in the welcoming drawing room. Carol and Gordon provide outstanding hospitality which is appreciated by their many regular guests.

Rooms: 3 en suite **S** fr £130 **D** fr £170* **Facilities:** STV DVD Lounge tea/coffee WiFi ⚓ Summerhouse **Extras:** Speciality toiletries, fruit, chocolates – complimentary **Parking:** 6 **Notes:** LB No children 12 years Closed 15 December to 14 January

| INVERNESS | Map 23 NH64 |

Achnagairn Estate

★★★★★ ❀❀ ☒ GUEST ACCOMMODATION

tel: 01463 831878 **Kirkhill IV5 7PD**
email: enquiries@perfect-manors.com **web:** www.perfect-manors.com
dir: *From Inverness on A862 follow Beauly signs. In Inchmore turn right signed Kirkhill. Pass through Kirkhill, entrance on left immediately on leaving village.*

Achnagairn lives up to the owners, Perfect Manors, motto to 'Escape the ordinary'. Opulence and luxury are the watchwords at this listed heritage building, which features an impressive vaulted ballroom, wood-panelled walls, tastefully decorated rooms and modern colour schemes that give the venue its unique character. Set amid breathtaking scenery, the property is the epitome of luxury design style. Each room offers great views across the surrounding countryside. Diners are treated to the best local produce in creative dishes.

Rooms: 20 en suite **S** fr £80 **D** fr £100* **Facilities:** TVL Dinner available **Parking:** 20 **Notes:** Closed (dates vary) November through to early March

Daviot Lodge

★★★★★ ☒ GUEST ACCOMMODATION

tel: 01463 772215 **Daviot Mains IV2 5ER**
email: margaret@daviotlodge.co.uk **web:** www.daviotlodge.co.uk
dir: *Exit A9, 5 miles south of Inverness onto B851 signed Croy. 1 mile on left.*

Standing in 80 acres of peaceful pastureland, this impressive establishment offers attractive, well-appointed and well-equipped bedrooms. The master bedroom is furnished with a four-poster bed. There is a tranquil lounge with deep sofas and a real fire, and a peaceful dining room where hearty breakfasts featuring the best of local produce are served. Full disabled access for wheelchairs is provided.

Rooms: 6 en suite (1 GF) **S** fr £75 **D** fr £115* **Facilities:** FTV DVD Lounge TVL tea/coffee Licensed WiFi **Extras:** Speciality toiletries, snacks **Parking:** 10 **Notes:** LB No children 10 years Closed 23 December to 2 January

INVERNESS *continued*

Premier Collection

Trafford Bank

★★★★★ GUEST HOUSE

tel: 01463 241414 **96 Fairfield Road IV3 5LL**
email: info@traffordbankhotel.co.uk web: www.traffordbankhotel.co.uk
dir: *Exit A82 at Kenneth Street, 2nd left into Fairfield Road, 600 yards on right.*

This impressive Victorian house lies in a residential area close to the canal. Lorraine Pun has made great use of her interior design skills to blend the best contemporary styles with the house's period character and the results are simply stunning. Delightful public areas offer a choice of lounges, while breakfast is taken in a beautiful conservatory featuring eye-catching wrought-iron chairs. Each en suite bedroom is unique in design and has a TV, DVD and CDs, hospitality tray, silent mini-fridges and much more.

Rooms: 5 en suite (2 fmly) **Facilities:** STV FTV TVL tea/coffee WiFi **Parking:** 10 **Notes:** LB

See advert opposite

Moyness House

★★★★ GUEST HOUSE

tel: 01463 233836 & 236624 **6 Bruce Gardens IV3 5EN**
email: stay@moyness.co.uk web: www.moyness.co.uk
dir: *Off A82 (Fort William Road), almost opposite Highland Regional Council headquarters.*

Situated in a quiet residential area just a short distance from the city centre, this elegant Victorian villa dates from 1880 and offers beautifully decorated, comfortable bedrooms and well-appointed bathrooms. There is an attractive sitting room and an inviting dining room, where traditional Scottish breakfasts are served. Guests are welcome to use the secluded and well-maintained back garden. Free, secure private parking is provided for guests.

Rooms: 6 en suite (1 fmly) (2 GF) **S** fr £85 **D** fr £98* **Facilities:** FTV Lounge tea/coffee WiFi **Extras:** Speciality toiletries, robes **Parking:** 10 **Notes:** LB

Heathcote B&B

★★★★ BED AND BREAKFAST

tel: 01463 236596 & 07833 730849 **59 Glenurquhart Road IV3 5PB**
email: info@heathcotebandb.co.uk web: www.heathcotebandb.co.uk
dir: *On A82, 1 mile from city centre.*

Only a few minutes' walk from the Eden Court Theatre and the centre of Inverness, this Victorian townhouse is ideally situated for touring the city and beyond, whether you are searching for the Loch Ness monster or just castle-hunting. The modern bedrooms and bathrooms offer spacious and comfortable accommodation. Friendly hospitality and memorable breakfasts are offered here. Ample off-street private parking is provided.

Rooms: 3 en suite **Facilities:** FTV tea/coffee WiFi 🐾 **Extras:** Bottled water **Parking:** 6

Lyndon Guest House

★★★★ GUEST HOUSE

tel: 01463 232551 **50 Telford Street IV3 5LE**
email: lyndon@invernessbedandbreakfast.com web: www.invernessbedandbreakfast.com
dir: *A9 onto A82, over Friars Bridge, right at roundabout into Telford Street. House on right.*

A warm Highland welcome awaits at Lyndon Guest House, family-run accommodation close to the centre of Inverness. All bedrooms are en suite and are equipped with plenty of useful facilities including full internet access. Gaelic is spoken here.

Rooms: 6 en suite (2 fmly) (2 GF) **Facilities:** FTV TVL tea/coffee WiFi 🐾 **Parking:** 7 **Notes:** Closed 20 December to 5 January

Trafford Bank
Guest House

Koshal and Lorraine Pun purchased Trafford Bank in 2002 with the vision to make it into one of the top boutique guest houses in Scotland.

From the paintings on our walls to the cushions on our beds, these are all from local highland businesses. Our breakfast menu is all locally sourced, we have a variety of options which caters for all guests.

This former Bishop's home has been refurbished from top to bottom and mixes antique and contemporary furniture, some of which has been designed by Lorraine herself — an accomplished interior designer.

The guest house is non-smoking throughout, and is surrounded by mature gardens that the guests can enjoy and has ample parking.

AA Breakfast Award

AA ★★★★★

Trafford Bank Guest House
96 Fairfield Road, Inverness, Highland IV3 5LL
Tel: 01463 241414
E-Mail: info@traffordbankhotel.co.uk

www.traffordbankhotel.co.uk

KINGUSSIE
Map 23 NH70

The Cross

★★★★ ◉◉◉ ♨ RESTAURANT WITH ROOMS

tel: 01540 661166 **Tweed Mill Brae, Ardbroilach Road PH21 1LB**
email: relax@thecross.co.uk **web:** www.thecross.co.uk
dir: *From lights in Kingussie centre take Ardbroilach Road, 300 yards left into Tweed Mill Brae.*

Built as a water-powered tweed mill in the late 19th century, The Cross is situated in the picturesque Cairngorms National Park and surrounded by four acres of riverside grounds that teem with an abundance of wildlife, including red squirrels. Comfortable lounges and a selection of well-appointed bedrooms are offered, and award-winning dinners are served by an open fire in the stone-walled and wood-beamed restaurant.

Rooms: 8 en suite **S** fr £90 **D** fr £100* **Facilities:** FTV DVD Lounge tea/coffee Dinner available Direct dial WiFi Riding ♨ **Extras:** Bottled water, speciality toiletries **Conf:** Max 20 Thtr 20 Class 20 Board 20 **Parking:** 20 **Notes:** LB Closed January and Christmas

LAGGAN
Map 22 NN29

The Rumblie Guest House

★★★★ ♨ GUEST HOUSE

tel: 01528 544766 **Gergask Avenue PH20 1AH**
email: mail@rumblie.com **web:** www.rumblie.com
dir: *A9 at Dalwhinnie onto A889. Right on A86, left at church after bridge, follow sign.*

Comfortable, eco-friendly accommodation and a warm welcome await you here, with evening meals available if pre-booked. The guest house is licensed, giving you a chance to try some of the wide range of whiskies available. In the morning, a fine breakfast, making good use of local organic produce, will set you up for the day. The Rumblie is situated in the Cairngorms National Park and on the long-distance East Highland Way.

Rooms: 3 en suite (1 GF) **S** fr £97 **D** fr £97 **Facilities:** FTV Lounge tea/coffee Dinner available Licensed WiFi ♨ **Extras:** Fruit, flowers, home-made shortbread, filtered water **Parking:** 5 **Notes:** No children 13 years Closed 20 November to 27 December

POOLEWE
Map 22 NG88

Premier Collection

Pool House

★★★★★ ♨ ⚘ GUEST HOUSE

tel: 01445 781272 **IV22 2LD**
email: stay@pool-house.co.uk **web:** www.pool-house.co.uk
dir: *6 miles north of Gairloch on A832 in the centre of village by bridge.*

Set on the shores of Loch Ewe where the river meets the bay, the understated roadside façade gives little hint of its splendid interior, nor of the views facing the bay. Memorable features include delightful public rooms and stunningly romantic suites, each individually designed and with feature bathrooms. Pool House is run very much as a country house – the hospitality and guest care by the Harrison family are second to none.

Rooms: 3 en suite **S** fr £175 **D** fr £225* **Facilities:** FTV DVD iPod docking station Lounge tea/coffee Dinner available Direct dial Licensed WiFi Snooker **Extras:** Sherry, speciality toiletries – complimentary **Parking:** 10 **Notes:** LB No children 12 years Closed November to mid March RS Monday evening closed

ROY BRIDGE
Map 22 NN28

Homagen

★★★★ BED AND BREAKFAST

tel: 01397 712411 **PH31 4AN**
email: stay@homagen.co.uk **web:** www.homagen.co.uk
dir: *On A86, opposite Roy Bridge Hotel.*

Homagen is a family-run property in a great location for touring the Highlands, with links to Fort William, Aviemore and beyond. Bedrooms feature modern decor and comfortable beds. Hearty breakfasts are served in the dining room at a communal table. Free WiFi is provided. Packed lunches are available for guests taking day trips.

Rooms: 4 rms (3 en suite) (1 pri facs) (4 GF) **S** fr £50 **D** fr £90 **Facilities:** FTV Lounge tea/coffee WiFi ♨ **Parking:** 6 **Notes:** LB No children 10 years Closed December to 1 February

SPEAN BRIDGE
Map 22 NN28

Distant Hills Guest House

★★★★ ♨ GUEST HOUSE

tel: 01397 712452 **Roy Bridge Road PH34 4EU**
email: enquiry@distanthills.com **web:** www.distanthillsspeanbridge.co.uk
dir: *From A82 onto A86 signed Newtonmore. 0.5 mile on right. From A86 1st house on left when entering Spean Bridge.*

Distant Hills Guest House in the heart of the Highlands offers stylish bedrooms, award-winning breakfasts and friendly hospitality. Set amid wonderful scenery, the house enjoys a quiet setting in its own impressive grounds. This is an ideal base for touring Fort William, Oban, Inverness and the Highlands whether walking, climbing or driving. Off-road parking and free WiFi are some of the numerous features here.

Rooms: 7 en suite (7 GF) **S** fr £79 **D** fr £94* **Facilities:** FTV DVD TVL tea/coffee WiFi ♨ **Extras:** Speciality toiletries, teacakes **Parking:** 10 **Notes:** No children 12 years Closed November to 15 March

Smiddy House

★★★★ ◉◉ ♨ RESTAURANT WITH ROOMS

tel: 01397 712335 **Roy Bridge Road PH34 4EU**
email: enquiry@smiddyhouse.com **web:** www.smiddyhouse.com
dir: *In village centre, A82 onto A86.*

Set in the Great Glen which stretches from Fort William to Inverness, this was once the village smithy and is now a very friendly restaurant with rooms. The attractive bedrooms, named after places in Scotland, are comfortably furnished and well equipped. A relaxing garden room is available for guests' use. Delicious evening meals are served in the award-winning Russell's restaurant.

Smiddy House

Rooms: 4 en suite 1 annexe en suite (1 GF) **D** fr £120* **Facilities:** FTV Lounge tea/coffee Dinner available WiFi **Extras:** Speciality toiletries – complimentary **Parking:** 15 **Notes:** No children 12 years Closed Monday RS November to March limited opening

---

STRATHPEFFER
Map 23 NH45

Inver Lodge

★★★ GUEST HOUSE

tel: 01997 421392 & 07895 030713 **IV14 9DL**
email: inverlodgebandb@gmail.com **web:** www.inverlodgestrathpeffer.com
dir: *A834 through Strathpeffer centre, turn beside Spa Pavilion signed Bowling Green, Inver Lodge on right.*

You are assured of a warm welcome at this Victorian lodge, secluded in its own tree-studded gardens yet within easy walking distance of the town centre. Bedrooms are comfortable and well equipped, and the cosy lounge is ideal for relaxation. Breakfasts are served at a communal table.

Rooms: 2 rms (1 fmly) **S** fr £35 **D** fr £52* **Facilities:** FTV Lounge tea/coffee WiFi **Parking:** 2 **Notes:** LB Closed Christmas and New Year

---

ULLAPOOL
Map 22 NH19

The Arch Inn

★★★ INN

tel: 01854 612454 **10-11 West Shore Street IV26 2UR**
email: info@thearchinn.co.uk **web:** www.thearchinn.co.uk
dir: *Into Ullapool, continue along Shore Street. Pass pier, inn on right.*

The Arch Inn is situated on Ullapool's waterfront on the shores of Loch Broom, only a two-minute walk from the Outer Hebrides ferry terminal. The accommodation provided is comfortable, and most rooms have stunning views over the loch to the mountains in the distance. The relaxed bar and grill offers a selection of fresh local produce including seafood.

Rooms: 10 en suite (1 fmly) (2 GF) **Facilities:** STV FTV tea/coffee Dinner available WiFi **Extras:** Sweets **Conf:** Max 60 Thtr 40 Class 30 Board 35 **Parking:** 5

INVERCLYDE

INVERKIP
Map 20 NS27

The Inverkip

★★★ INN

tel: 01475 521478 **Main Street PA16 0AS**
email: hello@inverkip.co.uk **web:** www.inverkip.co.uk
dir: *Just off A78, near Inverkip Marina.*

This family-run property enjoys a great location at the centre of the historic village of Inverkip and is only a short stroll from the popular Inverkip Marina. This is just the place for those with an interest in good pub food and a passion for cask ales, whiskies (over 200 on offer) or gins. The small public bar and a larger restaurant are very atmospheric; the friendly staff are always on hand and eager to please. Bedrooms and bathrooms are modern and well presented. Ample parking is provided on site.

Rooms: 5 en suite (2 fmly) **Facilities:** STV FTV Lounge tea/coffee Dinner available WiFi **Parking:** 33 **Notes:** Closed 24–25 and 31 December to 1 January (accommodation); 1–2 January and 25 December closed for accommodation and food

---

NORTH LANARKSHIRE

MOTHERWELL
Map 20 NS75

Innkeeper's Lodge Glasgow

★★★ INN

tel: 03451 551551 **1 Hamilton Road ML1 3RB**
email: info@innkeeperslodge.com **web:** www.innkeeperslodge.com
dir: *Phone for directions.*

This Innkeeper's Lodge (The Toby Carvery Strathclyde Park in Motherwell) enjoys a good location for those travelling to and from Scotland, or as a base for visiting anywhere in the central belt. The inn is located just off the M74 with links to nearby Glasgow and Edinburgh. Modern, spacious bedrooms occupy an attractive building where friendly service, wide-ranging breakfasts, free WiFi and complimentary parking are provided. Next door to the accommodation is the popular Toby Carvery where food and real ales are available all day.

Rooms: 28 en suite (13 fmly) (14 GF) **Facilities:** FTV tea/coffee Dinner available WiFi **Conf:** Max 35 **Parking:** 150

EAST LOTHIAN

ABERLADY   Map 21 NT47

Ducks Inn

★★★★ ◎◎ ⊛ RESTAURANT WITH ROOMS

tel: 01875 870682 **Main Street EH32 0RE**
email: info@ducks.co.uk **web:** www.ducks.co.uk
dir: *A1 (Bankton junction) take 1st exit to North Berwick. At next roundabout 3rd exit onto A198 signed Longniddry, left towards Aberlady. At T-junction, facing river, right to Aberlady.*

The name of this restaurant with rooms is referenced around the building – Ducks Restaurant for award-winning cuisine, Donald's Bistro and the Ducklings informal coffee shop. The warm and welcoming public areas include a great bar, full of collected objets d'art, offering real ales, a range of malt whiskies and Cuban cigars kept in a large humidor. The comfortable bedrooms are well appointed and have stylish en suites. The team are informal and friendly, taking the time to chat to their guests.

Rooms: 23 en suite (1 fmly) (6 GF) **S** fr £85 **D** fr £110* **Facilities:** STV FTV Lounge TVL tea/coffee Dinner available Direct dial WiFi ⅃ 🔒 **Conf:** Max 100 Thtr 100 Class 60 Board 30 **Parking:** 15

WEST LOTHIAN

EAST CALDER   Map 21 NT06

Ashcroft Farmhouse

★★★★ 🍽 GUEST HOUSE

tel: 01506 881810 & 07788 926239 **East Calder EH53 0ET**
email: ashcroftinfo@aol.com **web:** www.ashcroftfarmhouse.com

(For full entry see Livingston)

Whitecroft Bed & Breakfast

★★★★ BED AND BREAKFAST

tel: 01506 882494 **7 Raw Holdings, East Calder EH53 0ET**
email: lornascot@aol.com **web:** www.whitecroftbandb.co.uk

(For full entry see Livingston)

LINLITHGOW   Map 21 NS97

Premier Collection

Arden Country House

★★★★★ 🍽 GUEST ACCOMMODATION

tel: 01506 670172 **Belsyde EH49 6QE**
email: info@ardencountryhouse.com **web:** www.ardencountryhouse.com
dir: *1.3 miles southwest of Linlithgow. A706 over Union Canal, entrance 200 yards on left at Lodge Cottage.*

Situated in the picturesque grounds of the Belsyde country estate and close to the Royal Burgh of Linlithgow, Arden Country House offers immaculate, stylishly furnished and spacious bedrooms. There is a cosy ground-floor lounge and a charming dining room where delicious breakfasts feature the best local produce.

Rooms: 3 en suite (1 GF) **S** fr £80 **D** fr £95 (room only)* **Facilities:** FTV iPod docking station Lounge tea/coffee WiFi 🔒 **Extras:** Savoury snacks, chocolates **Parking:** 4 **Notes:** LB No children 12 years Closed 25–26 December

Bomains Farm Guest House

★★★★ GUEST HOUSE

tel: 01506 822188 & 07974 736480 **Bo'ness EH49 7RQ**
email: bunty.kirk@onetel.net **web:** www.bomains.co.uk
dir: *A706, 1.5 miles north towards Bo'ness, left at golf course crossroads, 1st farm on right.*

From its elevated location, this friendly farmhouse has stunning views of the Firth of Forth. The bedrooms, which vary in size, are beautifully decorated and well equipped with many thoughtful extra touches. Delicious home-cooked food, featuring the best local produce, is served in a stylish lounge-dining room.

Rooms: 6 rms (4 en suite) (1 pri facs) (1 fmly) (2 GF) **Facilities:** STV FTV DVD Lounge TVL tea/coffee WiFi ⅃ Fishing 🔒 **Extras:** Sweets **Parking:** 12

Kirkland House

★★★★ BED AND BREAKFAST

tel: 01506 822188 & 07974 736480 **Bomains Farm EH49 7RQ**
email: bunty.kirk@onetel.net **web:** www.bomains.co.uk
dir: *A706, 1.5 miles north towards Bo'ness, left at golf course crossroads, 1st farm on right.*

Kirkland House is a purpose-built property adjacent to the family-run Bomains Farm Guest House, where a number of guest services are provided. The large bedrooms come with high quality fixtures and fittings, and patio doors that lead onto the garden which has a children's play area and views onto the River Forth. This is a peaceful location within striking distance of Linlithgow and Edinburgh.

Rooms: 3 en suite (1 fmly) (3 GF) **Facilities:** FTV TVL tea/coffee WiFi ⅃ Fishing **Parking:** 6

LIVINGSTON   Map 21 NT06

Ashcroft Farmhouse

★★★★ 🍽 GUEST HOUSE

tel: 01506 881810 & 07788 926239 **East Calder EH53 0ET**
email: ashcroftinfo@aol.com **web:** www.ashcroftfarmhouse.com
dir: *From A71 follow East Calder/B7015 signs. Farmhouse 0.5 mile east of East Calder.*

With over 40 years' experience in caring for guests, Derek and Elizabeth Scott ensure a stay at Ashcroft will be memorable. Their modern home sits in lovely, award-winning landscaped gardens and provides attractive and well-equipped ground-floor bedrooms. The comfortable lounge includes a video and DVD library. Breakfast, featuring home-made sausages and the best local produce, is served at individual tables in the stylish dining room. Free WiFi is available, and a Park and Ride facility is nearby.

Rooms: 6 en suite (2 fmly) (6 GF) **D** fr £80* **Facilities:** FTV TVL tea/coffee WiFi 🔒 **Parking:** 8

Whitecroft Bed & Breakfast

★★★★ BED AND BREAKFAST

tel: 01506 882494 **7 Raw Holdings, East Calder EH53 0ET**
email: lornascot@aol.com **web:** www.whitecroftbandb.co.uk
dir: A71 onto B7015, establishment on right.

A relaxed and friendly atmosphere prevails at Whitecroft, a charming, modern bed and breakfast. The bedrooms, all on the ground floor, are attractively colour co-ordinated, well-equipped and contain many thoughtful extra touches. Breakfast is served at individual tables in the smart dining room.

Rooms: 3 en suite (3 GF) **Facilities:** FTV DVD tea/coffee WiFi **Parking:** 5
Notes: No children 12 years

MIDLOTHIAN

DALKEITH
Map 21 NT36

The Sun Inn

★★★★ ⚛ ☐ INN

tel: 0131 663 2456 **Lothian Bridge EH22 4TR**
email: thesuninn@live.com **web:** www.thesuninnedinburgh.co.uk
dir: On A7 towards Galashiels, opposite Newbattle Viaduct.

The Sun Inn dates back to 1697 and is situated within easy striking distance of Edinburgh. It has boutique-style bedrooms (one featuring a copper bath) and modern bathrooms. High quality, award-winning food is served in stylish surroundings; drinks can be enjoyed in the terraced garden area.

Rooms: 6 en suite **S** fr £75 **D** fr £95* **Facilities:** STV FTV Lounge tea/coffee Dinner available WiFi ⚓ Fishing **Conf:** Max 80 Thtr 80 Class 50 Board 40 **Parking:** 100 **Notes:** LB

MORAY

FORRES
Map 23 NJ05

Cluny Bank

★★★★ ⚛ RESTAURANT WITH ROOMS

tel: 01309 674304 **69 St Leonards Road IV36 1DW**
email: info@clunybankhotel.co.uk **web:** www.clunybankhotel.co.uk

Historic, listed Cluny Bank occupies a quiet location within walking distance of the centre of Forres, and is an ideal base for exploring the north-east of Scotland. Family-run, the building retains many original architectural features. Public areas include the Altyre Bar with a wide range of whiskies, and Franklin's Restaurant where a real taste of Moray can be experienced. Room service, complimentary WiFi and memorable breakfasts are also provided for guests.

Rooms: 6 en suite 1 annexe en suite (2 GF) **S** fr £85 **D** fr £122.50* **Facilities:** FTV iPod docking station Lounge tea/coffee Dinner available Direct dial WiFi **Parking:** 7 **Notes:** LB

PERTH & KINROSS

ABERFELDY
Map 23 NN84

Errichel House

★★★★ ⚛⚛ ☐ RESTAURANT WITH ROOMS

tel: 01887 829562 & 07921 507458 **Errichel Farm, Crieff Road PH15 2EL**
email: paulnewman@errichel.co.uk **web:** www.errichel.co.uk
dir: 2 miles from Aberfeldy on Crieff Road (A826).

The accommodation on this family-run working farm occupies a stunning location in an elevated location above Aberfeldy, with breathtaking views of the Perthshire hills. The beautiful grounds, with a duck pond, are home to an array of wildlife. Bedrooms and public areas are luxuriously presented and deeply comfortable. A stay here is not complete without sampling the food on offer at the restaurant 'Thyme at Errichel' or taking home some of the many home-made delicacies from their 'Thyme to Eat' shop. In fact, all the lamb, beef and pork sold here comes from the farm itself.

Rooms: 4 en suite (1 fmly) **D** fr £129* **Facilities:** FTV iPod docking station Lounge tea/coffee Dinner available WiFi ⚓ **Conf:** Max 40 Thtr 40 Class 16 Board 20 **Parking:** 12 **Notes:** LB Closed 23–26 December RS 12 January to 1 March restaurant open Thursday to Friday and Saturday evening Civ wed 120

ALYTH
Map 21 NO24

Tigh Na Leigh Guesthouse

★★★★★ ☐ ⚘ GUEST ACCOMMODATION

tel: 01828 632372 **22–24 Airlie Street PH11 8AJ**
email: book@tighnaleigh.com **web:** www.tighnaleigh.co.uk
dir: In town centre on B952.

Situated in the heart of this charming country town, Tigh Na Leigh (Gaelic for 'The House of the Doctor') is an equally charming property. It has an imposing, yet welcoming appearance, and inside, the Victorian architecture blends with contemporary interior design. Bedrooms, including a superb suite, have state-of-the-art bathrooms and spa baths. There are three lounges, and delicious meals are served in the conservatory-dining room overlooking a spectacular landscaped garden. Free WiFi is provided.

Rooms: 5 en suite (1 GF) **S** fr £57 **D** fr £97* **Facilities:** FTV DVD iPod docking station Lounge TVL tea/coffee Dinner available Licensed WiFi ⚓ **Extras:** Fruit, mineral water **Parking:** 5 **Notes:** No children 12 years Closed December to January

BLAIR ATHOLL   Map 23 NN86

The Firs

★★★★ GUEST HOUSE

tel: 01796 481256 **PH18 5TA**
email: kirstie@firs-blairatholl.co.uk **web:** www.firs-blairatholl.co.uk
dir: *A9 follow signs to Blair Atholl, 1st left after Blair Atholl garage.*

The Firs is located in the peaceful village of Blair Atholl, home of Europe's only legal private army, the Atholl Highlanders. This is a well-presented property with lovely gardens. Bedrooms are comfortable and have quality decor. Public areas are warm and welcoming and are enhanced by a log fire, while breakfast is served in the conservatory at individual tables.

Rooms: 6 en suite (3 fmly) (2 GF) **S** fr £55 **D** fr £75* **Facilities:** FTV DVD Lounge tea/coffee WiFi ⚓ **Extras:** Speciality toiletries **Parking:** 7 **Notes:** LB Closed November to February

CALVINE   Map 23 NN86

The Struan Inn

★★★★ GUEST ACCOMMODATION

tel: 01796 483714 **PH18 5UB**
email: thestruan.calvine@btinternet.com **web:** www.thestruan-inn.co.uk
dir: *From north: A9 turn right onto B847, turn right for Kinloch Rannoch. Under bridge, 1st right. From south: A9 turn left onto B847, turn right for Kinloch Rannoch, then as for from north.*

Located on the edge of the Cairngorms National Park in a peaceful location yet just two minutes from the A9, this historic inn is comfortable and welcoming. Inside there is a residents' bar with a log fire, a lounge for relaxing in and a restaurant serving hearty dinners. The bedrooms are well appointed with modern amenities. The hospitality is warm and friendly.

Rooms: 5 en suite (2 fmly) (1 GF) **S** fr £55 **D** fr £70 **Facilities:** STV DVD iPod docking station TVL tea/coffee Dinner available Licensed WiFi ⚓ **Parking:** 8 **Notes:** Closed 17 December to January

MEIKLEOUR   Map 21 NO13

Meikleour Arms

★★★★ INN

tel: 01250 883206 & 883406 **PH2 6EB**
email: contact@meikleourarms.co.uk **web:** www.meikleourarms.co.uk
dir: *North of Perth on A93.*

The popular country estate inn with stylish, boutique accommodation welcomes both locals and visitors who come to the area for fishing and shooting. The elegant, contemporary bedrooms and cottages all have super-king or king-sized beds with luxurious hypoallergenic bedding, impressive bathrooms and quirky French furnishings; ground-floor rooms have baths and separate walk-in showers. An attractive restaurant, with a private dining room, serves high quality local produce, and the residents' sitting room, with its attractive fireplace, is perfect for enjoying the property's own real ale or the extensive wine list. Dogs are allowed in rooms with wooden floors.

Rooms: 11 en suite 9 rms annexe (5 en suite) (3 fmly) (14 GF) **Facilities:** FTV Lounge tea/coffee Dinner available WiFi ⚓ Fishing ⚓ Drying room for anglers, Tayside police-licensed gun cabinets **Extras:** Speciality toiletries, bottled water, sherry, fruit – complimentary **Parking:** 40

SCOTTISH BORDERS

EDDLESTON   Map 21 NT24

The Horseshoe Restaurant with Rooms

★★★★ 🍴 RESTAURANT WITH ROOMS

tel: 01721 730225 **Edinburgh Road EH45 8QP**
email: reservations@horseshoeinn.co.uk **web:** www.horseshoeinn.co.uk
dir: *A703, 5 miles north of Peebles.*

The Horseshoe is five miles north of Peebles and only 18 miles south of Edinburgh. Originally a blacksmith's shop, it has a very good reputation for its delightful atmosphere and excellent cuisine. There are eight luxuriously appointed and individually designed bedrooms. Please note: children are welcome, but dinner is not served to under fives except in the private dining room.

Rooms: 8 en suite (1 fmly) (6 GF) **Facilities:** FTV Lounge tea/coffee Dinner available Direct dial WiFi **Extras:** Speciality toiletries, fruit, mineral water – complimentary **Parking:** 20 **Notes:** LB Closed 25 December, 1st 2 weeks January and 2 weeks July RS Monday and Tuesday closed

INNERLEITHEN   Map 21 NT33

Caddon View

★★★★ 🍴 🍷 GUEST ACCOMMODATION

tel: 01896 830208 **14 Pirn Road EH44 6HH**
email: stay@caddonview.co.uk **web:** www.caddonview.co.uk
dir: *Signed from A72 in Innerleithen.*

Set in its own landscaped gardens, this well-presented Victorian house was originally built in the 1850s. Caddon View offers high standards of accommodation along with wonderful hospitality and customer care. Located in the beautiful Tweed Valley, it's ideally placed for all the border areas as well as Edinburgh. The property is licensed and serves quality evening meals (by prior arrangement), in a bright, welcoming and well-appointed dining room.

Rooms: 8 rms (7 en suite) (1 pri facs) (2 fmly) (2 GF) **S** fr £55 **D** fr £65 **Facilities:** FTV DVD Lounge tea/coffee Dinner available Licensed WiFi ⚓ **Parking:** 7 **Notes:** Closed 25–26 December RS Sunday to Monday no dinner available

JEDBURGH   Map 21 NT62

Ferniehirst Mill Lodge

★★ GUEST HOUSE

tel: 01835 863279 **TD8 6PQ**
email: ferniehirstmill@aol.com **web:** www.ferniehirstmill.co.uk
dir: *2.5 miles south of Jedburgh on A68, onto private track to end.*

Reached by a narrow farm track and a rustic wooden bridge, this chalet-style house has a secluded setting by the River Jed. Bedrooms are small and functional, and there is a comfortable lounge in which to relax. Home-cooked and hearty breakfasts are served in the cosy dining room.

Rooms: 7 en suite (1 GF) **Facilities:** TVL tea/coffee WiFi Fishing Riding ⚓ **Parking:** 10

MELROSE
Map 21 NT53

Premier Collection

Fauhope Country House

★★★★★ GUEST HOUSE

tel: 01896 823184 & 07906 184266 **Gattonside TD6 9LU**
email: info@fauhopehouse.com **web:** www.fauhopehouse.com
dir: *From roundabout on A6091 (west of Melrose) take B6360 signed Gattonside. Left signed Gattonside (over River Tweed bridge). Right signed Gattonside. 1 mile, through Gattonside, left into Monkswood Road just before derestriction sign. Immediately right into private road.*

It's hard to imagine a more complete experience than a stay at Fauhope Country House, set high on a hillside on the north-east edge of the village. Hospitality is first class, breakfasts are excellent, and the delightful property has a splendid interior. The bedrooms are luxurious, each is individual and superbly equipped, and the public areas are elegantly appointed and enhanced by beautiful floral arrangements; the dining room is particularly stunning.

Rooms: 3 en suite **Facilities:** FTV DVD Lounge tea/coffee Dinner available WiFi ⚘ Riding Treatment room **Extras:** Speciality toiletries, fruit, sherry – complimentary **Parking:** 10 **Notes:** LB

PEEBLES
Map 21 NT24

Premier Collection

Kingsmuir House

★★★★★ BED AND BREAKFAST

tel: 01721 724413 & 07776 405842 **Springhill Road EH45 9EP**
email: malcolm@kingsmuirhouse.co.uk **web:** www.kingsmuirhouse.co.uk
dir: *From High Street, over bridge then 2nd right into Springhill Road. 0.25 mile opposite tennis court.*

Kingsmuir House was built in 1855 and is set in a slightly elevated position to the south-west of Peebles, just a few minutes' walk from the high street. This period building still boasts many original features and the decor and furnishings are in keeping with its character. Hospitality is warm and genuine. The bedroom suites are generous in size and beautifully presented with many thoughtful extras provided as standard. The en suites are also a feature, with walk-in showers and free-standing roll-top baths. The gardens are delightful and include a charming summer house.

Rooms: 2 en suite **S** fr £90 **D** fr £140* **Facilities:** FTV DVD iPod docking station tea/coffee WiFi ⚘ **Extras:** Home-made shortbread and truffles, fruit **Parking:** 5 **Notes:** No children 12 years

WALKERBURN
Map 21 NT33

Premier Collection

Windlestraw

★★★★★ ◉◉ RESTAURANT WITH ROOMS

tel: 01896 870636 **Galashiels Road EH43 6AA**
email: stay@windlestraw.co.uk **web:** www.windlestraw.co.uk
dir: *East of Innerleithen on A72. On left, just before leaving the village.*

The present owners are breathing fresh life into this beautiful Edwardian manor situated in two-acre grounds in the rolling hills. It's in a peaceful location yet Edinburgh is easily accessible. The house was built in 1906 for the wife of a Scottish cashmere mill owner and many detailed architectural features remain. The smart, spacious bedrooms come with Egyptian cotton bed linen, TVs and WiFi. Expect a warm welcome and relaxed atmosphere together with superb Scottish cooking at breakfast and in the evening (please note, no children under 11 years at dinner). Windlestraw is an AA Restaurant with Rooms of the Year runner up for 2018–19.

Rooms: 6 en suite **S** fr £175 **D** fr £200* **Facilities:** FTV Lounge tea/coffee Dinner available Direct dial WiFi ⚘ **Extras:** Speciality toiletries **Parking:** 10 **Notes:** LB Closed 20 December to 10 February Civ wed 25

STIRLING

STIRLING
Map 21 NS79

Premier Collection

Victoria Square Guest House

★★★★★ 🅰 GUEST HOUSE

tel: 01786 473920 **12 Victoria Square FK8 2QZ**
email: info@vsgh.co.uk **web:** www.victoriasquareguesthouse.com
dir: *M9 junction 10 into Stirling, at Smith Museum 1st right into Victoria Place. 1st left into Victoria Square.*

This classic Victorian building is situated in the peaceful and prestigious Kings Park area of Stirling, just a short walk from the castle, the golf club, the Smith Museum & Art Gallery and other attractions. The spacious and well-appointed bedrooms ensure a peaceful and relaxing stay; they combine contemporary elegance with historical charm. A warm welcome is guaranteed.

Rooms: 10 en suite (1 GF) **Facilities:** FTV iPod docking station Lounge tea/coffee WiFi ⚘ **Extras:** Speciality toiletries, mini-fridge, robes **Parking:** 5 **Notes:** No children 12 years Closed 23–29 December

Follow the AA

twitter: @TheAA_Lifestyle
facebook: www.facebook.com/TheAAUK

SCOTTISH ISLANDS

ISLE OF ARRAN

BRODICK   Map 20 NS03

Dunvegan House

★★★★ GUEST HOUSE

tel: 01770 302811 **Dunvegan Shore Road KA27 8AJ**
email: dunveganhouse1@hotmail.com **web:** www.dunveganhouse-arran.co.uk
dir: *Turn right from ferry terminal, 500 yards along Shore Road.*

Situated close to the shore and enjoying spectacular views of the bay, this establishment is a popular choice for visitors to the island. The property benefits from having a hands-on approach from the friendly owner while public areas and bedrooms have great views.

Rooms: 9 en suite (3 GF) **S** fr £60 **D** fr £90* **Facilities:** FTV Lounge tea/coffee Licensed WiFi 🛁 **Parking:** 8 **Notes:** Closed 23 December to 3 January

WHITING BAY   Map 20 NS02

AA GUEST ACCOMMODATION
OF THE YEAR FOR SCOTLAND 2018–19

Premier Collection

Cruickshanks Boutique B&B

★★★★★ 🛡 BED AND BREAKFAST

tel: 01770 700190 **Benview, Golf Course Road KA27 8QT**
email: info@cruickshanksarran.co.uk **web:** www.cruickshanksarran.co.uk
dir: *From Ardrossan take ferry to Brodick. From ferry terminal turn left onto A841 south for 8 miles, turn right at The Coffee Pot. Follow signs for Whiting Bay Golf Club, turn right into Golf Course Road, Cruickshanks on left.*

Cruickshanks Boutique B&B lies above Whiting Bay village with commanding views over the Firth of Clyde towards the Scottish mainland. All bedrooms feature luxurious Hypnos mattresses, Egyptian cotton bedding and comfortable hypo-allergenic duvets. Each has a comfortable seating area, WiFi, TV and DAB clock radio with Bluetooth. Bathrooms feature rain showers, bathrobes, hairdryers and toiletries from Arran Aromatics. The large and well-appointed sitting room has a wide range of books, maps and journals. Breakfast offers home-made muesli, jams and marmalades and artisan breads, in addition to cooked options including the traditional Scottish breakfast, local smoked haddock and French toast with maple syrup. Afternoon tea, featuring Nanette's home baking, is available at 4pm every day. Cruickshanks is close to Whiting Bay Golf Course and there are several walks that take you to the dramatic Glenashdale Falls and imposing Neolithic standing stones known locally as 'The Giants Graves'.

Rooms: 3 en suite **S** fr £100 **D** fr £120* **Facilities:** FTV iPod docking station Lounge tea/coffee WiFi 🛁 **Extras:** Speciality toiletries, fresh fruit, afternoon tea **Parking:** 3 **Notes:** No children 16 years Closed December to February

ISLE OF ISLAY

GLENEGEDALE   Map 20 NR35

Premier Collection

Glenegedale House

★★★★★ 🛡 GUEST HOUSE

tel: 01496 300400 & 07554 669664 **PA42 7AS**
email: info@glenegedalehouse.co.uk **web:** www.glenegedalehouse.co.uk
dir: *From Port Askaig ferry take A846, through Bridgend. In Bowmore left at crossroads. House on left in 5.5 miles.*

The strength here is that the hosts who go out of their way to ensure guests enjoy both the house and all that the island has to offer. Situated halfway between Bowmore and Port Ellen, this luxury guest house boasts some of the best views on the island, with the Mull of Oa and the glory of the Atlantic Ocean in full view. The modern accommodation is complemented by a range of comfortable lounges. Memorable breakfasts are served in the stunning dining room.

Rooms: 4 en suite (1 GF) **S** fr £110 **D** fr £205 **Facilities:** FTV Lounge tea/coffee Licensed WiFi 🎣 Fishing 🛁 **Parking:** 8 **Notes:** LB No children 12 years Closed December

ISLE OF MULL

CRAIGNURE   Map 20 NN11

Pennygate Lodge

[U]

tel: 01680 812333 **PA65 6AY**
email: info@pennygatelodge.scot **web:** www.pennygatelodge.scot
dir: *From ferry in Craignure left, 1.25 miles. Left at police station, next right. Pennygate Lodge at top of driveway.*

Currently the rating for this establishment is not confirmed. This may be due to a change of ownership or because it has only recently joined the AA rating scheme.

Rooms: 6 en suite **S** fr £100 **D** fr £130* **Facilities:** Lounge tea/coffee Dinner available Licensed WiFi 🛁 **Extras:** Speciality toiletries, fresh milk **Parking:** 10 **Notes:** Closed January

TOBERMORY
Map 22 NM55

Highland Cottage
★★★★ ◎◎ 🍽 RESTAURANT WITH ROOMS

tel: 01688 302030 **24 Breadalbane Street PA75 6PD**
email: davidandjo@highlandcottage.co.uk **web:** www.highlandcottage.co.uk
dir: *From A848 at Craignure/Fishnish ferry terminal, pass Tobermory signs, straight on at mini roundabout, across narrow bridge, turn right. On right opposite fire station.*

Providing the highest level of natural and unassuming hospitality, this delightful little gem lies high above the island's capital. Don't be fooled by its side street location, a stunning view over the bay is just a few metres away. 'A country house in town', it is an Aladdin's Cave of collectables and treasures, as well as masses of books and magazines. There are two inviting lounges, one with an honesty bar. The cosy dining room offers memorable dinners and splendid breakfasts. Bedrooms are individual in design; some have four-posters and all are comprehensively equipped including TVs and music centres.

Rooms: 6 en suite (1 GF) **D** fr £145* **Facilities:** FTV Lounge tea/coffee Dinner available Direct dial WiFi 🛁 **Extras:** Speciality toiletries, fruit, phone/tablet charger **Notes:** No children 10 years Closed November to March

Follow us on twitter
@TheAA_Lifestyle

Symbols and abbreviations
explained on pages 6–7

ISLE OF SKYE

STRUAN
Map 22 NG35

Premier Collection

Ullinish Country Lodge
★★★★★ ◎◎◎ 🍽 RESTAURANT WITH ROOMS

tel: 01470 572214 **IV56 8FD**
email: ullinish@theisleofskye.co.uk **web:** www.theisleofskye.co.uk
dir: *From Skye bridge take A87 north, then left onto A863. Lodge signed after Struan on left.*

Set in some of Scotland's most dramatic landscape, with views of the Black Cuillin and MacLeod's Tables, this lodge has lochs on three sides. Samuel Johnson and James Boswell stayed here in 1773 and were impressed with the hospitality even then — hosts, Brian and Pam hope to extend the same welcome to their guests today. As you would expect, all bedrooms have amazing views; each room has a half-tester bed and some of the en suites have roll-top baths. Modern, award-winning Scottish dishes are created with skill and precision and served in the candelit dining room. Free WiFi is available.

Rooms: 6 en suite **S** fr £125 **D** fr £190* **Facilities:** FTV Lounge tea/coffee Dinner available WiFi **Extras:** Sherry, sweets, mineral water – complimentary **Parking:** 8 **Notes:** LB No children 16 years Closed 24 December to January

UIG
Map 22 NG36

Woodbine House
GUEST ACCOMMODATION

tel: 01470 542243 & 07985 660382 **IV51 9XP**
email: contact@woodbineskye.co.uk **web:** www.woodbineskye.co.uk
dir: *From Portree to Uig Bay, pass Ferry Inn, right onto A855 (Staffin Road), house 300 yards on right.*

Built in the late 19th century, Woodbine House occupies an elevated position overlooking Uig Bay and the surrounding countryside, and is well suited for walking and bird-watching enthusiasts. The ground-floor dining room has lovely sea views, as do the front-facing bedrooms.

Rooms: 5 en suite (1 fmly) (1 GF) **S** fr £50 **D** fr £70* **Facilities:** FTV TVL tea/coffee WiFi **Parking:** 5 **Notes:** LB RS November to February long stays or group bookings only

Wales

ISLE OF ANGLESEY

BEAUMARIS
Map 14 SH67

Premier Collection

The Bull - Beaumaris
★★★★★ @@ 🛏 INN

tel: 01248 810329 **Castle Street LL58 8AP**
email: info@bullsheadinn.co.uk **web:** www.bullsheadinn.co.uk
dir: *On main street in town centre.*

Both Charles Dickens and Samuel Johnson visited this inn, and the interior still features exposed beams and antique weaponry. Bedrooms are richly decorated and traditional, while The Townhouse, just across a side street, offers additional boutique bedrooms, each with vibrant decor. The food continues to attract high praise in both the Loft Restaurant and the less formal Brasserie, and cask-conditioned ales are served in the traditional bar. Meetings and functions can be catered for. (Please note, no children under 7 years in fine dining restaurant).

Rooms: 25 en suite (2 fmly) (5 GF) **S** fr £100 **D** fr £110* **Facilities:** FTV Lounge tea/coffee Dinner available Direct dial Lift WiFi ⚓ **Extras:** Speciality toiletries, Welsh Cakes, Aberffraw biscuits – complimentary **Parking:** 1 **Notes:** LB Closed 24–26 December

HOLYHEAD
Map 14 SH28

Blackthorn Farm
★★★★ ⚑ GUEST ACCOMMODATION

tel: 01407 765262 **Penrhosfeilw, Trearddur Bay LL65 2LT**
email: enquiries@blackthornfarm.co.uk **web:** www.blackthornleisure.co.uk
dir: *A55 to Holyhead, take 1st exit at roundabout, turn immediately right between two pubs. At end of road, turn right, 0.5 mile on left.*

Blackthorn Farm is a family-run establishment that is also a camping and touring site. Set in 18 peaceful acres on Holy Island, the farm enjoys outstanding panoramic views of the Irish Sea, Snowdonia and the Anglesey coast. A beach and coastal trails are within easy reach. A full Welsh breakfast is served. Please note, pets are welcome here.

Rooms: 8 rms (6 en suite) (3 fmly) (1 GF) **S** fr £72 **D** fr £85* **Facilities:** FTV DVD tea/coffee Licensed WiFi ⚓ **Parking:** 10 **Notes:** LB Closed 22–31 December

MENAI BRIDGE
Map 14 SH57

Anglesey Arms
★★★★ INN

tel: 01248 712305 **Mona Road LL59 5EA**
email: anglesey.arms@jwlees.co.uk **web:** www.anglesey-arms.co.uk
dir: *Phone for directions.*

There are many reasons to stay at the Anglesey Arms – a welcoming friendly team, real craft ales on tap, locally-sourced, delicious food and comfortable bedrooms. Located just as you come over the Thomas Telford Bridge from the mainland, it's one of the first buildings in Anglesey. The smart bedrooms have TVs, WiFi, tea- and coffee-making facilities and complimentary mineral water. Alfresco dining on the elevated terrace is a real treat in the summer months.

Rooms: 16 en suite **S** fr £85 **D** fr £150* **Facilities:** Dinner available WiFi **Parking:** 45

RHOSNEIGR
Map 14 SH37

Cefn Dref
★★★★ 🛏 BED AND BREAKFAST

tel: 01407 810714 & 07834 340854 **LL64 5JH**
email: bookings@cefndref.co.uk **web:** www.cefndref.co.uk
dir: *A55 junction 5 (signed Rhosneigr), onto A4080 to Llanfaelog. Turn right signed Rhosneigr, 1st house on right after 30mph sign.*

Enjoying stunning coastal views, this welcoming Edwardian shooting lodge is a very comfortable and inviting bed and breakfast. Bedrooms, complemented by smart, stylish bathrooms, are very well equipped with extras including WiFi and luxury toiletries. Breakfast is a memorable experience, with home-made or locally-sourced produce from an extensive and imaginative menu. The town centre, with many dining options, is a short walk away, as is the sea.

Rooms: 3 en suite (1 fmly) **S** fr £74 **D** fr £89* **Facilities:** FTV DVD iPod docking station tea/coffee WiFi ⚓ ⚓ **Extras:** Speciality toiletries, fridges in rooms **Parking:** 10 **Notes:** Closed November to Easter

BRIDGEND

BRIDGEND
Map 9 SS97

Hazelwood Guest House
★★★★ GUEST HOUSE

tel: 01656 647780 **Tondu Road CF31 4LJ**
email: info@hazelwood-house.co.uk **web:** www.hazelwood-house.co.uk
dir: *Phone for directions.*

Located just outside Bridgend, this popular guest house offers a range of well-equipped bedrooms and bathrooms including some on the ground floor. Breakfast is taken in the comfortable conservatory and a large car park is also provided. There are several options for dinner – all within a short walk of Hazelwood, including a pleasant inn.

Rooms: 8 en suite (3 GF) **Facilities:** FTV TVL tea/coffee WiFi ⚓ **Parking:** 14 **Notes:** LB Closed 24–27 December

CARDIFF

CARDIFF
Map 9 ST17

Innkeeper's Lodge Cardiff
★★★★ INN

tel: 03451 551551 **The Beverley Hotel, 75–77 Cathedral Road CF11 9PG**
email: info@innkeeperslodge.com **web:** www.innkeeperslodge.com
dir: *M4 junction 29 (from east) onto A48. Left onto A4119, 0.5 mile left again (Cathedral Road). Lodge on right.*

Located in the Pontcanna district of Cardiff, this Victorian villa has been tastefully restored as an inn. The modern bedrooms are equipped to a good standard, offering a range of extras for both the business and leisure guests. The popular bar and restaurant serve home-cooked classics plus a number of real ales on tap. Just a short walk away are the Swalec Stadium, Cardiff University and the Millennium Centre.

Rooms: 17 en suite (9 fmly) **Facilities:** FTV tea/coffee Dinner available WiFi

FELINGWM UCHAF
Map 8 SN52

Allt Y Golau Farmhouse

★★★★ 🛏 FARMHOUSE

tel: 01267 290455 **Allt Y Golau Uchaf SA32 7BB**
email: alltygolau@btinternet.com **web:** www.alltygolau.com
dir: A40 onto B4310, north for 2 miles. 1st on left after Felingwm Uchaf.

This delightful Georgian farmhouse has been furnished and decorated to a high standard by the present owners, and enjoys panoramic views over the Tywi Valley to the Black Mountains beyond. Guests are welcome to take a relaxing walk through the two acres of mature garden. Many thoughtful extras are provided in the comfortable bedrooms, and there is a separate lounge. Breakfast is provided in the cosy dining room and served around a communal table.

Rooms: 3 rms (2 en suite) (1 pri facs) (2 GF) **S** fr £45 **D** fr £70 **Facilities:** TVL tea/coffee WiFi 🛁 **Extras:** Speciality toiletries, snacks — complimentary **Parking:** 3
Notes: No children 12 years Closed 20 December to 2 January 2 acres small holding

LLANARTHNE
Map 8 SN31

Premier Collection

Llwyn Helyg Country House

★★★★★ 🛏 BED AND BREAKFAST

tel: 01558 668778 & 07464 106085 **SA32 8HJ**
email: enquiries@llwynhelygcountryhouse.co.uk
web: www.llwynhelygcountryhouse.co.uk
dir: A48 onto B4310, at roundabout at entrance of National Botanic Gardens of Wales take 1st exit (B4310). After 0.3 mile turn right at farm along lane then sharp left, 1 mile on left.

The owners of Llwyn Helyg, a modern 'country house', have used the finest quality materials to create this luxury bed and breakfast accommodation. Situated in three acres of landscaped gardens and surrounded by countryside, it's on the outskirts of Llanarthne, midway between Carmarthen and Llandeilo. All the individually designed, en suite bedrooms have 6-foot wide beds and luxurious Vi-Spring mattresses. Private parking is available.

Rooms: 3 en suite **S** fr £105 **D** fr £135 **Facilities:** FTV DVD iPod docking station Lounge TVL tea/coffee WiFi 🛁 Therapy/Holistic treatment room **Extras:** Speciality toiletries, fruit, snacks — complimentary **Conf:** Max 6 Board 6 **Parking:** 10
Notes: LB No children 16 years Closed Christmas and New Year

LLANDOVERY
Map 9 SN73

Llanerchindda Farm

★★★ 🛏 GUEST HOUSE

tel: 01550 750274 **Cynghordy SA20 0NB**
email: info@cambrianway.com **web:** www.cambrianway.com
dir: A483 (Llandovery to Builth Wells road), after 40mph sign turn left at brown tourist sign (Llanerchindda), 2.75 miles to farm.

Set in 50 acres of Welsh countryside with spectacular views over the Black Mountains and the Brecon Beacons, this farmhouse-style accommodation is the ideal base for various activities including walking, fishing, quad-bike riding and birdwatching. Bedrooms and bathrooms are comfortable and guests also have use of the lounge. In addition to a substantial breakfast, dinner is available by prior arrangement and features delicious home cooking.

Rooms: 9 en suite (1 fmly) (2 GF) **S** fr £42.50 **D** fr £85* **Facilities:** FTV Lounge TVL tea/coffee Dinner available Licensed WiFi ⚓ Fishing 🔫 Clay pigeon shooting, 4x4 driving experience **Parking:** 31 **Notes:** LB Closed 2–16 January

See advert on page 326

LLANSTEFFAN
Map 8 SN31

Mansion House Llansteffan
★★★★ ◉◉ RESTAURANT WITH ROOMS

tel: 01267 241515 & 07768 194539 **Pantyrathro SA33 5AJ**
email: info@mansionhousellansteffan.co.uk **web:** www.mansionhousellansteffan.co.uk
dir: *From Carmarthen on B4312 towards Llansteffan, follow brown signs.*

Mansion House has been lovingly restored by the current owners, and is set in five acres of grounds with enviable views over the Towy Estuary and Carmarthen Bay. While bedrooms differ in size and style, all are well-equipped and complemented by smart bathrooms. With a wealth of quality produce right on the doorstep it's not surprising that the head chef focuses on using seasonal, local and home-grown produce on the constantly changing, interesting menu. Pre-dinner drinks can be taken in the bar, where there is an excellent range of gins.

Rooms: 8 en suite (1 fmly) (2 GF) **S** fr £110 **D** fr £120* **Facilities:** FTV Lounge tea/coffee Dinner available Direct dial WiFi ⚓ **Extras:** Speciality toiletries, robes, home-made cookies **Conf:** Max 200 Thtr 150 Class 80 Board 40 **Parking:** 50
Notes: LB Civ wed 120

LLANYBYDDER
Map 8 SN54

Glasfryn Guest House
★★★★ GUEST HOUSE

tel: 01570 481400 & 07398 139084 **Glasfryn SA40 9TY**
email: ron@glasfrynguesthouse.co.uk **web:** www.glasfrynguesthouse.co.uk
dir: *On A485. On entering Llanybydder from Carmarthen, guest house on right.*

Glasfryn is a spacious, double-fronted Victorian villa standing in the centre of market town of Llanybydder. Renowned for its livestock markets and monthly pony sales, the location is ideal for exploring the nearby Cardigan Bay, the Brecon Beacons, and shopping centres of Carmarthen and Aberystwyth. The friendly owners welcome you into their home, and bedrooms are of a good size; most have en suite facilities. A wealth of original features has been retained, with high ceilings, original woodwork and architraves. Dinners can be provided on request, or there are several good quality eating places within a short drive.

Rooms: 4 rms (3 en suite) (1 pri facs) (1 fmly) **Facilities:** FTV DVD tea/coffee Dinner available WiFi ⚓ **Parking:** 6

ST CLEARS
Map 8 SN21

Coedllys Country House
★★★★★ ⚱ BED AND BREAKFAST

tel: 01994 231455 **Coedllys Uchaf, Llangynin SA33 4JY**
email: coedllys@btinternet.com **web:** www.coedllys.co.uk
dir: *A40 at St Clears roundabout, take 3rd exit, at lights turn left. After 100 yards turn right, 3 miles to Llangynin, pass village sign. 30mph sign on left, turn immediately down track (private drive).*

Set in a peaceful valley, Coedllys is the home of the Harbers who make visitors feel like honoured guests. Bedrooms are lavishly furnished, and the thoughtful and useful extras make a stay very memorable. There is a cosy, well-furnished lounge, and an extensive breakfast choice is served in the pleasant dining room. A further cottage-style annexe, suitable as a self-catering let, is also available.

Rooms: 2 en suite **D** fr £100* **Facilities:** FTV DVD iPod docking station Lounge tea/coffee WiFi ⚓ **Extras:** Speciality toiletries, home-made biscuits – complimentary **Parking:** 6 **Notes:** LB No children 12 years Closed 22–28 December

CEREDIGION

ABERAERON	Map 8 SN46

Premier Collection

Feathers Royal

★★★★★ 🛏 INN

tel: 01545 571750 **Alban Square SA46 0AQ**
email: enquiries@feathersroyal.co.uk **web:** www.feathersroyal.co.uk
dir: *A482 (Lampeter Road), Feathers Royal opposite recreation grounds.*

This is a family-run inn, ideally located in the picturesque Georgian town of Aberaeron. It is a charming Grade II listed property, built in 1815 as a traditional coaching house, and later transformed to coincide with the town's bicentenary celebrations. Accommodation is very comfortable with modern fittings and accessories provided, and the public areas are well appointed. There is a large suite available for private or business functions.

Rooms: 13 en suite (2 fmly) **S** fr £79 **D** fr £125* **Facilities:** FTV Lounge tea/coffee Dinner available Direct dial WiFi 🔒 **Conf:** Max 200 Thtr 200 Class 100 Board 50 **Parking:** 20 **Notes:** LB Civ wed 200

The Castle

★★★★ 🛏 INN

tel: 01545 570205 **Market Street SA46 0AU**
email: castle_hotel@btconnect.com **web:** www.the-castlehotel.co.uk
dir: *On A487, in centre of town.*

The Castle is a Grade II listed building right in the centre of the pretty harbour town of Aberaeron. Pastel coloured houses are a feature of this Georgian town, ideally situated for many walks, including the Llanerchaeron Trail and Wales Coastal Path. A smart café bar serves very good quality home-cooked dishes throughout the day. The modern bedrooms have TVs, WiFi, Egyptian linen and duck-down duvets.

Rooms: 8 en suite (1 fmly) **Facilities:** FTV tea/coffee Dinner available WiFi 🔒 **Conf:** Max 45 Thtr 30 Class 40 Board 20 **Notes:** LB

ABERYSTWYTH	Map 8 SN58

Bodalwyn Guest House

★★★★ GUEST HOUSE

tel: 01970 612578 **Queen's Avenue SY23 2EG**
email: enquiries@bodalwyn.co.uk **web:** www.bodalwyn.co.uk
dir: *500 yards north of town centre. Exit A487 (Northgate Street) into North Road to T-junction into Queen's Avenue. House opposite.*

Located a short walk from the promenade, this imposing Edwardian house, built for a college professor, has been appointed to provide high standards of comfort and good facilities. Smart modern bathrooms complement the spacious bedrooms, which are equipped with a wealth of thoughtful extras; family rooms are available. Welsh breakfasts are served in the elegant conservatory-dining room.

Rooms: 7 en suite (2 fmly) **S** fr £48 **D** fr £75* **Facilities:** FTV DVD tea/coffee WiFi **Notes:** Closed 22 December to 2 January

Yr Hafod

★★★★ GUEST HOUSE

tel: 01970 617579 **1 South Marine Terrace SY23 1JX**
email: johnyrhafod@aol.com **web:** www.yrhafod.co.uk
dir: *On south promenade between harbour and castle.*

Yr Hafod is an immaculately maintained end of terrace Victorian house with commanding views overlooking South Bay. The spacious bedrooms are comfortable, some with delightful sea views and many have particularly well-appointed bathrooms. Breakfast is served in the front-facing dining room.

Rooms: 6 rms (3 en suite) **S** fr £38 **D** fr £76 **Facilities:** STV FTV TVL tea/coffee WiFi 🔒 **Extras:** Chocolates, mineral water – complimentary **Notes:** Closed Christmas and January

Glyn-Garth

★★★★ GUEST HOUSE

tel: 01970 615050 & 07890 401498 **South Road SY23 1JS**
email: glyngarth@aol.com **web:** www.glyngarth.pages.qpg.com
dir: *In town centre. Exit A487 into South Road, off South Promenade.*

Privately owned and personally run by the same family for over 50 years, this immaculately maintained guest house provides a range of thoughtfully furnished bedrooms with smart modern bathrooms. Breakfast is served in the attractive dining room and a lounge is also available.

Rooms: 10 rms (6 en suite) (2 fmly) (1 GF) **S** fr £39 **D** fr £66* **Facilities:** STV FTV TVL tea/coffee WiFi ♿ 🔒

Y Gelli

★★★ GUEST HOUSE

tel: 01970 617834 **Dolau, Lovesgrove SY23 3HP**
email: pat@plasdolau.co.uk **web:** www.plasdolau.co.uk
dir: *Off A44, 2.75 miles east of town centre.*

Set in spacious grounds on the town's outskirts, this modern detached house contains a range of practical furnished bedrooms, with three further rooms available in an adjacent Victorian property. Comprehensive breakfasts are served in the attractive dining room, with evening meals available on request. A comfortable lounge is also available for guests' use.

Rooms: 6 rms (3 en suite) 3 rms annexe (1 en suite) (3 fmly) (1 GF) **Facilities:** FTV DVD TVL tea/coffee Dinner available Snooker Table tennis, stabling can be provided **Parking:** 20 **Notes:** LB

CARDIGAN
Map 8 SN14

Premier Collection

Caemorgan Mansion

★★★★★ ⊕ ≋ GUEST HOUSE

tel: 01239 613297 **Caemorgan Road SA43 1QU**
email: guest@caemorgan.com **web:** www.caemorgan.com
dir: North of Cardigan on A487 towards Aberporth. Left into Caemorgan Road, entrance in 200 metres.

Caemorgan Mansion stands in its own peaceful grounds, a haven for local wildlife, on the fringes of Cardigan, and is ideally located for visiting the glorious local beaches. Bought in a derelict state, the owners have breathed new life into the property. The bedrooms are spacious and have high quality bathrooms; several have feature showers and baths. The smart dining room overlooking the gardens is the ideal place to sample the innovative cuisine made from locally sourced produce at breakfast and dinner. The friendly hosts are on hand to offer suggestions for places to visit during your stay.

Rooms: 5 en suite **S** fr £90 **D** fr £90 **Facilities:** FTV DVD iPod docking station Lounge tea/coffee Dinner available Licensed WiFi ⚿ **Extras:** Robes, slippers, speciality toiletries, safe **Conf:** Max 20 Thtr 20 Class 10 Board 10 **Parking:** 10 **Notes:** No children 15 years Closed 23–29 December

EGLWYS FACH
Map 14 SN69

Premier Collection

Ynyshir

★★★★★ ⊕⊕⊕⊕⊕ RESTAURANT WITH ROOMS

tel: 01654 781209 **SY20 8TA**
email: info@ynyshir.co.uk **web:** www.ynyshir.co.uk
dir: Exit A487, 5.5 miles south of Machynlleth, signed from main road.

Set in beautifully landscaped grounds and surrounded by the RSPB Ynys-hir Nature Reserve, Ynyshir is a haven of calm. The house was once owned by Queen Victoria and is surrounded by mountain scenery. Lavishly styled bedrooms, each individually themed around a great painter, provide high standards of luxury and comfort. The lounge and bar, adorned with an abundance of fresh flowers, have different moods. The dining room offers highly accomplished cooking using the best, locally sourced ingredients including herbs, soft fruit and vegetables from the hotel's own kitchen garden, and wild foods gathered nearby. This restaurant with rooms makes an idyllic location for weddings.

Rooms: 7 en suite 3 annexe en suite (4 GF) **S** fr £130 **D** fr £150* **Facilities:** FTV DVD Lounge tea/coffee Dinner available Direct dial WiFi ⚿ RSPB Bird Reserve **Extras:** Speciality toiletries, bottled water **Parking:** 15 **Notes:** Closed 6 weeks in year, Sunday, Monday and Tuesday Civ wed 40

LLECHRYD
Map 8 SN24

Hammet @ Castell Malgwyn

★★★★ ⊕⊕ GUEST ACCOMMODATION

tel: 01239 682382 **SA43 2QA**
email: chrismason-watts@hotmail.co.uk **web:** www.hammethouse.co.uk
dir: From A40 in St Clears at Penblewin roundabout, take A478 towards Cardigan. Right on B4332 signed Boncath. Left signed Llechryd. Left before river bridge in Llechryd.

Dating back in part to 1450, this property has 15 light and airy Georgian bedrooms with contemporary furnishings and facilities that create a pleasing mix of old and new. Drinks tray with whole-leaf teas, freshly-ground WaDo coffee and home-baked Hammet House goodies are some of the little home comforts on offer. The bathrooms are stocked with luxury toiletries and fluffy soft towels. With the addition of award-winning, modern food, including vegetarian and tasting menus, and a very well-stocked bar, this is certainly a great spot to linger awhile if visiting this beautiful part of Wales.

Rooms: 15 en suite (1 fmly) **S** fr £100 **D** fr £125* **Facilities:** FTV Lounge TVL tea/coffee Dinner available Direct dial Licensed WiFi ⚿ Fishing **Extras:** Home-made biscuits **Conf:** Max 160 Thtr 160 Class 20 Board 20 **Parking:** 40 **Notes:** LB Civ wed 100

NEW QUAY
Map 8 SN35

The Swallows Bed and Breakfast

★★★★ BED AND BREAKFAST

tel: 07516 905548 **Blaenwaun Fawr SA44 6JD**
email: theswallowsbandb@gmail.com **web:** www.the-swallows-bed-and-breakfast.com
dir: South of New Quay on A487. Through Synod Inn hamlet turn opposite parking sign for layby.

The Swallows Bed and Breakfast, a short distance from the coast, is set just off the main coastal road with stunning views of the countryside near Cardigan Bay. This relaxed and friendly property offers three spacious bedrooms, with large walk-in showers, that are separate from the main house, allowing guests total privacy and their own front door. Each room has a conservatory which acts as a dining room for breakfast and dinner. Hearty home-made dinners, after a day exploring the nearby coastal path or perhaps spotting dolphins, are delivered to your door to enjoy at your leisure.

Rooms: 3 annexe en suite (3 fmly) (3 GF) **S** fr £70 **D** fr £85* **Facilities:** FTV DVD tea/coffee Dinner available WiFi ⚿ **Extras:** Fresh milk, fruit – complimentary **Parking:** 3 **Notes:** LB

TREGARON
Map 9 SN65

Y Talbot

★★★★ ⊕⊕ INN

tel: 01974 298208 **The Square SY25 6JL**
email: info@ytalbot.com **web:** www.ytalbot.com
dir: From Lampeter or Aberystwyth on A485, in Tregaron turn opposite NatWest, 100 yards to inn.

Located in the heart of this quiet town, Y Talbot has been appointed to provide a range of very high-quality bedrooms and bathrooms with luxury showers; some smaller, standard rooms are also available. There is a traditional bar serving real ales and a contemporary main restaurant and lounge. Dinner offers a very good selection of dishes using quality produce.

Rooms: 11 en suite 2 annexe en suite (3 fmly) (1 GF) **S** fr £70 **D** fr £115* **Facilities:** FTV iPod docking station Lounge tea/coffee Dinner available WiFi ⚿ ⚿ Drying room **Extras:** Speciality toiletries, mineral water, cafetière **Conf:** Max 120 Thtr 80 Class 120 Board 40 **Parking:** 7 **Notes:** LB Civ wed 140

CONWY

ABERGELE
Map 14 SH97

Premier Collection

The Kinmel Arms

★★★★★ ◎◎ RESTAURANT WITH ROOMS

tel: 01745 832207 **The Village, St George LL22 9BP**
email: info@thekinmelarms.co.uk **web:** www.thekinmelarms.co.uk
dir: From A55 junction 24a to St George. East on A55, junction 24. 1st left to Rhuddlan, 1st right into St George. 2nd right.

This converted 17th-century coaching inn stands close to the church in the village of St George. The restaurant specialises in skilfully prepared produce from Wales and north-west England. Friendly, helpful staff will ensure you have a relaxing stay. The four attractive suites are kitted out with small kitchenettes where continental breakfasts are placed each day to enjoy at your leisure. Each suite is individually designed in a natural style with luxurious bathrooms to match.

Rooms: 4 en suite (2 GF) **S** fr £115 **D** fr £135 **Facilities:** STV Lounge tea/coffee Dinner available ⚘ 🔒 **Extras:** Speciality toiletries, fruit, snacks, bottled water – complimentary **Conf:** Max 12 Board 12 **Parking:** 50 **Notes:** LB No children 16 years Closed 25 December and 1 January RS Monday closed (excluding bank holidays)

BETWS-Y-COED
Map 14 SH75

Premier Collection

Penmachno Hall

★★★★★ 🍽 GUEST ACCOMMODATION

tel: 01690 760410 **Penmachno LL24 0PU**
email: stay@penmachnohall.co.uk **web:** www.penmachnohall.co.uk
dir: 4 miles south of Betws-y-Coed. A5 onto B4406 to Penmachno, over bridge, right at Eagles pub signed Ty Mawr. 500 yards at stone bridge.

Set in more than two acres of mature grounds including a mountain stream and woodland, this impressive Victorian rectory provides high standards of comfort and good facilities. Stylish decor and quality furnishings highlight the many original features throughout the ground-floor areas, and the bedrooms have a wealth of thoughtful extras. Alongside the main building is a superb two-bedroom, self-catering unit in a former coach house. Pre-booked, set menu, party-style evening meals are served on Saturday nights, while buffet-style meals are served Tuesday through Friday.

Rooms: 3 en suite **D** fr £95* **Facilities:** STV DVD Lounge tea/coffee Dinner available Licensed WiFi 🔒 **Extras:** Fruit – complimentary, robes **Parking:** 5 **Notes:** LB Closed Christmas and New Year RS Sunday to Monday no evening meals

Afon View Guest House

★★★★ GUEST HOUSE

tel: 01690 710726 **Holyhead Road LL24 0AN**
email: welcome@afon-view.co.uk **web:** www.afon-view.co.uk
dir: On A5, 60 yards west of Rockbottom Shop.

A warm welcome is assured at this elegant Victorian house, located between Waterloo Bridge and the village centre. Bedrooms are equipped with lots of thoughtful extras, and day rooms include an attractive dining room and comfortable guest lounge.

Rooms: 7 en suite (1 fmly) **S** fr £65 **D** fr £75* **Facilities:** FTV Lounge tea/coffee WiFi 🔒 **Parking:** 7 **Notes:** LB No children 8 years Closed 20–27 December

Bryn Bella Guest House

★★★★ GUEST HOUSE

tel: 01690 710627 **Lon Muriau, Llanrwst Road LL24 0HD**
email: welcome@bryn-bella.co.uk **web:** www.bryn-bella.co.uk
dir: A5 onto A470, 0.5 mile right onto driveway signed Bryn Bella.

Located in an elevated position on the outskirts of the village, with stunning views of the surrounding countryside, this elegant Victorian house provides a range of thoughtfully-equipped bedrooms and smart, modern bathrooms. Their eco-friendly approach is to be commended and this ethos runs through the whole operation from local sourcing, reducing the food-miles to water reclamation. A warm welcome is assured, and guest services include a daily weather forecast.

Rooms: 5 en suite (1 GF) **S** fr £85 **D** fr £85* **Facilities:** FTV DVD TVL tea/coffee WiFi 🔒 **Extras:** Robes, microwave **Parking:** 6 **Notes:** LB No children 16 years

Cwmanog Isaf Farm

★★★★ FARMHOUSE

tel: 01690 710225 & 07808 421634 **Fairy Glen LL24 0SL**
email: h.hughes165@btinternet.com **web:** www.cwmanogisaffarmholidays.co.uk
dir: 1 mile south of Betws-y-Coed off A470 before stone bridge, 500 yards on farm lane.

Peacefully located in 30 acres of undulating land, where the Fairy Glen (a well known beauty spot on the River Conwy) can be found, this 200-year-old house on a working livestock farm has been restored to provide comfortable, thoughtfully furnished bedrooms. Breakfasts use home-reared or organic produce. The property's elevated position provides stunning views of the surrounding countryside.

Rooms: 3 en suite (1 GF) **S** fr £55 **D** fr £65* **Facilities:** STV Lounge tea/coffee 🔒 **Parking:** 4 **Notes:** No children 15 years Closed November to Easter 30 acres sheep

Park Hill

★★★★ GUEST HOUSE

tel: 01690 710540 **Llanrwst Road LL24 0HD**
email: welcome@park-hill.co.uk **web:** www.park-hill.co.uk
dir: 0.5 mile north of Betws-y-Coed on A470 (Llanrwst Road).

A warm welcome is assured at this guest house, which benefits from a peaceful location overlooking the village of Betws-y-Coed and the valley beyond. Well-equipped bedrooms, including one with a four-poster, offer comfortable beds and modern extras. There is a sun lounge to the front, a heated swimming pool, sauna and whirlpool bath for guests' use. Ample on-site parking is provided.

Rooms: 8 en suite **S** fr £78 **D** fr £85 **Facilities:** FTV Lounge tea/coffee WiFi 🏊 ⚘ Sauna 🔒 **Parking:** 11 **Notes:** LB No children 8 years

CAPEL CURIG · Map 14 SH75

Bryn Tyrch Inn

★★★★ ⊛ INN

tel: 01690 720223 & 07855 762791 **LL24 0EL**
email: info@bryntyrchinn.co.uk **web:** www.bryntyrchinn.co.uk
dir: *On A5 at top end of village.*

Dating from the 19th century, this former posting house has public areas of real character together with stylish, modern bedrooms with smart en suite bathrooms. Hog and lamb roasts are a feature on certain days throughout the year and the award-winning restaurant also impresses. The enthusiastic proprietors, assisted by a friendly team are constantly making improvements to ensure a visit to Bryn Tyrch is worth the trip.

Rooms: 11 en suite **Facilities:** FTV Lounge tea/coffee Dinner available WiFi ⌔ Drying facilities **Extras:** Home-made biscuits **Parking:** 30 **Notes:** LB Closed 15–27 December and 3–20 January RS February to March open weekends only and school holidays Civ wed 75

COLWYN BAY · Map 14 SH87

The Northwood

★★★★ GUEST HOUSE

tel: 01492 549931 **47 Rhos Road, Rhos-on-Sea LL28 4RS**
email: welcome@thenorthwood.co.uk **web:** www.thenorthwood.co.uk
dir: *Exit at A55 junction 22 (Old Colwyn). At T-junction right, to next T-junction (facing sea). Left, pass pier, opposite harbour left into Rhos Road. On left adjacent to church.*

A short walk from the seafront and shops, this constantly improving guest house has a warm and friendly atmosphere and welcomes back many regular guests. The bedrooms are en suite, comfortable and well equipped for the modern traveller.

Rooms: 9 en suite (4 fmly) (2 GF) **Facilities:** FTV DVD TVL tea/coffee Licensed WiFi ⌔ **Conf:** Max 20 Class 20 Board 20 **Parking:** 12 **Notes:** LB No children 16 years

CONWY · Map 14 SH77

Premier Collection

The Groes Inn

★★★★★ ⊜ INN

tel: 01492 650545 **Tyn-y-Groes LL32 8TN**
email: groes.inn@jwlees.co.uk **web:** www.groesinn.com
dir: *A55, over Old Conwy Bridge, 1st left through Castle Walls on B5106 (Trefriw Road), 2 miles on right.*

Located in the picturesque Conwy Valley, this historic inn dates from 1573 and was the first licensed house in Wales. The exterior and gardens have an abundance of shrubs and seasonal flowers that create an impressive welcome, which is matched by the friendly and professional staff. Public areas are decorated and furnished with flair to highlight the many period features. The spacious bedrooms, in renovated outbuildings, are equipped with a wealth of thoughtful extras; many have balconies overlooking the countryside.

Rooms: 18 en suite (1 fmly) (7 GF) **Facilities:** FTV tea/coffee Dinner available Direct dial WiFi ⌔ Petanque **Parking:** 100 **Notes:** LB Civ wed 100

Premier Collection

Sychnant Pass Country House

★★★★★ ⌔ GUEST ACCOMMODATION

tel: 01492 596868 **Sychnant Pass Road LL32 8BJ**
email: office@sychnantpasscountryhouse.co.uk **web:** www.sychnant-pass-house.co.uk
dir: *Phone for directions.*

A warm welcome is assured on arrival at Sychnant Pass Country House from the friendly team here. Located on the northern edge of the Snowdonia National Park and within minutes of Conwy and Llandudno, it enjoys a secluded position and is ideally situated for visiting the many attractions in north Wales. There is a relaxing, comfortable lounge, and for more energetic guests there is an indoor swimming pool, sauna and gym. Dinner, using the finest local seasonal produce, is served in the smart dining room overlooking the gardens. A range of bedrooms styles is offered, including one room with its own hot tub.

Rooms: 12 en suite (4 fmly) (2 GF) **S** fr £95 **D** fr £135 **Facilities:** FTV Lounge tea/coffee Dinner available Licensed WiFi ⌔ Sauna Gym ⌔ Outside heated hot tub **Parking:** 20 **Notes:** Civ wed 45

DWYGYFYLCHI · Map 14 SH77

The Gladstone

★★★★ INN

tel: 01492 623231 **Ygborwen Road LL34 6PS**
email: thegladstonepub@hotmail.co.uk **web:** www.thegladstone.co.uk
dir: *A55 junction 16 turn left, then left again towards Dwygyfylchi, 0.25 mile on right.*

The Gladstone is first and foremost a great pub enjoying a superb sea-facing outlook with views of Puffin Island and Great Orme. Guests can sit inside or out to take in the sunset with drinks and an extensive menu served in a friendly, informal style. Comfortable, stylish bedrooms are individually designed, equipped with plenty of modern extras and luxurious bathrooms. Off-road parking is available.

Rooms: 6 en suite **S** fr £75 **D** fr £75* **Facilities:** FTV Lounge TVL tea/coffee Dinner available WiFi ⌔ **Conf:** Max 20 Board 20 **Parking:** 25 **Notes:** LB Civ wed 40

LLANDUDNO · Map 14 SH78

Premier Collection

Bryn Derwen

★★★★★ BED AND BREAKFAST

tel: 01492 876804 **34 Abbey Road LL30 2EE**
email: brynderwen34@btinternet.com **web:** www.bryn-derwen.co.uk
dir: *A470 into Llandudno, left at The Parade promenade to cenotaph, left, over roundabout, 4th right into York Road, Bryn Derwen at top.*

Bryn Derwen is located in a quiet area of Llandudno, just a short walk from the main shopping area and local restaurants. A friendly welcome is assured at this impressive Victorian house, which retains many original features such as tiled floors and fine stained-glass windows. Decor and furnishings highlight the historic charm of the property, which is most apparent in the sumptuous lounges and attractive dining room. A choice of individually styled bedrooms is offered, and all are equipped with many thoughtful extras.

Rooms: 9 en suite (1 fmly) **Facilities:** FTV DVD iPod docking station Lounge TVL tea/coffee Licensed WiFi ⌔ ⌔ **Extras:** Speciality toiletries, water, chocolates – complimentary **Parking:** 9 **Notes:** LB No children 12 years Closed mid December to mid January

Brigstock House

★★★★ GUEST HOUSE

tel: 01492 876416 **1 St David's Place LL30 2UG**
email: brigstockguesthouse@gmail.com **web:** www.brigstockhouse.co.uk
dir: *A470 into Llandudno, left into The Parade promenade, left into Lloyd Street, left into St David's Road and left into St David's Place.*

This impressive Edwardian property in a quiet residential corner of the town is within easy walking distance of the seafront and central shopping area. The atmosphere is relaxed and refined. Attractive, modern bedrooms are tastefully decorated with suites available for those who like to spread out. A comfortable lounge is also available with honesty bar. Substantial breakfasts are served in the elegant dining room.

Rooms: 8 en suite **Facilities:** FTV DVD TVL tea/coffee Licensed WiFi 🐾 **Parking:** 6 **Notes:** LB No children 12 years Closed December to January

The Cliffbury

★★★★ GUEST ACCOMMODATION

tel: 01492 877224 **34 St David's Road LL30 2UH**
email: info@thecliffbury.co.uk **web:** www.thecliffbury.co.uk
dir: *Phone for directions.*

Located on a leafy avenue within easy walking distance of the town centre, this elegant Edwardian house sets high standards. Bedrooms, furnished in a bright, modern style, provide a range of practical and thoughtful extras; two popular suites are available. A warm welcome is guaranteed, and comfort is at the heart of everything the hosts provide. Off-street parking is available.

Rooms: 6 en suite **D** fr £72* **Facilities:** FTV DVD tea/coffee WiFi **Parking:** 6 **Notes:** LB No children 14 years Closed January

St Hilary Guest House

★★★★ GUEST ACCOMMODATION

tel: 01492 875551 **16 Craig-y-Don Parade, The Promenade LL30 1BG**
email: info@sthilaryguesthouse.co.uk **web:** www.sthilaryguesthouse.co.uk
dir: *0.5 mile east of town centre. On B5115 (seafront road) near Venue Cymru.*

Anne-Marie and Howard offer a warm and personal welcome at their house sitting at the more peaceful Craig-y-Don end of The Promenade. Many of the elegant bedrooms have sea views and all are equipped with modern facilities such as WiFi and large TVs. The attractive front-facing dining room is the scene for hearty breakfasts. A bright and comfortable guests' lounge with an honesty bar is also available.

Rooms: 9 en suite (1 GF) **S** fr £56 **D** fr £80* **Facilities:** FTV DVD iPod docking station Lounge tea/coffee Licensed WiFi **Notes:** LB No children 18 years Closed mid December to mid January

Stratford House B&B

★★★★ GUEST ACCOMMODATION

tel: 01492 877962 **8 Craig-y-Don Parade, The Promenade LL30 1BG**
email: stratfordhtl@aol.com **web:** www.thestratfordbandb.com
dir: *A470 at roundabout take 4th exit, on Queens Road signed Craig-y-Don to promenade, on right.*

This immaculately presented, spacious house is located on the seafront with spectacular views. Bedrooms are attractively decorated, some with four-poster beds, and all have an excellent range of accessories including TVs. The traditionally decorated dining room is also beautifully presented. The friendly owners are very welcoming.

Rooms: 9 en suite (1 fmly) (1 GF) **S** fr £60 **D** fr £70 **Facilities:** FTV tea/coffee WiFi **Extras:** Chocolates, fruit teas, hot chocolate, bottled water – complimentary **Notes:** LB No children 10 years Closed January to February RS December and March

Britannia Guest House

★★★★ GUEST HOUSE

tel: 01492 877185 & 07890 765071 **15 Craig-y-Don Parade, The Promenade LL30 1BG**
email: info@thebritanniaguesthouse.co.uk **web:** www.thebritanniaguesthouse.co.uk
dir: *A55 onto A470 to Llandudno, at roundabout take 4th exit signed Craig-y-Don, right at promenade.*

This family-run Victorian guest house offers a warm welcome and friendly service. The bedrooms are very comfortable and well equipped, and many have fantastic views of Llandudno's bay. Ground-floor rooms are available, and hearty breakfasts are served in the dining room that has sea views.

Rooms: 10 en suite (2 GF) **D** fr £78* **Facilities:** FTV tea/coffee WiFi **Extras:** Speciality toiletries **Notes:** LB No children 10 years Closed 28 October to 20 March

Can-Y-Bae

★★★★ GUEST ACCOMMODATION

tel: 01492 874188 **10 Mostyn Crescent, Central Promenade LL30 1AR**
email: canybae@btconnect.com **web:** www.can-y-baehotel.com
dir: *A55 junction 19, A470, signed Llandudno/Promenade. Can-Y-Bae on seafront promenade between Venue Cymru Theatre and bandstand.*

A warm welcome is assured at this tastefully renovated house, centrally located on the Promenade. Bedrooms are equipped with both practical and homely extras and upper floors are serviced by a modern lift. Public rooms include a panoramic lounge, cosy bar with souvenirs of famous guests and an attractive ground-floor dining room.

Rooms: 16 en suite (2 GF) **S** fr £45 **D** fr £80* **Facilities:** FTV Lounge tea/coffee Dinner available Direct dial Lift Licensed WiFi **Extras:** Speciality toiletries, mineral water – complimentary **Notes:** LB No children 12 years

LLANDUDNO *continued*

The Epperstone

★★★★ GUEST ACCOMMODATION

tel: 01492 878746 & 07749 304394 **15 Abbey Road LL30 2EE**
email: epperstonehotel@btconnect.com **web:** www.theepperstone.co.uk
dir: *A550, A470 to Mostyn Street. Left at roundabout, 4th right into York Road. Epperstone at junction of York Road and Abbey Road.*

This delightful property is located in wonderful gardens in a residential part of town, within easy walking distance of the seafront and shopping area. Bedrooms are attractively decorated and thoughtfully equipped. Two lounges and a Victorian-style conservatory are available.

Rooms: 8 en suite (4 fmly) (1 GF) **S** fr £45 **D** fr £90* **Facilities:** FTV Lounge tea/coffee Dinner available Direct dial Licensed WiFi 🐾 **Parking:** 7 **Notes:** LB No children 8 years Closed January to April

Glenavon Guest House

★★★★ GUEST HOUSE

tel: 01492 877687 **27 St Mary's Road LL30 2UB**
email: postmaster@glenavon.plus.com **web:** www.glenavon-llandudno.co.uk
dir: *From A470 signed Llandudno, left at lights into Trinity Avenue. 3rd right into St Mary's Road. Glenavon on right.*

The owners of Glenavon Guest House extend a warm welcome to all their guests, but supporters of Liverpool Football Club will find themselves particularly at home here – they can admire the extensive range of club memorabilia throughout the comfortable day rooms. The bedrooms are equipped with thoughtful extras and Welsh breakfasts provide a good start to the day.

Rooms: 7 en suite (1 fmly) **Facilities:** FTV TVL tea/coffee WiFi 🐾 **Parking:** 4 **Notes:** LB

The Lilly Restaurant with Rooms

★★★★ ◉ ♨ RESTAURANT WITH ROOMS

tel: 01492 876513 **West Parade, West Shore LL30 2BD**
email: thelilly@live.co.uk **web:** www.thelilly.co.uk
dir: *Phone for detailed directions.*

Located on the seafront on the West Shore with views over the Great Orme, this establishment has good facilities and bedrooms that offer high standards of comfort. Children are very welcome here, and a relaxed atmosphere is found in Madhatter's Brasserie which takes its name from Lewis Carroll's *Alice in Wonderland* – part of the book may have been written while the author was staying on the West Shore. The Lilly also has a fine-dining restaurant.

Rooms: 5 en suite **Facilities:** FTV iPod docking station Lounge tea/coffee Dinner available Direct dial WiFi **Extras:** Speciality toiletries **Conf:** Max 35 Thtr 25 Board 20 **Notes:** LB

No. 9 Guest House

★★★★ BED AND BREAKFAST

tel: 01492 877251 & 07950 445524 **9 Chapel Street LL30 2SY**
email: m.hartill69@gmail.com **web:** www.no9llandudno.co.uk
dir: *See B&B's website for detailed directions.*

No. 9 Guest House is centrally located in Llandudno with the promenade, shopping areas and restaurants all within a few minutes' walk. This Victorian building is traditionally styled, with a warm welcome assured from the friendly owner. Bedrooms vary in size and offer comfortable facilities for guests. A hearty breakfast is provided that includes home-made jams and seasonal dishes in addition to the traditional breakfast.

Rooms: 8 en suite (2 fmly) **S** fr £35 **D** fr £64* **Facilities:** FTV DVD TVL WiFi 🐾

The Oasis

★★★★ BED AND BREAKFAST

tel: 01492 877822 **4 Nevill Crescent LL30 1AT**
email: info@theoasiswales.co.uk **web:** www.theoasiswales.co.uk
dir: *A470 to Llandudno, right at roundabout onto B5115 (Clarence Crescent). On Promenade.*

The Oasis is a family-run bed and breakfast run by hosts Carole and Ed who always look forward to welcoming their guests. Situated on the main promenade with beautiful views of the Great Orme, the Victorian Pier and the Irish Sea, a stay here will prove relaxing and enjoyable. The en suite bedrooms are tastefully decorated and equipped with tea- and coffee-making facilities and hairdryers. Free WiFi is available too. A home-cooked full English breakfast is served each morning. The Oasis is an AA Friendliest B&B of the Year runner up for 2018–19.

Rooms: 15 en suite (5 fmly) (3 GF) **S** fr £50 **D** fr £60* **Facilities:** FTV TVL tea/coffee WiFi 🐾 **Parking:** 1

The Trevone

★★★ GUEST ACCOMMODATION

tel: 01492 876314 **10 St Georges Crescent LL30 2LF**
email: info@trevone.net **web:** www.trevone.net
dir: *From A55 follow signs for Llandudno and central promenade.*

The Trevone is in a splendid location at the heart of the Llandudno seafront and a friendly welcome and good service is assured. Bedrooms and bathrooms come in a range of shapes and sizes; some have excellent sea views. Guests can relax in a choice of lounges and a well-stocked bar is provided.

Rooms: 24 en suite (5 fmly) (1 GF) **Facilities:** FTV Lounge TVL tea/coffee Lift Licensed WiFi 🐾 **Notes:** LB Closed December to February

Gwesty Links

[U]

tel: 01492 879180 **77 Conway Road LL30 1PN**
email: gwestylinks@jwlees.co.uk **web:** www.linkshotelllandudno.co.uk
dir: *A55 junction 19 onto A470, signed Llandudno. Continue for 3 miles, left at roundabout into Maesdu Road.*

Currently the rating for this establishment is not confirmed. This may be due to a change of ownership or because it has only recently joined the AA rating scheme.

Rooms: 15 en suite (1 fmly) **Facilities:** FTV tea/coffee Licensed WiFi

RHOS-ON-SEA Map 14 SH88
See also Colwyn Bay

Premier Collection

Plas Rhos
★★★★★ ⬧ GUEST ACCOMMODATION

tel: 01492 543698 **Cayley Promenade LL28 4EP**
email: info@plasrhos.co.uk **web:** www.plasrhos.co.uk
dir: *A55 junction 20 onto B5115 for Rhos-on-Sea, right at roundabout into Whitehall Road to promenade.*

Stunning sea views are a feature of this lovely Victorian house, which provides high standards of comfort and hospitality. Cosy bedrooms are filled with a wealth of thoughtful extras, and public areas include a choice of sumptuous lounges featuring smart decor, quality soft furnishings and memorabilia. Breakfast is served in the attractive dining room, overlooking the patio garden.

Rooms: 5 en suite **S** fr £70 **D** fr £90* **Facilities:** FTV Lounge TVL tea/coffee Licensed WiFi ⬧ **Parking:** 4 **Notes:** LB No children 12 years Closed November to March

Whitehall Guest House
★★★★ GUEST HOUSE

tel: 01492 547296 **51 Cayley Promenade LL28 4EP**
email: tony@whitehall-hotel.co.uk **web:** www.whitehall-hotel.co.uk
dir: *A55 onto B5115 (Brompton Avenue), right at roundabout into Whitehall Road to seafront.*

Overlooking the Rhos-on-Sea promenade, this popular, family-run establishment is convenient for the shops and local amenities. Attractively appointed bedrooms include family rooms and a room on the ground floor; all benefit from an excellent range of facilities such as TVs with DVD as well as air conditioning. Facilities include a bar and a foyer lounge.

Rooms: 12 en suite (4 fmly) (1 GF) **S** fr £40 **D** fr £75* **Facilities:** FTV Lounge TVL tea/coffee Licensed WiFi ⬧ **Parking:** 4 **Notes:** LB

TAL-Y-CAFN Map 14 SH77

Premier Collection

Bodnant Welsh Food Centre
★★★★★ ⬧ RESTAURANT WITH ROOMS

tel: 01492 651100 & 651102 **Furnace Farm LL28 5RP**
email: reception@bodnant-welshfood.co.uk **web:** www.bodnant-welshfood.co.uk
dir: *A55 junction 19, follow signs for A470, 4 miles towards Tal-y-Cafn.*

Overlooking the River Conwy and neighbouring Bodnant Gardens, this 18th-century farm has been fully restored and is now the home to Bodnant Welsh Food Centre. It is ideally placed to explore the North Wales coastline, Snowdonia and the nearby surf park. The Hayloft Restaurant serves interesting lunches and dinners, including a seven-course tasting menu. A range of bedroom types and sizes is offered plus a guest lounge and kitchen. The buildings include a tea room, farm shop and a wine merchant with a focus on Welsh products. There is a cookery school on site, and small conferences and weddings can be catered for here.

Rooms: 6 en suite (1 GF) **Facilities:** FTV Lounge TVL tea/coffee Dinner available Lift WiFi **Conf:** Max 80 Thtr 80 Class 18 Board 22 **Parking:** 80 **Notes:** LB Closed 25–26 December Civ wed 80

TREFRIW Map 14 SH76

Premier Collection

Yr Hafod Country House
★★★★★ ⬧ BED AND BREAKFAST

tel: 01492 642444 **LL27 0RQ**
email: enquiries@hafod-house.co.uk **web:** www.hafod-house.co.uk
dir: *From north: A470 onto B5279, after 1 mile left onto B5106. 5.5 miles to Trefriw, over bridge 200 metres on left. From south: A470 into Llanrwst, left over bridge onto B5106. 1.5 miles on right.*

Situated in tranquil countryside and ideally located for the Conwy Valley and Snowdonia National Park, this cosy, family-run bed and breakfast offers four smartly appointed bedrooms, which are tastefully designed and comfortable; each has separate access and its own balcony. A hearty breakfast is served in the traditional dining room and not to be missed – dishes are freshly prepared using as much home-grown and local produce as possible. The well-stocked bar and lounge are also part of the package. Bespoke dinner menus are designed on request for groups of 6–12 people when three or more bedrooms are booked. There is a number of quality local eating establishments, some within easy walking distance.

Rooms: 4 en suite **S** fr £70 **D** fr £90* **Facilities:** FTV DVD TVL tea/coffee Licensed WiFi ⬧ **Extras:** Speciality toiletries, sweets, bottled water – complimentary **Parking:** 4 **Notes:** Closed December to 13 February

Ty Newydd B&B
★★★ GUEST ACCOMMODATION

tel: 01492 641210 **Conwy Road LL27 0JH**
email: tynewyddtrefriw@aol.com **web:** www.tynewyddtrefriw.co.uk
dir: *In village centre, near post office.*

Situated in a small village in the unspoilt Conwy Valley, Ty Newydd is just a short drive from Llandudno. The hosts of this large Victorian house offer a genuine warm Welsh welcome on arrival. Comfortable rooms are well equipped, and the property is within easy walking distance of a number of pubs and restaurants.

Rooms: 4 rms (2 en suite) (2 pri facs) (1 fmly) **S** fr £40 **D** fr £70* **Facilities:** STV FTV TVL tea/coffee WiFi ⬧ **Extras:** Safe **Notes:** LB

DENBIGHSHIRE

CORWEN
Map 15 SJ04

Bron-y-Graig
★★★★ GUEST HOUSE

tel: 01490 413007 **LL21 0DR**
email: info@north-wales-hotel.co.uk web: www.north-wales-hotel.co.uk
dir: *On A5 on east edge of Corwen.*

A short walk from the town centre, Bron-y-Graig is an impressive Victorian house that has retained many original features including fireplaces, stained glass and a tiled floor in the entrance hall. Bedrooms, complemented by luxurious bathrooms, are thoughtfully furnished; two are to be found in a coach house. Ground-floor areas include a traditionally furnished dining room and a comfortable lounge. A warm welcome and attentive service are assured.

Rooms: 7 en suite 2 annexe en suite (4 fmly) **S** fr £49 **D** fr £69* **Facilities:** STV FTV DVD Lounge tea/coffee Direct dial Licensed WiFi **Conf:** Max 20 Class 20 Board 15 **Parking:** 15 **Notes:** LB

DENBIGH
Map 15 SJ06

Guildhall Tavern
★★★★ INN

tel: 01745 816533 **Hall Square LL16 3NU**
email: info@guildhalltavernhotel.co.uk web: www.guildhalltavernhotel.co.uk
dir: *Phone for directions.*

Standing in the centre of a medieval town, this 16th-century inn has had a number of different uses over the years including a stint as a military HQ in 1646, when it was taken over by Generals Mytton and Myddleton. A wealth of historic features is still evident throughout including the ornate carved staircases. The bedrooms are individually decorated and complemented by good quality bathrooms – with baths or showers. There is a friendly bar area frequented by guests and locals, that serves a range of local ales and ciders alongside home-cooked dishes.

Rooms: 10 rms **Facilities:** Dinner available

LLANDYRNOG
Map 15 SJ16

Pentre Mawr Country House
★★★★★ GUEST ACCOMMODATION

tel: 01824 790732 **Llandyrnog LL16 4LA**
email: info@pentremawrcountryhouse.co.uk web: www.pentremawrcountryhouse.co.uk
dir: *From Denbigh follow Bodfari/Llandyrnog signs. Left at roundabout to Bodfari, 50 yards, left into country lane, Pentre Mawr on left.*

Expect a warm welcome from Graham and Bre at this superb family country house, set in nearly 200 acres of meadows, park and woodland. The property has been in Graham's family for over 400 years. Bedrooms are individually decorated, very spacious, and each is thoughtfully equipped. Breakfast is served in the conservatory-restaurant overlooking the salt water swimming pool on the terrace. A formal private dining room is available for larger parties. There is a range of diverse accommodation options in addition to the main house, including six luxury safari lodges and two suites, all with private hot tubs.

Rooms: 3 en suite 8 annexe en suite (7 GF) **Facilities:** FTV DVD iPod docking station Lounge tea/coffee Dinner available Licensed WiFi ✃ 🦢 Fishing **Extras:** Robes **Conf:** Max 20 Class 20 Board 20 **Parking:** 14 **Notes:** LB No children 13 years

LLANGOLLEN
Map 15 SJ24

See also Corwen

Tyn Celyn Farmhouse
★★★★ BED AND BREAKFAST

tel: 01978 512428 **Tyndwr LL20 8AR**
email: info@tyncelyn-bnb-llangollen.co.uk web: www.tyncelyn-bnb-llangollen.co.uk
dir: *A5 to Llangollen, pass golf club on right, next left signed Tyndwr Hall, 0.5 mile sharp left into Tyndwr Road, past Tyndwr Hall on left. Tyn Celyn 0.5 mile on left.*

This 300-year-old timber-framed farmhouse has stunning views over the Vale of Llangollen. Bedrooms, one of which is located on the ground floor, provide a range of thoughtful extras in addition to fine period furniture. Breakfast is served at a magnificent carved table in a spacious sitting-dining room.

Rooms: 3 en suite (1 fmly) (1 GF) **Facilities:** FTV DVD TVL tea/coffee WiFi **Parking:** 5 **Notes:** LB

RUTHIN
Map 15 SJ15

Premier Collection

Firgrove Country House B&B
★★★★★ 🛏 🍽 BED AND BREAKFAST

tel: 01824 702677 & 07710 251606 **Firgrove, Llanfwrog LL15 2LL**
email: meadway@firgrovecountryhouse.co.uk **web:** www.firgrovecountryhouse.co.uk
dir: *0.5 mile southwest of Ruthin. A494 onto B5105, 0.25 mile past Llanfwrog church on right.*

Standing in immaculate mature gardens in a peaceful rural location, this well-proportioned house retains many original features, highlighted by the quality decor and furnishings throughout. Bedrooms, complemented by smart, modern bathrooms, are equipped with a wealth of thoughtful extras. Memorable breakfasts, using home-made or local produce, are served in an elegant dining room. Imaginative dinners are also available by prior arrangement and a warm welcome is assured.

Rooms: 2 en suite 1 annexe en suite (1 GF) **S** fr £80 **D** fr £100* **Facilities:** FTV Lounge tea/coffee Dinner available WiFi 🅿 **Extras:** Mineral water, fresh milk – complimentary; fridge **Parking:** 4 **Notes:** No children Closed November to February

ST ASAPH
Map 15 SJ07

Premier Collection

Tan-Yr-Onnen Guest House
★★★★★ 🛏 GUEST HOUSE

tel: 01745 583821 **Waen LL17 0DU**
email: tanyronnenvisit@aol.com **web:** www.northwalesbreaks.co.uk
dir: *West on A55 junction 28, turn left in 300 yards.*

A warm welcome is assured at Tan-Yr-Onnen Guest House, which is quietly located in six acres of gardens, conveniently close to the A55. The very well-equipped accommodation includes four ground-floor rooms with French windows that open onto the terrace. Upstairs, there are two luxury suites with lounge areas. Hearty breakfasts are served in the dining room overlooking the gardens, and a conservatory-lounge and WiFi access are also available.

Rooms: 6 en suite (1 fmly) (4 GF) **Facilities:** FTV Lounge tea/coffee Licensed WiFi 🅿 **Parking:** 8

GWYNEDD

ABERDYFI
Map 14 SN69

Premier Collection

Penhelig Arms
★★★★★ ◎ INN

tel: 01654 767215 **Terrace Road LL35 0LT**
email: info@penheligarms.com **web:** www.penheligarms.com

Originally a collection of fishermen's cottages, the charming Penhelig Arms overlooks the picturesque Dyfi Estuary within the Snowdonia National Park. Bedrooms in the main house are charming, with many taking in the impressive views. Award-winning cuisine is a real feature at the inn; local produce is a key factor on menus in the popular dining room and bar, where bookings are essential to avoid disappointment.

Rooms: 11 en suite 4 annexe en suite **D** fr £99* **Facilities:** Dinner available WiFi **Parking:** 5

BARMOUTH   Map 14 SH61

See also Dyffren Ardudwy

Llwyndu Farmhouse

★★★★ 🍴 🛏 GUEST ACCOMMODATION

tel: 01341 280144 **Llanaber LL42 1RR**
email: intouch@llwyndu-farmhouse.co.uk **web:** www.llwyndu-farmhouse.co.uk
dir: *A496 towards Harlech where street lights end, on outskirts of Barmouth, next right.*

This converted 16th-century farmhouse offers warm hospitality and traditional guest accommodation. Many original features have been retained, including inglenook fireplaces, exposed beams and timbers. There is a cosy lounge and meals can be enjoyed in the licensed restaurant. Bedrooms are well equipped; some have four-poster beds and extraordinary views over Cardigan Bay. Some bedrooms are in the old dairy building.

Rooms: 3 en suite 3 annexe en suite (2 fmly) **S** fr £110 **D** fr £110* **Facilities:** FTV TVL tea/coffee Dinner available Licensed WiFi 🛁 **Extras:** Speciality toiletries, fruit, snacks – complimentary **Conf:** Max 10 **Parking:** 10 **Notes:** LB Closed 24–27 December RS Sunday and Wednesday no dinner

BEDDGELERT   Map 14 SH54

Tanronnen Inn

★★★★ INN

tel: 01766 890347 **LL55 4YB**
email: tanronnen@btconnect.com **web:** www.tanronnen.co.uk
dir: *In village centre opposite river bridge.*

This delightful village inn offers comfortable, modern and attractively appointed accommodation, including rooms suitable for families. There is a selection of pleasant and relaxing public areas. The wide range of bar food and good selection of real ales prove popular with tourists and locals alike. More formal meals are served in the restaurant.

Rooms: 7 en suite (3 fmly) **Facilities:** FTV tea/coffee Dinner available Direct dial 🛁 **Parking:** 9 **Notes:** LB

CAERNARFON   Map 14 SH46

Plas Dinas Country House

★★★★★ 🍴 🛏 GUEST ACCOMMODATION

tel: 01286 830214 **Bontnewydd LL54 7YF**
email: res@plasdinas.co.uk **web:** www.plasdinas.co.uk
dir: *3 miles south of Caernarfon, off A487, 0.5 mile down private drive.*

Situated in 15 acres of beautiful grounds in Snowdonia, this delightful Grade II listed building dates back to the mid-17th century, but has many Victorian additions. It was once the home of the Armstrong-Jones family, and there are many family portraits, memorabilia and original pieces of furniture on view. The bedrooms are individually decorated and include four-poster beds along with modern facilities. There is a stylish drawing room where a fire burns in the winter, and fresh local produce features on the dinner menu.

Rooms: 10 en suite (2 fmly) (1 GF) **S** fr £109 **D** fr £109* **Facilities:** FTV Lounge tea/coffee Dinner available Licensed WiFi **Extras:** Speciality toiletries, mini-bar **Conf:** Max 14 Board 14 **Parking:** 16 **Notes:** No children 12 years Civ wed 32

Black Boy Inn

★★★★ INN

tel: 01286 673604 **LL55 1RW**
email: office@black-boy-inn.com **web:** www.black-boy-inn.com
dir: *A55 junction 9, A487, follow signs for Caernarfon. Inn within town walls between castle and Victoria Dock.*

Located within Caernarfon's historic town walls, this fine 16th-century inn has low ceilings, narrow staircases and thick wooden beams originally from old ships. It is one of the oldest inns in north Wales, and has a wealth of charm and character. The bedrooms provide modern accommodation, and hearty meals are available in both the restaurant and bar area. On-site parking is available.

Rooms: 16 en suite 10 annexe en suite (5 fmly) (3 GF) **Facilities:** FTV tea/coffee Dinner available Direct dial WiFi ⌧ ☎ **Conf:** Max 40 Thtr 40 Class 20 Board 30 **Parking:** 26 **Notes:** LB

| **CRICCIETH** | Map 14 SH43 |

Bron Rhiw

★★★★ ☕ GUEST ACCOMMODATION

tel: 01766 522257 **Caernarfon Road LL52 0AP**
email: clairecriccieth@yahoo.co.uk **web:** www.bronrhiwhotel.co.uk
dir: *From High Street onto B4411, Bron Rhiw 300 yards on right.*

A warm welcome and high standards of comfort and facilities are assured at Bron Rhiw, a constantly improving Victorian property just a short walk from the seafront. Bedrooms are equipped with lots of thoughtful extras and ground-floor areas include a sumptuous lounge, a cosy bar, and an elegant dining room, the setting for imaginative breakfasts.

Rooms: 9 en suite **S** fr £53 **D** fr £85* **Facilities:** FTV Lounge tea/coffee Licensed WiFi ☎ **Parking:** 3 **Notes:** LB No children 10 years Closed October to March

| **DOLGELLAU** | Map 14 SH71 |

Premier Collection

Tyddynmawr Farmhouse

★★★★★ FARMHOUSE

tel: 01341 422331 **Cader Road, Islawrdref LL40 1TL**
email: olwynevans@btconnect.com **web:** www.wales-guesthouse.co.uk
dir: *From town centre left at top of square, left at garage into Cader Road for 3 miles. 1st farm on left after Gwernan Lake.*

A warm welcome is assured at this 18th-century farmhouse which lies at the foot of Cader Idris amid breathtaking scenery. The bedrooms are spacious and have Welsh oak furniture; the upper room has a balcony and the ground-floor room has a patio area. The bathrooms are large and luxurious. Breakfast offers an excellent choice of home-made items including bread, preserves, muesli or smoked fish. Self-catering cottages are also available.

Rooms: 2 en suite (1 GF) **S** fr £70 **D** fr £88 **Facilities:** Lounge TVL tea/coffee WiFi ☎ **Parking:** 8 **Notes:** No children Closed December to January 800 acres beef/ sheep

DOLGELLAU *continued*

Dolgun Uchaf Guesthouse

★★★★ GUEST HOUSE

tel: 01341 422269 **Dolgun Uchaf LL40 2AB**
email: dolgunuchaf@aol.com **web:** www.guesthousessnowdonia.com
dir: *Exit A470 at Little Chef just south of Dolgellau. Dolgun Uchaf 1st property on right.*

Located in a peaceful area with stunning views of the surrounding countryside, this 500-year-old property was a rich history including a time as a Quaker meeting place. The house retains many original features including exposed beams and open fireplaces. The bedrooms, some in the house and others with external access are well equipped. Ample parking is provided on site plus a lounge for guests and a spacious breakfast room complete the facilities.

Rooms: 3 en suite 1 annexe en suite (1 GF) **Facilities:** TVL tea/coffee Dinner available WiFi **Parking:** 6 **Notes:** No children 5 years

DYFFRYN ARDUDWY
Map 14 SH52

Cadwgan Inn

★★★★ INN

tel: 01341 247240 **LL44 2HA**
email: cadwgan.hotel@virgin.net **web:** www.cadwganhotel.co.uk
dir: *In Dyffryn Ardudwy into Station Road, over railway crossing.*

Privately-owned Cadwgan Inn stands in its own grounds, a stone's throw from Dyffryn Ardudwy station, between Barmouth and Harlech. With the beach just a short walk away, this well-equipped and modern accommodation includes family rooms and a luxury four-poster bedroom. Public areas include an attractive dining room and popular bar, serving honest pub food. Families are ably catered for.

Rooms: 6 en suite (3 fmly) **Facilities:** TVL tea/coffee Dinner available Sauna Gym **Notes:** LB Civ wed 60

LLANBEDR
Map 14 SH52

Victoria Inn

★★★★ INN

tel: 01341 241213 **LL45 2LD**
email: junevicinn@aol.com **web:** www.vic-inn.co.uk
dir: *In village centre.*

A former coaching inn, the Victoria Inn lies beside the River Artro in a very pretty village. Many original features remain, including the Settle Bar with its flagstone floor, black polished fireplace and unusual circular wooden settle. The menu is extensive and is supplemented by blackboard specials. Bedrooms are spacious and thoughtfully furnished.

Rooms: 5 en suite (1 fmly) **Facilities:** FTV tea/coffee Dinner available **Conf:** Max 40 **Parking:** 75 **Notes:** LB

PWLLHELI
Map 14 SH33

Premier Collection

The Old Rectory

★★★★★ BED AND BREAKFAST

tel: 01758 721519 **Boduan LL53 6DT**
email: theashcrofts@theoldrectory.net **web:** www.theoldrectory.net
dir: *From Pwllheli take A497 signed Nefyn. Continue 3 miles, after village sign for Boduan turn left. 1st house on right, opposite the AA box.*

The Old Rectory is a lovely Georgian property set in delightful grounds. Ideally located for the marina in Abersoch, it is centrally placed for walkers on the Welsh Coast Path. The proprietors take great pride in their home and provide very well-appointed bedrooms, spacious public areas and super gardens. Breakfast is also a delight, featuring local produce and taken at a large communal table in the dining room.

Rooms: 4 en suite (1 fmly) **S** fr £85 **D** fr £100* **Facilities:** FTV tea/coffee WiFi **Extras:** Chocolates, sherry **Conf:** Max 8 Board 8 **Parking:** 6 **Notes:** LB Closed 24–27 December

MERTHYR TYDFIL

MERTHYR TYDFIL
Map 9 SO00

The Mount Pleasant Inn

★★★★ GUEST HOUSE

tel: 01443 693555 & 07918 763640 **Mount Pleasant CF48 4TD**
email: jwacmorgan@aol.com **web:** www.themountpleasantinn.co.uk
dir: A470 at Abercynnon roundabout onto A4054 towards Aberfan. 2.5 miles to Mount Pleasant.

With pleasant views across the valley, this friendly and welcoming guest house provides a relaxed and homely ambience. Bedrooms come in a range of shapes and sizes but all are well equipped. Mount Pleasant is fully licensed and dinner is available to residents; good quality, home-cooked dishes are on offer. Guests may enjoy a drink on the outdoor seating terrace to the rear of the property or choose to laze in the outdoor spa pool.

Rooms: 5 en suite (1 fmly) **Facilities:** STV FTV DVD Lounge TVL tea/coffee Dinner available Licensed WiFi ⌂ Heated spa pool **Extras:** Speciality toiletries – complimentary **Notes:** Closed 23 December to 2 January

PONTSTICILL
Map 9 SO01

Penrhadw Farm

★★★★ GUEST HOUSE

tel: 01685 723481 & 07733 327871 **CF48 2TU**
email: treghotel@aol.com **web:** www.penrhadwfarm.co.uk
dir: 5 miles north of Merthyr Tydfil.

Expect a warm welcome at this 19th-century former farmhouse in the glorious Brecon Beacons National Park. The house is appointed to provide quality modern accommodation. The well-equipped, spacious bedrooms include two large suites in cottages adjacent to the main building. There is also a comfortable lounge. Separate tables are provided in the cosy breakfast room.

Rooms: 5 en suite 5 annexe en suite (5 fmly) (1 GF) **Facilities:** FTV TVL tea/coffee Dinner available WiFi ⌂ **Conf:** Max 10 Thtr 10 Class 10 **Parking:** 22 **Notes:** LB

MONMOUTHSHIRE

ABERGAVENNY
Map 9 SO21

The Abergavenny

★★★★ GUEST ACCOMMODATION

tel: 01873 859050 **21 Monmouth Road NP7 5HF**
email: mail@abergavennyhotel.com **web:** www.abergavennyhotel.com
dir: Phone for directions.

Located just a few minutes' stroll from the sister accommodation (the popular Angel Hotel), this relaxing property offers high-quality bedrooms and bathrooms in a range of shapes and sizes. Guests can enjoy a drink in the bar where a good selection of wines, beers and cocktails is available before wandering up the High Street to find one of the many restaurants. Breakfast here is a self-service, continental-style operation. The adjacent car park is a welcome addition.

Rooms: 20 en suite **Facilities:** Licensed

LLANDOGO
Map 4 SO50

The Sloop Inn

★★★★ INN

tel: 01594 530291 **NP25 4TW**
email: thesloopinn@btinternet.com **web:** www.thesloopinn.co.uk
dir: On A466 in village centre.

This welcoming inn is centrally located in the village of Llandogo, close to the River Wye in an outstandingly beautiful valley. The Sloop Inn offers a selection of traditional food, as well as friendly hospitality. The dining room has delightful views over the valley, and the spacious bedrooms and bathrooms are equipped for both business and leisure guests.

Rooms: 4 en suite (1 fmly) **Facilities:** tea/coffee Dinner available WiFi **Parking:** 50 **Notes:** LB RS Monday to Friday closed 3–6pm

MONMOUTH
Map 10 SO51

Inn at Penallt

★★★★ INN

tel: 01600 772765 **Penallt NP25 4SE**
email: enquiries@theinnatpenallt.co.uk **web:** www.theinnatpenallt.co.uk
dir: Phone for directions.

This village inn offers traditional-style, relaxed and welcoming hospitality. Along with a good range of real ales and ciders, popular menus based on quality local suppliers are available in the bar or the conservatory. Bedrooms are well decorated and are located above the inn. The pleasant rear garden includes seating where the delightful views over the surrounding countryside can be enjoyed.

Rooms: 4 en suite **Facilities:** Dinner available

Church Farm Guest House

★★★ GUEST HOUSE

tel: 01600 712176 **Mitchel Troy NP25 4HZ**
email: info@churchfarmguesthouse.eclipse.co.uk **web:** www.churchfarmmonmouth.co.uk
dir: From A40 south, left onto B4293 for Trelleck before tunnel, 150 yards turn left and follow signs to Mitchel Troy. Guest House on main road on left, 200 yards beyond campsite.

Located in the village of Mitchel Troy, this 16th-century former farmhouse retains many original features including exposed beams and open fireplaces. There is a range of bedrooms and a spacious lounge, and breakfast is served in the traditionally furnished dining room.

Rooms: 8 rms (6 en suite) (2 pri facs) (3 fmly) **S** fr £38 **D** fr £76 **Facilities:** FTV Lounge TVL tea/coffee WiFi ⌂ **Parking:** 12 **Notes:** LB Closed Christmas

| ROCKFIELD | Map 9 SO41 |

The Stonemill & Steppes Farm Cottages

★★★★ ◉◉ RESTAURANT WITH ROOMS

tel: 01600 775424 **NP25 5SW**
email: bookings@thestonemill.co.uk **web:** www.steppesfarmcottages.co.uk
dir: A48 to Monmouth, take B4233 to Rockfield. 2.6 miles.

Located in a small hamlet just west of Monmouth, close to the Forest of Dean and the Wye Valley, this restaurant with rooms offers six very well-appointed cottages. The comfortable rooms (available for self-catering or on a B&B basis) have been lovingly restored to retain many original features. In a separate, converted 16th-century barn is the award-winning Stonemill Restaurant with its oak beams, vaulted ceilings and an old cider press. A breakfast hamper is delivered to each cottage. This establishment's location proves handy for golfers wishing to play on the many courses in the area.

Rooms: 6 en suite (6 fmly) (6 GF) **S** fr £80 **D** fr £160* **Facilities:** FTV DVD TVL tea/coffee Dinner available WiFi ♨ ⛳ Free golf **Conf:** Max 60 Thtr 60 Class 56 Board 40 **Parking:** 53 **Notes:** LB Civ wed 120

| USK | Map 9 SO30 |

Newbridge on Usk

★★★★★ ◉◉ ⬛ RESTAURANT WITH ROOMS

tel: 01633 451000 & 410262 **Tredunnock NP15 1LY**
email: bookings@celtic-manor.com **web:** www.celtic-manor.com
dir: M4 junction 24, signed Newport, onto B4236. At Ship Inn turn right, over mini roundabout onto Llangybi/Usk road. Turn right opposite Cwrt Bleddyn Hotel, signed Tredunnock, through village and down hill.

This cosy country inn is tucked away in a beautiful village setting alongside the River Usk. The well-equipped bedrooms, in a separate building, provide comfort and a good range of extras. Guests can eat at rustic tables around the bar or in the upstairs dining room where award-winning, seasonal food is served; there is also a small private dining room. Breakfast is one of the highlights of a stay, with quality local ingredients offered in abundance.

Rooms: 6 en suite (2 fmly) (4 GF) **Facilities:** STV FTV DVD tea/coffee Dinner available Direct dial WiFi ♨ ♨ ♨ Fishing Sauna Gym Facilities available at Celtic Manor Resort **Extras:** Speciality toiletries – complimentary **Conf:** Max 14 Thtr 14 Class 14 Board 14 **Parking:** 60 **Notes:** LB Civ wed 80

| WHITEBROOK | Map 4 SO50 |

The Whitebrook

★★★★★ ◉◉◉◉ ⬛ RESTAURANT WITH ROOMS

tel: 01600 860254 **NP25 4TX**
email: info@thewhitebrook.co.uk **web:** www.thewhitebrook.co.uk
dir: 4 miles from Monmouth on B4293, left at sign to Whitebrook, 2 miles on unclassified road, on right.

Peacefully located and surrounded by woods and rivers, this delightful restaurant with rooms offers a tranquil escape. The bedrooms are located above the main restaurant and come in a range of shapes and sizes – all are very comfortably decorated and furnished. The outstanding, four AA Rosette award-winning food makes great use of the finest local produce and the relaxing surroundings and friendly service provide a memorable dining experience.

Rooms: 8 en suite **S** fr £187 **D** fr £265* **Facilities:** FTV Lounge tea/coffee Dinner available Direct dial WiFi **Extras:** Speciality toiletries, Welsh cakes **Parking:** 20 **Notes:** No children 12 years Closed 2–15 January

| NEATH | Map 9 SS79 |

Cwmbach Cottages Guest House

★★★★ GUEST HOUSE

tel: 01639 639825 **Cwmbach Road, Cadoxton SA10 8AH**
email: l.morgan5@btinternet.com **web:** www.cwmbachguesthouse.co.uk
dir: 1.5 miles northeast of Neath. A465 onto A474 and A4230 towards Aberdulais, left opposite Cadoxton church, guest house signed.

This terrace of former miners' cottages has been restored to provide a range of thoughtfully furnished bedrooms, with one on the ground floor for easier access. Spacious public areas include a comfortable lounge and a pleasant breakfast room with separate tables. A superb decked patio overlooks a wooded hillside, rich with wildlife.

Rooms: 5 en suite (2 fmly) (1 GF) **Facilities:** FTV DVD iPod docking station Lounge TVL tea/coffee WiFi ♨ ⛳ **Parking:** 13 **Notes:** LB

PEMBROKESHIRE

EGLWYSWRW
Map 8 SN13

Premier Collection

Ael y Bryn
★★★★★ 🕮 🍴 BED AND BREAKFAST

tel: 01239 891411 **SA41 3UL**
email: stay@aelybrynpembrokeshire.co.uk **web:** www.aelybrynpembrokeshire.co.uk
dir: *In Eglwyswrw at junction of B4332 and A487 turn right signed Cardigan. Left after car park, 0.5 mile on left.*

Set in beautiful countryside between Cardigan and Fishguard, a mere four miles from the coastal path, Ael y Bryn is a long, single-storey building that offers impressive levels of accommodation. Obviously, all rooms are on the ground floor, meaning access is easy for all. Alongside the four luxurious bedrooms, guests have use of a conservatory, a lounge/music room, a library, an inner courtyard and a delightful garden. Breakfast, and evening meals (available with prior notice) are served in the attractive dining room. Cyclists and walkers are welcome and safe storage and drying space is provided.

Rooms: 4 en suite (4 GF) **D** fr £105* **Facilities:** FTV Lounge tea/coffee Dinner available WiFi 🔒 **Extras:** Fresh milk, mini-fridge – complimentary **Parking:** 4 **Notes:** No children 14 years Closed mid December to mid January

FISHGUARD
Map 8 SM93

Premier Collection

Erw-Lon Farm
★★★★★ 🍴 FARMHOUSE

tel: 01348 881297 **Pontfaen SA65 9TS**
email: lilwenmcallister@btinternet.com **web:** www.erwlonfarm.co.uk
dir: *5.5 miles southeast of Fishguard on B4313.*

Located in the Pembrokeshire Coast National Park, with stunning views of the Gwaun Valley, this attractive farmhouse has been converted to provide modern well-equipped bedrooms with a wealth of homely extras. The McAllisters give the warmest of welcomes, and their memorable dinners feature the finest local produce.

Rooms: 3 en suite **S** fr £60 **D** fr £85 **Facilities:** FTV TVL tea/coffee WiFi 🔒 **Parking:** 5 **Notes:** LB No children 10 years Closed December to March 128 acres beef/sheep

Cefn-y-Dre
★★★★ 🍴 BED AND BREAKFAST

tel: 01348 875663 **Cefyn-y-Dre House SA65 9QS**
email: welcome@cefnydre.co.uk **web:** www.cefnydre.co.uk
dir: *On A40 in Scleddau turn opposite Gate Inn. Pass garden centre on left, 200 yards turn right into No Through Road.*

Perched in delightful countryside along the end of a winding lane, this peaceful B&B is located approximately a mile from Fishguard town and harbour. Bedrooms and bathrooms are very well decorated and furnished and include some welcome extras. Breakfast makes use of high quality ingredients and includes a number of daily specials. The owners offer a very friendly and relaxed style of accommodation with tea and cake offered on arrival. Guests are welcome to use the lounge and play the piano if the mood takes them.

Rooms: 3 rms (2 en suite) (1 pri facs) **Facilities:** FTV Lounge tea/coffee Dinner available Licensed WiFi 🔒 **Parking:** 8 **Notes:** LB

HAVERFORDWEST
Map 8 SM91

Premier Collection

Roch Castle

★★★★★ ⚉ GUEST ACCOMMODATION

tel: 01437 725566 **Roch SA62 6AQ**
email: stay@rochcastle.com **web:** www.rochcastle.com
dir: *Phone for directions.*

Be the king of the castle at Roch Castle, a unique property dating back to the
12th century. Ideally located with 360-degree views over St Brides Bay and the
Preseli Hills, it is just a short drive from the smallest city in Wales, St Davids,
and the larger town of Haverfordwest. Sympathetically restored, the quality here
is unrivalled, and it is fully hypo-allergenic throughout. Staying at Roch Castle
is a unique experience and the professional team are on hand to make the
most of your stay. Complimentary transfers are available each evening to the
award-winning two AA Rosette, Blas Restaurant at their sister hotel, Twr y Felin,
St Davids.

Rooms: 6 en suite **D** fr £230 **Facilities:** STV FTV DVD iPod docking station Lounge
TVL tea/coffee Direct dial Licensed WiFi **Extras:** Speciality toiletries –
complimentary; honesty bar – chargeable **Conf:** Max 18 Class 12 Board 18
Parking: 10 **Notes:** LB No children 12 years Civ wed 18

Premier Collection

Slebech Park Estate

★★★★★ ◉◉ ⚉ RESTAURANT WITH ROOMS

tel: 01437 752000 & 752002 **SA62 4AX**
email: enquiries@slebech.co.uk **web:** www.slebech.co.uk
dir: *East of Haverfordwest on A40, take exit signed Picton Castle.*

A delightful and peaceful retreat located on the shores of Dau Gleddau Estuary
– one of Europe's largest natural harbours. The estate covers 650 acres, with an
array of walks leading from the door through meadows and woodlands and by
the river. Guests are ensured a warm welcome and excellent service throughout
their stay. Bedrooms come in a range of shapes and sizes – all have quality
fittings, organic toiletries and deeply-comfortable beds with Egyptian cotton
sheets. Both the award-winning dinner and breakfast are served in a separate
restaurant – the range of carefully prepared dishes makes good use of top
quality, local produce; lunch and afternoon tea are also available. Dogs are
welcome here too. Slebech Park is an AA Unique B&B of the Year runner up for
2018–19.

Rooms: 19 en suite (5 fmly) (7 GF) **S** fr £75 **D** fr £85* **Facilities:** STV FTV Lounge
tea/coffee Dinner available Direct dial WiFi ⚉ ⚉ ⚓ Fishing ⚓ Shooting
Extras: Speciality toiletries, home-made cakes **Conf:** Max 200 Thtr 200 Class 180
Board 160 **Parking:** 60 **Notes:** LB Civ wed 120

See advert opposite

College Guest House

★★★★ GUEST HOUSE

tel: 01437 763710 **93 Hill Street, St Thomas Green SA61 1QL**
email: colinlarby@aol.com web: www.collegeguesthouse.com
dir: *In town centre, along High Street, pass church, keep in left lane. 1st exit by Stonemason Arms pub, follow signs for St Thomas Green/Leisure Centre/Police Station. 300 metres on left by No Entry sign.*

Situated in a mainly residential area within easy walking distance of Haverdfordwest's attractions, this impressive Georgian house offers good levels of comfort and facilities. There is a range of practically equipped bedrooms, along with public areas that include a spacious lounge (with internet access) and an attractive pine-furnished dining room – the setting for comprehensive breakfasts.

Rooms: 8 en suite (4 fmly) **Facilities:** FTV DVD TVL tea/coffee WiFi

---

KILGETTY	Map 8 SN10

The Begelly Arms

★★★ INN

tel: 01834 812601 **New Road SA68 0YF**
email: info@begellyarms.co.uk web: www.begellyarms.co.uk
dir: *On A40 at St Clears roundabout onto A477, signed Tenby/Pembroke Dock. At next roundabout take 3rd exit signed Kilgetty, into village, on left.*

Being located very close to Oakwood Theme Park, this is a popular inn with families. Bedrooms are located in two areas – some above the main inn and others in an adjacent block. Food is served throughout the day and children are well catered for in terms of menus and a garden to play in at the rear of the building. Function rooms are also available and a large car park is provided.

Rooms: 7 en suite (1 fmly) **Facilities:** STV FTV DVD tea/coffee Dinner available WiFi ⚓ **Parking:** 60 **Notes:** LB

MANORBIER
Map 8 SS09

Castlemead

★★★★ ⊜ RESTAURANT WITH ROOMS

tel: 01834 871358 **SA70 7TA**
email: castlemeadhotel@aol.com **web:** www.castlemeadhotel.com
dir: *A4139 towards Pembroke, B4585 into village, follow signs to beach and castle, establishment on left.*

Benefiting from a superb location with spectacular views of the bay, the Norman church and Manorbier Castle, this family-run business is friendly and welcoming. Bedrooms, including some in a converted former coach house at ground floor level, are generally quite spacious and have modern facilities. There is a sea-view residents' lounge, a cosy bar and a restaurant accessed by stairs which is also open to non-residents. There are extensive gardens to the rear of the property.

Rooms: 5 en suite 3 annexe en suite (2 fmly) (3 GF) **S** fr £75 **D** fr £110 **Facilities:** FTV Lounge tea/coffee Dinner available Direct dial WiFi ⚓ **Parking:** 20
Notes: Closed January to February RS November maybe bed and breakfast only

NEWPORT
Map 8 SN03

Llys Meddyg

★★★★ ◉◉ ♨ RESTAURANT WITH ROOMS

tel: 01239 820008 **East Street SA42 0SY**
email: info@llysmeddyg.com **web:** www.llysmeddyg.com
dir: *On A487 in centre of town.*

Llys Meddyg is a Georgian townhouse offering a blend of old and new, with elegant furnishings, deep sofas and a welcoming fire. The owners of the property employed local craftsmen to create a lovely interior that has an eclectic style. The focus of the quality restaurant menu is on fresh, seasonal, locally sourced ingredients. The spacious bedrooms are comfortable and contemporary in design; the bathrooms vary in style.

Rooms: 5 en suite 3 annexe en suite (3 fmly) (1 GF) **S** fr £70 **D** fr £100*
Facilities: FTV iPod docking station Lounge tea/coffee Dinner available WiFi Riding ⚓ **Extras:** Speciality toiletries – complimentary; mini-bar – chargeable **Conf:** Max 20 Class 20 Board 20 **Parking:** 8 **Notes:** LB Civ wed 90

ST DAVIDS
Map 8 SM72

Premier Collection

Penrhiw

★★★★★ GUEST ACCOMMODATION

tel: 01437 725588 & 725555 **SA62 6PG**
email: stay@penrhiwhotel.com **web:** www.penrhiwhotel.com
dir: *Phone for directions.*

Penrhiw was originally built as a vicarage in 1884 and is a fine example of Victorian architecture – over the years it has been used for many things including a retreat. Ideally located in the centre of St Davids, the smallest city in Wales, the property offers calming and relaxing, luxury accommodation. The property has been designed to be completely hypo-allergenic. Transfers are offered to the sister hotel, Twr Y Felin where guests can enjoy an excellent dining experience before being driven back. Breakfast is a treat and not to be missed.

Rooms: 6 en suite 2 annexe en suite (1 GF) **S** fr £190 **D** fr £190* **Facilities:** STV FTV DVD iPod docking station Lounge TVL tea/coffee Direct dial Licensed WiFi **Extras:** Speciality toiletries, fridge – complimentary; honesty bar – chargeable **Conf:** Max 18 Thtr 18 Class 18 Board 18 **Parking:** 8 **Notes:** LB No children 12 years Civ wed

Premier Collection

Ramsey House

★★★★★ GUEST HOUSE

tel: 01437 720321 & 07795 575005 **Lower Moor SA62 6RP**
email: info@ramseyhouse.co.uk **web:** www.ramseyhouse.co.uk
dir: *From Cross Square in St Davids towards Porthclais, house 0.25 mile on left.*

This pleasant guest house, under the ownership of Suzanne and Shaun Ellison, offers the ideal combination of professional management and the warmth of a family-run establishment. The property is quietly located on the outskirts of St Davids and is surrounded by unspoilt countryside. It provides modern, well-equipped bedrooms, most with en suite bathrooms, along with a good range of welcome extras. Breakfast provides a choice of home-made items, including breads and preserves.

Rooms: 6 rms (5 en suite) (1 pri facs) (3 GF) **S** fr £80 **D** fr £100* **Facilities:** FTV Lounge tea/coffee Licensed WiFi **Extras:** Speciality toiletries – complimentary: Fruit, wine, flowers – chargeable **Parking:** 10 **Notes:** LB No children 16 years Closed November to 13 February

The Waterings

★★★★ BED AND BREAKFAST

tel: 01437 720876 **Anchor Drive, High Street SA62 6QH**
email: enquiries@waterings.co.uk **web:** www.waterings.co.uk
dir: *On A487 on east edge of St Davids.*

Situated a short walk from the centre of St Davids, The Waterings offers spacious bedrooms that are accessed from a courtyard garden; most bedrooms have their own separate seating area. Breakfast, made from a good selection of local produce, is served in a smart dining room in the main house.

Rooms: 2 en suite 5 annexe en suite (4 fmly) (5 GF) **Facilities:** FTV tea/coffee Licensed WiFi Table tennis **Conf:** Max 15 Board 15 **Parking:** 20 **Notes:** No children 5 years

The City Inn

★★★ INN

tel: 0845 347 3102 *(Calls cost 7p per minute plus your phone company's access charge)* & 01437 720829 **New Street SA62 6SU**
email: info@cityinnstdavids.co.uk **web:** www.cityinnstdavids.co.uk
dir: *Phone for directions.*

Located just a 10-minute walk from St Davids Cathedral and even closer to the main town, this well-furnished inn provides a relaxed and informal atmosphere. Guests can choose from a range of bar and restaurant menus at both dinner and lunch; meals are served in the spacious lounge or the main dining room. The car park is a welcome feature.

Rooms: 9 en suite (5 fmly) **S** fr £53 **D** fr £78 **Facilities:** FTV Dinner available WiFi **Parking:** 12 **Notes:** Closed 23–26 December

SOLVA
Map 8 SM82

Premier Collection

Crug Glas Country House

★★★★★ @@ ☺ RESTAURANT WITH ROOMS

tel: 01348 831302 **Abereiddy SA62 6XX**
email: janet@crug-glas.co.uk **web:** www.crug-glas.co.uk
dir: *From Solva to St Davids on A487. From St Davids take A487 towards Fishguard. 1st left after Carnhedryn, house signed.*

This house, on a dairy, beef and cereal farm of approximately 600 acres, is situated about a mile from the coast on the St Davids Peninsula. Comfort, relaxation and flawless attention to detail are provided by the charming host, Janet Evans. Each spacious bedroom has the hallmark of assured design plus a luxury bathroom with both bath and shower; one suite on the top floor has great views. In addition there are two suites in separate buildings.

Rooms: 7 en suite (1 fmly) (2 GF) **S** fr £110 **D** fr £150 **Facilities:** FTV Lounge tea/coffee Dinner available WiFi **Extras:** Speciality toiletries **Conf:** Max 200 Thtr 200 Class 200 Board 200 **Parking:** 10 **Notes:** Closed 22–29 December Civ wed 220

TENBY
Map 8 SN10

Premier Collection

Trefloyne Manor

★★★★★ @ GUEST ACCOMMODATION

tel: 01834 842165 & 844429 **Trefloyne Lane, Penally SA70 7RG**
email: tom.benyon@trefloyne.com **web:** www.trefloyne.com
dir: *A478 to Tenby onto A4139 signed Penally. Turn right opposite Kiln Park Garage, then 1st right to Trefloyne, 150 metres along Trefloyne Lane turn left into Trefloyne Manor.*

Delightfully located in a peaceful valley and surrounded by an 18-hole golf course, this relaxing property offers an excellent range of high quality bedrooms and bathrooms. Some rooms are in the main house while others are in an adjacent coach house – all are decorated to very high standards and include a number of suites. Both dinner and breakfast use local produce and are served in the light and airy conservatory overlooking the golf course.

Rooms: 5 en suite 7 annexe en suite (4 fmly) (3 GF) **S** fr £75 **D** fr £90* **Facilities:** FTV iPod docking station Lounge TVL tea/coffee Dinner available Licensed WiFi ⅃ **Extras:** Speciality toiletries, home-made biscuits **Conf:** Max 60 Thtr 60 Class 60 Board 40 **Parking:** 150 **Notes:** LB Closed 25 December Civ wed 110

Esplanade

★★★★ GUEST ACCOMMODATION

tel: 01834 842760 & 843333 **1 The Esplanade SA70 7DU**
email: esplanadetenby@googlemail.com **web:** www.esplanadetenby.co.uk
dir: *Follow signs to South Beach, exit South Parade into St Florence Parade. Premises on seafront adjacent to town walls.*

Located beside the historic town walls of Tenby, with stunning views over the sea to Caldey Island, the Esplanade provides a range of standard and luxury bedrooms, some ideal for families. Breakfast is offered in the elegant front-facing dining room, which contains a comfortable lounge-bar area.

Rooms: 14 en suite (4 fmly) (1 GF) **Facilities:** FTV DVD Lounge tea/coffee Direct dial Licensed WiFi **Extras:** Mineral water – complimentary **Notes:** LB Closed 15 December to 6 January

POWYS

BRECON
Map 9 SO02

Premier Collection

Peterstone Court

★★★★★ @ ☺ RESTAURANT WITH ROOMS

tel: 01874 665387 **Llanhamlach LD3 7YB**
email: info@peterstone-court.com **web:** www.peterstone-court.com
dir: *3 miles from Brecon on A40 towards Abergavenny.*

Situated on the edge of the Brecon Beacons, this establishment affords stunning views overlooking the River Usk. The atmosphere is friendly and informal, with no unnecessary fuss. No two bedrooms are alike, but all share comparable levels of comfort, quality and elegance. Public areas reflect similar standards, eclectically styled with a blend of the contemporary and the traditional. Quality produce is cooked with care in a range of enjoyable dishes.

Rooms: 8 en suite 4 annexe en suite (2 fmly) **Facilities:** FTV DVD iPod docking station Lounge tea/coffee Dinner available Direct dial WiFi ⊰ Fishing Riding Sauna Gym **Pool open mid April to 1 October, spa facilities **Conf:** Max 100 Thtr 100 Class 100 Board 60 **Parking:** 60 **Notes:** LB Civ wed

BUILTH WELLS
Map 9 SO05

AA GUEST ACCOMMODATION OF THE YEAR FOR WALES 2018–19

Rhedyn Guest House

★★★★ ☺ ☺ GUEST HOUSE

tel: 01982 551944 & 07703 209721 **Rhedyn, Cilmery LD2 3LH**
email: info@rhedynguesthouse.co.uk **web:** www.rhedynguesthouse.co.uk
dir: *From Builth Wells on A483 towards Garth. Rhedyn Guest House on right, through farm gate, closing all gates once through.*

This detached property stands just off the main road outside Cilmery, which is a short drive from Builth Wells. Three comfortable bedrooms provide all the modern facilities including WiFi and a range of guest extras. Two bedrooms are on the ground floor and have their own entrances. Dinner, bookable at the time of reservation, offers imaginative menus. A hearty breakfast, including a selection of home-made preserves, is served in the delightful dining room around a communal table. Access to the guest house is via two gates through a field.

Rooms: 1 en suite 2 annexe en suite (2 GF) **S** fr £90 **D** fr £100* **Facilities:** STV FTV DVD iPod docking station Lounge tea/coffee Dinner available WiFi **Extras:** Sherry, Welsh cakes – complimentary **Parking:** 3 **Notes:** No children except babies

CEMMAES
Map 14 SH80

The Penrhos Arms

★★★★ INN

tel: 01650 511243 & 07808 589349 **SY20 9PR**
email: dawndavies8@hotmail.com **web:** www.penrhosarms.com

The Penrhos Arms provides a warm welcome to new and returning guests alike – it is a historic inn with a charming and comfortable interior. The bedrooms are smartly appointed and have very comfortable beds. A hearty range of menu choices, using local produce whenever possible, is offered.

Rooms: 5 en suite 2 annexe en suite (1 fmly) **Facilities:** FTV DVD TVL tea/coffee Dinner available WiFi ⅃ **Conf:** Max 40 **Notes:** LB Civ wed 50

CRICKHOWELL
Map 9 SO21

The Bear
★★★★ ◎ INN

tel: 01873 810408 **High Street NP8 1BW**
email: info@bearhotel.co.uk **web:** www.bearhotel.co.uk
dir: *Town centre, off A40 (Brecon road). 6 miles from Abergavenny.*

The Bear is a favourite with locals as well as visitors; the character and friendliness of this 15th-century coaching inn are renowned. The bedrooms come in a variety of sizes and include some with four-posters. The bar and restaurant are furnished in keeping with the style of the building, and provide comfortable areas in which to enjoy some of the very popular dishes that use the finest locally-sourced ingredients, served from a menu to suit all tastes.

Rooms: 34 en suite (4 fmly) (6 GF) **S** fr £90 **D** fr £112* **Facilities:** FTV Lounge tea/coffee Dinner available Direct dial WiFi Fishing ⚓ **Conf:** Max 50 Thtr 50 Board 20 **Parking:** 40 **Notes:** Closed 25 December

CRIGGION
Map 15 SJ21

Brimford House
★★★★ FARMHOUSE

tel: 01938 570235 **SY5 9AU**
email: info@brimford.co.uk **web:** www.brimford.co.uk
dir: *Exit B4393 after Crew Green left for Criggion, Brimford 1st on left after pub.*

This elegant Georgian house stands in lovely open countryside and is a good base for touring central Wales and the Marches. The bedrooms are spacious, and thoughtful extras enhance guest comfort. A cheery log fire burns in the lounge during colder weather; the hospitality is equally warm and creates a relaxing atmosphere throughout.

Rooms: 3 en suite **S** fr £55 **D** fr £80* **Facilities:** FTV TVL tea/coffee WiFi Fishing **Parking:** 4 **Notes:** LB 250 acres arable/beef/sheep

ERWOOD
Map 9 SO04

Hafod-y-Garreg
★★★★ ◠ BED AND BREAKFAST

tel: 01982 560400 **LD2 3TQ**
email: johnanniehafod@gmail.com **web:** www.hafodygarreg.co.uk
dir: *1 mile south of Erwood. Exit A470 at Trericket Mill, sharp right, up track past cream farmhouse towards pine forest, through gate.*

This remote Grade II listed farmhouse dates in part from 1401 and has been confirmed, by dendrochronology, as the 'oldest dwelling in Wales'. As you would expect, the house has tremendous character, and is decorated and furnished to befit its age; even so, the bedrooms have all the modern facilities. There is an impressive dining room and a lounge with an open fireplace. Warm hospitality from John and Annie is a major strength here.

Rooms: 2 en suite **S** fr £92 **D** fr £95* **Facilities:** STV iPod docking station tea/coffee Dinner available WiFi ⚓ **Extras:** Speciality toiletries, sherry, magazines/books – complimentary **Parking:** 6 **Notes:** No children Closed Christmas

HAY-ON-WYE
Map 9 SO24

See also Erwood

Old Black Lion Inn
★★★★ ◎ INN

tel: 01497 820841 **26 Lion Street HR3 5AD**
email: info@oldblacklion.co.uk **web:** www.oldblacklion.co.uk
dir: *From B4348 in Hay-on-Wye into Lion Street. Inn on right.*

This fine old coaching inn, with a history stretching back several centuries, has a wealth of charm and character. It was occupied by Oliver Cromwell during the siege of Hay Castle. Privately owned and personally run, it provides cosy and well-equipped bedrooms, some located in an adjacent building. A wide range of well-prepared food is provided, and the service is relaxed and friendly.

Rooms: 6 rms (5 en suite) (1 pri facs) 4 annexe en suite (2 GF) **Facilities:** FTV Lounge TVL tea/coffee Dinner available Direct dial WiFi ⚓ **Parking:** 12 **Notes:** RS 3–12 January Limited services

LLANDRINDOD WELLS
Map 9 SO06

Holly Farm
★★★★ FARMHOUSE

tel: 01597 822402 **Holly Lane, Howey LD1 5PP**
email: ruth@hollyfarmbandb.co.uk **web:** www.hollyfarmbandb.co.uk
dir: *On A483 2 miles south of Llandrindod Wells near Howey.*

This working farm dates from Tudor times and is situated with easy access to the larger towns of Builth Wells and Llandrindod Wells. The bedrooms are homely and full of character. A comfortable lounge has a warming log fire in cooler months, and the pleasant gardens offer a peaceful area to sit in the warmer summer months. A hearty farmhouse breakfast can be enjoyed in the quaint dining room.

Rooms: 3 en suite (1 fmly) **S** fr £45 **D** fr £75* **Facilities:** FTV DVD TVL tea/coffee WiFi ⚓ **Parking:** 4 **Notes:** LB 70 acres beef/sheep

LLANGAMMARCH WELLS
Map 9 SN94

The Cammarch
★★★★ GUEST ACCOMMODATION

tel: 01591 620545 **LD4 4BY**
email: mail@cammarch.com **web:** www.cammarch.com
dir: *Exit A483 at Garth, signed Llangammarch Wells, opposite T-junction.*

This property dates from the 1850s and was built as a railway hotel. Owner Kathryn Dangerfield offers a warm welcome to all guests and the establishment provides modern, well-equipped bedrooms that are tastefully decorated. There is a comfortable, spacious bar and lounge with a log-burning fire, ideal for colder evenings. The conservatory dining room, overlooking the attractive gardens and pond, offers fresh local produce on the dinner menu and the hearty Welsh breakfast makes a good start to the day. Parking is provided at the side of the property.

Rooms: 12 en suite (3 fmly) **Facilities:** FTV DVD Lounge TVL tea/coffee Dinner available Licensed WiFi ⤳ Fishing ⚓ **Extras:** Speciality toiletries **Conf:** Max 20 Thtr 20 Class 15 Board 15 **Parking:** 16 **Notes:** LB RS Christmas to New Year

LLANGEDWYN
Map 15 SJ12

Plas Uchaf Country House

★★★★ ♀ 🛏 GUEST HOUSE

tel: 01691 780588 & 07817 419747 **SY10 9LD**
email: info@plasuchaf.com **web:** www.plasuchaf.com
dir: *Mile End services Oswestry A483/Welshpool. After 2 miles right at White Lion public house, 4.5 miles to Llangedwyn. 150 yards after school on right.*

Located in an elevated position in extensive mature parkland, this elegant Queen Anne house provides high standards of comfort and facilities. The interior flooring was created from recycled ship timbers taken from the Armada fleet of 1588, and furnishing styles highlight the many period features. Imaginative dinners are available, and a warm welcome is assured.

Rooms: 6 en suite (1 fmly) (1 GF) **S** fr £75 **D** fr £105* **Facilities:** FTV iPod docking station Lounge tea/coffee Dinner available Licensed WiFi ☺ 🏊 🔒 **Extras:** Speciality toiletries – complimentary **Conf:** Max 15 Thtr 15 Class 15 Board 15 **Parking:** 30 **Notes:** LB

LLANGURIG
Map 9 SN97

The Old Vicarage

★★★★ GUEST HOUSE

tel: 01686 440280 **SY18 6RN**
email: info@theoldvicaragellangurig.co.uk **web:** www.theoldvicaragellangurig.co.uk
dir: *A470 onto A44, signed.*

Located in pretty, mature grounds, which feature a magnificent holly tree, this elegant Victorian house provides a range of thoughtfully furnished bedrooms, some with fine period objects. Breakfast is served in a spacious dining room, and a comfortable guest lounge is also available.

Rooms: 4 en suite (1 fmly) **S** fr £42 **D** fr £74* **Facilities:** DVD TVL tea/coffee Licensed WiFi 🔒 **Parking:** 6 **Notes:** LB No children 6 years

LLANWRTYD WELLS
Map 9 SN84

Lasswade Country House

★★★★ 🌸🌸 RESTAURANT WITH ROOMS

tel: 01591 610515 **Station Road LD5 4RW**
email: info@lasswadehotel.co.uk **web:** www.lasswadehotel.co.uk
dir: *Exit A483 into Irfon Terrace, right into Station Road, 350 yards on right.*

This friendly establishment on the edge of the town has impressive views over the countryside. Bedrooms are comfortably furnished and well equipped, while the public areas consist of a tastefully decorated lounge, an elegant restaurant with a bar, and an airy conservatory which looks towards the neighbouring hills. The kitchen makes good use of fresh, local produce to provide an enjoyable, award-winning dining experience.

Rooms: 8 en suite (1 fmly) **D** fr £90* **Facilities:** FTV Lounge TVL tea/coffee Dinner available WiFi 🔒 **Conf:** Max 20 Thtr 20 Class 20 Board 20 **Parking:** 6 **Notes:** LB Closed Christmas and New Year

Carlton Riverside

★★★★ 🌸🌸 RESTAURANT WITH ROOMS

tel: 01591 610248 **Irfon Crescent LD5 4SP**
email: carltonriverside@hotmail.co.uk **web:** www.carltonriverside.co.uk
dir: *Phone for directions.*

Located riverside as the name suggests, this pleasant restaurant with rooms offers friendly and personal hospitality and service in a relaxed and comfortable setting. Bedrooms come in a range of shapes and sizes but are all comfortably furnished. The real highlight here however is the food; carefully sourced, mainly local and seasonal produce is expertly combined under the guidance of talented head chef Luke Roberts. An interesting wine list accompanies the menu, with an especially good selection by the half bottle.

Rooms: 4 en suite **S** fr £50 **D** fr £75* **Facilities:** FTV Lounge tea/coffee Dinner available WiFi **Notes:** LB Closed 15–30 December

MONTGOMERY	Map 15 S029

The Nags Head Inn

★★★★★ INN

tel: 01686 640600 **Garthmyl SY15 6RS**
email: jdrestaurantsltd@outlook.com **web:** www.nagsheadgarthmyl.co.uk
dir: *On A483 between Welshpool and Newtown.*

Once a coaching inn, the Grade II listed Nags Head continues to offer accommodation but has been bought right up to date. A warm welcome is assured from the friendly team here. Log fires in the winter and a sun-soaked terrace for alfresco dining make this a great destination at any time of the year. Meals here should not be missed – a range of imaginative dishes including their own take on pub classics is on offer. To complement the food, a range of local beers is stocked in addition to a well-chosen wine list.

Rooms: 5 en suite **S** fr £60 **D** fr £80* **Facilities:** FTV Lounge TVL tea/coffee Dinner available WiFi ♿ **Conf:** Max 16 **Parking:** 40

SWANSEA

LLANGENNITH	Map 8 SS49

Kings Head

★★★★ INN

tel: 01792 386212 **Town House SA3 1HX**
email: info@kingsheadgower.co.uk **web:** www.kingsheadgower.co.uk
dir: *M4 junction 47 follow signs for Gower A483. At next roundabout, 2nd left follow signs to Gowerton. At lights right onto B495, through old walls, keep left at fork. Kings Head on right.*

The Kings Head is made up of three 17th-century buildings set behind a splendid rough stone wall; it stands opposite the church in this coastal village. The well-equipped bedrooms, including some on the ground floor, are in two of the buildings. This is an ideal base for exploring the Gower Peninsula, whether for walking, cycling or surfing. Evening meals and breakfasts can be taken in the inn.

Rooms: 27 en suite (3 fmly) (14 GF) **D** fr £125 **Facilities:** FTV tea/coffee Dinner available Direct dial WiFi ♿ **Conf:** Max 50 **Parking:** 35 **Notes:** LB Closed 25 December RS 24 December closed for check-in

PARKMILL (NEAR SWANSEA)	Map 8 SS58

Parc-le-Breos House

★★★★ FARMHOUSE

tel: 01792 371636 **SA3 2HA**
email: info@parclebreos.co.uk **web:** www.parc-le-breos.co.uk
dir: *On A4118, right 300 yards after Shepherds shop, next left, signed.*

This imposing, early 19th-century house is at the end of a forest drive and set in over 60 acres of delightful grounds. Many charming, original features have been retained in the public rooms which include a lounge and a games room. The bedrooms have comfortable furnishings, and many are suitable for families. The freshly prepared dinners should not be missed, and afternoon tea on the terrace is a highlight during the summer months.

Rooms: 10 en suite (7 fmly) (1 GF) **S** fr £99 **D** fr £106* **Facilities:** FTV Lounge TVL tea/coffee Dinner available Licensed WiFi Fishing **Conf:** Max 30 Thtr 30 **Parking:** 12 **Notes:** LB Closed 25–26 December 65 acres arable/horses/pigs/chickens

SWANSEA	Map 9 SS69

Hurst Dene Guest House

★★★ GUEST HOUSE

tel: 01792 280920 **10 Sketty Road, Uplands SA2 0LJ**
email: hurstdenehotel@yahoo.co.uk **web:** www.hurstdene.co.uk
dir: *1 mile west of city centre. A4118 through Uplands shopping area into Sketty Road, Hurst Dene on right.*

This friendly guest house has a private car park and provides soundly maintained bedrooms with modern furnishings and equipment. Facilities include an attractive breakfast room with separate tables and a small comfortable lounge.

Rooms: 10 rms (8 en suite) (3 fmly) (1 GF) **Facilities:** FTV TVL tea/coffee WiFi **Parking:** 7 **Notes:** Closed 22 December to 1 January

TORFAEN

PONTYPOOL
Map 9 SO20

The Lion

[U]

tel: 01495 792516 **41 Broad Street, Blaenavon NP4 9NH**
email: info@thelionhotelblaenavon.co.uk web: www.thelionhotelblaenavon.co.uk
dir: *North of Pontypool, in centre of Blaenavon.*

Currently the rating for this establishment is not confirmed. This may be due to a change of ownership or because it has only recently joined the AA rating scheme.

Rooms: 12 en suite (2 fmly) **Facilities:** FTV DVD TVL tea/coffee Dinner available Direct dial WiFi Sauna steam room **Notes:** LB

VALE OF GLAMORGAN

HENSOL
Map 9 ST07

Premier Collection

Llanerch Vineyard

★★★★★ ◎ ♀ GUEST ACCOMMODATION

tel: 01443 222716 **CF72 8GG**
email: info@llanerch-vineyard.co.uk web: www.llanerch-vineyard.co.uk
dir: *M4 junction 34, follow brown tourist signs.*

Llanerch Vineyard is delightfully set on a working vineyard with views over the vines to the countryside beyond. Bedrooms and bathrooms come in a range of shapes and sizes including sumptuously appointed suites in the main building. The Cariad Restaurant & Bistro is open for lunch, afternoon tea and dinner, with outdoor seating on the terrace in the warmer months. The vineyard's own wines are available to purchase in the small shop area and also appear on the wine list at dinner.

Rooms: 3 en suite 8 annexe en suite (4 fmly) (7 GF) **Facilities:** FTV TVL tea/coffee Dinner available Direct dial Licensed WiFi ♪ Wine tasting and vineyard tour **Extras:** Bottled water – complimentary **Conf:** Max 150 Thtr 150 Class 80 Board 40 **Parking:** 100 **Notes:** LB Civ wed 150

LLANCARFAN
Map 9 ST07

The Fox & Hounds

★★★★ ◎ INN

tel: 01446 781287 **CF62 3AD**
email: enquiries@fandhllancarfan.co.uk web: www.fandhllancarfan.co.uk
dir: *A48, east of Cardiff, towards Cowbridge. Through St Nicholas village, left at lights onto A4226 signed Barry. After 1.5 miles turn right signed Llancarfan and follow brown tourist sign to Fox & Hounds, over ford on left.*

This whitewashed inn has a picture-postcard setting in the centre of the village, next to the stream and overlooking the church. The smart terrace is ideal for alfresco dining in the summer, and in the winter, the log fires inside the pub are equally inviting. The bar and restaurant are popular not only with guests but also with the friendly locals – an ideal environment to spend a relaxing evening, sampling the local ales. Dinner, showcasing locally-sourced, seasonal ingredients, is served by the friendly team and really shouldn't be missed. The bedrooms are tastefully decorated and well equipped for the modern guest.

Rooms: 8 en suite (1 fmly) **Facilities:** FTV Lounge tea/coffee Dinner available WiFi **Extras:** Speciality toiletries, robes, fresh milk **Conf:** Max 20 **Parking:** 20

PENARTH
Map 9 ST17

Premier Collection

Restaurant James Sommerin

★★★★★ ◎◎◎◎ RESTAURANT WITH ROOMS

tel: 029 2070 6559 **The Esplanade CF64 3AU**
email: info@jamessommerinrestaurant.co.uk
web: www.jamessommerinrestaurant.co.uk
dir: *Phone for directions.*

Restaurant James Sommerin stands proudly by the pier in Penarth with unrivalled views across the bay and is just a short distance from the centre of Cardiff. The cuisine is outstanding and exciting, with three different tasting menus offered in addition to the à la carte – all showcase the passion for food from this innovative chef and his team. It's a great idea to stay in one of individually styled, elegant bedrooms after taking full advantage of the interesting and extensive wine list. This is truly a family business – the friendly front-of-house team are under the watchful eye of Louise Sommerin and James and Louise's oldest daughter can be seen assisting in the kitchen too.

Rooms: 9 en suite **S** fr £130 **D** fr £150* **Facilities:** FTV tea/coffee Dinner available Lift WiFi **Extras:** Bottled water, fresh milk, slippers **Conf:** Max 60 **Notes:** LB Closed 25–26 December, 1 January RS Monday closed

See advert opposite

Restaurant James Sommerin with Rooms

The restaurant opened in May 2014 with its 9 bedrooms only opening in February 2016.

The family run Restaurant with Rooms is situated on the Esplanade in Penarth with panoramic views over the Severn Estuary. James and eldest daughter, Georgia, can be found cooking up a storm in the kitchen and Louise, front of house.

There are 9 en-suite bedrooms, elegantly decorated with 5 benefiting from unobstructed sea views and 4 with views over the courtyard. All rooms benefit from flat screen Freeview TVs, hot drinks tray, complimentary water and toiletries. All rooms are accessible via a lift, one room has complete disabled access and facilities, and another is dog friendly (there is an additional £25 charge per dog staying in the room).

The restaurant offers A la Carte and Tasting Menus, all dietary requirements are catered for.

Free wifi access available.

The Esplanade, Penarth CF64 3AU   Tel: 029 2070 6559
jamessommerinrestaurant.co.uk   info@jamessommerinrestaurant.co.uk

WREXHAM

LLANARMON DYFFRYN CEIRIOG   Map 15 SJ13

The Hand at Llanarmon

★★★★ @@ INN

tel: 01691 600666 **Ceiriog Valley LL20 7LD**
email: reception@thehandhotel.co.uk **web:** www.thehandhotel.co.uk
dir: *Exit A5 at Chirk onto B4500 signed Ceiriog Valley, 11 miles to village.*

Appointed to a high standard, this inn provides a range of thoughtfully furnished bedrooms, with smart modern bathrooms. Public areas retain many original features including exposed beams and open fires. Imaginative food makes great use of the finest local produce. A warm welcome and attentive service ensure a memorable guest experience.

Rooms: 13 en suite (4 GF) **S** fr £79 **D** fr £99* **Facilities:** STV FTV Lounge tea/coffee Dinner available Direct dial WiFi **Extras:** Speciality toiletries **Conf:** Max 15 Thtr 10 Class 10 Board 15 **Parking:** 19 **Notes:** LB

WREXHAM   Map 15 SJ35

The Lemon Tree

★★★ ⌂ RESTAURANT WITH ROOMS

tel: 01978 261211 **29 Rhosddu Road LL11 2LP**
email: info@thelemontree.org.uk **web:** www.thelemontree.org.uk
dir: *A483 junction 5 follow signs for town centre, pass university and football stadium. Keep left, left at 1st roundabout.*

A modern and stylish restaurant setting awaits within this unassuming Gothic, Grade II listed building in the heart of Wrexham. The owners have a relaxed approach and offer locally sourced, modern British cuisine in the evenings. Straightforward and good-value bedrooms, in a range of sizes, are smartly appointed and comfortable.

Rooms: 12 en suite **Facilities:** FTV TVL tea/coffee Dinner available WiFi **Conf:** Max 40 Thtr 40 Class 20 Board 20 **Parking:** 15 **Notes:** LB

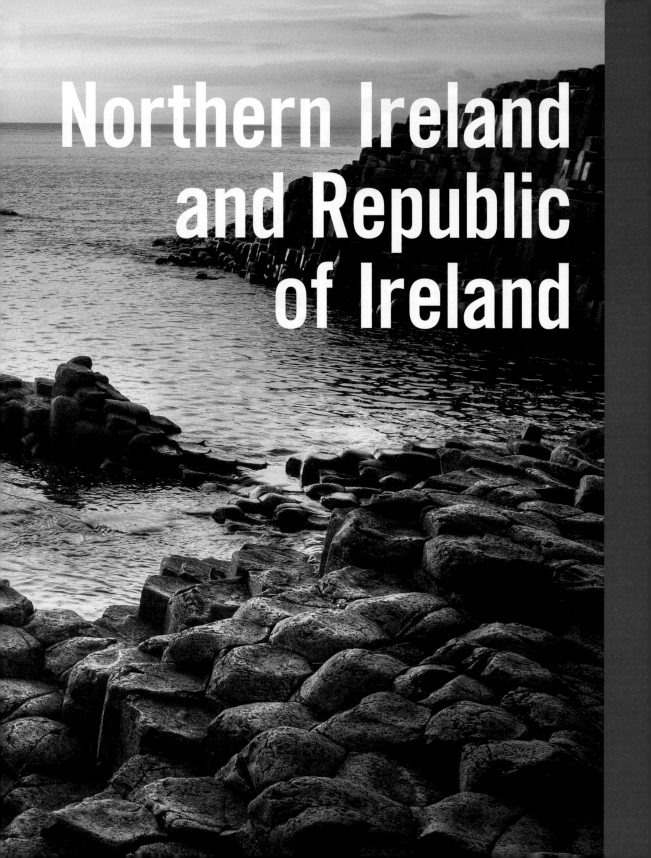

Northern Ireland and Republic of Ireland

NORTHERN IRELAND

COUNTY ANTRIM

BUSHMILLS — Map 1 D6

AA GUEST ACCOMMODATION OF THE YEAR FOR NORTHERN IRELAND 2018–19

Premier Collection

Causeway Lodge

★★★★★ GUEST HOUSE

tel: 028 2073 0333 **52 Moycraig Road, Dunseverick BT57 8TB**
email: stay@causewaylodge.com **web:** www.causewaylodge.com
dir: *Phone for directions.*

Causeway Lodge offers high-quality, contemporary accommodation in an idyllic setting on the north Antrim coast. Each of the individually designed bedrooms is thoughtfully presented and the Causeway Suite is very stylish. The house is close to the Giant's Causeway, Carrick-A-Rede rope bridge and the famous Bushmills Distillery. WiFi is available and a warm welcome is assured from the friendly owners.

Rooms: 4 en suite 1 annexe en suite (2 fmly) (1 GF) **S** fr £100 **D** fr £120*
Facilities: STV FTV iPod docking station TVL tea/coffee WiFi Sauna Gym ◈ Hot tub **Extras:** Speciality toiletries, fridge, bottled water, fresh milk, robes, slippers **Parking:** 6 **Notes:** Closed February

Premier Collection

Whitepark House

★★★★★ GUEST ACCOMMODATION

tel: 028 2073 1482 **150 Whitepark Road, Ballintoy BT54 6NH**
email: bob@whiteparkhouse.com **web:** www.whiteparkhouse.com
dir: *On A2 at Whitepark Bay, 6 miles east of Bushmills.*

Whitepark House sits above a sandy beach and has super views of the ocean and Scotland's Western Isles. The house features objets d'art gathered from Far Eastern travels, while the traditional bedrooms are homely. Breakfasts are served around a central table in the open-plan hallway, and hospitality is warm and memorable.

Rooms: 3 en suite **S** fr £90 **D** fr £130 **Facilities:** Lounge tea/coffee WiFi
Extras: Bottled water, robes **Parking:** 6 **Notes:** No children 10 years Closed December to February

BELFAST

BELFAST — Map 1 D5

Tara Lodge

★★★★ GUEST ACCOMMODATION

tel: 028 9059 0900 **36 Cromwell Road BT7 1JW**
email: sinead@taralodge.com **web:** www.taralodge.com
dir: *M1 onto A55, left onto A1, right into Fitzwilliam Street, left into University Road, proceed to Botanic Avenue.*

Friendly staff and comfortable bedrooms make Tara Lodge popular for both leisure or business guests. The stylish dining room is the scene for memorable breakfasts, while secure off-road parking is a bonus so close to the city centre.

Rooms: 19 en suite 15 annexe en suite (3 GF) **S** fr £75 **D** fr £80* **Facilities:** STV FTV DVD TVL tea/coffee Direct dial Lift WiFi **Parking:** 19 **Notes:** LB Closed 24–28 December

Springfield B&B

★★★ BED AND BREAKFAST

tel: 07711 971188 **16 Springfield Road BT12 7AG**
email: k.obrien@live.co.uk **web:** www.bnbbelfast.com
dir: *Phone for directions.*

Located just 10–15 minutes' walk from the city centre, Springfield B&B offers budget accommodation and genuine hospitality. Bedrooms and en suites are generally compact but cater well for guests. Complimentary, super-fast WiFi and good-sized TVs feature throughout. Breakfast offers a great start to the day with the traditional Ulster Fry – not for the faint-hearted, but not to be missed.

Rooms: 5 en suite **Facilities:** WiFi

COUNTY FERMANAGH

ENNISKILLEN — Map 1 C5

Belmore Court & Motel

★★★★ GUEST ACCOMMODATION

tel: 028 6632 6633 **Tempo Road BT74 6HX**
email: info@motel.co.uk **web:** www.motel.co.uk
dir: *On A4, opposite Tesco on corner of Tempo Road (B80).*

Situated in the centre of Enniskillen, Belmore Court is in an ideal location for visiting the north-west and Fermanagh lakes. The accommodation comes in a range of styles – from rooms with a small kitchen area to executive suites. These stylish rooms have TVs and free WiFi; some include a coffee maker. The public areas are also modern, and the breakfast room catches all the morning sun. Parking is available.

Rooms: 30 en suite 30 annexe en suite (17 fmly) (12 GF) **S** fr £60 **D** fr £70 (room only) **Facilities:** FTV DVD iPod docking station TVL tea/coffee Direct dial Lift WiFi ⌁ ◈ **Extras:** Speciality toiletries **Conf:** Max 45 Thtr 45 Class 25 Board 16 **Parking:** 60 **Notes:** LB Closed 24–28 December

COUNTY LONDONDERRY DERRY

MAGHERA — Map 1 C5

Ardtara Country House

★★★★ ◈◈ RESTAURANT WITH ROOMS

tel: 028 7964 4490 **8 Gorteade Road BT46 5SA**
email: info@ardtara.com **web:** www.ardtara.com
dir: *Take M2, M22, A6 towards Derry. 7 miles past Castledawson roundabout take A29 through Maghera. Continue on A29 towards Coleraine for 3 miles. Right onto B75 for 1 mile. Ardtara located on left.*

Set in its own extensive gardens, Ardtara Country House enjoys a secluded location just a short drive from the beautiful north Antrim coast and the famous Giant's Causeway. This fine 19th-century house offers guests spacious bedrooms with views over the landscaped gardens. There is a comfortable lounge, a cosy bar and many original features have been sympathetically restored. The award-winning restaurant offers the best fresh seasonal produce and the hearty breakfasts served in the conservatory are not to be missed. The city of Derry is a short drive away as is the challenging Royal Portrush golf course.

Rooms: 9 en suite (1 GF) **Facilities:** Lounge tea/coffee Dinner available Direct dial WiFi ⌁ Fishing Riding ◈ **Extras:** Robes, slippers **Conf:** Max 50 **Parking:** 100 **Notes:** LB Civ wed 65

REPUBLIC OF IRELAND

COUNTY CLARE

BALLYVAUGHAN   Map 1 B3

Hazelwood Lodge

★★★★ ☕ GUEST ACCOMMODATION

tel: 065 7077092
email: info@hazelwoodlodge.ie **web:** www.hazelwoodlodge.ie
dir: *1 kilometre from village, south on N67. 1st property on left.*

Located just one kilometre south of the coastal village of Ballyvaughan, Hazelwood Lodge is the family home of three generations of the Sweeney family and their dog, Donny. The unassuming frontage belies the airiness and quality that lies within. Bedrooms are spacious, with high quality furnishings and wonderfully comfortable beds. There is a relaxing lounge area with a terrace at the rear to catch the last of the evening sun. Having two experienced chefs in the family ensures that breakfast here is a real highlight, featuring some interesting and healthy options, together with home-baking and hand-made preserves. Dinner can be served to groups by prior arrangement.

Rooms: 8 en suite (4 fmly) (2 GF) **S** fr €70 **D** fr €90 **Facilities:** STV FTV Lounge tea/coffee WiFi 🌳 **Extras:** Still water, fresh milk in fridge, home-made biscuits **Parking:** 10 **Notes:** Closed 31 October to 10 February

Ballyvaughan Lodge

★★★ ☕ GUEST HOUSE

tel: 065 7077292 & 086 2511512
email: ballyvaughanlodge@yahoo.ie **web:** www.ballyvaughanlodge.com
dir: *From Galway take N6. Exit at junction 8 onto N18 onto N69 signed Ennistimon. Lodge on right on entering Ballyvaughan.*

This is the warm and welcoming home of the O'Sullivans and makes the ideal base for touring the wonderful Burren region and Galway Bay. The village has a number of craft shops and atmospheric pubs, most of which serve evening meals. Bedrooms are comfortably appointed, and the relaxing lounges include a sun room with reading material, guides and interesting pieces of original art. Breakfast is a delight – an array of fresh and poached fruits and local farmhouse cheeses followed by a selection of options, cooked to order by Pauline.

Rooms: 11 en suite (1 fmly) (5 GF) **S** fr €60 **D** fr €90 **Facilities:** FTV Lounge TVL tea/coffee Direct dial WiFi 🌳 **Extras:** Bottled water, snacks, chocolates – complimentary **Parking:** 11 **Notes:** Closed December to January

DOOLIN   Map 1 B3

Cullinan's Guesthouse

★★★ ☕ GUEST HOUSE

tel: 065 7074183
email: info@cullinansdoolin.com **web:** www.cullinansdoolin.com
dir: *In town centre at crossroads between McGanns Pub and O'Connors Pub.*

A charming guest house and restaurant, where excellent food is served in the conservatory dining room (in season; closed Wednesdays and Sundays) overlooking the River Aille. Chef-patron James Cullinan features locally caught fresh fish on the dinner menu, which also includes steaks, lamb and vegetarian dishes, and there is a popular Early Bird menu. Bedrooms are attractively decorated in a traditional style. There is a cosy guest lounge and ample off-street parking.

Rooms: 8 en suite 2 annexe en suite (3 fmly) (3 GF) **Facilities:** STV FTV Lounge TVL tea/coffee Dinner available Direct dial WiFi **Parking:** 15 **Notes:** No children 4 years Closed mid December to mid February

LAHINCH   Map 1 B3

Premier Collection

Moy House

★★★★★ ⊚⊚ ☕ GUEST HOUSE

tel: 065 7082800
email: moyhouse@eircom.net **web:** www.moyhouse.com
dir: *1 kilometre south from Lahinch on Miltown Malbay road, signed from Lahinch, N67.*

Moy House, an 18th-century former hunting lodge, overlooks Lahinch Bay, the world-famous surfing beach and championship golf links. Individually designed bedrooms and suites are decorated with luxurious fabrics and fine antique furniture. The elegant drawing room has an open turf fire and guests can enjoy breathtaking views of the ocean while enjoying a pre-dinner drink from the honesty bar. The Conservatory Restaurant adjoins the elegant dining room and features award-winning cuisine. The menu is based on local seafood and seasonal produce from small independent farmers; a gourmet tasting menu is served on selected nights. Dinner must be pre-booked. Breakfast is also a treat, with several healthy options on offer together with the traditional Irish selection.

Rooms: 9 en suite (2 fmly) (4 GF) **S** fr €130 **D** fr €165* **Facilities:** STV FTV DVD Lounge Dinner available Direct dial Licensed WiFi ♪ 🌳 Private access to beach **Extras:** Speciality toiletries **Conf:** Max 16 Board 16 **Parking:** 30 **Notes:** LB Closed November to February Civ wed 35

COUNTY CORK

BALTIMORE
Map 1 B1

Rolfs Country House

★★★ RESTAURANT WITH ROOMS

tel: 028 20289 **Baltimore Hill**
email: info@rolfscountryhouse.com **web:** www.rolfscountryhouse.com
dir: *Before village turn sharp left up hill. House signed.*

Situated on a hill above the fishing village of Baltimore, these 400-year-old stone buildings have been successfully converted by the Haffner family. There are 10 traditionally furnished en suite bedrooms in an annexe, a cosy bar with an open fire and a rustic restaurant set on two levels. Dinner is served nightly during the high season and at weekends in the winter; the menu features quality meats, artisan cheeses and fish landed at the busy pier. This is a lovely place to stay and the hosts are very friendly.

Rooms: 10 annexe en suite (4 GF) **Facilities:** FTV Lounge tea/coffee Dinner available WiFi **Parking:** 60 **Notes:** LB Closed 20–26 December

CLONAKILTY
Map 1 B2

Duvane House

★★★★ 🐿 FARMHOUSE

tel: 023 8833129 **Ballyduvane**
email: duvanefarm@eircom.net **web:** www.duvanehouse.com
dir: *1 kilometre southwest from Clonakilty on N71.*

This Georgian farmhouse is on the N71, Skibbereen road. Bedrooms are comfortable and include four-poster and brass beds. There is a lovely sitting room and dining room, and a wide choice is available at breakfast (dinner is available by arrangement). Local amenities include Blue Flag beaches, riding and golf.

Rooms: 4 en suite (1 fmly) **Facilities:** TVL tea/coffee Dinner available WiFi ⚓ Fishing ⚓ **Parking:** 20 **Notes:** LB Closed November to March 100 acres beef/dairy/mixed/sheep/horses

DURRUS
Map 1 A2

Blairscove House & Restaurant

★★★★ 🐿🐿 RESTAURANT WITH ROOMS

tel: 027 61127
email: mail@blairscove.ie **web:** www.blairscove.ie
dir: *From Durrus on R591 towards Crookhaven, 2.4 km, blue gate on right.*

Blairscove comprises four elegant suites located in the courtyard of a Georgian country house outside the pretty village of Durrus near Bantry; each room is individually decorated in a contemporary style and has stunning views over Dunmanus Bay and the mountains. The restaurant is renowned for its wide range of hors d'oeuvres and its open wood-fire grill. The piano-playing and candlelight add to a unique dining experience.

Rooms: 4 annexe en suite (1 fmly) **Facilities:** FTV DVD tea/coffee Dinner available Direct dial WiFi ⚓ **Extras:** Speciality toiletries, sherry – complimentary; wine – chargeable **Parking:** 30 **Notes:** Closed November to mid March Civ wed 35

GOLEEN
Map 1 A1

The Heron's Cove

★★★★ 🔅 🐿 BED AND BREAKFAST

tel: 028 35225 & 0868 073072 **The Harbour**
email: suehill@eircom.net **web:** www.heronscove.com
dir: *By harbour in Goleen.*

There are charming views of the harbour, fast-flowing stream and inland hills from The Heron's Cove, at Ireland's most south-westerly point near Mizen Head. Bedrooms are comfortably furnished and some have balconies. The restaurant and wine bar are run by chef-patron Sue Hill, where the freshest fish and local produce feature on the menus and guests can choose their own wines from the cocktail bar shelves. Breakfast is a special treat and the best West Cork ingredients can be enjoyed while watching the famous herons.

Rooms: 4 en suite (1 fmly) **S** fr €50 **D** fr €90 **Facilities:** STV FTV tea/coffee Dinner available Direct dial Licensed WiFi ⚓ **Extras:** Bottled water – complimentary **Parking:** 10 **Notes:** Closed mid November to mid February RS October to April bookings essential

KINSALE
Map 1 B2

Premier Collection

Friar's Lodge

★★★★★ GUEST HOUSE

tel: 086 2895075 & 021 4777384 **5 Friars Street**
email: mtierney@indigo.ie **web:** www.friars-lodge.com
dir: *In town centre next to parish church.*

This family-run and owned lodge was purpose-built and is near the Carmelite Friary on a quiet street just a short walk from Kinsale, renowned for its restaurants and bars. Bedrooms and suites are particularly spacious and furnished with comfort in mind. Being close to The Old Head Golf Club, and many others, there is storage for clubs and a drying room, with secure parking to the rear. A wine and snack menu is available; the elegant dining room is the setting for imaginative Irish breakfasts.

Rooms: 18 en suite (2 fmly) (4 GF) **Facilities:** STV tea/coffee Direct dial Lift WiFi **Parking:** 20 **Notes:** Closed Christmas

Long Quay House

★★★★ GUEST ACCOMMODATION

tel: 021 4709833 **Long Quay**
email: info@longquayhousekinsale.com **web:** www.longquayhousekinsale.com
dir: *Follow R600 from Cork to Kinsale, on entering the town, house on right.*

Located at the entrance to the picturesque coastal town of Kinsale, Long Quay House is a Georgian residence and the home of Rasa and Peter Deasy. Many of the comfortable rooms retain the original proportions of the building but don't miss out on today's creature comforts. Breakfast is a particularly noteworthy with beautiful presentations of interesting options. Kinsale is renowned for its restaurants and is also an ideal base for touring west Cork.

Rooms: 8 en suite (2 fmly) (1 GF) **Facilities:** FTV TVL Direct dial WiFi ⚹
Notes: Closed 15 November to 27 December

The White House

★★★★ ⚹ RESTAURANT WITH ROOMS

tel: 021 4772125 **Pearse Street, The Glen**
email: info@whitehouse-kinsale.ie **web:** www.whitehouse-kinsale.ie
dir: *In town centre.*

Centrally located among the narrow, twisting streets of the charming maritime town of Kinsale, this restaurant with rooms dates from 1850. It is a welcoming hostelry with smart, comfortably appointed, contemporary bedrooms. The atmospheric bar and bistro are open for lunch and dinner, with Restaurant d'Antibes also open during the evenings. The varied menu features local fish and beef. The courtyard at the rear makes a perfect setting in summer and there is regular entertainment in the bar.

Rooms: 10 en suite (2 fmly) **S** fr €70 **D** fr €120* **Facilities:** STV tea/coffee Dinner available Direct dial WiFi **Notes:** LB Closed 24–25 December

The Old Bank House

Ⓤ

tel: 021 4772206 **10/11 Pearse Street**
email: info@oldbankhousekinsale.com **web:** www.oldbankhousekinsale.com
dir: *On main road into Kinsale from Cork Airport (R600). House on right at start of Kinsale, next to Post Office.*

Currently the rating for this establishment is not confirmed. This may be due to a change of ownership or because it has only recently joined the AA rating scheme.

Rooms: 17 en suite (3 fmly) **Facilities:** STV FTV TVL tea/coffee Direct dial Lift WiFi
Extras: Nespresso machine, cookies on arrival **Notes:** LB Closed 25 December

---

SHANAGARRY | Map 1 C2

Premier Collection

Ballymaloe House

★★★★★ ◉◉ ⚹ GUEST HOUSE

tel: 021 4652531
email: res@ballymaloe.ie **web:** www.ballymaloe.ie
dir: *N25 onto R630 at Midleton roundabout. After 0.5 mile, left onto R631 to Cloyne. 2 miles after Cloyne on Ballycotton road.*

This charming country house is on a 400-acre farm, part of the Geraldine Estate in east Cork. Bedrooms upstairs in the main house retain many original features, and the ground-floor and courtyard rooms have garden patios. The relaxing drawing room and dining rooms have enchanting old-world charm. Ballymaloe House is renowned for excellent meals that use many ingredients produced on the farm. There is a craft shop, café, tennis courts and a small golf course on the estate.

Rooms: 20 en suite 9 annexe en suite (2 fmly) (3 GF) **Facilities:** Lounge TVL Dinner available Direct dial Licensed WiFi ⚹ ⚹ ⚹ ⚹ Children's sand pit/slide **Conf:** Max 200 Thtr 200 Class 50 Board 50 **Parking:** 50 **Notes:** LB Closed 23–26 December, 8–28 January RS January to February Closed Sunday to Tuesday rooms and dinner Civ wed 170

COUNTY DONEGAL

BALLYLIFFIN | Map 1 C6

Ballyliffin TownHouse

★★★★ ⚹ GUEST ACCOMMODATION

tel: 074 9378300
email: info@ballyliffintownhouse.ie **web:** www.ballyliffintownhouse.ie
dir: *Phone for directions.*

A popular spot with golfers, this warm and welcoming property is located at the top of the village of Ballyliffin on the Inishowen Peninsula. Family owned and operated, you can be assured of a friendly welcome and extensive knowledge of the visitor activities in the area. Bedrooms and en suites, of hotel standard, are spacious and very comfortably appointed. There is a large lounge for resident guests, together with an atmospheric pub. Breakfast is the highlight of a stay and features an attractive and appetising cold buffet selection and interesting choice of hot options.

Rooms: 13 en suite (5 fmly) **Facilities:** STV FTV DVD Lounge TVL tea/coffee Direct dial Lift Licensed WiFi ⚹ Riding **Extras:** Home-made cakes and biscuits **Parking:** 31 **Notes:** LB

CARRIGANS · Map 1 C5

Mount Royd Country Home

★★★★ ⚲ BED AND BREAKFAST

tel: 074 9140163
email: jmartin@mountroyd.com web: www.mountroyd.com
dir: *From Letterkenny on N14. At Dry Arch roundabout 2nd exit onto N13. At next roundabout 2nd exit onto N14 towards Lifford. Left at R236 to Carrigans. Or from Derry take A40 to Carrigans.*

Mount Royd is a creeper-clad house with beautifully maintained gardens in the pretty village of Carrigans, a short distance from the city of Derry. The friendly Martins take hospitality to new heights – nothing is too much trouble for them; it's no wonder so many of their guest return. Breakfast is a feast of choices including home-baking and eggs from their own hens. Each of the individually designed bedrooms is very comfortable, with lots of personal touches.

Rooms: 4 en suite (1 fmly) (1 GF) **Facilities:** FTV TVL tea/coffee WiFi **Parking:** 7 **Notes:** LB No children 12 years RS November to February

DONEGAL · Map 1 B5

The Red Door Country House

★★★★ ◉ RESTAURANT WITH ROOMS

tel: 074 9360289 **Fahan, Inishowen**
email: info@thereddoor.ie web: www.thereddoor.ie
dir: *In Fahan village, church on right, The Red Door signed on left.*

Situated amidst mature trees and landscaped gardens, this warm and welcoming restaurant with rooms stands proudly on the shore of Lough Swilly, in the historic village of Fahan just south of Buncrana. Dating from 1789, the original features of the house are cleverly combined with contemporary styling. Bedrooms are cosy and comfortable, each individually decorated and en suite. The house has a fine reputation in the region for the quality of its evening meals and alfresco lunches. Breakfast is also a highlight and is designed to be lingered over.

Rooms: 4 en suite **Facilities:** FTV Lounge tea/coffee Dinner available WiFi ⚲ **Conf:** Max 100 Thtr 100 Board 100 **Parking:** 40 **Notes:** RS Monday to Tuesday closed Civ wed 160

DUBLIN

DUBLIN · Map 1 D4

Premier Collection

Cliff Townhouse

★★★★★ ◉◉ RESTAURANT WITH ROOMS

tel: 01 6383939 **22 St Stephens Green D02 HW54**
email: vbracken@clifftownhouse.ie web: www.clifftownhouse.ie
dir: *Phone for directions.*

This fine Georgian property is located on one of the quieter areas of St Stephens Green, very much at the heart of the government district with both the Concert Hall and Grafton Street shopping district within walking distance. The bedrooms, some with park views, are comfortably appointed with really cosy, top-quality beds and bedding. The public spaces include an award-winning restaurant where seafood is a speciality. There is also an atmospheric bar in the basement serving authentic Spanish tapas.

Rooms: 9 en suite (3 fmly) **Facilities:** STV FTV iPod docking station Dinner available Direct dial Lift WiFi **Extras:** Speciality toiletries **Conf:** Max 50 Thtr 50 Class 25 Board 20 **Notes:** LB Closed 25–27 December

Premier Collection

Glenogra Town House

★★★★★ GUEST HOUSE

tel: 01 6683661 **64 Merrion Road, Ballsbridge**
email: info@glenogra.com web: www.glenogra.com
dir: *Opposite Royal Dublin Showgrounds and Intercontinental Hotel.*

This fine 19th-century red brick house is situated across from the RDS and close to the Aviva Stadium. The bedrooms are comfortably appointed and include many thoughtful extras; three bedrooms are on the ground floor. There is an elegant drawing room and dining room, and the interesting breakfast menu offers a range of dishes. Secure parking is available, and The Aircoach and city-centre buses stop in Merrion Road; the DART rail is around the corner.

Rooms: 13 en suite (1 fmly) (3 GF) **S** fr €69 **D** fr €99* **Facilities:** STV TVL tea/coffee Direct dial WiFi ⚲ **Parking:** 10 **Notes:** LB Closed 23–28 December

Premier Collection

Harrington Hall

★★★★★ GUEST HOUSE

tel: 01 4753497 **69–70 Harcourt Street**
email: harringtonhall@eircom.net web: www.harringtonhall.com
dir: *St Stephen's Green via O'Connell Street, in Earlsfort Terrace pass National Concert Hall and right into Hatch Street, right into Harcourt Street.*

Harrington Hall is a Georgian house on a one-way street, just off St Stephen's Green in the centre of the city. The spacious bedrooms are well appointed and include comfortable suites. A lovely plasterwork ceiling adorns the relaxing drawing room, and an extensive breakfast menu is served in the basement dining room. A lift, porter service and limited off-street parking are available.

Rooms: 28 en suite (3 fmly) (3 GF) **Facilities:** STV FTV tea/coffee Direct dial Lift Licensed WiFi ⚲ **Parking:** 14 **Notes:** LB Closed 24–26 December

Charleville Lodge Guest House

★★★★ GUEST HOUSE

tel: 01 8386633 **268/272 North Circular Road, Phibsborough**
email: info@charlevillelodge.ie web: www.charlevillelodge.ie
dir: *North from O'Connell Street to Phibsborough, left fork at St Peter's Church, house 250 metres on left.*

Situated close to the city centre near Phoenix Park, this elegant terrace of Victorian houses provides accommodation of a high standard. The two interconnecting lounges are welcoming, and the smart dining room offers a choice of breakfasts. Bedrooms are very comfortable with pleasant decor, and there is a secure car park.

Rooms: 30 en suite (2 fmly) (4 GF) **Facilities:** STV FTV Lounge TVL tea/coffee Direct dial Licensed WiFi ⚲ **Conf:** Max 10 Thtr 10 Class 10 Board 10 **Parking:** 18 **Notes:** LB

Ardagh House

★★★ GUEST HOUSE

tel: 01 4977068 **1 Highfield Road, Rathgar**
email: enquiries@ardahouse.com **web:** www.ardahouse.com
dir: *South of city centre through Rathmines.*

Ardagh House is an early 19th-century building with modern additions, and stands in a premier residential area on the outskirts of the city, close to local restaurants and pubs. It retains many original features and has a relaxing lounge that overlooks a delightful garden. There is an attractive dining room where hearty breakfasts are served at individual tables. The comfortable bedrooms vary in size. Ample off-street parking is available.

Rooms: 19 en suite (4 fmly) (1 GF) **Facilities:** FTV TVL tea/coffee Direct dial WiFi
Parking: 20 **Notes:** Closed 22 December to 3 January

Leeson Bridge Guest House

★★★ GUEST HOUSE

tel: 01 6681000 & 6682255 **1 Upper Leeson Street**
email: info@leesonbridgehouse.ie **web:** www.leesonbridgehouse.ie
dir: *At junction of N11 and N7, Leeson Street.*

This guest house is located right by Leeson Street Bridge, close to the city centre and is easily accessible from the ferry ports. Centred around a Georgian house, many of its original architectural features are retained. It offers a range of en suite bedroom styles, some with spa baths, sauna or galley kitchenette. Residents have access to ample parking at the rear. A take-away breakfast is offered to guests departing early in the morning.

Rooms: 20 en suite (1 fmly) (2 GF) **Facilities:** STV FTV TVL tea/coffee Direct dial Lift WiFi Fishing **Parking:** 18 **Notes:** LB

COUNTY GALWAY

CLIFDEN Map 1 A4

Ardmore House

★★★★ FARMHOUSE

tel: 095 21221 & 076 6030227 **Sky Road**
email: info@ardmore-house.com **web:** www.ardmore-house.com
dir: *N59 from Galway to Clifden. Just north of Clifden centre follow signs on left for 'Sky Road', 5 kilometres, house on left.*

Ardmore House is set in the wild scenery of Connemara, between hills and the sea on the Sky Road. Bedrooms are attractively decorated and the house is very comfortable throughout. A good hearty breakfast is provided and features home baking. A path leads from the house to the coast.

Rooms: 6 en suite (1 fmly) (5 GF) **Facilities:** STV FTV Lounge tea/coffee WiFi
Parking: 8 **Notes:** LB Closed October to March 25 acres non-working

Faul House

★★★★ FARMHOUSE

tel: 095 21239 & 087 9285287 **Ballyconneely Road**
email: info@ireland.com **web:** www.faulhouse.com
dir: *1.5 kilometres from town right at rugby pitch.*

Faul House, a fine modern farmhouse, stands on a quiet and secluded road overlooking Clifden Bay. It is smart and comfortable with large, well-furnished bedrooms that have good views. Kathleen offers a hearty breakfast with home baking. Connemara ponies are available for trekking.

Rooms: 6 en suite (3 fmly) (3 GF) **Facilities:** FTV Lounge TVL tea/coffee WiFi
Parking: 10 **Notes:** Closed November to 26 March 35 acres sheep/ponies/hens/ducks

Mallmore House

★★★★ BED AND BREAKFAST

tel: 095 21460 **Ballyconneely Road**
email: info@mallmore.com **web:** www.mallmorecountryhouse.com
dir: *1.5 kilometres from Clifden towards Ballyconneely take 1st right.*

Mallmore House, overlooking Clifden Bay, is a charming and lovingly maintained 17th-century house. It is situated close to the town and has a beautiful garden and mature woodland. The bedrooms are spacious and very well appointed with antique furniture. The drawing room with a turf fire is a delightful place to relax. There is a wide choice at breakfast including home baking and locally smoked fish. Mallmore is a lovely place to stay and enjoy the peace and quiet of Connemara.

Rooms: 6 en suite (1 fmly) (6 GF) **Facilities:** FTV DVD Lounge tea/coffee WiFi
🔒 **Parking:** 15 **Notes:** Closed October to 1 April

Ben View House

★★★ GUEST HOUSE

tel: 095 21256 **Bridge Street**
email: benviewhouse@ireland.com **web:** www.benviewhouse.com
dir: *Enter town on N59, opposite Esso fuel station.*

This house is well located in the centre of the town with ample on-street parking. Dating from 1824, it offers good quality accommodation at a moderate cost. The breakfast room and lounge have an old world atmosphere, with antique furniture and sparkling silverware in everyday use.

Rooms: 10 rms (9 en suite) (3 fmly) **Facilities:** TVL tea/coffee **Notes:** LB

| GALWAY | Map 1 B3 |

Premier Collection

Screebe House

★★★★★ RESTAURANT WITH ROOMS

tel: 091 574110 **Rosmuc**
email: booking@screebe.com **web:** www.screebe.com
dir: Phone for directions.

This house was a hunting and fishing lodge in the 19th century and is situated right on the edge of Camus Bay – it cannot get any closer to the Atlantic. Each of the spacious bedrooms is designed with relaxation and comfort in mind – unusually, there are no TVs in the rooms. The public rooms retain their original charm, most have real fires in the cooler months. Dinner is a particular highlight; the daily-changing, seven-course set menu is driven by the season and the market. Breakfast is also noteworthy for its range and quality. An ideal base for country pursuits, with an adjacent pool and sauna for the less sporty.

Rooms: 10 rms (8 en suite) (2 pri facs) (2 GF) **Facilities:** Lounge TVL Dinner available Direct dial WiFi 🛇 Fishing Sauna Gym **Conf:** Max 20 Thtr 20 Class 20 Board 20 **Parking:** 10 **Notes:** No children 16 years Closed 30 November to 10 February RS Monday to Tuesday closed

Marian Lodge Guest House

★★★★ GUEST HOUSE

tel: 091 521678 **Knocknacarra Road, Salthill Upper**
email: celine@marian-lodge.com **web:** www.marian-lodge.com
dir: From Galway to Salthill on R336, through Salthill, 1st right after Spinnaker Hotel into Knocknacarra Road.

This large modern house just 50 metres from the seafront, is an ideal base for both the city of Galway and the wilderness landscapes of Connemara. The comfortable bedrooms have orthopaedic beds and en suite facilities. There is also a cosy lounge and separate breakfast room where the welcoming host, Celine, is on hand to make recommendations for what to do with your day. Plenty of parking is available.

Rooms: 6 en suite (4 fmly) **Facilities:** STV TVL tea/coffee Direct dial **Parking:** 10 **Notes:** LB No children 3 years Closed 23–28 December

| COUNTY KERRY |

| DINGLE (AN DAINGEAN) | Map 1 A2 |

Premier Collection

Castlewood House

★★★★★ ♨ GUEST HOUSE

tel: 066 9152788 **The Wood**
web: www.castlewooddingle.com
dir: R559 from Dingle, 0.5 kilometre from Aquarium.

Less than a 10-minute stroll from the bustling centre of Dingle, Castlewood House is the perfect place to stop and take in all the delights the town has to offer. Quality standards exceed the expectations of many a hotel, but it is the personal attention that proprietors, Helen and Brian, give their guests that really impresses here. Wonderfully spacious bedrooms are well-appointed and accessed by a lift. Breakfast is a real highlight – so many options are available that choosing can be difficult. The drawing room is a great place to relax after a day's walking and to plan the next day's activities.

Rooms: 12 en suite (3 fmly) (4 GF) **S** fr €80 **D** fr €96* **Facilities:** STV tea/coffee Direct dial Lift **Parking:** 15 **Notes:** LB Closed 4–27 December and 4 January to 4 February Civ wed 20

Premier Collection

Gormans Clifftop House & Restaurant

★★★★★ ◉ GUEST HOUSE

tel: 066 9155162 & 083 0033133 **Glaise Bheag, Ballydavid**
email: info@gormans-clifftophouse.com **web:** www.gormans-clifftophouse.com
dir: R559 to An Mhuirioch, turn right at T-junction, north for 3 kilometres.

Sile and Vincent Gorman's guest house and restaurant is perched over the cliffs on the western tip of the Slea Head peninsula near Ballydavid, with bracing walks starting from the doorstep. The beauty of the rugged coastline, rhythm of the sea and the sun going down on Smerwick Harbour can be enjoyed over a delicious dinner in the smart dining room. The menu includes produce from the garden, local seafood and lamb. The bedrooms, with breathtaking views of the ocean or mountains, are comfortably proportioned and thoughtfully equipped; the ground-floor rooms are adapted for the less mobile.

Rooms: 8 en suite (2 fmly) (4 GF) **Facilities:** tea/coffee Dinner available Direct dial Licensed WiFi Bikes for hire **Parking:** 15 **Notes:** LB Closed 24–26 December RS October to March reservation only

KENMARE — Map 1 A2

Muxnaw Lodge

★★★★ BED AND BREAKFAST

tel: 064 6641252 & 087 2922895 **Casletownbere Road**
email: muxnaw@eircom.net **web:** www.muxnawlodge.eu
dir: *Phone for directions.*

Located on the Castletownbere Road, within easy walking distance of Kenmare town, this warm and friendly house is a former hunting lodge dating from the early 19th century. It is set on an elevated site in mature gardens. Bedrooms and en suites are individually decorated, with some enjoying views of the Kenmare River. The lounge retains much of its original character, in addition to the bright and airy sun room. Ample parking is available to the rear.

Rooms: 5 en suite (1 fmly) **Facilities:** STV DVD TVL tea/coffee WiFi ☺ 🔒 **Parking:** 5
Notes: No children Closed 24–25 December

Sea Shore Farm Guest House

★★★★ GUEST HOUSE

tel: 064 6641270 & 6641675 **Tubrid**
email: seashore@eircom.net **web:** www.seashorekenmare.com
dir: *1.6 kilometres from Kenmare off N70 (Ring of Kerry /Sneem road). Signed at junction N70 and N71.*

Overlooking Kenmare Bay on the Ring of Kerry road, this modern farm guest house is close to town and has spacious bedrooms. Ground-floor rooms open onto the patio and have easier access. Guests are welcome to enjoy farm walks through the fields to the shore, and nearby salmon and trout fishing on the Roughty River. There is a comfortable sitting room and dining room and a delightful garden.

Rooms: 6 en suite (2 fmly) (2 GF) **Facilities:** FTV Lounge tea/coffee Direct dial WiFi 🔒 **Extras:** Speciality toiletries, snacks – complimentary **Parking:** 10
Notes: No children 5 years Closed November to 19 March

KILGARVAN — Map 1 B2

Birchwood B&B

★★★★ GUEST ACCOMMODATION

tel: 064 6685473 & 087 9172504 **Churchground**
email: birchwood1@eircom.net **web:** www.birchwoodkilgarvan.com
dir: *600 metres east of Kilgarvan off R569.*

This family-owned property is set in 1.5 acres of gardens in a peaceful location just outside the village of Kilgarvan and overlooks a birch tree forest. The large and comfortable bedrooms include double, twin and family rooms and there's free WiFi throughout. The breakfast menu features fruits and juices together with home-made breads and preserves. Guests are welcome to use and enjoy the large gardens.

Rooms: 5 en suite (1 fmly) **S** fr €45 **D** fr €80 **Facilities:** FTV WiFi **Parking:** 5
Notes: Closed 16 December to 6 Janaury

KILLARNEY — Map 1 A2

Fairview Guest House

★★★★★ 🍽 GUEST HOUSE

tel: 064 6634164 **College Street**
email: info@fairviewkillarney.com **web:** www.killarneyfairview.com
dir: *In town centre off College Street.*

Great attention to detail is demonstrated in the design of this smart guest house, handily located in the town centre close to the bus and railway station. Bedrooms include some with air conditioning and jacuzzi baths, and all are comfortable, with quality furnishings and fittings. There is a lift to all floors, and the impressive penthouse suite enjoys views over the town towards the Kerry mountains. There is a relaxing sitting area and the breakfast menu offers a selection of dishes cooked to order. Local attractions and excursions include lake cruises, championship golf courses and the Killarney National Park.

Rooms: 29 en suite (2 fmly) (1 GF) **Facilities:** STV DVD TVL tea/coffee Dinner available Direct dial Lift Licensed WiFi ♿ Jacuzzi suites available **Parking:** 11
Notes: LB

Ashville House

★★★★ GUEST HOUSE

tel: 064 6636405 & 6636778 **Rock Road**
email: info@ashvillekillarney.com **web:** www.ashvillekillarney.com
dir: *In town centre. Exit at north end of High Street into Rock Road.*

This inviting house is just a stroll from the town centre and near the N22 (Tralee road). Bedrooms are comfortably furnished, and there is a pleasant sitting room and dining room. There is a private car park, and tours can be arranged.

Rooms: 12 en suite (4 GF) **S** fr €50 **D** fr €70 **Facilities:** STV FTV TVL tea/coffee Direct dial WiFi ♿ 🔒 **Parking:** 13 **Notes:** LB Closed November to 1 March

Kingfisher Lodge Bed & Breakfast

★★★★ GUEST HOUSE

tel: 064 6637131 & 086 3741379 **Lewis Road**
email: info@kingfisherlodgekillarney.com **web:** www.kingfisherlodgekillarney.com
dir: *Dublin link straight through 1st roundabout. Right at next roundabout towards town centre. Lodge on left.*

This welcoming, modern guest house is home to the Carroll family. It is situated within walking distance of the town centre, and has comfortable and well-appointed bedrooms, all of which are en suite. Breakfast is served in the attractively decorated dining room and there is also a relaxing lounge and conservatory with WiFi. A drying room is available for fishing and wet gear. Golf, walking and fishing trips can be arranged. There is ample parking, and a complimentary pick-up from the bus and train station is offered.

Rooms: 10 en suite (1 fmly) (2 GF) **Facilities:** STV FTV Lounge TVL tea/coffee Direct dial WiFi ♿ Walking, fishing, horseriding, golf can be booked **Parking:** 12
Notes: LB Closed 31 October to 9 March

KILLORGLIN — Map 1 A2

Premier Collection

Carrig House Country House & Restaurant

★★★★★ ◎◎ ⬱ GUEST HOUSE

tel: 066 9769100 **Caragh Lake**
email: info@carrighouse.com **web:** www.carrighouse.com
dir: N70 to Killorglin.

Located on the shores of Lake Caragh, a short drive from Killorglin and amid woodlands, this family-run house is the perfect retreat for a relaxing break. The bedrooms, some with lake views, come in a range of styles but each is decorated to a high standard with guest comfort in mind. Public rooms include elegant drawing rooms and cosy nooks. There is a true passion for food in evidence at dinner, where local seafood and seasonal produce are cooked and presented with care in the Lakeside Restaurant. Many outdoor pursuits can be found in the area — golf, hill walking, horse riding, cycling and water activities to name but a few.

Rooms: 16 en suite **Facilities:** Lounge TVL Dinner available Direct dial Licensed WiFi ⬱ ⬱ Fishing **Extras:** Bottled water **Parking:** 20 **Notes:** LB No children 8 years Closed October to February Civ wed 63

COUNTY KILKENNY

KILKENNY — Map 1 C3

Butler House

★★★★ GUEST HOUSE

tel: 056 7765707 & 7722828 **Patrick Street**
email: res@butler.ie **web:** www.butler.ie
dir: In centre near Kilkenny Castle.

Once the dower house of Kilkenny Castle, this fine Georgian building fronts onto the main street, with wonderful secluded gardens at the rear, through which you stroll to take breakfast in the Kilkenny Design Centre. Many of the spacious bedrooms retain architectural features of the period, together with contemporary furnishings and minimalist decor. There is a comfortable foyer lounge and a number of conference and event spaces. Secure parking is provided.

Rooms: 13 en suite (4 fmly) **Facilities:** STV FTV Lounge tea/coffee Direct dial WiFi ⬱ **Extras:** Bottled water – complimentary; safe in all rooms **Conf:** Max 120 Thtr 120 Class 40 Board 40 **Parking:** 24 **Notes:** LB Closed 24–29 December Civ wed 80

COUNTY LAOIS

PORT LAOISE — Map 1 C3

Mahers B&B

★★★★ BED AND BREAKFAST

tel: 087 212 9236 **Beech Avenue, Rathleague**
email: mahersbandb@rathleague.com **web:** www.mahers-bnb.com
dir: Phone for directions.

This Georgian home has been creatively appointed with attention paid to the details – original features sit happily alongside the modern facilities. Built in the late 18th century, this property has been in the Maher family for over 100 years. Outbuildings include storage for bikes, fishing tackle and hiking gear, and there is even an ornamental plant nursery on the site. Above all, it is the natural warm welcome from the family that endears visitors to this fine family home. There is a comfortable guest lounge, and breakfast is a real treat with several options always on offer.

Rooms: 4 rms (2 en suite) (2 pri facs) (3 fmly) **Facilities:** STV FTV TVL tea/coffee WiFi ⬱ ⬱ **Conf:** Max 20 Thtr 20 Class 16 Board 20 **Parking:** 10

COUNTY LOUTH

CARLINGFORD — Map 1 D4

Ghan House

★★★★ ◎◎ ⬱ GUEST ACCOMMODATION

tel: 042 9373682
email: info@ghanhouse.com **web:** www.ghanhouse.com
dir: M1 junction 18 signed Carlingford, 5 metres on left after 50kph speed sign on entering Carlingford.

Dating from 1727, Ghan House oozes charm and comfort. Set in a two-acre walled garden, the house is within 50 metres of Carlingford's centre, making it an ideal base for walking and touring the Cooley peninsula. The bedrooms, either in the house or a converted barn in the grounds, are warm and well appointed. Comfortable public rooms feature log fires and relaxing armchairs. Food is an important element of the business, and a successful cookery school has operated here for many years. Dinner has an emphasis on artisan produce and the renowned Cooley lamb. Breakfast is a treat and includes a choice of fruit compôtes and preserves.

Rooms: 4 en suite 8 annexe en suite (3 fmly) (4 GF) **S** fr €85 **D** fr €170 **Facilities:** FTV iPod docking station Lounge tea/coffee Dinner available Licensed WiFi ⬱ Riding ⬱ **Extras:** Home-made biscuits **Conf:** Max 50 Thtr 50 Class 26 Board 32 **Parking:** 35 **Notes:** LB Civ wed 50

COUNTY MAYO

CASTLEBAR   Map 1 B4

Lough Lannagh Lodge

★★★ GUEST ACCOMMODATION

tel: 094 9027111 **Old Westport Road**
email: info@loughlannagh.ie **web:** www.loughlannagh.ie
dir: *N5/N60/N84 to Castlebar. At ring road follow signs for N5 Westport, signed Lough Lannagh village approaching Westport roundabout.*

Lough Lannagh Lodge is in a delightful wooded area within walking distance of Castlebar. There is a conference centre, fitness centre, tennis, table tennis, laundry and drying facilities, a private kitchen and many activities for children. The bedrooms are well appointed and breakfast is served in the café. Dinner is available by appointment for groups.

Rooms: 24 en suite (24 fmly) (12 GF) **Facilities:** FTV Lounge TVL Dinner available Direct dial WiFi ⌕ ↕ ♿ Bicycle hire, water sports **Conf:** Max 100 Thtr 100 Class 54 Board 34 **Parking:** 24 **Notes:** LB Closed mid December to mid January RS Sunday no arrivals Civ wed 100

WESTPORT   Map 1 B4

Bertra House

★★★ FARMHOUSE

tel: 098 64833 & 086 0667233 **Thornhill, Murrisk**
email: bertrahse@eircom.net **web:** www.bertrahouse.com
dir: *West of Westport off R335, near Croagh Patrick on L1833.*

This attractive bungalow overlooks the Bertra Beach of Clew Bay, at the foot of Croagh Patrick, locally known as 'The Reek'. Located about a 10-minute drive from Westport, it is an ideal location for browsing the shops and touring north Mayo. Four bedrooms are en suite with the fifth having a dedicated bathroom. Breakfasts are generous and features Margaret Gill's home baking, some of which might just be available with a cup of tea in the cosy lounge on your arrival.

Rooms: 5 rms (4 en suite) (1 pri facs) (1 fmly) (5 GF) **S** fr €50 **D** fr €70*
Facilities: FTV Lounge TVL tea/coffee WiFi **Parking:** 7 **Notes:** LB No children 6 years Closed 15 November to 15 March 40 acres beef/sheep

COUNTY MEATH

SLANE   Map 1 D4

Premier Collection

Tankardstown

★★★★★ ◉◉ ♨ GUEST ACCOMMODATION

tel: 041 9824621
email: info@tankardstown.ie **web:** www.tankardstown.ie
dir: *N51 (Navan-Slane road), take turn directly opposite main entrance to Slane Castle, signed Kells. Continue for 5 kilometres.*

Tankardstown is a magical place. Set in 80 acres of parkland, it has many strings to its bow. The main house is host to elegant rooms, with others in cottages in the converted stableyard. Each is individually decorated to a very high standard. The cottages have the benefit of spacious kitchens and living areas, ideal for longer stays. The property is also host to the award-winning Brabazon, a fine dining restaurant, and there's a bistro for more casual fare. Excellent breakfasts are served in the main house, with the option of having it delivered to the cottages. This fine property is ideal for family gatherings and intimate wedding celebrations.

Rooms: 7 en suite 15 annexe en suite (6 fmly) (2 GF) **S** fr €105 **D** fr €210*
Facilities: STV FTV DVD Lounge TVL tea/coffee Dinner available Direct dial Licensed WiFi ↕ Fishing ♨ Hot tub **Extras:** Still water – complimentary; mini-bar – chargeable **Conf:** Max 150 Thtr 150 Class 80 Board 50 **Parking:** 200 **Notes:** Civ wed 200

COUNTY MONAGHAN

GLASLOUGH   Map 1 C5

Premier Collection

The Castle at Castle Leslie Estate

★★★★★ GUEST HOUSE

tel: 047 88100
email: info@castleleslie.com **web:** www.castleleslie.com
dir: *M1 junction 14, N2 to Monaghan then N12 onto R185 for Glaslough.*

Set in 1,000 acres of rolling countryside, The Castle is the centre of the Leslie Estate which has been in the family since the 1660s. Bedrooms are decorated in keeping with the age and style of the period, and are ideal for relaxing breaks where guests enjoy the peace and tranquillity of the property without any interference from TVs or other distractions. With a successful equestrian centre and a private fishing lake, this is an ideal location for those who enjoy country pursuits.

Rooms: 20 rms (19 en suite) (1 pri facs) **D** fr €220* **Facilities:** Lounge TVL Direct dial Lift Licensed WiFi ⌕ ↕ Fishing Riding Snooker Private cinema, falconry, clay target shooting **Extras:** Speciality toiletries **Conf:** Max 280 Thtr 260 Class 150 Board 65 **Parking:** 100 **Notes:** LB Closed 22–27 December Civ wed 90

COUNTY SLIGO

BALLYSADARE
Map 1 B5

Seashore House

★★★ BED AND BREAKFAST

tel: 071 9167827 & 086 2224842 **Lisduff**
email: info@seashoreguests.com **web:** www.seashoreguests.com
dir: N4 onto N59 west at Ballisadare, in 4 kilometres Seashore signed on right. Turn down road, 600 metres on right.

Seashore House is an attractive dormer bungalow in a quiet seashore location. A comfortable lounge with open turf fire and sunny conservatory-dining room look out over attractive landscaped gardens and further sea and mountain views. Bedrooms are attractively appointed and comfortable, and there is also a tennis court and bike storage. Credit cards are only accepted during high season.

Rooms: 4 en suite (1 fmly) (2 GF) **S** fr €55 **D** fr €90 **Facilities:** STV FTV TVL WiFi ⚘ ⚓ **Parking:** 6 **Notes:** LB No children Closed 31 October to April

STRANDHILL
Map 1 B5

Strandhill Lodge and Suites

★★★★ GUEST HOUSE

tel: 071 9122122 **Top Road**
email: info@strandhilllodgeandsuites.com **web:** www.strandhilllodgeandsuites.com
dir: From Sligo onto R292 for Strandhill.

Located in the centre of Strandhill, just five kilometres from Sligo, this property offers particularly spacious accommodation, finished to a very high standard; many of the rooms have stunning views of the bay. Public areas are open plan in design, with a bright and airy breakfast room where continental breakfast is served. This is an ideal property for those playing golf or participating in the many other leisure pursuits in the region. There is a meeting room on the first floor, and ample parking to the rear. A number of cosy pubs and good restaurants are located in the village.

Rooms: 21 en suite 1 annexe en suite (7 fmly) (8 GF) **Facilities:** STV FTV DVD iPod docking station Lounge TVL tea/coffee Direct dial Lift WiFi ⚘ ⚓ Fishing Riding ⚓ **Extras:** Bottled water **Conf:** Max 20 Thtr 20 Class 10 Board 8 **Parking:** 22 **Notes:** LB Closed January to 5 February

COUNTY TIPPERARY

CASHEL
Map 1 B3

Ashmore House

★★★ BED AND BREAKFAST

tel: 062 61286 & 0861 037010 **John Street**
email: info@ashmorehouse.com **web:** www.ashmorehouse.com
dir: M8 exit 8 to town centre, into John Street opposite Cashel Palace Hotel, house 100 metres on right.

Ashmore House is a Georgian building set in a colourfully planted walled garden, right in the centre of the town, within walking distance of the Rock of Cashel. Guests have use of a large sitting and dining room, and bedrooms come in a variety of sizes from big family rooms to a more compact double. Children are welcome and WiFi is available. There is secure parking at the rear.

Rooms: 5 en suite (2 fmly) **Facilities:** FTV TVL tea/coffee Dinner available WiFi **Parking:** 10

THURLES
Map 1 3

The Castle

★★★★★ BED AND BREAKFAST

tel: 0504 44324 **Twomileborris**
email: bookings@thecastlecountryhouse.com **web:** www.bandbthurles.com
dir: 7 kilometres east of Thurles. On N75, 200 metres west of Twomileborris at Castle.

Pierce and Joan offer a very welcome to their fascinating house that is sheltered by a 16th-century tower house – it has been in the Duggan family for over 200 years. The bedrooms are comfortable and spacious, there is a relaxing lounge and the dining room overlooks the delightful garden. Golf, fishing, hill walking, and traditional pubs and restaurants are all nearby. Dinner is available by arrangement.

Rooms: 4 en suite (3 fmly) **Facilities:** STV FTV TVL tea/coffee Dinner available WiFi ⚘ ⚓ ⚓ Fishing ⚓ **Conf:** Max 40 Board 20 **Parking:** 30 **Notes:** LB

TIPPERARY
Map 1 C3

Aisling

★★★ BED AND BREAKFAST

tel: 087 2278230 & 062 33307 **Glen of Aherlow**
email: ladygreg@oceanfree.net **web:** www.aislingbedandbreakfast.com
dir: From town centre R664 for 2.4 kilometres, past golf club.

Aisling is close to Tipperary on the R664, the Glen of Aherlow road. The bedrooms are well furnished and attractively decorated. There is a comfortable guest sitting room and a delightful garden with patio seating. Marian and Bob are helpful hosts, happy to arrange day trips and provide maps and information on the locality.

Rooms: 5 rms (3 en suite) (2 pri facs) (2 fmly) (5 GF) **S** fr €40 **D** fr €80* **Facilities:** STV FTV Lounge TVL WiFi ⚓ **Extras:** Snack on arrival – complimentary **Parking:** 5 **Notes:** LB

COUNTY WATERFORD

TRAMORE
Map 1 C2

Seacourt

★★★★ BED AND BREAKFAST

tel: 051 386244 **Tivoli Road**
email: seacourthouse@gmail.com **web:** www.seacourt.ie
dir: From Waterford City on R675 to Tramore. Over 2 roundabouts, at 3rd roundabout (boat in middle) straight over, 1st bed and breakfast on left.

Seacourt is a very comfortable house situated in a seaside town close to Splashworld, the beach and Tramore Racecourse, with many other tourist attractions to be found locally. The bedrooms, including a spacious ground-floor family room, are comfortably furnished. There is a cosy guest sitting room, a wide choice of cooked breakfasts, served in the dining room and ample off-street parking.

Rooms: 5 rms (5 pri facs) (1 fmly) (1 GF) **Facilities:** STV TVL tea/coffee WiFi ⚓ **Parking:** 10 **Notes:** No children 6 years Closed October to 2 April

Westcliff House

★★★★ GUEST ACCOMMODATION

tel: 051 381365 & 0876 655723 **5 Newtown Hill**
web: www.westcliffhouse.ie
dir: *Just off R675 (coast road).*

Westcliff House, the warm and inviting home of Evelyne Power and her family, is located in a quiet, elevated position in a residential area just a short drive from the town centre. Each of the bedrooms is comfortably appointed. Guests are welcome to make themselves at home in the cosy sitting room or the bright and airy sunroom at the rear overlooking the gardens – just the place to enjoy some refreshments and Evelyne's renowned baking.

Rooms: 4 en suite **Facilities:** FTV Lounge TVL tea/coffee WiFi 🔒 **Parking:** 4
Notes: No children Closed 30 September to 1 April

COUNTY WEXFORD

GOREY
Map 1 D3

Premier Collection

Clonganny House

★★★★★ ◉◉ GUEST ACCOMMODATION

tel: 053 948 2111 **Ballygarrett**
email: info@clonganny.com **web:** www.clonganny.com
dir: *Just off R742 between Ballygarrett and Kilmuckridge.*

Located three kilometres south of Ballygarrett, Clonganny House was painstakingly restored to its former glory by Brona and Phillippe Brillant. The breakfast room and lounge retain many original architectural features and are beautifully presented with guest comfort and relaxation in mind. Four individually designed, ground-level double rooms are offered; some have French windows overlooking the walled garden. The breakfast menu reveals some real treats, with options sure to please the most discerning palates; dinner is available on certain dates by prior arrangement. Guests can enjoy the walks set among the 10 acres of woodland grounds.

Rooms: 4 annexe en suite (4 GF) **S** fr €160 **D** fr €195* **Facilities:** FTV iPod docking station Lounge tea/coffee Dinner available Licensed WiFi ♨ 🔒 **Extras:** Speciality toiletries, snacks **Parking:** 13 **Notes:** No children 16 years Civ wed 20

WEXFORD
Map 1 D2

Premier Collection

Killiane Castle Country House & Farm

★★★★★ 🏠 FARMHOUSE

tel: 053 9158885 **Drinagh**
email: info@killianecastle.com **web:** www.killianecastle.com
dir: *Off N25 between Wexford and Rosslare.*

This 17th-century house, run by the Mernagh family, is on a working dairy farm at Drinagh, south of Wexford town; the house is part of a 13th-century Norman castle. There are elegant reception rooms and beautifully furnished bedrooms that include bottled water from their own artesian well. Breakfast is a real treat and includes farm produce and home-made baking and preserves.

Rooms: 9 en suite (2 fmly) (2 GF) **Facilities:** STV FTV DVD iPod docking station Lounge TVL Dinner available Licensed WiFi ♨ 🏌 🔒 Driving range, 18-hole pitch and putt **Extras:** Speciality toiletries, honesty bar **Parking:** 10
Notes: Closed December to February 230 acres dairy/sheep

Aldridge Lodge Restaurant and Guest Accommodation

★★★★ ◉◉ RESTAURANT WITH ROOMS

tel: 051 389116 **Duncannon**
email: info@aldridgelodge.com **web:** www.aldridgelodge.com
dir: *Phone for directions.*

Just a 45-minute drive from Rosslare, Aldridge Lodge is an ideal first night stop following a ferry crossing. It makes a great base for exploring the many attractions and activities of the Hook Peninsula. Hosts Joanne and Billy, who is also the chef, take a keen interest in their guests and it's no wonder so many return – weekend reservations are essential. While each of the three guest rooms is warm and cosy, what brings most visitors here is the food; Billy has a strong reputation for his use of local, seasonal ingredients. The breakfast experience is noteworthy too – quality dishes cooked with skill and care and enjoyed in a relaxed environment.

Rooms: 3 en suite **S** fr €60 **D** fr €100* **Facilities:** FTV tea/coffee Dinner available WiFi 🔒 **Parking:** 20 **Notes:** No children Closed 1st week January, 1st week May RS Monday to Wednesday closed Civ wed 30

COUNTY WICKLOW

DUNLAVIN
Map 1 C3

Tynte House

★★★★ FARMHOUSE

tel: 045 401561
email: info@tyntehouse.com **web:** www.tyntehouse.com
dir: *N81 at Hollywood Cross, right at Dunlavin, follow finger signs for Tynte House, past market house in town centre.*

This 19th-century farmhouse stands in the square of the quiet country village of Dunlavin, in the west of County Wicklow. The friendly hosts have carried out a lot of restoration resulting in cosy bedrooms and a relaxing guest sitting room. Breakfast, featuring Caroline's home baking, is a highlight of a visit to this house. An all-weather tennis court is located in the grounds, together with an indoor games room. This house is an ideal base for touring the Wicklow and Kildare areas with their many sporting attractions.

Rooms: 7 en suite (2 fmly) **S** fr €50 **D** fr €80* **Facilities:** Lounge TVL tea/coffee Direct dial WiFi ♨ Playground, games room **Parking:** 16 **Notes:** LB Closed 16 December to 9 January 200 acres beef/arable

COUNTY MAPS

England

1 Bedfordshire
2 Berkshire
3 Bristol
4 Buckinghamshire
5 Cambridgeshire
6 Greater Manchester
7 Herefordshire
8 Hertfordshire
9 Leicestershire
10 Northamptonshire
11 Nottinghamshire
12 Rutland
13 Staffordshire
14 Warwickshire
15 West Midlands
16 Worcestershire

Scotland

17 City of Glasgow
18 Clackmannanshire
19 East Ayrshire
20 East Dunbartonshire
21 East Renfrewshire
22 Perth & Kinross
23 Renfrewshire
24 South Lanarkshire
25 West Dunbartonshire

Wales

26 Blaenau Gwent
27 Bridgend
28 Caerphilly
29 Denbighshire
30 Flintshire
31 Merthyr Tydfil
32 Monmouthshire
33 Neath Port Talbot
34 Newport
35 Rhondda Cynon Taf
36 Torfaen
37 Vale of Glamorgan
38 Wrexham

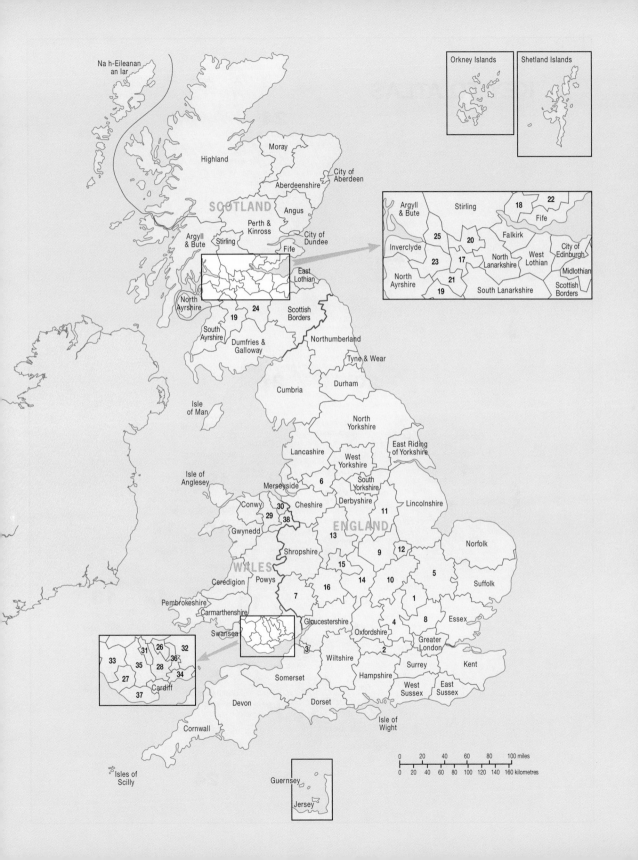

Na h-Eileanan
an Iar

Orkney Islands

Shetland Islands

Highland

Moray

Aberdeenshire

City of
Aberdeen

SCOTLAND

Angus

Perth &
Kinross

City of
Dundee

Argyll &
Bute

Stirling

Fife

Argyll
& Bute

Stirling

18

22

Fife

Inverclyde

25

20

Falkirk

West
Lothian

City of
Edinburgh

23

17

North
Lanarkshire

Midlothian

North
Ayrshire

21

Scottish
Borders

19

South Lanarkshire

North
Ayrshire

East
Lothian

19

24

Scottish
Borders

South
Ayrshire

Dumfries &
Galloway

Northumberland

Tyne & Wear

Cumbria

Durham

Isle
of Man

North
Yorkshire

Lancashire

West
Yorkshire

East Riding
of Yorkshire

Isle of
Anglesey

Merseyside

6

South
Yorkshire

Conwy

30

Cheshire

Derbyshire

Lincolnshire

29

38

Gwynedd

ENGLAND

11

13

Shropshire

9

12

Norfolk

WALES

15

Ceredigion

Powys

16

14

10

5

Pembrokeshire

7

1

Suffolk

Carmarthenshire

Gloucestershire

4

8

Essex

Swansea

31

26

32

3

Oxfordshire

Greater
London

33

35

28

36

Wiltshire

2

Surrey

Kent

27

34

Somerset

Hampshire

37

Cardiff

West
Sussex

East
Sussex

Devon

Dorset

Isle of
Wight

Cornwall

0   20   40   60   80   100 miles

Isles of
Scilly

0   20 40 60 80 100 120 140 160 kilometres

Guernsey

Jersey

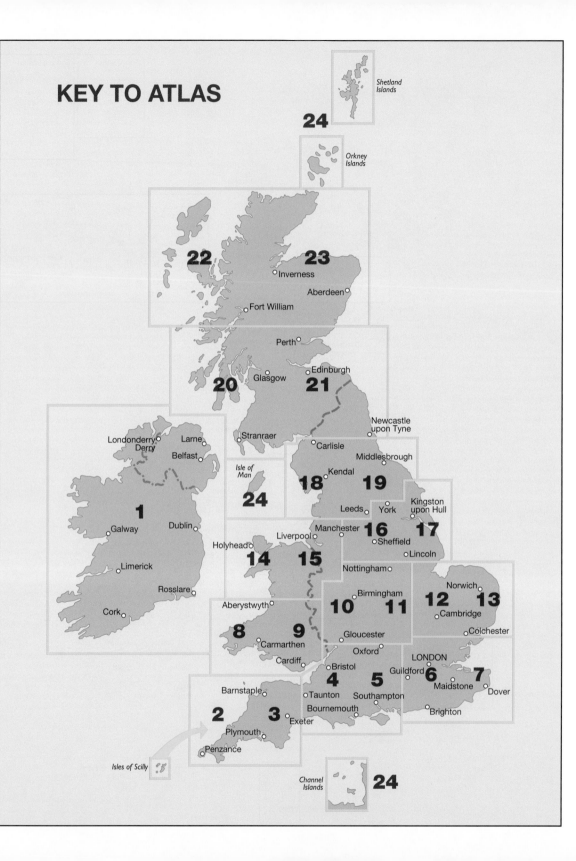

KEY TO ATLAS

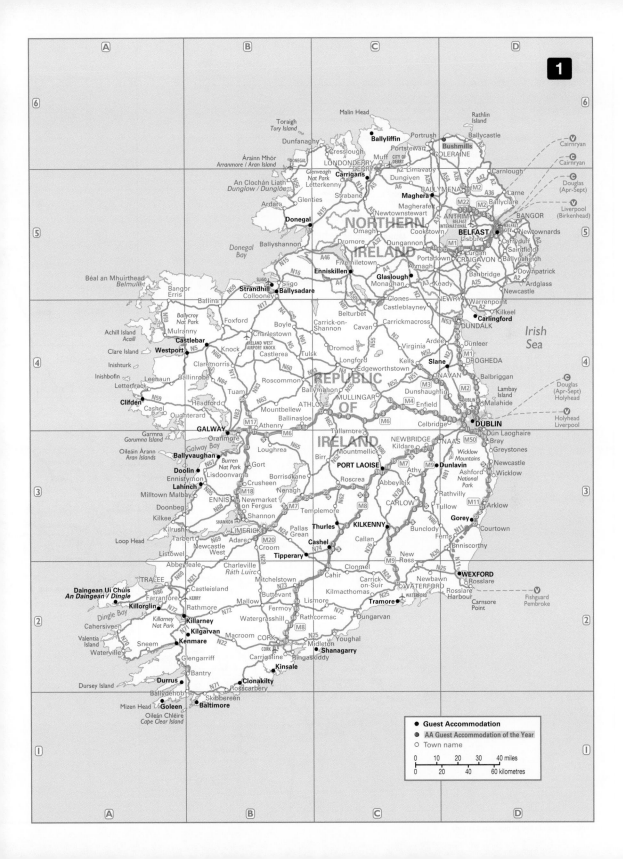

Legend

M6	Motorway/toll motorway	• Stamford	Guest Accommodation
⑤ ⓤ	Motorway junction full/restricted	• Castle Combe	AA Guest Accommodation Award Winners
A33	Primary route single/dual carriageway	○ King's Cliffe	Town/Village name
Ⓢ Ⓢ Ⓡ	Service area/rest area		National boundary
A34	Other A road single/dual carriageway	ESSEX	English county name & boundary
B3400	B road	CONWY	Welsh county name & boundary
	Unclassified road	MORAY	Scottish county name & boundary
Ⓥ — Ⓒ	Vehicle ferry/fast catamaran		National Park

ISLES OF SCILLY

Bryher · Tresco · St Martin's
New Grimsby · Higher Town
Hugh Town · St Mary's
Middle Town · Old Town · ISLES OF SCILLY (ST MARY'S)
St Agnes

SV

SW

Lundy

Hartland Point
Hartland
Meddon
Morwenstow
Kilkhampton
Bude
Bude Bay · Stratton
Widemouth Bay
Crackington Haven · Week St Mary
Boscastle
Tintagel
Delabole
Port Gaverne · Camelford
Port Isaac
Polzeath · St Kew
Harlyn · Rock · St Tudy · Bolventor
Padstow · Wadebridge · Blisland · BODMIN MOOR
Porthcothan
A389
CORNWALL · St Cleer
Mawgan Porth · St Mawgan · Lanivet · Bodmin · Dobwalls
St Columb Major · Liskeard · St Keyne
Newquay · A392 · Roche · Bugle · Lostwithiel · Wic
West Pentire · Luxulyan · St Blazey · Par · Pelynt
Perranporth · Summercourt · St Austell · Bodinnick · Loo
Mitchell · Ladock · St Stephen · Fowey · Polperro
St Agnes · Marazanvose · Polruan
Porthtowan · Grampound · Pentewan
Portreath · St Day · Tregony · Mevagissey
St Ives · Gwithian · Carnon Downs · Truro · Gorran Haven
St Ives Bay · Redruth · Ruan High Lanes · Portloe
Zennor · Lelant · Camborne · Veryan
Hayle · Leedstown · St Just-in-Roseland
St Just · Marazion · Penryn · Portscatho
Penzance · Perranuthnoe · Falmouth · St Mawes
Newlyn · Helston · Constantine
Land's End · St Buryan · Praa Sands · Gweek · Mawnan Smith
Sennen · Mousehole · Porthleven · Manaccan
Porthcurno · Treen · Mount's Bay · St Keverne
Mullion · Coverack
Lizard · Cadgwith
Lizard Point

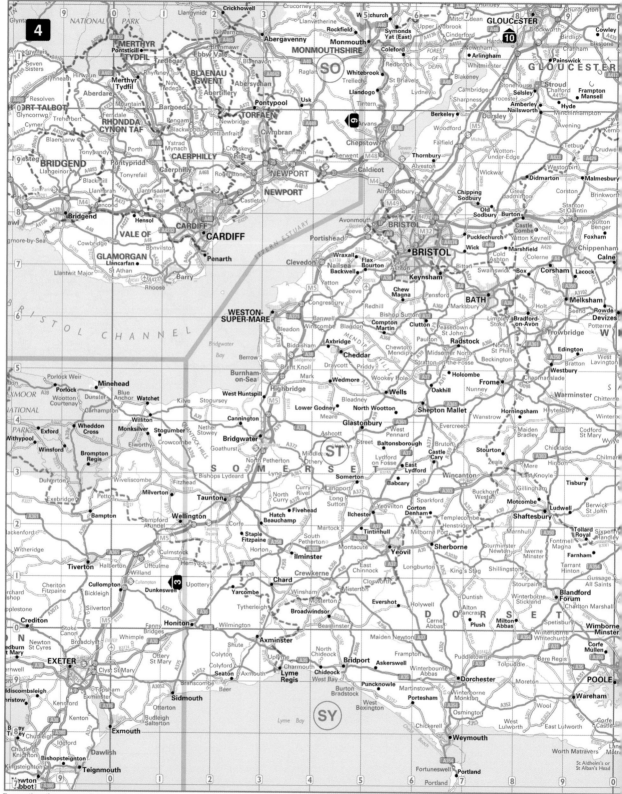

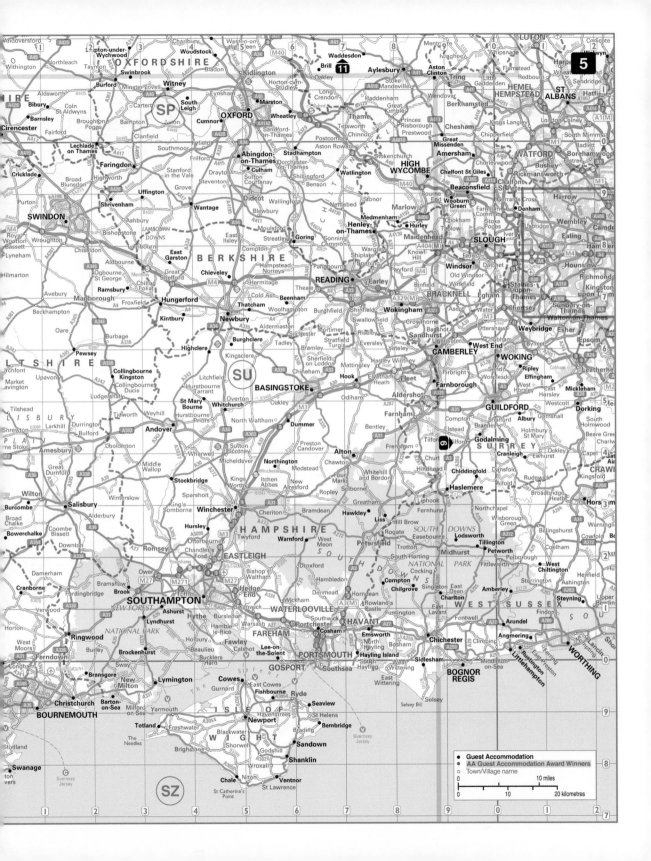

Guest Accommodation
AA Guest Accommodation Award Winners
Town/Village name

0   10 miles
0   10   20 kilometres

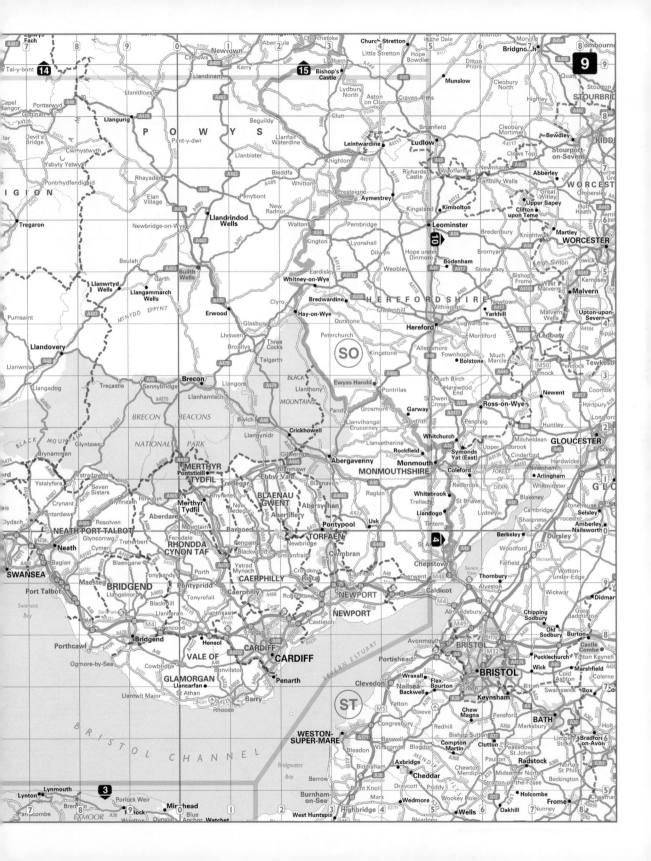

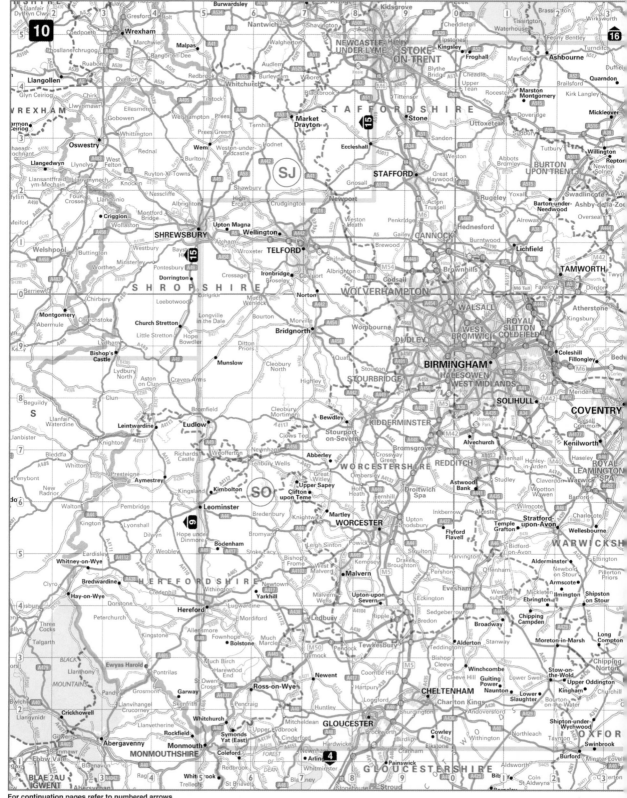

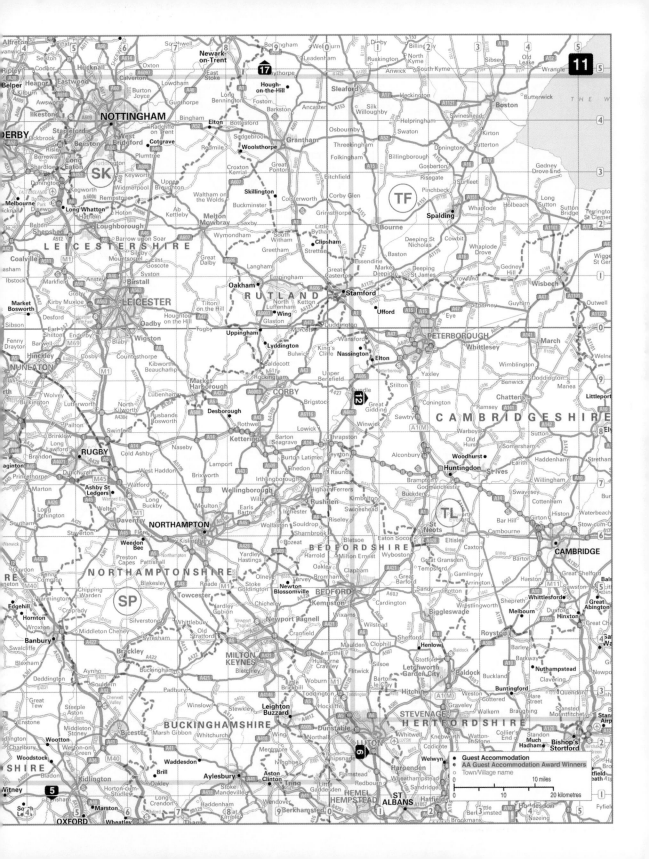

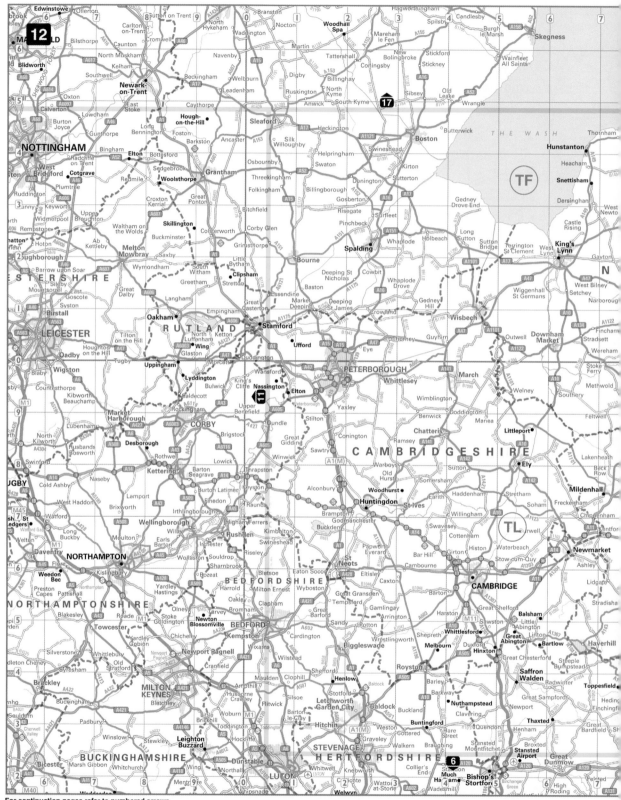

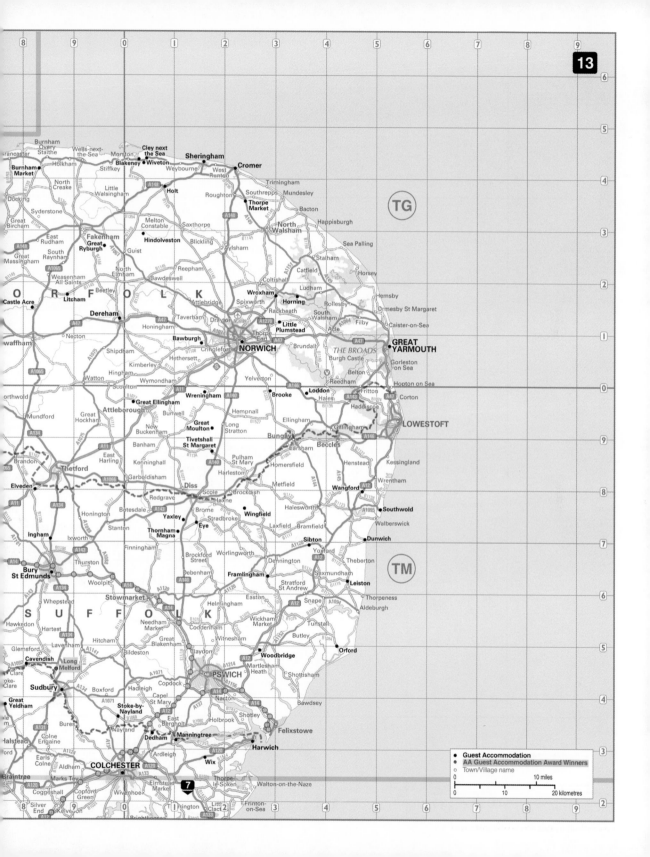

IRISH

SEA

Dublin
Dublin

Cemaes
Amlwch

ISLE OF
ANGLESEY

Llanerchymedd
Holyhead
Benllech
Red
Wharf Bay
Llanfachraeth
Llangoed

Trearddur Bay
Pentraeth

Llandudno
Rhôs-on-Sea
Colwyn Bay
Abergel
Rhy

Deganwy
Llanddulas

Holy
Island
Llangefni
Dwygyfylchi
Conwy
Llansanffraid
Glan Conwy
Betws-yn-Rhos

Rhosneigr
Beaumaris
Penmaenmawr
Menai
Bridge
Bangor
Llanfairfechan
Tal-y-Cafn
Llanfair
Talhaiarn
Llansannan

Aberffraw
Y Felinheli
LlanfairP.G.
Llanllechid
Tal-y-Bont
Trefriw
Llangernyw
Bylchau

Newborough
Bethesda
CONWY

Caernarfon
Llanrug
Llanrwst

Bethnewydd
Llanberis
Capel Curig

Llanwnda
Betws-y-Coed

Caernarfon
Bay
Llandwrog
Dolwyddelan
Penmachno
Pentrefoelas

Penygroes
Rhyd-Ddu
Cerrigydrudion

Clynnog-fawr
SH
Beddgelert
Blaenau Ffestiniog
Y Maen

Morfa Nefyn
Llanaelhaearn
Prenteg
Ffestiniog

Nefyn
Llanystumdwy
Tremadog
Maentwrog

Bodfuan
Porthmadog
Penrhyndeudraeth

Criccieth
Borth-y-Gest
Talsarnau
Llandder

Pwllheli
Trawsfynydd
SNOWDONIA

Sarn
Harlech
GWYNEDD
NATIONAL

Llanbedrog
Llanuwchllyn
PARK
Bala

Aberdaron
Y Rhiw
Abersoch
Llanbedr
Ganllwyd

Bardsey
Island
Dyffryn Ardudwy
A470
A494

Tal-y-bont
Dinas-Mawddwy

Barmouth
Dolgellau
Llangadfa

Fairbourne
Mallwyd

Llwyngwril
Corris

Cemmaes
Road
Cemmaes
Llanbrynmair

Tywyn
Bryncrug
Pennal
Machynlleth
Carno

SN
Aberdyfi
Eglwys
Fach

Borth

Tal-y-bont
9

Llandre
Llanidloes

Aberystwyth
Capel
Bangor
Ponterwyd
Goginan

For continuation pages refer to numbered arrows

Guest Accommodation
AA Guest Accommodation Award Winners
Town/Village name

0 ——————— 10 miles
0 ——— 10 ——— 20 kilometres

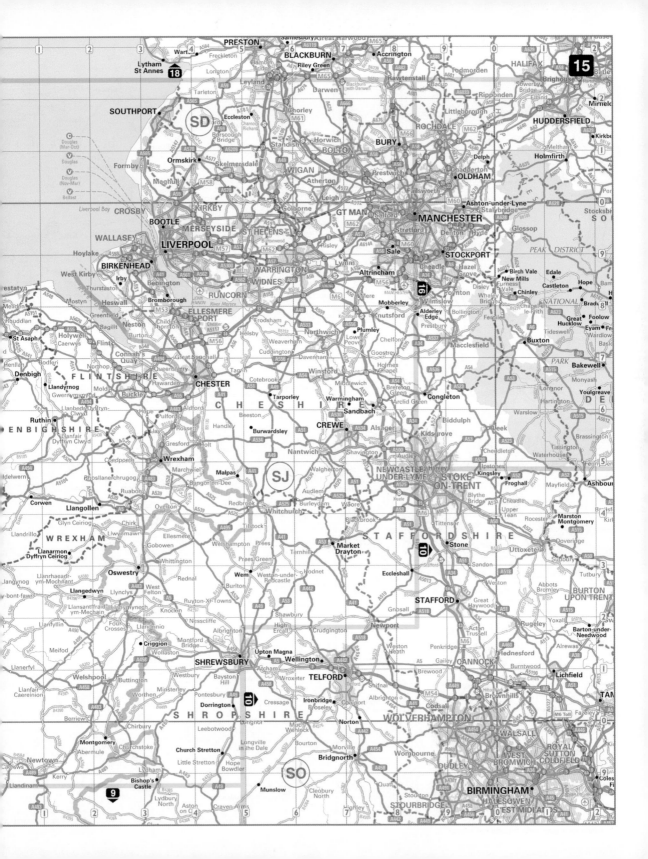

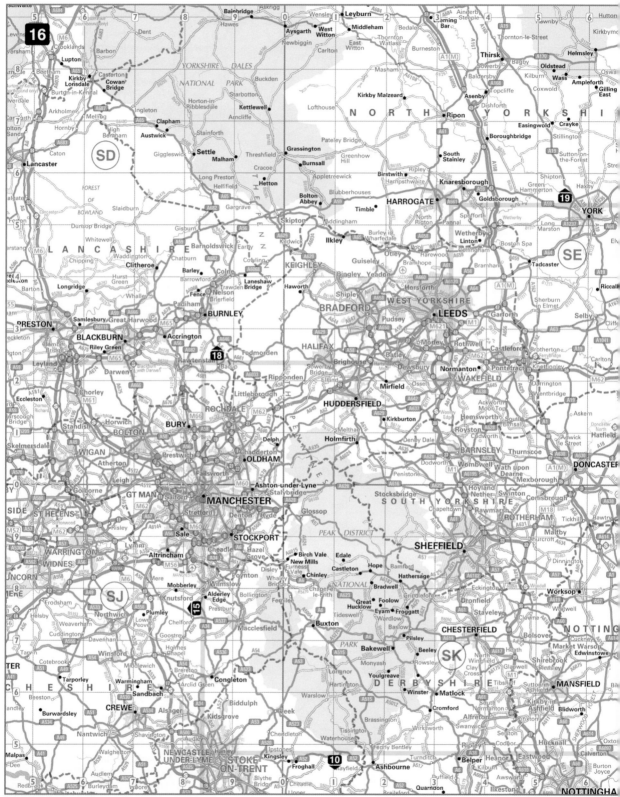

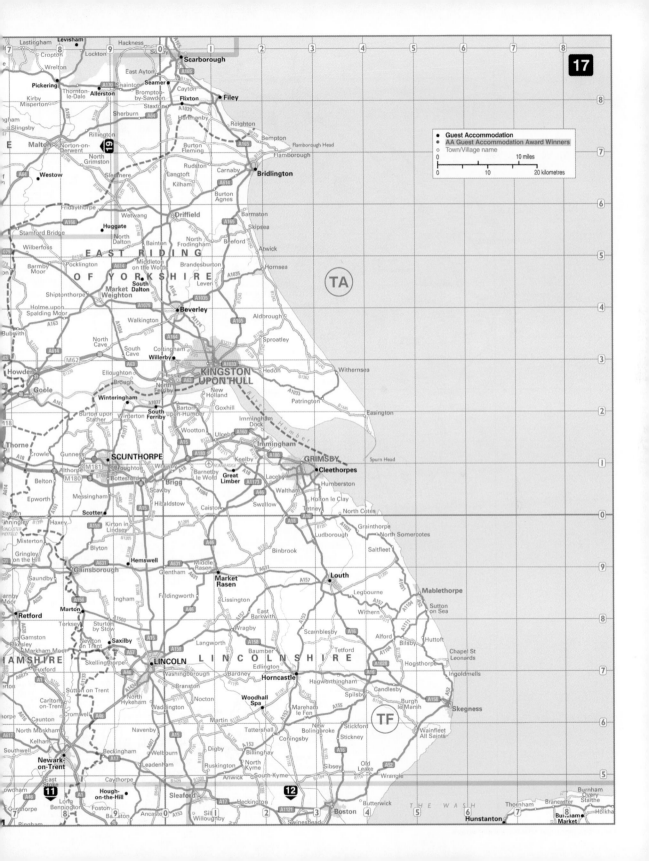

17

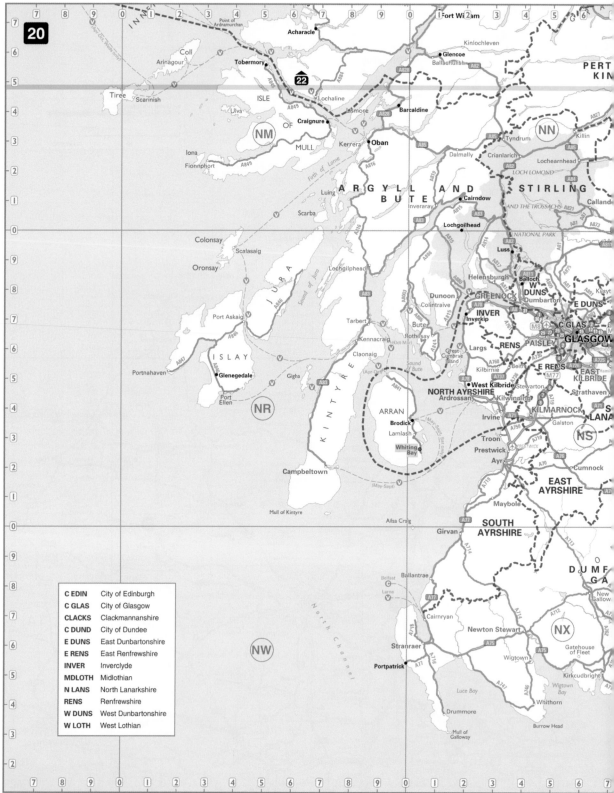

20

C EDIN	City of Edinburgh
C GLAS	City of Glasgow
CLACKS	Clackmannanshire
C DUND	City of Dundee
E DUNS	East Dunbartonshire
E RENS	East Renfrewshire
INVER	Inverclyde
MDLOTH	Midlothian
N LANS	North Lanarkshire
RENS	Renfrewshire
W DUNS	West Dunbartonshire
W LOTH	West Lothian

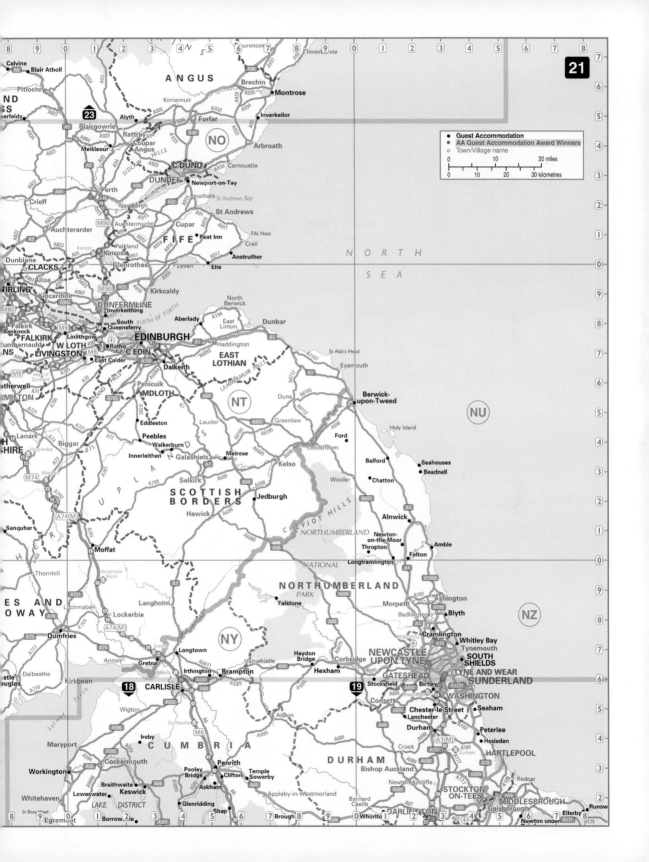

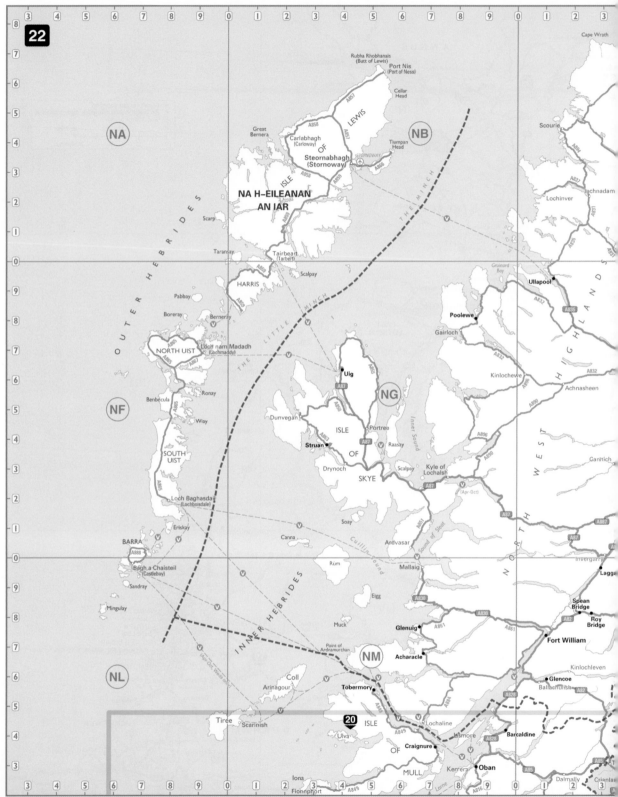

Guest Accommodation
AA Guest Accommodation Award Winners
Town/Village name

0   10   20 miles
0   10   20   30 kilometres

PENTLAND FIRTH

Stromness V   Dunnet Head   St Margaret's Hope
Scrabster   A836 Gills   Duncansby Head   John o' Groats
Thurso

Durness

Strathy Point

Bettyhill   Melvich

Tongue

A838

A836

Wick

NC

Altnaharra

ND

A9   A99

Dunbeath   Lybster

A838   Helmsdale

Lairg   Brora

Golspie

A839   A949   Dornoch

Bonar Bridge

HIGHLAND   Tain

NH   Alness

Strathpeffer   Dingwall   Invergordon   Cromarty

Fortrose   Nairn

Muir of Ord   INVERNESS   MORAY

Brachla   Forres   Lossiemouth   Buckie   Cullen   Portsoy   Banff   Fraserburgh

Drumnadrochit   Elgin   Rothes   NJ   Aberchirder   Turriff

Foyers   Grantown-on-Spey   Keith   Huntly   Peterhead

Invermoriston   Carrbridge   Aberlour   Dufftown   NK

Fort Augustus   Aviemore   Tomintoul   Oldmeldrum   Ellon

Monadhliath Mountains   CAIRNGORMS   Kildrummy   Alford   Inverurie   Kintore   Kirkwall V

Kingussie   CAIRNGORM MOUNTAINS   Tarland   ABERDEENSHIRE   Peterculter   CITY OF ABERDEEN   ABERDEEN

Newtonmore   NATIONAL   Aboyne   Banchory   Lerwick V

GRAMPIAN   Braemar   Ballater

PARK   Stonehaven

MOUNTAINS   Laurencekirk   Inverbervie

NN   Calvine   Blair Atholl   NO

PERTH AND KINROSS   Pitlochry   ANGUS   Brechin

Aberfeldy   Kirriemuir   Montrose

Blairgowrie   Alyth   Forfar   Inverkeilor

Meikleour   Rattray   21

Coupar Angus   Arbroath

Killin   SIDLAW HILLS   C DUND   Carnoustie

Loch   rnhead   Crieff   Perth   DUNDEE   Newport-on-Tay

St Andrews Bay

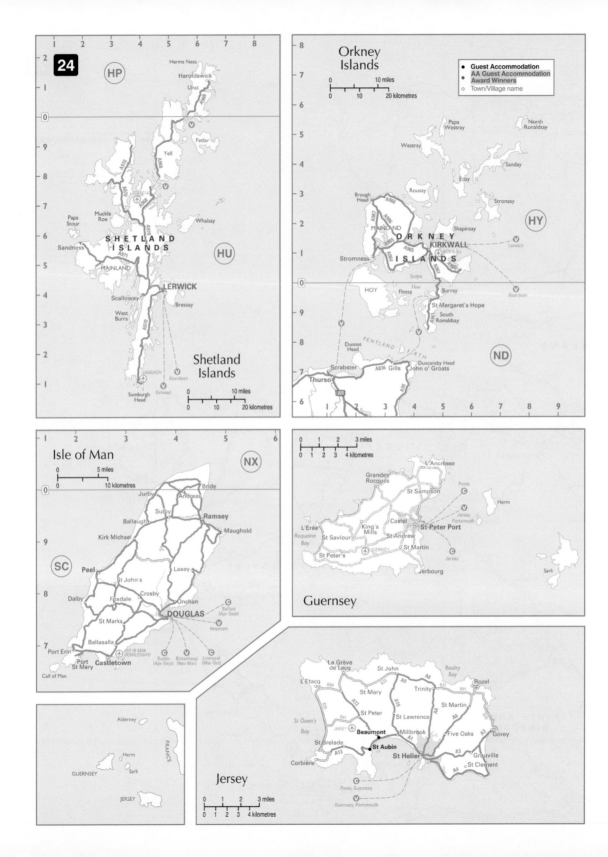

Central London

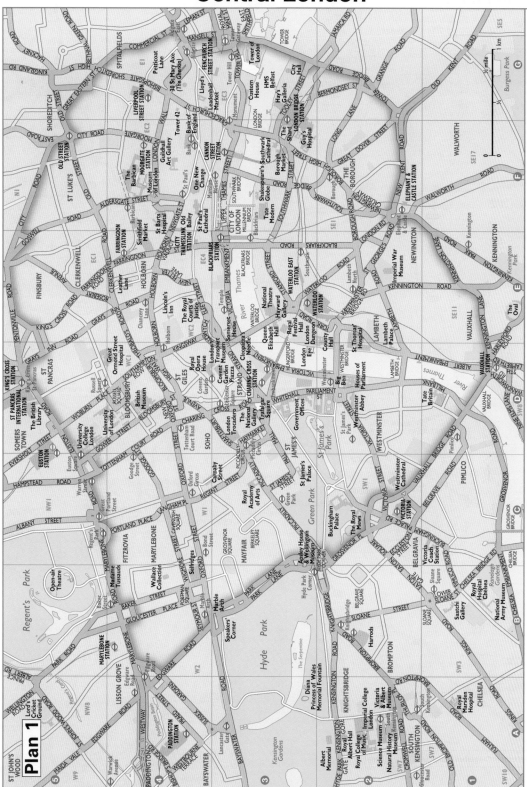

KEY TO B&B LOCATIONS

Each B&B in London has a map reference, eg C2. The letter 'C' refers to the grid square located at the bottom of the map. The figure '2' refers to the grid square located at the left hand edge of the map. For example, where these two intersect, Buckingham Palace can be found. Due to the scale of the map, only a rough guide to the location of a B&B can be given. A more detailed map will be necessary to be precise.

— Congestion Charge and T-Charge Zone boundary

London Plan 2

0 — 1 — 2 miles
0 — 1 — 2 — 3 kilometres

Central London Congestion Charge and T-Charge Zone

Index of Bed & Breakfasts

Readers' Report Form

Please send this form to:–
Editor, The B&B Guide,
Lifestyle Guides,
AA Media,
Fanum House,
Basingstoke RG21 4EA

e-mail: lifestyleguides@theAA.com

Please use this form to recommend any guest house, farmhouse or inn where you have stayed, that is not currently listed in the guide. If you have any comments about your stay at an establishment listed in the guide, please let us know, as feedback from readers helps to keep our guide accurate and up to date. If you have a complaint during your stay, we recommend that you discuss the matter with the establishment.

Please note that the AA does not undertake to arbitrate between you and the establishment, or to obtain compensation or engage in protracted correspondence.

Date

Your name (BLOCK CAPITALS)

Your address (BLOCK CAPITALS)

Post code

E-mail address

Name of establishment

Location

Comments

(please attach a separate sheet if necessary)

Please tick here ☐ if you DO NOT wish to receive details of AA offers or products   PTO

Readers' Report Form *continued*

Have you bought this guide before?   ☐ YES   ☐ NO

Do you regularly use any other accommodation, restaurant, pub or food guides?   ☐ YES   ☐ NO
If YES, which ones?

Why did you buy this guide? (tick all that apply)

Holiday ☐   Short break ☐   Business travel ☐   Special occasion ☐
Overnight stop ☐   Find a venue for an event e.g. conference ☐
Other (please state)

How often do you stay in B&Bs? (tick one choice)

More than once a month ☐   Once a month ☐   Once in 2-3 months ☐
Once in six months ☐   Once a year ☐   Less than once a year ☐
Other (please state)

Please answer these questions to help us make improvements to the guide:

Which of these factors are the most important when choosing a B&B? (tick all that apply)

Price ☐   Location ☐   Awards/ratings ☐   Service ☐
Decor/surroundings ☐   Previous experience ☐   Recommendation ☐
Other (please state)

Do you use the location atlas?   ☐ YES   ☐ NO

What elements of the guide do you find most useful when choosing somewhere to stay? (tick all that apply)

Description ☐   Photo ☐   Advertisement ☐   Star rating ☐

Is there any other information you would like to see added to this guide?

Readers' Report Form

Please send this form to:–
Editor, The B&B Guide,
Lifestyle Guides,
AA Media,
Fanum House,
Basingstoke RG21 4EA

e-mail: lifestyleguides@theAA.com

Please use this form to recommend any guest house, farmhouse or inn where you have stayed, that is not currently listed in the guide. If you have any comments about your stay at an establishment listed in the guide, please let us know, as feedback from readers helps to keep our guide accurate and up to date. If you have a complaint during your stay, we recommend that you discuss the matter with the establishment.

Please note that the AA does not undertake to arbitrate between you and the establishment, or to obtain compensation or engage in protracted correspondence.

Date

Your name (BLOCK CAPITALS)

Your address (BLOCK CAPITALS)

Post code

E-mail address

Name of establishment

Location

Comments

(please attach a separate sheet if necessary)

Please tick here ☐ if you DO NOT wish to receive details of AA offers or products

PTO

Readers' Report Form *continued*

Have you bought this guide before? ☐ YES ☐ NO

Do you regularly use any other accommodation, restaurant, pub or food guides? ☐ YES ☐ NO
If YES, which ones?

_____

_____

Why did you buy this guide? (tick all that apply)

Holiday ☐   Short break ☐   Business travel ☐   Special occasion ☐

Overnight stop ☐   Find a venue for an event e.g. conference ☐

Other (please state)
_____

How often do you stay in B&Bs? (tick one choice)

More than once a month ☐   Once a month ☐   Once in 2-3 months ☐

Once in six months ☐   Once a year ☐   Less than once a year ☐

Other (please state)
_____

Please answer these questions to help us make improvements to the guide:

Which of these factors are the most important when choosing a B&B? (tick all that apply)

Price ☐   Location ☐   Awards/ratings ☐   Service ☐

Decor/surroundings ☐   Previous experience ☐   Recommendation ☐

Other (please state)
_____

Do you use the location atlas? ☐ YES ☐ NO

What elements of the guide do you find most useful when choosing somewhere to stay? (tick all that apply)

Description ☐   Photo ☐   Advertisement ☐   Star rating ☐

Is there any other information you would like to see added to this guide?

_____

_____

_____

_____

_____

_____

Readers' Report Form

Please send this form to:–
Editor, The B&B Guide,
Lifestyle Guides,
AA Media,
Fanum House,
Basingstoke RG21 4EA

e-mail: lifestyleguides@theAA.com

Please use this form to recommend any guest house, farmhouse or inn where you have stayed, that is not currently listed in the guide. If you have any comments about your stay at an establishment listed in the guide, please let us know, as feedback from readers helps to keep our guide accurate and up to date. If you have a complaint during your stay, we recommend that you discuss the matter with the establishment.

Please note that the AA does not undertake to arbitrate between you and the establishment, or to obtain compensation or engage in protracted correspondence.

Date

Your name (BLOCK CAPITALS)

Your address (BLOCK CAPITALS)

Post code

E-mail address

Name of establishment

Location

Comments

(please attach a separate sheet if necessary)

Please tick here ☐ if you DO NOT wish to receive details of AA offers or products

PTO

Readers' Report Form *continued*

Have you bought this guide before? ☐ YES ☐ NO

Do you regularly use any other accommodation, restaurant, pub or food guides? ☐ YES ☐ NO
If YES, which ones?

....

....

Why did you buy this guide? (tick all that apply)

Holiday ☐   Short break ☐   Business travel ☐   Special occasion ☐

Overnight stop ☐   Find a venue for an event e.g. conference ☐

Other (please state) ....

How often do you stay in B&Bs? (tick one choice)

More than once a month ☐   Once a month ☐   Once in 2-3 months ☐

Once in six months ☐   Once a year ☐   Less than once a year ☐

Other (please state) ....

Please answer these questions to help us make improvements to the guide:

Which of these factors are the most important when choosing a B&B? (tick all that apply)

Price ☐   Location ☐   Awards/ratings ☐   Service ☐

Decor/surroundings ☐   Previous experience ☐   Recommendation ☐

Other (please state) ....

Do you use the location atlas? ☐ YES ☐ NO

What elements of the guide do you find most useful when choosing somewhere to stay? (tick all that apply)

Description ☐   Photo ☐   Advertisement ☐   Star rating ☐

Is there any other information you would like to see added to this guide?

....

....

....

....

....